Professional XML

Richard Anderson
Mark Birbeck
Michael Kay
Steven Livingstone
Brian Loesgen
Didier Martin
Stephen Mohr
Nikola Ozu
Bruce Peat
Jonathan Pinnock
Peter Stark
Kevin Williams

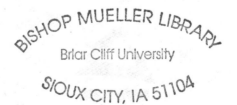

Wrox Press Ltd. ®

Professional XML

First Published January 2000

Latest Reprint April 2000

Published by Wrox Press Ltd
Arden House, 1102 Warwick Road, Acock's Green, Birmingham B27 6BH, UK
Printed in USA
ISBN 1-861003-11-0

Trademark Acknowledgements

Wrox has endeavored to provide trademark information about all the companies and products mentioned in this book by the appropriate use of capitals. However, Wrox cannot guarantee the accuracy of this information.

Credits

Authors
Richard Anderson
Mark Birbeck
Michael Kay
Steven Livingstone
Brian Loesgen
Didier Martin
Stephen Mohr
Nikola Ozu
Bruce Peat
Jonathan Pinnock
Peter Stark
Kevin Williams

Contributing Authors
David Baliles
Alex Homer

Technical Editors
Jon Duckett
Peter Jones
Karli Watson

Development Editor
Peter Morgan

Managing Editor
Victoria Hudgson

Project Manager
Chandima Nethisinghe

Technical Reviewers
Richard Anderson
Curt Arnold
Barclay Blair
Robert Chang
Michael Corning
Steven Danielson
Gerry Fillery
Lars Marius Garshol
John Granade
Chris Harris
Paul Houle
Michael Kay
Eve Maler
Bruce Martin
Michael Mason
Craig McQueen
John Montgomery
Paul Spencer
David Thompson
Keith Visco

Design / Layout
Tom Bartlett
Mark Burdett
William Fallon
Jonathan Jones
John McNulty

Index
Andrew Criddle

Cover Design
Chris Morris

About the Authors

Didier Martin

Didier PH Martin has worked with computers for the last 21 years. Even so, he still enjoys playing with new technologies and XML tools are like new toys at Christmas for him. After developing an accounting package, building robots, and even creating video games, he encountered the SGML world, and later the world of XML and this was the beginning of his passion for markup technologies. He is currently CEO of Talva Corp and enjoys working with his colleagues, creating the next generation of XML tools. Didier lives near a mountain and, when he's not creating tools or working on new standards, don't be surprised to see him on his skis in winter and on his bike in summer. His favorite thought: "a different point of view is worth a thousand points of IQ".

Mark Birbeck

Mark Birbeck has been a professional programmer for over 18 years. He's twiddled bits with Z80 and 6502 assembly language and written in C on early Unix systems. He remembers the day Windows actually became something worth using to write programs, and the day Microsoft made their C compiler speak C++. And he'll never forget the first time he saw a web server serve. But for him, none of this compares to the day he stumbled across XML – and he hasn't looked back. His company – x-port.net – specialise in the development of XML tools that help with the building of portal sites.

Mark would like to apologise to all the people he neglected when writing his chapter, even though none of them have got the faintest idea what he's talking about.

Michael Kay

Michael Kay works for the IT services company ICL, where he holds the post of ICL Fellow, responsible for investigating new technologies and advising clients on their exploitation, especially in the information management arena. He is known in the XML world as the author of SAXON, an open source XSL processor. His background (and Ph.D) is in database management: in the past he has designed a number of ICL software products from object-oriented databases to text search engines, and has served on standards committees including the ANSI X3H2 group responsible for SQL. His most recent XML project was the design of a messaging backbone for a cable TV company, to exchange data between a wide variety of systems operated internally and by suppliers. In a personal capacity, he has also been promoting the use of XML for exchanging family history data. Michael is based in Bracknell, England.

Brian Loesgen

Brian Loesgen is a Senior Software Engineer at Stellcom Inc., a San Diego-based leader in Internet solutions. At Stellcom Brian is involved in some of the most advanced web application development projects being built today. Brian has spoken at numerous technical conferences worldwide, and has been known to seize every opportunity possible to promote new technologies. He enjoys playing with bleeding edge software and translating those new technologies into real world benefits.

When not otherwise pre-occupied, Brian enjoys outdoor activities such as hiking in the mountains or going to the beach with his wife Miriam and children Steven and Melissa.

Brian can be reached at bloesgen@msn.com

Stephen Mohr

Stephen Mohr is a senior systems architect with Omicron Consulting. Over the last ten years, he has specialized in the PC computing platform, designing and developing systems using C++, Java, JavaScript, COM, and various internetworking standards and protocols. His latest efforts include the use of XML for application integration. Stephen holds BS and MS degrees in computer science from Rensselaer Polytechnic Institute. His research interests include distributed object-based computing and the practical applications of artificial intelligence.

Jonathan Pinnock

Jonathan Pinnock started programming in Pal III assembler on his school's PDP 8/e, with a massive 4K of memory, back in the days before Moore's Law reached the statute books. After turning his back on computers for three years in order to study Mathematics at Cambridge University, he was forced back into programming in order to make a living, something that he still does from time to time. These days, he works as an independent developer and consultant, mainly in the City of London. He is the author of *Professional DCOM Application Development*, but hopes that this will not be held against him.

Jonathan lives in Hertfordshire, England, with his wife, two children and 1961 Ami Continental jukebox. His moderately interesting web site is located at http://www.jpassoc.co.uk, and he can be contacted on jon@jpassoc.co.uk.

Steven Livingstone

Steven is based in Glasgow, Scotland and specialises in developing distributed web applications for business, as well as the creation of e-commerce applications using Site Server and XML. He also maintains the citix.com and deltabiz.com web sites. At deltabiz.com, he is currently working on an exciting project in developing a range of next generation electronic commerce products using BizTalk and SOAP. Watch this space.

I would like to thank everyone at Wrox for their help as well as my fellow authors who gave me some good advice when it was needed. Mostly, I would like to thank Donna for the patience she has shown for the last few months (told you we would go on holiday!).

I would be glad to hear from anyone at ceo@citix.com.

Peter Stark

Peter Stark works as an architect at Phone.com. He has been working in the WAP Forum from the day it was founded: the first year in the protocol's group, and the last year in the application's group, where WML and WMLScript is being specified. He also represents Phone.com in the W3C HTML working group, which specifies the XML variant of HTML, XHTML. He is originally from Sweden, but lives currently lives in San Francisco, California.

Kevin Williams

Kevin's first experience with computers was at the age of 10 (in 1980) when he took a BASIC class at a local community college on their PDP-9, and by the time he was 12, he stayed up for four days straight hand-assembling 6502 code on his Atari 400. His professional career has been focussed on Windows development – first client-server, then onto Internet work. He's done a little bit of everything, from VB to Powerbuilder to Delphi toC/C++ to MASM to ISAPI, CGI, ASP, HTML, XML, and any other acronym you might care to name, but these days, he's focusing on XML work. Kevin is currently working with the Mortgage Bankers' Association of America to help them put together an XML standard for the mortgage industry.

Richard Anderson

Richard Anderson is an established software developer who has worked with Microsoft technologies for nearly 10 years. He works for a small yet globally known software house in Peterborough (England), where he currently holds the position of "Research and Development Manager". What that means is that he plays with lots of great new technologies, and then tells people how they work, ensuring they are correctly understood and adopted correctly and successfully in new applications. He also writes applications too, and is responsible for mentoring and managing C++ and VB developers. Richard can be contacted via his private email account rja@arpsolutions.demon.co.uk.

Nikola Ozu

Nikola Ozu is a systems architect and consultant who lives in Wyoming. Currently he is working on an XML vocabulary for architects and designers. Recent work includes the use of XML as the basis for production and indexing systems for a publisher of medical and veterinary reference books and databases. Previous work has ranged from library systems on mainframes to embedded microsystems (telecom, robotics, toys, arcade games). In the early 90s, he was the designer and lead developer of the Health Reference Center and InfoTrac CD-ROM products. When not surfing the 'net, he surfs the Tetons and the Pacific, backpacks, and/or climbs anywhere there is rock – often accompanied by his 12-year-old son.

To: Noah, may we always think of 2^3 generations, instead of just our ownselves.

Bruce Peat

Bruce Peat is co-founder of the XML/edi Group, a grass roots advocacy organization interested in improving electronic business. The Group's efforts since July 1997 in promoting XML for global commerce solutions have brought much excitement to the industry – more information can be found at http://www.XMLedi.org. His passion with the Group coupled with positive feedback on the Group's efforts inspired him to start-up eProcess Solutions, a management and technology consulting firm focused on development of XML-based business exchange processes and pipelines (http://www.eProcessSolutions.com).

David Baliles

David Baliles works for Microsoft Corporation and specializes in the support and development of their Site Server and IIS products. In addition to Microsoft, David has worked with Electronic Data Systems (EDS) at the Center for Disease Control & Prevention in Atlanta and Equifax E-Business Solutions, where he deployed the latest Microsoft server products and web development technologies into existing corporate infrastructures. In addition to his job at Microsoft, David enjoys working with new XML-based technologies, as well as developing his own audio markup language, AUML. Off-hours, he tries to spend as much time as possible with his wife and friends. David would like to thank his wife for her enduring patience throughout this project, and for giving him the inspiration to continue giving 110% in everything he does.

David welcomes e-mail and can be reached at dbaliles@dndconsulting.com.

Table of Contents

Introduction

The Extensible Markup Language (XML) has emerged in just a few short years as nothing less than a phenomenon in computing. It is a concept, elegant in its simplicity, driving dramatic changes in the way Internet applications are written.

What Does This Book Cover?

This book explains and demonstrates the essential techniques for designing, using, and displaying XML documents. First and foremost, this book covers the fundamentals of XML as they are codified by the **World Wide Web Consortium** (W3C). The W3C is the standards body that originated XML in a formal way and continues to develop specifications for XML. Although the wider XML community is increasingly jumping in and offering new XML-related ideas outside the control of the W3C, the W3C is still central and important to the development of XML.

The focus of this book is on learning how to use XML as an enabling technology in real-world applications. It presents good design techniques, and shows how to interface XML-enabled applications with Web applications and database systems. It explores the frontiers of XML and previews some nascent technologies. Whether your requirements are oriented toward data exchange or visual styling, this book will cover all the relevant techniques in the XML community.

Each chapter contains a practical example. As XML is a platform-neutral technology, the examples cover a variety of languages, parsers, and servers. All the techniques are relevant across all the platforms, so you can get valuable insight from the examples even if they are not implemented using your favorite platform.

Who Is This Book For?

This book is for anyone who wants to use XML to build applications and systems. Web site developers can learn techniques to take their sites to the next level of sophistication, while programmers and software architects can learn where XML fits into their systems and how to use it to solve problems in application integration.

XML applications are usually distributed in nature and are commonly Web oriented. This is not a book specifically about distributed systems or Web development, so you do not need deep familiarity with those areas. A general awareness of multi-tier architectures and internetworking via the Web will be sufficient.

The examples in this book use a variety of programming languages and technologies. An important part of XML's appeal is the fact that it is platform and language neutral. If you have done some Web development, chances are you will find some examples written in your favorite language. If you don't see any examples specific to your platform, take heart. Tools for working with XML are available for Perl, C++, Java, JavaScript, and any COM-enabled language. Microsoft Internet Explorer (mainly version 5.0 and later) has strong XML capabilities built into it, and the Mozilla browser (the community source successor to Netscape's proprietary browser) is gaining similar support. XML tools are also turning up in major relational database management systems, as well as Web and application servers. If your platform isn't covered in this book, learn the fundamentals of XML and study the techniques presented in the examples, and you will be able to apply the lessons you learn here on any common computing platform.

How is this Book Structured?

Each chapter of this book takes up a separate topic pertaining to XML. Chapter 1 provides a conceptual introduction to the main aspects of XML. Chapters 2 and 3 are closely related as they cover the fundamentals of XML. Chapter 2 gets you started by covering the basic syntax and rules of XML. Chapter 3 takes you forward by providing tools for formally defining your own problem-specific XML vocabulary. The remaining chapters, however, are largely self-contained in terms of the techniques and technologies they present.

The main chapters are tied together with a unifying example. The example will assume a publisher wants to present their catalog of books in XML form. We will start by devising rules for describing books in a catalog, then build on those rules to show how each technology takes a turn in helping us build XML applications. You will see how book catalogs can be turned into documents, how such documents can be manipulated and accessed in code, and how their content can be styled for human readers. Since such an application would not, in practice, exist in a vacuum, you will also see how XML applications interface with databases.

There are several threads that run through this book which are outlined in the next section. This should allow you to read through the book focusing only on those issues that are important to you, skimming other sections.

Learning Threads

XML is evolving from its simple roots as a document markup language to a large, wide-ranging field of related markup technologies. It is this growth that is powering XML applications. With growth comes divergence. Different readers will come to this book with different expectations. XML is different things to different people. While we hope that you will read this book cover to cover, that is not necessary. Indeed, that may not even be the best way for everyone to approach this book.

This book has three threads springing from a common core. While you can certainly start at the first chapter and work your way sequentially through to the last, you can follow a more direct path to the knowledge you need. Everyone should read the core chapters to gain a common understanding of what XML encompasses. From there, you can approach XML as data or as content for visual presentation and styling.

Core

Chapters 2 (Well-formed XML) and 3 (DTDs) cover the fundamentals of XML 1.0. Chapter 2 gives you the basic syntax, while Chapter 3 tells you how to formally specify an XML vocabulary in a way that every XML programmer is expected to understand. These chapters form the irreducible minimum you need to understand XML and begin working with it. Chapter 4 (on Data Modeling) gives you effective guidelines and lessons in creating good XML structures. It's hard to recover from a bad XML vocabulary, but a good one will forgive a lot of programming mistakes. Chapter 5 teaches you the Document Object Model (DOM), the W3C's API for XML documents, among other things. This takes you out of the realm of documents and into the world of applications.

These four chapters are enough for you to begin XML applications programming. When you are finished with them, you will know what XML is, how to structure it, and how to manipulate XML documents in code. Although a wealth of XML techniques lies ahead, you will have a firm foundation upon which to build.

So the 'Core' thread includes:

- Chapter 2: Well-formed XML
- Chapter 3: Document Type Definitions
- Chapter 4: Data Modeling
- Chapter 5: Document Object Model

XML as Data

As you will see in the core chapters, XML, unlike HTML, clearly separates the content of a document from its visual representation. In fact, for the purposes of many applications, visual rendering of XML documents is not important. These applications treat XML as *data.* The concern here is with using XML as an interface between programs and systems. This may be the most exciting area of XML today – especially where XML can enable e-commerce as a technique for Web applications that negotiate commercial transactions.

Chapter 6 starts this thread. It discusses an event driven API (called SAX) for manipulating XML documents. As such, the API is especially useful for processing very large quantities of XML, streams of XML, or for when you need the smallest possible footprint in a parser. Chapter 7 introduces Namespaces and Schemas, two areas that let us express concepts more creatively and effectively than we can with DTDs. They are the emerging core for describing data in XML.

Chapter 8 will show you how to link documents and query within a document for a particular element. The querying technology used in the examples actually stems from the styling side of XML, and this chapter does double duty by appearing in the 'Presentation' thread as well as this one. It is useful in this thread for demonstrating how queries can be used in quickly finding elements we need, and for showing how we can relate different XML documents. Chapter 9 (Manipulating XML) also covers techniques for transforming XML documents for various purposes. It is interesting from the standpoint of data because it is presents some very powerful techniques for translating between vocabularies. It will prove useful for the interchange of data, particularly in e-commerce and business-to-business situations. Again, this chapter also has a bearing on the 'Presentation' thread as it introduces the idea of transforming XML documents into other languages which can help when it comes to presenting XML for a user to view.

Chapter 10 (XML and Databases) is all about data. Relational databases and XML are two approaches to capturing data for computing although they play different roles. This chapter teaches you how to interface the traditional approach to data storage to the use of XML. Chapter 11 (Server to Server) will show you how to reach out to another server when you don't have the data locally. This is a novel technique that is going to become common as web applications move to the forefront of computing. Chapter 12 then draws on the information in these two preceding chapters in its discussion of the use of XML as the messaging medium for e-commerce interactions. In this case, the other server belongs to a business partner. They examine the issues of exchanging data in this context, where XML fits into this picture, and details of how it is used.

Wrapping up this thread is the discussion of WAP (the Wireless Application Protocol) and it's associated use of XML in the Wireless Markup Language (WML), in Chapter 14. Much of WAP is concerned with the metamorphosis of data from the verbose form of XML to a compact binary representation without losing the benefits of the former for use on mobile devices. Considering this problem and seeing WAP's solution will let you better appreciate the benefits of XML as a data exchange medium. In addition, if XML is going to be used to store and transfer data, you'll want to put your data on all the common data devices, which will increasingly include wireless devices like cell phones and dedicated Web devices.

So our XML-as-data thread consists of:

Chapter 6: SAX: The Simple API for XML

Chapter 7: Namespaces and Schemas

Chapter 8: Linking and Querying

Chapter 9: Manipulating XML

Chapter 10: XML and Databases

Chapter 11: Server to Server

Chapter 12: eBusiness

Chapter 14: WAP and WML

Visual Presentation of XML

The data thread is great for moving data about between machines, but if you plan to pass XML to a human, you will be interested in the styling thread. Unlike more traditional computing fields that have focused on data, such as relational databases, the XML community has given quite a bit of thought to how data can be rendered efficiently. XML's solution is, appropriately, data-driven. Whether we use CSS or XSL, we apply the data in style sheets to the data in an XML document to produce a visual representation for the human consumer of our data.

Chapter 8, Linking and Querying, starts this thread. This is because a subset of the querying technology lets a programmer specify a set of criteria that is used in to select a part of a document that has to be styled. Styling can be as precise as specifying how to render particular elements depending on the context in which they are found. The same type of element can be rendered differently depending on who its parent is, or what else appears near it. With the context in place, Chapter 9 tells programmers the knowledge for transforming XML, if needed, into some other format suited to presentation. This is at the heart of data-driven styling.

Chapter 13 (Styling) builds on Chapters 8 and 9 to teach you styling for XML. Our style sheets become powerful sets of rules that are applied to the data in XML documents to create a visual presentation. From one set of data, you can quickly and efficiently produce multiple views for presentation. This is where the benefits of separating data from presentation are fully realized.

Chapter 14 (WAP) is included in the presentation thread because styling is an important consideration for small devices, and small devices are the primary users of wireless communications. It addresses how designers can compress the visual representation to fit the constraints of a very small display. This parallels the consideration our data counterparts have to give to compressing the data to fit through a low bandwidth network connection. Because your styling is driven by a style sheet and not embedded with the data, you can create an effective presentation format specifically for the wireless device.

To recap, our presentation thread is comprised of:

Chapter 8: Linking and Querying

Chapter 9: Manipulating XML

Chapter 13: Styling

Chapter 14: WAP

What You Need to Use this Book

The book assumes that you have some knowledge of HTML, JavaScript, Java, and ASP. If you are not familiar with Java or ASP it will not prevent you learning the concepts behind the topics where they are used, and they are kept to a minimum. But, in order to work with *all* of the examples in the book you will need to have a browser, an ASP compatible web server such as Microsoft's Personal Web Server, and (as a minimum for running Java programs) the Sun Java Runtime Environment (JRE) installed.

Personal Web Server (for Windows 9x machines) can be downloaded for free as part of the NT4 Option pack from:
http://www.microsoft.com/ntserver/nts/downloads/recommended/
NT4OptPk/default.asp

This is the same address that you can download IIS for Windows NT4. Windows 2000 Professional comes with a web server that supports ASP, though you have to select for it to be installed in the custom, rather than typical, install.

The JRE can be obtained for free from:
http://www.java.sun.com/products/jdk/1.2/jre/index.html

The complete source for larger portions of code from the book is available for download from:
http://www.wrox.com

Conventions

To help you get the most from the text and keep track of what's happening, we've used a number of conventions throughout the book.

For instance:

> **These boxes hold important, not-to-be forgotten information which is directly relevant to the surrounding text.**

While the background style is used for asides to the current discussion.

As for styles in the text:

When we introduce them, we **highlight** important words.

We show keyboard strokes like this: *Ctrl-A*.

We show filenames and code within the text like so: `doGet()`

Text on user interfaces and URLs are shown as: Menu.

We present code in three different ways. Definitions of methods and properties are shown as follows:

```
protected void doGet(HttpServletRequest req, HttpServletResponse resp)
                     throws ServletException, IOException
```

Example code is shown:

```
In our code examples, the code foreground style shows new, important,
    pertinent code
while code background shows code that's less important in the present context,
    or has been seen before.
```

Tell Us What You Think

We've worked hard to make this book as useful to you as possible, so we'd like to know what you think. We're always keen to know what it is you want and need to know.

We appreciate feedback on our efforts and take both criticism and praise on board in our future editorial efforts. If you've anything to say, let us know on:

feedback@wrox.com

Or via the feedback links on:

http://www.wrox.com

1

Introducing XML

In this chapter we will take you through from a brief discussion of the historical origins of XML to an understanding of how the key aspects of XML-related technology fit together. Along the way we will discuss the nature of XML in general, and its impact on web architectures past and future. We hope this will provide you with a good foundation for digging into the rest of the material in the book.

Markup Languages

Ever since the invention of the printing press, writers have made notes on manuscripts to instruct the printers concerning typesetting, and other production issues. These notes were called **markup**, and a collection of such notes that conform to a defined syntax and grammar can be called a **language**. For example, proofreaders use a hand-written **markup language (ML)** to communicate corrections to authors. Even the modern use of punctuation is a form of markup that remains with the text to advise the reader how to interpret that text. Most of these MLs use a distinct appearance so as to differentiate markup from the text to which it refers. Proofreaders' marks use a combination of cursive handwriting and special symbols to distinguish markup from the typeset text. Similarly, punctuation uses special symbols that cannot be confused with the alphabet and numbers that represent the textual content. Some punctuation symbols are so necessary to the understanding and production of printed English that they were included in the ASCII character set, the basis of the character sets used in almost all modern computers. Therefore these symbols also became part of modern programming language syntaxes, the standardization of the symbol set driving their re-appropriation for roles other than the punctuation of English.

The ASCII standard also defined a set of symbols (the "C0 control characters", with hexadecimal values `00` to `1F`) that were intended to be used to markup the structure of data transmissions. Only a few of these symbols found wide-spread acceptance, and their use was often inconsistent. The most common example is the character(s) used to delimit the end of a line of text in a document.

Teletype machines used the physical motion-based character pair `CR-LF` (carriage-return, line-feed), that was later used by both MS-DOS and MS-Windows. In contrast, Unix uses a single `LF` character, and the MacOS uses a single `CR` character. Because of these conflicting and non-standard uses of ASCII, document interchange between these systems often requires a translation step – a simple text file cannot be shared without conversion – and this is just the simplest of markup issues that doesn't even address the question of what constitutes a "line" of text. Most word-processing programs have eliminated the use of a text "line", and have instead treated end-of-line markup as "end-of-paragraph", with the ASCII period-space (". ") or period-space-space (". ") strings being used to delimit sentences (though this method is imperfect).

Various forms of delimiters have been used to define the boundaries of containers for content, special symbol glyphs, presentation style of the text, or other special features of a document. For example, the C and C++ programming languages use braces `{...}` to delimit units of data or code, such as functions, data structures, and object definitions. A typesetting language, intended for manual human editing, might use more readable strings like `.begin` and `.end`. Other languages use other characters, or literal strings of characters – commonly called **tags**. Of course, there has often been conflict between different sets of tags and their interpretation. Without common delimiter vocabularies, much less common internal data formats, it has been very difficult to convert data from one format to another, or otherwise share data between applications and organizations.

In 1969, a person walked on the Moon for the first time. In the same year, Ed Mosher, Ray Lorie, and Charles F. Goldfarb of IBM Research invented the first modern markup language, **Generalized Markup Language (GML)**. GML was a self-referential language for marking the structure of an arbitrary set of data, and was intended to be a meta-language – a language that could be used to describe other languages, their grammars and vocabularies. GML later became **Standard Generalized Markup Language (SGML)**. In 1986, SGML was adopted as an international data storage and exchange standard by the International Organization for Standardization (ISO), designated **ISO 8879** (see http://www.iso.ch). With the major impact of the World Wide Web (WWW) upon human commerce and communications, it could be argued that the quiet invention of GML was a more significant event in the history of technology than the high adventure of that first trip to another celestial body.

> **"Markup" is a method of conveying metadata (that is, information about a dataset). Markup languages use string literals, or "tags", to delimit and describe this data.**

Here is an extremely simple example of an SGML document:

```
<!DOCTYPE email [
<!ELEMENT email O O ((to & from & date & subject?), text) >
<!ELEMENT text - O (para+) >
<!ELEMENT para O O (#PCDATA) >
<!ELEMENT (to, from, date, subject) - O (#PCDATA) >
]>
<date>10/12/99
<to>you@yours.com
<from>me@mine.com
<text>I just mailed to say...
```

SGML is an extremely powerful (and rather complicated) markup language that has been widely used by the U.S. government and its contractors, large manufacturing companies, and publishers of technical information. Publishers often construct paper documents, such as books, reports, and reference manuals in SGML. These SGML documents are then transformed into a presentable format, and then sent to the typesetter and printer. SGML is also used to exchange technical specifications for manufacturing. However, its complexities and the high cost of its implementation have meant that most businesses and individuals cannot afford to embrace this useful technology.

More information about SGML can be found at http://www.oasis-open.org/cover

With advances in the development of the World Wide Web there was a drive for a simpler approach.

Origins and Goals of XML

In 1996, the **World Wide Web Consortium (or W3C**, `http://www.w3.org`) began the process of designing an extensible markup language that would combine the flexibility and power of SGML with the widespread acceptance of HTML. The language that became XML drew on the specification of SGML, and indeed, was specified to be a subset of this language. Using SGML as a starting point allowed the design team to concentrate on making what already worked simpler. SGML already provided an open-ended language that could be extended by anyone for their own purposes. The intention that XML should be simpler than SGML was driven by the consideration of ease-of-use: in part the reading and writing of markup by persons using simple and commonly available tools, but also the simplifying of computer processing of documents and interchange datasets. Due to its many optional features, SGML is so complex that it is difficult to write generic parsers, whereas XML parsers are much simpler. In addition, XML leverages existing Internet protocols and software for easy data processing and transmission. Being a proper subset of SGML, XML also retains backwards compatibility with existing SGML-oriented systems, so data marked up in XML could still be used in these systems, saving SGML-based industries a lot of money in conversion costs, whilst leveraging the greater accessibility provided by the Web.

XML 1.0 became a **W3C** Recommendation in February 1998. The formal specification, including the grammar in Extended Backus-Naur Form (EBNF) notation, is readily available on the Web from the W3C (at http://www.w3.org/TR/REC-xml); and there is also an excellent annotated version by Tim Bray, one of the co-editors of the XML specification (at http://www.xml.com/axml/testaxml.htm).

An XML 1.0 FAQ maintained by Peter Flynn et al. *on behalf of the W3C's XML Special Interest Group at* http://www.ucc.ie/xml/ *provides extensive links to other topics related to XML.*

XML is a simple, standard way to delimit text data. It has been described as "the ASCII of the Web". It is as if you could use your favorite programming language to create an arbitrary data structure, and then share it with anyone using any other language on any other computing platform. XML tags name the concept you are describing, and named attributes modify the tagged structures. So, you can formally describe the syntax you have devised and share it with others.

Let's take a look at a simple example:

```
<?xml version="1.0"?>
<books>
   <book category="reference">
      <author>Nigel Rees</author>
      <title>Sayings of the Century</title>
      <price>8.95</price>
   </book>
   <book category="fiction">
      <author>Evelyn Waugh</author>
      <title>Sword of Honour</title>
      <price>12.99</price>
   </book>
</books>
```

Without worrying too much about the particulars of the syntax, we can immediately see how powerful a mechanism the simple addition of tags *describing* the information they envelop is.

This data description mechanism in XML means it is a great way to share information over the Internet, because:

- It is open; XML can be used to exchange data with other users and programs in a platform-independent way.
- Its self-describing nature makes it an effective choice for business-to-business and extranet solutions.
- You can share data between programs without prior coordination. As we shall see shortly, mechanisms in XML allow you to discover the structure of a class of XML documents.

To work with XML documents, the W3C has standardized an API (Application Programming Interface) for XML, so it is easy to create programs that read and write XML, while the developer community has devised a popular, complimentary, event-based alternative API. In addition, XML was designed for ready support of non-European languages and internationalization. Like HTML 4.01, XML is based upon the Universal Character Set (UCS), defined in the **ISO/IEC 10646 character set** standard (which is currently congruent with the somewhat better-known **Unicode** standard, `http://www.unicode.org`). All the features that propelled HTML to popularity are present in XML.

However, XML is not, directly, a replacement for HTML. You can read every word of the XML Recommendation (the World Wide Web Consortium's equivalent of a standard) and not find a single word related to visual presentation. Unlike HTML, which fuses data and presentation, XML is about data alone.

Although XML itself *is* data, the XML community has not forgotten presentation. Unlike traditional methods of presenting data, which relied on extensive bodies of code, the presentation techniques for styling XML are data driven. These range from the simple to the extremely complex. Regardless of the technique chosen, however, XML styling is accomplished through another document dedicated to the task, called a **style sheet**. In it a designer specifies formatting styles and rules that determine when the styles should be applied. The same style sheet can then be used with multiple documents to create a similar appearance.

The styles and rules are applied to an XML document's data at the time of presentation and can even be used to transform it into HTML – or even some other data format. One of the main threads of this book will cover the techniques for visually rendering data marked up in XML. They are powerful enough to surpass the styling features in HTML, but XML is not, at its heart, about visual styling.

Lastly, in spite of the hype on the Web, XML is not an apocalypse that will sweep away all that came before it. It is going to enable programmers to do many interesting things simply and flexibly, but XML is not a programming language, nor an object-based system, nor an operating system. It is a powerful, elegant technique for thinking about, exchanging, and presenting data in a platform-independent manner.

Now that we know a bit about what XML is, let's look at where it fits into the architecture of web applications.

Web Architectures: Past and Future

First generation web applications followed the traditional client-server model of software architecture. Some made use of a third tier in the form of a relational database, but all tiers were held together by arbitrary and inflexible methods. Ironically, this is contrary to the spirit of the Web – a loose, open confederation of resources held together by simple protocols. XML, by contrast, is a great enabler. It provides programmers with the tools to build true multi-tier distributed systems held together by open standard, self-describing data. Let's contrast the past style of web architecture with an XML-driven architecture.

Classic Web Architecture

Consider the classic web application architecture. The client application is a web browser acting on behalf of a human agent. The browser transmits a request for a page to an HTTP server. The request is accompanied by a series of parameter names and values. These may be appended to the page URL (HTTP GET) or sent separately (HTTP POST). (For more information on HTTP see `http://www.w3.org/Protocols/`.) The parameters and their names are determined by the application and must be made known to the client by including them in the page that requests them. Consequently, the developer of the server application must also create the client page. Anyone who wishes to make use of the server must use the client page or reverse engineer the request structure from the client page. Such reverse engineering is subject to failure whenever the server changes the structure of the request.

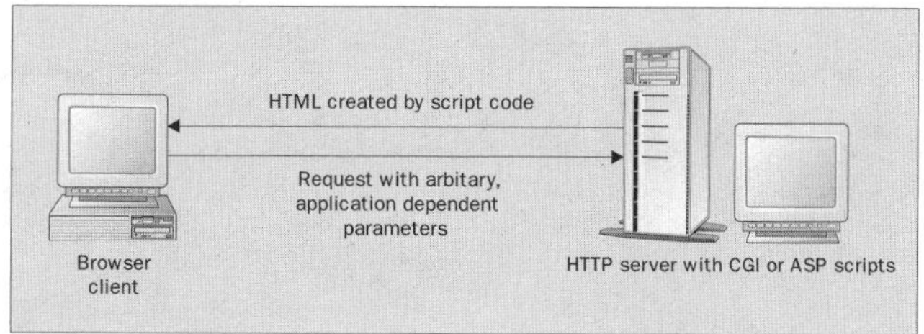

In this arrangement, the server satisfies the request by dynamically creating HTML via a CGI script or ASP. Such scripts may make use of a database or may do some processing of their own. There is rarely, if ever, any cooperation between HTTP servers to complete a request.

This architecture works well enough, of course, although it does have some notable limitations:

- We are restricted to a browser client.
- No one builds server pages to communicate with a programmatic agent or with another application. The structure of the request is implicit. You must either have the cooperation of the server application development team or reverse engineer the structure. As a result, parties other than the server side development team seldom build client applications.
- All content is delivered as HTML. This limits the ability of the client to do any post-processing, and the user is limited to the view determined by the server application at the time of delivery.
- If you want a different presentation, say a graph instead of a table, or perhaps a different sort order, you must make another round-trip to the server.
- The application is brittle; the client and the server must be in close synchronization. The slightest malformation of a request will typically break the server application.

So, how can XML help us with these problems?

Web Architecture with XML

Now we'll peek ahead and see what XML can enable in the future. A client – browser or program – sends an XML document as a request to a server. It contains named parameters much the way a traditional web application does. Unlike a traditional client, however, the structure of the request may be formally specified using a standardized mechanism obtained at runtime from the server. This mechanism documents the structure expected by the server and also allows the client to verify the correctness of the request before transmission. The server may also perform validity checking upon receipt.

Once the request arrives, the server may proceed in the fashion of traditional web applications, or may bring in some help. The XML doesn't address server-to-server communication per se, but innovative parties within the XML community have used XML to formalize such communication. Since the data a server would receive in such an exchange is also XML, it is quite easy for the first server to merge several documents together or transform a document into another format to satisfy a request. The same mechanism the client can use to discover structure is available to servers. Since XML is inherently hierarchical, it can readily encode non-relational sources of data. However, since most data maintained formally on servers is relational in nature, the XML community has given a great deal of thought and effort to matching relational data to XML structures. All these points make XML an excellent medium for exchanging data between servers and server-side applications. Once XML is chosen as the data exchange mechanism for a particular organization, programmers can quickly acquire or build components and libraries of utility routines for manipulating that data. These are equally useful for processing requests coming from client applications.

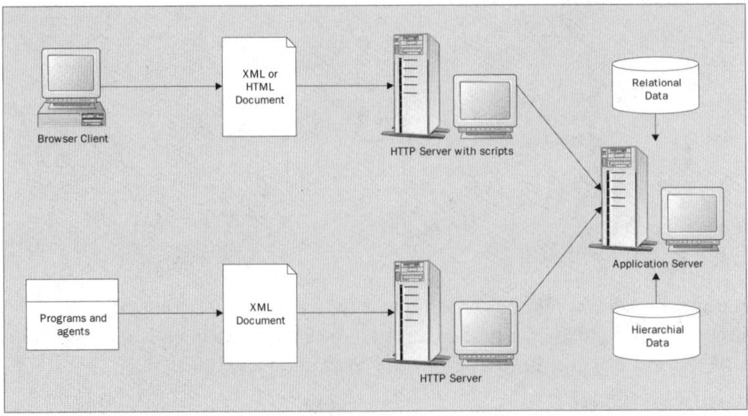

What does this do for us? To start, we are not limited to browser-based clients. XML is data and readily manipulated by programs. The same data can be styled for browser presentation or subjected to post-processing by an agent. The exchange mechanism – XML documents – makes no assumptions about the final use of the data. If the client is known to require HTML, a data driven transformation may be applied to an XML document to create the HTML page. The underlying application that created the XML need not be modified.

The coupling between the server application and the client is considerably looser because of the ability of a program to discover the structure of an XML document. Thus ambitious applications can be written to create documents with novel structures depending on the state of the application, which can still be interpreted without having to write custom software for each new type of document structure. More typically, industry standard tag sets will be created, and applications will use the structure discovery mechanism to protect against errors due to version changes.

In this vision of the future, every element of processing in our network of servers, clients, and applications is using the same mechanism for the exchange of data. Fortunately, that mechanism is extensible and subject to runtime discovery of structure. It is also supported on virtually every platform, is quite easy to use, and is able to process markup data from very different sources. Application developers are able to use data from nontraditional sources, and data from other servers to satisfy a client's request. This takes web development from client-server computing to a true multi-tier model.

This vision is not far from being realized.

The Nature of XML

Now that we have an idea of what we can do once we adopt XML, let's take a closer look and see how XML lets us attain our objectives. As we saw briefly earlier, XML is a simple approach to marking up content with tags to convey information. The tags delimit the content and the XML syntax lets us define structures of arbitrary complexity. It is all done with ordinary text, not binary data formats, making this a great solution for exchanging information between platforms. Virtually every general-purpose operating system that is not intended for embedded use handles text in some form. This helped HTML become so popular in such a short period of time. XML takes this to a new level because we can extend XML arbitrarily to meet new needs and uses. Because the extension mechanism is standard, we can automatically describe our extensions to anyone–programmer or machine–who reads our data. XML has several facets you should understand in order to fully appreciate and effectively use it for applications.

Self-Describing Data

The tags that delimit XML content name the specific element of data that they delimit. Named attributes are found in the tags that provide additional data about the element described. For example:

```
<car>
   <tyre_pressures>
      <front_pressure  units="psi">28</front_pressure>
      <back_pressure  units="psi">32</back_pressure>
   </tyre_pressures>
</car>
```

The data is self-describing to the extent that each item carries its own name that may be related to an external model for the real-world problem the document describes. So far, we have something that looks a lot like HTML. The meaning of HTML tags, though, is fixed by the W3C. If you want to describe something that is not covered by the HTML Recommendation, you will quickly find yourself talking to an audience of one. Consider a bit of XML and the same content presented as HTML:

```
<Person>
   <Name>
      <First>Thomas</First>
      <Last>Atkins</Last>
   </Name>
   <Age>30</Age>
</Person>
```

```
<TABLE>
   <TR>
      <TD>Thomas</TD><TD>Atkins</TD>
   </TR>
   <TR>
      <TD>age:</TD><TD>30</TD>
   </TR>
</TABLE>
```

Both forms describe a person in terms of his name and age. In the first form, XML, we can relate each bit of content to the real-world concept of a person. The parts of a person's name are delimited, and we know which name is the first name and which is the last. Provided we know something about people, the data's meaning is clear to us. The HTML form, by contrast, formats the data visually as a table, but there is no explicit way of knowing that we are dealing with people. One bit of organizational information, age, is hidden as content rather than structure. A human reading this might infer the proper context, but a computer will not, no matter how much we tell it about the rules of describing people.

The "eXtensible" part of XML involves a standard mechanism for defining new tags and their usage. Because it is standard, we have a fixed and formal way to describe these new tags and communicate them to other XML users. The same is true of the attributes you can apply to tags. The most recent proposals for defining an XML tag set for a document use XML syntax to write out the metadata – data about data – that communicates the structure of tags in a particular family of XML documents. Not only is our data self-describing, but the data *about* the data can be self-describing as well.

Let's now consider sets of XML tags to use in specific contexts.

Vocabularies

As we've hinted earlier, the most significant feature of XML is its inherent extensibility. In comparison, HTML began as a simple markup language (with a fixed tag set) for scientific papers to enable their exchange over the Internet, but it quickly evolved as browser developers added new features and tags to their software. Many of these additions to HTML were to provide for the delivery of multimedia features and flashy commercial web pages. Unfortunately, these tags were the semi-proprietary creations of individual companies, and often caused problems for other browsers. Some additions have become a formal part of HTML, but many remain proprietary. Regrettably, these additions have added little to HTML in the way of improved data modeling, semantic markup, or structured information exchange protocols.

In contrast, XML has always been intended to allow the easy and rapid construction of custom tag-sets specific to corporations, scientific disciplines, and other such domains. Whilst every corporation (or even individual!) could choose to define its own XML tag sets, one of the strengths of XML is the sharing of such "**vocabularies**", all of which use the same basic syntax, parsers, and other tools. Shared XML vocabularies provide more easily searchable documents and databases, and a way to exchange information between many different organizations and computer applications.

An XML "vocabulary" is a description of XML data that is used as the medium for information exchange, often within a specific domain of human activity (business, chemistry, law, music, for example).

An excellent resource for researching current XML vocabulary development is Robin Cover's "The SGML/XML Web Page" to be found at http://www.oasis-open.org/cover/.

Now would be a good time to introduce you quickly, without digging into the details of syntax, to some of the XML vocabularies around at the moment.

Scientific Vocabularies

The first real use of XML was with Peter Murray-Rust's "JUMBO" browser for the **Chemical Markup Language (CML)** (see http://www.xml-cml.org). CML has been referred to as "HTML with Molecules", but CML also provides for the conversion of various proprietary file formats without semantic loss, and the creation of structured documents suitable for professional publication.

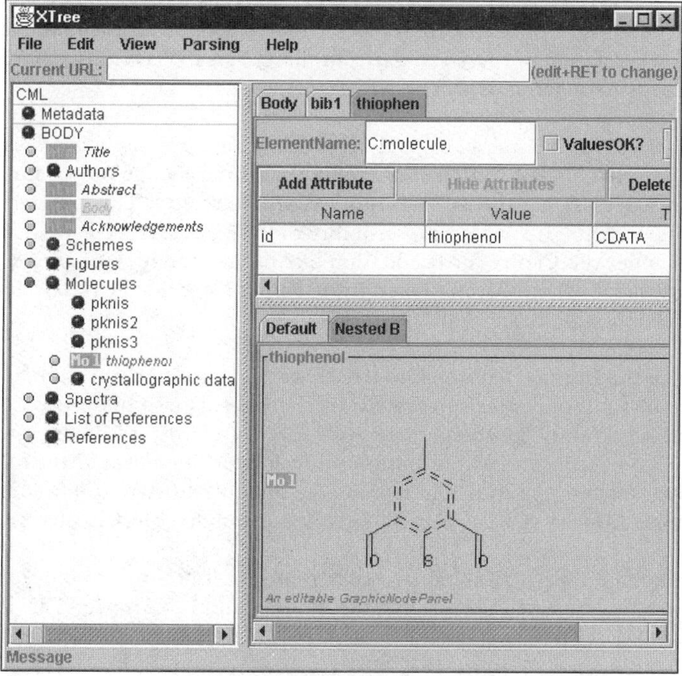

© (LGPL) Peter Murray-Rust

The fundamental language of science is mathematics, and there is an XML vocabulary named **MathML** that provides a way of exchanging mathematical expressions. MathML will replace the display of equations as mere pictures and/or ugly ASCII approximations allowing sophisticated rendering with suitable browsers, and provides an interchange format for symbolic algebra, geometry, statistics, and other math software tools. (For more information on MathML see http://www.w3.org/Math/.)

Other scientific vocabularies include the **Bioinformatic Sequence Markup Language (BSML)**, for the massive quantity of information produced by gene-mapping and sequencing (see http://www.visualgenomics.com/bsml/index.html); and NASA's **Instrument Markup Language (IML)** for the control of lab instruments and its first implementation, **Astronomical Instrument Markup Language (AIML)** – see http://pioneer.gsfc.nasa.gov/public/aiml/. These MLs are classic uses of XML vocabularies for structured technical documents, and the precise dissemination of scientific and technical information. Such use of XML has great promise for very powerful educational tools, as well.

Business Vocabularies

The most popular application of computing is commerce. The financial lifeblood of the world flows through computer networks using a variety of data formats. Most of these data formats are proprietary; indeed common public knowledge of international monetary wire-transfer protocols is probably undesirable! However, much fiscal and business information does need to be exchanged between companies, and this information benefits greatly from common information standards.

Businesses exchange both products and money, and such exchanges are described as transactions. These transactions often involve the exchange of legally binding documents on paper. Often, these documents can be exchanged electronically, using **Electronic Data Interchange (EDI)** standards. EDI defines a format for many of the business-to-business transactions that are the basis for most commerce. The origin of EDI in North America may be traced to the Transportation Data Coordinating Committee (TDCC) in the early 1970s. In the early 1990s, ANSI released the X12 standards (commonly known as "ASC X12"). The development of these standards in the U.S. is overseen by the not-for-profit **Data Interchange Standards Association (DISA)**.

Of course, like so many North American standards, X12 is not commonly used elsewhere in the world. Most of the world uses the **United Nations/Electronic Data Interchange for Administration, Commerce and Transport (UN/EDIFACT)** standard (see http://www.unece.org). The maintenance, development, and promotion of UN/EDIFACT is the responsibility of the **UN/EDIFACT Working Group (EWG)**, an empowered group under the Centre for Facilitation of Administration, Commerce and Trade (CEFACT). The European Commission's **Open Information Interchange (OII)** service is another resource for information regarding UN/EDIFACT.

The **Open Buying on the Internet Consortium (OBI)** is a non-profit organization that is developing open standards for business-to-business procurement over the Internet (see http://www.openbuy.org). Although OBI v2.0 is currently based upon the ASC X12 standards, it is being reworked as an XML vocabulary. Meanwhile, Ariba and Microsoft have developed **CommerceXML (cXML)** for similar purposes (http://www.cxml.org/home), and CommerceOne (http://www.commerceone.com) provides the **Common Business Library (CBL)**. We will look at e-commerce in Chapter 12.

Microsoft has also initiated the **BizTalk Framework** initiative (http://www.biztalk.org), which has support from companies like SAP, CommerceOne, Boeing and BP/Amoco. This library of XML schemas and message descriptions is intended "to enable electronic commerce and application integration".

Another industry initiative, with widespread support, is the **RosettaNet** organization (http://www.rosettanet.org/), which is describing business-to-business information exchange using XML, UML and other common protocols. The foundation of this is two master dictionaries: firstly, a set of technical specifications for all product categories; and secondly, descriptions of companies and business transactions.

A few years ago, Microsoft, Intuit, and CheckFree joined to develop an open specification for the online transfer of financial data, called **Open Financial Exchange (OFE, or OFX)**, based upon SGML. However, OFX was never fully valid SGML since it allowed the inclusion of undefined elements. In 1998, migration to XML was stated as a goal of OFX. As of Spring 1999, OFX and its related standards are being migrated to a newer ML, called **Interactive Financial Exchange (IFX)** – at http://www.ifxforum.org/.

Legal Vocabularies

Digital representation of paper forms remains a problem for the business, legal, and medical communities. One possible solution is UWI.Com's **Extensible Forms Description Language (XFDL)**. This XML vocabulary supports precision layout, computations, input validation, digital signatures, and legally binding transaction records and audit trails. (For more information see http://www.uwi.com/xfdl/).

Medical Vocabularies

Medical information covers the gamut of XML's uses. Medical reference materials and related scientific papers using XML markup can be easily translated for presentation in various forms; and they are also more readily found and retrieved using structured searches that are more focused and powerful than simple Boolean free-text searches. Clinical, financial and administrative information must be exchanged between numerous independent computer systems, at numerous different organizations ranging from hospitals to pharmacies to insurance companies and/or government agencies. In 1987, an ANSI X12 initiative produced the **Health Level 7 (HL7)** standard that is used in the majority of large U.S. hospitals today, and which is also used in Australia, Western Europe, Israel and Japan. Although this standard is not currently implemented using XML, progress is being made toward an XML version.

Computer Vocabularies

The Internet and the WWW also require ways to describe the exchange of information from disparate sources and of various formats. Here we list just a few.

One of the earliest XML vocabularies is the **Channel Definition Format (CDF)**, a format that was proposed by Microsoft to permit web sites to offer frequently updated collections of information (called "channels") for automatic delivery to subscribers. Unfortunately, the submission of CDF to the W3C is over 2½ years old, and is no longer XML-compliant (as it was based upon an early draft of the XML specification and includes now-illegal syntax).

There is **Structured Graph Format (SGF)**, an XML format for describing the structure of web sites, based upon the formal mathematics of structure graphs (http://www.isl.hiroshima-u.ac.jp/projects/SGF/index.html).

Netscape's Mozilla project is using an **XML-based User interface Language (XUL)**, as a cross-platform way of describing user interfaces. XUL can contain element types for UI controls, HTML4 markup for content data, and JavaScript for user event handling (http://www.mozilla.org/xpfe/xptoolkit/xulintro.html).

IBM's **Bean Markup Language (BML)** is an XML-based component configuration ML that is customized for the JavaBean component model. BML can be used to describe the creation of new JavaBeans, access and/or configure existing JavaBeans, bind events from one JavaBean to another, and call arbitrary methods in other JavaBeans (http://www.alphaworks.ibm.com/formula/bml).

Software distribution over a network could be controlled using the **Open Software Description (OSD)** format, proposed by Marimba and Microsoft (http://www.marimba.com/products/whitepapers/osd-wp.html).

Modern database design uses a rigorous design process that is based upon data modeling, often using the Unified Modeling Language (UML, which is *not* an XML-based markup language despite ending in "ML"). The Meta Object Facility (MOF) is an Object Management Group (OMG) standard for distributed data repositories and metadata management. The OMG, large systems companies (such as IBM, and Unisys) and database software companies (like Oracle, Rational, and Sybase) have promoted the merger of XML, UML, and MOF in the form of the **XML Metadata Interchange (XMI)** specification. Whilst this isn't strictly an XML vocabulary (since it's a superset of XML), XMI is a good example of the power of XML for non-document purposes (http://www-4.ibm.com/software/ad/features/xmi.html).

One of the most conservative technology domains is the switched public telephone network. For years, this network has used a rather complex protocol, Signaling System 7 (SS7). Recently, several XML-based alternatives have been proposed, including the **Call Policy Markup Language (CPML** – see http://www.dticorp.com/ESP%20white%20paper.htm). This is a by-product of a trend toward more open standards in the traditionally proprietary telecom industry. Voice-over-IP is another indication of the coming convergence between the voice and packet-switched networks, with key support from Lucent Technologies (formerly Bell Labs), Nortel Networks, and Cisco Systems.

As you might have noticed, many of these vocabularies are being defined collaboratively by groups of companies solely for the purpose of being able to exchange data readily. Let's now take a look at what that means in more detail.

The Main Features of XML Technology

Now that we have seen where XML came from and why, where it fits into distributed application architectures on the Web, and the names of a few of the specialised vocabularies that have been developed using it, let's take a closer look at the features and specifications involved in providing the core functionality of XML, in order of the chapters in this book.

Well-Formed XML

The rules of XML syntax are fundamental to everything we want to do with it. In the next chapter, we will help you to understand the features of "**well-formed**" XML. You'll find out what elements are, how to use them, and how attributes modify them. The idea of XML vocabularies will come up again as we start talking about the uses of XML. We'll also start thinking about standard **parsers** for manipulating XML documents in our applications. Basically, well-formed XML conforms to the syntax requirements of the W3C's XML 1.0 Recommendation. Parsers are processing tools that check that a document conforms to the syntax rules of XML (more on these in just a moment). Here is a simple well-formed document (don't worry about the precise details of the syntax yet):

```
<?xml version="1.0" ?>
<pet_store  store_ID="11218976">
   <purchases customer_ID="334343">
      <creature>
         <creature_type>llama</creature_type>
         <species>Vicuna</species>
      </creature>
      <feed>
         <daily feed>Ruminant grain feed</daily feed>
         <daily_feed_quantity>2</daily_feed_quantity>
      </feed>
   </purchases>
</pet_store>
```

Through practical examples in the next chapter, you'll start to see the advantages of separating content from presentation. HTML, which is related to XML, has definite limitations. That is why the common web browser is the only common HTML application. For all its utility, HTML has inherent problems, and XML provides a solution while retaining the simplicity and power that HTML used to change the face of computing. The basics of XML are the starting point for your migration to the next generation of web architecture.

Document Type Definitions

Once you sit down to write an XML vocabulary, you immediately run up against a pressing need: how do you specify the rules by which XML documents are written? If anyone can use the Extensible Markup Language to create their own markup vocabulary, how can we use XML documents in applications with any confidence? The answer is a set of information called a Document Type Definition (DTD). These definitions capture the rules a designer adds to extend the core rules of XML syntax and create a vocabulary to describe some problem or situation. This is the first mechanism you will encounter for the discovery of an XML vocabulary's structure. Many of the advantages we outlined for the coming web application architecture rely on this mechanism. By learning about DTDs, you become equipped with the tool to validate the documents your applications exchange, and you begin to have a chance to discover new vocabularies at runtime. Later on we will look at other mechanisms to express the structure of XML documents, but DTDs are currently the only officially approved way to do this.

Here is our pet store example from above, but this time with a DTD. (Again, don't worry too much about the syntax just yet):

```
<?xml version="1.0" ?>
<!DOCTYPE pet_store [
<!ELEMENT pet_store  (purchases?) >
<!ATTLIST    pet_store  storeID  CDATA  #IMPLIED >
<!ELEMENT  purchases  (creature*, feed*) >
<!ATTLIST    purchases  customer_ID  CDATA  #IMPLIED >
<!ELEMENT  creature  (creature_type, species)+  >
<!ELEMENT  creature_type  (#PCDATA) >
<!ELEMENT  species  (#PCDATA) >
<!ELEMENT  feed          (daily_feed, daily_feed_quantity)+ >
<!ELEMENT  daily_feed  (#PCDATA) >
<!ELEMENT  daily_feed_quantity  (#PCDATA) >
]>
<pet_store  store_ID="11218976">
   <purchases customer_ID="334343">
      <creature>
         <creature_type>llama</creature_type>
         <species>Vicuna</species>
      </creature>
      <feed>
         <daily feed>Ruminant Grain Feed</daily feed>
         <daily_feed_quantity>2</daily_feed_quantity>
      </feed>
   </purchases>
</pet_store>
```

As you can see, DTDs follow their own syntactic rules, but they enable you to make very definite statements about what is and is not a permissible document in a particular class of XML documents. This leads us directly to the distinction between validating and non-validating parsers. A non-validating parser only checks the document for well-formedness against the core rules of XML syntax. A validating parser also checks a document against a DTD to decide if it is legitimate according to the rules in the DTD. But, why would you ever want a non-validating parser? How do you point a validating parser to its DTD? How do you express a problem or application in terms of a DTD? These questions will be answered in Chapter 3.

Data Modeling

One key to success in an XML application is an effective XML vocabulary. A vocabulary is the specification of elements, their attributes, and the structure of documents that conform to your plan. You can no more create a good XML-enabled application without an effective vocabulary than you can write a database application with a weak database schema.

An effective vocabulary describes the relevant objects in your problem in a way that is expressive of the problem while permitting easy access to your data. Not only do you have to capture the essence of the objects you want to talk about, you have to do so in a way that works with, not against, the processing you will do. Creating a good vocabulary is an exercise in data modeling. There are no hard and fast rules, nor are there rote algorithms. There are, however, best practices and techniques. You'll learn these in Chapter 4 and get some practice defining DTDs. Working through this chapter is like learning about software design and good programming practices. You don't need it to start writing applications, but the applications you write will be better for having studied this material.

Document Object Model

Once you have the vocabulary designed for your needs, you can then start to decide on other aspects of your application. In the new web application architecture, applications must manipulate XML documents, and parts of those documents. Clients will build requests. Servers will parse those requests, construct new requests, and compose responses. The **Document Object Model** is one API for doing this. This specifies a set of objects and interfaces for manipulating HTML and XML documents. The W3C maintains the **Document Object Model** (DOM) Recommendation, and it is one of the two most widely supported APIs for working with XML documents (the other being the Simple API for XML, as we'll see in the next section).

The DOM provides a tree-structured view of the document. A DOM-compliant parser reads the entire document and offers a view of the document by constructing a 'tree' of objects in memory. The major component structures of the document are nodes in the object tree. Accessing items and manipulating them is a matter of navigating the parse tree using the DOM interfaces. Chapter 5 will explain the DOM object model and teach you how to work with XML documents in code using the DOM interfaces.

Simple API for XML

The other major API for working with XML documents is the Simple API for XML (SAX). Unlike the DOM, SAX is not the product of a standards organization. It is the ad hoc product of a number of XML developers who needed an effective API early in the development of XML. SAX remains popular because it takes a different approach to providing access to XML documents. Instead of presenting applications with a tree view of the complete document, SAX offers events as it parses the document. Events are of the form of, "here is a start tag; here is some element content; here is an end tag," and so forth. A SAX-compliant parser makes no effort to retain the document; instead, it notifies the using program as it processes each part of the document. What happens in response to an event is up to the program using the parser. A program has complete responsibility for maintaining state about the document. It can keep as much or as little information around as it needs in order to satisfy the requirements motivating the application.

As you might imagine, this makes for a fairly compact parser that makes minimal demands on system resources. This makes it ideal for handling very large XML documents. If you have a parts catalog that consists of a single 16 megabyte XML document, you won't want to read it all into memory. Although the DOM is the most commonly encountered API for XML today, SAX parsers are available. Chapter 6 will show you what SAX is, how to work with it, and when to use it. You'll get a practical introduction to working with an XML document using a SAX-compliant parser.

Namespaces and Schemas

Hopefully, as you learn more about XML and the advantages it provides to applications, you will be ready to build more sophisticated documents and vocabularies. You may be eager to do more in terms of automatically discovering structure. If you try this with DTDs, you will encounter some limitations. The answer to these limitations is already under development in the form of XML **Schemas** and **Namespaces**.

More and more XML vocabularies are being developed as the popularity of XML grows. One consequence is that developers are starting to encounter vocabularies from other developers that are useful to a problem on which they are working. Such vocabularies don't answer all their needs, but they do provide concepts that greatly simplify the task of developing a new vocabulary. If you are working on a new application for a common problem, chances are that someone has thought about the problem and written an XML vocabulary. If you can't use it whole, you'd like to build on it by borrowing the interesting bits. Even if you are working in isolation, you will want to build things in pieces; big problems are solved by breaking them down into a series of smaller problems.

The XML community recognized this problem and devised namespaces as an answer. A namespace is a source of names on which a document designer wishes to draw. By attributing the source, you can borrow from other sources and use partial vocabularies without ambiguity. If you are tackling a big problem, you can write a series of vocabularies covering small parts of the overall problem, then mix XML from the various vocabularies using namespaces.

A problem with this is that DTDs – the way we specify vocabularies in XML 1.0 – don't let you use namespaces. DTDs have other problems, as Chapter 7 will show you. The emerging solution is schemas, a replacement for DTDs using the syntax of XML. This chapter will explain several different approaches to schemas and demonstrate the benefits of schemas using our book catalog example. The DTD developed in Chapter 3 will be converted into schema form. You will see some of the benefits that schemas offer over DTDs. Finally, you'll gain exposure to working with schemas in code as we build a simple element concordance utility using browser-based script code.

Linking and Querying

One of the defining characteristics of HTML is linking. It is probably the most popular single feature of that markup language. When you think about it, relational databases do a form of linking themselves, using foreign keys to bring in data from another table. Any technology that expects to be part of robust applications must have some provision for linking bodies of data together. XML isn't immune to the charms of linking. Many developers wish to link to one XML document to another, or link non-XML content to an XML document. Images and other binary data could accompany an XML document if we had links in XML. Linking is a major area of investigation for the XML community. Several proposals are working their way through the W3C, notably XLink and XPointer. Chapter 8 will fill you in on these proposals. You'll see how you can use XML linking in your applications. Since there is no standard support for linking in XML parsers, you'll see how the common forms of links might be implemented.

Another area of some interest to the XML community is querying. There should be some way to pass some criteria to an XML parser and receive a collection of the document pieces that meet those criteria. With such capability, large XML documents can become a sort of database. Quite apart from the database-like aspects of querying, you will find that querying is central to transformations, a key model for manipulating and changing XML. Chapter 8 will give you knowledge of XML query syntax drawn from the major proposals set forth for XML.

Transforming XML

One very powerful XML technique is transformation. Transformations allow a programmer to map an XML document in one form into another form based on a set of rules that are applied to the first document. XML transformations are used to translate between similar XML vocabularies as well as translating XML documents into other text-based file formats like comma separated values. This is an important tool for web developers. If you are merging existing resources, you may need to perform some efficient transformations to get to a common format. If you are working between partners, say in a business-to-business setting, you will almost certainly need to transform documents from one format to another. Chapter 9 shows you how to achieve this. The interesting thing about transformations is that the mapping is specified in a separate document rather than code. If you need to dynamically translate between a series of related formats, you can develop a series of rule documents. At runtime, you determine which transformation is needed and simply apply the appropriate set of rules to the document at hand. This is particularly useful for business-to-business and supply chain applications.

Transformations in their most recent form are part of a styling language for XML called the Extensible Style Language (XSL). In fact, the transformation language is called XSL Transformations (XSLT). XSLT is intended primarily to organize an XML document for use with XSL styling. Even though it is not designed as a general-purpose transformation language, XSLT is quite flexible and will allow you to perform most translation, sorting, and organization tasks in XML without writing your own procedural code. Instead, you write rules for transforming XML based on the context in which elements appear. In Chapter 9, you will get a look at the XSLT syntax programmers can use to specify transformation rules. You will learn techniques for locating a particular element in a document based on criteria you supply. You will then learn how to specify the transformation to perform on the source XML document. When you are finished, you will have a good grasp of performing data driven manipulation of XML documents using XSLT.

XML and Databases

Web front ends to relational databases are quite common. The XML data model is inherently hierarchical, though, making for some difficulties matching it to the relational model used by most common databases. Although interfacing XML with relational data doesn't directly make use of the unique features of XML, it allows existing data to be introduced into new systems. Since XML is a popular and platform-neutral way to connect two parties together, programmers need a way to interface XML and databases. Many database vendors are adding native support for XML into their engines in recognition of this fact.

XML is primarily hierarchical in nature, while most common database systems in use today are relational. This leads to some issues in mapping one to the other. Chapter 10 explores effective strategies for mapping XML vocabularies to relational tables and back again. After examining the different degrees to which XML can be used to change the way applications interface with the data tier, the chapter will move on to develop a generic script that can be used to define tables in a relational database that will map to your XML schema. With these tools in hand, you will be positioned to construct the part of your application that connects the server application to data on the back end.

Server to Server

XML-enabled web applications can be connected to build systems. Until recently, most programmers viewed web applications as strictly client-server. A web client got its information from a web server. While the server might access a database, it did not request support from another web server. As time goes by and you have more and more application resources hosted by web servers, though, the ability to enlist more than one server to solve a problem becomes important. Letting one server call on another for data and processing lets us build sophisticated distributed applications from pre-existing applications. Since these systems often utilize differing server software and distributed computing technologies, XML is needed to provide a layer of abstraction in order to integrate dissimilar systems. Obtaining XML from another server, manipulating it, then passing the results to the client may satisfy a client request. A number of techniques for doing this efficiently using XML are under development. Some of these are XML-RPC, the Simple Object Access Protocol (SOAP), and Web Distributed Data Exchange (WDDX).

XML-RPC is a convention for remotely executing a procedure that resides on a server. It is similar to conventional RPCs in that it lets us name a procedure to execute and provide a list of parameter values. It uses XML as the format for doing this, thereby eliminating platform-specific problems. Because it is XML, it is very easy for a programmer to make a local resource available for remote execution. Implementations of XML-RPC are available for a number of common platforms.

SOAP is similar to XML-RPC and also uses XML to permit access to an object's methods and properties over HTTP. XML is used to describe the methods invoked and the parameters passed so as to avoid dependencies on any particular distributed object technology.

WDDX is a technique for serializing data structures using XML. It can be used as a low-level mechanism for returning database results across the Internet, for example.

Chapter 11 will equip you with knowledge of these and other methods of server-to-server communication using XML. XML-RPC, SOAP, and WDDX are clever applications of XML to the problem of network communication. With these technologies in hand, you will be better positioned to build multi-tier, distributed systems from your existing and future web-based resources.

When you are finished with Chapter 11, you will have a better appreciation of when different techniques are most effective. You will see a practical example of server-to-server communication when we see how one server gets book catalog information from another server regarding a book that is unavailable on the first server.

eBusiness and XML

XML is widely touted as a solution for the problem of exchanging data between applications. E-commerce, particularly business-to-business buying, is on the forefront of this use of XML. For many years, Electronic Data Interchange (EDI) was the standard for business-to-business data exchange (see http://www.geocities.com/WallStreet/Floor/5815/ for more information). EDI, however, has a number of drawbacks that effectively limit its use to large businesses and high-volume transactions. It uses proprietary networks and data formats for the exchange of data. As a consequence, implementing EDI systems has been costly and time-consuming. Small businesses typically couldn't afford the expense. The benefits of XML over the public Internet are changing that. Appropriate XML vocabularies are being defined to match the original EDI structures. This permits XML EDI implementations to leverage the availability of third party XML tools and parsers.

In Chapter 12, you'll see how XML is being applied to EDI to create a common, low cost infrastructure for electronic buying. This is quite a jump compared to the server-to-server communications we considered in the last chapter. In going from one partner to another, we are jumping formats as well as physical servers. The tools for vocabulary discovery become more important. The tools for data transformation become essential. Chapter 12 ties this information together.

The popularity and power of XML is also gaining it a foothold in data exchange situations beyond EDI. Simplicity, it seems, is a virtue. Whether you are interested in XML for EDI, some other standard, or simply for exchanging data between two proprietary applications, the lessons illustrated in Chapter 12 will better equip you for solving your own computing problems. Consider our book catalog example. What do we do when we want to present our catalog to a bookseller? We cannot assume they will use our vocabulary exclusively, and we must have a commerce mechanism if they are to buy any of our books. The answer lies in standard commercial vocabularies for the exchange of such data.

Styling

Although we've stressed the importance of separating data from presentation and the value of directly connecting one application to another, you will eventually want to present XML format data to a human user. Browser-based delivery will always be important, even in the new web architecture. Over the near term future, browser-based clients will continue to dominate. Some applications are even primarily about the display of such data. If this describes your requirements, you need to know about styling. I stressed that the XML community has devised several data-driven techniques for converting raw XML into richly formatted visual presentations. This data-driven approach stands in contrast to the traditional method of hard coding styling into script code. XML styling is an important tool for web developers. It is how user interfaces are quickly implemented for XML data, and how many interfaces can be applied to a single body of data delivered to a client. It is what enables a web server to deliver HTML to a restrictive client without modifying the code that creates the data. It is how web clients can let users switch between views without making another round-trip to the server for essentially the same information.

The techniques used for XML styling vary in their complexity and sophistication, and we cover the most important in Chapter 13. Perhaps the simplest technique is **Cascading Style Sheets** (CSS). These are not strictly from the XML community; rather, their use has been extended as XML developers borrowed them from the HTML-specific web development world. They are a basic yet capable means of assigning specific styling information to named XML elements. This is much in the way your favorite word processor assigns font, pitch, color, and other styling details to named styles in your document.

Another way of addressing styling is the **Extensible Stylesheet Language** (XSL). This outgrowth of XML marries the style assignment concerns of CSS with the expressive nature of XML. Programmers use XSL to specify the mapping of XML data into visual content. Unlike CSS, XSL lets you assign styling based on the context of the XML data, and even perform processing by embedding script code in your XSL style sheets.

Wireless Application Protocol and WML

Data marked up with XML tends to take more space than the same data encoded in a native binary format. This is generally not a problem with web applications as the bandwidth available from even a dialup connection is sufficient to move routine volumes of XML data. New wireless devices, however, typically support much lower data rates. These devices are the first step away from a homogeneous web composed of browsers to an exciting, heterogeneous web made up for traditional and non-traditional clients. These clients will have varying capabilities, so varying techniques must be used to deliver data and content. Can we use XML with unconventional clients such as cell phones and pocket organizers?

A novel approach to the problem is the **Wireless Application Protocol** (WAP). It makes clever use of a tokenized binary representation of XML to match the compact form of binary data with the standardized, self-describing form of XML. Unlike XML, though, WAP operates at a number of levels. It specifies components for various layers of networking protocols as well as the application layer. An industry association called the WAP Forum is the main driver behind this initiative. It coordinates its activities with the W3C, IETF, and other standards groups to promote this protocol.

Chapter 14 will show programmers what constitutes WAP, what constitutes the **Wireless Markup Language** (WML) and how the pieces work together to deliver self-describing data over low-bandwidth wireless networks.

An Example Application of XML

In the following two chapters we will work on the development of a marked up version of a publisher's book catalog (by sheer coincidence it just happens to be a Wrox one). This marking up of the catalog and its schema will then be used throughout the book to demonstrate the various aspects of the use of XML technologies that we cover in each of the subsequent chapters. These illustrations of the use of XML are largely independent of one another, relating strongly to the topic of the chapter, but each example does draw on what you will have learnt in earlier chapters. For integrated studies of the use of XML for applications, however, we will refer you to the case studies at the back of the book. The Book Catalog application it is a fairly straightforward example in which we show how XML can be used for both traditional document markup and general data modeling. In it we'll develop an XML vocabulary that includes typical publishing metadata. Such a vocabulary can be used as the basis for sending structured information relating to any type of transaction between publisher and clients/consumers: searching for titles; listings of titles with pricing information; requests for more deliveries of a title; monitoring the stocking of books in bookstores; publishing data or content to the Web; and so on. The resulting XML document frees up information to be used anywhere in the business process where pertinent information needs to be exchanged in a platform independent fashion.

Summary

In this chapter we have discussed the reasons underlying the development of markup languages in general, and said a little about the motivations for XML. We then discussed the effects of XML on the architecture of web applications. Some of these effects are potential, some have already been realized, but the overall evolution towards using open standards of data interchange to build distributed applications with loosely coupled components seems clear.

We then looked in more detail at the features of XML that are permitting this evolution to take place. The crucial fact being that that XML is a meta-language syntax standard that allows the production of task-specific vocabularies that can nonetheless be used with generic APIs. We then listed some of the most important standard-based vocabularies that are in use in, or are in development for, networked communication systems of many types.

Lastly, we briefly discussed the main XML technologies surrounding the core W3C XML 1.0 Recommendation.

Now let's move on to look at the core syntax of XML.

2

XML Syntax

In this chapter we will take a detailed look at the basics of XML syntax, covering the essential aspects of a basic document instance. By the end of this discussion you will be able to author basic XML documents for your own purposes. As part of the explanation we'll also begin developing the foundations for a **Book Catalog application** using XML to describe/model the data required for both bibliographic description of books and a dynamic database that supports all the features of a traditional printed catalog. This can then be used as the basis for providing e-commerce features that are only possible on the Internet.

> *You can find the XML 1.0 Recommendation (and other information) via* `http://www.w3.org/XML`. *There is also an annotated version of the specification at* `http://www.xml.com/axml/axml.html`

Markup Syntax

XML markup describes and provides structure to the content of an XML file or data packet, more generally known as an **XML entity**. This markup is comprised of tags that delimit different sections of content, provide references to special symbols and text macros, or convey special instructions to the application software and comments to the document's editors.

Hopefully you are familiar with the markup tags of HTML elements:

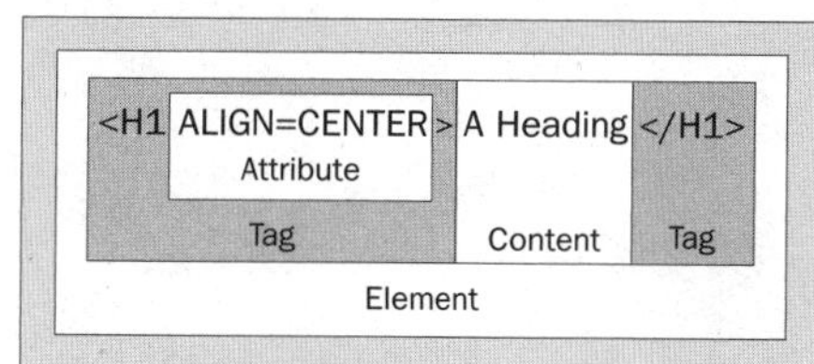

The structure of XML elements is essentially the same as in HTML, and XML markup has the same angled brackets to delimit tags beginning with a less-than (<) character and ending with a greater-than (>) character, but that is about as far as things go.

Unlike HTML, nearly all XML markup is case-sensitive, including element tag names and attribute values; that is:

```
Book ≠ BOOK ≠ book ≠ bOoK
```

XML's design goals of internationalization and simplified processing are the reasons for this case-sensitivity. Most non-English languages don't divide the alphabet into separate cases, and many letters (even within the Roman alphabet) may not have an upper or lower-case equivalent. For example, in French, the upper-case equivalent of "ç" is not necessarily "Ç" (it may just be "C"). The Greek letter "sigma" has one upper-case form, but two lower-case forms; Arabic uses multiple forms of the same "letter"; and so on. Case folding has numerous pitfalls, particularly with non-ASCII encodings, and XML's designers wisely chose to avoid these problems.

Let's look at how XML allows for internationalization.

Characters

Because XML is intended for worldwide use, characters are not limited to the 7-bit ASCII character set. XML specifies that characters are the numbers defined in the 16-bit+ Unicode 2.1 character set (at `http://www.unicode.org` – currently congruent with ISO/IEC 10646 – see also `http://www.iso.ch`). These are relatively new standards, and so much of the world's text isn't yet stored in Unicode. However, it was designed to be a superset of most existing character encodings, and so the conversion of legacy data to Unicode is straightforward. For example, converting ASCII to Unicode merely requires stuffing a zero into the high-order byte of the 16-bit character (while preserving the low-order byte as is).

Another bit of computer character history involves ligatures (e.g. combined "fi" or "ff" characters inherited from various typesetting systems), and "half-width katakana" from early attempts to handle Japanese text. Although these relics are included in the Unicode standard, their use must be discouraged – ligatures, for instance, are not really characters, they're a form of print styling that are best handled during the presentation of text, not embedded within the text data.

> *For a good introductory tutorial on character code issues see this page* `http://www.hut.fi/u/jkorpela/chars.html` *by Jukka Korpela.*

Legal XML characters include three ASCII C0 control characters, all normal ASCII display characters, and almost all other Unicode character values (shown in hexadecimal):

Character values (hexadecimal)	Description
`09`	Horizontal tab (HT)
`0A`	Line-feed (LF)
`0D`	Carriage-return (CR)
`20..7E`	ASCII display characters
`80..D7FF`	Unicode characters (inc. "Latin-1")
`E000..F8FF`	"Private Use Area"
`F900..FFFD`	CJK (Chinese-Japanese-Korean) Compatibility Ideographs
`10000..10FFFF`	Surrogate equivalents and "High Private Use Area"

Unicode has provided blocks of over 137,000 characters called the "Private Use Areas" for application-specific characters. Of course, any exchange of XML data using these private characters requires a separate agreement as to the interpretation of these characters, and thus this portion of Unicode should not be used for XML data objects that are intended to be widely exchanged.

Names

Structures used in XML are almost always named. All XML **names** must begin with a letter, underscore (_), or colon (`:`); and are continued using valid **name characters**. Valid name characters include the preceding, plus digits, hyphens (`-`), or full stops (periods). In actual practice, the colon character should not be used, except as a namespace delimiter (see Chapter 7). It is important to remember that letters are not limited to ASCII characters, so that non-English-speaking users of XML may use their own language for markup.

> *The XML specification also defines a related concept called a **name token** (typically abbreviated to **nmtoken**) that is any mixture of name characters without restriction on the initial characters. We won't need to talk about name tokens in this chapter, except insofar as they can be used in attribute values (see later), but they become important when we move on to the discussion of valid XML documents in the next chapter.*

The one other restriction upon names is that they may not begin with the string "`xml`", "`XML`", or any string which would match any variation of those three characters, in that sequence ("`xMl`" or "`Xml`", for example). Names beginning with these characters are reserved for W3C use only.

The following are legal names:

```
Book
BOOK
Wrox:Book_Catalog
ΑΓΔ
Conseil_Européen_pour_la_Recherche_Nucléaire_(CERN)
```

Note that the first two names are *not* equivalent – as discussed earlier, XML names are case-sensitive (unlike HTML). The third is an example of a name that uses the proposed namespace delimiter (the colon) – see Chapter 7 for more information about XML Namespaces. The last two examples are reminders that Greek and French are just as acceptable as English for XML names.

The following are *not* legal names:

```
-Book
42book
AmountIn$
E=mc²
XmlData
XML_on_NeXt_machines
```

The first two examples use characters that are not legal at the beginning of a name, even though these characters are legal name characters ('-' and '4'). The third and fourth examples use characters that are never legal in a name ('$' and the superscript '2'). The last two examples violate the "xml-is-reserved" restriction (unless, of course, these were defined by the W3C). In both this case and the first two examples, if the first character were, say, an underscore (e.g., "_42book", "_xml", or "_XML"), then these names would be legal.

Now that we know how to properly construct names in XML syntax, let's see how we make use of them.

Document Parts

A **well-formed** XML document is comprised of three parts:

- An optional **prolog.**
- The **body** of the document, consisting of one or more **elements,** in the form of a hierarchical tree that may also contain **character data**.
- An optional "miscellaneous" **epilog**, comprised of comments, processing instructions (or PIs), and/or white space that follows the end of the element tree.

More details of these aspects will be given soon.

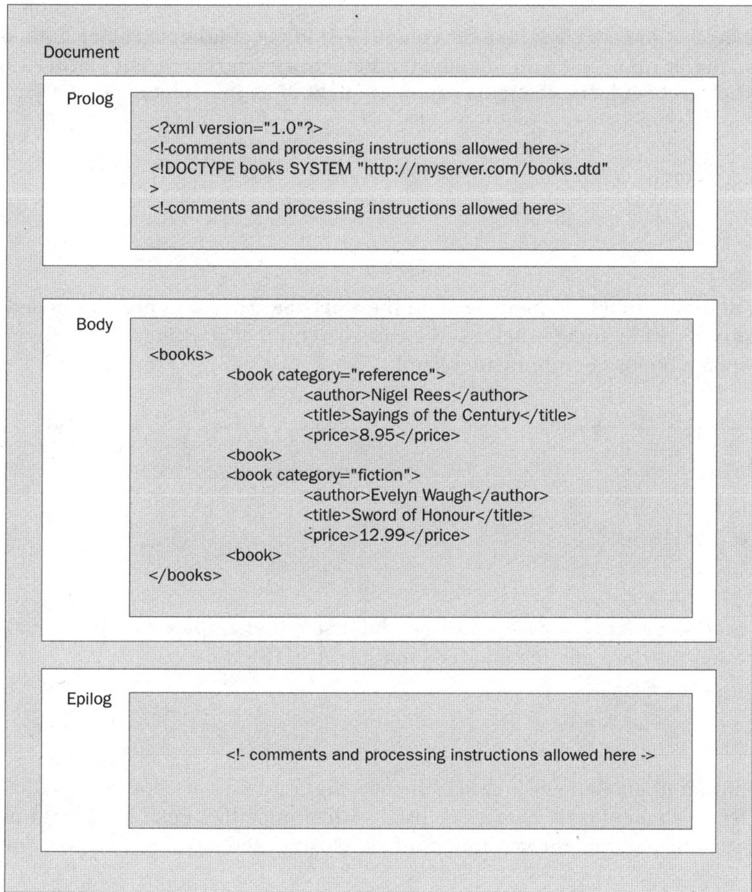

Document
Prolog
<?xml version="1.0"?>
<!-comments and processing instructions allowed here->
<!DOCTYPE books SYSTEM "http://myserver.com/books.dtd"
>
<!-comments and processing instructions allowed here>
Body
<books>
<book category="reference">
<author>Nigel Rees</author>
<title>Sayings of the Century</title>
<price>8.95</price>
<book>
<book category="fiction">
<author>Evelyn Waugh</author>
<title>Sword of Honour</title>
<price>12.99</price>
<book>
</books>
Epilog
<!- comments and processing instructions allowed here ->

Since data objects may be well-formed XML without including a prolog and/or epilog, we'll wait to look into the details of those parts until after we've described the all-important middle part – elements and character data.

Elements

Elements are the basic building blocks of an XML markup. They may contain other elements, **character data**, character references, entity references, PIs, comments, and/or CDATA sections – these are collectively known as **element content**. (Don't worry as to what all these terms mean just yet as we'll explain them later. Just focus on the idea that the elements are the containers.) All XML data (except for comments, PIs, and white space) must be contained within elements.

Elements are delimited using tags, which consist of the **element type name** (a string literal) enclosed within a pair of angle brackets ("< >"). Every element must be delimited with a **start-tag** and an **end-tag, unlike loose HTML the end tag cannot be missed out**. The only exception to this rule is an element that has no content, known as an **empty element**, which may be represented with either a start-tag/end-tag pair, or using an abbreviated hybrid form, the **empty-element tag**. We will see examples of tags in the following sections.

An "element" is XML's container for content —it may contain character data, other elements, and/or other markup (comments, PIs, entity references, etc.). Since they represent discrete objects, elements can be thought of as the "nouns" of XML.

Let's look at tags in more detail.

Start-tags

The beginning delimiter of an element is called the **start-tag**. Start-tags are comprised of an **element type name**, enclosed within angle brackets. We can also think of start-tags as "opening" an element, much as we'd open a file or communications link.

The following are legal start-tags:

```
<Book>
<BOOK>
<Wrox:Book_Catalog>
<ΑΓΔ>
```

Do remember that, since XML is case-sensitive, the first two examples are *not* equivalent tags; also, element type names may use any legal letters, not just ASCII letters.

End-tags

The ending delimiter of an element is called the **end-tag**. End-tags are comprised of a forward slash ("/") followed by an element type name, enclosed within angle brackets. Every end-tag must match a corresponding start-tag, and might be thought of as "closing" the element that was opened by the start-tag.

The following are legal end-tags, corresponding to the start-tags in the prior example:

```
</Book>
</BOOK>
</Wrox:Book_Catalog>
</ΑΓΔ>
```

So a complete element with start- and end-tags would look like:

```
<some_tag> content goes here </some_tag>
```

Let's now take a look at the abbreviation for elements without content.

Empty-Element Tags

Empty elements may not have any content whatsoever. Let's say that we wanted to explicitly indicate certain points in our XML document (we'll see an example in the next section). We could just add a start- and end-tag pair without any text between:

```
<point1></point1>
```

Of course, if we only want to indicate a point, not provide a container, it would be better if we didn't have to waste space. So, XML specifies that an empty element may also be represented in an abbreviated form that is a hybrid of the start- and end-tags. This has the advantages of both brevity and giving an explicit indication that element content is neither expected nor permitted.

Empty-element tags are comprised of an element type name followed by a forward slash ("/"), enclosed within angle brackets:

```
<point1/>
```

It is possible for an XML data object to contain nothing but a single document element and some empty elements (probably with attributes)! Such a file might be used to include a program's configuration settings, or a C++ object template.

Tags: A Simple Example

Any simple ASCII text file is a singular container (the file), holding a sequence of smaller containers (the text lines), which in turn contain characters. The file is implicitly contained by its physical existence within its parent file system. But, while there is usually no explicit "beginning-of-file" delimiter, the "end-of-file" is often marked with a special control character ("*Ctrl-Z*" or its hexadecimal equivalent "`1A`", for example). The text line begins implicitly with the physical beginning of its parent (the file), but each text line does have an "end-line" delimiter in the form of carriage-return and/or line-feed character(s).

For example, here is our basic ASCII file (note: the line numbers are *not* part of the file's content):

```
A Simple Example
   by Yours Truly
This is the 3rd line of a simple 5-line text file.
...the 4th line...
And lastly, a final line of text.
```

When the same text is represented as an XML document, the implicit structure of the data is now made explicit (again, the line numbers are not part of the document):

```
<textfile>
   <line>A Simple Example</line>
   <line>   by Yours Truly</line>
   <line>This is the 3rd line of a simple 5-line text file.</line>
   <line>...the 4th line...</line>
   <line>And lastly, a final line of text.</line>
   <EOF/>
</textfile>
```

In this example, we've explicitly marked the beginning and end of the entire file content (lines 1 and 8), the beginning and end of each line of text therein (lines 2-6), and included a representation of the end-of-file marker (line 7). This is an explicitly described and verifiable structure, comprised of seven elements (one of which contains the rest) that are represented by three different element types (`<textfile>`, `<line>`, and `<EOF/>`).

Now that we know the requirements for element type names and how tags are used in elements, let's stand back a bit and take a look at the structure of XML documents.

Document Element

Well-formed XML documents are defined as being in the form of a simple hierarchical tree, each document having one, and only one, root node, called the **document entity** or the **document root**. This node may contain PIs and/or comments, and will always contain a sub-tree of elements, the root of which is called the **document element**. This element is the parent of all other elements in the tree, and it may not be contained in any other element. Because the document root and the document element are *not* the same thing, it is better not to refer to the document element as the "root element" (even though it is the root of the element sub-tree).

The beginning of the maximum document tree for any XML data object is:

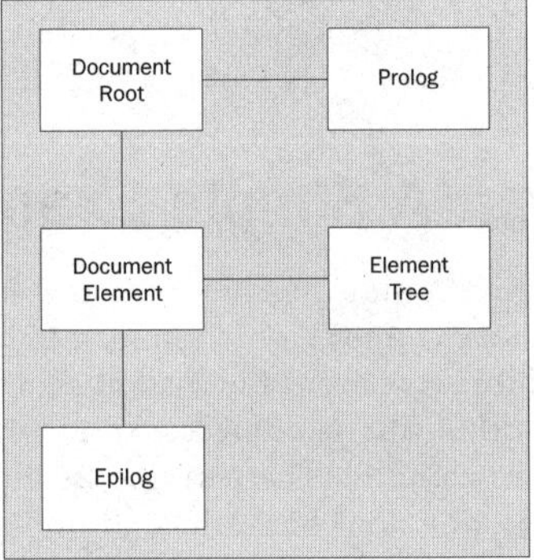

The beginning of the document tree that is implied by the last "textfile" example is:

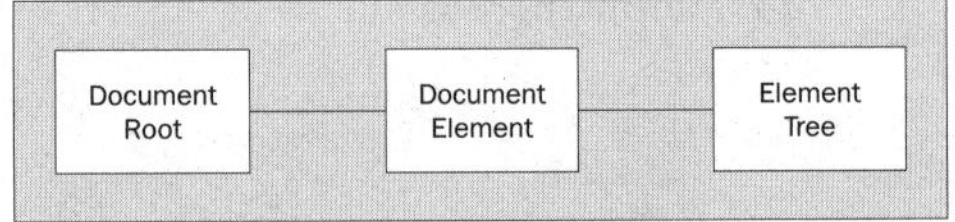

The document root of each XML document is also the point of attachment for the document's description using a DTD or Schema (see Chapters 3 and 7 for more information about these).

> **Any well-formed XML document must be comprised of elements that form a simple hierarchical tree, with a singular root node, called the "*document root*". This contains a secondary tree of elements, also with a singular root node, called the "*document element*".**

Now let's take a look at how the elements within the body of the document are arranged.

Child Elements

All other elements in an XML document are descendants ("children") of the document element. In the text file example earlier, the document element is the `<textfile>` element, and the `<line>` and `<EOF>` elements are its children.

The element tree that is implied by the last "textfile" example is:

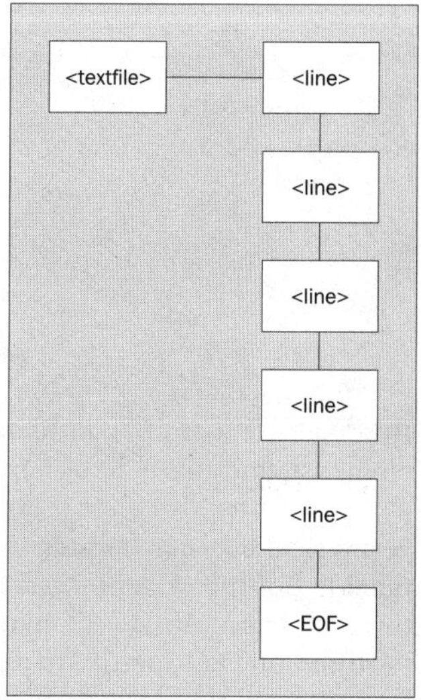

The element tree and its parent-child relationships are an important feature of XML.

Any element type may have one of four kinds of content. If the element type is only permitted to contain other elements or markup, but no character data, it is said to have **element content**. An element type that can contain both character data and other elements is considered to have **mixed content**. A subset of mixed content is an element that contains nothing but character data, which might informally be called "character content". Lastly, an "empty element" is one that may have no content whatsoever, although the empty-element tag may include attributes (which we'll come to shortly).

Element Nesting

XML imposes a key constraint upon elements – they must be properly nested. An analogy to physical objects helps illustrate what is meant by "properly nested". In fact, one might even claim that XML elements are things ("nouns") that must follow the same rules as any material thing.

Consider how this book might have been transported to you. After printing, this book and 23 others like it were packed into a box. Two boxes were packed into a carton, and cartons were loaded onto a truck and delivered to a bookstore. This could be represented by the following XML elements:

```
<truck>
   <carton>
      <box>
         <book>...</book>
         <book>...</book>
         <book>...</book>
```

```
            ...
            <book>...</book>
         </box>
         <box>
            <book>...</book>
            ...
            <book>...</book>
         </box>
      </carton>
      <carton>
      ...
      </carton>
      ...
      <carton>
      ...
      </carton>
   </truck>
```

In the above example, indentation is only to emphasize the hierarchical structure of these nested elements, and many books and cartons have been omitted for brevity.

A physical box can contain complete books, but can't have part of the book inside the box and part outside (for the sake of this example, let's ignore that moment in time when we're placing the book into the box – and sub-atomic particle behavior as well!). Likewise, a book can only be in one box, not partly in one and partly in another (again, I plead, let's not tear the books in half). And the boxes must be contained within cartons, which are in turn contained within the truck (please, no open doors and bumps in the road). XML elements must also follow this basic law of physical containment.

The tree that is implied by this example is:

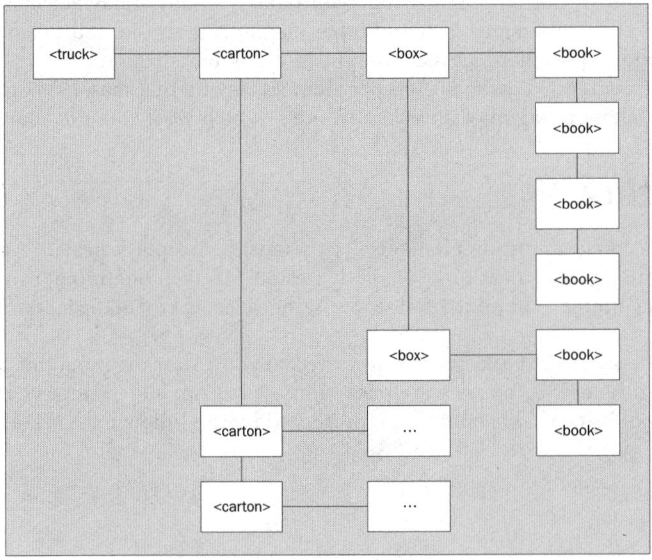

Improper Nesting

HTML and many word processing formats are not nearly so rigorous as XML when it comes to element structure. The following is an all-too-common example of overlapping HTML tags that works in most browsers but is *illegal* in XML:

```
<B>...some bold text, with <I>bold-italic</B> followed by plain italic text...</I>
```

Most HTML browsers have no trouble displaying this, but different browsers often do so in different ways:

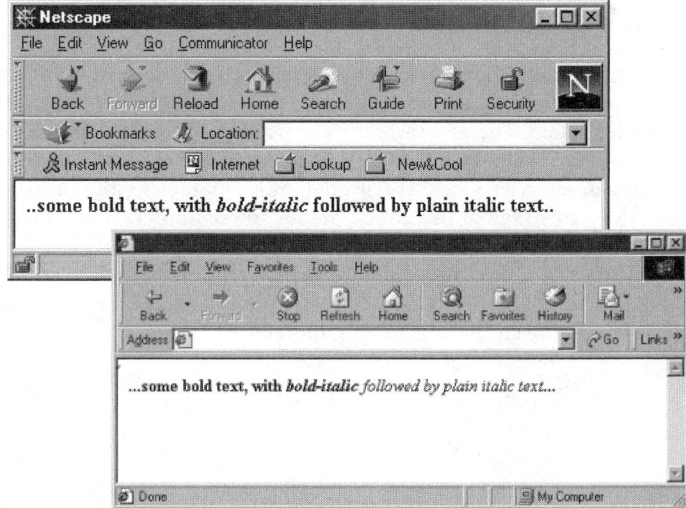

This situation might be fine for trivial text formatting, but when the tags are intended to describe real content, such as a name and address, this kind of overlap is ambiguous, or worse. Imagine trying to interpret the following (illegal in XML) construct:

```
<name>Joe Lee<address>Park Lane</name>Anytown</address>
```

The "tree" that would be implied by this example is:

```
name --- {name ∩ address} --- address
```

Since tags are not properly nested, a simple hierarchical tree of elements cannot be constructed. The middle element type hasn't been defined and doesn't really exist, it's just a synthetic placeholder to indicate the intersection of the two properly defined element types. While set theory and non-hierarchical trees would certainly allow us to use this sort of structure, its actual programming implementation would be a nightmare.

Since there's no way to differentiate between presentable and ambiguous overlaps, and the manipulation of the tree that is created by these overlaps would be so complex, XML simply prohibits any overlapping tags. The first time an improperly nested tag is encountered, the XML parser must report a "not well-formed" error, and will usually quit processing the document and report a "fatal" error (see the section on Parsers later in this chapter for more about fatal errors).

> ***HTML/SGML note**: HTML browsers will usually render even seriously broken tags, and SGML tools often attempt to continue processing a document, even after encountering errors. By design, XML doesn't allow this behavior.*

Before we move on to discuss attributes for our element types we need to say a few words about string literals in XML.

String Literals

String literals are used for the values of attributes, internal entities, and external identifiers. All string literals in XML are enclosed by a pair of delimiters, using either apostrophe (`'`) or quotation mark (`"`) characters. The one restriction upon these literals is that the character used for the delimiters may not appear within the literal – if an apostrophe appears in the literal, the quotation mark delimiter must be used, and vice versa. If both delimiter characters must appear in the literal, the one being used within the string (and at the same time for the delimiters) must be escaped, using an appropriate entity reference (`'` or `"`, which are both described later in this chapter, in the section on Character and Entity References).

The following are legal string literals:

```
"string"
'string'
'...his friend&apos;s cow said "moo"'
```

The following are illegal string literals:

```
"string'
'...his friend's cow said "moo"'
```

Technically speaking, in terms of the XML specification, the text between the string literal delimiters is part of the **character data** of the document, and we need to take a look at what this means before we deal with attributes.

Character Data

Character data is any text that isn't markup, and is the text content of an element or an attribute value.

The ampersand (&) and less-than (<) **characters** are markup delimiters, and thus may never appear in their literal form within character data (except in a CDATA section, which, again, we'll see later). If these characters are needed within character data, they must be escaped using the `&` or `<` entity references. These two escape sequences are part of the set of five such strings defined by the XML specification, and implemented in all compliant XML parsers (see the section on Character and Entity References later).

Remember, too, that because XML is intended for worldwide use, text means Unicode, not just ASCII (see the Characters section earlier in this chapter).

Now let's look at attributes.

Attributes

If elements are the "nouns" of XML, then attributes are its "adjectives".

Often there is some information about an element that we wish to attach *to* it, as opposed to the information that is contained within the element. This can be done using **attributes**, each of which is comprised of a name-value pair, using one of these two formats:

```
attribute_name="attribute_value"
attribute_name='attribute_value'
```

Attribute values must always be delimited strings (the rules for string literals apply) that may contain entity references, character references (explained later in this chapter), and/or text characters. However, as we have just explained, neither of the protected markup characters (< and &) may be used as simple characters within the attribute value – they must always be escaped using the `<` or `&` entity references.

> ***HTML note**: HTML permits numeric attributes, such as `<IMG WIDTH=300...>`; or undelimited attributes, like `<P ALIGN=LEFT>` – but neither is allowed in XML.*

Only one instance of an attribute name is allowed within the same start-tag or empty-element tag. For example, the following would *not* be legal in XML, as `src` occurs twice within the tag:

```
<img src="image1.jpg" src="altimage.jpg">
```

This restriction greatly simplifies the XML parser's handling of attributes.

As we've just hinted, both start-tags and empty-element tags may include attributes within the tag. For example, going back to our books, boxes, cartons, and trucks example from before, if we wished to attach a number to each carton of our book shipment, we could use the following attributes:

```
<carton number="0-666-42-1">
   ...
</carton>
<carton number='0-666-42-2'>
   ...
</carton>
```

In this example, the attribute name is "`number`" and the values are "`0-666-42-1`" and "`0-666-42-2`" in their respective element start-tags. Note that both the legal string literal delimiter characters (`"` and `'`) are illustrated in this example.

Similarly, our "<EOF/>" empty-element tag, from our earlier <textfile> example, could perhaps include the hex value of the original text file end-of-file character:

```
<EOF char="1A"/>
```

In this example, the attribute name is "char" and the value is "1A" (MS-DOS's infamous *Ctrl-Z*).

In addition to the attributes that you can define for yourselves, there are a couple of special attributes that have fixed roles within XML.

Special Attributes

Two special attributes have been defined by the XML 1.0 recommendation: xml:space and xml:lang.

These attributes may be used by the XML document author (or generating software) to pass a signal to the XML application (the browser, for example). Both of these use the XML Namespace syntax, that is, a namespace prefix ("xml"), followed by a colon (:), and then the attribute name ("space" or "lang"). See Chapter 7 for more information about Namespaces.

xml:space Attribute

This attribute exists because of the widespread use of HTML's <pre> tags to preserve text formatting, including any embedded white space characters. However, applications using XML might not, as a default, preserve the white space within a given element, depending on their purpose.

Instead of relying on the application's implicit behavior, the XML document author (or generating software) may use the xml:space attribute to tell the application that it should preserve the white space (though what the application actually does in response to this signal is defined by the application – there is no requirement within the XML Recommendation in this respect).

The value of this attribute is applied to the element and all of its children – not just to the element with the xml:space attribute. This isn't consistent with XML's general treatment of attributes, but this deviation is indeed formally specified.

If a validating parser is used, the xml:space attribute is constrained to use one of two enumerated values: "preserve" or "default" – no other values are valid (more on this issue in Chapter 3, on DTDs).

Now let's look at the other special attribute.

xml:lang Attribute

This attribute exists because of the XML design goal of internationalization. The use of Unicode only provides a standard method of *encoding* the characters used by a given human language – Unicode is mostly silent about the *rendering* of the text (there are some special display characters and the "BIDI" algorithm used to render bi-directional Semitic text, as well as cues for composite Asian characters). There are several other language-specific considerations: the sorting order of characters and symbols; how to delimit words for full-text indexing; spell-checking; hyphenation; and gender-specific pronouns or phrases.

If a validating parser is used, the `xml:lang` attribute (like all other attributes) must be declared in the DTD (see Chapter 3 for more details). Furthermore, in this case, the values of this attribute are constrained to use the following:

One of three types of language codes:

- ISO 639 – `http://sunsite.berkeley.edu/amher/iso_639.html`
- The IETF's RFC 1766 – `http://www.ietf.org/rfc/rfc1766.txt`
- User-defined language code

The ISO 3166 country codes – `http://sunsite.berkeley.edu/amher/iso_3166.html`

And one of the following basic formats:

- A 2-letter ISO 639 language code; for example, French or Japanese are represented by:

```
fr
ja
```

- A 2-letter ISO 639 language code, followed by one or more sub-codes. If the first sub-code exists and it consists of two letters, then those letters *must* be an ISO 3166 country code (the first two examples below). Otherwise, the sub-code(s) may describe the language's script, a dialect, a regional variation, etc. (the last five examples below); for example, language variants, such as those for English ("`en`") or Norwegian ("`no`"), or script variations, such as those used for Azerbaijani ("`az`"):

```
en-US
en-GB
en-cockney
no-bokmaal
no-nynorsk
az-arabic
az-cyrillic
```

- The string literal "`I-`" or "`I-`", followed by a 3- to 8-letter IANA-registered language code (`http://www.isi.edu/in-notes/iana/assignments/languages`); for example, the Native American language, Cherokee:

```
I-cherokee
```

- The string literal "`x-`" or "`X-`", followed by a user-defined language code; for example, the invented language, Klingon, from Star Trek would be represented by:

```
X-klingon
```

User-defined language codes must *begin with "`x-`" or "`X-`" to avoid possible conflicts with IANA-registered codes.*

There is a strong custom in the Internet community to use lower-case letters for language codes, and upper-case letters for country codes. Even though these attribute values are *not* case-sensitive (unlike most XML names), it would be best to adhere to this custom (remember the XML design goal of the easy use of existing Internet protocols).

The following snippet illustrates a few more possibilities:

```
<example>
   <song xml:lang="de">Sagt mir wo die Blumen sind</song>
   <question xml:lang="en-GB">
      What is your favourite colour of flower?
   </question>
   <question xml:lang="en-US">
      What is your favorite color of flower?
   </question>
   <question xml:lang="X-INVERSE">
      What flower is your color?
   </question>
</example>
```

An application (or style sheet) could use the `xml:lang` attribute to decide which `<question>` to present, based upon some user language configuration setting.

Like the `xml:space` attribute, the value of the `xml:lang` attribute is not just applied to the element including the attribute; it also applies to all child elements and attributes of that element. Also, there is no obligation for the application to pay any attention to the `xml:lang` attribute. While the `xml:space` attribute is likely to be more useful when styling the XML data, it is likely that the `xml:lang` attribute will be an essential feature of almost all international XML documents.

An aside about the words used to describe this feature: most people who handle multilingual text like to refer to this sort of labeling of content as "language tagging". Of course, this conflicts with the XML terminology: the `xml:lang` attribute is a not an XML "tag", so it will be necessary to mentally filter/invert these labels when discussing multilingual XML text.

Now that we've covered the syntax of elements and attributes, the basic building blocks of XML, you should be equipped to construct simple XML documents for yourself. But before we move on to discuss another key topic – entities – in depth, let's look briefly at two issues that you will need to know about before you process documents in your applications: white space and end-of-line handling.

White Space

In talking about the `xml:space` attribute we used the term white space without really defining what the term meant. But white space is an important linguistic concept for both human and computer languages. Only four characters are treated as white space in XML data:

Character values (in hexadecimal)	Description
`09`	Horizontal tab (HT)
`0A`	Line-feed (LF)
`0D`	Carriage-return (CR)
`20`	ASCII space character

There is no expansion of tabs to more than one character, so each of these is simply treated as a single character. Similarly, any formatting that might be implied by an LF and/or CR is left to the application and/or style sheet.

Also, Unicode defines a variety of different kinds of spaces, but none of these are considered white space within the context of XML markup.

The XML specification requires that the XML parser pass all characters, including all white space characters, to the application. If a validating parser is used, it is required to inform the application if white space characters appear within element content (and thus, by implication, those white space characters that are part of an element's character data). It is therefore always up to the application to handle white space.

XML's rule for handling white space is very simple: all white space characters within the content are preserved by the parser and passed unmodified to the application, while white space within element tags and attribute values may be removed.

Indenting tags and other markup is a common practice in writing both SGML and HTML documents, but when processing a document HTML browsers often remove all but a single white space character between words and other identifiable units of text, even within the document's content. This means that when the document is written the author can add as much white space as he/she wants to make the markup easier to read and emphasize the structure of the document, but that this will be lost when the document is processed. In addition, different browsers are allowed to have different default rules for white space removal, so many HTML authors must use the `<pre>` tag, the ` ` (non-breaking space) entity and/or the table tags to force more deterministic spacing of text. Elimination of this HTML processing approach, with its contradictory attitudes to white space, and avoiding the complexity of SGML's white space rules, were XML design goals.

***HTML/SGML note**: White space between markup is usually ignored by an HTML browser. SGML has a bunch of complex rules for deciding whether or not to preserve white space "caused by markup" – whatever that means (these rules have never been very clear or concise).*

Now let's look at how XML deals with the ends of lines within the document.

End-of-line Handling

XML data objects will often be stored in discrete computer files that are divided into "lines" of text. Two of the four XML white space characters are the standard ASCII end-of-line control characters. As we noted before, there are three common combinations of these two characters that are used to indicate end-of-line: CR-LF, LF only, and CR only.

In an effort to simplify coding of XML applications, XML parsers were required to convert all end-of-line strings to a single LF (line-feed) character. Naturally, this pleased Unix programmers, and befuddled many MS-Windows programmers (MacOS users have already been conditioned to handle multiple end-of-line strings). Tim Bray has stated that there were some second thoughts (given the MS-Windows market-share), but the fact remains that XML forces the use of Unix-style end-of-line characters.

Having dealt with white space and end-of-line handling we are now in a position to deal properly with the question of character and entity references.

Character and Entity References

Like SGML and HTML before it, XML provides two simple methods of representing characters that don't exist in the ASCII character set:

- character references
- entity references

Let's tackle character references first.

Character References

In XML, character references are typically used as a substitute for the literal form of a character in places where the direct processing of the literal form would result in a violation of the well-formedness constraints of XML syntax (see the "Well-formed Documents" section later in this chapter).

Character references represent a displayable character, and are comprised of a decimal or hexadecimal number, preceded by "`&#`" or "`&#x`" string literals (respectively), and followed by a semi-colon (`;`) character:

```
&#NNNNN;
&#xXXXX;
```

The "`NNNNN`" and "`XXXX`" strings above may be one or more digits that correspond to any Unicode character value that is allowed by XML. Although decimal numbers are more commonly used in HTML, the hex form is preferred for XML, since Unicode character encodings are defined using hex numbers.

For example:

```
&#169;
```

or

```
&#xA9;
```

would be displayed (in an HTML-aware browser) as:

and

```
&#174;
```

or

```
&#xAD;
```

would be displayed as:

Let's compare these with entity references.

Entity References

Entity references allow the insertion of any string literal into element content or attribute values, as well as providing mnemonic alternatives to character references.

Entity references are a legal XML name, preceded by an ampersand (&) and followed by a semi-colon (;) character:

```
&name;
```

Five entities are defined as an integral part of XML, and are used as escape sequences for the XML markup delimiter characters:

Entity	Usage
&	Always used to escape the & character (except within CDATA sections – more on these later).
<	Always used to escape the < character (except within CDATA sections).
>	May be used to escape the > character – within a CDATA section, the entity must always be used if the > follows a "]]" string literal.
'	May be used to escape the ' character in string literals.
"	May be used to escape the " character in string literals.

Except for the five entities shown above, all entities must be defined prior to their use in a document (just like traditional programming macro definition and use). Entities are defined in the document's DTD, which is a separate object external to the document called the "external subset" (see Chapter 3); and/or within the document itself using a section of the `<!DOCTYPE...>` declaration, called the "internal subset" (see the "Document Type Declaration" section later in this chapter). If an XML parser encounters an undefined entity reference, the parser is obligated to report a fatal error as defined in the terms of the XML specification (again, see the "Well-formed Documents" section later in this chapter).

For example:

```
AT&amp;T
```

would be displayed (in an XML-aware browser) as:

```
AT&T
```

and

```
&quot;Jack&apos;s Tracks&quot;
```

would be displayed as:

```
"Jack's Tracks"
```

Entity references may also be used as general text macros ("boilerplate"). For example, the following text includes a pair of entity references:

```
NOTE: &Disclaimer; [per &WROX;]
```

that might be presented, when the reference is replaced by the value it represents, as:

```
NOTE: This information is not to be used for navigation! [per Wrox Press, Ltd.]
```

Of course, we're assuming for the moment that these entities have already been defined.

When the replacement text for an entity is declared to include another entity reference, that reference is expanded in turn, and so on, until all such nested references are resolved. However, a nested "name" must not contain a recursive reference to itself, either directly or indirectly. (We will see how this might come about when we look at the declaration of entities in the section on the "Document Type Declaration" later on.)

Now let's move on to look at processing instructions.

Processing Instructions (PIs)

Since XML, like SGML before it, is a descriptive markup language, it does not presume to try to explain how to handle an element, or its contents. This is a powerful advantage in that it provides presentation flexibility, and OS- and application-independence. However, there are times when it is desirable to pass hints to an application along with the document. The **Processing Instruction (PI)** is the mechanism that XML provides for this purpose.

PIs use a variation of XML element syntax:

```
<?target ...instruction... ?>
```

The PI `target` is required, and must be a valid XML name that is used to identify the application (or other object) to which the PI is directed. The `...instruction...` portion of the PI is merely a string literal that may include any valid character string, except the "`?>`" string literal (the PI's ending delimiter). There is no further definition of PI syntax in the XML 1.0 Recommendation.

The other example of a nearly ubiquitous PI is the one used to associate a style sheet with an XML data object:

```
<?xml-stylesheet ... ?>
```

This PI was not included in the XML 1.0 Recommendation, but instead rated its very own W3C recommendation: "Associating Style Sheets with XML Documents, Version 1.0", dated 29 June 1999 – to be found at `http://www.w3.org/TR/xml-stylesheet`. See Chapter 13 for more about the use of this PI.

Note that the style sheet association PI has a name that begins with the string "`xml`"; this would be illegal for any non-W3C-defined PI, since its use is reserved for W3C specifications.

There has been something of a debate in the XML developer community as to whether or not PIs are truly useful, or are a bit of special syntax that will hinder the acceptance of XML (because of lack of support for PIs in existing browsers, or by allowing incompatible markup to be generated due to the lack of standardized target names). Another argument against PIs is that many of the hints that might be conveyed using a PI are better kept in external style sheets.

On the other hand, there are several possible advantages of PIs: as a hook for scripts or server-side includes (without resorting to abuse of HTML's "`<!-- -->`" comment syntax!); a mechanism for extending schemas that cannot otherwise be modified; a method of extending documents without altering DTD validation; or another way to pass document presentation information (such as line- or page-breaks) embedded in the document, but without affecting that document's structure.

In passing we've just mentioned HTML's commenting syntax. Let's now look at the same mechanism in XML.

Comments

It can be useful to insert notes, or **comments**, into a document. These comments might provide a revision log, historical notes, or any other sort of metadata that would be meaningful to the creator and editors of a document, but wasn't truly part of the document's content. Comments may appear anywhere in a document outside of other markup.

The basic syntax of an XML comment is:

```
<!--...comment text...-->
```

where the "`...comment text...`" portion can be any character string that doesn't include the "`--`" string literal (this restriction is for SGML compatibility). Furthermore, the "`...`" portion cannot end with a hyphen ("`-`") since this could cause misinterpretation of the closing delimiter.

Comments are not part of a document's character data! Within a comments section, entities are not expanded, nor is any markup interpreted.

The XML 1.0 specification allows, *but does not require*, an XML processor to provide a method for the application to retrieve the text of comments. Therefore, an XML application may never rely on using comments to transmit special instructions (an all-too-common HTML trick).

Let's see some examples:

```
<tag> ...some content... </tag> <!-- this is a legal comment -->
<!--======= Beginning of some more comments =======-->
<!--
   this is a comment containing unexpanded <tag> and &entity_reference;'s..
   that is continued on another line..
-->
<!--======= End of comments =======-->
```

The following are illegal comments (they can't appear within an element tag; and the literal "`--`" may not be used unless it is part of the comment's delimiters):

```
<tag> ...some content... </tag <!-- this is an illegal comment --> >
<!-- this is an illegal comment -- because of the double hyphen within -->
```

Now let's take a look at a means for escaping large chunks of text.

CDATA Sections

CDATA sections are a method of including text that contains characters that would otherwise be recognized as markup. This feature is primarily useful to authors who wish to include examples of XML markup in their documents, like the examples in this book. This is probably the only good reason to include CDATA sections in a document, since almost all the advantages of XML are lost when using these sections.

CDATA sections are *not* a good way to include binary data within an XML file! Such data could never include the three-byte sequence "5D 5D 3E" (hex for "]]>"), as this sequence would be interpreted as the end of the CDATA section. The binary data could be encoded with **Base64**, or some other technique that can assure that the encoded data never contains a greater-than (>) character. However, if this method is used, the Base64-encoded binary data could be included in any element's content, and thus a CDATA section would be unnecessary.

CDATA sections may occur anywhere that character data may occur, but they *cannot be nested.* The only markup string that's recognized within a CDATA section is its end delimiter ("]]>") – less-than characters (<) and ampersands (&) may occur in their literal form; they need not (and cannot) be escaped.

The basic syntax of a CDATA section is:

```
<![CDATA[...]]>
```

where the "..." portion can be any character string that doesn't include the "]]>" string literal.

If we wanted to include a piece of markup containing entity references in an XML document as uninterpreted markup (without letting the XML parser expand entities or interpret element tags), we could use either of the following methods:

```
<![CDATA[
<Catalog>
   <Legalese> &copy; 1999 Wrox Press, Ltd. &reg;</Legalese>
</Catalog>
]]>
```

Or:

```
&lt;Catalog>
   &lt;Legalese>&amp;nbsp;&amp;copy; 1999 Wrox Press, Ltd.
   &amp;reg;&lt;/Legalese>
&lt;/Catalog>
```

The string output to the application from the parser would be the same in both cases:

```
"<Catalog><Legalese> © 1999 Wrox Press, Ltd. ® </Legalese></Catalog>"
```

The first approach is obviously easier to read and write, and has the additional advantage of permitting the direct cutting-and-pasting of XML examples from elsewhere. The latter method merely replaces the two markup characters with the appropriate entity references, so that they will not be misinterpreted as element tags or entity references during parsing (more on parsing and parsers in a later section).

Document Structure

Now that we're equipped with some knowledge of the various pieces of syntax that can be used in an XML document depending on what you want to do, let's take a look at the overall logical structure of a document.

Prolog

An XML document starts with a prolog. The prolog is used to signal the beginning of XML data, describe its character encoding method, and provide some other configuration hints to the XML parser and application.

The prolog consists of an optional XML declaration (which we'll look at next), followed by zero or more comments, PIs, and white space characters, followed in turn by an optional document type declaration (with more optional comments, PIs, and white space characters). Since all these parts are effectively optional, this entails that the prolog may be omitted, and the document can still be well-formed (see section 2.8 of the XML 1.0 Recommendation).

Let's look at the first component of the prolog.

XML Declaration

All XML documents may (and should!) begin with a single **XML Declaration**. Although the XML declaration uses a similar syntax to a processing instruction, technically speaking within the terms of the XML recommendation it is not one, since it has a reserved role within XML.

```
<?xml version="1.0" ?>
```

If this XML declaration is included, it must be as the very first characters of the document – no preceding white space or comments are allowed. Strictly speaking, this declaration is not required in XML documents, but its use does permit some optimizations when processing the document, as we shall see.

> *Early drafts of XML did not specify case sensitivity for names, and many early implementers, including Microsoft, used an upper-case version of this declaration ("`<?XML... ?>`"). However, the final W3C recommendation specified case sensitivity, and defined the "`xml`" name as lower-case. Thus some so-called XML documents are no longer legal XML 1.0 data.*

The following is an example of the complete syntax of the XML Declaration (including the optional attributes `encoding` and `standalone`):

```
<?xml version="1.0" encoding="UTF-8" standalone="yes"?>
```

The attributes have been defined by the XML 1.0 specification:

- `version` – compulsory; value must be "`1.0`"; this attribute enables support of future versions of XML.
- `encoding` – optional; value must be a legal character encoding, such as "`UTF-8`", "`UTF-16`", or "`ISO-8859-1`" (the Latin-1 character encoding). All XML parsers are required to support at least UTF-8 and UTF-16. If this attribute is not included, "`UTF-8`" or "`UTF-16`" encoding is assumed, depending upon the format of the initial "`<?xml`" string. See Character Encodings later in this chapter.
- `standalone` – optional; value must be either "`yes`" or "`no`"; where "`yes`" means that all required entity declarations are contained within the document, and "`no`" means that an external DTD is required. (See Chapter 3 for more on DTDs.)

Unlike most XML attributes, these must be in the order shown above. On the other hand, but also unlike most XML attributes, the `encoding` attribute values are *not* case-sensitive. This inconsistency is due to XML's dependence upon existing ISO and Internet Assigned Numbers Authority (IANA) standards for character encoding names.

The most commonly supported character encoding names for XML use are:

- Unicode: "`UTF-8`", "`UTF-16`"
- ISO 10646: "`ISO-10646-UCS-2`", "`ISO-10646-UCS-4`"
- ISO 8859: "`ISO-8859-n`" (where "`n`" is a digit from "`1`" to "`9`")
- JIS X-0208-1997: "`ISO-2022-JP`", "`Shift_JIS`", and "`EUC-JP`"

Although HTTP provides a method for a server to tell the client (browser) what encoding is being used, sometimes there is no server (as when viewing files on a local file system). Using the `encoding` attribute is also more reliable than trying to rely upon auto-detection of the character encoding (this technique can get close, but can't distinguish UTF-8 from ISO-8859-1, or reliably detect the UTF-7 encoding).

Let's take a more detailed look at what we mean by an encoding.

Character Encodings

Unicode was originally designed as a simple set of 16-bit scalar values, since this would include most of the special symbols or characters needed for any modern language. Even though not all of these 65,535 characters have yet been used, it became clear that more characters would be needed, and Unicode has added the **surrogate block** mechanism to allow another 1,048,576 additional characters (this will be described in more detail a little further on).

Although Unicode identifies characters using scalar values (numbers), there are different acceptable ways of storing those numbers. The XML design goal of widespread network use demands that various encoding methods be allowed.

The **UTF-8** encoding treats 7-bit ASCII normally, but requires 2 to 5 bytes (each within the range of hex 80 to FF) for everything else – this is great for predominately ASCII text, but is not very nice for the rest of the world. Given the inefficiency of UTF-8 for non-ASCII data, and that Java has been built upon 16-bit Unicode characters, UTF-8 isn't a very good choice for international use. Incidentally, "UTF" means "Unicode Transformation Format" (in Unicode documentation), or "UCS Transformation Format" (in ISO 10646).

The **UTF-16** encoding is the simplest, storing 16-bit characters in one of the two traditional ways (big-endian and little-endian depending on the computer's processor architecture).

> *Phased out circa 1996, a big-endian architecture was one in which the most significant byte of a multi-byte numeric representation had the lowest address (in memory).*

Additional characters may be encoded using surrogate blocks (see below). The main concern about UTF-16 comes from East Asia, where sometimes two code units may be required to represent a single character. However, the vast majority of Asian characters only require single code units. According to the Unicode FAQ, the use of surrogate pairs should be much less than 1% of all text storage. Thus, most Unicode-conformant software uses the UTF-16 encoding.

The **UTF-32** encoding (nearly identical to the ISO 10646 **UCS-4** encoding) has the advantage of programming simplicity – all Unicode characters (and about 4 billion additional characters) can be encoded using this method. Although easier to program with (in some languages/systems), this is a less than ideal option, because such an encoding again doubles the storage space required by each individual character (and thus requires quadruple the amount of storage space of ASCII characters).

> *The relationship between ISO 10646 and Unicode is described at* `http://consult.cern.ch/cnl/215/node47.html`*, and ISO 8859 is discussed at* `http://ppewww.ph.gla.ac.uk/~flavell/iso8859/iso8859-pointers.html`

Surrogate Blocks

It became obvious that while 65,535 characters might be enough to support most current languages, the needs of scholars and historians, coupled with the dynamic nature of ideographic languages, demanded a larger number space. For example, about 14,500 composite characters were added for compatibility with existing character sets; and there are many mathematical symbols, Asian ideograms, and historical characters that have not yet been included in Unicode. Thus, Unicode added the **surrogate blocks**.

Surrogate blocks are Unicode's method of expanding its character number space beyond that provided by 16-bit numbers. Two blocks of 1,024 characters have been reserved (hex D800 to DBFF and DC00 to DFFF) to allow for 1,048,576 additional characters. A 16-bit value from the first block is the high-order part of the 32-bit number, the second is the low-order part. This allows a program that doesn't understand these combined characters to simply show one or two placeholders. These extended characters can be used for modern ideographic languages (such as Chinese or Japanese), ancient languages (Egyptian hieroglyphics, Phaistos Disk Script), and even invented languages (Klingon, Tolkien's Dwarvish runes).

For better or worse, surrogate block character pairs are *not* legal XML characters.

Byte-Order Marks (BOMs)

Unicode data can use a BOM as a signature to specify the encoding that is being used. For example:

Bytes	Encoding Form
`00 00 FE FF`	UTF-32/UCS-4, big-endian
`FF FE 00 00`	UTF-32/UCS-4, little-endian
`FE FF 00 ##`	UTF-16, big-endian
`FF FE ## 00`	UTF-16, little-endian
`EF BB BF`	UTF-8

Although these values are not legal within XML data, they may immediately precede the valid XML data in a transmitted data object and can provide valuable (albeit usually redundant) encoding information to the XML parser and/or application. An XML parser must be about to handle BOMs prior to the XML data, since support of both UTF-8 and UTF-16 encodings is a requirement.

Now let's look at the second optional component of the prolog.

Document Type Declaration

This is *not* to be confused with the Document Type Definition (more commonly known as the DTD!) Rather, the Document Type Declaration contains the internal subset of, and/or refers to the external subset of, the Document Type Definition (DTD).

All *valid* XML documents must include this declaration, but simple well-formed documents do not require its inclusion, as long as they do not contain any entity references (other than the five standard XML entities). If additional character entities are used, in a well-formed but not valid document that will be parsed with a non-validating parser, they may be declared in an internal subset of a standalone XML data object, without requiring the use of an external DTD or schema.

External Subset References

There are two forms of the Document Type Declaration that refer to the external subset of the DTD:

```
<!DOCTYPE root_element_name SYSTEM "system_identifier">
<!DOCTYPE root_element_name PUBLIC "public_identifier" "system_identifier">
```

The `root_element_name` is the point-of-attachment for the DTD. All children in the XML Document's element tree will thus inherit the DTD's declarations from this root node.

Both the `SYSTEM` identifier ("`system_identifier`" in the above example) and the `PUBLIC` identifier ("`public_identifier`" above) values are **URIs** (**Uniform Resource Identifiers**). At the time of writing this, a URI can be considered equivalent to a URL for all practical purposes; that is, it is of the form "`http://www.wrox.com/myfile.dtd`" – although it can be any unique name that is recognized by the processing application.

The `PUBLIC` identifier is used to reference a DTD that is catalogued and referenced using some method that is not defined in XML, but rather is the result of a standard within an organization, or an agreement between parties exchanging the XML data. This method has the result of not being a blind reference like a URL, but the disadvantage of not being portable beyond the organization and its associates.

An XML parser may try to generate a URI using the `PUBLIC` identifier. If it is unable to do so, the `SYSTEM` identifier URI must be used. The disadvantage of this form is that a URI can become stale (the domain name or file path can change, or become obsolete) and the DTD will no longer be located.

Since the commonly used fragment identifier (the # character) is not actually part of the URI, the parser may signal an error if a fragment identifier is encountered in a `SYSTEM` identifier. Any URI that contains non-ASCII characters must represent the characters in UTF-8 (as one or more bytes), and then use the standard URI "`%HH`" escape sequence for each of these bytes (where "`HH`" is the byte's value in hex).

An example of a reference to an external DTD:

```
<?xml version="1.0" standalone="no"?>
<!DOCTYPE Catalog SYSTEM "http://www.wrox.com/DTDs/PubCatalog.dtd">
<Catalog>
   ...
</Catalog>
```

Or:

```
<?xml version="1.0" standalone="no"?>
<!DOCTYPE Catalog PUBLIC "-//PubCatalog"
   "http://www.wrox.com/DTDs/PubCatalog.dtd">
<Catalog>
   ...
</Catalog>
```

These "identifiers" are yet another bit of XML that has been inherited from SGML.

> ***SGML note**: The SGML "public identifiers" provided a method of letting a document reference a local catalog (or use some other magical method) to find the DTD. This was certainly a very useful technique, but when XML was designed, there was no consensus on a general method of resolving these public identifiers. As a result, XML allows the use of public identifiers, but also requires a system identifier as a backup reference.*

Internal Subset Declarations

If no external DTD is available, an XML data object can still use entity references, provided that they are declared in the internal subset of the DTD, which is done using an expanded form of the `<!DOCTYPE...>` declaration. DTD syntax is the subject of the next chapter, so this will be covered in much more detail there. For the basic use shown below, it is sufficient to know that the internal subset declarations are delimited within the `<!DOCTYPE...>` declaration using brackets "`[ ... ]`", and that the `<!ENTITY...>` declarations are used to define the expansion of entity references.

The following is a simple example of an internal subset declaration for three symbolic character entities and two "text macro" or "boilerplate" entities:

```
<?xml version="1.0" encoding="utf-8" standalone="yes"?>
<!DOCTYPE Catalog [
   <!ENTITY copy "&#169;">
   <!ENTITY nbsp " ">
   <!ENTITY reg "&#174;">
   <!ENTITY COPYDATE "1999">
   <!ENTITY WROX "Wrox Press, Ltd.">
]>
<Catalog>
   <Legalese> &copy; &COPYDATE; &WROX; &reg;</Legalese>
</Catalog>
```

The above example would be displayed in IE5 (if the user has not specified a style sheet to use) as:

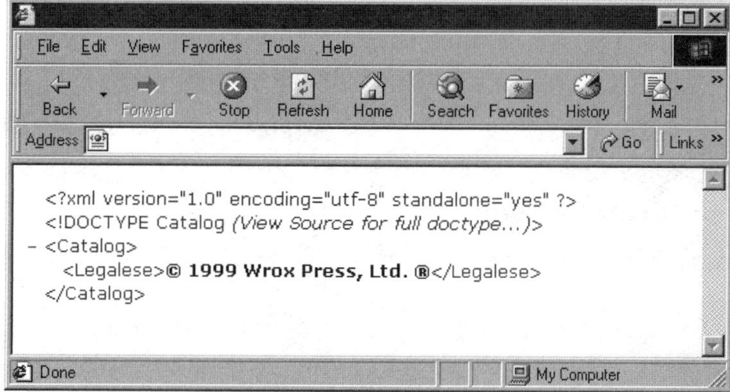

An XML document may use a DTD that has an internal and/or an external subset. If both subsets are used, and there two declarations for the same element type or entity, the internal subset will have precedence.

Now that we've dealt with the syntax of the prolog and the core syntax of a well-formed document, we'll quickly mention the third portion of an XML document.

Epilog

The XML epilog may include comments, PIs, and/or white space. It is unclear whether the PIs should be applied to the elements in the document preceding the Epilog, or the following data (if any).

This may well be a solution in search of a problem, or it may just be a problem in and of itself. Since XML does not define any end-of-document indicator, most applications will use the end-tag of the document element for this purpose. Thus, a network link is likely to be closed after encountering the root element end-tag, without any handling of an epilog. Also, the presence of processing instructions between documents is somewhat ambiguous, at best.

The epilog is considered a "real design error" by Tim Bray (one of the authors of the XML 1.0 Recommendation) – it is probably inadvisable to use it without a very compelling reason, and you should do so in the knowledge that it is unlikely be inter-operable with other XML applications.

At this point it would be a good idea to recap on the XML syntax we've learnt so far.

Summary of XML Syntax

The XML tag forms:

Syntax	Component
`<tagname>`	Element start-tag
`<tagname attribute="value" >`	Start-tag with an attribute
`</tagname>`	End-tag
`<tagname/>`	Empty-element tag
`<tagname attr1="value1" attr2="value2"/>`	Empty-element tag with two attributes

Special XML instructions and declarations:

Syntax	Component
`<?xml version="1.0" encoding="UTF-8" standalone="yes" ?>`	The XML declaration
`<?name string ?>`	Processing Instruction (PI), for the XML application
`<!-- string -->`	Comment, for the human writer/editor
`<![CDATA[ string... ]]>`	Unparsed Character Data (CDATA) Section
`<!DOCTYPE string... >`	Document Type Declaration (*not* the "DTD")

XML entity references:

Syntax	Component
`&#decimal;` Example: `®`	Reference to a character number, using its decimal value
`&#xHEX;` Example: `૴`	Reference to a character number, using its hexadecimal value
`&ref;`	Reference to a pre-defined XML entity (such as a text macro)

Now that we know all the parts that can be used in a well-formed document, let's discuss what the term "well-formed" actually means.

Well-formed Documents

All data objects (documents) that conform to the XML syntax specification are **well-formed XML documents**. Such documents can be used without a DTD or schema to describe their structure, and are also known as **standalone** XML documents. These documents cannot rely upon external declarations, and attribute values will receive no special processing or default values.

A well-formed XML document contains one or more elements (delimited by start- and end-tags) that nest properly within each other. There is one element, the document element, which contains any and all other elements within the document. All elements form a simple hierarchical tree, and so the only direct element-to-element relationship is that of parent-child. Sibling relationships can often be inferred using data structures internal to the XML application, but these are neither direct, nor reliable (due to the possibility of elements being inserted between the common parent and one or more of its children). Document content can include markup and/or character data.

Data objects are well-formed XML documents if:

- syntax conforms to the XML specification
- elements form a hierarchical tree, with a single root node
- there are no references to external entities, unless a DTD is provided

Any XML parser that encounters a construct within the XML data that is not well-formed must report this error to the application as a "fatal" error. Fatal errors need not cause the parser to terminate – it may continue processing in an attempt to find other errors, but it may not continue to pass character data and/or XML structures to the application in a normal fashion.

This approach to error-handling is the result of XML's design goal of compactness, and the intention that XML be used for much more than just document display – it's just not that hard to make an XML data object well-formed. Hopefully, this rather brutal error handling will prevent the creation of bloated software like Internet Explorer and Navigator (which have all sorts of special code to figure out how to handle ambiguous HTML).

> ***HTML/SGML note**: Tools for both of these are much more forgiving than XML. An HTML browser can usually render most of a seriously broken web page, a fact that contributed to the rapid acceptance of HTML. Yet, the actual rendering varies from browser to browser. Similarly, SGML tools usually try to continue processing a document even after encountering errors.*

The existence of well-formed documents allows use of XML data without the burden of constructing and referencing an external description of that data. The term "well-formed" has a similar meaning in formal mathematical logic – an assertion is well-formed if it meets grammatical rules, without any concern as to whether the assertion is "true" or not.

Parsers

In addition to specifying the syntax of XML, the W3C Recommendation described some of the behavior of the lower tier of XML's client architecture (the **XML processor** or **parser**). There are two types of parsers:

- **non-validating** – the parser merely ensures that a data object is well-formed XML
- **validating** – the parser uses a DTD to ensure the validity of a well-formed data object's form and content

Some parsers support both types, with configuration switches that determine whether or not the document will be validated.

Some of the behavior of XML parsers has been defined with the intent of easing the burden upon an application's handling of XML data. For example, as previously described, the character sequences used to delimit the end of text records are often operating system-specific. However an XML application needn't be concerned with this, because the XML parser will normalize all standard text record delimiters to a single line-feed (hex `0A`) character. White space handling is another area where parsers are constrained – unlike HTML or SGML, all white space must be passed from the document to the application. Also, general (character) entity strings are expanded by the parser, as defined by the internal or external DTD subset.

XML parsers are required to normalize attribute values (the "AttValue" below) before passing them to the XML application. This means that the parser will handle the following references and characters thus:

- character references – append the referenced character to the AttValue
- entity reference – recursively expand the replacement text of that entity, appending it to the AttValue
- white space characters – replace any carriage-return/line-feed pairs that are part of an external parsed entity or the literal entity value of an internal parsed entity, or any single white space character with the space character (hex 20), and then append the space to the AttValue
- all other characters – append the character to the AttValue

The AttValue is then processed further by removing any leading and/or trailing spaces, and converting sequences of multiple spaces to single spaces. The exception to this last rule is if the attribute value has been declared as CDATA in the DTD, and a validating parser is being used (see Chapter 3 for a description of DTDs and this specific declaration).

There are two approaches to implementing an XML parser. Much quasi-religious argument has occurred about this dichotomy, but each approach has its merits. Like so many other real-world problems, XML processing may have vastly different requirements, and thus different approaches may be best for different situations.

Event-driven Parsers

One approach to processing XML data is the use of an event-driven parser, the model of which is probably quite familiar to programmers of modern GUIs (Graphical User Interfaces) and OSs (Operating Systems). In this case, the XML parser executes a call-back to the application for each class of XML data: element (with attributes), character data, processing instructions, notation, or comments. It's up to the application to handle the XML data as it is provided via the call-backs – the XML parser does not maintain the element tree structure, or any of the data after it has been parsed. The event-driven method requires very modest system resources, even for extremely large documents; and because of its simple, low-level access to the structure of the XML data, provides great flexibility in handling the data within the XML application.

One of the earliest, best-known, and most elegant examples of this type of parser is James Clark's **expat**, written in ANSI-C. It is also available with C++ (**expatpp**), Perl (**XML::Parser**), and Python (**Pyexpat**) wrappers. Clark was the Technical Lead for the XML 1.0 Recommendation, and has also written another parser in Java, called **xp**.

Members of the XML-DEV mailing list, led by David Megginson (author of Microstar's **AElfred** parser), have developed a standard interface for event-based XML parsing, called **SAX 1.0: The Simple API for XML (SAX)**, with current implementations in Java, Perl, and Python, and support for more than a dozen different XML parsers. SAX was the result of Peter Murray-Rust's experiences integrating three different XML parsers (with proprietary APIs) into JUMBO – he proposed the creation of a common Java event-based API for parsing XML. He initiated the design discussion with Tim Bray and David Megginson (conducted in public on XML-DEV), and the latter wrote the initial Java implementation in about a month at the beginning of 1998. SAX has since been extended with the contributions of many people, and represents a very powerful approach to processing XML data (most event-driven parsers now support/use this API). We cover SAX in detail in Chapter 6.

Tree-based Parsers

One of the most widely used structures in software engineering is the simple hierarchical tree. All well-formed XML data is defined to be such a tree, and thus common and mature algorithms may be used to traverse the nodes of an XML document, search for content, and/or edit the document tree. These tree algorithms have the advantage of years of academic and commercial development. The XML parsers that use this approach generally conform to the W3C's **Document Object Model (DOM)**. The DOM is a platform- and language-neutral interface that allows manipulation of tree-structured documents. On the other hand, the DOM tree must be built in memory before the document can be manipulated – high-performance virtual memory support is imperative for larger documents! Once the tree is built, an application may access the DOM via a related API. The DOM will be discussed in detail in Chapter 5. Many of these "parsers" are actually built upon an event-driven XML parser that provides all the information needed to build the DOM tree.

Microsoft developed an early Java-based XML parser, called **MSXML**. Later, XML support was included as part of **Internet Explorer 5 (IE5)**, using a different parser. Microsoft recommends the **XJParser** supplied by DataChannel (it "tracks the functionality" of IE5's parser) as a retrofit component for **IE4**. In addition, Microsoft's **Office 2000** uses XML extensively as its data interchange format, which will greatly hasten the adoption of XML. At the same time, it should be clear that since many aspects of XML have not yet made their way to final recommendation status, Microsoft is working ahead of these standards and there may be differences between Microsoft's implementation and the formal W3C standards.

Netscape has promised full XML 1.0 and XSL support in its next generation browser, which is being built as an open-source project by the **Mozilla** organization. The current code-name for the browser is "**SeaMonkey**" (using the **NGLayout/Gecko** layout engine). The browser is still in development (not yet at the beta-test stage), and recent corporate changes are still causing confusion about the future of AOL/Netscape's browsers.

Fujitsu Laboratories has developed **HyBrick**, an advanced SGML/XML browser. It supports advanced linking and formatting capabilities, using a DSSSL (ISO 10179) renderer and XLink/XPointer engine. This browser is based upon James Clark's SP and Jade, and handles both valid and well-formed XML documents. As might be expected, this browser works well with Japanese, as well as English, text.

Parser Benchmarks

Two developers have recently done XML parser benchmark tests that look at several different parsers on Linux and Solaris systems. The (perhaps expected) results indicate that those written in C (specifically James Clark's expat) are still the fastest, followed by Java, and then the scripting languages (Perl and Python, both of which are actually just wrappers for the expat parser).

The Linux benchmark was performed and reported by Clark Cooper, who tested these six parsers:

- Expat (in C, by James Clark)
- RXP (in C, by Richard Tobin)
- XP (in Java, by James Clark)
- XML4J (in Java, by IBM)
- XML::Parser (in Perl, by Clark Cooper)
- Pyexpat (in Python, by Jack Jansen)

The Solaris benchmark was performed and reported by Steven Marcus, who tested the above (minus RXP), plus Sun's "xml-tr2" parser (in Java, by Javasoft). These can be found at:

- **Linux tests** – `http://www.xml.com/pub/Benchmark/exec.html`
- **Solaris tests** – `http://www.awaretechnologies.com/XML/xmlbench/solaris.html`

Now let's move on to look at an application of XML to a specific problem.

The Book Catalog Application

The Book Catalog application is a simple example of how XML can be used for both traditional document markup and more generic (and powerful) data modeling. This XML vocabulary includes typical bibliographic metadata, but also provides the basis for sending structured pricing information to a customer's search-bot, making book sales over the WWW, producing packing lists and shipping labels for the physical movement of books to stores, and exchanging accounting and order data between a publisher and bookstores. We'll be spending more time analyzing this application in the next chapter, eventually devising a DTD that comes a lot closer to meeting the catalog goals. For now we'll approach the problem in a simpler way.

Let's begin with the more or less atomic unit of this application – the book. We'll ignore the actual content of the book for the purpose of this example, but of course text markup is the traditional use of SGML and its descendants, such as XML. Books have some common bibliographic metadata such as author, publisher, publication date, copyright, etc.

Once we've developed a reasonable structure for books, we'll later wrap it in another layer – the catalog. This layer is more like a traditional database than a text document, and will therefore illustrate some of XML's data modeling capabilities.

The <Book> Element

At first, we'll construct a `<Book>` element using only simple child elements:

```
<?xml version="1.0" encoding="utf-8" standalone="yes"?>
<!--======== The Wrox Press Book Catalog Application ========-->
<Book>
   <Title>Professional XML</Title>
   <Author>Mark Birbeck, Steven Livingstone, Didier Martin,
      Stephen Mohr, Nikola Ozu, et al.
   </Author>
   <Publisher>Wrox Press, Ltd.</Publisher>
   <PubDate>November 1999</PubDate>
   <Abstract>XML 0-500kmh in 3 seconds</Abstract>
   <Pages>750</Pages>
   <ISBN>1-861003-11-0</ISBN>
   <RecSubjCategories>
      <Category>Internet</Category>
      <Category>Web Publishing</Category>
      <Category>XML</Category>
   </RecSubjCategories>
</Book>
```

There's one glaring mistake in the above example: all the co-authors have been lumped together in just one element.

Let's expand our structure a little more:

```
<?xml version="1.0" encoding="utf-8" standalone="yes"?>
<!--======== The Wrox Press Book Catalog Application ========-->
<Book>
   <Title>Professional XML</Title>
   <Authors>
      <Author>Mark Birbeck</Author>
      <Author>Peter Stark</Author>
      <Author>Steven Livingstone</Author>
      <Author>Didier Martin</Author>
      <Author>Stephen Mohr</Author>
      <Author>Michael Kay</Author>
      <Author>Nikola Ozu</Author>
   </Authors>
```

```
    <Publisher>Wrox Press, Ltd.</Publisher>
    <PubDate>November 1999</PubDate>
    <Abstract>XML 0-500kmh in 3 seconds</Abstract>
    <Pages>750</Pages>
    <ISBN>1-861003-11-0</ISBN>
    <RecSubjCategories>
       <Category>Internet</Category>
       <Category>Web Publishing</Category>
       <Category>XML</Category>
    </RecSubjCategories>
</Book>
```

Now we've explicitly separated the authors, so let's look at some of the specifics of how we're representing the bibliographic metadata. For example, we could argue that the title, ISBN, etc. are all properties of the <book> element, rather than parts of its content.

For the sake of illustration, we'll change these elements to attributes (although the prior approach is equally valid), and change some of the other <Book> child elements to attributes (based on the "it's a property" argument). We'll also add a <Price> element to further illustrate the use of attributes:

```
<?xml version="1.0" encoding="utf-8" standalone="yes"?>
<!--======= The Wrox Press Book Catalog Application =======-->
<Book title="Professional XML"
   publisher="Wrox Press, Ltd."
   pubdate="November 1999"
   pages="750"
   isbn="1-861003-11-0">

   <Authors>
      <!-- 'Author' elements deleted for brevity -->
   </Authors>
   <Price currency="USD">49.99</Price>
</Book>
```

There's obviously still a lot missing from this example. A lingering deficiency is the use of string literals for the publisher attribute and <Author> elements. This problem and others will be addressed in the next chapter, when the book catalog concept will be greatly expanded.

The preceding examples illustrate a common convention for dealing with the element vs. attribute decision: elements are "nouns" that represent objects, whilst attributes are the "adjectives" that describe the properties of those objects.

You may also note that we've used a code-style convention to help differentiate these two objects: element type names use the proper noun form (the first letter is capitalized); and attribute names are all lower-case. This helps reinforce what's being named, particularly when we're discussing these names in comments or other text.

The decision to use an element vs. an attribute is not a simple one. Much discussion and argument has occurred about this topic on both the XML-L and XML-DEV lists. Some argue that attributes should never be used – that they add unnecessary processing complexity, and that anything that can be represented as an attribute would be better contained within a child element. Others extol the advantage of be able to validate attribute values and assign default values using a DTD. Recent experiments have shown that, despite superficial appearances, use of generic data compression (such as gzip, LZW, or zlib) means that neither form has an inherent advantage for data storage or transmission (that is, the compressed XML data object's size is comparable).

Two of the editors of the XML 1.0 Recommendation and some other SGML/XML experts have written on this topic – see the following links for these articles (most are deep links to copies on Robin Cover's SGML/XML webpages).

- **"XML Syntax Recommendation for Serializing Graphs of Data"** by Andrew Layman – `http://www.w3.org/TandS/QL/QL98/pp/microsoft-serializing.html`
- **"Elements or attributes?"** by Eliot Kimber – `http://www.oasis-open.org/cover/attrKimber9711.html`
- **"Elements vs. Attributes"** by Michael Sperberg-McQueen – `http://www.oasis-open.org/cover/attrSperberg92.html`
- **"SGML/XML: Using Elements and Attributes"** by Robin Cover – `http://www.oasis-open.org/cover/elementsAndAttrs.html`
- **"When is an attribute an attribute?"** by Tim Bray – `http://www.oasis-open.org/cover/brayAttr980409.html`
- **"When to use attributes as opposed to elements"** by G. Ken Holman – `http://www.oasis-open.org/cover/holmanElementsAttrs.html`

Summary

In this chapter, we've shown the basic syntax that is required for all XML data. We can create simple well-formed documents without any other knowledge or tools, but this wouldn't begin to take advantage of much of the power of XML.

For example, nothing in this basic syntax provides for the "HT" in HTML – hypertext. Improved linking syntax is a very important aspect of some of the pending XML extensions (such as XLink and XPath) that are discussed later in this book (see Chapter 8).

Well-formed documents may be adequate for some applications, but this implies that any interpretation or validation of the data must be hard-coded in the XML application(s). A more portable approach is to provide a second document that is used to validate the first (or others of its general type). This validation document may be in the form of a DTD (see Chapter 3) or a Schema (see Chapter 7).

In its simplest form, XML is a powerful medium of data exchange. When extended with DTDs or schemas, namespaces, linking, and style sheets, XML is the basis for a new era of a much more powerful Internet. Coupled with Java, or another portable language, XML will lead to many more widespread and portable computing applications.

3

Document Type Definitions

The last chapter equipped you to write well-formed XML documents. However, when developing document structures that conform to XML 1.0, an interesting question arises: how do you communicate your structures to another party? The dominant browsers have or are developing native XML support, but this is limited to displaying the XML content. If you are developing the programs that consume the XML as well as generate it, your intentions are implicit in the code – *this* element follows *that* element, which means *this*, simply because you said so. There needs to be a common way for the designer of an XML vocabulary to communicate the syntactic rules of his vocabulary so that any other user of XML 1.0 can interpret the structure of documents that conform to the vocabulary – *this* element follows *that* element because it is specified right *here*. XML 1.0 provides such a mechanism as part of the specification; the Document Type Definition (DTD). A DTD uses a formal grammar to specify the structure and permissible values of XML documents. The XML you saw in the last chapter is **well-formed** XML. It conforms to the basic syntax rules of XML, but there are no other syntactic guarantees. In this chapter we're going to create **valid** XML: XML that conforms to the syntactic rules of XML as well as the rules of a vocabulary you create.

When you have a DTD, you gain several benefits. First, creating the DTD formally and precisely documents the vocabulary. All the rules of the vocabulary are contained in the DTD. Anything that isn't there isn't part of the vocabulary. Many parsers can use a DTD to **validate** a document instance. A simple declaration in the document instance allows the parser to retrieve the DTD and compare the document instance to the rules in the DTD. Authoring tools for XML can use DTDs for a similar purpose. Once a DTD has been selected, tools can enforce the DTD's rules, permitting an author to add only those elements or attributes that are permitted by the DTD, and according to the structure dictated by the DTD.

The XML 1.0 Recommendation is quite specific in how to construct a DTD and associate it with a document written according to the rules in the DTD. It also specifies what a parser is expected to do with a DTD. In this chapter, we'll consider why you would want to use DTDs. You'll learn the syntactic rules of XML 1.0 DTDs and how to associate a document instance with a DTD. With those tools in hand, we'll set out to create a DTD for our book catalog example.

Why Formal Structure?

Whenever you write code that operates against documents of a particular vocabulary, you are implicitly creating documentation. You have encoded rules about that vocabulary in the source code. The code enforces a certain structure; when the structure changes, the code must change. Often, this is perfectly acceptable. A designer can explain his intentions to a small group of programmers, and all the code in the application gets written with those assumptions in mind. It is very hard to write code that is completely data driven, after all.

Without explicit documentation, however, you have no way to reliably trap errors in documents. Your only error detection mechanism is to run the code. If your code is permissive or the document deviates from the designer's intentions in an unexpected way, the error may not be detected. Your application may behave in ways you didn't expect.

The answer is a clear, precise set of syntactic rules that capture everything that is permitted in the vocabulary. With such a document, programmers do not need to interview the vocabulary designer to make sure they understand the vocabulary. If the document is itself written in a formal (the rigorous form of "precise") grammar a parser can read the rules. That way, you can have a single error detection mechanism. The parser can indicate any vocabulary errors detected, and your application can respond appropriately before going into your program logic.

Document the Domain

Your XML documents are like a snapshot of the data structures in a program. They communicate some information from one program to another. That information pertains to the application domain – the problem you are trying to solve. If your XML vocabulary is a good model for the problem at hand, applications will be easier to write and maintain. In the course of devising an effective XML vocabulary, you learn a good deal about the business problem your application is intended to solve. If your XML is merely well-formed, your documentation of the business process is purely anecdotal. You can't assume your XML samples cover every possible case. Even if they do, they aren't an efficient way to pass on your knowledge.

A DTD, by contrast, captures all the information in your vocabulary by definition. Everything you learned that went into the design of the vocabulary must be in the DTD. Consequently, someone else can pick up your DTD and learn what you know (or at least captured) about the business problem. A DTD solves two problems at once: you get something a program can use, and you get documentation.

Validating Documents

A well-formed document written to implicit rules cannot be checked for errors. You are relying on the integrity of the applications that create and consume the XML for the integrity of the overall system. Errors in the code might not be caught. They could either cause another program to break, or cause bad data to get into the system. The XML 1.0 Recommendation, however, specifies the expected behavior of a validating parser. If an XML document references a DTD, a validating parser is expected to retrieve the DTD and ensure the document conforms to the grammar the DTD describes. If robust error checking is important to you, you simply use DTDs and a validating parser. The parser will find any errors in the document syntax, vocabulary, and any specified values. If the document gets past the parser's validity checks, you can safely pass the document on to the application logic. This won't protect you from faulty application logic, of course, but it does filter out bad data with very little effort on the part of your code.

This is particularly important to Internet applications. You cannot assume that you are dealing with applications subject to the same quality control your code went through. A programming team working for another organization may be implementing a public XML vocabulary for a particular business or industry. Their interpretation of the vocabulary may not be the same as yours. Their testing may not be as thorough as yours. With a DTD and a validating parser, you have an immediate and ironclad check of a document's integrity. Of course, the validity check is only as good as the DTD. With that in mind, let's find out what we need to know to write effective DTDs.

Writing DTDs: General Principles

XML documents, to grossly simplify, consist of elements and their attributes. There are some other items we need to be able to define, but documents support those two main concepts. In addition, an element's content is defined in terms of other elements or some basic types defined in the XML standard. A DTD, then, must be able to define all the elements in a document, the attributes that can be assigned to them, and the relationships between elements.

Associating a DTD with an XML Document

DTDs are associated with documents. When a validating parser reads the instruction by which documents are associated with a DTD, that tells the parser to get the DTD and validate the document according to the rules provided therein. Let's see how we tie DTDs to document instances.

The DOCTYPE Tag

We saw this briefly in Chapter 2. XML 1.0 provides the special `DOCTYPE` declaration to connect DTD declarations to a document instance. A `DOCTYPE` declaration must follow the XML declaration and precede any elements in the document. However, comments and processing instructions may appear between the XML declaration and the `DOCTYPE` declaration.

The DOCTYPE declaration contains the keyword DOCTYPE followed by the name of the root element of the document, followed by a construction that brings in the content declarations. Before I clarify that somewhat cryptic statement, let's see an example of the placement of the DOCTYPE declaration in the document instance. Here are the first three lines of an XML document:

```
<?xml version="1.0?>
<!DOCTYPE Catalog ...>
<Catalog>...
```

After saying that this document conforms to the syntax of XML 1.0 using the XML declaration at the top, we declare that this document falls into the Catalog vocabulary – the Document Type "Catalog". More specifically, the very first, or **root**, element of the document had better be Catalog or the parser will declare an error. In this case that happens to be true.

That ellipsis concealing the rest of the DOCTYPE declaration isn't very satisfying. Where are the declarations? As it happens, there are two ways to provide declarations. You can provide an **external subset** of declarations in a separate DTD file, or include an **internal subset** within the body of the DOCTYPE declaration, or both. In the last instance (mixing internal and external DTDs), the internal DTD may add declarations or override declarations found in the external DTD. (Parsers read the internal subset first and declarations therein take priority, by definition of the XML specification.)

There is one further variation to consider before we see how to provide declarations. The XML declaration can have a standalone attribute, as we saw in Chapter 2. This attribute can have one of two values: yes or no. If the value of that attribute is yes, then there are no declarations external to the document instance that would affect the information in the document passed to the application using it. A value of no indicates that there are external declarations that contain values that are necessary to properly define the document content – specific defaults values, for example.

Here's a variation on the preceding example that tell us that all the declarations we need will be found within the document:

```
<?xml version="1.0" standalone="yes" ?>
<!DOCTYPE Catalog ...
```

The optional standalone attribute is seldom seen in practice. The presence of the attribute with a value of yes does not guarantee that the document has no external dependencies of any *type, merely that it has no external declaration dependencies that, if not included in the processing, would make the document erroneous as far as the receiving application is concerned (even though the document might be well-formed XML). Its chief use is thus as a flag for parsers and other applications to indicate whether they need to retrieve external content.*

Now let's clear up that ellipsis we left earlier. A DOCTYPE declaration formally consists of the keyword, followed by the name of the document's root element (in this case Catalog), followed by an optional external identifier, followed by an optional block of markup declarations. The external identifier names and locates an external DTD (an external subset), while the markup declaration block physically contains markup declarations (an internal subset). Let's look at the markup declaration block first.

The Internal DTD Subset

If we want, we can bundle all the declarations we need in an internal subset, as we saw briefly in the last chapter. The markup declaration block within a DOCTYPE tag consists of a left square bracket, a list of declarations, and a right square bracket. Here's a simple example:

```
<!DOCTYPE Catalog [ ...internal subset declarations here... ]>
```

Internal DTDs are very useful. There is never a question about getting the DTD you need for the document. For all but the simplest XML vocabularies, however, an internal DTD can add substantial size to the document. Also, authoring sources (whether human authors or programs) must include the same internal DTD in every document instance. Even if the consumer of the document has no intention of validating the document, the declarations must be transmitted with the document. We won't use internal DTDs very often, but they are useful for simple vocabularies – particularly when testing prototypes of markup.

In some cases, authors might want to use both an internal DTD and an external DTD. The internal DTD adds declarations. When an internal DTD declares some item that was also declared in the external DTD, the internal declaration supersedes the external declaration. This permits some fine-tuning of declarations for particular document needs, but care must be exercised. If we override the external DTD too often it starts to lose relevance – a sign of a poor initial design.

External DTDs

An external DTD is more flexible in certain respects. The last chapter included a section on referencing one; in this section we'll recap and expand on what we learnt there. In this case, the DOCTYPE declaration consists of the usual keyword and root element name, followed by another keyword denoting the source of the external DTD, followed by the location of that DTD. Declaring the source has a few twists. The keyword for this can be either SYSTEM or PUBLIC. If the keyword is SYSTEM, the parser should be able to find the DTD given the URL alone – the DTD is directly and explicitly located by a URL. In that case, what follows "SYSTEM" is a URL naming the DTD file.

URLs used to locate DTDs should not contain fragment identifiers (the character # followed by a name). XML 1.0 indicates that parsers may signal an error if the URL contains such an identifier.

Here are two examples:

```
<!DOCTYPE Catalog SYSTEM "http://myserver/decs/PubCatalog.dtd">
```

and:

```
<!DOCTYPE Catalog SYSTEM
   "http://www.universallibrary.org/publishing/PubCatalog.dtd">
```

All the declarations needed to validate the document containing the first DOCTYPE declaration will be found in the file PubCatalog.dtd. In the second case, the DTD file is found on a Web server operated by a hypothetical universal library organization. In both cases an element declaration for the Catalog element is expected to be found within the PubCatalog.dtd file.

If, however, the source is PUBLIC, matters are slightly more involved. The PUBLIC keyword is provided for well-known vocabularies. For example, suppose considerable consensus had built up in the publishing industry around the book catalog DTD. An application parsing a document from this vocabulary might employ some strategy for locating the DTD. If it is very common, the application might have a local copy. Using it would be preferable to making a roundtrip to a Web server. The declarations might be in a database, or some other application-specific technique. By using the PUBLIC keyword with a URI, applications are given the opportunity to locate the DTD using their own algorithms.

A Uniform Resource Identifier (URI) may be a URL or simply a unique name.

For example:

```
<!DOCTYPE Catalog PUBLIC "universal/Publishing/Book">
```

If the URI universal/Publishing/Book is well known to the application processing documents of this type, the application can go find the DTD on its own in some efficient manner. Perhaps we have an XML parser geared to this particular vertical industry. It might have a local copy of the DTD, or it might access a DTD maintained on a local database server. The point is that the means of finding the DTD is left primarily to the application processing the DOCTYPE declaration.

Of course, the term "well-known" is frequently relative. In consequence, XML 1.0 permits a PUBLIC declaration to have both a public URI and a system identifier. If the application or parser consuming the document cannot locate a DTD from the URI provided with the PUBLIC keyword, it must use the system identifier.

```
<!DOCTYPE Catalog PUBLIC "universal/Publishing/Book"
   "http://www.universallibrary.org/publishing/PubCatalog.dtd">
```

In this example, the author of the document gave the receiving application a chance to find the DTD based on the public URI. If that fails, as would be expected of a general-purpose parser with no knowledge of our publishing domain, the application would be expected to request the named file from the Web server at www.universallibrary.org.

Basic Markup Declarations

The allowable content of an XML document is defined in terms of four kinds of markup declarations used in the DTD. The keywords associated with these declarations and their meanings are shown in the table below. The first two declarations deal with the information we expect to find in an XML document – elements and attributes:

DTD construct	Meaning
ELEMENT	Declaration of an XML element type
ATTLIST	Declaration of the attributes that may be assigned to a specific element type and the permissible values of those attributes

DTD construct	Meaning
ENTITY	Declaration of reusable content
NOTATION	Format declarations for external content not meant to be parsed (binary data, for example), and the external application that handles the content

The last two types may be thought of as supporting players. Entities, in particular, are designed to make an XML vocabulary designer's life easier. They normally consist of content that recurs sufficiently often in the DTD or document to warrant creating a special declaration. You use that declaration like an `include` statement in C/C++, repeating the name as a placeholder for the content.

Notations deal with content other than XML. A notation is used to declare a particular class of data and associate it with an external program. That external program becomes the handler for the declared class of data. For example, if you associated a JPEG image with a document you would want to have a viewer to accept and render the JPEG binary data. Of course, your document now depends on the handler being present on the receiving system. Some authors will forgo the handler reference in the interests of portability. In that case, the notation simply becomes a typing mechanism.

We will look at notations and entities in more detail in the next section.

Formal DTD Structure

Now you know what a DTD is and how to associate one with a document. I hope that the examples have whetted your appetite for learning how to declare document structure. In addition to the four markup declarations mentioned earlier, there are several other constructs that DTDs use. First, though, we'll tackle **entities**.

All the syntax we are going to discuss is precisely specified in the XML 1.0 Recommendation (`http://www.w3.org/TR/REC-xml/`). As that can sometimes be a bit cryptic, you may wish to have a look at the Annotated XML Specification, written by Tim Bray, a co-author of the Recommendation. This document can be found at `http://www.xml.com/axml/testaxml.htm`. It was originally created in XML, so it is also an interesting example of an XML application.

Entities

XML provides a facility for declaring chunks of content and referencing them as many times as you like where they are needed, saving space and sparing document authors a lot of typing. With the declaration of an entity in the DTD you define a name and the content it refers to. When you need it, you refer to it by name with a particular syntax indicating that the name is an entity reference. This is similar to a `define` directive in C/C++, or any sort of replaceable, boilerplate text or content. An entity used within the contents of a document is a **general entity**. We can refine our definition depending on whether or not the content of the entity is parsed. A **parsed entity** is XML content. The value of the entity is known as the replacement text. In contrast, an **unparsed entity** need not even be text.

If it is text, it need not be XML. This is where the terms come from. If you know that the replacement content may not be XML, or perhaps not even text, there is little point in turning a parser on it. On the other hand, a parsed entity is XML you are pasting into the document content, so you must pass it through the parser.

Let's look at the types of entity more closely, again recapping and expanding on the information in the last chapter.

Predefined Entities

XML must reserve some characters, such as the angle brackets, for its own use. In addition, some characters are non-printable. XML therefore provides some predefined entities so that authors may use these characters in their documents without conflict. So in the text content of an element, for example, certain characters can be referred to without them being confused with markup by the document processor at parse time.

Any character may be referred to by a numeric reference. This is done by writing the characters `&#` followed immediately (without white space) by the numeric value of the character and a semicolon. The greater than symbol, then, could be written `>`. Some characters are so prevalent that XML provides some predefined entities to deal with them:

Character	Entity Reference
<	<
>	>
&	&
' (apostrophe)	'
" (quotation mark)	"

So you might see for example:

```
<some_math>We have Arthur&apos;s variable x, where 10 &lt; x &gt; 46 </some_math>
```

General Entities

The simplest form of an entity is the general entity. It lets us declare a chunk of parsed text associated with a name by which we shall refer to the text. You declare such an entity with the keyword `ENTITY`, a name, and a replacement value. Here's a simple one:

```
<!ENTITY copyright "© MegaTrouble Toys, Inc., 1999">
```

With this declaration in place, we can plug in the copyright text anywhere in a document's content that we need it simply by referring to the name "copyright". Of course, a parser needs to be told when we are making an entity reference so that it won't confuse the entity name with markup text. To signal this intent, we delimit the name with an ampersand in front of the name and a semicolon following. There cannot be white space between the name and its delimiters:

```
&copyright;
```

Note that since the ampersand character is reserved for this role in XML, if we need to use an ampersand for something else in a document, we must use the predefined entity (shown earlier) for the character.

> **When the replacement text for an entity reference is substituted at parse time, the result must be well-formed XML.**

General entities also have an external form, where the replacement text is given in an external file. The declaration takes the form:

```
<!ENTITY myEntity  SYSTEM  "http://www.wrox.com/boilerplate/copyrighttext.txt" >
```

The keyword SYSTEM is used to indicate an external source, followed by the URL for the file. The combination of the PUBLIC keyword, URI identifier, and a fallback URL can also be used. There is a restriction on the use of external entities within a document in that references to *parsed* external entities cannot be made within the value of an attribute in case the character encoding of the entity is different from that of the main document.

Note that non-validating parsers are not required to read and include the content of entities with external content.

Lastly, entities must not contain references to themselves, either directly or indirectly. So the following declarations are illegal:

```
<!ENTITY badSelfRef    "Dancing with my&badSelfRef;" >
<!ENTITY referToOther  "Talking about &referBack;" >
<!ENTITY referBack    "Talking about &referToOther; >
```

Now let's look at another type of entity: parameter entities.

Parameter Entities

Parsed entities that are used solely within the DTD are called **parameter entities**. They let us easily reference and/or change commonly used constructs in the DTD by keeping them in one place. This is easier than changing a construct everywhere it appears in a DTD, but it still requires us to edit the DTD when we extend a construct. They are declared with the ENTITY keyword, a percent sign, a name, and the replacement value. It looks like this:

```
<!ENTITY  % peopleParameters  "age  CDATA #IMPLIED weight CDATA #IMPLIED height
   CDATA #REQUIRED">
```

The keyword CDATA refers to character data; more on this in the section on Attributes later.

The replacement text above is part of an attribute list declaration containing three common attributes. It is intended to be processed just as if it had been written into the DTD. Whenever this set of attributes turns up in our DTD, we can simply refer to the entity peopleParameters.

All parameter entities must be declared before they are referred to within a DTD. This means that a parameter entity declared in the external subset of the DTD cannot be referred to in the internal subset as the latter is read first by the parser – thus the reference will be seen before the declaration.

A parameter entity reference consists of the name delimited by a percent sign in front of the name and a semicolon following. There can be no white space between the delimiters and the name. Thus, we would reference the above entity like this:

```
<!ATTLIST   InsuredPerson
   %peopleParameters;
   carrier   CDATA   #REQUIRED >
```

For the moment, you'll have to take my word for it, but the `InsuredPerson` element is declared to have four attributes: one, `carrier`, that is explicitly declared, and the three (`age`, `weight`, and `height`) that appeared in our parameter entity and are declared when the replacement text is substituted for the entity reference by the parser. Thus, the example above is equivalent to the following:

```
<!ATTLIST   InsuredPerson
      age   CDATA #IMPLIED
      weight CDATA #IMPLIED
      height CDATA #REQUIRED
      carrier   CDATA   #REQUIRED >
```

This type of substitution – *within* a declaration – only works within the external subset of the DTD. In the internal subset, parameter entity references can only be made between other declarations; thus the replacement text for such an entity reference must be a complete declaration, otherwise the DTD will not be well formed.

All the rules for well-formed documents apply to parameter entities. The document must be well-formed after the replacement text has been substituted for the entity reference. Be careful when constructing parameter entities that you take this into account. In general, use markup within a parameter entity's replacement text only with extreme care. The following violates the well-formedness constraint:

```
<!ENTITY % myParm  "<!ENTITY genEnt 'some replacement text here'  ">
%myParm;
```

The replacement text for `%myParm;` is an incomplete declaration missing a terminating >, so when the substitution of `%myParm;` is made the DTD is no longer well-formed.

As was the case for general entities, parameter entities can have replacement text that resides in an external file:

```
<!ENTITY % myParam SYSTEM  "http://www.wrox.com/declarationsets/Wroxdecls1A.ent">
```

It should be clear from the discussion thus far that entities are a very useful tool to help us in our definition of XML document vocabularies. Now let's look at how we define the element types in our vocabulary.

Elements

The heart and soul of XML is the element. Element types are declared in DTDs using the ELEMENT tag. In addition to the keyword, the tag provides a name for the declared type and a content specification. Element type names have some restrictions on them that apply to names throughout XML, as we saw in Chapter 2. Names may use letters, digits, and the punctuation marks colon (:), underscore (_), hyphen (-), and period (.). Names may not, however, begin with a digit. They may only begin with a letter, underscore, or colon.

Although colons may be used with names, we will find a reserved use for them in a subsequent chapter when we take up the topic of namespaces. For this reason, it is best to avoid their use in element names.

Element content falls into four categories: **empty**, **element**, **mixed**, and **any**. An empty element has neither text nor child elements contained within it. It may have attributes. It is denoted with the keyword EMPTY. Element (a better term might be element-only) content denotes the situation in which an element contains child elements, but no text. Mixed content, as the name implies, is a mix of elements and parsed character data (#PCDATA), or text, content. These two types are where we can use structure to express meaning. Mixed and element content is indicated with a **content model**. A content model is a specification of the internal structure of an element's content. If you wish to leave the content of an element wide-open to any content that does not violate XML well-formed syntax, you declare it with the keyword ANY.

```
<!ELEMENT SomeData   EMPTY>
<!ELEMENT AnyOldThing   ANY>
```

The element type SomeData has no content. Here's an instance of the type:

```
<SomeData/>
```

There are a number of reasons why you might want to use an empty element. The mere appearance of the element in a document might signify something to an application. HTML does this with the <BR/> element. You might use this approach to signify that your application should change processing modes, for example. You might use empty element content if you wanted to insert a group of related parameters into a document that are too simple to have structure of their own. A related use is to express relationships. As we will see later when we discuss attributes, XML has some attribute types that are useful for expressing one-to-one and one-to-many relationships. If the relationship is all that is of interest, an empty element with such attributes is valuable.

The declaration of AnyOldThing as having ANY content would let us use any combination of elements and text. Generally speaking, you should use the ANY content model with extreme care, as the parser will provide very little validity checking for you.

Content models are where element structure gets declared. A **content model** consists of a set of parentheses enclosing some combination of child element names, operators, and the #PCDATA keyword. The operators are used to denote cardinality and indicate how elements and character data may be combined.

Order operators	Meaning
,	(comma) strict sequence
|	(pipe) choice

Taking the first of these, elements may be combined in sequence using a comma-delimited list. Here's a declaration for a PersonName element:

```
<!ELEMENT PersonName (First, Middle, Last)>
```

The elements First, Middle, and Last must appear, and they must appear in the order specified. Suppose you want to leave a document author some choice. Here's a declaration for a FruitBasket element type that could contain Apple or Orange, but not both:

```
<!ELEMENT FruitBasket (Apple | Orange)>
```

You may also nest content models for greater expression. Here is a modified FruitBasket that has Cherry followed by a choice of Apple or Orange:

```
<!ELEMENT FruitBasket (Cherry, (Apple | Orange))>
```

This variation must have Cherry and a choice between Apple and Orange. The elements will appear in that order. That is, the following two examples are the only permutations that are valid according to the declaration:

```
<FruitBasket>
   <Cherry>...</Cherry>
   <Orange>...</Orange>
</FruitBasket>
```

```
<FruitBasket>
   <Cherry>...</Cherry>
   <Apple>...</Apple>
</FruitBasket>
```

The operators we have seen so far lack something important: **cardinality**. How many instances of an element type are permitted? Here are the cardinality operators:

Cardinality operators	Meaning
?	Optional; may or may not appear
*	Zero or more
+	One or more

If no cardinality operator is used, the cardinality is one. These operators can be used with elements or content model groups to form very complicated structures. Let's do one more variation of the `FruitBasket` element type declaration:

```
<!ELEMENT FruitBasket (Cherry+, (Apple | Orange)*)>
```

This content model group says our basket contains one or more instances of the element type `Cherry`, followed by zero or more instances of the choice between `Apple` and `Orange`. Notice that all `Cherry` elements must appear together. Here's a conforming instance of `FruitBasket`:

```
<FruitBasket>
   <Cherry>...</Cherry>
   <Cherry>...</Cherry>
   <Apple>...</Apple>
   <Orange>...</Orange>
   <Orange>...</Orange>
</FruitBasket>
```

If you want to indicate mixed content, include `#PCDATA` in the content model. The elements in the content model must then be separated by the | operator, and the group as a whole declared as having 'zero or more' cardinality:

```
<!ELEMENT MixedBag (#PCDATA | ItemA | ItemB)*>
```

When using mixed content models, the `#PCDATA` keyword must be the first choice in the model according to the syntax specified in the XML 1.0 Recommendation, section 3.2.2.

This would indicate zero or more choices from `ItemA`, `ItemB`, and `#PCDATA`. This could lead to an instance such as this:

```
<MixedBag>
  <ItemA>...</ItemA>
  Here is some text I wanted to include as pcdata
  <ItemA>...</ItemA>
  <ItemB>...</ItemB>
</MixedBag>
```

Consider the content models below and think about what they are trying to express:

```
<!ELEMENT foo (A, (B | C)>
```

The element `foo` has two child elements, the first of which is always the element `A`. The second is a choice between `B` and `C`.

```
<!ELEMENT foo (A, B?, C)>
```

Now foo has two or three children in strict sequence. B is optional.

```
<!ELEMENT foo (A?, ((B, C) | D), E?)>
```

Our foo element has become a lot more complicated. The first child element can now be A, B, or D. It can have one to four child elements depending on the choices made. A is optional, B and C, or D will appear, and E is optional.

```
<!ELEMENT foo ((A, B) | (C | D))>
```

The element foo now has one or two children. Either A and B appear in that order, or C appears, or D appears. Now let's make a slight change to this model:

```
<!ELEMENT foo ((A, B)+ | (C | D))>
```

In the above example, we can have a repeating list of the pair A and B, or we can have a single occurrence of either C or D. Content models can produce strikingly different instances of child content. For instance:

```
<!ELEMENT foo (A, (B, C)*, D+)>
```

gives an A followed by zero or more pairs of B *then* C, followed by at least one D.

I hope the above examples have provoked you to try more involved models. Very rich and flexible structures can be composed from the simple rules offered by content models. Try writing out some documents conforming to the definitions above and running them through a validating parser using a DTD that contains one of the fragments above.

> *There are several parsers accessible as web pages on the Internet. I often use the validating one at* `http://www.stg.brown.edu/service/xmlvalid/` *to check out my DTD structures.*

Now let's look at attributes.

Attributes

Attributes complement and modify elements by providing a means of associating simple properties with elements. They are a particularly rich feature of XML that allows us to tie in a lot of information. In an HTML IMG tag, SRC is an attribute, for example. Attributes are declared in XML DTDs with the ATTLIST tag. Each element that has attributes declared for it will have at least one ATTLIST tag declaring an attribute list for the element. An ATTLIST declaration consists of the ATTLIST keyword followed by the name of the element to which the list applies, followed by zero or more attribute definitions. For readability, we often place each attribute definition on a separate line.

Each attribute definition consists of the name of the attribute, its type, and a default declaration:

```
<!ATTLIST myElement AttributeName CDATA #REQUIRED >
```

In this case we are declaring a single attribute `AttributeName` that must occur (`#REQUIRED` – default setting) in the start-tag of every instance of a `myElement` element, and that the value of the attribute is a character data string (`CDATA`).

An attribute declaration can have one of several different defaults that define the way the attribute appears in the document. Before we look at declaring the *types* of value for an attribute let's look at how defaults work in attribute declarations.

Default Values

There are four defaults for attribute declarations. These are shown in the following table:

Attribute defaults	Meaning
`#REQUIRED`	The attribute must appear on every instance of the element
`#IMPLIED`	The attribute may optionally appear on an instance of the element
`#FIXED` plus default value	The attribute must always have the default value; if the attribute does not appear, the value is assumed by the parser
Default value only	If the attribute does not appear, the default value is assumed by the parser. If the attribute appears it may have another value

If a default attribute value is provided in an `ATTLIST` declaration and the attribute is omitted in some instance of the element in a document, an XML parser behaves as though the attribute appeared with the default value. Thus, for the attribute declaration that appears below, the two element instances are equivalent:

```
<!ATTLIST SomeElt color "blue">

<SomeElt color="blue">...</SomeElt>
<SomeElt>...</SomeElt>
```

As you can see from the example, the declaration of the `color` attribute gave us a default value: `blue`. We explicitly declared this in the first instance, but left the attribute off in the second instance of the element. A parser would treat both as having a value of `blue` for the attribute `color`.

As an additional example let's consider a `Book` element with a `level` attribute. Now consider what happens if we decide that the `level` attribute should default to `Professional`:

```
<!ATTLIST Book
   level   CDATA  "Professional"
   >
```

If a Book element appears in the document without a level attribute, any application processing this element will assume that level appears with the value Professional. This is useful in cases where a default value predominates. In such cases, we declare the default value and omit the attribute from any element whose value matches the default.

However, this technique can also present a problem for your applications. Be sure that you select a default value that is safe in terms of your application's processing. It is easy to forget and omit an attribute. In that case, the DTD's default takes over. If you intend to write code that relies on the proper setting of an attribute's value, you should use the #REQUIRED keyword (or an enumeration of values, which we discuss later) and force values to be explicitly set.

Without worrying about the meaning of the various parts just yet, take a look at a sample attribute list for an element named Book:

```
<!ATTLIST Book
    ISBN       ID     #REQUIRED
    level      CDATA  #IMPLIED
    pubDate    CDATA  #REQUIRED
    pageCount  CDATA  #REQUIRED
    authors    IDREFS #IMPLIED
    threads    IDREFS #IMPLIED
    imprint    IDREF  #IMPLIED >
```

Note how we specify the element name, Book, followed by an attribute name, its type, and whether or not it is required. Optional attributes are denoted by the keyword #IMPLIED. Attributes that must always appear in every Book element are denoted by the keyword #REQUIRED.

Several XML types categorize attributes. These are shown in the table below:

Attribute Type	Meaning
CDATA	Character data (string)
ID	Name unique within a given document
IDREF	Reference to some element bearing an ID attribute possessing the same value as the IDREF attribute
IDREFS	Series of IDREFs delimited by white space
ENTITY	Name of a pre-defined external entity
ENTITIES	Series of ENTITY names delimited by white space
NMTOKEN	A name
NMTOKENS	A series of NMTOKENs delimited by white space
NOTATION	Accepts one of a set of names indicating notation types declared in the DTD
[Enumerated Value]	Accepts one of a series of explicitly user-defined values that the attribute can take on

Let's examine each of these attribute types in turn.

CDATA

Ultimately, all of our content turns up as text. When you have an attribute type whose value consists of just text, you may declare it as `CDATA`:

```
<!ATTLIST  SomeElt  someText CDATA  #IMPLIED>
```

The value of that attribute may be any character data string of any length. The only restriction is that the attribute value cannot contain markup. The declaration above might give us the following example:

```
<SomeElt someText="This is valid">...</SomeElt>
```

So long as the attribute value is simple text, the parser will declare it to be valid.

ID, IDREF, IDREFS: Relationships within Documents

An attribute that is an `ID` type is intended to have, not surprisingly, a value that is a unique identifying name. Values must follow the rules for names in XML. The value of an `ID` attribute on a given element must be unique throughout the document. This lets us uniquely name an element. No element may have more than one attribute of type `ID`. Finally, an attribute of type `ID` must be `#IMPLIED` or `#REQUIRED`, but never `#FIXED` *or* defaulted. When you think about it, it makes no sense to provide a default value, particularly a fixed default, for an `ID`. That would immediately violate the uniqueness constraint. For example, here a declaration that attaches a person's SSN (Social Security Number) to their details within a file as a unique identifier:

```
<!ATTLIST Person
   SSN ID  #REQUIRED>
```

What can we do with an `ID` type attribute to make it useful? Refer to it, of course. We can use it to model a one-to-one relationship between two objects modeled by elements in our vocabulary. The `IDREF` type allows us to create links and cross-references within documents. *Values* of `IDREF` attributes must meet the same constraints as `ID` types. They must also be the same as the value of some `ID` attribute value within the document. You can't use an `IDREF` value to point to an `ID` that isn't in the document (but there are other mechanisms for doing this, as we shall see in Chapter 8). In applications, then, we can use `ID` and `IDREF` to cross reference information instead of repeating it. If a document contained the declaration above, we could have the following declarations elsewhere in the DTD:

```
<!ELEMENT Customer EMPTY>
<!ATTLIST Customer
   id IDREF  #REQUIRED>
```

We have to know implicitly that the attribute `id` refers to the `SSN` attribute on `Person`. Then in a document:

```
<Person SSN="111-22-3333">
   <Name>...</Name>
   ...
</Person>
...
<Customer id="111-22-3333"/>
```

Rather than duplicate the entire `Person` element within `Customer`, we have an empty element with an `IDREF`. When we need `Person` information, our application can search for a `Person` element with the `SSN` attribute whose value matches the `id` attribute in a specified `Customer`.

Sometimes we want to link one element to many other elements. That is the purpose of the `IDREFS` type. It allows us to model a one-to-many relationship. The value of this type of attribute is a series of `ID` values separated by white space. The individual `ID`s must meet the `ID` type constraints, of course, and must match up with `ID` attribute values elsewhere in the document.

```
<!ELEMENT  Team  EMPTY>
<!ATTLIST  Team
   members IDREFS #REQUIRED>
```

Here, we've declared an empty element that specifies a relationship between individual members who form a project team. The `members` attribute will give us the identities of the team members by referring to `Person` elements declared elsewhere in the DTD with an `ID` type attribute. For example:

```
<Team members="111-22-3333 222-11-4444 123-45-6789"/>
```

This gives us a team composed of the people whose social security numbers are `111-22-3333`, `222-11-4444`, and `123-45-6789`.

`ID`, `IDREF`, and `IDREFS` attribute types give us the tools we need to express relationships commonly encountered in relational databases. This is particularly useful if you are using XML as an exchange format on top of a local database with a proprietary schema.

ENTITY, ENTITIES: Replaceable Content

Entities can be used within attribute declarations for the usual reasons of efficiency and reuse of common constructions. You have a construction that appears several times, so you declare an entity representing the construction, and then refer to it wherever you need the construction. Entities may additionally be used to include unparsed entities as valid attribute values. This is the mechanism by which a document author can point to data other than XML markup. If we have an image file that we wish to include with some XML data, a standard illustration for example, we can do this with an entity. We start by declaring the attribute to be of type `ENTITY`:

```
<!ATTLIST  SalesResults
      month_graph  ENTITY  #IMPLIED>
```

Elsewhere in the DTD, we declare the entity:

```
<!ENTITY  sales_chart  SYSTEM  "sales_chart.gif"  NDATA  gif>
```

The NDATA (notation data) keyword indicates that the data for the entity has an associated notation type (see the section on NOTATION-type attributes later).

Then, in the XML document, we can refer to the image in our attribute:

```
<SalesResults month_graph="sales_chart">...</SaleResults>
```

This associates the GIF file `sales_chart.gif` with the `SalesResults` element.

This works well for small numbers of entities that are commonly reused. In our example, for instance, you would reuse `sales_chart.gif` by overwriting the file each month. It is impractical for cases in which the entity values must change frequently.

To use `ENTITY` as an attribute type, then, you need to do four things. Three of them are declarations in the DTD (recall this can be either an external DTD or an internal subset). The fourth involves a specific document instance. Here, in summary, are the four steps:

- Declare a notation (which we will take up shortly)
- Declare one or more entities for use with the attribute
- Declare an attribute of type `ENTITY` for some element
- Create an instance of the element type in a document, providing the attribute and an entity name as the value

Just as we were able to use multiple `IDREF` values as a single attribute value (`IDREFS`), we can do the same with entities. The type is `ENTITIES`, and it works similarly to `IDREFS`. Each name in the attribute value must conform to the rules for the `ENTITY` type, and individual entity names are separated by white space. Thus (omitting the notation declaration for the time being):

```
<!ELEMENT  AccidentScene (#PCDATA)>
<!ATTLIST  AccidentScene
   photos  ENTITIES  #IMPLIED>
<!ENTITY  site  SYSTEM  "http://someserver/photos/scene.jpg" NDATA  JPEG>
<!ENTITY  auto_pic  SYSTEM  "http://someserver/photos/auto145.jpg" NDATA JPEG>
<!ENTITY  victims  SYSTEM  "http://someserver/photos/victims.jpg" NDATA JPEG>
...
<AccidentScene photos="site auto_pic victims">Accident Scene report...
</AccidentScene>
```

Now our insurance report pertaining to an accident scene has an element, `AccidentScene`, associated with photos of the scene, the car, and the victims related to it.

NMTOKEN, NMTOKENS: Name Tokens

On some occasions you will want to treat the value of an attribute as a discrete token rather than text. We could use an enumeration (which we'll tackle soon), but suppose we wanted to leave the list of values open-ended? XML has a type called **name token** that fits the bill. These are abbreviated in DTDs as NMTOKEN. NMTOKEN types must conform to the rules for names that we discussed under elements, although they are free of one restriction. They must be composed of letters, digits, and the punctuation marks colon, underscore, period, and hyphen. Unlike element and attribute names, though, any of these characters may be used for the first character of an NMTOKEN. Here's an example of how to declare an NMTOKEN attribute:

```
<!ATTLIST Employee
   security_level NMTOKEN  #REQUIRED>

<Employee security_level="trusted">...
```

This says that an Employee element may have an attribute named security_level whose value conforms to the rules for XML name tokens. We could use this to control access to confidential documents, for example. By choosing NMTOKEN over an enumeration, document authors will be able to accommodate new security level designations as they are created without editing the DTD every time. Any value that conforms to the rules we just stated for composing valid NMTOKEN values will be accepted as the value for this attribute.

Of course, this puts the burden of ensuring that permissible or meaningful values are used on the application. With an enumeration, a validating parser can provide this check for you.

As with IDREFS and ENTITIES, we can declare attributes of type NMTOKENS that have values composed of multiple name tokens. Each name must be a valid name token, and the items are separated by white space:

```
<!ATTLIST Employee
   security_compartments NMTOKENS  #IMPLIED>

<Employee security_compartments="red green mega ultra">...
```

This employee has access to the security compartments named red, green, mega, and ultra. These are valid NMTOKEN values in respect of their type, which is all that matters in this case. Unlike an enumeration, there is no checking performed on the value. It is up to the author to ensure he has provided an appropriate name.

NOTATION: Data Other than XML

We referred to notations back when we were considering entity type attributes. We gave some examples in which GIF and JPEG image files were associated with elements by using an entity name as the value of an attribute. However, an XML parser is not equipped to deal with binary formats. What is the parser to do? Notations are used to identify the format of external data items that we want to link to XML documents. We need a notation declaration to declare a name for the format and associate that name with an external handler. The parser refers the foreign data to the handler for processing. The handler declaration works like the DOCTYPE declaration did in locating DTD files. It can be PUBLIC or SYSTEM, and it must include the name of the external handler:

```
<!NOTATION  jpg  SYSTEM "jpgviewer.exe">
<!NOTATION  gif  SYSTEM "gifviewer.exe" >
```

Now we know that anytime the name `jpg` is used as a notation name, the data associated with the name should be sent off to `jpgviewer.exe` for processing. With notations, XML documents can now be the unifying document of a collection of dissimilar data types. This is useful for reports, medical records, legal and scholarly exhibits, and any rich multimedia presentation. XML, however, only gives you the minimal set of tools. Considerable effort is needed to build the proper presentation semantics into an application.

An attribute may be typed as a notation name by using the keyword `NOTATION`. For example:

```
<!ATTLIST  Image  type  NOTATION  (gif|jpg) "gif" >

<Image type="jpg">...
```

The above declaration says that an `Image` element may have an attribute `type` that is a notation. Acceptable values for the attribute are `gif` and `jpg`. If we were to leave the type attribute off an instance, the parser would assume that the attribute appeared with the default value, `gif`. In the instance shown, however, the value `jpg` overrides the default.

Enumerations: Choices

Name tokens are open-ended. The name rules restrict the format of values of `NMTOKEN` and `NMTOKENS` attributes, but leave the set of permissible values open otherwise. In many cases, we have a small set of character string values we want to permit: `yes` and `no` are useful enumerations for decision making; `red`, `yellow`, and `green` are important for traffic signals in the United States; and so forth. In such cases we resort to enumerated attributes.

An attribute is declared to be an enumeration by placing a group of values where the type keyword normally appears. A group consists of parentheses enclosing the permitted values separated by the pipe symbol (|). The values are not enclosed by quotation marks but, like names in XML, values are case sensitive. An instance of an attribute in the document must include one and only one of the permitted values exactly as it appears in the attribute declaration. Like any other attribute value, the enumerated value must be enclosed by quotation marks. Here are some examples:

```
<!ATTLIST Employee
   manager (yes | no)  #REQUIRED>

<!ATTLIST ClassifiedDoc
   security_level (unclassified | secret | Top_Secret) #REQUIRED>
```

In the first case only the value `yes` or `no` is permitted; `Yes`, `NO`, and `maybe` will all be rejected as invalid. It is every bit as important to respect case sensitivity as it is to stick to the values provided in the enumeration declaration. When composing an enumeration for values that may be manually entered by a user, consider including all the variations produced by modifying the case of the values.

Now let's look at one more technique we can use with our DTDs.

Conditional Sections

Programmers in many languages are accustomed to being able to specify material that should be parsed by the compiler only if certain conditions are met. DTDs provide a similar feature, albeit more restrictive than you may be accustomed to in programming languages – there is no conditional expression to be evaluated at run time. DTDs may include conditional sections that instruct the parser to include a section of declarations or ignore them. These sections are useful for controlling blocks of related declarations in a DTD. However, conditional sections are *not* allowed in the internal subset of the DTD.

Conditional sections consist of an exclamation mark, a square left bracket, and a keyword followed by a block of declarations delimited by square brackets. If the keyword is `INCLUDE`, the declarations in the block are considered part of the DTD for validation purposes. If the keyword is `IGNORE`, the declarations in the block are read but bypassed by the processor:

```
<![INCLUDE
   [<!ELEMENT AuditEntry  (#PCDATA)>
   <!ATTLIST AuditEntry
      timestamp CDATA #REQUIRED
      userID   IDREF #REQUIRED>
   ]]>

<![IGNORE
   [<!ELEMENT DebugEntry  (#PCDATA)>
   <!ATTLIST DebugEntry
      serial ID #REQUIRED
      page  CDATA #IMPLIED>
   ]]>
```

Note that we've closed both brackets. In this example, `AuditEntry` and its attributes will be part of the DTD and `DebugEntry` and its attributes will not. A document conforming to this DTD would be able to use `AuditEntry` elements but would be invalid if `DebugEntry` elements appeared.

This doesn't seem terribly useful at first glance. Why bother adding declarations to a DTD if you can't use them? Why say `INCLUDE` when the declarations are already there? The practical use of conditional sections is to use them in conjunction with parameter entities. Let's try that example again with a couple of additions. Imagine that we write a couple of entity declarations into the `DOCTYPE` declaration of the document instance when the document is created:

```
<!DOCTYPE MixedBag SYSTEM "testCONDSECT.dtd" [
<!ELEMENT MixedBag (foo)>
<!ELEMENT foo (A, B?, stuff)>
...
<!ELEMENT stuff (#PCDATA| AuditEntry|DebugEntry)*>
<!ENTITY % accountsDept "INCLUDE">
<!ENTITY % codeDept  "IGNORE">
]>
```

And then imagine that the document contains either debug information or accounting information as required when created. If we have the following in our external subset of the DTD:

```
<?xml encoding="UTF-8" ?>
<![%accountsDept;
   [<!ELEMENT AuditEntry  (#PCDATA)>
   <!ATTLIST AuditEntry
      timestamp CDATA #REQUIRED
      userID    IDREF #REQUIRED>
   ]]>

<![%codeDept;
   [<!ELEMENT DebugEntry  (#PCDATA)>
   <!ATTLIST DebugEntry
      serial ID #REQUIRED
      page  CDATA #IMPLIED>
   ]]>
```

then assuming that the document instance is one destined for the accounts department:

```
...
<stuff>We have Arthur&apos;s variable x, where 10 &lt; x &gt; 46
<AuditEntry timestamp="1999-11-29" userID="ref222">blahblah taxes
blahblah</AuditEntry>
</stuff>
...
```

the document should validate correctly.

Remember that declarations in the internal subset of the DTD are read first, so the parameter entity declarations occur before the entities are referred to in the external DTD subset.

This example assumes I want to write some elements for auditing in a production environment, but a different set of elements for debugging purposes during testing or in the case of error detection earlier in the process. The declarations surrounding `AuditEntry` will be included, and the declarations around `DebugEntry` will be ignored. It is a comparatively simple operation to swap the replacement text for the parameter entities, to make `DebugEntry` elements valid for documents with that purpose. If used carefully, conditional sections can provide substantial functionality and promote code reuse.

The Shortcomings of DTDs

DTDs are good enough to have propelled XML through its early adoption phase. However, they suffer from a few limitations. For one thing, they use a syntax all of their own, distinct from that of document instances. Importantly, it would be beneficial if XML parsers could give an application easy access to the declarations in DTDs they process. Few, if any, at present do so. This restricts our use of DTDs in practice to validating documents and conveying domain information to human programmers. Our applications have no opportunity to explore the declarations and learn structure.

Similarly, we can't use parsers to dynamically build DTDs. This might not seem like such a big limitation. After all, a DTD is supposed to be an immutable definition against which documents, some of which are dynamically created, are checked for validity. Even so, we might have some conditional situation in which we wanted to vary the vocabulary rules based on some value. We could read the current value from a database and construct the DTD as we went along. This DTD could be used to create a series of documents that are valid given the current status. The DTD would accompany the documents, thereby allowing the receiver to check the validity of the documents according to the state of the environment when the documents were created. The conditional constructs provided by DTDs don't permit this sort of thing, so we would be forced to dynamically create the DTD. Without parser support, we are forced to implement DTD creation by hand.

DTDs are a closed constructs. The rules of an XML vocabulary are wholly contained in the DTD. What is there is the vocabulary, and nothing else. That doesn't seem like a limitation until you want to borrow a useful declaration or construct from someone else's DTD. What efforts toward extensibility have been made are awkward given the low-level nature of entities. There is no simple and clear way to promote extensibility in DTDs. For extensible markup tools, DTDs aren't terribly cooperative. There is no way to segment declarations so that each declaration is a cohesive whole limited to concepts and objects that are closely related. If we had that feature, we could create a number of DTDs to describe our business domain, then stitch them together by reference to meet the needs of actual applications. When we reach the chapter on namespaces and schemas (Chapter 7) we'll see all sorts of possibilities for borrowing information. We'll have to move beyond DTDs to make use of them.

DTDs are also short on data type information. The only tool they provide is the notation. This does little to allow us to define our own types based on existing types. Notations allow us to flag a name as denoting a type other than parsed text, but that is not the same as a robust typing mechanism. We want to be able to denote some values as being of a simple type, such as numeric, other than text and be able to deal with those values appropriately.

In Chapter 7, we'll examine some proposals for other schema mechanisms before the W3C that seek to address the shortcomings of DTDs. However, irrespective of the shortcomings of DTDs, at the time of writing DTDs are the only formally recognized method for declaring the structure and content of an XML vocabulary. Understanding DTDs is essential to understanding other schema proposals and to using XML with the expectation of exchanging documents in some standard way.

A DTD for the Book Catalog Domain

It is time to take our tools and attempt to define an XML vocabulary for book publishing. More specifically, in the example that follows we want to specify the syntax for describing catalogs of books. At its most general, our vocabulary will deal with a single catalog containing many books. At the most precise, the vocabulary will allow us to describe a book in summary. We'll stop short of permitting a document author to include book content. That seems to be outside the scope of what we are trying to do. If we need to bridge the gap, we might provide some sort of link to a book document, but we really have no need to include content to meet the needs of a book catalog.

Formal Definition of the Book Catalog Domain

Let's take a few moments to describe the business process we are trying to model. We won't worry about the DTD immediately. You can make a good model once you understand the process, but rushing to create rules seldom leads to understanding. We'll begin by blocking out the main objects in our domain and look at how they relate to one another.

The Domain Model

We know coming into the problem that we need to talk about a catalog – whatever that is. Just one, though – everything we want to describe is inside it. We won't deal with relationships between catalogs, but rather with what is inside one catalog. This will sharpen our focus, something I believe is the key to writing a good XML vocabulary.

One catalog containing one or more books – that could be the entire vocabulary right there. What might we be missing if we stop here? Books are brought out by publishers, so perhaps we should include a publisher in the catalog somewhere. Is one enough? The obvious answer is yes. That would lead us to a model in which you need at least one Book Catalog document for each publisher. You might have more than one, though. Publishers sometimes have more than one line or specialty. Does this change things? How are these organized? Catalogs are usually organized around some theme. By default, the theme is everything the publisher prints. A publisher with many books might distribute catalogs more narrowly organized around some topic or area of knowledge.

By itself, that doesn't require us to include more than one publisher. But having raised the issue, you might start thinking who else might do things that way. A library or collector would have the same need to describe books according to a theme. A bookseller could do this, too. The last three catalog users suddenly need to include more than one publisher in their catalogs. Making this change throws open the doors to new opportunities. Such a change usually means you have a problem. It might be expected to stand the model on its head, which means you are pursuing a different problem. This time, though, that isn't the case. We can still satisfy the needs of a single publisher. The flow of the document following the publisher information would be the same: a sequence of book summaries. Going from "one and only one" publisher to "one or more" publishers makes our model a good deal more flexible without interfering with our ability to describe what we started out trying to describe.

What is a theme? It is some organizing thread of knowledge or discussion. Threads in a newsgroup are similar to this. The theme or thread will often be apparent from its name and its contents, but I don't think we should assume this. Threads should have descriptive information of their own. Here's an organizing diagram of what we have so far:

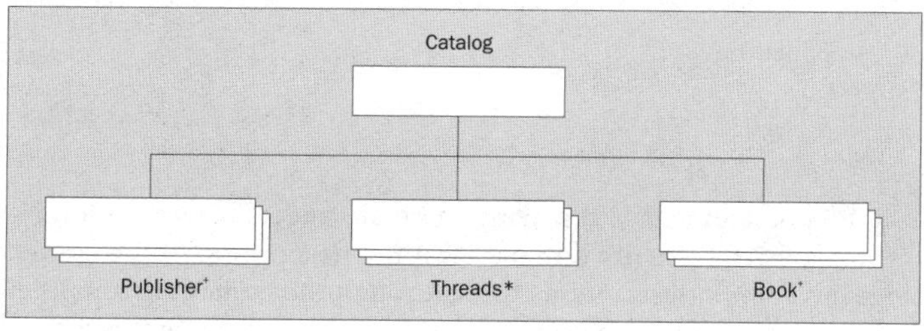

A catalog in our model has one or more publishers, zero or more threads, and one or more books. There are two issues I should discuss at this point. Both are assumptions I am making about the domain of discussion. First is the issue of cardinality. How did I decide that books and publishers should be present in "one or more" cardinality, while threads may not even appear? Well, a book catalog with zero books is an extreme situation only a mathematician could love. The rest of us generally aren't interested in empty sets – if they're empty, why talk about them? This will be a practical, rather than a theoretical vocabulary. However, there might not be any publisher thread to unite titles as such.

The issue isn't quite so clear-cut with respect to publishers. In some situations, we might be happy to just talk about the books in the catalog. Should we make the cardinality on publishers "zero or more"? You might feel differently – there are no immutable rules for building DTDs – but each book has a relationship to a publisher. Even in the simple case – a catalog from a single publisher – we should anchor that relationship. We can skip over publisher information, but we'll need it there for e-commerce applications. I'll make the call and say "one or more" publishers for our cardinality.

The other issue is how to relate threads and books. If we return to our analogy with newsgroup threads, we should make books children of threads. That is a little limiting, though. One book might find its way into multiple threads depending on the nature of the threads in the catalog and the book's generality. Some users of the catalog might not be interested in the organizing information implicit in threads. Many programs will fall into this area. A simple inventory program is one example. It would be interested in all the books, possibly in alphabetical order, or perhaps ordered by ISBN. Folding books into threads would force such programs to follow threads to get to the books. We'll make threads a distinct structure, then. Of course, to make the relationship between books and threads, we're going to need some mechanism for defining the link between the two. Keep this in mind for later.

Let's go one level further and glimpse the structure of our objects before we start in on the mechanics of writing our DTD. Since this is a catalog about books – publishers and threads are important only in how they relate to books – I'll start with them first.

Books

Rather than an organizational chart, I'll use an illustration indicative of a containment relationship because I want to stress that relationship. We are going through this exercise to find the child elements of a book, and that is a containment relationship. What do we have in a book (as concerns a catalog entry)?

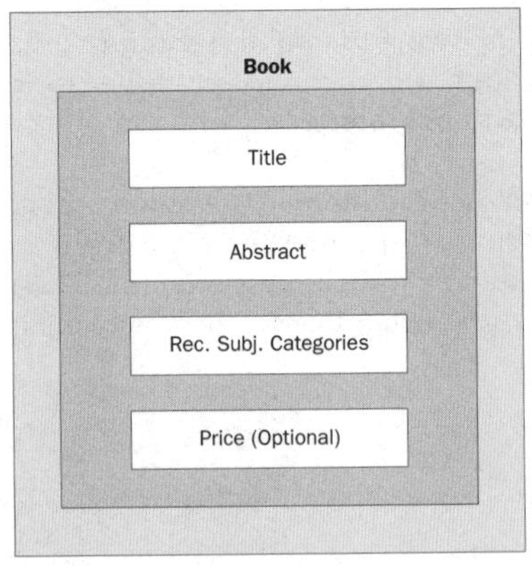

A book always has a title, of course. I'm throwing in an abstract. That's a notion from the academic world, and it just means a brief – usually one paragraph – description of the contents of the book. Printed retail catalogs have book descriptions too, although the content is usually lighter than an academic abstract. A short description is useful either way. In fact, since it is a condensed summary of the book, it would be a prime target for searches. If you get a hit on a keyword here you're much more likely to be interested in the book than if you got the same hit in the body of the book. In the body, you have room for digression. The abstract, however, is restricted to the main topic of the book. Whatever the motivation, a book abstract seems to be a good idea for a catalog.

If you look at the back of many commercially published books, you will find three recommended subject areas. These are provided by the publisher to help booksellers shelve the book appropriately. Catalog documents intended for commercial use should have this information.

Virtually every book that appears in a catalog is intended for sale. There are a few exceptions to this rule. The hypothetical book collector we considered while considering the cardinality of publishers might not be interested in discussing the price of the books in his collection. A museum or library might find price to be a moot point; the book has a value, but it is not catalogued for the purposes of sale. A publisher might put out a catalog in advance of settling on a retail price. For these reasons, let's allow price to be optional.

That seems short – four child items, no more? Remember, though, we explicitly ruled out body content in setting the boundaries of our vocabulary. If you think for a while, you'll realize that you get into the realm of content if you go much further. Chapter headings are content. Let's stop here for the moment, then, and move to one of our other major objects, the publisher.

Publishers

Here's our containment diagram for a publisher:

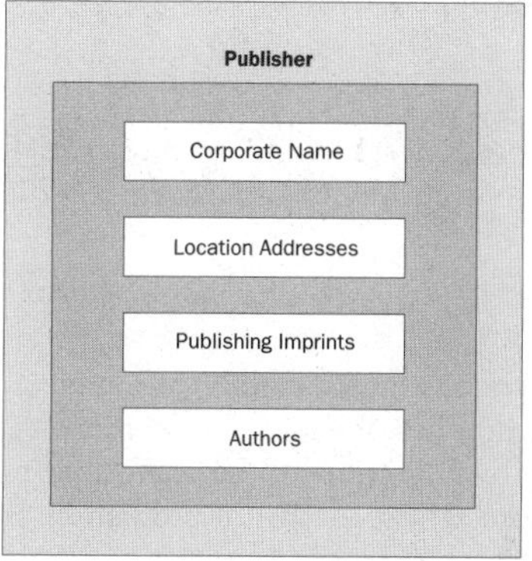

A publisher is a corporate entity. It is a company in the business of causing the creation, publication, and distribution of books. Our model of a publisher should reflect this commercial nature. A name, obviously, is essential. Because it is a company, it might – often does, in fact – have multiple operating locations. It is not unusual, for example, for a major publisher to have a physical presence on each continent on which it does business. The Internet might change this situation, but many publishers need to provide a list of locations – addresses, really. Publishers also often put together multiple imprints. This is similar to threads in catalogs. A better analogy is to brands in marketing. Imprints usually have a name and logo as if they were publishers. Describing a publisher fully necessitates listing its various imprints.

The last thing I've included is a bit more controversial. Authors write books. We might include author information inside books. Authors, however, often write more than one book. It makes sense to describe them outside of books and specify a relationship between the two. This is yet another call for some sort of linking mechanism. We noted this need when we discussed placing books outside threads. We'd better underline that mental note we made. Should authors be outside the scope of the publisher? While authors do jump from one publisher to another, this is the exception rather than the rule. A publisher's stable of authors is an important part of its intellectual capital, so I think we should include author information here.

Threads

What about threads? This is a somewhat elusive concept. It has no explicit parallel in the physical world we are describing. It is just something useful we have noted. It is hard, therefore, to define some formal structure that will apply to all catalogs. I believe that some brief textual content – `#PCDATA` – will be sufficient to describe a thread.

> *The Wrox Press web site (`http://www.wrox.com`) is organized by eight threads. Other publishers have similar concepts, sometimes expressed as a series, or according to the target audience. In the area of computer books, the idea of threads is particularly relevant as books are often organized according to a particular technology, language, or product family.*

The Publishing Catalog DTD

Now that we have some idea of what we are attempting to describe, let's get into the mechanics of specifying the markup to be used in book catalog documents. Objects are modeled in XML through elements. Information they contain will usually be child elements, although some simple properties will be described through attributes.

Catalog

Our upper, most general boundary makes it clear that the catalog element should be the root of a catalog document. From our organizational diagram, we can say the following about catalogs:

```
<!ELEMENT Catalog (Publisher+ , Thread* , Book+ )>
```

The content model is fairly simple. We have an ordered sequence of publishers, threads, and books. We specify the cardinality of each: one or more `Publishers`, zero or more `Threads`, and one or more `Books`. This shows `Threads` to be useful but not essential. Because of the cardinality of threads, we might have cases where the list of publishers is immediately followed by the list of books.

There are no attributes for the catalog element. It is singular, so there is no real need to provide it with its own identity. Everything we need to discuss in the catalog is contained within the other objects in the catalog.

Publisher

With that in mind, we can move on and dive into the definition for the publisher element:

```
<!ELEMENT Publisher (CorporateName , Address+ , Imprints , Author* )>
```

This corresponds to the diagram we saw earlier. We have a corporate entity with a name, one or more locations, some imprints, and zero or more authors. Some publishers may occasionally wish they had zero authors when dealing with a particularly troublesome one, but this is here for a catalog of anonymously authored books, perhaps monographs for a conference.

Wait just one moment, though; there's no cardinality for `Imprints`. This isn't an oversight. Rather than list them all at the same level as the other properties, I made a stylistic decision to provide a collection element at that level. It will have a collection of `Imprint` elements as its children. This doesn't change the meaning at all, but it helps application programmers. It is easy to ignore if that is your wish – simply move to the next element. If you are interested, you can get the number of imprints by checking the parser for the number of child elements belonging to the `Imprints` element.

Before moving on, there is one attribute of the `Publisher` element, and that is `isbn`:

```
<!ATTLIST Publisher isbn CDATA #REQUIRED >
```

We need a unique designator for the `Publisher` element, and we can't rely on the corporate name. A book's ISBN contains a unique number assigned to the publisher. For example, all Wrox Press books have ISBNs that contain the sequence 1861. This fragment of the overall ISBN is what I intend authors to provide as the value for this attribute.

Now let's quickly look at the child elements that make up the `Publisher` element:

```
<!ELEMENT CorporateName (#PCDATA )>
<!ELEMENT Address (Street+ , City , PoliticalDivision , Country , PostalCode )>
<!ELEMENT Imprints (Imprint+ )>
<!ELEMENT Imprint (#PCDATA )>
<!ELEMENT Author (FirstName , MI? , LastName , Biographical , Portrait )>
```

This is about what you would expect. Most of the subordinate elements resolve to `#PCDATA`.

A full listing of the Book Catalog DTD appears at the end of this section.

`Imprints` is composed of one or more `Imprint` elements – the latter being `#PCDATA` – as promised earlier. The `Author` element looks a bit more promising, but before diving into that content model, I'd like to point out a few novelties introduced by the attributes of the `Address` and `Imprint` elements:

```
<!ATTLIST Address headquarters (yes | no ) #IMPLIED >
<!ATTLIST Imprint shortImprintName ID #IMPLIED >
```

Since a publisher can have more than one physical location, it might be useful to distinguish between the headquarters location and the rest. I use a simple enumeration for this, but I don't insist on having this attribute present. The `#IMPLIED` keyword, you'll remember, let's an author leave this attribute off without compromising validity. If it is present, the value must be either `yes` or `no`, exactly.

Now look at the attribute list for the `Imprint` element. Since this element has `#PCDATA` for its content, there is no length restriction on the name of the `Imprint`. I need to associate books with imprints, and it would be nice if I had a short key with which to do this. That's what the `shortImprintName` attribute is for. Thus, Our Incredibly Wonderful Children's Book Division might become IncredChild. We still haven't imposed a length restriction, only suggested one in the name. There is no provision in the DTD grammar for setting lengths on strings.

More important than the problem of string length is the use of the `ID` type for this attribute. If the attribute appears, it is a unique key that may be referenced elsewhere in the document. In our case, we know implicitly that this will occur with the `Book` element, but the DTD doesn't provide a mechanism for stating this explicitly.

Returning to the Author element, here is the declaration of that element and all its children:

```
<!ELEMENT Author (FirstName , MI? , LastName , Biographical , Portrait )>
<!ATTLIST Author authorCiteID ID #REQUIRED>

<!ELEMENT FirstName (#PCDATA )>
<!ELEMENT MI (#PCDATA )>
<!ELEMENT LastName (#PCDATA )>
<!ELEMENT Biographical (#PCDATA )>
<!ELEMENT Portrait EMPTY>
<!ATTLIST Portrait picLink CDATA #IMPLIED >
```

The child elements of Author are relatively mundane and contain the sort of textual information you might expect. We have name and biographical information. The real work in this element comes in the attributes. The authorCiteID attribute of the Author element acts as a short-hand reference in the same way that shortImprintName worked for Imprint. It is an ID type attribute that serves to link an author to one or more books.

The Portrait element is intended to associate an image of the author with the textual information about the author. We cannot simply include the binary data with the XML markup, so we need a linking mechanism. An entity won't do here because we will have many image files to deal with in a long catalog with many authors, most of which will be dynamically named when the document is generated. The XML community is working on many proposals for linking, but there is no Recommendation and little or no support from parser vendors. Rather than drag in the syntax of XLink or XPointer, then, I'll simply provide a URL to the image as the value of the picLink attribute. We will have to create support for any sort of linking mechanism in our applications anyway. If the application consuming the catalog document uses a browser, we can generate an HTML document for the browser that contains an IMG tag. The picLink value would become the value of the IMG tag's SRC attribute in such an application. A non-visual consumer of the document would simply ignore this attribute.

The use of notations suggests itself here. I have chosen not to use this approach though, as I don't want to restrict the behavior of applications using this DTD. Without a handler, a notation will simply give a name to the data type. If I specify a handler, I have committed any applications that consume catalog documents to a particular behavior, such as displaying the link. I want this DTD to be equally useful to applications without a visual interface as well as more conventional, browser-based applications.

Thread

We've explored the content of the Publisher element all the way down to the bottom. Returning to the Catalog content model once more, we find that Thread is the next object in our model. Here is the declaration for that element:

```
<!ELEMENT Thread (#PCDATA )>
<!ATTLIST Thread threadID ID #IMPLIED >
```

The content of the element is just some text describing the thread. It might be a list of keywords (for Wrox this would be ASP, Database, XML and Scripting, etc.) or a longer description. The threadID attribute allows us to link a book to a thread.

Book

Returning once more to Catalog, we finally arrive at the Book element. This is the whole reason for writing this DTD in the first place. The element declaration is straight out of the diagram that we saw while considering the business domain:

```
<!ELEMENT Book (Title , Abstract , RecSubjCategories , Price? )>
```

As you might expect, Title and Abstract are composed of #PCDATA. RecSubjCategories is a bit more detailed:

```
<!ELEMENT RecSubjCategories (Category , Category , Category )>
```

Category is #PCDATA. Remember that we said that each book has three recommended subject areas. In fact, books have exactly three recommended subject areas. The simplest way to express this using the cardinality tools given us by DTDs is to spell out the content model as three instances of the Category element.

> *As we will see in Chapter 7, the proposed XML Schema draft allows us much more precise control. We could use Schema syntax to say that* Category *appears at least three times and at most three times without physically repeating the* Category *name.*

Price has a currency attribute to denote what currency the price value applies to. In this DTD, we are restricting the choices to the US and Canadian dollars and the British pound:

```
<!ATTLIST Price currency (USD | GBP | CD ) #REQUIRED>
```

It wouldn't be difficult to add other currencies and expand the scope of our dealings. This attribute is why Price is itself an element and not an attribute. Normally, I would model a simple atomic property like this as an attribute. Since we are potentially dealing with international trade, we must specify the currency for the Price content to make any sense to the consuming application. I want to make it clear that currency applies to Price. That is why I didn't simply have price and currency attributes associated with Book. By making Price an element with #PCDATA content, I can make currency an attribute and explicitly show what it pertains to.

Speaking of attributes of the Book element, let's look at the declaration for the Book attribute list:

```
<!ATTLIST Book ISBN    ID    #REQUIRED
   level    CDATA  #IMPLIED
   pubDate   CDATA  #REQUIRED
   pageCount CDATA  #REQUIRED
   authors   IDREFS #IMPLIED
   threads   IDREFS #IMPLIED
   imprint   IDREF  #IMPLIED >
```

This is substantially more complicated than anything we have dealt with so far. Many of these attributes are what you might expect, however. `ISBN` is of course the unique ISBN of the book, and we've made it an `ID` in case we want to make any associations later. The level attribute allows a publisher to assign a level of difficulty. The book you are reading is designated Professional. The value of this attribute will be publisher-specific. While most publishers have some concept similar to this, it isn't a universal concept, so I've made it an optional attribute. If it appears, though, it could become a useful key so that the attribute can be used in a sort or filter. The `pubDate` and `pageCount` attributes are the date of publication and count of pages for the book, respectively.

DTD syntax doesn't permit us to define date and numeric types, yet it would be very useful to do so here. An application might perform simple arithmetic to show how old a book is, or how many pages are contained in a multi-volume set. DTDs don't allow us to pass on the information that would enable this. The information must be implicit knowledge in our vocabulary. The XML Schemas proposal addresses this issue.

We've specified a number of `ID` type attributes so far in this DTD. Here is where we finally make use of them. The `authors` attribute has as its value one or more references to the `authorCiteID` values forming the `ID` of particular authors. For example:

```
<Book authors="smohr mkay mbirbeck" ...>
```

This would tell us that the authors whose `authorCiteID` values are `smohr`, `mkay`, and `mbirbeck` are the authors of this book. The `threads` attribute works similarly, associating a book with one or more threads of knowledge:

```
<Book threads="COM database XML" ...>
```

By allowing multiple `ID` references to threads, I allow the catalog to be parsed along multiple paths. A user could consult a catalog document and filter it from one or more threads dictated by his interests. A publisher might offer custom reading lists using the catalog as the base and extracting books according to thread and level.

Finally, `imprint` refers to the publisher's imprint. A book can only be issued by one imprint, so this attribute is of the singular type `IDREF`. Why not have an attribute for the book's publisher? The ISBN of the book contains the publisher's number. This number is always found in the same location of the ISBN, so we could readily extract the publisher's number and search all our `Publisher` elements for the one whose `isbn` attribute had the same value. To make things even easier, we could simply search according to the value of `imprint`. That would give us the `Publisher` without having to extract any substring from an attribute value as we had to do with the ISBN. Either approach is less than completely obvious to a reader, but they constitute useful and practical trade-offs.

As with any design work, multiple results are possible. You are invited to consider book publishing and catalog information from your own experience or requirements. See what sort of DTD you can develop; and see if there are any concepts you need that I have omitted. Try to express the same ideas presented here in a different way and see if that form has more meaning for you. A common source of debate is whether some item of interest should be modeled as an element or an attribute. Make some changes from my decisions and see what happens. Good DTD designs come from experience and experimentation.

The Complete DTD

Here is the complete listing `PubCatalog.dtd`. We'll be using it for the rest of this book:

```
<!ELEMENT Catalog (Publisher+ , Thread* , Book+ )>

<!-- Publisher section -->
<!ELEMENT Publisher (CorporateName , Address+ , Imprints , Author* )>
<!ATTLIST Publisher isbn CDATA #REQUIRED >
<!ELEMENT CorporateName (#PCDATA )>

<!ELEMENT Address (Street+ , City , PoliticalDivision , Country , PostalCode )>
<!ATTLIST Address headquarters (yes | no ) #IMPLIED >
<!ELEMENT Street (#PCDATA )>
<!ELEMENT City (#PCDATA )>

<!--State, province, canton, etc.-->
<!ELEMENT PoliticalDivision (#PCDATA )>
<!ELEMENT Country (#PCDATA )>
<!ELEMENT PostalCode (#PCDATA )>

<!ELEMENT Imprints (Imprint+ )>

<!ELEMENT Imprint (#PCDATA )>
<!ATTLIST Imprint shortImprintName ID #IMPLIED >

<!-- Author section -->

<!ELEMENT Author (FirstName , MI? , LastName , Biographical , Portrait )>
<!ATTLIST Author authorCiteID ID #REQUIRED>

<!ELEMENT FirstName (#PCDATA )>
<!ELEMENT MI (#PCDATA )>
<!ELEMENT LastName (#PCDATA )>

<!ELEMENT Biographical (#PCDATA )>

<!ELEMENT Portrait EMPTY>
<!ATTLIST Portrait picLink CDATA #IMPLIED >

<!-- Organization of the catalog -->
<!ELEMENT Thread (#PCDATA )>
<!ATTLIST Thread threadID ID #IMPLIED >

<!-- Book summary information (no content) -->

<!ELEMENT Book (Title , Abstract , RecSubjCategories , Price? )>
<!ATTLIST Book ISBN   ID   #REQUIRED
        level   CDATA  #IMPLIED
        pubDate  CDATA  #REQUIRED
        pageCount CDATA  #REQUIRED
        authors  IDREFS #IMPLIED
        threads  IDREFS #IMPLIED
        imprint  IDREF  #IMPLIED >
```

```
<!ELEMENT Title (#PCDATA )>
<!ELEMENT Abstract (#PCDATA )>
<!ELEMENT RecSubjCategories (Category , Category , Category )>
<!ELEMENT Category (#PCDATA )>
<!ELEMENT Price (#PCDATA )>
<!ATTLIST Price currency (USD | GBP | CD ) #REQUIRED>
```

Solving the Relationship Problem

Note how we used attributes of the `ID`, `IDREF`, and `IDREFS` types to denote relationships between objects in our model. These types are simple constructs, yet allow us to address a powerful problem. They are simple in that XML 1.0 is mute on the subject except to say that `ID`s must be unique throughout the document. The Recommendation does not mandate any programming semantics. We must provide our own programming support in applications that use this feature. We cannot expect an XML 1.0 compliant parser to do the linking for us.

> *At the time of writing, preliminary support for XSL, as provided by some parsers, gives us the ability to easily implement this capability without much programming. This is part of XSL, however, not XML, so many parsers on the market today won't provide this feature.*

Nevertheless, `ID` and `IDREF` is an important construct in XML. It enables us to provide relations similar to those modeled in a relational database within a document composed entirely of text. This is particularly important if you are designing a vocabulary some of whose applications are unknown. Whenever you know that a relationship exists, consider including the appropriate attribute list declarations to capture this information. An application can make good use of the information.

Not Quite There Yet

There are a few limitations imposed by the DTD grammar that are worth mentioning. These fall into three areas:

- Everything must be included in one DTD: No segmentation, except insofar as a DTD can be constructed to logically include sub-DTDs using suitable declarations and the parameter entity mechanism. However, the declarations needed for validation of a document cannot be drawn from logically separate schema entities at parse time.
- DTD syntax is different to XML document syntax (so we need a separate parsing mechanism to read from an application).
- Some things can't be expressed well: types and cardinality.

Our book catalog DTD isn't long or overly complex. Even so, we have two concepts – publishers and authors – that might be useful in other areas. We would need to define overarching DTDs to include DTD components for each instance of declaration set reuse across areas. This could become a problem in a longer, more complex domain. Everything that is acceptable in an XML vocabulary must be logically included in the DTD if you want to validate documents, making it difficult to construct content dynamically across areas with provision for a similarly dynamically constructed validation schema.

DTDs are written according to a grammar completely different to that used for XML documents. A validating XML parser can handle this, but there is no requirement for the parser to expose the DTD itself to the calling application. This is not a problem so long as we want the parser to use the DTD solely to validate documents. If we want to examine the DTD itself, we will require a custom parser to read the DTD and tell us about it. Suppose we want to know what the content model is for the `Catalog` element. This would be useful if we wanted to write a general-purpose tool that would create a template document from a DTD and allow authors to fill in the blanks. We could also use this feature if we wanted to tell an author what his options were when faced with an invalid tag in a document. If we ever want to dynamically create DTDs, say in response to some run-time condition that modifies content, we are unable to do so without a special API for the DTD. DTDs are read-only as far as present XML 1.0 parsers are concerned. These might seem like esoteric needs, but requirements have a way of growing. Sometime soon we will want to build automated tools that can discover the content of DTDs (or validation schemas in general) and do something with that information.

We've already seen one case where the DTD grammar let us down. The content model for the `RecSubjCategories` element required us to repeat the `Category` element three times because the cardinality declarations of DTDs aren't sufficiently fine-grained. Earlier in the chapter, we saw some very sophisticated content models, but they required some ingenuity on the designer's part. Many times, a complex content model is the result of working around the limitations of DTD cardinality tools. In the book catalog example, we saw the need for strong typing of attributes where `pubDate` and `pageCount` were concerned. The `Price` element itself could use strong typing. This will be very important when we start to write applications that work from the data included in an XML document rather than simply displaying it. There are some things that DTDs are just not well suited to expressing.

Summary

Document type definitions bring rigor and precision to the rules of well-formed XML presented in the previous chapter. A few simple markup declarations allow us to define the structure and permitted content of our XML documents. DTDs bring three key features to XML applications:

- Precise and unambiguous documentation of the business domain model
- A standard way to communicate the model to XML parsers
- Single point error trapping of XML documents from validating parsers

The first point essentially uses DTDs as an analysis and design tool. You need a DTD to validate XML, and a DTD forces designers to make precise and unambiguous decisions regarding the XML vocabulary. An XML application communicates on the basis of the vocabularies it understands, so the DTD tells programmers and testers what the application can describe.

Internal and external DTDs give us a standard way for applications to retrieve these models. If an application cares to use validation, the parser looks for either an internal set of declarations or makes the appropriate request to retrieve an external DTD.

The very idea of validation makes validating XML parsers a convenient single point for detecting many errors in XML-based applications. Structural and content errors will be detected by the parser, thereby greatly reducing the number of cases the application logic must check. Put as much detail and precision into the declarations in your DTDs as you can. The more effort you put into your DTD, the less error checking you will need to provide and maintain in your application.

4

Data Modeling and XML

The success of any XML application will depend on how well you have designed the actual XML documents you use: they not only need to be able to carry the information that people want to communicate today, but they need to be flexible enough to accommodate future requirements as well. This chapter looks at the factors you need to take into account when designing XML document structures.

We'll look at three aspects of the design process:

- Information modeling, which is about understanding the structure and meaning of the information carried in documents
- Document design, which is about translating your information model into a set of rules (or a schema) for creating actual documents
- Schema notations: techniques for recording your document design so it is accessible both to processing software and to human users

Information Modeling

We did some simple information modeling in the previous chapter when we introduced the book catalog domain. In this chapter we're going to look at modeling in more detail, and show some practical examples of its role in the design of XML-based information systems.

The first rule of information modeling is to focus on the "real world", not the technology. An information model is a description of the information used in an organization, independent of any IT systems.

- How is it structured?
- What does it mean?
- Who "owns" it, and who is responsible for its timeliness and quality?
- Where does it come from and what happens to it in the end?

So by definition, a discussion of information modeling will not be very specific to XML. We'll get on to the XML specifics later in the chapter.

So does modeling have a place in this book? We think so, because if you're working on an XML project, having an understanding of information modeling is essential. Also, although information modeling is technology-independent, it is usually covered in books on relational database design, which distorts the perspective. In a book on XML we can give an alternative and perhaps complementary perspective on the subject.

Why is information modeling important? Without a model, there is no information, only data. The information model defines the meaning of the data. In fact, there will always be an information model; the only choice is whether to have a shared information model that is written down and agreed on, or to take the risk of everyone having a different information model in their own heads, with the inevitable misunderstandings that result. If we have a shared information model, the opportunities are immense. To quote from a paper by Adam Bosworth, Andrew Layman, and Michael Rys of Microsoft (http://biztalk.org/Resources/canonical.asp):

> *...we are already well along the road to what had once been a futuristic possibility: a world in which any consumer of data has the tools to talk to any data producer, wherever located, and communication [is] based on the meaning of the data, not the accidents of its representation.*

We'll focus on general principles here, rather than on some specific formalism. If you want to read about methodologies such as UML (Unified Modeling Language) there are plenty of books on the subject, and full specifications on the web at http://www.rational.com/. There are two objectives in an information modeling exercise that are not always easy to reconcile:

- To achieve absolutely precise definitions
- To communicate effectively with users

The formal methodologies are often rather stronger on technical precision than on communicating with lay people, so we'll try to redress the balance a little by using terminology and simplified diagrammatic notations that speak for themselves.

A word of warning about terminology: in information modeling practice, words like *entity* and *attribute* have a quite different meaning from their use in the XML specification. We'll try and avoid this confusion by using different words. In particular, we'll call the things in the information model **objects** rather than **entities**, and we'll call their characteristics **properties** rather than the more usual **attributes**. That way we can keep the XML technical terms for the XML concepts.

Static and Dynamic Models

There are two main types of information model: **static** models and **dynamic** models.

Static models concentrate on describing the permissible states of the system. They are full of statements like "a customer may have one or more accounts", "a chapter may have zero or more footnotes", "every book has an ISBN". They describe the types of object in the system, their properties, and their relationships. As well as describing them, of course, they also define agreed names for these objects: names like *customer*, *account*, *chapter*, and *footnote*. Agreeing names for things is half the battle, which is why XML information models are sometimes referred to as **vocabularies**.

Dynamic models concentrate on describing what happens to information: examples of such models are process and workflow diagrams, data flow models, and object life histories. Dynamic models contain statements like: "The pathology department will send the results of the test to the consultant responsible for the patient episode". Dynamic models describe a set of information exchanges: data that is sent from one place to another for a particular purpose.

In general, static models are immediately relevant to the design of a database, where information is stored for long periods of time to serve a variety of purposes; while dynamic models are most directly relevant to the design of messages, which have only transient existence and a very specific purpose.

XML, of course, can be used to represent both kinds of data – documents and messages – in a system. But any system design needs to consider both static and dynamic models, and both are equally important. Some people prefer to start with one or the other, but it would be a mistake to say that either should be finished before the other is started. My own preference is to start with the static model, partly because that is where the basic terminology is established, and partly because the static information model tends to be the most enduring aspect of any information system – the thing that is still there twenty years later when all the code has been rewritten several times.

In practice, of course, the boundary between static long-term information and transient messages is often blurred: many objects in the static information model are actually events (a sale of a product, for example) and many documents that start off as a transient communication (a customer complaint, say) are then archived for a long period of time. Whether you model such objects as static or dynamic is again a personal choice that depends on the circumstances.

Documents and Data

Traditionally the worlds of documents and data were very separate. Commercial data processing was concerned with highly structured and formalized information – managing the ledger books of the enterprise. The aim was to codify data to allow processes to be automated, and to allow information to be aggregated and summarized so that senior managers could find out how much money they were making or losing. Document publishing, by contrast, was concerned with organizing the creation and production of text to be read by people, while emulating and preferably enhancing the effectiveness of the printed page as a vehicle for human communication.

So in one sense, the thrust in the data world has been to automate, to analyze, to codify, and to make systems more uniform; while in the document world the pressure has been to provide the flexibility to enable information authors to communicate with their readers as creatively as possible.

The Web has forced these two worlds together. XML is probably the first example of a technology that is equally at home in both camps. And the convergence is welcome to both sides, because information systems designers have for some time been striving for ways to increase the flexibility of their systems, while document designers have been looking for ways to capture more structure. The common goal today is "knowledge management", harnessing the collective knowledge of an organization, which includes everything on the spectrum from the highly-structured and organized to the ad-hoc and informal. And there are many "multimedia" applications nowadays that cross the traditional divide: an example, which we will use in this chapter, is the production of a holiday catalog.

Another place the two worlds come together is in the transactional documents that form part of an information processing system: orders, invoices, letters offering dates for a hospital appointment, expense claims, and accident reports, for example.

But the traditions remain separate, and it is easy to spot the difference between someone who has learnt the information modeling trade in the world of databases and someone whose background is in document design. We will try to tread a neutral path, in the knowledge that both groups have something to learn from the other.

Where Do You Start?

There is an old story about a traveler in London who asks for directions to Trafalgar Square, and is offered the advice: "If I was you, guv, I shouldn't start from here". It's the same with information modeling: in practice, you don't usually get a choice where to start, so the question is rhetorical.

In practice you start where you are, so the first step is to find out where this is. Is the scope and purpose of the system already defined? Is there a well-defined set of business processes in place, or are new ones being developed? Is the systems architecture already decided? How much influence do you have on the outcome; what are your terms of reference? Who are the people who are going to make the decisions; are there opposing camps with different perspectives?

The traditional approach, both in data processing and in document design, was to start with the existing paperwork. Find the documents that are relevant, determine their structure by a process of generalization and abstraction, talk to users about where the information in the documents comes from, how it gets from one document into another, and how it is used, then shake the whole thing up and come up with a data model.

Often today this isn't good enough, because people don't want to create systems that simply reproduce the existing way of doing things. An electronic commerce system needn't precisely mirror the traditional buying process, and an online holiday catalog needn't be an exact replica of the paper brochure. This requires a higher level of understanding of what the business is trying to achieve, what it is that motivates the users. You have to understand not only what information exists, but why, and to be more creative and imaginative in suggesting better ways of meeting the business objectives. But whether you can do this, of course, depends on the job you have been asked to do, and on the amount of influence you have with the people who run the show.

The Static Information Model

In this section we'll take a step-by-step approach to defining a static information model. These steps are:

- Step 1 – Identify things, name them, and define them
- Step 2 – Organize things into a class hierarchy
- Step 3 – Define relationships, cardinality and constraints
- Step 4 – Add properties to flesh out the details of values associated with the objects

Step 1: Naming Things

A good way to start any information modeling exercise is by establishing the names of the things in the system. The "things" are generally referred to as Entities, Objects, Classes, or Data Elements; it isn't really important. We'll call them **Object Types**.

Start by making a list of things relevant to the system: customer, account, holiday, hotel, resort, country, reservation, or payment for example. Some people recommend going through a textual description of the system and highlighting all the nouns. However you do it, this stage isn't difficult; it can usually be done in a relatively short time.

The next stage, which can sometimes take much longer, is to produce definitions of the object types. The definition of a term like "holiday" needs to ensure that you can recognize a holiday when you see one, and that there is no room for disputes about whether something is a holiday or not. Examples of the questions you should ask:

- If two people travel together, is that one holiday or two?
- Is an unsold holiday still a holiday, or is it something else?
- If a customer makes a reservation for a holiday and then switches to different date, is it still the same holiday or is it a different one?

There are two kinds of question I always find useful in establishing these definitions. The first is a question of the form:

- Is X a holiday?

Here we are testing, by giving examples of dubious cases, where people draw the boundaries around the concept. The second kind is to ask:

- Are X and Y the same holiday or different holidays?

Here we are no longer arguing about whether X and Y are indeed holidays, we are looking for rules that enable us to distinguish a particular holiday without ambiguity. This sort of question is particularly important with intangible objects, such as a flight, a channel, a service, or an advertising campaign.

You might find you get very different answers to these questions from different people. Some may have a completely different view as to what a holiday is, for example they may think that Easter 2001 is a holiday. This is why information modeling is so valuable: it flushes out the possible sources of misunderstanding. In one organization I worked with, data was being lost because one department thought that a retailer meant a single shop at a particular location, while another department thought a retailer was a company that might own any number of shops. Asking the question "Is QuickFood in Dallas the same retailer as QuickFood in Pittsburgh?" would have exposed the misunderstanding.

After this process you will probably end up with a rather longer list of object types, and some of them are likely to have rather longer names, for example holiday-inventory-item and party-holiday-reservation. If at all possible, it's important to choose names that people in the business will recognize and interpret correctly, because they won't always be checking with your carefully written definitions.

As well as naming the object types at this stage, because we're focusing on identity it's also worth thinking about how the individual instances will be identified. How is an individual holiday identified? There may be an existing code used in the business which you need to know about; or you may have to invent one; or you may decide to use a combination of properties – for example a holiday might be identified by the combination of customer number and start date. At this stage it's not uncommon to discover problems with the existing coding schemes used in the business, for example the corporate travel department might identify all employees of a particular company under a single customer code, while the customer service department identifies each traveling employee with a separate customer number.

So at the end of this step, we will have a list of object types with agreed names and definitions.

Step 2: Taxonomy

Taxonomy is a term used in biology to refer to a system of classification; in information modeling, we also call it a type hierarchy (some people like to call it an *ontology*). Having listed and named the object types, we now want to organize them into a hierarchical classification scheme. Often these hierarchical relationships will emerge while we are writing the definitions of the object types. We will often find definitions such as:

- A flights-only-holiday is a holiday that does not include booking for accommodation
- There are three types of accommodation: hotel accommodation, self-catering accommodation, and campsite accommodation

The key phrase here is "is a" (or "is a kind of"). A group-holiday is a holiday, a cancellation is a transaction, a deposit is a payment, a vegetarian-menu-selection is a no-cost-option. If you can write a sentence such as "A is a kind of B" or "Every A is a B", then you have identified a subtype relationship in your taxonomy.

This is sometimes called the *is-a* test: but be careful, because in English we also use *is-a* for the relationship between an individual **instance** and its **type**: "Benidorm is a resort". Writing *is-a-kind-of* is safer.

Identifying subtypes is useful when it comes to document design, as we'll see later, but more importantly, it is a great aid to understanding the object type definitions. For example, if your class hierarchy wrongly identifies customer as a subtype of traveler, hopefully someone will spot the error very quickly and point out, for example, that IBM is a customer but has yet to board a plane.

If you're used to object-oriented programming, you have a head start in defining type hierarchies, but you are also exposed to a possible danger, because programmers often think of object classes primarily in terms of modules of functionality inside the system, rather than the things they represent in the world outside. If you find yourself using verbs rather than nouns to name your object types then you are probably falling into this trap.

Here's an example of part of the type hierarchy we might use for our holiday business. This uses the UML notation, in which an arrow points from a sub-type to its super-type:

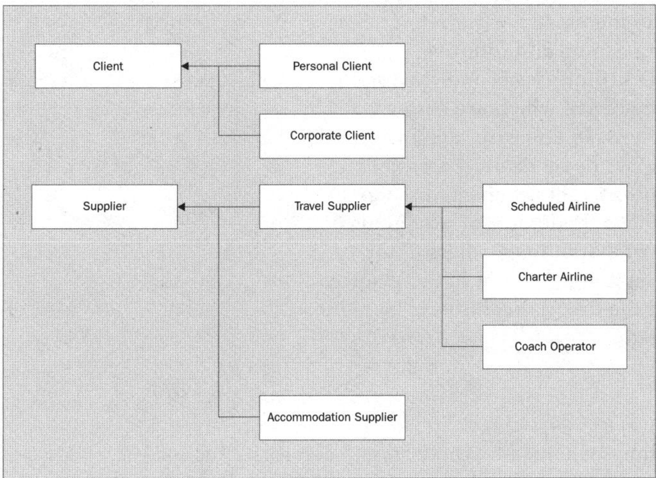

For more information on UML and its notation, see Instant UML *(ISBN: 1-86100-087-1).*

There's a lot more detail you can add to these diagrams, but for this stage, keeping them uncluttered helps to get the key messages across and helps you get feedback from users as to whether you've understood the concepts correctly. It's useful to draw the diagrams using a tool such as Visio, which allows you to expand or reduce the level of detail so you can present the same diagram in different ways to different audiences.

So step 2 is to organize your object types into a type hierarchy.

Step 3: Finding Relationships

Having named the object types, the next stage in static information modeling is to determine the relationships that exist among them.

English sentences are again a good way to start:

- A customer books one or more holidays
- Each holiday involves one or more travelers
- Each holiday involves zero or more journeys
- Each holiday involves one or more accommodation-bookings
- Each accommodation-booking is at one hotel

These relationships (or associations, as UML calls them) can then be shown diagrammatically, as in the next diagram. There are many different notations for these object-relationship diagrams, and everyone has their own preferences. We'll use UML notations in this chapter, because they are widely accepted in the IT industry, though I sometimes find when talking to users that there are more natural ways of showing, for example, that a relationship is one-to-many. My own preference is to keep the diagrams simple and intuitive, concentrating on the key messages and leaving the detail to textual documents, which are easier to maintain than diagrams. In any case, the level of detail that's appropriate depends on the project: if you have three months to get a web site up and running, you don't have the luxury of producing detailed definitions of all the finer points of the data model, and even if you attempt it, the chances are no-one will find the time to read them, let alone to keep them updated.

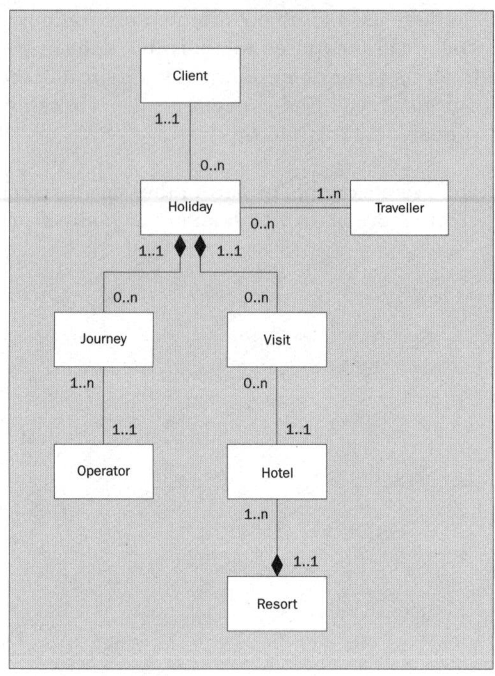

There are several things we need to know about each relationship.

The **cardinality** of a relationship describes how many of each kind of object can take part in it:

- The most common kind is a one-to-many relationship: one chapter has many paragraphs, one person takes many holidays, one book has many editions, one order contains several order-items. On the diagram we've labeled most of the one-to-many relationships as having exactly one object at one end ("1..1" means minimum one, maximum one) and from zero to n ("0..n") objects at the other end. Sometimes it makes more sense to use "1..n"; for example a resort that contains no hotels hardly counts as a resort.

- Many-to-many relationships also occur: one author may write several books but a book also has several authors. We've got one such relationship on our diagram: several travelers may travel together on the same holiday, but an individual traveler may also take several holidays (and an enterprising travel company would want to track this). In such cases it is often useful to name each pairing as an object in its own right: we've done this by referring to the pairing of one holiday and one hotel as a visit. The reason for doing this is that it gives you somewhere to put the properties that belong to the relationship rather than to either of the objects: each visit has dates and a room number associated with it, for example.

- One-to-one relationships are less common: an example is the relationship between a person and a job, where a person can only hold one job at any one time, and the job can only be held by one person.

In modeling information for eventual XML representation, a particularly important kind of relationship is the **contains** relationship. This is always one-to-many or one-to-one. There is no hard-and-fast rule as to exactly what constitutes a contains relationship, though the English use of the word gives a reasonable guide: a chapter contains paragraphs; a resort contains hotels; a hotel contains visitors. UML defines two forms of containment: **aggregation**, which is a fairly loose assembly of objects to allow a group of things to be treated for the time being as a whole (for example, a tour party, where the same people might belong to different tour parties at different times), and **composition**, which is a much stronger relationship where the parts have no independent existence of their own (for example, the rooms in a hotel cannot exist independently of the hotel). In UML, aggregation is indicated diagrammatically by a diamond at the aggregate end of the relationship.

It's quite possible to stretch the concept of aggregation: a holiday contains several flights; a schedule contains events; a telephone service package contains several products. But when we do this, we need to be careful, because we can easily lose sight of the fact that the relationship is actually many-to-many rather than one-to-many. For example, many schedules can contain the same event. Although the concept can be stretched, it's best to ensure that each object is only "contained in" one other object: this matches the intuitive understanding of the idea, and it also maps well to XML's data model, which, although it is capable of representing arbitrary links, is primarily hierarchical. To get concrete about it, where you see a diamond on the relationship diagram, you should be able to model it in XML as a containing element and a repeated child element, so in our example we could have an XML structure such as:

```
<HOLIDAY>
   <JOURNEY>
      <FROM>London Gatwick</FROM>
      <TO>Orlando, Florida</TO>
      <DATE>2000-02-15 11:40</DATE>
      <FLIGHT>BA1234</FLIGHT>
   </JOURNEY>
   <JOURNEY>
      <FROM>Orlando, Florida</FROM>
         <TO>London Gatwick</TO>
         <DATE>2000-03-01 18:20</DATE>
         <FLIGHT>BA1235</FLIGHT>
   </JOURNEY>
   <VISIT>
      <HOTEL>Orlando Hyatt Regency</HOTEL>
      <ARRIVAL>2000-02-15</ARRIVAL>
      <DEPARTURE>2000-03-01</DEPARTURE>
   </VISIT>
</HOLIDAY>
```

Finding good names for relationships is often tricky: it's not something that the English language is good at. It's easy to end up with a lot of rather unspecific names like includes, uses, or has. To make matters worse, the relationship generally has a different name depending which side you are looking at it from. In writing about relationships, it's often useful to use a full phrase hotel is-located-in resort, person is-an-author-of book. Fortunately we don't usually need to use these names as XML markup tags: they appear only in the system documentation. For this reason, we haven't included relationship names on the diagram.

So at the end of Step 3, we've defined the relationships that exist between the object types in our model.

Step 4: Defining Properties

Object types and relationships form the skeleton of the static information model; properties put the flesh on the bones. Properties are simply values associated with the objects. A person has height, weight, a nationality, and an occupation; a hotel has a certain number of rooms, a star rating, and a price category.

In listing the properties of an object, we don't need to include the relationships again: we don't need to treat "location" as a property of a hotel if we've already modeled this as a relationship to a resort.

The main thing we need to know about properties is the data type. Is there a fixed range of values, is it numeric, what units is it measured in? Is it optional or mandatory, and is there a default value?

If you are used to designing relational databases, you have probably absorbed the discipline of normalizing property values: you will have learnt that a table is in first normal form if all the property values are atomic, and if you find non-atomic properties, your instinct will be to invent additional tables to put them in. For XML design, it's a good idea to unlearn this discipline. Composite property values in XML are not a problem that needs to be designed away. An example of a composite property might be any measurement that includes both a numeric amount and a unit of measure (such as meters or gallons), or a monetary value that includes the amount and the currency. Other examples are an address, a geographic location, and a salary history. Eventually you will want to break these up into their component parts, but the great thing about a hierarchic model is that you can keep the parts together. This also means that you can leave the details of the internal structure until a later stage of design, which helps to keep the high-level model uncluttered and easy to understand.

In UML you can show the properties of an object within the box describing the object, as shown in the diagram below. In my own experience I have usually found it easier to maintain the lists of properties in textual form, perhaps in a spreadsheet. But it can sometimes be useful to show a few properties on the diagram as illustrative examples, to make it clearer what kind of information this object represents:

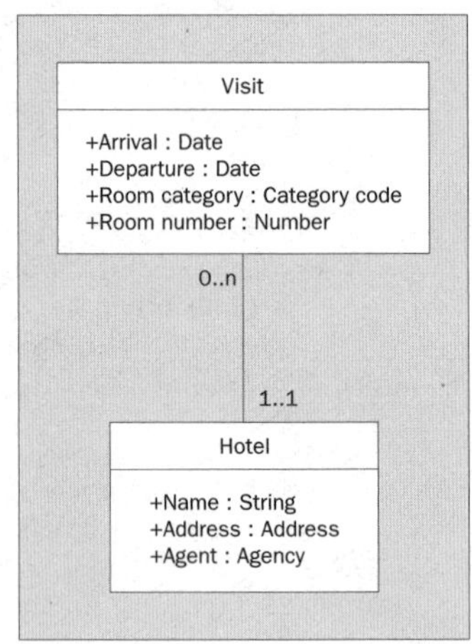

So at the end of step 4 we have completed the static information model: we have a complete definition of the types of object in the system, their relationships to each other, and their properties.

We'll now return to the other important aspect of information modeling: dynamic modeling, which is about describing what happens to the information as the system goes into operation.

Dynamic Modeling: What Happens to the Data?

So far we've looked at static information models. If we're going to use XML for representing the messages that flow around the system, we also need to understand what happens to the data, where it comes from, and where it goes next.

There are several approaches you can take to dynamic modeling. It's very unlikely that you would want to do all of them in a single project, so we're not going to define a simple step-by-step approach as we did for static modeling. Rather, we'll outline some of the techniques available, and leave you to choose which are worth doing on your particular project. We'll look at:

- Process and workflow models
- Data flow models
- Object models
- Object life histories
- Use cases
- Object interaction diagrams

Remember that the goal is to get agreement and common understanding: create the models that will help everyone understand what the system is supposed to be doing. You only need to model the parts of the system that are causing difficulty, not the whole thing.

Process and Workflow Models

Process models and **workflow models** focus on the roles of people and organizations in getting work done, with the information stores and processing stages playing a secondary role. A process model will describe, for example, what happens when a traveler has an accident while on holiday: it defines the responsibilities of the local representative in the resort, the agent in the local country, and the head office, making it clear who is responsible for arranging medical care, for arranging transport home, and for informing relatives. It probably prescribes various forms that are filled in and sent from one party to another to make the whole process run smoothly, and it may well involve no computer systems at all. Process models typically focus more on the roles, responsibilities, and tasks of each actor in the system, while workflow models focus more on the documents that move between the actors.

Data Flow Models

Data flow models are very similar, but focus more on the information system rather than the business. A data flow model describes *data stores* where information is held persistently (it might be a computer database, or just a filing cabinet), *processors* which manipulate the data, and *data flows* which transfer data from one processor or data store to another. This relies heavily on the static information model; the static model describes what we mean by concepts such as a traveler or a hotel, but says nothing about where the information is stored. In contrast, the data flow model might say that information about holidays is held in the bookings database until the holiday is complete and all accounts are settled, at which stage a summary of the holiday details is moved to the marketing information system and the rest is transferred to archive storage.

Object Models

Object models have a dynamic component as well as a static component. The dynamic or behavioral part of an object definition concentrates on describing what each object can do (or have done to it), as a set of operations or methods that define its actions.

I personally don't find behavioral object models very useful at the modeling stage; they are much more useful as a design tool. This is because many of the events that occur are associated with several objects (for example, a traveler checking in at a hotel), and associating them with one of these objects rather than another is actually a design decision.

Object Life Histories

Object life histories (or object lifelines, as UML calls them) also focus on individual objects, but take a more holistic approach: they describe what happens to each object throughout its lifetime – how it gets created, what events can happen to it during its life, what it does in reaction to these events, and what conditions cause it eventually to be destroyed.

I find object life histories very useful in testing the completeness of the model. There is often a tendency to focus on some events at the expense of others – how to handle a holiday booking, for example, but not how to handle a cancellation or a claim for a refund. Until you have defined how each object gets into the system and (preferably) how it gets removed from the system, there are gaps in your understanding, and there is probably implementation work that you have not included in your estimates.

Use Cases

Use cases analyze how specific user tasks are accomplished, for example, how does someone who has bought a holiday cancel their order? A use case can be rather similar to a process model, but it generally focuses on the activities of one particular user.

Use cases can be useful both in modeling the business and in describing the internal behavior of the IT system. One of the dangers is in mixing the two levels; it's best to keep them apart because they are interesting to different audiences. Practice varies, but the most useful use cases I've seen worked mainly at the level of the interaction of the user with the system – a description of a dialog such as "The user clicks on a map to indicate the desired holiday destination. The system responds with a list of hotels, each illustrated by a photograph and annotated with its name and price category. The user can click on any hotel to get further information about the hotel. The screen giving this information has a button allowing the user to make a reservation..." and so on.

UML provides graphical notations for describing use cases, but the best way to show users what is really intended is often with an interactive prototype, or what the media people call a **storyboard**.

A user interface dialog described as a use case will concentrate on describing what information is exchanged between the user and the system, rather than how it is presented on the screen. This leads naturally to an XML implementation in which the information content is separated from the presentation details.

Object Interaction Diagrams

Object interaction diagrams analyze the exchange of messages between objects at a finer level of detail than the data flow model. Whereas the data flow model might simply identify that the online bookings system sends transaction information to the credit card clearer and gets authorization in response, the interaction diagram will describe all the messages that make up this conversation in fine detail.

Object interaction diagrams are invaluable when you need to describe interactions between separate systems, for example a travel agent's systems and an airline's systems. They help you define what information goes into which message. Since these will often be XML messages, the object interaction diagram provides the context that we need before we can start designing the XML structure of each individual message.

Choosing a Dynamic Modeling approach

Some of the systems design methodologies that were advocated in the 1980s encouraged you to believe that you had to define all these models in full detail before you could start coding anything. That certainly isn't the case; life in the Internet world simply moves too fast for that. But it's useful to have a repertoire of techniques in your kit-bag for use when the situation demands it, hence the above descriptions illustrating where each of the models can be useful.

Don't necessarily think of these models as things that have to be done in meticulous detail and placed under change control – all of these models can be useful as working tools, for sketching out on a whiteboard when you meet with your users (or with other members of the design team) to try and reach a consensus on how things should work. As we've already mentioned, they really come into their own on an XML project when you are defining the messages that flow around from one subsystem to another; or in electronic commerce, when you define the messages that flow from your system to those of your suppliers and customers.

Designing XML Documents

The first section of this chapter concentrated on analyzing the real-world information that needs to be represented, so that everyone has a shared understanding of its meaning. But enough of analysis – it's time we focused back on XML. In this section we'll assume that we understand the information requirements in the system, and look at how to design XML documents that meet the need. We'll start by looking at the different roles XML can play in the system architecture.

Two Roles for XML

In discussing data flow models we saw that there are two kinds of data in the system: data stores, which hold long-term persistent data for reference purposes, and message flows, which move transient information from one subsystem (or person, or data store) to another.

XML is useful for both kinds of data, but the design considerations are rather different, so we'll look at each one in turn.

XML for Messages

Using XML for the messages in the system poses fewer design problems than using it for persistent data. This is because each message is generally fairly self-contained, and the question of what to include in a message usually falls out naturally from the process model.

We're using the term *message*, of course, in a very general sense. The message might be an EDI-style message sent between organizations to represent a transaction such as a hotel reservation. Or it might be data passed when one subsystem calls another, for example in a bank the fraud detection system might ask the operational banking system for a transaction history on a particular account, and get the answer back in the form of an XML message. It might also be a message intended for display to people, for example when you use your browser to get a weather forecast for a particular holiday resort. In this case the answer to your enquiry might come back from the back-end database system as an XML message, for the front-end system (or the browser) to turn into a visible page by rendering it using an appropriate style sheet. It might also be a message that originates from a person, such as a sales enquiry created using a form on your web site.

There are some general design principles that can be applied to all XML messages, whatever their precise role:

- The design should reflect the information content and not the intended use. The use that is made of the information will probably change over time, whereas the information content is more likely to remain stable. This particularly applies to presentation details: if the message is intended for human consumption, avoid including presentation information such as screen layouts and font sizes.
- The design should anticipate change. The design of XML itself, of course, gives a head start in this area, by avoiding traditional pitfalls such as fixed sized fields and fixed column ordering. But the document designer also has a responsibility to structure information in a way that anticipates change.
- Use a standard message type if there is one, rather than inventing one of your own. There is an increasing range of standardized message types available, for example from the Biztalk initiative http://www.biztalk.org/ sponsored by Microsoft, or the independent OASIS consortium http://www.oasis-open.org/. Other useful sites are http://www.ontology.org/, http://www.rosettanet.org/ and http://www.commercenet.org/. Some of the industry initiatives to create standard XML vocabularies and message types for particular application domains are described in Chapter 1. Even if you can't use them unchanged, you can probably get lots of ideas from them, or incorporate them into your own extended models by using namespaces and schemas, as we will see in Chapter 7.
- The data encoding should be as close to the natural encoding as you can achieve within performance constraints. Avoid codes such as `W` for `Withdrawn` unless the codes are deeply rooted in current business practice. Use identifiers and codes that are already used in the business (like credit card numbers) rather than artificial identifiers of your own invention, and (in particular) avoid identifiers that create an intimate dependency between the message and some existing database. The message should stand on its own.

One design decision that can sometimes be difficult is knowing whether to include unnecessary information just in case it is ever wanted in the future. There is no universal answer to this. If it's easier to include all the properties of an object than to select out those which you know the recipient is interested in, then include them all and let the recipient decide which to ignore. On the other hand, it would be foolish to send vastly more data than is needed, and there may also be security or privacy reasons for holding things back. The decision has to be pragmatic.

It is often a good idea to include "red tape" information in the message, even if it duplicates information available from whatever messaging system is used to carry the data. Date and time, identity of sender, and intended recipient are obvious values to include; a serial number can be useful to check that no messages have been lost in transit or transmitted twice. There are several reasons for including everything in the XML message: the recipient might find it easier to extract the information from the message rather than use a separate API to get it from elsewhere; and, more importantly, when the message is archived for purposes such as auditing, it's much easier to store it if everything is together in one place.

XML For Persistent Data

The design of messages is determined primarily by the dynamic information model. By contrast, when you use XML for persistent data, it is the static model that is important.

How Big is a Document?

The most difficult part of the design is to decide what the granularity of the data should be: what needs to go together in one document?

There are a few applications where it makes sense to have a single XML document containing gigabytes of data, but they are the exception rather than the rule. XML is not well suited for direct access; to access any part of such a large document with current technology, it will be necessary to parse the whole thing, which may take hours.

At the opposite extreme, having a very large number of tiny documents is usually not ideal either, because it makes it impossible to use the rich structure of XML to represent the relationships in the information model.

Sometimes, where business objects have a significant size and internal complexity, there is a natural mapping of one XML document to one business object. For example, in a human resources system it may be natural to use one XML document for each employee's record, or in a medical records system there might be one XML document for each patient episode.

When you use XML documents to hold persistent data, finding information will always be a two-part operation: first find the right document, then find the facts you are interested in within it. The tools and techniques available for the two parts of this operation are quite different, so the choice of what information to put in each document is of critical importance.

To locate the right document, there are four main options:

- Use the directory structure in the operating system filestore to locate documents by name. The filename of the document might relate to an object identifier used in the system, for example a personnel file might be named using the employee's personnel number.
- Index the documents from each other, like a traditional web site where documents are always found by following links, but typically in a more structured way. For example if you have a collection of reports of soccer matches each comprising one XML document, you could have another XML document that acts as an index, listing all the matches, the dates and venues, and the participating teams. You don't have to maintain this index by hand, of course. You can arrange it so that whenever a new match report is submitted it is automatically analyzed, and the relevant information is added to the index document. XSLT is ideal for writing an application to do this.

- Index the documents from a relational database. In this case you have the choice of holding the XML documents in files referenced from the database, or of holding them within the database itself. An increasing number of relational databases support this explicitly, and if necessary there is always the option of using a "blob" (binary large object) field. Using a relational database to index your XML documents allows you to use arbitrary SQL queries to identify them, but only using those properties that you have chosen to include explicitly in the database. For more information on using XML with relational databases, see Chapter 10.
- Index the documents using a free-text search engine. Again, an increasing number of search engines offer native support for XML. Using this approach allows you to search for documents using words that appear anywhere in the source. Although free text searching is often thought of mainly as a way of supporting end-user queries on unstructured data, as documents acquire more structure through markup it becomes even more powerful. For applications where the volume of updates is modest, this is a very effective alternative to using relational queries.

Another option is to use a so-called "XML Server". An XML server typically holds XML data not in its raw unparsed form, but in the form of a persistent DOM – that is, it stores the nodes of the Document Object Model as objects in an object database. This gives the ability to access the data using DOM interfaces without first reading the entire document from disk and parsing it. A major benefit of this is that it makes data access smoother, avoiding the use of one API to locate the right document and a different API to find the information within it. However, an XML server that stores every DOM node as a separate database object can be inefficient, especially when loading or updating very large databases. Also, because the standard DOM interface has no facilities to find data except by navigating to it, the query facilities are proprietary to each vendor.

Another way of reducing the cost of parsing large documents is to cache the documents in memory. For example, with Microsoft ASP pages or Java Server Pages you have the ability to store data with application scope, which essentially means you read it into memory when the web server is started and leave it there until it is closed down. Holding a gigabyte-sized document in memory like this would be expensive (most DOM implementations use around ten bytes of memory for each byte in the source XML file), but for data in the megabyte range it can be a practical approach – and buying memory is probably cheaper than buying XML Server software.

One rule of thumb I use to decide the right size of documents is the concept of a "screenful". Intellectually it's rather unsatisfactory, after all this talk of XML being presentation-independent, to make a key design decision on the basis of how much information we want to show the user at a time, but in practice it provides a good test. If a stored XML document contains much more data than a single user will ever want to see on the screen, then you are going to end up parsing a lot of data that the user never looks at; while if you need to access hundreds of stored XML documents to build up a single screenful of information, you are going to incur a substantial processing overhead on each user page access.

But what if the user wants to see a different small part of the data set each time? One technique is to keep the whole DOM document in memory on the server, as an object with application scope, and respond to the user request by filtering it to create a smaller XML document that meets the user request more precisely. You can then send this smaller document to the client for processing.

We'll be looking at XML and databases in more detail in Chapter 10.

How Many Document Types Should I Have?

Surprisingly, this is not as simple a question as it seems, because the concept of a document type in XML is not very rigidly defined. In particular there are two separate concepts, which don't have to correspond one-to-one: the DTD, and the top-level element type.

Where you conceptually have several different document types in your model, there are several ways you can represent them in XML:

- You can have a different DTD for each one. If the different document types have parts in common, you can define external parameter entities which are shared between the different DTDs.
- You can use the same DTD for all of the document types, but using a different top-level element tag for each section. There is nothing in a DTD that says which element should be the document element, so it is quite possible to define several document types in the same DTD. Components used in multiple document types can then easily be referenced in each one.

A DTD itself doesn't have to be a monolithic entity; a DTD can incorporate definitions from other DTDs by using external parameter entities, and can be parameterized using conditional sections, so it can be made very flexible indeed. Unfortunately this is often at the cost of complexity: it's not uncommon for an organization to find that no one understands the DTD any more, because it has become over-complex.

Whichever approach you choose, you should aim for your different document types to have as much as possible in common. That means standardizing common components such as name and address, standardizing conventions on naming of elements and attributes, and standardizing on red-tape data such as message timestamps and sequence numbers.

We'll have more to say on DTD design later.

Mapping the Information Model to XML

In this section we'll look in more detail at how you map the different parts of your information model to an XML document structure.

Representing Object Types

Generally an object type in your information model will translate into an element type in the XML structure.

You can use the name of the object type as the element name, or if you are concerned about the amount of space used, you can abbreviate it. Most people use short names as their element tags, not just to save space, but also because XML seems to be more readable that way: perhaps it avoids the tags distracting too much from the content.

Where the object type is part of a type hierarchy, you have a choice of which level in the hierarchy to base your XML elements on. For example, if `deposit` is a subtype of `payment`, you could either use `<deposit>` as the element tag, or use `<payment>` and indicate some other way that it is a deposit, perhaps by use of an attribute: `<payment type="deposit">`.

The advantage of using the most specific type (deposit) is that the DTD can define more precisely exactly what attributes and child elements are associated with this element. The advantage of using the more general type (payment) is that it is a little easier to write application code that doesn't care what all the different kinds of payment are.

As always, try to avoid designing data structures just for the convenience of the programmer writing the first application. The data structure will probably be there long after that first program has disappeared.

Representing Relationships

Some of the relationships in your model can be represented by using nested elements in the XML document structure. The obvious ones to represent this way are the "contains" relationships, for example `<footnote>` elements can be nested within a `<chapter>` element, and `<hotel>` elements can be nested within a `<resort>` element.

Obviously, an element can only be contained by one parent element, so the other relationships in the model must be handled in some other way. In practice this means by some kind of link.

There are several ways of representing a link from one element to another in XML:

- You can use `ID` and `IDREF` attributes. An `ID` attribute contains a value that identifies the element uniquely within its document; an `IDREF` attribute contains a value that must be the same as the `ID` of some other element in the document. So an `ID` acts like a primary key in a relational database, while an `IDREF` acts like a foreign key. And don't forget the handy `IDREFS` data type, which has no direct parallel in a relational database: an `IDREFS` attribute contains a space-separated list of `IDREF` values, so it is useful at the "one" end of a one-to-many relationship, or at either end of a many-to-many relationship.

- You can use XPointer references. These are the XML equivalent of the familiar HREF attribute in HTML. You can use an XPointer value to refer to an element in the same document or in a different document.

- You can use application-defined primary keys and foreign keys in your XML documents, without declaring them as being anything special. Your application knows the significance of the values as representing a relationship, but the XML software treats them as ordinary data.

All three approaches have their merits. The main advantage of using the `ID/IDREF` facility is that the XML parser will do the validation for you. Unfortunately, the standard DOM interface doesn't help you find an element given its `ID`, but many DOM implementations have plugged this gap with proprietary interfaces, for example Microsoft provides a `nodeFromID()` method. There are facilities in XSLT to exploit `ID` values, but you can just as easily use a non-`ID` value as a key for accessing elements by value. There are other limitations to using `ID`s, for example the fact that they have to be unique within the whole document (not just unique to an element type), the fact that you can only have one `ID` attribute in each element, and the fact that they have to conform to the syntax of XML names (which means that "234", "I18/296", and "ABC 123" are not valid as `ID`s). So the case for using the facility is not overwhelming.

Here's an example where using IDs might make sense. In a holiday itinerary for a party traveling together, there are optional events and excursions, but we recognize that not all members of the party will always take the same options. For example, Mum and Dad might want to go to the Casino while the kids go off to the Zoo. In an itinerary for a holiday, we'll represent this by giving each traveler an ID value, and against each excursion we'll include an IDREFS field that lists the travelers taking part, something like this:

```
<itinerary>
   <traveler id="t01">
      <name>Mrs Mary Higgins</name>
   </traveler>
   <traveler id="t02">
      <name>Mr John Higgins</name>
   </traveler>
   <traveler id="t03">
      <name>Rory Higgins</name>
      <age>12</age>
   </traveler>
   <traveler id="t03">
      <name>Kylie Higgins</name>
      <age>9</age>
   </traveler>
   <excursion participants="t01 t02">
      <venue>Casino</venue>
      <date>2000-06-15</date>
   </excursion>
   <excursion participants="t03 t04">
      <venue>Zoo</venue>
      <date>2000-06-15</date>
   </excursion>
</itinerary>
```

We've chosen here to make the link one-way, from the excursion to the traveler. We could equally have made it the other way, with an excursions attribute on the <traveler> element, or we could include both. I generally prefer to avoid the two-way link, because it only means that someone has to check that they're consistent and work out what to do if they aren't. If it's one way it's arbitrary which way you do it. Instinct might tell you to implement a one-to-many relationship using an IDREF attribute at the "many" end, because that's where you would put a foreign key in a relational table, but using an IDREFS attribute at the "one" end works just as well.

XPointer references are a lot more flexible than ID/IDREF, but unfortunately they are not fully standardized yet, and not very widely implemented either. Hopefully this is about to change – the XPath standard has been designed as a replacement for the previous XPointer syntax, and now has the status of a W3C Recommendation, so most of the work has been done. It's an advantage that XPointer allows cross-references from one document to another, though you need to know the detailed structure of the target document. XPointers are not identified as such in the DTD, so the parser will not validate them. If your chosen XML software supports XPointer values directly, it's worth considering them, but this is probably a future technology to watch out for rather than one that is really viable today.

The simplest kind of XPointer, of course, is simply a URL, and using a URL to represent a relationship is invaluable whenever there's a good reason for keeping separate things in separate documents.

Let's suppose, for example, that our holiday company is getting into the conferences business. Part of the arrangements for a conference include arranging an individual itinerary for each conference delegate. So it makes sense to have one XML document for the conference, and one for each delegate itinerary. It might look something like this:

```
<conference>
   <title>13th Annual High Achievers' Celebration</title>
   <resort>Honolulu</resort>
   <delegates>
      <delegate>
         <name>Jane Sales</name>
         <itinerary>http://high-speed.com/itinerary/JS0002.xml</itinerary>
      </delegate>
      <delegate>
         <name>John Pusher</name>
         <itinerary>http://high-speed.com/itinerary/JP0008.xml</itinerary>
      </delegate>
   </delegates>
</conference>
```

Here we are only linking to an XML document, but once the XPointer specification stabilizes it will become quite viable to link to an individual element within a document. For example, all the menus on offer at a hotel might be in one document and a menu selection for each delegate might be an XPointer to an individual menu.

Meanwhile the option of handling relationships using keys at application level is a perfectly viable approach, and gives you the maximum flexibility to manipulate the relationship in any way you want. The only disadvantage is that the XML parser software won't give you any help. The availability of the `key()` function in XSLT stylesheets means that processing relationships implemented in this way can be quite straightforward.

See Chapter 8 for more information on linking.

Representing Properties

Where you have identified a property in your information model, a classic dilemma arises: should you represent it in the XML document using an XML attribute, or using a nested (child) element? Once you have decided this there are other areas that need to be looked into.

Elements or Attributes?

Here is an example where the properties of a book are represented as XML attributes:

```
<book
   author="Nelson Mandela"
   title="Long Walk to Freedom"
   publisher="Abacus"
   isbn="0-349-10653-3" />
```

Here is the same information, this time representing the properties as child elements:

```
<book>
   <author>Nelson Mandela</author>
   <title>Long Walk to Freedom</title>
   <publisher>Abacus</publisher>
   <isbn>0-349-10653-3</isbn>
</book>
```

Which representation is best? This is one of the questions most frequently asked by those designing XML documents for the first time, and although some would say "do either, it doesn't make much difference", it is worth discussing the options in a little detail so you can decide the pros and cons for yourself. But we should start by saying that even the experts disagree, and sometimes they disagree passionately.

Firstly, let's try to dispose of the argument that there are philosophical reasons for choosing one approach or the other. Some would try and argue that a child element represents a contained object – something with its own existence and identity independent of its container – while an attribute represents a value associated with the object that has no separate life of its own (in the terminology of classical metaphysics, an *accident*). This is murky water to get into, and if you want to adopt arguments along these lines you had better read up your Aristotle before someone challenges you. If you follow this logic to its inevitable conclusion, you will end up deciding that `age` should be represented as an attribute, but `place-of-birth` as a child element (because a place is an object in its own right). This outcome doesn't seem particularly intuitive or helpful, and it leaves you with unproductive debates over each separate property.

Another line of reasoning is to look at the intentions of the designers of the XML standard. The distinction between child elements and attributes goes back to the early days of SGML, so we can ask an obvious question: how did the original SGML designers see the roles of the two constructs?

SGML, as we have seen, was in its origins a markup language for preparing text for publication. Other applications as a general purpose data interchange format came later. In its original role as a markup language there was a clear distinction between **content** (the text that the eventual reader was supposed to see on the page) and **metadata** (information about the content, intended for use by the software performing the various stages of processing). Quite simply, content was represented by text within element tags, and metadata was represented by attributes. This distinction was retained in HTML, and has caused many problems as HTML has evolved: client-side JavaScript sections, for example, couldn't be handled comfortably as attributes, so they were placed in a `<script>` element; but because this was not intended for the user to see, it also had to be commented out: a gross abuse of the intended purpose of comments.

So the distinction between element content and attributes in SGML was essentially a distinction as to who the information was intended for: element content was destined for the readers of the document, attributes for the typographers or their software. Of course, once SGML or XML is applied to the role of data interchange between software systems this distinction loses any meaning. Even where there are human readers, as with a spreadsheet, the question of what is there for the software and what is there for the user can be difficult to decide.

So looking at the history gives us no *right* answer either. We can therefore conclude that we are free to do it whichever way we like based on purely utilitarian considerations.

So let's look at the practical pros and cons of each approach.

	Advantages	Disadvantages
XML Attributes	DTD can constrain the values: useful when there is a small set of allowed values, such as "yes" and "no".	Simple string values only.
	DTD can define a default value.	No support for metadata (or "attributes of attributes").
	`ID` and `IDREF` validation.	Unordered.
	Lower space overhead (makes a difference when you are sending gigabytes of data over the network).	
	White space normalization is available for certain data types (such as `NMTOKENS`), which saves the application some parsing effort.	
	Easier to process using DOM and SAX interfaces.	
	Access to unparsed external entities, such as binary data.	
Child Elements	Support arbitrarily complex values and repeating values.	Slightly higher space usage.
	Ordered.	More complex programming.
	Support "attributes of attributes".	
	Extensible when the data model changes.	

How these factors balance out will vary from one application to another. For many experienced designers the most important factor is *potential for change*: the ability to extend the document or message formats as the application evolves. This factor leads inexorably towards using child elements rather than attributes, because one of the most frequent changes seen in practice is for a simple property such as "author" to expand into a complex structured property (a list of authors, say, each identified by first name and last name). But whether this is the right choice for your application is something only you can decide. It's worth mentioning that Biztalk, the influential Microsoft-sponsored initiative, makes exactly the opposite recommendation, so you're in good company whatever you choose.

Encoding Property Values

Whether you represent the properties of an object using elements or attributes, you have to make a decision on how to encode their values.

Some of the common situations encountered are listed here:

Quantities, such as Height, Width, and Weight

The first question is whether to standardize the unit of measure (all lengths in meters, for example) or to allow different units of measure. If the unit is included as part of the data, there is the option of making it part of the value (`height="1.86m"`) or making it a separate item (`<height units="m">1.86</height>`). Finally, the decimal number format must be defined, for example which symbols are used for the decimal point and thousands separator. Once XML Schemas become established it should be possible simply to reference a standard numeric data type and not worry about the lexical encoding, but for the moment this burden still falls on the document designer.

See Chapter 7 for more information on XML Schemas.

Yes/No Values

An obvious representation, in an English-speaking context, is to use the strings `yes` and `no`, or `y` and `n` if space is at a premium. If attributes are used, an alternative is to use the SGML convention, also encountered in HTML – for example `border="border"` means `yes`, and an absent border attribute means `no`. This convention had advantages in an SGML world but it is only of historic interest with XML. For SGML interoperability, XML discourages you from having two attributes on the same element with overlapping sets of values, having two attributes both with the permitted values `yes` and `no` for example.

Other Small Value Sets

The basic decision is whether to use full names or codes, such as `W` or `Withdrawn`, `uk` or `United Kingdom`. Apart from space considerations, the main benefit of using an expanded name is that it avoids misunderstanding – it is surprisingly common for the user community to assume that a code means something different from what the designer intended, and for confusion about the meaning of the data to occur as a result.

Dates and Times

Many would advocate standardizing on the ISO 8601 date format (`YYYY-MM-DD`) to avoid ambiguity. ISO 8601 also allows times to be represented, including the time zone.

There are actually many standards available for particular types of property. The International Organization for Standardization (ISO) have published a good many, among them the following:

Standard	Scope	Description
ISO 2955	Metric measurements (Système Internationale)	Method for representing SI and other units in information systems with limited character sets (without using Greek letters).
ISO 3166	Country codes	Specification of codes for the representation of names of countries; a set of two letter and three letter codes. The two letter codes are most familiar as internet domain names, such as de for Germany.
ISO 4217	Currency codes	Codes for national currencies.
ISO 5218	Human sexes	Codes to represent male and female (surely this must be the shortest international standard ever published?).
ISO 6093	Numeric values	Three presentations of numerical values, represented in character strings in machine readable form, and recognizable by humans
ISO 6709	Location of points	A format and representation for unique identification of points on, above, or below the earth's surface by longitude, latitude, and altitude.
ISO 8601	Dates and Times	Expression of dates, including calendar dates, ordinal dates, week numbers and times in numeric form, with punctuation to avoid ambiguity.

Of course there is no obligation to use any of these standards, but there are two great advantages if you do. Firstly, someone else has given more thought to the difficulties than you probably have time for, and secondly, telling people you're going to conform to a standard is a good way of cutting short unproductive debate.

There are many other sources of standards: Internet RFC 1766 for example defines a widely-used coding scheme for natural languages; the X.500/LDAP standards define a carefully researched scheme for representing personal names in use throughout the world (no, it isn't first name, middle initial, and surname); and of course there are many domain-specific standards such as ISBNs in the publishing world, airport codes in the travel industry, and so on.

In due course we can expect some of the more common data types to be standardized as part of the XML Schemas activity. At that stage it is likely that XML parsers will start to take over the job of parsing and validating data that uses these types, which will take some of the load off applications.

Property Names

When you use elements to represent properties in the information model, and to a lesser extent also when you use attributes, the question arises as to what names to use. This may seem obvious, but in fact there are two choices: you can name either the data type, or its role in the parent object. To take a couple of simple examples, the date of a document's creation can be named either `date-created` or `date`; the address of a customer can be named either `address` or `billing-address`.

Of course if there is more than one date or one address you have no choice but to use the longer form, and you might think of this simply as removing ambiguity, which in a sense it is. Unfortunately, at the same time you are also removing the implicit data type information. How is the application software to know that billing-address has the same validation constraints as service-address? Also, DTDs become much more complicated if every element is distinguished in this way.

A related question is whether to overload names of properties that appear in more than one object type. For example, a resort, a hotel, and a customer all have a name – is it reasonable to use the `<name>` tag in the XML document to represent all three? Essentially, in XML the philosophy is that element names are global (they should mean the same thing regardless where they appear) whereas attribute names are local to a particular element type. This isn't a hard-and-fast rule; you can get away with overloading of element names, in particular where the element is being used to represent a simple text property such as `NAME` or `TITLE`, and equally there are some contexts (particularly XSLT stylesheets) where attribute names can be treated as if they have global significance. As a general design principle, it's probably best in both cases to avoid using the same name to mean completely different things: for example, don't use `STATUS` to mean both the creditworthiness of an individual and the property that a flight has been confirmed.

There are several options you might want to consider for naming:

- Use a systematic convention for names, for example `<Billing.Address>` and `<Creation.Date>`. This might be useful to keep things nice and tidy, and you might even exploit the convention in your application software, but of course it won't mean anything to the XML software – and in particular, there's no way of exploiting such structured names in XSLT. (A dot in an XML name is allowed, but it has no more significance than any other character.) Other common options include using underscores between the words, and camelCase notation (where the first letter of the second word is capitalized), however the dot notation may be more significant to the processing application.
- Use the qualified name as the element name and use an attribute for the data type, for example `<BillingAddress type="Address">`. This means the data type is still available to the application. In fact, because every `BillingAddress` is an `Address`, the `type` attribute doesn't need to be present on each instance, but can be a `FIXED` attribute value defined in the DTD. However, this approach can't automatically define structural rules in the DTD that say every element with `type="Address"` conforms to the same pattern.
- Do the opposite: use the data type as the element name and an attribute for the role, for example `<Address role="Billing">`. From the point of view of writing a DTD, this is probably better, although there are still limitations: you can now define the rules for an address, but you can no longer say that each customer must have a billing address, which was possible with the first approach.
- Use an extra layer of nested elements:

```
<Customer>
   <BillingAddress>
      <Address>
      </Address>
   </BillingAddress>
</Customer>
```

From a theoretical point of view, this is probably the best so far: you can now define that the `Customer` must have a `BillingAddress`, that the `BillingAddress` must contain an `Address` (and nothing else), and that the Address follows the same rules as an Address appearing anywhere else. The only downside is, if you apply the principle rigorously to every property in your model, you'll end up with an awful lot of tags to worry about. Given how limited the data type validation in DTDs is anyway, it seems a lot of trouble to go to.

Binary Data

Not all properties of objects can be conveniently represented as character strings: multimedia data, in particular, is binary in nature. How should binary data such as images be represented in your XML design?

There are two main approaches: the binary objects can be **internal** or **external**. Internal means they are represented as part of the XML data stream, external means they are in a separate file.

For internal storage, most people use Base64 encoding. This is a technique of encoding each sequence of binary digits as an ASCII character. It works well with XML, because the ASCII characters used do not clash with the markup sequences (such as "<" and "`]]>`") that have a special meaning in XML. This means there is no risk of having a delimiter accidentally present in the data. Of course, the translation of the binary data to and from Base64 character strings is entirely the job of the application.

For external storage, the "pure XML" way of doing it is to use external unparsed entities and notations. For example, to include a reference to the image file `picture1.gif`, you would write in the DTD (typically in the internal subset):

```
<!NOTATION gif SYSTEM "gifeditor.exe">
<!ENTITY picture1 SYSTEM "picture1.gif" NDATA gif>
```

Here `gifeditor.exe` is supposed to be the name of an application that can handle data in this particular format. In practice, unless your chosen XML toolset defines otherwise, it is anything you want to use to identify the format uniquely. The reference to an unparsed entity appears as the value of an attribute of type `ENTITY`, so the DTD will also include a declaration such as:

```
<!ELEMENT picture EMPTY>
<!ATTLIST picture name ENTITY #REQUIRED>
```

Finally, at the place where you want the image to appear in the document, you can refer to it by means of an unparsed entity reference, for example:

```
<picture name="picture1"/>
```

Note that there is no "&" in the entity reference: the parser knows it's an entity reference because it is declared as such in the ATTLIST declaration in the DTD.

Finally, if all this seems rather cumbersome, you can simply use a URL link in the same way as HTML does:

```
<IMG SRC="picture.gif"/>
```

As far as the XML parser is concerned, this is just an ordinary CDATA attribute, but at application level you can interpret it as a URL pointing to a GIF file.

It should be stressed that whereas only one of these techniques (unparsed entities and notations) makes use of special XML facilities for handling binary data, that doesn't mean it is the only approved way of solving the problem: the other techniques mentioned are just as much correct XML.

If your main aim is to render the XML into HTML for display in a browser, the approach based on URL links is by far the simplest. If you are transmitting transient data between applications, using internal objects with Base64 encoding is probably the most resilient, because it avoids all problems concerning the integrity of the cross-reference, for example what happens if the linked object is updated.

When XLink is standardized and supported, it will be possible to embed some binary data, such as images, which will appear within the source document. We discuss XLink in Chapter 8.

Using XML Entities

In discussing how to translate the information model into an XML design, we haven't so far described many uses for XML entities.

This isn't really surprising, because entities in XML are supposed to be part of the physical document structure, not part of its logical structure. An entity reference is supposed to mean exactly the same thing as if the entity were expanded inline.

So it's natural to regard entities as part of the physical design stage – the XML design equivalent of the physical design stage in relational database design, where we worry about indexes and partitioning.

There are however some logical uses for entities. The main advantage of extracting something from the body of a document into an external entity is that it can then be updated separately from the rest of the document. This makes it useful for text or other document components that have a different update cycle or update authority from the main body. This control aspect is far more important than any space saving obtained by sharing common content. The same argument applies to a complex DTD where different parts are under the control of different people.

We mentioned in the discussion of information modeling (and then conveniently forgot) that it includes questions of ownership of information and the information lifecycle. Perhaps it is these aspects of the information model that should lead to design decisions on how to separate documents into separate physical entities.

Schema Languages and Notations

In the final part of this chapter we'll look at how to represent your document design on paper, or in electronic form, to make it accessible both to human users and to software. We'll look at two main schema notations: DTDs, and the various XML Schema proposals.

Let's start by looking at the objectives: what are we trying to achieve?

The Role of a Schema

The concept of a schema has been present for many years in both the database and the document worlds – perhaps it is one of the few things they have in common! The formal role of the schema is to define the set of all possible valid documents; or to look at it more negatively, to define what constraints, beyond those of XML itself, documents must meet for them to be meaningful.

We need to be careful in using the word **validity** here. In the XML standard, being "valid" means something quite specific. Informally, it means that a document conforms to the rules in its DTD. We are interested in many constraints that cannot be expressed in a DTD, and some that cannot be expressed in an XML Schema either – like a rule that the sequence number at the start of a message must be one greater than the sequence number at the start of the previous message. In the rest of this chapter we'll use the word "valid" in this user-oriented sense rather than in the strict XML sense: a document is valid if it satisfies all the constraints defined by the information model.

Why Do We Need Schemas?

This is what the current draft of the W3C XML Schema proposal has to say on the matter:

> *The purpose of a ... schema is to define and describe a class of XML documents by using these [markup] constructs to constrain and document the meaning, usage, and relationships of their constituent parts: datatypes, elements, and their content, attributes and their content, entities and their contents and notations. Schema constructs may also provide for the specification of additional information such as default values. Schemas are intended to document their own meaning, usage, and function through a common documentation vocabulary. Thus, XML Schema Structures can be used to define, describe, and catalogue XML vocabularies for classes of XML documents.*

Which, we would argue, says what schemas do but doesn't say why. There are really two separate purposes in a schema that we can find in this description: to **constrain** and to **explain**.

The Schema as a Set of Constraints

One purpose of a schema is to define the difference between a valid document and an invalid one. As far as possible the rules should be expressed in such a way that software can decide whether a document is valid or not; but there will always be room as well for rules that in practice only human beings can interpret. For example, a rule for a scientific journal that the author's address should include the city and country only, or that the abstract must be in French.

We need such constraints for two reasons: stylistic reasons (every publication wants to maintain its brand image, its house style, and its design integrity), and processing reasons. The processing reasons define the information requirements of the next stage in the process that is handling the document, whether this is a business process such as dealing with a job application form, a typographical process, or an internal systems process such as updating a database. The constraints can be seen in both cases as a kind of quality control.

Of course, constraints are not always a good thing. There is a great temptation, given the ability to impose rules, to use this ability thoughtlessly to make the system unnecessarily rigid. Information systems have a bad reputation for inflexibility, and the aim should be to use constraints sensibly to allow the humans in the process the maximum scope for using their intelligence. Used naively, constraints can even have a negative effect on information quality: I have in the past been forced to supply wrong data to an e-commerce system because the web page insisted that my address must be in a US State.

Also, the fact that we can define unambiguous rules and check them by software does not necessarily mean we have to validate a document against the rules at every conceivable stage of processing. For example, checking a document at the time it is delivered from your web server is completely futile: it should be validated when it is placed on the web server in the first place. Yet some people will blindly use a validating parser regardless. Similarly, when XML documents are sent from one software system to another one within the same organization, validation is useful during the testing stage, but once everything is running smoothly there is scope for one piece of software to trust another to get things right.

The Schema as an Explanation

The second purpose of a schema is to explain – to document the interpretation and usage of the constructs provided, so that the sender and the recipient share a common understanding of the meaning of the message.

In both the document and database traditions, this role of a schema has tended to play second fiddle, though potentially it is the more important. Part of the problem is that the schema doesn't usually reach the person who needs to know, namely the person entering the data on the screen. This is why many systems suffer from what has been called **semantic drift**, a tendency for the user community over time to change the way in which they use the system and the meanings they attach to the data fields, even though the software structure remains unchanged. In one example I encountered, users were deliberately entering data that they knew the system would reject, because the file of records awaiting correction was a convenient place to keep notes of phone calls that needed to be made the next day. In another system, I found that a news agency was sending invoices to its customers under the guise of dummy news articles.

You can't stop these things happening, any more than an architect can stop the occupants of a building from watching television in the kitchen. What you can do is to try to explain the purpose of the structures you are providing, to make them flexible enough for the users to achieve their purposes without abusing your designs, and as far as possible to make them intuitive and natural so that no-one will feel obliged to go down a different route deliberately.

The fact that end users won't look at the schema directly means there is a need for the schema to be application-readable: for example, it should be possible to extract explanations of data fields and display them as advisory text on data entry screens. This concept of a schema was fashionable in the 1970s and 1980s under the title of a **data dictionary**: another term that emphasizes its role in defining the meaning of names in the system's vocabulary, though it eventually dropped out of favor through abuse by software companies whose data dictionary was little more than an internal system catalog.

The DTD as a Schema

If the purpose of a schema is to constrain and explain, the limitations of the XML DTD become very quickly apparent. Let's look at some of the difficulties.

What Constraints can you Express in a DTD?

As a constraint language, DTDs are very limited. They provide some control over which elements can be nested within each other, but say nothing about the text contained within the elements. They offer slightly more control over attributes, but even this is very limited, for example there is no way of saying that an attribute must be numeric. This inevitably means that much of the real validation has to be done in the application; in fact, I have often found that DTD validation adds so little value, that it isn't worth bothering with.

Can you Rely on DTD Validation?

Even within the limits of the rules you can define in a DTD, there is the odd ability in XML for a document to set its own agenda: it is the document itself that decides whether it is going to reference a DTD or not, which DTD it is going to reference, and whether it is going to override any of the declarations in the DTD in its private internal subset. Even if the application knows it is using a validating parser, the constraints it is enforcing are those that the document chooses to obey, not those that the application wishes to impose.

For example, let's suppose you've defined a DTD for a holiday itinerary, and have called it `itinerary.dtd`. You have an application that's designed to print the itinerary so it can be mailed to the customer. If the application is going to avoid doing validation itself, it needs to be sure that the input document conforms to the DTD called `itinerary.dtd`. To do this, it needs to be sure:

- That the parser it is using is a validating one. (Obvious, but whether your application is written in SAX or DOM or XSLT, there's no easy way to find out.)
- That the document contains a reference in its `<!DOCTYPE>` declaration to `itinerary.dtd`. (Again, unfortunately most standard APIs don't provide this information.)
- That the parser is using what the application considers to be the right version of `itinerary.dtd` (this is getting hard).
- That the document element in the input document is the correct element type (the DTD doesn't say which element should be at the top level, but fortunately the application can do this check very easily).
- That the input document doesn't contain an internal DTD subset that overrides any of the key validation rules in the external DTD. For example, if the external DTD subset contains the definitions

```
<!ELEMENT PAYMENT EMPTY>
<!ATTLIST PAYMENT MEANS (check | credit-card) #REQUIRED>
```

  then the application might reasonably expect that a `<PAYMENT>` element in a valid input document would contain a `MEANS` attribute whose value was one of the strings "`check`", or "`credit-card`". But if the input document contained an internal DTD subset containing the declaration:

```
<!ATTLIST PAYMENT MEANS (check | credit-card | cash ) #IMPLIED>
```

then this would override the declaration in the external DTD. So the MEANS attribute could be omitted, or take the value "cash", and the input document would still be perfectly valid as far as the parser is concerned.

Writing DTDs

The syntax of DTDs does not conform to the XML syntax, and can be difficult to read and even harder to write, betraying its late 1960s SGML legacy with every choice of delimiter. A DTD as an explanation of the meaning of elements and attributes is about as useful as explaining a business process by showing compiled Java bytecodes: there are even places in the syntax where comments are not allowed.

There are editing tools on the market to make the writing of DTDs easier, but in the end, anyone who wants to fully understand a DTD will probably end up having to learn the syntax. This is inconvenient and architecturally inelegant, especially as there is no way of parsing DTDs in the same way as XML files.

DTDs and Namespaces

The final nail in the coffin is the fact that DTDs are almost impossible to use in conjunction with XML Namespaces. Namespaces are supposed to allow you to mix elements from more than one information model in the same document, for example to use chemical formulae as well as geographical coding in a document about the spread of pollution. The intent is that you can choose your own prefixes for names without changing the meaning, for example you could use <GEO:LI> to refer to Lithuania and <CHEM:LI> for Lithium.

There are two problems with this. Firstly, your document can only refer to one external DTD. Secondly, the renaming of elements by adding prefixes is not recognized by the DTD, so if you do this, in effect you will need to create a new version of the DTD each time.

But despite the limitations of DTDs, for the time being they are the only standard we have, so we will look at the question of how to create a DTD from your information model.

Deriving a DTD from the Information Model

We've already looked at the question of how the concepts of the information model should be translated into the design of XML documents, and some of these decisions will be reflected directly in the DTD. For example, the choice of whether to represent properties of objects as elements or as attributes.

But some other issues only become apparent when we actually try to write the DTD, and we'll take a look at these now.

Although the modeling capabilities of the DTD are limited, a great deal can be achieved by exploiting the very flexible mechanism of parameter entities. Although on paper parameter entities simply allow text to be shared between different definitions in the DTD, in practice they can be used as definitions in their own right, and a great deal of the art of writing effective DTDs depends on creative use of parameter entities.

Most of the DTD consists of two kinds of definition: **element definitions**, which define the content of elements; and **attribute definitions**, which define the attributes that can appear in each element. We'll therefore look at each of these in turn.

Defining the Content of Elements

A DTD allows the definition of five possible element structures:

Content model	Example
EMPTY content	`<!ELEMENT confirmed EMPTY >`
ANY content	`<!ELEMENT description ANY >`
Element content	`<!ELEMENT payment (currency?, amount, date, mode-of-payment?)>`
Mixed content	`<!ELEMENT estimated-cost (#PCDATA | note)* >`
PCDATA content	`<!ELEMENT color (#PCDATA) >`

The XML specification actually identifies only four structures: syntactically PCDATA content is simply a special case of mixed content, but from the modeling point of view it is quite different. Let's look at how each of these can be used.

Elements with EMPTY Content

An EMPTY element essentially represents a boolean value: it is either there, or it is not. If you want to flag that a particular booking has been confirmed, using an empty <CONFIRMED/> child element might be a reasonable way to model it.

EMPTY elements are also useful when you decide to represent properties of objects in the form of attributes rather than child elements. (Remember that EMPTY means there are no child elements or text nodes: it doesn't mean there are no attributes.) When you choose this approach, you can find that nearly all the elements in your document are empty: a document might contain thousands of elements of the form:

```
<payment from="1234" to="5678" amount="230.45" date="1999-10-15"/>
```

If you wanted you could even construct a document consisting of a single XML element with no children and lots of attributes: this might be a perfectly reasonable structure for certain kinds of message.

Another (admittedly unusual) way of using EMPTY elements is to represent the values of an enumerated data type. For example, you could write:

```
<TRAVELER>
   <GENDER><FEMALE/></GENDER>
</TRAVELER>
```

This allows the element declaration for GENDER to specify the list of valid values in the form of a structure with element content, thus:

```
<!ELEMENT GENDER ( MALE | FEMALE ) >
```

Elements with ANY Content

The ANY option is unlikely to arise in a DTD derived from an information model; on the contrary, it is most often used when the information model is not fully known. It doesn't actually allow an element to contain child elements of any type, only of types that are defined in the DTD, so it is equivalent to listing all the element types in the DTD. Since some of these will almost certainly make no sense, this can only be regarded as laziness: better to use element or mixed content and list those elements that do make sense in the context.

Elements with Element Content

Element content defines which elements may act as children to the element being defined, and also defines what order they may appear in, whether they are mandatory, and whether they may repeat. Of all the options, this one gives the designer the most precise control over validation. Consider the following definition:

```
<!ELEMENT RESORT (
   NAME,
   COUNTRY,
   REGION?,
   HOTEL+) >
```

This declaration defines that a RESORT must have a name, must be in a particular country, may be in a particular region, and must contain one or more hotels. Syntactically the child elements may be separated by white space, but by convention the white space is insignificant.

The biggest drawback to using this kind of declaration is that as well as saying which child elements can appear and how often, it also imposes an ordering on the elements: with this declaration in the DTD it would be invalid for the country to precede the resort name. There is no way of listing twenty optional but non-repeatable child elements without constraining them to appear in a particular order. Whether this is a problem depends on how the documents are actually generated. For documents written by human authors, you may feel that it is unreasonable to ask them to specify all the child elements in the right order just so that you can delegate the validation to the XML parser.

Elements with Mixed Content

Mixed element content arises most often with document structures, where you are using tags to mark particular words in text. The tags might of course be semantic tags rather than purely presentation tags, for example:

```
<resumé>
   <languages>
      I am fluent in <lang>English</lang>, <lang>Spanish</lang>, and to
      a lesser extent in <lang>Chinese</lang>.
   </languages>
</resumé>
```

Such structures do not tend to emerge from a formal information modeling approach of the kind we have described in this chapter – which does not mean they are necessarily a bad thing. On the contrary, they are an excellent way of representing information, particularly the fuzzier kind of information where we want to capture all the subtleties and ambiguities that can be expressed in natural language. It is not necessarily always right to try and formalize and codify everything.

Mixed element content can also arise where we want to represent not just facts, but properties of facts. Again, this isn't a concept found in most popular information modeling approaches, though it has many practical uses, particularly in fields such as medical notes, historical studies, or fraud investigation, where we want to record not just bold assertions such as "Thomas Wilson suffered from lead poisoning", but also observations relating to the facts: who stated this opinion and when? What was their evidence? How certain were they? Does someone else disagree? This can lead to this kind of structure:

```
<weight>182.3
   <plus-or-minus>0.5</plus-or-minus>
   <measured-by>John Smith</measured-by >
   <date-of-measurement>1991-10-15</date-of-measurement>
   <instrument>567421</instrument>
   <alternative-value>186.1
      <measured-by>Mary Jackson</measured-by>
      <date-of-measurement>1993-01-21</date-of-measurement>
   </alternative-value>
</weight>
```

Mixed element content isn't ideally suited to this purpose, because it always allows any of the child elements to appear any number of times and in any order, and in particular it allows more than one unit of text content. There are several alternatives which might work better: one is to represent the "facts" as elements and the "properties of facts" as attributes of these elements; another is to place another level of element tag around the value, so the above example would become:

```
<weight>
   <value>182</value>
   <plus-or-minus>0.5</plus-or-minus>
   <measured-by>John Smith</measured-by >
   <date-of-measurement>1991-10-15</date-of-measurement>
   <instrument>567421</instrument>
   <alternative-value>
      <value>186.1</value>
      <measured-by>Mary Jackson</measured-by>
      <date-of-measurement>1993-01-21</date-of-measurement>
   </alternative-value>
</weight>
```

But this would be rather unwieldy if the vast majority of so-called facts had only a value, with no additional commentary.

Elements with PCDATA Content

Finally, we come to PCDATA content. PCDATA elements form the atoms of the document, the units from which the higher-level structures are built, and if you are representing properties by elements, then most of them will be PCDATA elements.

Modeling the Object Type Hierarchy

There is no explicit concept in XML of a type hierarchy, but it is possible to use parameter entities to simulate it, and experienced DTD designers do this quite instinctively.

A specialized type is always defined by adding things to the definition of the type it is derived from. For example, the object type `<refund>` is a specialization of the type `<payment>` that has extra properties such as `<reason>` and `<authorized-by>`. If we define types in the DTD using parameter entities, this extension can be done in a natural way.

The following example uses child elements to represent properties:

```
<!ENTITY % payment "amount, date, account, notes?" >
<!ELEMENT payment ( %payment; ) >
<!ENTITY % refund "%payment;, reason?, authorised-by" >
<!ELEMENT refund ( %refund; )
```

When Several Properties Have the Same Data Type

In our modeling discussions earlier we raised the question of how to name the elements used to represent the two separate properties `Billing-Address` and `Service-Address`. Very often you will end up with several element types that have exactly the same data type, that is, the same validation rules. Again, you can represent this naturally in a DTD by using a parameter entity to represent the underlying data type:

```
<!ENTITY % address "address-line+, postcode, country" >
<!ELEMENT billing-address ( %address; ) >
<!ELEMENT service-address ( %address; ) >
```

Defining Attributes in the DTD

When the time comes to define attributes, there are typically rather fewer choices to make, and they follow fairly directly from the information model.

Deciding whether attributes should be optional or mandatory is generally straightforward. The decision whether to have a default value is typically a pragmatic one – it should really be based on whether you, as the document designer, want to decide the value to use if the document author doesn't care. Default values, of course, can be very valuable when you extend the DTD to include attributes that were not present in a previous version.

The notion of `FIXED` attribute values (that is, attributes whose declaration in the DTD states that every instance of the attribute will have the same value) often seems rather alien to people from a database background, but they are potentially a very powerful mechanism. Some possible uses are as follows:

- Use them in the same way as static fields in Java, to represent attributes of the element type as distinct from attributes of an instance. For example, you could use a fixed attribute to identify the data type of the element: so a `date-of-birth` field might have a fixed attribute `datatype="date"`; or you could have a fixed attribute that names a Java class used to validate the values of the element instances.

- Use them to identify the supertype. For example if you use many different element tags to record different events in the life of a customer (for example, `open-account`, `close-account`, `start-session`, `make-order`, `cancel-order`, or `make-payment`) then you may have some programs that want to analyze all events for a particular customer. Rather than hard-coding the list of element types that represent events, you can give each of them a fixed attribute `is-event="yes"`, and your program can use this attribute to select the relevant elements. For example in the DTD you might write:

```
<!ELEMENT CLOSE-ACCOUNT ...>
<!ATTLIST CLOSE-ACCOUNT is-event FIXED "yes">
```

And then in an application written in XSLT, for example, you could process all the element types classified as events by writing:

```
<xsl:for-each select="*/@is-event='yes'">
```

- Use them for an attribute that is constant today, but which might vary in the future: for example a version number.
- Use them in conjunction with conditional sections or parameter entities to provide an attribute that is only really fixed for a particular run of the program. For example, you could arrange to define a FIXED attribute called access-rights in an external parameter entity that takes a different value depending on who the user is. You could then use this in an XSLT application to filter out the data that the user is allowed to see, by using a condition such as:

```
<xsl:for-each select="data[@access-rights &gt;= @security-level]">
```

Choosing an Attribute Type

There is a tendency to use CDATA as the default type for all attributes, because it allows any string as the value, but in fact the majority of attributes are likely to conform to the NMTOKEN or NMTOKENS types. An NMTOKEN is any sequence of one or more letters, digits, or certain punctuation characters, including . and -, while NMTOKENS is a list of NMTOKEN values separated by white space. So:

```
1999-10-31
```

is a valid NMTOKEN value, and:

```
Defining attributes in the DTD
```

is a valid NMTOKENS value. The extra validation you get by using these types may be of marginal value, but the fact that the parser will normalize white space for you can be a useful convenience, particularly for applications written in XSLT.

As with element structure, parameter entities in the DTD can be a useful way of expressing commonality between attributes, or sets of attributes, used in many different elements.

The XML Schema Proposal

The limitations of DTDs have been recognized in W3C for some time, but it has taken considerable time to come up with an answer, partly because there were several rival proposals on the table, none of which seemed to solve the whole problem. One of the formative proposals was Microsoft's proprietary XML-Data specification, described at http://biztalk.org/Resources/schemasguide.asp.

The current ideas of the XML Schema Working Group are summarized in two working drafts, both dated 5th November 1999:

- Part 1, Structures (http://www.w3.org/TR/xmlschema-1) deals with facilities to control and describe the structural rules for a document
- Part 2, Datatypes (http://www.w3.org/TR/xmlschema-2) deals with the definition of data types for items of content

These proposals are very unfinished, with many sections described as work-in-progress, and strong caveats advising against using the specifications in their current form. Nevertheless, they give a good idea of the concepts that will probably emerge in the eventual specification, and it is worth gaining some familiarity with these, as even without XML Schema software, the ideas can be useful to you as a document designer.

The general idea of an XML Schema is that it is a document that describes (and constrains) a set of XML document instances. An XML Schema is itself an XML document: this is important because it means that XML applications (for example XSLT stylesheets) can easily interrogate the schema. SQL programmers will have no difficulty with this concept: it is exactly the same idea as having an SQL schema accessible in system tables that can be read using SQL. It also allows you to embellish the schema with information that's only there for application use – for example you might add information to each element definition regarding its privacy classification, and use this in your application to decide which data is shown to which users.

XML Schema, in its current draft form, has been split into two specifications. Part 1, Structures, deals primarily with constraints on the structure of elements. It introduces the concept of an **Archetype** which is essentially a compound data type. An element type can be declared to conform to a particular archetype, in which case the archetype defines all the constraints as to which child elements and attributes it may contain. The advantage of separating the archetype definition from the element definition is that several element types can then conform to the same archetype (`Billing.Address` and `Service.Address` can both conform to the archetype `Address`). This corresponds to one of the main uses of parameter entities in DTDs.

The XML Schema working group also intends to provide a mechanism for one archetype to refine another, as required to implement a type hierarchy. In the current drafts, however, the syntax for meeting this requirement is undefined.

Part 2 of the specification discusses data types: essentially the primitive data types such as strings, numbers, booleans, and dates, and the mechanisms for defining new data types by combining or restricting existing data types or simply by enumerating the values in the data type. These data types may be used to constrain the values of attributes or of text content in elements. The built-in data types are essentially those of modern programming languages or SQL, though the facilities for defining constraints such as minimum and maximum values are rather stronger than in most languages. The specification also retains the "legacy" XML data types such as `NMTOKENS`. They have clearly separated the definition of the values in the data type from their lexical representation in an XML document, so it is quite possible to have many different lexical representations of the same value (for example `3`, `3.0`, and `03.00`). As with Part 1, the definition of a data type is separated from the definition of the elements and attributes that use it, so many different elements and attributes can share the same data type.

In the current state of XML Schema there are still many integrity constraints that cannot be expressed in the schema and that will have to be enforced by the application. For example, there is currently no way of defining cross-attribute constraints (date of death must be later than date of birth), or structural constraints on an element other than the definition of its immediate children (for example: "in a dictionary entry, either the headword or at least one of its variants must have an etymology"). This will probably always be true: there will always be some validation that can only be done at application level, just as there is with the much more mature constraint definitions in relational databases.

We take a further look at XML Schemas in Chapter 7.

Summary

We started with a discussion of some basic principles of information modeling as they typically apply in an XML project, distinguishing in particular the roles of static information models (understanding the things in the world and their relationships) and dynamic information modeling (understanding what information has to get from A to B in the course of a business process). Both kinds of model are relevant to XML, and it is useful to classify XML documents into those that hold static, persistent data, and those that hold transient messages.

Then we looked at how to translate the conceptual information model into the design of XML documents. We examined some of the design decisions that need to be made: how to represent a type hierarchy, whether to use elements or attributes, and how to encode binary properties.

Finally we looked at how to express the design in an XML DTD or schema, both to specify the formal constraints to enable automatic checking of document instances, and to communicate the meaning of the documents to the people who will create the documents and process their information content.

5

The Document Object Model

By now, you should be starting to get a handle on the structure of XML documents and the ways they can be used to describe hierarchical information. Next, we need to look at the ways you may access an XML document from your programs. One of those ways is via the **Document Object Model**. In this chapter, we'll take a look at the Document Object Model and demonstrate its functionality with a few sample programs.

What is the Document Object Model?

The term Document Object Model has been applied to web browsers for some time. Objects such as window, document, and history have been considered part of the browser object model. Anyone who has done any web development, however, will know that the way in which this has been implemented has varied in different browsers. In order to create a more standardized way of accessing and manipulating document structure over the web, the W3C produced specifications resulting in the current W3C DOM.

The W3C DOM is a **language-** and **platform-neutral** definition, that is, interfaces are defined for the different objects comprising the DOM, but no specifics of implementation are provided, and it could be done in any programming language. This allows, for example, legacy data stores to be accessed using the DOM by implementing the DOM as a thin wrapper around the legacy data accessor functions. The objects in the DOM allow the developer to read, search, modify, add to, and delete from a document. The DOM lays out a standard functionality for document navigation and manipulation of the content and structure of HTML and XML documents.

XML Document Structure

Developers new to XML often assume that the main purpose of XML is to enable pieces of information in a file to be named so that others may easily understand them. As a result, documents prepared by novice XML developers often resemble "tag soup" – an unordered list of data elements with meaningful tag names, but containing about the same level of information as a flat file:

```
<INVOICE>
   <CUSTOMER>Homer J. Simpson</CUSTOMER>
   <ADDRESS>142 Evergreen Terrace</ADDRESS>
   <CITY>Springfield</CITY>
   <STATE>VA</STATE>
   <ZIP>00000</ZIP>
   <PRODUCT1>Plutonium</PRODUCT1>
   <UNITS1>10</UNITS1>
   <PRODUCT2>Donuts</PRODUCT2>
   <UNITS2>937</UNITS2>
   <PRODUCT3>Beer</PRODUCT3>
   <UNITS3>1028</UNITS3>
   <PRODUCT4>Peanuts</PRODUCT4>
   <UNITS4>1</UNITS4>
</INVOICE>
```

The ability of XML that many developers overlook is its ability to show relationships between elements – specifically, the ability to imply a parent-child relationship between two elements. The above file could be better expressed in XML this way:

```
<INVOICE>
   <CUSTOMER NAME="Homer J. Simpson"
             ADDRESS="142 Evergreen Terrace"
             CITY="Springfield"
             STATE="??"
             ZIP="00000">
   <LINEITEM PRODUCT="Plutonium"
             UNITS="10"/>
   <LINEITEM PRODUCT="Donuts"
             UNITS="937"/>
   <LINEITEM PRODUCT="Beer"
             UNITS="1028"/>
   <LINEITEM PRODUCT="Peanuts"
             UNITS="1"/>
</INVOICE>
```

In this form of the document, it becomes immediately apparent that the invoice element has four children: the line item elements. It also makes it easier to search the document – if we're looking for all orders for plutonium, we can do so by looking for `LINEITEM` elements with a `PRODUCT` attribute value of "`Plutonium`" – instead of having to look at the `PRODUCT1` element, `PRODUCT2` element, and so on.

The above document structure may be represented by a **node tree** that shows all elements and their relationships to one another:

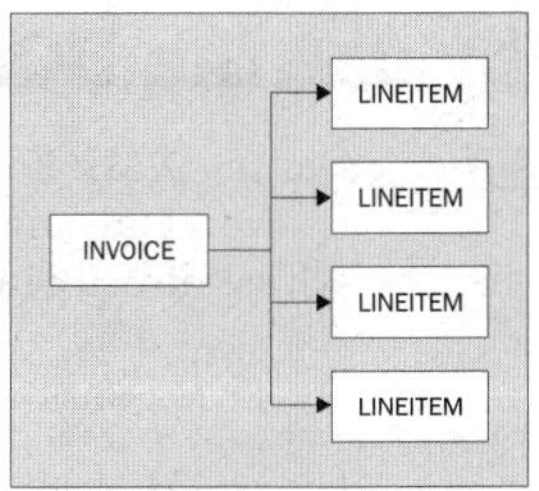

To add another line item to the invoice in the text file, we would have to read through the file until we got past the last line item element of the invoice, insert our new line item text, and then proceed with the rest of the document. As you can imagine, this technique becomes tricky quickly, especially if the node tree starts to become deep. However, if we could operate on the document in the node form with its tree structure, we'd be able to add the line item easily – we would simply create a new `LINEITEM` node and attach it as a child to the `INVOICE` node.

This is exactly how the DOM works.

When the DOM is used to manipulate an XML text file, the first thing it does is parse the file, breaking the file out into individual elements, attributes, comments, and so on. It then creates (in memory) a representation of the XML file as a node tree. The developer may then access the contents of the document through the node tree, and make modifications to it as necessary.

In fact, the DOM goes one step further and treats every item in the document as a node – elements, attributes, comments, processing instructions, and even the text that makes up an attribute. So, for our example above, the DOM representation would actually be:

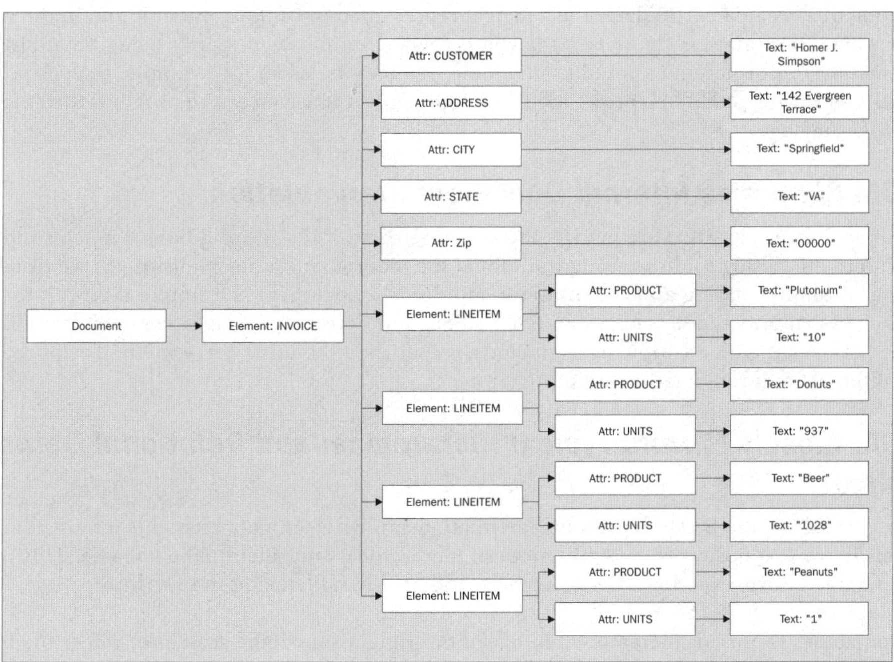

The DOM provides a robust set of interfaces to facilitate the manipulation of the DOM node tree.

Why use the DOM?

When accessing XML files, the DOM should almost always be the access method of choice. Using the DOM has several advantages over other available mechanisms for the generation of XML documents, such as writing directly to a stream:

- The DOM ensures proper grammar and well-formedness.
- The DOM abstracts content away from grammar.
- The DOM simplifies internal document manipulation.
- The DOM closely mirrors typical hierarchical and relational database structures.

Let's look at each of these in turn.

The DOM Ensures Proper Grammar and Well-Formedness

Because the DOM transforms the text file into an abstract representation of a node tree, problems like unclosed tags and improperly nested tags can be completely avoided. When manipulating an XML document with the DOM, the developer doesn't need to worry about the text expression of the document – only the parent-child relationships and associated information. In addition, the DOM will prevent improper parent-child relationships in the document. For example, an `Attr` object will never be allowed to be the parent of another `Attr` object.

The DOM Abstracts Content Away from Grammar

The node tree created by the DOM is a logical representation of the content found in the XML file – it shows what information is present and how it is related without necessarily being bound to the XML grammar. The information exposed by the node tree may be used, for example, to update a relational database, or create an HTML page – and developers need not concern themselves with the specifics of the XML language.

The DOM Simplifies Internal Document Manipulation

A developer using the DOM to modify the structure of an XML file will have a much simpler task than one who is attempting to do so using traditional file manipulation mechanisms. As we discussed in the previous example, adding an element to the middle of a document is a simple task with the DOM. In addition, global operations (such as deleting all elements with a particular tag name from a document) can be performed with a couple of commands, rather than the brute force method required to perform a scan of the file and remove the offending tags.

The DOM Closely Mirrors Typical Hierarchical and Relational Database Structures

The way in which the DOM represents the relationship between data elements is very similar to the way that this information is represented in modern hierarchical and relational databases. This makes it very easy to move information between a database and an XML file using the DOM.

Most databases represent hierarchical information using a **snowflake** structure, where the information in the database radiates out from a central "top-level" table much like the spokes of a wheel:

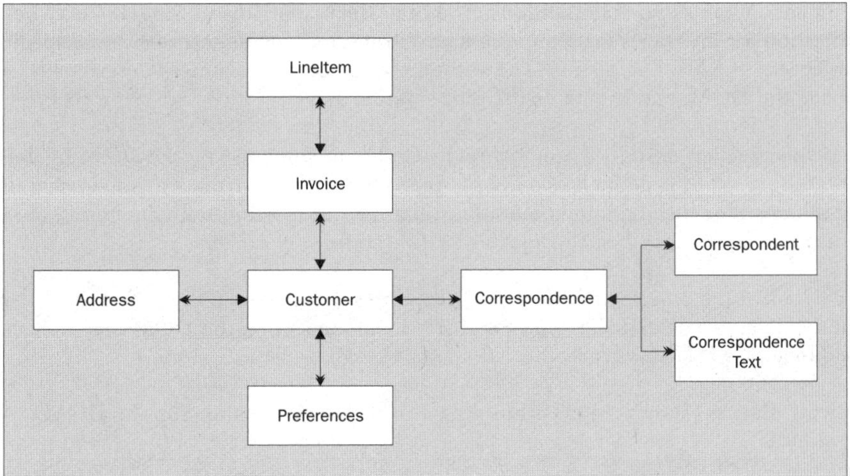

Note that for each customer, there may be multiple invoices, which may in turn have multiple line items. XML allows us to include multiple copies of a child element to support this behavior. Each of the above elements roughly corresponds to a table, which will then have columns associated with it (which will appear in the XML as attributes).

The XML equivalent of this structure would be:

```
<CUSTOMER>
   <INVOICE>
      <LINEITEM/>
   </INVOICE>
   <ADDRESS/>
   <CORRESPONDENCE>
      <CORRESPONDENT/>
      <CORRESPONDENCETEXT/>
   </CORRESPONDENCE>
   <PREFERENCES/>
</CUSTOMER>
```

Using the DOM to build the tree structure of a document allows information to be easily transferred between systems.

The DOM specification

As with other Internet standards, the DOM specification is maintained by the W3C. As of press time, the W3C has prepared two documents on DOM – the Level 1 and Level 2 documents.

DOM Level 1

The W3C document for DOM Level 1 has a status of Recommendation. This means that the W3C has reviewed it, accepted member comment on it, revised it, and is now promoting it as a standard on the World Wide Web. The full text of the recommendation may be found at http://www.w3.org/TR/REC-DOM-Level-1/.

This document contains two main sections. The first, **Document Object Model (Core) Level 1**, contains the specification for interfaces that can access any structured document, with some specific extensions that allow access to XML documents. The second section of the document describes HTML-specific extensions to the DOM, and is outside the scope of this book.

The DOM specification describes how strings are to be manipulated by the DOM by defining the datatype `DOMString`. It is defined as a double-byte character set string, encoded using the UTF-16 encoding scheme. For specific implementations, the interfaces will usually be bound to system datatypes that are also UTF-16 encoded, such as Java's `String` type.

Let's take a look at the objects, methods, and properties that make up the DOM level 1 specification. Note that the behavior described is that for XML documents only; the DOM may behave differently when used to access HTML documents.

The following diagram shows the class hierarchy for the objects making up the DOM:

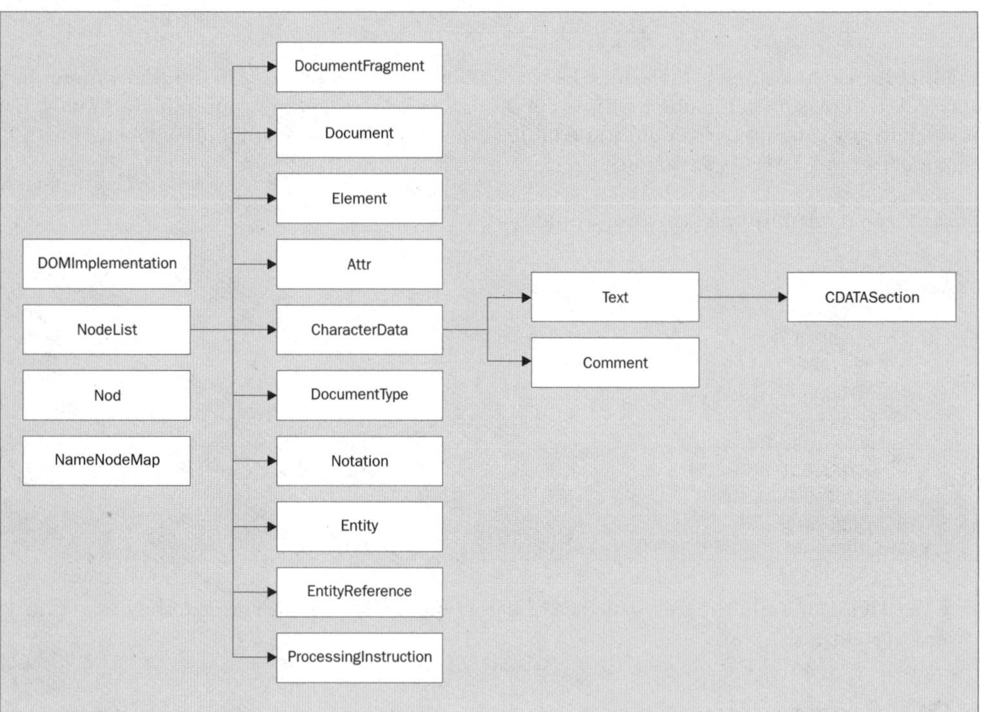

Full documentation for the DOM objects may be found in Appendix B.

DOM Level 2

As of press time, the W3C DOM level 2 specification currently has the status of Candidate Recommendation. This means that it has received significant review from its immediate technical community, and now requires implementation and technical feedback from parties external to the W3C. The level 2 specification contains all of the objects above, and adds the following:

- **Support for namespaces** – as we will see in Chapter 7, namespaces are used to distinguish discrete data elements with the same name in XML. They usually provide a link back to the original source of the XML structure that will have information about the elements in some format. The level 2 DOM will provide mechanisms for interrogating and modifying the namespace for a document.
- **Style sheets** – the level 2 DOM includes an object model for style sheets, as well as methods to query and manipulate the style sheet for a particular document.
- **Filtering** – the level 2 DOM adds methods for filtering the content in an XML document.
- **Event model** – an event model for XML is planned for level 2 of the DOM.
- **Ranges** – the level 2 DOM includes functions for manipulating large blocks of text that will be useful to those working with more traditional documents in XML.

The W3C Candidate Recommendation for the DOM level 2 specification may be found at http://www.w3.org/TR/DOM-Level-2/.

Understanding IDL and Bindings

When reading the DOM specifications, many developers may be unfamiliar with the way the interfaces are defined. Remember that the DOM as specified by the W3C is platform-neutral, that is, the W3C specifies what methods and properties need to be made available by a system-specific implementation, but not the details of how that implementation is achieved. To that end, the W3C has chosen to express the interfaces to the DOM in several ways: via OMG IDL, which is part of the CORBA 2.2 specification, and via Java and ECMAScript bindings. When implementing an application using the DOM, rather than using the W3C specifications, developers should refer to the implementation-specific documentation that should be provided with the libraries. For example, Microsoft provides implementation-specific documentation for their version of the XML DOM at http://msdn.microsoft.com/xml/reference/xmldom/start.asp

The DOM in the real world

So far, we've been looking at the DOM from a purely theoretical perspective – discussing it in terms of the general recommendation from the W3C. Next, let's take a look at the way the DOM is implemented in the real world.

The DOM in Current Browsers

As this book goes to press, only Internet Explorer 5 comes with native DOM libraries and support for XSL. Client side code may reference a data island – an XML document embedded within an HTML document – in a page using the `XMLDocument` property, accessible from the data island object in the document, which in turn exposes all the functionality supported by the Microsoft libraries. These libraries support all the required functionality of the DOM Level 1 specification, as well as some extended functions to make accessing XML data easier and to manipulate XSL style sheets.

Netscape does not yet offer built-in access to the DOM (as of version 4.7), but if you have a set of ActiveX or Java DOM libraries, you can access XML documents and manipulate them on the client side using Java or JavaScript. Note that your client will need to download and install these libraries before attempting to access XML documents. The next version of Netscape, currently under development, will include native support for XML and XSL.

The Microsoft implementation of the DOM as ActiveX and Java libraries may be downloaded free of charge from http://msdn.microsoft.com/downloads/tools/xmlparser/xmlparser.asp.

Grace and the Art of Degradation

Unless you have control over the target browser for your application (for example, if you're building an Intranet application for your company, and your company requires the use of Internet Explorer), it's important that any code you write executes cleanly on any browser. One way of doing this without sacrificing functionality is to interrogate the browser type in your code before attempting to perform browser-specific functions.

Let's look at an example, where you are authoring your application in JavaScript. You might include this fragment of code in your website's default page:

```
<SCRIPT>
   var agent = window.navigator.userAgent;
   var explorer = agent.indexOf ("MSIE 5");
   if (explorer > 0)
   {
      window.location.href = "http://www.mycompanywebsite.com/defaultie.htm";
   }
   else
   {
      window.location.href = "http://www.mycompanywebsite.com/defaultns.htm";
   }
</SCRIPT>
```

This code checks the value of the `userAgent` property on the navigator object to see what kind of browser is attempting to access the page. Only Microsoft Internet Explorer 5.X will have the string "`MSIE 5`" embedded in its `userAgent` property. By checking to see if the property contains that string, the script can determine whether the browser is Internet Explorer 5 or some other browser, and then redirect the user appropriately. For example, the `defaultie.htm` page (for IE 5 browsers) might have JScript code that takes advantage of the client-side XML DOM features in IE 5, while the `defaultns.htm` page (for non-IE 5 browsers) might rely on server-side forms processing to achieve the same results. Note that this code will need to change to accommodate the userAgent strings being passed by the various browser clients as newer versions become available.

The HTML DOM as a Special Case of the XML DOM

To understand the differences between HTML and XML, it's important to understand their evolution from a common parent: SGML.

HTML Isn't XML

SGML is an acronym for **Standard Generalized Markup Language**. SGML was the first markup language system to become widely used, and it is still heavily used in many businesses today, especially those that handle documents frequently (such as publishing firms). Rather than being a markup language like HTML, SGML is actually a way to *define* markup languages. This is much like XML, but with more freedom in the way tags are nested and information is specified. HTML is a particular implementation of SGML, that is, it abides by the grammar rules of SGML, but contains a specific definition of elements and attributes that are permissible in an HTML document. In fact, there is a DTD (document type definition) for SGML of HTML, describing the vocabulary and rules. It may be found at http://www.w3.org/TR/html40/sgml/dtd.html

XML, on the other hand, is a direct subset of SGML. One of the major goals behind the design of XML was to create a markup definition language that would retain much of the flexibility of SGML, but would be easier to parse. As a result, many of the constructs that were valid in SGML (and hence HTML) are invalid in XML documents.

Problems with the HTML DOM

The HTML DOM is not particularly flexible in the way it allows developers to access the contents of an HTML document. In particular, it is hampered by the need to support what is informally referred to as "DOM level 0" – functionality implemented in version 3.0 of Internet Explorer and version 3.0 of Netscape before any effort to standardize an object model for the behavior of HTML pages. This requires the HTML DOM to implement several functions simply for the purposes of backwards compatibility. Additionally, the HTML DOM supports a specific implementation of SGML (relying on the presence of a predefined DTD that governs the possible layout of the document).

The Future of the Internet: XHTML

The W3C is currently working on a proposed recommendation for an implementation of XML known as XHTML. This implementation will obey all of the grammar rules of XML (properly nested elements, quoted attributes, and so on), while conforming to the vocabulary of HTML (the elements and attributes that are available for use and their relationships to one another). While browsers that specifically support XHTML are not yet available, both an HTML parser and an XML parser will parse a properly written document in XHTML. When authoring HTML, a good practice is to follow the list of rules below to ensure that the document will also parse properly under the rules of XHTML:

- Documents must be well-formed, all elements must be properly closed (each `<TAG>` must have a corresponding `</TAG>`, or in the case of empty elements, may be closed by ending the start tag with "/").
- Elements must be properly nested – that is, each closing tag must close the most recent open tag (no overlap is permitted).
- Element and attribute names must be in lower case.
- Empty elements must either have an end tag or their start tag must end with "/".
- Attribute-value pairs must be explicitly defined.
- Script elements and style elements should be enclosed in a CDATA section to avoid improper parsing.
- The `id` attribute should be used to store element identifiers.

Let's look at each of these rules in more detail.

Documents Must be Well-Formed, All Elements Must be Properly Closed, and Elements Must be Properly Nested

HTML has certain elements that do not need to be explicitly closed, such as the **paragraph** element `<P>`. The parser determines where the element should be closed by examining the elements that follow. For example, the following HTML fragment is invalid in XHTML:

```
<p>This is the first paragraph.
<p>This is the second paragraph.
```

Instead, the following code (which is functionally equivalent in HTML) should be used:

```
<p>This is the first paragraph.</p>
<p>This is the second paragraph.</p>
```

Element and Attribute Names Must be in Lower Case

XML is case-sensitive, and treats tags with different cases as different tags. In the XHTML DTD, it was decided that lowercase tags should be used for all elements and attributes, and XHTML documents must follow this rule.

So instead of using this code:

```
<INPUT TYPE="button" ID="button1" VALUE="Click me!" />
```

use:

```
<input type="button" id="button1" value="Click Me!" />
```

Note that we added a slash at the end of the corrected version. This brings us to our next rule:

Empty Elements Must Either Have an End Tag or Their Start Tag Must End with "/"

In XML, all elements must be closed; if they are defined as `EMPTY` (having no information associated with them except attributes), they may be closed either by a separate end tag or by including the slash at the end of the start tag. In HTML, of course, not specifying an end tag for some elements is permitted, such as `<P>` – the next start tag encountered implies the end of the previous tagged block. For the greatest level of compatibility with older browsers, terminate tags with a separate end tag, rather than a trailing slash – some browsers do not parse trailing slashes correctly.

Attribute-Value Pairs Must be Explicitly Defined

If there is a default attribute for an element, it may no longer be specified without the attribute name.

Instead of:

```
<dl compact>
```

use:

```
<dl compact="compact">
```

Script Elements and Style Elements Should be Enclosed in a CDATA Section to Avoid Improper Parsing

Because `script` and `style` elements are declared as `#PCDATA` elements in the XHTML DTD, parsers will treat `<` and `&` as the start of markup. To avoid this, `script` and `style` elements should be enclosed in a CDATA element to allow them to contain unescaped text.

Rather than:

```
<script>
   ...
</script>
```

use:

```
<script>
   <![CDATA[
      ...
   ]]>
</script>
```

The id Attribute Should be Used to Store Element Identifiers

In the XHTML DTD, the `id` attribute is given a type of `ID`; therefore, it should be used to identify the element instead of the `name` attribute. In future implementations of XHTML, the `name` attribute is likely to be phased out.

Because XHTML is still an emerging standard, many current visual HTML tools do not follow its rules, and may inadvertently destroy XHTML documents if used to edit them. Keep this in mind when creating XHTML documents. When in doubt, use a text editor to modify your documents rather than a tool like FrontPage or Microsoft Visual InterDev.

By following these instructions, you will ensure the highest level of compatibility possible with future browsers that make the move to XHTML. Additionally, the XHTML documents you create may be sent to the client with a `mime-type` of HTML or XML, allowing the greatest flexibility in rendering and manipulation at the client end. The XML DOM may then be used to manipulate the contents of the XHTML document directly.

Working with the DOM

We've discussed how the DOM is structured, taking XML documents and transforming them into node trees that may be accessed programmatically. We've also talked about how the specification provided by the W3C is only a description of access mechanisms, and not a particular implementation. But how can we take this information and apply it to a particular problem? To do so, we'll need to use the DOM API.

DOM APIs

When writing a piece of software that accesses XML files using the DOM, a particular implementation of the DOM must be used. The implementation is a library of some kind, designed to be run on a particular hardware and software platform and to access a particular data store (such as a text file, a relational database, and so on).

What is an API?

The acronym **API** stands for **Application Programming Interface**. Don't be misled by the use of the word *interface* here – an API is actually a set of libraries that are used by a component to instruct another component to carry out lower-level services. As such, an API must be an *implementation* of an interface, with the appropriate code to connect to the other components and instruct them to carry out their functions.

The DOM is not an API

As we've seen before, the W3C DOM specification only provides the interface definition for the DOM libraries, not the specifics of their implementation. It then falls to third parties to provide implementations of the DOM that may be used by programmers. When planning to use the DOM to manipulate XML structures in your application, you will need to obtain platform-specific implementations of the DOM for each platform your application targets. In most cases, these libraries will need to be bundled with your application and deployed along with your application binaries.

Be aware that implementations of the DOM, just like implementations of HTML parsers, need to assert a compliance level to the W3C specifications. Given the state at press time of the W3C specifications (DOM level 1 is a recommendation, level 2 is a Candidate Recommendation), all implementations of the DOM should provide at least the functionality described in the level 1 document. Many implementations of the DOM will also provide additional functionality – either behavior described in the level 2 document, or additional behavior that the developers of the implementation felt would be useful. For example, the Microsoft DOM supports all of the level 1 specification, as well as additional navigation methods, methods and properties to support style sheets, and so on. As with any other development effort, you need to take into account your target platform(s) before deciding whether or not to take advantage of additional functionality provided in a particular implementation of the DOM.

Programming for XML Data Structures

When using the DOM to access information in an XML node tree, it is helpful to design your system around the access mechanisms the DOM provides. For example, if you are using an object-oriented database, you might tailor your objects to correspond to XML elements. If you know what elements you are expecting, you can create objects that encapsulate other objects, replicating the XML tree in memory in the most useful way possible – we saw an example of this earlier with the snowflake database design.

Also, you should bear in mind that XML files can be extremely large, so memory management becomes very important. A good implementation of the DOM will provide just-in-time extraction for elements where necessary (the trade-off is additional seek and retrieve time when reading element information), but it's crucial that your program manages memory well to avoid excessive swapping or failure. System resources should be monitored and certain thresholds should be set, beyond which the DOM may not be used to access any more files until system resources free up. If the file is simply too large to be handled by your implementation of the DOM, you may need to fall back to an event-driven parser like SAX (discussed in Chapter 6).

Client Side and Server Side

While there are many applications for the DOM and XML, they can be loosely grouped into two types: those deployed on a server (or in a controlled environment, such as a client-server system), and those deployed on a client. We'll take a look at some potential applications for DOM for each of these types.

DOM on the Server Side

Since Internet developers have much more control over the software deployed to their servers, the first applications of DOM have typically been on the server side. The DOM can be used to greatly simplify data interchange between disparate business systems, as well as providing an ideal mechanism for the archiving and retrieval of data.

Document Interchange

One of the first applications of XML in the enterprise will be to facilitate inter-process or inter-business communications. XML has many advantages over other transmission formats such as flat files or database dumps:

- XML files are **platform-independent** – unlike an Access database or a SQL Server dump, an XML file can be read and understood by virtually any system simply by reading the text and parsing it into a node tree using the DOM implementation on that system.
- XML files are **self-describing** – unlike a flat file (which requires a programmer to sit down with a format description and do a translation), a well-designed XML file needs little external documentation to decipher – each element that describes an author is clearly marked `<author>`, and so on.
- XML files show **hierarchical information** – unlike flat files, which may contain repeating groups for child elements (such as the books an author has written), XML files are designed to represent hierarchical information in a natural way – via a node tree. If the XML file contains seven authors and 22 books, for example, it's immediately obvious which books are associated with which authors simply by walking the node tree created by the DOM.

There is a strong trend in the software industry at the moment to standardize XML formats for business-to-business transfers of information. Groups like BizTalk (www.biztalk.org) and XML Mortgage Partners (www.xmlmortgage.org) are creating DTDs, schemas, and data dictionaries that will help businesses communicate with each other more effectively.

Archiving

XML is an ideal storage medium for archived information – especially if it comes from an object-oriented or hierarchical database. Relational databases may often (but not always) be easily represented as XML node trees as well. XML files compress very well due to their text-based nature and their tendency to repeat text (tags). A typical, fairly large XML file will compress to a tenth or twentieth of its original size. By walking the hierarchical or relational tree in a database and using the DOM to construct the appropriate node tree, entire sets of information may be easily archived to one XML file.

A typical example might be an invoicing system that removes invoices older than a year. An automated process might run once a night, scanning the database for invoices that are ready to be archived. Using the DOM, the process could then navigate through the hierarchical or relational tree of information associated with the invoice. Customer information, shipping information, line item information, and so on would all be packaged together in one file that would represent the invoice as a whole. That file could then be compressed and stored to tape or some other archival medium. If there was a question about a particular invoice, the XML file associated with it could be retrieved and decompressed. Someone could then visually scan the file looking for the information needed, or the information could be loaded back into the database using the DOM for manipulation there.

DOM on the Client Side

While at press time only the Microsoft Internet Explorer 5.0 client comes with DOM functionality built-in, Netscape and other browser developers are in the process of adding support for DOM level 1 to their systems. Once DOM-capable browsers are in common use, Internet developers will be able to take advantage of the DOM on the client to improve the way information is rendered and decrease round-trips to the server.

Flexible Client Rendering

It is becoming more and more important for documents to be viewable by a variety of different clients. These clients may need to render the document in various ways, depending on the type of client and the purpose of the file. For example, various cellular telephone providers are starting to provide a limited form of browsing from the tiny LCD screen on the telephone itself. HTML is not ideal for this purpose, since it doesn't include information about the meaning of the content in the various tags, only how to render it. Thus, a rendering engine on a telephone might not know whether it was important to tell the user what color a snake is, or whether it's poisonous. XML solves this problem by including information about the content as part of the markup. A customized browser might use the DOM to walk the node tree of the document received by such a device, and selectively identify information that could be discarded.

Client Data Entry

As the DOM is integrated into the major browsers, it will be possible to use client-side DOM manipulation of XML documents to provide a greater level of interaction with the user. Structured information may be collected from the client and shipped back to the server in one transaction, rather than a series of form calls spanning several HTML pages.

Scenarios for Using the DOM in the Publishing Process

Let's take a look at some ways the DOM can be used to generate and manipulate XML documents in enterprise environments.

The DOM and Databases

XML provides an ideal mechanism for transferring information between different databases. By their nature, databases are proprietary – each database has a different naming structure for elements, a different normalization level, and even different methods of describing enumerated information. Using the DOM, we can simplify the way information is passed between various databases.

Normally, when data is transferred between databases, a customized translator must be built for each transfer:

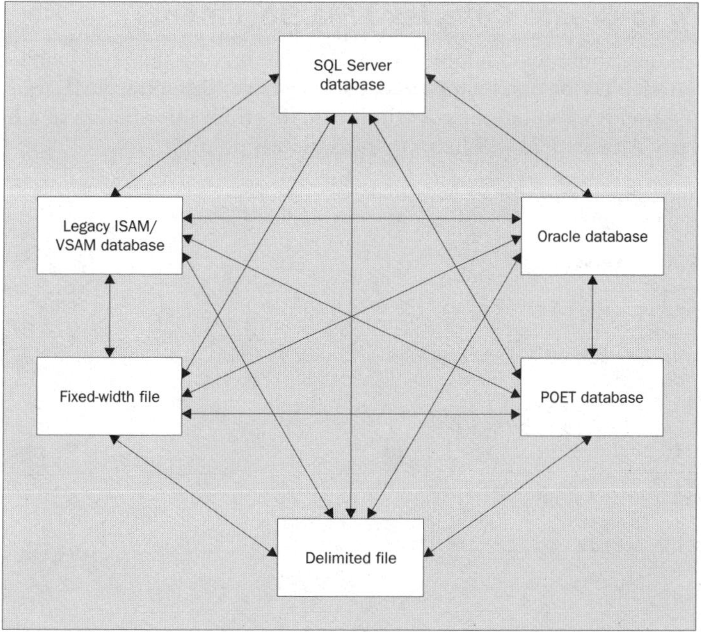

By using XML as the common transfer mechanism, the number of translators that need to be written is greatly reduced – each database needs only to be able to import and export from a common, agreed-upon XML structure:

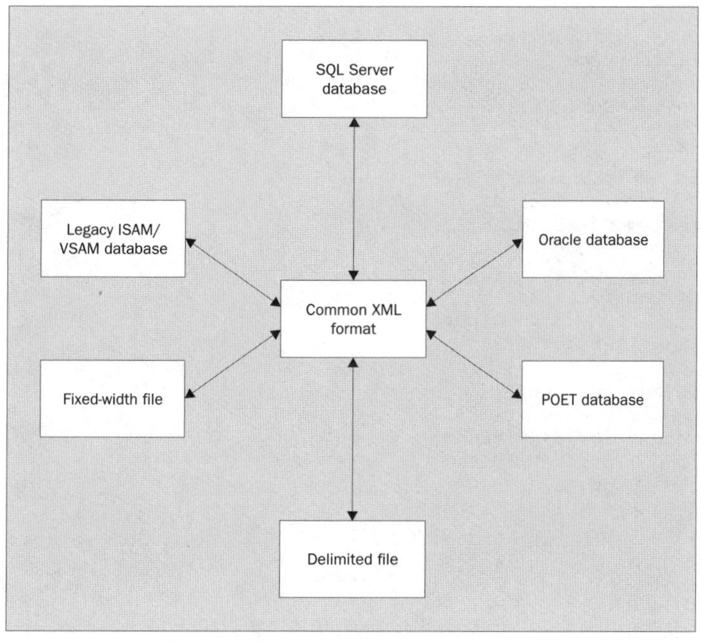

The DOM can be used to create these translation mechanisms.

Using the DOM to Create Complex XML Documents

One of the nice things about manipulating XML documents with the DOM is that the DOM is **random-access**, that is, a node may be created or attached anywhere within the XML tree at any time. This proves to be quite useful when building XML documents from information in a hierarchical or relational database. An example will help to illustrate this point.

Let's suppose we have the following database:

```
CREATE TABLE customer(
   customerid int,
   customername varchar(100),
   city varchar(50),
   state char(2),
   zip varchar(10))

CREATE TABLE invoice(
   invoiceid int,
   customerid int,
   invoicedate datetime)

CREATE TABLE lineitem(
   lineitemid int,
   invoiceid int,
   product varchar(50),
   units int)
```

We'd like to produce an XML file for a particular customer ID from the information stored in these tables, which should look like the following:

```
<customer id="customer1"
          customername="Homer J. Simpson"
          address="142 Evergreen Terrace"
          city="Springfield"
          state="VA"
          zip="00000">
   <invoice id="invoice1"
            invoicedate="11/7/1999">
      <lineitem id="lineitem1"
                product="Plutonium"
                units="17"/>
      <lineitem id="lineitem2"
                product="Donuts"
                units="8726"/>
   </invoice>
   <invoice id="invoice2"
            invoicedate="11/9/1999">
      <lineitem id="lineitem3"
                product="Beer"
                units="37816"/>
      <lineitem id="lineitem4"
                product="Peanuts"
                units="1"/>
   </invoice>
</customer>
```

To write this to an XML file manually, we'd have to perform the following steps:

- Get the information for the customer from the customer table
- Write the information for the customer to the XML file
- Get all the invoices for the customer from the invoice table
- For each invoice retrieved this way:
  - Write the information for the invoice to the XML file
  - Get all the line items for this invoice from the lineitem table
  - For each line item retrieved this way:
    - Write the information for the line item to the XML file
  - Write the close tag for the invoice object
- Write the close tag for the customer object

Whereas, using the DOM, we could generate the node tree this way:

- Generate the customer root node
- Get all the invoices for the customer
- Create a node for each invoice and append it to the customer node
- Get all the line items for the customer
- Create a node for each line item and append it to the appropriate invoice node

This is a simple example, but it should be clear that building an XML document using the DOM is much more straightforward than doing so by writing the information to a text file. Rather than jumping back and forth between tables to obtain the information needed, all the information in each table may be written at the same time. As the depth of the node tree increases, the first method becomes more and more cumbersome, while the second method scales easily. Also, generating the document using the DOM guarantees that it will be well-formed. In our first example, say we had forgotten to write the close tag for the invoice object – our XML document would no longer parse.

Sample Application Using DOM and XML

Next, we'll take a look at a couple of ways the DOM can be used in real-world applications.

A Simple Client Side Example

In this section, we'll be using JScript and the DOM objects on the client side to create an XML document representing a book. Because the DOM objects are being used on the client, this sample must be run using Internet Explorer 5. This example allows the user to enter information about a book, its authors and its categories. It generates the XML on-the-fly using the DOM and shows the entered information using XSL style sheets. The user interface for the application looks like the following:

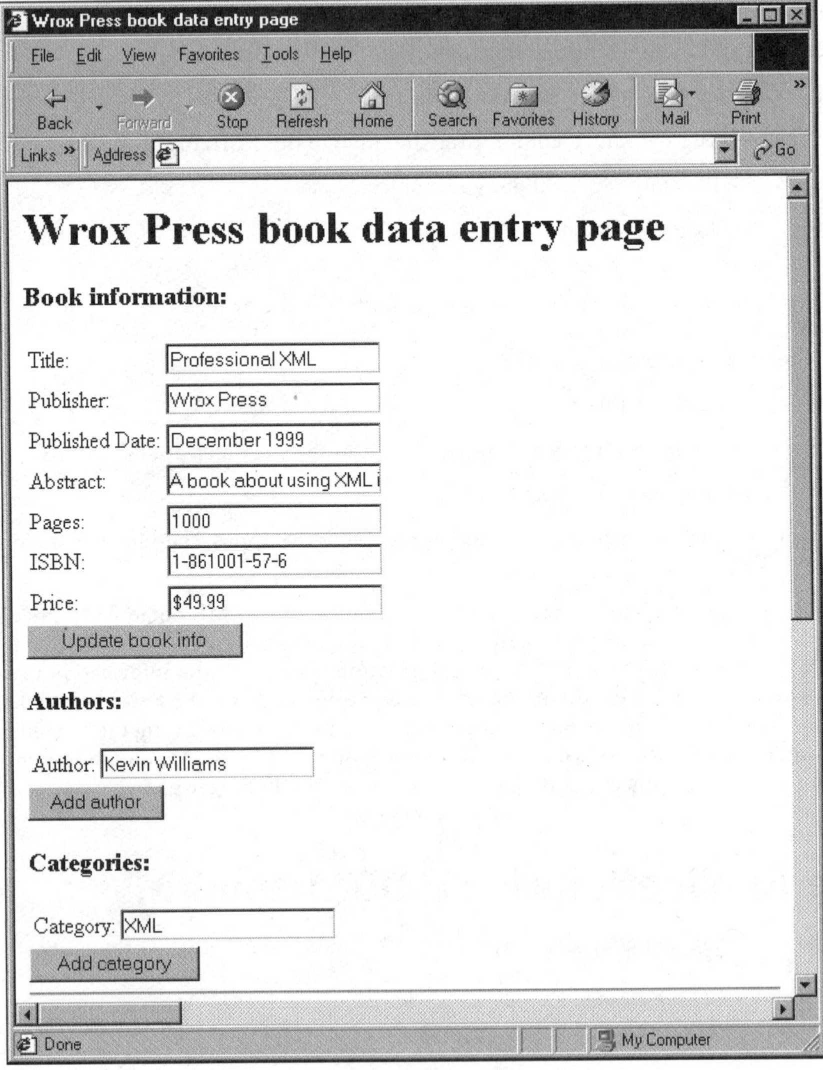

When the user adds items using the buttons, they will be displayed like so:

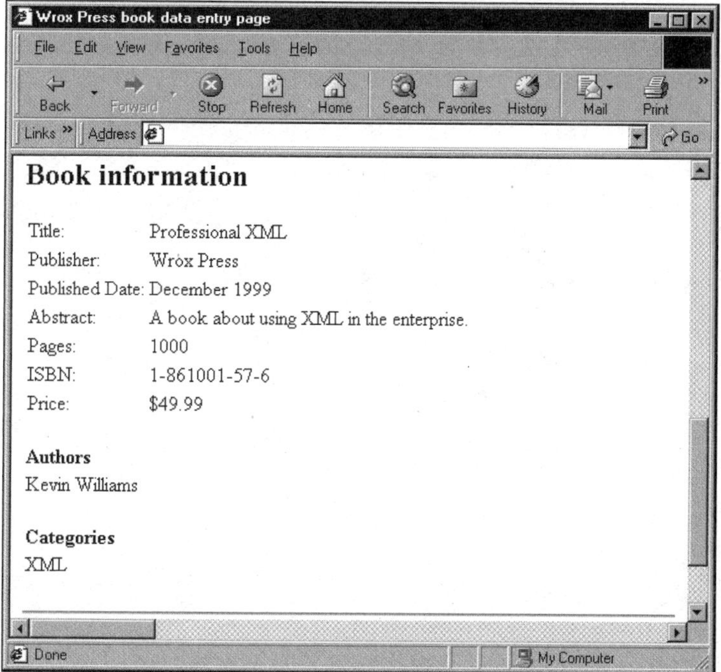

You can see an HTML representation of the book information below the form (as shown in the second screen shot), and the created XML across the bottom of the page. This demonstrates using the DOM to create an XML document programmatically.

Using the DOM to Let the User Modify the Page

The sample file for this section may be found with the download code for the rest of the book at http://www.wrox.com in the directory for this chapter.

First, let's create an HTML page that will be our book data-entry page – `BookClient.htm`. We'll start the page with a form allowing the user to enter general information for the book:

```
<HTML>
<HEAD>
   <TITLE>Wrox Press book data entry page</TITLE>
</HEAD>
<BODY onload="initializeBook()">
   <H1>Wrox Press book data entry page</H1>
   <H3>Book information:</H3>
   <TABLE>
      <TR>
         <TD>Title:</TD><TD><INPUT id=txtTitle></TD>
      </TR>
      <TR>
```

```
      <TD>Publisher:</TD><TD><INPUT id=txtPublisher></TD>
   </TR>
   <TR>
      <TD>Published Date:</TD><TD><INPUT id=txtPubDate></TD>
   </TR>
   <TR>
      <TD>Abstract:</TD><TD><INPUT id=txtAbstract></TD>
   </TR>
   <TR>
      <TD>Pages:</TD><TD><INPUT id=txtPages></TD>
   </TR>
   <TR>
      <TD>ISBN:</TD><TD><INPUT id=txtISBN></TD>
   </TR>
   <TR>
      <TD>Price:</TD><TD><INPUT id=txtPrice></TD>
   </TR>
</TABLE>
<INPUT id=btnUpdate type=button value="Update book info"
       onclick="updateBookInfo()">

<H3>Authors:</H3>
<TABLE>
   <TR>
      <TD>Author:</TD><TD><INPUT id=txtAuthor></TD>
   </TR>
</TABLE>
<INPUT id=btnAddAuthor type=button value="Add author"
       onclick="addAuthor()">
<H3>Categories:</H3>
<TABLE>
   <TR>
      <TD>Category:</TD><TD><INPUT id=txtCategory></TD>
   </TR>
</TABLE>
<INPUT id=btnAddCategory type=button value="Add category"
       onclick="addCategory()">
```

In the above code, we have four calls to JScript functions: `initializeBook()`, `updateBookInfo()`, `addAuthor()`, and `addCategory()`. These functions are used to initialize and modify the document information using the DOM, as we'll see in a moment. There are three groups of controls. First, we have inputs for general book information and an update button (since the general book information will only appear once in our book XML). Next, we have a form that allows authors to be added to the book (since authors may appear more than once), and finally a form that allows categories to be added to the book.

Next, we'll create the XML **data island** that will contain our finished book:

```
<XML id=docBook>
   <Book>
   </Book>
</XML>
```

In this case, we are using the data island as a signal to Internet Explorer 5 that we want to manipulate an XML document called docBook from within our code. Note that we have chosen to specify the root object for the XML document, an empty element called Book. If we chose, we could have left the data island completely empty, or we could have populated it with some initial information (like a book ID) before sending it to the client.

The next section of the code contains the script for manipulating the book:

```
<SCRIPT>

var docBook;
```

We specify docBook as a global here so that we don't have to keep accessing the XML document by its fully qualified name, document.all("docBook").XMLDocument. This syntax, new for IE 5, allows the XML DOM operations to be used from JScript on the client side – it exposes all the functionality of the XMLDOMDocument object. We'll initialize its value in the initializeBook() function, which as you'll recall is called in the onload event for the <BODY> tag:

```
function initializeBook()
{
   docBook = document.all("docBook").XMLDocument;
   docBook.async = false;
   renderElements();
}
```

Here, we're initializing the docBook variable to point to the docBook document. We're also setting the async property on the document to false. This forces all operations on the document to be performed **synchronously** – returning only when they have completed. This allows us to avoid accessing the document when it's still in the process of being updated. (Alternatively, you can code an event handler that will wait for the ondataavailable event to fire – but if there's nothing else the code can be working on, we might as well have it wait.) Finally, we call a procedure that will show the contents of the DOM – both in a raw format and using XSL style sheets.

Next, we have a helper function. This helper function will take an element name and create or replace that element for a given parent. That way, when our user decides to change the name of his book from "XML for Professionals" to "Professional XML", there won't suddenly be two <Title> child elements within the <Book> element.

This function introduces some new properties and methods from the DOM. Before we continue, let's take a quick look at what's new.

The createElement() method, run against a document, allows an Element object to be instantiated. The name of the new element to be created is passed as the only parameter. The method returns the created Element object. When an Element object is created this way, it is created as an orphan; that is, it is not attached to any specific parent. An additional call to a function like appendChild() (see below) is required to link this element to the appropriate place in the XML node tree.

The `createText()` method, run against a document, allows a `Text` object to be created. The text that makes up the content of the `Text` object is the only parameter passed to this method, and it returns the created `Text` object. Much like `createElement()`, the node created with `createText()` is orphaned until it is specifically added to the node tree. `Text` objects represent unformatted text in a document; typically, they will be found as the children of `Element` objects. For example, in this brief code snippet:

```
<Book>
   <Title>Professional XML</Title>
</Book>
```

We have a `<Book>` element, which has as its child a `<Title>` element; that element has as its child a `<Text>` object containing the string "`Professional XML`".

The `appendChild()` method, which may be run against any node, is used to attach one node to another in a parent-child relationship. It takes the element to be attached as a parameter, and returns the added node.

The `getElementsByTagName()` method, which may be run against any node, is used to locate elements that are children of this node and whose tag matches the string passed to the `getElementsByTagName()` method. It returns a `NodeList` object, which is basically an unordered collection of the nodes that match the query.

The `replaceChild()` method, which may be run against any node, is used to replace a particular child node of a node with another child node. The new and old nodes are passed as parameters to this method, and it returns the old (deleted) node.

```
function createOrReplaceElement(sElementName, sElementValue, elementParent)
{
   var elementItem;
   var textValue;
   var nodelistOldItem;

   elementItem = docBook.createElement(sElementName);
   textValue = docBook.createTextNode(sElementValue);
   elementItem.appendChild(textValue);

   nodelistOldItem = elementParent.getElementsByTagName(sElementName);
   if (nodelistOldItem.length > 0)
   {
      elementParent.replaceChild(elementItem, nodelistOldItem.item(0));
   }
   else
   {
      elementParent.appendChild(elementItem);
   }
}
```

In this code, we create the new element and text nodes representing the element to be added. We then make the text node a child of the element node. Finally, we check to see if there are any child nodes of this parent with the same name. If so, the new child node is used to replace the old node; otherwise, the new child node is simply added to the parent.

Next, we implement the function that allows us to update the general book information in our document:

```
function updateBookInfo()
{
   createOrReplaceElement("Title",
                          txtTitle.value,
                          docBook.documentElement);
   createOrReplaceElement("Publisher",
                          txtPublisher.value,
                          docBook.documentElement);
   createOrReplaceElement("PubDate",
                          txtPubDate.value,
                          docBook.documentElement);
   createOrReplaceElement("Abstract",
                          txtAbstract.value,
                          docBook.documentElement);
   createOrReplaceElement("Pages",
                          txtPages.value,
                          docBook.documentElement);
   createOrReplaceElement("ISBN",
                          txtISBN.value,
                          docBook.documentElement);
   createOrReplaceElement("Price",
                          txtPrice.value,
                          docBook.documentElement);

   renderElements();
}
```

This code simply takes the values specified in the input controls on the form and uses them to create or replace child elements of the documents with new elements with the given values.

The next function adds an author to the book:

```
function addAuthor()
{
   var elementAuthor;
   var textAuthor;
   var nodelistAuthors;
   var elementAuthors;

   elementAuthor = docBook.createElement("Author");
   textAuthor = docBook.createTextNode(txtAuthor.value);
   elementAuthor.appendChild(textAuthor);
   nodelistAuthors = docBook.getElementsByTagName("Authors");
   if (nodelistAuthors.length == 0)
   {
      elementAuthors = docBook.createElement("Authors");
      docBook.documentElement.appendChild(elementAuthors);
   }
   else
   {
      elementAuthors = nodelistAuthors.item(0);
   }

   elementAuthors.appendChild(elementAuthor);

   renderElements();
}
```

This procedure creates an element and a text object, as before, and relates them in a parent-child relationship. It then checks the document to see if the container element `<Authors>` already exists. If it doesn't, it creates it. Finally, it attaches the element created at the beginning of the procedure to either the new object or the existing `<Authors>` object, as appropriate. We then refresh the document again to update our style-sheet formatted book and our raw XML section.

Next, we have a similar function that adds a category to a book:

```
function addCategory()
{
   var elementCategory;
   var textCategory;
   var nodelistRecSubjCategories;
   var elementRecSubjCategories;

   elementCategory = docBook.createElement("Category");
   textCategory = docBook.createTextNode(txtCategory.value);
   elementCategory.appendChild(textCategory);
   nodelistRecSubjCategories =
      docBook.getElementsByTagName("RecSubjCategories");
   if (nodelistRecSubjCategories.length == 0)
   {
      elementRecSubjCategories = docBook.createElement("RecSubjCategories");
      docBook.documentElement.appendChild(elementRecSubjCategories);
   }
   else
   {
      elementRecSubjCategories = nodelistRecSubjCategories.item(0);
   }

   elementRecSubjCategories.appendChild(elementCategory);

   renderElements();
}
```

Up to this point, the XML document exists only as a tree of nodes in memory in the XML DOM. In order for the user to see the changes, we need to **render** the document. The next function does just that, both using style sheets and in a raw form:

```
function renderElements()
{
   document.all("divRawXML").innerText = docBook.xml;
   bookInfo.innerHTML = docBook.transformNode(bookXSL.documentElement);
   authorTable.innerHTML = docBook.transformNode(authorXSL.documentElement);
   categoryTable.innerHTML =
      docBook.transformNode(categoryXSL.documentElement);
}

</SCRIPT>
```

Using the `xml` property of the document, we can get the raw text-output XML for the entire document. This is what most people think of when they think about XML "files". Note that the `xml` property is a Microsoft extension to the DOM – the W3C is planning to include input and output functionality in Level 3 when it is released. When we talk about the server-side use of the DOM, we'll see an example of how to generate an XML file using only the DOM level 1 functions.

We set the `divRawXML` element's text (at the bottom of the file) to be the raw text output. Next, we transform the XML document using style sheets for a more human-readable output. More information on XSL may be found in Chapter 9.

Finally, we have the three in-line style sheets and the rest of the HTML page, containing the `DIV` elements that are populated by the `renderElements()` function:

```
<XML id=bookXSL>
   <DIV xmlns:xsl="http://www.w3.org/TR/WD-xsl">
      <xsl:choose>
         <xsl:when test="/Book/Title[. $ne$ '']">
            <TABLE BORDER="0" CELLPADDING="1">
               <TR>
                  <TD>Title:</TD>
                  <TD><xsl:value-of select="/Book/Title"/></TD>
               </TR>
               <TR>
                  <TD>Publisher:</TD>
                  <TD><xsl:value-of select="/Book/Publisher"/></TD>
               </TR>
               <TR>
                  <TD>Published Date:</TD>
                  <TD><xsl:value-of select="/Book/PubDate"/></TD>
               </TR>
               <TR>
                  <TD>Abstract:</TD>
                  <TD><xsl:value-of select="/Book/Abstract"/></TD>
               </TR>
               <TR>
                  <TD>Pages:</TD>
                  <TD><xsl:value-of select="/Book/Pages"/></TD>
               </TR>
               <TR>
                  <TD>ISBN:</TD>
                  <TD><xsl:value-of select="/Book/ISBN"/></TD>
               </TR>
               <TR>
                  <TD>Price:</TD>
                  <TD><xsl:value-of select="/Book/Price"/></TD>
               </TR>
            </TABLE>
         </xsl:when>
         <xsl:otherwise>
            Book information not yet specified.
         </xsl:otherwise>
      </xsl:choose>
   </DIV>
</XML>
```

```
        <XML id=authorXSL>
           <DIV xmlns:xsl="http://www.w3.org/TR/WD-xsl">
              <TABLE BORDER="0" CELLSPACING="1">
                 <TR>
                    <TD><STRONG>Authors</STRONG></TD>
                 </TR>
                 <xsl:for-each select="/Book/Authors/Author">
                    <TR>
                       <TD><xsl:value-of select="text()"/></TD>
                    </TR>
                 </xsl:for-each>
              </TABLE>
           </DIV>
        </XML>

        <XML id=categoryXSL>
           <DIV xmlns:xsl="http://www.w3.org/TR/WD-xsl">
              <TABLE BORDER="0" CELLSPACING="1">
                 <TR>
                    <TD><STRONG>Categories</STRONG></TD>
                 </TR>
                 <xsl:for-each select="/Book/RecSubjCategories/Category">
                    <TR>
                       <TD><xsl:value-of select="text()"/></TD>
                    </TR>
                 </xsl:for-each>
              </TABLE>
           </DIV>
        </XML>

        <HR>
        <H2>Book information</H2>
        <P><DIV id=bookInfo></DIV></P>
        <P><DIV id=authorTable></DIV></P>
        <P><DIV id=categoryTable></DIV></P>
        <HR>
        The text expression of the current contents of the DOM tree is:
        <PRE><DIV id=divRawXML></DIV></PRE>
     </BODY>
     </HTML>
```

Although it's beyond the scope of this example, the XML document created on the client this way can now be passed back to the server for manipulation. The easiest way to do so is to set an input element, typically a hidden one, to the value of the `xml` property of the document; then, when the form is submitted, the information will be part of the submitted elements. XML documents already present on the client that are too large to be transmitted as part of a form submission may be transmitted via FTP, via HTTP using Posting Acceptor or some other HTTP file submitter, via `xmlhttp` transactions (a Microsoft-specific construct), or via Microsoft's SOAP protocol (discussed in Chapter 11).

A More Complex Programmatic Example

Next, let's take a look at how the DOM might be used on the server side. We'll build an ASP page that takes a fixed-width text file submitted via Posting Acceptor, parses it, builds a data island using the DOM, and sends the result back to the client.

Creating XML Documents from Text Using the DOM

For this sample, instead of entering book data into an HTML page, the user has a fixed-width text file that represents a book. We'll assume that it is sent to the server to the `/uploads` directory via some mechanism (FTP, Posting Acceptor, or whatever). The ASP page parses the uploaded file, generates a data island in an HTML page, and sends it back to the user to view.

The sample files for this section may be found with the other files for this chapter, downloadable from the Wrox website http://www.wrox.com.

The book file we will be submitting is this:

```
Professional XML              Wrox Press          December 1999
800       1861001576   49.99
This book is a definitive, practical guide to XML.
AMichael Kay
ASteven Livingston
ABrian Loesgen
ADidier Martin
AStephen Mohr
ANikola Ozu
AMark Seabourne
APeter Stark
AKevin Williams
CXML
CInternet Development
CClient-server Development
```

This is a fixed-width text file, like many still used to export data by legacy systems. We can see that the book title, publisher, and publication date may be found on the first line; the book price and ISBN number are on the second line; and the abstract is on the third line. The rest of the file lists authors (prefaced by the letter A) and categories (prefaced by the letter C). In a real situation, the system issuing the file would have documentation describing the format and content of the file.

We'll use this form, `BookForm.htm`, to request that the file be parsed:

```
<HTML>
   <BODY>
      <FORM action="/DisplayBook.asp"
            method="post">
         <INPUT type="submit" value="Parse the uploaded file">
      </FORM>
   </BODY>
</HTML>
```

The `DisplayBook.asp` page looks like this:

```
<%@ Language=VBScript %>
<HTML>
<HEAD>
   <TITLE>Thank you for submitting your book information!</TITLE>
```

We'll steal the `renderElements()` JScript procedure from our client example so we can see the results on the client using style sheets; however, what's important here is the way the file is parsed. Once it is parsed, it could easily be stored in a relational database or other repository.

```
<SCRIPT>
function renderElements()
{
   bookInfo.innerHTML =
      docBook.transformNode(bookXSL.documentElement);
   authorTable.innerHTML =
      docBook.transformNode(authorXSL.documentElement);
   categoryTable.innerHTML =
      docBook.transformNode(categoryXSL.documentElement);
}
</SCRIPT>
```

Next, we implement a couple of helper subroutines. The first one, `AddElementToParent()`, will add a given element with a given value to a specified parent in the DOM specified:

```
<%
   Sub AddElementToParent (domBook, elemParent, sChild, sValue)
      Dim elemSubelement
      Dim textSubelement

      Set elemSubelement = domBook.CreateElement(sChild)
      Set textSubelement = domBook.CreateTextNode(sValue)
      elemSubelement.appendChild(textSubelement)
      elemParent.appendChild(elemSubelement)

      Set elemSubelement = Nothing
      Set textSubelement = Nothing
   End Sub
```

The next helper subroutine generates an XML stream from the DOM. Note that some implementations of the DOM, such as Microsoft, include convenience properties that will generate this text for you, but if you don't have access to these non-level 1 shortcuts, you can use a subroutine like this one. Also note that most node types, such as attributes, comments, and so on, are not handled by the sample here. Later, we'll revisit this code and look at how some other node types might be exported by it. For now, though, the subroutine only handles node types of `element` or `text`:

```
   Sub WriteNodeXML (nodeTarget)
      Dim i

      If nodeTarget.NodeType = 1 Then
         ' Element
         Response.Write "<" & nodeTarget.tagName & ">"
         For i = 0 to nodeTarget.childNodes.Length - 1
            WriteNodeXML nodeTarget.childNodes.item(i)
         Next
         Response.Write "</" & nodeTarget.tagName & ">"
      ElseIf nodeTarget.NodeType = 3 Then
         ' Text Node
         Response.Write nodeTarget.data
      End If

   End Sub
%>
```

Note that recursion is used to generate the nested tags for the file – as always, when recursion is being used you should be on the lookout for stack problems. For most XML documents, though, this technique should work just fine.

We actually perform the parse of the submitted file inside the data island that will hold the XML. Once the parse is completed, we can do a `Response.Write` of the generated XML (from the `WriteNodeXML()` procedure), and it will create the data island in the HTML that is returned to the client:

```
<XML id=docBook>
   <%
      Dim fileInvoice
      Dim tsInvoice
      Dim domInvoice
      Dim elemInvoice
      Dim elemLineItem

      Dim sFilename
      Dim sPath
      Dim sLine
      Dim sWork

      Const ForReading = 1
```

Note that we've hard-coded the filename here for the sake of this example – in a real environment, the file would have come from Posting Acceptor or some other source:

```
      sFilename = "e:\web\book.txt"
```

Next, we create an instance of the Microsoft XML DOM object and set it to synchronous operation:

```
      ' create the instance of the DOM and the root Book element
      Set domBook = CreateObject("Microsoft.XMLDOM")
      domBook.async = false
```

Then we create the `Book` element and add it to our new document:

```
      Set elemBook = domBook.CreateElement("Book")
      domBook.appendChild elemBook
```

We'll now open the file and start parsing it:

```
      ' open the file
      Set fileBook = CreateObject("Scripting.FileSystemObject")
      Set tsBook = fileBook.OpenTextFile(sFilename, ForReading)
```

For each piece of general information associated with the book, we use the `AddElementToParent()` subroutine we wrote to add the appropriate subelement to the `Book` element. This subroutine will create an element node and a text node with the appropriate tagname and data, and then chain them together and to the parent node specified:

```
' process the title and publisher line
sLine = tsBook.ReadLine

sWork = Trim(Mid(sLine, 1, 30)) ' Title
AddElementToParent domBook, elemBook, "Title", sWork

sWork = Trim(Mid(sLine, 31, 20)) ' Publisher
AddElementToParent domBook, elemBook, "Publisher", sWork

sWork = Trim(Mid(sLine, 51, 20)) ' PubDate
AddElementToParent domBook, elemBook, "PubDate", sWork

' process the number of pages, ISBN, and price line
sLine = tsBook.ReadLine

sWork = Trim(Mid(sLine, 1, 10)) ' Number of pages
AddElementToParent domBook, elemBook, "Pages", sWork

sWork = Trim(Mid(sLine, 11, 13)) ' ISBN
AddElementToParent domBook, elemBook, "ISBN", sWork

sWork = Trim(Mid(sLine, 24, 10)) ' Price
AddElementToParent domBook, elemBook, "Price", sWork

' process the abstract line
sLine = tsBook.ReadLine

AddElementToParent domBook, elemBook, "Abstract", sLine
```

Each line remaining in the file either corresponds to an `Author` element or a `Category` element. The file has an indicator in the first column to indicate which is which – an `A` indicates an author, and a `C` indicates a category. First, we'll need to generate the `RecSubjCategories` and `Authors` container elements and add them as children of the `Book` element:

```
Set elemRecSubjCategories = domBook.CreateElement("RecSubjCategories")
Set elemAuthors = domBook.CreateElement("Authors")

elemBook.appendChild(elemRecSubjCategories)
elemBook.appendChild(elemAuthors)
```

Next, we'll read all the remaining lines in the file. For each one, we determine if it's a category or an author, and then add it as a child of the appropriate container element:

```
        While Not tsBook.AtEndOfStream
           sLine = tsBook.ReadLine
           If Left(sLine, 1) = "A" Then
              AddElementToParent domBook, elemAuthors, "Author", Mid(sLine, 2)
           Else
              AddElementToParent domBook, elemRecSubjCategories, "Category", _
                 Mid(sLine, 2)
           End If
        Wend
        tsBook.Close
```

Now, we write the raw XML to our response. Since our code executes within the data island, the data that is written will be embedded in the data island:

```
        WriteNodeXML elemBook

        ' and clear our objects
        Set fileBook = Nothing
        Set tsBook = Nothing
        Set domBook = Nothing
        Set elemBook = Nothing
        Set elemAuthor = Nothing
        Set elemRecSubjCategories = Nothing
        Set elemAuthors = Nothing
     %>
  </XML>
```

The three style sheets and body fragment below are taken from our first example. The only change is that the `BODY` element now has an `onload` event that renders the XML data island using the three style sheets:

```
  <XML id=bookXSL>
     <DIV xmlns:xsl="http://www.w3.org/TR/WD-xsl">
        <xsl:choose>
           <xsl:when test="/Book/Title[. $ne$ '']">
              <TABLE BORDER="0" CELLPADDING="1">
                 <TR>
                    <TD>Title:</TD>
                    <TD><xsl:value-of select="/Book/Title"/></TD>
                 </TR>
                 <TR>
                    <TD>Publisher:</TD>
                    <TD><xsl:value-of select="/Book/Publisher"/></TD>
                 </TR>
                 <TR>
                    <TD>Published Date:</TD>
                    <TD><xsl:value-of select="/Book/PubDate"/></TD>
                 </TR>
                 <TR>
                    <TD>Abstract:</TD>
                    <TD><xsl:value-of select="/Book/Abstract"/></TD>
```

```
                </TR>
                <TR>
                   <TD>Pages:</TD>
                   <TD><xsl:value-of select="/Book/Pages"/></TD>
                </TR>
                <TR>
                   <TD>ISBN:</TD>
                   <TD><xsl:value-of select="/Book/ISBN"/></TD>
                </TR>
                <TR>
                   <TD>Price:</TD>
                   <TD><xsl:value-of select="/Book/Price"/></TD>
                </TR>
             </TABLE>
          </xsl:when>
          <xsl:otherwise>
             Book information not yet specified.
          </xsl:otherwise>
       </xsl:choose>
    </DIV>
</XML>

<XML id=authorXSL>
   <DIV xmlns:xsl="http://www.w3.org/TR/WD-xsl">
      <TABLE BORDER="0" CELLSPACING="1">
         <TR>
            <TD><STRONG>Authors</STRONG></TD>
         </TR>
         <xsl:for-each select="/Book/Authors/Author">
            <TR>
               <TD><xsl:value-of select="text()"/></TD>
            </TR>
         </xsl:for-each>
      </TABLE>
   </DIV>
</XML>
<XML id=categoryXSL>
   <DIV xmlns:xsl="http://www.w3.org/TR/WD-xsl">
      <TABLE BORDER="0" CELLSPACING="1">
         <TR>
            <TD><STRONG>Categories</STRONG></TD>
         </TR>
         <xsl:for-each select="/Book/RecSubjCategories/Category">
            <TR>
               <TD><xsl:value-of select="text()"/></TD>
            </TR>
         </xsl:for-each>
      </TABLE>
   </DIV>
</XML>

</HEAD>
<BODY onload="renderElements()">
```

```
    <H2>Book information</H2>
    <P><DIV id=bookInfo></DIV></P>
    <P><DIV id=authorTable></DIV></P>
    <P><DIV id=categoryTable></DIV></P>

    </BODY>
</HTML>
```

The output of `DisplayBook.asp` looks like this:

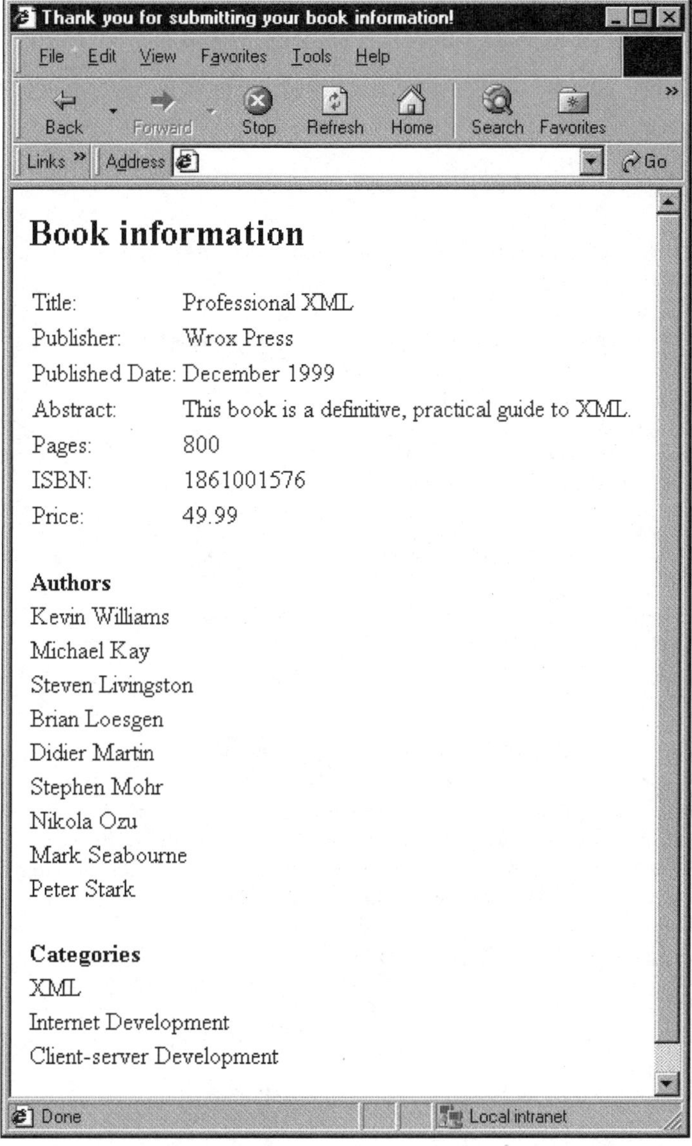

This simple example illustrates the ease with which the DOM may be used on the server to process information. For example, an online invoicing system might receive invoice files via FTP to some directory; a scheduled job could then run early in the morning to parse all the files in the directory, convert them to XML, and archive them for later use. Or a dynamic request for invoicing information from a database could read the appropriate information, convert it to XML using the DOM, and return it to the client for manipulation there.

Modifying Information Using the DOM

You might have noticed in the example above that the ISBN was poorly formatted. Normally, an ISBN has dashes in specific locations:

```
1-861001-57-6
```

However, what we receive in the file is the unformatted digits only:

```
1861001576
```

We can add code to our script to resolve this problem. Let's add some code to our previous example that reformats the ISBN.

After the file is closed and the XML DOM tree has been constructed, we'll add the following code:

```
Dim nodelistISBN
Dim i

Set nodelistISBN = elemBook.getElementsByTagName("ISBN")
For i = 0 to nodelistISBN.length - 1
   sWork = nodelistISBN.item(i).childnodes(0).data
   sWork = Left(sWork, 1) & "-" & Mid(sWork, 2, 6) & "-" & _
           Mid(sWork, 8, 2) & "-" & Mid(sWork, 10, 1)
   nodelistISBN.item(i).childnodes(0).data = sWork
Next

Set nodelistISBN = Nothing
```

This code searches the entire descendant tree of the `Book` element for elements called `ISBN`. Now, we know that every `ISBN` element has one child node – a text node containing the improperly-formatted string. We take that value, insert dashes as appropriate, and update the value with the properly-formatted one. Note that we're walking through all of the elements in the `NodeList`, so if there were more than one `ISBN` element, this block of code would catch them all – making this a handy technique for modifying deeply-embedded elements in large XML files.

The output of `DisplayBook.asp` now looks like this:

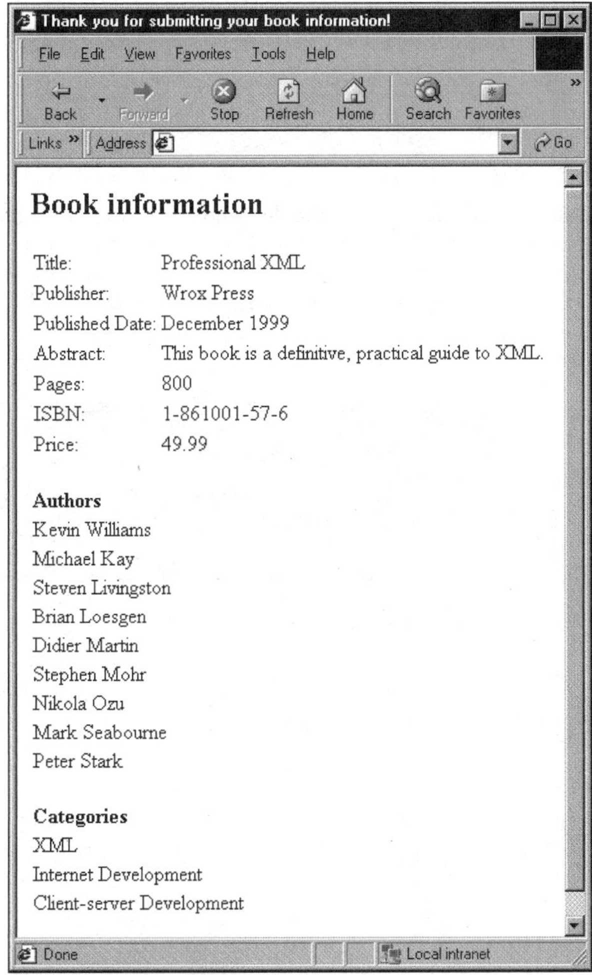

Deleting Elements Using the DOM

The DOM may also be used to delete elements from the node tree. Say, for example, that the author Kevin Williams is no longer an author on the book – but all the files still say that he is. We can use the DOM to delete any author called Kevin Williams.

Again, we'll build on the previous example.

After the ISBN code we added in the previous example, let's add the following block of code:

```
Dim nodelistAuthors

Set nodelistAuthors = elemBook.getElementsByTagName("Author")
For i = 0 to nodelistAuthors.length - 1
   If nodelistAuthors.item(i).childnodes(0).data = "Kevin Williams" Then
      ' we'll delete this node
```

```
            nodelistAuthors.item(i).parentnode. removeChild( _
                                                nodelistAuthors.item(i))
         End If
      Next

      Set nodelistAuthors = Nothing
```

Basically, we scan for all `Author` elements in the descendants of the `Book` element; then any that have the text Kevin Williams are removed as children of their parents (effectively, they are deleted). Note that there's no additional cleanup required; even though the nodes are still valid, they are not attached to any other nodes, and as a result will not be expressed in the generated XML.

The output of `DisplayBook.asp` now looks like this:

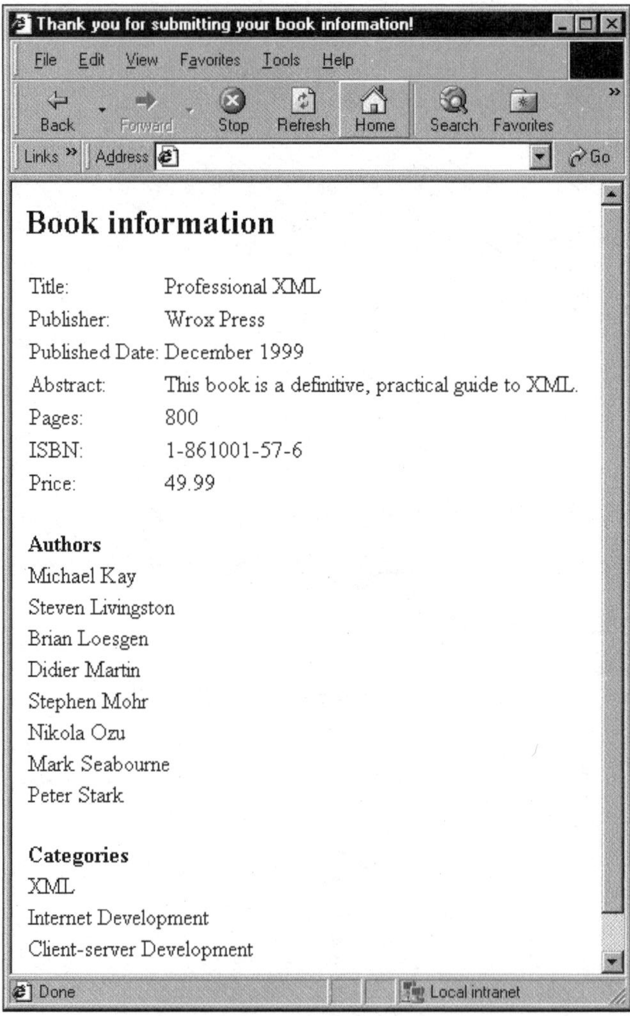

Generation of an XML Stream, Revisited

Recall the recursive subroutine, `WriteNodeXML()`, that generated the XML for a node tree:

```
Sub WriteNodeXML (nodeTarget)
   Dim i

   If nodeTarget.NodeType = 1 Then
      ' Element
      Response.Write "<" & nodeTarget.tagName & ">"
      For i = 0 to nodeTarget.childNodes.Length - 1
         WriteNodeXML nodeTarget.childNodes.item(i)
      Next
      Response.Write "</" & nodeTarget.tagName & ">"
   ElseIf nodeTarget.NodeType = 3 Then
      ' Text Node
      Response.Write nodeTarget.data
   End If

End Sub
```

While this works for our sample XML for our book, it won't handle all possible DOM permutations. While a description of a function that will properly express all the different node types is beyond the scope of this chapter, let's take a look at how we would go about expressing attributes (the next most important node type).

Because attributes are special nodes, they are not found as child nodes of the element to which they are attached; rather, they may be found in the `attributes` property of their element. This property returns a `NamedNodeMap` that may be iterated against to express all of the attribute information for a particular element. Adding code to do this to the previous version of the `WriteNodeXML()` function results in this code:

```
   Select Case nodeTarget.NodeType
      Case 1
         ' Element node
         Response.Write "<" & nodeTarget.tagName
         For i = 0 to nodeTarget.attributes.Length - 1
            Response.Write " " & nodeTarget.attributes.item(i).Name & "="
            Response.Write chr(34) & _
               nodeTarget.attributes.item(i).nodeValue & chr(34)
         Next
         Response.Write ">"
         For i = 0 to nodeTarget.childNodes.Length - 1
            WriteNodeXML nodeTarget.childNodes.item(i)
         Next
         Response.Write "</" & nodeTarget.tagName & ">"
      Case 3
         ' Text node
         Response.Write nodeTarget.data
      Case Else
   End Select
```

The name-value pairs for the attributes will now be embedded in the start tag of the element. In order to completely represent the DOM's contents as a file, we would also need to handle comments, processing instructions, CDATA sections, and so on.

It should be clear by now that the DOM provides a simple, flexible way to access the contents of an XML document. The DOM may be used on the client (provided you know the client browser) or on the server to manipulate, add to, and delete from XML structures.

Future of the DOM and XML

XML is still in the early stages of development. If you were doing HTML work when the HTML 1.0 specification was released, you know that the language has changed dramatically since then – and you can expect XML to follow the same pattern. In this section, we'll take a look at the ways the DOM and XML are expected to change, and some of the implications those changes will have for our industry.

Work by the W3C

The W3C is still in the process of defining XML and the DOM. As of press time, the level 1 specification of the DOM is a Recommendation and the level 2 specification is a Candidate Recomendation. In addition, the W3C has already begun to discuss level 3 of the DOM specification. In level 3, the W3C will formalize the mechanisms for document loading and saving XML structures to file (many of which are provided informally by implementations of the DOM already in place), as well as document validation issues. This release will also formalize document views and formatting mechanisms. Beyond level 3, the W3C plans to add user interaction mechanisms such as prompts, as well as a query language.

Applications

There are myriad third-party developers that are building tools to access and modify XML files. These developers are likely to take advantage of the DOM functionality to do so. In many instances, these tools will form a layer wrapping the DOM that allows developers to access information at a higher level (rather than having to traverse the node tree manually). One such application would be XPath – a query language that is used to control the traversal of the node tree and retrieval of data. As the DOM changes over the next year or two, you can expect the tools that facilitate access to XML documents to change as well.

Databases, Schemas, and the DOM

The line between databases and XML documents is becoming more and more narrow. As query languages become available to access XML documents, and XML schemas are used to strongly type the content of those documents, the transfer of information between databases and the DOM will become more and more error-free. Microsoft and Oracle, for example, are already building native XML support into their database server applications.

Summary

We have seen that the DOM provides a natural, object-oriented mechanism for traversing the node tree that makes up an XML document and retrieving the information stored there. In particular, we have seen that:

- The DOM provides a programmatic means of processing XML documents.
- The DOM allows us to modify XML data structures on both the client and the server.
- The DOM provides an ideal mechanism for transferring information between databases.
- The DOM may be implemented differently on different platforms.
- The DOM is very memory-intensive, and may not be the best platform for the manipulation of large XML files.

In short, when reading and manipulating XML documents, using the DOM will ensure the greatest level of interoperability between various platforms. However, using the DOM is not necessarily the best strategy, especially when working with very large files. To avoid the overhead of loading the entire document into memory, large XML files can be processed using an event-driven parser like SAX – as we'll see in the next chapter.

6

SAX 1.0: The Simple API for XML

In Chapter 5 we looked at how to write applications using the Document Object Model. In this chapter we'll look at an alternative way of processing an XML document: the SAX interface. We'll start by discussing why you might choose to use the SAX interface rather than the DOM. Then we'll explore the interface by writing some simple applications. We'll also discuss some design patterns that are useful when creating more complex SAX applications, and finally we'll look at where SAX is going next.

SAX is a very different style of interface from DOM. With DOM, your application asks what is in the document by following object references in memory; with SAX, the parser tells the application what is in the document by notifying the application of a stream of parsing **events**.

SAX stands for "Simple API for XML". Or if you really want it in full, the Simple Application Programming Interface for Extensible Markup Language.

As the name implies, SAX is an interface that allows you to write applications to read the data held in an XML document. It's primarily a Java interface, and all of our examples will be in Java. (Since we don't have the space to explain Java in this chapter we will assume knowledge of it for the purposes of this exposition. See Beginning Java 2, Wrox Press ISBN 1861002238, or the documentation at `http://www.java.sun.com` for more information.)

The SAX interface is supported by virtually every Java XML parser, and the level of compatibility is excellent. For a list of some of the implementations see `http://www.xmlsoftware.com` or David Megginson's site at `http://www.megginson.com/SAX/`

To write a SAX application in Java, you'll need to install the SAX classes (in addition to the Java JDK, of course). In most cases you'll find that the XML Parser does this for you automatically (we'll tell you where you can get parsers shortly). Check to see that classes such as `org.xml.sax.Parser` are present somewhere on your classpath. If not, you can install them from `http://www.megginson.com/SAX/`

We'll say a few words later on about where SAX came from and where it's going. But for the moment, we'll just mention a most remarkable feature: SAX doesn't belong to any standards body or consortium, nor to any company or individual; it just exists in cyberspace for anyone to implement and everyone to use. In particular, unlike most of the XML family of standards it has nothing to do with the W3C.

SAX development is coordinated by David Megginson, and its specification can be found on his site: `http://www.megginson.com/SAX/`. The specification, with trivial editorial changes, is reproduced for convenience in Appendix C of this book.

An Event-Based Interface

There are essentially three ways you can read an XML document from a program:

1. You can just read it as a file and sort out the tags for yourself. This is the hacker's approach, and we don't recommend it. You'll quickly find that dealing with all the special cases (different character encodings, escape conventions, internal and external entities, defaulted attributes and so on) is much harder work than you thought; you probably won't deal with all these special cases correctly and sooner or later someone will feed you a perfectly good XML document that your program can't handle. Avoid the temptation: it's not as if XML parsers are expensive (most are free).

2. You can use a parser that analyses the document and constructs a tree representation of its contents in memory: the output from the parser passes into the Document Object Model, or DOM. Your program can then start at the top of the tree and navigate around it, following references from one element to another to find the information it needs.

3. You can use a parser that reads the document and tells your program about the symbols it finds, as it finds them. For example it will tell you when it finds a start tag, when it finds some character data, and when it finds an end tag. This is called an **event-based** interface because the parser notifies the application of significant events as they occur. If this is the right kind of interface for you, use SAX.

Let's look at event-based parsing in a little more detail.

You may have come across the term 'event-based' in user interface programming, where an application is written to respond to events such as mouse-clicks as they occur. An event-based parser is similar: in particular, you have to get used to the idea that your application is not in control. Once things have been set in motion you don't call the parser, the parser calls you. That can seem strange at first, but once you get used to it, it's not a problem. In fact, it's much easier than user-interface programming, because, unlike a user going crazy with a mouse, the XML parsing events occur in a rather predictable sequence. XML elements have to be properly nested, so you know that every element that's been opened will sooner or later be closed, and so on.

Consider a simple XML file such as the following:

```
<?xml version="1.0"?>
<books>
   <book>Professional XML</book>
</books>
```

As the parser processes this, it will call a sequence of methods such as the following (we'll describe the actual method names and parameters later, this is just for illustration):

```
startDocument()
startElement( "books" )
startElement( "book" )
characters( "Professional XML" )
endElement( "book" )
endElement( "books" )
endDocument()
```

All your application has to do is to provide methods to be called when the events such as `startElement` and `endElement` occur.

Why Use an Event-Based Interface?

Given that you have a choice, it's important to understand when it's best to use an event-based interface like SAX, and when it's better to use a tree-based interface like the DOM.

Both interfaces are well standardized and widely supported, so whichever you choose, you have a wide choice of good quality parsers available, most of which are free. In fact many of the parsers support both interfaces.

The Benefits of SAX

The following sections outline the most obvious benefits of the SAX interface.

It Can Parse Files of Any Size

Because there is no need to load the whole file into memory, memory consumption is typically much less than the DOM, and it doesn't increase with the size of the file. Of course the actual amount of memory used by the DOM depends on the parser, but in many cases a 100Kb document will occupy at least 1Mb of memory.

A word of caution though: if your SAX application builds its own in-memory representation of the document, it is likely to take up just as much space as if you allowed the parser to build it.

It Is Useful When You Want to Build Your Own Data Structure

Your application might want to construct a data structure using high-level objects such as books, authors, and publishers rather than low-level elements, attributes, and processing instructions. These "business objects" might only be distantly related to the contents of the XML file; for example, they may combine data from the XML file and other sources. If you want to build up an application-oriented data structure in memory in this way, there is very little advantage in building up a low-level DOM structure first and then demolishing it. Just process each event as it occurs, to make the appropriate incremental change to your business object model.

It Is Useful When You Only Want a Small Subset of the Information

If you are only interested, say, in counting how many books have arrived in the library this week, or in determining their average price, it is very inefficient and quite unnecessary to read all the data that you don't want into memory along with the small amount that you do want. One of the beauties of SAX is that it makes it very easy to ignore the data you aren't interested in.

It Is Simple

As the name suggests, it's really quite simple to use.

It Is Fast

If it's possible to get the information you need from a single serial pass through the document, SAX will almost certainly be the fastest way to get it.

The Drawbacks of SAX

Having looked at the benefits it is only fair to address the potential drawbacks in using SAX.

There's No Random Access to the Document

Because the document is not in memory you have to handle the data in the order it arrives. SAX can be difficult to use when the document contains a lot of internal cross-references, for example using `ID` and `IDREF` attributes.

Complex Searches Can Be Difficult to Implement

Complex searches can be quite messy to program as the responsibility is on you to maintain data structures holding any context information you need to retain, for example the attributes of the ancestors of the current element.

The DTD Is Not Available

SAX 1.0 doesn't tell you anything about the contents of the DTD. Actually the DOM doesn't tell you much about it either, though some vendors have extended the DOM interface to do so. This isn't a problem for most applications: the DTD is mainly of interest to the parser; and as we'll see towards the end of the chapter the problem is fixed in SAX 2.0.

Lexical Information Is Not Available

The design principle in SAX is that it doesn't provide you with **lexical information**. SAX tries to tell you what the writer of the document wanted to say, and avoids troubling you with details of the way they chose to say it. For example:

- You can't find out whether the original document contained "
" or "
" or whether it contained a real newline character: all three are reported to the application in the same way.
- You don't get told about comments in the document: SAX assumes that comments are there for the author's benefit, not for the reader's.
- You don't get told about the order in which attributes were written: it isn't supposed to matter.

These restrictions are only a problem if you want to reproduce the way the document was written, perhaps for the benefit of future editing. For example, if you are writing an application designed to leave the existing content of the document intact, but to add some extra information from another source, the document author might get upset if you change the order of the attributes arbitrarily, or lose all the comments. In fact, most of the restrictions apply just as much to the DOM, although it does give you a little more information in some areas: for example, it retains comments. Again, many of the restrictions are fixed in SAX 2.0; though not all, for example the order of attributes is still a closely guarded secret, as is the choice of delimiter (single or double quotes).

SAX Is Read-Only

The DOM allows you to create or modify a document in memory, as well as reading a document from an XML source file. SAX, by contrast, is designed for reading XML documents, not for writing them.

Actually it turns out that the SAX interface is quite handy for writing XML documents as well as reading them. As we'll see later, the same stream of events that the parser sends to the application when reading an XML document can equally be sent from the application to an XML generator when writing one.

SAX Is Not Supported in Current Browsers

Although there are many XML parsers that support the SAX interface, At the time of writing there isn't a parser built into a mainstream web browser that supports it. You can incorporate a SAX-compliant parser within a Java applet, of course, but the overhead of downloading it from the server may strain the patience of a user with a slow Internet connection. In practice, your choice of interfaces for client-side XML programming is rather limited.

The Origins of SAX

The history of SAX is unusually well documented, because all the discussion took place on the public XML-DEV mailing list, whose archives are available at `http://www.lists.ic.ac.uk/hypermail/xml-dev/`. David Megginson has also summarized its history at `http://www.megginson.com/SAX/history.html`.

The process started late in 1997 as a result of pressure from XML users such as Peter Murray-Rust, who was developing XML applications and struggling with the needless incompatibility of different parsers. Suppliers of early XML parsers, including Tim Bray, David Megginson, and James Clark contributed to the discussion, and many other members of the list commented on the various drafts. David Megginson devised a process, rather in the spirit of the original Internet "Request for Comments", whereby comments and suggestions could be handled promptly yet fairly, and he eventually declared the specification frozen on 11 May 1998.

One of the major reasons for the success of SAX was that along with the initial specification, Megginson supplied front-end drivers for several popular XML parsers, including his own Ælfred, Tim Bray's Lark, and Microsoft's MSXML. Once SAX was established in this way, other parser writers such as IBM, Sun, and ORACLE were quick to incorporate native SAX interfaces into their own parsers, to enable existing applications to run with their products.

The definitive SAX specification is written in terms of Java interfaces. It has been adapted to other languages, though the only one we know of that is actively supported is an interface for the Python language, produced by Lars Marius Garshol (see `http://www.stud.ifi.uio.no/~larsga/download/python/xml/saxlib.html`). Of course, the Java interfaces can be used from other languages that interoperate with Java, for example by using Microsoft's Java VM that interfaces Java to COM. In this chapter, however, we'll stick to the original Java.

The Structure of SAX

SAX is structured as a number of Java **interfaces**. It's very important to understand the difference between an interface and a class:

- An interface says what methods there are, and what kind of parameters they expect. It is purely a specification; it doesn't provide any code to execute when the methods are called. But it is a concrete specification, not just a scrap of paper, and the Java compiler will check that a class that claims to implement an interface does so correctly.
- A class provides executable methods, including public methods that can be called by the code in other classes.
- A class may implement one or more interfaces. In many cases SAX specifies several interfaces which could theoretically be implemented by separate classes, but which in practice are often implemented in combination by a single class. To implement an interface, a class must supply code for each of the methods defined in the interface.
- Several classes may implement the same interface. Of course this is the whole point of the SAX exercise – there are lots of implementations of the SAX Parser interface for you to choose from, and because they all implement the same interface, your application doesn't care which one it is using.

Some of the interfaces in SAX are implemented by classes within the parser, and some must be implemented by classes within the application. There are some classes supplied with SAX itself, though you don't have to use these. And there are some classes (such as the error handling classes), which the parser must provide, but which your application can override if it wishes.

The Basic Structure

The components of a simple SAX application are shown in the following diagram:

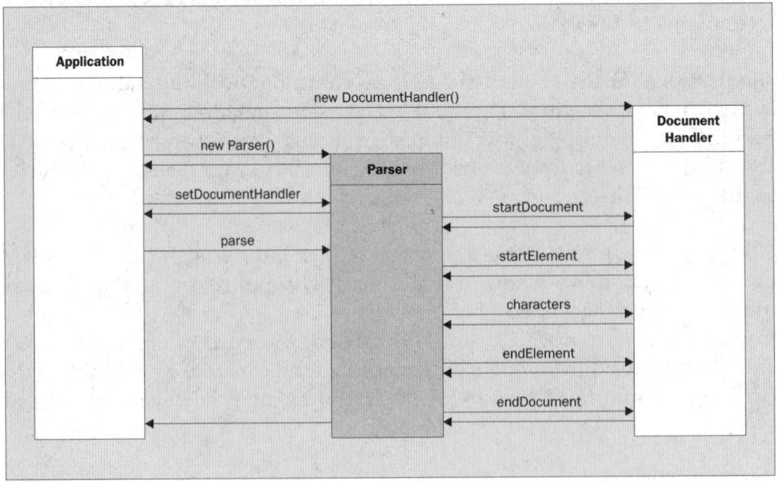

In the diagram:

- The **Application** is the "main program": the code that you write to start the whole process off.
- The **Document Handler** is code that you write to process the contents of the document.
- The **Parser** is an XML Parser that conforms to the SAX standard.

The job of the application is to create a parser (more technically, to instantiate a class that implements the `org.xml.sax.Parser` interface); to create a document handler (by instantiating a class that implements the `org.xml.sax.DocumentHandler` interface); to tell the parser what document handler to use (by calling the parser's `setDocumentHandler()` method); and to tell the parser to start processing a particular input document (by calling the `parse()` method of the parser).

The job of the parser is to notify the document handler of all the interesting things it finds in the document, such as element start tags and end tags.

The job of the document handler is to process these notifications to achieve whatever the application requires.

A Simple Example

Let's look at a very simple application: one that simply counts how many `<book>` elements there are in the supplied XML file (shown later).

In this example we will simplify the structure shown in the diagram above by using the same class to act as both the application and the document handler. The reason we can do this is that one Java class can implement several interfaces, so it can perform several roles at once.

The first thing the application must do is to create a parser:

```
import org.xml.sax.*;

...

Parser p = new com.jclark.xml.sax.Driver();
```

This is the only time you need to say which particular SAX parser you are using. We have chosen the `xp` parser produced by James Clark, and available from `http://www.jclark.com`. Like any other Java class you use, it must, of course, be on the Java classpath.

The chosen parser must implement the SAX Parser interface `org.xml.sax.Parser` (if it doesn't, Java will complain loudly), so it can be assigned to a variable of type `Parser`. Because of the import statement at the top, `Parser` is actually a shorthand for `org.xml.sax.Parser`.

So you need to know the relevant class name of your chosen parser. Oddly, many of the available SAX parsers don't advertise their parser class name in bright lights. So here is a list of some of the more popular parsers, with the class name you need to use to instantiate them. (Note however that this may change with later versions of the products.)

Product	Details	
Ælfred	**from:**	http://www.microstar.com/aelfred.html
	parser class:	com.microstar.xml.SAXDriver
Datachannel DXP	**from:**	http://www.datachannel.com/products/xjparser.html
	parser class:	com.datachannel.xml.sax.SAXDriver
IBM xml4j	**from:**	http://alphaworks.ibm.com/tech/xml4j
	parser class (non-validating):	com.ibm.xml.parsers.SAXParser
	parser class (validating):	com.ibm.xml.parsers.ValidatingSAXParser
Oracle	**from:**	http://www.oracle.com (requires TechNet registration)
	parser class:	oracle.xml.parser.v2.SAXParser
Sun Project X	**from:**	http://java.sun.com/products/xml/
	parser class (non-validating):	com.sun.xml.parser.Parser
	parser class (validating):	com.sun.xml.parser.ValidatingParser
xp	**from:**	http://www.jclark.com/xp
	parser class:	com.jclark.xml.sax.Driver

So, you've created a parser. Now you can start telling it what to do.

First you need to tell the parser what document handler to call when events occur. This can be any class that implements the SAX `org.xml.sax.DocumentHandler` interface. The simplest and most common approach is to make your application itself act as the document handler.

`DocumentHandler` itself is an interface defined in SAX. You could make your application program implement this interface directly, in which case you would have to provide code for all the different methods required by that interface. In our example, however, we want to ignore most of the events, so it would be rather tedious to define lots of methods that do nothing. Fortunately SAX supplies an implementation of `DocumentHandler` that does nothing, `HandlerBase`, and we can make our application extend this, so it inherits all the "do nothing" methods. Let's do this:

```
import org.xml.sax.*;

...

public class BookCounter extends HandlerBase
{
   public void countBooks()
   {
      Parser p = new com.jclark.xml.sax.Driver();
      p.setDocumentHandler(this);
   }
}
```

The call on `setDocumentHandler()` tells the parser that "this" class (your application program) is to receive notification of events. This class is an implementation of `org.xml.sax.DocumentHandler`, because it inherits from `org.xml.sax.HandlerBase`, which in turn implements `DocumentHandler`.

The parser is now almost ready to go; all it needs is a document to parse, and the Java `main()` method that lets it operate as a standalone program. Let's give it a file to parse first:

```
import org.xml.sax.*;
...

public class BookCounter extends HandlerBase
{

   public void countBooks() throws Exception
   {

      Parser p = new com.jclark.xml.sax.Driver();
      p.setDocumentHandler(this);
      p.parse("file:///C:/data/books.xml");
   }
}
```

Note that the argument to `parse()` is a URL, supplied as a string. We'll show you later how to supply a filename rather than a URL. Because the program now involves data input and output we must also add "`throws Exception`" to the `countBooks()` method to alert if there are errors.

We need to make one more addition to get the program to run as a standalone application: the Java `main()` method. In the `main` method we create an instance of the class, with `new BookCounter()`, and then call the object's `countBooks()` method; we also trap exceptions again for the new object as a whole. Our code should then look like this:

```
import org.xml.sax.*;
...

public class BookCounter extends HandlerBase
{

   public static void main (String args[]) throws Exception
   {
      (new BookCounter()).countBooks();
   }

      public void countBooks() throws Exception
      {
         Parser p = new com.jclark.xml.sax.Driver();
         p.setDocumentHandler(this);
         p.parse("file:///C:/data/books.xml");
      }
}
```

The program can now be run: it will parse the document and run to completion (assuming, of course, that the document is there to be parsed).

The only snag is that the program currently produces no output. To make it useful, we need to add a method that counts the <book> start tags as they are notified, and another that prints the number of books counted at the end of the document. These methods make use of the global variable count.

The final version of the application is shown below. You can find it on our web site on the pages for this book at http://www.wrox.com/ in the code for this chapter.

```
import org.xml.sax.*;

public class BookCounter extends HandlerBase
{

   private int count = 0;

   public static void main (String args[]) throws Exception
   {
      (new BookCounter()).countBooks();
   }

   public void countBooks() throws Exception
   {
      Parser p = new com.jclark.xml.sax.Driver();
      p.setDocumentHandler(this);
      p.parse("file:///c:/data/books.xml");
   }

   public void startElement(String name, AttributeList atts) throws SAXException
   {
      if (name.equals("book"))
         count++;
   }

   public void endDocument() throws SAXException
   {
      System.out.println("There are " + count + " books");
   }

}
```

You can now run this application from the command line, with a command of the form:

```
java BookCounter
```

and it will print the number of <book> elements in the supplied XML file. Suppose the file c:\data\books.xml contains the following file (available for download with the code for the chapter from http://www.wrox.com):

```
<?xml version="1.0"?>
<books>
   <book category="reference">
      <author>Nigel Rees</author>
      <title>Sayings of the Century</title>
      <price>8.95</price>
   </book>
```

```
    <book category="fiction">
        <author>Evelyn Waugh</author>
        <title>Sword of Honour</title>
        <price>12.99</price>
    </book>
    <book category="fiction">
        <author>Herman Melville</author>
        <title>Moby Dick</title>
        <price>8.99</price>
    </book>
</books>
```

Then the output displayed at the terminal will be:

```
>java BookCounter
There are 3 books
```

The DocumentHandler Interface

As the example above shows, the main work in a SAX application is done in a class that implements the `DocumentHandler` interface. Usually we'll be interested in rather more of the events than in the simple example above, so let's look at the other methods that make up this interface.

Document Events

First, there's a pair of methods that mark the start and end of document processing:

- ❑ `startDocument()`
- ❑ `endDocument()`

These two methods take no parameters and return no result. In fact, you can usually get by without them, since anything you want to do at the start can generally be done before you call `parse()`, and anything you want to do at the end can be done when `parse()` returns. However, in a more complex application you may want to make the application that calls `parse()` a different class from the `DocumentHandler`, and in this case these two methods are useful for initializing variables and tidying up at the end.

Note that a SAX parser (a single instance of the `Parser` class) should only be used to parse one XML document at a time. Once it has finished, you can use it again to parse another document. If you want to parse several documents concurrently, you need to create one instance of the `Parser` class for each. You'll almost certainly want to apply the same one-document-per-instance rule to a `DocumentHandler`, because there's nothing in the event information that tells you what document the event came from.

Element Events

As with document events, there is a pair of methods that are called to mark the start and end tags of each element in the document:

- ❑ `startElement(String name, AttributeList attList)`
- ❑ `endElement(String name)`

The `name` is the name that appears in the start and end tag of the element.

If the document uses the abbreviated syntax for an empty element (that is, "<tag/>"), the parser will notify both a start and end tag, exactly as if you had written "<tag></tag>". This is because XML defines these two constructs as equivalent, so your application shouldn't need to know which was used.

The attributes appearing in the start tag are bundled together into an object of class `AttributeList` and handed to the application all at once. This is a departure from the event-based model, in which you might expect each attribute to be notified as it occurs. `AttributeList` is another interface defined by SAX. It's up to the parser to define a class that implements this interface: all the application needs to know is the methods it can call to get details of individual attributes. The most useful one is:

- `getValue(String name)`

which returns the value of the named attribute as a `String`, if it is present, or null if it is absent.

One thing to remember about the `AttributeList` is that it's only valid for the duration of the `startElement()` method. Once your method returns control to the parser, it can (and often does) overwrite the `AttributeList` with different information. If you want to keep attribute information for later use, you'll need to make a copy. One convenient way to do this is to use the SAX "helper" class `AttributeListImpl`: this allows you to create another `AttributeList` as a private copy of the one you were given.

Character Data

Character data appearing in the XML document is usually reported to the application using the method:

- `characters(char[] chars, int start, int len)`

This interface was defined for efficiency rather than convenience. If you want to handle the character data as a String, you can easily construct one by writing:

```
String s = new String(chars, start, len);
```

The parser could have constructed this `String` for you, but creating new objects can be expensive in Java, so instead it just gives you a pointer to its internal buffer where the characters are already held.

One advantage of using Java for XML processing is that Java and XML both use the Unicode character set as standard. The characters passed in the `chars` array are always native Java Unicode characters, regardless of the character encoding used in the original source document. This means you never need to worry about how the characters were encoded.

One important point to remember is that the parser is allowed to break up character data however it likes, and pass it to you one piece at a time. This means that if you are looking for "gold" in your document, the following code is wrong:

```
public void characters(char[] chars, int start, int len) throws SAXException
{
   String s = new String(chars, start, len);
   if (s.indexOf("gold") >= 0) ...
}
```

Why? Because the string "gold" might appear in your document, but be notified to your application in two or more calls of the `characters()` method. In theory, there could be four separate calls, one for the "g", one for the "o", one for the "l", and one for the "d".

The worst aspect of this problem is that you will probably not discover your program is wrong during testing, because in practice parsers very rarely split the text in this way. They might split it, for example, only if the text happens to straddle a 4096-byte boundary (if there is some reason the memory should happen to be limited in this way at the time), and this might not happen until after months of successful running. Be warned.

There is one circumstance in which parsers are obliged to split the text, and that is when external entities are used. The SAX specification is quite explicit that a single call on `characters()` may not contain text from two different external entities.

If you want to do anything with character data other than simply copying it unconditionally to an output file, you are probably interested in knowing what element is belongs to. Unfortunately the SAX interface doesn't give you this information directly. If you need such contextual information, your application will have to maintain a data structure that retains some memory of previous events. The most common is a stack. In the next section we will show how you can use some simple data structures both to assemble character data supplied piecemeal by the parser, and to determine what element it is part of.

There is a second method for reporting character data, namely:

- `ignorableWhitespace(char[] chars, int start, int len)`

This interface can be used to report what the SAX specification rather loosely refers to as "ignorable white space". If the DTD defines an element with "element content" (that is, the element can have children but cannot contain PCDATA), then XML permits the child elements to be separated by spaces, tabs, and newlines, even though "real" character data is not allowed. This white space is probably insignificant, so a SAX application will almost invariably ignore it: which you can do simply by having an `ignorableWhitespace()` method that does nothing. The only time you might want to do anything else is if your application is copying the data unchanged to an output file.

The XML specification allows a parser to ignore information in the external DTD, however. A non-validating parser will not necessarily distinguish between an element with element content and one with mixed content. In this case the ignorable white space is likely to be reported via the ordinary `characters()` interface. Unfortunately there is no way within a SAX application of telling whether the parser is a validating one or not, so a portable application must be prepared for either. This is another limitation that is remedied in SAX 2.0.

Processing Instructions

There is one more kind of event that parsers report, namely processing instructions. You probably won't meet these very often: they are the instructions that can appear anywhere in an XML document between the symbols "<?" and "?>". A processing instruction has a name (called a **target**), and arbitrary character data (instructions for the target application concerned).

Processing instructions are notified to the `DocumentHandler` using the method:

- `processingInstruction(String name, String data)`

By convention, you should ignore any processing instruction (or copy it unchanged) unless you recognize its name.

> *Note that the XML declaration at the start of a document may look like a processing instruction, but it is not a true processing instruction, and is not reported to the application via this interface – indeed, it is not reported at all.*

Processing instructions are often written to look like element start tags, with a sequence of `keyword="value"` attributes. This syntax, however, is purely an application convention, and is not defined by the XML standard. So SAX doesn't recognize it; the contents of the processing instruction data are passed over in an amorphous lump.

Error Handling

We've glossed over error handling so far, but as always, it needs careful thought in a real production application.

There are three main kinds of errors that can occur:

- Failure to open the XML input file, or another file that it refers to, for example the DTD or another external entity. In this case the parser will throw an `IOException` (input/output exception), and it is up to your application to handle it.
- XML errors detected by the parser, including well-formedness errors and validity errors. These are handled by calling an error handler which your application can supply, as described below.
- Errors detected by the application: for example, an invalid date or number in an attribute. You handle these by throwing an exception in the `DocumentHandler` method that detects the error.

Handling XML errors

The SAX specification defines three levels of error severity, based on the terminology used in the XML standard itself. These are:

Error	Description
Fatal errors	These usually mean the XML is not well-formed. The parser will call the registered error handler if there is one; if not, it will throw a `SAXParseException`. In most cases a parser will stop after the first fatal error it finds.
Errors	These usually mean the XML is well-formed but not valid. The parser will call the registered error handler if there is one; if not, it will ignore the error.
Warnings	These mean that the XML is correct, but there is some condition that the parser considers it useful to report. For example this might be a violation of one of the "interoperability" rules: input that is correct XML but not correct SGML. The parser will call the registered error handler if there is one; if not, it will ignore the error.

The application can register an error handler using the parser's `setErrorHandler()` method. An error handler contains three methods, `fatalError()`, `error()`, and `warning()`, reflecting the three different error severities. If you don't want to define all three, you can make an error handler that inherits from `HandlerBase`: this contains versions of all three methods that take the same action as if no error handler were registered.

The parameter to the error handling method, in all three cases, is a `SAXParseException` object. You probably think of Java Exceptions as things that are thrown and caught when errors occur; but in fact an Exception is a regular Java object and can be passed as a parameter to methods just like any other: it might never be thrown at all. The `SAXParseException` contains information about the error, including where in the source XML file it occurred. The most common thing for an error handler method to do is to extract this information to construct an error message, which can be written to a suitable destination: for example, a web server log file.

The other useful thing the error handling method can do is to throw an exception: usually, but not necessarily, the exception that the parser supplied as a parameter. If you do this, the parse will typically be aborted, and the top-level application will see the same exception thrown by the `parse()` method. It then has another opportunity to output diagnostics. Whether you generate a fatal error message from within the error handler, or do it by letting the top-level application catch the exception, is entirely up to you.

Application-Detected Errors

When your application detects an error within a `DocumentHandler` method (for example, a badly formatted date), the method should throw a `SAXException` containing an appropriate message to explain the problem. After this, the parser deals with the situation exactly as if it had detected the error itself. Typically, it doesn't attempt to catch the exception, but exits immediately from the `parse()` method with the same exception, which the top-level application can then catch.

Identifying Where the Error Occurred

When the parser detects an XML syntax error, it will supply details of the error in a `SAXParseException` object. This object will include details of the URL, line, and column where the error occurred (a line number on its own is not much use, because the error may be in some external entity not in the main document). When you catch the `SAXParseException` in your application, you can extract this information and display it so the user can locate the error.

If the problem with the XML file is detected at application level (for example, an invalid date), it is equally important to tell the user where the problem was found, but this time you can't rely on the `SAXParseException` to locate it. Instead, SAX defines a `Locator` interface. The SAX specification doesn't insist that parsers supply a `Locator`, but most parsers do.

One of the methods you must implement in a document handler is the `setLocator()` method. If the parser maintains location information it will call this method to tell the document handler where to find the `Locator` object. At any subsequent time while your document handler is processing an event it can ask the `Locator` object for details of the current coordinates in the source document. There are three coordinates:

- The URL of the document or external entity currently being processed
- The line number within that URL
- The column number within that line

This is of course exactly the same information that you can get from a SAXParseException object, and in fact one of the things you can do very easily when your application detects an error is to throw a SAXParseException that takes the coordinates directly from the Locator object – just write:

```
if ( [data is not valid] )
{
   throw new SAXParseException("Invalid data", locator);
}
```

Why wasn't the location information simply included in the events passed to the document handler, such as startElement()? The reason is efficiency: most applications only want location information if something goes wrong, so there should be minimal overhead incurred when it is not needed. Supplying location information with each call from the parser to the document handler would be unnecessarily expensive.

Another Example: Using Character Data and Attributes

After this excursion into the world of error handling, let's develop a slightly more complex example SAX application.

The task this time is for the application to print the average price of fiction books in the catalog. We'll use the same data file (books.xml) as in our previous example.

We are interested only in those <book> elements that have the attribute category="fiction", and for these we are interested only in the contents of the <price> child element. We add up the prices, count the books, and at the end divide the total price by the number of books.

Here's our first version of the application:

```
import org.xml.sax.*;

public class AveragePrice extends HandlerBase
{

   private int count = 0;
   private boolean isFiction = false;
   private double totalPrice = 0.0;
   private StringBuffer content = new StringBuffer();

   public void determineAveragePrice() throws Exception
   {
      Parser p = new com.jclark.xml.sax.Driver();
      p.setDocumentHandler(this);
      p.parse("file:///c:/data/books.xml");
   }

   public void startElement(String name, AttributeList atts) throws SAXException
   {
```

```
         if (name.equals("book"))
         {
            String category = atts.getValue("category");
            isFiction = (category!=null && category.equals("fiction"));
            if (isFiction) count++;
         }
         content.setLength(0);
      }

      public void characters(char[] chars, int start, int len) throws SAXException
      {
         content.append(chars, start, len);
      }

      public void endElement(String name) throws SAXException
      {
         if (name.equals("price") && isFiction)
         {
            try
            {
               double price = new Double(content.toString()).doubleValue();
               totalPrice += price;
            }
            catch (java.lang.NumberFormatException err)
            {
               throw new SAXException("Price is not numeric");
            }
         }
         content.setLength(0);
      }

      public void endDocument() throws SAXException
      {
         System.out.println("The average price of fiction books is " +
              totalPrice / count);
      }

      public static void main (String args[]) throws java.lang.Exception
      {
         try
         {
            (new AveragePrice()).determineAveragePrice();
         }
         catch (SAXException err)
         {
            System.err.println("Parsing failed: " + err.getMessage());
         }
      }
   }
```

There are three main points to note in this code:

- The application needs to maintain one piece of context, namely whether the current book is fiction or not. It uses an instance variable to remember this, setting `isFiction` to true when a start tag for a fiction book is encountered, and to false when a start tag for a non-fiction book is read.
- See how the character content is accumulated in a Java `StringBuffer` and is not actually processed until the `endElement()` event is notified. This kills two birds with one stone: it solves the problem that the content of a single element might be broken up and notified piecemeal; at the same time, it means that when we handle the data, we know which element we are dealing with. The `StringBuffer` is emptied whenever a start or end tag is read, which means that when the application gets to the end tag of a PCDATA element (one that contains character data only) the buffer will contain the character data of that element.
- The application needs to do something sensible when the price of a book is not a valid number. (Until XML Schemas become standardized, we can't rely on the parser to do this piece of validation for us: DTDs provide no way of restricting the data type of character data within an element.) This condition is detected by the fact that the Java constructor `Double(String s)`, which converts a String to a number, reports an exception. The relevant code catches this exception, and reports a `SAXException` describing the problem. This will cause the parsing to be terminated with an appropriate error message.

When the code is run on our example XML file it produces the following output:

```
>java AveragePrice
The average price of fiction books is 10.99
```

But the program isn't yet perfect.

Firstly, it can easily fail if the structure of the input document is not as expected. For example, it will give wrong answers if the `<price>` element occurs other than in a `<book>`, or if there is a `<book>` with no `<price>`, or if a `<price>` element has its own child elements. Such things might happen because there is no DTD, or because a non-validating parser is used that doesn't check the DTD, or because a document is submitted that uses a different DTD from that expected, or because the DTD has been enhanced since the program was written.

Secondly, the diagnostics when errors are detected are rather unfriendly. The user will be told that a price is not numeric, but there may be hundreds of books in the list: it would be more helpful to say which one. Even more helpful would be to report all the errors in a single run, so that the user doesn't have to run the program once to find and correct each separate error. (Actually, most XML parsers will only report one syntax error in a single run, so there's a limit to what we can achieve here.)

In the next section we'll look at how to maintain more information about element context, which is necessary if we're to do more thorough validation. Before that, we'll make one improvement in the area of error handling. We'll use the `Locator` object to determine where in the source document the error occurred, and report it accordingly. In order to show what happens clearly, we've switched from James Clark's xp parser to IBM Alphaworks' xml4j, which provides clearer messages. Here is the revised program:

```
import org.xml.sax.*;

public class  AveragePrice extends HandlerBase
{

    private int count = 0;
    private boolean isFiction = false;
    private double totalPrice = 0.0;
    private StringBuffer content = new StringBuffer();
    private Locator locator;

    public void determineAveragePrice() throws Exception
    {
        Parser p = new com.ibm.xml.parsers.SAXParser();
        p.setDocumentHandler(this);
        p.parse("file:///c:/data/books.xml");
    }

    public void setDocumentLocator(Locator loc)
    {
        locator = loc;
    }

    public void startElement(String name, AttributeList atts) throws SAXException
    {
        if (name.equals("book"))
        {
            String category = atts.getValue("category");
            isFiction = (category!=null && category.equals("fiction"));
            if (isFiction) count++;
        }
        content.setLength(0);
    }

    public void characters(char[] chars, int start, int len) throws SAXException
    {
        content.append(chars, start, len);
    }

    public void endElement(String name) throws SAXException
    {
        if (name.equals("price") && isFiction)
        {
            try
            {
                double price = new Double(content.toString()).doubleValue();
                totalPrice += price;
            }
            catch (java.lang.NumberFormatException err)
            {
                if (locator!=null)
                {
                    System.err.println("Error in " + locator.getSystemId() +
                                " at line " + locator.getLineNumber() +
```

```
                                  " column " + locator.getColumnNumber());
                    }
                    throw new SAXException("Price is not numeric", err);
                }
            }
            content.setLength(0);
        }

        public void endDocument() throws SAXException
        {
            System.out.println("The average price of fiction books is " +
                 totalPrice / count);
        }

        public static void main (String args[]) throws java.lang.Exception
        {
            try
            {
                (new AveragePrice()).determineAveragePrice();
            }
            catch (SAXException err)
            {
                System.err.println("Parsing failed: " + err.getMessage());
            }
        }

    }
```

This version of the code improves the diagnostics with very little extra effort. The revised application does three things:

- It keeps a note of the `Locator` object supplied by the parser.
- When an error occurs, it uses the `Locator` object to print information about the location of the error before generating the `SAXException`. Note that the application has to allow for the case where there is no `Locator`, because SAX doesn't require the parser to supply one.
- It also includes details of the original "root cause" exception (the `NumberFormatException`) encapsulated within the `SAXParseException`, again allowing more precise diagnostics to be written.

This is the output we got from the xml4j parser, after modifying the price of *Moby Dick* from "8.99" to "A.99":

```
>java AveragePrice
Error in file:///c:/data/books.xml at line 16 column 22
Parsing failed: Price is not numeric
```

In this example the application produces a message containing location information before throwing the exception, and then produces the real error message when the exception is caught at the top level. An alternative is to pass the location information as part of the exception, which could be done by throwing a `SAXParseException` instead of an ordinary `SAXException`. However, the application still has to deal with the case where there is no `Locator`, in which case throwing a `SAXParseException` is not very convenient. An alternative here would be for your application to create its own default locator (containing no useful information) for use when the parser doesn't supply one.

Maintaining Context

We've seen in both the examples so far that the `DocumentHandler` generally needs to maintain some kind of context information as the parse proceeds. In the first case all that it did was to accumulate a count of elements; in the second example the `DocumentHandler` kept track of whether or not we were currently within a `<book>` element with `category="fiction"`.

Nearly all realistic SAX applications will need to maintain some context information of this kind. Very often, it's appropriate to keep track of the current element nesting, and in many cases it's also useful to know the attributes of all the ancestor elements of the data we're currently processing.

The obvious data structure to hold this information is a `Stack`, because it's natural to add information about an element when we reach its start tag, and to remove that information when we reach its end tag. A stack, of course, still requires far less memory than you would need to store the whole document, because the maximum number of entries on the stack is only as great as the maximum nesting of elements, which even in large and complex documents rarely exceeds a depth of ten or so.

We can see how a stack can be useful if we modify the requirements for the previous example application. This time we'll allow our book catalog to include multi-volume books, with a price for each volume and a price for the whole set. In calculating the average price, we want to consider the price of the whole set, not the price of the individual volumes.

The source document might now look like this (it's also available via the web site at `http://www.wrox.com`):

```
<?xml version="1.0"?>
<books>
    <book category="reference">
        <author>Nigel Rees</author>
        <title>Sayings of the Century</title>
        <price>8.95</price>
    </book>
    <book category="fiction">
        <author>Evelyn Waugh</author>
        <title>Sword of Honour</title>
        <price>12.99</price>
    </book>
    <book category="fiction">
        <author>Herman Melville</author>
        <title>Moby Dick</title>
        <price>8.99</price>
    </book>
    <book category="fiction">
        <author>J. R. R. Tolkien</author>
        <title>The Lord of the Rings</title>
        <price>22.99</price>
        <volume number="1">
            <title>The Fellowship of the Ring</title>
            <price>8.95</price>
        </volume>
        <volume number="2">
            <title>The Two Towers</title>
            <price>8.95</price>
```

```
        </volume>
        <volume number="3">
            <title>The Return of the King</title>
            <price>8.95</price>
        </volume>
    </book>
</books>
```

One way of handling this would be to introduce another flag in the program, which we set when we encounter a `<volume>` start tag, and unset when we find a `</volume>` end tag; we could ignore a `<price>` element if this flag is set. But this style of programming quickly leads to a proliferation of flags and complex nesting of if-then-else conditions. A better approach is to put all the information about the currently open elements on a stack, which we can then interrogate as required.

Here's the new version of the application:

```
import org.xml.sax.*;
import org.xml.sax.helpers.AttributeListImpl;
import java.util.Stack;

public class AveragePrice1 extends HandlerBase
{

   private int count = 0;
   private double totalPrice = 0.0;
   private StringBuffer content = new StringBuffer();
   private Locator locator;
   private Stack context = new Stack();

   public void determineAveragePrice() throws Exception
   {
      Parser p = new com.jclark.xml.sax.Driver();
      p.setDocumentHandler(this);
      p.parse("file:///c:/data/books1.xml");
   }

   public void setDocumentLocator(Locator loc)
   {
      locator = loc;
   }

   public void startElement(String name, AttributeList atts) throws SAXException
   {
      ElementDetails details = new ElementDetails(name, atts);
      context.push(details);
      if (name.equals("book"))
      {
         if (isFiction()) count++;
      }
      content.setLength(0);
   }
```

```
public void characters(char[] chars, int start, int len) throws SAXException
{
   content.append(chars, start, len);
}

public void endElement(String name) throws SAXException
{
   if (name.equals("price") && isFiction() && !isVolume())
   {
      try
      {
         double price = new Double(content.toString()).doubleValue();
         totalPrice += price;
      }
      catch (java.lang.NumberFormatException err)
      {
          if (locator!=null)
          {
                 System.err.println("Error in " + locator.getSystemId() +
                                    " at line " + locator.getLineNumber() +
                                    " column " + locator.getColumnNumber());
          }
          throw new SAXException("Price is not numeric", err);
      }
   }
   content.setLength(0);
   context.pop();
}

public void endDocument() throws SAXException
{
   System.out.println("The average price of fiction books is " +
       totalPrice / count );
}

public static void main (String args[]) throws java.lang.Exception
{
   (new AveragePrice1()).determineAveragePrice();
}

private boolean isFiction()
{
   boolean test = false;
   for (int p=context.size()-1; p>=0; p--) {
      ElementDetails elem = (ElementDetails)context.elementAt(p);
      if (elem.name.equals("book") &&
          elem.attributes.getValue("category")!=null &&
          elem.attributes.getValue("category").equals("fiction"))
      {
         return true;
      }
   }
   return false;
}
```

```
    private boolean isVolume()
    {
        boolean test = false;
        for (int p=context.size()-1; p>=0; p--) {
            ElementDetails elem = (ElementDetails)context.elementAt(p);
            if (elem.name.equals("volume"))
            {
                return true;
            }
        }
        return false;
    }

    private class ElementDetails
    {
        public String name;
        public AttributeList attributes;
        public ElementDetails(String name, AttributeList atts)
        {
            this.name = name;
            this.attributes = new AttributeListImpl(atts); // make a copy
        }
    }

}
```

Here is the expected output:

```
>java AveragePrice1
The average price of fiction books is 14.99
```

It might seem that maintaining this stack is a lot of effort for rather a small return. But it's a worthwhile investment. All real applications become more complex over time, and it's worth having a structure that allows the logic to evolve without destroying the structure of the program. Note how the condition tests, such as `isFiction()` and `isVolume()`, have now become methods applied to the context data structure rather than flags that are maintained as events occur. As the number of conditions to be tested multiplies, we can write more of these methods without increasing the complexity of the `startElement()` and `endElement()` methods.

Advanced SAX features

The features we've covered so far are probably enough for 90% of SAX applications. But it's useful to know something of the rest of the features, for those occasions when they are needed. This section of the chapter gives a survey of these features and their intended purpose.

Alternative Input Sources

In our examples so far, the XML document to be parsed has been described in the form of a URL. This is usually adequate, given the range of resources that a URL can describe. It allows the document to be held in a file locally or remotely, or for it to be generated dynamically by a web server.

Taking Input from a Byte Stream or Character Stream

Sometimes you want to supply the parser with a stream of XML that is generated by another program rather than being held in a file. For example, the XML might be stored in a relational database, or it might be output by an EDI message translation program, or it might be an XML section embedded within a file or message in some non-XML format. You don't want to have to write the XML to the file store (or to install a web server) just so that the parser can read your document.

To handle this situation, SAX allows you to supply the XML input in the form of a character stream or a byte stream. It provides the `InputSource` class to generalize all these possible sources of input.

For example, let's suppose your program wants to parse XML held in a character string that has just been read from a relational database using JDBC. The following code will do the job:

```
public void parseString(String s) throws SAXException, IOException
{
   StringReader reader = new StringReader(s);
   InputSource source = new InputSource(reader);
   parser.parse(source);
}
```

`InputSource` is a class (not an interface) provided with the SAX distribution. The application can set various details of the input source, some of which are mutually exclusive. These include supplying a URL, a Reader (as here), an InputStream, an encoding name, or a "public identifier". (Public identifiers, however, are as enigmatic in SAX as in the XML specification itself: there are no clues as to what the parser should actually do with the public identifier. But as we will see later, the application can use it.)

Why does SAX need to provide two options for in-memory data, an InputStream and a Reader?

An InputStream is a stream of bytes. The XML standard provides many rules about how a stream of bytes can be translated into a stream of Unicode characters, including for example the encoding attribute (which is part of the xml declaration at the start of the document content). To translate bytes to characters, it's not good enough to leave the work to the standard Java libraries, because they don't understand these rules, and they certainly can't be expected to read the `encoding attribute`. If the XML comes from a binary source, complete with encoding attribute, we want to hand the stream of bytes to the parser for it to interpret directly.

A Reader, by contrast, is a stream of Unicode characters. If we already have the data in the form of characters, we don't want to have to encode it first as a stream of bytes (say in the UTF-8 encoding) just so that the parser can decode it again. Better to hand the character stream to the parser directly. (Actually, there was some debate about the desirability of providing this option in SAX. While it's obviously useful, it's not entirely in the spirit of the XML specification, which defines an XML document strictly as sequence of bytes. It's perhaps best to think of the input character stream not as an XML document, but as a preprocessed XML document in which the first stage of processing, namely character decoding, has already been done.)

Whether we use a byte stream or a character stream, there is one snag you need to be aware of: the parser has no way of resolving a relative URL that appears in the document source. Suppose the document source contains the line

```
<!DOCTYPE books SYSTEM "books.dtd">
```

Where is `books.dtd` to be found? The XML specification says (in effect) that it should be found in the same directory as the source document, but of course we don't have a directory for the source document because it was in memory when parsing started.

SAX gets round this by allowing a system identifier (in other words, a URL) to be supplied *as well as* a byte stream or character stream. This URL is not used to read the source document, only as a base for resolving any relative URLs found in the source document.

Specifying a Filename rather than a URL

Another common source of input is a file name: for example, command-line interfaces generally use file names as arguments rather than URLs, and you may well want to use this form of argument in the interface to your application.

The SAX `InputSource` class does not directly allow you to specify a filename for the input; you have to convert the filename into a URL so that the parser can process it. If you are using Java 2, this is simplicity itself: the Java `File` class has a suitable method. So to parse the file `c:\sample.xml`, you can write:

```
parser.parse((new File("c:\sample.xml")).toURL().toString());
```

(Note that the `parse()` method expects the URL as a string, not as a Java URL object, hence the need to call `toString()` to achieve the conversion.)

With Java 1.1, the translation of a filename to a URL is a little more difficult than you might expect if you want the code to work equally on Windows and on UNIX, because of the wide variety of filename formats. Here's a method that handles most cases, though the error handling leaves something to be desired:

```
public String CreateURL(File file)
{
   String path = file.getAbsolutePath();
   try
   {
      return (new URL(path)).toString();
   }
   catch (MalformedURLException ex)
   {
      String fs = System.getProperty("file.separator");
      char sep = fs.charAt(0);
      if (sep != '/') path = path.replace(sep, '/');
      if (path.charAt(0) != '/') path = '/' + path;
      return "file://" + path;
   }
}
```

Input from Non-XML Sources

One of the more surprising ways in which SAX has been used is to feed applications with data that is not stored in XML at all. So long as the data is in a hierarchical format that can be mapped reasonably well to the XML data model, you can write a driver that behaves in every way like an XML parser. Your driver sends events such as `startElement()` and `endElement()` to the application's `DocumentHandler` just as if the data originated in an XML document, when in reality there is no XML document there to be parsed.

Why would you want to do this? It allows you to take advantage of applications that were written to accept XML data, without going through the clumsy process of writing your data in XML format and then parsing it again. For example, if you have an application designed to process incoming XML-EDI messages for electronic commerce transactions, you might want also to write a translator that feeds this application with messages arriving in older proprietary formats. One way to do this is for your translator to create an XML file and supply this file to the application. But a neat shortcut, if the target application is written to use SAX, is for your translator to call the application directly, pretending to be an XML parser.

The section below on SAX Filters discusses some of the possibilities using this approach.

Handling External Entities

We often think of XML entities as the markers like `äaut;` appearing in the text of a document. That's not quite accurate: `äaut;` isn't strictly an entity, but an *entity reference.* The entity is the thing that `äaut;` refers to, that is the definition in the DTD that associates the name "aumlaut" with its expanded text "ä".

There are many different kinds of entity in XML and we need to be very careful which kinds we are talking about. As we saw in Chapter 3, they include:

Entity	**Description**
Character references	Characters specified in terms of a numeric code (decimal or hexadecimal), for example `
` or `
` (these are not technically entities at all but we include them here for completeness).
Predefined entities	The special entity references defined in the XML standard, such as `<` and `&` These are the only entity references you can use that do not need a matching definition (either internal or external) in the DTD.
Internal entities	Entities whose expanded text is defined in the DTD (and not as a reference to some external storage object).
External parsed entities	Entities whose expanded text is well-formed XML defined in a separate file referenced from the main XML document by a system identifier or URL.
Unparsed entities	Entities containing non-XML data (for example, binary encoded images): these are always external. The actual format may be identified by a notation.

Entity	Description
Parameter entities	Entities containing parts of a DTD, rather than parts of a document body.
Document entity	The main source XML document is itself an entity.
External DTD	If the document references an external DTD, the DTD is also an entity.

The facilities in SAX for handling entities are concerned with resolving references to external entities, that is, to data held in separate "files" – more strictly, in containers identified by a system or public identifier. Internal entities, character references, and predefined entities are dealt with automatically by the parser and the application gets no chance to intervene in the way they are expanded.

External entities in XML are always identified by a system identifier (which is a URI, which is for most practical purposes the same thing as a URL) and, optionally, by a public identifier. Public identifiers are a carry-forward from SGML: the XML standard (and SAX for that matter) doesn't really say what public identifiers are or how they should be used, though there are conventions based on established SGML practice.

There are various situations where the standard rules for resolving an external entity reference by interpreting its system identifier or URL are not really adequate. These include:

- When the entities are held in a database (or any other place where they are not directly addressable by URL, for example a phrase library in a word processing system).
- When the same entity reference is to be interpreted differently depending on context. For example, the entity reference `¤tUser;` might expand to the name of the currently logged-in user.
- Where there is a versioning system in use, with multiple versions of the same entity, and rules for determining which version to use in given circumstances.
- Where there are many copies of a list of standard entities and the system wants to locate the nearest copy, for performance reasons.
- Where entities are referenced by public identifier rather than URL. Public identifiers have become popular in the SGML world and many publishing shops want to carry on using them with XML too. Traditionally in SGML, public identifiers are mapped to actual files using a lookup table known as a catalog. There is no such mechanism defined in XML, but SAX allows the application to use such a mechanism if it wishes.

Where external entities cannot be found simply by URL, a SAX application should provide an EntityResolver: that is, a class that implements the `org.xml.sax.EntityResolver` interface. The application can register an EntityResolver with the parser by calling the parser's `setEntityResolver()` method.

An EntityResolver needs to implement only one method: `resolveEntity()`. This is called by the parser with two parameters, a system identifier (or URL) and a public identifier. The public identifier will be null if no public identifier was specified in the entity declaration. The task of the `resolveEntity()` method is to return an `InputSource` object, which the parser will use to read the content of the external entity.

There is a simple example of an EntityResolver in the SAX specification, reproduced in Appendix C.

Unparsed Entities and Notations

In general SAX does not provide any information to the application about the contents of the DTD. During the definition phase of SAX, it was decided that this fell outside the needs of most applications, and it was therefore shelved. (As we will see, SAX 2.0 extends the facilities available in this area.)

However, a total ban on access to DTD contents would have made it impossible for a SAX application to deal with a document containing references to unparsed entities and notations. As it happens, these are features of XML that have been very little used, but no-one could predict that at the time, and they still have their enthusiasts. Unparsed entities allow an XML document to contain references to non-XML objects such as binary images or sound, and notations allow the format of such objects to be registered and accurately identified. When an unparsed entity is encountered, the parser (by definition) won't touch it with a barge-pole, so the job of interpreting it is left to the application. But the application can only deal with it if it can identify the external entity and notation, and for this it needs access to the relevant declarations from the DTD.

So the SAX interface `DTDHandler`, whose name suggests that it might provide access to all kinds of goodies in the DTD, actually provides only this minimal and very specialized information concerning unparsed entities and notations. If you need this information, you use the `DTDHandler` just like the other event-handling interfaces: you write a class that implements `org.xml.sax.DTDHandler`, and register it with the parser using the `setDTDHandler()` method. The parser will then tell you about the system identifiers and public identifiers used in unparsed entity and notation declarations in the DTD, and you can use this information later on when you encounter references to these objects (in the form of attributes of type `ENTITY`, `ENTITIES`, or `NOTATION`) in the body of the document.

But don't be disappointed that `DTDHandler` offers less than the name appears to promise!

Choosing a Parser

Under this heading we can usefully consider two separate questions:

- As a designer, how do you decide which product to use?
- As a programmer, how do you make your application configurable so that the parser can be selected at run time?

The first question is really outside the scope of this book. We have listed some of the SAX parsers available, and to be honest there is little to choose between them. They are all effectively free, though the small print of the licensing conditions varies from one to another: try them all and take your pick.

The parsers broadly fall into two categories, those produced by individuals and those produced by corporations. The products in both categories are equally reliable. Those produced by corporations may be better documented and supported, and they are also likely to contain a lot more ancillary features (like support for Mandarin Chinese character encoding, or a COBOL/CICS interface module). Fine if you happen to need that feature; a waste of disk space and download time if you don't.

If you want a parser that does SAX parsing and nothing else, that is fast, reliable and highly conformant to the standard, and if you don't want technical support, there are few products that can beat James Clark's xp parser available from `http://www.jclark.com/xp`. Ælfred (see `http://www.microstar.com/aelfred.html`) is smaller, which makes it a good choice for embedding in your own application, especially in applets where download time is important. The Sun and IBM parsers probably produce more helpful diagnostics for incorrect XML files, so they can be useful in an XML authoring environment. For the other parsers, the main consideration is the environment they run in: the Oracle parser, for example, is an obvious choice in an application that makes heavy use of Oracle products.

In practice it is a good idea to keep your options open: you don't know what parsers will come along in the future, and you don't know whether potential purchasers of your applications might have policies such as "No unsupported software" or "No software that doesn't have French error messages". This means you want to write your application in a way that avoids the crucial statement

```
Parser p = new com.jclark.xml.sax.Driver();
```

which locks you and your customers into one particular product.

If you were running in a distributed object environment such as CORBA (Common Object Request Broker Architecture – see `http://www.omg.org`), the correct architectural approach to this problem would be for your application to delegate the task of finding a parser to the Trader, which could use all sorts of rules to find one that met your run-time needs. The designers of SAX understandably wanted to avoid being dependant on such a run-time environment. Instead they left you with a number of choices:

- You can use the simple helper class `ParserFactory` that comes with the SAX distribution. Your application calls the static method `ParserFactory.makeParser()`. This reads the system property `org.xml.sax.parser` and interprets it as a class name. You can set a system property using the `–D` option on the Java command line, and hence, by writing a command script, from an environment variable.
- You can implement your own mechanism for instantiating a Parser class whose name is determined at run-time. You might hold the name in a configuration file or in the Windows registry. Provided you can read the name as a String, you can use a Java sequence such as the following to create a Parser instance. In practice, you will need to add some error handling to catch the various exceptions that can be thrown.

```
String parserName = [*** read name of parser ***];
Parser p = (Parser)(Class.forName(parserName).newInstance());
```

- You could also build a list of known parsers into your application, and try loading them in turn until you find one that you can load successfully. This allows your users to install any one of these parsers on their classpath, but of course it doesn't allow them to substitute a parser that you didn't know about.

An example of the second technique can be found in the `ParserManager` class from Michael Kay's SAXON package (see `http://users.iclway.co.uk/mhkay/saxon/`). This class instantiates a parser from information in a configuration file called `ParserManager.properties` (provided in the SAXON package). To run the application with a different parser, all that is needed is a quick edit to the configuration file (instructions for this are written in the file). `ParserManager` is a free-standing class which can be used independently of the rest of the SAXON package, and is freely distributable. Once you have installed `ParserManager` and its properties file on the classpath, you can create a SAX Parser simply by writing:

```
Parser = ParserManager.makeParser();
```

We will do this in our subsequent examples.

Some SAX Design Patterns

Our example SAX applications have only been interested in processing one or two different element types, and the processing has been very simple. In real applications where there is a need to process many different element types, this style of program can quickly become very unstructured. This happens for two reasons: firstly, the interactions of different events processing the same global context data can become difficult to disentangle, and secondly, each of the event-handling methods is doing a number of quite unrelated tasks.

So there is a need to think carefully about the design of a SAX application to prevent this happening. This section presents some of the possibilities. We'll look at two commonly used patterns: the filter pattern and the rule-based pattern.

The Filter Design Pattern

In the filter design pattern, which is also sometimes called the pipeline pattern, each stage of processing can be represented as a section of a pipeline: the data flows through the pipe, and each section of the pipe filters the data as it passes through. This is illustrated in the diagram below:

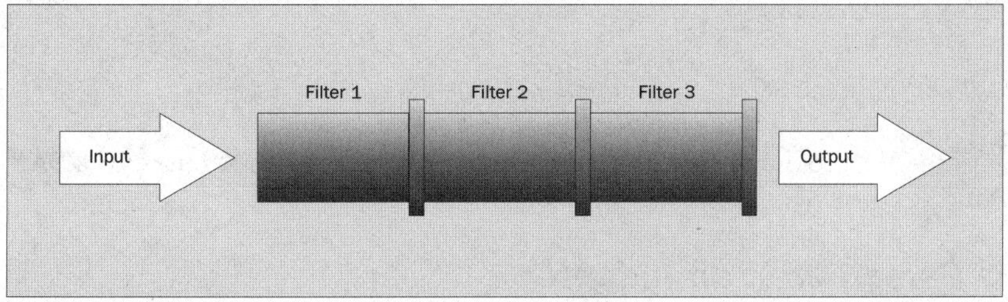

There are many different things a filter can do, for example:

- Remove elements of the source document that are not wanted
- Modify tags or attribute names
- Perform validation
- Normalize data values such as dates

The important characteristic of this design is that each filter has an input and an output, both of which conform to the same interface. The filter implements the interface at one end, and is a client of the same interface at the other end. So if we consider any adjacent pair of filters, the left-hand one acts as the Parser, the right-hand one as the DocumentHandler. And indeed, the filters in this structure will generally implement both the SAX `Parser` and `DocumentHandler` interfaces. ("Parser," of course, is a misnomer here. The characteristic of a SAX Parser is not that it understands the lexical and syntactic rules of XML, but that it notifies events to a DocumentHandler. Any program that performs such notification can implement the SAX Parser interface, even though it doesn't do any actual parsing.)

It is also possible for a filter to have more than one output, notifying the events to more than one recipient, or less commonly, for a filter to have more than one input, merging events from several sources.

The power of the filter design pattern is that the filters are highly reusable, because just like real plumbing, the same standard filters can be plugged together in many different ways.

The ParserFilter class

There are a number of tools around for constructing a pipeline of this form. The simplest is John Cowan's `ParserFilter` class, available from `http://www.ccil.org/~cowan/XML/`. This is an abstract class: it does the things that every filter needs to do, and leaves you to define a subclass for each specific filter needed in your own pipeline.

As you might expect, `ParserFilter` implements both the SAX `Parser` and `DocumentHandler` interfaces; in fact, for good measure, it implements the other SAX event-handling interfaces as well (`DTDHandler`, `ErrorHandler`, and `EntityResolver`). All that the event-handling methods in this class do is to pass the event on to the next filter in the pipeline: it's up to your subclass to override any methods that need to do useful work.

The `ParserFilter` class has a constructor that takes a `Parser` as its parameter: the effect is to create a piece of the pipeline and connect it to another piece on its left. To construct our three-stage pipeline in the diagram above, we could write:

```
ParserFilter pipeline = new Filter3(
                  new Filter2 (
                     new Filter1 (
                        new com.jclark.xml.sax.Driver())));
pipeline.setDocumentHandler(outputHandler);
```

The initial input to the pipeline is of course a SAX `Parser` and the final output is a SAX `DocumentHandler`.

An Example ParserFilter: an Indenter

Here is a complete working example of a `ParserFilter` called `Indenter`. This filter takes a stream of SAX events, and massages the data by adding white space before start and end tags to make the nested structure of the document visible on display. It then passes the massaged data to the next `DocumentHandler` (which might, of course, be another filter).

The code should be self-explanatory. Note how it relies on the methods in the superclass to actually send the events to the `DocumentHandler`:

```
import java.util.*;
import org.xml.sax.*;
import org.ccil.cowan.sax.ParserFilter;

/**
* Indenter: This ParserFilter indents elements, by adding white space where
appropriate.
* The string used for indentation is fixed at four spaces.
*/
```

```
public class Indenter extends ParserFilter {

    private final static String indentChars = "    ";   //indent by four spaces
    private int level = 0;                          // current indentation level
    private boolean sameline = false;               // true if no newlines in
                                                    //element
    private StringBuffer buffer = new StringBuffer();// buffer to hold character
                                                     //data

    /**
    * Constructor: supply the underlying parser used to feed input to this filter
    */

    public Indenter(Parser p) {
        super(p);
    }

    /**
    * Output an element start tag.
    */

    public void startElement(String tag, AttributeList atts) throws SAXException
    {
        flush();                        // clear out pending character data
        indent();                       // output white space to achieve indentation
        super.startElement(tag, atts);  // output the start tag and attributes
        level++;                         // we're now one level deeper
        sameline = true;                 // assume a single line of content
    }

    /**
    * Output element end tag
    */

    public void endElement(String tag) throws SAXException
    {
        flush();                            // clear out pending character data
        level--;                            // we've come out by one level
        if (!sameline) indent();  // output indentation if a new line was found
        super.endElement(tag);              // output the end tag
        sameline = false;                   // next tag will be on a new line
    }

    /**
    * Output a processing instruction
    */

    public void processingInstruction(String target, String data) throws
                                                            SAXException
    {
        flush();                            // clear out pending character data
        indent();                           // output white space for indentation
        super.processingInstruction(        // output the processing instruction
                           target, data);
    }
```

```
/**
* Output character data
*/

public void characters(char[] chars, int start, int len) throws SAXException
{
    buffer.append(chars,        // add the character data to a buffer for now
        start, len);
}

/**
* Output ignorable white space
*/

public void ignorableWhitespace(char[] ch, int start, int len) throws
                                                         SAXException
{
  // ignore it
}

/**
* Output white space to reflect the current indentation level
*/

private void indent() throws SAXException
{
                           // construct an array holding a newline
                           //character
                           // and the correct number of spaces
    int len = indentChars.length();
    char[] array = new char[level*len + 1];
    array[0] = '\n';
    for (int i=0; i<level; i++)
    {
        indentChars.getChars(0, len, array, len*i + 1);
    }
                           // output this array as character data
    super.characters(array, 0, level*len+1);
}

/**
* Flush the buffer containing accumulated character data.
* White space adjacent to markup is trimmed.
*/

public void flush() throws SAXException
{
                           // copy the buffer into a character array
    int end = buffer.length();
    if (end==0) return;
    char[] array = new char[end];
    buffer.getChars(0, end, array, 0);
                           // trim white space from the start and end
    int start=0;
```

```
        while (start<end && Character.isWhitespace(array[start])) start++;
        while (start<end && Character.isWhitespace(array[end-1])) end--;
                                // test to see if there is a newline in the buffer
        for (int i=start; i<end; i++)
        {
            if (array[i]=='\n') {
                sameline = false;
                break;
            }
        }
                                // output the remaining character data
        super.characters(array, start, end-start);
                                // clear the contents of the buffer
        buffer.setLength(0);
    }
}
```

To actually run this example, we will need a `DocumentHandler` that outputs the XML; let's suppose this exists and is called `XMLOutputter` (we'll show how `XMLOutputter` is written in the next section). We can then write a main program as follows:

```
public static void main(String[] args) throws Exception
{
    Indenter app = new Indenter(ParserManager.makeParser());
    app.setDocumentHandler(new XMLOutputter());
    app.parse(args[0]);
}
```

And you will also have to add an import statement for the `ParserManager` class at the top of the file:

```
import java.util.*;
import org.xml.sax.*;
import com.icl.saxon.ParserManager;
import org.ccil.cowan.sax.ParserFilter;
```

We've made the program a bit more realistic by making the input file an argument that you can specify on the command line (retrieved from `args[0]`), and by creating the underlying SAX Parser using the `ParserManager` class that we introduced earlier. It's still not a production-quality program, for example it falls over if called without an input argument, but it's getting closer. Once you have set up the classpath (remember that to use `ParserManager`, the file `ParserManager.properties` must also be on the classpath), you can run this program from the command line, for example:

```
java Indenter file:///c:/data/books.xml
```

The output appears nicely indented. Because the argument is a URL, you can format any XML file on the web.

The End of the Pipeline: Generating XML

Very often, as in the previous example, the final output of the pipeline will be a new XML document. So you will often need a `DocumentHandler` that uses the events coming out of the pipeline to generate an XML document: a sort of parser in reverse.

Surprisingly we couldn't find a `DocumentHandler` on the web that does this, so we've written one and included it here.

Here is the class. It's reasonably straightforward, except for the code that generates entity and character references for special characters, which uses some of Java's less intuitive methods for manipulating strings and arrays:

```
import org.xml.sax.*;
import java.io.*;

/**
  * XMLOutputter is a DocumentHandler that uses the notified events to
  * reconstruct the XML document on the standard output
  */

public class XMLOutputter implements DocumentHandler
{

    private Writer writer = null;

    /**
    * Set Document Locator. Provided merely to satisfy the interface.
    */

    public void setDocumentLocator(Locator locator) {}


    /**
    * Start of the document. Make the writer and write the XML declaration.
    */

    public void startDocument () throws SAXException
    {
        try
        {
            writer = new BufferedWriter(new PrintWriter(System.out));
            writer.write("<?xml version='1.0' ?>\n");
        }
        catch (java.io.IOException err)
        {
            throw new SAXException(err);
        }
    }

    /**
    * End of the document. Close the output stream.
    */
```

```
public void endDocument () throws SAXException
{
    try
    {
        writer.close();
    }
    catch (java.io.IOException err)
    {
        throw new SAXException(err);
    }
}

/**
* Start of an element. Output the start tag, escaping special characters.
*/

public void startElement (String name, AttributeList attributes)
                                            throws SAXException
{
    try
    {
        writer.write("<");
        writer.write(name);

        // output the attributes

        for (int i=0; i<attributes.getLength(); i++)
        {
            writer.write(" ");
            writeAttribute(attributes.getName(i), attributes.getValue(i));
        }
        writer.write(">");
    }
    catch (java.io.IOException err)
    {
        throw new SAXException(err);
    }
}

/**
* Write attribute name=value pair
*/

protected void writeAttribute(String attname, String value) throws
                                                      SAXException
{
    try
    {
        writer.write(attname);
        writer.write("='");
        char[] attval = value.toCharArray();
        char[] attesc = new char[value.length()*8];  // worst case scenario
        int newlen = escape(attval, 0, value.length(), attesc);
        writer.write(attesc, 0, newlen);
        writer.write("'");
    }
```

```
        catch (java.io.IOException err)
        {
            throw new SAXException(err);
        }
    }

    /**
    * End of an element. Output the end tag.
    */

    public void endElement (String name) throws SAXException
    {
        try
        {
            writer.write("</" + name + ">");
        }
        catch (java.io.IOException err)
        {
            throw new SAXException(err);
        }
    }

    /**
    * Character data.
    */

    public void characters (char[] ch, int start, int length) throws SAXException
    {
        try
        {
            char[] dest = new char[length*8];
            int newlen = escape(ch, start, length, dest);
            writer.write(dest, 0, newlen);
        }
        catch (java.io.IOException err)
        {
            throw new SAXException(err);
        }
    }

    /**
    * Ignorable white space: treat it as characters
    */

    public void ignorableWhitespace(char[] ch, int start, int length)
    throws SAXException
    {
        characters(ch, start, length);
    }

    /**
    * Handle a processing instruction.
    */
```

```
public void processingInstruction (String target, String data)
                                              throws SAXException
{
    try
    {
        writer.write("<?" + target + ' ' + data + "?>");
    }
    catch (java.io.IOException err)
    {
        throw new SAXException(err);
    }
}

/**
* Escape special characters for display.
* @param ch The character array containing the string
* @param start The start position of the input string within the character
*             array
* @param length The length of the input string within the character array
* @param out Character array to receive the output. In the worst case,
* this should be
* 8 times the length of the input array.
* @return The number of characters used in the output array
*/

private int escape(char ch[], int start, int length, char[] out)
{
    int o = 0;
    for (int i = start; i < start+length; i++)
    {
        if (ch[i]=='<')
        {
            ("&lt;").getChars(0, 4, out, o); o+=4;
        }
        else if (ch[i]=='>')
        {
            ("&gt;").getChars(0, 4, out, o); o+=4;
        }
        else if (ch[i]=='&')
        {
            ("&amp;").getChars(0, 5, out, o); o+=5;
        }
        else if (ch[i]=='\"')
        {
            ("&#34;").getChars(0, 5, out, o); o+=5;
        }
        else if (ch[i]=='\'')
        {
            ("&#39;").getChars(0, 5, out, o); o+=5;
        }
        else if (ch[i]<127)
        {
            out[o++]=ch[i];
        }
        else
        {
```

```
                    // output character reference
                    out[o++]='&';
                    out[o++]='#';
                    String code = Integer.toString(ch[i]);
                    int len = code.length();
                    code.getChars(0, len, out, o); o+=len;
                    out[o++]=';';
                }
            }

            return o;
        }

    }
```

Now you can see how SAX can be used to write XML documents as well as read them. In fact, you can run SAX back-to-front: instead of the Parser being standard software that someone else writes, and the DocumentHandler being your specific application code, you can write an implementation of `org.xml.sax.Parser` that contains your application logic for generating XML, and couple it to this off-the-shelf `DocumentHandler` for writing XML output!

Other ParserFilters

Let's take a look at some other useful ParserFilters.

NamespaceFilter

This `ParserFilter` implements the XML Namespaces recommendation, described in Chapter 7. It is available from John Cowan's web site at `http://www.ccil.org/~cowan/XML/`.

SAX was defined before the XML Namespaces recommendation was published, and takes no account of it. If an element name is written in the source document as `<html:table>`, then the element name passed to the `startDocument()` method will be `"html:table"`. There is no simple way for the application to determine which namespace `"html"` is referring to.

The `NamespaceFilter` solves this problem. It keeps track of all the namespace declarations in the document (that is, the "`xmlns:xxx`" attributes), and when a prefixed element or attribute name is reported by the SAX parser, it substitutes the full namespace URI for the prefix before passing it on down the pipeline. For example, if the element start tag is `<html:table xmlns:html="http://www.w3.org/TR/REC-html40">` then the element name passed on to the next DocumentHandler will be `"http://www.w3.org/TR/REC-html40^table"`. The circumflex character was chosen to separate the namespace URI from the local part of the element name because it's a character that can't appear in URIs or in XML names.

Sometimes applications want to know the prefix as well as the namespace URI (for example, for use in error messages). `NamespaceFilter` doesn't provide this information, but it could easily be extended to do so.

InheritanceFilter

This is also available from John Cowan's web site at `http://www.ccil.org/~cowan/XML/`.

Many XML document designs use the concept of an **inheritable attribute**. The idea is that if a particular attribute is not present on an element, the value is taken from the same attribute on a containing element. The XML standard itself uses this idea for the special attributes `xml:lang` and `xml:space`, and it is extensively used in some other standards such as the XSL Formatting Objects proposal.

`InheritanceFilter` is a `ParserFilter` that extends the attribute list passed to the `startElement()` method to include attributes that were not actually present on that element, but were inherited from parent elements. The `InheritanceFilter` needs to be primed with a list of attribute names that are to be treated as inherited attributes.

XLinkFilter

This ParserFilter provides support for the draft XLink specification for creating hyperlinks between XML documents. It is published by Simon St. Laurent on `http://www.simonstl.com/projects/xlinkfilter/`.

Unlike most ParserFilters, an `XLinkFilter` passes all the events through unchanged. While doing so, however, it constructs a data structure reflecting the XLink attributes encountered in the document. This data structure can then be interrogated by subsequent stages in the pipeline.

One kind of link defined in the XLink specification is a so-called "inclusion" link where the linked text is designed to appear inline within the main document – rather like a preprocessor `#include` directive in C. The XLink syntax for this is `show="parsed"`. This is very similar to an external entity reference, except that the application has some control over the decision whether and when to include the text: for example, the user might have a choice to display the long or short forms of a document. It would be quite possible, of course, to implement a filter that expanded such links directly, presenting an included document to subsequent pipeline stages as if it were physically embedded in the original document.

Pipelines with Shared Context

One potential difficulty with a pipeline is that each filter in the pipeline has to work out for itself things that other filters already know; a common example is knowing the parent of the current element. If one filter is already maintaining a stack of elements so that it can determine this, it is wasteful for another filter to do the same thing.

You can get round this by allowing one filter to access data structures set up by a previous filter, either directly or via public methods. However, this requires that the filters in the pipeline know rather more about each other than the pure pipeline model suggests, which reduces your ability to plug filters together in any order. Arguably, when processing reaches this level of complexity, it might be better to forget event-based processing entirely and use the DOM (with a navigational design pattern) instead.

The Rule-Based Design Pattern

An alternative way of structuring a SAX application, which again has the objective of separating functions and keeping the structure modular and simple, is a **rule-based** approach.

In general rule-based programs use an "Event-Condition-Action" model: they contain a collection of rules of the form "if this event occurs under these conditions, perform this action". Rule based programming can thus be seen as a natural extension of event-based programming.

The processing model of XSL (discussed in Chapter 9) can be seen as an example of rule-based programming. Each XSL template constitutes one rule: the event is the processing of a node in the source document, the condition is the pattern that controls which template is activated, and the action is the body of the template. We can use the same concepts in a SAX application.

The diagram below illustrates the structure of a rule-based SAX application. The input from the XML parser is fed into a switch, which evaluates the events against the defined conditions, and decides which actions to invoke. The actions are then passed to processing modules each of which is designed to perform one specific task.

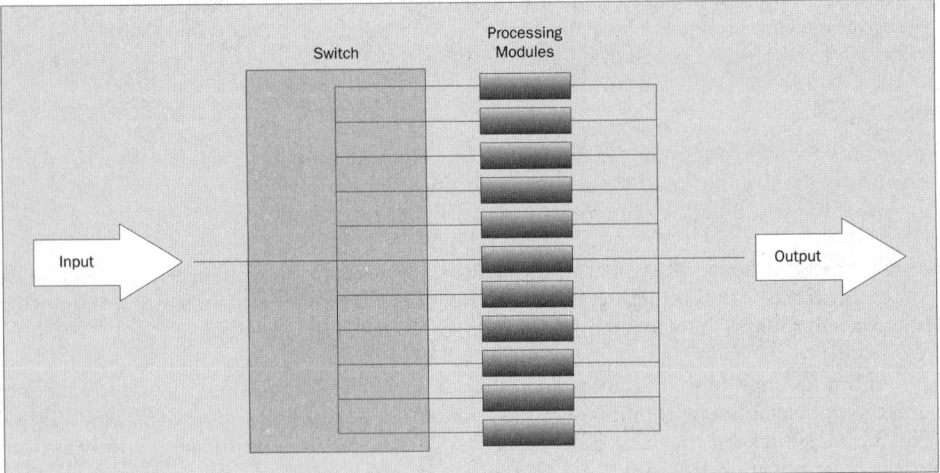

There are all sorts of ways conditions and actions could be implemented, but we'll describe a very simple implementation, where the condition is based only on element type.

Firstly, let's write the DocumentHandler. We'll call it `Switcher` because its job is to switch processing to a piece of code that handles the specific element type.

What `Switcher` does is to maintain a set of rules as a `Hashtable`. The set of rules is indexed by element type. The application can nominate a class called an `ElementHandler` to process a particular element type. When the parser notifies an element start tag, the appropriate ElementHandler is located in the set of rules, and it is called to process the start tag. At the same time, the ElementHandler is remembered on a stack, so that the same ElementHandler can be used to process the end tag and any character data occurring immediately within this element.

Here's the `Switcher` code:

```
import org.xml.sax.*;
import java.util.*;

/**
  * Switcher is a DocumentHandler that directs events to an appropriate element
  * handler based on the element type.
  */
```

```
public class Switcher extends HandlerBase
{

    private Hashtable rules = new Hashtable();
    private Stack stack = new Stack();

    /**
    * Define processing for an element type.
    */

    public void setElementHandler(String name, ElementHandler handler)
    {
        rules.put(name, handler);
    }

    /**
    * Start of an element. Decide what handler to use, and call it.
    */

    public void startElement (String name, AttributeList atts) throws
                                                            SAXException
    {
        ElementHandler handler = (ElementHandler)rules.get(name);
        stack.push(handler);
        if (handler!=null)
        {
            handler.startElement(name, atts);
        }
    }

    /**
    * End of an element.
    */

    public void endElement (String name) throws SAXException
    {
        ElementHandler handler = (ElementHandler)stack.pop();
        if (handler!=null)
        {
            handler.endElement(name);
        }
    }

    /**
    * Character data.
    */

    public void characters (char[] ch, int start, int length) throws SAXException
    {
        ElementHandler handler = (ElementHandler)stack.peek();
        if (handler!=null)
        {
            handler.characters(ch, start, length);
        }
    }

}
```

An ElementHandler is rather like a DocumentHandler, but it only ever gets to process a subset of the events: element start and end, and character data. So although we could use a DocumentHandler here, we've defined a special class. This serves both as a definition of the interface and as a superclass for real element handlers: good Java coding practice might suggest using a separate interface class, but this will do for now:

```
import org.xml.sax.*;

/**
  * ElementHandler is a class that process the start and end tags and
  * character data
  * for one element type. This class itself does nothing; the
  * real processing should
  * be defined in a subclass
  */

public class ElementHandler {

    /**
    * Start of an element
    */

    public void startElement (String name, AttributeList atts) throws
                                                          SAXException {}

    /**
    * End of an element
    */

    public void endElement (String name) throws SAXException {}

    /**
    * Character data
    */

    public void characters (char[] ch, int start, int length) throws
                                                         SAXException {}

}
```

So far this is all completely general. We could use the `Switcher` and `ElementHandler` classes with any kind of document, to do any kind of processing. Now let's exploit them for a real application: we want to produce an HTML page showing selected data from our list of books.

Here's an application that does it. We'll start with the main control structure. What this does is to create a `Switcher` and register a number of `ElementHandler` classes to process particular elements in the input XML document. It then creates a `Parser`, nominates `Switcher` as the `DocumentHandler`, and runs the parse:

```
import org.xml.sax.*;
import com.icl.saxon.ParserManager;

public class DisplayBookList
{

   public static void main (String args[]) throws Exception
   {
      (new DisplayBookList()).go(args[0]);
   }

   public void go(String input) throws Exception
   {
      Switcher s = new Switcher();
      s.setElementHandler("books", new BooklistHandler());
      s.setElementHandler("book", new BookHandler());
      s.setElementHandler("author", new AuthorHandler());
      s.setElementHandler("title", new TitleHandler());
      s.setElementHandler("price", new PriceHandler());
      s.setElementHandler("volume", new VolumeHandler());
      Parser p = ParserManager.makeParser();
      p.setDocumentHandler(s);
      p.parse(input);
   }

//...rest of code goes in here...
}
```

The actual element handlers can be defined as inner classes within the `DisplayBookList` class: this is useful because it enables them to share access to data.

The ElementHandler for the outermost element, "books", causes a skeletal HTML page to be created:

```
   private class BooklistHandler extends ElementHandler
   {

      public void startElement(String name, AttributeList atts)
      {
         System.out.println("<html>");
         System.out.println("<head><title>Book List</title></head>");
         System.out.println("<body><h1>A List of Books</h1>");
         System.out.println("<table>");
         System.out.println("<tr><th>Author</th>");
         System.out.println("<th>Title</th><th>Price</th></tr>");
      }

      public void endElement(String name)
      {
         System.out.println("</table></body></html>");
      }

   }
```

The ElementHandler for the repeated "book" element starts and ends a row in the generated HTML table, and initializes some variables to hold the data:

```
private String author;
private String title;
private String price;
private boolean inVolume;

private class BookHandler extends ElementHandler
{

   public void startElement(String name, AttributeList atts)
   {
      author = "";
      title = "";
      price = "";
      inVolume = false;
   }

   public void endElement(String name)
   {
      System.out.println("<tr><td>" + author + "</td>");
      System.out.println("<td>" + title + "</td>");
      System.out.println("<td>" + price + "</td></tr>");
   }
}
```

Finally, the element handlers for the fields within the <book> element update the local variables holding the data. We're being careless about performance here in the interests of clarity – it would be better to use StringBuffers rather than Strings for the variables.

```
private class AuthorHandler extends ElementHandler
{

   public void characters (char[] chars, int start, int len)
   {
      author = author + new String(chars, start, len);
   }
}

private class TitleHandler extends ElementHandler
{

   public void characters (char[] chars, int start, int len)
   {
      if (!inVolume)
      {
         title = title + new String(chars, start, len);
      }
   }
}
```

```
private class PriceHandler extends ElementHandler
{

   public void characters (char[] chars, int start, int len)
   {
      if (!inVolume)
      {
         price = price + new String(chars, start, len);
      }
   }
}

private class VolumeHandler extends ElementHandler
{

   public void startElement(String name, AttributeList atts)
   {
      inVolume = true;
   }

   public void endElement(String name)
   {
      inVolume = false;
   }
}
```

The flag `inVolume` is used to track whether the current element is within a containing `<volume>` element, in which case it is ignored. Once you've put all this together (the full code can be found in the download for the book at `http://www.wrox.com`) you can run this on a sample XML file with a command like this:

```
>java DisplayBookList file:///c:/data/books2.xml
```

The following output should then appear:

```
<html>
<head><title>Book List</title></head>
<body><h1>A List of Books</h1>
<table>
<tr><th>Author</th><th>Title</th><th>Price</th></tr>
<tr><td>Nigel Rees</td>
<td>Sayings of the Century</td>
<td>8.95</td></tr>
<tr><td>Evelyn Waugh</td>
<td>Sword of Honour</td>
<td>12.99</td></tr>
<tr><td>Herman Melville</td>
<td>Moby Dick</td>
<td>8.99</td></tr>
<tr><td>J. R. R. Tolkien</td>
<td>The Lord of the Rings</td>
<td>22.99</td></tr>
</table></body></html>
```

You can elaborate on this design pattern as much as you like. Possible enhancements include:

- Providing element handlers with access to a stack containing details of their context
- Selecting element handlers based on conditions other than just the element name
- Using element handlers as part of a pipeline, by allowing them to fire events into another DocumentHandler

The advantage of this design pattern is that it avoids a great deal of if-then-else programming. It removes the need to change the DocumentHandler to add conditional logic every time a new element type is introduced. Instead all you need to do is to register another element handler.

SAX 2.0

SAX 1.0 has been very widely implemented and has been in widespread use almost since the day the first draft appeared on 12January 1998 – a month earlier than the date of the final XML 1.0 recommendation. It has met user needs well, in spite of a few criticisms, some of which are hinted at in this chapter.

So it is perhaps unsurprising that the development of a successor, SAX 2.0, has been comparatively leisurely. Requirements were discussed on the XML-DEV mailing list during the early months of 1999, and an alpha version of a revised spec was published by David Megginson (though not widely advertised) on 1 June 1999. There has been little adverse comment, and it seems likely that the final specification of SAX 2.0 will be close to its current form, which can be found on `http://www.megginson.com/SAX/SAX2/`.

Whether the specification will be widely implemented is another matter. Time will tell.

The way in which the original SAX interface has been extended is in itself quite interesting. A standard mechanism has been defined to allow the application to ask the parser to support particular features or to set particular properties; the parser in all cases has the option to refuse. The set of features and properties that can be requested is itself entirely open-ended. SAX2 defines a core set, but additional features and properties can be invented by anyone at any time. To make this possible, the features and properties are identified by a URI, in rather the same way as XML namespaces.

The Configurable Interface

The key new interface in SAX2 is named `Configurable.` A SAX2 parser must implement the `org.xml.sax.Configurable` interface as well as the `org.xml.sax.Parser` interface. The `Configurable` interface contains four methods:

Method	Description
`getFeature(featureName)`	Allows the application to ask the parser whether or not it supports a particular feature.
`setFeature(featureName, boolean)`	Allows the application to request that the parser should turn a particular feature on or off.
`getProperty(featureName)`	Allows the application to request the current value of some particular property.
`setProperty(featureName, object)`	Allows the application to set some particular property to the supplied value.

In each case, if the parser does not recognize the feature or property name, it must throw a `SAXNotRecognizedException`. This means in general that the application will not know whether the parser supports the feature or not. If the parser recognizes the name of the feature or property, but cannot set it to the requested value, it must throw a `SAXNotSupportedException`.

To make this more concrete, consider one of the new core features, whose name is `http://xml.org/sax/features/validation`. This feature is provided to fix the problem in SAX 1.0 whereby an application has no way of discovering or controlling whether the parser is a validating one. With SAX 2.0, if this feature is on, the parser must validate the XML document; if it is off, it must not do so (in other words, the parse must succeed so long as the document is well-formed).

An application that explicitly requires a validating parser may call:

```
parser.setFeature("http://xml.org/sax/features/validation", true);
```

This is a core feature, so every SAX2 parser should recognize its name. A parser that can perform validation will return normally, while a parser that cannot perform validation will throw a `SAXNotSupportedException`.

Equally, an application that explicitly requires the parser *not* to do validation may call:

```
parser.setFeature("http://xml.org/sax/features/validation", false);
```

This time, a parser that insists on doing validation must respond to this request with a `SAXNotSupportedException`.

On the other hand, an application that simply wants to know whether the parser is performing validation or not may call:

```
if (parser.getFeature("http://xml.org/sax/features/validation")) ...
```

Core Features and Properties

The following core features and properties are defined in SAX2. A feature is simply shorthand for a property whose value is a Boolean:

Name (prefixed `http://xml.org/sax`)	Value	Meaning
`/features/validation`	boolean	Perform validation.
`/features/external-general-entities`	boolean	Expand general (parsed) external entities.
`/features/external-parameter-entities`	boolean	Expand the external DTD subset and external parameter entities.
`/features/namespaces`	boolean	Process namespace declarations. Element and attribute names with a prefix will have the prefix replaced by the URI of the namespace
`/features/normalize-text`	boolean	Normalize character data, by ensuring that all consecutive pieces of character data are passed in a single call of the `characters()` method.
`/features/use-locator`	boolean	Supply the application with a `Locator` object by calling the `setDocumentLocator()` method.
`/properties/namespace-sep`	String	Separator to be used between the URI and the local part of a name when the namespaces feature is enabled.
`/properties/dom-node`	`org.w3c.dom.Node`	Read-only property: if the DOM for the source document exists in memory, this property identifies the DOM node relating to the current event.
`/properties/xml-string`	String	Read-only property: a character string giving the XML representation of the current event.
`/handlers/DeclHandler`	`org.xml.sax.misc.DeclHandler`	Set a handler to process element and attribute declarations encountered in the DTD.
`/handlers/LexicalHandler`	`org.xml.sax.misc.LexicalHandler`	Set a handler to process lexical events. These include CDATA sections, entities, and comments.
`/handlers/NamespaceHandler`	`org.xml.sax.misc.NamespaceHandler`	Set a handler to process namespace declarations.

The core properties in SAX2 thus include three new event-handling interfaces: `features`, `properties`, and `handlers`. (Remember, however, that "core" simply means every parser must recognize a request for these features; it still has the right to refuse the request.)

The **declaration handler**, `DeclHandler`, meets the requirement for access to the structural definitions in the DTD. It provides access to element declarations in the simplest possible way, as a string that the application must parse.

The **lexical handler**, `LexicalHandler`, meets the requirement for access to information that was suppressed in SAX 1.0 because it was considered to be of no interest to applications. This includes the boundaries of internal entities, the boundaries of CDATA sections, and the existence of comments. Many application writers asked for these features because they enable the application to minimize the changes made to a document as it is being copied. Comments are needed for other reasons as well: for example, the XSLT recommendation allows a style sheet to say what should happen to comments in the source document, so an XSLT interpreter written using the SAX interface needs access to this information.

The **namespace handler**, `NamespaceHandler`, meets more advanced namespace handling requirements than the namespaces feature. Whereas the namespaces feature simply expands element and attribute prefixes using the namespace definitions currently in force, a namespace handler allows the namespace definitions themselves to be processed as events in their own right. This is useful in several circumstances:

- Where the application uses prefixes in contexts other than element and attribute names (for example, it might use them in attribute values)
- Where the application needs to know the prefix that was used (for example, for use in error messages, or in attempting to copy parts of the original document)

As remarked earlier, the SAX 2.0 specification cannot yet be regarded as stable, so even if you find a parser that supports it, use it with care.

Summary

We've presented some information about the origins of the SAX interface, which is implemented by a wide variety of parsers.

The thing that characterizes SAX, and that distinguishes it from the DOM interface, is that it is event-based. We discussed some of the factors that might cause you to use an event-based interface in preference to the DOM.

We discussed the structure of a simple SAX application, and the relationship of the three main classes, the application, the parser, and the document handler. We showed several examples of how to write SAX applications using these classes.

We presented some of the important design patterns for SAX applications, in particular, the filter or pipeline pattern, and the rule-based pattern.

Finally, we gave a preview of the features that are expected to appear in SAX 2.0 when it stabilizes.

We should end with a word of caution. All the examples shown in this chapter could be coded much more easily in XSLT, which we will discuss in Chapter 9. Of course that doesn't mean there is no need for SAX: Java applications can do many things that XSL style sheets can't – for example, loading data into a relational database; and they will usually be much faster. But it's worth thinking twice about your problem before you rush into assuming that SAX is the answer, because in many cases an XSL approach, or a hybrid approach using XSL for preprocessing, may be preferable.

7

Namespaces and Schemas

The tools for defining XML vocabularies that you've seen so far in this book – the basic rules of well-formed XML as well as DTDs – are the ones provided in the W3C XML 1.0 Recommendation. They are the fundamental parts of the XML world and define the core power of XML for application developers, allowing us (and others) to create markup vocabularies that describe the problem domain we are working in. But as we get to grips with using these technologies, especially in large real world applications, it is common to start to wish that we had a bit more functionality at our disposal.

Before we get stuck into the chapter, let's look at some of the problems with what we have available. However, don't let these worry you, as soon as we have seen what we are missing in the first couple of pages, we will spend the rest of the chapter addressing solutions to all of the problems we outline. Some of the problems you might have already come across, and identifying others will prevent you from spending fruitless hours chasing dead ends.

Firstly, in Chapter 3 we identified some drawbacks with DTDs. These mainly focused around them being written in a syntax other than XML (namely Extended Backus Naur Form) and that they are not expressive enough. So, the first thing to add to our list of problems will be to re-visit these shortcomings of DTDs and look at some attempts to solve them. This will also help us focus on some of the other problems associated with defining your own markup.

Another problem you may have thought of concerns everyone having the ability to create their own tags. You can easily imagine cases of people using the same element names to mean different things. For example, if you consider the use of an element such as `monitor`, it could have several meanings in different circumstances. If you had a DTD for computer peripherals, then monitor may refer to the screen, while in a music studio speakers are often called monitors. If there were a school DTD the monitor element may refer to a student who is given special responsibilities, whereas in a nuclear power plant monitors may be in place to report faults. Even if the meanings were the same, the possible content for the elements may change between definitions. With all of these different potential uses for elements, we need a way to distinguish the particular use of the element, especially if we mix different vocabularies in one XML document. To help solve this problem, there is a specification called XML Namespaces, from the W3C, which allows you to define the context of an element within a namespace.

Furthermore, there are likely to be situations where we need to combine XML documents from different sources, which conform to different DTDs. This may be when we are describing a large body of information, and a single DTD could be unwieldy and hard for human readers to understand, or it could be for an e-commerce application where we need to combine a business partner's data with our own. Unfortunately, the XML recommendation provides no way to mix DTDs in a single document without modifying, or creating a new, DTD (using external references).

Taking this line further, as more and more industry standard DTDs are created, there is an increasing chance that someone will already have created one that will relate to a problem domain you come to work in. If the existing DTD is not perfect for you to use immediately, rather than completely creating a new version, it might be helpful to add your own customizations in a separate DTD, which would still allow you to exchange a certain subset of information in the standard format. As we have just suggested, though, we cannot easily do this with DTDs.

These issues are becoming increasingly important especially considering the promise that XML offers in the realm of electronic commerce, where different companies and users will want to exchange data in formats that make sense to each other. While it is *possible* to read a DTD from code and to reconcile the documents, it is not a simple matter. So, we need some means to discover the differences and similarities of the competing vocabularies so we can establish a connection. To this end, the W3C are working on an alternative type of schema to DTDs, which will be written in XML called **XML Schemas**.

This alternative schema language will address these problems, and a number of other shortcomings of DTDs, which we shall look at later in the chapter. We will start, however, with a look at some of the problems with creating single XML documents from multiple sources.

The problems with creating single documents from sources that are written according to different DTDs and of different schemas using the same element names, concern data about vocabularies – how they are built and where the rules come from. The XML community and its supporters have been working on these problems, and the results are coming to fruition just in time to enable an emerging generation of XML-based electronic commerce. If you are interested in using XML to connect heterogeneous systems developed by disparate teams, you need to understand these new extensions to the XML world.

This chapter will cover the results of some of the XML community's efforts to solve these problems. It will provide you with knowledge of the two tools: **namespaces** and XML **Schemas**. Namespaces help XML vocabulary designers to break complex problems into smaller pieces and mix multiple vocabularies as needed to fully describe a problem in a single XML document. Schemas permit vocabulary designers to create a more precise definition of the vocabulary than is possible with DTDs, and do so using XML syntax.

The two tools answer some of the problems that may arise when using XML to tackle ambitious problems. In particular, namespaces and schemas allow XML designers and programmers to do the following:

- Better organize the vocabularies surrounding a complex problem
- Provide a way to retain strong typing of data when converting it to and from XML
- Describe vocabularies with more precision and flexibility than DTDs permit
- "Read" vocabulary rules in XML, permitting access to vocabulary definitions without increasing parser complexity

XML Namespaces reached W3C Recommendation status on January 14, 1999. Schemas are working their way through the standards process, but a Recommendation is expected soon. The demand for schemas within the application development community is so great, however, that technology previews of schema support are making their way into shipping parsers. This being the case, the schema draft is well worth studying in order to be ready for the rapid transition to schemas expected when a Recommendation is issued.

Mixing Vocabularies

Recall the Book Catalog DTD that we met in Chapter 3. After building a site that exposes your book catalogs as XML written to the `PubCatalog.dtd` vocabulary, you might decide to sell the books on-line. This means that you need to be able to take orders for the books in the catalog. So, you need a DTD that covers ordering of books.

If you continue in the vein of the DTD chapter, you might start adding to the `PubCatalog.dtd` file, because the two areas address different parts of the same problem domain: sharing data about books. They can, however, also be seen as different problem domains because the one addresses the whole of the catalogs details, while the other addresses sale of items from the catalog. While there is some overlap in the information conveyed by the two topics, if you tried to use one DTD to cover both areas, you might end up with one very large or confusing DTD.

DTDs that are large or that contain information about different topics are hard for programmers to read and understand. More importantly, if you're already using the catalog DTD in production, making changes to it now might affect that application. There is a better solution, however, merging data that conforms to separate catalog and order DTDs in a single document using namespaces, so we should explore this possibility. But first, let's take a closer look at the problems you face.

Segmenting a Problem

To begin with, why would you want to mix order details with the catalog DTD? You have at least two areas you're discussing, catalogs of all books and the sales of individual titles. If you think about when you're writing a large program, you break the overall problem into smaller pieces. Modules, classes, components, packages and functions are some of the constructs programming languages offer for this purpose. Designing a vocabulary can be seen as a similar problem to writing a program. You need ways to segment a large problem into multiple vocabularies. However, the problem we have to overcome isn't really one of writing individual DTDs to describe multiple vocabularies, we have already seen how we can do that in Chapter 3. The real problem lies in integrating the DTDs into the body of one document if we segment the definitions into catalog and order DTDs.

Reuse

In our PubCatalog.dtd we made use of the book element. This makes perfect sense in the way that we have talked about marking up our data in a way that describes contents of the element. However, as we are considering taking on-line orders for books, we are likely to want to use the same element name again, when referring to the book that a customer wants to order. Indeed, it is likely that the two would be described differently in the two DTDs. After all, the book element in the order might be a child of an order element, whereas it is a child of catalog in the PubCatalog.dtd.

As we have already suggested, this is a problem that will occur time and again as we create XML vocabularies. When describing real world concepts, we will continually find that common constructs keep appearing. After all, complex creations are built from simple building blocks – color, shape, price, and dimensions, for example – and simple things don't go undefined for long, so there will be many instances of element names that already have definitions and content models.

If either you, or someone else, has already created a DTD that uses these elements, your task will be made easier by borrowing from proven DTDs (indeed code to handle constructs defined in your vocabularies may even be available), this is the concept of **reuse**.

If you are programming for a corporation, you may be confronted with an existing body of DTDs. Borrowing from them can, in fact, make your life easier; while ignoring them makes everyone else's job harder as the DTDs represent an intellectual investment in a particular set of definitions by the programmers involved. These DTDs describe the business problem as others know it. As in real life, building on the DTDs related to books in our example, means that your task is to extend it in a way that flows naturally from the concepts that are already known and defined.

Indeed, if you are programming an application that must connect to an external partner's programs, you have little choice but to reuse existing concepts. The DTDs already in use form a common language you need to speak in order to be understood. Whenever concepts already exist, you should work to be understood in terms of those concepts. The users of pre-existing definitions have made an effort to develop and internalize them. Convincing them to adapt to your view of the problem may be insurmountably difficult. Even if you can accomplish this feat, additional cost is incurred in terms of building new definitions and code, or mapping from an existing DTD to your new one. Reuse saves time, effort, and money.

Ambiguity and Name Collision

Whether you're reusing useful definitions from another designer's DTD or combining segmented DTDs to create a document describing a composite problem, you risk the problems of **ambiguity** and **name collision** if the documents you are using feature elements of the same name. For example, books are a pretty common concept. You can be sure there are several DTDs that declare a Book element, at least for publishers and printers, retailers and libraries. A single usage of the name Book in a document needs resolution to match it with the proper Book element declaration. In our example Book is a name common to both catalogs and orders.

A document marked up using the PubCatalog.dtd may include the following use of the element <Book>:

```
<Book>
   <Title>Professional XML</Title>
   <Abstract>Compendium book containing everything you need to learn to use
            XML in your programming solutions today.</Abstract>
   <RecSubjCategories>
      <Category>XML</Category>
      <Category>Programming</Category>
      <Category>Internet</Category>
   </RecSubjCategories>
</Book>
```

Whereas an order for a book may require the following use of a `<Book>` element:

```
<Order>
...
   payment and shipping information
...
   <Item>
      <Book>
         <Title>Professional XML</Title>
         <ISBN>1-861003-11-0</ISBN>
      </Book>
      <Quantity>3</Quantity>
      <Price US$="49.99" />
      <Discount US$="10.00" />
      <SubTotal US$="119.97" />
   </Item>
</Order>
```

If I'm reading an XML document that includes data from both of the vocabularies, how do I know which definition it refers to?

The problem becomes acute when you use instances of a name drawn from multiple DTDs. Assume we have an application for civil engineers involved in town planning. When talking about lighting, we want to draw on pre-existing DTDs for traffic lights and street lights. Working in isolation, the respective vocabulary designers each chose the word `<Light>` as an element name. Had they known of the eventual use of their DTDs, they might have chosen `<TrafficSignal>` and `<StreetLamp>`, but this future use was not known at the time the DTDs were written. Now we are faced with the specter of documents that have ambiguous `Light` elements.

The declarations for the two uses of `<Light>` are very different. The first declaration covers traffic signals and has an enumeration for its `color` attribute. This enumeration is very important, as there are only three valid colors for our traffic signals. An application can be expected to do some error checking based on the value of this attribute:

```
<!ELEMENT Light EMPTY>
<!ATTLIST Light color (red | yellow | green) #REQUIRED>
```

The second declaration has no such restriction on its `color` attribute's value. Indeed, lamps are often chosen on the basis of cost, not color, although the color is still specified:

```
<!ELEMENT Light EMPTY>
<!ATTLIST Light color CDATA    #REQUIRED>
```

Now consider the following XML document written by an application that mixes the two DTDs:

```
<Inventory>
  <Light color="red"/>
  . . .
  <Light color="white"/>
  ...
</Inventory>
```

From this, we cannot tell whether the `Light` elements refer to traffic lights or street lamps (without checking the constraints on colors implied in the DTD). So, how would a receiving application know whether the `color` attribute's values are acceptable? We don't know which element refers to which DTD, and the value of the second `Light` element's `color` attribute would not be valid for the purposes of traffic lights. The problem is known as **ambiguity** for well-formed documents. Furthermore if the names `Light` and `color` required validation we could make a very big mess of our application, this is referred to as the problem of **name collisions**.

Namespaces

XML **namespaces** are the solution to the problems of ambiguity and name collisions. According to the W3C's Recommendation 'Namespaces in XML' (14 January 1999), a namespace is

> *...a collection of names, identified by a URI reference, which are used in XML documents as element types and attribute names.*

A collection of names that has structure; this sounds like a DTD and indeed, a DTD can be a namespace. In this case the URI could be the address of the DTD on your server, for example:

```
http://www.wrox.com/xmldtds/PubCatalog.dtd
```

The URI need not be a URL, though. (If you are unsure of the differences between the two, we describe them shortly.) In this case the namespace refers to the names used in the `PubCatalog.dtd`. So, if we were to link the use of the `Book` element with this namespace in some way, we would know that any reference to `Book` in a document that was linked with this namespace would refer to the usage as laid out in our `PubCatalog.dtd`.

Where a DTD dictates the entire structure of a document (and does so exclusively), a namespace is no more and no less than a resource from which we can draw just what definitions we need. Having said this, a namespace need not be a formal structural definition like a DTD, and the limited scope of this definition makes namespaces broadly applicable in XML. If the namespace is a DTD or schema, the definitions we use must remain consistent with the structure and syntax specified therein. We are free, however, to use just those names that we need or desire, and use a namespace as a way of distinguishing between the uses of an element.

So, in order to use the namespaces effectively in a document that combines elements from different sources, we need two parts:

- A reference to the URI that defines the use of the element
- An alias that we can use to identify which namespace our element is taken from, this takes the form of a prefix for the element (for example `<catalog:Book>` where `catalog` is the alias for the ambiguous `Book` element.)

Using and Declaring Namespaces

Having seen the advantages that Namespaces offer us in XML, we need to look in more detail at how we actually use them. We will start by looking at how we declare the namespace in a document, and then look at how we can use the namespace within the document, ending up with some examples.

Generally speaking, simple descriptive properties are often modeled as attributes and that is in fact how namespaces are declared in XML. There are a few twists and turns, however, so we'll proceed step by step to learn about what we can specify when we declare a namespace in an XML document.

Declaring a Namespace

If everyone is going to recognize a namespace declaration when they see one, we'll need a reserved word for them. The Namespaces Recommendation gives us `xmlns`. The value of the attribute is the URI that uniquely defines the namespace in use. This URI is often a URL pointing to a DTD, but it doesn't have to be. A URI, managed in such a way as to uniquely differentiate the namespace, is sufficient. Here are some simple namespace declarations:

```
xmlns="http://www.wrox.com/bookdefs/book.dtd"
xmlns="urn:wrox-publishing-orderdefs"
```

The nomenclature surrounding Web resources can be confusing. A Uniform Resource Identifier (URI) is a unique name for some resource. A Uniform Resource Locator (URL) locates the resource in terms of an access protocol and network location. This first example is a URL because it allows a browser to retrieve a resource from a particular location using HTTP. The second example names the resource but provides no location. The literal urn derives from an effort to develop permanent URIs.

Since one of our prime motivations for using namespaces was to be able to mix names from different sources, it might be useful for you to be able to provide an alias you could use throughout a document that would refer to the declaration. You do this by appending a colon and your alias to the `xmlns` attribute. Thus, the examples above become:

```
xmlns:catalog="http://www.wrox.com/bookdefs/PubCatalog.dtd"
xmlns:order="urn:wrox-publishing-sales-orderdefs"
```

Here the prefix `catalog` will refer to elements from the `PubCatalog.dtd`, while `order` will refer to elements declared in the `order.dtd`. After these declarations appear, we can just use `book` to refer to the first namespace declaration, and `order` to refer to the other one (without the URI). How we use these declarations and their aliases lets us provide even more information.

Here are the parts that make up a namespace declaration:

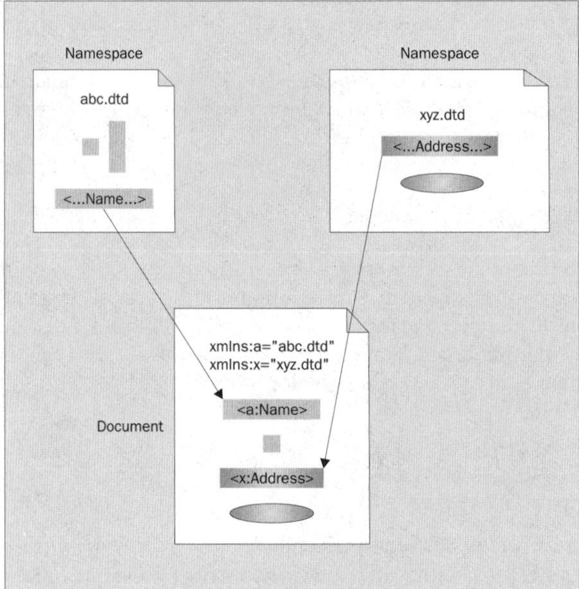

Qualified Names

It does us no good to declare a namespace if we can't tie it to a specific name we want to use. This is done through the use of **qualified names**. This is just what you might suppose it to be – a name qualified by the namespace from which it is drawn. You create a qualified name by taking the alias, known properly as a **namespace prefix**, and tack it on to the beginning of the name. Going back to the question of including a `Book` element in both catalog and ordering DTDs, assume that we declare a catalog namespace with the prefix `catalog` like so

```
xmlns:catalog="http://www.wrox.com/bookdefs/PubCatalog.dtd"
```

we can now use the prefix `catalog` to make it clear which namespace the element came from. So,

```
<catalog:Book />
```

would tell us that the name `Book` comes from the `catalog` namespace declaration. There could be a name `Book` in the `order` namespace as well, yet this qualified name avoids the possibility of ambiguity or collision. The name `Title` is unambiguously qualified as coming from a particular namespace. The namespace prefix is often referred to simply as the **prefix**, and the name itself is the **base name**.

Qualified names can apply to both element and attribute names. Here's an example that mixes some namespaces:

```
<catalog:Book order:ISBN="1-861003-11-0">
```

The element `<Book>` is drawn from the first namespace we saw above, while the attribute `ISBN` is drawn from the `order` namespace.

Scope

Namespace declarations have scope in the same way that variable declarations do in programming languages. This is important because it is not always the case that namespaces are declared at the beginning of XML documents, they can be included within a later section of the document. A namespace declaration therefore applies to the element in which the declaration appears, as well as children of that element even if it is not explicitly specified in the element. A name can refer to a namespace only if it is used within the scope of the namespace declaration.

However, we will also need to mix namespaces where elements would otherwise inherit the scope of a namespace, so there are two ways in which scope can be declared, **default** and **qualified**.

Default

As you might suspect, it could quickly get tiresome to have to add a prefix to every name in a document. In fact, by introducing the concept of name scope to our tool set, we can dispense with a lot of prefixes. If we define a default namespace, all unqualified names within the scope of the declaration are presumed to belong to that default. So, if you declare a default namespace in the root element, it is treated as the default namespace for the whole document, and can only be overridden by a more specific namespace declared within the document.

> **We declare a namespace to be the default for some scope by omitting the prefix declaration.**

Here's how you might use this to embed some HTML within an XML document marked up according to a DTD designed for book content, called `BookContent.dtd`:

```
<Chapter xmlns="http://www.wrox.com/bookdefs/BookContent.dtd">
   <Title number="7">Namespaces and Schemas</Title>
   <Author>I. M. Named</Author>
   <Content>
      <Paragraph>
         Let's have a table:
         <table xmlns="http://www.w3.org/TR/REC/REC-html40">
            <tr>
               <td>A tisket</td><td>A tasket</td>
```

```
            </tr>
            <tr>
               <td>One fish</td><td>Two fish</td>
            </tr>
         </table>
      </Paragraph>
      <Paragraph>This is a very short paragraph</Paragraph>
   </Content>
</Chapter>
```

The elements `<Title>`, `<Author>`, `<Content>`, and `<Paragraph>` and the attribute `number` come from the default namespace defined in the `<Chapter>` element. Within the `Chapter` element, however, you can see the `table` element and its children – `tr` and `td`. These belong to the HTML namespace declared in the `table` element. Note that the scope of the HTML namespace declaration in this example ends when the `table` element closes. The second occurrence of `Paragraph` does not come from the HTML namespace.

When a prefix is declared and then used with a name, the namespace is explicitly stated. For an unqualified name to be reconciled to a namespace, a default namespace must have been declared with a scope that includes the unqualified name (without the prefix).

Qualified

All this is well and good if you can clearly separate your namespaces. But sometimes, you'll want to sprinkle names from foreign namespaces throughout a document. You need a finer degree of granularity. Rather than declaring namespaces all over the place, you can make use of qualified names. Declare the namespaces you will need at the beginning of the document and then qualify them at the point of use.

```
<Measurements xmlns="urn:mydecs-science-measurements"
  xmlns:units="urn:mydecs-science-unitsofmeasure"
  xmlns:prop="urn:mydecs-science-thingsmeasured">
  <OutsideAir units:units="Fahrenheit">86</OutsideAir>
  <FuelTank>
    <prop:Volume units:units="liters">120</prop:Volume>
   <prop:Temperature units:units="Celsius">20</prop:Temperature>
  </FuelTank>
</Measurements>
```

In the root element, `Measurements`, I've declared three namespaces. The default takes care of the elements `<OutsideAir>`, `<FuelTank>`, and `<Measurements>`. However, I need to qualify some readings with units of measure, which I've done with the `units` namespace and the attribute `units:units` drawn from that namespace. Being able to qualify that name is very useful as this attribute pops up throughout the document. Finally, I needed to differentiate between some types of measurements, `prop:Volume` and `prop:Temperature`. Although I could have declared the `prop` namespace in the `<FuelTank>` element, I am free to use this namespace repeatedly (perhaps in a longer document) by declaring the namespace at the beginning and using qualified names.

Take a closer look at the namespace declarations and compare it to the namespace declaration in the `<Chapter>` element of the preceding section. That declaration was tied to a DTD, potentially making it possible to validate the names used against the DTD. In this example, we have unique names, but no DTD URL. Namespaces exist primarily to organize names into distinct sets and avoid name collisions. The W3C Namespace Recommendation says nothing about their use in validation. Indeed, the XML 1.0 Recommendation says nothing whatsoever about namespaces. The XML Schema effort (which we meet later) does more, but any current use of namespaces for validation will strictly remain an artifact of an individual parser's implementation until XML Schemas are an official W3C recommendation.

Using Namespaces in a Well-Formed Book Example

Let's try to markup the content of this book and see if we can use our new tool, namespaces, in a useful way. Assume a content DTD has been created, as in Chapter 3. We'll borrow names from the existing catalog DTD. Rather than recreate markup that exists in HTML, we'll borrow from that namespace, as well. We'll leave aside the issues of validation for now and assume this document need only be well-formed. Pay close attention to the scoping issues. Here's a start on marking up this book, showing the start of this chapter:

```
<Book xmlns="urn:wrox-pubdecs-content"
     xmlns:cat="urn:wrox-pubdecs-catalog"
     cat:ISBN="1-861003-11-0"
     cat:level="Professional"
     cat:pubdate="1999-11-01"
     cat:thread="WebDev"
     cat:pagecount="450">
  <cat:Title>Professional XML</cat:Title>
  <cat:Abstract>The W3C positions on namespaces and schemas are
   presented, together with a review of commercial support.</cat:Abstract>
  <Author>
   <FirstName>Iye</FirstName>
   <MI>M</MI>
   <LastName>Named</LastName>
   <Biographical>
     Iye M. Named is a researcher with the Adaptive Content
     division of Wrox Press. He has many good ideas, which he
     is too shy to mention.
   </Biographical>
   <Portrait piclink="inamed.jpg"/>
  </Author>
  <Chapter>
   <Title>Namespaces and Schemas</Title>
   <Section SectionAuthor="inamed">
     <Paragraph> The tools for defining XML vocabularies that you've seen so far
in this book - the basic rules of well-formed XML as well as DTDs - are the ones
provided in the W3C XML 1.0 Recommendation...
     </Paragraph>
     <Paragraph>Both problems ...</Paragraph>
     <Paragraph>This chapter ...</Paragraph>
     <Paragraph>The two ...
      <UL xmlns="http://www.w3.org/TR/REC/REC-html40">
        <LI>Better organize...</LI>
        <LI>Provide...</LI>
        <LI>Describe vocabularies...</LI>
        <LI>"Read" vocabulary rules...</LI>
      </UL>
```

```
      </Paragraph>
      <Paragraph>XML Namespaces...</Paragraph>
    </Section>
    <Section SectionAuthor="imnamed">
      <Title>Mixing Vocabularies</Title>
      <Paragraph>Recall the Book Catalog DTD...</Paragraph>
      ...
    </Section>
    ...
  </Chapter>
  ...
</Book>
```

I declared two namespaces in the root element. The content namespace is the default as I expect to rely heavily on that namespace and want to qualify as few names as possible. I found it useful to borrow a few names from the catalog namespace, so I declared that namespace with the prefix `cat`. This allowed me to bring in some attributes from the catalog namespace and include them in the root element, which is drawn from the default content namespace. Later, I needed to include a bulleted list. This is well-established in HTML, so I declared another namespace:

```
<UL xmlns="http://www.w3.org/TR/REC/REC-html40">
```

I haven't provided a prefix, so HTML becomes the default namespace, but only for the `UL` element and its children, the list items (`LI`). As soon as we emerge from that scope, with the closing tag for the `UL` element, we revert to the content namespace as our default.

I started this example by advising you that this is a well-formed example. Indeed, if I provided URLs in the namespace declarations that pointed to DTDs and asked you to run it through a validating parser, you'd be in for something of a shock. The XML 1.0 Recommendation makes no provision for more than one DTD per document. Here, although the DTDs are being used as unique names they are not being read for validation, the original DTD has no concept of the names from the HTML namespace. As soon as you try to bring in a foreign name, the parser will indicate an error as the element or attribute you have brought in is not permissible under the first DTD. I hope I've shown you that namespaces are useful. Validation is useful, too. Reconciling the two is just one of the benefits of XML schemas.

Schemas

The first thing to make clear is that a DTD is actually a type of schema. However, when people in the XML community refer to schemas they often mean a replacement for DTDs written in XML syntax, a term that we use in this chapter. There have been a number of proposals for alternatives to DTDs, and the W3C is currently working on creating a standard alternative drawing inspiration from these efforts. In a sense we can think of schemas as a constraint mechanism, in that, while they declare the allowed elements, attributes, etc. we are constraining the users choice of tags and their content models.

Generically, we can refer to schemas as **metadata**, or data about data, and as we shall see some of the schema efforts are not just concerned with defining a vocabulary, they go beyond this attempting to explain the relationships between certain types of data.

If you want to replace DTDs, you need to offer at least the same abilities as they provide. You need to specify the nature and structure of XML documents. Like a DTD, a schema is a description of the components and rules of an XML vocabulary. Schemas refine DTDs by permitting more precision in expressing some concepts in the vocabulary. In addition, schemas make some radical changes. They use a wholly different syntax than DTDs. They permit us to borrow from other schemas, thereby solving the validation problem you encountered in the final namespaces example. They offer datatyping of elements and attributes. Overall schemas really are a better answer to the problem of specifying vocabularies.

XML has done well with DTDs. At the same time, there has been considerable interest in improving on them. This interest has taken many forms with many proposals having been suggested (several of which are available from the W3C site as notes). While this has made for a richer body of work, it has also delayed the adoption of a Recommendation that covers the most common features desired of schemas. In particular, many developers have wanted strong typing, the ability to validate across multiple namespaces, and the use of XML syntax for some time. Fortunately, that situation is now being resolved. As of this writing (January 2000), the W3C Working Group on Schemas is well on the way to reconciling the many contributing proposals for a schema language into a single, useful specification. The improvements schemas bring, as we will see shortly, are of enormous value in enabling the automated exchange of XML documents.

The Problem with DTDs

You may have invested a lot in learning the syntax and rules of DTDs, and the lack of a schema specification shouldn't prevent you from exploring the many avenues of XML and working with some interesting examples. So you might wonder what's so wrong with DTDs that you have to learn a new method. Firstly, it is well worth learning DTDs because (at the time of writing) they provide the only standard for describing your own markup. In addition, there are many markup languages that have already been defined using DTDs, and the ability to read them is very helpful for adopting the markup.

However, as we suggested in Chapter 3, DTDs have a few shortcomings that become apparent as we try to do more with XML:

- they are difficult to write and understand
- programmatic processing of their metadata is difficult
- they are not extensible
- they do not provide support for namespaces
- there is no support for datatypes
- there is no support for inheritance

Let's take a look at each of these problems in turn.

DTDs are Difficult to Write and Understand

DTDs use a syntax other than XML, namely Extended Backus Naur Form (EBNF), and many people find it difficult to read and use. The proposed XML schemas, however, actually use XML to describe the languages they define, removing the difficulty of learning EBNF before learning to read and write them.

Programmatic Processing Of Metadata Is Difficult

The use of EBNF also makes the automated processing of metadata in DTDs difficult. There are, of course, parsers for DTDs. You probably already have one; it's your favorite validating parser. Validating parsers have to load and read a DTD before they can validate a conforming document. However, it is not possible to inquire into the DTD from a program using the DOM. The DOM makes no provision for gaining access to a vocabulary's metadata written in EBNF. Your validating parser reads the DTD and keeps its information to itself. Wouldn't it be nice if DTDs were written in XML so we could explore them as easily as we explore the documents written according to their rules? That feature would allow us to use the DOM to investigate the structure of newly encountered vocabularies or even modify a vocabulary's rules for validation depending on runtime conditions.

DTDs Are Not Extensible And Do Not Provide Support For Namespaces

As we've seen in our examination of namespaces, a DTD is *it.* All rules in a vocabulary must exist in the DTD. You put everything you need into the DTD and you live with it. You can't borrow from other sources without creating external entities.

Having written our `catalog.dtd`, should you want to add a new section to the code, say for a new `<releaseDate>` element, the whole DTD would have to be re-written. Even if you did just copy and paste the majority of it, you would have to be careful to make sure that your existing documents were still valid.

Furthermore, creating and maintaining your own subsets of markup declarations isn't as flexible as simply referring to an existing definition. You can't permit document authors to include something interesting later that isn't found in the DTD. Of course, we don't always want to give document authors this much freedom, but it would be nice to have the option of using parts of an existing schema when designing a new vocabulary.

Again, because all rules in a vocabulary must exist in the DTD, as we have seen you cannot mix namespaces. While you can use a namespace to introduce an element type into a document, you cannot use a namespace to refer to an element declaration in a DTD. If a namespace is used all elements from the namespace must be declared in the DTD.

DTDs Do Not Support Datatypes

One of the greatest strengths of XML is the fact that documents are completely written with a single, common data type – text. When we have our programming hats on, however, we often need to talk about types other than text. DTDs offer few datatypes other than text, which is a serious shortcoming when using XML in certain kinds of applications.

Because DTDs provide no standard mechanism for including the non-textual type of the data we markup, this means we have to share information about data types implicitly, performing the conversion for ourselves as we parse documents. For example, if we wanted to perform a calculation on some numeric element content, we would have to transfer the text into the appropriate datatype before the application could be expected to work with the data.

DTDs Do Not Support Inheritance

With DTDs there is no way of expressing inheritance, so if you imagine that we have a class called `books`, there is no way that we can say that books is a subclass of, say, `publications`, and have `books` inherit from `publications`.

In addition if we divide our books up into three types: Professional level, Programmer's Reference, and Beginners guides, we cannot say that they are sub-classes of books, and get them to inherit the properties of the books class.

In summary, DTDs are fine for defining document structures, and it is easy to understand the choice of DTDs in the XML 1.0 specification when we consider that XML was born out of SGML, which also uses DTDs. However, as we see XML being used in more programmatic situations, rather than just document markup, these limitations become increasingly important.

These, then, are the principal objections that schemas seek to address. Before looking at the current state of the XML Schemas draft, we should review some of the other metadata efforts in the XML community so that we can appreciate the direction in which they are going.

An Abundance of Help Creating Schemas

The academic world wasn't sitting around waiting for the invention of XML before taking on the topic of metadata. Metadata – data about data – is about describing information. This may be as simple as establishing a database schema or as ambitious as discussing the meaning behind the definitions in such a schema.

The academic community – and some of the XML-related metadata proposals – tends toward the ambitious end of this spectrum. One example is **Resource Description Framework** (RDF), a W3C backed effort for describing resources so that they may be discovered automatically. Other proposals have been aimed more at replacing DTDs or representing data in the manner of relational database schemas.

Because of the desire for an XML-based schema language to replace and extend DTDs, a number of proposals were put forward. These include:

- XML-Data
- Document Content Description (DCD)
- Schema for Object-Oriented XML (SOX)
- Document Definition Markup Language (DDML previously known as XSchema)

None of these have directly received formal work backed by the W3C, however each has been considered in the W3C work on XML Schemas.

Our needs fall somewhere in the middle of RDF and a simple XML version of DTDs. We need a way to express structure and content in a simple yet expressive form. While we would certainly appreciate as much expressive power as we might be offered, we are mindful of the fact that simplicity is also a strong factor in getting a proposal implemented in software and accepted by the community. XML itself, after all, is a simplified version of SGML. By reducing the feature set to a core of powerful yet simple features, XML's authors created a simple standard that quickly won wide acceptance.

So, in this section about XML Schemas we will look at some XML-based metadata proposals. First we will look at the ambitious RDF effort, and then two of the other schema proposals, namely XML-Data and DCD. This will give us the background to the work on schemas from the W3C. While looking at these, we will point out some of the major themes in XML-based schemas. The W3C schema group has looked at each of these, and they are intriguing in their range, as a basis for their work upon which the XML Schemas effort builds, drawing inspiration and useful concepts into the latest generation of metadata definition for XML.

After looking at these areas, we will see how the W3C work in progress on XML Schemas is shaping up, and will end the chapter with a look at using the early namespaces and schema support in MSXML.

> *The three proposals we review in this chapter are by no means the only influences on the current W3C XML Schema effort, nor the only metadata efforts progressing in the XML community. You are encouraged to review the efforts on* http://www.w3.org/Metadata/ *and* http://www.w3.org/TR/. *Some other efforts outside the W3C are referenced on Robin Cover's XML site whose index is found at* http://www.oasis-open.org/cover/siteIndex.html. *The three proposals I cover in the limited space below are in the main stream of the XML Schema effort and are sufficient to suggest some of the contributions to XML Schemas. Others of note include Schema for Object Oriented XML (SOX) and Document Definition Markup Lanuage, (DDML, previously known as XSchema).*

Note that we are not trying to teach each of these proposals, rather we are introducing some of the key concepts that are addressed in some of these metadata proposals. As the W3C XML Schema effort has not yet been fully ratified, there are no applications that support it yet for the purpose of examples. However, we will look at a specific syntax that is implemented as a technology preview by Microsoft in their MSXML parser (which ships with IE5 and is available as a standalone component). MSXML uses a subset of the XML Data proposal called XML Data – Reduced. These examples will come nearer the end of the chapter. So let's get on and look at the first of the proposals we will be introducing.

Resource Description Framework

The Resource Description Framework (RDF) is at the more ambitious end of the spectrum in the metadata efforts. It allows a designer to describe objects, add properties to define and describe them, and also to make complicated statements about the objects, such as statements about relationships between resources. Its proposed uses include sitemaps, content ratings, stream channel definitions, search engine data collection (web crawling), digital library collections, and distributed authoring. The specifications come in two sections:

- Model and Syntax
- RDF Schemas

The basic RDF model is a full Recommendation (22nd February 1999). It covers the descriptive data model that can be expressed in XML, as well as other syntaxes. RDF Schemas are a Proposed Recommendation (3rd March 1999) covering an XML vocabulary for expressing RDF data models. RDF draws on the experience of developing the Platform for Internet Content Selection (PICS), a scheme for defining Web content and implementing rating systems, and also draws on earlier academic work in metadata.

Schemas developed with RDF can define not only names and structure, but can also make assertions such as relationships about the things under discussion. RDF can be complicated, but it offers such tremendous expressive power and depth, that its complexity is required for it to be so descriptive.

RDF is oriented around three concepts: **resources**, **properties**, and **statements**.

Resources

Resources can be almost anything – any tangible entity in a conceptual domain that can be referred to by a URI, from an entire web site to a single element in an HTML or XML page. It could even include something that is not available on the web, such as a printed book.

Resources are typed; a class system is used to define categories from which specific resource instances are drawn. Class inheritance is supported, so a designer can specify levels of definition ranging from highly general to narrowly specific. Here are two simple class definitions, the first defines a general `Rocket` class, and the second refines that class through inheritance into a `ChemicalRocket` class. The `rdfs` and `rdf` namespaces are part of the RDF Recommendation:

```
<rdfs:Class rdf:ID="Rocket">
   <rdfs:subClassOf
      rdf:resource="http://www.w3.org/TR/WD-rdf-schema#Resource"/>
</rdfs:Class>

<rdfs:Class rdf:ID="ChemicalRocket">
   rdfs:ClassOf rdf:resource="#Rocket" />
</rdfs:Class>
```

Properties

Resources are said to have properties that define and describe them. Constraints are placed on properties to give them shape. These constraints limit the types of values that can be assigned to a property and the range of literal values from the type that can be chosen. Let's give our chemical rocket some fuel:

```
<rdfs:Class rdf:ID="Fuels">
   <rdfs:subClassOf rdf:resource="http://www.w3.org/TR/
                                    WD-rdf-schema#Resource"/>
</rdfs:Class>

<rdf:Property ID="fuel">
   <rdfs:range rdf:resource="#Fuels" />
   <rdfs:domain rdf:resource="#ChemicalRocket" />
</rdf:Property>
```

Our `fuel` property is typed as being of the `Fuels` class, and the property can take on values from this range. To do this, we would have to make a class declaration similar to the ones above somewhere else in our schema to define this, perhaps providing literal values for the rocket fuels we wish to discuss. The fuel property applies to the `ChemicalRocket` class, its domain.

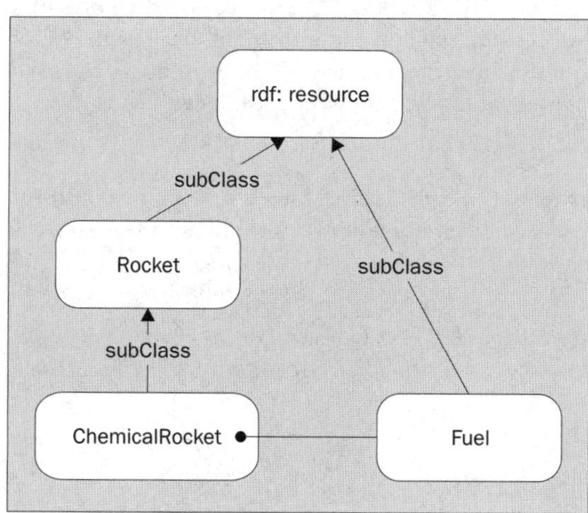

Statements

Once names and structure are defined through resources and properties, statements about the conceptual domain can be made. This is done by composing triplets of **subject** resources, **property** predicates, and **value** objects. The values can be literals for specific statements, or resources for powerful and sweeping statements about entire classes. Let's make a simple statement about a particular rocket in a document conforming to our RDF schema. First, you begin by declaring an instance of the `ChemicalRocket` class and giving it a name:

```
<?xml version="1.0" ?>
<rdf:RDF xmlns="http://www.w3.org/1999/02/22-rdf-syntax-ns#">
   <ChemicalRocket ID="Moonship" xmlns="urn:my-rdf-rocket-schema"/>
   <rdf:Description about="Moonship">
      <fuel>hydrogen</fuel>
   </rdf:Description>
</rdf:RDF>
```

Once we've declared our rocket instance, `Moonship`, using the `ID` attribute of the resource, we proceed to an RDF `Description` element. I've provided a particular value, `hydrogen`, to the fuel property (remember, `Moonship` is an instance of `ChemicalRocket`, and that class uses the `fuel` property). This may seem like a lot of work to do something very simple, but we can use this same syntax to make statements about classes, as well. As you make more statements within this schema, you will develop a rich body of explicit knowledge about the problem domain.

RDF is powerful, permitting tremendously expressive and sweeping statements. It answers the strong typing limitation of DTDs; indeed, strong typing is central to an RDF schema. Unfortunately, designing an RDF schema is a laborious process involving the declaration of many classes and properties. The ability to make meaningful statements, while appreciated, is probably a more powerful feature than we need for the purposes of defining XML vocabularies.

This is not to say that they are not useful in other situations. RDF statements let us formally describe facts in a machine-readable format. Normally, the XML vocabularies we write rely implicitly on commonsense understanding of the underlying real-world concepts. With RDF statements we could, at least in theory, provide enough information that an application could discover additional facts about a vocabulary. This would enable it to make better use of a new vocabulary and decide when it is applicable to a problem at hand. RDF will let an application drill down to the basic facts of a domain, at least to the point where we must engage in metaphysical discussions of whether a machine can understand the way people do. In short, then, RDF gives a tool for providing a description of the environment surrounding a vocabulary, one which tools can use to place a vocabulary in its proper context.

For a designer laboring over the task of defining names, structure, and relationships, though, this might be one burden too many. Our next metadata proposal takes a few steps down on the scale of expressiveness and generality.

Further information regarding RDF may be found at http://www.w3.org/TR/REC-rdf-syntax *(basic model) and* http://www.w3.org/TR/PR-rdf-schema *(RDF Schemas).*

XML Data

XML Data aims for a more modest scope than RDF. This proposal was submitted to the W3C by ArborText, DataChannel, Inso, and Microsoft, and is clearly focused toward automated documents and processing, but is still more ambitious than DTDs.

XML-Data makes a distinction between **syntactic** and **conceptual** schemas. While both use the same language, they provide different ways for us to think about the data we are marking up.

A syntactic model is a set of rules describing how to write documents using markup, as such DTDs are an example of syntactic schemas. In an XML document marked up according to our catalog DTD, a `<Book>` element can legally contain `<Title>`, `<Abstract>`, `<RecSubjCategories>`, and `<Price>` elements. A syntactic XML Data schema of this would represent similar constraints on the structure of the vocabulary.

Conceptual models, however, describe relationships between concepts or objects and as such they are ideal for modeling relational databases. We could use an XML Data schema to suggest the relationships that books have titles and prices, in a manner separate from the syntax of any XML document. In this sense XML Data was intended to broaden XML's reach to readily encompass information from relational databases. The principal relationships captured by the keys in a relational database can be captured formally in an XML Data schema. With namespaces, we can capture ad hoc relationships such as those in an ad hoc join by declaring namespaces for the joined tables and qualifying the columns in the query according to the table from which they come. We discuss the use of schemas with databases in Chapter 10.

XML Data provides some interesting tools that make it more powerful than DTDs. These tools address several of the problems we found in DTDs, so let's take a look at some of them and how they can be used:

Written in XML

XML Data uses an XML vocabulary for the construction of schemas, which allows users to read and write schemas without having to learn a new syntax first. It also means that we can use the DOM and existing parsers to peruse a schema or create a new one dynamically.

Continuing the conceptual schema metaphor, we could dynamically create a schema for an ad hoc SQL query based on the query itself. The recipient of the data would have both data and formal structure and would never know that this was dynamically generated.

Data Typing

XML Data adds strong typing of elements and attributes, thereby answering one of our prime objections to DTDs. These may be basic types defined by the datatypes namespace, or complex, user-defined types provided in a schema provided by the designer. There is no longer a need for applications to implicitly understand the datatype of some element or attribute and convert the strings of text into the appropriate format before using the data. This information can be explicitly specified in the schema, and parsers can perform the conversion on behalf of the application.

Constraints on Allowed Values

XML Data allows constraints on the range of values for elements and attributes to be defined, such as minimum and maximum. This can be extremely helpful in a lot of situations where you are validating XML documents. If you imagine an ordering scenario where you only accepted minimum orders worth over one hundred dollars, but to a maximum value of one thousand dollars, you could impose these constraints in an order schema written in XML Data. In an alternative sense you could use constraints to prevent people from spending any money if their account has no funds, or prevent them from inputting values that were not valid.

Inheritance of Types

An interesting reuse mechanism is XML Data's support for inheritance of types. This lets us evolve and extend elements as we describe the entities in the problem we are trying to solve with XML. We can write some generally expressive supertypes, then refine them into more specific classes of elements by adding members to or replacing members of the supertype declaration. Entities may be used this way in DTDs, but type inheritance formalizes the process. Without a formal set of semantics, entities can be misused to the point where they confuse rather than enlighten the user. A formal inheritance mechanism gives us a tool for promoting reuse while keeping some control of how the tool is used.

Open and Closed Content Models

Another powerful feature of XML Data is the notion of **open** and **closed content models**. A classical DTD is a closed model. Documents conforming to it must adhere to the rules and may not include anything that does not follow the rules, because all rules in a vocabulary must exist in the DTD.

If a schema is open, documents conforming to it may include other information not declared in the DTD. The parts that conform to the schema must obey the rules laid down in the schema, but we can insert other items without restriction from the current schema. These items may be defined in another schema or may be completely unconstrained. We might insert ad hoc values. More importantly from the standpoint of our current discussion, open model documents are the way we can mix namespaces. We can embed a chunk of information conforming to one schema right in the middle of a document conforming to another. More formally, individual elements may be explicitly declared to have open or closed content models. This is done through the `content` attribute. The default value for this attribute is open. Here is an example:

```
<elementType id="Person" content="closed">
   <element type="#name"/>
   <element type="#address"/>
</elementType>

<!-- This document fragment is invalid due to the added Telephone element -->
<Person>
   <Name>John Doe</Name>
   <Address>123 Anywhere Street Blasted Rock, NV</Address>
   <Telephone>555-1212</Telephone>
</Person>
```

Had the `content` attribute in the above example been given the value open, the fragment would have been valid.

Expanded ID and IDREF constructs

XML Data extends `ID` and `IDREF` constructs with relations. In a **relation**, one element acts as a key or index into another element's content. This is directly applicable to the primary and foreign keys of relational databases. It is also particularly useful in bilingual documents. Two are of particular interest: aliases and correlatives.

An **alias** is used to define an equivalent element, so in our example we may have `<Book>` in the English document and want to translate the tags to `<Livre>` in the equivalent French elements.

Other times we will want to suggest that two tags describe identical things, this is done using a **correlative**.

To think about this in a different way we may have a shopping document, in which we have a `<Purchaser>` element, which refers to a `<Customer>` element elsewhere. The correlative for `<Purchaser>` is `<Customer>`, indicating that `<Purchaser>` is an alias for `<Customer>`. This will be familiar to database designers from their work with entity relationship diagrams.

As you can see, XML Data directly answers all our objections to DTDs. We will not go further with practical information on XML Data quite yet, as a reduced form of the proposal appears in the schema support provided by the XML parser that comes with Microsoft Internet Explorer 5.0. We will study that support in depth later in this chapter.

> *More information on XML Data may be found at http://www.w3.org/TR/1998/NOTE-XML-data/.*

Document Content Description

The Document Content Description (DCD) proposal followed on the heels of the XML Data proposal. It was submitted by IBM, Microsoft, and Textuality. It is an RDF vocabulary expressly designed for the purpose of declaring XML vocabularies. Its backers used the expressive power of one metadata standard – RDF – to create a proposed standard with more modest scope. This is in the same spirit as XML's creation as a simplified subset of SGML.

DCD is syntactically similar to XML Data, although some of the more advanced features of XML Data are gone. DCD has no mention of relations and correlatives. It is strictly focused on defining XML vocabularies. It does, however, retain the strong data type support of XML Data, as well as element inheritance. Like XML Data, DCD permits a vocabulary designer to declare a schema model either open or closed. Unlike XML Data, DCD uses the same mechanism for declaring schemas open or closed as it uses for element definitions. Like XML Data, DCD permits the specification of constraints on the value of element content. For example, an element named `<SmallInvestment>` may be declared to be a fixed numeric type with constraints on its permissible values, say greater than zero and less than or equal to ten thousand.

```
<ElementDef Type="SmallInvestment" Datatype="fixed14.4" MinExclusive="0.00"
Max="10000.00">
```

DCD, while drawing from the rich body of RDF, is a direct assault on the problems of DTDs. It exchanges broad power for focused simplicity. Since it is so similar to both XML Data and the schema support in Internet Explorer, we will not go into greater depth on DCD. For the purposes of understanding the W3C schema efforts, however, remember that DCD is the simple end of the metadata spectrum. It focuses with sharp precision on the immediate problems of DTDs and forgoes depth in order to provide a readily implemented standard for XML schemas.

> *The W3C Note concerning the Document Content Description proposal may be found at http://www.w3c.org/TR/NOTE-dcd/.*

Finding the Right Balance

These proposals represent a selection of the spectrum of metadata capabilities. They are by no means the only efforts that have had an influence on XML Schemas.

Consider them, though, in the context of this book. Ask yourself "What is really needed to facilitate the use of XML in networked applications?" Answers to our earlier objections are a minimum set of requirements. In fact, for intranet applications, we might even get along without the ability to read schemas with XML parsers. I would argue for another requirement: simplicity. Application integration, particularly over the public Internet, cries out for simple, reliable solutions. Complexity is an invitation to failure, and delayed delivery. Just as simple XML rapidly outstripped complex SGML in popularity and rate of adoption, I believe a simple yet effective metadata proposal will best answer our needs.

RDF is admirable in its scope. It will likely find use in specialized arenas that require its powerful range of expression. It is unreasonable to expect, however, that a standard this complicated is going to become an integral part of the Web application developer's tool kit anytime soon. XML Data and DCD are closer to the mark; they have stripped out complexity in favor of what their promoters perceive to be the essentials. This is a difficult line to draw. Are the relations of XML Data necessary or not? Much depends on the nature of XML-based applications in the next few years.

We need something sooner than that. Metadata activity at the W3C has gathered momentum, perhaps in response to the many competing contributions from all sources. A working group devoted to XML Schemas has been hard at work and is hoping to reach Recommendation status during 2000. XML Schemas owe much to RDF, XML Data, DCD, and several other proposals. The current effort seems to be gravitating toward the simple end of the spectrum, which bodes well for timely completion of the initial effort (although it may well be extended at a later date). As this hoped to be an approved Recommendation of the W3C soon after the release of this book, we will examine this draft in depth.

W3C Work on XML Schemas

The W3C XML Schema Working Group has a two part working draft for XML Schemas dated 17 December 1999. As with any working draft, particular features and syntax are subject to change in later versions. These schemas answer our main objections to DTDs that we talked about earlier in the chapter. They are written in XML syntax, they permit the use of multiple namespaces, and they provide for strong typing of content. They are, moreover, a superset of the capabilities of XML 1.0 DTDs. Their expressive power is greater than DCD, but it is far less abstract than RDF. In short, this is a promising metadata effort.

The Working Draft of 17 December 1999 is divided into two sections: **structures** and **datatypes**.

The structures section, XML Schema Part 1: Structures, deals with the description and declaration of elements and attributes. The material provided therein allows an XML designer to specify complex element structure and set constraints on the permitted values of the content of those elements. This part of the specification can be found at http://www.w3.org/TR/xmlschema-1/

The second part, XML Schema Part 2: Datatypes, sets forth a standard set of content datatypes as well as the rules for generating new types from them. This part of the specification can be found at http://www.w3.org/TR/xmlschema-2/.

DTD vs. XML Schema: A Contrast

Hopefully, you are by now eager to learn about the formal syntax of XML Schemas. Just to make sure that this is so, let me provide a very simple DTD and its translation into XML Schema form. For all that I've talked about schemas and their features, I haven't let you see an example. Seeing the contrast between current practice – DTDs – and what we hope will become future practice – schemas – will show you how dramatically things will change. It may also give you some insight into some of the things we have been talking about so far. Don't worry too much about the syntax of the schema. We will explore that at length in the sections to come. Try to take in the big picture and use it as a frame of reference going forward.

Consider the following DTD for naming a person:

```
<!ELEMENT   Name         (Honorific?, First, MI?, Last, Suffix?)>
<!ELEMENT   Honorific    (#PCDATA)>
<!ELEMENT   First        (#PCDATA)>
<!ELEMENT   MI           (#PCDATA)>
<!ELEMENT   Last         (#PCDATA)>
<!ELEMENT   Suffix       (#PCDATA)>
```

We must minimally have first and last names, but we may optionally have a middle initial, honorific (Mr., Ms., Dr., etc.) and a suffix (Jr., III, etc.). Here is what it looks like in a schema:

```
<Schema ...>
   <element name="Name">
      <type>
         <element name="Honorific"
                  type="string" minOccurs="0" maxOccurs="1"/>
        <element name="First" type="string"/>
         <element name="MI"
                  type="string" minOccurs="0" maxOccurs="1"/>
         <element name="last" type="string"/>
         <element name="suffix"
                  type="string" minOccurs="0" maxOccurs="1"/>
      </type>
   </element>
</Schema>
```

The schema form is somewhat longer, but you will notice we specify a bit more information. To start with, we have a <Schema> element as the root of the schema. Then we have an element called Name, the name of which is set in the name attribute of the <element> tag, so:

```
   <element name="Name">
```

declares a <name> element. What is that for? I've used it in its simplest form here, but you should know it can be given a name and enclose element declarations. In such a form, it is suitable for reuse elsewhere, and specifies the content model of the <Name> element. Note how the elements contained within <Name> are declared. Since they are simple types (such as strings or PCDATA), we can declare them within the body of the <Name> declaration without further elaboration. You'll see that XML Schemas provide a longer list of basic types than we have with DTDs today.

Note how the optional elements are specified. With schemas we can specify the minimum and maximum number of times an element appears. This can lead to content models of greater complexity than we can specify in a DTD.

Above all, though, note the obvious – the schema is XML. The DOM manipulations you learned in previous chapters can be used to walk through this schema in a program and take it apart. This cannot be said for the DTD form.

Structures

Everything we can define with a DTD is accounted for in the Structures portion of XML Schemas. As XML Schemas are written in XML syntax, structures refer to the XML constructs that we can use to define our markup. Of course, this means that XML Schemas are really just another application of XML (an XML vocabulary for defining classes of XML document), and as such could have a schema to describe itself (in fact both a Schema and a DTD are provided in the appendices for the Structures section of XML Schemas to describe the schema vocabulary).

So the structures section of the specification is the part where the elements and attributes for defining schemas are set out. More importantly, the **content model** for elements is described in this part. Content models explicitly specify the allowable internal structure of elements. Structures are the heart of XML Schemas. So, let's consider these in detail.

Writing Schemas

A schema consists of a **preamble** and zero or more definitions and declarations. The next few sections discuss these definitions, so let's start with the preamble.

Preamble

The preamble is found within the root element, `schema`. This must include at least three pieces of information in attributes:

- `targetNS`, which is the namespace and URI of the schema you are using
- `version` to specify the version of this schema
- `xmlns` which provides the namespace for the XML Schemas specification
- optionally, `finalDefault` and/or `exactDefault`, to provide defaults for two types of extension that we shall take up much later

It may also include export, import, and include constructs, which we shall discuss later. Here is a sample schema showing the preamble:

```
<?xml version="1.0"?>
<schema targetNS="http://myserver/myschema.xsd"
        version="1.0"
        xmlns="http://www.w3.org/1999/XMLSchema">
   ...
</schema>
```

Here, our hypothetical schema is residing on `myserver`, and is called `myschema.xsd`, `.xsd` being the file extension for XML Schemas. It is in its first version. The default namespace declaration is the schema reference to *XML Schemas: Structures*, and this is a closed model schema, which means that all documents conforming to this schema will be completely defined by the schema and must not have any outside content.

Simple Type Definitions

The structures defined for XML Schemas rely heavily on type definitions. These allow a schema designer to declare extended types that can be used throughout a schema. They will be used to specify the content and type of elements and attributes. Let's start simply, though. A **simple type definition** is used to constrain information that does not include elements. It consists of a name and a specification that is either a reference to another type definition or consists of a series of **facets**. Facets will be described fully in the datatypes section, later in this chapter. A free-standing simple type definition is found in a datatype element:

```
<datatype name="smallInt" source="integer"/>
   <minExclusive value="0"/>
   <maxExclusive value="10"/>
</datatype>
```

We'll discuss this construction at length under datatypes. We can also have a simple type definition within other declarations, such as attributes. This is done with the `type` attribute, `type="smallInt"`, for example, which tells us the type of the declared item.

Complex Type Definitions

These are essential constructions in XML schemas. Without them, we would be unable to compose nontrivial content models for elements. The `<type>` element encloses a complex type definition. Nested within it, we have declarations for elements and attributes, or references to model groups. For example:

```
<type name="someContent">
   <element .../>
   <attribute .../>
</type>
```

Complex Type Definitions may become much more involved. This will be difficult to understand until we have learned how to declare attributes and elements. Pay attention to the `<type>` elements you see as we move forward and you will see what I mean.

Attributes and Attribute Groups

Attribute declarations consist of an `<attribute>` element, which must minimally include a `name` attribute. The `<attribute>` element also has optional cardinality attributes, `minOccurs` and `maxOccurs`, which are used to indicate whether the attribute must appear, and if so, how often. A `type` attribute specifies the datatype of the attribute, such as string or integer. An attribute declaration may also have `default` and `fixed` attributes. These function much like the `IMPLIED` and `FIXED` keywords in DTDs. The value of the `fixed` attribute is the value the attribute must always have. The value of the `default` attribute is the value which is assumed if the attribute does not explicitly appear in an element within an XML document. Here are a couple of sample attribute declarations:

```
<attribute name="simpleAttr"/>

<attribute name="sequenceNo" type="integer" default="0"/>
```

We will often encounter a group of related attributes that are applied to multiple element declarations in a schema. XML schema structures accommodate this with the idea of attribute groups. This is a named collection of attribute declarations:

```
<attributeGroup name="troopParameters">
   <attribute name="serialNum" type="string"/>
   <attribute name="rank" type="string"/>
</attributeGroup>

<type name="officerParms">
   <attributeGroup ref="troopParameters"/>
</type>
```

Here we've declared the `troopParameters` attribute group, then used it within the `officerParms` type definition.

Content Models

We won't get far without content models, and XML Schemas provide us with mechanisms for describing content models with a lot more accuracy than DTDs. These use complex type definitions and a new structure, the `<group>` element, to build the internal contents of an element declaration.

We now need another attribute for type elements, the `content` attribute. The `content` attribute tells us what elements can be contained (although it says nothing about permitted attributes):

Content attribute value	meaning
`unconstrained`	Content of any kind
`empty`	Empty element
`mixed`	Elements and character data

For example:

```
<type name="WideOpen" content="unconstrained"/>

<type name="NothingHere" content="empty"/>

<type content="mixed">
   <element ... />
</type>
```

Things become more interesting when we get to element-only content. Now we need some content operators – termed **compositors** in the Schema draft – to show how content may be composed. These compositors are the value of the `order` attribute of a `<group>` element. This new element gives us a way to provide ordered bodies of elements in a declaration. The compositors are shown in the following table:

Compositor keyword	Meaning	DTD equivalent
`seq`	Elements must follow in exact order	, (comma)
`choice`	Exactly one of the model elements appears	| (pipe)

Element Declarations

Here, we can immediately see how XML is used to make the syntax of schemas an XML application, where we had to use the `<!ELEMENT` syntax to declare a `<Book>` element in a DTD we now put element declarations inside an XML element, so we use:

```
<element name="Book" />
```

Here the `<element />` element is used to declare an element (the element is describing its content in keeping with the idea of self-describing data). The `name` attribute simply takes a value of the element we are creating.

Simple elements are composed of a reference to a data type and a series of attribute declarations or a reference to an attribute group. This is analogous to a DTD declaration where the element contains only PCDATA, except that the content is strongly typed. For example:

```
<element name="ZIP" type="string"/>
<element name="windspeed" type="float"/>
```

These would correspond to:

```
<!ELEMENT ZIP #PCDATA>
<!ELEMENT windspeed #PCDATA>
```

Of course, there would be no notion of the string and floating-point numeric types from the DTD declarations. When we want to define an element with structure, we replace the data type reference with a content model. Let's leave that aside for a moment and see how we make an element declaration by adding references to other declarations. Let's specify the schema for this simple fragment of XML:

```
<Name>
   <First>John</First>
   <MI>A.</MI>
   <Last>Doe</Last>
</Name>
```

Here are the required element declarations:

```
<element name="First" type="string"/>

<element name="MI" type="string"/>

<element name="Last" type="string"/>
```

```
<element name="Name">
   <type>
      <group order="seq">
         <element type="First" type="string" minOccurs="1"/>
         <element type="MI" type="string" minOccurs="0"/>
         <element type="Last" type="string" minOccurs="1"/>
      </group>
   </type>
</element>
```

This starts out simply enough. `First`, `MI`, and `Last` are strings. Note that I've made `MI` a string to accommodate long middle initials, such as `O'M` or `A. G.` Now we'll wrap them together into the composite element `<Name>`.

Examples are often the best way to learn, so here are some more examples and their DTD equivalents:

```
<element name="ListOfNames">
   <type>
      <group order="seq">
         <element type="CustomerName"/>
         <element type="SalesName"/>
         <element type="ProductName"/>
      </group>
   </type>
</element>

<!ELEMENT  (CustomerName, SalesName, ProductName)>
```

```
<element name="PickOne">
   <type order="choice">
      <group order="choice">
         <element type="ColumnOne"/>
         <element type="ColumnTwo"/>
      </group>
   </type>
</element>

<!ELEMENT  PickOne  (ColumnOne | ColumnTwo)>
```

Now, we'll want to be able to specify multiple occurrences of element content. To do this, we use the `minOccurs` and `maxOccurs` attributes on the element references. When we get to model groups in a little while, we'll see that we can apply these attributes there as well to build more complicated content models.

Model Groups

Some other schema constructs give us the ability to compose building blocks of definitions and declarations. As we have seen, we can have a **model group** within a particular type, to which we can then give a name. This construct enables us to build complex content models as we can refer to a **named model group** to build some part of an element content model for reuse in types and element declarations by putting a name to a model group, thereby allowing us to reference it elsewhere. Here are some samples:

```
<type minOccurs="1" maxOccurs="2">
   <group order="seq">
      <element type="A"/>
      <element type="B"/>
   </group>
   <group order="choice" minOccurs="3" maxOccurs="7">
      <element type="C"/>
      <element type="D"/>
   </group>
</type>
```

In this model, every document will start with a sequence of AB. This will occur at least once, perhaps twice. Next, we can choose between C and D and make the choice three to seven times. Finally, we bring all our elements back one last time in any order. The following would be a legal document fragment conforming to this content model.

```
<A/><B/><A/><B/>   <!-- sequence -->
<C/><C/><D/><C/>   <!-- choice -->
```

You can also nest groups to form complex content models. For example:

```
<group order="seq">
   <group order="choice">
      <element type="A"/>
      <element type="B"/>
   </group>
   <group order="choice">
      <group order="choice">
         <element type="A"/>
         <element type="B"/>
      </group>
      <group order="seq">
         <element type="B"/>
         <element type="C"/>
         <element type="D"/>
      </group>
   </group>
</group>
```

The equivalent DTD content model for some element <foo> is:

```
<!ELEMENT foo ((A | B), ((A | B) | (B, C, D)))>
```

Now consider how we can use content model groups if we can refer to them by name:

```
<group name="partsGroup" order="seq">
   <element type="BigParts"/>
   <element type="LittleParts"/>
</group>

<element name="PartsAndTheirMeasures">
   <type>
      <group ref="partsGroup"/>
      <attribute name="count" type="integer"/>
      <attribute name="size" type="integer"/>
   </type>
</element>
```

In the preceding example, I defined a content model, then incorporated it into an element declaration. The combination of these constructs gives schema designers flexible reuse and permits the specification of vocabularies with great economy.

```
<attributeGroup name="partMeasures">
   <attribute name="count" type="integer"/>
   <attribute name="size" type="integer"/>
</attributeGroup>

<element name="PartsAndTheirMeasures">
   <type>
      <group ref="partsGroup"/>
      <attributeGroup ref="partMeasures"/>
   </type>
</element>
```

This is a variation on the first example. Instead of building the attribute declarations into the `<element>`, I created an attribute group containing the declarations, then created the element declaration using references to the element group and the attribute group. Here's another way to use attribute groups.

```
<element name="PairedFasteners">
  <type>
     <group order="seq">
         <element type="Nut"/>
         <element type="Bolt"/>
     </group>
  </type>
  <attributeGroup ref="partMeasures"/>
</element>
```

This time, I wanted to reuse the attribute group with different element content. I was able to do this in an element declaration by explicitly specifying the content model, then using a reference to the attribute group. Note that my content model includes elements of the types `Nut` and `Bolt`. These are types I would have had to declare elsewhere in the schema.

Wildcards

XML schemas provide the `any` element that allows us to introduce a wildcard into a schema at any particular point. Schemas provide for departures from the written schema in any of the following four ways:

- Any well-formed XML element construction
- Any well-formed element construction so long as it is in any namespace other than the one in which the wildcard appears
- Any well-formed element construction, provided it is from a specific namespace
- Any well-formed element construction provided it is from the current namespace

Wildcards may also be used in conjunction with attributes, in which case we can use the `anyAttribute` element. Here are examples for each of the four cases:

```
<any/>

<any namespace="##other"/>

<any namespace=http://www.myserver.com/OtherSchema/>

<any namespace="##targetNamespace"/>
```

Note the use of the `other` and `targetNamespace` keywords. Now, here's an example of using a wildcard in conjunction with attributes within an element declaration:

```
<element name="someElement">
   <type>
      <anyAttribute namespace=http://www.w3.org/1999?XMLSchema/>
      <element name="someNum" type="integer"/>
   </type>
</element>
```

Here we've declared an element that has a single child element, `<someNum>`, and may have any attribute declared in the W3C schema for XML Schemas.

Deriving Type Definitions

When we use the source attribute on a type, we are in effect deriving a new type from an existing one. XML schemas provides some formal rules for type derivation that we will now examine. Specifically, we can extend a type or restrict it. The value of the `derivedBy` attribute specifies which method is used.

Derivation

A new type extends another when it adds additional content to its source type. In this case, all the content declared in the source type will appear in the derived type. For example, we extend a `PersonName` type declaration by adding an honorific element to the existing content:

```
<type name="PersonName">
   <element name="FirstName" type="string"/>
   <element name="MI" type="string"/>
   <element name="LastName" type="string"/>
</type>

<type name="FormalPersonName" source="PersonName" derivedBy="extension">
   <element name="honorific" type="string"/>
</type>
```

If, however, we wish to somehow restrict a type when we derive a new type from it, we can give the `derivedBy` attribute the value restriction and add a `<restrictions>` element:

```
<type name="ShortName" source="PersonName" derivedBy="restriction">
   <restrictions>
      <element name="MI" maxOccurs="0"/>
   </restrictions>
</type>
```

Here, we've restricted the type so that the <MI> element no longer appears. When deriving types, be sure the constraints on elements and attributes are more restrictive than those on the same declaration in the source type.

Types may control derivation from themselves as well as their appearance in instance documents through the use of three attributes, `abstract`, `exact`, and `final`. If `abstract` has the value `true`, no instance of the declared type may appear in an instance document. The default for this implied attribute is `false` as one might expect. If `exact` has the value `true`, no derived type may appear in an instance document in its place. Only the type so declared may be used. If `final` is given the value `true`, then no further derivation of the type is permitted.

Composition

We can combine schemas and namespaces together to allow users to build document instances from multiple schemas. Schemas also allow designers to use other schemas in building their own schema document. This is termed **composition**.

Import

You can import parts of another schema for use in yours provided the namespace of the other schema is referenced in an <import> element. This element has the `namespace` attribute whose value is a URI for the schema you want to use. You may also provide a `schemaLocation` attribute to point to the schema file desired. Once you have imported a namespace, you can use some construction from the other schema within your schema:

```
<schema name="SomeOtherSchema.xsd"
        xmlns:other=" http://www.OtherOrg.org/schemas/Useful.xsd" >
   <import namespace="http://www.OtherOrg.org/SomeUsefulSchema"
           schemaLocation="http://www.OtherOrg.org/schemas/Useful.xsd"/>
   ...
  <element ref="other:stuff" name="someName"/>
</schema>
```

When a construct is imported into a schema, it remains an external resource. We are composing a new schema, in effect, by linking in parts of another schema rather than including them whole in the new schema. When a validating parser validates a document according to a schema, it must retrieve the other schema to validate material in the document against the external resource.

Inclusion

Inclusion is specified with the <include> element. This appears in a schema after the <import> element and before the <export> element, if any. The <include> element is an empty element with the required attribute `schemaLocation`, whose value is a URI to the included schema. When this element appears in a schema, the schema is understood to consist of its declared types as well as all the types declared in the included schema provided several criteria are met: The URI must resolve to another schema, and the schema thus designated must have a `targetNamespace` attribute identical to the containing schema's `targetNamespace` attribute value.

Annotating Schemas

No body of computing definitions or code is complete without a mechanism for providing additional comments or processing information. Schemas provide for this with the <annotation> element. This element may contain <info> elements, which consist of character data intended for human consumption, or <appinfo> elements, which do the same for schema processors. Either element may have an `infoSource` attribute that provides a URI reference to further information.

```
<element name="HardToRemember">
   <annotation>
      <info>
         I want to remember the following about this element declaration...
      </info>
   </annotation>
   ...
</element>
```

Datatypes

The real world relies on concepts of numbers, strings, and sets, so programs written in modern programming languages support elaborate systems of built-in types and procedures for defining new types. Therefore the addition of data types to XML Schemas will be a great asset to programmers using XML for data in their applications. This support for data types includes the ability to check the validity of a value in a document as well as aiding an appropriate conversion from text to the native type when processing an XML document. So, we need to capture the data types of the information we markup if we are going to use XML documents as the basis for integrating programs and systems.

This is what the second part of the XML Schemas specifications, *XML Schemas: Datatypes*, aims to do. Not only does it provide a means of capturing the basic type of data, but it also gives us a means of recording the constraints imposed on the data in our problem domain. It will let us record numeric bounds, sets and list ordering. It will also let us specify masks for the permissible string representations of our data.

Schema datatypes are said to have a set of distinct values called their **value space**. This is the abstract collection of values the type can take on. For example, the set of integral numerics is the value space for the integer type. Constraining properties and operations on the values in the space characterize this space. When we go to represent a data type for our users, we require a **lexical representation**, the literal string representation of the type. A real number might be represented a string of digits, a decimal point, and a specified number of digits after that point. A date is represented by YYYY-MM-DD. This is the ISO 8601 format, which XML adopts for datetime representations.

XML Schemas: Datatypes is all about specifying value spaces, then listing the constraining properties of the type. It provides a set of primitive data types, and then elaborates a mechanism for generating new types derived from those primitives. The draft includes a number of generated types of wide utility, but schema designers are welcome to generate their own types intended for application-specific use.

Some properties, termed **facets**, are provided to specify datatypes. Facets refine the value space to give us the permissible values for the new type. Facets are either **fundamental** or **constraining**. Fundamental facets define some fundamental property of the datatype. Constraining facets place restrictions on the value space but do not define its nature. Strings, for example, have length. Length doesn't tell you about the nature of strings, but they define what string values are permitted. Each type provided in XML Schemas lists its specific facets. One very important facet is lexical representation. Since we are speaking in terms of XML, a text-based system, we must specify the text representation of non-text types. The particular meaning of this facet depends on the datatype. The more important ones are listed in the following tables.

Primitive Types

Primitive datatypes are those that are not defined in terms of other types. They are axiomatic. We proceed from an intuitive concept of the type described. It is natural for the XML Schemas proposal to include the classic XML 1.0 types, but it also adds some types of its own.

Here are the primitive types introduced by XML Schemas:

Schema Primitive Type	Definition
`string`	Finite sequence of ISO 10646 or Unicode characters, such as `"thisisastring"`.
`boolean`	The set {`true`, `false`}.
`float`	Standard mathematical concept of real numbers, corresponding to a single precision 32 bit floating point type.
`double`	Standard mathematical concept of real numbers, corresponding to a double precision 64 bit floating point type; doubles consist of a decimal mantissa, followed optionally by the letter `E` and an integer exponent, for example `6.02E23`.
`decimal`	Standard mathematical concept of a real numeric type; it covers a smaller range than double, and consists of a sequence of digits separated by a period, such as `9.06`.
`timeInstant`	The combination of date and time to define a specific instant in time, encoded as a string, `2000-01-01T08:12:00.000` represents 8:12 on 1 Jan 2000, expressed with seconds and fractional seconds. This type is always expressed `YYYY-MM-DDThh:mm:ss.sss`, but can be immediately followed by a `Z`, to specify that the time is a Coordinated Universal Time. Alternatively, the time zone can be specified by supplying a difference from CUT, using a + or a – followed by `hh:mm`. For example, the above date and time string could be followed by `-04:00`.
`timeDuration`	A combination of date and time to define a period, interval, or duration of time. For example, one month is represented as `P0Y1M0DT0H0M0S`, where the lexical pattern is `PnYnMnDTnHnMnS`, and can be preceeded by a + or `-`. The representation may be truncated on the right when the finer time intervals are not needed, for example `P2Y3M` for 2 years and three months. Note that the number precedes the character representing the interval. Seconds may be expressed by a number including a decimal to represent fractional seconds. A minus sign preceding the lexical representation indicates a negative duration.
`recurringInstant`	An instant of time that recurs with some regular frequency, such as, every day; represented by substituting a dash for any period not provided in the lexical pattern for `timeInstant`. For example, an instant that occurs at 08:00 every day would be expressed as `----T08:00:00.000`.
`binary`	Arbitrarily long bodies of binary data.
`uri`	URI reference.

Generated and User Defined Types

As the name suggests, a generated datatype builds from an existing type. The type on which it builds is the **basetype**. XML Schemas specify some generated types that are broadly useful. These are shown in the following table:

Generated type	Base type	Meaning
`language`	`string`	Natural language identifiers; a token that meets the `LanguageID` production in XML, for example "`en`"
`NMTOKEN`	`NMTOKENS`	XML 1.0 `NMTOKEN`
`NMTOKENS`	`string`	XML 1.0 `NMTOKENS`
`Name`	`NMTOKEN`	XML 1.0 name
`Qname`	`Name`	XML 1.0 qualified name
`NCNAME`	`Name`	XML 1.0 "non-colonized" name
`ID`	`NCName`	XML 1.0 attribute type `ID`
`IDREF`	`IDREFS`	XML 1.0 attribute type `IDREF`
`IDREFS`	`string`	XML 1.0 attribute type `IDREFS`
`ENTITY`	`ENTITIES`	XML 1.0 `ENTITY`
`ENTITIES`	`string`	XML 1.0 `ENTITIES`
`NOTATION`	`NCName`	XML 1.0 `NOTATION`
`integer`	`decimal`	Standard mathematical concept of a discrete numeric type (discrete here separates it from the definition of number)
`non-negative-integer`	`integer`	Standard mathematical concept of non-negative integers
`positive-integer`	`integer`	Standard mathematical concept of positive integers
`non-positive-integer`	`integer`	Standard mathematical concept of a negative integer, or zero
`negative-integer`	`integer`	Standard mathematical concept of a strictly negative integer
`date`	`recurringInstant`	Standard concept of a day, that is, an interval beginning at midnight and lasting 24 hours
`time`	`recurringInstant`	Same as the left-truncated representation for `timeInstant`, `hh:mm:ss.sss`.

We declare a new type with a `datatype` element. This element has `name` and `source` attributes. The `source` attribute's value indicates the type from which the new type is derived. Here's a minimal example:

```
<datatype name="height" source="decimal"/>
```

We further specify a new datatype by adding facets. These must be appropriate to the basetype, that is, only ordered facets may be applied to datatypes generated from an ordered basetype. Typically, we would specify constraining facets for a new type by providing specific values for the constraining facets of the basetype. For example, let's declare some generated types denoting large and small orders of products:

```
<datatype name="largeOrder" source="integer">
   <minExclusive value="1000"/>
</datatype>

<datatype name="smallOrder" source="integer">
   <minExclusive value="0"/>
   <maxInclusive value="1000"/>
</datatype>
```

The `integer` type has constraining facets denoting bounds named `minInclusive`, `minExclusive`, `maxInclusive`, and `maxExclusive`. The example above takes advantage of these to establish that a small order is anything that has between 1 and 1000 units, inclusive. A large order in our type system is anything over 1000 units.

XML Data – Reduced

XML Schemas aren't yet a recommendation at the time of this writing (Janurary 2000), so we cannot provide an example here of them in use. However, to see how we will be able to utilize the power of XML Schemas we can look at a different implementation of schemas written in XML syntax called XML Data – Reduced, a subset of XML Data implemented in Microsoft's MSXML parser, which we can use within IE5 or as a standalone component. While the syntax of XML Data – Reduced does differ from the working draft of XML Schemas available at the time of writing, it helps show how we can use the benefits that XML Schemas bring in our applications.

Not only is MSXML one of the more widely used parsers, but Microsoft is actively using XML Data – Reduced for a number of their initiatives, notably BizTalk. This includes an effort to share vertical market vocabularies for e-commerce. While Microsoft promises to adopt XML Schemas when the draft becomes a Recommendation, the result right now is that a lot of people are building prototypes and even products using XML Data – Reduced, as an intermediary measure until the W3C schema recommendation.

As this is an implementation we are able to work with now, and which is being used in several areas for prototyping, in this penultimate section of the chapter we shall take a look at the syntax of XML Data – Reduced. Once we have looked at the syntax we will then develop some examples that show you the power of these new schemas.

IBM has introduced partial support for XML Schemas in a beta edition of their XML4J parser. However, since MSXML has richer support and is a shipping tool, we will focus on XML Data – Reduced.

What is XML Data – Reduced?

As we have said, XML Data – Reduced (XML-DR) is a subset of the full XML Data proposal, In terms of how much the subset covers, it provides roughly the same functionality as the Document Content Description specification containing those constructs needed to perform the tasks of a DTD. It also provides a few extensions to the capabilities DTDs offer. It is implemented as a **technology preview** in the XML parser that ships with Internet Explorer 5.0. It is also supported in some commercial tools, notably DTD/Schema editors such as Extensibility's XML Authority. It is definitely investigating because it is available for experimentation and is being used in a number of initiatives.

Schema Support

Conceptually XML Data – Reduced is similar to the core constructs of XML Schemas, even though the syntax is slightly different. The more complicated constructs, such as types, are not reproduced, but everything you need to define a vocabulary in XML is here, often using very similar syntax. Here are the elements specified in XML Data – Reduced and their XML Schemas equivalents:

Note carefully the case of the names as there are subtle differences between XML Schemas and XML-DR schemas:

XML Schemas construct	XML-DR construct
`schema`	`Schema`
`element`	`ElementType`
`elementRef`	`element`
`attribute`	`AttributeType`
`none`	`attribute`
`datatype`	`datatype`
`none`	`description`
`ModelGroup, group`	`group`

The entire reference for XML-DR schemas may be found online at http://msdn.microsoft.com/xml/reference/schema/start.asp.

Schemas

The `Schema` element in XML-DR is quite similar to the `schema` element in XML Schemas. This element performs the following functions:

- Contains element and attribute declarations
- Names the schema
- Declares namespaces used in the schema

Unlike XML Schemas, schemas in XML-DR do not use a preamble containing `import`, `export`, and `include` elements. Instead, they use namespace declarations. Every XML-DR schema must declare the XML Data and Microsoft datatypes namespaces. If a certain naming convention is observed (which will be introduced below when we discuss parser support for XML-DR), external content from another namespace may be used and validated in a schema. Here is a sample schema omitting the content:

```
<Schema name="ShortSchema.xml" xmlns="urn:schemas-microsoft-com:xml-data"
        xmlns:dt="urn:schemas-microsoft-com:datatypes">
   ... <!-- Declarations here -->
</Schema>
```

Elements and Attributes

Elements and attributes are declared in `ElementType` and `AttributeType` elements, respectively.

```
<elementType name="myElement" />
```

The `<ElementType>` element has five important attributes.

ElementType Attribute	Meaning
`name`	Name of the element
`content`	Describes the content that may be contained by the element: `empty`, `textOnly` (PCDATA only), `eltOnly` (element content only), `mixed` (PCDATA and elements)
`dt:type`	Denotes the type of the element. This attribute corresponds to the `<datatype>` element in XML Schemas. Valid values are taken from the XML Data Types Preview implementation.
`model`	Open or closed content model
`order`	Basic ordering of child elements: `one` (one chosen from a list of elements), `seq` (a specified sequence of elements), `many` (specified elements may appear or not appear, in any order)

Again, elements can contain one of four types of content described in the value of the `content` attribute of the `<ElementType>` element:

- no content: `empty`
- text only: `textOnly`
- subelements only: `eltOnly`
- a mix of text and sub elements: `mixed`

We can use the `<element>` and `<attribute>` elements to constrain the content of the declared element. These elements declare the child elements and attributes that may be applied to an element.

The <element> element can take three attributes:

Attribute	Description
type	Corresponds to the value of the name attribute of the <ElementType> defined in the schema.
minOccurs	Minimum number of times the reference element type can occur on the element, takes the values 0 where the minimum value is zero, and the element is optional or 1 where the element must occur at least once (default is 1)
maxOccurs	Maximum number of times the element can occur on the element, takes the values 1 where it can occur once at the most, or * where the occurrences are unlimited (default is 1)

The <attribute> element also can also take three attributes:

Attribute	Description
default	Default value for the attribute, overrides any default provided in <AttributeType> element it refers to.
type	Corresponds to the value of the name attribute of the <AttributeType> element defined in this schema.
required	Indicates whether the attribute must be present on the element, takes the value yes if it is required. Not needed if specified in the <AttributeType> element.

Let's take a look at some simple element declarations and their DTD equivalents. First we have a parent element called <Fex>, which can contain a child element called <Tex>.

```
<ElementType name="Fex" content="mixed" order="many">
   <element type="Tex"/>
</ElementType>
```

Here, some <ElementType> declaration for <Tex> would have been included elsewhere in the schema. In a DTD, the declaration we have just seen would be:

```
<!ELEMENT Fex (#PCDATA | Tex)*>
```

Next, we have a <Person> element, which has the child elements <FirstName>, <MI> and <LastName>:

```
<!ELEMENT Person (FirstName, MI, LastName)>
```

Using XML-DR this would look as follows:

```
<ElementType name="Person" content="eltOnly" order="seq">
   <element type="FirstName"/>
   <element type="MI"/>
   <element type="LastName/>
</ElementType>
```

Content models are composed using the `order` attribute and the `group` element. So, if we want to get more complicated, we need to look at the attributes of the `<group>` elements and use the attributes of the `<element>` element that we have already seen:

`<group>` attributes	Meaning
`maxOccurs`	Maximum number of times the group may occur. May be `0` or `*` (many).
`minOccurs`	Minimum number of times the group may occur. May be `0` (optional) or `1` (must occur at least once).
`order`	Ordering of contained elements and groups. May be `one` (select one element from the group), `seq` (each element in sequence), or `many` (any element in the group may or may not appear, in any order).

So, if we wanted to declare the following content model in terms of XML-DR:

```
<!ELEMENT Foo ((X | Y) | (A, B?, C))>
```

It would look like this:

```
<ElementType name="Foo" content="eltOnly" order="one">
    <group order="one">
       <element type="X"/>
       <element type="Y"/>
    </group>
    <group order="seq">
       <element type="A"/>
       <element type="B" minOccurs="0"/>
       <element type="C"/>
    </group>
</ElementType>
```

To declare attributes, we need the `<AttributeType>` element, which has one required attribute and four optional attributes. We associate an attribute with an element through the inclusion of an `<attribute>` element as a child of the `<ElementType>` used to declare the element, just as we did with elements. The `type` attribute of the `<attribute>` element refers to the `<AttributeType>` that declares the attribute.

`<AttributeType>` attributes	Meaning
`name`	Required; name of the attribute
`default`	Default value of the attribute; must be consistent with `dt:type`
`dt:type`	Data type of the attribute defined
`dt:values`	A list of possible values when `dt:type` is enumeration
`required`	Indicates whether the attribute must appear on all instances of the element; true or false

On versions of the IE 5 parser prior to Windows 2000, `dt:type` may only take on the XML 1.0 primitive types: `entity`, `entities`, `enumeration`, `id`, `idref`, `idrefs`, `nmtoken`, `nmtokens`, `notation`, and `string`. The full range of data types discussed below is supported for the version of the parser that ships with Windows 2000.

Here is how we might go about adding a required age attribute to the <Person> element we declared previously in a DTD:

```
<!ELEMENT Person (FirstName, MI, LastName)>
<!ATTLIST Person age CDATA #REQUIRED>
```

While in XML-DR this becomes:

```
<AttributeType name="age" required="yes"/>

<ElementType name="Person" content="eltOnly" order="seq">
   <attribute type="age">
   <element type="FirstName"/>
   <element type="MI"/>
   <element type="LastName/>
</ElementType>
```

The <attribute> element can also be used to declare a default value or indicate whether the attribute is required. If the associated <AttributeType> provided a required attribute, we need not repeat that attribute in the <attribute> element.

Another interesting variation is that an <AttributeType> element may appear within the bounds of an <ElementType> instance. In that case, the attribute type declared is only valid within the scope of the <ElementType> declaration and may not be referenced elsewhere in the schema. Here's the same <Person> and age declaration with age being defined for use solely with <Person>:

```
<ElementType name="Person" content="eltOnly" order="seq">
   <AttributeType name="age" required="yes"/>
   <element type="FirstName"/>
   <element type="MI"/>
   <element type="LastName/>
</ElementType>
```

Groups

We saw the <group> element used with <ElementType> element declarations. Its usage is fairly straightforward, but the values permitted on the attributes of this element differ from those we saw under XML Schemas. For one thing, it is not as flexible in its cardinality support. The all enumerated type for ordering is also not supported. <Group> takes the maxOccurs, minOccurs and order attributes, which we met in the previous section.

Comments

XML-DR provides the description element for inline documentation.

```
<description>This is how you use the description element</description>
```

Of course, XML-style comments <!-- Some comment here --> work as well. However, we can use the description element for capturing schema-related comments, such as usage notes, that could be read by a particular tool. XML-DR itself does not differentiate between the two forms of comments, but merely provides this alternative form.

Data Types

XML-DR makes use of the datatypes technology preview in IE 5.0 to provide strong typing for elements and attributes. This is in addition to the `dt:type` attribute used with `<AttributeType>` elements. This element, `<datatype>`, takes the single attribute `dt:type` to indicate the type of the parent element.

```
<ElementType name="Age">
   <datatype dt:type="int"/>
</ElementType>
```

The strong typing support in IE 5.0 provides not only the XML 1.0 primitives, but a wide variety of derived types common to PC applications. Here are the additional types supported:

Data type	Meaning
`bin.base64`	MIME style base64 encoded binary
`bin.hex`	Hexadecimal digits representing octets
`boolean`	0 (false) or 1 (true)
`char`	Single character
`date`	ISO 8601 date without the time
`dateTime`	ISO 8601 date time, with optional time and fractional seconds to nanosecond resolution
`dateTime.tz`	`dateTime`, but with optional time zone added
`fixed.14.4`	Numeric type with no more than 14 digits to the left of the decimal point and no more than four to the right
`float`	Real number with optional sign, fractional digits, and exponent
`int`	Integral numeric type
`number`	General numeric type with no limit on digits; may have optional sign, fractional digits, and exponent
`time`	ISO 8601 format time group
`time.tz`	As for time, but with time zone added
`i1`	One byte signed integer
`i2`	Two byte signed integer
`i4`	Four byte signed integer
`r4`	Four byte real number
`r8`	Eight byte real number
`ui1`	Single byte unsigned integer
`ui2`	Two byte unsigned integer
`ui4`	Four byte unsigned integer
`uri`	URI string
`uuid`	Hexadecimal digits denoting octets and composing a COM-style UUID; hyphens are optional and ignored if present.

In versions of the parser prior to Windows 2000, the derived datatypes described in the table above are restricted to use with well-formed XML documents. Validation with XML-DR schemas is not supported by those versions.

Namespaces and Schema Support in MSXML

MSXML features previews of Namespaces and XML Data – Reduced schemas. You have to use the Microsoft COM-based XML Parser, MSXML, which ships with Internet Explorer 5.0 or can be downloaded from their site if you want support for XML-DR in code. It is important to re-iterate that XML-DR is a Microsoft technology preview, not a creation of the W3C. *This is strictly a proprietary implementation supported by Microsoft alone.* As one of the first attempts to support schemas, however, MSXML's XML-DR support is potentially quite useful to programmers who want to jump into the frontiers of XML metadata.

MSXML supports XML-DR and namespaces through extensions to the XML DOM.

An early access version (EA2) of IBM's XML4J parser is partially supporting the September 1999 draft of XML Schemas. IBM indicates this support may appear in later, released versions of the parser. Given the state of flux of XML Schemas, however, it is difficult to provide working examples that will be valid by the time you read this book.

Namespaces

Support for namespaces in MSXML quite robust. When accessing a node in the DOM that is namespace-qualified, you can use the `basename`, or `prefix`, and `namespaceURI` properties to obtain namespace-related information.

Property	Meaning
`basename`	Returns a string whose value is the unqualified basename of the node
`prefix`	Returns a string with the namespace prefix
`namespaceURI`	Returns a string with the namespace URI corresponding to the node's namespace prefix

There are two methods of interest to programmers that deal with namespaces. If you want to create a namespace qualified node using the extended Microsoft XML DOM, you cannot use `createElement()` to create it directly. Instead, you must use the document object's `createNode()` method. It takes an enumerated value to indicate the type of node to create, the qualified name, and the associated URI:

```
qualifiedNode = doc.createNode(1, "pub:Book", "urn:myschemas-pub");
```

Alternately, you can create a default namespace by using `createElement()` followed by setting the `xmlns` attribute:

```
qualifiedNode = doc.createElement("Book");
qualifiedNode.setAttribute("xmlns", "urn:myschemas-pub");
```

Note, however, that in the latter case you then lose the ability to qualify other names using the declared namespace.

The JavaScript line above creates an element with the qualified name `<pub:Book>` in the `myschemas-pub` namespace. Here is a partial list of the node type enumerations supported by MSXML that are of interest to namespaces:

Enumeration	Value
NODE_ELEMENT	1
NODE_ATTRIBUTE	2
NODE_ENTITY_REFERENCE	5
NODE_ENTITY	6
NODE_NOTATION	12

The `attributes` collection of a node supports the `getQualifiedItem()` method, allowing you to search for attributes by their qualified name. This method takes the basename and prefix of the desired attribute and returns a node object if the attribute is found. To search for an attribute `pub:isbn`, you would make the following call:

```
FoundAttr = nodeAttrs.getQualifiedItem("isbn", "pub");
```

Validation

MSXML will validate a document against a DTD like any other validating parser. In addition, if a schema is provided with the prefix `x-schema`, MSXML assumes that the name that follows the colon is an XML-DR style schema and will attempt to load it and use it to validate the document.

```
<Book xmlns="x-schema:PubCatalog.xml">
        <!-- PubCatalog is assumed to be a schema -->
```

If you have validated your document against an XML-DR schema, you have the opportunity to gain access to the schema node that defines a particular node in your document. This is done with the `definition` property. If called with a node corresponding to an element or attribute, you will receive a node containing the applicable `<ElementType>` or `<AttributeType>` element:

```
SchemaNode = node.definition;
```

Datatypes

The data type support in MSXML is separate but complementary to the XML-DR preview. Even if you do not use schemas, you can use strongly typed elements and attributes in well-formed XML. To do this, you must declare the Microsoft data type namespace in your document:

```
<MyRootElement xmlns:dt="urn:schemas-microsoft-com:datatypes">
```

Once this is done, you can use the supported types in code. Where you might previously have used `nodeValue()` to get the value of an element or attribute, you can call `nodeTypedValue()` to obtain the strongly typed value. Assume you have some XML that includes the element:

```
<PageCount dt:dt="int">350</PageCount>
```

You could then do the following in JavaScript:

```
sCount = node.nodeValue;        <!-- returns the string "350" -->
Count = node.nodeTypedValue;    <!-- returns the numeric value 350 -->
```

If you had two nodes, `<node1>` and `<node2>`, that represented the `<PageCount>` elements from two different documents, you could get the total page count like this:

```
TotalCount = node1.nodeTypedValue + node2.nodeTypedValue;
```

The property `nodeTypeString` returns a fixed string denoting the data type. For our `<PageCount>` example, this property would return "int".

Variations on the Book Catalog

By now, I hope you are eager to apply namespace and schema information to our book catalog example. Although we won't follow this schema through the rest of the book, I'm going to show how we can use what I've presented in this chapter to improve our understanding and organization of book publishing information.

Why Bother?

What is wrong with our Book Catalog DTD? Nothing, really, but it is starting to get long. Everything about book catalogs has to go into the one DTD if we are to properly validate a catalog document. All the criticisms leveled against DTDs earlier in the chapter in general apply to our particular DTD.

The first this we will do is break up the publishing catalog domain into two separate schemas, one reflecting a namespace dealing with authors, the other catalog information. Additionally, we can provide strong typing on some of our attributes and elements, thereby making our life easier when it comes time to write applications that process catalogs. Since XML Schemas is in a state of flux as it nears Recommendation status, we will use the XML-DR version of schemas as implemented in MSXML.

Segmentation

Our `catalog.dtd` that we met in Chapter 3 gave us a number of concepts. A catalog certainly needs books, but wouldn't it be better if the authors live outside the catalog? After all, if we need to write a schema for marking up the actual content of individual books, we will probably want to include author information there as well. This is one of the main motivations in splitting up our Book Catalog DTD into two separate schemas: `Catalog` and `Author`. When we want to create a catalog document, we can declare a default namespace for the `Catalog` schema and then use a qualified namespace to bring in the `Author` schema.

Additional Expression

In our bookCatalog.dtd we had a few attributes that could benefit from strong typing. If we included data types, it would make it easier to total up page counts, and we would certainly like to be able to be able to calculate order totals given an order from the catalog. So, we need to go through the Catalog schema and see what attributes should be qualified with type information.

Metadata Discovery

Creating a schema in XML syntax is useful to programmers, in that we give them a little bit of support for writing programs that manipulate book catalog documents marked up according to our schema. The greatest support we provide is simply taking the DTD into schema form. Once it is in XML syntax, programmers can use the same parser that they use with XML document instances to discover the meaning behind the metadata.

Suppose you were unfamiliar with our schema. You could investigate individual elements with the <definition> element. This would be useful in a document browser. A user might click for additional information on a particular item and see the metadata associated with it. We wouldn't present the XML definition, of course, though we might show that an item is a numeric type. In the case of enumerations, we would certainly show the range of values the item could take. Cardinality information is certainly important to see, as is the knowledge of whether an attribute is required or not. All these could be discovered at the time a document instance is read as long as we provide a schema in XML syntax to go with it. After we've turned our catalog DTD into a schema I'll show how we can use the DOM to generate a concordance of elements in a schema. This will take a schema and provide you with a cross-reference of elements and how they are used.

Recasting the DTD

Let's take a closer look at our DTD. We'll work through a translation into XML-DR format showing incremental improvements to our definition as we go.

There is no clear consensus on what file extension to use for XML-DR schema files. Microsoft sources tend to use xml*, while one commercially available tool uses* xdr*. The W3C Schema working group, as we have seen, favors* xsd *for their version of schemas. I will use* xml *for the examples that follow. In any case, a schema is XML, so its MIME type remains* text/xml.

As you may remember, the catalog was split into three sections:

- Publisher information about the publisher
- Threads that contain descriptive information
- Books containing the information about the books

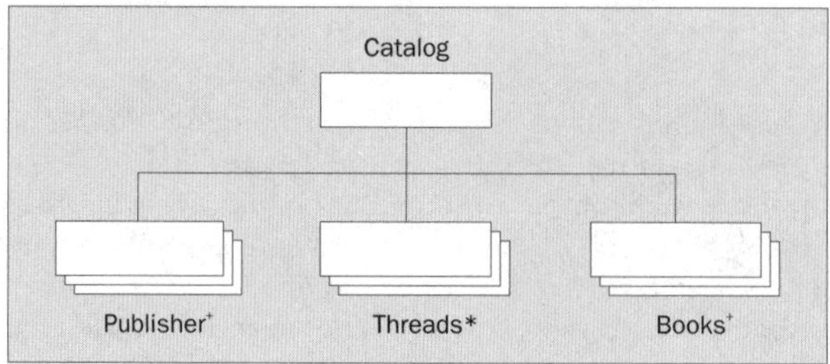

The publisher section also included the author details, however we are going to remove the author details and place them in the separate author schema so that we can borrow from it in the catalog schema, and make use of it in other areas as well. So let's start with the author schema, before coming back to the rest of the catalog.

Author Schema

We ought look at the authors schema first, because the catalog schema we develop next will borrow from it. The first thing to do is cut out the declaration of the <Author> element and everything subordinate to it and create a new schema file, authors.xml. The top of the file should declare conformance to XML 1.0, name the schema, and declare the XML-DR and datatypes namespaces:

```
<?xml version ="1.0"?>
<Schema name = "authors.xml"
        xmlns = "urn:schemas-microsoft-com:xml-data"
        xmlns:dt = "urn:schemas-microsoft-com:datatypes">
```

Note that the default namespace is XML-DR and the datatypes namespace will be aliased with the prefix dt. The Author element is our starting place. It contains only element content consisting of the name-related, <Biographical>, and <Portrait> elements in sequence:

```
<!ELEMENT Author  ((FirstName, MI?, LastName, Biographical, Portrait)>
<!ATTLIST Author authorCiteID ID  #REQUIRED>
```

In XML-DR, this becomes:

```
<AttributeType name = "authorCiteID" dt:type = "ID" required = "yes"/>
<ElementType name = "Author" content = "eltOnly" order = "seq">
   <attribute type = "authorCiteID"/>
   <element type = "FirstName"/>
   <element type = "MI" minOccurs = "0" maxOccurs = "1"/>
   <element type = "LastName"/>
   <element type = "Biographical"/>
   <element type = "Portrait"/>
</ElementType>
```

We've retained the XML ID type for authorCiteID to preserve the link between authors and books. Note especially the cardinality on MI. It can occur either zero times or once, that is, it is optional. Now declare the child elements of <Author>:

```
<ElementType name = "FirstName" content = "textOnly"/>
<ElementType name = "MI" content = "textOnly"/>
<ElementType name = "LastName" content = "textOnly"/>
<ElementType name = "Biographical" content = "textOnly"/>
<AttributeType name = "picLink"/>
<ElementType name = "Portrait" content = "empty">
  <attribute type = "picLink"/>
</ElementType>
```

Close the top level <Schema> element and you are done. Now you have a reusable schema that can be brought in wherever we markup author information.

Catalog Schema

Having removed the author elements from the catalog DTD and placed them in a separate schema, we now turn our attention to recreating the catalog data in XML. We will call this schema PubCatalog.xml. This will borrow from the author schema when we need to contain author details. Here's the opening information:

```
<?xml version ="1.0"?>
<Schema name = "PubCatalog.xml"
        xmlns = "urn:schemas-microsoft-com:xml-data"
        xmlns:dt = "urn:schemas-microsoft-com:datatypes"
        xmlns:athr = "x-schema:authors.xml">
```

Note how we've added a namespace declaration for our newly created author schema authors.xml with the alias prefix athr.

Let's dig right in: we start with the <Catalog> element, which contains other elements. This contains the <Publisher>, <Thread>, and <Book> elements, just as we had in the earlier catalog.dtd, each of which may occur many times.

```
<ElementType name = "Catalog" content = "eltOnly" order = "seq">
   <element type = "Publisher" minOccurs = "1" maxOccurs = "*"/>
   <element type = "Thread" minOccurs = "0" maxOccurs = "*"/>
   <element type = "Book" minOccurs = "1" maxOccurs = "*"/>
</ElementType>
```

Next we need to declare the isbn attribute, which will be used within both the <Publisher> and <Book> elements that we have just declared:

```
<AttributeType name = "isbn" required = "yes"/>
```

Publisher

The next section that we need to address is the content of the <Publisher> element we just declared. This still contains the same first three child elements that we saw in the DTD, however we have created a separate schema for the author details, so we need to refer to that namespace and borrow from it.

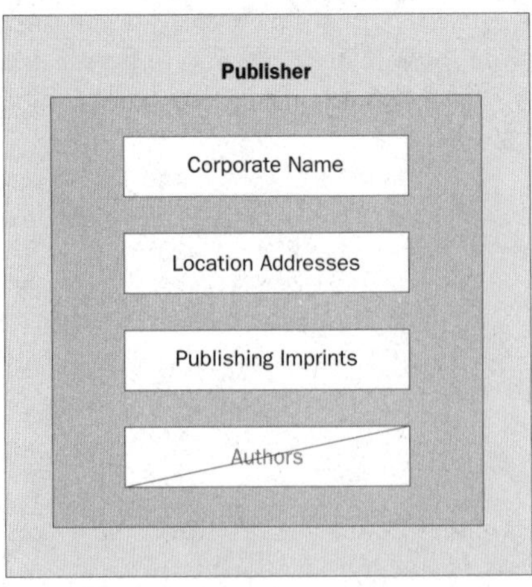

As we mentioned, we can make use of the `<description>` element to make information about the DTD available to a processing application, and that is just what we do, here we are using it to specify that the `<Publisher>` element is used for publishers information.

```
<ElementType name = "Publisher" content = "eltOnly" order = "seq">
   <description> Publisher section </description>
   <attribute type = "isbn"/>
   <element type = "CorporateName"/>
   <element type = "Address" minOccurs = "1" maxOccurs = "*"/>
   <element type = "Imprints"/>
   <element type = "athr:Author" minOccurs = "0" maxOccurs = "*"/>
</ElementType>
```

Drilling down in to the schema, the `<CorporateName>` element that is simple an element that contained PCDATA in the DTD, so we specify that it's content is text only:

```
<ElementType name = "CorporateName" content = "textOnly"/>
```

Next we have the address information, which you may recall contained a `yes/no` enumeration for the attribute `headquarters`, which we define first:

```
<AttributeType name = "headquarters"
               dt:type = "enumeration" dt:values = "yes no"/>
<ElementType name = "Address" content = "eltOnly" order = "seq">
   <attribute type = "headquarters"/>
   <element type = "Street" minOccurs = "1" maxOccurs = "*"/>
   <element type = "City"/>
   <element type = "PoliticalDivision"/>
   <element type = "Country"/>
   <element type = "PostalCode"/>
</ElementType>
```

Note the form of the `enumeration` datatype in XML-DR. Continuing, we declare the elements used in the address elements:

```
<ElementType name = "Street" content = "textOnly"/>
<ElementType name = "City" content = "textOnly"/>
<ElementType name = "PoliticalDivision" content = "textOnly">
   <description>State, province, canton, etc.</description>
</ElementType>
<ElementType name = "Country" content = "textOnly"/>
<ElementType name = "PostalCode" content = "textOnly"/>
```

The third child element of the `<Publisher>` element is about the publisher imprints:

```
<ElementType name = "Imprints" content = "eltOnly" order = "seq">
   <element type = "Imprint" minOccurs = "1" maxOccurs = "*"/>
</ElementType>

<AttributeType name = "shortImprintName" dt:type = "ID"/>
<ElementType name = "Imprint" content = "textOnly">
   <attribute type = "shortImprintName"/>
</ElementType>
```

The fourth child of the `<Publisher>` element held the author details in the DTD, but seeing as we have removed it, we can move on to the `<Thread>`.

Thread

<Thread> was used to specify the category area of the book. If you look above the bar code on the back of the book, you can see three different threads that are used to categorize the book, these are used, for example, by bookstores when deciding which section to put the book in.

```
<AttributeType name = "threadID" dt:type = "ID"/>
<ElementType name = "Thread" content = "textOnly">
   <description>
      Subject threads consist of one or more books
      related by some thread of study
   </description>
<attribute type = "threadID"/>
</ElementType>
```

Again we have used a <description> element to explain what threads are used for.

Book

The final section is the one that deals with the books themselves. As we noted in the DTD chapter, this must include title, abstract, recommended subject categories and price:

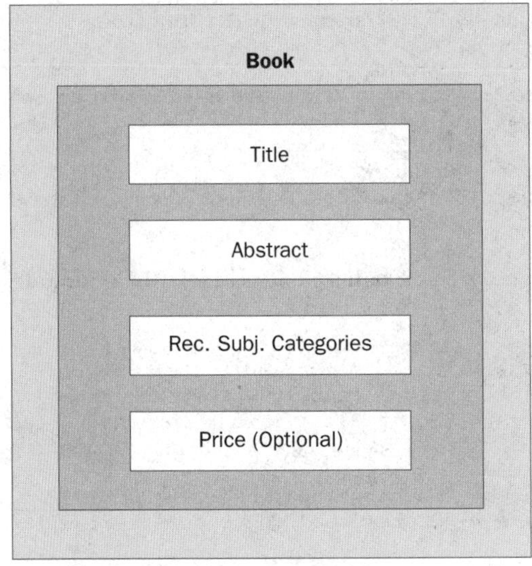

Before we define the elements, we must define several attributes:

```
<AttributeType name = "ISBN" dt:type = "ID" required = "yes"/>
<AttributeType name = "level"/>
<AttributeType name = "pubdate" required = "yes"/>
```

Next we reach the pageCount attribute. This was one place we decided we could really use strong typing of data. We'll make the attribute an integer type:

```
<AttributeType name = "pageCount" dt:type="int" required = "yes"/>
```

Then we continue with the various references:

```
<AttributeType name = "authors" dt:type = "IDREFS"/>
<AttributeType name = "threads" dt:type = "IDREFS"/>
<AttributeType name = "imprint" dt:type = "IDREF"/>

<AttributeType name = "shortImprintName" dt:type = "ID"/>
```

Having set the attributes that we will be using, we declare the content of `<Book>`, which uses the attributes we have just declared and several child elements:

```
<ElementType name = "Book" content = "eltOnly" order = "seq">
   <description> Book summary information (no content) </description>
   <attribute type = "ISBN"/>
   <attribute type = "level"/>
   <attribute type = "pubdate"/>
   <attribute type = "pageCount"/>
   <attribute type = "authors"/>
   <attribute type = "threads"/>
   <attribute type = "imprint"/>
   <element type = "Title"/>
   <element type = "Abstract"/>
   <element type = "RecSubjCategories"/>
   <element type = "Price" minOccurs = "0" maxOccurs = "1"/>
</ElementType>
```

Then we can describe the contents of these child elements:

```
<ElementType name = "Title" content = "textOnly"/>
<ElementType name = "Abstract" content = "textOnly"/>
<ElementType name = "RecSubjCategories" content = "eltOnly" order = "seq">
   <element type = "Category"/>
   <element type = "Category"/>
   <element type = "Category"/>
</ElementType>
<ElementType name = "Category" content = "textOnly"/>
```

The `<Price>` element declaration again brings us to datatype support. The currency attribute requires an enumeration, while the text value of the element itself should be a numeric type suitable for representing currency:

```
   <AttributeType name = "currency" dt:type = "enumeration"
                  dt:values = "USD GBF CD" required = "yes"/>
   <ElementType name = "Price" dt:type="fixed.14.4" content = "textOnly">
      <attribute type = "currency"/>
   </ElementType>
</Schema>
```

And that's it, with a bit of translation from DTD syntax to XML-DR and the addition of some strong typing, we have created a new catalog schema that reuses the authors schema through namespace support. It gives us the same sort of validation support as the DTD provided we change the root element of the sample `catalog.xml` file to reflect the use of the schema:

```
<?xml version ="1.0"?>
<Catalog xmlns = "x-schema:PubCatalog.xml">
```

Note that the namespace declaration eliminates the need for a `DOCTYPE` declaration.

Schema Concordance

It would be nice to have a simple listing of all the elements in a schema and their contents. That is, for each element declaration, we'd like a list of the permissible child elements and attributes used by that element. That way, we'd be able to gauge the impact of changing any particular element or attribute. Since XML-DR schemas use XML syntax, we can use MSXML and some JavaScript to produce this utility. Here's what it will look like when it is finished and pointed at our `PubCatalog.xml` schema file:

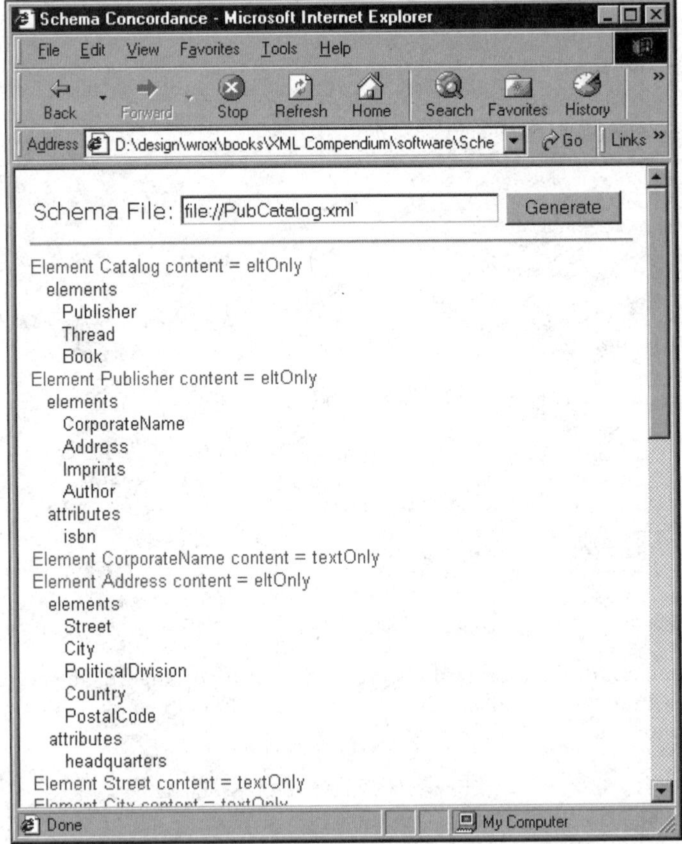

The source code for `SchemaConcordance.html` is available from our Web site at `http://www.wrox.com`. There are no configuration requirements other than to provide an appropriate URL to the file you wish to cross-index.

Finding the Elements

We know that a schema document starts with a root `<Schema>` element. Its child elements will be `<ElementType>` and `<AttributeType>` elements. The elements are declared with `<ElementType>` elements, and each such element contains a list of the elements and attributes it contains. This simplifies our task somewhat. All we have to do is walk the list of the `<Schema>` element's child nodes and process each `<ElementType>` element we find. Here is the heart of the code we need:

```
if (parser.documentElement.nodeName == "Schema")
{
   for (var ni=0; ni < parser.documentElement.childNodes.length; ni++)
   {
      if (parser.documentElement.childNodes(ni).nodeName == "ElementType")
         CrossRefElement(parser.documentElement.childNodes(ni));
   }
}
```

We know the number of child elements, so walking the entire document can be performed in a simple loop. The `nodeName` property of the element nodes lets us find the element declarations by looking for the name `<ElementType>`.

Processing an Element Declaration

The function `CrossRefElement()` accepts an `<ElementType>` element node and lists its contents. This is where we encounter a complication. There is no guarantee that `<element>` and `<attribute>` elements will be sorted. A schema could list attributes before elements in one `ElementType`, then reverse it in another, or even intermix the two. We need a consistent order so we can add the appropriate title in our output. We will have to create two arrays, one for element names and one for attribute names and then display the results when we are finished with the element declaration. Here is the part of `CrossRefElement()` that extracts element declaration information:

```
var rChildElements = new Array();
var rAttributes = new Array();
var WorkNode;
var nEltCount = 0;
var nAttrCount = 0;

for (ni = 0; ni < eltNode.childNodes.length; ni++)
{
   WorkNode = eltNode.childNodes(ni);
   switch (WorkNode.nodeName)
   {
      case "element":
         rChildElements[nEltCount++] =
                              WorkNode.attributes.getNamedItem("type").text;
         break;

      case "attribute":
         rAttributes[nAttrCount++] =
                              WorkNode.attributes.getNamedItem("type").text;
         break;

      case "group":
         SqueezeGroup(WorkNode, rChildElements, rAttributes);
         nEltCount = rChildElements.length;
         nAttrCount = rAttributes.length;
         break;
   }
}
...
```

When we encounter an `<element>` or `<attribute>` schema element, we get the value of the `type` attribute, which we know to be the name of an associated `<ElementType>` or `<AttributeType>` element. We do this by making use of the `getNamedItem()` function, which is specific to the extensions of the DOM implemented by Microsoft in MSXML to retrieve an attribute by name. If schemas didn't contain groups, our work would be done. Since groups do contain element and attribute information we need, we must call another function; `SqueezeGroup()`. This function looks almost the same as what we see above:

```
function SqueezeGroup(node, rElts, rAttrs)
{
   var nEltCt = rElts.length;
   var nAttrCt = rAttrs.length;
   var childNode;

   // Fix up indices for empty arrays
   if (nEltCt < 0)
      nEltCt = 0;
   if (nAttrCt < 0)
      nEltCt = 0;

   for (var nj = 0; nj < node.childNodes.length; nj++)
   {
      childNode = node.childNodes(nj);

      switch (childNode.nodeName)
      {
         case "element":
            rElts[nEltCt++] = childNode.attributes.getNamedItem("type").text;
            break;

         case "attribute";
            rAttrs[nAttrCt++] =
                                 childNode.attributes.getNamedItem("type").text;
            break;

         case "group":
            SqueezeGroup(childNode, rElts, rAttrs);
            nEltCt = rElts.length;
            nAttrCt = rAttrs.length;
            break;
      }
   }
}
```

`SqueezeGroup()` is passed the `group` node and the arrays containing the element and attribute names. Since there may be some names in the arrays by the time we get here, we have to set our array indices based on the current length of the array:

```
var nEltCt = rElts.length;
var nAttrCt = rAttrs.length;
```

Since `SqueezeGroup()` can add to the count, `CrossRefElement()` must reset its indices when control returns to it from `SqueezeGroup()`:

```
case "group":
   SqueezeGroup(WorkNode, rChildElements, rAttributes);
   nEltCount = rChildElements.length;
   nAttrCount = rAttributes.length;
   break;
```

Finally, since groups may contain other groups, we call `SqueezeGroup()` recursively to make sure we get all the information out of a group:

```
case "group":
   SqueezeGroup(childNode, rElts, rAttrs);
   nEltCt = rElts.length;
   nAttrCt = rAttrs.length;
   break;
```

Displaying the Results

Once an `<ElementType>` element is completely processed, we can use DHTML to display the results in a named DIV. The last part of `CrossRefElement()` does this for us:

```
sEltHeader = "Element " + eltNode.attributes.getNamedItem("name").text +
             "  content = " + eltNode.attributes.getNamedItem("content").text;
ListLine(sEltHeader , "green");
tabsize += 12;
// List all child elements
if (rChildElements.length > 0)
{
   ListLine("elements", "blue");
   tabsize += 12;
   for (ni = 0; ni < rChildElements.length; ni++)
      ListLine(rChildElements[ni], "black");
   tabsize -= 12;
}
// List all attributes
if (rAttributes.length > 0)
{
   ListLine("attributes", "blue");
   tabsize += 12;
   for (ni = 0; ni < rAttributes.length; ni++)
      ListLine(rAttributes[ni], "black");
   tabsize -= 12;
}
tabsize -= 12;
```

`ListLine()` is a utility function that takes some text and a color literal string and inserts the text into the DIV in the appropriate color. The variables `tabsize` and `listline` are global variables used to control relative placement of text.

Summary

We have seen that namespaces and schemas written in XML provide us with some powerful new tools for expression. They help us get over problems associated with creating single document instances that relate to several schemas. This ability means that we can extend existing schemas when necessary or separate out large complex schemas into smaller more manageable ones. At the same time, schemas in XML provide a number of other benefits that address the shortcomings associated with DTDs.

RDF is quite powerful, though that very power may make it too complex for everyday use. The W3C Schemas effort is bringing metadata into focus for working XML programmers, but is not yet a standard. In the mean time, until W3C XML Schemas are standardized XML-DR and its associated datatypes give us an implementation that is close to XML Schemas in construction, and allow us to roll up our sleeves and write some code immediately. While XML-DR doesn't offer the full range of capabilities promised in XML Schemas, we were able to make some improvements to our working example. In particular, we have brought the following benefits to our Book Catalog example:

- Better organization and reuse of a complex domain through vocabulary segmentation
- Strong typing of data when converting it to and from XML
- Retained the precision of the DTD (Schemas promise greater flexibility in cardinality)
- Expressed our problem in XML syntax, allowing us to use conventional XML parsers to read and process our schemas

Metadata is moving from the exclusive province of the academic community to the everyday toolbox of XML programmers. The rich research efforts in metadata are giving birth to a focused, practical standard in the hands of the W3C. Indeed, XML Schemas will do as much for programmers when they are supported as the DOM did. The XML-DR support in MSXML hints at the possibilities. Perhaps by the time you read this the W3C will have issued a Schemas Recommendation.

8

Linking and Querying

While the XML 1.0 specification has been around and stable for a while now, there are other specifications currently being created by the W3C that will round out the functionality of XML. We've seen some of these in the last chapter, but for XML to reach its full potential, we need a way to implement linking between, pointing into, and querying into XML documents.

As we begin to store more and more of our information in XML document repositories, we will need to gain access to the information in a structured manner. We need a way of specifying relationships between parts of documents, and a way of accessing the portions (or *resources*) within the document that have relationships to other resources. These resources can be portions of the same document, portions of different documents, or even items that are not XML at all!

In this chapter we will look at six different key areas that address linking and querying:

- **The XML Information Set** – the W3C document that defines the various pieces of information which go together to make up an XML document. A good understanding of the Infoset is crucial before tackling the other topics in this chapter.
- **XLink** – the W3C's mechanism for linking to other resources from within an XML document. Roughly analogous to a hyperlink, XLink also allows non-XML documents to be linked together.
- **XPath** – The W3C's general language specification for addressing parts of an XML document.
- **XPointer** – The W3C's mechanism for pointing to a particular location in, or portion of, an XML document. Note that XPointer wraps XPath – XPath is used to define the addressing mechanism, while XPointer provides a standard way to use that mechanism in references. XPointers may be used to point to XML documents from non-XML sources, such as HTML.

- **XML Fragment Interchange** – the W3C specification for the transmission of partial XML documents. It provides a way to specify contextual information for a fragment of a document without transmitting the entire document.
- **Querying XML documents** – we'll take a look at XSLT (which is covered more in depth in the next chapter) and how it may be used to query XML documents.

XML Information Set

The **XML Information Set**, or **Infoset**, is a working draft created by the W3C to describe the various bits of information that go together to create a well-formed XML document. The latest version of the W3C document on the Infoset may be found at http://www.w3.org/TR/xml-infoset.

Don't get lost in the jargon in this specification – basically, the purpose is to provide a common vocabulary to describe the contents of an XML document. Any XML processor that returns information about the content of an XML document will describe that content in terms of these information types. This vocabulary forms the basis for all other W3C specifications in progress that allow programmatic access to the internals of an XML document, while older specifications will have to adhere to it in their next iterations. As we'll see, the Document Object Model (discussed in Chapter 5) also manipulates XML content in terms of the information types described here.

Information Types

There are fifteen distinct types of information that together comprise a well-formed XML document. Some of these items are required to be in a parsed representation of an XML document in order for it to be congruent (by the W3C standards) to the original document, and others may be optionally discarded, and some that say 'required' are only required when present (we'll come back to this in a moment). The fifteen types of information are:

- exactly one document information item (required)
- one or more element information items (required)
- attribute information items (required)
- processing instruction information items (required)
- character information items (required)
- reference to skipped entity information items (required)
- comment information items (optional)
- a document type declaration information item (optional)
- entity information items (required for unparsed entities, optional for parsed entities)
- notation information items (required)
- entity start marker information items (optional)
- entity end marker information items (optional)
- CDATA start marker information items (optional)
- CDATA end marker information items (optional)
- namespace declaration items (required)

Each well-formed XML document must have exactly one document information item, and at least one element information item representing the root element of the document. Take for example the following smallest-possible well-formed XML document:

```
<Catalog/>
```

This document has a document information item representing information about the document as a whole (because every XML document has a document information item), and a `Catalog` element information item representing the `<Catalog>` element.

The items defined as optional above are optional in the sense that they are not necessary in a parsed representation of a document for it to be sufficiently congruent to the original by the W3C's Infoset definition. So, say for example you had the following XML document:

```
<Catalog>
   <Book>
      <Title>Professional XML</Title>
      <!-- We are missing some information for this book! -->
   </Book>
</Catalog>
```

When fully parsed, this document consists of a document information item, three element information items (`Catalog`, `Book`, and `Title`), and a comment information item. According to the Infoset specification, the comment information item may be discarded without loss of information in the original document – but you are required to keep the document information item and the three element information items.

Let's take a quick look at each information item type that is specified in the Infoset, and the properties that are defined for each one.

Document

There must always be exactly one **document** information item that contains information about the document as a whole. It has the following properties:

- A list of child information items in the order they occurred in the original document. This list will contain at least one element information item. Additionally, it must contain any processing instruction information items that are defined outside the context of the document's root element. At the developer's discretion, this list may also include comment information items that fall outside the document's root element, as well as the document type declaration information item (if one is specified in the original document).
- An unordered set of notation information items for all notations within the document.
- An unordered set of entity information items for all unparsed entities within the document. This list may also include entity information items for parsed entities, the document entity, and the external DTD subset, if the developer chooses.
- The developer may choose also to include the URI of the document being processed.

Element

There must be one **element** information item for each element in the XML document. The two variations of the syntax for an element should be familiar by now:

```
<Book/>
```

and

```
<Book>
   ...
</Book>
```

Element information items have the following properties:

- An ordered list of child **elements, processing instruction, reference to skipped entity**, and **character** information items, in the order they appear within the element. This list may be empty. At the developer's discretion, **comment** information items may also be included in this list. This list may also contain **entity start marker, entity end marker, CDATA start marker,** and **CDATA end marker** information items – if these are included, they must always be included in matching pairs (no start marker without an end marker, and vice-versa).
- An unordered set of **attribute** information items, one for each of the attributes of this element. Default attributes are also included in this set. Note that if a namespace attribute is provided for this element, and the parser is not namespace-aware, an attribute will be included in this list for the namespace specification; otherwise, it will not be included here. This set may be empty.
- The uniform resource identifier (URI) portion of the element name provided by the namespace processor. If there is no namespace processing being performed by the parser, or if no namespace is specified for the element, the URI should be null.
- The local portion of the element name. If no namespace processing is being performed by the parser, this name will be the stated name (including the namespace and colon if the element name contains a namespace identifier). Otherwise, this will be the local portion of the name only (the part after the colon), or the entire name if no namespace is specified.
- An unordered set of references to **namespace declaration** information items. These correspond to the namespaces declared as part of this element.
- At the developer's discretion, an unordered set of references to **namespace declaration** information items that correspond to the namespace declarations that are in scope for this element (that is, they are declared in this element or one of its ancestors).

I realize that the namespace handling process may be a bit unclear, so here's a couple of examples:

XML without namespaces:

```
<Catalog>
   <Book>
      ...
   </Book>
</Catalog>
```

For namespace-aware and non-namespace-aware parsers, the <Book> element would have:

```
URI = (null)
Local name = Book
```

Whereas, if the XML were to have namespaces:

```
<Catalog xmlns:wrox='http://www.wrox.com/Catalog'>
   <wrox:Book>
      ...
   </wrox:Book>
</Catalog>
```

For a namespace-aware parser, the <Book> element would have the properties:

```
URI = http://www.wrox.com/Catalog
Local name = Book
```

While for a non-namespace-aware parser it would have the properties:

```
URI = (null)
Local name = wrox:Book
```

See Chapter 7 for more information on namespaces.

Attribute

There must be one **attribute** information item for each attribute in the document. If the processor is namespace-aware, attributes used to define namespaces will not appear as information items. For example:

```
<Book color='red'>
   ...
</Book>
```

Here, `color` is an attribute.

Attribute information items have the following properties:

- The URI part, if any, of the attribute's name. See the previous definition of an element for an explanation of how the URI is treated by namespace-aware and non-namespace-aware parsers.
- The local part of the attribute's name. Again, see the definition of element to understand how namespaces are parsed.
- An ordered list of **character** information items for each character appearing in the (normalized) attribute value. Optionally, **entity start marker** and **entity end marker** information items for each entity reference in the attribute value may also be included in this list.
- At the developer's discretion, a flag indicating whether the value for this attribute was specified or set by default in a DTD or schema.
- At the developer's discretion, the default value for this attribute from the DTD.
- At the developer's discretion, the type declared for this attribute in the DTD – `ID`, `IDREF`, `IDREFS`, `ENTITY`, `ENTITIES`, `NMTOKEN`, `NMTOKENS`, `NOTATION`, `CDATA`, or `ENUMERATED`.

Processing Instruction

There must be one **processing instruction** information item for each processing instruction in the document. For the purposes of the Infoset, the XML declaration and external parsed entity declarations are not considered processing instructions *per se.* The syntax for a processing instruction is:

```
<?operation foo?>
```

Processing instruction information items have the following properties:

- The target of the processing instruction. This is the first token immediately following the "<?" in the processing instruction tag.
- The content of the processing instruction. This is the remaining text in the tag before the closing"?>", with leading white space removed. It may be an empty string.
- The developer may also include the URI of the entity that originally contained this processing instruction (if the processing instruction was declared in-line, this will be the URI of the document being processed, if known).

Reference to Skipped Entity

There must be one **reference to skipped entity** information item for each reference to an entity that a non-validating parser has not interpreted, either because the declaration for the unknown entity was not read (if it was not available, for example) or the parser does not include external parsed entities.

Say, for example, that the entity reference:

```
&Book;
```

was read by a non-validating parser, but the parser chose not to expand external parsed entities. This information would be represented as a **reference to unknown entity** information item.

Reference to unknown entity information items have the following properties:

- The name of the entity being referenced.
- At the developer's discretion, a reference to the entity information item for the unexpanded external parsed entity, if the parser has read the declaration.

Character

There must be one **character** information item for each non-markup character in the document. That's right – one information item per *character.*

For example, in the following fragment:

```
<Book>
   <Title>ABC</Title>
</Book>
```

there would be three **character** information items: one for the letter A, one for the letter B, and one for the letter C. In practice, implementations will combine adjacent characters into a text or string construct rather than listing each character separately (and this is permissible, according to the W3C Infoset specification).

Character information items have the following properties:

- The ISO 10646 (Unicode) character code for the character.
- A flag indicating whether this character is white space within content or not. Validating parsers must always set this flag; non-validating parsers may optionally set this flag to false.
- The developer may choose to indicate whether this character was included as part of a predefined XML entity.

Comment

There may be one **comment** information item for each comment in the document. Here is a comment:

```
<!-- We need more information on this book! -->
```

Comment information items have the following property:

- The content of the comment.

Document Type Declaration

There may be one **document type declaration** information item, if the developer chooses, and if there is a document type declaration in the document, such as:

```
<!DOCTYPE catalog SYSTEM "http://www.wrox.com/Catalog/Catalog.dtd">
```

A document type declaration information item may have the following properties:

- A reference to the **entity** information item for the external DTD subset.
- An ordered list of references to the **comment** and **processing instruction** information items that appear in the DTD.

Entity

Unparsed external entities are required to appear as **entity** information items. There may be an entity information item for each other entity in the document. If an entity is declared more than once, only the first declaration is used to create an **entity** information item.

An example of an internal entity declaration:

```
<!Entity Version "1.0">
```

An example of an external entity declaration:

```
<!Entity ProXMLBook SYSTEM "http://www.wrox.com/Catalog/ProXMLBook.xml">
```

An example of an external entity declaration for a non-XML data type:

```
<!Entity ProXMLCover SYSTEM "http://www.wrox.com/Catalog/ProXMLCover.gif"
   NDATA gif>
```

Entity information items have the following properties:

- The type of entity (internal parameter entity, external parameter entity, internal general entity, external general entity, unparsed entity, document entity, or external DTD subset).
- The name of the entity. Null if the **entity** information item is the document or external DTD entity. In the examples above, the entity name would be `Version`, `ProXMLBook`, and `ProXMLCover`, respectively.
- The system identifier of the entity. For internal entities, this property is null; for the document entity, it may be null or it may contain the system identifier for the document. For the examples above the system identifiers would be null, `http://www.wrox.com/Catalog/ProXMLBook.xml`, and `http://www.wrox.com/Catalog/ProXMLCover.gif`.
- The public identifier of the entity, if one exists. Null for internal entities.
- A reference to the **notation** information item associated with the entity, if the entity is an unparsed entity. Null for other entity types.
- The base URI of the entity. If this entity is an internal entity, this value must be null.
- At the developer's discretion, the text of the entity if it is an internal entity.
- The developer may also include the name of the character encoding set in which the entity is expressed.
- Optionally, the developer may also include an indication of the standalone status of the entity. Valid values are "`yes`", "`no`", and "`not present`".

Notation

There is one **notation** information item for each notation declared in the DTD. Such as:

```
<!NOTATION gif SYSTEM "gifviewer.exe">
```

Notation information items have the following properties:

- The name of the notation.
- The system identifier of the notation, or null if no system identifier was specified.
- The public identifier of the notation, or null if no public identifier was specified.
- The base URI that corresponds to the notation.

Entity Start Marker

There is one entity start marker to indicate the beginning of inserted text from a parsed general entity. They are not used for parameter entities.

Entity start marker information items have the following property:

- A reference to the **entity** information item for the inserted text.

Entity End Marker

There is one entity end marker to indicate the end of inserted text from a parsed general entity. They are not used for parameter entities.

Entity end marker information items have the following property:

- A reference to the **entity** information item for the inserted text.

CDATA Start Marker

There is one entity start marker to indicate the beginning of text embedded in a CDATA section.

CDATA start marker information items have no properties.

CDATA End Marker

There is one entity end marker to indicate the end of text embedded in a CDATA section.

CDATA end marker information items have no properties.

Namespace Declaration

There is one namespace declaration for each namespace that is declared (or implied) as an attribute of an element.

Namespace declaration information items have the following properties:

- The namespace being declared. This is the portion of the attribute name following the `xmlns:` prefix.
- The absolute URI of the namespace being declared. Either this property or the children property (described next) or both must be reported.
- An ordered list of character references to the character information items that make up the content of the attribute value. This may also include entity start and entity end markers to indicate the location of entity references. Either this property or the absolute URI property (or both) must be present. The W3C has added this property to allow for the possibility of non-URI namespaces in future implementations.

Importance of the Information Set

If these "information items" and "properties" sound familiar, they should – they're virtually identical to the objects in the DOM (which we discussed in Chapter 5). In fact, all of the various technologies the W3C has specified for accessing XML documents – the XML DOM, XLink, XPath, XPointer, and XSLT – derive from the basic structure outlined in the XML Information Set. In order to take full advantage of the functionality provided by these technologies, you need to stop thinking of XML documents as streams of text and start thinking of them in terms of these objects.

Finally, note that while the Information Set provides details for the connections between objects, it doesn't specify any particular implementation. While the various technologies we'll be discussing all interpret these objects as a tree structure, it's also perfectly acceptable to interpret them as a stream of objects with pointers to one another – and in fact, this is how most event-driven processors behave. Let's take a look at an example.

Say you have this document (which you should be familiar with by now) – I'll throw in my `color` attribute to spice things up a little bit:

```
<Catalog>
   <Book color="red">
      <Title>IE5 XML Programmer's Reference</Title>
      <Pages>480</Pages>
      <ISBN>1-861001-57-6</ISBN>
      <RecSubjCategories>
         <Category>Internet</Category>
         <Category>Web Publishing</Category>
         <Category>XML</Category>
      </RecSubjCategories>
      <Price>$49.99</Price>
   </Book>
</Catalog>
```

A tree-based representation of this document would look like this:

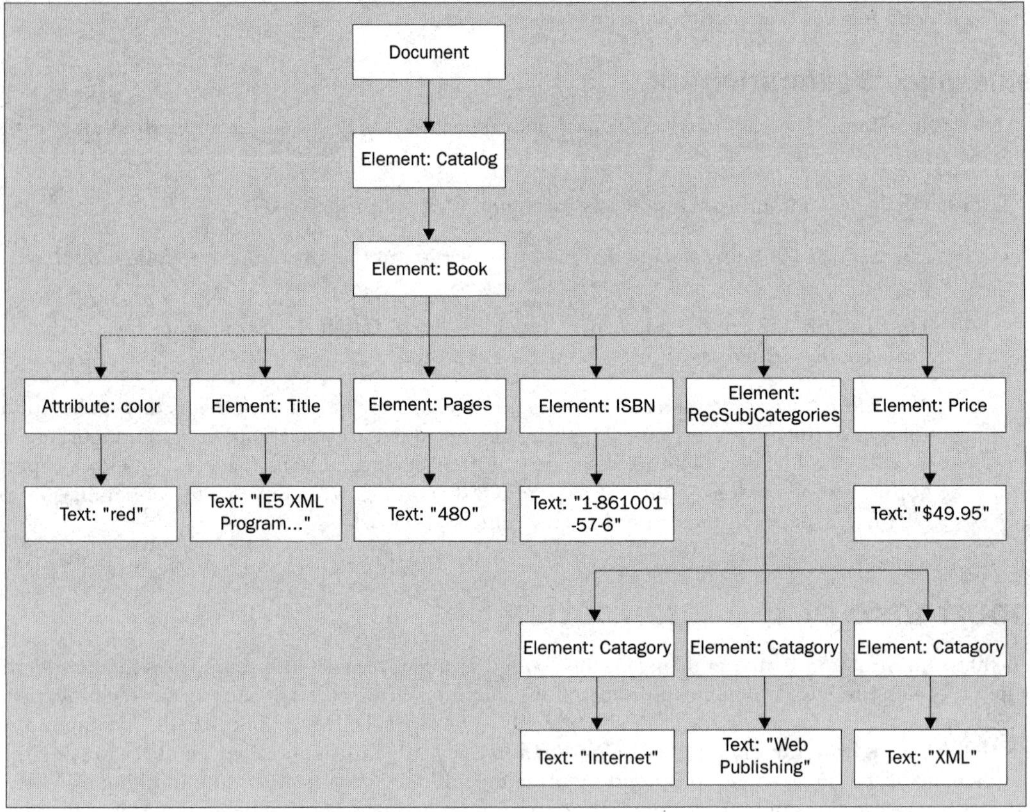

However, the Infoset would also allow the document to be represented like this:

Information Item ID	Information Item Type	Properties
1	Document	List of children: 2
2	Element	URI: Null Local name: Catalog List of children: 3 Set of attributes: Empty
3	Element	URI: Null Local name: Book List of children: 6, 8, 10, 12, 19 Set of attributes: 4
4	Attribute	URI: Null Local name: color Text of attribute: 5
5	Text	Value: "red"
6	Element	URI: Null Local name: Title List of children: 7 Set of attributes: Empty
7	Text	Value: "IE5 XML Programmer's Reference"
8	Element	URI: Null Local name: Pages List of children: 9 Set of attributes: Empty
9	Text	Value: "480"
10	Element	URI: Null Local name: ISBN List of children: 11 Set of attributes: Empty
11	Text	Value: "1-861001-57-6"
12	Element	URI: Null Local name: RecSubjCategories List of children: 13, 15, 17 Set of attributes: Empty
13	Element	URI: Null Local name: Category List of children: 14 Set of attributes: Empty
14	Text	Value: "Internet"
15	Element	URI: Null Local name: Category List of children: 16 Set of attributes: Empty
16	Text	Value: "Web Publishing"
17	Element	URI: Null Local name: Category List of children: 18 Set of attributes: Empty
18	Text	Value: "XML"
19	Element	URI: Null Local name: Price List of children: 20 Set of attributes: Empty
20	Text	Value: "$49.99"

Summary

In order to use the various technologies specified by the W3C to access and manipulate XML documents, you first need to understand the compartmentalization defined by the W3C in the Infoset specification. Once you can make the switch from thinking about XML documents in terms of text to thinking about them in terms of linked information items, you'll find that using the linking and querying mechanisms to access XML documents becomes very intuitive and natural. These technologies use the information set items described in the Infoset to manipulate and address XML documents, relying on the parent-child information represented in the items to navigate through those documents.

Linking

Let's take a look at how we can extend the functionality of XML by including links to external resources such as other XML documents, HTML documents, or even images. As we will see, we may use links to define relationships between similar documents, to define a sequence in which documents should be navigated, or even to embed non-XML content in an XML document.

What is Linking?

If you've used HTML, you are no doubt familiar with the concept of a **hyperlink**. You can specify an anchor that acts as a link to another document:

```
<A HREF="www.wrox.com/Catalog/Catalog.html">Book catalog</A>
```

This declaration tells us two things. First, it says that the text Book catalog is the start of a connection between two resources (because it's wrapped in an `A` tag that contains an `HREF` attribute). Second, it says that the URL `www.wrox.com/Catalog/Catalog.html` is the destination of that same connection. This is a simple example of a link – a connection between resources. XML linking is similar to HTML linking, but with greater functionality and flexibility (as we'll see a little later).

The Distinction Between Conceptual Linking and Rendering

Note that the above content is typically rendered by highlighting the start of the connection in some way (underlining it, changing its color, and so on), with a click of the mouse causing navigation to the destination content. However, this behavior is not explicitly defined in the HTML specification – a content rendering engine is free to render it any way it sees fit. One has only to think about a browser for a visually impaired user to understand why. Understanding the difference between linking and rendering is important if you are to understand the way XML linking works, since the XML linking specification only provides a conceptual model.

The Problem with HTML Links

We mentioned earlier that HTML links are fairly inflexible compared with XLink. In particular, HTML anchor links have the following drawbacks:

HTML Links are Embedded in the Source Document

This limitation prevents us from creating a link out of document whose markup we cannot edit, for example, or a document that doesn't provide native markup capacity (such as an image file). If we could somehow take our links out of the documents they reference, we could also construct a store for our links (in a link database or file) that connects our content together but is managed from a central location. We'll revisit the subject of link databases later.

HTML Links Only Allow Navigation in One Direction

If we have a sequence of pages we want the user to be able to navigate between, we need to explicitly define hyperlinks between all of them. For example, we might have a document called `page1.htm` that contains the word Next, hyperlinked to `page2.htm`. If we want to define a hyperlink (say for the word Previous) that allows us to navigate back to `page1.htm`, we need to explicitly define the link in the other direction here. It would be nice if we could state that the two pages are linked once, without worrying about the direction of the navigation.

HTML Links Only Connect Two Resources

We've all seen sites on the Internet where multiple pages of information are connected by lists of links, or by Previous and Next links:

```
<H3>Joe's Grill - Menu</H3>

Breakfast:
   Two eggs, any style..............$1.95
   Bacon............................$1.25
   Sausage..........................$1.25
   Pancakes.........................$3.00

<P><A HREF="http://www.joesgrill.com/beverages.htm">Beverages</A></P>
<P><A HREF="http://www.joesgrill.com/appetizers.htm">Appetizers</A></P>
<P><A HREF="http://www.joesgrill.com/sandwiches.htm">Sandwiches</A></P>
<P><A HREF="http://www.joesgrill.com/grill.htm">From the Grill</A></P>
<P><A HREF="http://www.joesgrill.com/dessert.htm">Desserts</A></P>
<P><A HREF="http://www.joesgrill.com/main.htm">Return to main menu</A></P>
```

Of course, each other page of the menu has a similar list of hyperlinks on it, making maintenance of the menu a nightmare. If Joe's Grill decides to add a pasta menu, for example, every page will need to have a link added to the pasta page. It would be nice if we could specify that all the resources were linked in one place and let the browser take care of navigating between them.

HTML Links Do Not Specify the Behavior of the Rendering Engine

It would be nice to be able to specify some additional conceptual behavior for the engine rendering the content. Should the rendering engine automatically traverse the link, or should it wait for user interaction before doing so? Should the rendering engine create a new context (for a browser, a window) to render the linked content, or should it even be embedded in with the current content? With HTML links, only the target named window may be specified, and the browser will behave differently based on the browser's current state (if a window with the specified name is already open, for example, it will replace that content; otherwise, it will create a new window).

The W3C's specification for XML linking addresses all of these issues, as we will see.

The W3C Specification: XLink

The specification for XML linking is known as XLink. It currently has a status of working draft, which means details of its implementation may change by the time it becomes a W3C recommendation. The latest version of this document may be found at http://www.w3.org/TR/WD-xlink. (At the time of writing the latest version was from the 20th December 1999.)

Since the XLink specification still has a status of working draft, there aren't any serious implementations of its functionality as of press time. Gaining a good understanding of these concepts now, however, will enable you to take full advantage of XLink when it enters the mainstream.

XLink Declarations

The namespace declared by the W3C for the December Working Draft of XLink is:

http://www.w3.org/1999/xlink/namespace/

To assert a link from an XML document, this namespace must be defined for the sub-tree in which the link is asserted. There are two ways of declaring a link:

- You may create an XLink element
- You may add XLink attributes to an element of your own

A XML link element looks something like this in an `<xlink:type>` element (note that there are two possible values in place of *type*, which we shall meet shortly):

```
<xlink:simple href="authors.xml" role="author list" title="Author list"
              show="replace" actuate="onRequest">
   List of authors
</xlink:simple>
```

And an element that has XLink attributes associated with it would look like this with an `xlink:type` attribute:

```
<Authors xmlns:xlink="http://www.w3.org/XML/XLink/0.9" xlink:type="simple"
         xlink:href="authors.xml" xlink:role="author list"
         xlink:title="Author list" xlink:show="replace"
xlink:actuate="onRequest"/>
```

Of course, the normal rules for namespaces apply – if you define the namespace on a parent, you don't have to declare it again for the linking element.

Note that if you choose to add XLink attributes to one of your own elements and you're using a DTD, you'll need to define the attributes in the `<!ATTLIST>` for the linking element. Otherwise, your validating processor will complain that it doesn't recognize the `xlink:*` attributes! For the above example, you would need this element definition in your DTD:

```
<!ELEMENT Authors EMPTY>
<!ATTLIST Authors
   xmlns:xlink   CDATA #FIXED "http://www.w3.org/1999/xlink/namespace/"
   xlink:type    (simple|extended|locator|arc) #FIXED "simple"
   xlink:href    CDATA #REQUIRED
   xlink:role    CDATA #IMPLIED
   xlink:title   CDATA #IMPLIED
   xlink:show    (new|embedded|replace) "replace"
   xlink:actuate (onLoad|onRequest) "onRequest" >
```

Link Types

As we just said, the `xlink:type` elements and attributes can take one of two values in the place of *type*: `simple` and `extended`. `Simple` links offer similar functionality to HTML hyperlinks, while `extended` links offer greater capabilities. As we'll see later, simple links are really just a subset of extended links – even though a different syntax is used for simple links. We'll take a look at each type of link in this section. Let's start with simple links.

Simple links

Simple links are very similar to the HTML `<A HREF=...>` link you may already be familiar with. The following attributes are used when declaring a simple link:

xlink:type

For simple links, this attribute is always `simple`. If you are declaring a simple XLink element, then the element name should be `xlink:simple`.

xlink:href

The destination URI of the link.

xlink:role

A string that describes the function of the link's content. While the W3C does not specify what the `role` may be used for, some implementations of XLink may use the `role` string to control rendering of the document.

xlink:title

A human-readable string that describes the link. Again, the W3C does not specify how this is to be used in an XLink-aware renderer, but it could be used to provide a visual indicator to the user that the element is a link.

xlink:show

This attribute defines how the target content is to be rendered for the user. It may take one of three values:

- `new` – the target content is to be rendered in a separate context (in a browser, this might be a new browser window).
- `replace` – the target content should replace the source content in its original context (in a browser, this would be normal hyperlink behavior).
- `embedded` – the content will be embedded in the source document at the link position.

xlink:actuate

This attribute defines when the link should be triggered. It may take one of two values:

- `onRequest` – the user must take some action to trigger the link. This is analogous to the way HTML hyperlinks work, where a user must click the linked text to activate the link.
- `onLoad` – the link will automatically be activated when the source document is loaded. This is most useful when the `xlink:show` attribute is `embedded`, but might also have some applications when it is `new` (to automatically open an additional context window with the destination information when the source document is opened, for example).

Simple links are functionally equivalent to HTML hyperlinks – they link two locations in one direction, and the start of the link is always the declaration of the link itself:

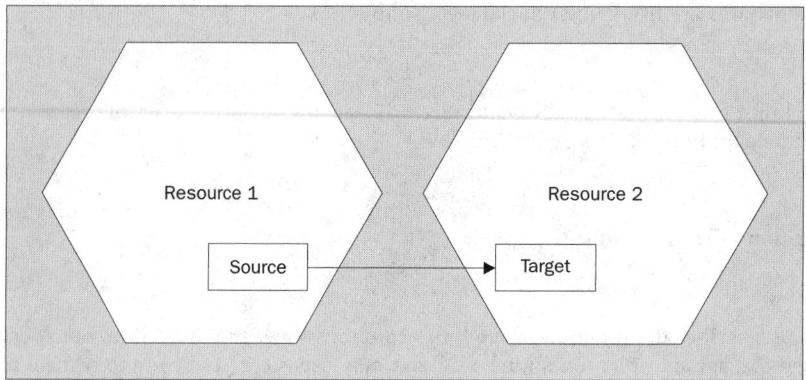

Note that even though we show the resources as being different, it's perfectly acceptable for both resources to be the same:

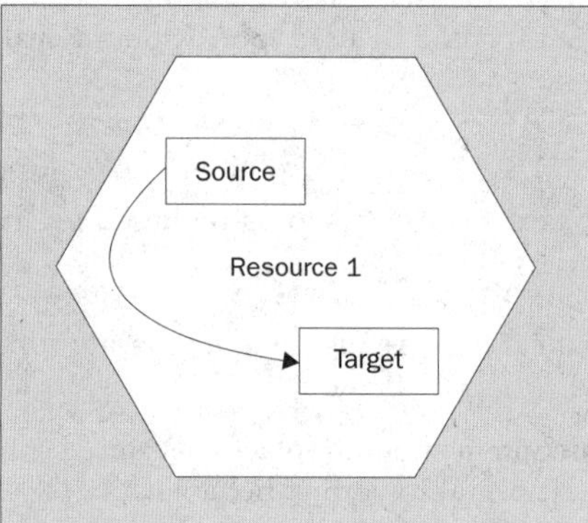

This will be an important point to remember later, when we're discussing extended links. XLink operates on locations, not resources – with the default location for a resource being the "top", however that happens to be defined for the type of resource.

Simple Link Examples

Let's take a look at a couple of quick examples before we move on:

```
<xlink:simple xmlns:xlink="http://www.w3.org/1999/xlink/namespace/"
              xlink:href="authors.xml"
              xlink:role="author list"
              xlink:title="Author list"
              xlink:show="new"
              xlink:actuate="onRequest"/>
```

This example creates a link with the title Author list, and makes the user aware that there is link information associated with it (perhaps by underlining it, as in an HTML document). When the user activates the link, the `authors.xml` document is opened in a new context.

```
<authors xmlns:xlink="http://www.w3.org/1999/xlink/namespace/"
                xlink:type="simple"
                xlink:href="authors.xml"
                xlink:role="author list"
                xlink:title="Author list"
                xlink:show="embedded"
                xlink:actuate="onLoad"/>
```

This example indicates that the authors.xml document should be rendered at the link position in the source document when the source document is initially rendered (remembering that it is actually up to the user agent how it treats the link, so it may vary).

Note that there are some combinations of show and actuate that don't make a great deal of sense, such as xlink:show = "replace" and xlink:actuate = "onLoad". This could potentially serve as a redirection from one document to another, but what will the renderer do if two such links are in the source document? As with all specific rendering behavior, the W3C specification makes no attempt to clarify what a renderer's behavior should be in circumstances like these, and only time will tell how specific implementations deal with the problem.

Extended Links

The other way links may be defined for XLink is as extended links. Extended links allow more than one resource to be linked together, and they may be specified out-of-line (that is, in a document other than the source document). Let's take a look at the syntax for extended links.

Here is the definition for an extended link:

```
<!ELEMENT xlink:extended
   (xlink:title*, xlink:arc*, xlink:locator, (xlink:arc | xlink:locator)*,
    xlink:resource*)>
<!ATTLIST xlink:extended
   role            NMTOKEN               #IMPLIED
   title           CDATA                 #IMPLIED>
```

Note that we may now have four types of sub-elements: <xlink:title>, <xlink:arc>, <xlink:locator>, and <xlink:resource>. We'll discuss these in a minute. The following attributes may be associated with an extended link element:

xlink:type

For extended links, this attribute is always extended. If you are declaring an extended XLink element, then the element name should be <xlink:extended>.

xlink:role

This attribute performs the same function as in the simple link element.

xlink:title

This attribute performs the same function as in the simple link element.

Note that there's no specification for the destination of the link – the href attribute is missing. Actually, the source isn't defined either – unlike simple links, extended links do not imply that their source is the document in which the link is located. To specify the various locations participating in an extended link and the connections between the links, we'll need to use the two sub-elements: <xlink:location> and <xlink:arc>.

The <xlink:title> Element

This element is used to associate semantic information with an extended link. For example, a link that associates the different pages of a menu might have an `<xlink:title>` element with the value "Menu". How this information is used is up to the processor – the XLink specification does not define the use of the information. Multiple titles may be specified (for example, if an XML document is being internationalized).

Here's the definition for the `<xlink:title>` element:

```
<!ELEMENT xlink:title ANY>
<!ATTLIST xlink:title
   xml:lang        CDATA             #IMPLIED
>
```

The one attribute, `xml:lang`, is used to specify the language for internationalization purposes.

The <xlink:locator> Element

These elements should always appear as sub-elements of an extended link. They are used to specify the locations that are participating in an extended link. For example, if we were implementing a link between five different resources (say, five pages of a menu), we would have one locator child element for each of the five resources participating in the link.

Here's the definition for the `<xlink:locator>` element:

```
<!ELEMENT xlink:locator ANY>
<!ATTLIST xlink:locator
   href  CDATA   #REQUIRED
   role  NMTOKEN #IMPLIED
   title CDATA   #IMPLIED >
```

As you can see, here we can specify the URI of the location, as well as its text name and approximate function. These attributes perform the same functions that they did for simple link elements.

Note that a locator does not explicitly indicate a link – it only specifies a location that is participating in the extended link. To define explicit connections between locators, we need to use the `<xlink:arc>` element.

The <xlink:arc> Element

These elements also appear as sub-elements of an extended link, and are used to define connections between two locators participating in an extended link.

Here's the definition for the `<xlink:arc>` element:

```
<!ELEMENT xlink:arc ANY>
<!ATTLIST xlink:arc
   from    NMTOKEN                #REQUIRED
   to      NMTOKEN                #REQUIRED
   show    (new|embedded|replace) "replace"
   actuate (onRequest|onLoad)     "onRequest" >
```

The show and actuate attributes perform the same function as they do for simple links: they define how the link is to be initiated and rendered. If these attributes are not specified, it is up to the particular implementation to decide how the arcs are to be traversed. In addition, there are two new attributes:

xlink:from

This attribute is the value of the role attribute of the <xlink:locator> or <xlink:resource> element that defines the start point of the link. Being able to explicitly define the source of a link allows us to create out-of-line link databases, as we'll see later in the chapter.

xlink:to

This attribute is the value of the role attribute of the <xlink:locator> or <xlink:resource> element that defines the end point of the link.

Note that if more than one locator or resource in an extended link has the same role, an arc defined on that role will connect all locators with that role. For example, say we have the following document:

```
<xlink:extended xmlns:xlink="http://www.w3.org/1999/xlink/namespace/"
                role="family"
                title="John Smith's family">
   <xlink:locator href="johnsmith.xml"
                role="parent"
                title="John Smith"/>
   <xlink:locator href="marysmith.xml"
                role="parent"
                title="Mary Smith"/>
   <xlink:locator href="billysmith.xml"
                role="child"
                title="Billy Smith"/>
   <xlink:locator href="kateysmith.xml"
                role="child"
                title="Katey Smith"/>
   <xlink:locator href="johnsmithjr.xml"
                role="child"
                title="John Smith Jr."/>
   <xlink:arc from="parent"
                to="child"
                show="replace"
                actuate="onRequest"/>
</xlink:extended>
```

The following connections are defined by the extended link:

```
John Smith to Billy Smith
John Smith to Katey Smith
John Smith to John Smith Jr.
Mary Smith to Billy Smith
Mary Smith to Katey Smith
Mary Smith to John Smith Jr.
```

The <xlink:resource> Element

These elements appear as sub-elements of an extended link, and are used to define local (inline) participants in the link (as opposed to the <xlink:locator> element, which is used to specify the out-of-line participants in the link). These elements have a role and title, and have a content type of ANY; the usage of that content is not defined by the XLink specification.

Here's the definition for the <xlink:resource> element:

```
<!ELEMENT xlink:resource ANY>
<!ATTLIST xlink:resource
   role           NMTOKEN         #IMPLIED
   title          CDATA           #IMPLIED
>
```

Implicit versus Explicit Arcs

Note that some connection information may be determined by looking at the list of locations that are participating in an extended link. Say we have the following extended link declaration:

```
<xlink:extended xmlns:xlink="http://www.w3.org/1999/xlink/namespace/"
                role="menu pages"
                title="Joe's menu">
   <xlink:locator href="menu1.xml"
                role="menu page 1"
                title="Beverages"/>
   <xlink:locator href="menu2.xml"
                role="menu page 2"
                title="Appetizers"/>
   <xlink:locator href="menu3.xml"
                role="menu page 3"
                title="Sandwiches"/>
   <xlink:locator href="menu4.xml"
                role="menu page 4"
                title="Desserts"/>
   <xlink:arc from="menu page 1"
                to="menu page 2"
                show="replace"
                actuate="onRequest"/>
   <xlink:arc from="menu page 2"
                to="menu page 3"
                show="replace"
                actuate="onRequest"/>
   <xlink:arc from="menu page 3"
                to="menu page 4"
                show="replace"
                actuate="onRequest"/>
</xlink:extended>
```

The explicit links in this declaration are those defined by <xlink:arc> elements:

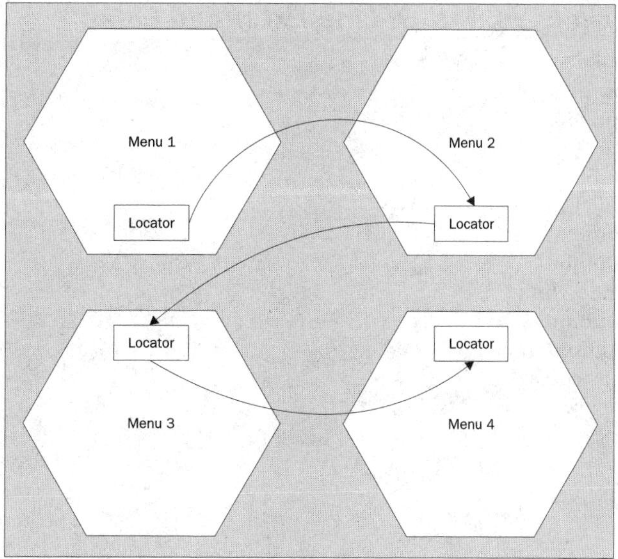

However, if we did not include the <xlink:arc> elements, there would be an implicit arc between each of the locators defined as part of the extended link definition:

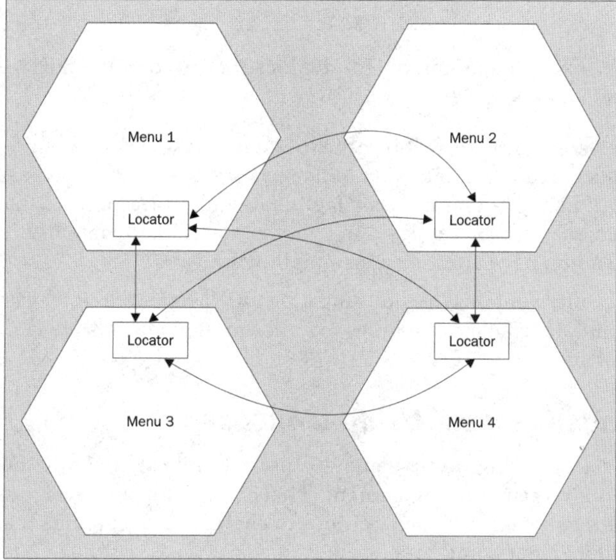

The W3C doesn't specify whether an XLink-aware parser needs to handle implicit links, or if they are to be handled differently than explicit links. Again, it remains to be seen how implementations of XLink deal with the issue.

By defining an extended link with locators and arcs, any number of resources may be connected together in as complex a fashion as is necessary. We'll take a look at some ways extended links may be used a little later, but first let's take a look at the difference between **inline** extended links and **out-of-line** extended links.

Inline Extended Links vs. Out-Of-Line Extended Links

Extended links may be embedded in one of the resources participating in an extended link (if that resource happens to be an XML document). The link definition doesn't imply anything about any of the locators in the extended link – it's parsed by the XLink-aware processor and used in whatever way that processor sees fit to render the arcs between the locators.

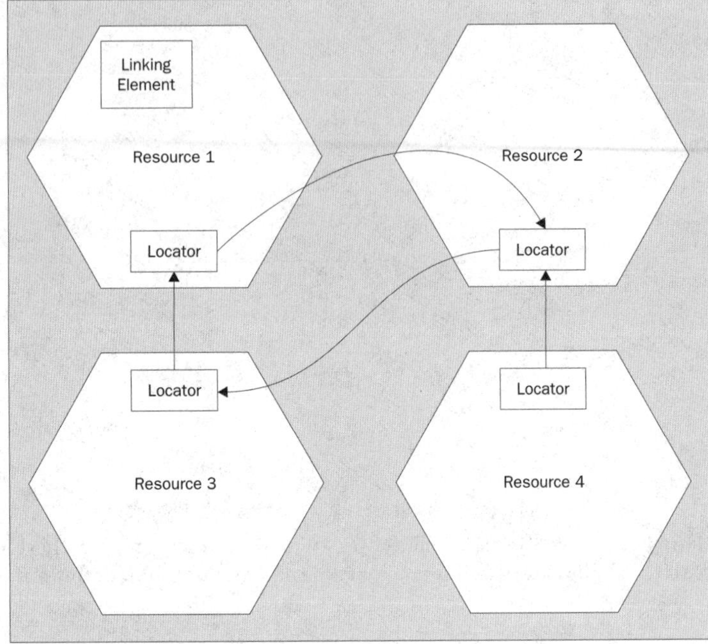

While embedding the extended link in one of the locations used in the link will work, this approach has a couple of problems:

- An XLink-aware processor will be able to navigate the links if the resource containing the extended link is read first, but what happens if, say, Resource 2 is read first? The processor has no way of knowing that there's a legitimate link to Resource 3 that may be navigated. The link information could be repeated in every resource that contains a locator in the extended link, but then you have a maintenance nightmare.
- The resource that contains the links must be an XML resource. What happens, for example, if we want to link four image resources together in the pattern shown above? Where can we put the link information?

Out-Of-Line Extended Links – Using Linkbases

A special type of `<xlink:extended>` element is used to indicate to an XLink-aware processor that out-of-line links exist for a particular document. Their `role` attribute must be set to `xlink:external-linkset`. The locator sub-elements then define external XML documents that may contain XLink information for the document being processed:

```
<xlink:extended
   xmlns:xlink="http://www.w3.org/1999/xlink/namespace/"
   role="xlink:external-linkset">
   <xlink:locator
      href="http://www.wrox.com/Catalog/linkdb.xml"
      role="linkdatabase"
      title="Out-of-line catalog links" />
</xlink:extended>
```

When an XLink-aware processor encounters an extended link with a role of `xlink:external-linkset`, it reads the documents indicated in the locator sub-element(s) of that extended link element, looking for extended links that reference the document being processed. It then "remembers" that information as if it were included in the original document. This makes it much easier to maintain linkages between items – in effect, solving the "Joe wants to add a pasta menu" problem we ran into earlier.

Here's our separate XML document containing out-of-line link information connecting our resources:

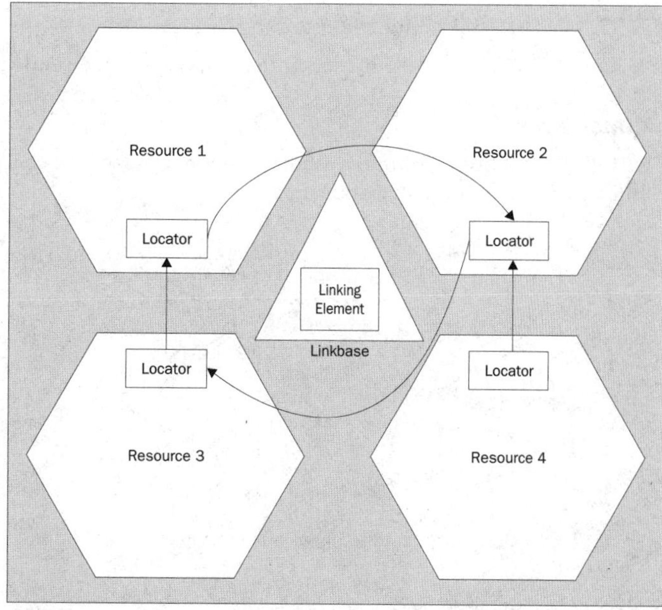

If we then add `xlink:external-linkset` extended links to the four linked documents, information for the external link will then be available when any of the documents is the current document:

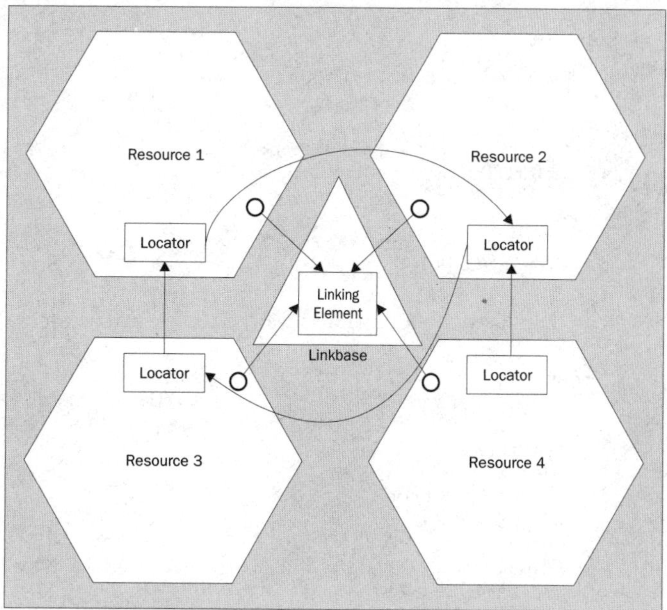

Some Examples of Extended XLinks

Let's take a look at the way extended links solve some of the problems we mentioned before with HTML links:

- HTML links must be embedded in the source document
- HTML links only allow navigation in one direction
- HTML links only connect two resources
- HTML links do not specify the behavior of the rendering engine

Link Databases

Using extended link groups, we can maintain a list of links between documents. We might have the following link document, `menulink.xml`:

```
<xlink:extended xmlns:xlink="http://www.w3.org/1999/xlink/namespace/"
                role="menu links"
                title="See other parts of menu">
   <xlink:locator href="menu1.xml"
                role="menu page 1"
                title="Beverages"/>
   <xlink:locator href="menu2.xml"
                role="menu page 2"
                title="Appetizers"/>
   <xlink:locator href="menu3.xml"
                role="menu page 3"
                title="Sandwiches"/>
   <xlink:locator href="menu4.xml"
                role="menu page 4"
                title="Desserts"/>
   <xlink:arc from="menu page 1"
                to="menu page 2"
                show="replace"
                actuate="onRequest"/>
   <xlink:arc from="menu page 2"
                to="menu page 3"
                show="replace"
                actuate="onRequest"/>
   <xlink:arc from="menu page 3"
                to="menu page 4"
                show="replace"
                actuate="onRequest"/>
</xlink:extended>
```

We can then have the following `menu1.xml` (the same general format applies to all the menu pages):

```
<menupage xmlns:xlink="http://www.w3.org/1999/xlink/namespace/">
   <xlink:extended role="xlink:external-linkset">
      <xlink:locator href="menulink.xml"/>
   </xlink:extended>
   <menuitem>
      <name>Coffee</name>
      <price>$0.99</price>
   </menuitem>
   <menuitem>
      <name>Tea</name>
      <price>$1.09</price>
```

```
    </menuitem>
    <menuitem>
       <name>Soda</name>
       <price>$1.25</price>
    </menuitem>
</menupage>
```

When menu1.xml is opened, an XLink-aware processor will read the extended link information from the menulink.xml document and render the document in a way that will make it clear that this document links to menu2.xml. A browser might choose to render the information this way (of course, this is a mockup – no browser directly supports XLink as of press time):

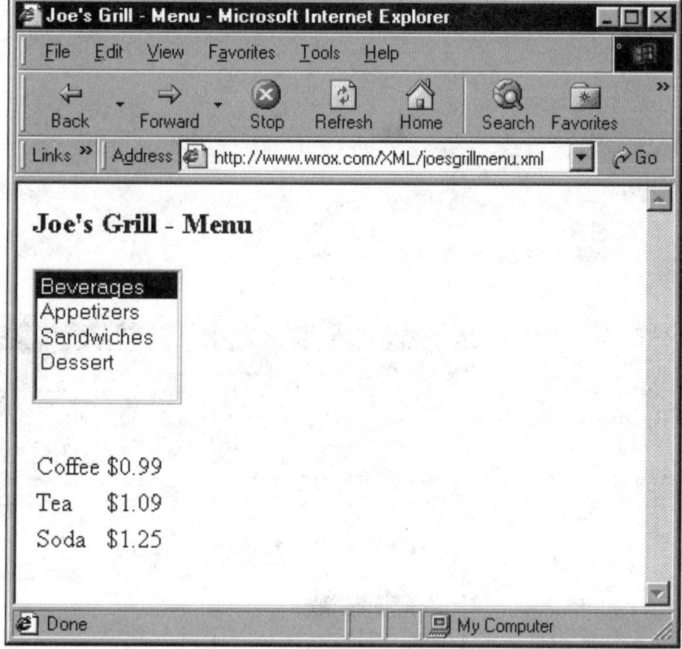

If Joe now wants to add a pasta menu, all we need to do is modify the link database document:

```
<xlink:extended xmlns:xlink="http://www.w3.org/1999/xlink/namespace/"
                role="menu links"
                title="See other parts of menu">
   <xlink:locator href="menu1.xml"
                role="menu page 1"
                title="Beverages"/>
   <xlink:locator href="menu2.xml"
                role="menu page 2"
                title="Appetizers"/>
   <xlink:locator href="menu3.xml"
                role="menu page 3"
                title="Sandwiches"/>
   <xlink:locator href="menu4.xml"
                role="menu page 4"
                title="Desserts"/>
```

```
    <xlink:locator href="menu5.xml"
                   role="menu page 5"
                   title="Pasta"/>
    <xlink:arc from="menu page 1"
                   to="menu page 2"
                   show="replace"
                   actuate="onRequest"/>
    <xlink:arc from="menu page 2"
                   to="menu page 3"
                   show="replace"
                   actuate="onRequest"/>
    <xlink:arc from="menu page 3"
                   to="menu page 4"
                   show="replace"
                   actuate="onRequest"/>
    <xlink:arc from="menu page 3"
                   to="menu page 5"
                   show="replace"
                   actuate="onRequest"/>
    <xlink:arc from="menu page 5"
                   to="menu page 4"
                   show="replace"
                   actuate="onRequest"/>
  </xlink:extended>
```

We then create the menu5.xml document for the pasta items, and that's it – we don't have to go back and modify any of the other menu pages! Our browser would reflect the change automatically:

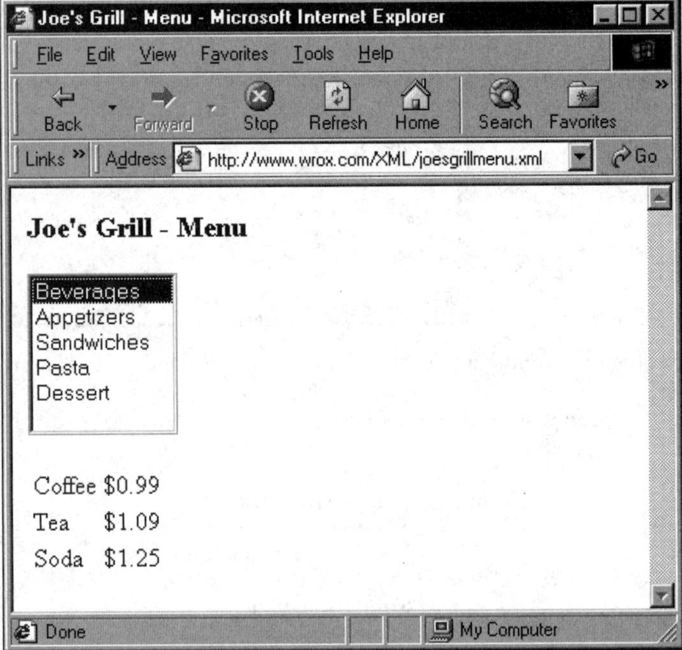

If we wanted to change the order the menu pages were traversed, we could do so by modifying the link database document (instead of touching each participating document in the link, as we would need to with HTML). As you can see, the abstraction of link information away from content is a powerful way of controlling and maintaining links between documents, as well as allowing others who do not control your content to link to (and from!) it – as we'll see in the next section.

Marking Up Read-Only Documents

Using out-of-line links is also great way to annotate read-only documents from another source. Let's take a look at a brief example of how this might be done.

Say we have the following, read-only document, called `quotelist.xml`, which contains quotes, which we can then annotate to clarify:

```
<quotelist>
   <quote>
      Now is the time for all good men to come to the aid of their country.
   </quote>
</quotelist>
```

We want to add to this document in another document, `comments.xml`:

```
<comment>
   By men, the author obviously meant all people, not the male gender.
</comment>
```

We can specify a link document, `commentlink.xml`, which asserts a linkage between `comments.xml` and the read-only `quotelist.xml`:

```
<xlink:extended xmlns:xlink="http://www.w3.org/1999/xlink/namespace/"
                role="quote comments"
                title="Comments">
   <xlink:locator href="quotelist.xml"
                role="quotes"
                title="Famous quotes"/>
   <xlink:locator href="comments.xml"
                role="comments"
                title="Commentary"/>
   <xlink:arc from="quotes"
                to="comments"
                show="new"
                actuate="onRequest"/>
</xlink:extended>
```

An XLink-aware processor would open the link document, read the extended link, and see that there is a link between the `quotelist` document and the comments document. It might then bring up the `quotelist` content and allow links back from it to the comments document:

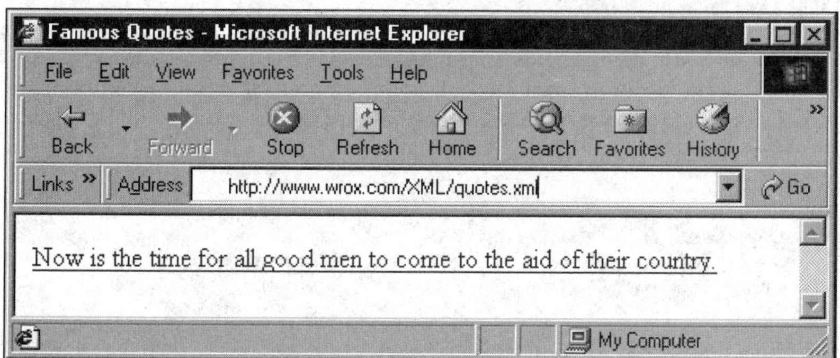

Clicking on the linked element would bring up the comment information:

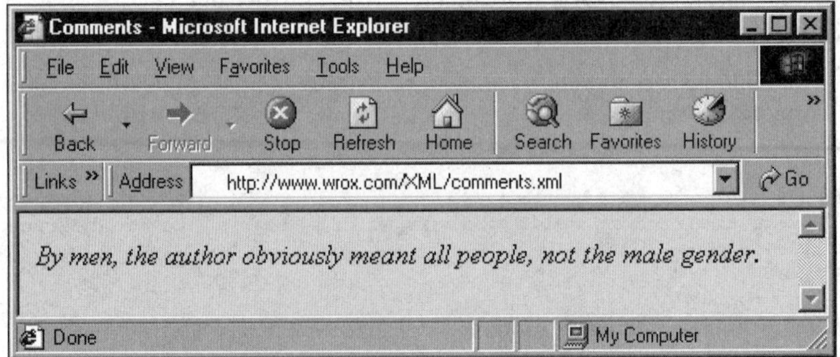

It would be even better if we could link to the precise location in the `quotelist.xml` document that corresponds to the word we are commenting on, "men" – but that's the job of **XPointer**, which we'll discuss next.

XLink Summary

XLink provides a flexible mechanism for defining links in XML documents that connect various resources together. These resources may even be resources that don't normally have the ability to contain links, like image files. XLink may be used to link one document to another, much as HTML hyperlinks work, or it may be used to link many different resources together. It may also be used to abstract link information away from content, allowing linkage information to be easily updated. However, XLink is not implemented in any serious fashion in the toolsets most commonly in use at this time – although some form of XLink will undoubtedly be available soon for use by XML developers.

XPointer

We mentioned earlier that it would be nice if we could point not to an entire XML document, but to some portion of it – individual sub-trees, attributes, or even individual characters that are part of text content. The W3C has defined a mechanism that allows us to do just that.

HTML Pointers

Again, the concept of XML Pointers has an analogue in HTML: the `<A NAME=...>` markup. This markup indicates that the position marked by the `<A>` element may be linked to using the HTML pointer syntax. For example, if we have the following document, `content.htm`:

```
<HTML>
   <BODY>
      <A NAME="sentence1">This is the first sentence.</BR></A>
      <A NAME="sentence2">This is the second sentence.</BR></A>
      <A NAME="sentence3">This is the third sentence.</BR></A>
   </BODY>
</HTML>
```

We can link to this document from another document, `index.htm`, using this syntax:

```
<HTML>
  <BODY>
    <A HREF="content.htm#sentence1">Go to the first sentence</BR></A>
    <A HREF="content.htm#sentence2">Go to the second sentence</BR></A>
    <A HREF="content.htm#sentence3">Go to the third sentence</BR></A>
  </BODY>
</HTML>
```

HTML uses the # character to indicate that the text following it refers to a named anchor point in the target document. A browser will typically render the content by positioning the viewer at the marked position in the target document. Note that, like HTML anchors, the targeted document does not need to be directly specified; if it is not, all XPointer locations are relative to the base URI of the document (usually the document containing the XPointer). XPointer expressions may be used anywhere a URI is used, and an XPointer-aware processor should handle them properly. For example, an XPointer might be used to further refine the URI of a locator in an extended XLink.

The Problem With HTML Pointers

Like HTML links, HTML pointers have shortcomings.

HTML Anchor Points Must Be Declared

In order to point to a specific location in an HTML document, that document must contain an `<A NAME=...>` anchor reference. HTML pointers may not point to a location in an HTML document that does not have this declaration, making it impossible to point into a read-only document that doesn't already have anchor points declared.

HTML Anchor Points Must Link to the Entire Target Document

There is no way to specify an HTML pointer that points to part of a target document – all that may be specified is an anchor point in the full document. It would be nice if we could define a pointer that points to only a portion of a target document, so the processor could render only that section instead of the full target.

The XML pointing mechanism addresses both of these issues, as we'll see later.

The XPointer Specification

The W3C specification for XML pointers is known as XPointer. It may be found at http://www.w3.org/TR/xptr.

As of the time of writing, the XPointer specification is a Working Draft in last call status. This means it is likely to become a Recommendation within the next couple of months, and the information found in the specification is unlikely to change very much.

Note that the XPointer specification essentially extends another specification, XPath. XPath is the W3C's common mechanism for addressing individual information items in an XML document, and is also a major component of XSLT. XPointer provides a syntax for stating address information in a link to an XML document, as well as extending XPath with a few additional features. We'll discuss XPath briefly a little later.

Specifying XPointers in a URI

XPointers are referenced in a similar way to HTML pointers. When working with an XPointer-aware processor, URIs may contain a reference to a position in an XML document by appending an XPointer fragment identifier to the URI of the document itself. Unlike HTML anchor references, the pointing mechanism being used in the URI must be identified by putting the pointing mechanism name and parentheses around the locator – for XPointers, this will always take the form `xpointer()`.

For example:

```
http://www.wrox.com/Catalog/catalog.xml#xpointer(book1)
```

would point to the element with the ID `book1` in the `catalog.xml` document. We'll talk about the way fragment identifiers may be specified in some real depth a little later.

In the previous example, the document is being pointed into in the same way that an HTML pointer would – the fragment identifier specifies a position to which the document should be moved when rendered. It's also possible to request that only the specified fragment be rendered and the rest of the document be discarded. This is done by using the "|" fragment specifier rather than "#":

```
http://www.wrox.com/Catalog/catalog.xml|xpointer(book1)
```

This URI would only render the element with the ID `book1` (and anything contained in that element, such as its child elements and attributes) and discard the rest of the document. This provides a great way to sift through large XML documents and only return information that is relevant to the situation at hand.

How May Fragment Identifiers be Specified?

There are three ways of specifying fragment identifiers in XPointer. One of them, the full specification, is quite complex and allows a great deal of flexibility in pointing into an XML document. It builds on the W3C XPath Recommendation, which we'll discuss when we talk about the full specification mechanism. First, we'll talk about the two other ways fragment identifiers may be specified in XPointer.

Bare Name Fragment Identification

To provide a similar functionality to that we are used to in HTML pointers, a shorthand notation is provided for pointing to elements with specific IDs. For example, let's say we had the following document, `catalog.xml`:

```
<Catalog>
   <Book color="red" ID="book1">
      <Title>IE5 XML Programmer's Reference</Title>
      <Pages>480</Pages>
      <ISBN>1-861001-57-6</ISBN>
      <RecSubjCategories>
         <Category>Internet</Category>
         <Category>Web Publishing</Category>
         <Category>XML</Category>
      </RecSubjCategories>
      <Price>$49.99</Price>
   </Book>
</Catalog>
```

We may point to the Book element with the ID book1 using the following syntax:

```
#book1
```

If the fragment is simply an ID value, the pointer points to the element with that ID value. Note that for this shorthand to work, the document being pointed into must have a schema that specifies the ID attribute for the element.

Child Sequence Fragment Identification

Child sequence fragment identifiers, or **tumbler** fragment identifiers, allow a document to be pointed into by walking through the child element tree. Some examples may be helpful. In our sample catalog document, catalog.xml:

```
<Catalog>
   <Book color="red" ID="book1">
      <Title>IE5 XML Programmer's Reference</Title>
      <Pages>480</Pages>
      <ISBN>1-861001-57-6</ISBN>
      <RecSubjCategories>
         <Category>Internet</Category>
         <Category>Web Publishing</Category>
         <Category>XML</Category>
      </RecSubjCategories>
      <Price>$49.99</Price>
   </Book>
</Catalog>
```

We may point to the second Category element with the URI:

```
#/1/1/4/2
```

This syntax may be understood this way:

- Go to the first element in the document (the Catalog element)
- Then go to the first child element of that element (the book1 <Book> element)
- Then go to the fourth child element of that element (the <RecSubjCategories> element)
- Then go to the second child element of that element (the Web Publishing <Category> element)

Tumblers may also start from a named node, specified as in the bare name fragment identification method. The following URI is equivalent to the one above:

```
http://www.wrox.com/catalog/catalog.xml#xpointer(book1/4/2)
```

The Full XPointer Specification

The full XPointer specification is built on the XPath Recommendation. XPath provides a universal way of specifying some portion of an XML document. It is a base technology for both XPointer and XSLT, which we'll cover in a later chapter. The next section looks at the way XPath expressions are constructed and how they may be used to point into XML documents.

The W3C XPath Recommendation

XPath is a specification that was worked on jointly by members of the XSL and XPath Working Groups, as they realized that both required a way of selecting a part of an XML document. Both groups use and build upon the functionality offered by XPath. The specification for XPath has a status of Recommendation, meaning that it's ready to be implemented and will not change from its current status in this version. It may be found at http://www.w3.org/TR/XPath. In this section we will look at XPath is some depth; which will equip you with more than enough information to implement XPointers.

Location Steps

Location steps are the construct you will be using the most when constructing XPointers. They provide a way to select nodes from an XML document. They all operate with respect to the **context node**, which is simply the current node in the XML document as the location step is being evaluated (if a node is not specified in some other way, the current node is the root element of the document). Note that if we have more than one location step in an XPointer, there may be more than one current node being evaluated. This will make more sense when we get to some examples later.

Location nodes are constructed from three types of information: the **axis**, the **node test**, and zero or more **predicates**. Let's take a look at each of these and their role in locating nodes in the target document.

Axis

The axis partitions the document based on the context node. It is used to define a starting region to apply the node test and predicate(s) to when evaluating the expression. The possible axes are:

Axes	Definition
`child`	contains all the children of the context node.
`descendant`	contains all the children, grandchildren, and so on of the context node.
`parent`	the parent of the context node.
`ancestor`	the parent node, grandparent node, and so on of the context node.
`following-sibling`	the following siblings of the context node.
`preceding-sibling`	the preceding siblings of the context node.
`following`	all of the nodes that come after the context node in document order. This axis does not include the descendants of the context node, or attribute and namespace nodes.
`preceding`	all of the nodes that come before the context node in document order. This axis does not include the ancestors of the context node, or attribute and namespace nodes.
`attribute`	the attribute nodes of the context node.
`namespace`	the namespace nodes of the context node.
`self`	the context node only.
`descendant-or-self`	the union of the descendant node and the self node.
`ancestor-or-self`	the union of the ancestor node and the self node.

Once we have specified a partition of the document to analyze, we may further narrow it down by using a node test.

Node Tests

Node tests allow specific elements or node types to be selected from the specified axis. There are several types of node tests:

- Specifying an element name matches only those nodes that have that name. A node test of `Book` would only match elements called `<Book>` within the specified axis.
- Specifying the wildcard character, `*`, matches all elements in the specified axis.
- The `node()` node test matches all nodes in the specified axis.
- The `text()` node test matches all text elements in the specified axis.
- The `comment()` node test matches all comment elements in the specified axis.
- The `processing-instruction()` node test matches all processing instruction elements in the specified axis. In addition, a name may be specified in the parentheses; the test will then only match those processing instruction elements that have the specified name.

Predicates

Predicates allow further filtering of the node set identified by the axis and the node test. A predicate is a Boolean expression that is evaluated for each node in the resultant node set after filtering using the axis and node test.

XPath provides a number of functions that you can use to test for the nodes you require. These functions return values of various forms, such as strings and numbers, which you can compare using the comparative operators =, !=, <=, <, >=, and >, either with each other or with constants that you provide. Larger expressions can also be separated by the Boolean operators `and` and `or`. In this case, the expressions in question (on either side of the Boolean operator) are passed to the `Boolean()` function, which processes expressions in the following way:

- **numbers**– true if and only if they are neither zero, positive zero, nor NaN (see below)
- **node-sets** –true if and only if they are non-empty
- **strings** – true if and only if their length is non-zero
- **objects** – if these are of a type other than the four basic types (number, node set, Boolean, and string) they are converted to a Boolean in a way that is dependent on that type

Numbers are double-precision 64-bit format IEEE 754 values, and fall into the following categories:

- positive numbers
- negative numbers
- positive zero
- negative zero
- positive infinity ("`Infinity`")
- negative infinity ("`-Infinity`")
- not-a-number ("`NaN`")

The operators +, -, *, div, and mod can be used with numbers, along with parentheses, to influence the order of mathematical operations.

The simplest function provided by XPath is `Position()`, which simply evaluates to the position of the element in question. We could use this, for example, to select only the first `<Book>` child element of the context element, using the predicate:

```
position() = 1
```

We'll see how predicates fit into complete XPath expressions later.

As this function is used so often, it is used implicitly where functions result in numbers, or numerical constants are used, so the above predicate can simply be expressed as:

```
1
```

The complete set of predicate functions are divided up into the following types in the XPath specification:

- **node set** functions
- **string** functions
- **Boolean** functions
- **number** functions

We'll look at each of these types in turn, but before we list the functions we should examine some of the fundamental definitions they require.

Definitions

Many functions operate on the current **expression evaluation context** in some way. The context consists of the context node (which, as we have already seen, is the current node being evaluated, or the root node if none is specified) along with the following:

- **context size** – the total count of nodes within the context, determined using the context node and the axis
- **context position** – the current position within the nodes in the context, which is less than or equal to the context size
- **variable bindings** – mappings between variable names and values, where values are objects
- **function library** – mappings between function names and functions
- **namespace declarations** – mappings from namespace prefixes to URIs

Any given node has a **string-value**. String-values exist for every type of node, and may come from part of the node in question, or may be made of the string-values of its descendants.

Some types of node have an **expanded-name**, of the form `MyNamespace:MyName`. The `MyNamespace` part is the **namespace-uri**, the `MyName` part is the **local** part.

Now, let's go on and look at the functions.

Node Set Functions

These functions concern multiple nodes, and are shown in the table below:

Function (Return Type, Name, and Parameters)	Description
`number last()`	Returns the context size of the expression evaluation context.
`number position()`	Returns the context position of the expression evaluation context.
`number count( node-set)`	Returns the number of nodes in the argument node set.
`node-set id( object)`	Returns a node set containing nodes with `ID` attributes matching those in the `object` parameter. `object` can be a white space separated string of `ID`s, or a node-set in its own right, in which case the set of `ID`s is constructed from the **string-value**s of those nodes.
`string local-name( node-set?)`	Returns the local part of the expanded-name of the first node in the node set supplied (in document order), or of the context node if this parameter is omitted. Empty strings are returned for empty node sets or nodes with no expanded-name.
`string namespace-uri( node-set?)`	Returns the namespace part of the expanded-name of the first node in the node set supplied (in document order), or of the context node if this parameter is omitted. Empty strings are returned for empty node sets or nodes with no namespace.
`string name( node-set?)`	Returns a `QName` representing the expanded-name of the first node in the node set supplied (in document order), or of the context node if this parameter is omitted.

String Functions

String functions are those that operate on or return strings:

Function (Return Type, Name, and Parameters)	Description
`string string( object?)`	Returns a stringified version of the object specified, or the string-value of the context node if none is specified. If the object is a node set then the string-value of the first node in the set (in document order), is returned. Numbers return their string representation, Booleans return `true` or `false`, and other types of object return values dependant on their type.
`string concat( string, string, string*)`	Returns the concatenation of its arguments.
`boolean starts-with( string, string)`	True if the first string starts with the second string, otherwise false.

Table Continued on Following Page

Function (Return Type, Name, and Parameters)	Description
`boolean contains( string, string)`	True if the first string contains the second string, otherwise false.
`string substring-before( string, string)`	Returns the portion of the first string that occurs before the second string, if the first string contains the second string, otherwise returns an empty string.
`string substring-after( string, string)`	Returns the portion of the first string that occurs after the second string, if the first string contains the second string, otherwise returns an empty string.
`string substring( string, number, number?)`	Returns the portion of the string from the character indexed by the first number, with the length specified by the second number. If the second number is omitted, the returned string will contain all the characters in the original string from the indexed character to the end of the string. Characters are indexed from the beginning where the first character is character 1.
`number string-length( string?)`	Returns the number of characters in the specified string, or of the string-value of the context node if no string is supplied.
`string normalize-space( string?)`	Strips leading and trailing white space and replaces sections of white space with single spaces. Operates on the string-value of the context node if no argument is used.
`string translate( string, string, string)`	Replaces characters in the first string supplied according to the second and third strings. Each character in the first string is compared with the characters in the second string, and is replaced if there is a match. The replacement character is the one in the third string whose position matches that of the matched character in the second string. If there is no character at this position in the third string (which may occur if the third string is shorter than the second string) then the character is simply removed.

Boolean Functions

Boolean functions all return Boolean values:

Function (Return Type, Name, and Parameters)	Description
`boolean boolean( object)`	Returns a Boolean dependant on the supplied object. The rules governing this transformation were discussed earlier.
`boolean not( boolean)`	Returns true if its argument is false, and false otherwise.
`boolean true()`	Returns true.

Function (Return Type, Name, and Parameters)	Description
`boolean false()`	Returns false.
`boolean lang( string)`	Returns true if the language of the context node (as specified by its xml:lang attribute) is the same as (or is a sub-language of) the language specified. Returns false if the languages are different or if this attribute does not appear in the node.

Number Functions

These return numbers based on their arguments:

Function (Return Type, Name, and Parameters)	Description
`number number( object?)`	Converts strings to their numerical equivalent (according to the IEEE 754 round-to-nearest rule) or to `NaN`, Booleans to 1 (true) or 0 (false), uses the string-value of the first node (in document order) of a node set into its numerical equivalent (in the same way as a string), or other objects into numbers depending on their type.
`number sum( node-set)`	Returns the sum of the numbers represented by the string-values of the nodes in the node set.
`number floor( number)`	Returns the largest number (closest to positive infinity) that is not greater than the argument and is an integer.
`number ceiling( number)`	Returns the smallest number (closest to negative infinity) that is not less than the argument and is an integer.
`number round( number)`	Returns the integer that is closest to the value of the argument, using the value closest to positive infinity if two integers fit this statement.

We'll see some examples later that make the use of predicates more clear.

Putting It All Together

A location set specification takes the form:

```
axis::node test[predicate]
```

So, to select the first three `<Book>` child elements of the context element we would use:

```
child::Book[position() <= 3]
```

Note that if this expression is embedded in a tag (such as an XLink pointing to an XPointer), the characters `<` and `&` will need to be escaped:

```
child::Book[position() &lt;= 3]
```

An XPointer fragment identifier may be defined as a sequence of location sets separated by a forward slash. It should start with some expression that establishes the context node – either a single forward slash, indicating that the context node starts at the document element, or an abbreviated absolute location (which we'll cover when we talk about abbreviations). An ID locator may also be used to establish the context node.

So, to navigate to the second `<Category>` element in the `<RecSubjCategories>` element in the first `<Book>` element of our example, we would use the locator:

```
Catalog.xml#/
    child::Book[position() = 1]/
    child::RecSubjCategories/
    child::Category[position() = 2]
```

Whew! That's a mouthful. Let's take a look at some abbreviations we can use to shorten fragment identifier expressions.

Abbreviations

There are some shorthand ways to specify commonly used constructs in XPath, which you may take advantage of when defining XPointer fragment identifiers.

If no axis is specified, the child axis is assumed. Both of the following fragments select the first `<Book>` child element of the document element:

```
Catalog.xml#/child::Book[position() = 1]
Catalog.xml#/Book[position() = 1]
```

The attribute axis may be abbreviated as well – instead of `attribute::`, we may use `@`. Therefore, these two fragments both select the `color` attribute of the first `<Book>` element:

```
Catalog.xml#Book[position() = 1]/attribute::color
Catalog.xml#Book[position() = 1]/@color
```

One common construct is `/descendant-or-self::node()/` which selects every descendant node of the context node for further manipulation. However, this construct may be abbreviated to `//`. Both of the following examples select every `<Title>` node in the document:

```
Catalog.xml#/descendant-or-self::node()/Title
Catalog.xml#//Title
```

The `"."` abbreviation is the same as `self::node()`. The following two locators specify all the `<Title>` descendants of the context node:

```
self::node()//Title
.//Title
```

Similarly, the `..` abbreviation is the same as `parent::node()`. So, the following two locators specify all the `<Title>` children of the parent of the context node:

```
parent::node()/Title
../Title
```

Finally, in a predicate, the phrase `position() = X` may be replaced by *X*. The following two locators specify the second `<Title>` child of the context node:

```
Title[position() = 2]
Title[2]
```

If we apply our new abbreviations to the example we used above:

```
Catalog.xml#/
    child::Book[position() = 1]/
    child::RecSubjCategories/
    child::Category[position() = 2]
```

We see that we may now express this as:

```
Catalog.xml#/Book[1]/RecSubjCategories/Category[2]
```

XPath provides a flexible mechanism for addressing individual portions of an XML document to any granularity you like, even down to individual characters in text elements. XPointer leverages this technology to allow XML documents to be pointed into as part of URI locators. In addition, XPointer extends the functionality of XPath in a couple of important ways.

XPointer Extensions to XPath

XPointer extends XPath to allow for some additional functionality. It introduces the concepts of points and ranges as positional declarations within a document (in addition to the node construct in XPath), and provides some functions for manipulating these new position references.

Points

XPointer defines the concept of a **point** location, as distinct from a node. While a point location may be a node, it may also be a particular location within character content (for example, at the third character of the text value of the `<Title>` element). Points are useful in the definition of **ranges**, which we will look at next.

Ranges

XPointer also defines the concept of a **range** location, which is defined to be the XML structure and content between two points. Note that this might result in a section that is not well-formed, as only part of some elements may be enclosed in the range. The ability to specify ranges would allow, for example, a pointer to point to all the occurrences of a particular word in a target document (as the result of a search engine's output, for example). Ranges may be declared this way:

```
#xpointer(<locator> to <locator>)
```

So, a range that selects the range starting from the element with the ID `book1` and ending with the element with the ID `book3`, inclusive, including all of the content in document order that falls between them, would be specified as:

```
#xpointer(book1 to book3)
```

Additional Functions

There are some additional functions defined in the XPointer specification to allow for the generation and manipulation of point and range locations. Let's take a look at the three most important ones: `string-range()`, `here()`, and `unique()`.

The `string-range()` function searches the text in the target document and returns range locations for each discovered instance of a target string. For example, this locator would return all of the instances of the string `XML` in the `catalog.xml` document:

```
catalog.xml#xpointer(string-range(/, "XML"))
```

This function might be used, for example, in a search engine – each instance of the word would be a range in the XPointer, allowing an application to show contextual text around the instance and perhaps allowing the user to jump to that location in the document via an XLink.

The `here()` function returns the element that contains the XPointer itself. This function allows XPointers to point to other locations relative to the XPointer's location in the pointing document itself. For example, the following XPointer would point to the parent of the XPointer element itself:

```
#xpointer(here()/..)
```

The `unique()` function is a Boolean function that determines if a location set only contains one item. This is important in XPointer to ensure that a single location is pointed to by an XPointer expression (for example, if automated processing is interpreting the file). These two predicates are synonymous:

```
[unique()]
[count() = 1]
```

XPointer Errors

There are three errors that may be caused by an improper XPointer. Any parser that is XPointer-aware will need to handle these errors in some way (the XPointer specification leaves the exact mechanism up to the developer designing the XPointer-aware processor).

Syntax Error

A fragment identifier that does not correspond to the syntactical constraints of the XPointer specification results in a **syntax error**.

Resource Error

A fragment identifier that is syntactically correct, but is attached to an improper resource (such as a document that is not a well-formed XML document), causes a **resource error**.

Sub-Resource Error

A fragment identifier that is syntactically correct and is attached to a well-formed XML document but does not result in any valid locations causes a **sub-resource** error.

Any processing application that is XPointer-aware should catch these errors and handle them in an orderly way.

Summary

XPointers provide a mechanism for a URI to point to some portion of an XML document. While there are not any serious implementations of XPointers at this time, the specification is currently in last call status, and processor implementations using XPointers will be available very soon.

XML Fragment Interchange

As our XML document repositories grow, and our average document size increases, manipulating the documents becomes more and more unwieldy. It would be nice if we could just work with a small portion of the document instead of needing to transfer and load the full version of it every time. To address this need, the W3C has created a specification for **XML Fragment Interchange** (which we'll refer to as XFI, although this acronym is not used in the current working draft) that defines some mechanisms for the creation and transfer of a portion of an XML document. At this time, the specification still has the status of Working Draft – while the workgroup has concluded its work, the W3C has decided to hold off promoting this specification until the other XML specifications have matured somewhat.

The W3C specification for XML Fragment Interchange may be found at http://www.w3.org/TR/WD-xml-fragment.

What are Document Fragments?

A **document fragment** is defined by this specification to be any **well-balanced** subset of the original document. Well-balanced subsets of documents contain whole information items – but they do not necessarily need to be well-formed in the sense that an XML document is well-formed. Specifically, well-balanced subsets must contain complete tags (no partial tags are allowed), and if a well-balanced subset contains a start tag, it must contain the corresponding end tag. We'll see some examples of this later.

It is up to the application that serves the fragments to decide which pieces of information are useful to the receiver. The most common example would be to transmit only elements that are necessary for the receiver's function, but other types of fragments are possible. To help us understand what portion of a document may be a fragment, let's take a look at the diagram from earlier in the chapter:

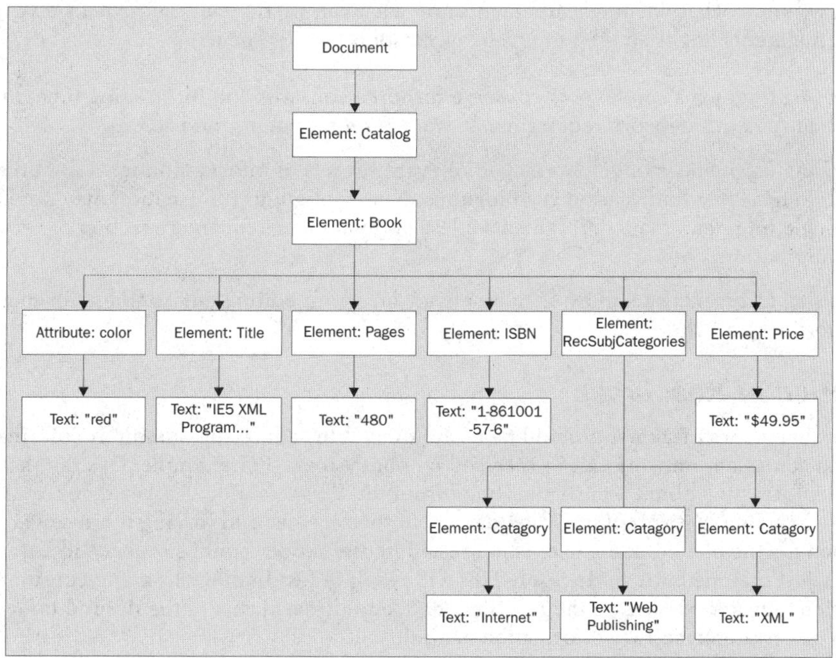

In the tree representation, any of the branches connected to the main tree by a solid line may be thought of as a possible fragment, because each branch is guaranteed to be contiguously defined within the original document. Attributes may not be defined as fragments, because they are embedded in tags and thus do not qualify as well-balanced. In addition, adjacent siblings (and their children) may be defined together as a fragment, since they occur together in the original document. It may also help to think in terms of the original (serialized text) document: a valid fragment will appear as a contiguous block of text in the original document, while non-contiguous text may never be a valid fragment. Note, however, that we may have a contiguous block of text that is not a valid fragment – the above rules still apply.

Some valid fragments for the above diagram might be:

- The `<RecSubjCategories>` element and all of its children
- The text item "`480`"
- The first two `<Category>` elements and their children

However, the following would not be valid fragments:

- The first `<Category>` element and the third `<Category>` element
- The `<color>` attribute
- The `<Price>` start tag, but not the `</Price>` end tag
- The `<Book>` element without its text child

Some uses for document fragments

Now that we know what document fragments are, what can we do with them? Let's take a look at a few ways that fragments might be useful to us in application development:

- Using fragments can help us conserve resource consumption (processing time, memory requirements, network requirements, storage requirements, and so on).
- Using fragments can help us isolate relevant subsets of information from a source document – as long as that information is contiguous. Non-contiguous information may not be sent in a single fragment, making fragments a less optimal choice for the redaction of certain pieces of information.
- Using fragments can allow us to create a concurrent editing environment for our large XML documents.

Conservation of Resources

The most obvious way fragments could be useful to us is to reduce the amount of information that is transferred across our networks and processed by our systems. For example, let's say that a user has requested information about a particular book from the Wrox catalog. Rather than transmitting the entire Wrox catalog (with all of the book details) to the receiver and forcing the receiver to fish out the information for the one book the user is interested in, the sender could simply send a fragment containing just the one book to the user. This will result in less bandwidth being consumed by the transmission, quicker parsing on the receiving end, and direct access to the desired information without having to traverse unnecessary information as well.

Collecting a Subset of Information

Let's extend our example XML from earlier in the chapter. Say that Wrox included private information about royalties, distribution numbers, and so on in their XML catalog document. Unfortunately, unless that information is contiguous, XFI does not allow us to pass that information as a fragment, making XFI a poor solution to this problem. Let's take a look at an example:

```
<Catalog>
   <Book color="red">
      <Title>IE5 XML Programmer's Reference</Title>
      <Pages>480</Pages>
      <ISBN>1-861001-57-6</ISBN>
      <RecSubjCategories>
         <Category>Internet</Category>
         <Category>Web Publishing</Category>
         <Category>XML</Category>
      </RecSubjCategories>
      <Price>$49.99</Price>
      <Royalties>...</Royalties>
      <DistributedCopies>...<DistributedCopies>
   </Book>
</Catalog>
```

If someone asked for information about the *IE5 XML Programmer's Reference* book, a fragment could be created that only included the sibling elements for public information about the book, but did not include the private information:

```
      <Title>IE5 XML Programmer's Reference</Title>
      <Pages>480</Pages>
      <ISBN>1-861001-57-6</ISBN>
      <RecSubjCategories>
         <Category>Internet</Category>
         <Category>Web Publishing</Category>
         <Category>XML</Category>
      </RecSubjCategories>
      <Price>$49.99</Price>
```

Unfortunately, fragments are not a good choice for **redaction** of information (editing a subset of information that can be published), since only contiguous nodes may be specified – if we wanted to send the entire catalog with private information removed, we wouldn't be able to use a fragment to do so. A much better choice for this type of manipulation would be XPath and XSLT, as we'll see later when we talk about those technologies.

Concurrent Editing and Version Control

Taking our example from above, let's presume that the catalog document goes a little deeper and actually contains the text of each book in question:

```
<Catalog>
   <Book color="red">
      <Title>IE5 XML Programmer's Reference</Title>
      <Pages>480</Pages>
      <ISBN>1-861001-57-6</ISBN>
      <RecSubjCategories>
         <Category>Internet</Category>
         <Category>Web Publishing</Category>
         <Category>XML</Category>
```

```
        </RecSubjCategories>
        <Price>$49.99</Price>
        <Chapter id="chap1">...</Chapter>
        <Chapter id="chap2">...</Chapter>
        <Chapter id="chap3">...</Chapter>
        <Chapter id="chap4">...</Chapter>
        ...
    </Book>
</Catalog>
```

Let's see how we could implement a crude form of concurrent editing and version control for the different chapters in this book.

We'll need some sort of database to track the current status of each chapter in a book:

Book	Chapter	Status
IE5 XML Programmer's Reference	1	Not checked out
IE5 XML Programmer's Reference	2	Checked out to "jond"
IE5 XML Programmer's Reference	3	Checked out to "kevinw"
IE5 XML Programmer's Reference	4	Not checked out

Of course, if we had control over the content, we could implement this as a status attribute on the <Chapter> elements as well.

We would then write an application to allow the various authors and editors to check out and check in each chapter. When a chapter is checked out to a particular author, only that fragment is sent to the author:

```
    <Chapter id="chap3">...</Chapter>
```

This allows one author to work on a chapter at the same time as another author is editing a different chapter, without them overwriting each other's work. When the author is finished making changes to the chapter, he would send the modified fragment back to Wrox, who would then integrate it into the original document. It would be a simple matter at that point to update a version table in our database to indicate who had edited the document and when. There are commercial XML servers available that already implement this kind of functionality.

The Problem: Bare Document Fragments Aren't Always Enough

Having said that we can use XFI to retrieve a subsection of an XML document, there are times when a receiver needs more information than that included in the document fragment to do its job; it often requires some kind of context. We'll examine some situations where bare document fragments don't provide enough information, and then we'll take a look at the W3C's solution to the problem.

What Do I Describe?

Often, in a well-designed XML document, elements are reused with different meanings depending on where they are located in the document structure. Take the following example:

```
<Bookstore>
   <Book>
      <Title>IE5 XML Programmer's Reference</Title>
      <Price>$49.95</Price>
   </Book>
   <Coffee>
      <CoffeeType>Double mocha latte</CoffeeType>
      <Price>$2.99</Price>
   </Coffee>
</Bookstore>
```

Now, let's say we received the following fragment of this document:

```
      <Price>$2.99</Price>
```

Is this the price of a programming book, or of a double mocha latte? Without any additional information, it's hard to tell. The sender could send the entire parent element:

```
   <Coffee>
      <CoffeeType>Double mocha latte</CoffeeType>
      <Price>$2.99</Price>
   </Coffee>
```

But now we've received information that we didn't necessarily want or need. It would be nice if we could get some context information for our fragment without necessarily receiving all of the content of the context.

Using IDREF and IDREFS

Say that Wrox has implemented the version control management software described in the earlier example. An author is writing Chapter 4 when she realizes she wants to include a reference back to something she had written in Chapter 1. She remembers that she had assigned an ID to that paragraph, but she doesn't remember what it was. Since she only has the Chapter 4 fragment to work with, she can't map to an ID in Chapter 1 using an IDREF. It would be nice if she could have some sort of information about the content in Chapter 1 – such as the section titles tagged with IDREFS – without needing to download an entire copy of the book.

Validating Processors

Imagine that we're using a DTD to specify the content in our catalog example:

```
<!DOCTYPE catalog SYSTEM "www.wrox.com/XML/Catalog.dtd">
<Catalog>
   <Book color="red">
      <Title>IE5 XML Programmer's Reference</Title>
      <Pages>480</Pages>
      <ISBN>1-861001-57-6</ISBN>
      <RecSubjCategories>
         <Category>Internet</Category>
         <Category>Web Publishing</Category>
         <Category>XML</Category>
```

```
        </RecSubjCategories>
        <Price>$49.99</Price>
        <Chapter id="chap1">...</Chapter>
        <Chapter id="chap2">...</Chapter>
        <Chapter id="chap3">...</Chapter>
        <Chapter id="chap4">...</Chapter>
        ...
    </Book>
</Catalog>
```

Again, an author wants to check one chapter out. If the author is using a validating processor to verify the structure of his chapter, she is going to have a problem using the original DTD to do so – the original DTD will be expecting a `<Catalog>` element, a `<Book>` element, and so on. An ideal version of the document would include placeholders to satisfy the DTD, but not include their content to minimize bandwidth consumption and processing time.

The Solution: Context Information

Fortunately, the W3C anticipated these problems when specifying XFI, and provided a mechanism for the transmission of **context information** along with the fragment to the receiver.

What is Context Information?

Context information is information that is sent to a receiver to help describe the fragment's structural position within the original document. The XFI specification allows a lot of flexibility in exactly what information is provided for context to the user; this information should be delivered based on the receiver's needs. It might be as little as the fragment's ancestors up to the document element, or as much as all the various element tags in the original document – it's up to the XML server to decide what context information would be useful to the receiving processor.

While the specification does not explain exactly how the context information should be transported, it provides two suggestions. This first involves sending the requestor two files:

- The fragment context specification file, which contains all of the necessary information around the element, and a reference to the file that contains the fragment
- The fragment itself in a separate file

While this requires two files to be generated, and that one of them be cached in some way (via a file persisted to disk or some other mechanism), it does mean that the receiving processor can provide information that would surround the fragment.

The other option is that it might be transferred in one single file using namespaces to separate the context information from the actual fragment content. To illustrate some examples of fragment interchange we will use the first of the two proposals (we will revisit the second shortly).

What is Allowed to be Part of Context Information?

The W3C specifies that the following information may be provided for the purposes of context for a fragment:

- The URI of the DTD used for the original document
- The URI of the internal subset for the document
- The URI of the original document this fragment was taken from
- A specification of the location of the fragment in the original document
- Ancestor information for the fragment body
- Sibling information for the fragment body
- Sibling information for any of the ancestors
- Descendant information for any of the ancestors or siblings
- Attribute information for any of the elements specified above

Note that this covers all of the nodes in our node tree except for those included in the specified fragment; the author of the XML server can design the fragment generator to include whatever portion of this information is relevant to the receiver for the purposes of interpreting the fragment.

How are Fragments Represented?

The W3C has created the following namespace for fragment declarations:

```
http://www.w3.org/XML/Fragment/1.0
```

The `<fcs>` element (short for Fragment Context Specifier) is the wrapper element for the specification of fragment contexts. All fragment contexts should be wrapped in an `<fcs>` element. It has the following four attributes:

- `extref` – the URI of the DTD for the original document
- `intref` – the URI of the "externalized" internal subset
- `parentref` – the URI of the original document itself
- `sourcelocn` – a specification of the location of the fragment within the original document

Note that no encoding scheme is specified for this locator by the W3C at this time, although one might expect the W3C to use XPointer to specify this location.

The children of the `<fcs>` element should be some portion of the element tree (possibly including attributes) for the original document. Again, the portion of the element tree represented is decided by the sending application, and should be dependent on the needs of the receiving application. At the position in the sub-tree where the fragment body should belong, a `<fragbody>` element should be included in its place. This element has one attribute – `fragbodyref` – that should be a URI reference to the actual fragment.

Let's look at an example. Say we have this catalog file:

```
<Catalog>
   <Book color="red">
      <Title>IE5 XML Programmer's Reference</Title>
      <Pages>480</Pages>
      <ISBN>1-861001-57-6</ISBN>
      <RecSubjCategories>
         <Category>Internet</Category>
         <Category>Web Publishing</Category>
         <Category>XML</Category>
      </RecSubjCategories>
      <Price>$49.99</Price>
      <Chapter id="chap1">...</Chapter>
      <Chapter id="chap2">...</Chapter>
      <Chapter id="chap3">...</Chapter>
      <Chapter id="chap4">...</Chapter>
      ...
   </Book>
</Catalog>
```

We want to transmit just the ISBN for the book to the receiver. We would create a fragment context specification that looks like this:

```
<f:fcs xmlns:f="http://www.w3.org/XML/Fragment/1.0"
       parentref="http://www.wrox.com/Catalog/Catalog.XML"
       xmlns="http://www.wrox.com/Catalog/">
   <Catalog>
      <Book>
         <f:fragbody fragbodyref="http://www.wrox.com/Catalog/ISBN.XML"/>
      </Book>
   </Catalog>
</f:fcs>
```

Here you can see that the fragment context specification file contains the `<Catalog>` and `<Book>` elements to provide context for the fragment, and a reference to the second file, which actually contains the requested fragment. In the fragment file itself, which is referenced in the `<fragbody>` element as `http://www.wrox.com/Catalog/ISBN.XML`, we have the following fragment:

```
<ISBN>1-861001-57-6</ISBN>
```

Examples, Revisited

Let's take a look at our three examples again and see how we would use fragments and contexts to send the information to the receiver.

What Do I Describe?

Earlier, we were trying to figure out how to indicate that the price sent to the receiver was associated with coffee and not a book. If we transmitted the following fragment context specification:

```
<f:fcs xmlns:f="http://www.w3.org/XML/Fragment/1.0"
       parentref="http://www.wrox.com/Bookstore/Bookstore.XML"
       xmlns="http://www.wrox.com/Bookstore/">
   <Bookstore>
      <Coffee>
         <f:fragbody fragbodyref="http://www.wrox.com/Bookstore/Price.XML"/>
      </Coffee>
   </Bookstore>
</f:fcs>
```

the user would know that the following fragment is a child of the `<Coffee>` element, and a grandchild of the `<Bookstore>` element:

```
   <Price>$5.99</Price>
```

so it would be obvious to the receiver what the `<Price>` element in the `Price.xml` file represented.

Using IDREF and IDREFS

OK, so how about the author that wanted to reference back to an `ID` for a paragraph in Chapter 1, if all she has to edit is Chapter 4? If we sent this fragment context specification:

```
<f:fcs xmlns:f="http://www.w3.org/XML/Fragment/1.0"
       parentref="http://www.wrox.com/FullText/FullText.XML"
       xmlns="http://www.wrox.com/FullText/">
<Catalog>
   <Book>
      <Chapter id="chap1">
         <para ID="IntroXML">
         <para ID="IntroChap1">
         <para ID="IntroChap2">
         <para ID="IntroChap3">
         <para ID="IntroChap4">
         ...
      </Chapter>
      <Chapter id="chap2">
         <para ID="XMLKeywords">
         ...
      </Chapter>
      <Chapter id="chap3">
         <para ID="XMLDTDs">
         ...
      </Chapter>
      <f:fragbody fragbodyref="http://www.wrox.com/FullText/IE5XMLChapter4.xml"/>
   </Book>
</Catalog>
</f:fcs>
```

The author would have a reference to the context of their chapter, which is a fragment in the `IE5XMLChapter4.xml` file:

```
<Chapter id="chap4">
   ...
</Chapter>
```

now the author would have the `ID`s of the various positions in each chapter to refer back to in the fragment context specification file – and she could add an `IDREF` to, say, `IntroChap4` to point back to information given in the first chapter about chapter 4.

Validating Processors

In order to keep a validating processor happy, we can include a copy of all required elements with character data removed – optional elements may be discarded. So, for our example, we might transmit the following fragment context specification:

```
<f:fcs xmlns:f="http://www.w3.org/XML/Fragment/1.0"
       extref="http://www.wrox.com/XML/Catalog.dtd"
       parentref="http://www.wrox.com/FullText/FullText.XML"
       xmlns="http://www.wrox.com/FullText/">
<Catalog>
   <Book>
      <Title></Title>
      <Pages></Pages>
      <ISBN></ISBN>
      <RecSubjCategories>
      </RecSubjCategories>
      <Price></Price>
      <f:fragbody fragbodyref="http://www.wrox.com/FullText/IE5XMLChapter4.XML"/>
   </Book>
</Catalog>
</f:fcs>
```

Which provides the processor with the required elements for the following fragment to be valid:

```
<Chapter id="chap4">
   ...
</Chapter>
```

Note that we dropped the <Category> elements (because we're assuming that <Category> is declared as optional in the DTD) and the additional <Chapter> elements (because <Chapter> is specified as having one or more occurrences in the DTD). On receiving these two files, the processor would parse the fragment body in place as if it were an external parsed entity, discard the context wrapper on the context piece, and be able to validate the document against the DTD.

How Fragments May Be Transmitted

Now that we've defined some fragments and fragment context specifications, how do we go about sending them to a receiver? The W3C doesn't constrain the transmission of fragments in the XFI specification, but it does offer a couple of different possible ways a fragment-aware receiving processor might accept transmissions.

The Separate File Mechanism

We've already seen the way fragments work with two separate files. One file contains the fragment itself and the other contains the fragment context specification file. To send this information to a receiver, the fragment context specification file is sent. The fragment-aware processor parses the fragment context specification file and goes to the location in the `fragbodyref` attribute to read the fragment body itself:

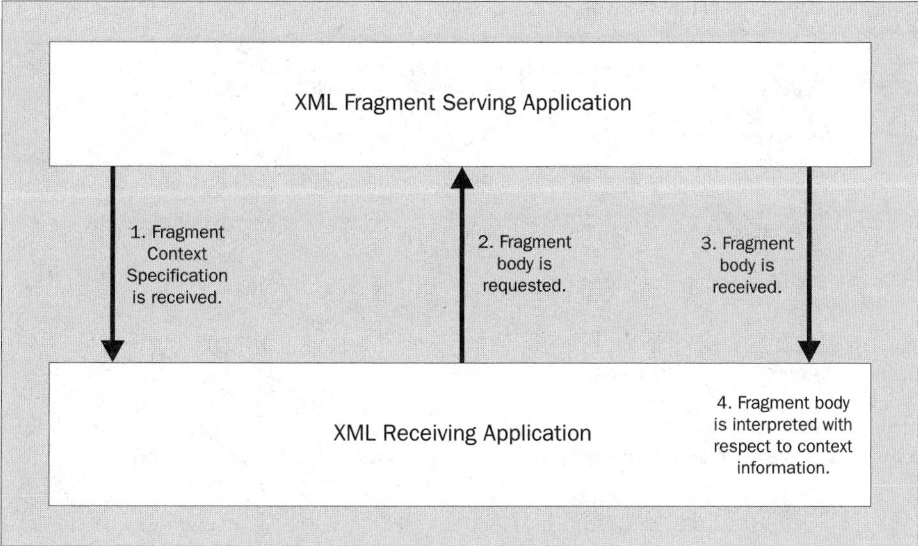

Unfortunately, this requires two files to be generated by the fragment serving application, and that one of them be cached in some way (via a file persisted to disk or some other mechanism). In addition, this requires an extra round trip across the network, which we'd like to avoid if possible.

The Proposed Package Mechanism

While the W3C declares that the transmission of fragments is outside the scope of the XFI specification, it does provide a **non-normative** (W3C code for suggested but not required) way that a fragment and a fragment body may be packaged together and sent as one file. Basically, a new namespace is proposed that would provide an element that would contain a fragment body. Then, instead of two files with a fragment context specification like so:

```
<f:fcs xmlns:f="http://www.w3.org/XML/Fragment/1.0"
       parentref="http://www.wrox.com/Bookstore/Bookstore.XML"
       xmlns="http://www.wrox.com/Bookstore/">
   <Bookstore>
      <Coffee>
         <f:fragbody fragbodyref="http://www.wrox.com/Bookstore/Price.XML"/>
      </Coffee>
   </Bookstore>
</f:fcs>
```

and a fragment body such as this:

```
   <Price>$5.99</Price>
```

we would have just one file:

```
<p:package xmlns:p=http://www.w3.org/XML/Package/1.0
           xmlns:f="http://www.w3.org/XML/Fragment/1.0"
           xmlns="http://www.wrox.com/Bookstore/">
   <f:fcs parentref="http://www.wrox.com/Bookstore/Bookstore.XML">
      <Bookstore>
         <Coffee>
            <f:fragbody/>
         </Coffee>
      </Bookstore>
   </f:fcs>
   <p:body>
      <Price>$5.99</Price>
   </p:body>
</p:package>
```

Note that we no longer specify a location for the fragment body – it is assumed to fall in the `<p:body>` element. In this scenario, only one trip to the server would be required:

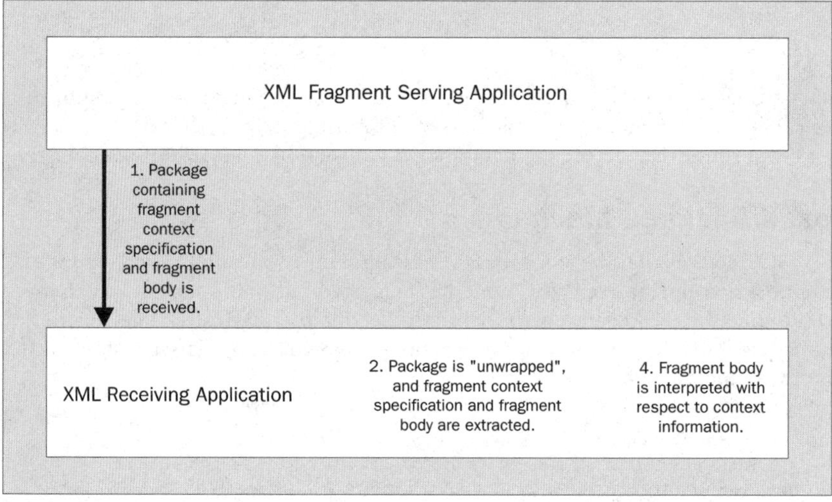

This technique allows us to reduce round-trips to the server, and also reduces the complexity of the serving application itself.

Summary

The XML Fragment Interchange provides a way to send a portion of an XML document to a receiver, along with enough context information to make the document usable by the receiver. We've taken a look at some ways fragments might be useful – allowing us to manage multiple authors for a document, for example, or decreasing the amount of unused information that is transmitted across our networks and processed by our XML processors. However, fragments returned must correspond to contiguous elements in the source document, making sophisticated manipulation of the original content impossible. While there aren't any widely-available fragment-aware processors yet, being comfortable with the concepts of fragment and context will prepare you for fragments when they do start hitting the streets. As the various XML technologies converge, XFI is likely to be the method used to transfer partial documents generated by queries or fragmentary links created using XLink.

Querying

We've seen how we may link out of XML documents and point to specific portions of them. It would also be nice to be able to use a query language to access a portion of an XML document and process it. In this section, we'll take a look at some mechanisms for querying XML files and retrieving content from them.

What Is a Query Language?

If you've ever worked with a relational database, you'll probably be familiar with one form of a querying language: SQL. The Structured Query Language allows a user to access information contained in the database, and manipulate it in several ways. Before we delve into the topic of querying XML documents and sources, we should have a look at what a query language should be able to do. So, let's look at some of the operations that are possible with SQL, and that should ideally be possible using some hypothetical query language for XML.

Row-wise Restriction of Returned Information

One of the most basic things we need to do when returning information from a database is to restrict the information returned by filtering the rows to only return rows matching certain criteria. This is achieved through SQL by using the `WHERE` sub-clause of a `SELECT` statement:

```
SELECT *
   FROM Book
   WHERE Title = "Professional XML"
```

Column-wise Restriction of Returned Information

We should also be able to restrict the information returned by restricting the columns returned from the database to only the columns we are interested in. These are specified in the `SELECT` statement:

```
SELECT Title, Price
   FROM Book
```

Summarizing Returned Information

We also need to be able to summarize returned information, aggregating several pieces of information from several rows together into one piece of information. SQL provides some helper functions that provide this functionality:

```
SELECT AVG(Price)
   FROM Book
```

Sorting Returned Information

The ability to reorder the returned information from a query is very important. SQL provides the `ORDER BY` phrase as a means to perform sorting:

```
SELECT Book
   ORDER BY Price
```

Inner Joins

Because of the normalized nature of SQL tables, we often need to return information from more than one table in order to return a meaningful result. In SQL, this is implemented using an inner join, or equijoin, operation:

```
SELECT Book.Title, RecSubjCategories.Category
   FROM Book INNER JOIN RecSubjCategories ON Book.BookID =
      RecSubjCategories.BookID
   WHERE Book.Author = "Kevin Williams"
```

Outer Joins

When retrieving information from more than one place in SQL, often we want to return information from one table even if related information in another table doesn't exist. For example, we might want to return all books and the categories they fall into, but we might also want to return all books even if they have no categories. This may be done in SQL using an outer join operation:

```
SELECT Book.Title, RecSubjCategories.Category
   FROM Book
   LEFT OUTER JOIN RecSubjCategories
   ON Book.BookID = RecSubjCategories.BookID
   WHERE Book.Author = "Kevin Williams"
```

Manipulation of Table Content

It is possible to manipulate the information in a database using SQL commands, allowing information to be added, modified, or removed on a row-by-row basis. These commands are the `INSERT`, `UPDATE`, and `DELETE` commands:

```
INSERT RecSubjCategories (BookID, Category)
   VALUES (1, "XML")

UPDATE Book
   SET Title = "Pro XML"
   WHERE BookID = 1

DELETE Book
   WHERE BookID = 1
```

These functions are really outside the scope of what we'd like our hypothetical XML query engine to do – there are other ways of achieving these goals in XML, such as the DOM. This functionality would be convenient to have, but is not essential to a strong query language.

Returning Information From More Than One Source

Implementations of SQL often provide the ability to return information from more than one place – typically, this might be information stored in different databases on the same machine. In the SQL Server implementation of SQL, for example, this may be achieved by prefixing the table name with the database name:

```
SELECT WorkDB.Book.*
   FROM WorkDB.Book, PublishedDB.Book
   WHERE WorkDB.Book.BookID = PublishedDB.Book.BookID
```

Procedural Processing

In most implementations of SQL, some form of stored query or stored procedure may be created. These abide by the SQL syntax, but are processed in a procedural way. Take for example the following stored procedure:

```
CREATE PROC DefaultCategories (@BookID integer)
AS
BEGIN
   DELETE RecSubjCategories
      FROM RecSubjCategories INNER JOIN Book ON RecSubjCategories.BookID =
         Book.BookID
      WHERE Book.BookID = @BookID

   INSERT RecSubjCategories (BookID, Category)
      VALUES (@BookID, "No category specified")
END
```

This stored procedure performs two actions: first, it deletes all of the categories for the specified book; then, it inserts a default category for that book. There are more constructs that may be used, such as temporary tables, variables, and cursors, which make stored procedures very powerful tools to manipulate relational data.

We'll see later how technologies that are currently available for XML may be used to perform many of these same functions. Before we start looking at those technologies, though, we need to understand how XML documents are structured in a different way from relational databases.

The Differences Between Relational Databases and XML Documents

To understand the issues we'll be facing when we attempt to query XML documents, we need to briefly re-examine the structure of an XML document. First of all let's take a look at SQL structures for the sake of comparison.

SQL data structures consist of a series of tables. Each table may have one or more columns. For example, here is the SQL table generation script for the `Book` and `RecSubjCategories` tables we've been discussing:

```
CREATE TABLE Book (
   BookID int,
   Title varchar(100),
   Pages integer,
   ISBN varchar(15),
   Price varchar(15) )

CREATE TABLE RecSubjCategories (
   RecSubjCategoriesID int,
   BookID int,
   Category varchar(100) )
```

The next two tables show some sample data for these tables, first for the `Book` table:

BookID	Title	Pages	ISBN	Price
1	IE5 XML Programmer's Reference	480	1-861001-57-6	$49.99

Then the `RecSubjCategories` table:

RecSubjCategoriesID	BookID	Category
1	1	XML
2	1	Web Publishing
3	1	Internet

There are a few important points to make about these structures.

SQL Rows Have Unique Identifiers

The first element in each of our sample tables is the **primary key** for that table. A properly designed SQL database will always have a primary key defined for every table that uniquely defines each record in that table. Often, this primary key will be an arbitrary, system-assigned number (via a sequence or some other mechanism). In contrast, XML elements (which are the analogue of tables in the SQL structures) may be defined without unique keys (although there is a mechanism provided by XML, the `ID` attribute, that is designed to hold just that information). It is perfectly acceptable, for example, to have the following document in XML:

```
<NutritionHistory>
   <SingleDay>
      <Date>January 7, 2000</Date>
      <Beverage>Jolt Cola</Beverage>
      <Beverage>Jolt Cola</Beverage>
      <Beverage>Jolt Cola</Beverage>
      ...
   </SingleDay>
</NutritionHistory>
```

Note the three `<Beverage>` elements with exactly the same content. XML can distinguish between these elements by the order in which they were encountered when the document was parsed. This brings us to the next difference between relational databases and XML:

SQL Rows Do Not Imply Sequence

Relational databases do not imply any sort of order to the information found in their tables. For example, in the sample structures we examined before there are three `RecSubjCategories` specified for our book: `Internet`, `Web Publishing`, and `XML`. These subject categories are used on the back of a book, above the bar code, to indicate to book sellers which shelf the books should be placed on, and are intended to be used in the correct order. In an XML document, the order that these are encountered can imply a sequence – the book might primarily be best suited with books about XML, alternatively with some information on Web Publishing, or with books about the Internet if the first two are not available. This sequencing information is lost when storing this information in a SQL database. If the information is to be retained, some sort of column should be assigned to the `RecSubjCategories` record to show the priority of the category.

Our query language should be aware of the sequential nature of the information found in an XML document and preserve that information in the result of any query performed using that language. In addition, the position of elements should be available to a query engine so that it may use that information to filter the results – for example, a query engine should be able to return the second <Category> element for a given <Book> element.

SQL Structures Do Not Provide Hierarchical Encapsulation

Relational structures, by definition, are not hierarchical – they give us no way to encapsulate the <RecSubjCategories> elements in our previous example inside the <Book> element. Instead, the <RecSubjCategories> elements must contain pointers that refer back to the element to which they pertain – in our example, the column BookID in the RecSubjCategories table points back to the book record that "contains" the RecSubjCategories information. This pointing mechanism allows us to define one-to-one and one-to-many references, as we might in XML, but it goes beyond that – it allows us to point to any other element in the database structure if we choose.

All this talk of pointing should remind you of the equivalent mechanism in XML – the use of an IDREF or IDREFS attribute to point back to an element with a specific ID. One could imagine a DTD fragment for <Books> and <RecSubjCategories> that looked something like the following:

```
<!ELEMENT Catalog (Book*, RecSubjCategories*)>

<!ELEMENT Book (ID, Title, Pages, ISBN, Price)>
<!ELEMENT ID ID>
<!ELEMENT Title #PCDATA>
<!ELEMENT Pages #PCDATA>
<!ELEMENT ISBN #PCDATA>
<!ELEMENT PRICE #PCDATA>

<!ELEMENT RecSubjCategories (ID, BookID, Category)>
<!ELEMENT BookID IDREFS>
<!ELEMENT Category #PCDATA>
```

In this structure, our example from above would be:

```
<Catalog>
   <Book ID="B1">
      <Title>IE5 XML Programmer's Reference</Title>
      <Pages>480</Pages>
      <ISBN>1-861001-57-6</ISBN>
      <Price>$49.99</Price>
   </Book>
   <RecSubjCategories ID="R1" BookIDs="B1">
      <Category>XML</Category>
      <Category>Web Publishing</Category>
      <Category>Internet</Category>
   </RecSubjCategories>
</Catalog>
```

To find the list of categories for a particular book, we now need to look for the <RecSubjCategories> element that has a BookID which points back to that book. Conversely, to find the book that contains a particular list of categories, we would need to search for the book (or books) with the ID (or IDs) pointed to by the BookIDs of the <RecSubjCategories> element in question. Relational databases handle this natively with joins, making the transversal of the linkage between the elements transparent, whereas the traversal of linkages with standard XML tools (like the DOM or SAX) requires some additional work.

As we know, XML also allows information to be encapsulated as children of parents. This will typically only be used to represent a one-to-one or one-to-many relationship (as embedding the same child in more than one parent would lead to repetition of information, which is better represented in XML documents with the ID-IDREFS pointing mechanism). The original version of our example uses encapsulation to show that the category information is part of the book information. XML technologies such as the DOM, SAX, XLink, XPointer, XPath, and XSLT are designed to work best with node trees formed from parent-child relationships. Our XML query language should be able to navigate both parent-child relationships and ID-IDREF relationships – in either direction – and preserve that information in the result of the query.

XML Confounds Attributes and Text-Only Content

In an XML document, it's possible to have an attribute associated with a particular element that has text content and text-only content for an element itself. Thus, we can have the two possibilities shown below:

```
<Catalog>
   <Book Title="IE5 XML Programmer's Reference"
      Pages="480"
      ISBN="1-861001-57-6"
      Price="$49.99"/>
</Catalog>
```

```
<Catalog>
   <Book ID="B1">
      <Title>IE5 XML Programmer's Reference</Title>
      <Pages>480</Pages>
      <ISBN>1-861001-57-6</ISBN>
      <Price>$49.99</Price>
   </Book>
</Catalog>
```

These two formulations are syntactically different but semantically identical – books have titles, whether they are expressed as attributes of books or text-only child elements of books. The information in each example could be stored in the Book table we defined before:

```
CREATE TABLE Book (
   BookID int,
   Title varchar(100),
   Pages integer,
   ISBN varchar(15),
   Price varchar(15) )
```

The "text element vs. attribute" debate is ongoing – there are attempts to assert some canonical forms for XML content (Microsoft's canonical form for BizTalk objects, for example, may be found at http://www.biztalk.org/resources/canonical.asp), but the W3C specification does not constrain XML documents to one form or the other. Our XML query engine should be able to handle both cases.

XML Allows a Mixed Content Model for Elements

XML allows elements to be defined as having a mixed content model – they may contain both text information and sub-elements. Here's an example:

```
<!ELEMENT Book(#PCDATA, Title, Pages, #PCDATA, ISBN, #PCDATA)>
```

A <Book> element conforming to the previous specification might look like this:

```
<Book>
   Here's some random text.
   <Title>Professional XML</Title>
   <Pages>480</Pages>
   Some other text appears here.
   <ISBN>1-861001-57-6</ISBN>
   And finally another fragment of text.
</Book>
```

The need for this becomes obvious if you think about marking up a paragraph: certain words or phrases may be bold, or italicized, but the majority of the text in the paragraph appears with no additional markup. This may be somewhat counter-intuitive if you're used to working with data objects – to represent the above information in a relational database, some other semantic construct(s) might need to be added to a relational database (such as a `value1`, `value2`, and `value3` column in the `Book` table). The problem deepens if we have an even more flexible structure in XML:

```
<!ELEMENT Book((#PCDATA | Title | Pages | ISBN)*)>
```

In this case, we might have any number of text blocks inside the <Book> element.

Any querying language we use to access XML has to be able to handle content specifications like this.

So, having looked at what a query language must address, let's take a look at how the querying effort for XML has been going so far.

The History of Query Languages for XML

The early users of XML quickly identified a need for a query language. To that end, in 1998 a couple of groups started working on proposals to the W3C for a mechanism to query XML documents. Before we talk about the current state of querying technology, let's take a look at the history of query languages for XML.

XML-QL

One of the submissions to the W3C was a language called XML-QL. The authors of this submission approached the problem from a database perspective, adopting many of the same techniques used in accessing hierarchical and relational databases. XML-QL specifies a sample fragment of an XML document and provides a construction mechanism that allows the same information to be output however the developer desires. Let's take a look at an example before we continue.

Imagine that we want to create a document that lists all of the book titles in our sample XML catalog. The output should be formatted this way:

```
<Titles>
   <Title>IE5 XML Programmer's Reference</Title>
   <Title>Designing Distributed Applications</Title>
   ...
</Titles>
```

In XML-QL, we would use the following query:

```
CONSTRUCT <Titles> {
   WHERE
      <Book>
         <Title>$t</Title>
      </Book> IN "http://www.wrox.com/XML/catalog.xml"
   CONSTRUCT
      <Title>$t</Title>
} </Titles>
```

You can see the similarities to SQL here. We have a `WHERE` clause that allows us to restrict the information being manipulated, and the `CONSTRUCT` clause (similar to the `SELECT` clause in SQL) that we use to create the generated output. These clauses may be nested, allowing us a great deal of flexibility in the retrieval and presentation of information.

While XML-QL is very flexible, it has a couple of drawbacks:

- **XML-QL does not provide for the preservation of sequence** – in an XML-QL processor, the resultant output is not guaranteed to be in the same order as the original document. While this might not be a big problem for XML data documents, it's a serious problem for XML text markup documents (imagine trying to read a book where the paragraphs were out of order!).
- **XML-QL does not provide for the preservation of structure** – you may have noticed in our previous example that we had to generate the entire structure of the result document by specifying the tags to be used – in effect, recreating the structure in the query. If we were just trying to reduce a large document down to the portion we're interested in (for example, all the books by a particular author), it would be nice if the structural information were preserved – we don't want to have to build the entire book sub-structure just to mirror what's in the original document!

At about the same time the XML-QL proposal was submitted to the W3C, another proposal was submitted that took a more markup-oriented approach: XQL.

XQL

The XQL proposal approached the problem of querying from a structured document perspective. It is designed to preserve the structure and sequence of the original document as much as possible while providing a means to reduce content. Let's revisit our example from the previous section. (For those of you who are familiar with Microsoft's implementation of XSL, please remember that this discussion pertains only to the original version of XQL – we'll get to the modern state of affairs shortly.)

In XQL, a query to create a list of titles from our catalog would look like this:

```
//Title
```

And the resultant output would be:

```
<xql:result>
   <Title>IE5 XML Programmer's Reference</Title>
   <Title>Designing Distributed Applications</Title>
   ...
</xql:result>
```

Note that the sequence is guaranteed to be preserved from the original document by XQL. While the text document shown above has the <xql:result> container wrapped around it, an XQL processor that returns a node set would simply return an ordered list of <Title> element nodes.

XQL also preserves hierarchical information. For example, if we chose to retrieve only the book called "IE5 XML Programmer's Reference", we could do so with the following query:

```
//Book[Book.Title="IE5 XML Programmer's Reference"]
```

The output of the query would be the following:

```
<xql:result>
<Book>
   <Title>IE5 XML Programmer's Reference</Title>
   <Authors>
      <Author>Alex Homer</Author>
   </Authors>
   <Publisher>Wrox Press, Ltd.</Publisher>
   <PubDate>August 1999</PubDate>
   <Abstract>Reference of XML capabilities in IE5</Abstract>
   <Pages>480</Pages>
   <ISBN>1-861001-57-6</ISBN>
   <RecSubjCategories>
      <Category>Internet</Category>
      <Category>Web Publishing</Category>
      <Category>XML</Category>
   </RecSubjCategories>
   <Price>$49.99</Price>
</Book>
</xql:result>
```

Note that all of the nested content of the selected Book element is preserved, whereas with XML-QL we would have had to specify all of the sub-elements in the CONSTRUCT clause.

While XQL solves some of the problems with XML-QL, it also falls short in a couple of ways:

- **XQL cannot provide distinct information** – since XQL is designed to operate against the node, not the information, it does not have a native way to identify when two elements have the same content. For example, there is no way to generate a distinct list of the authors in our XML catalog using XQL – XQL will generate one <Author> node per <Author> node in the original document, regardless of the node's content.
- **XQL cannot pivot relationships** – a common technique when working with relational information is to pivot relationships. For example, we may have a list of books and their respective authors, but we want to generate a list of all authors and the books they have contributed to. Because XQL preserves hierarchy, this query is impossible using XQL as it was originally designed.

While XQL is a more natural way to access the hierarchical information in an XML document, it cannot manipulate the data in as flexible a way as XML-QL. The ideal query language, then, would combine the flexibility of XML-QL with the structured access mechanisms of XQL.

XSLT and XPath

Despite the lack of a querying standard, it is possible to use two existing W3C recommendations to create a solution to the querying problem: XSLT and XPath. You will no doubt have recognized the query patterns used in XQL – XQL is the direct ancestor of XPath. XPath is used to access individual nodes of an XML document while preserving the hierarchy and structure of the original document. XSLT (which you'll learn more about in the next chapter) is then used to manipulate the results of these queries, constructing new elements and rearranging the resultant elements when necessary (much in the same way that XML-QL allows). As we'll see, the XSLT-XPath combination allows the developer to easily manipulate and rearrange the information in a source document at will.

Using XPath and XSLT to Query XML Documents

The best technology currently available to query XML documents is XSLT. XSLT uses XPath to filter nodes out of documents, while XSLT is used to present the data in any number of forms. While you may be familiar with using XSLT to perform XML-to-HTML transformations (which you'll learn more about in Chapter 9 which covers XSLT and transformations), it may also be used to transform to any structure – including XML. In this section, we'll take a look at how XSLT may be used to transform one XML document into another, addressing some of the querying needs we discussed earlier in the chapter.

Testing XSLT and XPath Queries With XT

At the time of going to press, none of the commonly used XML libraries such as the Microsoft and Sun implementations include full XSLT and XPath support, as these Working Drafts had only just become Recommendations. Microsoft is promising full XSLT and XPath support in the next release of MSXML, a preview of which is expected sometime in January 2000. Until then, James Clark (the editor of the XSLT specification, and one of the editors of the XPath specification) has been kind enough to provide an implementation of XSLT in a set of Java libraries or packaged as a Win32 executable. These may be downloaded from:

```
http://www.jclark.com/xml/xt.html
```

All of the examples in this section of the chapter were tested using XT. Instructions for downloading and using XT may be found in Appendix G. All of the examples in this chapter operate on our standard `catalog.xml` file:

```
<?xml version="1.0" encoding="utf-8" standalone="yes"?>
<!--======= The Wrox Press Book Catalog Application =======-->

<Catalog>
<Book>
   <Title>IE5 XML Programmer's Reference</Title>
   <Authors>
      <Author>Alex Homer</Author>
   </Authors>
   <Publisher>Wrox Press, Ltd.</Publisher>
   <PubDate>August 1999</PubDate>
   <Abstract>Reference of XML capabilities in IE5</Abstract>
   <Pages>480</Pages>
   <ISBN>1-861001-57-6</ISBN>
   <RecSubjCategories>
      <Category>Internet</Category>
      <Category>Web Publishing</Category>
      <Category>XML</Category>
   </RecSubjCategories>
   <Price>$49.99</Price>
```

```
</Book>
...
<Book>
   ...
</Book>
</Catalog>
```

Row-wise Restriction of Returned Information

In XML, the equivalent of row-wise restriction of information would be the restriction of elements returned based on their content. As we've seen, an XPath expression may be used to look for a specific value in a field.

So, if we want to return all books in our catalog with an author called `Alex Homer`, we may use the following stylesheet:

```
<xsl:stylesheet xmlns:xsl="http://www.w3.org/1999/XSL/Transform" version="1.0">
   <xsl:template match="/Catalog">
      <xsl:copy>
         <xsl:for-each select="//Book[Authors/Author='Alex Homer']">
            <xsl:copy>
               <xsl:apply-templates name="childnodes"/>
            </xsl:copy>
         </xsl:for-each>
      </xsl:copy>
   </xsl:template>
   <xsl:template name="childnodes" match="*">
      <xsl:copy>
         <xsl:apply-templates name="childnodes"/>
      </xsl:copy>
   </xsl:template>
</xsl:stylesheet>
```

Note that there are two templates in this stylesheet. The template whose `name` is `"childnodes"` is used to recursively write all of the descendant elements of the node currently being written to the output XML document – `<xsl:copy>` is used to copy the current node, and the `childnodes` template is run against all of the children to copy them to the file as well. We'll be using this technique in the next few examples.

The portion of the template that performs the row-wise selection is the `<xsl:for-each>` block in the first template. This block selects only certain books in the document for output – those matching the XPath expression inside the square brackets (which, as we know, selects for `<Author>` elements with the text `Alex Homer`). The output of this script when run against our `catalog.xml` document returns three books that Alex has written on:

```
<?xml version="1.0" encoding="utf-8"?>
<Catalog>
<Book>
   <Title>IE5 XML Programmer's Reference</Title>
   <Authors>
      <Author>Alex Homer</Author>
   </Authors>
   <Publisher>Wrox Press, Ltd.</Publisher>
   <PubDate>August 1999</PubDate>
   <Abstract>Reference of XML capabilities in IE5</Abstract>
   <Pages>480</Pages>
   <ISBN>1-861001-57-6</ISBN>
   <RecSubjCategories>
      <Category>Internet</Category>
```

```
        <Category>Web Publishing</Category>
        <Category>XML</Category>
      </RecSubjCategories>
      <Price>$49.99</Price>
   </Book>
   <Book>
      <Title>Professional ASP 3.0</Title>
      ...
   </Book>
   <Book>
      <Title>Beginning Components for ASP</Title>
      ...
   </Book>
</Catalog>
```

Column-wise Restriction of Returned Information

For XML, column-wise restriction of returned information is achieved by restricting the text-level elements or attributes returned by a stylesheet. Say we only want to retrieve the titles of the books where Alex Homer was a contributing author, as opposed to the whole of the book details. We can use the following style sheet:

```
<xsl:stylesheet xmlns:xsl="http://www.w3.org/1999/XSL/Transform" version="1.0">
   <xsl:template match="/Catalog">
      <xsl:copy>
         <xsl:for-each select="//Book[./Authors/Author='Alex Homer']">
            <xsl:copy>
               <xsl:apply-templates select="Title" name="childnodes"/>
            </xsl:copy>
         </xsl:for-each>
      </xsl:copy>
   </xsl:template>
   <xsl:template name="childnodes" match="*">
      <xsl:copy>
         <xsl:apply-templates name="childnodes"/>
      </xsl:copy>
   </xsl:template>
</xsl:stylesheet>
```

Here, we've just added another XPath expression as a child to select titles from the selected books – it will only return the titles for the selected books. Obviously, the XPath in the second `select` statement may be modified to change the text elements – or columns – being returned.

The above query returns the following output:

```
<?xml version="1.0" encoding="utf-8"?>
<Catalog>
   <Book>
      <Title>IE5 XML Programmer's Reference</Title>
   </Book>
   <Book>
      <Title>Professional ASP 3.0</Title>
   </Book>
   <Book>
      <Title>Beginning Components for ASP</Title>
   </Book>
</Catalog>
```

Note that we've added white space to make the output from XT a little more readable.

Summarizing Returned Information

XML information may be summarized using XPath's built-in aggregation functions. For example, if we wanted to return the total number of pages in every book written in part by Alex Homer, we could use this style sheet:

```
<xsl:stylesheet xmlns:xsl="http://www.w3.org/1999/XSL/Transform" version="1.0">
   <xsl:template match="/Catalog">
      <xsl:copy>
         <xsl:element name="totalPages">
            <xsl:value-of select=
               "sum(//Book[./Authors/Author='Alex Homer']/Pages)"/>
         </xsl:element>
      </xsl:copy>
   </xsl:template>
</xsl:stylesheet>
```

Here, we're just using the `sum()` function to add together the numeric values of the `<Pages>` element(s) selected by the XPath expression in the `<xsl:value-of>` element. Note that we couldn't operate on the price the same way using an XPath expression, since the `<Price>` element, as defined in our catalog, has a leading `$`. While XPath provides some functionality for dealing with string manipulation, it cannot operate on sets in quite the same way that a SQL command can, making nested operations (such as trimming off that leading dollar sign and then adding the resulting numbers together) difficult.

After applying this style sheet to our `catalog.xml` document, we would have:

```
<?xml version="1.0" encoding="utf-8"?>
<Catalog>
   <totalPages>3036</totalPages>
</Catalog>
```

Sorting

Now let's extend our query for titles of books where Alex Homer is one of the authors. We'll also order the returned books by their title (in alphabetical order):

```
<xsl:stylesheet xmlns:xsl="http://www.w3.org/1999/XSL/Transform" version="1.0">
   <xsl:template match="/Catalog">
      <xsl:copy>
         <xsl:for-each select="//Book[./Authors/Author='Alex Homer']">
            <xsl:sort select="Title"/>
            <xsl:copy>
               <xsl:apply-templates select="Title" name="childnodes"/>
            </xsl:copy>
         </xsl:for-each>
      </xsl:copy>
   </xsl:template>
   <xsl:template name="childnodes" match="*">
      <xsl:copy>
         <xsl:apply-templates name="childnodes"/>
      </xsl:copy>
   </xsl:template>
</xsl:stylesheet>
```

We've simply added an <xsl:sort> element to the <xsl:for-each> element. It indicates that the node set returned by the select attribute in the <xsl:for-each> element should be sorted by Title.

Here's the output of our transformation:

```
<?xml version="1.0" encoding="utf-8"?>
<Catalog>
   <Book>
      <Title>Beginning Components for ASP</Title>
   </Book>
   <Book>
      <Title>IE5 XML Programmer's Reference</Title>
   </Book>
   <Book>
      <Title>Professional ASP 3.0</Title>
   </Book>
</Catalog>
```

Inner Joins

Because of the way XML documents have containment as well as pointing, the concept of an inner join is not necessarily directly applicable to them – there's no need to go looking for a piece of information if it's contained in the piece you already have. On the other hand, if we are linking our elements together using ID and IDREF attributes, we may need this ability. XPath allows a document to be traversed up and down the node tree, allowing us to create some behavior that is similar to that provided by the SQL inner join mechanism. For example, we may use this style sheet to select all the book-author pairs where one of the authors is Alex Homer:

```
<xsl:stylesheet xmlns:xsl="http://www.w3.org/1999/XSL/Transform" version="1.0">
   <xsl:template match="/Catalog">
      <xsl:copy>
         <xsl:for-each select="//Book[Authors/Author='Alex Homer']">
            <xsl:for-each select="Authors/Author">
               <xsl:element name="BookAuthor">
                  <xsl:element name="Title">
                     <xsl:value-of select="../../Title"/>
                  </xsl:element>
                  <xsl:element name="Author">
                     <xsl:value-of select="."/>
                  </xsl:element>
               </xsl:element>
            </xsl:for-each>
         </xsl:for-each>
      </xsl:copy>
   </xsl:template>
</xsl:stylesheet>
```

Here, we have two <xsl:for-each> blocks. The first one handles the filtering aspect of the question: Which books are we interested in? The second one then navigates back down the tree to get to the information we're interested in repeating: the <Author> element(s). We then navigate back up the tree using .. to get the other piece of information we're interested in, namely the title for the book. Here's the transformed output:

```
<?xml version="1.0" encoding="utf-8"?>
<Catalog>
   <BookAuthor>
      <Title>IE5 XML Programmer's Reference</Title>
      <Author>Alex Homer</Author>
   </BookAuthor>
   <BookAuthor>
      <Title>Professional ASP 3.0</Title>
      <Author>Alex Homer</Author>
   </BookAuthor>
   <BookAuthor>
      <Title>Professional ASP 3.0</Title>
      <Author>Brian Francis</Author>
   </BookAuthor>
   <BookAuthor>
      <Title>Professional ASP 3.0</Title>
      <Author>David Sussman</Author>
   </BookAuthor>
   <BookAuthor>
      <Title>Beginning Components for ASP</Title>
      <Author>Alex Homer</Author>
   </BookAuthor>
   <BookAuthor>
      <Title>Beginning Components for ASP</Title>
      <Author>Richard Anderson</Author>
   </BookAuthor>
   <BookAuthor>
      <Title>Beginning Components for ASP</Title>
      <Author>Simon Robinson</Author>
   </BookAuthor>
</Catalog>
```

Outer Joins

Again, since XML documents provide containment, outer joins aren't as important as they are in relational database queries – a processor can simply look at the children of an element to see if a piece of information is present or absent. However, it's possible to provide some of the same functionality as an outer join would provide by navigating the document tree. Say we wanted to provide a list of all books, indicating whether they were partially written by Alex Homer or not. In SQL, we could use an outer join – returning `NULL` if the book was not partially written by Alex Homer. In XSLT, we can use the `count()` function and the `<xsl:choose>` branching element to provide the same functionality:

```
<xsl:stylesheet xmlns:xsl="http://www.w3.org/1999/XSL/Transform" version="1.0">
   <xsl:template match="/Catalog">
      <xsl:copy>
         <xsl:for-each select="Book">
            <xsl:choose>
               <xsl:when test="count(./Authors[Author='Alex Homer']) > 0">
                  <xsl:element name="BookAuthor">
                     <xsl:element name="Title">
                        <xsl:value-of select="Title"/>
                     </xsl:element>
                     <xsl:element name="CowrittenByAlexHomer">Yes</xsl:element>
                  </xsl:element>
               </xsl:when>
```

```
                <xsl:otherwise>
                   <xsl:element name="BookAuthor">
                      <xsl:element name="Title">
                         <xsl:value-of select="Title"/>
                      </xsl:element>
                      <xsl:element name="CowrittenByAlexHomer">No</xsl:element>
                   </xsl:element>
                </xsl:otherwise>
             </xsl:choose>
          </xsl:for-each>
       </xsl:copy>
    </xsl:template>
 </xsl:stylesheet>
```

Here, we check to see if Alex Homer is one of the contributing authors on each book (the `count()` function is used to perform this check); we then create the element one of two ways depending on the path taken by the `<xsl:choose>` conditional element. The output of the above transformation is this:

```
<?xml version="1.0" encoding="utf-8"?>
<Catalog>
   <BookAuthor>
      <Title>IE5 XML Programmer's Reference</Title>
      <CowrittenByAlexHomer>Yes</CowrittenByAlexHomer>
   </BookAuthor>
   <BookAuthor>
      <Title>Designing Distributed Applications</Title>
      <CowrittenByAlexHomer>No</CowrittenByAlexHomer>
   </BookAuthor>
   <BookAuthor>
      <Title>Professional Java XML</Title>
      <CowrittenByAlexHomer>No</CowrittenByAlexHomer>
   </BookAuthor>
   <BookAuthor>
      <Title>XML Design and Implementation</Title>
      <CowrittenByAlexHomer>No</CowrittenByAlexHomer>
   </BookAuthor>
   <BookAuthor>
      <Title>Beginning ASP 3.0</Title>
      <CowrittenByAlexHomer>No</CowrittenByAlexHomer>
   </BookAuthor>
   <BookAuthor>
      <Title>Professional ASP 3.0</Title>
      <CowrittenByAlexHomer>Yes</CowrittenByAlexHomer>
   </BookAuthor>
   <BookAuthor>
      <Title>Professional Site Server 3.0</Title>
      <CowrittenByAlexHomer>No</CowrittenByAlexHomer>
   </BookAuthor>
   <BookAuthor>
      <Title>Professional ADSI Programming</Title>
      <CowrittenByAlexHomer>No</CowrittenByAlexHomer>
   </BookAuthor>
   <BookAuthor>
      <Title>Beginning Components for ASP</Title>
      <CowrittenByAlexHomer>Yes</CowrittenByAlexHomer>
   </BookAuthor>
</Catalog>
```

Manipulation of Table Content

Because XSLT performs operations on a transformed copy of the source document, rather than the source document itself, it is incapable of modifying the original document. As we discussed before, there are other tools that are better suited to this sort of manipulation of XML documents.

Returning Information From More Than One Source

XSLT provides the `xsl:document()` function to allow external documents to be processed at the same time as a base document is being transformed. This allows us to pull information from multiple sources together into one result. For example, let's say we have a document in the same directory as the style sheet called `status.xml` that describes the status of the information shown in `catalog.xml`:

```
<CatalogStatus>
   <GeneratedDate>December 17, 1999</GeneratedDate>
   <LastModifiedDate>December 12, 1999</LastModifiedDate>
   <LastUpdatedBy>Jon Duckett</LastUpdatedBy>
</CatalogStatus>
```

Now, let's see how we can add the `<GeneratedDate>` element from this document to the resultant structure when asking for the titles of all the books by Alex Homer:

```
<xsl:stylesheet xmlns:xsl="http://www.w3.org/1999/XSL/Transform" version="1.0">
   <xsl:template match="/Catalog">
      <xsl:copy>
         <xsl:copy-of select="document('status.xml')//GeneratedDate"/>
         <xsl:for-each select="//Book[./Authors/Author='Alex Homer']">
            <xsl:copy>
               <xsl:apply-templates select="Title" name="childnodes"/>
            </xsl:copy>
         </xsl:for-each>
      </xsl:copy>
   </xsl:template>
   <xsl:template name="childnodes" match="*">
      <xsl:copy>
         <xsl:apply-templates name="childnodes"/>
      </xsl:copy>
   </xsl:template>
</xsl:stylesheet>
```

We've directed the XSLT processor to open the document `status.xml` and insert any element called `<GeneratedDate>` into the transformed document inside the root `<Catalog>` element. Note that normal location steps may be used to filter the node set created by the `document()` function.

The generated XML document is:

```
<?xml version="1.0" encoding="utf-8"?>
<Catalog>
   <GeneratedDate>December 17, 1999</GeneratedDate>
   <Book>
      <Title>IE5 XML Programmer's Reference</Title>
   </Book>
   <Book>
      <Title>Professional ASP 3.0</Title>
   </Book>
   <Book>
      <Title>Beginning Components for ASP</Title>
   </Book>
</Catalog>
```

Procedural Processing

While some degree of procedural processing is possible with XSLT, it does not provide anything close to what may be achieved with either SQL Server or Oracle. For example, while a limited form of cursoring is supported with the `<xsl:for-each>` element (allowing the individual nodes in a node set to be manipulated one-at-a-time), it does not allow the cursor to be programmatically "walked" forward and back. Let's take a look at one last example – producing a list of all authors included in `catalog.xml` and the titles of the books each author has contributed to.

To refresh, in SQL we could use the following statement:

```
SELECT a.author, b.title
   FROM author INNER JOIN book ON author.bookID = book.bookID
   ORDER BY a.author
```

This would result in the following type of structure:

Author	Title
Alex Homer	IE 5 XML Programmer's Reference
Alex Homer	Professional ASP 3.0
Alex Homer	Beginning Components for ASP
Brian Francis	Professional ASP 3.0
...	

The system receiving the flattened structure would then present it in such a way as to eliminate the repeated author information. The other option would be to use the `DISTINCT` keyword on the `SELECT` statement to retrieve all the authors first, and then retrieve all the books written for each author.

Ideally, we'd like the output of our XSLT transform to look something like the following:

```
<?xml version="1.0" encoding="utf-8"?>
<Catalog>
   <Author>
      <Name>Alexander Nakhimovsky</Name>
      <Title>Professional Java XML</Title>
   </Author>
   <Author>
      <Name>Alex Homer</Name>
      <Title>IE5 XML Programmer's Reference</Title>
      <Title>Professional ASP 3.0</Title>
      <Title>Beginning Components for ASP</Title>
   </Author>
   ...
</Catalog>
```

To make this happen, we're going to have to use a new XSLT element type – a variable – and join back to another location in the document with it. Let's see how this would be done. The complete style sheet looks like this:

```
<xsl:stylesheet xmlns:xsl="http://www.w3.org/1999/XSL/Transform" version="1.0">
   <xsl:template match="/Catalog">
      <xsl:copy>
         <xsl:for-each select="//Author/text()">
            <xsl:sort select="."/>
            <xsl:variable name="thisAuthor" select="."/>
            <xsl:if test="count(preceding::Author[text()=$thisAuthor]) = 0">
               <xsl:element name="Author">
                  <xsl:element name="Name">
                     <xsl:value-of select="$thisAuthor"/>
                  </xsl:element>
                  <xsl:for-each select="//Book[./Authors/Author=$thisAuthor]">
                     <xsl:copy-of select="Title"/>
                  </xsl:for-each>
               </xsl:element>
            </xsl:if>
         </xsl:for-each>
      </xsl:copy>
   </xsl:template>
</xsl:stylesheet>
```

Let's break this up and look at each section in turn. First off:

```
<xsl:stylesheet xmlns:xsl="http://www.w3.org/1999/XSL/Transform" version="1.0">
   <xsl:template match="/Catalog">
      <xsl:copy>
         <xsl:for-each select="//Author/text()">
```

Here, we're first creating a cursor using `<xsl:for-each>` on all the author names found anywhere in the document. Note that we will have duplicates here – each time an author is mentioned on a book, that author's name will appear in the list. We'll see how we take care of making these names distinct in a minute.

```
            <xsl:sort select="."/>
```

We'll sort the names alphabetically (in this case, by first name).

```
            <xsl:variable name="thisAuthor" select="."/>
```

This statement stores the value of the author currently being reported in a variable. This is a great way to refer back to information once the context has changed, as we will see later.

```
            <xsl:if test="count(preceding::Author[text()=$thisAuthor]) = 0">
```

This is our sneaky way of getting around the distinctness problem. The nodes selected in the `<xsl:for-each>` element's `select` attribute will be repeated for each book the author has – for example, Alex Homer's name will appear three times. To ensure that we only operate on an author once, we perform this test. Translated from XPath into English, this test says: "Only proceed if there's no `<Author>` element that appears earlier in the (original) document with the same text." Naturally, this is only going to be true once for each discrete author name, and we have the distinctness we were looking for. (As an aside, the "traditional" method of keeping the previous author's name in a variable and comparing it to the current author's name to see if it's changed will not work due to the variable scope rules in XSLT.)

```
                <xsl:element name="Author">
                   <xsl:element name="Name">
                      <xsl:value-of select="$thisAuthor"/>
                   </xsl:element>
```

We create the <Author> wrapper element and a <Name> wrapper element with the name of our author (taken from the variable).

```
                   <xsl:for-each select="//Book[./Authors/Author=$thisAuthor]">
```

Here, we instantiate another cursor for all books anywhere in the document having an author that matches our current author. Note that we couldn't have used "." in place of $thisAuthor here – because the context being referenced inside the square brackets is the context of the <Book> element being checked, not the context of the first <xsl:for-each>. Understanding context is vital to avoid unexpected results when using XSLT.

```
                      <xsl:copy-of select="Title"/>
```

We write the <Title> element of the book to the output and continue looping:

```
                   </xsl:for-each>
                </xsl:element>
             </xsl:if>
          </xsl:for-each>
       </xsl:copy>
    </xsl:template>
 </xsl:stylesheet>
```

The output of this stylesheet is this:

```
<?xml version="1.0" encoding="utf-8"?>
<Catalog>
   <Author>
      <Name>Alexander Nakhimovsky</Name>
      <Title>Professional Java XML</Title>
   </Author>
   <Author>
      <Name>Alex Homer</Name>
      <Title>IE5 XML Programmer's Reference</Title>
      <Title>Professional ASP 3.0</Title>
      <Title>Beginning Components for ASP</Title>
   </Author>
   <Author>
      <Name>Brian Francis</Name>
      <Title>Beginning ASP 3.0</Title>
      <Title>Professional ASP 3.0</Title>
   </Author>
   <Author>
      <Name>Chris Ullman</Name>
      <Title>Beginning ASP 3.0</Title>
   </Author>
   ...
</Catalog>
```

The Future of Query Languages

While XSLT and XPath allow the developer a fair amount of control over the querying and presentation of XML content, the W3C acknowledges that the two technologies do not provide a final querying solution. Some queries (like our books-per-author query above) are quite difficult to perform in XSLT and XPath, and additional functionality normally found in query languages (such as the addition or updating of elements) is not available. The W3C has formed the **XML Query Working Group** to "provide flexible querying facilities to extract data from real and virtual documents on the Web." While this group had, at the time of writing, not yet generated any output, we can expect to see a working draft of a newer querying technology from them soon.

Summary

In this chapter, we've taken a look at some of the newest technologies for the access and manipulation of XML documents:

- We reviewed the W3C **Infoset**, where the W3C describes the pieces of information that together make up an XML document.
- We reviewed the **XLink** specification that defines the mechanisms for creating links in XML documents between resources.
- We reviewed the **XPointer** specification that defines the mechanism for pointing to a specific location, or range of locations, in an XML document.
- We took a look at the working draft specification for **XML Fragment Interchange** and how XML fragments could be passed with context information to aid in their interpretation.
- We took a look at some proposed query languages for XML and examined some examples using the latest querying technologies, **XSLT** and **XPath**.

While many of these technologies are not widely used as of press time, they will certainly be a part of the widely-used XML technology set soon enough. Understanding these technologies now will give you a jump on the competition when they become available.

9

Transforming XML

Some talk about XML as a document format. Some talk about it as an underlying hierarchical model for storing data. At another level, an XML document can be perceived as data traveling through a network of processing agents. Each network node stores or processes the data and transmits the result to a neighbor node. In this world, an XML document is data flowing through or between applications on a network. However we look at it, any XML document is a collection of elements organized in accordance to a certain schema (whether explicit, through the use of a DTD or other schema, or implicit, without a defined schema) and is also a potential hierarchical structure. We can also say that the XML document is a serialized version of a hierarchical structure – a plain text document used for information exchange between processing agents. However, internally these processing agent do not use the serialized version (the XML document) but a more workable internal representation.

If XML is to truly help us create flexible applications that will talk to each other across platforms and in different applications, and if we really want to re-use the data we mark up in XML and share that data using XML as a common format, we need to be prepared for people and applications that do not use the same structure for their data we do. In this chapter we will look at ways in which we can transform the structure of our data into another XML vocabulary, or just re-order our own data.

In this chapter, we will concentrate on the transformation aspect of processing XML. There are many reasons why we need to transform XML, so we will start this chapter with a look at why and when we might want to transform XML into other forms. The majority of the chapter will use XSL transformations, although we will have a discussion at the end of the chapter about other methods for transformations.

The different transformation methods that can be used have caused heated debate in the XML community. Different programmers often prefer different solutions to how they transform XML, so, we will look at some of the different viewpoints underlying their preferences to let you decide which method to use (we do assume that you are either familiar with the DOM having read Chapter 5, or are already using it).

After looking at some reasons why you need to transform your documents, we will go on to look at using XSLT as a transformation language. We will introduce you to the basic syntax to get you used to using XSL for transforming documents. This will include an example of transforming our book list into a new structure. Note that this transformation requires knowledge of XPath, which is a specification used within XSLT to specify a particular part of an XML file. XPath was detailed in the previous chapter. Once we have looked at XSLT, we will look at how to use the DOM and script to alter the structure of the same book list. This will be followed by a look at more dynamic documents; taking what we have learnt from the XSL section of this chapter and the DOM chapter earlier, we will create a document that re-orders the contents of a table based on a user's interaction. We will then compare these two approaches to transformation. To wrap up the transformations we will look at when you might like to consider using the different approaches. In all, this chapter will cover:

- Why XML transformations are necessary
- An introduction to the XSLT syntax
- An example of using XSLT to transform static documents
- Using XSLT to transform more dynamic XML documents

This will put you in a position to choose the type of transformation that you need for your XML documents, and teach you the core concepts behind different types of transformation.

Why Transform XML?

If we are using XML stored in a text-based file, or we are receiving XML generated by some other type of program, it is in a fixed format. While XML is platform independent, and can be transferred between different parts of applications, there will be times when people require the information in different structures. In addition, there will be times when we need to transform a document's structure on the fly in an interactive document. For example, so that the document is restructured based upon a user's request or preferences. Transformations generally fall into one of three categories:

- **Structural transformations** – where you are transforming from one XML vocabulary into another, which is like a translation. An example may be between two financial markup languages such as FPML and finML.
- **Creating dynamic documents** – allowing users to re-order, filter, and sort parts of a document, such as allowing users to click on table column headings to reorder the contents of a table.
- **Transformations into a rendition language** – ready for presentation to a user in some form of browser, such as Wireless Application Protocol, HTML, VOXML, or Scalable Vector Graphics.

Let's take a look at each of these in turn.

Translating Between Different Vocabularies

If we think again about the catalog of books we marked up in XML in Chapter 2, there are many potential uses for the catalog data. For example, Wrox may use a catalog of its books on its web site and on its intranet using the DTD we created in Chapter 3. Meanwhile, several bookstores require almost exactly the same information. This all sounds like a perfect job for XML. However, if the different bookstores mark up their data using a different DTD to describe the same data, we need a way to transform our data into a version compatible with theirs.

For example, the www.wrox.com site may use the data marked up using the following section of the `pubCatalog.dtd` that we met in Chapter 3:

```
<Book ISBN="1-861003-11-0" level="Professional" pubdate="11-21-99"
      pageCount="500" authors="multi">
   <Title>Professional XML</Title>
   <Abstract>XML is an important area that you must learn about</Abstract>
   <RecSubjCategories>
      <Category>XML</Category>
      <Category>Programming</Category>
      <Category>Internet Programming</Category>
   </RecSubjCategories>
   <Price>$49.99</Price>
</Book>
```

However, XYZBooks Inc. may require the data in a different form, such as:

```
<Book>
   <Title>Professional XML</Title>
   <ISBN>1-861003-11-0</ISBN>
   <Abstract>XML is an important area that you must learn about</Abstract>
   <Pubdate>11-21-99</Pubdate>
   <RecSubjCategories>
      <Category>XML</Category>
      <Category>Programming</Category>
      <Category>Internet Programming</Category>
   </RecSubjCategories>
   <Price>$49.99</Price>
</Book>
```

As you can see, two of the attributes of the `<Book>` element have become elements in their own right: `<ISBN>` and `<Pubdate>`. Again, rather than preparing and storing the data for the two formats, we can just transform one into the other.

This is just one example of where we may need to transform one XML vocabulary into another, I am sure you can think of many others. One area where this sort of transformation has been touted as being important is in e-commerce, where different companies may need their data in different formats. Alternatively, we may even decide to update one of our existing applications, and need to be able to transform legacy XML (now there's a thought for you) into the new structure.

Transformations are a valuable player in XML, bearing in mind the intention that we should be able to **re-purpose** our data once it is marked up in XML. After all, if we only need to perform a simple transformation, there is no need to maintain two versions of our data. The transformation capabilities of XSL are ideally suited to this sort of transformation.

Dynamic Transformations

The last section looked at offering the same data in different ways, where both parties require specific, static versions of an XML document. But there are also occasions where we might need to do more dynamic transformations. If you think about spreadsheets, which undoubtedly revolutionized desktop PC use nearly twenty years ago, users require that data is re-sorted on the click of a column heading. This requires a more dynamic transformation.

Any transformation that requires user interaction, or producing interactive documents, can be quite a different task compared with producing static documents. Dynamic transformations often require event handling, which involves the use of a programming language.

Because scripting languages and the DOM allow transformations without XSL, and because the Document Object Model (DOM) can be used in browsers through its binding to JavaScript and other languages (such as Java, C++, Perl, Visual Basic, or Python) some people prefer to do these dynamic transformations with DOM and script (without XSL). Later in the chapter we will see examples of both and reasons why you may want to use one approach over another.

Different Browsers

Many web developers have experienced the headache of having to develop parallel sites, or parts of sites for incompatible browser versions. The idea that XML can only be served to web browsers that understand XML may seem like just another area for browser incompatibility to occur. However, if we were to develop our site content in XML, we could then transform it into different markup languages, so we could create different versions of HTML from the core XML content. Let's see how this might work:

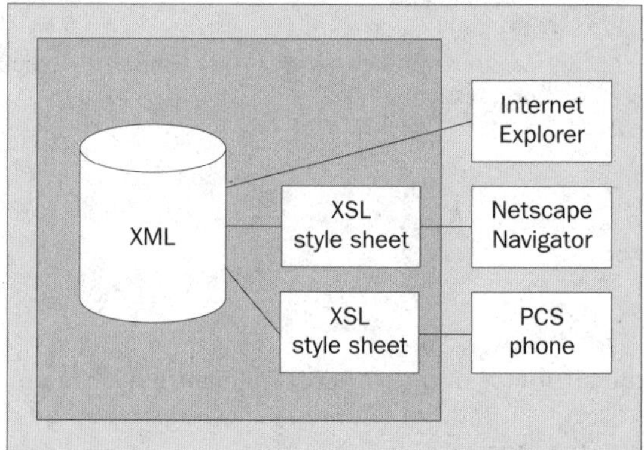

Here we are using three different style sheets to create three versions of the XML content. The version for Internet Explorer 5 may still be in XML, while the other two can be two different rendition languages. This approach avoids the need for replicating the content three times for the different browsers. By transforming the XML data, several pages could use the same XML content to render pages in the correct format for the requesting browser. In this example we are simply using XSL style sheets as templates for how the data should be displayed, one for each client. These style sheets act as templates for the underlying data, therefore we could use the same style sheet to transform the data for several pages.

Indeed, transforming XML into HTML is popular where display in a browser is required, due to the lack of an XML linking specification from the W3C.

This approach is set to become increasingly important as new types of browsers make their way onto the Internet. We are already seeing digital television services, games consoles, and a variety of mobile devices, from handheld personal digital assistants (PDAs) to mobile phones, offering Internet access. As these diverse clients increase their share in the browser market there will be pressure to serve pages that are designed for their different needs. For example, as we will see in Chapter 14, the facilities offered by mobile phones with limited screen size and lower bandwidth and processing power will require special services. These may involve transforming the XML into another markup language such as the Wireless Markup Language (WML), which is designed for mobile phones and PDAs. So, the ability to transform our content into different versions will become increasingly common.

XSL

The **eXtensible Stylesheet Language** is an XML based language designed to transform an XML document into another XML document or to transform an XML document into rendition objects. The original XSL language has been split into three separate languages:

- Transformation (XSLT)
- Rendition (XSLF – which can involve the use of XSLT)
- Accessing the XML underlying structure (XPath)

XSL has its roots in both Cascading Style Sheets (CSS) and a language called DSSSL (Document Style Semantics and Specification Language (DSSSL – pronounced 'deessel'). As it evolves, XSL's styling aspects are becoming increasingly closer to CSS and farther from DSSSL. Styling is covered in Chapter 13.

As you might have guessed, the key area we are looking at in this chapter is the transformation capabilities of XSL. The XSLT specification became a Recommendation on 16th November 1999. It also relies on the XPath specification, which became a recommendation on the same day, as a way of selecting the area of the document to transform.

XSLT

This section looks at how we can use XSLT to transform XML documents, and we will see where XPath is employed in XSLT. As the first sentence of the XSLT specifications explicitly states: "*[XSLT] is a language for transforming XML documents into other XML documents*". As we saw earlier, we may need to transform XML into another structure for many reasons. To do this we need an XSLT processor. We will discuss two of the commonly available ones as soon as we have seen what the XSLT processor actually does.

XSLT is a language written in XML. This means that an XSLT style sheet for transforming an XML document is actually a well-formed XML document. So, in this chapter we will be learning the syntax of XSLT and what it allows us to do.

First we have a very important point to clarify:

XSLT engines do not manipulate documents; they manipulate structure.

In order for an XSLT engine to be able to transform an XML document, the document must first be converted into a **structure** or an **internal model**. This internal model is a tree. This model is independent of any API used to access it. In the SGML world, this abstract model is called a **grove**. Because, actually, XML is a subset of SGML, it also inherits some of its basic concepts. Thus, the grove is simply the abstract tree structure independently of any API used to reach or manipulate the tree's entities. For instance, the DOM is the API recommended by W3C to access the grove. The DOM is the API, the grove is the abstract structure. Thus, a grove may have more than one API or could have different APIs for different languages. Throughout this chapter, we refer to the grove when we're talking about the abstract tree structure.

So the following XML:

```
<?xml version="1.0" ?>
<Book ISBN="1-861003-11-0" level="Professional" pubdate="11-21-99"
      pageCount="500" authors="multi">
   <Title>Professional XML</Title>
   <Abstract>XML is an important area that you must learn about</Abstract>
   <RecSubjCategories>
      <Category>XML</Category>
      <Category>Programming</Category>
      <Category>Internet Programming</Category>
   </RecSubjCategories>
   <Price>$49.99</Price>
</Book>
```

Can be represented in an abstract form of a tree something like this:

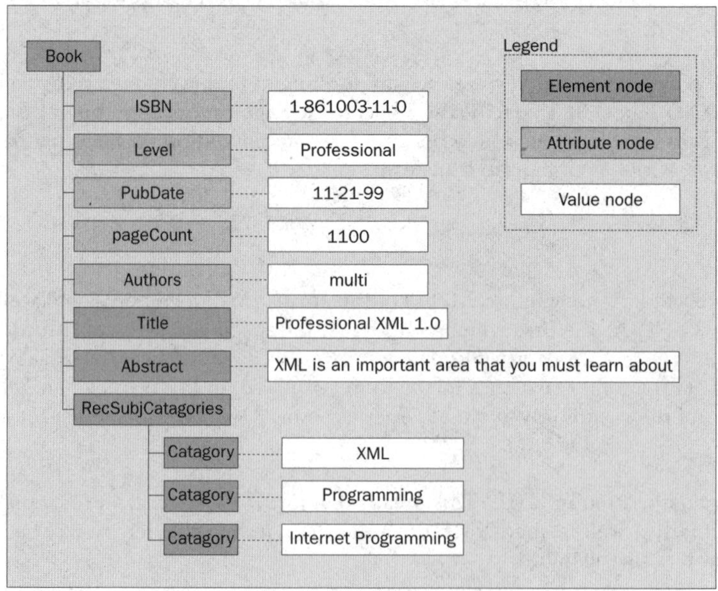

It doesn't matter how we choose to look at or process the file, <Title>, <Abstract>, <RecSubjCategories>, and <Price> are all children of <Book>, and <Category> is a grandchild of <Book> and a child of <RecSubjCategories>. This is why we say this abstract tree structure is a model that is independent of any API used to access it (such as the W3C DOM), and it is this **structure** that XSL processors use, to select the appropriate part of the structure. XPath is the language used to access any element of the tree structure.

How Does the XSL Processor Transform the Source Document?

As we said, XSLT operates on the document model not the syntax. Both the source and destination formats are applications of XML, and the underlying structure of both is a tree. In addition the XSL style sheet is an XML document, thus it too can be represented by a tree. So, in all, XSLT processors hold three trees.

XSLT is a **declarative** language, which means that you specify how you want the result to look, rather than saying how it should be transformed, and this is why we need the XSL processor to do the work. The XSL style sheet is made up of **templates** that specify how each node of the source tree should appear in the result tree.

The following diagram illustrates how the processor works:

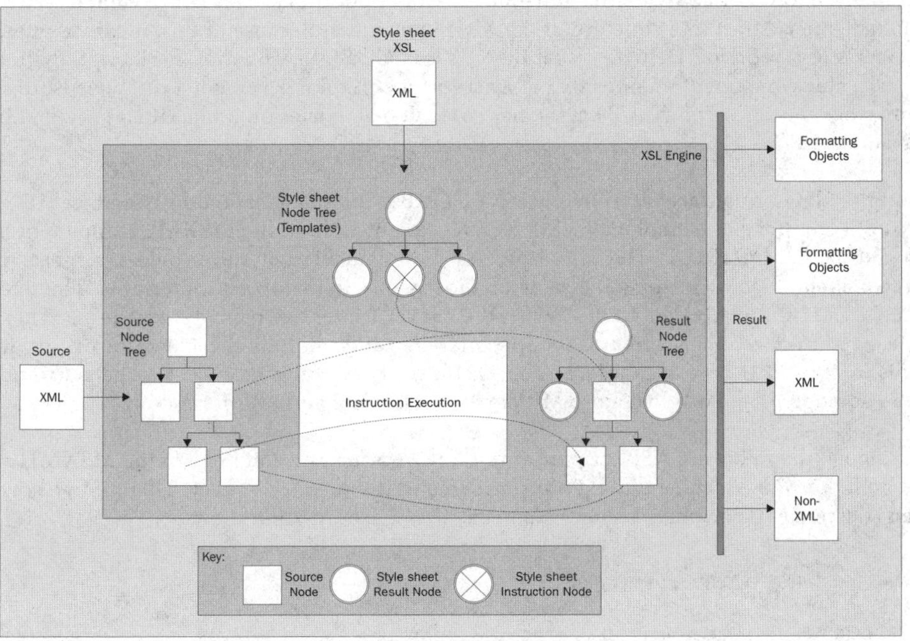

Here we can see that there are the three structures. Remember that the source and the result structures are abstract representations of the document. The processor goes through the source grove, starting with the root, and looks for a matching template in the style sheet tree. When it finds one, it uses the rules in the template to write an abstract representation of the result into the result tree. Then it moves through the source document, node by node, lead by the XSLT instruction <xsl:apply-template>, looking for a match in the style sheet. If there is no matching template, it moves on to the next one. We can say that it executes a default template, which has no output result. Then, the result tree is translated into an XML document, text, an HTML document, or whatever the desired result is.

This, at least in theory, is what should happen. But there are different variations on how XSLT engines are built. XSLT engines could be optimized, and the style sheet may not necessarily be stored as a grove or tree structure. However, this gives a general idea of their behavior.

Having taken an overview of what an XSL processor does in order to perform its transformation, you will need to make sure you have one installed on your machine to work with the examples in this chapter. As there are different ways of implementing an XSL processor, let's take a look at two of them:

- **MSXML** – the Microsoft XML parser with a DOM interface, which includes an XSLT engine in the form of a COM component. The MSXML engine included in IE5 is quite out of date compared to the recommendations. The technology preview version is more up to date.
- **XT** – James Clark's dedicated XSLT engine. This is written in Java and is therefore usable on several platforms. XT is more up to date concerning its conformance with the latest XSLT specifications.

The MSXML XSL Processor

MSXML is not just a parser; it also includes an XSL processor. MSXML is tightly integrated with Internet Explorer 5, but is also available as a standalone COM component from http://msdn.microsoft.com/xml/ for integration with applications. This component uses the DOM to manipulate the abstract tree structure of the XML document. Because of this, it can be interfaced to languages like JavaScript, Delphi, Visual Basic, VisualCOBOL, VBScript, PerlScript, PythonScript, C++, etc. This component requires that at least Internet Explorer version 4 or above is present on the system, since the Microsoft XSLT engine has some dependencies on other DLLs provided by this application.

The original DOM interface is defined using a CORBA Interface Definition Language (IDL), but Microsoft's component technology COM uses a different IDL, so the MSXML component interface is defined using the COM IDL. The Microsoft DOM implementation, nevertheless, respects the spirit of this recommendation by keeping the same method names in the object's interfaces. The interface `IXMLDocument` is equivalent to the W3C DOM level 1 interface named `document`. The W3C `document` interface inherits from the `node` interface, and similarly the `IXMLDocument` interface inherits from the `IXMLNode` interface. The `IXMLDocument` interface has also been extended to contain additional methods that aid XML document parsing and transformation.

For example, the following ASP script uses the `IXMLDocument` interface of the MSXML component to parse both the XML document to be transformed and the XSL style sheet. Then, it transforms the parsed source XML document using the parsed XSL transformation sheet:

```
<%@ LANGUAGE = VBScript %>
<%
   ' Set the source and style sheet locations
   sourceFile = Server.MapPath("catalog.xml")
   styleFile = Server.MapPath("catalog.xsl")

   ' Load the XML and get it parsed
   Set source = CreateObject("Microsoft.XMLDOM")
   source.async = false
   source.load(sourceFile)
```

```
    ' Load the XSLT and get it parsed
    Set style = CreateObject("Microsoft.XMLDOM")
    style.async = false
    style.load(styleFile)

    ' Transform the XML document using the XSL transformation sheet.
    Response.Write(source.transformNode(style))
%>
```

The general mechanism used to transform documents with MSXML is:

- Load the original document to be transformed. The `load()` method also parses the document so that the document is stored internally as a tree structure (like the one we saw earlier).
- Load the XSLT document. Again, the `load()` method parses the document and transforms it into a tree.
- Make the transformation by using the `transformNode()` function. This function returns a string (a `BSTR`). The returned string contains the transformed document. So, if the XSLT transformation sheet contains an XML to HTML transformation, then the document stored in the resultant string is an HTML document.

The MSXML component integrates in the same component:

- An XML parser
- An extended DOM level 1 interface to the tree
- An XSLT transformation engine

The XT XSL Processor

XT is another popular XSLT processor; written by James Clark, it is simple to use and can be downloaded for free from the author's site http://www.jclark.com/xml/xt.html. It is written in Java, and has been successfully tested on several Java Virtual machines. For the Win32 platform, it can be downloaded as a single executable, although this requires Microsoft's Java VM to be installed on the machine. This processor will be useful to experiment with the different transformations introduced throughout this chapter.

As opposed to MSXML, which includes its own XML parser, the XT engine can operate with any SAX-compliant parser (we discussed SAX in Chapter 6). As long as the SAX parser is implemented in Java, it will interface properly with the XT engine. The package also comes with a fast Java parser named XP.

- XT is used through the command line. On Windows, running XT is probably easier than on other platforms. The following command line transforms an XML document with an XSLT style sheet, resulting in an HTML document:

```
Xt booklist.xml booklist.xsl booklist.htm
```

XT also accepts XSLT parameters, for example:

```
Xt booklist.xml booklist.xsl booklist.htm result=HTML
```

In the example above, the `result` parameter is included in the XSLT style sheet as an XSLT variable. This variable can then be used in the XSLT templates.

A big advantage of XT is that it can run on platforms other than windows. However, not all platforms allow you to run a Java application as a stand-alone executable, and most platforms require that you run the Java application with the Java executable provided with the Java JDK. For instance, the following command line will run XT on Linux:

```
java -Dcom.jclark.xsl.sax.parser=xp.jar com.jclark.xsl.sax.Driver booklist.xml
booklist.xsl booklist.htm result=HTML
```

The XT engine speed depends a lot on the processing power of your machine, since Java is an interpreted language.

Using XSLT

To see how XSLT works, we are going to jump straight in with a simple example. Let's start with the details of a book marked up in XML and transform it into XHTML for display in a browser.

> *XHTML is an extended version of HTML 4.0 designed to be an application of XML. For more information, consult the latest W3C recommendation proposal at http://www.w3.org/TR/xhtml1.*

Here is some book catalog information marked up in XML, according to the DTD developed in Chapter 3:

```
<?xml version="1.0" encoding="utf-8" standalone="yes"?>
<!--======= The Wrox Press Book Catalog Application =======-->
<Catalog>
<Book>
   <Title>Designing Distributed Applications</Title>
   <Authors>
      <Author>Stephen Mohr</Author>
   </Authors>
   <Publisher>Wrox Press, Ltd.</Publisher>
   <PubDate>May 1999</PubDate>
   <Abstract>5 principles that will make your web applications more flexible
            and live longer</Abstract>
   <Pages>460</Pages>
   <ISBN>1-861002-27-0</ISBN>
   <RecSubjCategories>
      <Category>Internet</Category>
      <Category>Programming</Category>
      <Category>XML</Category>
   </RecSubjCategories>
</Book>
```

```
<Book>
   <Title>Professional Java XML</Title>
   <Authors>
      <Author>Alexander Nakhimovsky</Author>
      <Author>Tom Myers</Author>
   </Authors>
   <Publisher>Wrox Press, Ltd.</Publisher>
   <PubDate>August 1999</PubDate>
   <Abstract>Learn to utilize the powerful combination of Java and
            XML</Abstract>
   <Pages>600</Pages>
   <ISBN>1-861002-85-8</ISBN>
   <RecSubjCategories>
      <Category>Java</Category>
      <Category>Programming</Category>
      <Category>XML</Category>
   </RecSubjCategories>
</Book>
</Catalog>
```

Let's have a look at the simple XSLT style sheet that will be used to transform the source document into the required result document, which will be an XHTML document that displays the titles of the books in the catalog:

```
<?xml version="1.0"?>
<xsl:stylesheet version="1.0"
                xmlns:xsl="http://www.w3.org/1999/XSL/Transform">

<xsl:output method="html"/>

<xsl:template match="/">
   <html>
      <head>
         <title>The book catalog</title>
      </head>
      <body>
         <xsl:apply-templates select="//Book" />
      </body>
   </html>
</xsl:template>

<xsl:template match="Book">
   <DIV style="margin-left: 40pt;
         margin-bottom: 15pt;
         text-align: left;
         line-height: 12pt;
         text-indent: 0pt;" >
      <xsl:apply-templates select="Title" />
   </DIV>
</xsl:template>

<xsl:template match="Title">
   <DIV style="margin-left: 40pt;
         font-family: Arial;
         font-weight: 700;
         font-size: 14pt;" >
      <SPAN>
```

```
        <xsl:value-of select="."/>
      </SPAN>
   </DIV>
</xsl:template>

</xsl:stylesheet>
```

Caution: as it stands, this example can only be executed by an XSLT engine conformant to the XSLT version 1 recommendations. SAXON and XT fall into this category, IE5.0 doesn't – because it does not support XPath and some XSLT constructs. However, in this particular case it is possible to modify the above file such that IE5.0 can use it: you will have to change the namespace from http://www.w3.org/1999/XSL/Transform *to* http://www.w3.org/TR/WD-xsl *and remove the* `<xsl:output method="html"/>` *statement. Bear in mind, though, that this modification will not work for all the examples in this chapter, so until there a more up to date parser is supplied for IE you're better off using XT.*

Finally, the resulting XHTML document will look like this:

```
<!DOCTYPE html PUBLIC "-//W3C//DTD HTML 4.0 Transitional//EN">
<html>
<head>
   <title>The book catalog</title>
</head>
<body>
   <DIV style="margin-left: 40pt;
               margin-bottom: 15pt;
               text-align: left;
               line-height: 12pt;
               text-indent: 0pt;">
      <DIV style="margin-left: 40pt;
                  font-family: Arial;
                  font-weight: 700;
                  font-size: 14pt;">
         <SPAN>Designing Distributed Applications</SPAN>
      </DIV>
   </DIV>
   <DIV style="margin-left: 40pt;
               margin-bottom: 15pt;
               text-align: left;
               line-height: 12pt;
               text-indent: 0pt;">
      <DIV style="margin-left: 40pt;
                  font-family: Arial;
                  font-weight: 700;
                  font-size: 14pt;">
         <SPAN>Professional Java XML</SPAN>
      </DIV>
   </DIV>
</body>
</html>
```

The simple result looks like this:

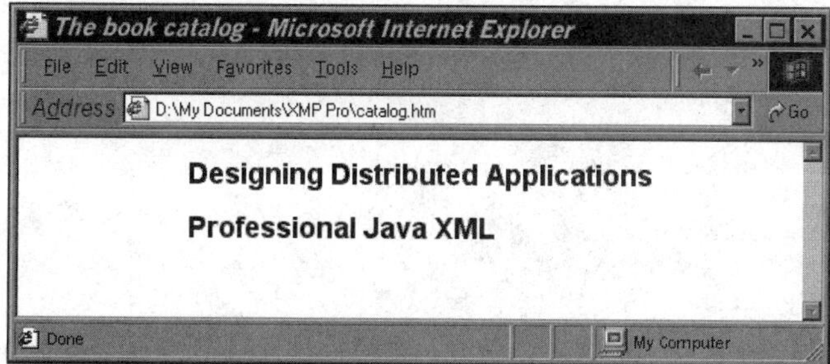

Getting Help with the Transformation

To better understand what's supposed to be going on in this example, pretend that you are an XSLT engine for a moment, and look at the world through its eyes (go on, no one is watching). First, as an XSLT engine, remember that you need the document structure not the text itself. After all, you can only process the structure not the text. So, somebody has to transform the text into the required abstract tree structure, the grove. As an XSLT engine, you may have one of these two friends:

- A parser with a DOM interface
- A parser just giving you an event for each element

If you use the services of a parser having a DOM interface, this implies that the parser encapsulates the tree and that you access any of the objects on the grove through the DOM interface.

If you interface with a parser giving you an event for each element, you manage the grove yourself and then store the document's structure the way you want. This is the approach in Java using a SAX interface.

Therefore, my dear XSLT engine, you have the choice of whether to get help from your parser with a DOM interface and outsource the grove management to them, or to manage it yourself.

The internal structure could be implemented in different ways; however, even if you use associative arrays or lists pointing to lists, the modeled structure is a tree. The DOM is the W3C recommendation that specifies how to interface to this structure.

If you remember back to the earlier diagram, you are holding three trees. One contains the representation of the source document, one will hold the representation of the result tree's structure, but what was the third tree for? Wasn't an XSLT document also an XML document? Yes. You're beginning to learn your role well. This is what the third tree is for. In the case of the XSLT document, its conversion to an internal tree structure may not imply a conversion from text into a hierarchical structure. The XSLT internal structure may be something else, something more optimized for XSLT processing.

So, the original XML document is first parsed then converted into an abstract tree structure, an internal representation of the hierarchical structure. The DOM is an interface to this internal structure. The XSLT document is also parsed and converted into an internal structure. It may be an abstract tree structure but may be also another kind of structure, optimized for template processing and pattern matching.

The `Catalog.xml` file:

```
<Catalog>
<Book>
   <Title>IE5 XML Programmer's Reference</Title>
   <Authors>
      <Author>Alex Homer</Author>
   </Authors>
   <Publisher>Wrox Press, Ltd.</Publisher>
   <PubDate>August 1999</PubDate>
   <Abstract>Reference of XML capabilities in IE5</Abstract>
   <Pages>480</Pages>
   <ISBN>1-861001-57-6</ISBN>
   <RecSubjCategories>
      <Category>Internet</Category>
      <Category>Web Publishing</Category>
      <Category>XML</Category>
   </RecSubjCategories>
</Book>
</Catalog>
```

will be represented by an abstract tree in the XSL processor as shown below:

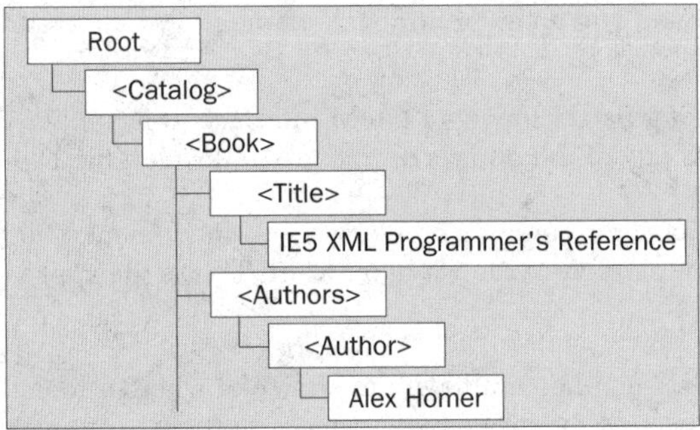

How the Style Sheet Transforms the Document

As we said, XSL is an application of XML, so the style sheet (or transformation sheet, if you prefer) is really an XML document. Because it is an XML document, it can start with the XML declaration, which indicates to a XML parser in which XML version this document is encoded.

The root element of our style sheet is the `<xsl:stylesheet>` element:

```
<xsl:stylesheet version="1.0"
                xmlns:xsl="http://www.w3.org/1999/XSL/Transform">
```

The first attribute of the `<xsl:stylesheet>` element is the XSLT version. The second is the attribute `xmlns:xsl`, which holds the namespace for the XSL transformation recommendation.

As you might remember from Chapter 7, on Namespaces and Schemas, this declares the namespace of XSLT. As you can see, the prefix associated with the namespace is `xsl`, so the root element is actually `<stylesheet>`, but it has been qualified by `xsl:`, its namespace prefix. Having declared the namespace, any element beginning with the prefix `xsl:` is part of the XSL vocabulary.

The `<stylesheet>` element contains three **templates**, each of which is nested within the `<template>` element, which is actually `<xsl:template>` in the style sheet because we included the namespace. You will notice that the `<template>` element has an attribute called `match`. The value of this attribute is a pattern that matches the node of the tree that the template should be applied to, in the form of an XPath expression.

The first task is to tell the XSLT engine the desired output. In the example, an HTML result is expected, and specified using:

```
<xsl:output method="html"/>
```

Knowing the expected output format, as a processor, you will start in the source document tree at the root node. You will then look for a template in the style sheet that matches the root node. Note that the root node is the document node, not the first element. In the example case, the root node is not the `<Catalog>` element, but rather the XML document itself. So, do we have a template matching the document root? The answer is yes. If you remember back to the XPath section in the last chapter, the root of a document can also be represented by a forward slash (/) symbol. This is exactly what we see in the first template:

```
<xsl:template match="/">
   <html xmlns="http://www.w3.org/TR/xhtml1/strict">
      <head>
         <title>The book catalog</title>
      </head>
      <body>
         <xsl:apply-templates select="//Book" />
      </body>
   </html>
</xsl:template>
```

So, you have found a template that matches the root element of the source document. What do you do now? To better represent what's happening in the head of an XSLT processor, imagine a cursor navigating in the original XML document nodes tree; its position is the **current node**, and right now the current node is the root element.

Step 1: You have positioned the current cursor on the root node and found a matching template in the XSLT structure. The template has a "/" pattern. So, output the following result. Remember, we are working with an abstract tree structure, represented in the diagrammatic part of the following figure, on the left:

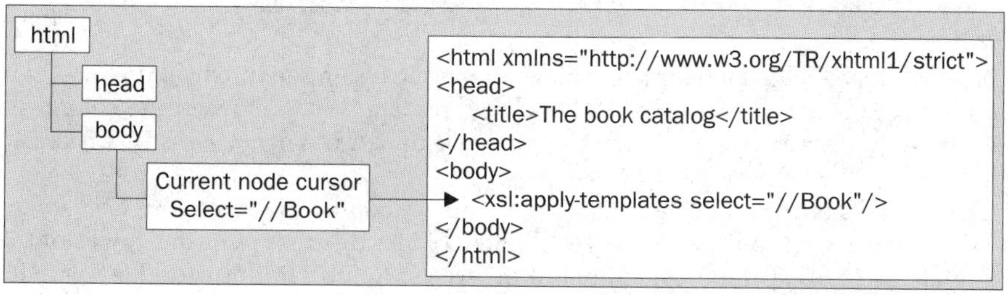

html
head
body
Current node cursor
Select="//Book"

```
<html xmlns="http://www.w3.org/TR/xhtml1/strict">
<head>
   <title>The book catalog</title>
</head>
<body>
   <xsl:apply-templates select="//Book"/>
</body>
</html>
```

In the middle of this first template, nested in the `<Body>` element, there is an `<xml:apply-templates />` construct. This is where we will be writing the content of the page. It has an attribute called `select`, whose value is an XPath expression. This construct means:

- "From the XPath query "`//Book`", obtain a node list. Then, for each node in this node list, try to match a template. If a match is found, apply the template."

But what does "`//Book`" mean? It means "select the `<Book>` elements that are descendants of the root node".

Step 2: Further down in our XSL file we find a template match for `<Book>` elements (`<xsl:template match="Book">`), so next we apply this template to the first `<Book>` element in our node list. Our current cursor is now on the first `<Book>` node.

Step 3: We then insert the `<Book>` matching template's content where the `<apply-templates select="//Book" />` construct is located. First we add the default CSS styling properties for the book data – any further elements that do not contain more specific CSS style properties will inherit these properties. Next, we find another `<apply-templates />`, this time with a `select` attribute of "`Title`". From the rule in Step 1, we know that this requires us to construct a node set of `<Title>` nodes. However, this time the current node is the first `<Book>` node, and our XPath expression dictates that our new node set will only contain the `<Title>` nodes that are children of the current node. This means that our node set will consist of the `<Title>` child of the first `<Book>` node.

> *This is where we start to see the versatility of the XPath expressions we use. If we were to substitute `<xsl:apply-templates select="//Title" />` for the existing element the node set would contain all `<Title>` descendants of the root node (the parent of the `<Book>` node) – which would mean all the `<Title>` nodes in the grove.*

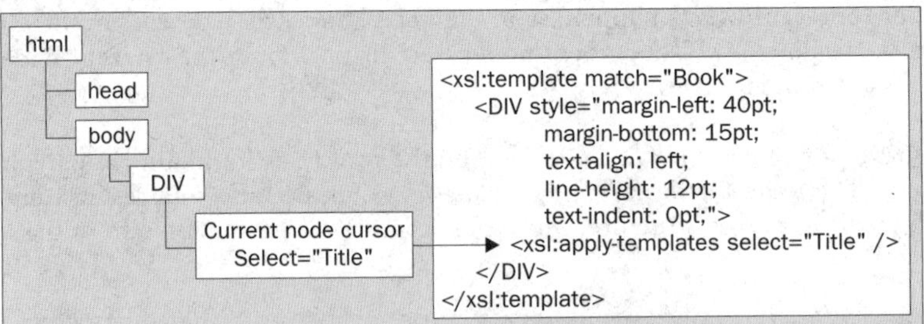

Step 4: Next we try to match a template against the `<Title>` node in our node set. Again we find a match: the `<xsl:template match="Title">` template. We then insert the contents of this template where the `<xsl:apply-templates select="Title" />` construct is located.

Step 5: The contents of the `<Title>` matching template consist of some more CSS styling properties and an `<xsl:value-of select="."/>` element. This construct pulls the values of the nodes specified by its `select` attribute XPath out of the tree structure. In this case the XPath is "`.`", meaning the `<Title>` node itself, so we write out the contents of the `<Title>` node.

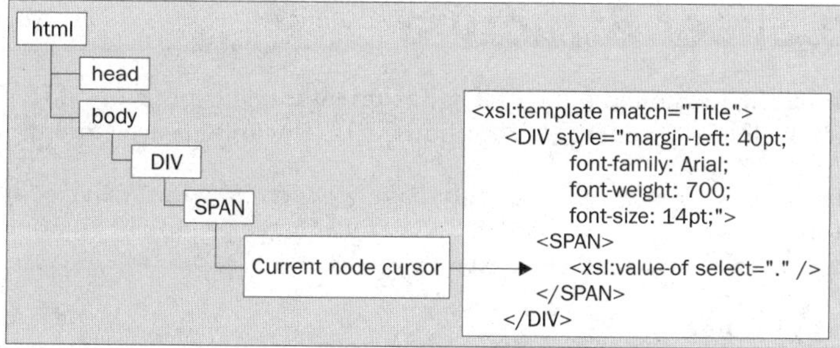
html
head
body
DIV
SPAN
Current node cursor
<xsl:template match="Title">
<DIV style="margin-left: 40pt;
font-family: Arial;
font-weight: 700;
font-size: 14pt;">
<SPAN>
<xsl:value-of select="." />
</SPAN>
</DIV>

Step 6: We have now applied templates to all the nodes in the node set we created in the `<Book>` matching template, so we move on to the next node in the first node set we created – which is the second `<Book>` node. This is treated in the same way as our first `<Book>` node, so we go through steps 4 and 5 again. We continue this process until we have processed all of the `<Book>` elements.

During this process we not only transformed an XML document form a certain document type to another, but also performed some editing in the process – only the `<Book>` and `<Title>` elements are transformed. Also, the transformation is not a one-to-one transformation. For each element of the original document there can be more than one element in the resultant document.

We should note something important here. The template matching the `<Title>` element does not insert elements into the result tree, it inserts text nodes. As we said earlier, a grove is an internal hierarchical structure. When the XML document is converted into this hierarchical structure, we transform the text document into a tree like model. In this tree, child elements are also the tree's child nodes. Data content is a child node too. For instance, the `<Book>` element contains one `<Title>` element. This `<Title>` element does not contain elements but contains data content, which becomes a child node.

So, what have we learned while pretending to be an XSL engine?

- First we build a grove that is an internal tree representation of the document. This grove always has a root element. The root element represents the XML document – it is not the document's top level element. Then, under that root element is the node hierarchy. Each node is typed. A node can be, for example, a node for the DTD, for the schema, or for a processing instruction. If an element has attributes, then each element also has a collection of attribute nodes. If the element has data content, then a data content node is added under the element node. Hence, an element node may have a collection of attribute nodes and a data content node as children.
- Secondly, we create a structure for the XSLT document. This may also be a grove but it may be any kind of structure optimized for template processing and pattern matching.
- Then, each time we encounter an `<xsl:apply-templates>` element we form a node list and continue processing with this list. If the `<xsl:apply-templates>` element contains a `select` attribute, we obtain the node list from the XPath query specified, Otherwise the node list will consist of all child nodes.
- Each time an `<xsl:value-of>` construct is encountered, we extract a value from the source tree based on the XPath expression in the `select` attribute.
- Transformation is not solely restricted to one-to-one translation, it also allows addition of new information content, one-to-many element translation, element addition, and element deletion.

XSLT Style Sheet Structure

So, we have seen our first example of an XSLT document transforming an XML document into a new structure. Now we shall take a general look at how XSLT documents are structured.

We learnt a lot from our first example; not only have we seen how the XSLT processor works through a document that it must transform – which will be very useful as we look at creating other elements – we have also used four of the key XSLT elements:

- `<xsl:stylesheet>`
- `<xsl:template>`
- `<xsl:apply-templates>`
- `<xsl:value-of>`

We started our first example document with the XML declaration because the style sheet is an XML document. Remembering that `xsl:` is used as a qualified name prefix for all elements that are part of the XSLT namespace, the `<stylesheet>` element is the document element that contains the other elements of the style sheet, and this is where the namespace is declared. Within this element we had three `<template>` elements, which are used to specify how the element, or other node, specified in the `match` attribute should be transformed. These can be seen as the main building blocks of most transformations. The `<xsl:apply-templates>` element is used to tell the processor to process all child elements of the current element if no `select` attribute is present. Otherwise, only the element nodes matching the selection criteria are processed. Finally, the `xsl:value-of` element is used to write out element content.

This illustrates the two types of element defined in the XSLT specification. Apart from the root element, there are **templates** and **instructions**. `<xsl:template>` is, obviously, a template, as it would appear underneath the root element in the abstract tree structure, while `<xsl:apply-templates>` and `<xsl:value-of>` are instructions that appear as children of the `<template>` element. Remember that an XSLT document is an XML document, and as such can be converted into a tree structure.

The following diagram shows the top-level elements, children of the `<xsl:stylesheet>` element:

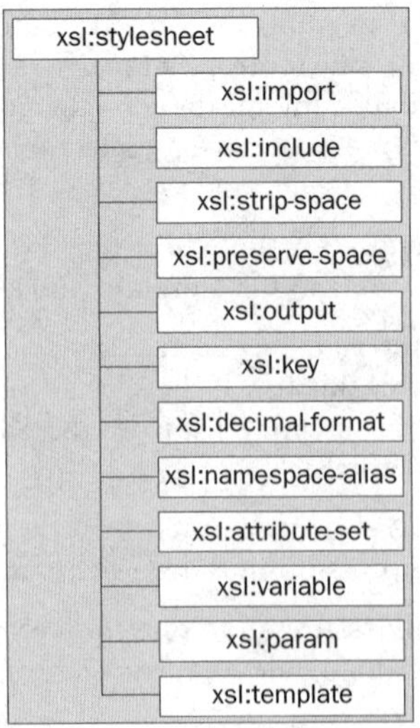

This illustrates how the <xsl:stylesheet> element is always the root element of any XSLT style sheet. Beneath this element we can have any of these top-level elements. So, the abstract structure that the XSLT processor works upon would be like this for the root and any top-level elements. Let's look through some of these.

Creating Templates

The key construct in any XSLT style sheet is the <template> element, which is used with a match attribute, whose value is a pattern – or XPath expression – saying which node the template should be applied to. More specifically, any XPath expression returning a node list is a candidate for a match attribute value. However, it's easier to remember that the pattern is an XPath expression indicating the nodes on which templates should be applied. Within the templates we can include elements, and element's content.

Dealing with White Space

To help us deal with white space, XSL provides two constructs, which are used as top-level elements:

- xsl:strip-space to remove selected nodes that are just white space
- xsl:preserve-space maintains any white space in the content

xsl:strip-space

The <xsl:strip-space> element removes text nodes that just consist of white space from the tree when the element name is included in the elements attribute. For instance, the following <xsl:strip-space> element will remove any <BOOKLIST> or <ITEM> element's text node that consist only of white space:

```
<xsl:strip-space elements="BOOKLIST ITEM" />
```

Thus, the above element tells the XSL engine that if the elements <BOOKLIST> and <ITEM> are made up of white space, their text node should be removed from the tree (though the element node remains).

xsl:preserve-space

Similarly, if we want instead to preserve some white space for certain element content, then we include the <xsl:preserve-space> element. Again, the elements attribute is used to specify the list of all elements that we want to add to the set of elements with their white space preserved. In the example below white space is preserved for the <CATALOG> and <PRICE> elements.

```
<xsl:preserve-space elements="CATALOG PRICE"/>
```

Output Format

The <xsl:output /> element can be used to specify the output format of a result tree (although it is not required that an XSL processor implement this function).

Again, this is a top-level element and should normally immediately follow the <xsl:stylesheet> element. This is not a mandatory element, and the XSL engine will have, in many cases, the default set to HTML if some conditions are met:

- The root node of the result tree should have a child
- The root's first child node should be an html element
- Any nodes preceding the first child node should contain only white space characters.

It is possible also to set the result tree to different formats like xml, html, or text. An interesting attribute of the <xsl:output> element is the encoding attribute. This latter allows us to translate from a certain encoding to another one if the target encoding is supported by the XLST engine. For instance, an ASCI encoded XML document can be transformed into a Unicode encoded document. Thus, to transform a XML document into a new XML document with a different encoding, you should include the <xsl:output> element immediately after the <xsl:stylesheet> element:

```
<?xml version="1.0"?>
<xsl:stylesheet version="1.0"
                xmlns:xsl="http://www.w3.org/1999/XSL/Transform">
<xsl:output method="xml" encoding="UTF-16"/>
```

Combining Style Sheets

One convenient way to re-use code is to create modules. These modules can then be re-used in other modules – XSLT can include or import external style sheets. Two constructs are used to this effect:

- The <xsl:include> element
- The <xsl:import> element

xsl:include

The <xsl:include> element simply allows us to include an external style sheet where the <xsl:include> element is located. The XSLT document referred by the URI is first parsed then the children of the included document's <stylesheet> element replace the <xsl:include> element in the including document. It is necessary that the <xsl:include> construct be located as child of the <stylesheet> element:

```
<?xml version="1.0"?>
<xsl:stylesheet version="1.0"
                xmlns:xsl="http://www.w3.org/1999/XSL/Transform">
<xsl:include href="Commontemplates.xsl">
```

xsl:import

<xsl:import> is quite different from <xsl:include> – <xsl:include> just means perform a file inclusion, while <xsl:import> modifies the document's tree. In fact, the <xsl:import> construct modifies the templates' order and processing precedence.

First and foremost, the element should precede any other top-level element – it should be the first child of the `<xsl:stylesheet>` element.

At first, all style sheets that are imported are included as text. Once they have all been collected, they are used to form an **import tree**. Thus, each style sheet imported is included in the host style sheet import tree. It is possible to have imported style sheets that themselves import other style sheets.

For example, the `booklist.xsl` style sheet might import a second style sheet like so:

```
<?xml version="1.0"?>
<xsl:stylesheet version="1.0"
                xmlns:xsl="http://www.w3.org/1999/XSL/Transform">
<xsl:import href="NewBooks.xsl">
```

Now let's say that the `newBooks.xsl` imports another style sheet:

```
<?xml version="1.0"?>
<xsl:stylesheet version="1.0"
                xmlns:xsl="http://www.w3.org/1999/XSL/Transform">
<xsl:import href="recentXML.xsl">
```

Then the resultant **import tree** would look like this:

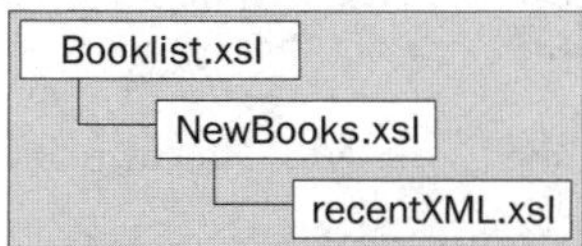

This forms a structure in which directives from one style sheet can take precedence over another, where instructions in `Booklist.xsl` take priority over both others. When templates are matched to a particular element, `Booklist.xsl` is processed first, then `NewBooks.xsl`, and finally `recent.xsl`. The `<xsl:import>` construct has direct impact on the style sheet processing. The XSL document tree is modified by this element, and the style sheets are assembled into a single unit – the import tree.

Embedding Style Sheets

A style sheet is not necessarily a separate document. It can also be embedded into another XML document. For instance, a dynamically constructed XML document may include its style sheet before transmitting the document to the user agent. In the example below, an XSL style sheet is embedded in a XML document:

```
<?xml version="1.0"?>
<?xml-stylesheet href="#BooklistStyle" type="text/xsl" media="screen"?>
<xsl:stylesheet version="1.0"
                id= "BooklistStyle"
                xmlns:xsl="http://www.w3.org/1999/XSL/Transform">
   ...
</stylesheet>
<BOOKLIST>
   ...
</BOOKLIST>
```

Here, the style sheet is included in the XML document. It is referenced using an XML `id` (indicated by the # symbol), so the XSL processor knows that the style sheet is within a document fragment uniquely identified by an `id` attribute on an element. The XSL processor will then extract the style sheet fragment from the document, parse it, and construct the internal structure necessary for XSL processing. The XML document itself is parsed, but the resultant document tree does not contain the style sheet tree. So, from a single XML document the user agent makes two document structures:

- A grove for the XML document excluding the `<xsl:stylesheet>` element (which encloses the whole style sheet). This structure is accessible using the DOM.
- A structure for the XSL document, which includes only the `<xsl:stylesheet>` element and its contents. The structure may or may not be a grove and may or may not be accessible using the DOM.

Examples of Using XSLT

As you have already seen, XSLT is a powerful tool for transforming an XML document with a certain structure or document type in to a new one – such as transforming an XML document into XHTML. Having seen an early example that taught us how the XSLT processor works, and having seen a reference section explaining the most commonly used elements available to us in XSLT, the second half of this chapter will look at some more examples of using XSLT in different situations. These will include:

- Structural transformation, from one XML vocabulary to another
- Repeated processing of elements using a loop – `xsl:for-each`
- Sorting order of elements to be processed
- Conditional processing using `xsl:if` and `xsl:choose`
- Creating dynamic documents

Structural Transformations

Let's have a look at an example that allows us to change the structure of the XML file into another XML structure, rather than XHTML. Say we need to re-order the elements of an XML document brought to you by a colleague, as shown below:

```
<?xml version="1.0"?>
<BOOKLIST>
   <ITEM>
      <CODE>16-048</CODE>
      <CATEGORY>Scripting</CATEGORY>
      <RELEASE_DATE>1998-04-21</RELEASE_DATE>
      <TITLE>Instant JavaScript</TITLE>
      <PRICE>$49.34</PRICE>
   </ITEM>
   <ITEM>
      <CODE>16-105</CODE>
      <CATEGORY>ASP</CATEGORY>
      <RELEASE_DATE>1998-05-10</RELEASE_DATE>
      <TITLE>Instant Active Server Pages</TITLE>
      <PRICE>$23.45</PRICE>
```

```
    </ITEM>
    <ITEM>
       <CODE>16-041</CODE>
       <CATEGORY>HTML</CATEGORY>
       <RELEASE_DATE>1998-03-07</RELEASE_DATE>
       <TITLE>Instant HTML</TITLE>
       <PRICE>$34.23</PRICE>
    </ITEM>
</BOOKLIST>
```

So far so good, but he also added some spice to your life by adding a number of requirements:

- The document must be published on a browser able to render XML documents with CSS style sheets
- Each item (which is a book) must be displayed as a block
- Each title should be displayed first (in that block)
- The category and the code should be displayed on the same line but with the category displayed first
- The last line of each block should contain first the release date and then the price

And, as if that was not enough, he mentions that the `<CATEGORY>` content should be indicated with a "Category:" string, and that the code should be enclosed in parentheses. Sounds like he's added enough spice to your life to make a hot Mexican meal? Well, the release date and the price should also be separated with a "-". And, the cherry on top of the sundae, you can use only CSS1 style sheets. At this point you may think that this is not your day. But XSLT is just waiting to help you.

So, the first thing that you need to do, so that you can style the document using CSS, is to transform the existing document structure into something that looks like this:

```
<?xml version="1.0"?>
<?xml-stylesheet
   type="text/css"
   href="catalog.css"
   media="screen"?>
<BOOKLIST>
   <ITEM>
      <TITLE>Instant JavaScript</TITLE>
      <DESCRIPTION>
         <CATEGORY>Category: Scripting</CATEGORY>
         <CODE>(16-048)</CODE>
      </DESCRIPTION>
      <LISTING>
         <RELEASE_DATE>Release date: 1998-04-21</RELEASE_DATE>
         <PRICE>Price: $49.34</PRICE>
      </LISTING>
   </ITEM>
   <ITEM>
      <TITLE>Instant Active Server Pages</TITLE>
      <DESCRIPTION>
         <CATEGORY>Category: ASP</CATEGORY>
         <CODE>(16-105)</CODE>
      </DESCRIPTION>
```

```
        <LISTING>
            <RELEASE_DATE>release date: 1998-05-10</RELEASE_DATE>
            <PRICE>Price: $23.45</PRICE>
        </LISTING>
    </ITEM>
    <ITEM>
        <TITLE>Instant HTML</TITLE>
        <DESCRIPTION>
            <CATEGORY>Category: HTML</CATEGORY>
            <CODE>(16-041)</CODE>
        </DESCRIPTION>
        <LISTING>
            <RELEASE_DATE>release date: 1998-03-07</RELEASE_DATE>
            <PRICE>Price: $34.23</PRICE>
        </LISTING>
    </ITEM>
</BOOKLIST>
```

To do this, we will be using the following style sheet, which we will study in more detail in a moment. It only contains two templates.

> *Note: The example can be processed with XT or SAXON. To run the following template on Microsoft Internet Explorer, you need a more recent version of the MSXML component than the one provided with Internet Explorer version 5.*

```
<?xml version="1.0"?>
<xsl:stylesheet version="1.0"
                xmlns:xsl="http://www.w3.org/1999/XSL/Transform">

<xsl:output method="xml"/>

<xsl:template match="/">
    <xsl:processing-instruction name="xml-stylesheet">
        href="catalog.css" type"text/css" media="screen"
    </xsl:processing-instruction>
    <BOOKLIST>
        <xsl:apply-templates/>
    </BOOKLIST>
</xsl:template>

<xsl:template match="ITEM">
    <ITEM>
        <TITLE>
            <xsl:apply-templates select="TITLE/text()" />
        </TITLE>
        <DESCRIPTION>
            <CATEGORY>
                Category:
                <xsl:apply-templates select="CATEGORY/text()" />
            </CATEGORY>
            <CODE>
                (<xsl:apply-templates select="CODE/text()" />)
            </CODE>
```

```
        </DESCRIPTION>
        <LISTING>
           <RELEASE_DATE >
              Release date:
              <xsl:apply-templates select="RELEASE_DATE/text()" />
           </RELEASE_DATE>
           <PRICE>
              - Price:
              <xsl:apply-templates select="PRICE/text()"/>
           </PRICE>
        </LISTING>
     </ITEM>
  </xsl:template>

  </xsl:stylesheet>
```

As we saw in the previous example, the source document has first to be transformed into a grove (an internal hierarchical structure). The elements are then matched (or not as the case may be) to templates after the XSLT document has been converted into an internal structure for processing.

The first template is matched to the document's root:

```
<xsl:template match="/">
   <xsl:processing-instruction name="xml-stylesheet">
      href="catalog.css" type"text/css" media="screen"
   </xsl:processing-instruction>
   <BOOKLIST>
      <xsl:apply-templates/>
   </BOOKLIST>
</xsl:template>
```

XML documents can be associated with style sheet documents using an `<?xml-stylesheet ... ?>` processing instruction. We want our resultant document to be associated with a CSS style sheet, so we have to write it into the template so that the resulting document includes the processing instruction.

To create the processing instruction in the result tree, we use a special XSL construct, the `<xsl:processing-intruction>` element. The attribute name provides the processing instruction name and the data content all the other attributes. Thus the following XSL element:

```
   <xsl:processing-instruction name="xml-stylesheet">
      href="catalog.css" type"text/css" media="screen"
   </xsl:processing-instruction>
```

is converted in the result tree to:

```
<?xml-stylesheet href="catalog.css" type"text/css" media="screen"?>
```

The other `<BOOKLIST>` elements included in this template will be inserted in the result tree. The now familiar `<apply-templates>` construct indicates to the XSLT processor that it should process all children without any selection criteria – the children to be processed are the current node children – then these children are matched with templates, or if a child consists of data content that is not matched to a template, it is inserted in the result tree. Otherwise, if the data content child is matched to a template, then this template is processed and its content included in the result tree.

As you may have noticed, there is no template matching the <BOOKLIST> element. XSLT engines have an implicit template matched to any element without an explicitly specified template. This implicit template allows successful recursive processing to continue in the absence of a successful pattern match with an explicitly specified template. The implicit template is defined as:

```
<xsl:template match="*|/">
   <xsl:apply-templates/>
</xsl:template>
```

Thus the <BOOKLIST> element, which does not have an explicitly defined template rule, is matched to the implicit template. This implicit template is also called the **default template**.

The <BOOKLIST> element contains <ITEM> elements, for which there is a template. In fact, this is the element that we want to reorganize. Reorganizing the <ITEM> elements is quite easy, we just include the elements sorted the way we want. If new elements have to be added, we simply include them in the template as well.

We use the <xsl:apply-templates> construct quite differently from how we used it in the first template. Earlier we used the `select` attribute to specify to the XSLT engine that only elements matching the selection criteria will be matched to an explicit template or to the default template.

The following expression includes the <TITLE> data content of the original XML document into the produced <TITLE> element in the output tree.

```
<TITLE><xsl:apply-templates select="TITLE/text()"/></TITLE>
```

The `select` attribute XPath expression indicates to the XSLT engine that the content of the text child node of the <TITLE> element will be inserted at the same position as the <xsl:apply-templates> construct is located.

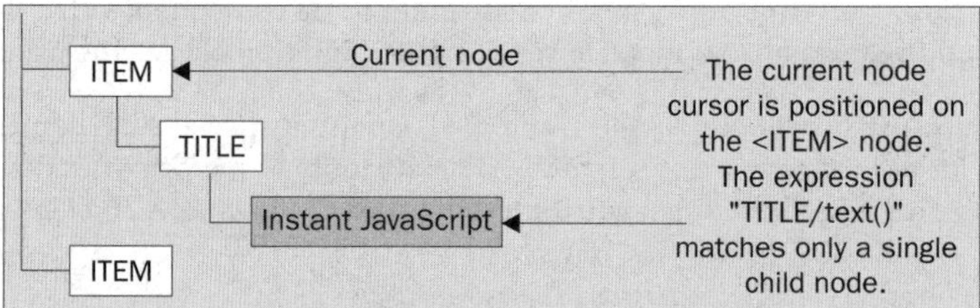

Note here that the template is matched to the <ITEM> element, and because the <TITLE> element is a child of this, the right XPath expression is "`TITLE/text()`". If we used "`//TITLE/text()`" instead then the data content of all the <TITLE> elements would have been inserted in the result tree as shown below:

```
<TITLE>Instant JavaScriptInstant Active Server PagesInstant HTML</TITLE>
```

This is because adding the "`//TITLE`" means "process all descendant nodes of the root node (of type "element") that are named <TITLE>". Note that the XPath expression "`.//TITLE/text()`" means "process all descendents of the currently selected node having the name <TITLE>". The `.` in front of the `//` makes all the difference.

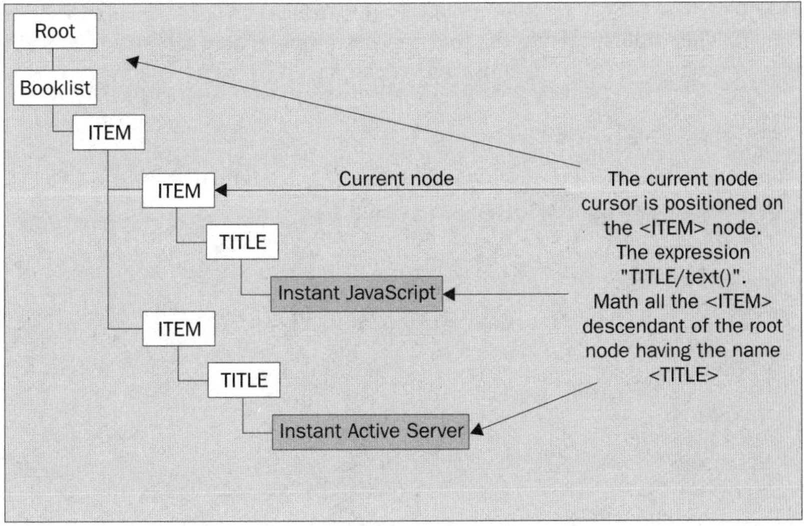

Thus, all the `<xsl:apply-template select...>` constructs contained in the template matching the `<ITEM>` node are relative to the currently selected node. In our case, this is the `<ITEM>` node. The current node cursor was moved to the `<ITEM>` element by the template's match attribute:

```
<xsl:template match="ITEM">
   <ITEM>
      <TITLE>
         <xsl:apply-templates select="TITLE/text()" />
      </TITLE>
      <DESCRIPTION>
         <CATEGORY>
            Category:
            <xsl:apply-templates select="CATEGORY/text()" />
         </CATEGORY>
         <CODE>
            (<xsl:apply-templates select="CODE/text()" />)
         </CODE>
      </DESCRIPTION>
      <LISTING>
         <RELEASE_DATE >
            Release date:
            <xsl:apply-templates select="RELEASE_DATE/text()" />
         </RELEASE_DATE>
         <PRICE>
            - Price:
            <xsl:apply-templates select="PRICE/text()"/>
         </PRICE>
      </LISTING>
   </ITEM>
</xsl:template>
```

As we saw earlier, there is also an alternative way to extract the right information from the original XML document. This is illustrated in the following example, where all `<xsl:apply-templates.../>` constructs are replaced by `<xsl:value of .../>` constructs:

```
<xsl:template match="ITEM">
   <ITEM>
      <TITLE>
         <xsl:value-of select=".//TITLE"/>
      </TITLE>
         <DESCRIPTION>
         <CATEGORY>
            Category:
            <xsl:value-of select=".//CATEGORY"/>
         </CATEGORY>
         <CODE>
            (<xsl:value-of select=".//CODE"/>)
         </CODE>
      </DESCRIPTION>
      <LISTING>
         <RELEASE_DATE >
            Release date:
            <xsl:value-of select=".//RELEASE_DATE"/>
         </RELEASE_DATE>
         <PRICE>
            - Price:
            <xsl:value-of select=".//PRICE"/>
         </PRICE>
      </LISTING>
   </ITEM>
</xsl:template>
```

We just saw that there are two ways to insert the right elements in the right place:

- With the `<xsl:apply-templates>` construct
- With the `<xsl:value-of>` construct

I recommend the second construct – `<xsl:value-of>` – which explicitly tells us that it is the value of the selection that is included in the output tree. As you noticed, we do not have to include the `"text()"` instruction in the selection expression since the value of an element is its data content.

New data content can also be added to the pulled content. For instance, we want to include the expression Category: at the beginning of the resultant data content so that we obtain something like:

```
<CATEGORY>Category: Scripting</CATEGORY>
```

Again, we use the `<xsl:value-of ... />` construct, again it is replaced by the `<CATEGORY>` element's data content, but we have also added the text Category:.

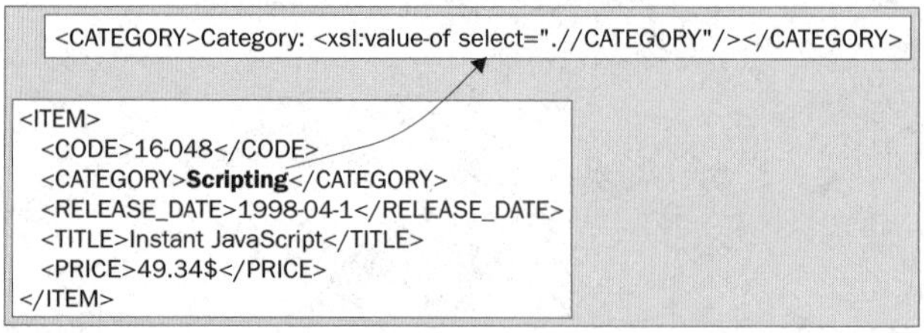

```
<CATEGORY>Category: <xsl:value-of select=".//CATEGORY"/></CATEGORY>

<ITEM>
  <CODE>16-048</CODE>
  <CATEGORY>Scripting</CATEGORY>
  <RELEASE_DATE>1998-04-1</RELEASE_DATE>
  <TITLE>Instant JavaScript</TITLE>
  <PRICE>49.34$</PRICE>
</ITEM>
```

Using XSLT to transform documents is very important for a number of areas. Here we have used it to transform one XML document into another structure so that we can display it in the appropriate way. While we were essentially using the same tags in the result document, we were re-inserting their content from the template using the `<value-of>` or the `<apply-templates>` construct to obtain the source document element data, and writing in the elements ourselves. We could just as easily be creating new tags so that the document would be transformed into a completely new vocabulary. We could also transform this document into the vocabulary used in the earlier example (which we developed in Chapter 2).

This kind of technique would therefore be ideal for transforming to presentation languages such as HTML and WML (Wireless Markup Language). It is also useful for translating to different vocabularies if people we exchange information with require a different XML structure. For example, if we were exchanging financial data, and one company used FPML while the other used FinXML, we could translate between the two.

Repetition

Loops are the kind of construct we often use in procedural programming languages. XSLT also supports a loop construct, in the form of the `<xsl:for-each ... />` element. Its content is repeated as long as there are elements in the original XML document that correspond to the value of the `select` attribute. As an example, we can use the `for-each` construct to transform the booklist XML document into an XHTML document where items are listed in a table. This is actually the whole XSLT style sheet – you will notice some interesting things about its use:

```
<?xml version="1.0"?>

<html xmlns="http://www.w3.org/TR/xhtml1/strict"
      xsl:version="1.0"
      xmlns:xsl="http://www.w3.org/1999/XSL/Transform">
   <head>
      <title>The book catalog listed in a table</title>
   </head>
   <body>
      <table border="1" cellspacing="0" cellpadding="5">
         <tbody>
            <xsl:for-each select="BOOKLIST/ITEM">
               <tr>
                  <th align="left"><xsl:value-of select=".//TITLE"/></th>
                  <td><xsl:value-of select=".//CATEGORY" /></td>
                  <td><xsl:value-of select=".//RELEASE_DATE" /></td>
                  <td><xsl:value-of select=".//PRICE" /></td>
               </tr>
            </xsl:for-each>
         </tbody>
      </table>
   </body>
</html>
```

The first thing you'll probably notice about this example is that it uses a format different from that in previous examples. This document only contains a single template, which *implicitly* matches the root element. Actually, there is no need in this alternative format to include the `<xsl:template>` construct. The implicit template is, in this case, `<xsl:template match="/">`.

The table that we are creating contains a row for each <ITEM> (or book). In this example we do not use the template matching mechanism, we loop through the document using the for-each construct, extracting element content with value-of constructs:

```
<xsl:for-each select="BOOKLIST/ITEM">
  <tr>
    <th align="left"><xsl:value-of select=".//TITLE"/></th>
    <td><xsl:value-of select=".//CATEGORY" /></td>
    <td><xsl:value-of select=".//RELEASE_DATE" /></td>
    <td><xsl:value-of select=".//PRICE" /></td>
  </tr>
</xsl:for-each>
```

We are telling the processor: "for each <ITEM> element nested in the root <BOOKLIST> element, write the contents of the <TITLE>, <CATEGORY>, <RELEASE_DATE>, and <PRICE> elements out into the table". The selection criterion for the loop construct is an XPath expression starting from the root; so we have to explicitly include all elements included in the document tree's branch up to the <ITEM> element. The loop finishes when no more elements satisfy the selection criterion.

To obtain the value included in a table cell, we use the <xsl:value-of ... /> element. As you may remember, this has the effect of extracting the data content from the node matching the XPath expression that is the value of the select attribute.

The resulting output is shown below:

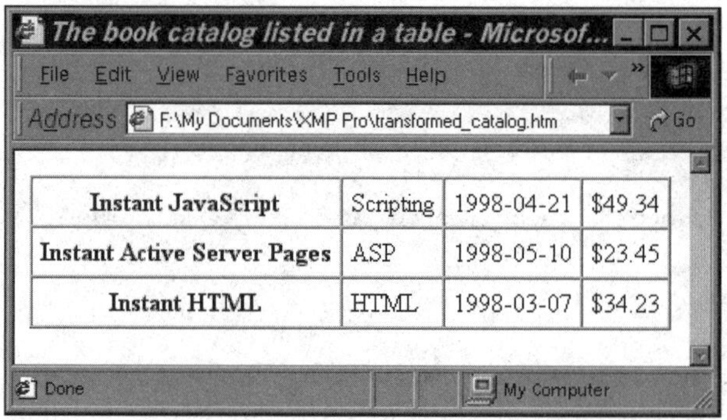

Sorting

After having moved elements in our booklist document, even having added new data content and linked the resultant document to a CSS style sheet, let's add sorting. The goal is to sort the booklist items first by category, then by title.

The XSL construct used for this task is the <xsl:sort> element. To tell the XSLT engine which element to sort, we include the select attribute set to an XPath value. For instance, to sort the items by title we would use the following construct:

```
<xsl:sort select=".//TITLE"/>
```

The question is: where can we include this element? It is an instruction element that can only be used inside the `<xsl:apply-templates ... />` or `<xsl:for-each ... >` elements, as illustrated in the following style sheet, which is a modification of the one in the *Repetition* section:

```
<?xml version="1.0"?>

<html xmlns="http://www.w3.org/TR/xhtml1/strict"
      xsl:version="1.0"
      xmlns:xsl="http://www.w3.org/1999/XSL/Transform">
   <head>
      <title>The book catalog listed in a table</title>
   </head>
   <body>
      <table border="1" cellspacing="0" cellpadding="5">
         <tbody>
            <xsl:for-each select="BOOKLIST/ITEM">
               <xsl:sort select=".//CATEGORY"/>
               <xsl:sort select=".//TITLE"/>
               <tr>
                  <th align="left"><xsl:value-of select=".//TITLE"/></th>
                  <td><xsl:value-of select=".//CATEGORY" /></td>
                  <td><xsl:value-of select=".//RELEASE_DATE" /></td>
                  <td><xsl:value-of select=".//PRICE" /></td>
               </tr>
            </xsl:for-each>
         </tbody>
      </table>
   </body>
</html>
```

Now, the `<xsl:for-each ... >` element contains new instructions on how to process selected nodes. The engine will sort the nodes before matching them with templates. In the above example, the nodes are sorted first by category, then by title – as shown below:

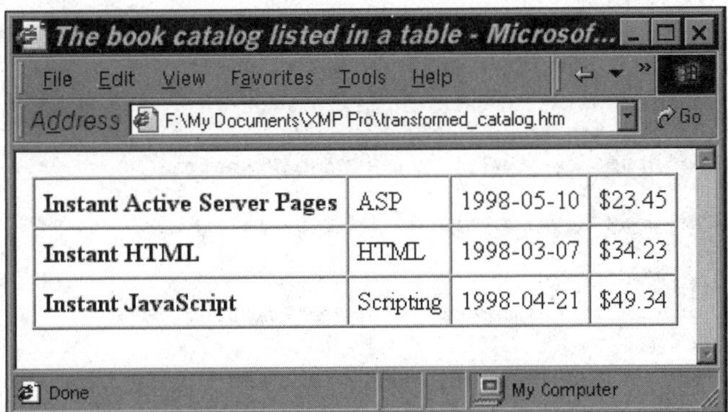

The sort order is dependent on the `<xsl:sort .../>` element order. For instance, the following construct will instead sort the nodes by `<TITLE>` and `<RELEAE_DATE>`:

```
<xsl:sort select=".//TITLE"/>
<xsl:sort select=".//RELEASE_DATE"/>
```

It is important to remember that the <sort> construct re-orders the nodes before any other processing is imposed on the node.

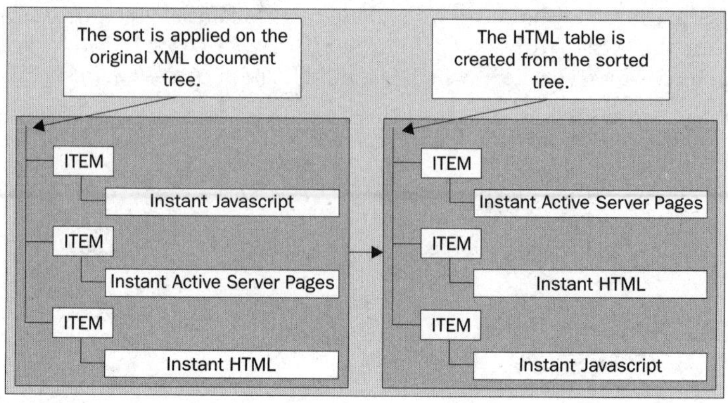

Conditional Processing

Other constructs often found in procedural languages are:

- The if construct, named <xsl:if> in XSLT
- The if/elseif construct, named <xsl:choose> in XSLT

At this point you may think that for a declarative language XSLT includes several procedural constructs. This is true; what makes it a declarative language is that you do not have to explicitly tell the XSLT engine to output a certain content. You specify a content or template to it, which will be included in the output result. Nonetheless, XSLT also has certain procedural characteristics.

Now, let's say that in our previous example we only wanted to include the <ITEMS> part of the Scripting category in the result tree. To do so, we need a filter, or an if construct, to indicate to the engine "if you encounter *this* pattern then do *this*". To achieve this result, we include the <xsl:if> instruction element in our template, as in the example below:

```
<?xml version="1.0"?>

<html xmlns="http://www.w3.org/TR/xhtml1/strict"
      xsl:version="1.0"
      xmlns:xsl="http://www.w3.org/1999/XSL/Transform">
   <head>
      <title>The book catalog listed in a table</title>
   </head>
   <body>
      <table border="1" cellspacing="0" cellpadding="5">
         <tbody>
            <xsl:for-each select="BOOKLIST/ITEM">
               <xsl:if test="contains(CATEGORY/text(), 'Scripting')">
                  <tr>
                     <th align="left"><xsl:value-of select=".//TITLE"/></th>
                     <td><xsl:value-of select=".//CATEGORY" /></td>
                     <td><xsl:value-of select=".//RELEASE_DATE" /></td>
                     <td><xsl:value-of select=".//PRICE" /></td>
                  </tr>
```

```
                </xsl:if>
            </xsl:for-each>
        </tbody>
    </table>
  </body>
</html>
```

Now, in the loop we included a condition to be satisfied. If the condition is true, then the template included in the `<xsl:if>` element is inserted in the result tree. If not, then the template is simply ignored.

In the `test` attribute, we compare the string `Scripting` to the `<CATEGORY>` element's data content. In fact, we use the `contains()` function to check if the `<CATEGORY>` element's text node contains the `Scripting` string. First, the `contains(string1, string2)` function returns a Boolean value of true if the first string (`string1`) contains the second string (`string2`), as we saw in the *Predicate* section in the last chapter. `string1` is obtained by the `CATEGORY/text()` XPath expression, which uses the address of the `<CATEGORY>` data content. An element's data content is also a string.

You probably noticed that inside an attribute's value, we used the expression `'Scripting'` instead of `"Scripting"` for our string – we used single quotes not double quotes. This is because only the whole attribute's value can be enclosed by double quotes. Thus, any expression that needs to be enclosed, for example a string, is to be enclosed by single quotes, as in the following expression:

```
                <xsl:if test="contains(CATEGORY/text(), 'Scripting')">
```

The next figure illustrates the HTML document produced using the transformation style sheet:

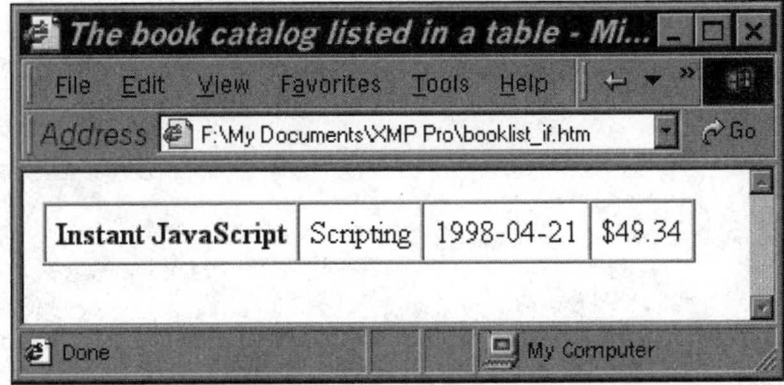

Sometimes we need a construct to perform some kind of action that is dependant on the item matched. For instance, in our previous example we filtered the original tree to transform only the `<ITEMS>` part of the Scripting category. In the next example, we will use a different transformation based on the category type.

In this example, we want to color code each table row with a different color, using a color for each category type. We can use a if/elseif pattern in the form of an `<xsl:choose>` element. This element is always used with its companion: the `<xsl:when>` element. Each condition is tested by the `<xsl:when>` construct, and more particularly by this element's test attribute:

```
<?xml version="1.0"?>

<xsl:stylesheet xsl:version="1.0"
                xmlns:xsl="http://www.w3.org/1999/XSL/Transform">

<xsl:template name="DoTableBody">
   <th align="left"><xsl:apply-templates select="./TITLE"/></th>
   <td><xsl:apply-templates select="./CATEGORY" /></td>
   <td><xsl:apply-templates select="./RELEASE_DATE" /></td>
   <td><xsl:apply-templates select="./PRICE" /></td>
</xsl:template>

<xsl:template match="/">
   <html xmlns="http://www.w3.org/TR/xhtml1/strict">
      <head>
         <title>The book catalog listed in a table</title>
      </head>
      <body>
         <table border="1" cellspacing="0" cellpadding="5">
            <tbody>
               <xsl:for-each select="/BOOKLIST/ITEM">
                  <xsl:choose>
                     <xsl:when test="contains(CATEGORY/text(),'HTML')">
                        <tr style="color:red">
                           <xsl:call-template name="DoTableBody"/>
                        </tr>
                     </xsl:when>
                     <xsl:when test="contains(CATEGORY/text(),'Scripting')">
                        <tr style="color:green">
                           <xsl:call-template name="DoTableBody"/>
                        </tr>
                     </xsl:when>
                     <xsl:when test="contains(CATEGORY/text(),'ASP')">
                        <tr style="color:blue">
                           <xsl:call-template name="DoTableBody"/>
                        </tr>
                     </xsl:when>
                     <xsl:when test="contains(CATEGORY/text(),'JavaScript')">
                        <tr style="color:yellow">
                           <xsl:call-template name="DoTableBody"/>
                        </tr>
                     </xsl:when>
                  </xsl:choose>
               </xsl:for-each>
            </tbody>
         </table>
      </body>
   </html>
</xsl:template>

</xsl:stylesheet>
```

In the example above, we created an `if/elseif` construct with the `<xsl:choose>` element. Then each condition was tested with a `<xsl:when>` element. You probably noticed that we used the same expression as in the last example, but this time used it to check each case separately. In the first case, we check if the `<CATEGORY>` element's data content contains the string 'HTML'. If this is true, then we set the row style to use the color red. We then continue this pattern, checking for other category types.

Unlike in the last example, where we checked for a single condition, we check for several conditions. The output is shown below:

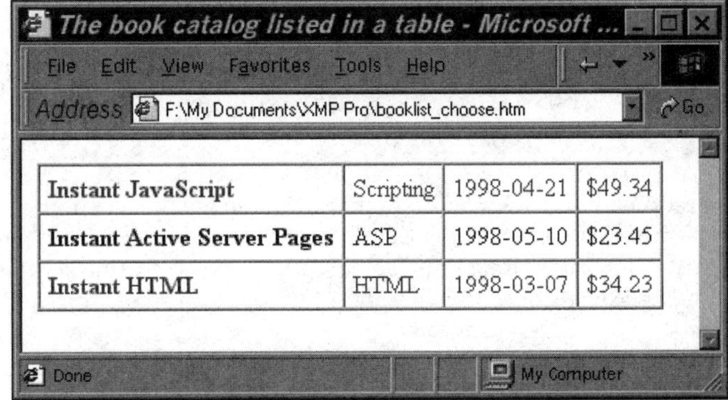

Instant JavaScript	Scripting	1998-04-21	$49.34
Instant Active Server Pages	ASP	1998-05-10	$23.45
Instant HTML	HTML	1998-03-07	$34.23

An important fact to note is that because we used a template as a kind of subroutine, the simplified form cannot be used in this case. Because of this, we used the usual `<xsl:stylesheet>` construct instead.

Named templates

In the previous example we used a named template that had no parameters:

```
<xsl:template name="DoTableBody">
   <th align="left"><xsl:apply-templates select="./TITLE"/></th>
   <td><xsl:apply-templates select="./CATEGORY" /></td>
   <td><xsl:apply-templates select="./RELEASE_DATE" /></td>
   <td><xsl:apply-templates select="./PRICE" /></td>
</xsl:template>
```

A named template can receive parameters. Let's say that in our example we want to pass, as a parameter, the row header alignment (which can be set to `left`, `right`, or `center`). To do so, we add the `<xsl:param ... >` element to the named template, as shown in the following listing fragment:

```
<xsl:template name="DoTableBody">
   <xsl:param name="alignment">left</xsl:param>
   <xsl:param name="color">green</xsl:param>
   <tr style="color:{$color}">
      <th align="{$alignment}">
         <xsl:apply-templates select="./TITLE"/>
      </th>
      <td><xsl:apply-templates select="./CATEGORY" /></td>
      <td><xsl:apply-templates select="./RELEASE_DATE" /></td>
      <td><xsl:apply-templates select="./PRICE" /></td>
   </tr>
</xsl:template>
```

One parameter is named `alignment`, and its default value is `left`. The other one is named `color`, and its default value is `green`. These default values can be overridden by a `call-template`, with the parameters' values passed to the named template:

```
<xsl:call-template name="DoTableBody">
   <xsl:with-param name="alignment">
      center
   </xsl:with-param>
   <xsl:with-param name="color">
      red
   </xsl:with-param>
</xsl:call-template>
```

The following illustrations show the two different HTML documents created by a `call-template` construct. The first figure was created using `call-templates` without any parameters, and thus has both the `alignment` value set by default to `left` and the `color` value set to `green`. The other figure was created by changing the attributes for the `call-templates` construct in the ASP category to `center` and `red`.

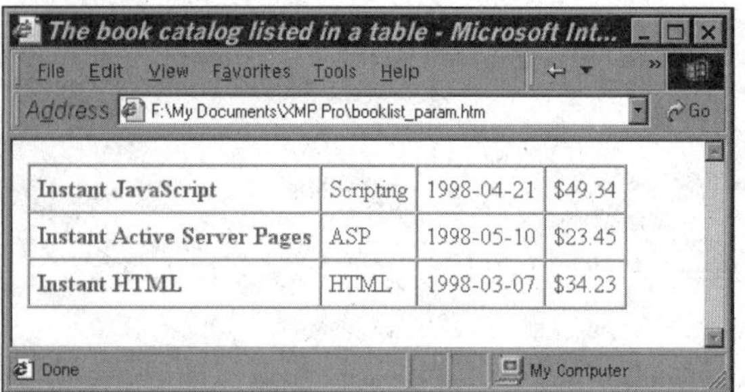

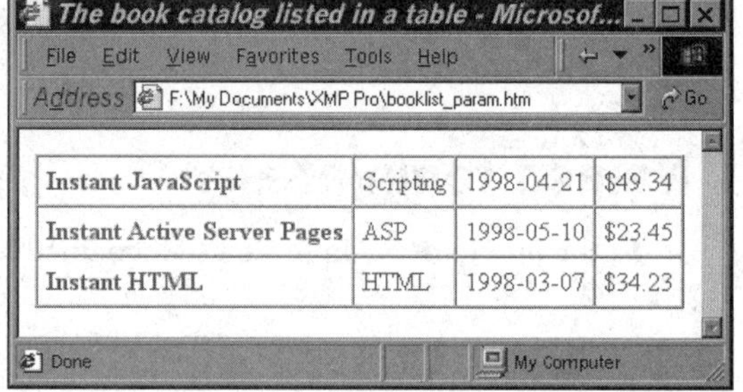

Numbering

Now, let's now add line numbering to our XSLT style sheet, so that we get the result illustrated below:

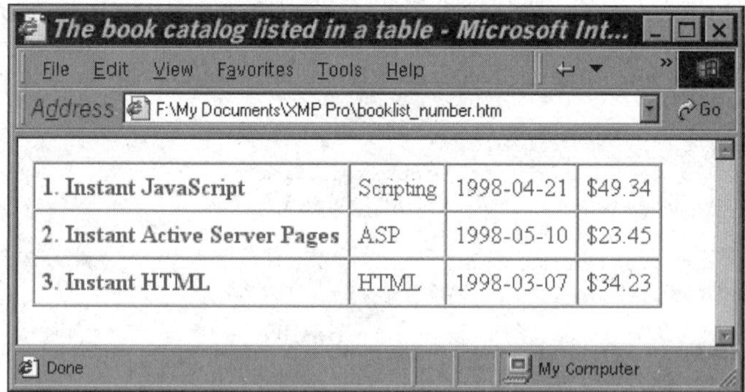

To obtain this result we use the same style sheet as for the previous example, but this time we add the `<xsl:number ...>` construct. The construct's attributes, `value` and `format`, respectively indicate the value to insert in the output tree and the format used as a mask for the output. In our case we set the `value` attribute to the actual cursor position within the container element (the `<ITEM>` element). This is illustrated by the following code fragment:

```
<xsl:template name="DoTableBody">
   <xsl:param name="alignment">left</xsl:param>
   <xsl:param name="color">green</xsl:param>
   <tr style="color:{$color}">
      <th align="{$alignment}">
         <xsl:number value="position()" format="1. "/>
         <xsl:apply-templates select="./TITLE"/>
      </th>
      <td><xsl:apply-templates select="./CATEGORY" /></td>
      <td><xsl:apply-templates select="./RELEASE_DATE" /></td>
      <td><xsl:apply-templates select="./PRICE" /></td>
   </tr>
</xsl:template>
```

The `<xsl:number ... >` element can also use several other attributes, increasing its flexibility. For more details see the XSLT Recommendation at http://www.w3.org/TR/xslt.

The listing below is a combination of the last 5 examples, and is applying the following XSLT constructs to the original `Booklist` XML document:

- **Repetition** – using the `<xsl:for-each ...>` element
- **Sorting** – using the `<xsl:sort ...>` element
- **Conditional processing** – using both the `<xsl:if ...>` and `<xsl:choose ...>` elements.
- **Named templates** – using the `<xsl:template name ...>`, `<xsl:param ...>`, `<xsl:with-param ...>`, and `<xsl:call-template ...>` elements
- **Numbering** – using the `<xsl:number ...>` element

```
<?xml version="1.0"?>

<xsl:stylesheet xsl:version="1.0"
   xmlns:xsl="http://www.w3.org/1999/XSL/Transform"
   xmlns="http://www.w3.org/TR/xhtml1/strict">

<xsl:output method="html"/>

<xsl:template name="DoTableBody">
   <xsl:param name="alignment">left</xsl:param>
   <xsl:param name="color">green</xsl:param>
   <tr style="color:{$color}">
      <th align="{$alignment}">
         <xsl:number value="position()" format="1. "/>
         <xsl:apply-templates select="./TITLE"/>
      </th>
      <td><xsl:apply-templates select="./CATEGORY" /></td>
      <td><xsl:apply-templates select="./RELEASE_DATE" /></td>
      <td><xsl:apply-templates select="./PRICE" /></td>
   </tr>
</xsl:template>
```

```
<xsl:template match="/">
   <html xmlns="http://www.w3.org/TR/xhtml1/strict">
      <head>
         <title>The book catalog listed in a table</title>
      </head>
      <body>
         <table border="1" cellspacing="0" cellpadding="5">
            <tbody>
               <xsl:for-each select="/BOOKLIST/ITEM">
                  <xsl:sort select=".//CATEGORY"/>
                  <xsl:sort select=".//TITLE"/>
                  <xsl:choose>
                     <xsl:when test="contains(CATEGORY/text(),'HTML')">
                        <xsl:call-template name="DoTableBody"/>
                     </xsl:when>
                     <xsl:when test="contains(CATEGORY/text(),'Scripting')">
                        <xsl:call-template name="DoTableBody">
                           <xsl:with-param name="color">
                              blue
                           </xsl:with-param>
                        </xsl:call-template>
                     </xsl:when>
                     <xsl:when test="contains(CATEGORY/text(),'ASP')">
                        <xsl:call-template name="DoTableBody">
                           <xsl:with-param name="alignment">
                              center
                           </xsl:with-param>
                           <xsl:with-param name="color">
                              red
                           </xsl:with-param>
                        </xsl:call-template>
                     </xsl:when>
                  </xsl:choose>
               </xsl:for-each>
            </tbody>
         </table>
      </body>
   </html>
</xsl:template>

</xsl:stylesheet>
```

The following figure was obtained by:

- Transforming the original XML document with XT
- Rendering the transformation result (an HTML document) in Microsoft Internet explorer

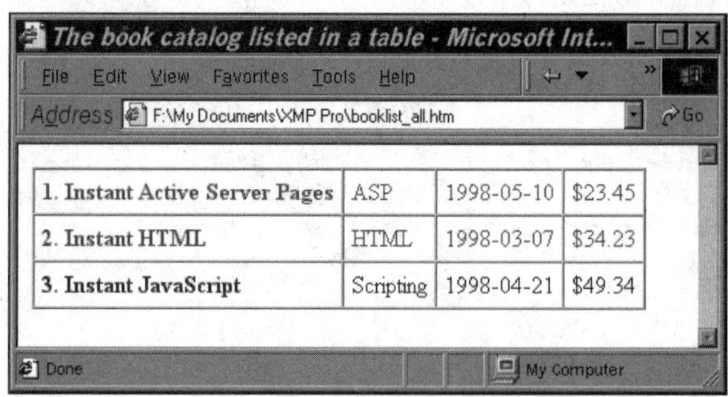

Any XML browser that is fully compliant with the W3C recommendations will transform and render the document if the original XML document contains an `<xsl:stylesheet ...>` element.

Copying

We will now perform a different kind of manipulation on the `Booklist` XML document. We will keep the same document structure in the transformed document as in the original XML document, and keep the resultant formant as XML. We will simply sort the `<ITEM>` elements by their `<CODE>` value (data content). The following listing will do the job:

```
<?xml version="1.0"?>

<xsl:stylesheet xsl:version="1.0"
   xmlns:xsl="http://www.w3.org/1999/XSL/Transform">

<xsl:output method="xml"/>

<xsl:template match="*">
   <xsl:copy>
      <xsl:apply-templates>
         <xsl:sort select=".//CODE"/>
      </xsl:apply-templates>
   </xsl:copy>
</xsl:template>

</xsl:stylesheet>
```

Firstly, the only template rule is matched with any element node. Then, the `<xsl:copy>` element indicates to the XSLT engine to copy the element node to the result tree. We also tell the XSLT engine to sort the elements by the `<CODE>` element's value. The result is illustrated by the following XML document – the original document keeps its structure, but the `<ITEM>` elements are now sorted by the value of `<CODE>`:

```
<BOOKLIST>
   <ITEM>
      <CODE>16-041</CODE>
      <CATEGORY>HTML</CATEGORY>
      <RELEASE_DATE>1998-03-07</RELEASE_DATE>
      <TITLE>Instant HTML</TITLE>
      <PRICE>$34.23</PRICE>
   </ITEM>
   <ITEM>
      <CODE>16-048</CODE>
      <CATEGORY>Scripting</CATEGORY>
      <RELEASE_DATE>1998-04-21</RELEASE_DATE>
      <TITLE>Instant JavaScript</TITLE>
      <PRICE>$49.34</PRICE>
   </ITEM>
   <ITEM>
```

```
        <CODE>16-105</CODE>
        <CATEGORY>ASP</CATEGORY>
        <RELEASE_DATE>1998-05-10</RELEASE_DATE>
        <TITLE>Instant Active Server Pages</TITLE>
        <PRICE>$23.45</PRICE>
    </ITEM>
</BOOKLIST>
```

Transformation of an XML Document with the DOM

An XML document can also be transformed using the DOM, which is an interface to the grove representation of the document. However, using the DOM to transform an XML document can be a dangerous path to follow, since most DOM implementations contain a lot of proprietary constructs. To excuse the architects of these implementations, however, you should consider that this is mainly due to deficiencies in the DOM Recommendation. For instance, even the DOM2 recommendations do not specify how to load or save an XML document, so a DOM implementer will have to invent methods for these fundamental operations. The result of this is that most scripts you use to transform XML documents are probably not portable, as in many cases they will include some proprietary constructs.

Structural Transformations with the DOM

In order to compare the XSLT and DOM ways of structurally transforming XML documents, let's use the same example as we did in the *Structural Transformations* section earlier in the chapter.

To recap, we want to transform an XML document of the form:

```
<?xml version="1.0"?>
<BOOKLIST>
    <ITEM>
        <CODE>16-048</CODE>
        <CATEGORY>Scripting</CATEGORY>
        <RELEASE_DATE>1998-04-21</RELEASE_DATE>
        <TITLE>Instant JavaScript</TITLE>
        <PRICE>$49.34</PRICE>
    </ITEM>
    <ITEM>
        <CODE>16-105</CODE>
        <CATEGORY>ASP</CATEGORY>
        <RELEASE_DATE>1998-05-10</RELEASE_DATE>
        <TITLE>Instant Active Server Pages</TITLE>
        <PRICE>$23.45</PRICE>
    </ITEM>
    <ITEM>
        <CODE>16-041</CODE>
        <CATEGORY>HTML</CATEGORY>
        <RELEASE_DATE>1998-03-07</RELEASE_DATE>
        <TITLE>Instant HTML</TITLE>
        <PRICE>$34.23</PRICE>
    </ITEM>
</BOOKLIST>
```

into an XML document of the form:

```
<?xml version="1.0"?>
<BOOKLIST>
   <ITEM>
      <TITLE>Instant JavaScript</TITLE>
      <DESCRIPTION>
         <CATEGORY>Category: Scripting</CATEGORY>
         <CODE>(16-048)</CODE>
      </DESCRIPTION>
      <LISTING>
         <RELEASE_DATE>Release date: 1998-04-21</RELEASE_DATE>
         <PRICE>Price: $49.34</PRICE>
      </LISTING>
   </ITEM>
   <ITEM>
      <TITLE>Instant Active Server Pages</TITLE>
      <DESCRIPTION>
         <CATEGORY>Category: ASP</CATEGORY>
         <CODE>(16-105)</CODE>
      </DESCRIPTION>
      <LISTING>
         <RELEASE_DATE>release date: 1998-05-10</RELEASE_DATE>
         <PRICE>Price: $23.45</PRICE>
      </LISTING>
   </ITEM>
   <ITEM>
      <TITLE>Instant HTML</TITLE>
      <DESCRIPTION>
         <CATEGORY>Category: HTML</CATEGORY>
         <CODE>(16-041)</CODE>
      </DESCRIPTION>
      <LISTING>
         <RELEASE_DATE>release date: 1998-03-07</RELEASE_DATE>
         <PRICE>Price: $34.23</PRICE>
      </LISTING>
   </ITEM>
</BOOKLIST>
```

The next section will show how VBScript can modify the structure of the `Booklist` XML document.

VBScript Example

VBScript can be used to obtain the same result that we got using XSLT. The script in this section is not portable (for the reasons outlined in the last section) and can only run on a Windows platform. This is the main difference between using XSLT and using a script language with the DOM. Why choose VBScript? Simple – because 3 million developers can understand it.

The following script can be run through the Windows Script Host (WSH). Assuming you have WSH installed, this is as simple as saving this in a file called `Transform.vbs` and double clicking on it:

```
Set xmldoc = CreateObject("Microsoft.XMLDOM")
XMLDoc.load("C:\My Documents\XML Pro\Booklist.xml")

Set oItem = xmlDoc.getElementsByTagName("ITEM")
Set oTitle = xmlDoc.getElementsByTagName("TITLE")
Set oCode = xmlDoc.getElementsByTagName("CODE")
Set oPrice = xmlDoc.getElementsByTagName("PRICE")
```

```
Set oRelease_Date = xmlDoc.getElementsByTagName("RELEASE_DATE")
Set oCategory = xmlDoc.getElementsByTagName("CATEGORY")

For i=0 To (oItem.length -1)
   Set oDescription = XMLDoc.createElement("DESCRIPTION")
   Set oTempDescription = oItem.item(i).appendChild(oDescription)
   oTempdescription.appendChild(oTitle.item(i))
   oTempDescription.appendChild(oCode.item(i))
   oTempDescription.appendChild(oCategory.item(i))
   Set oListing= XMLDoc.createElement("LISTING")
   Set oTempListing = oItem.item(i).appendChild(oListing)
   oTempListing.appendChild(oRelease_Date.item(i))
   oTempListing.appendChild(oPrice.item(i))
Next

XMLDoc.Save("sample.xml")
```

Let's examine this script in more detail. The first task is to create the DOM object with the `CreateObject()` method. We then load the source XML document into the DOM, parse it, and fill the internal tree structure – all with the `load()` method:

```
Set xmldoc = CreateObject("Microsoft.XMLDOM")
XMLDoc.load("C:\My Documents\XML Pro\Booklist.xml")
```

These last two lines are not part of the DOM recommendation, they are particular to the VBScript environment.

Because we are lucky enough not to have a complicated document structure, we can obtain the elements we need quite easily, using the `getElementsByTagName()` method. This would be more complicated if the document structure contained elements with the same name but located in different locations within the hierarchy. So, the next step is to obtain all the element objects needed for our transformation:

```
Set oItem = xmlDoc.getElementsByTagName("ITEM")
Set oTitle = xmlDoc.getElementsByTagName("TITLE")
Set oCode = xmlDoc.getElementsByTagName("CODE")
Set oPrice = xmlDoc.getElementsByTagName("PRICE")
Set oRelease_Date = xmlDoc.getElementsByTagName("RELEASE_DATE")
Set oCategory = xmlDoc.getElementsByTagName("CATEGORY")
```

Now we need to process any `<ITEM>` object element node contained in the booklist. To do this, we obtain the number of `<ITEM>` element node instances contained in the DOM, using the `length()` method. You would probably expect a `count()` method here, but the W3C recommendation uses the word `length()` to indicate an instance count. Notice here that the range of valid child node indices is `0` to `length-1` inclusive:

```
For i=0 To (oItem.length -1)
```

Because we have to add a new element as a child of the `<ITEM>` element, we create one with the object factory included in the DOM object:

```
   Set oDescription = XMLDoc.createElement("DESCRIPTION")
```

Then we append this new element as a child of the currently processed <ITEM> node. An element node object is returned, representing the <DESCRIPTION> element node:

```
Set oTempDescription = oItem.item(i).appendChild(oDescription)
```

At this stage, we have modified the internal structure by adding a new <DESCRIPTION> node as child of the <ITEM> element node as illustrated below:

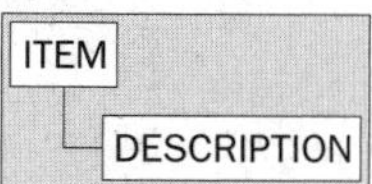

We then include the element nodes <TITLE>, <CODE>, and <CATEGORY> as children of the <DESCRIPTION> element node:

```
oTempdescription.appendChild(oTitle.item(i))
oTempDescription.appendChild(oCode.item(i))
oTempDescription.appendChild(oCategory.item(i))
```

In fact, we are moving these nodes from their actual position to a new one, as illustrated in the following figure:

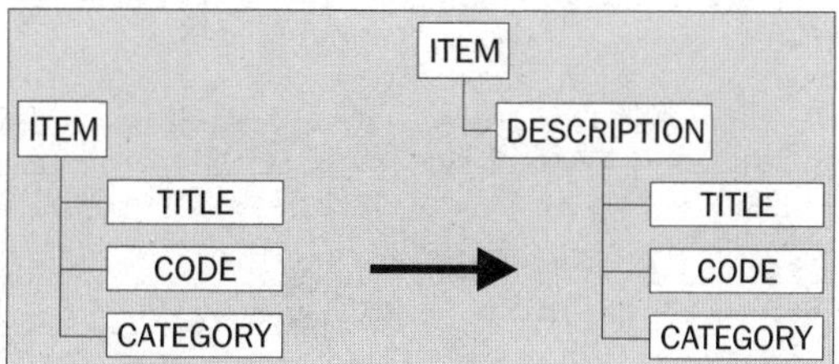

We then perform the same kind of operations for the new <LISTING> element node. We create it, insert it as child of the <ITEM> node element, and move the <RELEASE_DATE> and <PRICE> element nodes from their present position as children of the <ITEM> element node to their new position as children of the <LISTING> element node:

```
    Set oListing= XMLDoc.createElement("LISTING")
    Set oTempListing = oItem.item(i).appendChild(oListing)
    oTempListing.appendChild(oRelease_Date.item(i))
    oTempListing.appendChild(oPrice.item(i))
Next
```

Finally, we save the transformed structure as an XML document:

```
XMLDoc.Save("sample.xml")
```

Modifying an XSLT Document at Runtime

Up to now we have stayed within the boundaries of standards, and the previous examples can be executed with any XSLT processor that conforms to the W3C Recommendation. In this section, however, we'll use some proprietary Microsoft extensions to illustrate how XSLT can be used for user interactivity.

An XSL style sheet is activated by the inclusion of an `<xsl-stylesheet>` processing instruction within the XML document to be processed, or by interacting with it through a proprietary extension to the DOM. In all previous examples, we used the processing instruction as a link to the style sheet, but in this section, we'll use the Microsoft proprietary DOM extension to interface with the XSLT processor to show how XSLT can be used to sort the book list.

> *Several constructs used in this example are specific to Microsoft Internet Explorer version 5. Some constructs are simply outdated XSLT constructs and others are particular to this implementation and are not part of the W3C standard. Thus, the example listed will work only with the Microsoft Internet Explorer Version 5. Other XSLT engines such as XT will report errors.*

The XSLT script below can be used to render our `Booklist` XML document:

```
<xsl:stylesheet xmlns:xsl="http://www.w3.org/TR/WD-xsl">
<xsl:template match="/">
   <html>
      <head>
         <title>The book catalog</title>
         <script>
            <xsl:comment>
               <![CDATA[
                  var xslStylesheet = null;
                  var xmlSource = null;
                  var attribNode = null;
                  function sort(field)
                  {
                     attribNode.value = field;
                     Booklist.innerHTML =
                       xmlSource.documentElement.transformNode(xslStylesheet);
                  }
               ]]>
            </xsl:comment>
         </script>
         <script for="window" event="onload">
            <xsl:comment>
               <![CDATA[
                  xslStylesheet = document.XSLDocument;
                  xmlSource = document.XMLDocument;
                  attribNode =
                     document.XSLDocument.selectSingleNode("//@order-by");
                  sort('TITLE');
               ]]>
            </xsl:comment>
         </script>
      </head>
      <body>
         <div id="Booklist"></div>
```

```
        </body>
      </html>
   </xsl:template>

   <xsl:template match="BOOKLIST">
      <table border="0" frame="border" cellspacing="0" width="100%">
         <thead title="Alt-click sorts in descending order.">
            <tr style="background: brown;
                       color: white;
                       font-family: MS Sans Serif;
                       font-size:10pt">
               <th onclick="sort('TITLE')" width="33%" style="cursor:hand;">
                  <div>Title</div>
               </th>
               <th onclick="sort('CATEGORY')" width="20%" style="cursor:hand;">
                  <div>Category</div>
               </th>
               <th onclick="sort('CODE')" width="10%" style="cursor:hand;">
                  <div>Code</div>
               </th>
               <th onclick="sort('RELEASE_DATE')" style="cursor:hand;">
                  <div id="RELEASE_DATE">Release Date</div>
               </th>
               <th onclick="sort('PRICE')" width="10%" style="cursor:hand;">
                  <div>Price</div>
               </th>
            </tr>
         </thead>
         <tbody id="BOOKLIST_TABLE_BODY">
            <xsl:for-each select="//ITEM" order-by="//TITLE" >
               <tr>
                  <td><xsl:value-of select="TITLE"/></td>
                  <td><xsl:value-of select="CATEGORY"/></td>
                  <td><xsl:value-of select="CODE"/></td>
                  <td align="center"><xsl:value-of select="RELEASE_DATE"/></td>
                  <td><xsl:value-of select="PRICE"/></td>
               </tr>
            </xsl:for-each>
         </tbody>
      </table>
   </xsl:template>

   </xsl:stylesheet>
```

The first thing that the Microsoft Internet Explorer will do is to parse the XML and the XSL documents. The Microsoft parser creates a document model for both documents. Each of these documents can be accessed by an extended version of the DOM. Microsoft implemented the DOM with COM interfaces and added new functions. We can say that in some ways the Microsoft extended interface inherited from the W3C standard interfaces and added new properties or methods. It is these added methods, and not the standard W3C methods, that we will use in the example.

The elements implementing the run-time dynamic behavior are the `<script>` elements. At runtime the first script that is parsed and executed is the script not associated with any particular object. This script contains neither the `for` attribute nor the `event` attribute.

```
<script>
   <xsl:comment>
      <![CDATA[
         var xslStylesheet = null;
         var xmlSource = null;
         var attribNode = null;
```

The script itself is enclosed by the `<xsl:comment>` element, which is translated (in the output tree) into the XML comment element. The script is written in JavaScript, and you probably noticed that we declared three objects and set them to a `null` value.

At runtime one of the first events to be fired is the `window.onload` event. We attached a script to this event:

```
<script for="window" event="onload">
   <xsl:comment>
      <![CDATA[
         xslStylesheet = document.XSLDocument;
         xmlSource = document.XMLDocument;
         attribNode =
            document.XSLDocument.selectSingleNode("//@order-by");
         sort('TITLE');
      ]]>
   </xsl:comment>
</script>
```

First, we obtain the XSL style sheet document from the document object. Then, we obtain the XML document from the document object. In the XML object hierarchy, the document object contains two extended DOMs: the XML extended DOM and the XSL extended DOM:

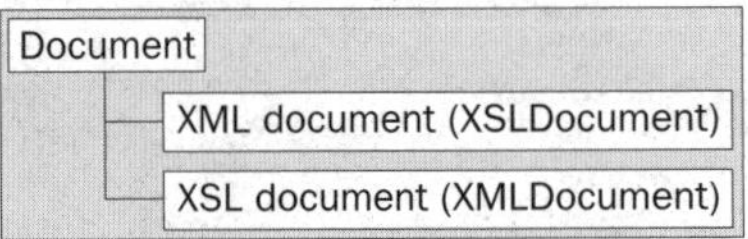

Both of these objects will useful to sort, transform, and display the XML document in Internet Explorer.

We also obtain the sort field object from the XSL tree. To get this object we ask the extended DOM to return the first object found that contains the `order-by` attribute. There is a single element containing this attribute: the `<xsl:for-each>` construct.

```
<xsl:for-each select="//ITEM" order-by="//TITLE" >
   <tr>
      <td><xsl:value-of select="TITLE"/></td>
      <td><xsl:value-of select="CATEGORY"/></td>
      <td><xsl:value-of select="CODE"/></td>
      <td><xsl:value-of select="RELEASE_DATE"/></td>
      <td><xsl:value-of select="PRICE"/></td>
   </tr>
</xsl:for-each>
```

We should mention that at the time of writing of this document, the latest specifications have changed the sorting mechanism, and this construct is no longer a standard one. The sort construct is now as we explained earlier. So, when Explorer becomes compatible with this specification, the sorting will be defined as:

```
<xsl:for-each select="//ITEM">
   <xsl:sort select="TITLE"/>
   <tr>
      <td><xsl:value-of select="TITLE"/></td>
      <td><xsl:value-of select="CATEGORY"/></td>
      <td><xsl:value-of select="CODE"/></td>
      <td><xsl:value-of select="RELEASE_DATE"/></td>
      <td><xsl:value-of select="PRICE"/></td>
   </tr>
</xsl:for-each>
```

Thus, the JavaScript line obtaining the sort object becomes:

```
attribNode =
  document.XSLDocument.selectSingleNode("xsl:sort/@select");
```

What is returned by `selectSingleNode()` is the attribute node, not the element node. Each element having one or more attributes is converted in the document tree to an element node with one or more attribute children. Thus, what the `attribNode` variable contains is the attribute node object.

Next, we sort and display the items by title order:

```
sort('TITLE');
```

Using the `sort()` function:

```
function sort(field)
{
   attribNode.value = field;
   Booklist.innerHTML =
     xmlSource.documentElement.transformNode(xslStylesheet);
}
```

First, the attribute node object value is set with the '`TITLE`' string. This, in effect, modifies the extended DOM. So here, instead of modifying a XML document with XSL, we used the extended DOM – at runtime the XSL style sheet document can be modified with the extended DOM and an appropriate script.

The second line requires more explanations. First, you may ask yourself where the `Booklist` object comes from. This object was created in the XSL script with the following construct:

```
<body>
   <div id="Booklist"></div>
</body>
```

As you can see, we created a uniquely identified object named `Booklist` when we created a `<DIV>` element. This is the HTML element that receives the result of the XML to HTML transformation. So, when the following expression is interpreted by the JavaScript interpreter:

```
Booklist.innerHTML =
    xmlSource.documentElement.transformNode(xslStylesheet);
```

we call the `transformNode()` method on the `documentElement` object of the original XML document. This is the extended DOM method used to transform a XML document into HTML. This method takes as a parameter the XSL extended DOM that we stored in the `xslStylesheet` variable. The result is then stored in the `innerHTML` attribute of the `Booklist` object. This causes a refresh of the HTML document, and therefore a display refresh. The sorted table then appears on the screen:

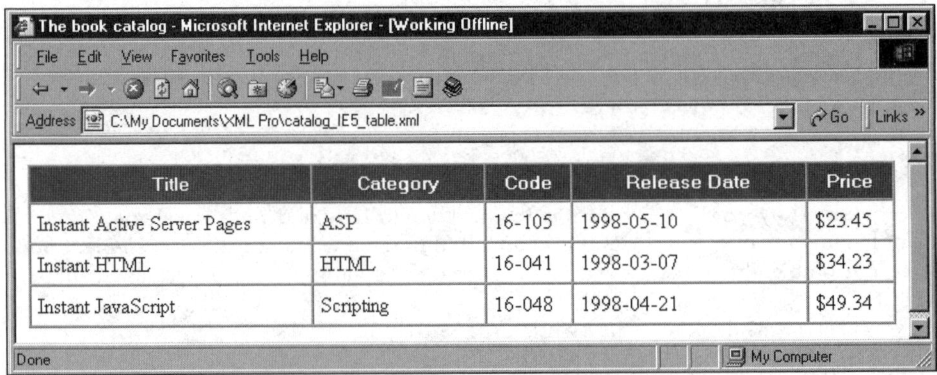

The table headers have been set with a CSS style that indicates to the browser to display a small hand each time the cursor is on the table's headers. The user is accustomed to identifying a small hand with something that can be clicked on. Each column header is associated with the `sort()` function, which, in this case, acts as an event handler for the `onclick` event. If, for instance, the user clicks on the Price column, then the sort function is called with the `<onclick="sort('PRICE')" ...>` construct. When the `sort()` function receives the `'PRICE'` string as a parameter it sets this string as a value for the `attribNode` variable. This, in fact, changes the XSL style sheet. The modification is equivalent to writing the following construct:

```
<xsl:for-each select="//ITEM" order-by="//PRICE" >
```

instead of:

```
<xsl:for-each select="//ITEM" order-by="//TITLE" >
```

as was originally in the XSL style sheet. After the XSL extended DOM has been modified, we transform the original XML document again, using the modified XSL style sheet, and set the result of this transformation as input to the `innerHTML` attribute of the HTML `Booklist` object (named this way because of the `<DIV>` id).

So, because the XSL document is transformed into a tree structure (and because the extended DOM is the interface that Microsoft provides to this tree) it is possible to modify the XSL script with this interface. The modified XSL script can then perform a different transformation on the original document. Thus, to obtain different results based on the user interaction, the XSL style sheet can be modified from within script languages.

Comparing XSL Transformations with DOM Transformations

One of the key differences between the XSL and DOM transformation processes is that XSL is a **declarative** language rather than a **procedural** language. As such, XSL describes the state of the transformed document in relation to the original document. The DOM is an API that allows the manipulation of the tree structure.

The WSH VBScript we saw above used the DOM to achieve the same kind of transformation we did with an XSLT style sheet. But we can say that more elaborate transformation engines (conformant to the DOM1 or DOM2 specifications) are more limited than XSLT engines. This is mainly because the DOM1 and DOM2 Recommendations do not incorporate XPath expressions to reach a particular tree structure node. So, under certain circumstances, it can be a lot harder to use the DOM to transform an XML document than to use XSLT. If future editions of the DOM Recommendations include the capability to reach a particular node with an XPath expression, then using the DOM may be as easy and as powerful as using XSLT.

As we saw in the other DOM usage example, an XSLT style sheet can transform an XML document into HTML. The resultant HTML document can contain scripts that further manipulate the internal tree structure. Script procedures can be triggered by user actions, and these procedures can contain code using the DOM API to manipulate the XSLT document associated to the original XML document. This is what we did when we changed the value of some XSLT elements (the sorting value) when the user clicked on a table header to sort on this column category. In this example the DOM is used to change the value of an XML element's attributes, and because XSLT is itself an XML document, it can be modified with the DOM API. In this case, the DOM adds value to the XSLT transformation by providing sorting without having to include sorting code in the script.

Generally, we can say that in the actual state of the art, XSLT style sheets can be made more portable than scripts that use the DOM API. We saw that right at the beginning – the actual DOM1 and DOM2 Recommendations do not contain any constructs to load or save XML documents. Because of all this, it is better to use XSLT style sheets to perform transformations than it is to use scripts including DOM constructs.

Summary

In this chapter we have taken a look at transforming XML document structures. In particular we have spent a lot of time focusing on XSLT (XSL Transformations). This required knowledge of XPath and XPointers, which we meet in Chapter 8.

We have seen that there are several reasons why we may need to transform XML documents. These include:

- Transforming XML into a presentation language
- Translating between different vocabularies of XML
- Creating dynamic documents

XSLT is actually a huge topic, and hopefully this chapter will have got you used to the syntax of this particular specification. While it would be quite possible to write a whole book on the subject (indeed, look out for *XSLT Programmer's Reference* from Wrox Press, ISBN 1-861003-12-9), this should get you used to the overall functionality available, and give you a firm grounding in writing your own transformation style sheets.

The implementation that is available in Internet Explorer 5 was introduced before the XSLT specification was completed, so there are some differences, and some extensions. However, there are also other XSLT processors that you can use in your applications:

- XT – http://www.jclark.com/xml/xt.html
- SAXON – http://users.iclway.co.uk/mhkay/saxon

10

XML and Databases

The future of XML is inseparable from database technology. The ability to generate XML documents automatically from data stored in diverse mediums, and the ability to exchange information from different data stores will be major facets of the future of an information-oriented Internet. Dynamic XML documents will increasingly become the norm as XML is used to convey everything from weather reports to invoices, film reviews to sports results, and photographs to sound.

The purpose of this chapter is to look at the relationship between databases and XML. We will do this from two sides. First we will look at the use of databases to store data that is to be treated as XML, then we will look at XML as a way of interchanging data between different database systems. The boundaries between these two approaches are obviously not drawn out clearly, but the first is more relevant to new systems in which you want to store your XML data, while the second relates more to legacy systems – where you have existing databases that need to interchange their data. We will then go on to look at an example. So, the chapter is divided into three sections:

- Storing XML
- XML for interchange
- Book catalog sample

In the storage section we will look at a number of alternatives that are used to store XML and examine why a straightforward file system just isn't adequate for the sorts of elaborate and sophisticated systems we all want to build. We'll look at what the limitations of a file system are, why we need to look beyond XML documents, and what types of software package might be best to store our XML in.

When looking at the ideal software for storing our XML, we may establish that not everything is possible yet (depending upon what you need to do), but we will at least have established a set of key requirements and considerations that we should bear in mind when evaluating products.

In the interchange part of the chapter, we will look at how data can be communicated between different server storage mediums using XML as an intermediate format. Although it is a significant step to use XML as a way of getting data out of one server and into another – for example, from an **relational database management system** (**RDBMS**) to an **object-oriented database management system** (**OODBMS**), or from Oracle to Sybase – we will see that consideration still has to be given to the structure of that XML.

Having looked at the ideal way to store XML data, and then the best way to retrieve legacy data as XML, we will illustrate some of the ideas we have developed by using the book catalog sample.

So, let's dive straight in and look at some of the issues surrounding storing XML.

Storing XML

Let's start by looking at the storage of XML, and the alternative means we can use to do this. To begin with, we'll address the issue of storage generally, and then move on to examine why we might want to use a database, rather than being content with disk files.

The Problem of Persistence

To ensure that the XML documents that you have met so far in this book can be used again, they will have been saved to some storage medium – usually a file system. Saving information for further use is called **persistence,** and refers to the act of making information available after a program has finished running. You may be happily editing a letter with a word processor, for example, but if you switch off your computer or close the program you will lose that letter. Persisting your letter means storing it so that it can be used again.

Our experience of XML so far in this book is of documents that can be persisted using an ordinary file system. These documents would be stored in the same way that you might store a word processing document or a spreadsheet – as files. Since they are XML, you could edit them with one of the many specialist XML editing tools that are available. However, unlike a Microsoft Word document or a sound file, XML files are also ordinary text files, so you can edit them with any text editor.

This technique is fine for many uses. For example, if we look at our book catalog, we can see that if there are only a few publishers, each with only a couple of books and authors, then the document would not be very large at all. Also, if the information in the document was only going to be used by one or two people – such as the CD collection XML file that I'm sure you have tucked away somewhere on your PC – then, once again, a single file will suffice.

Limitations of File Systems

For some purposes, the file-based approach is fine. For serious applications, however, this file system approach is simply not good enough. We'll summarize here some of the limitations of such an approach, and build up a wish-list as we go.

Size

The first limitation relates simply to the size of the document. What if there were 20 publishers in our book catalog list, and each publisher had 200 books and 50 authors? The XML document that we are passing around would become very unwieldy. Not only would it be large, but it would also be quite difficult to navigate through the information if you wanted to maintain different parts of the document.

- We want to be able to cope with extremely large documents, and we want to be able to examine parts of a document separately from others.

Concurrency

Just as we want to be able to move around different parts of our document quickly and easily, so too we may want different people to update those different parts at different times. Perhaps the book editors are responsible for adding new book titles and authors, while administrators look after the publishers. With only a single document in a file system, only one person could work on the information at a time. If an editor needed to add a new book title, while accounts wanted to update the information about an author, one would have to wait for the other to finish. Indeed, it is also possible that two people might try to edit the same file at the same time, and one of the sets of changes would be completely lost.

- We want to allow a number of people to work on a document at the same time.

The Right Tool for the Job

It is also the case that an XML editor may not be the right tool for dealing with different parts of a document. We might prefer the accounts department to maintain the authors without being distracted by other parts of the XML document, and the tool of choice for them might be a simple form. This form might provide other features, such as searching or phone number dialing. On the other hand, the tool for maintaining the list of books might need to contain the draft documents for the book itself.

- We want to be able to maintain sections of the document with whichever tool is most suitable for the data.

Versioning

An important issue that is often overlooked when handling documents of any type is control over different versions of the same document.

- We want to be able to keep track of different versions of a document.

Security

Using different tools for different parts of the document, and allowing different users to access different parts of the document at the same time raises issues of security.

- We want to control what parts of a document certain people can see or modify.

Integration: Centralization and Repetition

There are also issues to do with centralization and repetition of data. The accounts department may already have a database of authors, which is used to handle royalty payments. Should we repeat all of this information when we need to produce the author list in the catalog, or should we be able to produce XML documents that combine data from a number of sources?

- We want to be able to seamlessly integrate other external data into our document.

Reposing the Problem

It is very difficult to solve these problems using an ordinary file system. Although most operating systems allow files to be opened simultaneously by a number of users, most current text and XML editors do not have sufficient control over these files to allow users to edit different parts of the same document, and not corrupt each other's work. In addition, the security applied by the operating system is usually at the document level. This means that different people could be given different access rights to different documents, but not different *parts* of the same document.

To begin to solve the problems outlined above we need to take a different conceptual view of XML documents. In fact, we need to try to move away from imagining our basic XML unit as being a document, and instead begin to think about manipulating nodes.

Documents and Nodes

One of the confusions that those new to XML often have is in assuming that the basic unit of storage for XML documents must be ordinary text in a file. Because a document must be human readable, the assumption is that the document must be stored as a text file, either in a file system, or perhaps within a field in a database. This is actually a misunderstanding of the XML 1.0 specification.

An **application** – a computer program that you or I may write – is not intended to deal with XML files directly, but to act via a parser, or **XML processor**. The introduction (section 1) of the XML 1.0 specification says:

> *A software module called an* ***XML processor*** *is used to read XML documents and provide access to their content and structure. It is assumed that an XML processor is doing its work on behalf of another module, called the* **application**. *This specification* [XML 1.0] *describes the required behavior of an XML processor in terms of how it must read XML data and the information it must provide to the application*

In other words, although we spend a lot of time looking at XML documents and admiring their structure, the reality is that we should be thinking in terms of the node structure that a document would represent. The role of the DOM – whether written for Java or Visual Basic; whether written by IBM or Sun – is to hide the underlying document from us and allow us to operate on a tree of nodes. Of course when we're talking about data or representing it on the printed page as in this book, the easiest way to do this is to use the XML tag syntax; however, we should always try to bear in mind this separation:

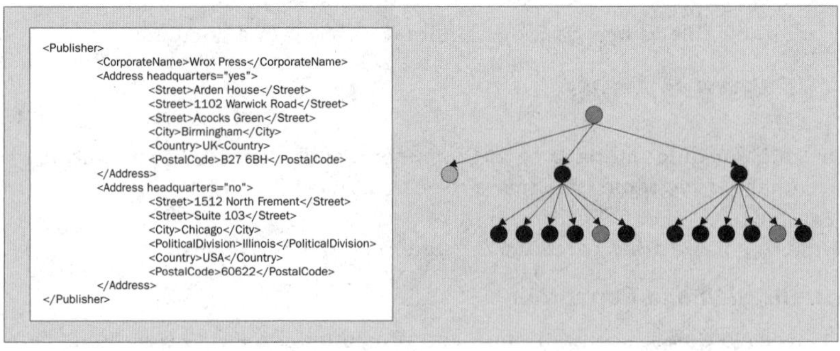

None of this will be new to you – the means of navigating these nodes is the role of the DOM, and that was discussed in Chapter 5 – so you might ask why I am repeating it. Well, what this means is that our understanding of the storage of our XML documents changes somewhat. Rather than simply looking for mechanisms that cope with text – say, file systems or text fields in a database – we need to understand how different tools and products cope with sets of hierarchical nodes. XML, as text, becomes simply a convenient means of conveying the information in those nodes from one system to another:

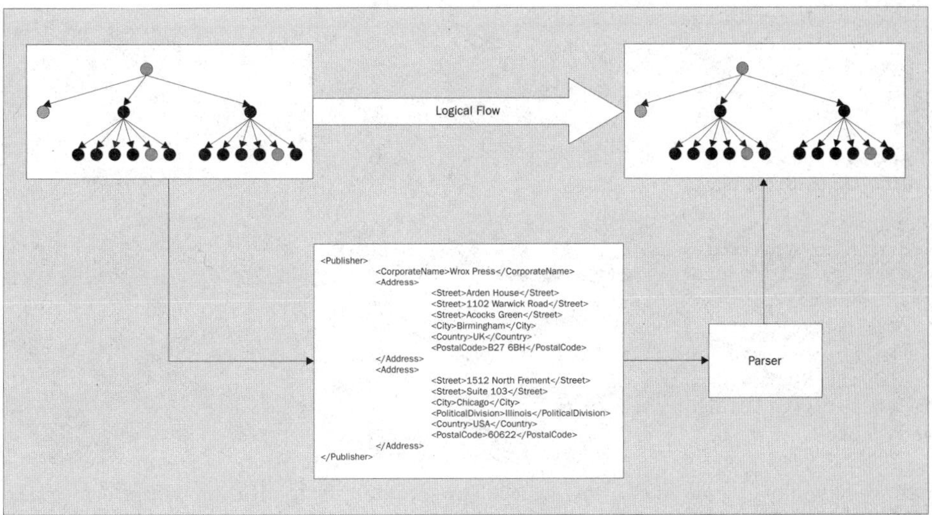

The means of transportation of our nodes is still XML documents; however, we are now saying that to a parser an XML document is nothing more than the unit of input. Take the document used in the previous diagrams:

```
<Publisher>
   <CorporateName>Wrox Press</CorporateName>
   <Address headquarters="yes">
      <Street>Arden House</Street>
      <Street>1102 Warwick Road</Street>
      <Street>Acocks Green</Street>
      <City>Birmingham</City>
      <Country>UK</Country>
      <PostalCode>B27 6BH</PostalCode>
   </Address>
   <Address headquarters="no">
      <Street>1512 North Frement</Street>
      <Street>Suite 103</Street>
      <City>Chicago</City>
      <PoliticalDivision>Illinois</PoliticalDivision>
      <Country>USA</Country>
      <PostalCode>60622</PostalCode>
   </Address>
</Publisher>
```

There is no reason why we cannot take the addresses out of this document and create two more perfectly acceptable XML documents. This is something we often do instinctively when discussing XML. For example, I might say that the UK address of Wrox Press is:

```
<Address headquarters="yes">
   <Street>Arden House</Street>
   <Street>1102 Warwick Road</Street>
   <Street>Acocks Green</Street>
   <City>Birmingham</City>
   <Country>UK</Country>
   <PostalCode>B27 6BH</PostalCode>
</Address>
```

and that the US address is:

```
<Address headquarters="no">
   <Street>1512 North Frement</Street>
   <Street>Suite 103</Street>
   <City>Chicago</City>
   <PoliticalDivision>Illinois</PoliticalDivision>
   <Country>USA</Country>
   <PostalCode>60622</PostalCode>
</Address>
```

Although we haven't yet worked out how we are going to do this, by dealing with *nodes* we have at least created the possibility for two people to be working simultaneously on the same XML document – by allowing them to work on separate nodes. Providing we can build a system that allows control of individual nodes, we can build a system that appears to allow control over different parts of an XML document. Different users can be given different sets of nodes to edit –in the form of valid XML documents. Working on our two addresses would involve the following:

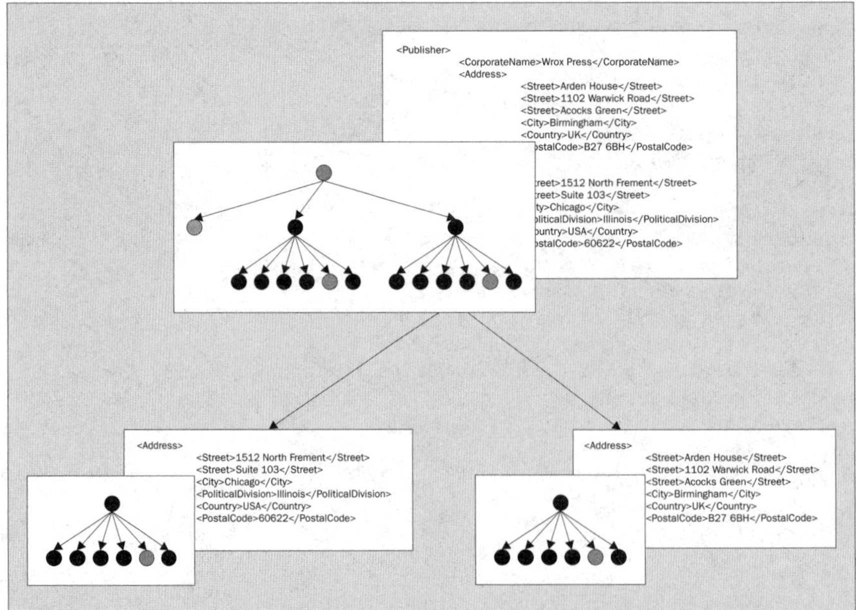

A server that is designed to make nodes available in this way – or XML documents that may themselves be part of a larger XML document – we will call an **XML server**. It is important to bear these concepts in mind when evaluating different products, since many applications will claim to cope with XML, but may not allow the sort of control that we are suggesting is desirable. We will discuss some of these applications later.

Some people argue that this 'node model' does not go far enough, because the nodes themselves do not relate to the elements they represent. For example, to access the `headquarters` *attribute on the* `<Address>` *element, we should be able to use:*

```
var hq = n.headquarters;
```

whereas with the DOM we must use:

```
var hq = n.attributes.getNamedItem("headquarters").value;
```

Each node should essentially be an object with its own defined properties and methods. This approach is called the ***Grove Paradigm****. See Robin Cover's site for more details, at* http://www.oasis-open.org/cover/topics.html#groves. *While the approach raises some important issues, it is furiously debated, and is unlikely to be appearing in your neighborhood any time soon.*

Summary

To really get control of our XML documents we need to be able to solve all of the problems that we discussed under *Limitations of File Systems*:

- We want to be able to cope with extremely large documents, and we want to be able to examine parts of a document separately from others.
- We want to allow a number of people to work on a document at the same time.
- We want to be able to maintain sections of the document with whichever tool is most suitable for the data.
- We want to be able to keep track of different versions of a document.
- We want to control what parts of a document certain people can see or modify.
- We want to be able to seamlessly integrate other external data into our document.

In order to address these points, we established that we must have the ability to manipulate any node within our documents.

Document Management

Before we look at the manipulation of nodes, it is worth spending a little time on an intermediate technique – the storage of documents in databases. Just to recap, we have established that using a file system to handle our documents is not a powerful enough technique to address security issues and large numbers of users. We've also seen that operating at the level of nodes – rather than documents – may go some way to solving this. Before we can look at addressing these problems I'll touch briefly on an 'in between' approach, which is to improve the way we deal with *documents* using techniques that are more flexible than a file system.

It may well be the case that for your project you can handle XML as a series of documents. Perhaps you just need something that is slightly better than a simple text file on a file system, but locking and securing individual nodes may be too elaborate. We'll therefore take a quick look at some products that handle the storage and retrieval of XML documents in their entirety. Some of these products address some of our requirements relating to group working and versioning, however because they deal with documents as their basic unit they cannot meet all of our needs. By looking at some of these limitations it should become clearer as to why we need something more sophisticated.

RDBMS Solutions

Storing an XML document in a text field of a relational database management system (RDBMS) is straightforward, and should be possible on any database product. However, once stored, the document is nothing more than a string of text – the XML is stored in much the same way as you might use a database to hold images or text documents. Oracle has added a feature to their database product *8i*, which allows XML documents that have been stored in a field to be queried as XML. This is achieved by extending the normal `SELECT` statement. This makes for a very powerful document storage technique; a record in a table could have a field to hold an XML document, and then other fields could be used to hold information about the document such as whether it is locked out, who last changed it, etc.

These features are most likely to be of use to someone building a full XML server of their own, rather than directly for the average development project. While it is essentially a mix of two data models – relational data and hierarchical, structured data – it would be possible to build either an XML document server or even an XML node server. Constructing such applications on top of an RDBMS like Oracle is obviously going to be easier than doing so on top of an RDBMS that does not have XML support.

> *Further information is available at* http://technet.oracle.com/tech/xml/xsql_servlet/. *A servlet is also available to convert ordinary SQL queries to XML. Microsoft have also announced a technology preview that allows database queries to be automatically converted to XML. For more information see* http://msdn.microsoft.com/workshop/xml/articles/xmlsql/default.asp.

OODBMS Solutions

Object-oriented database management systems (OODBMS) have been around for long time, and provide many of the features that we would like to see in our ideal XML server. However, the initial take from most vendors has simply been to use their database products as very powerful XML document repositories. Let's take a quick look at a few of these:

Inso Corporation DynaBase 3.1

DynaBase is based on *ObjectStore 4.0*, but doesn't seem to do anything clever with XML documents. They are stored much as an image or spreadsheet might be stored, although with all the advantages of an object-oriented database to manage them. (We discuss an application where *ObjectStore* is used to fuller effect later.) More details can be found at: http://www.inso.com/ and http://www.ebt.com/dynabase/.

Chrystal Astoria 3.0

Astoria allows the storage of components, which are documents of any type. Essentially a group editing product with XML/SGML awareness, *Astoria* can work with other authoring tools to control group access to components. It supports searching, authoring, editing, review and revision, translation, and multimedia distribution. For more information, visit: http://www.chrystal.com/.

DataChannel Rio 3.2

Rio stores XML documents in folders that users have varying levels of access to. The documents can also be Microsoft Office files, and conversion takes place automatically. The *Rio* product was primarily concerned with keeping users up to date with changes in files on an intranet. However, the latest release uses *X-Machine* from Software AG (See *Tamino,* later. Also, note that the DataChannel site refers to this as *XStore*, but there is no mention of *XStore* on Software AG's site. However, the description of *X-Machine* fits the bill for what DataChannel call *XStore.*) Data Channel's web site is at: http://www.datachannel.com/.

Vignette StoryServer

Generates dynamic content, and can deliver documents from other systems, including XML. Their recently announced *SyndicationServer* allows stories stored in their system to be exported in the ICE (Information & Content Exchange – there is more on ICE in Chapter 12) format, an XML grammar. Another important development for those considering using XML in a publishing environment is Vignette's collaboration with Quark, makers of the ubiquitous *QuarkXPress* product. See http://www.vignette.com/ for more details.

Conclusion

Document management techniques go some way towards addressing the limitations of storing XML documents in a file system. RDBMS and OODBMS products will allow for large volumes of information to be stored, while the object-oriented databases will allow control over different documents, with versioning, locking, and so on. This may be sufficient for many projects, but these products are most likely to find use as the foundation for XML node servers.

XML Storage and Databases

Let's return to the limitations of file systems for the storage of XML documents that we outlined in our discussion of the problems of persistence, and look at some of the features of databases that may help us to find a solution:

- **Size** – databases can usually cope with extremely large amounts of information. Since this information is accessible in a granular way – we can refer to one author or two books – then it is easy to navigate.
- **Concurrency** – databases are designed to allow more than one user to access information at the same time. Most products will allow one user to access authors while another accesses books, for example. They will also allow one user to edit one author, while another user edits a different author.
- **The right tool for the job** – databases are usually back-end products that are usable with many different types of application. Just as all applications can read and write from the file system, so they can access databases. Interfaces to a database include Microsoft Access forms, a web form, or even another database server retrieving information.
- **Versioning** – relational databases do not usually have native support for versioning, but many object-oriented databases do.
- **Security** – just as databases allow a fine degree of control over when information stored in them can be accessed, so too they usually allow different levels of access. One user might be able to view authors but not edit them, another might be able to add new books, but not delete them.
- **Integration** – databases are ideal for enabling the sharing of repeated information. Author data from the accounts department can be shared with author data for the book catalog.

It certainly seems that database technology will be ideally suited to our needs. Both relational and object databases allow control over small amounts of information. RDBMS and OODBMS will both allow two people to edit different pieces of information in the same area, as in the example we discussed above with two addresses. Object databases will further allow security to be set on individual objects (relational databases usually only allow control over all objects of a certain type).

In this section we will look at object and relational database techniques and see how good each of them is at modeling or storing hierarchies of nodes, as we discussed in the first part of this section.

Object-oriented Databases

For a number of years now, databases that model real-world information in the form of objects have been available. Although the speed with which information can be retrieved from these stores is rarely faster than from relational databases, their advantage is that they make information more easy to manage when using object-oriented programming techniques. Their main advantage from the point of view of our current discussion is that they very straightforwardly model our node hierarchy.

We'll look briefly at some OO concepts before discussing how objects might be a useful way of building XML documents.

Object-oriented Programming

Object-oriented programming – or **OOP** – provides a very efficient and reliable mechanism for writing well structured programs. An **object** can be anything the programmer desires, from the tangible, such as a car or an invoice, through to the more abstract, such as a list. A **class** definition would say how each object should look: what attributes it has; whether it contains any other classes; and what abilities the class has.

A class definition for authors, for example, would specify that an author has a first and last name, and a list of books that they have written. An object of type author, however, would have real values, such as "Stephen" and "Mohr". When an object is created from its class definition, the class is said to be **instantiated**.

One advantage of the OO approach for producing reliable code is that information pertinent to an object can be **encapsulated**. This has the effect of only exposing information at the level at which it should be used. By allowing classes to **inherit** from each other, encapsulation can be used to build on tried and tested code. For example, say we had a Java class `Person`, defined as follows:

```
public class Person
{
   public String FirstName;
   public String MI;
   public String LastName;

   public Person(String FirstName, String MI, String LastName)
   {
      this.FirstName = FirstName;
      this.MI = MI;
      this.LastName = LastName;
   }

   public String fullName ()
   {
      return this.FirstName + " " + this.MI + ". " + this.LastName;
   }
}
```

and that the `fullName()` routine had been thoroughly tested and found to be very reliable. We would therefore like to take advantage of this. When we come to define our `Author` class for a program at Wrox, we can build on the `Person` class by inheriting from it:

```
public class Author extends Person
{
   public int authorCiteID;
   public DCollection books;

   public Author(int authorCiteID, String FirstName, String MI,
                 String LastName)
   {
      super(FirstName, MI, LastName);
      this.authorCiteID = authorCiteID;
   }
```

```
    public void printBooks()
    {
       Enumeration elements;
       System.out.println("Books written by " + this.fullName() + ":");
       for (elements = books.elements(); books.hasMoreElements();)
       {
          System.out.println(elements.nextElement());
       }
    }
 }
```

We are now free to concentrate on the code to implement our `Author` class, having built on the work done by the designers of the `Person` class. Without us having to write any additional code, any `Author` that we create automatically inherits the features of a `Person`. We can therefore display the name of an author with the following:

```
Author a = new Author(1, "Stephen", "", "Mohr")
System.out.println(a.fullName());
```

OO and XML

It probably didn't take you long to notice the close affinity between objects and XML elements in the previous part. Recall from the schema defined in Chapter 7 that an author could look something like this:

```
<Author authorCiteID="4">
   <FirstName>Frank</FirstName>
   <MI />
   <LastName>Boumphrey</LastName>
   <Biographical>
      Frank Boumphrey currently works for Cormorant Consulting, a firm that
      specializes in medical and legal documentation. His main objective at
      the present is to help XML to become the language of choice in web
      documents.
   </Biographical>
   <Portrait
      picLink="http://webdev.wrox.co.uk/resources/authors/boumphreyf.gif" />
</Author>
```

To create such an element using the DOM would require numerous calls to `createElement()` and `setAttribute()`, with a lot of possibility for error. Using the basic object techniques we just introduced we saw that creating *objects* that are authors is more reliable. To illustrate, the following JavaScript creates the first part of the author document just listed:

```
oNode = oParser.createElement("Author");
oNode.setAttribute("authorCiteID", "4");

oTemp = oParser.createElement("FirstName");
oTemp.text = "Frank";
oNode.appendChild(oTemp);

oTemp = oParser.createElement("LastName");
oTemp.text = "Boumphrey";
oNode.appendChild(oTemp);
```

Of course, this could be tidied up a little with functions, but the advantage of the object approach is that we are dealing with a *model* of our data, rather than just nodes. In the Java example we saw earlier, we could say insert *an* author, rather than a *node* called 'author'.

Persistence

OO databases arose to fill the need to persist objects from programs such as the Java excerpt we have just discussed. While it is possible to represent our `Author` object on a disk file or in a relational database, the former is inefficient, and the latter requires programmers to constantly move between two data models – relational and hierarchical. Many tools do exist to perform the mapping between classes in languages like Java and C++, and relational databases, but to model hierarchical data in a relational database requires many joins on those tables (we'll look at joins and relational databases in the next section). If the object tree has a great deal of depth, this may end up being represented by many tables, and as a consequence could be quite slow.

Benefits

ODBMS have advantages then, when we really are dealing with objects that have complex relationships and depth. However, since they are not generally as fast as RDBMS, the latter can still be used to model object structures if the complexity is not great. We'll look now at two products that use object technology to deliver most of the advanced techniques that we discussed earlier.

Object Oriented Database Products

Let's take a look at two object-oriented databases:

Object Design – eXcelon 1.1

The *eXcelon* product is a well-respected OO database that has recently had XML support added. While the general behavior of *ObjectStore 4.0* – the database that underlies *eXcelon* – would be to store documents as a unit within the object hierarchy (see the section on *Document Management* earlier), *eXcelon* actually parses the XML input to create new objects. In other words, rather than each object in the database being a full XML document, it is instead a *node* from the document. These nodes can be retrieved using XQL queries (see Chapter 8):

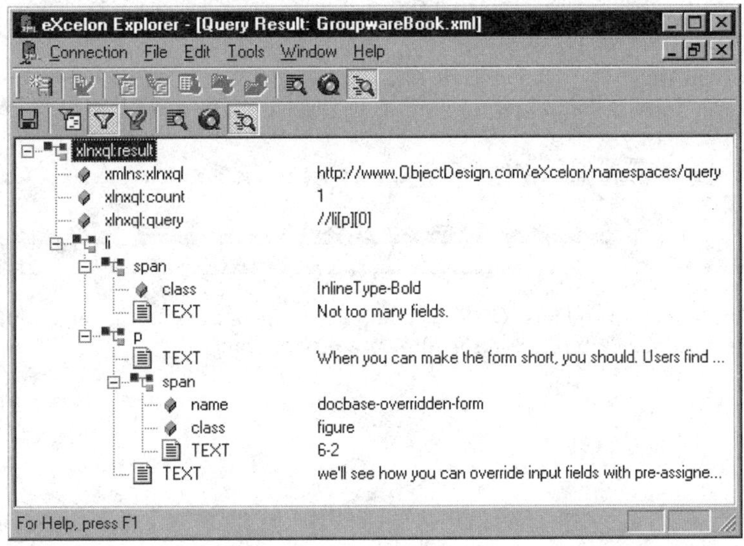

It is because of this parsing and then storing each node as a unique object that *eXcelon* is way ahead of other products. These nodes can be manipulated with the full power of the underlying OO technology of *ObjectStore*. An odd omission is that there is no validation when importing the source documents, although this is sure to be rectified soon. See http://www.odi.com/excelon/ for more information on Excelon.

POET – Content Management System 2.0

CMS is based on the *Object Server Suite (OSS) 6.0*, POET's own object-oriented database. In a similar manner to the conversion of incoming XML into objects in *eXcelon*, *CMS* allows nodes at any level to be delineated as 'components'. These components have independence from each other for checking out, version control, etc., which means that two people could edit different nodes in the same document at the same time.

Searching the structure can be carried out in two ways, either as a standard text wide search, or within tags. However, the latter does not distinguish at what level the tag is, so if elements called `<Title>` appear in many different documents they will all be found; it therefore certainly isn't as sophisticated as XPath, which we will look at later.

However, one very powerful feature is the ability to re-use content. A component can be referred to from other places, but only needs to be maintained once; the component acts as if it is actually at whatever position refers to it:

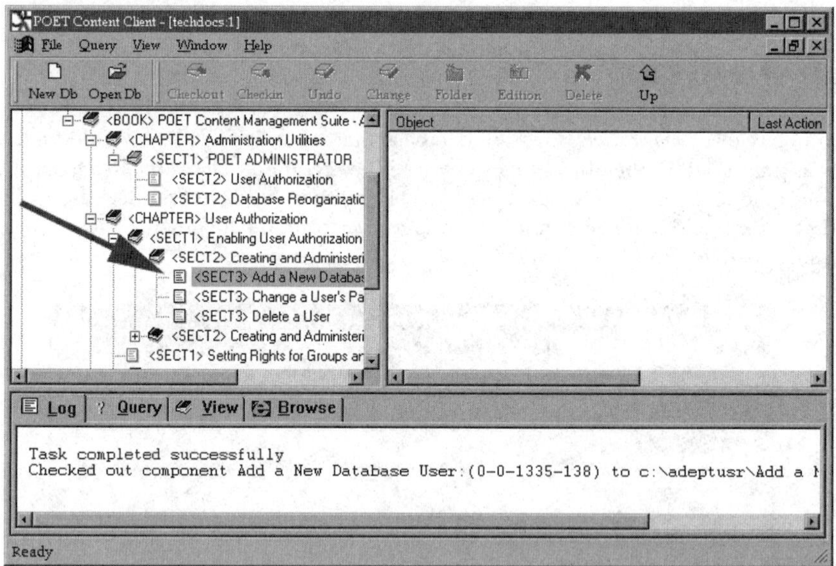

As with some of the other products, *CMS* has component check-in and out, versioning, and style transformations. For more information see http://www.poet.com/.

Summary

The native abilities of OO databases make them extremely promising candidates for powerful manipulation of XML documents. The ability to individually manipulate nodes – whether locking, securing, or versioning – gives them the potential to meet many of the advanced requirements we outlined earlier. Either of the two applications outlined here would provide a solid foundation for an XML-based project that needs advanced storage and retrieval.

If everything is so great, then you may be asking yourself what the catch is. In many ways it is cultural rather than technical; the installed base of OO database software is a tiny fraction of that for relational systems, and this is unlikely to change soon. It will certainly be possible for products such as the ones described here to make some headway because they manage XML well, but sales will have little to do with OO technology, and more to do with the ease with which stores of XML documents can be implemented.

That's not to say that there aren't technical issues as well. It may sound obvious, but OO databases are best for object data. They are often not as efficient as relational databases for modeling other types of structure, or for situations where the hierarchy is very flat – say a few objects that each contain tens of thousands of other objects.

So, although we have found a promising solution in OO databases, we must continue our quest, since the vast majority of you will be dealing with relational storage mediums.

Relational Databases

Relational Database Management Systems – or **RDBMS** – use the familiar **row** and **column** approach to storing data:

authorCiteID	FirstName	MI	LastName	Biographical	Portrait
1	Stephen	<NULL>	Mohr	Stephen began pro	http://webdev.wro
2	Kathie	<NULL>	Kingsley-Hughes	Kathie is the MD of	<NULL>
3	Alex	<NULL>	Homer	Alex is a software (	http://webdev.wro
4	Frank	<NULL>	Boumphrey	Frank Boumphrey c	http://webdev.wro

This illustration shows a **table** that will contain authors. Each author is represented by a row, and each attribute of an author is represented by a column.

Despite the many advantages of OO databases, RDBMSs continue to be by far the most popular because they can represent so many real-world problems, and for many of these problems give much better response time. Take invoices, for example. These fit neatly into this model as a collection of two-dimensional arrays, as do contact management systems, stock control packages, and so on:

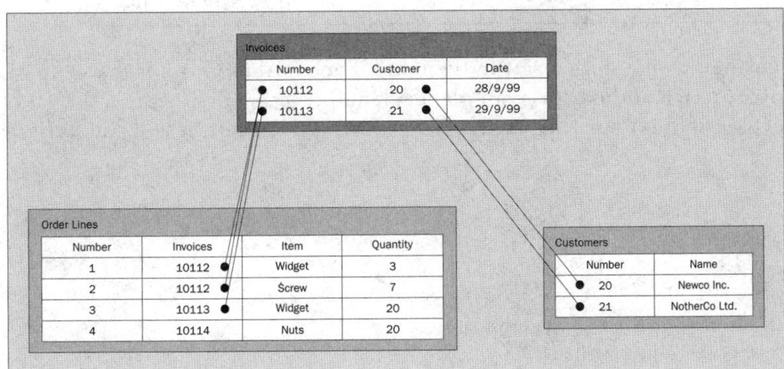

The basic relational database concepts are:

- Tables
- Queries
- Joins

The following few sections introduce these concepts, although can easily be skipped if you are experienced in using relational databases. After we have revised these basics, we will look at how we might use relational databases to model a hierarchy of nodes, and then how we might automate some of the conversion. You will need to be familiar with these concepts to follow how this modeling takes place.

Tables

A simple **table** of data to store authors of books might contain the following:

AuthorCiteID	FirstName	MI	LastName	Biographical
1	Stephen		Mohr	Stephen began programming in high school and is now a senior software systems architect with Omicron Consulting. He designs and develops systems using C++, Java, JavaScript, COM, and various internetworking standards and protocols.
2	Kathie		Kingsley-Hughes	Kathie is the MD of Kingsley-Hughes Development Ltd, a Training and Consultancy firm specialising in Web Development and visual programming languages.
3	Frank		Boumphrey	Frank Boumphrey currently works for Cormorant Consulting, a firm that specializes in medical and legal documentation. His main objective at the present is to help XML to become the language of choice in web documents.

Each author has their own entry or **row** in the table. Each of these rows is made up of a number of **fields** that are common to each author, for example, each author has a first name field, and a last name field. Even if a particular field is empty, as the `MI` field is for each author, it will still exist in each row.

The headings in the table correspond to the **columns** in the table definition. These could be defined as follows:

Column Name	Data Type	Allow Null
AuthorCiteID	Integer	No
FirstName	String	Yes
MI	String	Yes
LastName	String	No
Biography	String	Yes

With this definition we have specified the properties that we need to store for each author, and have indicated which of those must be present and which are optional. Since it means little to have an author without at least a unique ID and a surname, we have made that the minimum requirement for a record.

Having decided how to store this data in our table, we need a mechanism to retrieve it.

Queries

The common method of accessing data stored in relational databases is to use **Structured Query Language**, or **SQL**. Although there have been many improvements and enhancements over the years to the features available from SQL, at its core is the `SELECT` statement. Using this statement, a request to an RDBMS server to give us all the authors in the database would be written as follows:

```
SELECT * FROM Author;
```

A common mistake for those new to SQL is to read the asterisk as 'please retrieve all records'. This is understandable given the role the asterisk plays in situations such as finding files in directories, but in SQL it means 'please retrieve all columns'.

In the case of the author table we defined in the previous section that would mean returning the data for five columns. A query that retrieves only specified columns, rather than retrieving all known columns would look like this:

```
SELECT FirstName, LastName FROM Author;
```

The results of a `SELECT` statement form a **recordset** – a list of query results that can be stepped through, retrieving each row as you go – which in this example would contain the following:

FirstName	LastName
Stephen	Mohr
Kathie	Kingsley-Hughes
Frank	Boumphrey

As you can see, even without the asterisk we still get all rows back from the database, since this is the default behavior of the `SELECT` statement. One way to limit the records returned is to use a `WHERE` clause. If we wanted Stephen Mohr's biography, for example, we could write the following query:

```
SELECT Biographical FROM Author WHERE LastName = 'Mohr';
```

In this case we are asking the database to return all records that have the field `LastName` set to a value of `Mohr`, and then to give us back just the `Biographical` field. As you would expect the `WHERE` clause is quite rich. The following query for example, would return both Kathie and Stephen's biographies:

```
SELECT Biographical FROM Author WHERE LastName > 'K';
```

Joins

Relational databases are named that way because they handle relationships. The aim of a join is to establish these relationships between tables in a database. Although it would be possible to store data in one large table without joins, it would quickly become inefficient in terms of resource usage and response time. For example, there is nothing to stop us from building our system like this:

FirstName	LastName	Biographical	Title	ISBN
Stephen	Mohr	Stephen began...	XML Applications	1-861001-52-5
Stephen	Mohr	Stephen began...	Designing Distributed Applications with XML, ASP, IE5, LDAP and MSMQ	1-861002-27-0
Kathie	Kingsley-Hughes	Kathie is the MD of...	XML Applications	1-861001-52-5
Frank	Boumphrey	Frank Boumphrey currently...	Professional Style Sheets for HTML and XML	1-861001-65-7
Frank	Boumphrey	Frank Boumphrey currently...	XML Applications	1-861001-52-5

However, it should be obvious that there is no need to repeat an author's name and biographical details for each book they write, and equally there is no point in repeating the book's information for each author who was involved in writing the book. Not only is this inefficient, it is also difficult to maintain, since a change to an author's profile would need to be copied through to every place that it occurs.

To achieve a more efficient relationship between books and authors we need to establish a many-to-many relationship. This requires a special technique, which we will introduce in a moment. Before we do so, lets look at how one-to-one and one-to-many relationships can be established.

One-to-one and One-to-many Joins

You may remember from our book catalog that a book can have a price, and that each price can have a currency:

```
<AttributeType name="currency" dt:type="enumeration" dt:values="USD GBF CD"
               required="yes" />

<ElementType name="Price" dt:type="fixed.14.4" content="textOnly">
   <attribute Type="currency" />
</ElementType>
```

If we were to take the approach outlined a moment ago – where all data is placed in a large table – then this could be stored in our database as follows:

Title	ISBN	Currency	Price
XML Applications	1-861001-52-5	USD	49.99
Designing Distributed Applications with XML, ASP, IE5, LDAP and MSMQ	1-861002-27-0	USD	49.99
Professional Style Sheets for HTML and XML	1-861001-65-7	GBF	45.99

However, the schema says that there are only three currencies that can be used, and each price (and therefore book) can only have one currency, although this doesn't prevent each currency from being used many times over. We could therefore establish a one-to-many relationship between the entity `Book` and a new entity, `Currency`. This process of rationalizing the data is called **normalization**, and is discussed in more detail below. Separating off the currencies into another table gives us a few advantages:

- We can store additional information about a currency, such as a longer version of the currency name for use in drop boxes and reports, and perhaps an exchange rate.
- We can ensure that only currencies in our list are entered into the book table.

We achieve this by firstly adding a new table for the currency:

CurrencyID	ShortName	LongName
1	USD	United States Dollars
2	GBF	British Pounds
3	CD	Canadian Dollars

The `CurrencyID` column is the **primary key** of the table. It is used to ensure that each row is unique and is used as a means of addressing a record from another table. Although in this case we could have used the `ShortName` as the primary key and saved ourselves a column, it is fairly common practice to use integers to join tables since they are compact and comparisons will be quick.

After setting up our currency table, we alter our book table so that it refers to the currency table for its currencies:

Title	ISBN	CurrencyID	Price
XML Applications	1-861001-52-5	1	49.99
Designing Distributed Applications with XML, ASP, IE5, LDAP and MSMQ	1-861002-27-0	1	49.99
Professional Style Sheets for HTML and XML	1-861001-65-7	2	45.99

Here we see a reference being established by using the value of the primary key. Since the `CurrencyID` in the book table is doing a look-up on the primary key of the currency table, we say it is a **foreign key**. In some database systems it is possible to enforce this relationship between primary and foreign keys, such that we cannot, for example, put the number 10,000 into the field, since there is no corresponding record in the currency database. Setting columns to have a property of 'foreign key' is an important way of ensuring that the data stays consistent.

Now we can produce a recordset of books and their currencies using a further variant of the `WHERE` clause:

```
SELECT Title, ShortName, Price
   FROM Book, Currency
   WHERE Book.CurrencyID = Currency.CurrencyID;
```

As before, the columns we want to retrieve are listed between `SELECT` and `FROM`, but this time we are asking for data from two different tables, the book and currency tables. However, to make each row meaningful we are requesting that each row from the book table be matched with a row from the currency table. We don't want just any row though; we want the row that has the same currency number as the one we have in the book row. In effect, the `CurrencyID` column in the book table is performing a **look-up** into the currency table to obtain the details that it needs. The resulting recordset would be as follows:

Title	ShortName	Price
XML Applications	USD	49.99
Designing Distributed Applications with XML, ASP, IE5, LDAP and MSMQ	USD	49.99
Professional Style Sheets for HTML and XML	GBP	45.99

As you can see, despite having separated our data into different tables, we can bring it back together again at any time using joins, as if it was in one table.

This currency illustration models a one-to-many relationship – one currency relates to many books – but the same technique is also used to model one-to-one relationships. We might for example, store the price and currency in one table, and refer to the entire 'price' unit from a book. One book would therefore have one price.

Many-to-many Joins

The method just described, of placing a reference to a column in one table inside a column of another table, is fine for one-to-one or one-to-many relationships. However, it does not allow us to represent the many-to-many relationship that we need for our books-to-authors scenario. Just to remind ourselves, we are saying that a book can have many authors, and an author could have written many books. For this we will need a separate table that contains nothing but the relationships we are trying to establish.

Let's suppose that we have the following author table:

authorCiteID	FirstName	LastName	Biographical
1	Stephen	Mohr	Stephen began...
2	Kathie	Kingsley-Hughes	Kathie is the MD of...
3	Frank	Boumphrey	Frank Boumphrey currently...

Note that each author has a unique number – or primary key – to identify them, just like the currencies had, but that there is no reference to books in this table. Now lets look at the book table, which also has a unique ID for each book:

BookID	Title	ISBN
1	XML Applications	1-861001-52-5
2	Designing Distributed Applications with XML, ASP, IE5, LDAP and MSMQ	1-861002-27-0
3	Professional Style Sheets for HTML and XML	1-861001-65-7

Note once again that just as the author table has no reference to the book table, this table has no reference to the author table. Unlike with our one-to-one and one-to-many relationships which could be achieved with an extra column in a table, we need to establish a third table to maintain the many-to-many joins. The additional table will contain:

BookID	authorCiteID
1	1
1	2
1	3
2	1
3	3

The table contains nothing but the relationships between the two other tables. This technique could be extended to provide relationships between more tables if desired. How do we retrieve this information from the database? Well, to find all books written by Stephen Mohr, we would use the following SQL statement:

```
SELECT * FROM Author, Book, BookAuthor
   WHERE BookAuthor.authorCiteID = Author.authorCiteID
   AND Author.LastName = 'Mohr'
   AND Book.BookID = BookAuthor.BookID;
```

And to find all the authors of 'XML Applications', we would use this statement:

```
SELECT * FROM Author, Book, BookAuthor
   WHERE BookAuthor.BookID = Book.BookID
   AND Book.Title = 'XML Applications'
   AND Author.authorCiteID = BookAuthor.authorCiteID;
```

Note that the queries are joining all three tables together. The first query works as follows:

- The part of the WHERE clause that matches `BookAuthor.authorCiteID` to `Author.authorCiteID` is retrieving all authors that are referred to in the `BookAuthor` table.
- The part that compares `LastName` to `'Mohr'` narrows this list of authors to Stephen Mohr.
- The comparison between the two `BookID` fields looks up the books that Stephen has written.

With this join, then, we can ask questions about books and their relationships to authors. The complete table configuration looks as follows:

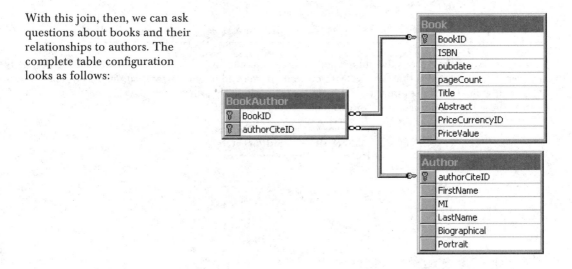

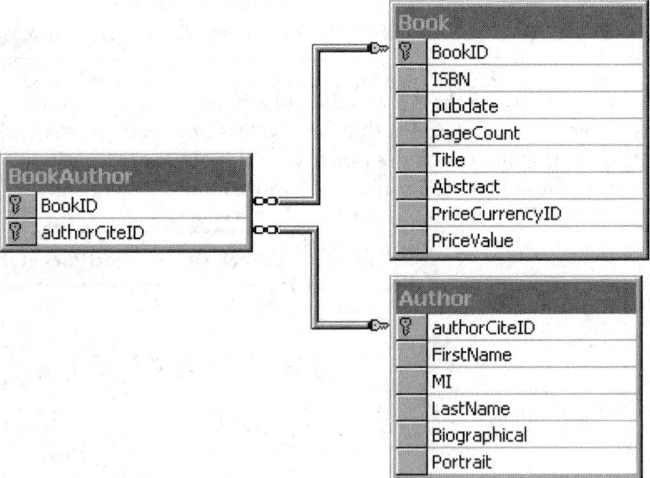

RDBMS and XML

To return to the central question that we are addressing in this section; given these features of relational databases, how good are they at providing the advanced capabilities for XML document manipulation? To establish this we need to examine how well relational databases model node information.

Remembering our discussion on tables we can see that a row can easily be used to represent an element, with the columns of the table holding the attributes. For example, the `Author` table in the table configuration diagram above would very easily hold `<Author>` elements from our book catalog schema.

We know that some elements contain text as well as attributes but this could be simulated by using an additional column with a known name, such as `PCDATA`. Since it has a known name we would know that when it comes to be output it should not be extracted as an attribute but as an element.

An example of this from the book catalog is the `<Imprint>` element, which might look something like this:

```
<Imprint shortImprintName="XMLAPP">XML Applications</Imprint>
```

The data in the `Imprint` table might represent this as follows:

attr_id_shortImprintName	pcdata
DDA	Designing Distributed Applications
XMLAPP	XML Applications
PROXML	Professional XML

Mapping elements to rows in a table is quite straightforward, but only half the battle; we still need to represent the relationships between the nodes. To do this we need to use the different types of joins we looked at in the previous section. We can model a parent/child relationship very simply by creating a join from a foreign key on the table that represents the child, to the primary key on the table that represents the parent. For example, the `Imprint` table we just created might be extended to look like this:

pk_Imprint	fk_Imprints	attr_id_shortImprintName	pcdata
1	1	DDA	Designing Distributed Applications
2	1	XMLAPP	XML Applications
3	1	PROXML	Professional XML

with the field `fk_Imprints` being a reference – or foreign key – for the primary key in the parent table `Imprints`. This table refers in turn to the publisher:

pk_Imprints	fk_Publisher
1	1

Limitations of RDBMS

At first sight this all seems pretty useful; the hierarchy of parent and child nodes is established by placing a reference in the child table to the parent. However, there is a major problem in that the parent/child relationships are too rigid. For example, with the approach we just outlined, it would not be possible to represent the following:

```
<A>
   <B>
      <C>
         <D />
      </C>
   </B>
   <C>
      <D />
   </C>
</A>
```

This is because the relationship between an element of type `C` and its parent is not fixed; it could have a parent of type `A` or of type `B`. If we were to use the simple primary key/foreign key technique that we have just described, this XML structure would need to have either one or the other. In other words, elements of type `C` would have a foreign key to the table for `A` or the table for `B` – but not both.

So, although RDBMS reasonably models nodes in its table structure, it doesn't seem to handle the relationships between those nodes very well. Having said that, we shouldn't dismiss RDBMS as a mechanism for storing XML nodes. There are many scenarios that this type of database will represent perfectly adequately. In fact, as we will see later, our book catalog example works fine because the schema does not contain situations like the one just described.

Later we will step through how we might convert a schema to a series of tables and relationships.

Products

Although the installed base of RDBMS is large, there is nothing in this sphere that compares to *POET* or *eXcelon*. The following product is probably the most advanced. After that we list a few utilities that may be of interest.

LivePage Corporation LivePage Enterprise 3.0

LivePage converts between XML and a relational database. This is achieved by placing a software layer over a relational database, which handles the conversions in and out. *LivePage* is not itself a database, but sits on top of one of the following:

- IBM DB2 2.1 or later
- Microsoft SQL Server 6.0 or later
- Oracle SQL 7 or later
- Sybase SQL Server 10 and 11
- Sybase SQL Anywhere 5.0 or later.

This product is not marketed and sold as an XML server since it provides many more facilities than just storing and delivering XML documents. However, it is important to mention since it shows that some of the limitations that we noted earlier with RDBMS can be worked around to produce an industrial-strength product. See http://www.livepage.com/ for more details.

Utilities

The following will be of interest when experimenting with legacy databases within an XML project, but are unlikely to meet the requirements of a large project.

Cerium Component Software Incorporated - XMLDB and XML Servlet

XMLDB takes an XML document and generates instructions to create the required tables and insert the data. *XML Servlet* is template-driven, using an XML-based language capable of specifying SQL queries and HTML forms. See http://ceriumworks.com/tech.html.

IBM - DataCraft

In their own words: "...an application generation tool targeted for RDF/XML applications in the context of Web-commerce applications. *DataCraft*, a facility capable of generating visual query skeletons and running the queries against *DB2*, is an excellent tool for Web-Database application generation using XML. *DataCraft* provides client tools visually navigating resource schema, and query language building queries visually from the schema based on XML and RDF. *DataCraft* uses RDF and XML to describe data collection structures and to exchange resource schema and query between the server and client." See http://www.alphaworks.ibm.com/formula/datacraft.

Intelligent Systems Research - ODBC2XML

A tool for transferring data from an ODBC database to an XML document. `SELECT` statements are embedded in a template as processing instructions. See http://members.xoom.com/gvaughan/odbc2xml.htm.

Mey & Westphal RIPOSTE Software - XOSL

A Microsoft Windows DLL for transferring data from a database to an XML document. This is template-driven, using XOSL-specific elements to embed queries. See http://www.riposte.com/xosl/.

Ronald Bourret - XML-DBMS

Java classes for transferring data between a relational database and an XML document, using a mapping language to determine which columns are attributes and which are elements. See http://www.informatik.tu-darmstadt.de/DVS1/staff/bourret/xmldbms/xmldbms.htm.

Stonebroom - ASP2XML

An OLE COM component for transferring data between an XML document and any ODBC or OLE-DB data source. The product is model-driven but both the input and output XML must use ASP2XML-specific tags. See http://www.stonebroom.com/.

Volker Turau - DB2XML

Java classes for transferring data from a relational database to an XML document, which may be returned as a file, stream, or DOM object. See http://www.informatik.fh-wiesbaden.de/~turau/DB2XML/index.html.

Conclusion

At the moment, OO databases have the edge in representing and maintaining XML documents. Their hierarchical structure conveniently represents the hierarchy contained in XML documents, and more importantly individual nodes in a document can be represented by objects in the database.

However, the popularity of both relational databases and XML means that the fight is far from over. Relational database vendors will continue to add XML features of ever increasing sophistication, while third-party suppliers will build XML servers on top of those databases. Given the amount of data that companies have tied up in relational systems, solutions that place an XML layer over the top of this information – such as *LivePage* – will become increasingly significant and cost-effective.

Before we move on, I'd like to just mention the following products that didn't easily fit into the categories we had above. They are all more or less being marketed as 'XML servers':

Bluestone – XML Suite

This is a Java-based product that allows XML documents to be sent from server to server, and at each server a document handler is invoked based on the document type. This is a very powerful approach, particularly in relation to legacy data. The XML-Server part of the suite uses DSIMs (Data Source Integration Modules) to allow XML documents to be retrieved from or stored in other systems. The following ship with the product:

- ODBC
- JDBC
- XML
- LDAP
- SMTP e-mail
- FTP

The following are obtainable separately:

- SAP R/3
- PeopleSoft
- Tuxedo
- CICS
- MQSeries

For more information see http://www.bluestone.com/xml/.

Software AG – Tamino

Tamino stores XML documents as XML. An important feature is that it provides a layer to sit over legacy database systems that will map the database to and from XML. This module is called *X-Node*. See http://www.softwareag.com/.

UserLand Software – Frontier

Frontier can dish up web pages from its object database-driven content management system, with special processing for XML in and out. See http://frontier.userland.com/.

XML for Interchange

Since the issue of legacy data is such an important one, we will now have a look at how this data might be extracted and represented as XML. In this section we will look at how XML:

- provides for a standard means to exchange information between different systems
- provides a standard way to query data from different systems
- gives a new lease of life to client/server technology

Standard for Data

As we discussed earlier, many people have trouble moving from a document view of XML to a data structure view. Although XML is often discussed as a powerful means of marking up documents, it should be remembered that when the XML 1.0 specification discusses 'XML documents' it means something very different to a word processing document or a spreadsheet.

Word processing and spreadsheet documents are clearly discernible on your hard drive, stored in a file within a directory. An XML document may also exist in this form, and many useful applications are being developed that make use of information stored in this way. However, these applications are ultimately quite limited, and usually involve something along the lines of marking up the text of the complete works of Shakespeare so that they can be represented in an interesting way.

An XML document need not exist in this fixed form, however. It can be created just at the point where it is needed, via a web server. It is possible then that two requests for the same 'document' might return different results. For example, a page that generates an XML document containing a list of Wrox authors may return one list today, and another tomorrow as new authors are added.

To illustrate this, let's create a basic ASP script to export a list of the Wrox authors as simple XML:

```
<%@ Language=VBScript %>
<%
   Response.ContentType = "text/xml"
   Dim dbConn
   Set dbConn = CreateObject("ADODB.Connection")
   dbConn.Open "DSN=XMLPRO;"

   Dim rs
   Set rs = Server.CreateObject("ADODB.Recordset")
   rs.Open "Select * from Author", dbConn, 0, 3
%>
<?xml version="1.0" encoding="UTF-8"?>
<Authors>
```

```
<%
   Do While Not rs.EOF
%>
   <Author authorCiteID="<%=rs("authorCiteID")%>">
      <FirstName><%=rs("FirstName")%></FirstName>
      <MI><%=rs("MI")%></MI>
      <LastName><%=rs("LastName")%></LastName>
      <Biographical><%=rs("Biographical")%></Biographical>
      <Portrait picLink="<%=rs("Portrait")%>" />
   </Author><%=vbCrLf%>
<%
      rs.MoveNext
   Loop
%>
</Authors>
<%
   rs.Close
   dbConn.Close
%>
```

The resulting XML document might look as follows:

```
<?xml version="1.0" encoding="UTF-8"?>
<Authors>
   <Author authorCiteID="1">
      <FirstName>Stephen</FirstName>
      <MI></MI>
      <LastName>Mohr</LastName>
      <Biographical>
         Stephen began programming in high school and is now a senior software
         systems architect with Omicron Consulting, he designs and develops
         systems using C++, Java, JavaScript, COM, and various internetworking
         standards and protocols.
      </Biographical>
      <Portrait picLink =
         "http://webdev.wrox.co.uk/resources/authors/mohrs.gif" />
   </Author>
   <Author authorCiteID="2">
      <FirstName>Kathie</FirstName>
      <MI></MI>
      <LastName>Kingsley-Hughes</LastName>
      <Biographical>
         Kathie is the MD of Kingsley-Hughes Development Ltd, a Training and
         Consultancy firm specialising in Web Development and visual
         programming languages, first going into CDF channels with The Dragon
         Channel.
      </Biographical>
      <Portrait picLink="" />
   </Author>
   <Author authorCiteID="3">
      <FirstName>Alex</FirstName>
      <MI></MI>
      <LastName>Homer</LastName>
```

```
        <Biographical>
           Alex is a software consultant and developer whose company, Stonebroom
           Software, specialises in office integration and Internet-related
           development. He works regularly with Wrox Press on a range of
           projects.
        </Biographical>
        <Portrait picLink =
           "http://webdev.wrox.co.uk/resources/authors/homera.gif" />
     </Author>
     <Author authorCiteID="4">
        <FirstName>Frank</FirstName>
        <MI></MI>
        <LastName>Boumphrey</LastName>
        <Biographical>
           Frank Boumphrey currently works for Cormorant Consulting, a firm that
           specializes in medical and legal documentation. His main objective at
           the present is to help XML to become the language of choice in web
           documents.
        </Biographical>
        <Portrait picLink =
           "http://webdev.wrox.co.uk/resources/authors/boumphreyf.gif" />
     </Author>
  </Authors>
```

That we have represented the relational data as a series of nodes, using XML, means that we can now distribute this data to any interested system, provided that the system can first convert the XML. For example, we can export an author list stored in *Oracle*, to be imported into a *POET* database, without anyone writing an Oracle-to-POET converter. In fact no-one even had to write a relational-to-object converter. All that was needed was to ensure that both sides could read and write a common XML grammar. It's worth remembering that ODBC was devised to try and bridge the gap between different database systems, yet what we have with XML is significantly more advanced.

An application that makes use of the information in the database directly – such as a Microsoft Access form or a Java application – might use the following structure if communication was taking place over the Internet:

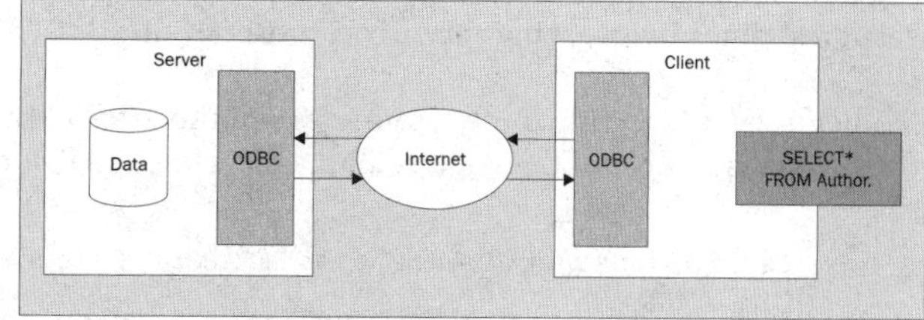

However, there are several problems with this approach:

- Only systems that understand ODBC can retrieve this information
- Many firewalls do not allow ODBC transactions
- ODBC is vulnerable to hackers, who may send unauthorized transactions that then need to be verified by the server

By putting an XML interface on both sides of the communications pipe we have removed the client's dependency on ODBC:

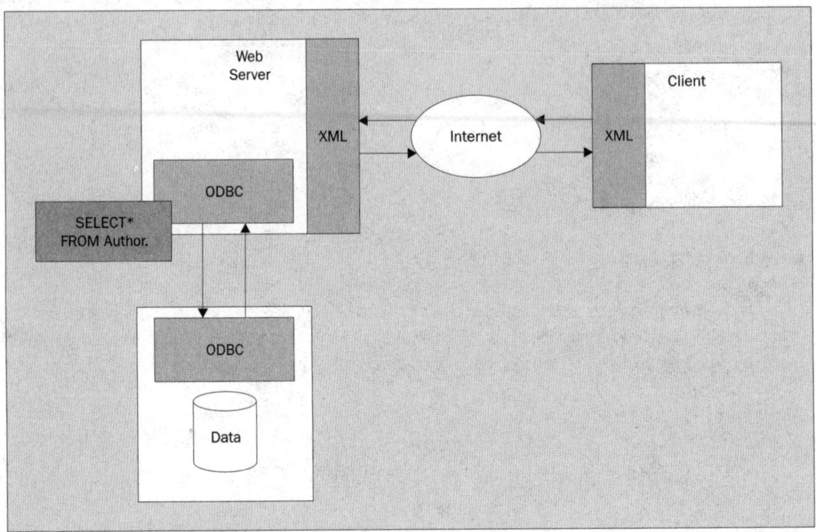

Also, if we encapsulate the XML in some way and transmit it over port 80 (the normal HTTP port), we can solve our firewall blocking issue. In fact, Microsoft has a new technology, SOAP (Simple Object Access Protocol), that does just that. For more information on SOAP see Chapter 11.

Standard for Querying

As it stands, the ASP script we just wrote to return an XML document containing authors will return all the authors in the database. While this is useful to us, we may want to reduce network traffic and response times by querying for only a subset of this data.

To begin with, lets just simply modify our authors-to-XML script so that it will accept a parameter of a `WHERE` clause. Most of the code remains the same, so I've only shown the new lines:

```
      Set rs = Server.CreateObject("ADODB.Recordset")
      Dim sQuery
      Dim sWhere
      sQuery = "SELECT * FROM Author"
      sWhere = Request.QueryString("WHERE")
      If Not IsEmpty(sWhere) Then
         sQuery = sQuery & " WHERE " & sWhere
      End If
      rs.Open sQuery, dbConn, 0, 3
   %>
```

This allows us to retrieve XML representations of different authors, simply by specifying a parameter in a URL. For example, say we were to request that the XML returned were placed in a Data Island inside an HTML page, that specification might look like the following:

```
<H1>Wrox Authors</H1>
<HR>
<XML ID="authors" SRC="xmlAuthor.asp?WHERE=LastName='Mohr'"></XML>
<TABLE BORDER=1 DATASRC="#authors">
   <THEAD>
      <TH>authorCiteID</TH>
```

Data Islands are currently implemented only by Microsoft, but that doesn't really affect this example. I am illustrating how the URL would look to request an XML document for a single author. The same script could also be used to retrieve all authors or just a few.

Querying XML vs Querying the Database

However, we have reached an interesting position now in that we are running queries that are formatted specifically for a relational database, but getting the results back as XML. Given how important it is that we are presenting the output data in a manner independent of the underlying data store, wouldn't it be better if we could query the data in a way that was also independent of the back-end database? Suppose for example, that we replaced our relational database with an object-oriented database. The query syntax that we have just used – `LastName='Mohr'` – may well be useless in an object environment. It would be ideal if the query that we were using to retrieve the data did not have to change.

As it stands then, although we have created a layer over our database that is XML, we are still querying as if we had access to the underlying database. In reality, our application structure is as follows:

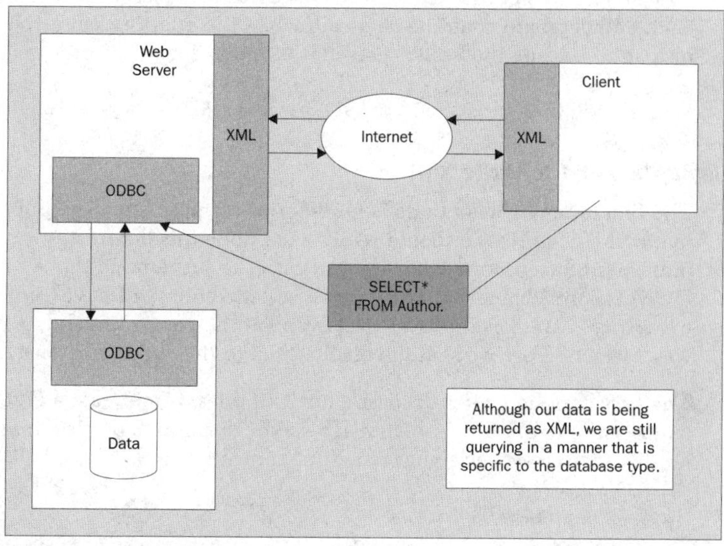

As we go to press Microsoft have announced exactly this; a layer that sits over SQL Server 7 *and returns queries specified with* `SELECT` *statements as XML.*

XML Query Languages

Let's recap. We have established a simple method of retrieving data from any relational database and presenting it as XML. In other words we have 'mapped' our relational data to the node structure of XML. As far as the outside world is concerned our database may as well contain XML, but to query that data in our current implementation the outside world would need to know what format that data is stored in – in this case a relational database. Instead we need to be able to query the nodes.

At the time of writing much work is being done on phrasing queries in XML syntax – this has already been discussed in Chapter 8. Since there has been no agreement on this, for the purposes of our illustration we will treat the database as one big XML document, and use XSL query syntax for our enquiries.

> *The query syntax of XSL has been broken off as XPath. The recommendation is available at http://www.w3.org/TR/xpath.*

I prefer XPath over many of the other proposals for querying XML because it allows a query to be expressed as a URL. This is an important consideration for a data-centric Internet.

So, given that we would like to use XPath for our queries, how exactly do we go about doing that? The best and most efficient solution would be to actually write code that converts XPath queries to queries of the right type for the underlying database. The specifics of this will depend on different database systems, but we will illustrate some of the issues in our sample later.

For now we will take a much simpler approach, which is to load our list of authors into an XML DOM (Document Object Model) and then use XSL to select the nodes. We then have the advantage that the back-end database could be changed, while the query remains the same. Let's modify our script so that instead of passing the `WHERE` part of a `SELECT` query, we pass in XPath syntax queries such as this:

```
http://www.wrox.com/xmlAuthors.asp?xsl=//Author[LastName='Mohr']
```

Using the DOM to Write XML

The first thing we need to do is modify our script to store the information we retrieve from the database in an XML DOM. We should really have done this before anyway, but for some documents, like the one we produced, it was quicker and easier to just embed the tag names using script. However, using the DOM ensures that all tags will match, all attributes will have quotes around them, and that all namespaces are correct. We could even get the parser to validate our resultant node tree, to make sure it was correct before we sent the results back to the caller, or transform the results.

The first step then, after declaring our variables, is to create a DOM to hold our results (note that IE 5 will need to be installed on your IIS server to run this particular script, although you could easily modify the script to use your parser of choice):

```
<%@ Language=VBScript %>
<%
   Response.ContentType = "text/xml"
   Dim dbConn
   Set dbConn = CreateObject("ADODB.Connection")
   dbConn.Open "DSN=WroxBookCatalog;"

   Dim oParser
   Set oParser = Server.CreateObject("Microsoft.XMLDOM")
```

This object gives us access to all of the features of the DOM (see Chapter 5 for a full discussion of the features that are available). Next we run our query on the database to retrieve all of the authors:

```
Dim rsAuthors
Dim sQuery
sQuery = "SELECT * FROM Author"
Set rsAuthors = Server.CreateObject("ADODB.Recordset")
rsAuthors.Open sQuery, dbConn, 0, 3
```

This establishes our recordset exactly as before, ready to be stepped through. Whereas before we would write out tags, this time we are going to use the DOM. The first step is to create an element called `<Authors>` that will hold all of the authors:

```
Dim oAuthors
Set oAuthors = oParser.createElement("Authors")
```

As you can see, creating this element is a lot easier than writing out `<Authors>` and `</Authors>` at the beginning and end, since the DOM guarantees that the hierarchy will be correctly maintained. Now we're ready to start looping through the data. Each time we get a record from the database we need to create a new element in the DOM, this time called `<Author>`:

```
Do While Not rsAuthors.EOF
   Dim oAuthor
   Set oAuthor = oParser.createElement("Author")
```

Note that a common mistake when new to using the DOM is to assume that the node we have just created is attached to something; it isn't! Although you have to call the element creation function via the parser object, the node is essentially free floating. We will attach it to the `<Authors>` node at the end of the loop when it has been completely configured.

The first thing to do with the `<Author>` element is to set its `authorCiteID` attribute. Note that the `setAttribute()` function will fail if the value in the database is `NULL`, so normally we would check for `NULL` first. However, in this situation we know that since this is the table key it will always be present:

```
   oAuthor.setAttribute "authorCiteID", rsAuthors("authorCiteID")
```

The next four fields in the record are represented by elements in the XML document. To make it easier to add elements to the `<Author>` node we've added a function called `FieldToElement()` which is detailed below:

```
   FieldToElement oAuthor, rsAuthors, "FirstName"
   FieldToElement oAuthor, rsAuthors, "MI"
   FieldToElement oAuthor, rsAuthors, "LastName"
   FieldToElement oAuthor, rsAuthors, "Biographical"
```

The `Portrait` field in the database maps to an attribute called `picLink` on an empty element called `<Portrait>`. Unlike with the `authorCiteID` attribute, we need to check that the database value is not `NULL` since it will abort our loop if it is. If it is `NULL` we will not bother creating a `<Portrait>` element:

```
      If Not IsNull(rsAuthors("Portrait")) Then
         Dim oNode

         Set oNode = oParser.createElement("Portrait")
         oNode.setAttribute "picLink", rsAuthors("Portrait")
         oAuthor.appendChild(oNode)
         Set oNode = Nothing
      End If
```

Before completing the loop and moving to the next record we append the `<Author>` node to the `<Authors>` node:

```
      oAuthors.appendChild(oAuthor)
      rsAuthors.MoveNext
      Set oAuthor = Nothing
   Loop
```

Once we have finished adding nodes to the `<Authors>` node, we can copy the node list we have built up into the XML document container of the parser object we created earlier. We need to do this, because at this point our `oAuthors` object is just a node that contains a set of nodes, and not a full XML document:

```
   rsAuthors.Close
   dbConn.Close
   Set oParser.documentElement = oAuthors
```

Once we have created our DOM we need to send it to the browser. We precede it with the necessary information to show that it's an XML document, and then use the DOM `xml` property that writes the textual equivalent of its internal structure. The DOM takes care of opening and closing tags, quotes on attributes and so on:

```
%>
<?xml version="1.0" encoding="UTF-8"?>
<%
   Response.Write oParser.xml
```

Finally, here is the function that we mentioned earlier which makes it easier to create nodes from fields in a recordset, and add them to another node. As with the `picLink` attribute, we don't bother creating anything if the value in the database is `NULL`. This is worth doing if the data set is large, since there could well be many empty elements which would take up space. However, we should only do this if we know that the DTD for the document allows the element to not exist if it is empty. In this case it does:

```
   Sub FieldToElement(oTargetNode, rs, sField)
      If Not IsNull(rs(sField)) Then
         Dim oTempNode : Set oTempNode = oParser.createElement(sField)
         oTempNode.text = rs(sField)
```

```
            oTargetNode.appendChild(oTempNode)
            Set oTempNode = Nothing
         End If
      End Sub
   %>
```

Adding the Query

The code we have just written simply outputs all the authors as XML, but uses the DOM rather than writing our own tags. In other words, we haven't added any additional functionality to what we had before. However, now that the data is in the DOM, we can do anything with it that we would do with XML. In particular, we can now add our XSL query statement.

The additional code is highlighted, and comes after we have converted the data from the database into a DOM. Only then can we apply the XSL statement:

```
<?xml version="1.0" encoding="UTF-8"?>
<%
   Dim sXSL
   sXSL = Request.QueryString("xsl")
   If IsEmpty(sXSL) Then
      Response.Write oParser.xml
   Else
      Set oNodeList = oParser.documentElement.selectNodes(sXSL)
```

If there was no query passed by the caller then we return the entire results set. However, if there is a query we use the `selectNodes` statement to apply a filter. The `selectNodes` statement can be applied to any node, so we could have written:

```
      Set oNodeList = oAuthors.selectNodes(sXSL)
```

However, because the `<Authors>` node that we have built up is not a proper XML document there is no root node, and queries that begin with a / – meaning start at the root and work from there – end up returning nothing. We therefore query the document element of the DOM object we created earlier, into which we stored the `<Authors>` node.

Outputting the Results

The result of a node selection in XSL is not necessarily a valid XML document. For example, the XSL query:

```
/Authors/Author/LastName
```

would return the following nodes:

```
<LastName>Mohr</LastName>
<LastName>Kingsley-Hughes</LastName>
<LastName>Boumphrey</LastName>
```

This would be invalid as an XML document since there is no root node – or *more than one* root node, depending on which way you look at it!

However, we can't simply wrap everything in an <Authors> node like we did before, because the results might not be authors. The previous query wrapped in the <Authors> tag would look like this:

```
<Authors>
   <LastName>Mohr</LastName>
   <LastName>Kingsley-Hughes</LastName>
   <LastName>Boumphrey</LastName>
</Authors>
```

which would break our DTD or schema, since <LastName> is only supposed to be a child of <Author> not <Authors>. Of course we could say that our search only returns authors, and stick to putting the results inside an <Authors> element, but this greatly reduces the flexibility of our script. For example, if someone wanted to find a list of all the references to pictures in the database so that they could make up a portrait gallery, they could use the following query:

```
/Authors/Author/Portrait[@picLink]
```

This query asks our server to find all <Portrait> elements that have an attribute called picLink which is set to something, that is, it is not empty. In addition, each <Portrait> element returned must be the child of an <Author> element, which in turn must be the child of the <Authors> element. That query would return the following results:

```
   <Portrait picLink =
      "http://webdev.wrox.co.uk/resources/authors/mohrs.gif"/>
   <Portrait picLink =
      "http://webdev.wrox.co.uk/resources/authors/boumphreyf.gif"/>
```

If we can't wrap it in <Authors>, and we can't just make up new container elements like <LastNames> and <Portraits> at will (because they also would fail validation), then we might consider wrapping the data in something generic. For example, we could design our own wrapper, and perhaps include in it information about how the data being returned was arrived at:

```
<wr:ResultsWrapper wr:query="/Authors/Author/LastName"
                   xmlns:wr="wroxresultsnamespace">
   <LastName>Mohr</LastName>
   <LastName>Kingsley-Hughes</LastName>
   <LastName>Boumphrey</LastName>
</wr:ResultsWrapper>
```

We might even go further and add timestamps and other information that help in handling the query results. In the next section we will look briefly at some methods of packaging up this data. For now we will return just the data requested – which means that we can possibly return results that are not technically XML documents – for example, there may be more than one element at the root of the document. Let's finish our script by writing out the results of our XSL query:

```
    Else
        Set oNodeList = oParser.documentElement.selectNodes(sXSL)
        Dim ix
        For ix = 0 To oNodeList.length - 1
            Response.Write oNodeList.item(ix).xml
        Next
    End if

    Sub FieldToElement(oTargetNode, rs, sField)
```

Note the use of a loop this time. Since we may have a number of top-level nodes, we need to loop through the resultant node list and output the XML for each node, rather than simply outputting the XML for the entire tree.

Optimization

The technique we have just outlined is extremely inefficient. It requires us to read all authors before we discover that we only want one of them. In our simple scenario this is no big deal, but in a database of thousands of items it could be very slow.

To make things more efficient we should take advantage of the querying capabilities of the underlying database, and combine them with the abilities of XSLT and XPath. Given that we are mainly looking at relational databases, we'll have a quick look at how XPath statements can be mapped to SQL statements. For example:

```
Author[@MI]
```

is a request for all authors that have an attribute called `MI`. This can straightforwardly be mapped to:

```
SELECT * FROM Author WHERE MI <> "";
```

Selecting a single author would be:

```
Author[LastName = 'Mohr']
```

Which could be mapped to:

```
SELECT * FROM Author WHERE LastName = 'Mohr';
```

XPath also allows nodes to be selected based on the values in nodes in other parts of the tree. For example, using the book catalog schema from Chapter 7, if you wanted to select all the books that were associated with a particular publisher you would need the following XPath query:

```
/Catalog/Book[imprint/@ID=/Catalog/Publisher[CorporateName="Wrox Press
Ltd."]/Imprints/Imprint/@shortImprintName]
```

This says that we want all <Book> elements that have imprint/@ID set to the same value as the shortImprintName attribute in the <Imprint> element in the <Imprints> element in the <Publisher> whose <CorporateName> is "Wrox Press Ltd.".

Modeling the hierarchical statements in SQL is straightforward. Recall that we can use simple join statements to retrieve parent/child relationships, so /Catalog/Book would just become:

```
SELECT *
   FROM Catalog, Book
   WHERE pk_Catalog = fk_Catalog
```

The part of the query that requests a specific publisher:

```
/Catalog/Publisher[CorporateName="Wrox Press Ltd."]
```

is not much more difficult:

```
SELECT *
   FROM Catalog, Publisher
   WHERE pk_Catalog = fk_Catalog
   AND CorporateName = "Wrox Press Ltd."
```

(This assumes we know that the text-only element <CorporateName> has been stored in a column and not a table. We will look at this later.)

The filter on Catalog/Book is more difficult. For this we need to introduce another aspect of the SELECT statement – **subqueries**. Subqueries allow the results of one query to be used as a list of values to test against in another query. In our case, we want to build up a list of all the shortImprintName values and then see which ones match with the ID values of the imprint elements, before then using *that* list to find the books that refer to that imprint. We can achieve this as follows:

```
SELECT *
   FROM Book
   WHERE imprint IN (
      SELECT *
      FROM Imprint
      WHERE ID IN (
         SELECT shortImprintName
         FROM Imprint
      )
   )
```

Note that I have conveniently 'omitted' the other filter we established earlier that selects only one publisher. However, I'm sure you can see that it is possible to model XPath queries with SQL queries. There are two problems though. The first is that XPath is not yet a standard, so anything you code now could change. The second is that you would need to parse the XPath statements and be able to understand the whole syntax. Quite how these issues become resolved is not yet clear, but we may well see the emergence of XPath parsers that sit on top of specific database layers, in much the same way as ODBC sits on top of different underlying data storage formats.

Conclusion

XML provides an extremely powerful means of exchanging data between different systems. This is particularly useful for databases since data interchange can take place between database types that are completely different.

While the data can be represented in a common format there is (as yet) no accepted standard for retrieval. Although not as flexible as we would desire, specifying our queries in XPath illustrates the potential of using a standard query syntax.

Standards You Might Need

We have already discussed the different possible query syntaxes for selecting XML data. Alongside the question of standards for queries, we also discussed the issue of how to return the results of the data. A couple of standards provide pointers as to how this might be done.

Fragment Interchange

The simplest and probably most powerful is the fragment interchange proposal at http://www.w3.org/TR/WD-xml-fragment. This proposal provides a mechanism by which 'loose nodes' might be given some context. We saw this in Chapter 8, but let's put it to use here and look at an example: retrieving of the bibliography of one author. We established code earlier to allow us to use the following syntax:

```
http://www.wrox.com/xmlAuthors.asp?xsl=//Author[LastName='Mohr']/Biographical
```

to retrieve:

```
<Biographical>
   Stephen began programming in high school and is now a senior software
   systems architect with Omicron Consulting, he designs and develops systems
   using C++, Java, JavaScript, COM, and various internetworking standards and
   protocols.
</Biographical>
```

The fragment interchange proposal suggests that we create a separate document that provides the context:

```
<f:fcs xmlns:f="http://www.w3.org/XML/Fragment/1.0"
       xmlns="http://www.wrox.com/authors.xdr">
   <Authors>
      <Author authorCiteID="1">
         <FirstName />
         <MI />
         <LastName />
         <f:fragbody fragbodyref="xmlAuthors.asp?xsl=//Author
                                 [LastName='Mohr']/Biographical"/>
         <Portrait />
      </Author>
```

```
        <Author authorCiteID="2" />
        <Author authorCiteID="3" />
      </Authors>
   </f:fcs>
```

Note that this fragment interchange document shows elements that are on the same level as elements that are needed for context, but it doesn't waste space with the full contents of those elements. So, you can see that all of the elements in the relevant <Author> element are named, but contain no data. Equally, all the other <Author> elements that represent other authors in the database have place-holders with no contents, although attributes are always passed for any element, no matter what position it is at. The data that is the result of the query is referenced by a URI at the position <fragbody>. To make this mechanism work you would need to create a script that outputs XML in the above format, and then refer to it with something like:

```
http://www.wrox.com/fcsAuthors.asp?xsl=//Author[LastName='Mohr']/Biographical
```

This fragment in turn refers to the <xmlAuthors> script we had earlier.

> *Previous drafts of the fragment interchange proposal allowed the fragment and its context to be packaged in the same XML document. This can still be done, but the proposal does not lay down a standard for this anymore. Instead it states that a packaging workgroup will address the issue.*

SOAP and XML-RPC

Another means by which we may return results is through SOAP or XML-RPC which are discussed in more depth in Chapter 11. Both of these protocols provide methods for wrapping up the results of calls to a server, although they don't inherently contain context information. It would be a simple matter to add this to your return documents.

Book Catalog Sample

Enough theory! We've established that databases can store XML and that we can exchange data from different databases by going via XML. It's time to start implementing the book catalog as a database.

In the following sample we will assume Wrox Press already has a relational database of author information, but that we need to create new databases for the publisher and book information. For the latter we will use the schema to define a relational database table structure.

Handling Existing Data and Applications

We'll imagine that long before XML was a twinkle in the eye of SGML, we had a database of the names and addresses of authors, and some notes about them. For the purposes of this illustration I have simply created an address book database using one of the database creation wizards in Microsoft Access. The sample data entry form has two pages, as follows:

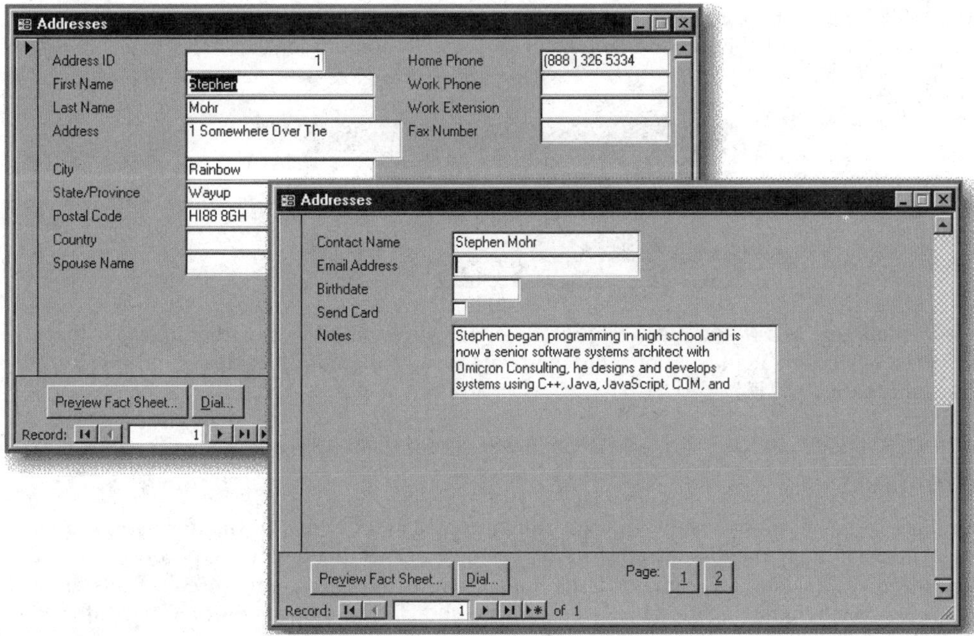

There are a number of points to make about this example scenario. The first is that the data *already exists.* This is important to take on board when planning a project that may be based on XML. Trying to get everyone in your company to move their storage medium from an existing database application to XML could be very tricky, particularly if there is a lot of commitment to that storage medium in the form of useful applications. Also, because of these applications, handling XML may not be the best way to deal with the information anyway. In this case we have a simple data entry form, where new records can easily be added and existing data edited. Should the user really be asked to edit this instead?:

```
<authors>
   <Author authorCiteID="1">
      <FirstName>Stephen</FirstName>
      <LastName>Mohr</LastName>
      <Address>1 Somewhere Over The</Address>
      <City>Rainbow</City>
      <State>WayUp</State>
      <PostalCode>HI88 8GH</PostalCode>
      <HomePhone>(888) 326 5334</HomePhone>
      <Notes>
         Stephen began programming in high school and is now a senior software
         systems architect with Omicron Consulting, he designs and develops
         systems using C++, Java, JavaScript, COM, and various internetworking
         standards and protocols.
      </Notes>
   </Author>
   <Author authorCiteID="2">
      <FirstName>Kathie</FirstName>
      <LastName>Kingsley-Hughes</LastName>
      ...
      <Notes>Kathie is the MD of Kingsley-Hughes Development Ltd, a...</Notes>
</authors>
```

Even if our users are given XML editors to maintain this data – and there are some good ones on the market – it still does not have the range of features that even our simple Microsoft Access form has. For example, clicking on the dial button while the cursor is in the home phone number field, would result in the following dialog box:

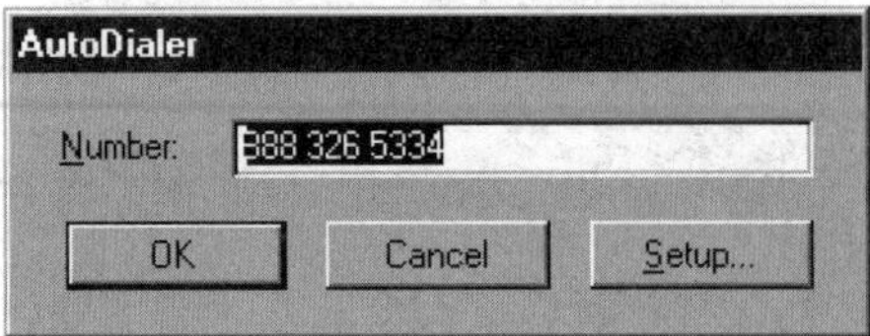

To move the data to XML would mean weakening our application, not strengthening it. In short, we already have a perfectly adequate application and data storage medium. Lets leave it there, but see if we can extract this data as XML.

XML Recordsets

The first thing we need to establish when exporting legacy data as XML, is what format it should be in. We saw earlier that many database products have been extended to allow the export of data as a set of relational records. The data is still an XML document, but the XML grammar used reflects the storage of that data in a relational database. Here's an example showing how our author address information might be exported to this type of structure:

```
<RecordSet name="authors">
   <Record name="Author">
      <Column name="authorCiteID" value="1" />
      <Column name="FirstName" value="Stephen" />
      <Column name="LastName" value="Mohr" />
      <Column name="Address" value="1 Somewhere Over The" />
      <Column name="City" value="Rainbow" />
      <Column name="State" value="WayUp" />
      <Column name="PostalCode" value="HI88 8GH" />
      <Column name="HomePhone" value="(888) 326 5334" />
      <Column name="Notes" value="Stephen began..." />
   </Record>
   <Record name="Author">
      <Column name="authorCiteID" value="2" />
      <Column name="FirstName" value="Kathie" />
      <Column name="LastName" value="Kingsley-Hughes" />
      ...
      <Column name="Notes" value="Kathie is..." />
   </Record>
</RecordSet>
```

To differentiate this from exporting XML with structure, we will call this **XML recordsets**. It is useful to us – just! – mainly because it is in XML. Once we have our data in XML we can obviously use all the tools that we have learned about in this book to manipulate that XML; we might use XSLT to transform the information into a set of tables in HTML, or we may change the column names so that the data can be inserted into another database.

But let's be honest, there are major weaknesses with this approach. The most obvious is that the only validation we can perform is to ensure that a `<RecordSet>` element contains only `Record` elements, and they in turn only contain `<Column>` elements. If we were hoping to transfer this information to another server to be placed in its database, that server would have no easy way of knowing that the highlighted column should not appear here:

```
<Record name="Author">
   <Column name="authorCiteID" value="1" />
   <Column name="FirstName" value="Stephen" />
   <Column name="LastName" value="Mohr" />
   <Column name="Address" value="1 Somewhere Over The" />
   <Column name="City" value="Rainbow" />
   <Column name="State" value="WayUp" />
   <Column name="PostalCode" value="HI88 8GH" />
   <Column name="HomePhone" value="(888) 326 5334" />
   <Column name="InvoiceNumber" value="1223" />
   <Column name="Notes" value="Stephen began..." />
</Record>
```

Of course, we could include information with the data that says what columns to expect. Microsoft's Active Data Objects (ADO) takes this approach. The following shows how the data in our Access database would be exported if the new features of ADO were used to persist a recordset:

Microsoft's ADO is now at version 2.5. More information is available at http://www.microsoft.com/data/ado.

```
<xml xmlns:s='uuid:BDC6E3F0-6DA3-11d1-A2A3-00AA00C14882'
     xmlns:dt='uuid:C2F41010-65B3-11d1-A29F-00AA00C14882'
     xmlns:rs='urn:schemas-microsoft-com:rowset'
     xmlns:z='#RowsetSchema'>
<s:Schema id='RowsetSchema'>
   <s:ElementType name='row' content='eltOnly'>
      <s:attribute type="authorCiteID" />
      <s:attribute type="FirstName" />
      <s:attribute type="LastName" />
      <s:attribute type="Address" />
      <s:attribute type="City" />
      <s:attribute type="State" />
      <s:attribute type="PostalCode" />
      <s:attribute type="HomePhone" />
      <s:attribute type="Notes" />
      <s:extends type='rs:rowbase'/>
   </s:ElementType>
   <s:AttributeType name='authorCiteID' rs:number='1' rs:nullable='true'
                    rs:write='true'>
      <s:datatype dt:type='string' dt:maxLength='255'/>
```

```
    </s:AttributeType>
    <s:AttributeType name='FirstName' rs:number='2' rs:nullable='true'
                     rs:write='true'>
      <s:datatype dt:type='string' dt:maxLength='255'/>
    </s:AttributeType>
    <s:AttributeType name='LastName' rs:number='3' rs:nullable='true'
                     rs:write='true'>
      <s:datatype dt:type='string' dt:maxLength='255'/>
    </s:AttributeType>
    <s:AttributeType name='Address' rs:number='4' rs:nullable='true'
                     rs:write='true'>
      <s:datatype dt:type='string' dt:maxLength='255'/>
    </s:AttributeType>
    <s:AttributeType name='City' rs:number='5' rs:nullable='true'
                     rs:write='true'>
      <s:datatype dt:type='string' dt:maxLength='255'/>
    </s:AttributeType>
    <s:AttributeType name='State' rs:number='6' rs:nullable='true'
                     rs:write='true'>
      <s:datatype dt:type='string' dt:maxLength='255'/>
    </s:AttributeType>
    <s:AttributeType name='PostalCode' rs:number='7' rs:nullable='true'
                     rs:write='true'>
      <s:datatype dt:type='string' dt:maxLength='255'/>
    </s:AttributeType>
    <s:AttributeType name='HomePhone' rs:number='8' rs:nullable='true'
                     rs:write='true'>
      <s:datatype dt:type='string' dt:maxLength='255'/>
    </s:AttributeType>
    <s:AttributeType name='Notes' rs:number='9' rs:nullable='true'
                     rs:write='true'>
      <s:datatype dt:type='string' dt:maxLength='255'/>
    </s:AttributeType>
  </s:Schema>
  <rs:data>
    <z:row authorCiteID="1" FirstName="Stephen" LastName="Mohr"
           Address="1 Somewhere Over The" City="Rainbow" State="WayUp"
           PostalCode="HI88 8GH" HomePhone="(888) 326 5334"
           Notes="Stephen began..." />
  </rs:data>
  </xml>
```

But even with this extra information we still have a 'flat' version of the data in our database; we have represented the data as a recordset, rather than with some structure. That said, this technique will probably find a great deal of use in situations where data is being transferred to other relational databases. Since all RDBMSs can converse in terms of tables, rows and columns, they will all be able to understand this format. With the additional information relating to how the columns should be defined provided by the schema element, this is quite a powerful technique. The code that uses ADO to generate this output is simple too (the following is Visual Basic):

```
Set con = New ADODB.Connection
con.ConnectionString = "DSN=XMLPRO;"
con.Open
```

```
Set rs = con.Execute("Select * FROM Addresses")

rs.save "AuthorsRS", adPersistXML
```

The advantages of this simplicity may make it the answer for your application.

XML Data: Using Transformations

Assuming, however, that we need to impose some structure on the flattened information, the simplest way to get structure into our data is to transform the output. An example of an XSLT stylesheet that would convert this 'flat' database book format to the format used by the book catalog sample (if we wanted to merge data from a flat structure into our structured catalog) would be as follows:

```
<xsl:stylesheet version="1.0"
                xmlns:xsl="http://www.w3.org/1999/XSL/Transform"
                xmlns:z='#RowsetSchema'>
   <xsl:template match="z:row">
      <xsl:element name="Author">
         <xsl:attribute name="authorCiteID">
            <xsl:value-of select="@authorCiteID" />
         </xsl:attribute>
         <xsl:element name="FirstName">
            <xsl:value-of select="@FirstName" />
         </xsl:element>
         <xsl:element name="LastName">
            <xsl:value-of select="@LastName" />
         </xsl:element>
         <xsl:element name="Biographical">
            <xsl:value-of select="@Notes" />
         </xsl:element>
      </xsl:element>
   </xsl:template>
</xsl:stylesheet>
```

The style sheet is simply taking each of the attributes from `<z:row>` and outputting them as elements, albeit with different names. The result of this transformation is the following simple XML file:

```
<Author authorCiteID="1">
   <FirstName>Stephen</FirstName>
   <LastName>Mohr</LastName>
   <Biographical>Stephen began...</Biographical>
</Author>
```

In a small system there is probably little to choose between this technique and just writing different scripts for the different targets for the data without going via the intermediary XML recordset. However, in larger systems that need to provide the information in many formats for many audiences, this technique might well be useful. For example, if we wanted to export the information is such a way that it could be understood by a completely different system we might either export it in the 'flat' format and let the target system deal with it, or we might produce another style sheet and use that to transform the 'flat' data once again.

Since these types of mappings are invariably one-to-one, it would even be possible to devise a document structure that says how to map records and fields to the required schema format. Style sheets like the one above could then be generated automatically and even provide information to allow the underlying database to be modified.

XML Data: Using Scripts

Another way to see the information as structured XML is to generate a list of authors as an XML page on a web server. We saw how to do this in an earlier section, so I'll only show the main loop here, with a small change to allow the author database we already have to be used:

```
<Authors>
<%
   Do While Not rs.EOF
%>
   <Author authorCiteID="<%=rs("authorCiteID")%>">
      <FirstName><%=rs("FirstName")%></FirstName>
      <MI><%=rs("MI")%></MI>
      <LastName><%=rs("LastName")%></LastName>
      <Biographical><%=rs("Notes")%></Biographical>
      <Portrait picLink="<%=rs("Portrait")%>" />
   </Author>
<%
      rs.MoveNext
   Loop
%>
</Authors>
```

Conclusion

Extracting data from legacy systems presents us with a number of problems. Although the neatest solution is to retrieve the data in a common format – an XML representation of relational structure – and then transform it to the desired format, this may well present performance issues. If the targets for the data are few, then specifically written scripts may well be the answer. If there are a large number of destination formats for the data then it may be best to cache the intermediate XML representation of the data and then only transform that as required.

The Book Catalog Schema

We've now established how to use the already existing author data, but we still need to represent the rest of the book catalog in a database. In this section we'll work through some of the key parts of the book catalogue schema definition, and as we go, we'll draw out some of the key points for building a relational database that would hold data that conforms to that schema. During the course of doing this we will establish some rules that we can later use to automate the process of creating a relational database from a schema. Finally we will discuss the main features of the code that will carry out that automatic conversion, the full listing being available on the source code, downloadable from http://www.wrox.com.

Defining The Catalog Database

In this discussion we will often convert each schema definition to a node structure. I will represent the node structures using the following simple conventions:

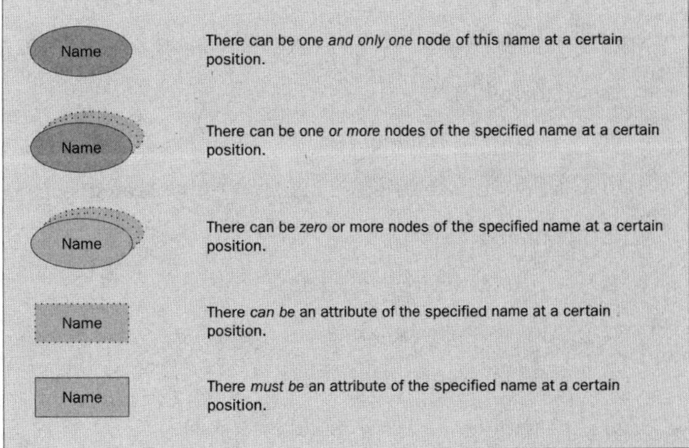

Name
There can be one *and only one* node of this name at a certain position.
Name
There can be one *or more* nodes of the specified name at a certain position.
Name
There can be *zero* or more nodes of the specified name at a certain position.
Name
There *can be* an attribute of the specified name at a certain position.
Name
There *must be* an attribute of the specified name at a certain position.

Structure is indicated by the position of the nodes. For example, the following would indicate that a node of type A has a required attribute called B, one node of type C, and zero or more nodes of type D:

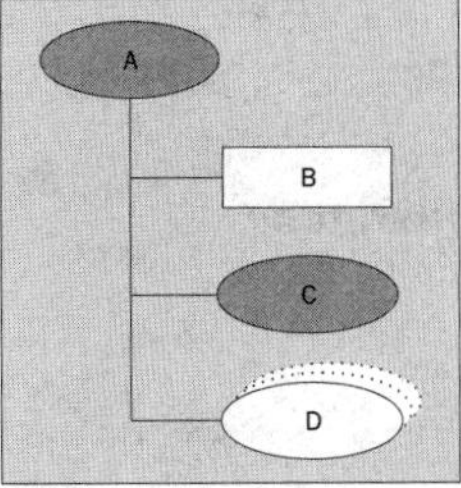

Examples of XML documents that would conform to this node structure include the following:

```
<A B="xyz">
   <C />
</A>
```

```
<A B="xyz">
   <C />
   <D />
</A>
```

```
<A B="xyz">
   <C />
   <D />
   <D />
   <D />
   <D />
   <D />
</A>
```

Lets begin to convert the schema definition to a relational database by drawing out some of the key features of schemas in general – and obviously XML documents – which are:

- Hierarchy
- Attributes
- Text-only elements
- Multiple occurrences of a text-only element
- Enumeration
- Attributes with the `id` data type
- Elements as containers
- `minOccurs` attributes
- Attributes with specific data types
- Attributes with the `idref` data type
- Attributes with the `idrefs` data type

Hierarchy

The book catlog schema from Chapter 7 begins as follows:

```
<?xml version="1.0"?>
<Schema name="PubCatalog.xdr"
        xmlns="urn:schemas-microsoft-com:xml-data"
        xmlns:dt="urn:schemas-microsoft-com:datatypes"
        xmlns:athr="x-schema:authors.xml">

   <ElementType name="Catalog" content="eltOnly" order="seq">
      <element type="Publisher" minOccurs="1" maxOccurs="*"/>
      <element type="Thread" minOccurs="0" maxOccurs="*"/>
      <element type="Book" minOccurs="1" maxOccurs="*"/>
   </ElementType>
```

This describes a `<Catalog>` element that can only contain other elements. This means that it is not allowable to have other text which is inside the element `<Catalog>`but which is not inside the elements that `<Catalog>` contains. (You'll remember from Chapter 7 that this means that `<Catalog>` cannot contain **mixed content**.) This greatly simplifies our database implementation.

The elements that `<Catalog>` can contain are of type `<Publisher>`, `<Thread>` and `<Book>`. All of these elements can appear any number of times, but there must be at least one `<Publisher>`, and at least one `<Book>`. Examples of XML documents that could be represented by this schema definition include:

```
<Catalog>
   <Publisher />
   <Book />
</Catalog>
```

```
<Catalog>
   <Publisher />
   <Publisher />
   <Thread />
   <Thread />
   <Book />
   <Book />
</Catalog>
```

```
<Catalog>
   <Publisher />
   <Thread />
   <Thread />
   <Thread />
   <Book />
   <Book />
   <Book />
   <Book />
   <Book />
</Catalog>
```

The node structure for this is:

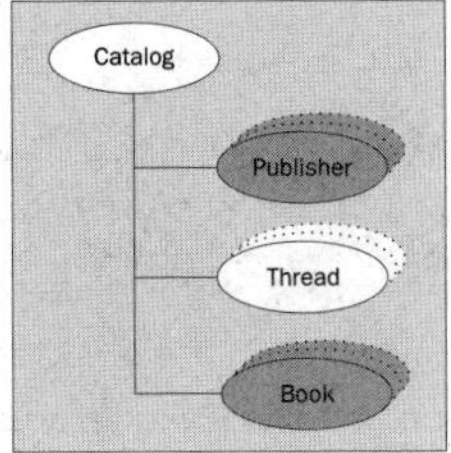

You will recall from the discussion on features of relational databases that this can easily be represented in our by four tables. You would be justified in saying "Why not three?", since there is only ever one `<Catalog>` and we could imply the relationship between the other tables and `<Catalog>`. However, since we want to produce a solution that can be easily generalized – and there is also the possibility that our database could expand in the future – we will create a `Catalog` table.

The hierarchical relationship between these tables can be established by creating joins between the lower tables and the containing table. For example, to make a connection between a `Publisher` record in the `Publisher` table and a `Catalog` record (in this case the only one) we would need the following:

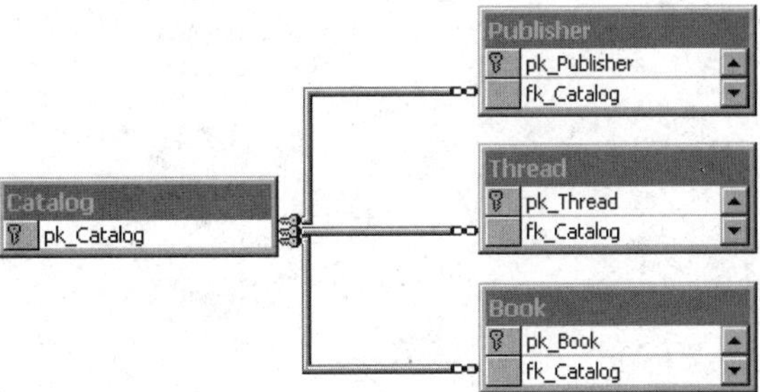

To find all the <Book> children of a <Catalog> we would simply query the Book table for all rows where the fk_Catalog column is set to the value of the <Catalog> we are searching for.

We are now in a position to define our first two rules. (Rule 1 is only to save us repeating ourselves in later rules):

- **Rule 1** – whenever we create a new table, create a primary key with the same name as the table, but with a prefix of pk_. This column should be an automatically-incremented integer.
- **Rule 2** – for each element node type, create a table with the same name as the element, then:
  - If the element node is a child node create a column with the same name as the parent element node, but with a prefix of fk_.
  - Create a foreign key relationship between the column just created and the column in the table with the same name as the parent element node, where the column name is the parent element name prefixed by pk_.

Attributes

The first of the three tables we need is the Publisher table. The schema definition tells us the information we need for the table:

```
<AttributeType name="isbn" required="yes"/>
<ElementType name="Publisher" content="eltOnly" order="seq">
   <description>Publisher section</description>
   <attribute type="isbn"/>
   <element type="CorporateName"/>
   <element type="Address" minOccurs="1" maxOccurs="*"/>
   <element type="Imprints"/>
   <element type="athr:Author" minOccurs="0" maxOccurs="*"/>
</ElementType>
```

As with the <Catalog> element, a <Publisher> element can only contain other elements – it can contain no mixed content. The elements are <CorporateName>, <Address>, <Imprints>, and <Author>:

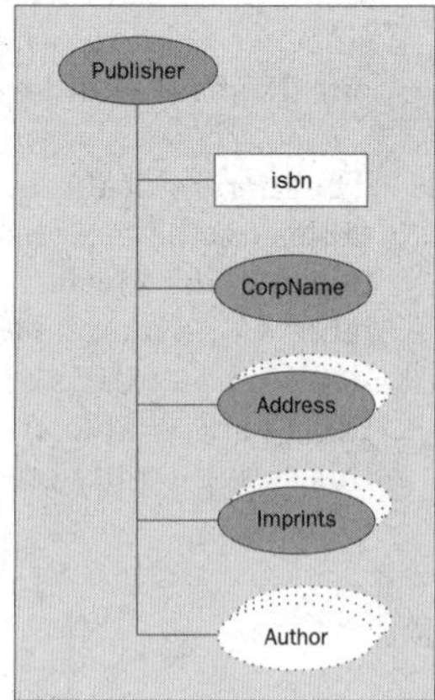

Applying our hierarchy rules we establish a further four tables and establish relationships between them. However, `<Publisher>` also has an attribute node, `isbn`. This can very easily be represented as a field in the `Publisher` table, and we'll give it the same name as the node. Note that our node structure says that the attribute node is required, so we should make it a required field on our table. We do this by not allowing `NULL` values, and can therefore define this column as follows:

Column Name	Datatype	Length	Precision	Scale	Allow Nulls	Default Value
isbn	varchar	255	0	0	☐	

We can now also define another rule:

- **Rule 3** – for each attribute node:
    - Create a column with the same name as the attribute node.
    - If the attribute is required then the column should not allow `NULL` values.

Text-only Elements

The next element that a `<Publisher>` element can contain is a `<CorporateName>`, defined as follows:

```
<ElementType name="CorporateName" content="textOnly"/>
```

As required by our first rule, we would ordinarily create a table called `CorporateName`. After the keys were set up by the rule, a one-to-one relationship between the `Publisher` table and the `CorporateName` table would exist, as follows:

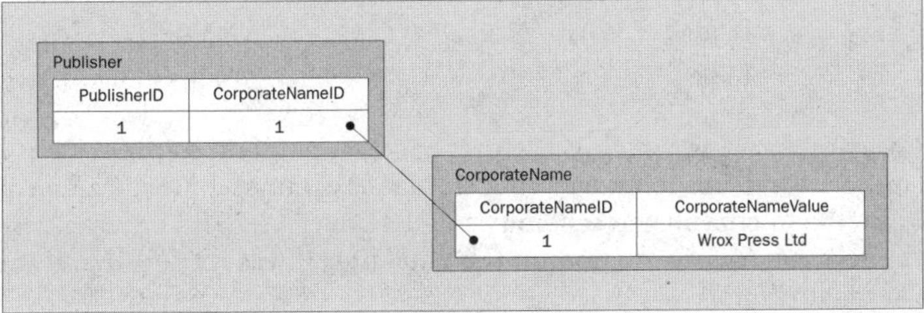

From a database viewpoint, an extra table for `CorporateName` is unnecessary, representing **over normalization**. This means that data has been taken out to another table which could just as easily sit in a column in the `<Publisher>` table. From an XML stand-point too, the extra table seems unnecessary. The content of the `<CorporateName>` element is only text – it cannot contain any children – so could just as easily be stored in a column on the `Publisher` table. Our `Publisher` table could therefore be more efficiently expressed as follows:

	Column Name	Datatype	Length	Precision	Scale	Allow Nulls	Default Value	Identity	Identity Seed	Identity Increment
🔑	pk_Publisher	int	4	10	0	☐		☑	1	1
	fk_Catalog	int	4	10	0	☐		☐		
	isbn	varchar	255	0	0	☐		☐		
	CorporateName	varchar	255	0	0	☑		☐		

This improves performance over having a table for each element, since it is not necessary to create a large number of joins to retrieve the data. To retrieve our `<Publisher>` information we only need the following query:

```
SELECT isbn, CorporateName FROM Publisher;
```

Whereas with a separate table for company names we would need to do the following:

```
SELECT p.isbn AS isbn, cn.CorporateName AS CorporateName
   FROM Publisher AS p, CorporateName AS cn
   WHERE p.CorporateNameID = cn.CorporateNameID;
```

Although this doesn't seem to be that much extra work, when we see the schema for addresses later we will see how complex – and potentially much slower – a query to retrieve a publisher's address would be.

The decision you would have to make when implementing a relational store for XML data is how easy it is to work out which field should be an attribute and which a text-only element. As it stands, the data in the `Publisher` table just described could be exported either as elements:

```
<Publisher>
   <isbn>1-86100</isbn>
   <CorporateName>Wrox Press Ltd.</CorporateName>
</Publisher>
```

or as attributes on an element:

```
<Publisher isbn="1-86100"
           CorporateName="Wrox Press Ltd."/>
```

We have no easy way of knowing which is the preferred output, and so the issue is how best to represent this in our database in such a way that storage is optimal, but we can easily recreate the XML. One technique would be to consult the schema as data is retrieved and before it is written. Another approach would be to use a transformation on the data after it was retrieved and then every field could be brought back as an attribute.

Both of these approaches may work in different situations, and are used by some of the tools described in the relational database section above. A simple approach we will use here is to name the columns in the database in such a way as to make it easy to regain lost information. If attributes are prefixed with `attr_` and text only elements with `elem_` then we should easily be able to tell the difference. We therefore need to modify rule three to include the prefix `attr_`:

- **Rule 3** – for each attribute node:
  - Create a column with the same name as the attribute node, *with the prefix* `attr_`.
  - If the attribute is required then the column should not allow `NULL` values.

We can also include another rule:

- **Rule 4** - if an element node can only contain text then create a column in the parent element table, and give that column the same name as the node, with a prefix of `elem_`.

Multiple Occurrences of a Text-only Element

Although placing text-only elements into a field is a useful optimization, there are situations where it cannot be used. One such situation is when the element can appear more than once. If we continue with the schema we can see that the `<Street>` element can contain only text, but that it can express multiple rows of the street part of an address:

```
<ElementType name="Address" content="eltOnly" order="seq">
   <attribute type="headquarters"/>
   <element type="Street" minOccurs="1" maxOccurs="*"/>
   <element type="City"/>
   <element type="PoliticalDivision"/>
   <element type="Country"/>
   <element type="PostalCode"/>
</ElementType>

<AttributeType name="headquarters"
               dt:type="enumeration"
               dt:values="yes no" />
<ElementType name="Street" content="textOnly"/>
```

Although `<Street>` has no children, the fact that it can have multiple values cannot be implemented in a relational database using one column. We will therefore need to add a table to hold the multiple `<Street>` values. First lets modify Rule four:

- **Rule 4** – if an element node can only contain text, *and has a maximum occurrence of 1*, then create a column in the parent element table, and give that column the same name as the node, with a prefix of `elem_`.

This means that we have all the rules we need to complete the `Address` table – with no `Street` column – which will look as follows:

	Column Name	Datatype	Length	Precision	Scale	Allow Nulls	Default Value	Identity	Identity Seed	Identity Increment
🔑	pk_Address	int	4	10	0	☐		☑	1	1
	fk_Publisher	int	4	10	0	☐		☐		
	attr_headquarters	varchar	255	0	0	☑		☐		
	elem_City	varchar	255	0	0	☑		☐		
	elem_PoliticalDivision	varchar	255	0	0	☑		☐		
	elem_Country	varchar	255	0	0	☑		☐		
	elem_PostalCode	varchar	255	0	0	☑		☐		

However, there is one more issue before we create our `Street` table. Up until now, all the tables that we have created to hold element information have simply referred to the parent element, and possibly had attributes. The `<Street>` element however, has no attributes but can contain its own data. It will therefore need a column in the table to hold it. But since the data is not an attribute or a text-only child element there is no name that we can give the data. In a relational database each column must have a name, so we'll call it `pcdata`. That is, after all, what it is, and will allow us to spot it easily when we are exporting the data as XML.

The `Street` table can now be defined as:

	Column Name	Datatype	Length	Precision	Scale	Allow Nulls	Default Value	Identity	Identity Seed	Identity Increment
🔑	pk_Street	int	4	10	0	☐		☑	1	1
	fk_Address	int	4	10	0	☐		☐		
	pcdata	varchar	255	0	0	☐		☐		

With this table, the data for the street part of addresses might be:

pk_Street	fk_Address	pcdata
1	1	Arden House
2	1	1102 Warwick Road
3	1	Acocks Green
4	2	1512 North Fremont
5	2	Suite 103

In this example there are two addresses, the first uses street records 1, 2 and 3, while the second uses records 4 and 5. We now need to modify rule two to cope with the situation where elements have their own text content:

- **Rule 2** – for each element node type, create a table with the same name as the element, then:
  - If the element node is a child node create a column with the same name as the parent element node, but with a prefix of `fk_`.
  - Create a foreign key relationship between the column just created and the column in the table with the same name as the parent element node, where the column name is the parent element name prefixed by `pk_`.
  - *If the content type of the element node is text only then create a column with the name* `pcdata`.

Another place where multiple occurrences of an element is defined is in `<RecSubjCategories>`:

```
<ElementType name="RecSubjCategories" content="eltOnly" order="seq">
   <element type="Category"/>
   <element type="Category"/>
   <element type="Category"/>
</ElementType>
<ElementType name="Category" content="textOnly"/>
```

The `<RecSubjCategories>` element itself is easy to model; we simply create a new table. There is some redundancy – since in this situation a `<Category>` can only be attached to one `<Book>` – but we have to retain this seemingly redundant table so that we can rebuild the correct XML structure when required. (We discuss this further below.)

The part that is more difficult to model is that the `<Category>` element occurs three times. This means that we cannot use our usual rules since we can neither create three tables called `Category` – if `Category` elements were not text-only – or create three columns called `Category` in the `RecSubjCategories` table – since `<Category>` is text only.

We already have a rule that if an element occurs more than once it must go in its own table, so we will create a table called `Category`. However, we can see that when we come to write the element processing code we need to:

- Count how many times the element being processed occurs at the current hierarchical level.
- Do not try to create a new table for subsequent occurrences of the same element.

The resulting tables look no different from how they would look if the definition had been as follows:

```
<ElementType name="RecSubjCategories" content="eltOnly" order="seq">
   <element type="Category" minOccurs="1" maxOccurs="*"/>
</ElementType>
<ElementType name="Category" content="textOnly"/>
```

The fact that there should only be three occurrences could be enforced by a trigger.

Note that this rule assumes that the sequence of the categories is not important. If it were important, we could add a position indicator to our SQL DDL to indicate what order the elements were encountered in.

Enumeration

While we were looking at the schema for addresses you may have noticed the `headquarters` attribute which can have only one of two values – `yes` or `no`. One way that we could deal with this would be to create `headquarters` as a boolean field. This could cause problems later though, if another option was introduced such as '`Used To Be`'. Instead, we will try to establish some general requirements for enumeration that we can use in any situation.

First we need to set-up the table that will hold the enumerated values. Let's call it `enum_headquarters` to try to reduce the possibility of the name we choose conflicting with other – genuine – element names:

	Column Name	Datatype	Length	Precision	Scale	Allow Nulls	Default Value	Identity	Identity Seed	Identity Increment
🔑	pk_enum_headquarters	varchar	50	0	0	☐		☐		

The table only needs one column because it only needs to contain the possible values that `headquarters` can have. Since these are unique they can also function as the primary key. The data in the table would be as follows:

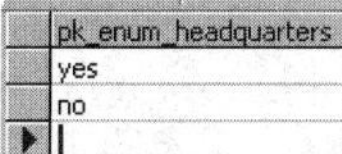

pk_enum_headquarters
yes
no

This gives us our enumeration rules:

- **Rule 5** – for each attribute node that has a type of enumeration, create a table with the same name as the attribute node, with a prefix of `enum_`. Include one variable-length string column with the same name as the attribute node, with a prefix of `pk_enum_`, and a datatype of `variable-length string`. Populate the table with the values in the enumeration.

We need to modify rule three again, to ensure that we don't lose the information about the attribute being enumerated:

- **Rule 3** – for each attribute node:
  - Create a column with the same name as the attribute node:
    – With the prefix `attr_` if the attribute is a normal attribute.
    – *With the prefix* `attr_enum_` *if the attribute is of type enumerated.*
  - If the attribute is required then the column should not allow `NULL` values.

Actually, we're still not finished with rule three! We'll see more of this later...

Attributes With the id Data Type

The next part of the definition of a publisher is a list of all their imprints:

```
<ElementType name="Imprints" content="eltOnly" order="seq">
   <element type="Imprint" minOccurs="1" maxOccurs="*"/>
</ElementType>
<ElementType name="Imprint" content="textOnly">
   <AttributeType name="shortImprintName" dt:type="id"/>
   <attribute type="shortImprintName"/>
</ElementType>
```

Each `<Publisher>` has an element called `<Imprints>` that in turn contains elements called `<Imprint>`. Each of these elements has some text, which is the title of the imprint and an attribute called `shortImprintName` which is of type `id`.

Using rule two we create two new tables, `Imprints` and `Imprint`, each referring to their parent elements. The first table looks like this:

	Column Name	Datatype	Length	Precision	Scale	Allow Nulls	Default Value	Identity	Identity Seed	Identity Increment
🔑	pk_Imprints	int	4	10	0	☐		☑	1	1
	fk_Publisher	int	4	10	0	☐		☐		

The second table – `Imprint` – has text content so requires a `pcdata` column. This is also handled now by rule two. The only thing that is not taken care of is the attribute `shortImprintName`. This attribute is of type `id`, which means that it will be used by another part of the XML document to refer to an element. The schema has in fact been set up in such a way that the `<Thread>` element – which we will see in a moment – can refer to an imprint by citing its short name. As with the enumeration we don't want to lose this information, so we retain it by prefixing the column name with `attr_id_`. We'll modify rule three accordingly:

- **Rule 3** – for each attribute node:
  - Create a column with the same name as the attribute node:
    – With the prefix `attr_` if the attribute is a normal attribute.
    – With the prefix `attr_enum_` if the attribute is of type enumerated.
    – *With the prefix* `attr_id_` *if the attribute is of type* `id`.
  - If the attribute is required then the column should not allow `NULL` values.

The `Imprint` table therefore looks like this:

Column Name	Datatype	Length	Precision	Scale	Allow Nulls	Default Value	Identity	Identity Seed	Identity Increment
pk_Imprint	int	4	10	0	☐		☑	1	1
fk_Imprints	int	4	10	0	☐		☐		
attr_id_shortImprintName	varchar	255	0	0	☐		☐		
pcdata	varchar	255	0	0	☐		☐		

Elements As Containers

Note that we have introduced some redundancy here that we cannot avoid. If we were designing this database with no view to exporting the data as XML then we would not need the `Imprints` table, since it only allows a number of imprints from the `Imprint` table to be connected to the `Publisher` table. A table structured like this one would normally only be used if we wanted each publisher to have a number of imprint collections, but in our schema each publisher has only one. If we represent this database structure from the standpoint of nodes, we are saying that there is essentially no difference between the following two structures:

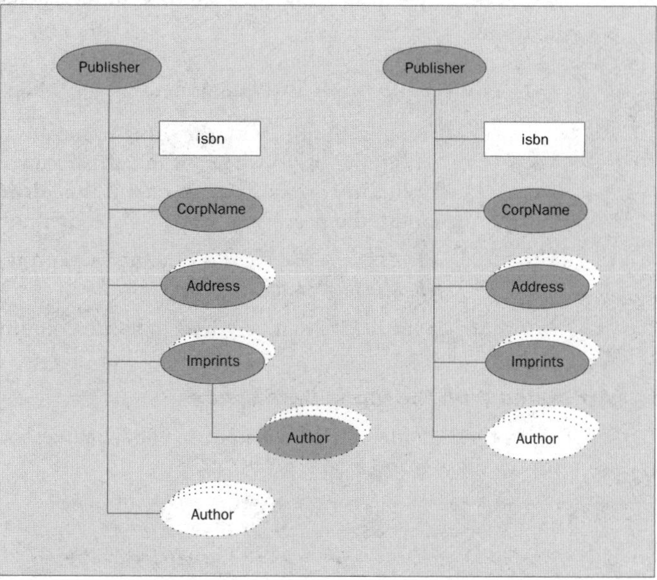

This is because `Imprints` has no data of its own – it is simply a container for other data. However, although we want to try to make our relational database as efficient as possible, we will have to leave this table in, and live with the unnecessary extra join. Otherwise when we export the XML we would have no way of knowing that that there is a containing element between `<Publisher>` and each `<Imprint>`.

minOccurs Attribute

In the `<Author>` element the element `MI` can be `NULL`. This is because `minOccurs` is set to zero in the schema, meaning that the element can be completely omitted if desired. Elements that cannot be omitted have been given a default value of an empty string, which is different to `NULL`. When we are exporting our data we can check to see if it's `NULL`, and if it is we won't bother emitting the element. Otherwise, even if the field is empty it should still be output. We'll add a rule for this:

- **Rule 6** – if an element has a `minOccurs` value of zero then make the column nullable.

Attributes With Specific Data Types

The last of the top-level elements in the `<Catalog>` is the `<Book>` element. The definition begins with the attribute types, which we have seen before, except for one:

```
<AttributeType name="pageCount" dt:type="int" required="yes"/>
```

The type of the attribute is being specified, rather than left as the usual text. Another example is in the <Price> element:

```
<ElementType name="Price" dt:type="fixed.14.4" content="textOnly">
   <attribute type="currency"/>
</ElementType>
```

We will therefore need to create a column of the correct type for the element. This requires us to modify rule three:

- **Rule 3** – for each attribute node:
  - Create a column with the same name as the attribute node:
    – With the prefix `attr_` if the attribute is a normal attribute.
    – With the prefix `attr_enum_` if the attribute is of type enumerated.
    – With the prefix `attr_id_` if the attribute is of type id.
  - *The data type should be a* `variable-length` *string with a length of 255, unless there is a data type specified in the* `dt:type` *attribute.*
  - If the attribute is required then the column should not allow *NULL* values.

Attributes With the idrefs Data Type

The next set of attributes are also of a type we have not met before, but these cannot simply be modeled with database storage types:

```
<AttributeType name="authors" dt:type="idrefs"/>
<AttributeType name="threads" dt:type="idrefs"/>
```

The purpose of these two attributes is to provide a white space separated list of references to <Author> and <Thread> elements. This is not something that is easy to maintain in one column of a table, so we will model this relationship by introducing tables of the same name as the attributes, with foreign keys that point into the `Author` and `Thread` tables. We'll create the tables in the same way as we would element tables, so `authors` would be like this:

Column Name	Datatype	Length	Precision	Scale	Allow Nulls	Default Value	Identity	Identity Seed	Identity Increment
pk_authors	int	4	10	0	☐		☑	1	1
fk_Book	int	4	10	0	☐		☐		
attr_idref_Author	varchar	255	0	0	☐		☐		

and `threads` would be like this:

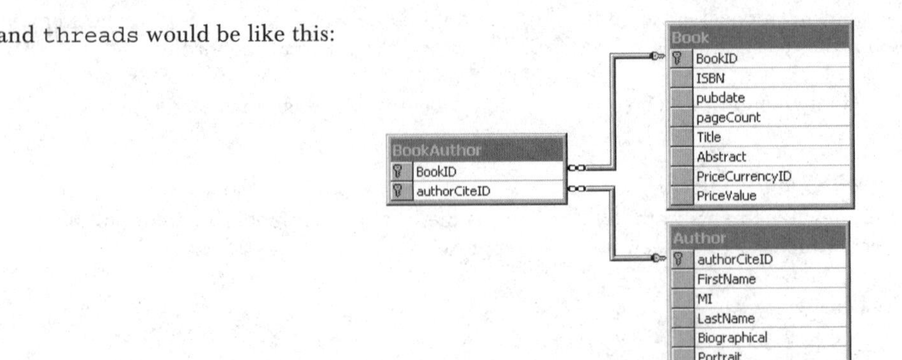

The rule we need to define is a little contrived, but it does the job:

- **Rule 7** – if an attribute is of type `idrefs` then:
  - Create a table of the same name as the attribute.
  - In it, create a column with the same name as the singular version of the element name capitalized, prefixed by `attr_idref_`.
  - Create a foreign key to the table of the same name as the singular version capitalized, using the `attr_id_` column on the target table.

Since this is a little complicated, let's go through the steps with the `authors` attribute. First, we create a table called `authors` with all of the usual characteristics. Then we add a column to that table; the name for the column is the singular of `authors` capitalised – `Author` – and then prefixed with `attr_idref_`. Finally, create a foreign key which connects this column to the `attr_id_` column in the target table (in this case `attr_id_authorCiteID` in the table `Author`). Note that this rule assumes that the `idrefs` attribute has the name, plural, of the element whose IDs are being referenced – a common practice when designing XML schemas.

An example of the data that the schema definition we have looked at so far will allow, might be:

```
<Book ISBN="1-861001-52-5"
      Level="Experienced"
      pubdate="1/10/99"
      pageCount="458"
      authors="1 2 4"
      threads="1 3 6"/>
```

You can see that the `authors` and `threads` attributes are simply lists of `ids` that occur elsewhere in the document.

Note that if the table structure we have created looks familiar to you, you are on the right track; we would have established exactly the same tables and relationships had we wanted to generate the following XML:

```
<Book ISBN="1-861001-52-5"
      Level="Experienced"
      pubdate="1/10/99"
      pageCount="458">
   <authors>
      <Author authorCiteID="1">
         <FirstName>Stephen</FirstName>
         <LastName>Mohr</LastName>
         <Biographical>
            Stephen began programming in high school and is now a senior
            software systems architect with Omicron Consulting, he designs and
            develops systems using C++, Java, JavaScript, COM, and various
            internetworking standards and protocols.
         </Biographical>
         <Portrait picLink="http://webdev.wrox.co.uk/resources/
                            authors/mohrs.gif" />
      </Author>
```

```
        <Author authorCiteID="2">
            <FirstName>Kathie</FirstName>
            <LastName>Kingsley-Hughes</LastName>
            <Biographical>
                Kathie is the MD of Kingsley-Hughes Development Ltd, a Training
                and Consultancy firm specialising in Web Development and visual
                programming languages, first going into CDF channels with The
                Dragon Channel.
            </Biographical>
            <Portrait picLink="" />
        </Author>
    </authors>
    <threads>
        <Thread threadID="1">Internet</Thread>
        <Thread threadID="3">Programming</Thread>
        <Thread threadID="6">XML</Thread>
    </threads>
</Book>
```

However, note that with this method, because each book contains its authors, there may be a lot of repetition – if an author wrote two books their details would appear twice, once under each book. The `idrefs` technique allows elements to *appear to* contain other elements without unnecessary repetition.

Attributes With the idref Data Type

Another type of attribute that we haven't defined a rule for is `idref`. An example of this type is used when referring to an imprint for a book:

```
    <AttributeType name="imprint" dt:type="idref"/>
```

Unlike `idrefs`, only one reference can occur within the attribute, so we don't need to use an additional table. All we need to do is create a column with a suitable name, and then construct a foreign key that connects this column to the `Imprint` table. Our rule would be:

- **Rule 8** – if an attribute is of type `idref` then:
  - Create a column with the same name as the attribute, prefixed by `attr_idref_`.
  - Create a foreign key relationship between that column and the `attr_id_column` of the table of the same name as the attribute name capitalised.

In this case we are creating a foreign key between the column `attr_idref_imprint` on the `Book` table, and `attr_id_shortImprintName` on the `Imprint` table. Note that this rule assumes that the `idref` attribute has the same name as the element whose `id` it points to – again, a fairly common practice when designing XML schemas.

Structure

The following is a representation of the tables and relationships that we would create with our rules for the `Publisher` hierarchy:

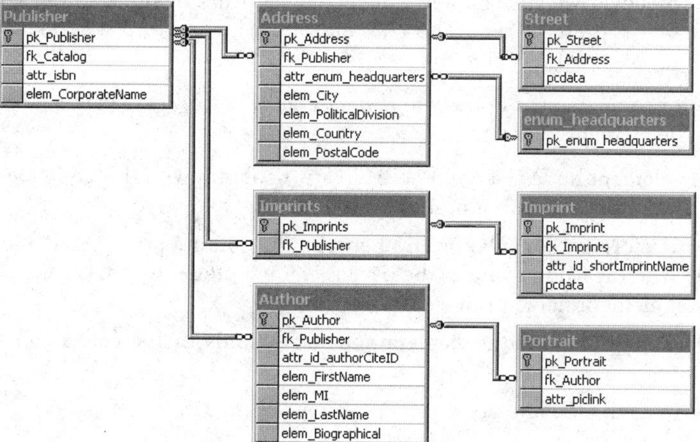

The following is a representation of the tables and relationships that we would create with our rules for the `Book` hierarchy:

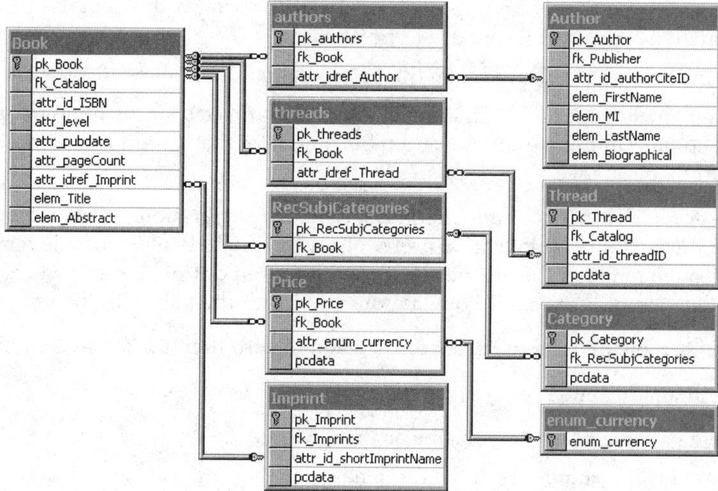

Summary

The benefits of using XML to define the structure of our XML documents – through XML schemas – means that we are able to automate many tasks. In this case we have created a set of rules that will allow us to create a relational database from the schema.

We'll summarize the rules that we have created so far, before we look at the code. Note that I've added some clauses to rules 2 and 3 that explicitly show rule priorities (some of the later rules take precedence in certain circumstances) – these are shown in italic:

- **Rule 1** – whenever we create a new table, create a primary key with the same name as the table, but with a prefix of `pk_`. This column should be an `automatically-incremented` integer.
- **Rule 2** – for each element node type *that does not match rule 4*, create a table with the same name as the element, then:
    - If the element node is a child node create a column with the same name as the parent element node, but with a prefix of `fk_`.
    - Create a foreign key relationship between the column just created and the column in the table with the same name as the parent element node, where the column name is the parent element name prefixed by `pk_`.
    - If the content type of the element node is text only then create a column with the name `pcdata`.
- **Rule 3** – for each attribute node *that does not match rules 5, 7 or 8*:
    - Create a column with the same name as the attribute node:
– With the prefix `attr_` if the attribute is a normal attribute.
– With the prefix `attr_enum_` if the attribute is of type enumerated.
– With the prefix `attr_id_` if the attribute is of type id.
    - The data type should be a `variable-length` string with a length of 255, unless there is a data type specified in the `dt:type` attribute.
    - If the attribute is required then the column should not allow `NULL` values.
- **Rule 4** – if an element node can only contain text, and has a maximum occurrence of 1, then create a column in the parent element table, and give that column the same name as the node, with a prefix of `elem_`.
- **Rule 5** – for each attribute node that has a type of enumeration, create a table with the same name as the attribute node, with a prefix of `enum_`. Include one variable-length string column with the same name as the attribute node, with a prefix of `pk_enum_`, and a datatype of `variable-length string`. Populate the table with the values in the enumeration.
- **Rule 6** – if an element has a `minOccurs` value of zero then make the column nullable.
- **Rule 7** – if an attribute is of type `idrefs` then:
    - Create a table of the same name as the attribute.
    - In it, create a column with the same name as the singular version of the element name capitalized, prefixed by `attr_idref_`.
    - Create a foreign key to the table of the same name as the singular version capitalized, using the `attr_id_` column on the target table.
- **Rule 8** – if an attribute is of type `idref` then:
    - Create a column with the same name as the attribute, prefixed by `attr_idref_`.
    - Create a foreign key relationship between that column and the `attr_id_column` of the table of the same name as the attribute name capitalized.

Automating Database Creation

The following script takes the rules that we devised in the previous section and creates a tree, which is a set of instructions to create a database. We have chosen to use a script to perform the translation because the equivalent XSLT style sheet to convert an XML-DR schema would be very complex, if not impossible, to create. The main problem is that creating relationships between tables in a relational database requires not only that those tables exist, but that the primary key on the target table exists. To ensure this is always the case we need to create relationships only after all tables and keys have been created. The safest way to do this is to build up a tree of nodes that represent those instructions since we can insert at any point in the hierarchy, at any stage of our processing.

Another advantage of using a node structure to build up our commands is that we have an opportunity to optimize the commands. For example, after establishing a command to create a table for each element we can remove the commands for those elements that could easily be stored as columns.

The script (`schematordb.asp`) begins with a form to identify the schema to process and two DIVs to hold the processing results. The first provides a quick way to see the tables and columns that will be created, while the second lists the actual SQL commands that will be generated:

```
<HTML>
<HEAD>
<TITLE>Schema to RDBMS Converter</TITLE>
</HEAD>
<BODY>
<TABLE>
   <TR>
      <TD><FONT face=Verdana>Schema File: </FONT></TD>
      <TD>
         <INPUT id="loadfile"
                name="loadfile"
                style="HEIGHT: 22px; WIDTH: 230px"
                value="file:c:/PubCatalog.xml">
      </TD>
      <TD>
         <FONT face=Verdana>
            <INPUT id="GenerateBtn"
                   name="GenerateBtn"
                   type="button"
                   value="Generate"
                   OnClick="OnGenerateClick()">
         </FONT>
      </TD>
   </TR>
</TABLE>
<HR>
<TABLE>
   <TR>
      <TD valign="TOP"><DIV id="infoResult"></DIV></TD>
      <TD valign="TOP"><XMP id="sqlResult"></XMP></TD>
   </TD>
</TABLE>
```

The script itself begins by creating XML DOMs for processing the XML Schema input, holding the SQL DDL output, and holding the style sheets. There are two style sheets involved in this process. The first transforms the list of commands created into a summary of properties of each column, ordered by the table on which the columns will appear. Primary and foreign keys are also shown.

The second style sheet converts the same creation nodes into the correct SQL statements to create a database that reflects the schema.

To begin with, we create some variables to hold various parts of the output:

```
<SCRIPT language="Javascript">
<!--
var COMPLETED = 4;

var parser = new ActiveXObject("microsoft.xmldom");
var oParsOut = new ActiveXObject("microsoft.xmldom");
var oStyle = new ActiveXObject("microsoft.xmldom");

var oDB, oDBT, oDBPK, oDBID, oDBFK, oDBDAT;
```

The function that is executed when the button is pressed does all the work:

```
function OnGenerateClick()
{
   parser.async = "false";
   oParsOut.async = "false";
   oStyle.async = "false";
```

First load the schema document, and check that it does actually contain a schema node:

```
   parser.load(document.all("loadfile").value);
   if (parser.readyState == COMPLETED && parser.parseError == 0)
   {
      oDE = parser.documentElement;
      // Minimal check for XML-DR validity
      if (oDE.nodeName == "Schema")
      {
```

Next create all of the elements that will hold the results of analyzing the schema:

```
         oDB = oParsOut.createElement("DB");
         oDBT = oParsOut.createElement("Tables");
         oDBPK = oParsOut.createElement("PrimaryKeys");
         oDBID = oParsOut.createElement("IDs");
         oDBFK = oParsOut.createElement("ForeignKeys");
         oDBDAT = oParsOut.createElement("Data");
```

Our first pass through the schema tries to create a list of all the tables that we might need. This will be a table for each element type, a table for any attribute type with a type of `idrefs`, and a table for each attribute type with a type of enumeration. The tables for the first two situations are named after the element or attribute type whose information they will hold:

```
// First we create a list of all the tables we might need.
//  We will optimise this later, so some may get deleted.
//  We need a table for:
//  - each ElementType
//  - each AttributeType which has a type of 'idrefs'
oNL = oDE.selectNodes(
   "//ElementType | //AttributeType[@dt:type='idrefs']"
);
for (var i = 0; i < oNL.length; i++)
{
   sTable = oNL(i).attributes.getNamedItem("name").value;
   CreateTABLE(sTable, true);
}
```

The tables for enumeration are prefixed with `enum_` to ensure they don't clash with anything else. We also have to create the necessary instructions to add the values in an enumeration to the enumeration table:

```
//  - each AttributeType which has a type of 'enumeration'
oNL = oDE.selectNodes("//AttributeType[@dt:type='enumeration']");
for (var i = 0; i < oNL.length; i++)
{
   sTable =
      "enum_" + oNL(i).attributes.getNamedItem("name").value;
   CreateTABLE(sTable, false);
   CreateDATA(
      sTable,
      oNL(i).attributes.getNamedItem("dt:values").value
   );
}
```

Although we have created a table for each element type, we know nothing about the hierarchical relationships that can exist between the elements. The next stage therefore is to step through each element and locate its definition in the matching element type:

```
// Next step through all the elements:
// - elements that are not text only, get attached to their parent
// - elements that are text only, but can occur more than once or
//   have attributes also get attached to their parent
// - other elements become columns
oNL = oDE.selectNodes("//element");
for (i = 0; i < oNL.length; i++)
{
   sType = getAttr(oNL(i), "type");
   bMulti = (getAttr(oNL(i), "maxOccurs") == "*");
   // Get the definition of the element (the ElementType)
   oET = oDE.selectSingleNode(
      "//ElementType[@name='" + sType+ "']"
   );
```

```
            if (oET != null)
            {
               // We leave the table intact and link to the parent if the
               //element is NOT text only
               //  OR there is more than one occurrence of the element
               bHasAttr = (oET.selectNodes("attribute").length != 0);
```

If the element is *not* text only, or there can be more than one occurrence of the element, or it has some attributes then we will leave it in its own table and create a join. However, if the element is text only, there can only be one occurrence and it has no attributes then it can safely be made into a column on the parent table:

```
               if ((getAttr(oET, "content") != "textOnly") || bMulti ||
                   bHasAttr)
               {
                  CreateLookup(sType, getAttr(oNL(i).parentNode, "name"));
               }
               // Otherwise mark the table for deletion from our create
               // table list, and add the
               // element as a column instead
               else
                  {
                  oTemp = oDBT.selectSingleNode("Table[@name='" + sType
                                                      + "']");
                  oTemp.setAttribute("Delete", "yes");
                  NewColumnDEF(getAttr(oNL(i).parentNode, "name"),
                               "elem_" + sType);
               }
            }
         }
```

Having finished with all of the elements we now step through all of the attributes:

```
         // Now put the attributes on. Those that refer to enumerations have a
         //  special syntax
         oNL = oDE.selectNodes("//attribute");
         for (i = 0; i < oNL.length; i++)
         {
```

For each attribute get the definition of that attribute:

```
            sType = getAttr(oNL(i), "type");
            // Get the definition of the attribute (the AttributeType)
            oAT = oDE.selectSingleNode("//AttributeType[@name='" + sType
                                             + "']")
            if (oAT != null)
            {
```

No matter what type of attribute we have we will need to do something with the parent table, so get its name:

```
            // Get information about the table that contains the attribute
            sContainer = getAttr(oNL(i).parentNode, "name");
```

Exactly what we do with the attribute depends on its type:

```
            switch (getAttr(oAT, "dt:type"))
            {
```

Enumerations are achieved by creating a column on the attribute's element table that refers to the enumeration table. The enumeration table would have been created earlier:

```
               case "enumeration":
                  CreateLookup(sContainer, "enum_" + sType);
                  break;
```

An `IDREF` also results in a column being added to the parent:

```
               case "idref":
                  CreateIDREF(sContainer, CapFirst(sType));
                  break;
```

`IDREF`s need a join to be established:

```
               case "idrefs":
                  CreateIDREFS(sContainer, sType);
                  break;
```

An `ID` means add a column to the parent:

```
               case "id":
                  CreateID(sContainer, sType);
                  break;
```

Specified data types mean that the column should be created but with a specific data type:

```
               case "fixed.14.4":
                  NewColumnMONEY(sContainer, "attr_" + sType);
                  break;

               case "int":
                  NewColumnINT(sContainer, "attr_" + sType);
                  break;

               default:
                  NewColumnDEF(sContainer, "attr_" + sType);
                  break;
            }
         }
      }
```

Now we can loop through our list of tables to create and remove the ones that we have optimized out. Note that if we remove the command to create a table we have to remove the corresponding instruction to create a primary key on that table:

```
// Finally, delete the tables we no longer need
oNL = oDBT.selectNodes("Table[@Delete='yes']");
for (i = 0; i < oNL.length; i++)
{
   oTemp = oDBT.removeChild(oNL(i));
   // If we delete a table we should delete its primary key too
   oCL = oDBPK.selectNodes("PK[@table='" + getAttr(oTemp, "name") +
                                "']");
   for (j = 0; j < oCL.length; j++)
   {
      oTemp = oDBPK.removeChild(oCL(j));
   }
}
```

We're done with the creation list, so add it to the containing node:

```
oDB.appendChild(oDBT);
```

Place all of the constraints – primary keys, foreign keys and so on – into another container, and place that in the containing node:

```
oNode = oParsOut.createElement("Constraints");
oNode.appendChild(oDBPK);
oNode.appendChild(oDBID);
oNode.appendChild(oDBFK);
oDB.appendChild(oNode);
```

Add in the list of instructions that will populate some of the tables with data:

```
oDB.appendChild(oDBDAT);
```

Finally, store the entire document ready for transformation and load the required style sheet (`DBCreateView.xsl`, available with the downloadable code for this book). You may need to edit the URL for this style sheet to locate it on your system. If the load is successful and the document parses correctly, then do the transform and place the result in the correct area on the web page:

```
oParsOut.documentElement = oDB;

oStyle.load("http://server/DBCreateView.xsl");
if (oStyle.parseError.errorCode != 0)
{
   sResult = reportParseError(oStyle.parseError);
}
else
{
   try
   {
      sResult = oParsOut.transformNode(oStyle);
   }
```

```
            catch (exception)
            {
               sResult = reportRuntimeError(exception);
            }
         }
         infoResult.innerHTML = sResult;
```

The first transformation created a summary of what will be created in the database, listing all the tables and their columns. This next transformation will actually send the series of instructions to a SQL database that will construct the databases elements (again, you'll need to change the URL shown for your system, in order to locate `DBCreateSQL.xsl` – available with the downloadable code):

```
         oStyle.load("http://server/DBCreateSQL.xsl");
         if (oStyle.parseError.errorCode != 0)
         {
            sResult = reportParseError(oStyle.parseError);
         }
         else
         {
            try
            {
               sResult = oParsOut.transformNode(oStyle);
            }
            catch (exception)
            {
               sResult = reportRuntimeError(exception);
            }
         }
         sqlResult.innerText = sResult;
      }
      else
         alert("The URL doesn't designate a schema file under XML-DR rules.");
   }
   else
      alert("Parser detects error: " + parser.parseError.reason);
}
```

The remaining code provides all the functions that are needed to set up the command instructions. The first creates a new table, which in turn requires a primary key:

```
function CreateTABLE(s, bAuto)
{
   var oTemp = oParsOut.createElement("Table");
   oTemp.setAttribute("name", s);
   oDBT.appendChild(oTemp);
   CreatePK(s, bAuto);
}
```

The next function creates an ID column in a table:

```
function CreateID(s, c)
{
   var oTemp = oParsOut.createElement("ID");
   c = "attr_id_" + c;
   oTemp.setAttribute("table", s);
   oTemp.setAttribute("name", c);
   oDBID.appendChild(oTemp);

   // Add the column to the create table node
   NewColumnDEF(s, c);
}
```

Creating data requires us to perform an insert on an already existing table:

```
function CreateDATA(sT, s)
{
   var ar = s.split(" ");
   for (var i = 0; i < ar.length; i++)
   {
      var oTemp = oParsOut.createElement("Insert");
      oTemp.setAttribute("table", sT);
      oTemp.setAttribute("value", ar[i]);
      oDBDAT.appendChild(oTemp);
   }
}
```

Primary keys are created with this function. Note that if the key's main purpose is as an end-point for references then it will probably have the bAuto parameter set. This sets the primary key to be an auto incrementing integer:

```
function CreatePK(s, bAuto)
{
   var oTemp = oParsOut.createElement("PK");
   oTemp.setAttribute("table", s);
   oTemp.setAttribute("name", "pk_" + s);
   oDBPK.appendChild(oTemp);
   if (bAuto)
   {
      NewColumnAUTOINC(s, "pk_" + s);
   }
   else
   {
      NewColumnDEF(s, "pk_" + s);
   }
}
```

A lookup is achieved by placing a foreign key on one table, referring to the primary key on another:

```
function CreateLookup(sT1, sT2)
{
   // Creating a lookup between one table and another requires the primary key
   //  of the second table
   var oTemp = oDBPK.selectSingleNode("PK[@table='" + sT2 + "']");
   CreateRel(sT1, "fk_" + sT2, sT2, getAttr(oTemp, "name"));
}
```

An `IDREF` column also creates a relationship between two tables, but not necessarily to the primary key of the designated table:

```
function CreateIDREF(sT1, sT2)
{
   // Creating an ID lookup between one table and another requires the
   // attribute that has a property of 'id' from the second table. We've
   // already created these in the 'unique values' list, so just look it up
   var oTemp = oDBID.selectSingleNode("ID[@table='" + sT2 + "']");
   CreateRel(sT1, "fk_attr_idref_" + sT2, sT2, getAttr(oTemp, "name"));
}
```

An `IDREFS` attribute would have caused an intermediate – or join – table to be created. We need to find this table and then refer to it from the two tables that are actually being joined via this intermediary:

```
function CreateIDREFS(sT1, sT2)
{
   // Creating an IDREFS lookup involves an intermediate table.
   //The instruction to
   //  create this will already be in our list, so find that first
   var oTemp = oDBT.selectSingleNode("Table[@name='" + sT2 + "']");
   CreateLookup(sT2, sT1);
   sT1 = sT2;
   sT2 = CapFirstSingular(sT2);
   CreateIDREF(sT1, sT2);
}
```

A relationship is created by adding an instruction to the list of foreign keys that need creating:

```
function CreateRel(sT1, sFK, sT2, sPK)
{
   // Create an instruction to generate a foreign key
   var oTemp = oParsOut.createElement("FK");
   oTemp.setAttribute("table1", sT1);
   oTemp.setAttribute("src", sFK);
   oTemp.setAttribute("table2", sT2);
   oTemp.setAttribute("dest", sPK);
   oDBFK.appendChild(oTemp);

   NewColumnDEF(sT1, sFK);
}
```

This function allows us to find an already existing instruction to create a table:

```
function getCreateTable(s)
{
   return oDBT.selectSingleNode("Table[@name='" + s + "']");
}
```

These two functions allow us to convert words like `author` to `Author` (`CapFirst`) and `authors` to `Author` (`CapFirstSingular`) for use when creating tables that can be referred to when an attribute has `IDREF` and `IDREFS` values:

```
function CapFirst(s)
{
   return s.substr(0, 1).toUpperCase() + s.substr(1);
}

function CapFirstSingular(s)
{
   return CapFirst(s).substr(0, s.length-1);
}
```

A new column of a particular data type is added with this function:

```
function NewColumn(sT, s, sType, bNull)
{
   var oTemp = oParsOut.createElement("Column");
   oTemp.setAttribute("name", s);
   oTemp.setAttribute("type", sType);
   oTemp.setAttribute("null", bNull ? "yes" : "no");
   getCreateTable(sT).appendChild(oTemp);
}
```

The function just described is then called with the following more specific functions:

```
function NewColumnDEF(sT, s)
{
   NewColumn(sT, s, "varchar(255)", false);
}

function NewColumnINT(sT, s)
{
   NewColumn(sT, s, "int", true);
}

function NewColumnAUTOINC(sT, s)
{
   NewColumn(sT, s, "int identity(1, 1)", false);
}

function NewColumnMONEY(sT, s)
{
   NewColumn(sT, s, "money", true);
}
```

This function allows us to retrieve an attribute's value from a node, and returns an empty string if the node does not have that attribute:

```
function getAttr(o, s)
{
   var sRet = "";
   if (o != null)
   {
      var n = o.attributes.getNamedItem(s);
      if (n != null)
      {
         sRet = n.value;
      }
   }
   return sRet;
}
```

Finally, our error reporting routines. The first is used after we have loaded other XML files, and reports any parse errors. The second is used if any runtime errors occurr:

```
// Parse error formatting function
function reportParseError(error)
{
   var s = "";
   for (var i=1; i<error.linepos; i++)
   {
      s += " ";
   }
   r = "<font face=Verdana size=2><font size=4>XML Error loading '" +
       error.url + "'</font>" +
       "<P><B>" + error.reason +
       "</B></P></font>";
   if (error.line > 0)
      r += "<font size=3><XMP>" +
           "at line " + error.line + ", character " + error.linepos +
           "\n" + error.srcText +
           "\n" + s + "^" +
           "</XMP></font>";
   return r;
}

// Runtime error formatting function
function reportRuntimeError(exception)
{
   return "<font face=Verdana size=2><font size=4>XSL Runtime Error</font>" +
          "<P><B>" + exception.description + "</B></P></font>";
}
//-->
</SCRIPT>

</BODY>
</HTML>
```

This list of commands is prepared first before actually creating the specific database instructions because it allows us to optimize and order the commands. For example, after creating a list of all the tables we need, we can go through and delete the tables that are text only. We can also ensure that all tables are present before relationships are established between them.

Once we have the list of commands a style sheet is applied that converts the commands to SQL statements. This two-stage process is advantageous because it separates the processing of the input schema from the creation of the output. If the commands to create tables or insert keys are different for another type of database then the transformation style sheet can be changed. If a different schema syntax is used, then the source processing code can be changed.

The following is the output from running the script on the book catalog schema:

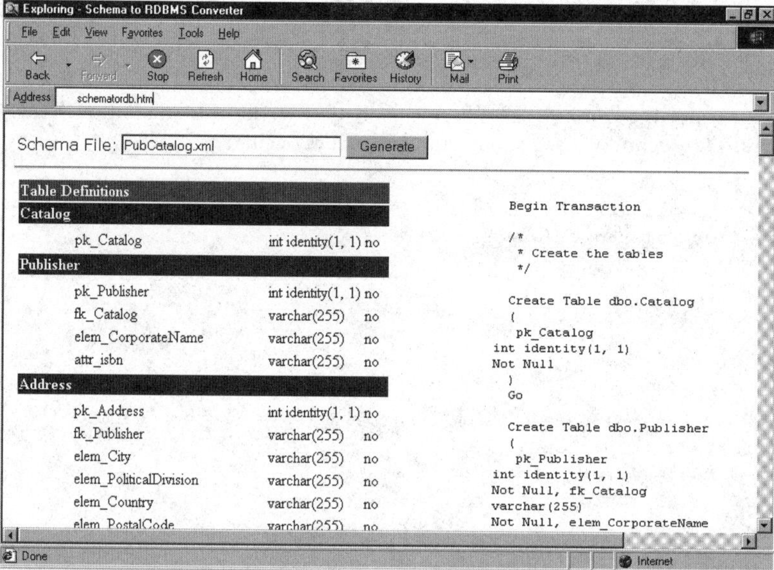

On the left is the list of the instructions that need to be carried out, and on the right are those instructions as a series of SQL statements.

Conclusion

The distance between XML and databases is still great. We have established that there are a number of ways to do things – sometimes too many ways. However, the early implementations from database vendors indicate that their commitment to bringing XML functionality to databases – and database functionality to XML – will continue apace.

XML will increasingly be the foundation for data interchange, display, indexing, and so on, it will find its way into just about every application and device we currently deal with. From mobile phones, to home entertainment systems, to satellite systems, mark-up based on XML will be used to allow clean and efficient communications.

And at the same time as the languages of communication are increasingly based on XML, so too will be the ubiquitous unit of information storage, the document. Images, faxes, sound recordings, video clips and spreadsheets, to name a few, will increasingly find their native file format being XML. Companies such as Macromedia and Quark have announced that the file formats for their well-known products will become XML. Microsoft has also shown that it is going in this direction with the recently launched Office 2000 suite of applications.

Given the inevitable spread of XML it is imperative that programmers and systems designers plan applications that can deliver dynamic XML documents, in large quantities with tight control. For this they will certainly need to look to database technology.

11

Server to Server

Traditional server and distributed communications rely on tightly coupled component model systems, such as COM or COBRA. These techniques are not really suitable for the Internet, and introduce a degree of dependency and/or platform issues. Indeed, even in an Intranet you will find yourself getting information on what component architecture remote objects were written in, and the platform they reside on. Would it not be easier if you could just write your client application without having to know anything about the architecture of participating distributed objects? On an Internet environment you probably won't have a choice.

Using XML as a distributed component model we can overcome many of the problems encountered over heterogeneous architectures and platforms. XML is, at its most basic, just text, and as this is understood by every platform and language in existence, it can be used to pass message requests and responses across any environment.

This chapter is going to look at the various technologies and techniques that can be employed for server-to-server communications, illustrating examples of their usage and how each can fit into our book catalog example.

Transporting XML

First off, let's look at an overview of a practical scenario where various methods, some traditional and some new, of transporting XML are used. We will consider passing XML using FTP, MSMQ, HTTP, and SMTP.

The following diagram illustrates the scenario of a central book publisher maintaining many thousands of books, an individual book reseller who buys hundreds of titles per week from the central publisher, and consumers who buy individual titles from the reseller:

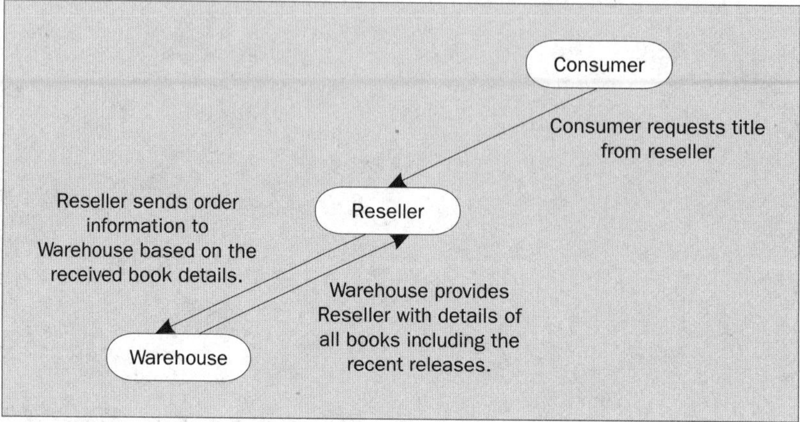

So far we have discussed the processes involved in the chain, but where does XML fit in? The diagram below outlines the methods used to transfer information between the various servers and the following commentary explains how XML is utilized in each step.

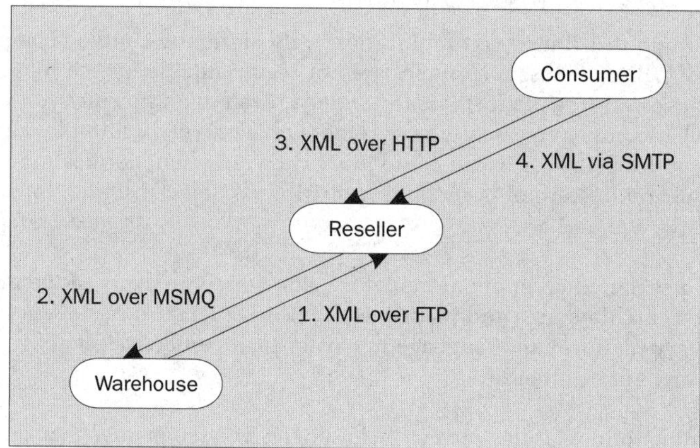

1. XML Over FTP

An automated process at the warehouse regularly sends XML documents to the reseller containing the latest book information for all the titles it has in its database. This document contains details such as title, subject, summary, price etc. Obviously, over time there are many thousands of titles, and so the size of the XML document can become large. It was decided the most efficient method to transfer these files was via FTP, which is suited to bulk data transfer.

As this is effectively an background automatic, asynchronous process we must run a process on the reseller destination server which scans the target directory for the arrival of the XML document and performs an appropriate action, such as indexing the information or inserting it into the business book database.

The diagram below shows how this process could work.

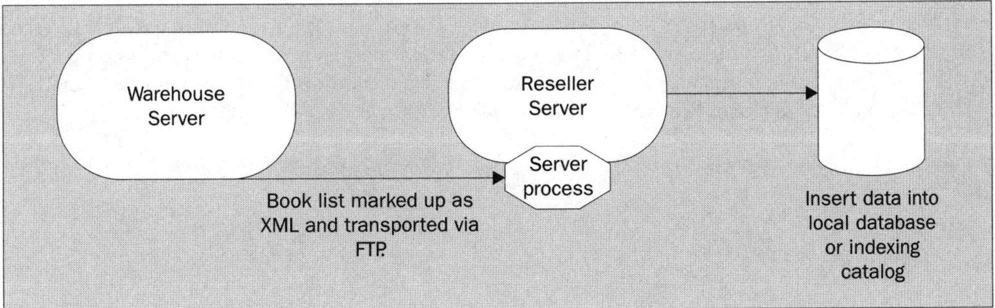

2. XML and Message Queuing

The actual order for the books requested by the reseller from the warehouse is also asynchronous, and is relatively lightweight when compared with the XML document transported over FTP. The order should be delivered sometime soon, and it is essential that the message arrives, so the best technology would be message queuing, such as Microsoft Message Queue (MSMQ), or IBM's MQSeries.

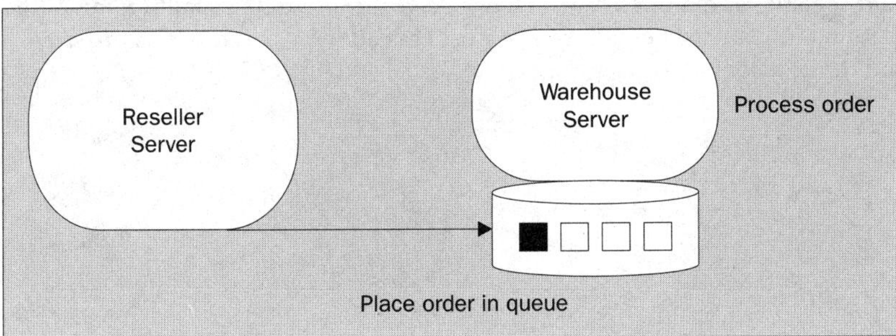

Rather than directly submitting the order request to the server application, the information is submitted to a message queue and dealt with at a later time. The order request can therefore be submitted in XML, which can be derived from the XML document that marks up the books that are available. This document is the one that was sent previously, via FTP.

3. XML Over HTTP

When a consumer buys a book from the reseller, he uses a web browser and submits an XML document corresponding to the request for the book. The request is dealt with synchronously, and could be sent as a MSXML POST to the web server, or, if we developed a custom component, we could use the MSXML component to perform the XML HTTP request within it.

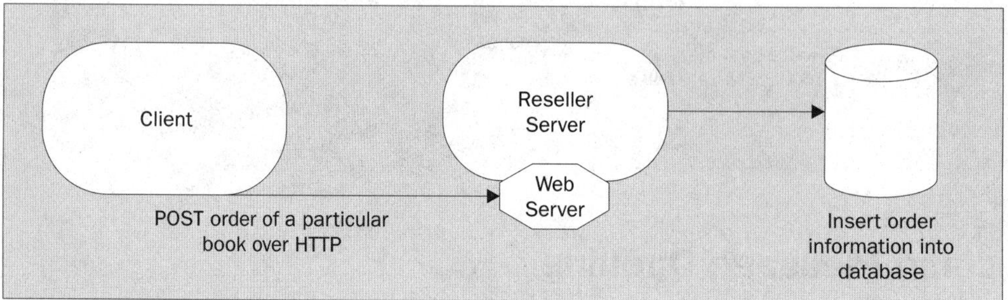

4. XML Over SMTP

The final method that a consumer can use to order a title is via SMTP (e-mail). An XML document can be sent according to a valid schema, and a process which checks a specific POP3 mailbox for valid XML book orders according a published schema for ordering. This allows asynchronous ordering between the consumer and the reseller.

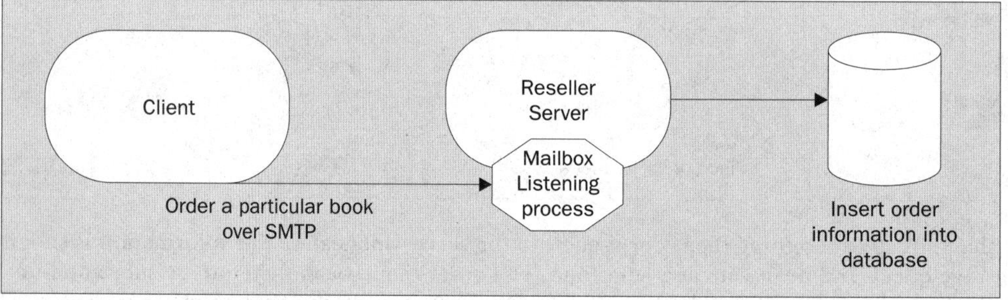

XML as a Distributed Component Model

As the previous section demonstrated, there are a number of ways in which XML can be sent as a message between systems. We are now going to look at some of the more popular methods and standards that are emerging for XML message transport.

Message Transfer and Serialization

Typical XML documents are built to represent structured, human-readable data to which some processing can be applied. We can extend this concept to machine-readable data, and use serialized (see over the page) data to pass messages that follow well-defined standards. This reduces platform dependencies and can be easily manipulated through code.

Message passing involves a process called **serialization** and it's inverse, **de-serialization**. Serialization is a process whereby a data term is structured in a simple one-dimensional format suitable for transport across the wire. For example, the data `Hello, World!` could be serialized into the format:

```
<string>Hello, World!</string>
```

Similarly, a recordset with the data:

Column Name	Value
FirstName	Steven
LastName	Livingstone
City	Glasgow

could be serialized as follows:

```
<recordset>
   <column>
      <columnName>
         FirstName
      </columnName>
      <columnValue>
         Steven
      </columnValue>
   </column>
   <column>
      <columnName>
         LastName
      </columnName>
      <columnValue>
         Livingstone
      </columnValue>
   </column>
   <column>
      <columnName>
         City
      </columnName>
      <columnValue>
         Glasgow
      </columnValue>
   </column>
</recordset>
```

Once we have the data serialized, we can easily pass it between other systems as simple text and use de-serialization at the destination to return the data to the desired system format. There are many protocols that can be used to pass serialized data, the more popular being HTTP, FTP, and SMTP (the protocol used to transfer e-mails).

Serialization With XML-RPC and SOAP

One of the main focuses of this chapter is **XML-RPC** (**XML Remote Procedural Calling**), which, as we will see, serializes simple and more complex data types into XML to transport over the Internet. Implementations allow types in many languages to be serialized (and de-serialized) and have a broad scope, fitting in well with the Internet. **SOAP**, or the **Simple Object Access Protocol**, which we will also discuss in some detail, is a more complex and mature version of XML-RPC. Both of these are (at the time of writing) completely open, and implementations are available for several platforms.

XML-RPC is probably the most popular and useful of the XML-based distributed communications protocols available, with SOAP being a likely successor in the longer term – particularly with more complex systems.

Coins (Combining XML & Java)

Some do not see Javabeans as the best way to write components in Java with its dependence on Java serialization. **Coins** combines both XML and Java to replace serialization with XML, and doesn't attempt to preserve object state. Its goals are to ease the transfer of information between programs.

Furthermore, the debugging process would be improved due to the simpler nature of XML (which is also less sensitive to change than traditional Javabeans), and there would be less of a limitation on processing – as data can be easily exchanged between applications when it is in XML format. Coins can also be returned to an XML document with only a reference to external components, because Coins supports links between elements in separate documents (as opposed to traditional Javabeans that have no support for hyperlinks and minimal support for component partitioning).

Coins, unlike XML-RPC that models static interfaces in XML, requires an arms-length relationship between XML documents and Java objects. One consequence of this is a lifting of dependencies between the programs that are interchanging information. Data elements can be added by an updated program without having to synchronize updates to the other programs.

> *Further information on Coins is available from* http://www.jxml.com/coins/index.html

Serialization With WDDX

As a middle ground we have **WDDX**, which stands for **Web Distributed Data eXchange** and is a technology for exchanging complex data structures between programming languages. It is basically a standard for language-independent representations of XML data, and includes a set of serializing/de-serializing modules as well. Modules are developed by Allaire, and, at present, are included for JavaScript 1.x, ColdFusion 4.0, COM, Perl, and Java. WDDX describes distributed objects using XML, but does not invoke remote calls as XML-RPC does.

> *You can download the WDDX SDK from* http://www.wddx.org/, *which also has some further detailed information on WDDX.*

WDDX applications produce packets describing local objects through serialization, which can then be transmitted to remote servers where an application can de-serialize the packet to provide useful information it understands.

WDDX doesn't concern itself with how the data is sent; only that it is POSTed to a web page that can access the serialized XML from the request object. A sample WDDX packet containing the name of a requested book title would look like the following:

```
<!DOCTYPE wddxPacket SYSTEM "wddx.dtd">
<wddxPacket version='0.9'>
   <header/>
   <data>
      <var name="title">
         <string>Professional XML</string>
      </var>
   </data>
</wddxPacket>
```

We would create this packet by serializing the information with a script such as the following Perl example:

> The Perl WDDX library is available in the downloadable SDK.

```
# Include WDDX library
use wddx;

# Include HTML-Encoding functions
use HTML::Entities;

# Set the $Title variable to the name of the book
$Title = "Professional XML";

# Create a new serializer "object"
$SerObj = new wddx();

# Serialize the $Title variable into a WDDX Packet
$BookPacket = $SerObj ->cfwddx
(
   "action" => 'perl2wddx',
   "input"  => {"string" => \$Title,}
);
```

This is a JavaScript example providing the same functionality:

```
<!-- Include JavaScript / WDDX functionality -->
<SCRIPT LANGUAGE="JavaScript" SRC="Wddx.js"></SCRIPT>

<!--- Create a custom function that serializes our message --->
<SCRIPT LANGUAGE="JavaScript">
   function SerializeMsg()
   {
      var Book = new Object;
      Book.title = "Professional XML"

      // Create a new serializer "object"
      SerObj = new WddxSerializer;
```

```
        // Serialize the Message variable into a WDDX Packet
        BookPacket = SerObj.serialize(Book);

        // Return the new WDDX packet
        return BookPacket;
    }
</SCRIPT>
```

We would then store the serialized WDDX message in a `HIDDEN` element, which then allows the message to be POSTed from a form submission – we called this hidden field "`WddxContent`". When this content is posted in the `WddxContent` field, we would want to de-serialize it to get our original WDDX message. We should use the WDDX de-serializer object to do this work for us.

```
<%@ LANGUAGE="Javascript" %>
<%
   strWDDXPacket = Request.Form("WDDXContent");

   // Create a new serializer "object"
   var ObjDeser = Server.CreateObject("WDDX.Deserializer.1");

   // Serialize the Message variable into a WDDX Packet
   Book = ObjDeser.deserialize(strWDDXPacket);

   //writes out our book title
   Response.write(Book.getProp("Title"));
%>
```

WDDX is a useful specification and works well with many languages. Indeed, it is already being used with some products produced by Allaire (its creators). However, it is a more closed specification than XML-RPC and SOAP, and doesn't command the same following these specifications have. It is also relatively limited (compared with SOAP), but works well with simple distributed communications.

Serializing With XMOP

XML Metadata Object Persistence has the goal of allowing technologies such as COM, Java, and CORBA to inter-operate by providing formal object serialization mechanisms that are not tied directly to any particular system object. Objects can therefore be marshaled between COM and Java, and even via different implementations of Java Virtual Machines.

The intention was/is to make XMOP complementary to XML-RPC or SOAP (as a way to serialize interface parameters in SOAP method calls, for example).

XMOP makes use of the **Simple Object Definition Language** (**SODL** at http://jabr.ne.mediaone.net/documents/sodl.htm) which is a XML IDL DTD allowing objects to be described in such a way that they remain compatible with the IDL's used in COM and CORBA. XMOP in fact uses the version 1.0 DTD of SODL.

> *You can find out more information on XMOP at http://jabr.ne.mediaone.net/documents/xmop.htm.*

KOALA Serialization

On the other hand, the **Koala Object Markup Language** (**KOML**) is a Java solution describing how to serialize and de-serialize Java Objects in an XML document, and conforms to the XML 1.0 standard and SAX 1.0. Some may find it useful, as it is a 100% Java solution, but as it only works for Java classes it has a narrow focus and may not fit all needs, particularly on the Internet.

The Koala project integrates with the Java class using the `Serializable` interface, providing a hook into the serialization stream itself.

A KOML serializable object must implement the interface `java.io.Serializable`, so a class named `Book` described in Java with the following code:

```
public class Book implements Serializable
{
   int id = 1642;
}
```

would be represented in KOML as the following XML:

```
<?xml version='1.0' encoding='UTF-8'?>
<!DOCTYPE koml SYSTEM "http://www.inria.fr/koala/XML/koml12.dtd">
<koml version='1.2'>
   <classes>
      <class name='Book' uid='-5510978188925784084'>
         <field name='i' type='int'/>
      </class>
   </classes>
   <object class='Book' id='i1'>
      <value type='int' name='id'>1642</value>
   </object>
</koml>
```

The namespace of a KOML document should point to the URL http://www.inria.fr/koala/XML/koml11.dtd, and further information on KOML can be found at http://www.inria.fr/koala/XML/serialization/.

Tightly Coupled Vs Loosely Coupled Systems

We are now going to consider the advantages and disadvantages of the loosely coupled systems offered by XML in comparison with more traditional tightly coupled systems. Tightly coupled systems offered by many of today's applications understand the form of messages being passed between them, such as whether they are using DCOM or CORBA (IIOP), for example. Loosely coupled systems, on the other hand, do not require such strict understanding between systems, and in the case of XML, it is simply text that is sent between them.

Disadvantages of Loosley Coupled Systems

Perhaps the two biggest disadvantages of using loosely coupled XML for a distributed component solution are bandwidth and speed. For example, although the creation of XML messages is made simpler, each is validated by a XML parser before being passed on to applications, and the overhead of this validation can become significant. Furthermore, the mark-up text added to the data to construct an XML document is significant, and increases the amount of network traffic caused by the transfer (although the method used for transport could implement compression techniques to reduce the level of traffic).

Tightly coupled systems understand the form of messages being passed between them, and this can provide a saving in network costs when compared to XML messages, which must be parsed. Of course, traditional tightly coupled systems often require handshakes, and can easily fail if the server or client has been upgraded to a new format.

Advantages of Loosley Coupled Systems

An XML based component framework can, in fact, be very scalable, as multiple method invocations can be wrapped in one request, as opposed to a traditional client-server model, where a request has to be made for each method that is called.

The diagram below shows traditional processes of remote method invocation:

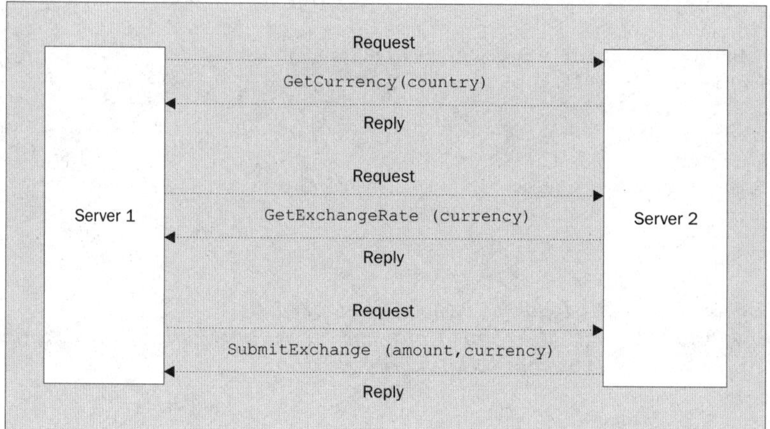

The next figure shows XML processes of remote method invocation:

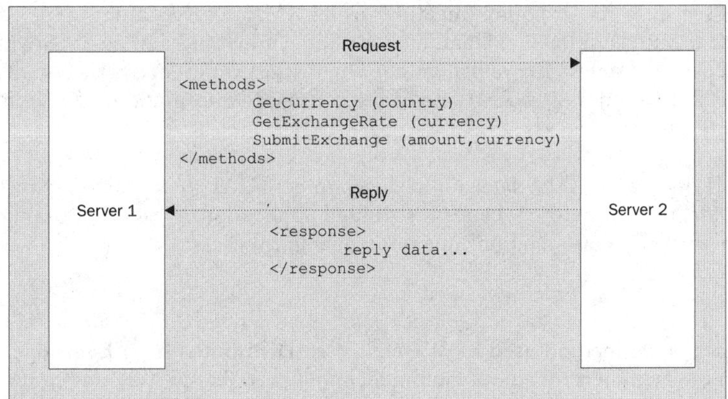

For high-reliability applications, it is possible to request that a series of calls are treated as one transaction. This technique guarantees that the calls are completed in an "all or none" fashion. If your application wishes to use transactions and you use the XML-RPC protocol, then you would have to build transactional capabilities into your applications yourself. However, the newer SOAP protocol (and many commercial XML server products) has capabilities to implement transactional-based applications if desired.

One can enforce a kind of version control amongst the various servers in a distributed application. Because each XML "document" can be validated against an appropriate DTD or schema, one can add functionality or make non-conflicting modifications. In the event that conflicts are found by a server, graceful error handling can be implemented. As long as XML tags are not removed, full functionality can effectively be maintained between distributed components that are effectively isolated. In fact, with the transformation languages available with XML the client structure doesn't even have to be in a fixed XML format, so long as the necessary data is included.

With loosely coupled systems it is relatively simple for documents created from different protocol specifications to send messages to each other. For example, we are going to discuss both the XML-RPC and SOAP protocols for distributed communications using XML. These systems are based on different XML specifications, but there is no reason (and it is in fact being discussed) why a method such as XSLT could not be used to 'translate' between the different specifications for particular versions of XML documents.

Methods of Communication

Servers that communicate with each other using XML can make use of a number of protocols and standards to provide the bridge between distributed components. The most popular is HTTP, as this is the most common standard protocol in use, although SMTP and FTP are similarly standardized enough to provide platform independent transport of the XML messages. However, more specific network interfaces such as CORBA/IIOP, Java RMI (Remote Method Invocation), and Microsoft DCOM/COM can be used with many dynamic XML application servers.

This chapter will focus on HTTP as the communications protocol for distributed applications, as it is the simplest and most independent protocol available, but we will also discuss some of the products available that can implement some of the alternative transport methods available towards the end of this chapter.

Remote Calls

The first method of server to server communications using XML is very similar to the traditional method of calling distributed applications, namely via calling a method and passing parameters to that method, which will provide you with a return value. The distinct difference is that all of these calls operate over pure HTTP and use only XML messages to provide information on what methods to invoke on the remote web server.

We will look at XML-RPC and SOAP later on in the chapter. SOAP offers the functionality detailed above, and is very effective for heterogeneous distributed applications – as well as being probably the most exciting of the server communications developments in progress.

Data Exchange

Data exchange, which is the method used by WDDX (Web Distributed Data Exchange, outlined above), differs slightly from the Remote Procedural calling technology in that it often does not account for a particular protocol and only provides assistance in creating XML based messages based on your data, rather than encapsulating the methods and parameters to be used on the distributed machine. There are initiatives for pure HTTP data exchange, where a particular page is invoked on the remote server and the data is POSTed to the page as XML. Other methods allow you to support XML data exchange via COM, CORBA SMTP and many other transport methods.

XML-RPC

XML-RPC, or eXtensible Mark-up Language Remote Procedural Call is a relatively new method of invoking methods on distributed machines and having information returned. It uses XML to transmit structured messages which encapsulate function calls that are 'executed' against remote systems, and so we can integrate remote systems with local systems seamlessly. In fact, as XML-RPC operates over pure HTTP, and uses XML (plain text) to pass messages, the entire specification is effectively language independent.

You may be suspicious of another declaration of a system which is platform independent, but this suspicion should be eased if you consider that the two main components, namely HTTP and XML, are simple but effective standards which have been accepted by the entire industry and run on virtually all platforms. Sure, XML-RPC may be simple, but it may be one of the most effective areas of all the new XML technologies to emerge over the next couple of years.

The current XML-RPC specification (available from http://www.xmlrpc.com) allows us to get a return value for a particular method using a set of parameters specified by a remote machine. We can use it to call methods on a remote server directly from a client or from a server. We will look more at the latter case in our discussion of server communications.

Exciting initiatives have been cropping up in the XML-RPC world, such as http://www.mailtothefuture.com, which allows you to use interfaces exposed from a remote server to send e-mail to yourself at a future date – kind of like a reminder system. You can remotely add a new message, remove a previous message, get the number of messages in a users queue as well as some other methods. All of these can be done without having to visit the site and use their interface. The following diagram illustrates how this works.

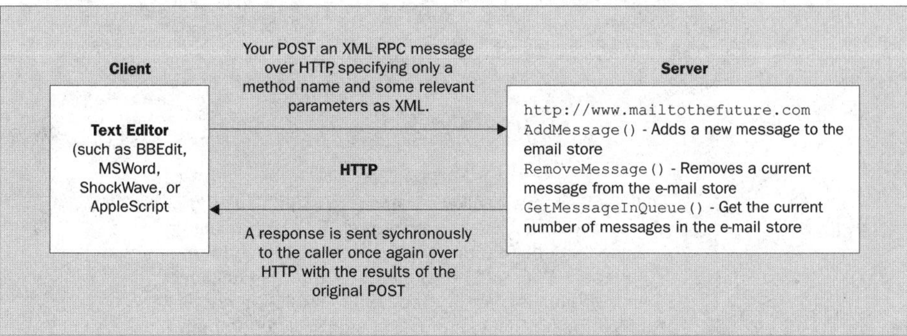

More recently, we have seen the discussion group editors from platforms like Frontier, AppleMacs, Unix, and Windows (among others) allowing users to add and modify messages at remote discussion groups. This can be done through a web browser or a client application (such as Microsoft Word). With this interface you can create a workstation editor that's not browser based, allowing you to create and edit messages with more advanced text editors than the ones built into web browsers.

XML-RPC allows you to post a message to the discussion forum, edit an existing message in the forum, and save your existing message. This can be done from *any* system that supports the HTTP protocol and any kind of text editor.

The possibilities are increasing weekly, and are continuously being pushed forward by Dave Winer at http://www.xmlrpc.com/.

Why Use XML-RPC?

Traditional methods of remote communication involve COM and CORBA techniques (such as DCOM or IIOP), and are well supported across many development communities. Although these techniques will undoubtedly remain popular in tightly integrated systems, the evolving world of distributed computing stresses these traditional methods. XML-RPC systems, in contrast, are much more adaptable to widely distributed networks. For example, XML systems do not require the server identities to be known before a method call. Instead, the server can be specified within the call, or even determined afterwards using a dynamic load-balancing process.

We then, traditionally, have to know the properties of the technologies involved, such as the platform types, whether they use COM or CORBA, if they are behind a firewall (many systems have problems with this), as well as many other considerations.

The following diagram illustrates how XML-RPC methods have no problems with a firewall as compared with traditional methods which have problems, particularly in the Internet scenario.

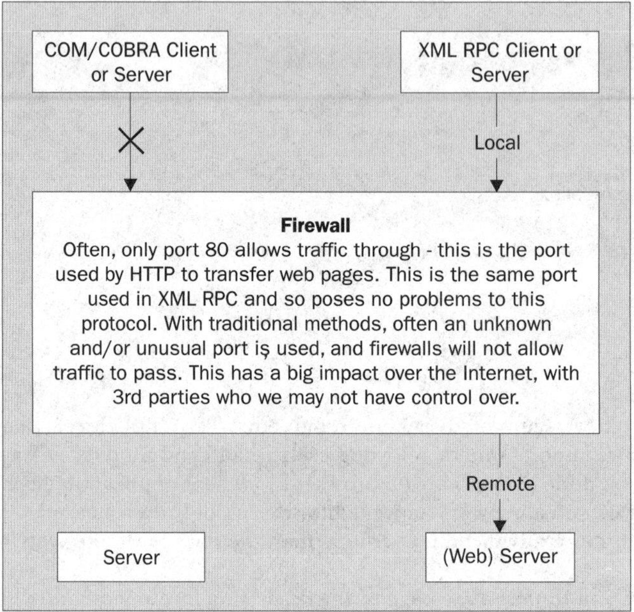

With the XML-RPC protocol, all communication works over HTTP, so there is no problem with transmitting information through firewalls (as almost all firewalls will allow HTTP to pass). Furthermore, as XML describes the interface as well as the data, there are less integration issues when compared with traditional more inflexible systems. In fact, all that is needed is a URL, interface descriptions, and the return value expected – it is this simple.

Some recent work at XMLRPC.com is perhaps the best illustration of this. Userland.com exposed some methods from their web site (running on Frontier) for modifying discussion group messages. This allows developers to remotely call the methods to perform actions such as create a new message on the discussion board and modify one of their existing messages – all via XML-RPC from any remote client systems supporting the HTTP protocol.

Userland provides one relatively short document with each method name; its expected parameters, its return value, and a short description of the method. Within a couple of days, people had editors on platforms such as Macs, Windows, and Unix, in a variety of programming languages including ASP, COM, PHP, Lingo, Java, and Applescript to name but a few.

There were very few problems. In fact, one of the more amusing e-mails from Dave Winer outlined that he thought he had a problem because no "success" messages had been posted 24 hours after the Discussion Group specification release. I wonder if any reader would ever consider 24 hours a long time when integrating multiple platforms and languages from across the world using traditional techniques? That's just how powerful XML-RPC is considered to be.

It is important to remember that XML-RPC is not always right for distributed computing. It is slower than traditional methods, which are most commonly used in closed networks for the reasons outlined above. However, the Internet is slower than most closed networks, and so you wouldn't really notice any latency problems using XML-RPC (as it would be the network latency rather than the processing time which would cause most delay). If you are calling methods on the same corporate network and are more interested in speed, without being worried about having to expose your application interfaces to remote servers, you would likely be better suited to using either COM or CORBA techniques such as DCOM or IIOP. As you will see, you can still expose many of the methods used in your COM/CORBA applications through XML-RPC with an HTTP wrapper on a web server.

The following diagram shows a possible structure for a distributed system with XML-RPC. This diagram should illustrate to you how any XML-RPC enabled client can call methods on XML-RPC servers on dissimilar platforms running various XML-RPC servers – there are many possible configurations. You can see that servers can invoke methods on other remote servers as well as provide services to client applications. Essentially there is no difference between a client invoking a call and a server invoking the same call.

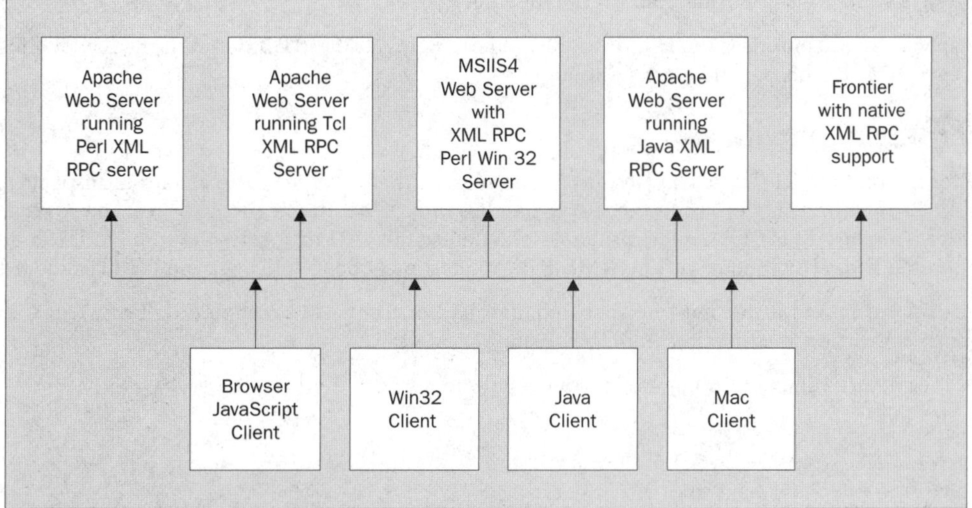

Where Does XML-RPC Fit In?

Previous chapters have described XML and its related technologies in some detail, so it may be surprising that XML-RPC currently utilizes only the most basic of these, namely the XML 1.0 standard and the XML Document Object Model.

These basic features of XML are supported on practically every platform and ensure that the XML-RPC specification can be supported across the board. Perhaps we will see other features of XML find its way into the XML-RPC specification in the future.

The XML-RPC Specification – A Technical Overview

The XML-RPC implementation is based around an HTTP POST where the body is marked up using XML containing the method to execute on the remote server and any parameters needed by the method. A response payload is returned which is also based on XML.

Parameters and return values to a procedure can be simple data types such as Boolean, integers, strings, floats and dates as well as more complex data structures such as complex record and list structures via arrays and structures. In fact, binary data can also be expressed using Base64 encoding, allowing, for example, images to be returned to method calls.

> *Base64 is used to convert binary data to ASCII text for transportation through SMTP servers, and other text based protocols, so that no data is misinterpreted. Base64 is also the standard to allow transfer of binary encoded information via XML-RPC, such as GIFs and JPEGs. We will look in more detail at this later in the chapter.*

Another important part of the specification is that there must only be one return value, although this could be a structure composing many resultant values.

The specification comprises the HTTP header requirements, XML-RPC Request, the Payload format, the XML-RPC Response, and error handling.

Header Requirements

The format of the URI (Universal Resource Identifier) in the first line of the header is unspecified, and could be empty or a single slash if the server handles only XML-RPC calls. However, if the server handles a mixture of HTTP requests, then we should use the URI to specify the route to the code that handles the XML-RPC requests. The XML-RPC request must be a POST via the HTTP standard.

A `User-Agent` and `Host` must be specified and the `Content-Type` should be `text/xml`. Finally, the correct `Content-length` should be given.

Let's look at an example fulfilling the header requirements:

```
POST /RPC2 HTTP/1.0
User-Agent: Frontier/5.1.2 (WinNT)
Host: betty.userland.com
Content-Type: text/xml
Content-length: 181
```

The above example specifies `RPC2` as the responder for the XML-RPC request from a Frontier client running on Windows NT to a server called `betty` at `userland.com`. The `Content-Type` is correctly specified as `text/xml` and of `Content-length 181`. This is a valid XML-RPC request.

Request Payload Format

The request specifies that the structure is XML and that version 1.0 of the XML specification is being used. The entire payload should then be wrapped in a `<methodCall>` element, which must contain a sub-element `<methodName>` containing a string describing the name of the remote method to be invoked. It is up to the sever to correctly interpret the characters in a method name, but valid identifiers are lower and upper case `A` to `Z`, `0` to `9`, underscore, dot, colon, and slash (with XML's usual restrictions on the first character).

If the method has parameters, the `<methodCall>` element must contain a `<params>` element, which in turn can contain one or more `<param>` elements, each having a `<value>` item in the order they appear as defined by the method interface. The following is an example template for a request:

```
<?xml version="1.0"?>
<methodCall>
   <methodName>mymethodname</methodName>
   <params>
      <param>
         <value><string>myParameter</string></value>
      </param>
   </params>
</methodCall>
```

Specifying Parameters

Values specified as parameters come under the umbrella of scalars, arrays and structures, where the scalar types are:

- integer
- Boolean
- string
- double
- date/time
- Base 64

We'll look at each of these types in turn.

Integers

An integer in XML-RPC is a four-byte signed integer denoted by the `<i4>` or `<int>` elements. Leading zeros are collapsed, and no white space is permitted. For example:

```
<?xml version="1.0"?>
<methodCall>
   <methodName>GetCelcius</methodName>
   <params>
      <param>
         <value><int>-5</int></value>
      </param>
   </params>
</methodCall>
```

You may find it strange that the datatype is not expressed as an attribute, and maybe by the lack of attributes in general in the XML-RPC specification. There is no real reason for this, other than the decision not to use them by the specification author.

There is a lot of debate in the XML-RPC community about whether attributes would really be any more useful than element definitions, but as yet there have been no moves to use them.

Boolean

A Boolean is denoted by the `<boolean>` element, and can be `0` for false or `1` for true. For example:

```
<?xml version="1.0"?>
<methodCall>
   <methodName>SetProductAvailability</methodName>
   <params>
      <param>
         <value><boolean>1</boolean></value>
      </param>
   </params>
</methodCall>
```

String

A string is enclosed in a `<string>` element, and can be any valid ASCII value, but as XML-RPC is valid XML special characters such as < and & must be encoded as `<` and `&` respectively. Encoding is currently not specified in XML-RPC, so the default encoding for your parser is used. The encoding type is not currently required to be specified in XML-RPC, although this is an issue that is currently gathering discussion at the XML-RPC discussion groups. Therefore the XML default UTF-8 encoding will be used, which is sufficient for most messaging. The following is an example showing the use of a sting type:

```
<?xml version="1.0"?>
<methodCall>
   <methodName>GetCompanyNumber</methodName>
   <params>
      <param>
         <value><string>Wrox Press</string></value>
      </param>
   </params>
</methodCall>
```

Double

A double is defined as double precision signed floating-point number in XML-RPC, and is denoted by the element `<double>`. A double cannot contain white space, and should consist of a plus or minus followed by any number of numeric characters, and then followed by a period and any number of numeric characters (the range is implementation-dependent and not specified). An example of this data type is shown below:

```
<?xml version="1.0"?>
<methodCall>
   <methodName>SetMyCurrentBankBalance</methodName>
   <params>
      <param>
         <value><double>-23435.87</<double></value>
      </param>
   </params>
</methodCall>
```

Date/Time

The date and time, denoted by <dateTime.iso8601>, is a subset of the iso8601 standard, and will be a crucial part of many Internet business systems. The format is this: YYYYMMDDTHH24:MM:SS which makes is very easy to transfer date and time specific information via XML-RPC. Information on the timezone should be specified either by the server or the documentation, and is not detailed within this element. An example is shown below:

```
<?xml version="1.0"?>
<methodCall>
   <methodName>GetInventoryLevel</methodName>
   <params>
      <param>
         <value>
             <dateTime.iso8601>19990912T13:54:12<dateTime.iso8601>
         </value>
      </param>
   </params>
</methodCall>
```

Base 64

We can use the Base64 standard to allow transfer of binary encoded information via XML-RPC, such as GISs and JPEGs, by specifying the binary file inside the wrapper (as in the example below). The <base64> element is used to specify encoded data. The example does not use a real encoded image!

```
<?xml version="1.0"?>
<methodCall>
   <methodName>InsertCompanySharesGraph</methodName>
   <params>
      <param>
         <value>
            <base64>Wk964jkf0skamllp97Okmk<base64>
         </value>
      </param>
   </params>
</methodCall>
```

Arrays

An <array> in XML-RPC has a single <data> element which contains *any number* of <value> elements containing the parameterized data. Different types can be mixed within an array, and they can even be recursive, with any <value> element containing an array or structure. This could be used when you wish to pass information (for example, state information on an object) that consists of a sequential number of parameters that you don't know at design time (or can vary), or if there are so many parameters that you would rather pass an array of them rather than pass each individual parameter separately. An example is shown below.

```
<?xml version="1.0"?>
<methodCall>
   <methodName>InsertCompanyInfo</methodName>
   <params>
      <param>
```

```
            <array>
               <data>
                  <value><string>Deltabiz Inc</string></value>
                  <value><int>8878</int></value>
                  <value><boolean>1</boolean></value>
                  <value>
                     <array>
                        <data>
                           <value><int>674</int></value>
                           <value><string>NoWhere Rd</string></value>
                           <value><string>Glasgow</string></value>
                        </data>
                     </array>
                  </value>
               </data>
            </array>
         </param>
      </params>
   </methodCall>
```

Structures

A structure allows you to assign some intelligent information to the order of values, unlike with arrays, where data is simply sequential. Structures are denoted by a <struct> element containing one or more <member> elements (a member limit is not specified). These, in turn, have both <name> and <value> elements to hold the data. Like arrays, structures can be recursive, and can also contain arrays. The following example illustrates an XML-RPC structure:

```
<?xml version="1.0"?>
<methodCall>
   <methodName>CreatePurchase</methodName>
   <params>
      <param>
         <struct>
            <member>
               <name>Product</name>
               <value><string>Silver Clock</string></value>
            </member>
            <member>
               <name>Cost</name>
               <value><i4>87</i4></value>
            </member>
            <member>
               <name>Purchase Date</name>
               <value>
                  <dateTime.iso8601>19990912T02:53:02</dateTime.iso8601>
               </value>
            </member>
            <member>
               <name>Purchase Order</name>
               <value><double>384793</double></value>
            </member>
         </struct>
      </param>
   </params>
</methodCall>
```

Looking at the above code, you may think that XML methods could eliminate much of the redundancy, as the following section illustrates:

```
<struct>
   <Product><string>Silver Clock</string></Product>
   <Cost><i4>87</i4></Cost>
   ...
</struct>
```

There may be many reasons for the XML-RPC specification not having been defined in this manner. One possible reason is that the way the XML-RPC structure is defined more closely resembles structures (or dictionary objects) in conventional programming languages, where we have explicit name/value pairs.

Response Header

The first line of the response should be a valid HTTP header of `200 OK` (unless there is a lower level error in the server itself), followed by a `Content-Type` of `text/xml` and a correct `Content-length`. An example is shown below (`Date` and `Server` are optional headers):

```
HTTP/1.0 200 OK
Connection: close
Content-length: 342
Content-Type: text/xml
Date: Fri, 17 Jul 1998 19:55:08 GMT
Server: Userland Frontier/5.1.2-WinNT
```

Response Format

The response payload must have a structure where a `<methodResponse>` element can contain a single `<params>` element, encapsulating a single `<param>` element with a single `<value>` element.

```
<?xml version="1.0"?>
<methodResponse>
   <params>
      <value>
         <array>
            <data>
               <value><string>www.deltabiz.com</string></value>
               <value><double>-76570</double></value>
            </data>
         </array>
      </value>
   </params>
</methodResponse>
```

In the case where there is a problem, the response can also contain error information. We will look at this now.

Response Faults

As an *alternative* to the successful response format detailed above, the response can return fault information. In this case the <methodResponse> element contains a <fault> element, which contains a <value> element. The <value> element contains a <struct> element with two members, one called faultCode with an <int> value, and another called faultString with a string denoting the reason for the error.

An example is shown below:

```
<?xml version="1.0"?>
<methodResponse>
   <fault>
      <value>
         <struct>
            <member>
               <name>faultCode</name>
               <value><int>873</int></value>
            </member>
            <member>
               <name>faultString</name>
               <value><string>An error message</string></value>
            </member>
         </struct>
      </value>
   </fault>
</methodResponse>
```

Implementing XML-RPC

XML-RPC can be broken into two components, namely client and server. The client is completely independent from the server, so that a COM client running on a Windows NT Server can invoke methods on a Unix Apache server written in Perl.

XML-RPC implementations are available for Python, Java, Perl, Tcl, ASP, COM, and PHP. Further detail on how to get each implementation is given in the XML-RPC section "*Where To Go From Here*".

A Simple Example

The following example illustrates some of the above languages and shows how to invoke a remote method returning the current balance of my savings account. We will break the example into the request XML, the client implementation, the response XML, and the server implementation.

The example is based on ASP and MS IIS, although the server can be called by a client written using another technology, or we could write the server using another technology and use one of these clients to call it – so long as the interface definition remains constant there will be no problems. That is the beauty of XML-RPC.

Before starting the examples, put all of the sample files into a directory <root>/xmlrpc/client/ on your web server. Also, download the ASP client/server files from the URL given in the section "*Where To Go From Here*" below, and ensure that the file xmlrpc.asp is also in the directory <root>/xmlrpc/client/.

Also, register the COM component, as outlined at the same URL, using the RegSvr32 utility. Ensure that you follow all the instructions (install IE5 etc.) detailed at this site to successfully install the RPC implementations.

Note that to register the component, simply open a command prompt, type

```
RegSvr32 <component name>.dll
```

and a message box will pop up telling you that the component has been successfully registered.

Request XML

The following code describes the XML-RPC HTTP request for the sample, where we want to call a local method called `GetCurrentBalance()`, which accepts an account number as the parameter.

```
<?xml version="1.0"?>
<methodCall>
   <methodName>GetCurrentBalance</methodName>
   <params>
      <param>
         <value>
            <double>873214</double>
         </value>
      </param>
   </params>
</methodCall>
```

We can see that the method we wish to invoke is called `GetCurrentBalance()`, and that we are passing the account number as a double.

Using the XML-RPC methods within the target platform, the developer will only need to provide the parameters and methods. The actual XML code will be, of course, expanded as part of the initial method invocation, and an HTTP POST will be made on behalf of the user. Let's look at how we would implement the above in four languages, namely ASP, COM (VB), Java, and PHP.

> *Note that if you want to try examples as you go, then you should consider looking at the section* "Where To Go From Here" *to download the appropriate XML-RPC implementations.*

Active Server Pages

```
<!--#include file="xmlrpc.asp" -->
<%
   ReDim paramList(1)
   paramList(0)=873214

   myresp = xmlRPC("http://localhost /xmlrpc/server.asp", _
                   "GetCurrentBalance", paramList)

   response.write(myresp & "<p>")
%>
```

COM (Visual Basic)

```
Dim obj As deltabiz.XMLRPCclient
Set obj = CreateObject("deltabiz.xmlrpcClient")

ReDim param(1)
Dim strArr
param(0) = 873214

retval = obj.xmlRPC("http://localhost/xmlrpc/server.asp", "", _
                    "", "", "GetCurrentBalance", param)

MsgBox retval
```

Java

```
XmlRpcClient xmlrpc =
   new XmlRpcClient("http://www.localhost.com/xmlrpc/server.asp");
Vector params = new Vector();

params.addElement(873214);
Integer retVal = (Integer) xmlrpc.execute("GetCurrentBalance", params);
```

PHP

```
$xclient=new xmlrpc_client("/xmlrpc/server.asp", .
                           "localhost",80);
$ret=$xclient->send(new xmlrpcmsg("GetCurrentBalance", .
                                  array(new xmlrpcval("873214","double"))));

$returnval=$ret->value();
$retVal=$returnval->scalarval();
```

Response XML

The response XML to the above request should follow the following structure:

```
<?xml version="1.0"?>
<methodResponse>
   <params>
      <param>
         <value>
            <int>7635</int>
         </value>
      </param>
   </params>
</methodResponse>
```

If there were a problem with the invocation, we would receive a response as shown below. The following XML would illustrate that there had been a problem contacting the XML-RPC server:

```
<?xml version="1.0"?>
<methodResponse>
   <fault>
      <value>
         <struct>
            <member>
               <name>faultCode</name>
               <value><int>345</int></value>
            </member>
            <member>
               <name>faultString</name>
               <value>
                <string>The server name or address could not be resolved.</string>
               </value>
            </member>
         </struct>
      </value>
   </fault>
</methodResponse>
```

Notice that the actual fault codes and fault strings are genuine Win32 errors, and so you should wrap you call in an error handling function. You should check error details for the specific XML-RPC implementation you are using.

An example for our call above would be:

```
<!--#include file="xmlrpc.asp" -->
<%
   ReDim paramList(1)
   paramList(0)=876

   On Error Resume Next

   myresp = xmlRPC("http://localhost/xmlrpc/server.asp", _
                   "GetCurrentBalance", paramList)

   If Err.Number<>0 Then
      response.write("Error Number: " & Err.Number & "<BR/>")
      response.write("Error Detail: " & Err.Description & "<P>")
   Else
      response.write(myresp & "<p>")
   End If
%>
```

Let's have a look at the server code to invoke these methods. Note again that the server implementations do not need to be written in the same language (or even platform) as the client, but we will look at equivalent implementations, as we did for the client.

Active Server Pages

```
<!--#include file="xmlrpc.asp" -->
<%
   rpcserver
%>

<SCRIPT LANGUAGE=JAVASCRIPT RUNAT=SERVER>
   function GetCurrentBalance(AccNumber)
   {
      var intBalance=7635;

      //return the amount to the client
      return intBalance;
   }
</SCRIPT>
```

Java

```
XmlRpcServer xmlrpc = new XmlRpcServer();
xmlrpc.addHandler("GetCurrentBalance", new BalanceHandler());

Integer result = xmlrpc.execute(request.getInputStream());
response.setContentType("text/xml");
response.setContentLength(result.length());
PrintWriter writer = response.getWriter();
writer.write(result);
writer.flush();
```

PHP

```
<?php
include("xmlrpc.inc"); include("xmlrpcs.inc");

function GetCurrentBalanceImpl($params)
{
   return new xmlrpcresp(new rpcval("873214","integer"));
}

$s = new xmlrpc_server(array("GetCurrentBalance" =>
                             "GetCurrentBalanceImpl"));
?>
```

Sample Book Application

The following example application (available via the Wrox website along with the rest of the code for this book) illustrates how to invoke remote methods to both receive information and update remote information stores. Wrox Books have decided to have 5 remote servers in different parts of the world that store book information locally as an XML file, although the files should be updateable directly from a Wrox local web server in Birmingham (we will assume that catalog maintenance is done centrally from this location). A user should be able to choose the locations to query and obtain the list of subjects available to view. When this list has been returned, the user should select one subject along with the areas to query, in order to receive detailed information about titles available at those locations.

Let's look at a schematic illustrating the process.

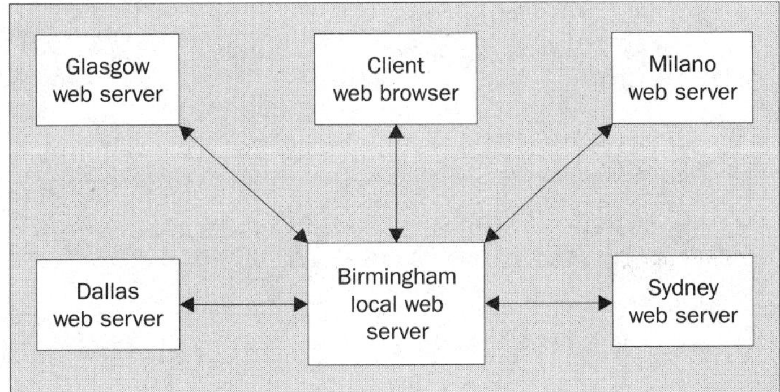

A user who wants to view book information at one or more of the servers is presented with a screen showing the choice of sites to search for a list of book subjects available. This is illustrated below.

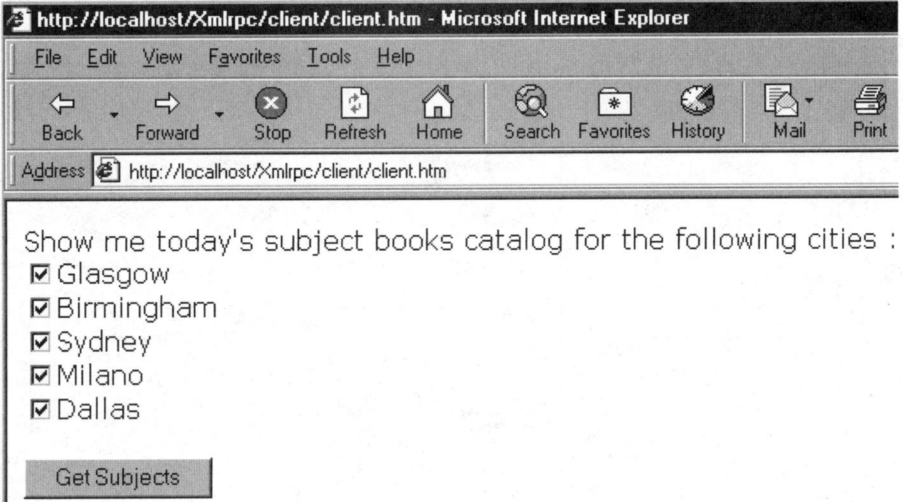

The HTML required to generate the screen is as follows, and is in the file `client.htm`:

```
<HTML>
<HEAD>
   <META NAME="GENERATOR" Content="Microsoft Visual Studio 6.0">
</HEAD>
<BODY>
   <form method="post" action="Subjects.asp" name=form1>
      Show me today's subject books catalog for the following cities :
      <BR/>
      <INPUT name="city" type=checkbox value="Glasgow"
             CHECKED>Glasgow
      <BR/>
      <INPUT name="city" type=checkbox value="Birmingham"
             CHECKED>Birmingham
      <BR/>
```

```
        <INPUT name="city" type=checkbox value="Sydney"
               CHECKED>Sydney
        <BR/>
        <INPUT name="city" type=checkbox value="Milano"
               CHECKED>Milano
        <BR/>
        <INPUT name="city" type=checkbox value="Dallas"
               CHECKED>Dallas
        <P/>
        <input type="hidden" name="Function" VALUE="GetSubjects">
        <input type="submit" value="Get Subjects">
     </form>
  </BODY>
  </HTML>
```

The response returns a list of the cities following by a drop down box of the available book subjects.

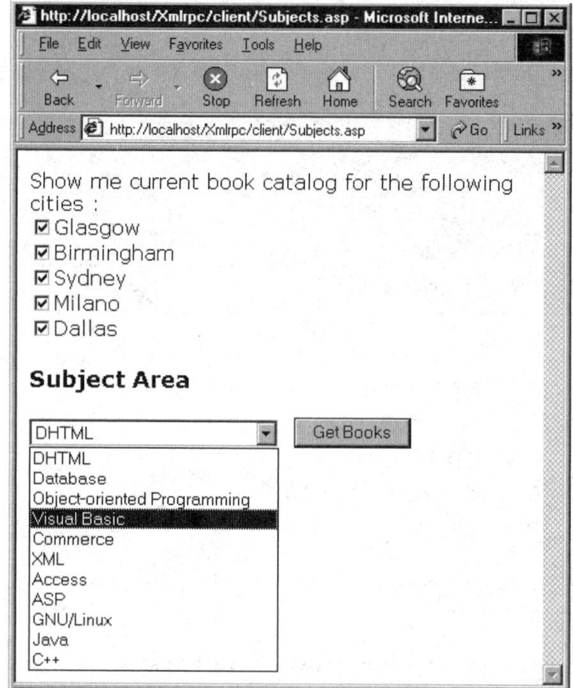

Data on books available at a particular remote site is stored within an XML file at that site. The XML file is called `CityNameBooks.xml`, and each file is queried depending on the cities selected. Therefore all the city data XML files are different and up to date for that site.

> *Note that this example illustrates the power of XML-RPC. Each XML store can be on a different remote server across the world. Equally, to use the example you can either put all of the XML stores in one directory on your web server or create numerous virtual servers by creating webs on different ports and referring to the XML store as* http://myserver:port/<citystore>.xml. *The location is entirely hidden to the clients.*
>
> *Further details on where you specify the location of the XML stores is given further on in the chapter.*

The following XML file is for the Glasgow bookstore. There can be many books, but each book entry must contain a book ID, a publication date, the title of the book, the authors of the book, and, finally, the subject domain of the book. The publication date (`pubdate`) is in UK date format, as all processing is carried out on the Birmingham UK web server. Obviously if this XML file was to be processed on several international servers, a format such as ISO 8601 (which is the format used internally for the XML-RPC specification) would be of more benefit.

```
<?xml version="1.0"?>
<books>
   <book bookid="1" pubdate="01/03/1999">
      <title>
         Instant Netscape Dynamic HTML Programmer's Reference NC4
         Edition
      </title>
      <authors>
         <author>Alex Homer</author>
         <author>Chris Ullman</author>
      </authors>
      <subject>DHTML</subject>
   </book>
   <book bookid="2" pubdate="11/10/2000">
      <title>Professional Visual Basic 6 Distributed Objects</title>
      <authors>
         <author>Rockford Lhotka</author>
      </authors>
      <subject>Visual Basic</subject>
   </book>
   <book bookid="3" pubdate="11/12/1999">
      <title>Beginning Active Server Pages 2.0</title>
      <authors>
         <author>Brian Francis</author>
         <author>John Kauffman</author>
         <author>Juan T Llibre</author>
         <author>David Sussman</author>
         <author>Chris Ullman</author>
      </authors>
      <subject>ASP</subject>
   </book>
   <book bookid="4" pubdate="11/10/2000">
      <title>Beginner's Guide to Access 2.0</title>
      <authors>
         <author>Wrox Author Team</author>
      </authors>
      <subject>Access</subject>
   </book>
   <book bookid="5" pubdate="11/12/1999">
      <title>Beginning Java 2</title>
      <authors>
         <author>Ivor Horton</author>
      </authors>
      <subject>Java</subject>
   </book>
</books>
```

Getting The Subjects List

The following diagram illustrates the process required to get a subject list from the XML data files.

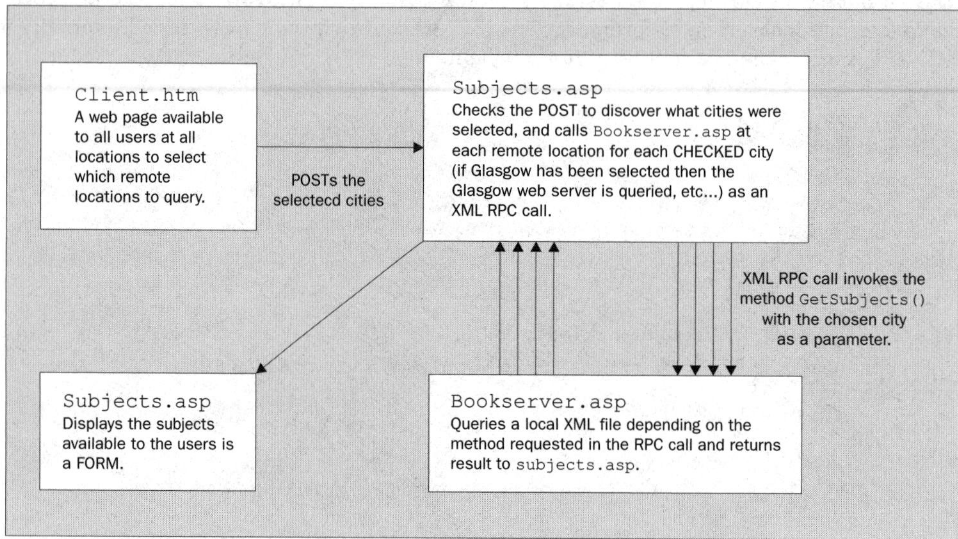

The form submission is actually posted to a page called `subjects.asp`, which is written in VBScript. We must first include the XML-RPC client/server file that contains the functions to convert your method invocations as defined in the specification (which, in the case of ASP, is currently written in VBScript).

```
<!--#include file="xmlrpc.asp"-->
```

We then have some HTML which simply writes the cities and checkboxes out as in the initial screen – this points to a file called `proxy.asp` which is used when requesting books for the chosen subject.

```
<HTML>
<HEAD>
   <META NAME="GENERATOR" Content="Microsoft Visual Studio 6.0">
</HEAD>
<BODY>
   <form method="post" action="proxy.asp" id=form1 name=form1>
      Show me current book catalog for the following cities :
      <BR/>
      <INPUT name="city" type=checkbox value="Glasgow"
             CHECKED>Glasgow
      <BR/>
      <INPUT name="city" type=checkbox value="Birmingham"
             CHECKED>Birmingham
      <BR/>
      <INPUT name="city" type=checkbox value="Sydney"
             CHECKED>Sydney
      <BR/>
      <INPUT name="city" type=checkbox value="Milano"
             CHECKED>Milano
```

```
    <BR/>
    <INPUT name="city" type=checkbox value="Dallas"
           CHECKED>Dallas
    <P/>
```

We then create an instance of a dictionary object to hold each of the subject names returned, which is then used in the function `CheckDuplicate()`. This function determines whether a subject instance has already been found, and if it hasn't, it is added to the collection – this prevents the user from seeing repeated subject areas in the drop down.

```
<%
   Dim objDict
   Set objDict = Server.CreateObject("Scripting.Dictionary")

   Function CheckDuplicate(strValue)
      If objDict.Exists(strValue) Then
         CheckDuplicate="TRUE"
      Else
         objDict.Add strValue,strValue
         CheckDuplicate="FALSE"
      End If
   End Function
```

We then reference the hidden element called `Function` on the previous page, `client.htm`, which defined the XML-RPC method to be invoked. The method we want to invoke is actually called `GetSubjects()`, and the desired city should be passed as a parameter, so we declare an array (the parameters must be passed as an array) called `paramList` as having one element.

```
   strFunction=Request.Form("Function")
   Dim paramList(1)
   Dim intNumCities
   intNumCities=0
   Dim intCounter
   intCounter=0
```

These values are inserted into a disconnected recordset, as it is simple to persist distributed systems data with the recordset object's `save()` (as XML) method. The recordset is set to use a client cursor to allow the recordset to be disconnected.

```
   'Create a local ADO RecordSet to store our data for manipulation
   Set objRS = Server.CreateObject("ADODB.RecordSet")
   objRS.CursorLocation=3
```

The fields are then created in the recordset object. We want to be able to identify each title by its location and its unique ID at that location. So, we append three such titles to the recordset, with the ID defined as an integer (an integer type is defined by a "3" for an ADO Recordset) and the title and city as strings (a string type is defined by a "8" for an ADO Recordset). We then `Open()` the recordset for manipulation.

```
'Create the Fields
objRS.Fields.Append "ID",3
objRS.Fields.Append "Title",8
objRS.Fields.Append "City",8
objRS.Open
```

For each of the cities we have our servers at, we then make XML-RPC calls to get the list of book subjects available. First we test whether the client had checked to search the Glasgow database. We do this by checking the FORM POST made by the user using the `Instr()` function, which returns a number greater than `0` if the first specified string contains an occurrence of the second string ("`Glasgow`" in the first case). If this is the case, then we define our XML-RPC parameter as `Glasgow` (as `GetSubjects()` expects one parameter). Then, the XML-RPC invocation is made to the remote server using the following format:

```
returnValue = xmlRPC(URL,MethodName,ParamaterArray)
```

Obviously, to make the application files accessible to those of us on a single server, the server queries are made to the local server by default. However, the URL in the XML-RPC call can be changed to any remote server supporting the XML-RPC interfaces for the application.

A simple way to test this on a single server is to set up 5 test web sites on different ports and change the URL in the XML-RPC invocation to reflect this.

The return value to the XML-RPC call is a comma-delimited array of the subjects available at the requested location, so we use the `Split()` method to get a one-dimensional array of the subjects. We then iterate through this array, adding each of the ID, subject title, and city details to our recordset. We repeat the XML-RPC calls for each of the distributed locations chosen by the user, which are all specified in the form request object.

```
If Instr(1,Request.Form("City"),"Glasgow")>0 Then
   paramList(0)="Glasgow"
   strGlas = _
      xmlRPC("http://LOCALHOST/xmlrpc/client/BookServer.asp", _
             "GetSubjects", paramList)
   arrTemp=split(strGlas,",")

   For k=0 To UBOUND(arrTemp)
      objRS.AddNew
      objRS.Fields("ID").Value=k
      objRS.Fields("Title").Value=arrTemp(k)
      objRS.Fields("City").Value=paramList(0)
      objRS.Update
      intCounter=intCounter+1
   Next
End If

If Instr(1,Request.Form("City"),"Birmingham")>0 Then
   paramList(0)="Birmingham"
   strBirm = _
      xmlRPC("http://LOCALHOST/xmlrpc/client/BookServer.asp", _
             strFunction, paramList)
   arrTemp=split(strBirm,",")
```

```
    For k=0 To UBOUND(arrTemp)
        objRS.AddNew
        objRS.Fields("ID").Value=k
        objRS.Fields("Title").Value=arrTemp(k)
        objRS.Fields("City").Value=paramList(0)
        objRS.Update
        intCounter=intCounter+1
    Next
End If

If Instr(1,Request.Form("City"),"Sydney")>0 Then
    paramList(0)="Sydney"
    strSyd = _
        xmlRPC("http://LOCALHOST/xmlrpc/client/BookServer.asp", _
                strFunction, paramList)
    arrTemp=split(strSyd,",")

    For k=0 To UBOUND(arrTemp)
        objRS.AddNew
        objRS.Fields("ID").Value=k
        objRS.Fields("Title").Value=arrTemp(k)
        objRS.Fields("City").Value=paramList(0)
        objRS.Update
        intCounter=intCounter+1
    Next
End If

If Instr(1,Request.Form("City"),"Milano")>0 Then
    paramList(0)="Milano"
    strMil = _
        xmlRPC("http://LOCALHOST/xmlrpc/client/BookServer.asp", _
                strFunction, paramList)
    arrTemp=split(strMil,",")

    For k=0 To UBOUND(arrTemp)
        objRS.AddNew
        objRS.Fields("ID").Value=k
        objRS.Fields("Title").Value=arrTemp(k)
        objRS.Fields("City").Value=paramList(0)
        objRS.Update
        intCounter=intCounter+1
    Next
End If

If Instr(1,Request.Form("City"),"Dallas")>0 Then
    paramList(0)="Dallas"
    strDal = _
        xmlRPC("http://LOCALHOST/xmlrpc/client/BookServer.asp", _
                strFunction, paramList)
    arrTemp=split(strDal,",")

    For k=0 To UBOUND(arrTemp)
        objRS.AddNew
        objRS.Fields("ID").Value=k
        objRS.Fields("Title").Value=arrTemp(k)
        objRS.Fields("City").Value=paramList(0)
```

```
            objRS.Update
            intCounter=intCounter+1
         Next
      End If
```

When we have iterated through each of the chosen subjects, we will have a complete disconnected recordset of our book subject details from all of our chosen locations. If the recordset is not empty and we have had a list of subjects returned, we write them into an HTML SELECT element by iterating through the recordset object. During this process, we call the `CheckDuplicate()` function, which ensures that we do not write out the same subject twice if it appears multiple times when all subjects are gathered from all cities. We will look at this function in more detail in the next section. If there are currently no subjects available (meaning that the chosen city has no current book store) then an appropriate message is displayed to the user.

```
      'get the values in Ascending order
      objRS.MoveFirst

      Response.Write "<h3>Subject Area</h3>"

      If NOT objRS.EOF Then
         Response.Write "<SELECT Name='Subject'>"
         Dim strValue
         strValue=""

         Do While NOT objRS.EOF
            If CheckDuplicate(objRS.Fields(1).Value)="FALSE" Then
               Response.Write "<OPTION VALUE='" & objRS.Fields(1).Value _
                              & "'>" & objRS.Fields(1).Value & vbNewLine
            End If

            objRS.MoveNext
         Loop
         Response.Write "</SELECT>"
      Else
         Response.Write "<H4>There are currently no subject(s) at " & _
                        "your chosen locations(s).</H4>"
      End If

      objRS.Close
      Set objRS = Nothing
   %>
```

Finally, we set up the function which will be called after the user chooses one of the subjects from the `SELECT` and clicks the "Get Books" submit button to POST to a file called `proxy.asp`, which we describe next.

```
         <input type="hidden" name="Function" VALUE="GetBooks">
         <input type="submit" value="Get Books" id=submit1 name=submit1>
      </form>
   </BODY>
   </HTML>
```

Retrieving Book Information

Now that we have retrieved the subjects available from our chosen cities we want to be able to select one of the subject areas and have all titles of that subject returned to us, along with the authors of the book. An example of what would be displayed is shown below. The example shows a case where the user chose Glasgow and Birmingham, selected the subject domain as Commerce, and clicked the "Get Books" button:

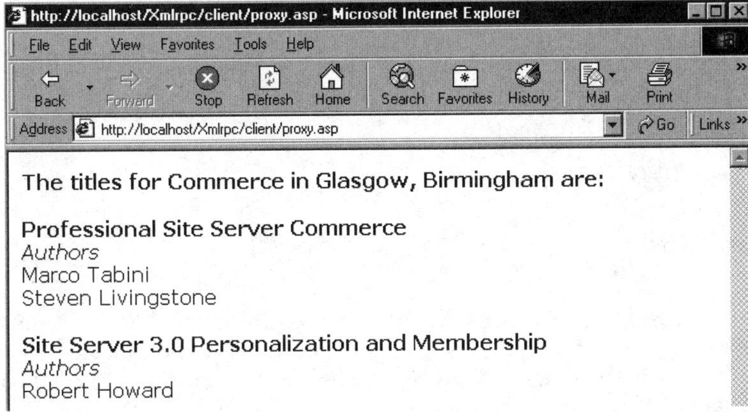

> **Make sure you have followed the instructions given at the start of the chapter and copied all of the Wrox downloaded files to the directory `<root>/xmlrpc/client/` on your web server.**

The following diagram illustrates how this part of the system links to the previous section where the user had to choose a subject domain.

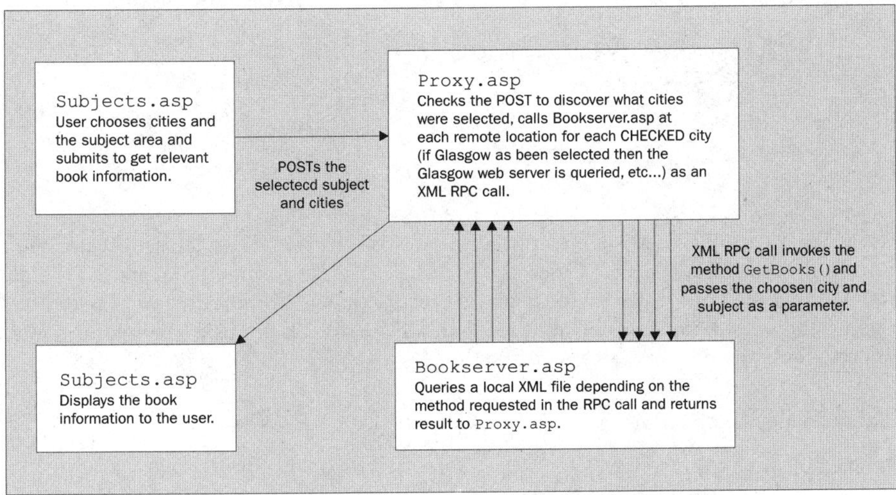

The script to create the above page (`proxy.asp`) is written almost exclusively in JavaScript. However, as the current implementation for ASP was designed to work with VBScript, we must have a function in VBScript which creates a `VBArray` object for passing to the XML-RPC method. This is needed, as the parameter list used in the XML-RPC method invocation described above requires an array of the parameters (which must be a `VBArray`). This is the first section we come to in `proxy.asp`:

```
<!--#include file="xmlrpc.asp"-->

<SCRIPT LANGUAGE=vbscript RUNAT=Server>
   Function CreateVBArray(a)
      Dim i, j, k
      Dim arr(2)
      arr(0)=Request.Form("Subject")
      arr(1)=a
      CreateVBArray = arr
   End Function
</SCRIPT>
```

We then change to use JavaScript. First we re-implement the `CheckDuplicate()` function we used in `subjects.asp` earlier using VBScript. This function basically takes the value to be added to the `Dictionary` object and checks whether it already exists (using the `Exists()` method of the object) – if it does not, it is added.

```
<SCRIPT LANGUAGE=JAVASCRIPT RUNAT=SERVER>
   var objDict = Server.CreateObject("Scripting.Dictionary")

   function CheckDuplicate(strValue)
   {
      var strRet="";

      if (objDict.Exists(strValue))
         strRet="TRUE";
      else
      {
         objDict.Add(strValue,strValue);
         strRet="FALSE";
      }

      return strRet;
   }
```

A function called `DrawScreen()` encapsulates the XML-RPC code which will create the HTML displaying the results of our search. Once again, we declare the parameter array and the dictionary object for holding the book data. We also create our disconnected recordset and create the fields to which we will append the response from the XML-RPC calls. This is listed below for comparison with the VBScript equivalent in `subjects.asp`:

```
   function DrawScreen()
   {
      var strFunction=Request.Form("Function");
      var paramList = new Array(2);
      var intNumCities=0;
```

```
var arrBookList = new Array(1);
var intCounter=0;
var objDictList=Server.CreateObject("Scripting.Dictionary");

//Create a local ADO RecordSet to store our data for manipulation
var objRS = Server.CreateObject("ADODB.RecordSet");
objRS.CursorLocation=3;

//Create the Fields
objRS.Fields.Append("ID",3);
objRS.Fields.Append("Title",8);
objRS.Fields.Append("City",8);
objRS.Open();
```

The section where we invoke the remote method is slightly different. We first check that at least one city has been selected and, if so, what city is being referenced:

```
if (Request.Form("City").Count>0 &&
    Request.Form("City").Item(1).indexOf("Glasgow")!=-1)
{
```

We then use the `CreateVBArray()` method to return an object of type `VBArray` that holds the parameters to the method. An XML-RPC invocation is then executed, calling the `BookServer.asp` file at the appropriate URL and passing the function to call (`GetBooks()`) and the `VBArray` list of parameters to pass to the call (the city and the subject in this case). Each book and its details (a `BookRecord`) are then returned, separated by commas (that is, of the form: `BookRecord1`, `BookRecord2`, `BookRecord3`, etc.) and the results are appended to the recordset.

Each ID is defined by the unique index `k`, which identifies a record containing the book title and authors of the book.

```
    paramList=CreateVBArray(Request.Form("City").Item(1));
    strGlas =
       xmlRPC("http://LOCALHOST/xmlrpc/client/BookServer.asp",
              strFunction, paramList);
    arrTemp = strGlas.split(",");

    for (k=0;k<arrTemp.length;k++)
    {
       objRS.AddNew();
       objRS.Fields("ID").Value=k;
       objRS.Fields("Title").Value=arrTemp[k];
       objRS.Fields("City").Value=Request.Form("City").Item(1);
       objRS.Update();
       intCounter++;
    }
}

// code repeating this for each city (as before) not shown.
```

We create a header that declares the subject area of interest and the cities queried. We then iterate through the recordset, and for each record where there is an entry (not "`no title`" which is returned when there are no books of a particular subject in the domain) we ensure that it has not already been written. If it has not yet been written, the split function creates an array, using a hash as the delimiter. This is because when the `BookRecord` is created during the RPC call, the book title is separated from its authors by a "#" character. Therefore, when the split function creates our array, the first element will always hold the title of the book, and the rest of the elements will be the authors of the book.

```
      Response.Write("<h4>The titles for " + Request.Form("Subject") +
                     " in " + Request.Form("City") + " is : </h4>");

      //get the values in Ascending order
      if (!objRS.EOF)
      {
         while (!objRS.EOF)
         {
            if (objRS.Fields(1).Value!="no titles")
            { //we should write it out
               if (CheckDuplicate(objRS.Fields(1).Value)=="FALSE")
               {
                  str = objRS.Fields(1).Value.split("#");
                  Response.Write("<P><B>" + str[0] + "</B>");
                  Response.Write("<BR><I>Authors</I><BR>");
                  for (i=1;i<str.length;i++)
                     Response.Write(str[i] + "<BR>");
               }
            }
            j++;
            objRS.MoveNext();
         }
      }
```

If there are no books available then the user is given a message to indicate this and the recordset resources are released.

```
      else
         Response.Write("<h4>There are currently no books for this "
                        + "subject at your chosen locations(s).</H4>");

      objRS.Close();
      var objRS = null;
   }
</SCRIPT>

<HTML>
<HEAD>
</HEAD>

<%DrawScreen()%>

</HTML>
```

Updating a Catalog

One important aspect to this kind of distributed system is the ability to update a catalog from the central server, independent of what kind of server is running on the distributed server. The HTML interface for updating a catalog is shown below. This file is `AddNew.asp` in the downloaded sample files.

> *In this section, you will have to be logged on as a user who has permissions to write to files, as you will be directly updating XML files. One way to do this is to enable challenge-response authentication and disable the anonymous users for the client directory. You can do this from within the IIS Management Console by right-clicking on the client directory and choosing Properties. Then, choose the* Directory Security *tab and click the* Edit *button. Ensure* Allow Anonymous Access *is unchecked and that* Windows NT Challenge/Response *is checked.*

Add a new Book

Choose a City and enter the appropriate details
- ○ Glasgow
- ○ Birmingham
- ○ Sydney
- ○ Milano
- ◉ Dallas

Publication Date
[05/08/1999]

Title
[Professional Active Serv]

Authors
[Alex Homer]
[David Sussman]
[Brian Francis]

Subject
[ASP]

[Add Book]

The following diagram shows how the catalog updating works.

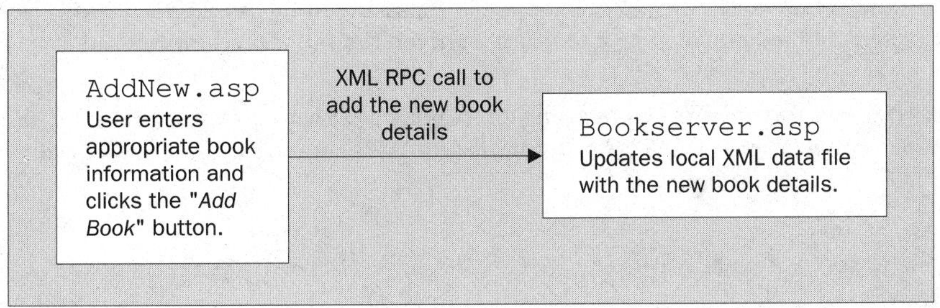

The file called `AddNew.asp` contains both the above HTML and the script to perform the XML-RPC request. The XML-RPC method we want to invoke exposes the following interface:

Method Name	Parameters
`AddNewBook()`	`city` – name of the city
	`PubDate` – publication date
	`Title` – book title
	`Authors` – list of authors of book
	`Subject` – subject domain of the book

The client page, `AddNew.asp` starts with the usual RPC include file and HTML header:

```
<!--#include file="xmlrpc.asp" -->
<HTML>
<HEAD>
<META NAME="GENERATOR" Content="Microsoft Visual Studio 6.0">
<TITLE></TITLE>
</HEAD>
<BODY>
```

We then check if an author has been posted from the above web page (which is always required for a book) and if so, we set the parameter array to each of the POSTed values:

```
<P>
<%
   If NOT Request.form("auth") = "" then
      Dim paramList(5)
      paramList(0)=Request.form("city")
      paramList(1)=Request.form("pubdate")
      paramList(2)=Request.form("title")
      paramList(3)=Request.form("auth")
      paramList(4)=Request.form("subject")
```

Now that we have defined the parameters to the method, we can invoke it using the COM object for XML-RPC, which will return the new ID of the book that has been added (more information on the XML-RPC COM implementation is given in the "*Where To Go From Here*" section). We do this by creating an instance of the `xmlrpcClient` object and passing in the method `AddNewBook()` with the array of parameters defined above. The client if then given the ID of the new book that has been added.

> *As an exercise, you may wish to try and extend this functionality by getting a new ID from a central repository with an XML-RPC call from the* `BookServer.asp` *file, rather than getting the ID from the local XML file.*

```
      Set objDB = Server.CreateObject("deltabiz.xmlrpcClient")
      myresp = _
        objDB.xmlRPC("http://LOCALHOST/xmlrpc/client/BookServer.asp", _
                     "","","","AddNewBook", paramList)
```

```
        Response.Write "<P><STRONG>The new book has been added to "
        Response.Write Request.form("city") & ".</STRONG></P>"
        Response.write(" The book has been given an ID of " & myresp & "<P>")
    Else
%>
```

Finally, here is the section we actually use to submit the request of the book update, with inputs for the city, the publication date, the book title, the authors and the subject of the book. The method `AddBook()` is added as a hidden element.

```
<P><STRONG>Add a new Book</STRONG></P>
<FORM action=AddNew.asp id=form1 method=post name=form1>
Choose a City and enter the appropriate details
<BR>
<INPUT CHECKED name=city type=radio value=Glasgow>Glasgow<BR>
<INPUT name=city type=radio value=Birmingham>Birmingham<BR>
<INPUT name=city type=radio value=Sydney>Sydney<BR>
<INPUT name=city type=radio value=Milano>Milano<BR>
<INPUT name=city type=radio value=Dallas>Dallas</P>
<P>
<P>Publication Date<BR><INPUT name="pubdate"></P>
<P> Title<BR><INPUT name="title"></P>
<P> Authors<BR>
<INPUT name="auth"><BR>
<INPUT name="auth"><BR>
<INPUT name="auth"><BR>
<INPUT name="auth"><BR>
<INPUT name="auth"><BR>
<INPUT name="auth"><BR>
<INPUT name="auth">
</P>
<P>Subject<BR><INPUT name="subject"></P>
<% End If%>
<INPUT name=Function type=hidden value=AddBook>
<INPUT id=submit1 name=submit1 type=submit value="Add Book">
</FORM></P>
</BODY>
</HTML>
```

The Wrox Books Server

The only part of the application we have not yet dealt with is the server implementation as provided by `BookServer.asp`. This is typical of XML-RPC implementations you would work with on the Internet. You will not have direct access to the server code, but an interface specification and semantics will be provided. However, this section is useful to understand the other side of the RPC application, and should be particularly helpful if you write you own RPC server applications.

This part of the application actually implements the remote methods we have been calling in the application.

In the ASP version of XML-RPC both the client and server implementations are in the same include file, although we call the procedure `rpcserver()` to invoke the XML server. This header section is required in ALL server implementations of XML-RPC – this simply initializes the server with the data POSTed from the client within the XMLRC call.

```
<!--#include file="xmlrpc.asp" -->
<%
   rpcserver
%>
```

The rest of the server has been developed using JavaScript, except the VB Array function we looked at earlier.

```
<SCRIPT LANGUAGE=vbscript RUNAT=Server>
   Function CreateVBArrayAddNewBook(a)
      Dim i, j, k
      Dim arr(1)
      arr(0) = a
      CreateVBArrayAddNewBook = arr
   End Function
</SCRIPT>
```

The first function was to get the subjects available for a particular city. We create an instance of the MSXML DOM object and open up the cities XML file. It then gets a `NodeList` object using the `getElementsByTagName()` method and creates a one dimensional array of the subjects available (which is the 3rd `childNode` of the book element).

```
<SCRIPT LANGUAGE=JAVASCRIPT RUNAT=SERVER>
   function GetSubjects(city)
   {
      var arrTitles = new Array();

      //'load the XML document
      var objXML = Server.CreateObject("Microsoft.XMLDOM");
      objXML.async = false;
      objXML.load(Server.MapPath(city + "books.xml"));

      //'get all the book titles in a Nodelist
      var objNodeList = objXML.getElementsByTagName("book");

      for (var i=0;i<objNodeList.length;i++)
      {
         arrTitles[i]=objNodeList.item(i).childNodes(2).text;
      }

      return arrTitles;
   }
```

When we had gathered a list of all subjects, we wanted a way to get all the books for a particular city of a specified subject. The `GetBooks()` function does this, and similarly loads the relevant city XML store.

```
   function GetBooks(subject,city)
   {
      var arrTitles = new Array();

      //'load the XML document
      var objXML = Server.CreateObject("Microsoft.XMLDOM");
      objXML.async = false;
      objXML.load(Server.MapPath(city+"books.xml"));
```

We then get all of the `<book>` elements in a `nodeList` object and walk through each element, checking whether the subject type of the specified book (the 3rd `childNode` of the book element) is the same as the one passed from the client. If there is a subject match then the title of the book is added as the first element of an array. An iteration is made through each `<authors>` element (the 2nd `childNode` of the `<book>` element), which itself may have multiple `<author>` `childNodes`. Each author is added to the second element of the array we have just added the book title to, with each author of that book delimited by a hash. The next book gets added to the next element of the array and so on. We end up with an array like the following:

```
arrTitles[0]="BookTitleA#Author1"
arrTitles[1]="BookTitleB#Author1# Author2# Author3"
arrTitles[2]="BookTitleC#Author1# Author2"
...
```

The code to do this is as follows:

```
//'get all the book titles in a Nodelist
var objNodeList = objXML.getElementsByTagName("book");

var j=0;
for (var i=0;i<objNodeList.length;i++)
{
   if (objNodeList.item(i).childNodes.length>0)
   {
      if (subject==objNodeList.item(i).childNodes(2).text)
      {
         arrTitles[j]=objNodeList.item(i).childNodes(0).text;

         for (k=0;
           k<objNodeList.item(i).childNodes(1).childNodes.length;
           k++)
         {
            if (k==0)
               arrTitles[j]+="#" +
         objNodeList.item(i).childNodes(1).childNodes(k).text;
            else
               arrTitles[j]+="#" +
         objNodeList.item(i).childNodes(1).childNodes(k).text;
         }

         j++;
      }
   }
}
```

If there are no titles for a particular city, then we simply return the text "no titles".

```
        if (arrTitles.length==0)
        {
            arrTitles[0]="no titles";
            return arrTitles;
        }
        else
        {
            return arrTitles;
        }
    }
```

To update a city's XML bookstore, we should call the `AddNewBook()` method, which takes the city to add the data to, the title of the new book, an array of authors and the subject domain of the book. We create an instance of the MXSML DOM and get the `documentElement` for the root of the XML file:

```
    //This function adds a new book to the specified city xml file
    //Authors is a list of authors separated by a |
    function AddNewBook(city,pubDate,title,Authors,subject)
    {
        var ret="";
        var arrTitles = new Array();

        //load the XML document
        var objXML = Server.CreateObject("Microsoft.XMLDOM");
        objXML.async = false;
        objXML.load(Server.MapPath(city+"books.xml"));
        var objRoot = objXML.documentElement;
```

The last `<book>` element of the document is found with the `lastChild()` method, and the book ID of the new element to be added is one greater than that of the last element book ID, defined by an attribute `bookid`.

```
        var objLastBookNode = objRoot.lastChild;

        //Get the next available ID number for a book
        var intNextNum =
            parseInt(objLastBookNode.getAttribute("bookid"))+1;
```

We create a new `<book>` element, using the `createElement()` method, to append to the document, and then we set both the ID attributes we have just obtained and publishing date attribute which was passed as a parameter in the RPC call.

The `<title>` element is also created and is appended as a `childNode` of the new `<book>` element, and the value of this `<title>` element is set from the parameters passed in the XML-RPC call.

```
        //Create a new book element and add attributes
        var objBookEl = objXML.createElement("book");

        //Add the Book Element Attributes
        objBookEl.setAttribute("bookid",intNextNum)
        objBookEl.setAttribute("pubdate",pubDate)
```

```
        //Add the Title Element
        var objTitleEl = objXML.createElement("title");
        objBookEl.appendChild(objTitleEl);
        objTitleEl.text=title;
```

We create an <authors> element and append each of the authors passed in the parameters (each author being delimited by a comma) as <author> elements that are children of the <authors> element. This <authors> element is then appended to the parent <book> element.

```
        //Add the Authors of the book Element
        var objAuthorsEl = objXML.createElement("authors");

        var arrAuthList = new Array();
        arrAuthList=Authors.split(",");

        for (var i=0;i<arrAuthList.length;i++)
        {
           if (arrAuthList[i].length>1)
           {
              var objAuthorEl = objXML.createElement("author");
              objAuthorEl.text=arrAuthList[i];
              objAuthorsEl.appendChild(objAuthorEl);
           }
        }

        objBookEl.appendChild(objAuthorsEl);
```

Finally the <subject> element is created and appended to the <book> element (which we created earlier), and the subject text is set per the XML-RPC parameter passed. After this, the <book> element itself is appended to the document root as a new book.

```
        //Add the Subject Element
        var objSubjectEl = objXML.createElement("subject");
        objBookEl.appendChild(objSubjectEl);
        objSubjectEl.text=subject;

        objRoot.appendChild(objBookEl);
```

Finally, we save the XML document, using the save() method of the Microsoft XML implementation, with its new updated structure and return the ID of the added book as the response to the XML-RPC call:

```
        //persist the new document
        var xmldoc = Server.CreateObject("Microsoft.XMLDOM");
        xmldoc.async = false;
        xmldoc.load(objXML);
        xmldoc.save(Server.MapPath(city+"books.xml"));

        var objXML = null;
        var xmldoc = null;

        return intNextNum;
    }
</SCRIPT>
```

Where to go from here

The following list shows the various implementations and where to get them:

- **XML-RPC client for Python**, by PythonWare – http://www.pythonware.com/products/xmlrpc/
- **XML-RPC client/server for Java**, by Hannes Wallnöfer – http://helma.at/hannes/xmlrpc/
- **XML-RPC client for Java**, by Josh Lucas – http://www.stonecottage.com/josh/rpcClient.html
- **XML-RPC client/server for Perl**, by Ken MacLeod – http://bitsko.slc.ut.us/~ken/xml-rpc/
- **XML-RPC in Tcl**, by Steve Ball – http://www.zveno.com/zm.cgi/in-tclxml/in-xmlrpc.tml
- **XML-RPC client/server for ASP**, by David Carter-Tod – http://www.wc.cc.va.us/dtod/XMLRPC/
- **XML-RPC client for COM**, by Steven Livingstone – http://www.deltabiz.com/xmlrpc/default.asp
- **XML-RPC client/server for PHP**, by Useful Inc – http://usefulinc.com/xmlrpc/

There is also built-in XML-RPC support in Frontier and Zope 2.0 (http://www.zope.org/Download/Releases/Zope-2.0.0/).

ASP

All files, client or server, which are to participate in XML-RPC method invocation require the file `xmlrpc.asp` to be included at the top. You invoke a method via XML-RPC using the following syntax:

```
xmlRPC("Server URI", "procedure or function name", array of arguments)
```

The current implementation requires MS Internet Explorer 5 and the free Softwing ASPTear component from http://www.alphasierrapapa.com/IisDev/Components/. The free Base64 Encoding Library by Alvaro Redondo must also be registered on the machine (use the regsvr32 utility from MS DOS).

COM

The XML-RPC COM client implementation was written by myself (Steven Livingstone) and is currently being tested within implementations throughout the XML-RPC community. The DLL is freely available from http://www.deltabiz.com/xmlrpc/default.asp and it should be registered using the regsvr32 utility.

Currently, the ProgID is `deltabiz.xmlrpcClient`, and you would execute a XML-RPC call in VBScript as follows:

```
Set objDB = Server.CreateObject("deltabiz.xmlrpcClient")
myresp = objDB.xmlRPC(URL, ProxyURL, ProxyUserName, ProxyPassword, _
                      methodName, ParameterArray)
```

where

Parameter	Meaning
`URL`	The location of the XML-RPC server
`ProxyURL`	The URL of the proxy server, should be set to `""` if you do not use a proxy
`ProxyUserName`	The username you access the proxy with, should be `""` for no proxy
`ProxyPassword`	The proxy password you use, should be `""` for no proxy
`methodName`	The name of the remote function to invoke
`parameterArray`	Holds the parameters for the method

The commercial version of ASPTear is needed for the Proxy version, but otherwise the free version is OK.

Java

There are two Java implementations, one client/server from Hannes Wallnöfer and one client from Josh Lucas.

The first of these comes with a built-in HTTP server. A XML parser must be available on the system and, as the XML-RPC library uses SAX, you should use one of the suggested parsers listed at the download area, although James Clark's popular XT parser is the default. API documentation and a mailing list are available from the site.

Josh Lucas has a Java XML-RPC client. The downloaded files should be within your classpath, and `com.barista.*` should be imported.

There are also implementations available in Python, Perl, Tcl, and PHP – all downloadable from the XML-RPC web site at http://www.xmlrpc.com/.

SOAP

XML-RPC has found support and popularity because of its great simplicity. A lot can be done with a little. Simple code written in almost any language – on many platforms – enables tasks to be initiated on remote servers. Since many web programmers are familiar with posting to server scripts or gateway applications, most will be able to devise the code required to use these powerful techniques.

In this section we will look at some enhancements to XML-RPC, many of which exist in the form of a new proposal called the Simple Object Access Protocol (SOAP). First off we'll look at what SOAP is and why it has come into being, which relates to how it addresses certain shortcomings of XML-RPC. Next we'll see a simple SOAP implementation using ASP scripts – although in the same manner as you saw with XML-RPC, a SOAP interface could be written in any language – before going on to look at a sample. Finally, we will discuss the range of problems for which SOAP is a useful solution, and those where it is not.

> *As we went to press the final release of the SOAP spec was at* http://msdn.microsoft.com/xml/general/soapspec-v1.asp. *Be wary of the fact that many articles – including one on Microsoft's site! – are still referring to the 0.9 version, which is very different to this final release.*

XML-RPC++

Initiating remote procedure calls through HTTP – using XML to define those calls – is flexible and powerful, because it builds on two widely used standards. This book will have convinced you – as if you needed it – that XML, as one of those standards, has strength because it can store or convey data from, to, or within many systems. But for interoperability in a standard, HTTP must be the granddaddy of them all. There are very few platforms around now that do not have web server software available for them.

The limitations we will discuss here in relation to XML-RPC are therefore not to do with the concepts it is based on; we're 110% convinced about those. Rather, on closer inspection of the *implementation* of those concepts we will see that we need to go one step further than XML-RPC. We need an XML-RPC++. We need SOAP.

> *Of course, the more observant among you will note that we are not really doing a 'plus plus', in the manner described in Stroustrop's original definition of C++. All I can say is that if you* did *spot that, then you should get out of the house more.*

So, where exactly does XML-RPC need improvements? The first area – although broad – relates to the manner in which information is tagged within XML-RPC, so to begin with we will look at XML-RPC's verbosity along with how it handles data in general, and see how SOAP addresses all of this. The second area relates to the control that administrators have over what can and cannot be passed into the systems they manage, so after looking at the data issues we will go on to examine how XML-RPC's 'all or nothing' approach can be solved.

> *You may ask why we have bothered with XML-RPC at all, if SOAP is so much better. The reason is that despite the short lifetime of XML-RPC it has already attracted a great deal of interest – and for good reason. Programmers all over the globe are interacting with Dave Winer's UserLand for example, using XML-RPC. And, as you will see in this section, XML-RPC is much simpler to implement than SOAP, so it is very likely that XML-RPC will exist for a while to come.*
>
> *However, I would very strongly advise anyone implementing a new RPC system to only use XML-RPC if they really cannot find or build a SOAP module for their platform. Industrial-strength applications are extremely unlikely to be possible using XML-RPC – despite the claims of its many fans. Microsoft was key to devising SOAP and is keen to push it, and soon it will very likely eclipse most other server-to-server techniques – or at least become the glue between them.*

Data

The main weaknesses of XML-RPC in data transfer relate to verbosity and data typing. First we will look at the amount of XML required to convey information in XML-RPC, and then at the way that this data is typed – by which we simply mean the means by which the difference between, say, an integer and a string is conveyed. We will then look at how SOAP allows complex structures and arrays to be transferred, before having a quick round up of some of the additional features that SOAP adds which have no parallel in XML-RPC.

Verbosity

The dictionary definition of **verbosity** is as follows:

> ***verbosity*** *– The quality or state of being verbose; the use of more words than are necessary; prolixity; wordiness; verbiage. (Source: Webster's Revised Unabridged Dictionary, © 1996, 1998 MICRA, Inc.)*

Which sums up exactly what I mean by this XML-RPC problem – the essence of what you convey in an XML-RPC message would not be lost if some other (smaller) set of symbols were used.

As you saw in the previous section, in XML-RPC every value is demarcated by a `<value>` element. Within this element is another element, which indicates the type of the value, and that element in turn contains the value itself. For example:

```
<value><int>7</int></value>
```

There are two problems with this. The first is that from a straight XML point of view, the data has no type. We simply have one element that contains another, which in turn contains a string. The fact that the data is an integer is not known until we begin to process the document at the level of XML-RPC – it certainly isn't available to the DOM since all we have is an element called `<int>`. Much of the work on data typing within XML is very recent, and so wasn't available to the original authors of XML-RPC. However, since this is beginning to firm up it makes sense to use it. We will look at this issue in a moment.

The second problem is that while this method of encoding might be fine for one or two pieces of information, it gets very long for larger quantities of data:

```
<value>
   <array>
      <data>
         <value><int>4</int></value>
         <value><int>5</int></value>
         <value><int>6</int></value>
         <value><int>7</int></value>
      </data>
   </array>
</value>
```

Since the range of possible elements – `<int>`, `<string>`, `<array>`, and so on – are known in advance, `<value>` and `<data>` serve little purpose here. For example, there is no reason the array could not be represented as follows:

```
<array>
   <int>4</int>
   <int>5</int>
   <int>6</int>
   <int>7</int>
</array>
```

Structures

The problem of XML-RPC verbosity is worse when we look at the encoding of *structures* of data. Recall from the XML-RPC section that a `<struct>` element is used to convey a structure, and that each part has a name and value pair, for example:

```
<value>
   <struct>
      <member>
         <name>Product</name>
         <value><string>Silver Clock</string></value>
      </member>
      <member>
         <name>Cost</name>
         <value><i4>87</i4></value>
      </member>
      <member>
         <name>Purchase Date</name>
         <value>
            <dateTime.iso8601>19990912T02:53:02<dateTime.iso8601>
         </value>
      </member>
      <member>
         <name>Purchase Order</name>
         <value><double>384793</double></value>
      </member>
   </struct>
</value>
```

Yet the same information could be conveyed like this (assuming for the moment that we still use the verbose type information):

```
<Order>
   <Product><string>Silver Clock</string></Product>
   <Cost><int>87</int></Cost>

<PurchaseDate><dateTime.iso8601>19990912T02:53:02</dateTime.iso8601></PurchaseDate>
   <PurchaseOrder><double>384793</double></PurchaseOrder>
</Order>
```

While this is still using elements such as `<string>` and `<int>` around the data to indicate the type of the data – which we will address in a moment – it has the advantage that it maps the structure directly to XML. This means that if we were to add this syntax to XML-RPC then we could pass XML straight through between client and server. As it stands, XML-RPC has no means of doing this without going via the `<struct>` arrangement, which 'hides' the data's structure. SOAP addresses this issue, but this is best explained by looking at data typing.

Data Typing

SOAP draws on a recent W3C Working Draft – XML Schema Part 2 – to help convey more information about the data it is handling. As you saw in Chapter 7 the draft provides a number of 'built in' data types, as well as a mechanism to add new ones. SOAP makes use of this feature to add new data types such as variants and arrays, which I will come to in a moment.

Using SOAP and the data types that are defined in the working draft, the final layout for our structure would be as follows:

```
<Order xsd:xmlns="W3C-Schemas-URI">
   <Product xsd:type="string">Silver Clock</Product>
   <Cost xsd:type="integer">87</Cost>
   <PurchaseDate xsd:type="timeInstant">19990912T02:53:02</PurchaseDate>
   <PurchaseOrder xsd:type="integer">384793</PurchaseOrder>
</Order>
```

This is probably much more like the original XML that we wanted to convey through our remote procedure call, and far better than XML-RPC's verbosity.

One problem with automating the production of structures such as this is that there may be no information about the name of an object or parameter, or the name may be irrelevant anyway. SOAP allows us to use one other abbreviation, reminiscent of the XML-RPC technique:

```
<Order>
   <string>Silver Clock</string>
   <integer>87</integer>
   <timeInstant>19990912T02:53:02</timeInstant>
   <integer>384793</integer>
</Order>
```

Deciding when to use this technique and when to use the type attribute is fairly straightforward. Most of the time you can use whichever you prefer; the SOAP specification simply says that whenever the name of the element is not enough to uniquely indicate the *type* of the data then the type attribute should be used. For example this is a float:

```
<velocity xsd:type="float">15.5</velocity>
```

while this is simply a string:

```
<velocity>15.5</velocity>
```

Although both techniques – setting the element name to the data type or using the `xsd:type` attribute – amount to the same thing, using the `xsd:type` attribute has the advantage that we are able to obtain correctly typed data from the parser. For example, if we were to ask our parser to read the contents of the `<PurchaseOrder>` element, we would obtain a time and date value, rather than a simple string. This of course requires that the XML parser makes the typed version of the element contents available, as discussed in Chapter 7.

Extending XML Schema Part 2

The valid element values – such as `string` and `integer` – are the same as those listed in the XML Schema Part 2 Working Draft. SOAP adds another – `variant` – to indicate elements that may contain one of a number of possible data types. Although Microsoft's Visual Basic makes extensive use of variants – and VB Script does not use any data type other than variants – the inclusion of variants in SOAP is only really useful for arrays that might contain a mixture of value types. In the following example we have a two-element array that contains an integer in element zero and a string in element one:

```
<ArrayOfvariant xsd:type="u:variant[2]">
    <variant xsd:type="int">23</variant>
    <variant xsd:type="string">some string</variant>
</ArrayOfvariant>
```

SOAP also extends the draft by adding arrays, in fact it provides two ways to encode arrays. The first requires that the information about the array's contents be encoded into the element name, for example:

```
<ArrayOfinteger xsd:type"u:int[4]">
    <integer>4</integer>
    <integer>5</integer>
    <integer>6</integer>
    <integer>7</integer>
</ArrayOfinteger>
```

This example is taken from the SOAP spec, but there is no data type called `int` in the XML Schema Part 2 Working Draft, from which SOAP data types must come. This means that the type `int` will come from the added user-defined types. The SOAP spec does not address exactly how this user-defined type information will be conveyed, since it explicitly says that SOAP packets will not have a schema. Also, the schema will in most useful cases need to be dynamically created with each packet since data types may be complex objects.

The element name is set to be `ArrayOf` followed by the basic type of each unit in the array. The element also has its `type` attribute set to indicate the size of the array, in this case `u:int[4]`. This means simply that it is an array of four integers.

The second method for indicating an array is to use a named element:

```
<Authors xsd:type="u:author[4]">
    <author>Stephen</author>
    <author>Kathie</author>
    <author>Eric</author>
    <author>Peter</author>
</Authors>
```

In this case we are saying that each element of the array is an author. Note that which technique you choose is not determined by the *contents* of the array; it is perfectly legitimate to have:

```
<ArrayOfauthor xsd:type="u:author[4]">
   <author>Stephen</author>
   <author>Kathie</author>
   <author>Eric</author>
   <author>Peter</author>
</ArrayOfauthor>
```

which uses the `ArrayOf` approach for `authors`, not `integers`. Which method you would use is actually set by the use to which you would put the array within the context of the other information that you are transferring. Since this concerns other information types as well, I'll come back to this point in a separate section – for now, I'll simply say that which method you use depends on whether the information in the array can be referred to from more than one place in the data being transferred.

Before we leave arrays however, I'll just throw out a couple of quick examples so that you can start to get a feel for the flexibility of the enhancements that SOAP has built onto XML-RPC.

This is a two dimensional array of strings:

```
<ArrayOfstring xsd:type="u:string[2,3]">
   <string>row 1 column 1</string>
   <string>row 1 column 2</string>
   <string>row 1 column 3</string>
   <string>row 2 column 1</string>
   <string>row 2 column 2</string>
   <string>row 2 column 3</string>
</ArrayOfstring>
```

Although all the elements of the array follow one after the other, they are to be interpreted as two rows, each containing three columns. A two dimensional array such as this is different to an array of arrays, which would be represented as follows:

```
<ArrayOfArrayOfstring xsd:type="u:string[][2]">
   <ArrayOfstring xsd:type="u:string[3]">
      <string>one</string>
      <string>two</string>
      <string>three</string>
   </ArrayOfstring>
   <ArrayOfstring xsd:type="u:string[2]">
      <string>one</string>
      <string>two</string>
   </ArrayOfstring>
</ArrayOfArrayOfstring>
```

Note that since the two arrays are separate it's perfectly valid for them to have different sizes.

Array elements can also indicate the position within the array that they are to be placed. In this example we can insert array elements out of sequence:

```
<ArrayOfstring xsd:type="u:string[3]">
   <string position="[1]">two</string>
   <string position="[2]">three</string>
   <string position="[0]">one</string>
</ArrayOfstring>
```

This ability to specify a location allows only part of an array to be passed. In this example we have missed an element out:

```
<ArrayOfstring xsd:type="u:string[3]">
   <string position="[0]">one</string>
   <string position="[2]">three</string>
</ArrayOfstring>
```

If you wanted to specify a consecutive set of elements that began at a certain position in the array, but did not want to specify the initial elements then it is possible to specify an offset from which to start loading the elements:

```
<ArrayOfstring xsd:type="u:string[3]" offset="[1]">
   <string>two</string>
   <string>three</string>
</ArrayOfstring>
```

If this looks wrong to you, don't forget that array elements are numbered from zero, and so the offset must be too.

Other Enhancements

So, SOAP has addressed the question of the type of the data, it has added better array handling and it now allows XML to be passed as XML, rather than being obscured in verbose structures. Is there anything else?

Well, the next neat feature that SOAP adds is a technique to allow one value to be referred to in a number of places. While there would be nothing essentially wrong with passing the following data structure:

```
<Authors>
   <author>
      <name>Steve</name>
      <City>Birmingham</City>
   </author>
   <author>
      <name>Fred</name>
      <City>Birmingham</City>
   </author>
</Authors>
```

you can see that if we had a few hundred authors lucky enough to live in Birmingham, there would be a fair amount of extra information. SOAP allows elements to be **multi-reference**, as the following shows:

```
<Authors>
<author>
      <name>Steve</name>
      <City href="#1" />
   </author>
   <author>
      <name>Fred</name>
      <City href="#1" />
   </author>
</Authors>

<City id="1">Birmingham</City>
```

Data that can only be referred to once is **single-reference**, which is essentially any element without an `id` attribute. This multi-reference technique finds many uses. For example, another way that we could encode the array of arrays that we looked at earlier would be like this:

```
<ArrayOfArrayOfstring xsd:type="u:string[][2]">
   <ArrayOfstring href="#array-1"/>
   <ArrayOfstring href="#array-2"/>
</ArrayOfArrayOfstring>

<ArrayOfstring id="array-1" xsd:type="u:string[3]">
   <string>one</string>
   <string>two</string>
   <string>three</string>
</ArrayOfstring>

<ArrayOfstring id="array-2" xsd:type="u:string[2]">
   <string>one</string>
   <string>two</string>
</ArrayOfstring>
```

Note that these multi-reference arrays must always use the `ArrayOf` syntax, and they must always be at the top level. (In the SOAP spec an element that is at the top level is called an **independent** element, and one that is contained by another element is called an **embedded** element. As with XML-RPC, SOAP has a payload that contains the information being passed to a procedure or returned from it. The 'top level' is the payload.

The following is not allowed since it breaks both of these rules:

```
<ArrayOfArrayOfstring xsd:type="u:string[][2]">
   <ArrayOfstring href="#array-1"/>
   <ArrayOfstring href="#array-2"/>
   <!—This should be at the top level -->
   <ArrayOfstring id="array-1" xsd:type="u:string[3]">
   <string>one</string>
      <string>two</string>
      <string>three</string>
   </ArrayOfstring>
</ArrayOfArrayOfstring>
```

```
<!-- This should use ArrayOf -->
<MyArray id="array-2" xsd:type="u:string[2]">
   <string>one</string>
   <string>two</string>
</MyArray>
```

To reiterate – `array-1` is in error because it should be at the top level, and `array-2` is incorrect because if it is going to be referred to from elsewhere then it should use the `ArrayOf` syntax.

Summary of Data Handling Enhancements

SOAP has added a number of sophisticated features to the data handling capabilities of XML-RPC. The addition of a method of data typing that promises to become a standard across XML applications gives SOAP a solid foundation. Also, a number of techniques, such as sparse arrays and multi-reference elements, contribute to reducing the quantity of information passed. Finally, the ability to pass XML 'as is', rather than encoded as name/value pairs, gives greater flexibility to data formats.

Now that we've established the enhancements to data handling, lets look at how methods are invoked.

Invokation

SOAP adds a number of new features to the way that calls are made. In particular, to allow site administrators greater control over what can and cannot be done with the servers that they have responsibility for, more information is provided in the header of the packets, as well as more flexible use of the HTTP verbs.

One problem with using standard HTTP as the transport mechanism for remote procedure calls is that it is difficult to then distinguish between a request that may be part of some sophisticated communications procedure, and one that is simply errant or malicious. As we saw with XML-RPC the POST verb is used to convey the information that determines which procedure to execute. But POST is also used to fill in forms, for anything from credit card details for purchases to specifying who your favourite Spice Girl is (or not). It can even be used for uploading files.

In some situations the use of the POST verb for RPC won't matter. For example, security might not be an issue, or – and this is more likely – we may have a situation where a developer wants to implement RPC functionality on a server, but does not have the ability to add new verbs or header information to that server. For this reason we would always want to try and convey our RPC information through a POST first.

However, imagine that for various reasons an administrator has prevented POSTs from reaching the servers that they manage by stopping them at a firewall. Although they want to allow RPC calls through, they don't want to allow any other POSTs. The only way of telling that the XML-RPC request is a remote procedure call being conveyed with POST – rather than a non-RPC POST – is by looking at the actual data being transferred. But this is more work than a firewall should have to do, since it requires that the firewall understand the payload, and so parse the XML. If the firewall is going to do that for SOAP, why not BizTalk, WebDAV, or any other protocol? It would be impossible to maintain the firewalls as new software would need to be continuously added as new standards were devised. In this situation then, we would prefer a verb that is distinguishable from POST.

Let's re-cap. The *power* of XML-RPC is that it uses HTTP as its transport mechanism. This is great because it means that just about any firewall will allow our procedure calls through – we don't need to configure special ports as we would if we were using Corba or DCOM. However, one *problem* with XML-RPC is that it doesn't advertise itself very precisely. It simply uses the verb POST with the content-type "`text/xml`", making it very difficult to control with any degree of granularity.

So, enough of the problems – what's the answer? Somehow we need to give the firewall more information.

Extending HTTP

It is neither possible nor desirable to simply add new verbs to HTTP. Imagine if everyone simply added their own verbs whenever they felt like it. Firewall and server administrators would have no way of knowing the purpose of a particular request, and no way of applying reliable filtering. What if two different services wanted to invent a new verb like RENAME? How would we tell them apart?

Rather than add new verbs every time the need arises, we want to be able to provide more information in the header. The *HTTP Extension Framework* provides a mechanism for adding additional header and verb information to HTTP requests, such that the nature of the information being conveyed can be inferred without having to delve into the request itself.

> *A complete description of the HTTP Extension Framework can be found at* *http://www.w3.org/Protocols/HTTP/ietf-http-ext/.*

The extension framework allows for a list of headers that *must* be understood by a server or some proxy before a message can be processed. Think of it in the same way that you might specify that a function call has required parameters; if the function were able to draw a line, it might require a start point parameter and an end point parameter. Without either of these it is not a valid call. With the extension framework we can specify something similar, and if the server doing the processing does not understand any of the mandatory parameters then it must reject the entire call, rather than try to do the best it can with whatever it is given.

So how is all this information specified? The first requirement is that whatever HTTP verb you want to use, you must prefix it with `M-` if there are any mandatory headers present. The second requirement is that these mandatory headers are grouped with a mechanism similar to that used for namespaces in XML. An example from the extension framework itself should help clarify this:

```
M-PUT /a-resource HTTP/1.1
Man: "http://www.copyright.org/rights-management"; ns=16
16-copyright: http://www.copyright.org/COPYRIGHT.html
16-contributions: http://www.copyright.org/PATCHES.html
Host: www.w3.org
Content-Length: 1203
Content-Type: text/html
```

Just to refresh you on what the standard HTTP parts mean, before we look at the extensions:

- The end of the first line indicates that we have submitted an HTTP version 1.1 request.
- The `Host` header says that the server that is to receive the request is `www.w3.org`.
- The middle of the first line has the URL that the request is for, `/a-resource`.

- The length of the request is 1203 bytes (Content-Length) and the MIME type of the request (Content-Type) is of type HTML.

Now let's look at the additional – extension framework – information:

- Since the verb on line one has the M- prefix then there must be a Man: header.
- Once the M- has been removed, then the request is actually using the HTTP verb PUT.
- The Man: header uses a URI to identify a namespace and 16 to name it (line two).
- The 16 can be used to identify all headers that are mandatory for this PUT.
- We therefore have two mandatory headers – copyright and contributions.

As you can see this allows anyone to use a header called copyright for their own purposes, as long as a unique namespace prefix is used to avoid confusion between some other copyright header and the one we have in this example – and maybe even thousands of others.

SOAP's Mandatory Headers

So lets look at the headers that are required for SOAP. In fact in the latest spec there is now only one, and that is the method that you would like executing. Previous releases of SOAP had an interface name as well as a method. However, the fact that the name of the method is itself prefixed with a namespace – in the example here, Some-Namespace-URI#GetLastTradePrice – probably made SOAP's authors think the interface name was redundant.

A properly formed header for a SOAP request might look like this:

```
M-POST /StockQuote HTTP/1.1
Host: www.stockquoteserver.com
Content-Type: text/xml
Content-Length: nnnn
Man: "urn:schemas-xmlsoap-org:soap.v1", ns=01
01-SOAPMethodName: Some-Namespace-URI#GetLastTradePrice
```

As you would expect we have the M- prefix to indicate that we have mandatory headers present. And as you already know this would cause a server (or perhaps a firewall) that can understand the *HTTP ExtensionFramework* to look for a header called Man:. On finding this header the processing software would see that there is a unique namespace declared – this namespace must be set to urn:schemas-xmlsoap-org:soap.v1, as in the example – and that this namespace is associated with the prefix 01. We therefore have a mandatory header called SOAPMethodName that resides in the namespace urn:schemas-xmlsoap-org:soap.v1, and no server should process this message unless it understands this header.

We have now created the possibility for a site administrator to filter out our requests. If the administrator wanted to prevent any SOAP requests from arriving at servers under their jurisdiction then devices could be configured not to forward messages with headers in the namespace urn:schemas-xmlsoap-org:soap.v1. If it was only certain requests that should be filtered then the configuration could be made to look for the header urn:schemas-xmlsoap-org:soap.v1:SOAPMethodName being set to some specific value. As I'm sure you can see, the whole point of *not* checking just for SOAPMethodName is that someone else might have used that header to mean something completely different. With the namespace there is no ambiguity.

What Happened to XML-RPC's Simplicity?

However, if we're not careful we will lose the very thing that has already made XML-RPC so successful – that you only need to be able to perform or process a POST instruction to implement remote control of a server. We need therefore to be able to execute calls using traditional POSTs, and then scale upwards if necessary. The same call as before would therefore look like this:

```
POST /StockQuote HTTP/1.1
Host: www.stockquoteserver.com
Content-Type: text/xml
Content-Length: nnnn
SOAPMethodName: Some-Namespace-URI#GetLastTradePrice
```

The verb prefix has gone, as has the prefix on the SOAP header that tells us which method is being executed.

The SOAP spec says that the format shown here should be tried by client software first – that is a straightforward POST with the method to be invoked in the `SOAPMethodName` header. If this is accepted by a server then our call doesn't look that much different to an XML-RPC call. All that has changed is that the header should now flag up which method is to be executed.

> *Note that the SOAP spec does not actually* require *this header, so you could actually submit a simple POST much like those used with XML-RPC. This is why a firewall administrator would most likely configure their systems to reject packages with a verb of POST and a content type of XML, since if all you do is check for the presence or absence of* `SOAPMethodName` *as a header you may let through a SOAP request.*

If an administrator wants to have more control then they can set their proxies to reject these POSTs by watching for a header of `SOAPMethodName`. Of course this might also reject some completely unrelated, non-SOAP requests that just happen to use `SOAPMethodName` as a header name, but there's nothing that can be done about that. A server set to reject these requests should indicate to the client that the method is not allowed with a `405 Method Not Allowed` return value.

If a client receives this error code then it should not automatically assume that SOAP is not supported, since as we have said it may be that the server wants more information before allowing the call through. In the event of a `405`, therefore, the client should re-submit the request, but this time use the M-POST format – including all mandatory headers.

> *If you are familiar with the 0.9 version of SOAP then note that the order in which you must try POST and M-POST has been reversed.*

Summary of Method Invokation

Hopefully I can make all of this clearer with a few sample requests. This first one comes from the SOAP spec itself, and makes a call to a server using an ordinary POST, as we would have done with XML-RPC. I'll explain the structure of the data passed when I look at the implementation of a SOAP server in the next section; for now we're really only interested in the header information:

```
POST /StockQuote HTTP/1.1
Host: www.stockquoteserver.com
Content-Type: text/xml
Content-Length: nnnn

<SOAP:Envelope xmlns:SOAP="urn:schemas-xmlsoap-org:soap.v1">
   <SOAP:Body>
      <m:GetLastTradePrice xmlns:m="Some-Namespace-URI">
         <symbol>DIS</symbol>
      </m:GetLastTradePrice>
   </SOAP:Body>
</SOAP:Envelope>
```

As far as the SOAP specification is concerned this request is perfectly valid, since the header does not have to contain the name of the method (although it should). Unfortunately for a firewall though, it has no idea what method is being invoked since it does not understand the body of the request, only the headers. It could just allow all methods through, or it could demand that the header information be provided. As we have seen, the aim of the `M-XXX` extensions in the *HTTP Extension Framework* is to provide a mechanism to do just that – demand certain headers. The framework provides a version of all the HTTP verbs that do the same as they would do normally, but they can only be acted upon if the mandatory header information is present.

So, let's re-cap on how our request would look if we were forced to re-submit it using a 'mandatory POST', or M-POST – which is what would happen if a server or proxy was set to ignore POSTs with a content type of XML. Our second request would look as follows, with the additional header information highlighted:

```
M-POST /StockQuote HTTP/1.1
Host: www.stockquoteserver.com
Content-Type: text/xml
Content-Length: nnnn
Man: "urn:schemas-xmlsoap-org:soap.v1", ns=01
01-SOAPMethodName: Some-Namespace-URI#GetLastTradePrice

<SOAP:Envelope xmlns:SOAP="urn:schemas-xmlsoap-org:soap.v1">
   ...
</SOAP:Envelope>
```

The `Man:` header is part of the extension framework, and indicates a prefix that will be used to group together all headers that are part of the mandatory requirement. In this case we are saying that any header that begins with "`01-`" is part of the same mandatory group. As we said before, the "`01`" functions much like a namespace prefix in XML, and in fact must be set to the same value as the SOAP namespace URI within the SOAP payload.

Now our firewall is much happier. It can see what we are trying to do with our request and can determine whether it wants to allow it through. By configuring the firewall to reject POSTs that have a content-type of "`text/xml`" the firewall can force a SOAP client to make all its method calls using M-POST. These requests are then guaranteed to have the necessary header information for the firewall to make a judgement about what to allow through and what to reject.

The SOAP spec does not quite describe things in the way I have done here. Rather it presents a scenario in which a firewall is configured to reject POSTs with a content-type of "`text/xml`" *and with a header of type* `SOAPMethodName`*. However, since the spec also says that the* `SOAPMethodName` *header* should *be provided, rather than* must *be provided, there seems no way that this can be a useful set up, since requests with no SOAP method header would therefore be allowed through.*

This means that all XML POSTs must be rejected by a firewall to enforce the use of M-POST. This may well turn out to be a problem in the future, since this combination is not unique to SOAP requests. For example, a server may support BizTalk or WebDAV, as well as SOAP, and both of these could use the verb POST with a content-type of "`text/xml`"*. A firewall may be preventing perfectly acceptable WebDAV requests in its attempts to force SOAP to use the mandatory syntax.*

Version 0.9 of SOAP used the content-type "`text/xml-SOAP`" *to resolve this ambiguity, but this has been dropped. Although a useful distinguisher, I think this was ultimately the right decision, since the aim of content types was never to invent them every time someone felt like it. Version 0.9 also had another solution, which was to make the SOAP method header compulsory. This has also been dropped in the final spec. This may have been a concession to XML-RPC fans, allowing a SOAP request to be initiated with nothing more than a simple POST. But as I have said, the unfortunate result is that there is no way of knowing that a request is without doubt a SOAP request.*

Implementation

We've looked at the improvements that SOAP makes over XML-RPC. Now, rather than going through the definition of the SOAP spec in isolation we'll actually step through building a SOAP client and server. During the course of this we can introduce key points from the spec.

The code for this section is included with the downloadable code for this book.

Module Structure

There are two main modules that we need to build – one for client systems and one for server systems. Since there are certain functions that we need to perform on both the client and the server – such as building payloads – then we also need to create a module of common procedures.

Client Module

We'll start with the code that puts a call together. Although the idea of a remote procedure call is to execute a function on another server, we still want to make that call look as much like a normal function call as possible. For example, a local call to get the name of the first author in a database might look like this:

```
name = getAuthorName(1)
```

So we would like our remote call to look something like this:

```
name = RemoteCall("ServerName", "getAuthorName", 1)
```

If you are implementing your SOAP client and server using a language such as C or C++ (see the case study later in this book for a C++ implementation) then you will easily be able to handle calls with a variable number of parameters. However, we are going to demonstrate building a SOAP implementation with ASP, so we are only able to pass a pre-determined number of parameters. To get round the limitations of this we will always pass one parameter, which will be an array. This array will then contain the actual parameters – and so there can be as many as you like.

A sample client request might look like this:

```
<!--#include virtual="X-Port/SOAP/SOAP.asp" -->
<!--#include virtual="X-Port/SOAP/SOAPClient.asp" -->

Dim paramList(2), oRet

if not Request.form("iAuthor") = "" then
   paramList(0) = CInt(Request.form("iAuthor"))
   paramList(1) = 1
   iRet = SOAP("http://server/SOAP/myServer.asp", _
               "myNamespace", _
               "getAuthor", _
               paramList, _
               oRet)
   '
   ' Check the return status and then maybe do something with the returned value
   '
end if
```

In this example we are passing two parameters to the remote procedure `getAuthor()`. Any values returned from the call will be in the variable `oRet`, and any status information about the success or failure of the call will be in `iRet`. The remote procedure is invoked with the function `SOAP()`, although if you are implementing your own system you can obviously use any name that you consider meaningful.

In case you're wondering what this procedure does on the remote server, it returns a set quantity of authors whose ID is *greater than or equal to* the first parameter. In the example, this value comes from a form variable. As for the actual number of authors returned, this is set by the second parameter – in this case 1. This routine will be used later in our sample.

> *You may have noticed that there are two include files and wondered why we don't include the base module – `SOAP.asp` – within the other – `SOAPClient.asp` – so that we need only include one file. In most situations we could do this, however, later I will show you a scenario where we want to build an application which is both a client and a server. In that situation we would have the base module included twice, so it is best to keep it out of both the client and server modules, and specifically request it. Of course if you are using a more sophisticated environment than ASP then you can use conditional includes to avoid this problem.*

The Call

Let's see what happens when we execute our call. The following code is in `SOAPClient.asp`:

```
function SOAP(sURL, sNamespace, sMethod, arrParam, ByRef oRet)
On Error Resume Next
   '
   'Create and send the XML request
   '
   Dim oSOAP : Set oSOAP = doRemoteCall(sURL, sNamespace, sMethod, arrParam)
   If Err.Number <> 0 Then
      Dim sTemp : sTemp = Err.Number & ": " & Err.Description
      Err.Clear
      Err.Raise 999, "SOAP", "Failed to call remote server (" & sTemp & ")"
   Else
      ...
   End If
end function
```

The call actually gets passed to another function – `doCall()` – which does the actual processing. The `SOAP()` routine only has to concern itself with letting the caller know whether that processing was successful or not.

So what does the actual remote call do? Here is the beginning of the routine, and as you can see the first task is to prepare a call payload:

```
function doRemoteCall(sU, sNS, sM, arP)
   On Error Resume Next
   '
   ' Create the request body from the method name and array of parameters
   '
   Dim oPL : Set oPL = CreateCallPayload(sNS, sM, arP)
   If Err.Number <> 0 Then
      Dim sTemp : sTemp = Err.Number & ": " & Err.Description
      Err.Clear
      Err.Raise 999, "SOAP", "Failed to create payload (" & sTemp & ")"
   Else
      ...
   End If
end function
```

Payloads

Creating a payload is a task that needs doing on both the client and server side, so the payload functions are in the common module – `SOAP.asp`.

As with XML-RPC, a payload consists of the real data that we want to have transferred, wrapped in a fairly strict package to ensure that the data can be extracted correctly. The actual format of a payload is slightly different for the different situations that payloads are needed for. For example, a payload that carries information for a method call will be different from one that conveys the results of that call. SOAP provides different payloads for calls, returns and error reporting.

Although there are three types of payload there are some common aspects of all payloads:

- They are all wrapped in an element with the name `<Envelope>`. This element must belong to the SOAP namespace.
- The `<Envelope>` element in turn contains a `<Body>` element, which is also in the SOAP namespace.

These conditions mean that we will *always* have at least the following pattern:

```
<SOAP:Envelope xmlns:SOAP="urn:schemas-xmlsoap-org:soap.v1">
   <SOAP:Body>
      ...
   </SOAP:Body>
</SOAP:Envelope>
```

We can now encode the payload function, which wraps up whatever sub element has been defined, whether a call, a response, or a fault:

```
function CreatePayload(oSubElem)
   Dim oPL : Set oPL = Server.CreateObject("Microsoft.XMLDOM")
   oPL.async = false

   Dim oRoot : Set oRoot = oPL.createNode(1, "SOAP:Envelope", NS_SOAP)
   oRoot.setAttribute "xmlns:xsd", NS_DATATYPES
   oRoot.setAttribute "xmlns:dt", NS_DATATYPES

   Dim oBody : Set oBody = oPL.createNode(1, "SOAP:Body", NS_SOAP)

   Dim oPI : Set oPI = oPL.createProcessingInstruction("xml", "version=""1.0""")

   oPL.appendChild(oPI)
   oBody.appendChild(oSubElem)
   oRoot.appendChild(oBody)
   oPL.appendChild(oRoot)

   Set CreatePayload = oPL
end function
```

Apologies to those on the XML-DEV mailing list who don't believe that the opening statement of an XML document is a processing instruction!

Note that the `<Envelope>` element also contains the namespace definition for data types, as discussed earlier. Normally we would only need to add the `xsd` namespace, but as an interim measure I have also added the namespace for XML-DR so that we can get typed data from the Microsoft XML DOM (see Chapter 7 for a fuller explanation.) The element can contain any number of namespace definitions if we want, and it can also contain other attributes provided that they are qualified with a namespace.

Now that we have a function that can create a payload that contains any sub-element, we need routines to create those sub-elements. We need one for a call, one for the response to calls, and one to indicate errors.

Method Calls and Responses

Calls and their responses use the name of the method, placed in whatever namespace is passed. Responses have "Response" appended to the name of the method, so we might make a call with:

```
<SOAP:Envelope xmlns:SOAP="urn:schemas-xmlsoap-org:soap.v1">
   <SOAP:Body>
      <m:getAuthor xmlns:m="Some-Namespace">
         ...
      </m:getAuthor>
   </SOAP:Body>
</SOAP:Envelope>
```

and get a response back, like this:

```
<SOAP:Envelope xmlns:SOAP="urn:schemas-xmlsoap-org:soap.v1">
   <SOAP:Body>
      <m:getAuthorResponse xmlns:m="Some-Namespace">
         ...
      </m:getAuthorResponse>
   </SOAP:Body>
</SOAP:Envelope>
```

The function that creates a call payload looks like this:

```
function CreateCallPayload(sNamespace, sMethod, arP)
   Dim oSubElem, i
   Set oSubElem = oDOM.createNode(1, "m:" & sMethod, sNamespace)
   for i = 0 to UBound(arP) - 1
      addChild oSubElem, "", arP(i)
   next
   Set CreateCallPayload = CreatePayload(oSubElem)
end function
```

and the call response function only needs to call the call payload function, with a modified method name:

```
function CreateCallResponsePayload(sNamespace, sMethod, arP)
   Set CreateCallResponsePayload = CreateCallPayload(sNamespace, _
                                                     sMethod & "Response", arP)
end function
```

A call payload has all the parameters one after the other. The `addChild()` routine is also in the common module `SOAP.asp`, and is used to add nodes to the output. The second parameter of `addChild()` is usually the name that should be given to the node, but in this case we are leaving it blank to indicate that we want to use the name of the data type as the node name (the `addChild()` function is discussed later):

Note that we are making each parameter 'anonymous' as a convenience; we are not required to do so by the spec. The following example from the spec shows another way that the call might be encoded, this time using named parameters:

```
<SOAP:Envelope xmlns:SOAP="urn:schemas-xmlsoap-org:soap.v1">
   <SOAP:Body>
      <m:GetLastTradePriceDetails xmlns:m="Some-Namespace-URI">
         <Symbol>DEF</Symbol>
         <Company>DEF Corp</Company>
         <Price>34.1</Price>
      </m:GetLastTradePriceDetails>
   </SOAP:Body>
</SOAP:Envelope>
```

However, with a simple ASP implementation, such as the one we are building here, it is more trouble than it is worth to encode parameter names as well as values (systems that define and name the interface will no doubt develop, as discussed below). Hence our naming the parameters with their data type for simplicity. In our system if we had an array containing three elements, with the same values as those in the example I just gave, we would get:

```
<SOAP:Envelope xmlns:SOAP="urn:schemas-xmlsoap-org:soap.v1"
               xmlns:xsd="Some-Schema-Namespace-URI">
   <SOAP:Body>
      <m:GetLastTradePriceDetails xmlns:m="Some-Namespace-URI">
         <String xsd:type="string">DEF</String>
         <String xsd:type="string">DEF Corp</String>
         <Float xsd:type="float">34.1</Float>
      </m:GetLastTradePriceDetails>
   </SOAP:Body>
</SOAP:Envelope>
```

Method Parameters

The SOAP specification says that parameters can be both 'in' and 'in/out', which means that they can be values that are passed to a routine as information, or values that are additionally intended to hold the results of the function. However, there is nowhere in SOAP to define the pattern that a function should take – that is, which parameters are for input and which should also return data.

This means that there is no way for a client implementation to discover what parameters are required in advance of making a call, and there is no way for a server to generalize the process of checking passed parameters before executing the method. Of course, you can check the parameters in each of your functions to see if you are receiving what you would expect to receive, but ideally the SOAP server layer should hide this from you.

Although this checking would be very useful, it is probably correct that this is not part of SOAP for two reasons. Firstly, it really would annoy the fans of XML-RPC! No longer would you be able to knock up a quick client and server module for any platform; you would now have to deal with the checking of parameter names and the data types of those parameters. But if both the client and server modules are under your control, you can ensure that the parameters are correct without having to be so elaborate.

The second reason is that there are already a number of other initiatives that exist for specifying the 'footprint' of a function. Some of these come from the world of software design, where objects and their methods can be defined automatically from various tools. Others are new, and specifically aim to cope with XML-based protocols such as SOAP and XML-RPC. One such initiative is the **Component Description Language** (**CDL**) from DevelopMentor, at http://www.develop.com/soap/cdl.htm, which allows the types of parameters to be specified, along with a function's return values.

Fault Responses

The final payload type is for errors. A fault response is returned if the SOAP layer is able to determine that something is wrong. There are a number of levels at which errors can occur; there may be a problem with the package, or with the XML passed, or the method name in the payload may not match that in the header. However, it will not always be possible for SOAP itself to spot these errors. If, for example, there is an error in the XML passed, or M-POST is used but no mandatory parameters have been passed then the package will not even get as far as being processed by SOAP. On the other hand, if the wrong namespace has been used to specify the SOAP elements then SOAP will be able to spot that, and act accordingly.

SOAP returns indications about faults that it can detect in the following way:

```
<SOAP:Envelope xmlns:SOAP="urn:schemas-xmlsoap-org:soap.v1">
   <SOAP:Body>
      <SOAP:Fault>
         <SOAP:faultcode>200</SOAP:faultcode>
         <SOAP:faultstring>SOAP Must Understand Error</SOAP:faultstring>
         <SOAP:runcode>1</SOAP:runcode>
      </SOAP:Fault>
   </SOAP:Body>
</SOAP:Envelope>
```

This example is from the SOAP spec itself, the only difference being we have stated the namespace prefixes explicitly on `<faultcode>`, `<faultstring>` and `<runcode>`. The spec tends to leave out namespace prefixes once inside the sub-element – in this case `<SOAP:Fault>` – but the code we are building prefixes anything to do with SOAP with the SOAP prefix.

The meaning of the various parts of the `<Fault>` structure are as follows:

- `<faultcode>` is the code number for the fault, such as 100 if the call was made using an unsupported version of SOAP.
- `<faultstring>` is the string version of the error, say "Version Mismatch" for error 100.
- `<runcode>` is used to indicate whether – despite the error being reported – the function was passed to the application. The current range of values are `0`, `1`, and `2`, indicating "Maybe", "No" and "Yes".

These three elements are required, but a fourth element is also possible – `<detail>` – which can contain anything the application might want to return, such as more detailed information about why the call failed. For example, if the application being called were to fail then it should return the SOAP error 400 but that doesn't tell the caller much; the application may also want to provide more information about the error:

```
<SOAP:Envelope xmlns:SOAP="urn:schemas-xmlsoap-org:soap.v1">
   <SOAP:Body>
      <SOAP:Fault>
         <SOAP:faultcode>400</SOAP:faultcode>
         <SOAP:faultstring>SOAP Application Failed Error</SOAP:faultstring>
         <SOAP:runcode>1</SOAP:runcode>
         <SOAP:detail>
            <errorcode>1001</errorcode>
```

```
            <message>No such record</message>
         </SOAP:detail>
      </SOAP:Fault>
   </SOAP:Body>
</SOAP:Envelope>
```

A fault payload is prepared with the following function:

```
function CreateFaultPayload(iFaultcode, sDetail)
   Dim oSubElem
   Set oSubElem = oDOM.createNode(1, "SOAP:Fault", NS_SOAP)
   addChild oSubElem, "faultcode", iFaultcode
   Select Case iFaultcode
      Case 100
         sFaultstring = "Version Mismatch"
      Case 200
         sFaultstring = "Must Understand"
      Case 300
         sFaultstring = "Invalid Request"
      Case 400
         sFaultstring = "Application Faulted"
   End Select
   addChild oSubElem, "faultstring", sFaultstring
   addChild oSubElem, "runcode", iRuncode
   if sDetail <> "" then
      addChild oSubElem, "detail", sDetail
   end if
   Set CreateFaultPayload = CreatePayload(oSubElem)
end function
```

The function only needs the fault code and a detail string to create a `<Fault>` structure. The fault string is the created from the code, and the run code is determined from a global variable. Note that the detail string is only returned if it is actually set to something.

As with all the payload functions, `addChild()` is used to create nodes within the tree that is being constructed. We'll now turn to this function.

addChild()

We met the `addChild()` function briefly in the previous section, but we will look at it here in more detail because it is quite central to our SOAP system. The purpose of `addChild()` is to add a node to an XML tree, with the node conforming to the data rules outlined in the SOAP spec. For example if we have an integer of value 7, we might want the following node to be created:

```
<integer>7</integer>
```

or:

```
<score xsd:type="int">7</score>
```

The function is very flexible, handling arrays and so on, and because it is recursive it can cope with arrays of arrays and other complex structures. It can also convert some VB objects to XML, such as recordsets that are the result of database queries. The function is quite long so for the full picture refer to the supplied files. Here I'll just show a small part of the routine.

The parameters passed are the node that we want to append to, the name that we would like the new node to have and the actual item to convert to a node. If the name of the node is blank then we use the type of the item passed as the element name:

```
Function addChild(oEl, sName, vItem)
   Dim bRet : bRet = False
   If sName = "" Then
      sName = TypeName(vItem)
   End If
```

Create the node that will contain the data. Note that if we have a variant array then we use the `ArrayOf` syntax:

```
   If sName = "Variant()" Then
      sName = "ArrayOfvariant"
   End If
   Dim oTemp : Set oTemp = oDOM.createElement(sName)
```

Depending on the type of the data, set the new element up correctly:

```
   Select Case TypeName(vItem)
      Case "Null"
         oTemp.setAttribute "xsd:null", "1"
      Case "Boolean"
         setTypedData oTemp, "boolean", vItem
      Case "Integer"
         setTypedData oTemp, "integer", vItem
      Case "Long"
         setTypedData oTemp, "integer", vItem
      Case "Single"
         setTypedData oTemp, "float", vItem
      Case "Double"
         setTypedData oTemp, "float", vItem
      Case "String"
         vItem = Replace(vItem, "&", "&amp;", 1, -1, 1)
         vItem = Replace(vItem, "<", "&lt;", 1, -1, 1)
         setTypedData oTemp, "string", vItem
```

The ability to provide a recordset as a parameter makes this a powerful function. Note that for each field we recursively call `addChild()` so that we get the correct data type for the entry. A by-product of this is that we can cope with nested recordsets:

```
      Case "Recordset"
         Do While Not vItem.EOF
            Dim oRec : Set oRec = oDOM.createElement("Record")
            Dim oField, oNodeField
            for each oField in vItem.fields
```

```
            Set oNodeField = oDOM.createElement(oField.name)
            addChild oTemp, oField.name, oField.value
         next
         oTemp.appendChild(oRec)
         vItem.MoveNext
      Loop
```

Finally, anything that doesn't match could be an array, or unrecognised. If it's an array we treat it as an array of variants:

```
   Case Else
      If VarType(vItem) > vbArray Then
         Set oTemp = Nothing
         Set oTemp = oDOM.createElement("ArrayOfvariant")
         oTemp.setAttribute "xsd:type", "u:variant[" & UBound(vItem) & "]"
         for i = 0 to UBound(vItem) - 1
            addChild oTemp, "variant", vItem(i)
         next
      Else
         setTypedData oTemp, "string", "Unrecognised: " & TypeName(vItem) & _
                         " [" & VarType(vItem) & "]"
      End If
   End Select
 oEl.appendChild(oTemp)
 addChild = bRet
end function
```

The final part of the payload functionality is the low-level routine that sets a node to a particular data type:

```
function setTypedData(ByRef oNode, sType, vData)
on error resume next
   oNode.setAttribute "xsd:type", sType
   oNode.dataType = sType
   oNode.nodeTypedValue = vData
   If Err Then
      oNode.setAttribute "xsd:type", "string"
      oNode.dataType = "string"
      oNode.nodeTypedValue = _
         "Error setting '" & oNode.nodeName & "' " & "(type " & sType & ") to " _
         & "'" & vData & "' " & "(type " & VarTypeText(vData) & "). " _
         & "[" & err.number & "-" & err.description& "-" & err.source & "]"
      Err.Clear
   End If
end function
```

In order to take advantage of the XML-DR facilities in the Microsoft XML DOM I have placed the values into the `nodeTypedValue` attribute, as well as setting the `xsd:type` value as required by XML Schemas Part 2. I would assume that when Microsoft release the next version of their XML DOM then the `dt:dt` syntax would have been replaced by the `xsd:type` syntax, in which case the first line of this function can be removed.

Posting the Payload

Having established how payloads are created, let's return to the remote call that we were looking at. To save you looking back, the code we have so far is here:

```
function doRemoteCall(sU, sNS, sM, arP)
   On Error Resume Next
   '
   ' Create the request body from the method name and array of parameters
   '
   Dim oPL : Set oPL = CreateCallPayload(sNS, sM, arP)
   If Err.Number <> 0 Then
      Dim sTemp : sTemp = Err.Number & ": " & Err.Description
      Err.Clear
      Err.Raise 999, "SOAP", "Failed to create payload (" & sTemp & ")"
   Else
      ...
   End If
end function
```

Provided that the call payload was created successfully we are now in a position to send the payload to the remote server. Remember from our discussion of the enhancements in SOAP that we must first try to do a POST, before trying an M-POST. So, here is the first section of code:

```
      Err.Raise 999, "SOAP", "Failed to create payload (" & sTemp & ")"
   Else
      sM = sNS & "#" & sM
      Dim oHTTP : Set oHTTP = Server.CreateObject("Microsoft.XMLHTTP")
      iStatus = doPost("POST", oHTTP, sU, sNS, sM, oPL)
      If iStatus = 405 Then
         iStatus = doPost("M-POST", oHTTP, sU, sNS, sM, oPL)
      End If
```

If you are writing your own SOAP modules then bear in mind that the SOAP spec lists a few other HTTP return codes that must be handled. For example, redirections with the code `302` must be honored. Some components that handle your HTTP requests will perform this for you without you having to do anything, but it is worth checking that this is the case.

After executing either a POST (or an M-POST) we can check the return value. If we receive a `200` then we know at least that HTTP processed our call – although there still may have been some errors at SOAP's level. Anything other than a `200` is an error. The most likely error codes will be `501 Not Implemented` or `510 Not Extended`:

```
      '
      ' A 200 means that the HTTP layer is all OK
      '
      If iStatus <> 200 Then
         Err.Raise 999, "SOAP", "HTTP error: " & iStatus
      Else
         Set doRemoteCall = oHTTP.responseXML
      End If
   End If
end function
```

The function that performs the POST or M-POST is as follows:

```
function doPost(sType, oHTTP, sURL, sNS, sMN, oB)
On Error Resume Next
   Dim sMethod : sMethod = sMN
   If sNS <> "" Then
      sMethod = sNS & "#" & sMethod
   End If
   oHTTP.open sType, sURL, false
   oHTTP.setRequestHeader "Content-Type", "text/xml"
   If sType = "M-POST" Then
      oHTTP.setRequestHeader "Man", """" & NS_SOAP & """,ns=01"
      oHTTP.setRequestHeader "01-SOAPMethodName", sMethod
   Else
      oHTTP.setRequestHeader "SOAPMethodName", sMethod
   End If
   oHTTP.send(oB.xml)
   doPost = oHTTP.status
end function
```

If the type of POST being performed is a mandatory one – an M-POST – then ensure that all the headers are present.

The only other task we need to perform is a check on the data that is returned. This is in the top level SOAP function. The `CheckPayload()` function is responsible for examining a payload to make sure that method names are consistent between headers and payload, namespaces are correct and so on. The function is used on the client side to check the payload returned from a call, and on the server side to check a payload that is instigating a call. The function returns the nodes of interest in the `oSOAP` parameter, or an error structure in the `dom` parameter:

```
      Err.Raise 999, "SOAP", "Failed to call remote server (" & sTemp & ")"
   Else
      Dim dom
      Dim iOK : iOK = CheckPayload(oSOAP, dom, sNamespace, sMethod &
                      "Response", 1)
      If iOK = False Then
         Set oSOAP = dom
      End If
```

Note that the selection begins at the root node. This is because we have to cope with two situations here; one is when the actual root node is a `<SOAP:Fault>` element, which would be the case if the remote server returned us a `<SOAP:Fault>` and `CheckPayload()` stepped through to it. The second is if there were any errors in the payload returned, in which case we will get a fault payload back from `CheckPayload()`. In that case, the root element would be a `<SOAP:Envelope>`. If we find a `<SOAP:Fault>` element then we should dig out the fault code and other information and display it:

```
      Dim oTemp : Set oTemp = oSOAP.selectSingleNode("//SOAP:Fault")
      If Not IsNull(oTemp) Then
         Set oSOAP = oTemp
         Dim iFC : iFC = oSOAP.selectSingleNode("faultcode").nodeTypedValue
         Dim sFS : sFS = oSOAP.selectSingleNode("faultstring").nodeTypedValue
         Dim sDet : sDet = oSOAP.selectSingleNode("detail").nodeTypedValue
```

```
            Err.Clear
            Err.Raise 999, sNamespace & "#" & sMethod, sFS & ": (" & sDet & ")"
         Else
```

If everything was OK then we can convert the XML returned to us into ordinary variables using `XMLToValue()` – effectively the reverse of our `addChild()` function:

```
            SOAP = True
            oRet = XMLToValue(oSOAP)
         End If
      End If
```

Server Module

Now let's build the server side. The first thing to do is create an XML DOM object and load it with the data that has been posted to us:

```
<%
On Error Resume Next
Set oXML = Server.CreateObject("Microsoft.XMLDOM")
oXML.async = false
oXML.load(Request)
```

Next obtain the method used by the caller. If it's an M-POST then we need to obtain the `Man` header, which contains the namespace that will be used to identify the mandatory headers. The namespace has quotes around it so remove them:

```
sMethod = Request.ServerVariables("REQUEST_METHOD")
Dim oBody
If sMethod = "M-POST" Then
   sMan = Request.ServerVariables("HTTP_Man")
   sMan = Trim(Replace(sMan, """", ""))
```

We should check that the namespace is the same as that defined in the SOAP spec, but at the moment nothing is done:

```
   iPos = Instr(sMan, ";")
   If Left(sMan, iPos - 1) <> NS_SOAP Then
   End If
```

The actual namespace identifier – similar to the prefix in XML – follows the "`ns=`". Once this has been retrieved we can create the header name so that we can retrieve the method name:

```
   iPos = Instr(sMan, "ns=")
   sManID = Mid(sMan, iPos + 1)

   sMethodName = Request.ServerVariables("HTTP_" & sManID & "-SOAPMethodName")
Else
   sMethodName = Request.ServerVariables("HTTP_SOAPMethodName")
End If
```

Now that we have the method name we need to split off the namespace since we will need to check it against the payload namespace value:

```
'
' Get the namespace and method
'
sNamespace = ""
iPos = Instr(sMethodName, "#")
if iPos <> 0 then
   sNamespace = Left(sMethodName, iPos - 1)
   sMethodName = Mid(sMethodName, iPos + 1)
end if
```

The following snippet is not part of the SOAP spec, but it is a useful piece of code for testing purposes. All it does is give back to the client exactly what was passed, when the method is `ECHO()` and the namespace is `SOAP`:

```
'
' If the namespace is "SOAP" and the method is "ECHO" then just send it
' all straight back as XML to help testing
'
If sNamespace = "SOAP" and sMethodName = "ECHO" Then
   Response.ContentType = "text/xml"
   Response.Write oXML.xml
Else
```

Before we actually execute the function being requested we need to check that the payload is consistent:

```
   Dim vRet
   Dim domServer
   iOK = CheckPayload(oXML, domServer, sNamespace, sMethodName)
   If iOK Then
```

If the payload is OK then `oXML` will contain the parameter nodes so convert them to variables, before passing them to the call-back routine:

```
      param = XMLToValue(oXML)
      SOAPCallback(param)
      Set oXML = Nothing
```

If the call was executed successfully then we can create a response payload that will be returned to the caller. On the other hand if there is an error, then create a fault payload:

```
      If Err Then
         Set domServer = CreateFaultPayload(400, err.number & ": " & _
                         err.description)
         Err.Clear
      Else
         Set domServer = CreateCallResponsePayload(sNamespace, sMethodName, vRet)
      End If
   End If
```

```
    Response.ContentType = "text/xml"
    Response.Write domServer.xml
    Set domServer = Nothing
End If
%>
```

The last piece of the jigsaw is the set of actual routines that should be executed. Recall that the actual call we made used the following syntax:

```
if not Request.form("iAuthor") = "" then
   paramList(0) = CInt(Request.form("iAuthor"))
   paramList(1) = 1
   iRet = SOAP("http://server/SOAP/myServer.asp", _
               "myNamespace", _
               "getAuthor", _
               paramList, _
               oRet)
   '
   ' Check the return status and then maybe do something with the returned value
   '
end if
```

We now need to create the `myServer.asp` module. The SOAP server module needs to be included to give us access to all the payload and data handling functions. To create links to your functions you need a single callback that the SOAP structure will call. Within this function you place case statements, which select on the namespace and methods. This allows the same method name to be used in different namespaces. Note that although the namespace and method values could be passed as parameters, currently they are global variables. Your function must always place its return value in the `vRet` variable, which is also global:

```
<!--#include virtual="/X-Port/SOAP/SOAP.asp" -->
<!--#include virtual="/X-Port/SOAP/SOAPServer.asp" -->
<%
'
' The main code calls a user-defined function and then wraps up the results.
' The results are then returned to the caller
'

Function SOAPCallback(param)
   '
   ' First check the namespace
   '
   Select Case sNamespace
      Case "myNamespace"
         '
         ' Can now check the method name
         '
         Select Case sMethodName
            Case "getAuthor"
               vRet = getAuthor(param(0), param(1))
            Case Else
               Err.Raise 1000, "Namespace '" & sNamespace & "' _
                                 has no method called '" _
```

```
                             & sMethodName & "'"
         End Select
      Case Else
         Err.Raise 1002, "There is no namespace called '" & sNamespace & "'"
   End Select
End Function
```

Finally we reach the function itself. The routine simply queries our `Author` table (see the last chapter) for `iCount` number of authors who have an `ID` greater than `iID`. The result of the query is placed into an array, with each row in the database being a further array:

```
function getAuthor(iID, iCount)
   Set dbConn = CreateObject("ADODB.Connection")
   dbConn.Provider = "MSDataShape"
   dbConn.Open "Data Provider=MSDASQL;DSN=SSMembership;user=sa;pwd=1998;"
   Dim rs : Set rs = Server.CreateObject("ADODB.Recordset")
   Dim sQuery
   sQuery = "SELECT * FROM Author WHERE pk_Author > " & iID
   rs.Open sQuery, dbConn, 0, 3
   If Err = 0 Then
      Dim a
      a = rs.GetRows(iCount)
      Dim aRow()
      ReDim aRow(UBound(a, 1) + 1)
      Dim aRows()
      ReDim aRows(UBound(a, 2) + 1)
      for i = 0 to UBound(a, 2)
         for j = 0 to UBound(a, 1)
            aRow(j) = a(j, i)
         next
         aRows(i) = aRow
      next
      getAuthor = aRows
   End If
end function
%>
```

Conclusion

While XML-RPC has deservedly achieved popularity because of its simplicity, it was ultimately *too* simple. XML-RPC was not defined tightly enough to cope with industrial-strength server-to-server applications, but SOAP as a major upgrade now makes it a viable choice, whilst hopefully retaining some of the ease of implementation within XML-RPC.

WebDAV

SOAP provides an important foundation for building RPC applications. It is likely that in the future other RPC standards will be devised for different purposes that build on the SOAP foundation.

However, while we have the possibility of standardizing on the *format* by which methods are conveyed, we have not standardized on the methods themselves. In many ways this is immaterial. The range of applications is so great that you couldn't possibly generalize the methods that should be used. However, there is one type of application that is extremely common on the Internet – the editing and uploading of files.

Much of the popularity of XML-RPC has come about through its imaginative use by the guys at UserLand. One of the many exciting applications that they have devised is a way for people to upload and edit messages on a bulletin-board. Another is the ability to maintain news items. Both of these programs use XML-RPC to allow a remote user to maintain their data, without the server needing to concern itself with how that data is edited.

While this is an impressive use of the technology, the problem is simply that the methods used to keep the information up to date are not standard. In other words, a client application written to edit information on the UserLand site could not be used to maintain information at another location. Equally, applications that can maintain information with other protocols, such as Microsoft FrontPage, could not be used to edit UserLand data.

WebDAV stands for *Web Document Authoring and Versioning* and provides a set of methods specifically geared towards the editing and control of any type of data that can be accessed through HTTP. WebDAV defines methods and their format for adding, deleting and browsing. Whereas SOAP defines how method calls should be *conveyed,* WebDAV defines the methods themselves.

Of course, it is perfectly possible to publish a set of methods that can be called with SOAP in much the same way that you might publish an API for some software package. This is likely to become increasingly common for systems that provide applications over the Internet.

Although WebDAV is the right solution for handling remote data manipulation, implementing a client and server is not a simple weekend's work like XML-RPC or SOAP. However, it does open up some important possibilities. For example, Microsoft have added a WebDAV compatible layer to their web server which provides the same functionality as their FrontPage Server extensions, but now in a standard way. This means that any client software that understands WebDAV can be use to edit documents stored behind such a server. A number of tools will emerge but currently FrontPage and Microsoft's WebFolders (an additional component for Internet Explorer 5) can communicate with any WebDAV server. Microsoft has also announced that they will provide a WebDAV interface to the next release of Exchange Server.

> *More information on WebDAV can be found at* *http://www.ietf.cnri.reston.va.us/rfc/rfc2518.txt*. *Other companies are working on WebDAV interfaces too. A good example of a significant use of the technique is at* *http://www.sharemation.com/*.

Summary

In this chapter we have looked at several methods of server-to-server communication, all of which have made some use of XML. We started by looking at situations where this communication is necessary, and then briefly considered some of the options available to developers. In this section we had our first look at XML-RPC and SOAP, as well as being introduced to Coins, WDDX, XMOP and KOALA.

Next, we had an in-depth look at XML-RPC – why it exists, what it can do, what its syntax is, and in what situations we might look elsewhere for communication solutions. We also looked at examples showing the use of XML-RPC in more detail, from a simple single method call to the use of XML-RPC in a more involved situation – the book catalog example that has been developed throughout this book. A list of URLs was also provided for tools and additional reading.

Moving on, we introduced SOAP as an enhanced XML-RPC. We've seen how this technology – in its infancy at the time of writing – may change the way we look at distributed computing. Its advantages are obvious – SOAP is a simple protocol enabling us to utilize the existing HTTP infrastructure in a powerful new way, without the inherent verbosity of XML-RPC. Again, we saw this technology at work first hand by the means of an educational example.

Finally, we saw how WEBDAV is attempting to standardize the more common method calls we might want to make over the web. WEBDAV is very much an up-and-coming technology, so links were provided to more up to date sources of information.

12

eBusiness and XML

Initially created to exchange and display static, human-readable documents, the World Wide Web has rapidly matured into an essential communication, advertising, and sales channel for organizations of all sizes around the world.

The functions of the Web that involve buying and selling typically fall under the banner of electronic commerce, better known as **e-commerce**. Because e-commerce is an over-used and often misused term, I've provided my personal interpretation of the term here:

> **e-commerce is the exchange of goods or services for money between two or more entities over the Web.**

There has been a rapid evolution on the Web; from exchanging scientific documents, to being able to purchase goods and services. The topic of setting up e-commerce sites deserves a whole book on its own, and this chapter does not attempt to teach you how to create e-commerce solutions. However, there are many misconceptions surrounding the use of XML in e-commerce, and the aim of this chapter is to explain some of the key issues regarding the role of XML in e-commerce. Unfortunately, e-commerce is extremely difficult, labor intensive, and expensive; indeed it is a long way from providing true returns in many areas of the market. XML will not instantly make e-commerce applications much easier to develop, although it will undoubtedly change the face of the way e-commerce applications are developed and it is these issues that we will address.

The chapter is divided into two halves. The first half is more theoretical and introduces the traditional EDI approach to e-commerce, showing how solutions that are implemented using XML syntax are, in fact, similar to existing EDI applications – although it will highlight the advantages and the reasons behind the increasing use of XML.

While we are looking at this, we will see some of the key issues in moving to an XML syntax, and address some common misconceptions. The first half then ends with a look at the future directions of XML in e-commerce, and how it will be able to offer a lot more than existing EDI standards. In the second half of the chapter, we get a lot more practical. This section looks at some of the existing DTDs and schemas that have been developed for use in horizontal industries, and more examples of messages. This is followed by a look at solutions for implementing this new era of e-commerce, including a look at Microsoft's BizTalk framework.

So, in this chapter we shall see:

- How existing EDI e-commerce solutions work
- How XML provides a mechanism for defining business vocabularies that let us share business data among different applications, even on different platforms
- Misconceptions, perceptions, and motivations behind using XML in e-commerce
- Some of the directions e-commerce is likely to take in the future
- Examples of implementations of XML in vertical industries
- Examples of solutions for horizontal industries
- An introduction to Microsoft's BizTalk framework

People want to know how XML fits in with their endeavors, how they can make the most of the current state of affairs, and where the technology is heading. This chapter attempts to look at the objectives, trends, misconceptions, vision, and initiatives involved in fulfilling the vision of global e-commerce solutions.

What is E-Commerce?

If we strip e-commerce down to its bare bones, we can see that it is simply about two or more parties exchanging some kind of information electronically for money. It doesn't really matter what is being sold, from compact disks, to automobile parts, to intellectual property; the underlying aim is to get some kind of message from one party to another in a form that means something to both parties.

Big businesses and banks have been involved in such electronic transactions for decades, with the need to support credit card merchant services, ATM machines, exchange of account details between offices, and so on. Traditionally, for these services, businesses had to use **Value Added Networks** (**VAN**s) to share this data. Since 1994, however, there has been a paradigm shift, as the Internet's popularity has resulted in new business models. This electronic information sharing is no longer the domain of large businesses, it is now within the reach of small and medium sized enterprises, collectively known as **SME**s, expanding the number of uses people have found for electronic information exchange.

The traditional method of communication for the large companies, who pioneered electronic information exchange, is a solution known as **EDI** (which simply stands for Electronic Data Interchange). However, such systems are notoriously expensive and difficult to implement, making the barriers to entry high. So, in this chapter, we will take a brief look at how EDI exchanges take place, then go on to look at how the Internet and XML are changing the shape of these communications.

We have only just begun to see how XML, delivered via the Internet, can change the way businesses interact with each other. The trend towards XML is expected to expand and diversify as more applications of available technologies are employed to help gain competitive advantage in the age of electronic information. In addition to e-commerce, one of the major emerging trends – adding another dimension to business – is to share an increasing amount and variety of other enterprise and organizational information, an area that is currently being defined and implemented alongside the new e-commerce applications. The term for this superset of exchanges that includes e-commence, plus the variety of supplemental messages, has been named **eBusiness**.

History is being made here and now, and developments thus far have proven useful, representing a fine start. Now it is time to take these tools and lessons learned, and expand the benefits gained from our new business languages, to a global audience of businesses worldwide. Many of these businesses have had the desire to automate their processes, but have not yet had the resources or tools to effectively express their language, or to maintain, search, and drive their development, workflow, or exchange business documents. Now they do.

When we think about e-commerce, a lot of us think about web sites that sell products and services to the public. However, many of the larger web sites' back-ends are being automated and process orders either via EDI or in proprietary protocols and formats. In addition there are also large areas of business that use e-commerce to trade with other businesses in a **supply chain**. (The supply chain is the coordination of a portfolio of assets, logistics, information, and operations, involved in fulfilling final customer demand, which may involve other autonomous companies.) There is also an increasing trend to share more information between departments, and completely separate businesses. Let's take a look at three models and what they involve in terms of eBusiness.

- Selling direct to customers
- Business to business transactions
- Information sharing and content syndication

There are many variations upon each of these models, however they give us a base upon which we can consider the areas in which XML will help eBusiness.

Selling Direct to the Customer

This is a model with which we are all familiar, and is the one that many people think of first when we talk about e-commerce. Typical examples are sites such as Amazon.com and Dell Direct. Using a standard web browser we can go to their web sites and view their products. If we see something we like, we can then purchase the items using credit cards, and get them delivered to our doors.

This model has not only helped big businesses, it can also offer a lifeline to many small companies that make or sell specialist products to a small potential market. Despite the images protrayed in commercials by companies such as Microsoft and IBM, there are still few small businesses that have taken advantage of the Internet as a direct sales channel. As we will see later in the chapter, new tools will help SMEs take advantage of the Internet.

The process of traditional manufacturers hawking their wares directly to potential consumers online, bypassing the middleman in search for higher profits, is known as **disintermediation**. The challenges facing these manufacturers include marketing directly to consumers, consumer response, small order processing, not to mention alienation of current sales channels. Some manufacturers, however, are modifying their disintermediation efforts by partnering with online retailers to enlist them as distribution and fulfillment centers.

Business to Business Transactions

This idea behind business to business (also known as **B2B**) transactions is similar to selling direct to the public, however the transactions are placed between trading partners. These big companies, however, will not be getting out their credit cards every time they place an order, and will more likely have accounts with their suppliers, and their transactions often take place using predefined, shared languages.

One of the key advantages for businesses that use these models is that there is often less paperwork to be processed, meaning orders can be fulfilled quicker. Some processes can even be automated in line with stock levels, which facilitates just-in-time ordering, and – in some cases – removes the need for someone to place each order manually. When automated processes take care of the day-to-day orders, fulfillment managers can focus on exceptions to the process.

Typically when businesses automate their transaction handling, either by choice or in reaction to customer demand, they find this has a rippling effect throughout their order department's processes. True cost savings are provided to organizations that modify their business practices. But automation comes with a cost, integration can require a large up-front expense, eliminating jobs, and requiring maintenance. As a result, some organizations turn to **rip and read** processing. Rip and read is where a transaction – once received – is printed out and processed via paper routing or rekeyed into the organizations computer. This process is not restricted to smaller organizations; some of the largest corporations perform this type of processing daily in parts of the organization. One of the promises of XML in eBusiness is to give organizations the tools that will allow automation with a decrease in technical complexity, removing the need for rip and read processing.

Information Sharing and Content Syndication

The final model we will look at is that of sharing information. This may take many forms, it may just be summaries of sales data being sent from satellite stores to a headquarters, or it may be syndication of intellectual property – such as music, video, news dispatch or a stock market company selling stock market analyst's reports. The supply chain metaphor can be applied to services in the same way as with physical goods – as demonstrated in the areas such as marketing.

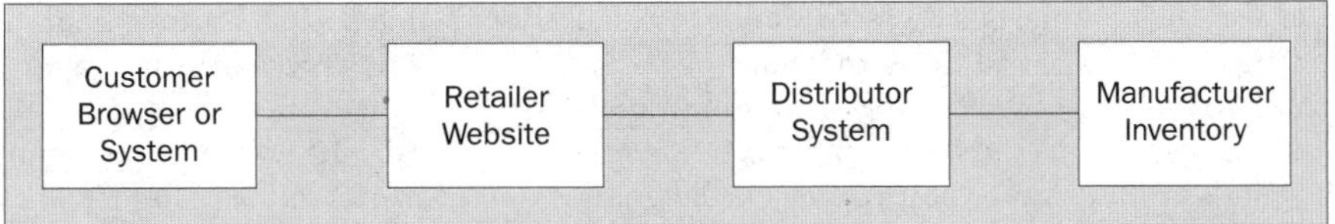

If 1990s was the decade of corporations executing **Enterprise Resource Planning** (**ERP** – integrated application software suites that addresses manufacturing, distribution and financial business functions, enabling enterprises to optimize their business processes, and allowing for necessary management analysis and appropriate decision making), the next decade will surely be focused on extending the enterprise and streamlining intra-enterprise processes. Automation of information sharing will provide corporations with distinct advantages over their unwilling counterparts as aggressive organizations move to developing partnerships and create new business models through information sharing.

Information sharing will also allow **infomediaries** or brokers to provide reintermediation services by gathering information from multiple suppliers on capability, pricing, availability or other metrics, such as online auctions.

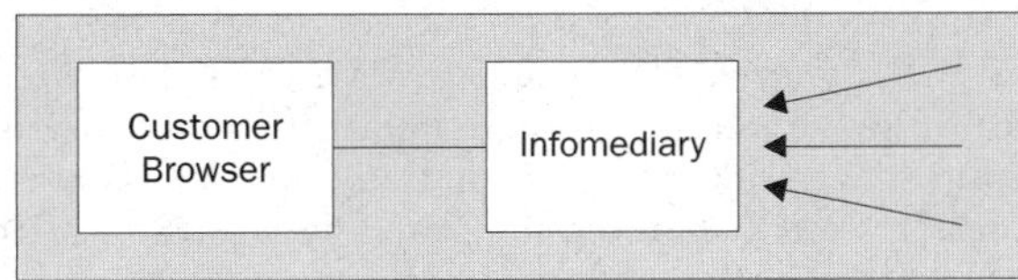

In order to understand how XML is changing the face of e-commerce, we should see how EDI paved the way for e-commerce.

EDI – Electronic Data Interchange

EDI has been around in one form of another for over 30 years. It helped pave the way for the looming breakthrough of eBusiness. Well before the Web and even the Internet as we know it existed, companies were exchanging data electronically using standardized transactions tailored for each industry. Many companies in the automotive, grocery, and electronics industries, for example, achieved significant savings and improved business processes using EDI. In the early 1980s, the American National Standards Institute (ANSI), seeing the benefits of standards in electronic business, established an accredited standards committee for EDI and gave it the designation **X12**.

No one knows the exact number of organizations implementing EDI, but it is likely that the number is above 100,000, and rising. Although, as we shall see, there is a focus on new EDI systems incorporating XML for **interoperability**.

Since the early 1970s in North America, EDI standards have been used by big business and governments to exchange financial, manufacturing, inventory, technical, and transport information. The most commonly known of such standard is X12, which is currently being maintained by the not-for-profit **Data Interchange Standards Association (DISA)** http://www.disa.org.

Much of the rest of the world is involved with the **United Nations Electronic Data Interchange for Administration, Commerce and Transport (UN/EDIFACT)** initiative. The EDIFACT standards are overseen by the Centre for Facilitation of Administration, Commerce and Trade (CEFACT) at the UN Economic Commission for Europe (UNECE), in Geneva, Switzerland. For more information on UN/EDIFACT see http://www.unece.org/trade/untdid/welcome.htm

There have also been numerous de facto standards for B2B exchanges, such as inter-bank financial protocols ("wire transfer"), and those that control the international networks of Automated Teller Machines (ATMs) and credit-card verification terminals. Various consortia of corporations have used X12 and UN/EDIFACT as the basis for industry-specific EDI standards. For example, many of the world's hospitals and insurance companies exchange medical information using the **Health Level Seven (HL7)** standard.

Since EDI technology pre-dates the commercial use of the Internet, EDI not only includes specifications for message formats, but also defines communications protocols, and even some hardware requirements. The expense of implementing such systems has limited the market for this technology; a lot of money has been spent on systems that use proprietary software and hardware, and which often mix EDI with other proprietary solutions used within the company. For all practical purposes, only government agencies and big business have had the resources to fully exploit the power of EDI. The explosion of the commercial use of the Internet in the 1990s, however, has created the demand for more modern and more easily implemented eBusiness standards. Thus, almost all of the current EDI standards are being revised to use XML as the new foundation for their required messages and transactions.

But how did EDI pave the way for this new era of eBusiness? This is an important question to answer; we need to know what EDI offered before XML so that we can see where XML is making an impact. We need to be aware that EDI already offered standard ways of marking up data in electronic messages, which allowed companies within an industry to share information electronically – before XML was even thought of. Because of limited bandwidth available on traditional VANs, these messages use a compact and difficult to understand syntax, transferred using proprietary protocols. However, EDI systems do offer features such as mature transaction handling, management of trading profiles, logging and archival, handling of business and legal requirements, and error handling. On top of this infrastructure are APIs for application integration, version control, and exception reporting. We don't need to focus on the software and hardware that EDI uses here, rather we will take a quick look at what is exchanged in an EDI transaction or **business conversation**.

Business Conversations

EDI provides the language required for exchanging business semantics. In rather the same way that industries can share common XML DTDs or schemas to ensure that they mark up data in a way that can be shared, EDI specifications offer standards for sharing business information.

Existing EDI standards are based upon the concept of **transactions**, which are comprised of **messages** in published, pre-defined and commonly-known **formats**, that are transmitted using pre-defined communications **protocols**. While protocols tend to be static, and often implemented directly in hardware, message formats tend to be more dynamic, and must be shared between multiple organizations, using commonly-accessible **schemas** that are usually stored in **repositories**. Schemas are detailed descriptions of the format of data objects that have been mutually agreed-upon by the various parties involved in the transactions. Most of the EDI repositories are managed by non-profit organizations or industry consortia to prevent any single company from exerting excessive influence upon the design and implementation of these important interchange data.

If you think that this sounds similar to the concept of industries agreeing on DTDs or other schemas that can be used to share data marked up in XML, you would be correct. The sets of messages and their schemas are a similar idea to XML documents that are validated against one or more standard DTDs or other schema. Indeed, as we shall see later in the chapter, there are a number of XML repositories springing up to provide a service where people can share their XML schemas. Anyway, let's continue and look at what happens in an EDI transaction.

EDI offers a large set of standard messages that can be used within transactions. The following diagram illustrates an exchange scenario between a buyer and supplier using X12 transactions. Each number represents the type of message that is being exchanged.

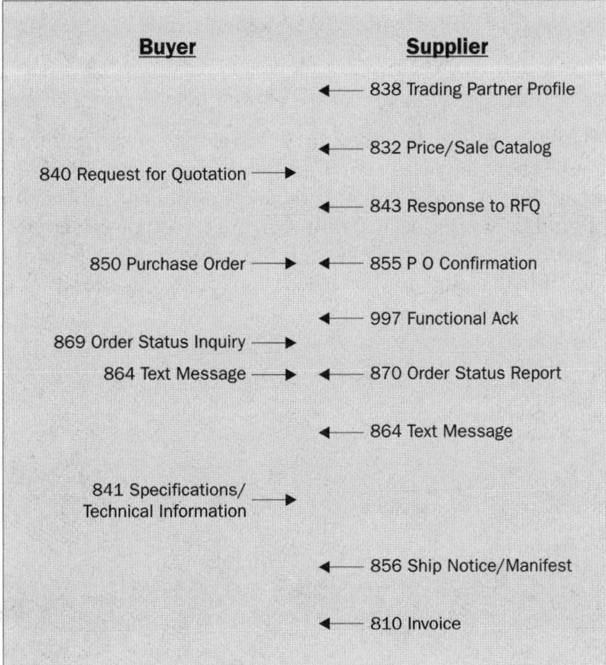

So, EDI offers these standard message types, indicated by their numbers or **codes**. As you can see, the supplier starts by sending a trading partner profile (838), and a catalog (832). The buyer then knows the products/services available and how to deal with the supplier, and can send a request for a quotation or RFQ (840) to the supplier, who can use a response to the RFQ. In this example, the result is a purchase order (850) being raised. And so it goes on, until the buyer receives an invoice (810).

There are hundreds of such standard messages each with its own purpose and identifying code in both X12 and EDIFACT that will help the two parties communicate. Some of these are developed for specific industries, and include messages especially tailored for car and health insurance, shipping, mortgages, and student loans, the list goes on. However, the development of the messages and vocabularies is extremely expensive, and remains one of the highest barriers to entry.

As you might guess, there are frequent occasions when industries customize these standard messages to specify additional information about the trading partners involved, which again involves further development. This may entail either the use of custom content (devised and agreed upon by trading partners), or the use of temporary identifiers allowed for in the EDI specifications. Ideally, when these extensions have been made, they should be submitted to a standards body for adoption in a future version of the standard. But, as you might imagine, once an exchange is implemented with the temporary code and in working order, there seems little gained from expending additional resources, so many real world systems employ non-standard syntax.

So, let's take a quick look at what an EDI message can look like. We will look at an example of two purchase orders in X12.

Structure of an EDI Message

An EDI message consists of data **segments** and **elements** that need to be interpreted. As we have already noted, the mechanism for specifying the order of the data segments is reminiscent of the functionality provided by XML DTDs. Segments can be mandatory, optional, or conditional, and can be repeated a predefined number of times. The collection of EDI Elements called out for each segment is also specified in the data standard, and includes datatyping attributes, along with minimum and maximum values.

Here we can see the purchase order is wrapped in an **envelope** consisting of a **header** at the top and **trailer** at the end. The interchange header includes the routing information, the version of the standard used, control counts, a timestamp, and a flag to indicate whether the transaction should be processed as normal or whether it should be treated as a test. Inside the envelope are control envelopes for identifying functional groups (transaction types) and the beginning and end of documents. The trailer contains the count of functional groups in the transaction along with the transaction identifier, which is matched to one found in the header.

There are two purchase orders in this message, each requesting four items:

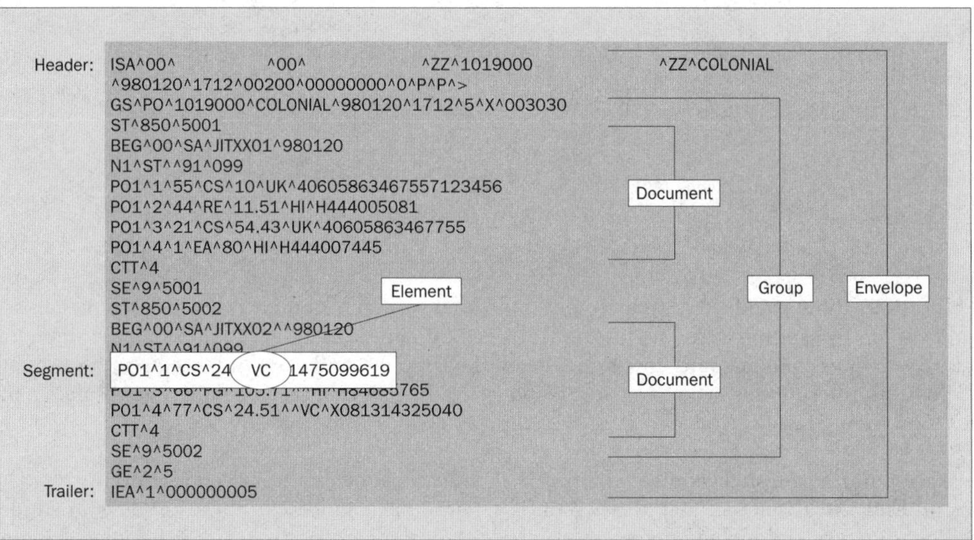

Unless you are familiar with X12, it is unlikely that this message made much sense – you would certainly have no chance of telling that this is a purchase order, let alone what the order is requesting. Those who have invested time learning the structure and constraint mechanisms relate this experience to learning a foreign language. End users, however, do not view the exchange in this form; they have a business application with a rich user interface, so it is not really of great concern to us, we are just using it as an example of the syntax. Although it is worth noting that companies who use EDI systems for sharing data with the outside world generally use a different language within the company, which means that tools called **mappers** are used in EDI to automatically translate the standard messages that are exchanged between partners from and into formats that are used inside the company.

Moving from EDI Syntax to XML

Let's look closer at one segment of this message, the Interchange Control Header, and see how we could implement the X12 approach in XML. The Interchange Control Header (also known as an ISA) is used to start and identify an interchange, we have chosen it as an example because it can be greatly enhanced when moving to XML. This example uses the control number as the ISA value that is simply assigned by the sender of the transaction. The ISA is the only segment that is fixed length, with positional reference to delimiters. The delimiters in X12 are user definable.

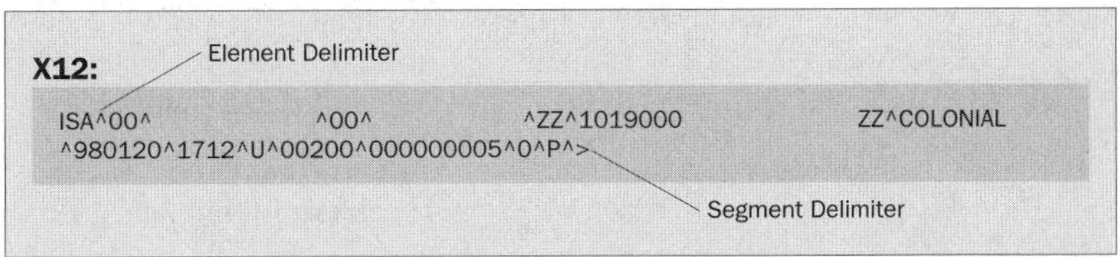

Here is an example of how we could implement this in XML:

```
<ISA AuthorizationQual= '00' Authorization= '' SecurityQual = '00' Security= ''
SenderQual= 'ZZ' Sender=' 1019000' ReceiverQual= 'ZZ' Receiver=' COLONIAL '
XchgDate=' 980120'  XchgTime=' 1712' StdAgency ='U' StdVersion =' 00200'
AckReq='0' Usage='P' >000000005</ISA>
```

As you can see, the X12 syntax is quite compact, and was developed due to the low availability and high cost of bandwidth. However, with bandwidth rising, and costs falling, it is no longer of such great concern. You can also see that the XML version is a lot easier to read and understand, which makes the vocabulary easier to learn than X12 syntax.

Note: with XML, attributes that contain null values are not required, they are only shown here for clarity – as we are matching the X12 syntax to XML.

Here is what the attributes we made up in the XML version would mean; they correspond with long names defined in the X12 syntax:

Attribute	Long Name	Purpose
`AuthorizationQual`	Authorization Information Qualifier	Identify the type of information in the Authorization Information
`Authorization`	Authorization Information	Additional identification or authorization of the interchange sender or the data in the interchange
`SecurityQual`	Security Information Qualifier	Identify the type of information in the Security Information
`Security`	Security Information	Identifying the security information about the interchange sender or the data in the interchange

Attribute	Long Name	Purpose
`SenderQual`	Interchange ID Qualifier	Designate the system/method of code structure used to designate the sender ID element being qualified
`Sender`	Interchange Sender ID	Identification code published by the sender for other parties to use as the receiver ID to route data to them
`ReceiverQual`	Interchange ID Qualifier	Designate the system/method of code structure used to designate the receiver ID element being qualified
`Receiver`	Interchange Receiver	Identification code published by the receiver of the data
`XchgDate`	Interchange Date	Date of the interchange
`XchgTime`	Interchange Time	Time of the interchange
`StdAgency`	Interchange Control Standards Identifier	Code to identify the agency responsible for the control standard used by the message that is enclosed by the interchange header and trailer
`StdVersion`	Interchange Control Version Number	Version for the interchange control segments
`AckReq`	Acknowledgment Requested	Code sent by the sender to request an interchange acknowledgment from the receiver
`Usage`	Usage Indicator	Flag to indicate whether data enclosed by this interchange envelope is test, production or information

It is not recommended that today's EDI standards should always be mapped so directly to XML implementations, rather, the important aim is to distill the rich semantics of the standards and combine this with applicable computing technology in XML syntax.

When implementing these eBusiness solutions with XML this fusion is called XML/EDI

Whether you understand EDI syntax or not, I'm sure that you can imagine XML being used to create a much more readable conversation about the procurement process... But there is another strength in applying XML to EDI-style messages, in that XML allows us to use tags to provide the hooks into parts of programs (scripts, components etc.) that allow us to have greater control over our processes to which our business rules can applied.

The XML tagging syntax is much more verbose, but simplifies integration of messages, allowing for smarter systems. It allows additional information to be used by the process in addition to the data itself.

But what is so important about a simple syntax? With XML/EDI we are looking for ways of tagging our information so that it does not need to be translated between internal formats and standards for information exchange.

Using XML we can develop vocabularies that can be used both inside the organization, from workflow to searching our databases, as well as for exchanges between trading partners.

Rather than having to map our internal representations into EDI syntax just for exchanges, with XML we can create rich vocabularies that are just as useful internally as they are for exchanges with external trading partners, so our XML/EDI formats need not be translated.

If we think about this, probably the most exciting aspect of XML/EDI is the possibility of a global framework with common mechanisms that can bring the various EDI and workflow standards together in XML syntax. In the next few years, hard decisions have to be made, and visionaries from all sides need to come to the same 'virtual' table and develop a single header and enveloping structure, repository exchanges, etc. The expected time to achieve our goal of a single global method for handling our eBusiness information and components is some years out, but is well worth the effort.

Applying XML in eBusiness

As we have seen already, XML offers a standard syntax for marking up data and allows us to add extra information to messages so that we can attach or relate scripts and business rules; this enables us to fully validate both the syntax and message structure. To see how we employ these advantages and how XML can be applied to eBusiness, let's look at another example of an eBusiness message in XML.

Even if you had never properly looked into using XML in eBusiness, you could probably guess that it involves XML travelling between a customer and a supplier. But what must this XML contain? We will be referring to the XML that is sent between trading partners as a **message**, though we use the term here independent of the way in which the information is transferred (not necessarily an email message or a message in a message queue-based application).

This section may seem more appropriate for those who are sending XML documents between participants. If you are filling out an HTML form, you will not always send an XML document. However, it is often advantageous to construct XML on the client if possible, because if you decide to re-write the application at the destination of the message, it will still be able to use the same client application. Indeed, once you have received an order from a web-based form, there will be the need to pass the order information along to whoever will fill the order, so it makes sense to use XML on ever step of the journey, from the point of origin through to order fulfilment.

Here is an example message that you can refer back to when looking at the following section. It is a sample message from Microsoft's BizTalk framework. We will meet the BizTalk framework at the end of the chapter; as it is a set of guidelines for how to publish schemas in XML and how to use XML messages for application integration and electronic commerce, its goal being to accelerate the rapid adoption of XML in eBusiness.

Note that the root <BizTalk> element has two direct descendant elements: a <Route> element, containing header information, and a <Body> element containing the message to send.

```
<?xml version="1.0"?>
<BizTalk xmlns:="urn:schemas-biztalk.org:BizTalk/biztalk-0.8xml">
<Route>
   <From Location ID="value" LocationType="value" Process="value"
         Path="value" Handle="value" />
   <To Location ID="value" LocationType="value" Address="value"
       Path="value" Handle="value" />
</Route>
<Body xmlns:= "urn:your-namespace-goes-here">
   <MessageType>
      -- Your XML document data goes here --
   </MessageType>
</Body>
</BizTalk>
```

This sample illustrates one of the main points about XML messages; that from a flow-control, debugging and audit standpoint, it is strongly advisable to include header information as part of our XML message, in addition to the data. The two sections are often referred to as a **header** and a **body**, so we shall look at each of these in turn.

> **One of the key differences between using XML to send data between parties, and EDI is that EDI takes a tightly-coupled approach to messages, whereas XML offers a far more loosely-coupled architecture, which is a lot more flexible and easy to extend.**

Message Headers

Header information – sometimes called an **envelope** – includes the additional information required to carry out the exchange (other than the payload itself of course). There isn't (as yet) a unified set of information or definition for what should be included in the header, though it often includes information regarding:

- Routing
- Security
- Batching
- Error process flagging
- Transaction identification
- Information that is legally required, such as tracking information associated with messages.

The ability to exchange and route transactions between XML servers in a set of standard methods is critical for global eBusiness.

> *In some applications this header information is not always stored as XML, for example, when you are ordering a CD on-line, from a browser with an HTML form, the header information of where the order information should be sent is kept in the HTTP headers. However, if you are using a system that just generates an XML document that contains the information, then you need to include information about who it is from and where it is going to. Depending upon the application, this may need to be kept in XML as well as other forms of header so that a receiving application can process it.*

Let's take a look at an example of this type of header information. ICE (Information and Content Exchange) is an application of XML for content syndication, which is a growing business, and much thought has been put to the headers which carry payloads of multimedia, catalogs, and provide for other solutions. The following depicts the header elements of the message. Note: the approach taken with ICE was a single DTD to cover all the exchanges to and from the subscriber.

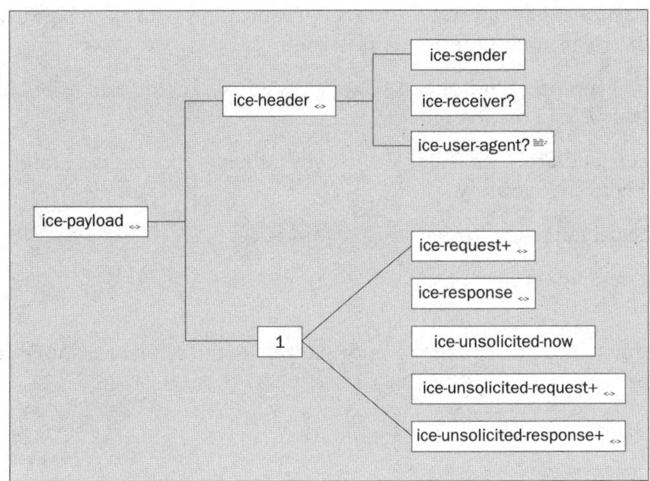

Here is the DTD Header Fragment:

```
<!ELEMENT ice-header  (ice-sender , ice-receiver? , ice-user-agent? )>
<!ELEMENT ice-sender EMPTY>
<!ELEMENT ice-receiver EMPTY>
<!ELEMENT ice-user-agent  (#PCDATA )>
```

`sender` takes the attributes: name, `role`, `sender-id`
`receiver` takes the attributes: name, `receiver-id`

This demonstrates how a simple mechanism can be very powerful and provide a general solution that can be applied to many eBusiness scenarios.

Multi-Layered Routing Issues

An important aspect of these messages is how to reference **local information** or **resources** concerning a message during a conversation with a trading partner. Local information is not stored in the message, however it is required by the processing application, so we need to provide **hooks** with which the application can work. As we have seen eariler in this chapter, with eBusiness we are dealing with business conversations, the thread for the conversation and all 'session' information requires a mechanism to keep the information related. For example, when receiving an invoice from a trading partner, we need to be able to relate this information to the purchase order, the trading partner transactions file, etc. As we noted earlier, this is an area where XML's syntax is of help to application developers. Sometimes it is also necessary to add information when your trading partner needs to pass the message downstream for further processing. At present there is no standard solution to dealing withlocal information, and there would be great benefit from one, but a common methodology for tagging such resources should aim to achieve the following goals:

- Support chained and nested workflows
- Allow for record linking (key) persistence through the life of a transaction
- Create transactions that can live within an organization (workflow) and/or be externally exchanged between trading partners (Internet, EDI)
- Allow for the keeping of individual system keys, for tracking and accessing information stored in hierarchical (XML) or relational form
- Allow for intermediaries, brokers, VANs, and other parties, to accurately relay the message easily, quickly and accurately
- Have a standard language for defining record access
- Transport independence

The following diagram shows persistence of information, as the eBusiness moves through the pipeline.

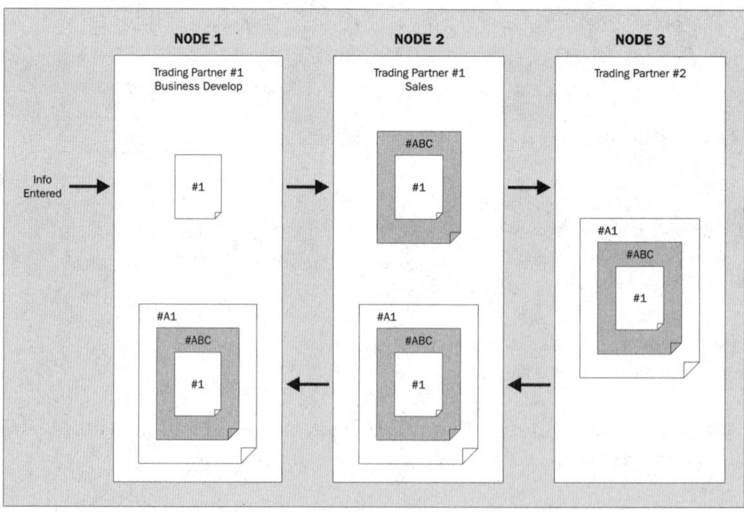

In this diagram, we can see that, as information enters the system and goes to the first trading partner's business development department, elements are added to the message header (indicated by #1). This information will help identify information that was in the message and which now has been stored locally in the first node (in case the message returns at a later point in the workflow or if there is a query about the message. It can also be used as a hook for processing in that node. The message – with its addition – is then passed on to node 2, where more elements are added to the header (this time indicated by #ABC). When the information reaches the trading partner at node 3, a third set of elements are added to the message header. Now, each node has added some key information that will allow it to identify the information regarding the message that is stored locally, or a process that should be performed when the message arrives at a node.

The following paragraphs depict one possible starting place for industry to begin work in this area; although much work still needs to be put into this issue, making sure all requirements are met from all angles.

The added information regarding *local information* or *resources* can be any logical set of elements. In the following example, we add `Echo` elements for each node (or trading partner) during the lifecycle of the resource, and new elements may be added for each process within that node. These hooks allows for drill back capability – each element having an identifier to say which node and process added the hook. The `Echo` elements are optionally assigned only at logical resource levels (for example, for each message) and are not intended at every element. The `Echo` element use is not for information exchange *per se* with trading partners but as a mechanism for a specific node owner to hook into their persistent storage format – the meaning of these elements are only of concern to the owners, and mean nothing to the other trading partners or nodes (note that each node could use different element names). `Echo` elements are intended to identify the resource owner, version of the resource process, resource location and key. Additional elements can be added as a sub resource of the `Echo` element using `EchoItems` elements nested within the `Echo` element. The structure of `EchoItems` is recursive allowing tree structures to be added to the resource, if required by the node owner. Here we can see how we use the `EchoItems` & an `Echo` element so that each resource can see the different processes following its `Echo` element, we will expand it with examples next:

```
<Resource biz='placeholder'>placeholder</Resource>
<Echo>placeholder</Echo>
<EchoItems>
   <Item>placeholder</Item>
   ...
   <EchoItems>
      <Item>placeholder</Item>
      ...
   </EchoItems>
</EchoItems>
...
```

Echo elements identify an ID of the owner as element content. The opening ID element can contain attributes, such as:

Attribute	Full Name	Meaning
q	qualifier	indicates the assigning authority of ID as adopted from the appropriate X12 qualifier values
t	token	contains a string of information that is used by the node's process and is owner independent. The token contains a string and can include index references, etc. using whatever format an organization desires to use to select a table (tree) and record (subtree)
c	configuration	indicates the version of the process and information store when the token was saved; typically this is a timestamp. The configuration can be used to interpret past tokens as processes and stores are updated

Routing Issue Example

Using the above approach, we will see how the Echo elements could be represented. The following scenario contains five Echo references assigned to a resource. The first entry is the minimum data that would be assigned. The qualifier (in this case q="01") indicates that: 109872721 is a DUNS number for the owner (a number allocated by Dunn and Bradstreet to companies outside of Europe), and the owner is keeping a reference key (ABC353) as the token.

```
<Resource.2 biz='43432432432'>
    <Echo q='01' t='ABC353'>109872721</Echo>
```

During processing of the resource, the following steps are taken:

- The system checks to see if there is one or more than one Echo elements whose content matches its identifier
- If there is more than one value, you look for the value of the q attribute, to find the Echo element that matches your company/process
- You then use the value of the t attribute to retrieve the record that needs to be processed from some kind of persistant storage device (db or file)

The second example shows a situation where the node owner has used the c attribute as a timestamp of the token. In addition, a User item is kept to identify the specific information about the node, this is used internally in the organization, which is identified as 109872721. The owner is also keeping an anchor token as well, typically used to refer to the original message in the conversation among the trading partners, for easy thread identification.

```
<Echo q='01' c='19991126:3443' t='345434'>109872721</Echo>
<EchoItems>
   <Item value='JonesGeorge@mycompany.com'>User</Item>
   <Item value='333444'>Anchor</Item>
</EchoItems>
```

The third, fourth and fifth `Echo` element examples provide other probable values for the `t` attribute. As you can see, they indicate parts of queries upon data sources, because this is the attribute used to recover the original records. As you can see, the information is highly specific to the node owner:

```
<Echo q='01' t='WHERE
    <CustProfile><UniqueID>ABCD123456789</UniqueID>
    <CustProfile>'>
    139878721
</Echo>
```

```
<Echo q='01' t='WHERE <CustProfile><GivenName>George</GivenName>
                <Phone>2233332222</Phone><CustProfile>'>
   6134478721
</Echo>
```

```
<Echo q='01' t='SELECT KEY(Record) FROM Travel_Header ch, Cust_Body csp
                WHERE csp.Approver='EDI' AND
                CONTAINS (Customer, "George Smith WITHIN Contact") > 0'>
    4137778721
</Echo>
...
```

Here you can see the type of information that can be used to add hooks into messages for processing applications to use. So, having considered the header, we should now look at the main part of the message.

Message Body

The body holds the main content of the message that needs to reach the destination specified in the header, it could be an order, a confirmation, some important information or sales data that needs to be shared etc. The body of the message can be written in any number of existing XML vocabularies, or we may choose to write our own for the specific task in hand, and we looked at how you might want to model this information in Chapter 4.

With the increasing number of XML industry standards already available, there may well be one that suits your needs already, or that is close enough to your needs that you can base your own schema on it. But how do you find the one that suits you? Start with your trading partner. Perhaps they can provide you with a schema or refer you to a web site that will. Their resource may include reference to one of the XML **repositories** (sites that hold a number of DTDs and other component schemas, codelists, and scripts for people to use) which we look at later in this chapter.

Using Existing Schemas

Remembering that the definition of a suitable vocabulary for EDI transactions was one of the major expenses in implementing an EDI system, if a vocabulary already exists for your problem domain, you would do well to study it carefully. Not only could it serve your purposes, ideally saving you from writing your own XML vocabulary, the chances are that the people who developed it have already spent a lot of effort on working out what information needs to be passed between parties. You can either consider adopting that industry standard directly, or base your own upon it. If you are only *basing* your vocabulary upon an existing standard, it is worth considering whether to replicate its functionality or whether you should actually use part of that standard incorporating *its* namespace with one of your own (we looked at this concept in Chapter 7 on Namespaces and Schemas).

Before we start using these schemas, remember the common misconception we met earlier:

> *If a community creates a standard definition that allows us all to read off the same page, then surely our systems will be interoperable.*

As we said, EDI has proved that this is not the case. EDI standards are just defined transaction structures, which industries have come together to agree on – common views of a business document. The standards have the loosest constraint in describing the exchange – they are just a superset of all the messages devised by the organizations involved in developing the standards. To trade based on these standards, supplemental agreements are developed to further define the specifics of the exchange based on the trading partner relationship, defining a subset and detailed use of the elements.

Registries and Repositories

There are several registries and repositories that hold industry specific information for users to share, and they vary in the amount and breadth of information they cover. Registries just contain DTDs and other schemas, while repositories contain further information, such as database schemas, software code or routines, and other objects needed to conduct business – a repository indexes business objects as well as transactions, registeries only store at items required at the transactional level. Both registries and repositories give organizations, particular smaller companies, information that helps them develop systems or expand their ability to conduct exchanges based on prior submissions more quickly by sharing the experience and code ofothers in their industry. Two of the main registries at the time of writing are:

- **BizTalk.org** – is an industry initiative started by Microsoft and supported by community of XML standards users. We'll be discussing BizTalk in more detail throughout this chapter (http://www.biztalk.org).
- **OASIS** – the Organization for the Advancement of Structured Information Standards, is a nonprofit, international consortium steered by XML.org (a vendor neutral consortium) dedicated to accelerating the adoption of product-independent formats (XML) based on public standards (http://www.oasis-open.org/cover and http://www.oasis-open.org/html/rrpublic.htm).

Because organizations rarely do business in a single industry, many will make use of the different sets of information in the repositories. For example, a company making automotive parts may choose to access BizTalk.org which contains information on AIAG, which is used to do business with auto manufacturers, VICS for selling to auto parts stores, and the Defense Logistics Agency for bidding on procurements from the Department of Defense.

The natural migration for registeries is to allow for the referencing of not only DTDs and Schema but also logic business fragments that are dynamically referenced at the resolution of a busienss unit. See *Repositories* under *Looking at the Future.*

Internationalization

Very few messaging protocols are global today. For global eBusiness, systems must be designed to be flexible enough to account for differences between various regions. Businesses must understand regulatory, legal, revenue, privacy, and tax guidelines faced by companies conducting exchanges with vendors and customers in each country.

That wraps up our brief overview of how EDI can be implemented using XML; so let's now look at some of the perceptions surrounding XML's use in eBusiness, we will start with some misconceptions, before looking at why it really is so important, and what kind of difference it makes.

Common Misconceptions

There are a lot of misconceptions surrounding XML's role in eBusiness, for example many people suggest that:

> *"Quite simply, with XML, we can create languages that are much easier to read, can be displayed in a browser with a simple style sheet, that can be exchanged across the Internet, and that use comparatively cheap interoperable software. And that's the simple answer to why XML is so important to e-commerce"*

However, they forget that we have this now with HTML and the Web, which has already changed e-commerce. Sure, XML may help the web developers implement back-ends that work with the Internet e-commerce sites, but the front end of most is still, and will remain for a while HTML (until there is widespread use of browsers that support XML). Others suggest that:

> *"It doesn't matter what information you are trying to exchange, as long as your partner understands the markup you are using, you will be able to exchange the data simply and easily"*

These people need to ask themselves what the difference is between their comment and EDI standards today. The answer as to why you should use XML in e-commerce doesn't lie in these two statements.

Let's look at some more concepts that are being taught to hundreds at conferences, in books and in other educational material today. They are all incorrect assumptions about XML's use with trading partner communication.

If We Agree on a DTD/Schema Then We Can All Exchange Documents

There is a misconception among many XML developers that if we agree on a DTD/Schema then documents can be exchanged. This is a nice digestible concept for everyone to grasp, the community creates a standard definition that allows us all to read off the same page, and then surely our systems will be interoperable. Unfortunately, EDI has proved that this is not the case. EDI standards already provide defined transaction sets which industries have come together to agree on – common views of a business document. In the real world, however, even with these standards, supplemental agreements are developed to further define the specifics of the exchange based on the trading partner relationship, extending the standards in a way that no longer fits the standard.

There is a real business reason why "standards" need to be extensible. In order to give themselves a leading edge over competitors, solution providers will continue to seek out differentiators that make their products or services stand out from their competitors. Because of this, our messages need to be able to handle new packages, or alternate non-standard methods will be developed to do so.

But how does one extend a DTD today? There are several options discussed below:

1. Copy and modify for the standard for each trading partner. (poor choice as we would end up with too many DTDs)

2. Use of a recursive tree. For instance, the recursive elements shown below in an `ice-item-group`, `ice-item`, and `ice-item-ref` allow ICE to be extended and carry packages to be defined later between trading partners. To extend the package a unique reference `id` qualifies the item, and with the ability for the tree to call itself, complete branches can be added at select points in the closed model of a DTD and validated if required. Thus trading partners would exchange codes to extend the message.

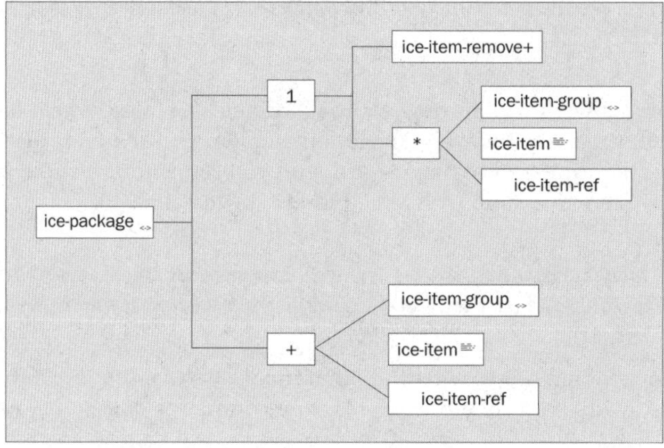

More information on the ICE initiative can be found at: http://www.gca.org/ice/default.htm

3. Use of a DTD stubbing mechanism. The standard DTD includes a call out, using parameter entities, to a DTD fragment either local to the receiving partner's server or a repository common to both trading partners. If the standard is all that is required, then the stub includes a null DTD. If extensions to the standard are required for any reason, elements are included in the stub DTD where allowed in the defined locations.

The community is looking to the W3C for XML Schemas (which we met in Chapter 7) that promise to allow for defining an open model for such additions to a 'standard' schema.

Note that in the case of vendor implementations, broken messages and mechanisms have always been an area to exploit. If a company has a fix to a problem, this gives the product an edge in serving the customer base, and in some cases can eliminate competition. This gives standard participating companies an edge; so smart vendors can skew the standards process to their advantage. Cases where the standard was designed to work with a particular vendors product, rather than for the overall good of the industry do occur. This jockeying on the issues, or intentional slow down of the process must be watched and monitored. However, the benefits of vendor participation outweigh this issue, in that vendors bring knowledge, investment, and marketing components to the groups.

We Can Build Processes Based on the DOM

Most XML developers learn about the DOM early on when starting to program with XML, and see it as an easy and ideal way to work with XML documents in eBusiness solutions. However, eBusiness messages can be many megabytes in length and it is not uncommon for an organization to have to deal with over 50 Gigabytes of information per month. While the DOM is fine for small messages, there can be problems when dealing with larger documents.

Because the DOM takes an "in memory" approach to dealing with XML documents, it will take up too many system resources when being used with larger files, and will only be able to handle smaller messages. Of course the actual amount of memory used by the DOM depends on the parser, but in many cases a 100Kb document will occupy at least 1Mb of memory.

A better approach for receiving larger documents is to use event driven process of SAX, the Simple API for XML which we met in Chapter 6, as it tends not cause applications to have memory management problems. Many EDI applications had "in memory" problems and forced companies to rewrite their engines. This isn't to say avoid the DOM, just beware of your situation.

Note that if your SAX application builds its own in-memory representation of the document, it is likely to take up just as much space as if you allowed the parser to build it.

EDI is a Format that isn't Particularly Human Readable; Unlike XML, Which Will Therefore be Easier to Use

eBusiness systems today, and for the most part in the future will not display the raw tags to the users, and only need to be understood by the system developers. Overly verbose tagging mechanisms slow down the automated production process. In fact, much of the information is passed as keys for the system to access local data. As we have already mentioned, the strength in applying XML is that it allows for additional information to be used by the system in addition to the data itself, and that the tags provide the hooks that can be attached to processes that enforce business rules.

Our Prime Objective is to Remove Process From Content

When using XML we are often encouraged to only include content in the XML file, for example style rules for displaying XML are kept in a separate style sheet. While this is a noble objective and applies generically, the truth is that messages in transactional eBusiness have to include the original directives, such as add, change, delete, etc. as well as the content. For processing reasons it is easier for these to appear as markup using `<noun.verb>` tagging. Only by understanding both the subject and the action to be invoked can the application instantiate the correct process.

We Can Validate Our Documents Using A Validating Parser

One thing that is absolutely vital to ensure system integrity is that the message arriving in the application can be processed successfully; any message entering a system from a trading partner must be checked fully before entering an enterprise's business critical system. This is the issue of **validation**. This is a three-step issue:

- The information must be marked-up in compliance with the proper DTD or schema
- Values of elements and character data may need to be checked for validity and/or compliance with business rules pertaining to the content (more about this in a moment). This is tied in with a company's business rules (such as not taking orders under $1000 or over $10,000 from ACME Corporation).
- There may be an additional process that converts the XML/EDI to an older EDI format (or some other internal message format), and this process may need to apply more validity checking.

XML document validation is vital to ensure that incoming data meets application requirements. Validation of the document against a DTD or schema can be used to ensure that the vocabulary and grammar is correct, and that it contains required elements. However, in EDI it has been common for validation to occur at the application level.

> **An important distinction must be made between syntax/structure validation and application validation. Application validation enforces business rules and must be done at the application level, for it is at this level that we have full understanding of the business objectives.**

Application validation allows system designers to enforce business rules and deal with different trading partner agreements. All messages entering any eBusiness system must be very carefully checked as any value that the system cannot process could cause the system to break down.

Because of this stringent requirement, full validations for eBusiness cannot take place at a standard parser. Even with the promise of XML schemas, that allow us to handle constraints, companies will tend to add rule processing and security mechanisms into specialized parsers to handle this requirement. As an alternative to burdening the application with the task of validation, you could have a separate "listener/dispatcher" application whose role would be to watch for and validate inbound messages, and pass them on to the application if they are valid.

Some of these misconceptions may sound familiar to you, as each has been suggested on many occasions. Having dispelled some of these misconceptions, let's turn our attention to what the real advantages of using XML are.

Perceptions Surrounding the Use of XML in eBusiness

As we are adding our page to the history books by applying XML to eBusiness, many are concerned that the page will be too much of a repeat of pages of the past. The quote *"Those who forget history are doomed to repeat it"* is applicable today as we converge the two worlds of XML and EDI. By now, you should have started to get the picture that XML's role in eBusiness is very similar to that of EDI, although we have already identified two of the key advantages in that:

- XML syntax offers greater control over our applications
- XML vocabularies can save us from using a different format for our exchanges compared with our internal representations of data

So what else is going to make the world of eBusiness that uses XML so different? To help us answer this question we should look at why EDI was not adopted by more organizations. Here is a list of the top 5 perceived barriers to entry into EDI:

- System cost
- Lack of standards
- Lack of training
- Company attitude
- Security

Let's look at each of these in turn.

System Cost

We have said that EDI is expensive to implement, but the process that involves the largest cost is a similar process to one involved in the XML world. Much of the expense in deploying an EDI system occurs because the problem domain is a hard nut to crack; defining the standards for the messages in the first place takes a lot of time and investment. In addition, it is necessary to create maps between internal data and messages with each trading partner. In fact, the labor cost for training and the development tools add up to a fraction of the total cost when integrating an EDI system within an organization. But it is important to note that simply changing the syntax of our messages into XML isn't necessarily going to make the development of schemas cheaper – and traditional EDI standards can be extended to include all the mechanisms of XML. So where are the cost savings with XML/EDI? The answer is often by leveraging the concept of:

> *"If we are selling at a loss, lets make it up in volume."*

XML/EDI is opening the niche market to the enterprise, allowing return on investment (ROI) from development costs in almost every aspect of the infrastructure of an organization. Because of this, the major software corporations who thought the EDI market too small and too labor intensive now see real growth in integration of sales and service on a large scale. The incorporation of XML in products is a key reason for the power of XML in eBusiness.

Coming from this software tool point of view and looking at the situation another way, the genie is out of the bottle, gone are the days of selling backend systems, databases, messaging, etc. that don't have a component that addresses interoperability.

> **Users/customers have grown to expect interoperability. XML provides interoperability, and vendors understand that by leveraging XML they gain a competitive advantage over their counterparts.**

Lack Of Standards

While it will take time for industries to create DTDs and other schemas for their XML exchanges, because of the increasing drive to interoperable systems, and the increasing use of XML within businesses applications, more companies are creating schemas that will be able to be used for exchanges. In addition there are a number of industry initiatives to create repositories for schemas, which we shall meet shortly. Indeed Microsoft's BizTalk strategy involves helping companies define schemas for their XML interchanges.

Lack of Training

With widespread adoption of XML in both the organizations and by product vendors, our labor talent can be used in flexible ways, training investment on the language and tools can be recouped. Before long, we may even see high schools teaching XML along with HTML. These factors reduce the risk for companies and protect their investment, no wonder then why company attitude is changing with XML/EDI.

Company Attitude

While EDI only gained a foothold in large corporations and government institutions, smaller businesses are becoming more aware of the power of the Web, and the availability of the Internet. There is increasing pressure for companies to have a presence on the Web, and the snowball effect that we can see starting will gain momentum, encouraging more and more businesses to harness the extra potential sales.

Security

With the increasing support for XML being built into software, there is reduced need to implement custom security mechanisms. Furthermore, there are a number of specifications in development for ensuring integrity, message authentication, and/or signer authentication services, such as the joint venture on XML Signatures being carried out by the W3C and IETF (for more information on XML Signatures, see http://www.w3.org/Signature).

As we have seen, EDI already offered the required functionality for electronic transactions, and this is a point that is often lost in the hype surrounding XML. The speed of XML's proliferation into all manner of business sectors has been astounding. Its rapid acceptance has led to a pervasiveness never achieved by EDI. We are already seeing XML being used to represent data in a huge variety of fields, from DNA sequences to astronomical data. This adds real value to the XML/EDI effort, with possibilities for broad adoption of XML in many business domains, we are rapidly heading towards common knowledge bases, and a bodies of tools that can be used across business systems. So, in summary, some of the key reasons as to why XML is making such an impact on eBusiness are that:

- XML syntax offers greater control over our applications
- XML vocabularies can save us from using a different format for our exchanges compared with our internal representations of data
- Support for XML is being built into software applications with a drive towards interoperability between products
- The use of XML internally within organizations is increasing
- There is no longer the need to translate between internal representations of data and interchange standards
- There are increasing numbers of programmers displaying skills in using XML
- There is increasing interest and understanding of the advantages eBusiness can bring – the hype surrounding XML and eBusiness

While these are undoubtedly some of the main reasons why XML is being adopted in eBusiness, there are more advantages that XML will bring in the future, we should be clear that the fusion of XML and EDI is more than a sum of its parts. It is this future that we shall look at next, because the fusion opens up new paradigms for eBusiness, not just warmed over 1970s concepts with XML.

Having said this, there are a lot of lessons we can learn from the EDI effort. It would be foolish not to take advantage of their experience. The lessons learnt from implementing EDI offer us a rich business language, business practices, trading partner management, logging, acknowledgements, and transaction expertise, which we can make use of when thinking about using XML in eBusiness solutions.

Looking to the Future

We have seen some of the key foundations of using XML and EDI, so let's take a look at some of the strategies in development that will help enhance e-commerce by making for the user and developer simpler and more flexible mechanisms. We will look at:

- Simple Markup Language
- Discovery & Mediation
- Repositories
- Bizcodes
- Agents
- Templates

Simple Markup Language

Much of the success of HTML has come from its broad accessibility and ease of use, but the gaining popularity of XML is partly due to the limitations of HTML's syntax. So, while there are temptations to add features to XML and surrounding standards to increase its flexibility, we should be careful not to make them too complicated. The reason behind this is simple: complexity raises the bar for vendor entry into the eBusiness world, and implementations are important for gaining acceptance and popularity. It is also important that general users get results as easily and consistently with XML as they do with HTML.

On this note, some companies investing in electronic commerce today have started to lobby the various policy and standards bodies to assure XML family of standards remain as simple and compact as possible, not overburdened with feature-creep. One such eBusiness vendor did so at the November 1999 W3C meeting of the XML Schemas Working Group; in an eloquent plea for keeping the specification simple, they offered the rule of thumb, 'If in doubt leave it out', which is echoed by many having to build products to support the recommendations. The vendors know that success tends to happen when the approach is smaller, lighter, faster, cheaper, easier and more accessible, and wants to protect their investment made in XML technology.

Why the feature-creep? The XML related-bodies are currently defining the needs for (1) in-house systems; such as document publishing, CD distribution, and information management and (2) external systems for electronic commerce, and the requirements of the two camps are often at odds. Broadly speaking, in-house systems developers want more flexibility and extra features in the standards, while those who are concerned with interoperability of systems want to keep the standards simpler. This has resulted in a new push for an even simpler standard; a stripped-down variant of XML called **Simple Markup Language** (**SML**).

Because there exists a strong inverse correlation between complexity and global acceptance, it is not out of the question that we will be living in a world of XML and SML. For every feature added to a XML family of recommendations, there is an increased strain on application's processing and footprint sizes. So, SML can be defined as an extracted, simpler, unambiguous subset of the broader scoped XML recommendations, although it may possibly be coupled with supplemental transaction mechanisms. Many see this as an unfortunate turn of events, but it might be the only direction offered to developers who are focused on determining XML syntax for machine-to-machine exchanges.

Discovery & Mediation

Typically, the exchange mechanisms used in today's eBusiness solutions have prior knowledge of the process, and have access to common information such as code lists, standards, constraints, etc. There are a number of situations, however, where end users or programs will need to discover the sort of resources available from a site and the vocabularies that a trading partner uses for themselves. This will allow a wide range of new features, from automatically being able to trade with new companies, to creating comparison shopping applications that will find prices of like products or services automatically for us.

In addition to defining "industry specific" messages, we need to define standard methods of exchanging this infrastructure-type of information as well. We need to be able to discover information about the languages used and products/services available from a trading partner, and this is where discovery and mediation are important. The work in these areas is still young, and there are several directions in which it could go.

It doesn't take much of a stretch of imagination to believe that we should/can have a business messaging infrastructure to simply ask "do you want your usual?" in a few parameters. Or indeed we should be able to put out a tender for goods and services and automatically get quotations returned without the need for human intervention. So, we need a way of "brokering" logical business units. As we will see, this work leads onto efforts such as agents acting on our behalf, which we meet shortly.

Applicability to Finding Resource Instances

With discovery mechanisms, a process (application, trading partner, etc.) can find out – from a trading partner – the format and version of vocabulary that the trading partner supports. Indeed, as part of the discovery process, when a customer asks for information about the language a trading partner speaks, the trading partner could offer a template – written in their chosen vocabulary – so that the customer only need fill in the details of what they are looking for.

For example, if you wanted to find out the details of a contact from a trading partner, the trading partner could send you the following template, which holds the information they need to run a query and return the information to you:

```
WHERE
      <CustProfile>
          <GivenName>$a</GivenName>
          <Contact><Phone>$b</Phone></Contact>
        </CustProfile>
      IN "www.orgname.com/custprofile.xml",
      $y >
```

Here, the trading partner only has to let the customer know what the parameters `$a` and `$b` represent, and the customer can fill in the details that will execute the query and return a result.

Having seen how things are supposed to happen in an eBusiness scenario, what do we do if something goes wrong? Discovery should also dictate to the trading partners possible contingency strategies and resources as well, depending on the environment and conditions at the time. One early move into this area has been the eCo Framework from CommerceNet.

eCo Framework

The eCo Framework is a recommended blueprint addressing discovery processes, published by the CommerceNet consortium. In a white paper they state:

> *"The eCo working group has determined that in order to promote business-to-business (B2B) interoperation between heterogeneous e-commerce systems on the Internet, there is a basic requirement that trading partners be able to:*

- Discover other businesses on the Internet
- Determine whether they want to do business and how they can participate within a market
- Determine what services are provided and consumed by other businesses
- Determine the underlying interactions and the documents and data used by interactions
- Determine if and how their e-commerce systems can communicate
- If necessary, determine what modifications need to be implemented to ensure interoperability between their systems
- If desired, establish communications through channels other than the Internet."

This insight and effort of refining the discovery processes is a step forward and provides an excellent framework on which to build. In order to allow a trading partner, web user, or searchbot to determine what can be harvested from a site, a method of **bootstrapping** the discovery of eCo Interfaces has been defined. The term bootstrapping refers to only assuming mimimum system requirements while learning more complex mechanisms. The eCo framework calls out an `eco.xml` document which is used to interrogate and discover the supported interfaces and properties at the site. The architecture also provides mechanisms for exposing existing e-commerce systems in eCo compliant terms. In order to support existing e-commerce systems that were not designed with the eCo specification in mind, there exists a mechanism for describing and providing information on interfacing with those systems.

Refer to the eCo Specification at http://eco.commerce.net/specs/index.cfm

eCo Framework Example

If a business that implemented the eCo Business Environment wanted to allow itself to be indexed as an eCo compliant business, it could place the following XML file at the root of its Web site. This example is for a company who offer catalog services:

```
<?xml version="1.0"?>
<EcoInterfaces xmlns = 'http://www.commerce.net/eco'>

   <Head>
      <Identifier>http://www.my_company.com/...</Identifier>
      <Creator>http://www.my_company.com/~BillSmith</Creator>
      <Date>19991118</Date>
      <Version>1.0</Version>
      <TimeToLive>86000</TimeToLive>
      <Description>...</Description>
      <Label>...</Label>
   </Head>

   <Interface type="Business">
      <Identifier>http://www.my_company.com.com/business</Identifier>
      <Creator>http://www.my_company.com.com/~WillSmith </Creator>
      <Version>1.0</Version>
      <Date>19991118</Date>
      <TimeToLive>86000</TimeToLive>
      <Description>Catalog Business</Description>
      <Label>My Company</Label>
   </Interface>

   <Interface type="Service">
      <Identifier>http://www.my_company.com.com/eco/OrderService</Identifier>
      <Creator>http://www.my_company.com.com /~JillSmith</Creator>
      <Version>1.0</Version>
      <Date>19991118</Date>
      <TimeToLive>86000</TimeToLive>
      <Description>My order service interface description.</Description>
      <Label>My Company Order Service</Label>
   </Interface>

   <Interface type="Service">
      <Identifier>
         http://www.my_company.com.com/eco/CatalogService
      </Identifier>
      <Creator>http://www.my_company.com.com/~GillSmith</Creator>
      ...

   </Interface>

</EcoInterfaces>
```

Comparison Shopping

Another area where discovery will be important is in the area of comparison shopping. If we have marked up our products and services in XML, it will be possible to create search engines that will compare prices of these products and services and show end users a number of alternatives of where to purchase their products from. While it is likely that these sites would start by just comparing prices and allowing you to select a location from where you purchase the product/service, it is expected that you would later be able to stipulate further choices about warranty, time of delivery etc. However, the concepts eliminate the need to manually trawl shops and e-commerce sites manually to find several resources from which to buy.

Repositories

There is a growing need for compatible processes and vocabularies to reduce **stovepipe** and redundant tasks. Stovepipe is a term for applications that are built solely for internal purposes to solve a specific problem and are therefore inflexible. In order for industries, associations, and individual enterprises to make XML work for their information exchange requirements, they need to establish standard mechanisms by which they can share their vocabularies.

Repositories may be as simple as a place where different DTDs and schemas are stored, to more complex scenarios where more information is made available. This information may include XML-based directory mechanisms, configuration management, topic maps, database structures, UML modeling tools, and more. They may also contain glossaries that explain generic-specific relationships, synonyms, and multiple senses of terms depending on context. It is even possible that they will contain software that can be used by parties using the vocabulary in question. As repositories develop, it is likely that there will be increasing amounts of information made available, both as the repositories try to make themselves an important player, and as competing standards vie for adoption as the de facto standard in that area.

It is worth noting here that enterprises have (1) internal concepts, (2) concepts they share with others in their industry, and (3) concepts which are common to their resident country or countries and (4) concepts which are global. By definition the domains of type 1, 2 and 3 are conceptualized in a different manner for each enterprise, perhaps by resolution of business needs or emphasis of concepts, and so our XML eBusiness systems must accommodate these differences. Our eBusiness systems must deal with these language differences in a standard manner; through negotiation, shared cross-references, and through mechanisms to repackage messages in a different vocabulary appropriate to the domain, etc.

Another issue has to do with the optimal version resolution of our business language. So, at what level does it make the most sense to share? Is it at the Schema or DTD level? If so, do we all share one purchase order, making it a generic "kitchen sink" of elements from which a layering of implementation conventions (ICs) can be drawn to describe an industry? Or perhaps a repository for the countless number of defined purchase orders, one for selling airplanes and one for selling pencils? How many would there be? Thousands, and then still all situations wouldn't be covered. Neither of these scenarios are ideal. So what is the answer? Historically, rolling the entire standard is costly, requires synchronization delays with proposed updates, and needs programmers to address the complete new version of the standard. These maintenance problems can be reduced substantially if we build proper configuration management into our processes – preferably at the logical unit level.

XML repositories are therefore likely to provide the means to:

- Access industry components and nomenclature as a guide when modeling (using UML), developing and testing systems through the life cycle.
- Extending the reach of electronic to include the mapping and processing of data directly into the organizations' business systems
- Covering a wider range of interactions among trading partners, such as real-time exchanges.
- Taking advantage of the next generation applications software that can interact directly with the transmitted data from trading partners

So repositories may eventually contain collections of standardized tags, business components (program code – both source and complied), objects, style sheets, and industry terms and codes.

To navigate the repositories, and find the appropriate information for the industry you are working in, there is a need for key new functionality using **glossaries** (information trees) that can be navigated based on **topics** (business domains) and required business functions. Glossaries are functionally directed; therefore an end-user would expect to navigate a glossary, in a directed domain path search, to locate the particular business action. This domain-based decision trees within topics on top of a semantic net provides an adjunct interface to the traditional keyword or dictionary style searches.

Put succinctly the concept is "select what you want to do from this list provided for your area of business, and the relevant logical business units will be displayed along with prompts for more information to help you further." For instance, a user may navigate one of the tree hierarchies to locate within a financial investment repository, the commodities section, and a BUY action, then find the items required to perform that task, and the standard transactions, times and schedules, special conditions (such as, limits and edge requirements) and events provided for it. Glossaries also then identify the individual data elements and detail their relationship with other elements both inside and outside their industries.

There are also a number of other initiatives that are helping in the development of repositories:

- **Directory Services Markup Language (DSML)** – for managing data about people, resources and processes which is very synergistic with LDAP. http://www.dsml.org
- **UDEF**, the Universal Data Element Framework, is an attempt to map various data standards (CALS, STEP, X12 EDI, etc.) into a single framework using sets of object classes and properties to define data elements. http://www.udef.com
- **BSR** (Basic Semantic Register) is an International Standards Organization (ISO) effort; with roots to the BSI/Beacon project. http://www.iso.ch/BSR
- **ISO/IEC 11179-1**, International Standards Organization's (ISO) / Framework for the Specification and Standardization of Data Elements composition, including metadata. http://www.sdct.itl.nist.gov/~ftp/l8/other/coalition/Ovr11179.html
- **UREP** – The Universal Repository from UNISYS is an XML-based extensible information system that defines, integrates and manages metadata and business data. http://www.unisys.com/marketplace/urep
- **XML Metadata Interchange Format** (XMI) "specifies an open information interchange model that is intended to give developers working with object technology the ability to exchange programming data over the Internet in a standardized way." http://www.omg.org
- **DII COE XML Registry** – To improve data interoperability within DOD communities; items to browse and use satisfy DOD system or database requirements. http://diides.ncr.disa.mil/xmlreg/index.cfm

Bizcodes

We are all familiar with barcodes, they contain reference identifiers to various items and products and provide input to collection devices that link the scanned item's identifier to an item in a backend database. Applications that use barcodes include inventory counting, asset/package tracking, log identification, sales order entry, meter reading, and parking tickets to name just a few. Barcodes are used both in the collection of data, and for querying systems for price checks and other standard business operations. Barcodes have always been a sister technology to EDI for collected information, and for the sharing of metadata.

Bizcodes extend barcodes, building on their success, adoption, and on the know-how already in place. They widen the scope to include all metadata references in the eBusiness community, and were proposed by the XML/EDI group (http://www.xmledi.com/). Bizcodes could become the key to the XML repositories, allowing for interrogation of information concerning items, picturemasks, appropriate values, default values, help, definitions, links to validation classes, and constraints. Bizcodes are also a simple mechanism that provide for automated mapping between XML vocabularies, dialects, schemas, and various standards for reuse.

For more information on bizcodes and repository linking using a reduced XLink and XPointer recommendation, see the XML/EDI Group's white paper at http://www.xmledi.com/repository/.

Just like the familiar UPC/EAN barcodes for products and items, that provide simple, semantically neutral numbers for manufacturers, distributors, and retailers to use for inventory control, bizcodes provide neutral identifiers for relating data elements among eBusiness metadata and the processes associated with elements.

The prime advantages of using bizcodes are:

- Cross-reference information is housed in the XML/EDI repositories
- Transformations are simplified through a linking process
- Allows for effective reuse of logical units
- Provides international language transformation for global eBusiness
- Simple one link linking mechanism in the DTD or in XML Schema archetypes
- The information "attached" is managed and extensible allowing for knowledge additions
- Attributes and relationships can be interrogated further
- Same mechanism for industry, international standards as well as for enterprise vocabulary; converting 'price' in German, Japanese, and Indian, a very much needed attribute for global eBusiness.
- Allows for transient definitions with lifetimes for transactions
- Allows for the collection of metrics on business language
- Allows the repository to learn business languages quickly, and subscribe to standards

Agents

Agent technologies, programs that act independently in attempt to accomplish a goal for a user or for another program, are already here today. They provide possibilities for more scalable and maintainable data exchanges. Agents will allow our XML/EDI systems to be self-adaptive and able to handle a large expansion of exchanges without excessive human interaction.

So, we need to understand how we integrate software agent technologies into XML systems. We are not talking about "Star Wars" style capabilities here, but simple functions like interfacing to legacy information systems that will only handle 2 address lines in an address, or no more than a fixed number of items per order.

This is so that when an order containing more items than accounted for, or 3 address lines come in to the system, the agent can handle the document. They can be used as a way of enforcing business logic, and handling situations where business logic is not met. To do this metadata rules are used, expressed as in XML (we will see more about an implementation of this shortly).

This use of agents removes the need for specifying hard-coded constraints – making it much easier to adapt the business logic. This means that developers building new XML implementations should avoid hard-coded constraints in the XML content to prevent such problems in process models, and begin to use adaptable metadata-driven state machines.

The metadata can be used in any number of situations from Rule Based Development Environments (RBDE) to comparison discovery mechanisms. For example, as illustrated in the following diagram, we could use agents to go out and compare details about a product we want to buy. In this example we are looking for travel goods. The agent is sent out to request details about the travel goods we require; it advertises what it is looking for; and comes back with exact matches from anyone who provides their details in a suitably marked up format. The agent may then go on to recommend a product based on parameters you have provided, such as price, time to deliver, warranty period, etc.

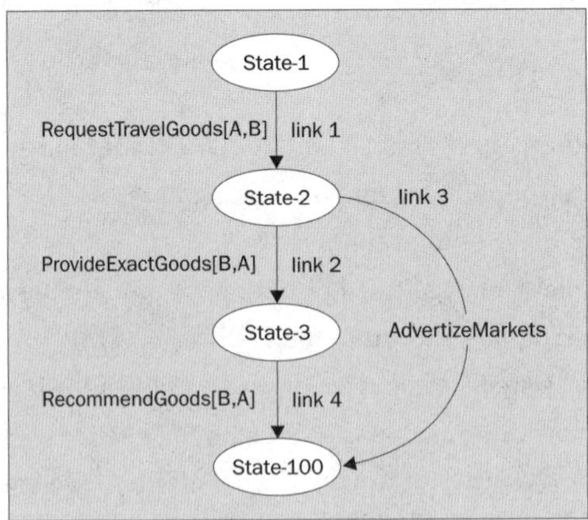

Perhaps the most immediate use for agent tools is in tracking XML transaction content to alert support staff to potential failure conditions in the information, particularly relating to versioning. Traditional EDI implementers have long understood the need to manage versioning between trading partners. In an XML-driven world, versioning must be at the concept level to allow for language updates, and our agent technology will provide the mechanism to handle updates to this level of resolution in the transaction content and structures.

Business Rules Markup Language (BRML)

Increasingly object-oriented developers are separating business logic from data access and application logic. This enables the same business logic to be used in different applications, and allows the business logic to be updated easily on its own (separate from the rest of the application code). IBM's **CommonRules** 1.0 release includes API's for developers to enhance Java or non-Java applications, allowing them to create executable business rules that can be exchanged between enterprises using heterogeneous rule systems across the Web, enhancing interoperability and conflict handling. CommonRules provides a common **interlingua** (international language for communication) to represent these rules for exchange, using an XML application called **Business Rules Markup Language (BRML)** to represent the interlingua. These rules may then be exchanged as XML, directly as Java objects, or in other string formats.

Using CommonRules, a seller website/application can communicate its business rules regarding pricing, promotions, refunds and cancellation policies, ordering lead time, and other contractual terms & conditions, to a customer application/agent, even when the vendor's rules are implemented using a different rule system, as it is designed to enhance the functionality of existing rule-based systems. Then when a conflict in rules is found an alarm can be raised.

Rules are a powerful way of specifying business logic, as they combine automatic executability with a relatively easy syntax, as they use "declarative" (rather than only procedural) semantics. It even allows non-programmers to modify the business rules at run-time.

> *For more information visit http://www.research.ibm.com/rules/home.html*

Templates

When we are exchanging data in business applications using new vocabularies, we must consider who is going to do the job of translating the message. Most developers agree that it is easier for a customer to format the message in the vocabulary that the receiver requires, rather than the receiving application having to work out what the request is for, and then translating it into their vocabulary. If you remember back to the example of a template in the Discovery and Mediation, you can get a good idea of the power of templates. If the receivers tell the sender where and how the information should be sent the task is much easier.

> *Offering details about the language in which you handle transactions is a good way of dealing with transactions; although some larger businesses that can better afford to implement systems will understand multiple vocabularies might choose to do so.*

The ideas behind templates build on repositories, discovery and mediation techniques, bizcodes, and agents. The concept being that it will be possible for to establish a common negotiation protocol at the business layer. The idea of templates extends upon the example we have already seen; they should be able to be dynamically created by agents. Because business interactions can be complex, and potentially require specialized knowledge, so XML/EDI data manipulation agents can ensure that users can express their requirements in high-level, natural language supplementing templates, possibly using an interlingua similar to that used by IBM's CommonRules. When an application makes a call to start a transaction, then eBusiness infrastructure components will automatically create the appropriate rule templates and XML syntax to match user requirements, for the requestor to fill in, and return to the supplier. These same agents would broker the entire interchange.

Wrapping Up The Theory

That look at the future brings us to the end of the first part of the chapter. So far we have seen that the Internet has changed the way in which we are able to exchange data electronically, no longer relying on expensive VANs, although the current uses of XML in eBusiness are not quite as radically different from existing EDI applications as some people might think. We have dispelled some of the common myths surrounding the use of XML in e-commerce and seen how the integration of XML into vendors products and existing skills in the area have really been at the root of XMLs success as a popular language for eBusiness transactions. We even met some of the issues in implementing an XML-based e-commerce application, although the subject is too large to go into in detail, it should have shown you where some of the key benefits lie.

One last thing to remember is that, big businesses who have spent large amounts of money investing in EDI applications are not likely to throw them out overnight. For many, traditional EDI has worked fine for several years and will continue to do so. However, it is the rising interest in interoperability that will eventually creep into their systems as they are updated, or the promise of added benefits that are to come in the future.

Some of the things we saw in the final section, such as metadata discovery and repositories are with us today, although they will no doubt move on from their current incarnations. Whereas work on agent technologies and templates is still in the early stages. However, the use of XML is spreading eBusiness in new directions, and the ability for a program to go out on the web, find a product you want, discover the language the supplier speaks, and get an order form directly from them might not be that far away...

eBusiness Solutions

Having looked at the theory of using XML in eBusiness, we will now take a look at some industry efforts that actually implement solutions that use XML. We will take a look at some of the many industry DTDs that have started to emerge, which we can learn a lot from. Obviously, we cannot attempt to cover every industry's efforts to implement schemas, however, we will look at some key examples, which will help us see some important features that other industries have decided to model. In particular we will look at some financial, healthcare, and travel industry initiatives.

In addition, we will be looking at ways of implementing some of the concepts that we have seen developed up to this point in the chapter. One particular solution we will look at is BizTalk. We will talk about the http://www.BizTalk.org web site, which is a schema repository, as well as their initiatives for creating XML schemas. However, the schema repository is only one part of the larger BizTalk framework, which also talks about products and services. Unfortunately, the explanation of the larger scheme of the BizTalk framework in the early stages was not clear, so we hope to explain how the parts fit together.

Overall we will look at:

- Some markup initiatives for vertical industry
- Dealing with horizontal industries
- The BizTalk framework

Industry Solutions

Most of the eBusiness solutions that have been developed already are in the area of business-to-business transactions. We can divide business-to-business transactions into two key areas:

- **Vertical Markets** – companies as part of the same process, someone who needs to supply a product or service to another company so that they can fulfill their task. For example, a car manufacturer and a tire manufacturer, or an airline and a package tour operator or travel agent.
- **Horizontal Markets** – complimentary products and services that are not required for the same product, for example a drug manufacturer and doctors who prescribe drugs

So, let's move on and look at some of these verticals.

Key Vertical Industry Solutions

Currently, suppliers, intermediaries, and customers find it difficult to share and exchange information. This difficulty has limited the variety of distribution channels available to suppliers. As many sales and marketing professionals are aware, current distribution channels make it very difficult for suppliers to differentiate their services, reach new categories of consumers, and create innovative offers. And it is the channels themselves that define the relationships between suppliers and customers.

Meanwhile, customers are limited in their ability to combine the services of suppliers, to select services that best match their needs, and to compare services from different sources. To either plan or arrange the services they want, customers must navigate a complex web of interrelationships, which in most cases they elect not to do.

Many experts consider the Internet and XML a way to overcome the limitations of traditional distribution channels. Several industries that have embraced this technology, taking their first steps into XML-based solutions, are becoming some of the largest participants in electronic commerce. Unfortunately, they are still wed to the older method of fixed transaction sets, setting down reworked ideas into XML syntax rather than expanding them to make full use of the potential new technologies; but once they have made the move to XML, there is an increased chance that they will start to exploit some of the possibilities that we laid out at the end of the last section.

The initiatives underway each address various aspects of eBusiness using XML in their own way, but there are so many XML and eBusiness standardization initiatives that we need to ask "Which horse should we hitch our wagon to?" Many businesses are currently asking themselves the following questions:

- Which effort(s) do I support?
- Which effort(s) do I monitor?
- What are the ramifications if I support the wrong effort?
- What are the ramifications if I wait until the hoopla dies down?
- Which direction is my industry heading in?
- Which direction are my business partners (and competitors) going in?

One of the benefits of XML is that it allows information to be transformed. If companies take the 'high road' and model their data robustly enough to support their own internal and external processes, they shouldn't have any problem 'playing' with any of the eventual lead initiatives; it will be possible to map their own internal structures onto the industry initiatives – transforming them into a format they can share with others. We looked at XSLT in Chapter 9 (although XSLT is not always the best solution in business situations – something we examine in Case Study 3). However, the current danger is for organizations to adopt a specific architecture that doesn't support their internal needs in order to work with an external entity.

Over the past 12 to 18 months there have been a number of businesses in the same industry who have got together to define the scenarios, messages, content models, and data elements needed for doing business electronically. These groups can represent the companies in their own industries, as well as those across complimentary industries and boundaries. But, if you look at the participants in the main efforts (RosettaNet, BizTalk, ebXML etc.), the same large players are involved. Small and medium enterprises (SMEs) can't afford this type of participation and/or effort, and are at somewhat of a disadvantage, unless they make use of Web-based collaborative tools, Web sites, Internet listservers, and member E-Mail. Where previous EDI standards exist, the consortia can build on this valuable experience, but they can also extend the reach beyond current EDI trading partners, as well as fill in the gaps that predefined EDI transactions have left out.

Let's take a quick look at a few of the initiatives involved in travel, human resources and healthcare, as examples of vertical industries that have developed their own applications of XML. These will also illustrate the variety of types of information that are exchanged using XML, not just traditional transaction sets like those used EDI, but also documents and other information. Then we shall take a closer look at one further example cXML. This section is not intended to teach you how to mark up the information for your specific industry, as it would take several books (more likely volumes) to do so, and would undoubtedly be out of date by the time it were published. However, it does give examples of some of the initiatives, along with some sample code so that you can see what type of information is being exchanged and the syntaxes that are being used.

Travel

Travel is the world's largest industry; it is global and interconnected. This characteristic allows travelers to create complex trips encompassing multiple destinations located hundreds or thousands of miles apart.

The ranks of the travel industry includes airlines, hotels, car rental companies, global distribution systems, and travel agencies, as well as many other businesses that provide products and services geared to the needs of travelers. The travel industry is diverse, and because of this the industry is fragmented by mode of transportation (air, car, rail, ship), by type of service (hotel, travel agency, distribution system), and even by type of traveler (business or pleasure). You may remember some of the issues surrounding marking up data for travel companies from the chapter on Data Modeling (Chapter 4). As a result of this fragmentation, most travel industry segments have evolved their own unique identities as well as separate rule-making bodies for formulating standards, processes, and procedures for reservations.

Open Travel Alliance (OTA)

The OTA is defining the future of the travel industry, defining a better strategy for the cost-effective communication of travel-related information.

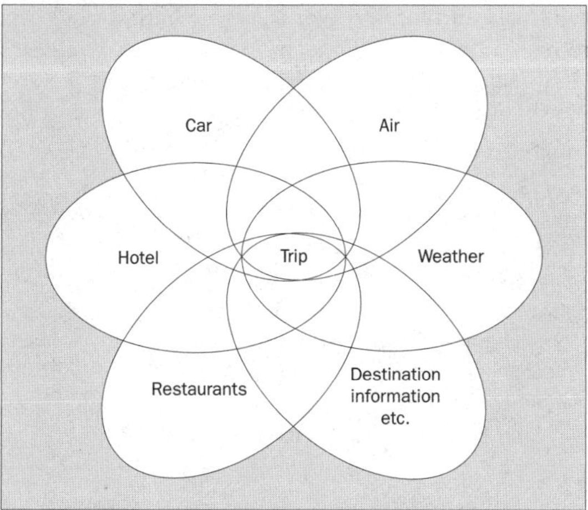

The Open Travel Alliance seeks to produce a standard capable of exploiting the almost universal access to low-cost, fast communications infrastructure that has arrived with the Internet. When implemented, the standard will facilitate the exchange of trip-centric information between all industry participants, regardless of how connected.

OTA is creating a *trip-centric* definition of the industry. The messages are moving beyond serving only the traditional segments and, to be truly useful, provide a comprehensive, cost-effective solution for the travelers themselves.

To ensure that the Alliance's goals are met effectively, they have subscribed to Data Interchange Standard Association (DISA)'s Collaborative Services program. The program provides services at all levels to support industry organizations interested in building business glossaries and messages. In partnership, the two groups have gained much momentum in addressing XML modeling as well as detailed exchange mechanism. A demonstration is scheduled in the beginning of 2000, with more messages to be added during the year.

> *For more information on OTA see* http://www.opentravel.com/.

This shows how vertical industries can come together to work with each other in defining languages that will allow different parts of one of the largest industries in the world to communicate with each other. This will not only help tour operators get sales, but will also help smaller vendors put together complete packages (to compete with larger travel operators), and will enable customers to book their whole travel arrangements on line with greater ease.

Human Resources

There are several companies deploying XML-based HR systems for résumés and time and attendance systems servicing thousands of employees at multiple companies on a global scale. Because of the nature of recruitment, a workflow is created that involves a stage where managers approval is required. This workflow means that there has to be a way of specifying the level of access for different parties that use the data. Unlike the travel industry, human resources is an area that doesn't appear to be a consensus on a common approach to defining how XML will be used or message sets, and in the short term multiple "standards" will exist.

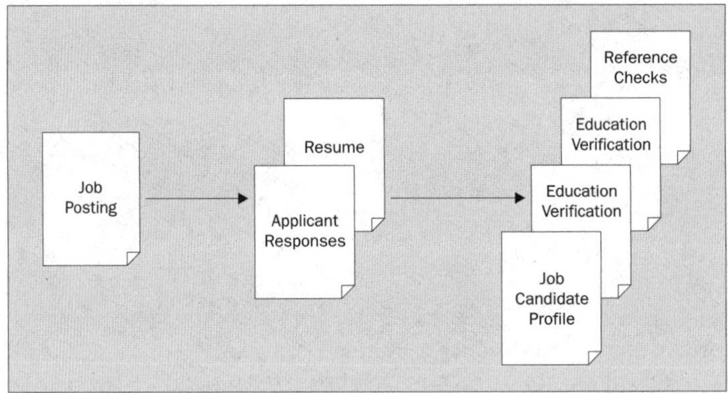

In this section we will take a look at the syntax of some of the messages that can be transferred in one of the markup languages that has been used with human resources: HR-XML, to give you an idea of what the messages look like.

HR-XML

The HR-XML Consortium is a non-profit organization dedicated to the development and promotion of standardized human resources-related XML vocabularies for enabling e-commerce and the automation of HR data exchange. It's members include companies such as Icarian Inc., SAP, IBM, Skills Village Inc., jobs.com Inc., Personic Software Inc., Lawson, Structured Methods, and J.D. Edwards (although at the time of writing PeopleSoft and Oracle were also evaluating it). The HR-XML Consortium has developed three provisional schemas, each of which is available as a DTD or an XML schema conforming to the BizTalk specification:

- Job posting
- Résumés
- Candidate profiles

Let's look at how these three steps are followed, with some examples of how they are used.

> **Note that the examples are provided to illustrate some of the lengthy and detailed standards listed in the Schema's available for HR-XML. You should explore each of the schema's in more details for a full idea of what is available.**
>
> **You can access the documentation for each of the the HR-XML Consortium schema standards at http://www.hr-xml.org/.**

Job Posting

Initially, a job is posted using the Job Posting schema, detailing the availability of a particular position and can be easily exchanged between employers, recruiters, career web sites, and workforce staffing solution providers. Information held in a job posting document would be who the hiring organization is, contact and a description of the job available as well as how to apply for it.

The sample document is available for downloaded along with the rest of the code for this book from http://www.wrox.com and is called `posting.xml`.

To illustrate how to use the Job Schema we will look an example for a posting. We first define the BizTalk header section, following the 0.81 BizTalk Framework specification to use the JobPosting schema (at the time of writing these schemas had not been updated to the 1.0 specification which had been released).

```
<?xml version="1.0" ?>
<BizTalk xmlns="urn:schemas-biztalk-org/biztalk-0.81.xml">
     <Body>
          <JobPosting xmlns="urn:schemas-biztalk-org:HR-XML-org/JobPosting">
```

We first declare information about the organization which will be hiring the employee within the `HiringOrg` element, with an attribute called `type` with value `agent` (the schema defines this value as an enumeration with values agent, principal or unspecified). We initially provide some general details about the hiring organization, and our example `Citix Agents Co` is the agency.

```
               <HiringOrg type="agent">
                    <OrgName>Citix Agents Co.</OrgName>
                    <Website>http://www.citix.com</Website>
                    <BusType>Technical Staff Provider
                         <SIC>99371234</SIC>
                    </BusType>
                    <EmployerDesc>Provide contract staff for international XML
                                   positions.
                    </EmployerDesc>
```

We then complete the information with some contact details, including the name of the contact (yours truly!) as well as a contact address (- please don't send anything as it will never get there), telephone number and email address.

```
            <Contact>
                <Name><First>Steven</First><Last>Livingstone</Last></Name>
                <JobTitle>Technical Director</JobTitle>
                <Address>
                    <AddressLine>1022 Brinlow Avenue</AddressLine>
                    <AddressLine>Yoker</AddressLine>
                    <City>Glasgow</City>
                    <PostalCode>G13A 999</PostalCode>
                    <Country>Scotland</Country>
                </Address>
                <PhoneNumbers>
                    <Voice>
                        <AreaCode>001</AreaCode>
                        <TelNumber>100000</TelNumber>
                    </Voice>
                </PhoneNumbers>
                <Email>ceo@citix.com</Email>
            </Contact>
        </HiringOrg>
```

Now, because we have stated that our Hiring Organization is an agency, they would act on behalf of the true employer. The schema defines this as the `PrincipalEmployer` and requires some basic information about the organization the employer will be working with. Our company is called `Global XML Inc.` and is a Software Development company as the following code section shows.

```
            <PrincipalEmployer>
                <OrgName>Global XML Inc.</OrgName>
                <Website>http://www.global-xml-inc.com</Website>
                <BusType>Software Development
                    <SIC>83648236</SIC>
                </BusType>
                <EmployerDesc>Global Software company specialising in
                             E-Commerce Internet Content Development.
                </EmployerDesc>
            </PrincipalEmployer>
```

The final section of the Job Posting document gives details on the actual position. Our example below is for an XML Developer, located in Glagow and describes some of the reasons as to why the job is being offered (as an unordered list) within the `JobPurpose` element. We can also outline the qualifications needed for the job (`QualifRequired`), such as Software packages used and general experience. Finally, the `HowToApply` element will contain any further information an applicant may need to be put forward for the job.

```
            <JobInformation>
                <JobTitle>XML Developer</JobTitle>
                <Location>Glasgow, Scotland</Location>
                <Description>
                    <JobPurpose>
```

```
                              <ul>
                                    <li>Develop XML Schema's representing the business
                                        processes of our E-Commcerce partners;
                                     </li>
                                    <li>To aid software developers with their
                                         implementation of XML techniques;
                                    </li>
                                    <li>Advise of the implementation and progression of
                                         XML techniques;
                                     </li>
                              </ul>
                             </JobPurpose>
                             <QualifRequired>
                             <SoftwareRequired>XML Wizard '99</SoftwareRequired>
                             <ExperienceRequired YearsOfExperience="1">
                                     You must have some commercial experience of XML.
                                </ExperienceRequired>
                             </QualifRequired>
                             <Preferences>
                                <p>Prefer candidate with prior experience in the
                                        banking or financial industry.
                                     </p>
                             </Preferences>
                             <Compensation>
                                 <p>You'll make a mint!</p>
                             </Compensation>
                           </Description>
                           <HowToApply>
                             <p>Send in a full CV and some examples of your work.</p>
                           </HowToApply>
                      </JobInformation>
                 </JobPosting>
            </Body>
       </BizTalk>
```

Now that we have looked at how a job could be marked up for posting, lets us look at an example resume sent by an applicant in response to the above position.

Résumés

The Resume schema allows a job candidate to create a rich resume, which can be used in databanks and is very searchable. The tags allow tags to have personal data secured at the tag level. The resume documents could then be returned to an employer or agency who are looking for candidates matching the criteria specified in their search.

The sample document is available as `resume.xml` in the download files. Our example resume starts with the usual mandatory BizTalk header tags.

```
<?xml version="1.0"?>
<BizTalk xmlns="urn:schemas-biztalk-org/biztalk-0.81.xml">
<Body>
<Resume xmlns="urn:schemas-biztalk-org:HR-XML-org/Resume">
```

The `ResumeProlog` section allows a person to specify the conditions around his employment, such as the availability date and compensation information such as your current contract rate and the required contract rate.

```
      <ResumeProlog>
          <RevisionDate>
            <Date><Day>5</Day><Month>January</Month><Year>1999</Year></Date>
          </RevisionDate>
          <AvailabilityDate>
            <StartDate><Day>15</Day><Month>January</Month>
                             <Year>2000</Year></StartDate>
            <EndDate><Day>5</Day><Month>Febuary</Month>
                             <Year>2000</Year></EndDate>
          </AvailabilityDate>
          <CompensationDetail>
            <Rate>
             <Current>£45 per hour</Current>
             <Required>£50 per hour</Required>
            </Rate>
            <Benefits>
              <Required>Travel Expenses and Lunch coupon desired.</Required>
            </Benefits>
          </CompensationDetail>
      </ResumeProlog>
```

The final section is the `ResumeBody` which should contain further information within the tags `PersonalData` and `ResumeSection`. The `PersonalData` tag, as its name suggests, contains contact information about the person's resume, such as the persons name, address, telephone and email addresses.

```
      <ResumeBody>
         <PersonalData>
                 <Name><First>Jane</First><Last>Doe</Last></Name>
                 <JobTitle>Primary Web Developer</JobTitle>
                 <Address>
                      <AddressLine>973 FunnyName Road</AddressLine>
                      <AddressLine>Anderton Place</AddressLine>
                      <City>SaddleWich</City>
                      <PostalCode>H77 8I9</PostalCode>
                 </Address>
                 <Email>ntw_uk@hotmail.com</Email>
                 <Voice>
                      <AreaCode>09772</AreaCode>
                      <TelNumber>980-0283</TelNumber>
                 </Voice>
                 <EmployeName>InterCo Internet Consultants Ltd.</EmployeName>
          </PersonalData>
     </ResumeBody>
   </Resume>
  </Body>
  </BizTalk>
```

There may be multiple ResumeSection's for each section type attribute (SecType) which can be one of the following of the enumerations defined in the schema.

- Objective
- Experience
- Personal
- References
- Education
- Certifications
- Licenses
- QualifSummary (summary of qualifications)
- Skills
- ProfAssociations (membership of professional associations)
- Unspecified

These sections are used to provide some detail on qualifications, skill sets and experience and would generally be publically available for searching on, with the personal data being secured. Each section contains a SectionTitle and appropriate details such as the summary of qualifications, as was done below.

```
        ...
        <ResumeSection SecType="QualifSummary">
          <SectionTitle>University Qualifications</SectionTitle>
          <SecBody>
               <P>BSc in Physics and a MSc in Information Technology Systems
               at Strathclyde University.</P>
          </SecBody>
        </ResumeSection>

        <ResumeSection SecType="Experience">
             <SectionTitle>Working with
             <EmployerName>InterCo Internet Consultants Ltd.</EmployerName> as the
             <JobTitle>Development Lead</JobTitle> which also involved being a
             <JobTitle>Technical Documenter</JobTitle> and
            <JobTitle>System Tester</JobTitle>.
             <StartDate>
              <Date><Month>June</Month><Year>1998</Year></Date>
             </StartDate>
             to present. Also gained my <CertificationQualif>Level 2 International
             Certification in XML</CertificationQualif>.
          </SectionTitle>
        </ResumeSection>
    </ResumeBody>
  </Resume>
  </Body>
  </BizTalk>
```

The resume section is similar to the candidate profile schema we will discuss below, but the latter is more concise and has a more consistent structure. We will now look at the final HR-XML standard schema describing a candidate profile.

CandidateProfile

The CandidateProfile allows the exchange of information about candidates among employers, recruiters, career web sites, and workforce staffing solution providers and can contain data related to the candidates job objectives, qualifications, and work and educational history. This related data could be

- Derived from a lexical parse of non-structured resume,
- Posted by the job candidate in an online application form,
- Collected by a recruiter in a telephone conversation, or
- Filtered directly from an XML-tagged resume.

The sample document is available as `profile.xml` in the download files. Our example below illustrates the initial mandatory elements for a candidate profile BizTalk compliant document.

```
<?xml version="1.0"?>
<BizTalk xmlns="urn:schemas-biztalk-org/biztalk-0.81.xml">
<Body>
<CandidateProfile xmlns="urn:schemas-biztalk-org:HR-XML-org/CandidateProfile">
```

The `PostDetail` elements can then contain information on the valid range of this profile of the candidate as shown in the section below.

```
<PostDetail>
    <StartDate>
        <Date><Month>January</Month><Day>05</Day><Year>2000</Year></Date>
    </StartDate>
    <EndDate>
        <Date><Month>Febuary</Month><Day>25</Day><Year>2001</Year></Date>
    </EndDate>
</PostDetail>
```

The `JobCandidateContact` element holds contact information about the candidate, such as the persons name, address, telephone number and email addresses.

```
<JobCandidateContact>
<Name>
    <First>Steven</First>
    <Last>Livingstone</Last>
</Name>
<Address>
   <AddressLine>973 FunnyName Road</AddressLine>
   <AddressLine>Anderton Place</AddressLine>
   <City>SaddleWich</City>
   <PostalCode>H77 8I9</PostalCode>
</Address>
```

```
<PhoneNumbers>
   <Voice>
        <AreaCode>09772</AreaCode>
        <TelNumber>980-0283</TelNumber>
   </Voice>
</PhoneNumbers>
<Email>ntw_uk@hotmail.com</Email>
</JobCandidateContact>
```

The Objective element may be used to show details which specify conditions or preferences a candidate may have about a potential position. In the example below, the desired location is the US, working 37 hours per week.

```
<Objective>
    <Location>US</Location>
    <Industry>Software Consulting</Industry>
    <Schedule>
        <FullTime>
          <HoursPerWeek>37</HoursPerWeek>
        </FullTime>
    </Schedule>
    <AvailabilityDate>
        <Date><Day>15</Day><Month>1</Month><Year>2000</Year></Date>
        <Comment>4 weeks notice is needed to my current employer.</Comment>
    </AvailabilityDate>
</Objective>
```

We then outline the qualifications, which can include skills qualifications, experience, software experience, programming languages, licenses, certificates, knowledge of equipment, knowledge of hardware and operating systems.

Each element may have attributes of YearsOfExperience, level (the level from 0 to 5 knowledge you have of the item) and the level of interest you have for the item or area outlined between the tags.

```
<Qualifications>
  <CertificationQualif>
        Level 2 International Certification in XML
    </CertificationQualif>
  <ExperienceQualif YearsOfExperience="2" level="4" interest="4">
        XML Commercial Development
    </ExperienceQualif>
    <PrgmLangQualif level="4" YearsOfExperience="6" interest="3">
        Visual Basic
    </PrgmLangQualif>
    <PrgmLangQualif YearsOfExperience="6" level="3" interest="2">
        C++
    </PrgmLangQualif>
    <SkillsQualif YearsOfExperience="2" level="3" interest="4">
       Development Lead
    </SkillsQualif>
    <SkillsQualif YearsOfExperience="4" level="4" interest="2">
       Technical Documenter
    </SkillsQualif>
```

```
        <SkillsQualif YearsOfExperience="7" level="3" interest="1">
           System Tester
        </SkillsQualif>
    </Qualifications>
```

Finally in our example, we outline the `History` of the candidate, including an `Education` profile and `Position` profile. The education profile should gives some detail on the University attended as well as degree qualifications and a timescope.

```
    <History>
        <Education>
            <School>Strathclyde University</School>
            <Location>Glasgow, Scotland.</Location>
            <Degree>BSc Physics</Degree>
            <StartDate>
              <Date><Year>1992</Year></Date>
            </StartDate>
            <EndDate>
              <Date><Year>1996</Year></Date>
            </EndDate>
        </Education>
```

We conclude the candidate profile by outlining the candidates work experience, with details such as the employer name, title of the job and a summary of work carried out.

```
        <Position>
            <EmployerName>InterCo Internet Consultants Ltd.</EmployerName>
            <Location>Milan, Italy.</Location>
            <JobTitle>Development Lead</JobTitle>
            <Industry>Software Development</Industry>
            <StartDate>
              <Date><Month>June</Month><Year>1998</Year></Date>
            </StartDate>
            <EndDate>
              <Date><Month>January</Month><Year>2000</Year></Date>
            </EndDate>
            <Summary>
              <p>Developed XML Software applications for the company Intranet.</p>
            </Summary>
        </Position>
    </History>
  </CandidateProfile>
  </Body>
  </BizTalk>
```

The above examples should give you a good idea of the HR-XML standards and the level of importance XML plays in allowing many employers, employees and agencies to exchange candidate and employment information. You should explore the schema's to see the full capabilities of the standards, however it shows how the different messages are split up and how XML makes the job of describing the information easier. Remembering that it is always possible to extend it internally if you required more information, though this extended information would not be understood by anyone who had not prepared for your extensions.

These have been designed both as DTDs and Microsoft BizTalk compatible schemas and so allow documents created following the above schemas to be interchanged among employees and employers seamlessly.

For more information visit http://www.hr-xml.org/

This is not the only initiative in the area of human resources, however. There are others including WorkForce Markup Language (WFML) developed by AppliedTheory Communications (ATC) and the America's Job Bank (AJB). AJB is a US federal government agency that consolidates and hosts résumés and job listings from state employment agencies. The purpose of the initiative is to collaborate on the creation and standardization of human resource/electronic recruiting XML definitions. For more information visit http://www.xml-hr.org/. In addition, there is Human Resources Markup Language (HRML), which was created by Datamain, Inc. HRML remains focused on job postings and has been used extensively as an internal representation for job listings and résumés at Datamain. A recent version has been added to the website to include envelopes, private tags, and job class tags. For more information on HRML visit http://www.hrml.com/.

Healthcare

Providers of Web-based applications for healthcare are flocking to implement XML coding, according to e-Healthcare Market Reporter, with companies such as Microsoft and Computer Sciences Corporation touting XML as a way to cut costs and time through increased workflow and e-commerce capabilities. During Windows on Healthcare V, the annual Microsoft Healthcare Users Group conference in San Diego, the company said it is developing a version of its Windows Distributed Internet Architecture (DNA) especially for healthcare, to be called Windows DNA for Healthcare. Meanwhile, Computer Sciences Corporation (CSC) released an XML tagging product the company developed in collaboration with the U.S. Department of Defense's Program Manager for the Joint Computer-Aided Acquisition and Logistics Support (JCALS) Office. XML has a lot to offer the Healthcare industry where multimedia is a requirement.

HL7 SGML/XML Special Interest Group

The name of the Healthcare Level 7 SGML/XML Special Interest Group's gives away that fact that this group has matured with XML technology. The SIG has addressed many of the issues involved with the medical industry, such as prescriptions, policy & procedures, clinical notes, and Electronic Patient Records (EPR), as well as addressing traditional HL7 messages in XML syntax.

> *HL7 - Health Level Seven is one of several ANSI-accredited Standards Developing Organizations (SDOs) operating in the healthcare arena. Most SDOs produce standards (sometimes called specifications or protocols) for a particular healthcare domain such as pharmacy, medical devices, imaging, or insurance (claims processing) transactions. Healthcare Level Seven's domain is clinical and administrative data. Reports such as billing abstracts, insurance claims, and epidemiological reports as well as the birth-to-death patient record are derived from the basic clinical documents by extraction, copying, linking or combination.*

Corporate Research Group (New Rochelle, NY) says that Internet pharmacy business will generate between $1.4 billion and $2.8 billion in revenues in 2001. And some day, physicians will enter prescribing instructions on the web via a secure system that will:

- Verify the physician's identity
- Check compliance with the patient's applicable formulary
- Check the patient's personal history for adverse drug reactions
- Enter the patient in any applicable disease management programs
- Shop for the drug at the best price available
- Have the medication delivered to the patient
- Deduct the cost from the patient's credit card
- Bill the health plan
- Adjust the inventory at the store

Below is a draft example of a prescription in XML:

```
<PRESCRIPTION>Viagra
   <FORM>50 mg. capsule</FORM>
   <DISPENSE>6</DISPENSE>
   <DOSAGE>1 cap(s)po</DOSAGE>
   <INSTRUCTIONS>As desired</INSTRUCTIONS>
   <REFILL>1</REFILL>
   <SUBSTITUTE>may substitute</SUBSTITUTE>
   <NUMBER NOTYPE="DEA">AB1234567</NUMBER>
</PRESCRIPTION>
```

The architectural approach taken by the SIG is well designed and implements highly granular (atomic) concepts, such as billing codes or controlled vocabulary terms that can be entered into text as markup at all levels of the architecture. For instance, the HL7 Patient Record Proposal provides coding and structure of highly granular markup, and will be defined in the architectural DTDs for each level:

- **Level 1 - Coded Header**. Level 1 compliance offers complete interoperability for human-readable content, but does not specify encoding for interoperable machine processing beyond the header.
- **Level 2 - Coded Context**. The document body is structured into sections to support minimal processing, such as entry into forms, and safe assumption of context to clinical content. It contains the same Coded Header as Level 1.
- **Level 3 - Coded Content**. The document body must be XML of sufficient structure and specificity to be consistent with the HL7 Reference Information Model (RIM) and be consistent with the coded header and coded context of levels 1 and 2.

For more information see http://www.mcis.duke.edu/standards/HL7/sigs/sgml/index.html.

Having taken a look at these three examples, you should be starting to get an idea of how XML can be used in vertical industries. We have shown how the Open Travel Alliance are using XML to integrate services offered by various sections of the travel industry. Companies that mark up their data according to the OTA schemas will be able to send their information to anyone who understands it. We have seen the type of syntax and messages that are used in HR-XML to give us a better idea of how business information can be marked up. And we have seen how HL7 initiatives will mean that we can share information about healthcare with a wider audience, which could not only make our lives easier when ordering prescription drugs, but also save our lives by allowing access to medical records in emergencies. It is not to say that much of this could not be done without XML, however the current surge in its popularity and the commitment of software vendors is making possibility into reality.

RosettaNet

RosettaNet's aim is to develop a set of industry-wide electronic business interoperability standards that help industries integrate their business conversations. RosettaNet's model is based around the concept of **language** and the requirements associated with spoken languages that are required for a complete understanding from business to business. If we think about the way that humans communicate business orders on the telephone, then we will start to understand the model. In order for a conversation to take place we need to be able to make and hear **sounds**. If we extend this metaphor, we need an **alphabet** to make up **words**. If we then take the words and and apply **grammar** we can create a **dialog**. That dialog can form a business process, which can be transmitted across some apparatus such as a **telephone**.

This model may *sound* simple, but is right on the mark and works. If you look at the following diagram, you can see how RosettaNet apply the model of the language to e-commerce.

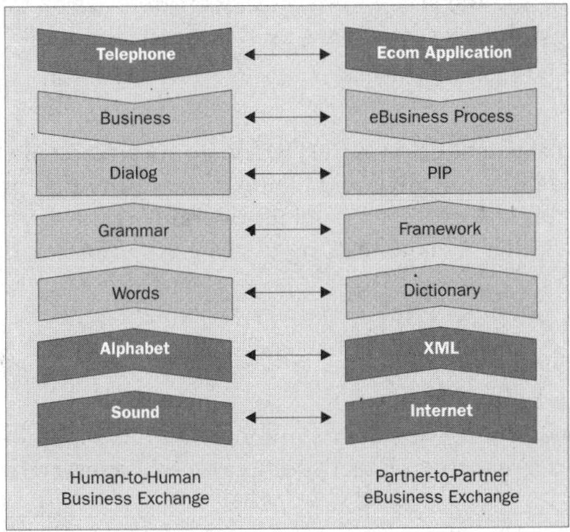

The Internet is compared with the process of making sounds. XML functions as alphabet in this model, and the e-commerce application is the instrument for the transmission of an electronic business process.

In order for eBusiness to achieve its potential, there is a need for dictionaries, the framework, the Partner Interface Processes and the eBusiness processes. RosettaNet attempts to fill the gaps by focusing on building a master dictionary that can be used to define properties for products, partners, and business transactions. This master dictionary, coupled with an established implementation framework (how the exchange is carried out), is used to support the dialog, which is known as the Partner Interface Process or PIP.

RosettaNet has already identified the following tasks and are currently working on them to fill in the picture:

- **Business Process Modeling** - to identify and quantify the individual elements of a current business process at every level of the supply chain, and then analyze them to identify any misalignments or inefficiencies.
- Through **Business Process Analysis** of the detailed "as is" model, a "generic to-be" process emerges, showing the opportunities for re-alignment in the form of a **Partner Interface Process** (**PIP**) target list, and estimating the business impact of implementing the resulting PIPs (savings as a function of time and money).
- A **PIP Blueprint** is created from this to-be process that specifies how partner roles (buyer, seller, assembler, catalog publisher, etc.) interactively perform interface activities that collaboratively achieve a business objective. This includes specifying the PIP Service(s), Transaction(s), and Message(s) - which includes dictionary properties, along with class and sequence diagrams in UML.
- A **PIP Protocol** is created for the PIP blueprint. The protocol specifies how networked applications that adhere to the RosettaNet implementation framework must interoperate to execute the process specified in a PIP blueprint. This includes an XML document (or documents) based on Implementation Framework DTDs, a Validation tool, and Implementation guides for each interface.
- In parallel, two **Data Dictionaries** are being developed to provide a common set of properties required by PIPs. The first is a technical properties dictionary (technical specifications for all product categories), and the second is a business properties dictionary that includes catalog properties, partner properties (attributes used to describe supply chain partner companies) and business transaction properties.

During the development of the data dictionaries, language specific elements more than tripled that of the X12 and EDIFACT code lists, segment and elements that provided priming the pump for the dictionary. The key to making the process more interoperable is making the language specific to the needs of the organizations, rather then attempting to use generic shared data definitions.

For more information on RosettaNet see
http://www.rosettanet.org/general/index_general.html

RosettaNet is producing real results – October's implementation activities featured the results of 42 PIPs, and 6 successful pilots between 15 RosettaNet partners, giving credit to the methodology taken by the initiative.

cXML – A Detailed Example of Vertical Industries

cXML version 1.0 is a protocol designed to allow XML driven business to business electronic commerce transactions across the Internet. There are two mechanisms available for application interchange, allowing Request-Response based transactions via the HTTP protocol, or one-way transports which are not limited to a particular method. At the time of writing, there were also plans to move cXML to a BizTalk compatible schema.

Why cXML?

Consumer to Businesses and Business to Business applications are becoming more global, and distributed integration is a must for successful electronic commerce applications. Until relatively recently it has been difficult and expensive to allow commerce application integration, but with initiatives such as BizTalk and cXML this should become much simpler and less costly in the future.

This section will look at exactly what cXML is and how it can already be used within your commerce applications to provide a very efficient and open system.

The cXML specification can be downloaded from http://www.cXML.org.

cXML Protocol Specification

The cXML specification offers three main options for the structure of an XML document instance. The first two separate the document into two logical sections, as we discussed earlier in this chapter – the header section within the `<Header>` element and the body section within either a `<Message>` or `<Request>` element – the third is a single `<Reponse>` element. The header section primarily controls transport information and the body can contain any XML, but more commonly, as cXML Business document definition – we will cover this shortly.

It is useful in this area to see a practical example of what the framework for a cXML documents looks like and then we will explain the concepts outlined in the document. So, an instance of a cXML document could be like the one defined below. It shows a message (within the `Request` element), uniquely defined by it's `payloadID`, being sent from `steven@somewhere.com` to the recepients `donna@anotherplace.com` and `kod@anotherplace.com`.

```
<cXML version="1.0" payloadID="19991001.8263.872344@somewhere.com"
timestamp="1999-10-01T01:11:03-05:35">
<Header>
    <From>
        <Credential domain="SomeUserIDForDomain">
            <Identity>steven@somewhere.com</Identity>
        </Credential>
    </From>
    <To>
        <Credential domain="RemoteDomainUserID">
            <Identity>donna@anotherplace.com</Identity>
        </Credential>
        <Credential domain="AnotherRemoteDomainUserID">
            <Identity>kod@anotherplace.com</Identity>
        </Credential>
    </To>
    <Sender>
        <Credential domain="SomeUserIDForDomain">
            <Identity>steven@somewhere.com</Identity>
            <DigitalSignature type="PK7 self-contained"
                     encoding="Base64">
            </DigitalSignature>
        </Credential>
```

```
        <UserAgent>Ariba ORMS 6.0</UserAgent>
    </Sender>
</Header>
<Request deploymentMode="test">
        cXML Business Document Definition ...
    </Request>
</cXML>
```

Let's look at the important parts of this document and how they fit into the cXML specification.

The cXML Envelope

The cXML envelope is a mandatory section of a cXML instance, which wraps around the header and body information to create a unique root element – in cXML's case this is `<cXML>`. The DTD representation of the cXML root element is:

```
<!ELEMENT cXML ((Header, Message) |
                (Header, Request) |
                (Response))>

<!ATTLIST cXML
    version    %uint;          "1.0"
    payloadID  %string;        #REQUIRED
    timestamp  %datetime.tz;   #REQUIRED
>
```

There are three attributes which can be applied to the cXML root element, namely:

Attribute	Description	Values
`Version`	States the version of the cXML protocol. At the time of writing, this was version 1.0.	`"1.0"`
`PayloadID`	A unique identifier with the prime purpose of being able to trace and identify messages if needed. Recommended form for this is shown.	`Datetime.process id.random number@hostname`
`timestamp`	The Timestamp attribute contains the data and time the message was sent in ISO8601 format. This means that our datetime must be of the format	`YYYY-MM-DDThh:mm:ssTZD`

The timestamp reads as follows:

`YYYY` = four-digit year
`MM` = two-digit month (01=January, etc.)
`DD` = two-digit day of month (01 through 31)
`hh` = two digits of hour (00 through 23) (am/pm NOT allowed)
`mm` = two digits of minute (00 through 59)
`ss` = two digits of second (00 through 59)
`TZD` = time zone designator

The value of the time zone designator is one of the following :

`Z` - indicates UTC (Coordinated Universal Time). The "Z" must be upper case.
`+hh:mm` - indicates that the time is a local time which is `hh` hours and `mm` minutes ahead of UTC.
`-hh:mm` - indicates that the time is a local time which is `hh` hours and `mm` minutes behind UTC.

> *More information about iso8601 can be found at the following locations :*
> *http://www.w3.org/TR/PR-html40/types.html#h-6.11*
> *http://www.saqqara.demon.co.uk/datefmt.htm*

So, in our example above, we have defined the root tag as follows:

```
<cXML version="1.0" payloadID="19991001.8263.872344@somewhere.com"
timestamp="1999-10-01T01:11:03-05:30">
```

The instance in our document above is of the date 1st October 1999, with a process id of `8263` and a random numer `872344` on the host `somewhere.com/`

The Header section

The header section must consist of three important constituents, as shown in the instance above. These are:

- `From` section
- `To` section
- `Sender` Section

It has a DTD as follows:

```
<!ELEMENT Header (From, To, Sender)>

<!ELEMENT From (Credential+)>
<!ELEMENT To (Credential+)>
<!ELEMENT Sender (Credential, UserAgent)>
<!ELEMENT UserAgent (#PCDATA)>
```

Notice that the entire `Header` section is wrapped in the element envelope (the `cXML` element), which contains several child elements to describe the transport of the document. We will now look at the role these sub-elements play in the cXML document.

From

The `From` element is really the same idea as From in an email – it simply identifies the source of the request. It can contain one or more `Credential` elements allowing the requestor to identify himself.

Our example of the From element identifies the user, whose email address is steven@somewhere.com and whose domain ID is SomeUserIDForDomain, as the originator of the message.

```
<From>
<Credential domain="SomeUserIDForDomain">
<Identity>steven@somewhere.com</Identity>
</Credential>
</From>
```

We will discuss the Credential element in details shortly.

To

Just in the same way that we used a From element to hold details of who the message is from, we have a To element to include information about the destination of the request. In our case, we have specified two domain IDs along with their email addresses to identify the destination users.

```
<To>
<Credential domain="RemoteDomainUserID">
    <Identity>donna@anotherplace.com</Identity>
</Credential>
<Credential domain="AnotherRemoteDomainUserID">
    <Identity>rambo@anotherplace.com</Identity>
</Credential>
</To>
```

Sender

The Sender element plays an important role in authenticating the transmitter of the cXML instance and is the only part of the header that changes as it is passed through the system. In general, it is the same as the From element, although the Sender element often contains the Credential element with authentication information to identify the sender. The Sender element often contains authentication and is the only one that changes as the cXML message is routed through the systems participating in delivering the message to its recipient.

In our sample instance, a user with domain id SomeUserIDForDomain and identity steven@somewhere.com is identified as the sender of the instance.

```
<Sender>
   <Credential domain="SomeUserIDForDomain">
      <Identity>steven@somewhere.com</Identity>
      <DigitalSignature type="PK7 self-contained" encoding="Base64">
      </DigitalSignature>
   </Credential>
   <UserAgent>Ariba ORMS 6.0</UserAgent>
</Sender>
```

Notice that in our example within the Credential element, we use the Identity tag to contain the email address of the sender as well a DigitalSignature element which acts in the same as a password does in conventional systems to act as an authentication mechanism. Rather than the DigitalSignature method, the SharedSecret element could be used when the Sender has a username/password combination that the Requester at the other end of the HTTP connection can understand.

Notice that we also define a `UserAgent` element within our `Sender` element – we discuss the use of this element below.

Credential

The `Credential` element is used to allow users to identify themselves in the same way as the From field works for SMTP (email) and has an attribute called `domain` which allows us to tie the instance to a particular sender of a domain. If necessary, more than one `Credential` element may be use to specify the sender allowing the requestor to identify themselves in multiple ways (analogous to sending both SMTP and X.400 email addresses in an email message).

Here is a snippet from the full DTD `Credential` element, for use in the `From` element:

```
<!ELEMENT Identity ANY>
<!ELEMENT Credential (Identity, (%cxml.authentication;)?)>
<!ATTLIST Credential
    domain  %string;   #REQUIRED
>
```

The DTD section above is typically sufficient for the `From` element of the cXML header as we saw above.

However, for the `Sender` element, it is common to include some authentication information as well as some user information. This brings us to the full DTD of the `Credential` element.

```
<!ELEMENT DigitalSignature ANY>
<!ATTLIST DigitalSignature
    type      %string;   "PK7 self-contained"
    encoding  %string;   "Base64"
>

<!ELEMENT SharedSecret ANY>
<!ELEMENT Identity ANY>
<!ENTITY % cxml.authentication  "SharedSecret | DigitalSignature">
<!ELEMENT Credential (Identity, (%cxml.authentication;)?)>
<!ATTLIST Credential
    domain  %string;   #REQUIRED
>
```

The `DigitalSignature` element can have two attributes as define below:

Attribute	Description	Value
`type`	The type of digital signature used and the recommended format is `PK7 self-contained`	Suggested: `PK7 self-contained` Can be other
`encoding`	How the signature should be encoded for streaming over HTTP. This will default top "base64" encoding which is becoming very popular on the web, although you can choose your own encoding format if you desire.	Default: `base64` Can be other

The `DigitalSignature` element would be used if the two cooperating parties agree on a common certificate format and authority as defined by the type attribute.

The other authentication method is to use the `SharedSecrect` element which can play the role of a password with the combination of an identity and `SharedSecrect` acting as a Username/Password combination. Typically, this would be securely exchanged before any transportation took place.

UserAgent

The `UserAgent` element should simply hold the string representation of the `UserAgent` who is receiving the cXML document, in the same way that we have a `UserAgent` in HTTP.

This completes our look at the Header and Envelope of a cXML document. We will now look at the various ways the message information is transported.

Message Transfer

In cXML, there are two methods implementations where information is transferred.

- Request/Response messaging
- Asynchronous or one-way transfer

Let's look at how these methods are implemented.

Request/Response Messaging

A cXML Request-Response scenario is shown in the following diagram. A client sends a cXML request to a server ensuring that a single request is made for each envelope, which simplifies server implementation. The XML data which is sent may be almost any type, but the main purpose of cXML is to use the request types specified in the cXML implementation.

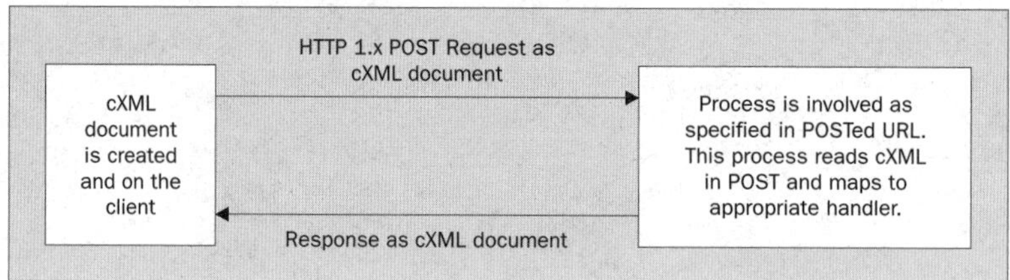

Request

An XML request instance would use the following framework

```
<cXML>
    <Header>
        Our header details here
    </Header>
    <Request>
        Our Request details here
    </Request>
</cXML>
```

The DTD for the framework is as follows:

```
<!ENTITY % cxml.requests  "OrderRequest |
                           PunchOutSetupRequest |
                           GetPendingRequest |
                           SubscriptionListRequest |
                           SubscriptionContentRequest |
                           SupplierListRequest |
                           SupplierDataRequest"
>

<!ELEMENT Request (%cxml.requests;)>
<!ATTLIST Request
    deploymentMode  (production | test)  "production"
>
```

The Request element has one attribute called deploymentMode which can be either production or test depending upon whether you are just testing the system or have deployed it for use. The Request values defined are part of the cXML specification and are dedicated to enabling open message transfer.

So, an example of a request during a test process for a list of suppliers with whom a buyer has an active relationship would be:

```
<Request deploymentMode="test">
     <SupplierListRequest/>
</Request>
```

Response

The Response element is sent back to inform the client of the application results of operations, even if there are no results to show. A cXML document which has been successfully processed would have a framework as below:

```
<cXML>
    <Header>
        Our header details here
    </Header>
    <Response>
       <Status code="200" text="OK"/>
        Our Request details here
    </Response>
</cXML>
```

So, if we now look at the DTD for a response instance, we have:

```
<!ELEMENT Status (#PCDATA)>
<!ATTLIST Status
    code  %uint;    #REQUIRED
    text  %string;  #REQUIRED
>
```

```
<!ENTITY % cxml.responses  "OrderResponse |
                            PunchOutSetupResponse |
                            GetPendingResponse |
                            SubscriptionListResponse |
                            SubscriptionContentResponse |
                            SupplierListResponse |
                            SupplierDataResponse"
>

<!ELEMENT Response (Status, (%cxml.responses;)?)>
```

The Response element must contain a Status child element, which indicates whether the instance has been successfully processed, and if not the reason why. This element has code and text attributes where the value of the code attribute follows on a similar model to the HTTP codes and text contains the textual representation of the code (for logs etc.). An error code of 500 would indicate and error and the XML parse error or application error should be represented within the returned XML context to aid debugging.

The Response may also conform to one of the cXML DTD specifications which we will look at shortly. A response to our previous SupplierListRequest sample may be illustrated by the following instance.

```
<Response>
  <Status code="200" text="OK"/>
  <SupplierListResponse>
     <Supplier corporateURL="http://www.citix.com"
           storeFrontURL="http://www.deltabiz.com">
        <Name xml:lang="en-US">Citix Co</Name>
        <Comments xml:lang="en-US">Our biggest customer</Comments>
        <SupplierID domain="DUNS">475435</SupplierID>
     </Supplier>
</SupplierListResponse>
</Response>
```

Note that you can view the SupplierListResponse DTD in the file supplier.mod in the cXML specification which can be downloaded from http://www.cxml.org.

The other kind of messaging available with cXML, is asynchronous or one-way messaging. We will look at that now.

Asynchronous Messaging

Asynchronous messaging is for situations where synchronous messaging (such as HTTP) is not available and so we are not guaranteed or will get a response to our request. The following diagram shows what an asynchronous response may logically look like.

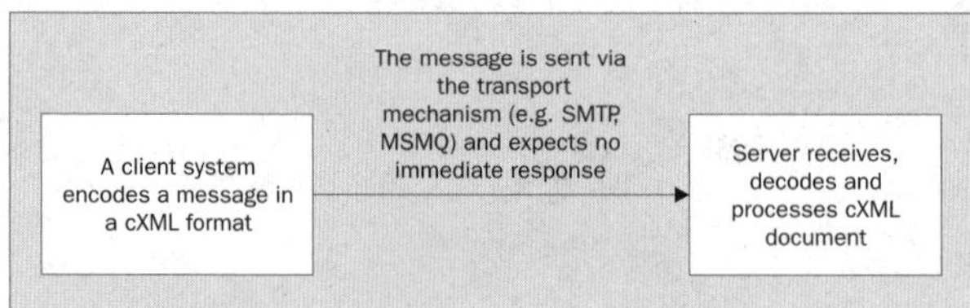

The structure of an asynchronous cXML message is not completely dissimilar to that for the Request/Response format.

```
<cXML>
    <Header>
        Our header details
    </Header>
    <Message>
        Our message details
    </Message>
</cXML>
```

In fact, the structure of the cXML one-way instance can only differed from the Request/Response scenario by the `Message` element rather than `Request` or `Response`. The DTD of this message element is shown below.

```
<!ENTITY % cxml.messages  "PunchOutOrderMessage |
                           PunchOutOrderAckMessage |
                           SubscriptionChangeMessage |
                           SupplierChangeMessage"
>

<!ELEMENT Message (Status?, (%cxml.messages;))>
<!ATTLIST Message
    deploymentMode  (production | test)  "production"
    inReplyTo       %string;  #IMPLIED
>
```

The `Message` element may optionally contain a status child element and cXML message as described above. There are also two attributes which can be applied – the `deploymentMode` attribute which we discussed above and the optional `inReplyTo` attribute.

In a bid to mimic asynchronous Request/Response functionality, the `inReplyTo` attribute can indicate a message to which this message is replying, having a value of the `payloadID` of the original message.

The following is an example of a asynchronous Request/Response action for changing a buyers content description.

```
<Message inReplyTo="19991001.8263.872344@somewhere.com">
     <SubscriptionChangeMessage type="update">
          <Subscription>
                <InternalID>6235</InternalID>
                <Name xml:lang="en-US">Annual Cost</Name>
                <Changetime>2000-01-13T11:33:01-28:10</Changetime>
                <SupplierID domain="DUNS">82735236</SupplierID>
                <Format version="2.1">CIF</Format>
          </Subscription>
     </SubscriptionChangeMessage>
</Message>
```

You can find the `SubscriptionChangeMessage` cXML module in `Subscription.mod` with the cXML download at http://www.cxml.org.

Asynchronous Transport

Currently, the most popular ways of transporting asynchronous messages in the cXML specification is via HTTP (if possible) or URL-Form-Encoding, although there is no reason why other methods such as SMTP or MSMQ should not be supported.

With HTTP one-way transport, the client simply POSTs the cXML message to the server and ends the connection without waiting for any kind of response. However, with URL encoding, the cXML document is not directly sent to the server, but instead is encoded as a hidden HTML form field, allowing the server web page to display some user-orientated information. More details on this method of transport is available in the cXML documentation.

Basic and Common Elements

There are some standards to which cXML entities align, notably:

- The isoLangCode representing the ISO Language Code 639
- The unitOfMeasure entity follows the UN/CEFACT Recommendation
- The HTTP/1.1 standard is used for URL definitions.

cXML Definitions

The cXML specification defines several standard documents coming under the following general headings.

- Order Definitions
- PunchOut Definitions
- Catalog Definitions
- Subscription Management Definitions
- Message Retrieval Definitions

The cXML 1.0 specification goes into great detail in defining all of the cXML documents, but we will briefly discuss the object of each of the above sections.

Order Definitions

This consists of the `OrderRequest` and `OrderResponse` documents, where `OrderRequest` is like a purchase order and `OrderResponse` is like a suppliers purchase order acknowlegdement.

PunchOut Definitions

The `PunchOut` documents within cXML allow shoppers to view and add items from a remote catalog to their current shopping cart without losing its state. The `PunchOutSetUp` document allows users to identify themselves to the remote system and setup the ability to redirect the current session to a remote browsing session.

This effectively allows us to support partners distributed catalogs without multiple purchase orders for each system.

Catalog Definitions

The cXML `Catalog` definitions contain the three elements `Supplier`, `Index` and `Contract` to describe persisted or cached data on a shoppers system. The buyer uses `Supplier` elements to get more information about the supplier such as address contact and ordering details.

`Index` elements describe goods and services inventory information about the supplier. Finally, `Contract` elements described flexible aspects of the contract between the consumer and the supplier, such as the cost of a particular item.

Subscription Management Definitions

The Subscription Management definitions allow an intermediate, 3rd party, to manage supplier information and catalog contents between a buyer and a supplier.

Message Retrieval Definitions

One of the more interesting definitions, this section describes how a system can queue messages when the server is unable to accept messages directly, perhaps due to a firewall or proxy scenario.

cXML Definition Documents

In addition to the above definitions, there are a series of documents which comprise the cXML standard and under which the above documents reside. These are available as `.mod` files in the cXML download and specify how to develop and deploy cXML 1.0-compliant applications.

These documents are listed with a brief summary on their purpose. Consult the cXML documentation for more specific information.

- `cxml.dtd`
  The DTD upon which all cXML documents are constructed.
- `Base.mod`
  Defines the basic elements used to build higher level constructs in cXML.
- `Common.mod`
  The common types used throughout the cXML definiton.
- `Contract.mod`
  A contact between a supplier and a list of items.
- `Index.mod`
  Allows us to update the list of goods and/or services which are being handled by the system.
- `Item.mod`
  Contains detailed information about an item.
- `Pending.mod`
  The data elements being carried back in the response. These are fully formed cXML messages being carried through the Request/Response channel.
- `Subscription.mod`
  Indicates that something changed in a buyer's content subscription. Since this is a Message, it can come at any time – no explicit Request needs to be send first.
- `Supplier.mod`
  Supplier of goods and services. Includes a list of SupplierIDs which indentify the Supplier.
- `Transaction.mod`
  Definition of transactional elements available within cXML.
- `Transport.mod`
  Describes the envelope transport used with cXML.

DoD's CatXML

The Department of Defense's Joint Program Electronic Commerce Program Office (JECPO), in support of DoD part vendors, is currently developing CatXML for the seamless electronic exchange of distributed catalog query and response for suppliers. It is an example of a large organization that is using cXML, which is key to CatXML's design. CatXML, defines how vendors can put themselves online and sell goods and services through collaborative catalogs. Collaborative catalogs are the current generation of catalogs based on highly scalable architectures that allows suppliers to sell their wares to very large procurement communities, such as portals. JECPO's objective with CatXML is to define an exchange specification that can make it easy for part and catalog vendors to integrate with today's generation of electronic commerce mechanisms.

Companies with on-line electronic catalogs are eligible to participate in the DoD EMall, and will be issued a blanket purchase agreement that allows companies to display their products and services to the DoD EMall customer. The customer can order items from the EMall using their VISA or Government purchase cards

That concludes our look at cXML as an example of a language that has been developed for use by vertical industries. So, we should move on to look at horizontal industries.

First Steps – Horizontal Industries

Today efforts are under way to apply EDI, XML, collaborative repositories, and agent technology to create XML/EDI frameworks that simplify the processes involved. This section will provide an overview of how eBusiness applications will use these frameworks.

ASC X12

At the last trimester X12 meeting of 1999 a specific XML steering committee was established to address issues regarding the possible impact XML would have on X12 standards and process at all levels. The work would extend the Technical Report Type 1; *X12-XML: Representation of X12 Semantics in XML Syntax*, from the X12C Subcommittee on XML, called X12CTG3.

For more information see: http://www.disa.org/x12/x12c/X12CTG3/x12ctg3.htm

The focus of the X12CTG3 subcommittee has been on the constructs required to preserve the semantics of the rich X12 standard – and not simply duplicate X12 in XML syntax. This also gives something to the X12 implementers for further experimentation, such as data transformations. In defining a methodology, the process uncovered that a simple conversion of X12 to XML/EDI isn't the most effective solution, and that any work done should feed into the next version of X12 itself. As expected, those looking for a simple algorithm were disappointed in the findings. The exercise X12CTG3 has underway has given X12 a list of lessons learned which needs to be adopted to make the X12 standard more agile.

For instance, too many of the semantics in an X12 message are buried in code lists. An example of this is where the `MEA` (measure segment) in an X12 message gives a weight – but a weight of what? If it is preceded by an `HL` (heirachical loop) segment the contents of the `HL03` element would inform the application that it was the weight of the shipment or truck or box.

Much work was put into what gets moved forward into XML/EDI, and the approach that makes the most sense. Little discussion took place on defining specific metadata container or additional routing and control mechanisms. The thinking was that these areas are immature and would be flushed out on the second go around.

The following is the example given in the technical report of an XML representation of the 850 Purchase Order transaction set, with parts omitted for clarity and brevity. Here is the X12 designation:

```
BEG*00*SA*1513339**19990621~
N1*ST**11*001786664W101~
PO1**10*CA*24.48**UI*XYZ05879000032~
PO4*72~
```

And here is the version in XML syntax:

```
<PurchaseOrder X12:PROMOTEDQUAL="Original" >
<Header>
     <BEG-BegSegPurchaseOrder>
          ...
     </BEG-BegSegPurchaseOrder >

     <Loop-H310-N1-Name X12:PROMOTEDQUAL="ShipTo">
          ...
     </Loop-H310-N1-Name >

     <Detail>
            < Loop-PO1-BaselineItemData >
                 ...
            </Loop-PO1-BaselineItemData >

            < Loop-PO1-BaselineItemData >
                 ...
            </Loop-PO1-BaselineItemData >
     </Detail>
</Header>

< Summary>
      < CTT-TransTotals>
        ...
      < AMT-MonetaryAmt>
        ...
</Summary>
```

So, what about the other main EDI language, UN/EDIFACT?

XML-EDIFACT

The XML-EDIFACT effort is an effort to experiment with different approaches in bringing UN/EDIFACT to XML/EDI. One of the outcomes from this initiative is a free perl module; **XML::Edifact** available under GNU general public license, able to translate any well formed UN/EDIFACT message into human readable and valid XML and vice versa, by using the original words from the UN/EDIFACT batch directories as markup and the defining document as namespace.

Below is a message fragment for line item:

```
<?xml version="1.0"?>
<!DOCTYPE teleord:message
  SYSTEM "http://www.xml-edifact.org/LIB/xml-edifact-03/teleord.dtd">

<!-- XML message produced by edi2xml.pl (c) Kraehe@Bakunin.North.De -->

<teleord:message
  xmlns:teleord='http://www.xml-edifact.org/LIB/xml-edifact-03/teleord.rdf'
  xmlns:trsd='http://www.xml-edifact.org/LIB/xml-edifact-03/trsd.rdf'
  xmlns:trcd='http://www.xml-edifact.org/LIB/xml-edifact-03/trcd.rdf'
  xmlns:tred='http://www.xml-edifact.org/LIB/xml-edifact-03/tred.rdf'
  xmlns:uncl='http://www.xml-edifact.org/LIB/xml-edifact-03/uncl.rdf'
  xmlns:anxs='http://www.xml-edifact.org/LIB/xml-edifact-03/anxe.rdf'
  xmlns:anxc='http://www.xml-edifact.org/LIB/xml-edifact-03/anxc.rdf'
  xmlns:anxe='http://www.xml-edifact.org/LIB/xml-edifact-03/anxe.rdf'
  xmlns:unsl='http://www.xml-edifact.org/LIB/xml-edifact-03/unsl.rdf'
  xmlns:unknown='http://www.xml-edifact.org/LIB/xml-edifact-03/unknown.rdf' >

<!-- SEGMENT LIN+16 -->
<trsd:line.item>
    <tred:line.item.number>16</tred:line.item.number>
</trsd:line.item>

<!-- SEGMENT PIA+5+1861081383:IB -->
<trsd:additional.product.id>
  <tred:product.id.function.qualifier uncl:code="4347:5">Product identification
  </tred:product.id.function.qualifier>
  <trcd:item.number.identification>
     <tred:item.number>1861081383</tred:item.number>
        <tred:item.number.type.coded uncl:code="7143:IB">ISBN (International
                          Standard Book Number)</tred:item.number.type.coded>
  </trcd:item.number.identification>
</trsd:additional.product.id>

<!-- SEGMENT IMD+F+BPU+:::CASS -->
<teleord:item.description>
  <tred:item.description.type.coded uncl:code="7077:F">Free-form
  </tred:item.description.type.coded>
  <teleord:item.characteristic.coded teleord:code="7081:BPU">Book Publisher
  </teleord:item.characteristic.coded>
  <trcd:item.description>
  <tred:item.description>CASS</tred:item.description>
  </trcd:item.description>
  </teleord:item.description>
```

```
<!-- SEGMENT QTY+21:3 -->
<trsd:quantity>
  <trcd:quantity.details>
    <tred:quantity.qualifier uncl:code="6063:21">Ordered quantity
    </tred:quantity.qualifier>
    <tred:quantity>3</tred:quantity>
  </trcd:quantity.details>
</trsd:quantity>

<!-- SEGMENT PRI+AAA:12.5:SR:DPR::LBR -->
<trsd:price.details>
  <trcd:price.information>
    <tred:price.qualifier uncl:code="5125:AAA">Calculation net
    </tred:price.qualifier>
    <tred:price>12.5</tred:price>
    <tred:price.type.coded uncl:code="5375:SR">Suggested retail
    </tred:price.type.coded>
    <tred:price.type.qualifier uncl:code="5387:DPR">DiscountPrice
    </tred:price.type.qualifier>
<tred:measure.unit.qualifier>LBR</tred:measure.unit.qualifier>
  </trcd:price.information>
</trsd:price.details>

</teleord:message>
```

For more information visit: http://www.xml-edifact.org

Electronic Business XML Working Group (ebXML)

At the beginning of December 1999 a joint 18-month effort of the United Nations body for Trade Facilitation and Electronic Business (UN/CEFACT) and the Organization for the Advancement of Structured Information Standards (OASIS) was launched to initiate a worldwide project to standardize XML business specifications. UN/CEFACT and OASIS have established the Electronic Business XML Working Group to develop a technical framework that will enable XML to be utilized in a consistent manner for the exchange of all electronic business data. The results of the Electronic Business XML Working Group will be placed in the public domain on XML.org and UNECE/CEFACT sites.

In addition to "Marketing, Awareness & Education", the following are the proposed technical project teams:

ebXML Requirements – Short and long term objectives:

Business Process Methodology – Framework and interoperability; model interchange (UML to XML schemas and vice versa), and design patterns for ebXML. IBM's 'XMI Toolkit', available from http://www.alphaworks.ibm.com/tech/xmitoolkit/ supports sharing and conversions between Java, Rational Rose, UML models; and includes an API to read and write XMI 1.0 files is a good harbinger of work in this area.

Transport/Routing and packaging - Enveloping for routing of message content, security, guaranteed message delivery, batch processing, related messages in a collection, quality of service. The deliverables are the technical rules and guidelines to eBusiness.

Core Components – Use existing semantics in some uniform way, reuse/compose existing elements/components, extensions of existing messages to cover new applications, identify core or horizontal data semantics. The deliverables are ebXML and EDIFACT Working Group D group message design rules

Technical Architecture – semantic equivalents between data elements, transformation of semantics, and internationalisation. The deliverables include ebXML and EDIFACT Working Group D group mapping design rules and Guideline to transform EDIFACT messages into XML messages.

Registry and Repository – Versioning, tool to tool, repository to repository, tool to repository and vice versa). The deliverables are the registry architecture, physical repositories, and interoperability guidelines.

Technical Coordination & Support – Maintain the ebXML web site, certification, test beds, developer starter kits and publish software compliance criteria.

The confirmed meeting attendees are from other XML initiatives, industry groups, standards organizations, vendor consortiums and individual enterprises. This mix of participants is the 'must have' if we are to have a chance for consensus at all levels for interoperability.

As we did in the earlier section on implementing solutions for horizontal industries, we will now take a more detailed look at one other effort: Microsoft's BizTalk.

First Horizontal Steps

The **BizTalk framework** was started by Microsoft, working with many major organizations spanning a wide range of industries, intent on guiding the creation and maintenance of XML data schemas to allow electronic commerce and application integration. These schemas are hosted at http://www.biztalk.org/ within the BizTalk library, and are available to anyone who wishes to use them to allow their systems to be integrated with other systems using the same schema. The schemas are effectively "read-only", so that once you start using a particular schema to integrate your systems it cannot be changed – although using versioning, schemas can be updated as required.

The goal is to create a library of schemas available for every industry, thereby allowing maximum reuse and interoperability with a minimum of offline communication. Trading partners should be able to exchange messages provided they adhere to schemas posted to the library. In theory, a prospective partner could prepare for data exchange with an organization simply by complying with the schema that organization posted to the library. No prior communication between the two parties would be required. Although, in practice, some prior communication offline will likely be required to establish trading agreements. The library provides a practical benefit however, in that it advertises the message schemas partners require for communications and helps prospective trading partners prepare for document exchange without lengthy coordination with a partner.

Unlike traditional efforts such as EDI, the BizTalk Framework makes no effort to impose business semantics on trading partners. While it does impose restrictions on tags, it is only so far as they promote message exchange. The core content of a BizTalk message is left up to the trading partners. This allows a BizTalk schema designer the freedom to specify his data exchange requirements at whatever level of detail his business requires.

The BizTalk library already contains schemas that are oriented to low-level exchanges, e.g., individual purchase orders, as well as high-level, business-specific content such as architectural construction. Each schema in the library is associated with a sample message and human-readable documentation. The intent is to permit a prospective trading partner to ready his software for the new schema without involving the schema poster. In addition to being a schema repository, BizTalk.org also provides a mechanism whereby you can register your interest in a given schema. This is a dual-purpose capability: you'll be notified of changes to the schema, and it also gives repository browsers an indication of the popularity and acceptance of a given schema by showing a usage count.

Now we have had an overview of BizTalk, let's look at the specification.

The BizTalk Tag Specification

The BizTalk framework tag specification is, at the time of writing, at version 1.0. Schemas posted to the library use Microsoft's XML Data-Reduced Schema (XML-DR) which is a cut down version of the XML Data proposal for schemas in XML syntax. This implementation tracked the W3C schema draft at the time it was introduced early in 1999. Since then, the W3C Schema effort has evolved and diverged somewhat from XML-DR. It is important to note, however, that the BizTalk team has made it clear that when the XML Schema specification is formalized and becomes a recommendation by the W3C, BizTalk will use this standard. Although schemas written to the XML-DR implementation will be supported for an indefinite period and tools will be provided to ease the transition.

The specification covers the following:

- Document Structure
- Document Identity
- Conforming to the BizTalk framework
- Document Routing Information

Goals and Current Constraints of the Specification

The BizTalk specification has the goal of allowing companies, businesses or developers to make use of the tags to interchange information without having to standardize on programming technologies or distributed computing technologies. It accomplishes this goal by requiring a minimal set of tags on all interchange messages. These tags are designed to facilitate the identification and routing of BizTalk messages.

Embedded within the required tags is an element that will serve as the container for user-defined XML documents. Organizations are thus able to design document types that adequately describe the desired business interchange. Because the design of messages is open-ended, organizations must have a means of discovering the schemas of their trading partners – and it is the public library of message schemas at the BizTalk.org web site that offers this service. This allows trading partners to search the library for schemas posted by their trading partners. Should developers wish to build upon existing schemas, they are free to do so, thereby promoting commonality within industries.

The common tags and schema library help solve the problem of establishing a common basis for communication. What is left is the task of putting two or more applications in communication with one another. We can use open protocols for message transport such as HTTP, SMTP and message queuing software to exchange BizTalk documents between computers, and these cover the most common forms of interprocess communication. They are certainly sufficient to deliver XML documents on a loosely coupled basis between processes. The combination of a nearly universal syntax – XML – and a readily discovered vocabulary (through the schema library), as well as loose, asynchronous communications provides a basis for communication sufficient for the automated exchange of business information. While slow by computing standards, such exchange is many orders of magnitude faster than manual business communication.

Document Structure

All documents and messages use document schemas written according to the XML-Data Reduced format devised by Microsoft and implemented in their MSXML parser. A generalized structure consisting of a set of mandatory elements is defined by the BizTalk Tag specification, all conforming to the World Wide Web Consortium XML 1.0 standard. The mandatory elements have the intention of providing a means to establish the identity of documents as well as the routing for the document via a set of definitions, codes and structure.

A document conforming to the BizTalk specification can have each of the following sections:

- The BizTalk document root – mandatory
- The BizTalk header element – optional
- The document body element – mandatory

The following code shows a generic sample for a BizTalk document:

```
<?xml version="1.0"?>
<bizTalk_1 xmlns:="urn:schemas-biztalk-org/biztalk_1.xml">
   <header>
      <delivery>
         <message>
            <messageID>12346</messageID>
            <sent>1999-12-31T23:59:59-05:00</sent>
            <subject>Generic Sample</subject>
         </message>
         <to>
            <address>http://www.generic_co.com/recv.asp</address>
            <state>
               <referenceID>1</referenceID>
               <handle>1</handle>
               <process>receiveProcess</process>
            </state>
         </to>
         <from>
            <address>
              http://www.bland_co.com/send.asp
            </address>
```

```
            <state>
               <referenceID>23</referenceID>
               <handle>2</handle>
               <process>orderProcess</process>
            </state>
         </from>
      </delivery>
      <manifest>
         <document>
            <name>bland_co_order</name>
            <description>Bland Sample Order Document</description>
         </document>
         <attachment>
            <index>1</index>
            <filename>whatIwant.jpg</filename>
            <description>picture of what I want</description>
            <type>jpg</type>
         </attachment>
      </manifest>
   </header>
   <body >
      <bland_co_order
            xmlns:= "x-schema:http://www.bland_co.com/schemas/order.xml">
         -- Your XML document data goes here --
      </bland_co_order>
   </body>
</bizTalk_1>
```

This sample may seem imposing at first glance. As we shall see, however, it consists of header information and your message. The header, which is responsible for the complexity in the sample shown above, actually imposes few restrictions on the message originator. BizTalk headers provide a number of optional elements to convey information to the message recipient. The values contained in those elements is left up to the implementing applications. The sample depicted uses all the optional elements. Depending on your specific application needs, your documents may be considerably simpler.

Two interesting features of the BizTalk tag specification should be noted. First, although XML-DR schemas support datatypes beyond those of XML 1.0, the BizTalk 1.0 schema does not make use of strong typing. Microsoft's XML parser, MSXML, supports these types in the version shipped with Internet Explorer 5.0, but the framework is explicitly platform independent. Avoiding these types makes the schema accessible to non-Microsoft platforms. Of course, the schema implementation itself is platform-specific, but this is unavoidable. Once the W3C issues an XML Schema recommendation, strong data types will be accessible to all XML platforms. Another interesting feature is that none of the BizTalk elements have attributes associated with them, with the exception of namespace declarations. All information except the namespaces in release 1.0 of the BizTalk framework is communicated through XML elements.

The BizTalk Document Root

All BizTalk documents must be enclosed in the following XML root element:

```
<bizTalk_1 xmlns:="urn:schemas-biztalk.org:bizTalk/biztalk_1.xml">
</bizTalk_1>
```

This element defines the BizTalk namespace and specifies the document as being a BizTalk version 1.0 document using elements from the BizTalk namespace. The namespace identifier shown is the well-known URN mandated for BizTalk 1.0, so a client could validate the document against this if necessary. Within this root element, the message header and the body elements must appear.

The Document Header

A BizTalk compliant message can consist of the document root and the document body. Before we get to the document body, however, let's look at the optional header element. The purpose of the header is to provide a variety of information that facilitates the routing, handling, and processing of the document. If a header element is used, it appears exactly once.

The header element may contain the following elements:

Element	Appears	Purpose
delivery	0 or once	Describes the message and its routing
manifest	0 or once	Describes what the message contains and what attachments are associated with the message

The delivery element describes the message in general terms, where it came from, and where it is going. The manifest element describes the contents of the message and any related files. Most of the information contained within a header's elements are intended for use by the sending and receiving applications. Most elements contained within the header are placeholders so far as the framework is concerned; they provide information to applications, but serve no purpose so far as the framework itself is concerned.

The manifest element describes the contents of the document in more detail. It provides elements for naming the document and associating one or more non-XML files with the message as attachments.

The delivery Element

This element identifies the message, who sent it, and who is to receive it. Here is the shell of the delivery element with its immediate child elements:

```
<delivery>
   <message>. . .</message>
   <to>. . .</to>
   <from>. . .</from>
</delivery>
```

More formally, the following elements are permitted within the delivery element:

Element	Appears	Purpose
message	once	Provides an identifier, timestamp, and human-readable label for the message
to	once	Provides the source URL and internal state information for the receiving process
from	once	Provides the source URL and internal state information for the sending process

The `message` element is useful for tracking sequences of BizTalk messages. The framework itself makes no use of the information contained within this element. It does, however, facilitate the construction of business processes involving multiple BizTalk messages or the implementation of auditing features in BizTalk-enabled processes. Here is the content model for the `message` element:

Element	Appears	Purpose
`messageID`	once	Sequential message number of GUID assigned by the application
`sent`	once	Timestamp generated at the time of message origination
`subject`	0 or once	Human-readable label describing the type of message

Note that while strong data types are not used in the BizTalk framework schema, the format of the `sent` element should be in accordance with the `dateTime.tz` data type of XML-DR (a subset of ISO 8601 format), i.e., YYYY-MM-DDTHH:MM:SS[+|-]HH:MM. Here, once again, is our sample message element:

```
<message>
   <messageID>12346</messageID>
   <sent>1999-12-31T23:59:59-05:00</sent>
   <subject>Generic Sample</subject>
</message>
```

In this case, the message identifier is a sequential number assigned by the message originator. This is useful for properly ordering a sequence of BizTalk messages or for developing an audit trail. The message was sent one second before midnight on December 31, 1999 in the time zone five hours behind Greenwich Mean Time (U.S. East Coast). The `subject` element, which is completely arbitrary so far as BizTalk is concerned, is used to identify the type of message when debugging a process.

The `to` and `from` elements share the same content model. This consists of the sending (or receiving) process' URL and a `state` element. The `state` element provides three items that an application can use to uniquely associate the message with some internal state information. Before getting into details, consider the content model for the `to` and `from` elements:

Element	Appears	Purpose
`address`	once	URL of the sending (receiving) process
`state`	0 or once	Holder of information used to associate a message with some state information held by the sending or receiving process.

The `address` element is a URI. It must be sufficient to denote the logical address of the message, but it need not be a URL. That is, given a logical URI such as `trading-partner-supplies:purchasing`, a BizTalk server implementation might map that into the URL specified for the purchasing process of the trading partner named by the URI. More commonly, the URL will be known and supplied by the sending process.

State information is used when a given business exchange consists of a series of related BizTalk messages. In such cases, a process will need to be able to associate a given message instance with some internal data, much as an Active Server Pages (ASP) Session variable can contain a list of properties. It is difficult to prescribe a generic mechanism for doing this, but BizTalk provides three levels of specificity in its content model:

Element	Appears	Purpose
`referenceID`	once	Unique identifier for the business interchange
`handle`	0 or once	Refines `referenceID` to specify a specific part of an interchange, e.g., step in a work flow
`process`	0 or once	Refines handle to provide a context for the handle, e.g., a security context.

Now that we have the entire contents of the `delivery` element, let's revisit the sample:

```
<delivery>
   <message>
      <messageID>12346</messageID>
      <sent>1999-12-31T23:59:59-05:00</sent>
      <subject>Generic Sample</subject>
   </message>
   <to>
      <address>http://www.generic_co.com/recv.asp</address>
      <state>
         <referenceID>1</referenceID>
         <handle>1</handle>
         <process>receiveProcess</process>
      </state>
   </to>
   <from>
      <address>http://www.bland_co.com/send.asp</address>
      <state>
         <referenceID>23</referenceID>
         <handle>2</handle>
         <process>orderProcess</process>
      </state>
   </from>
</delivery>
```

We've already worked through the `message` element, so let's focus on the `to` and `from` elements. The message, from which this delivery element is taken, is generated by a process implemented in an ASP page created by the Bland Company and hosted at `http://www.bland_co.com/send.asp`. The state information associated with this message in that process is denoted by the `orderProcess` module, in step 2 of the interchange, denoted by `referenceID` 23. This will mean nothing to the recipient, but can and should be copied by the receiving process into any reply message. The recipient of this message is the Generic Company process implemented by another ASP page at `http://www.generic_co.com/recv.asp`. This message is part of an extended series of BizTalk messages, so that process is keeping some state information alive for us. The `referenceID`, `handle`, and `process` shown allow the recipient to retrieve the proper local data for use in processing this message.

As you can see, the complexity of the delivery element in your BizTalk messages will depend on the complexity of your business interchange. Simple exchanges can omit the `state` elements.

The manifest Element

This element provides a receiving application with clues to the content of the transmission. The element itself is optional and is used when multiple documents must be associated with the interchange. There are two kinds of documents that may be transmitted: BizTalk messages and non-XML attachments. Not surprisingly, the content model for `manifest` has two child elements:

Element	Appears	Purpose
`document`	One or more	Describes a single XML message included in the interchange
`attachment`	0 or more	Describes a single non-BizTalk message included in the interchange.

You might have more than one BizTalk message (that is to say more than one instance of the part of the interchange written in your chosen vocabulary) within the `<body>` in a single interchange – if the business workflow semantics are such that more than one XML message must be bundled into the `<body>` of the BizTalk message. Such a BizTalk message is termed a **boxcar document**. Our sample is not a boxcar document. Suppose, however, that our sample message was intended to order supplies for a business meeting. It might be desirable in such a situation to package all the related purchase orders into a single BizTalk message. In that case, we would want a boxcar document composed of multiple purchase orders described by `document` elements. Here is the content model for that element:

Element	Appears	Purpose
`name`	once	Element name of the root of the included document
`description`	0 or once	Human readable description of the document

An attachment, by contrast, is an associated file that is not included in the body of the BizTalk document. This is useful for binary information such as pictures or data files in a proprietary format. Multi-part MIME transmissions are generally used to send documents with attachments. Here is the content model for the `attachment` element:

Element	Appears	Purpose
`index`	once	Identifier denoting this attachment
`filename`	once	Name of the attached file
`description`	0 or once	Human-readable description of the attachment
`type`	0 or once	Keyword identifying the document type

Let's take another look at the manifest element in our sample:

```
<manifest>
   <document>
      <name>bland_co_order</name>
      <description>Bland Sample Order Document</description>
   </document>
   <attachment>
      <index>1</index>
      <filename>whatIwant.jpg</filename>
      <description>picture of what I want</description>
      <type>jpg</type>
   </attachment>
</manifest>
```

In this case, the Bland Company is sending an order document in the body of the BizTalk message. That document has a root element named bland_co_order. It has a single attachment, a jpeg file named whatIwant.jpg.

The Document Body

The document body is mandatory. This is where schema designers get involved. You will need to develop schemas for your business processes, if there are no existing ones, or adapt them if they are not suitable for your purposes. XML documents written to conform to these schemas are included as child elements of the body element. The header element was needed to get the document to the destination with any associated data identified, but the body element is the reason why the message was sent in the first place. The body element has one or more child elements. Each child element is a document written according to a BizTalk schema. A boxcar document will have more than one such child element. The schema developed for the interchange determines the content of these elements.

Here is the body from our example:

```
<body >
   <bland_co_order
         xmlns:= "x-schema:http://www.bland_co.com/schemas/order.xml">
      -- Your XML document data goes here --
   </bland_co_order>
</body>
```

As we saw in the manifest for this message, our sample contains a single document rooted by the bland_co_order element. We've declared a namespace to allow BizTalk to validate the body. Normally, you would expect to find the schema in the BizTalk library, but the Bland Company has chosen to host the schema on its own server.

A BizTalk Document for Wrox Books

We will now define a sample XML document conforming to the rules of version 0.81 of the BizTalk framework. We will first define a document schema conforming to the XML Data - Reduced Schema (XML-DR) that could be stored in the BizTalk library for companies wishing to transmit data about books.

The schema could be used to request information on a specific book for a consumer on a commerce web site or from a remote server, as well as allow the administrator or a remote server to update or submit information about a book. The schema is shown below:

```
<?xml version="1.0"?>
<Schema name="BookInfo"
   xmlns="urn:schemas-microsoft-com:xml-data"
   xmlns:dt="urn:schemas-microsoft-com:datatypes">

<!--A book has a cost defined by both a currency and price-->
<ElementType name="Currency" content="textOnly" model="open" dt:type="string"/>
<ElementType name="Price" content="textOnly" model="open" dt:type="number"/>
<ElementType name="BookCost" content="eltOnly" model="closed">
   <element type="Currency"/>
   <element type="Price"/>
</ElementType>

<!--Information about the book-->
<ElementType name="Title" content="textOnly" model="open" dt:type="string"/>
<ElementType name="Author" content="textOnly" model="open" dt:type="string"/>
<ElementType name="ISBN" content="textOnly" model="open" dt:type="number"/>
<ElementType name="Subject" content="textOnly" model="open" dt:type="string"/>
<ElementType name="PubDate" content="textOnly" model="open" dt:type="date"/>
<ElementType name="RefURL" content="textOnly" model="open" dt:type="uri"/>
<ElementType name="TitleData" content="eltOnly" model="open">
   <element type="Title"/>
   <element type="Author" minOccurs="1" maxOccurs="*"/>
   <element type="ISBN"/>
   <element type="Subject"/>
   <element type="PubDate"/>
   <element type="RefURL"/>
</ElementType>

<!--Genaral Information about the book-->
<ElementType name="BookNumber" content="textOnly" model="open" dt:type="string"/>
<ElementType name="Summary" content="textOnly" model="open" dt:type="string"/>
<ElementType name="BookInfo" content="eltOnly" model="open">
   <element type="BookNumber"/>
   <element type="Description"/>
   <element type="TitleData"/>
   <element type="BookCost"/>
</ElementType>

</Schema>
```

Let's take a closer look at this schema. All BizTalk framework documents must use the current XML-DR Schema draft, and so we set the namespaces of the Microsoft XML-DR implementation as well as the schema datatypes which are heavily used throughout BizTalk documents.

```
<?xml version="1.0"?>
<Schema name="BookInfo"
   xmlns="urn:schemas-microsoft-com:xml-data"
   xmlns:dt="urn:schemas-microsoft-com:datatypes">
```

> *Note that, while the BizTalk specification avoids datatyping, there is nothing that prevents datatyping in the body of the message.*

Our published document should allow the cost of the book to be declared so that customers and resellers can determine its price. We first define a currency string to state the currency that the cost will be listed in – this could be potentially an enumeration of currencies if desired. We then define an element to contain the price of the book as a number type.

We then declare an `ElementType` named `<BookCost>` which will contain the elements `<Currency>` and `<Price>` and state that this is all that will be able to come under this element by setting the model to closed.

```
<!--A book has a cost defined by both a currency and price-->
<ElementType name="Currency" content="textOnly" model="open" dt:type="string"/>
<ElementType name="Price" content="textOnly" model="open" dt:type="number"/>
<ElementType name="BookCost" content="eltOnly" model="closed">
    <element type="Currency"/>
    <element type="Price"/>
</ElementType>
```

The next important part of our schema is to define a section for carrying details about the book. We define an `ElementType` of `<Title>` as a string for the book titles, as well as `<Author>`, `<ISBN>`, and `<Subject>` elements, the use of which is self-explanatory.

```
<!--Information about the book-->
<ElementType name="Title" content="textOnly" model="open" dt:type="string"/>
<ElementType name="Author" content="textOnly" model="open" dt:type="string"/>
<ElementType name="ISBN" content="textOnly" model="open" dt:type="number"/>
<ElementType name="Subject" content="textOnly" model="open" dt:type="string"/>
```

An element for the date of publication is declared using the date schema datatype, which uses the ISO 8601 format. This means the date should be specified in the format `YYYY-MM-DD`.

```
<ElementType name="PubDate" content="textOnly" model="open" dt:type="date"/>
```

A reference URL is a common addition when defining a book, and we use the `<RefURL>` element to allow for this, defined as a datatype of `uri` – a Universal Resource Identifier.

```
<ElementType name="RefURL" content="textOnly" model="open" dt:type="uri"/>
```

We then define a parent `<TitleData>` element to contain these elements. Notice that a book may have multiple authors, so we have allowed many `<Author>` elements.

```
<ElementType name="TitleData" content="eltOnly" model="open">
   <element type="Title"/>
   <element type="Author" minOccurs="1" maxOccurs="*"/>
   <element type="ISBN"/>
   <element type="Subject"/>
   <element type="PubDate"/>
   <element type="RefURL"/>
</ElementType>
```

To complete our document schema, we define a root element called `<BookInfo>` which is defined to contain our previously defined elements, as well as two new elements called `<BookNumber>`, to hold an internal ID of the book, and `<Summary>` to contain some overview detail on the book.

```
<!--Genaral Information about the book-->
<ElementType name="BookNumber" content="textOnly" model="open" dt:type="string"/>
<ElementType name="Summary" content="textOnly" model="open" dt:type="string"/>
<ElementType name="BookInfo" content="eltOnly" model="open">
   <element type="BookNumber"/>
   <element type="Summary"/>
   <element type="TitleData"/>
   <element type="BookCost"/>
</ElementType>
</Schema>
```

So, an XML document instance that conforms to this schema may look like the following:

```
<?xml version="1.0"?>
<BookInfo xmlns="x-schema:books.xml">
<BookNumber>423423</BookNumber>
<Summary>
   This book details Site Server Commerce 3.0 and can be used by beginners and
   experienced developers alike.
</Summary>
<TitleData>
   <Title>Professional Site Server Commerce 3.0</Title>
   <Author>Marco Tabini</Author>
   <Author>Steven Livingstone</Author>
   <ISBN>983479387</ISBN>
   <Subject>Commerce</Subject>
   <PubDate>1999-11-20</PubDate>
   <RefURL>http://www.wrox.com/</RefURL>
</TitleData>
<BookCost>
   <Currency>US$</Currency>
   <Price>59.76</Price>
</BookCost>
</BookInfo>
```

To be able to transport our document according to the rules defined in the BizTalk schema, there are a few additional tags we must add to our instance as we discussed earlier in the section. The BizTalk instance is shown below. Notice how we wrap our document schema within the BizTalk tags and define our routing details.

```
<biztalk_1 xmlns="urn:schemas-biztalk-org:biztalk/biztalk-1.0.xml">
<header>
   <header>
      <delivery>
         <message>
            <messageID>1</messageID>
            <sent>1999-12-31T18:24:00-05:00</sent>
            <subject>Book Information</subject>
         </message>
```

```
            <to>
               <address>http://www.deltabiz.com/biztalk/book.asp</address>
            </to>
            <from>
               <address>http://www.citix.com/biztalk/info.asp</address>
            </from>
         </delivery>
         <manifest>
            <document>
               <name>BookInfo</name>
               <description>Book Summary Information</description>
            </document>
         </manifest>
      </header>
   </header>
   <body>
      <BookInfo xmlns="urn:schemas-biztalk.org:deltabiz.com/books.xml">
         <BookNumber>423423</BookNumber>
            <Summary>
               This book details Site Server Commerce 3.0 and can be used by
               beginners and experienced developers alike.
            </Summary>
            <TitleData>
               <Title>Professional Site Server Commerce 3.0</Title>
               <Author>Marco Tabini</Author>
               <Author>Steven Livingstone</Author>
               <ISBN>983479387</ISBN>
               <Subject>Commerce</Subject>
               <PubDate>1999-11-20</PubDate>
               <RefURL>http://www.wrox.com/</RefURL>
            </TitleData>
            <BookCost>
               <Currency>US$</Currency>
               <Price>59.76</Price>
            </BookCost>
         </BookInfo>
      </body>
   </biztalk_1>
```

Note that we've omitted the state element within the `to` and `from` elements. This is a fairly simple transaction consisting of an informational reply to a request for information, so there is no interchange state information involved.

Implementing BizTalk Solutions

Currently, the BizTalk server which will work with the BizTalk framework (on the server side) is still under development, and so a Jumpstart kit has been released to allow you to work with BizTalk documents and get an idea of the power behind this kind of shared schema. It currently supports both COM and Perl implementations.

The Kit is currently in early implementation and you can encounter some problems, but it is a useful exercise to try it out. You will require certain software on your workstation, and you will need to build the tools with the build files provided. We will not be running through the entire kit due to it's size and complexity (that would require a few chapters on its own!), but an overview of it's components should give you a good start.

The Jumpstart Kit is available for free download from http://www.biztalk.org/Resources/tools.asp. *This compressed file contains instructions for building the tools and lists all the software prerequisites for the Kit.*

The BizTalk JumpStart Kit Overview

The Framework is simply a specification for the interface between two or more programs. Implementing the Framework requires a server to act as an intermediary between the programs. The server needs to receive a message from one program, examine its contents according to the tags mandated by the Framework, and route the message to the receiving application. If the Framework did not use such an intermediary server, we would be back to the current state of affairs in which all integration must be embedded in the code of the participating applications. Microsoft is indeed developing such a server, named Microsoft BizTalk Server, for the Windows platform at the time of writing (Winter 1999). Since the BizTalk Framework became active well prior to the release of BizTalk Server, it became necessary to have some sort of software for developers that would let them experiment with the Framework. This software is the BizTalk Jumpstart Kit. Under the kit, developers write application adapters to connect applications to the jumpstart server software.

While the BizTalk Server will require users to run Windows 2000, the Jumpstart Kit will work on Windows NT4.

The kit consists of the following components:

- Selector – a COM component that receives messages and routes them to the appropriate application adapter
- Timer Utility – a program that lets developers test asynchronous delivery by queuing messages for delivery at some later time
- Persistence Utility – a tool for maintaining state information that spans a work flow of several messages
- Plug-In Generator – an add-in for Visual Basic that reads a schema and generates a business object hiding the details of XML DOM manipulation from programmers
- Message Component – a COM component that hides the XML DOM details of constructing BizTalk tags from programmers
- Application Adapter project type – a project shell that helps programmers write components that integrate applications with the BizTalk Jumpstart components
- Namespace Server – an application that works like a directory of message types, matching message names to the application adapter that consumes messages of that type
- Property Manager – a configuration utility for the Jumpstart Kit

Applications use the message component and the classes generated by the plug-in generator to create BizTalk messages. The application then uses an adapter to pass the message to the selector. The selector, in turn, examines the message and determines its type. The type of message is used as a key into the table maintained by the namespace server to identify the recipient of the message. The selector, having determined the intended recipient, invokes the appropriate adapter to pass the message to the receiving application. That application then uses components to read the message. Some components – notably the Selector, Namespace Server, and Property Manager – stand in place of the equivalent BizTalk Server runtime components and are not, therefore, broadly useful to BizTalk Server users. The Timer utility is a testing tool and tightly tied to the Jumpstart Kit. The Persistence Utility could be useful, but an industrial-strength application will likely use other methods. This flow is a lightweight version of what is desired in a robust, production ready BizTalk Server. As such, the Jumpstart components are adequate to prototype BizTalk integration projects, but not sufficient for production purposes. Nevertheless, the Jumpstart Kit allows organizations to prepare for integration projects while BizTalk Server is under development.

BizTalk Server

Microsoft BizTalk Server is Microsoft's implementation of the BizTalk Framework for the Windows platform. It is a product that assists in enterprise application integration using the exchange of structured business documents through common interprocess protocols like HTTP. Like the Framework, BizTalk Server relies on the flow of structured business documents between applications. Working with BizTalk Server consists of several tasks:

- Defining structured messages formats
- Specifying the mapping between formats as required
- Organizing partners and work flow agreements
- Managing and configuring the server process

BizTalk Server uses the specifications and agreements to route documents between partners using the appropriate protocol. There is an API for BizTalk, but the server is also capable of working with unmodified legacy applications. The main advantage programmers gain from working with BizTalk Server is that most of the work needed to integrate two applications is performed by the server through configuration. This is a tremendous improvement over the current state of affairs in which the work is done by the programs themselves in code.

BizTalk Editor

The key to application integration using BizTalk is the exchange of structured messages. Whether those messages use XML or some other parsed text scheme, programmers must be able to specify the structure of messages. This is the function of BizTalk Editor. The Editor is a graphical tool that uses a tree-structure metaphor to build message specification files, or simply specifications. BizTalk Editor is influenced by database terminology, which is a reasonable approach given that much of the information used to compose messages will come from databases.

Programmers work with records and fields. A record corresponds to some object or entity, while fields are the properties of the object. This works nicely with a database-style table structure in which the rows are individual objects described by the values in the row's fields. Unlike a relational table, however, a specification can nest records within other records. This allows us to describe parent-child relationships such as are represented by a database join. The tree that represents a specification in BizTalk Editor also resembles a file directory structure, with records standing in for directories and fields replacing files.

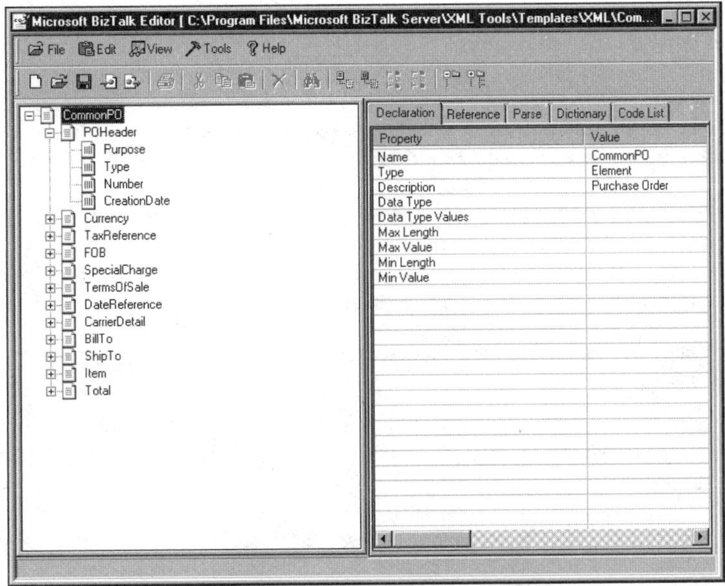

When writing an XML-based specification, a programmer may describe the records and fields in terms of the basic XML data types as well as the derived types permitted under XML – DR Schemas. All the options available in a schema are available to specification builders. BizTalk Editor permits programmers to take full advantage of XML without forcing them to become XML experts. Because the Editor allows the use of formats other than XML, the interface is carefully constructed so that XML terminology does not dominate.

Programmers need not start from scratch when defining specifications. There are initiatives underway to transform EDI commerce message formats and Health Level 7 medical message formats to XML. BizTalk Server includes a collection of basic XML template specifications for common business messages such as purchase orders and invoices. ADO, the mainstream Microsoft database access technology, allowed database recordsets to be persisted as XML since version 2.0. Programmers can use this feature to model their specifications on their existing database tables schemas.

Many legacy message formats are in forms other than XML. Both EDI formats, X12 and EDIFACT, use delimited message formats. Messages built around mainframe systems are frequently written in character delimited or fixed position formats. BizTalk Editor supports the use of these formats. To begin with, BizTalk includes specifications for both X12 and EDIFACT. A programmer can load these specifications and modify them as needed. More importantly, BizTalk Editor permits programmers to specify all aspects of delimited and positional flatfile formats. This information is retained and used by BizTalk server to properly parse an incoming message.

BizTalk Mapper

Mapping your own message formats to a partner's formats is a critical task in application integration. The BizTalk Mapper tool is supplied to help programmers deal with this task. It is a graphical editor that loads two specifications and permits a programmer to specify how the records and fields map to one another. These can be simple one-to-one relationships, 1-to-many or many-to-1 relationships, or mappings involving function or script-based conversions.

The interface consists of two panes for specifications and a mapping grid in between the specifications. The specification pane on the left contains the source specification. This is the incoming message that needs to be mapped to a new format. That new format is the destination specification, displayed in the other specification pane. The mapping grid shows relationships and any intermediate processing required to perform the mapping. Simple relationships are mapped by dragging a record or field in one specification to the appropriate record or field in the other. In such cases, BizTalk Server performs the translation from an incoming message to the corresponding local message type by copying the content of a record or field in the incoming message into the mapped record or field in the other message specification. Sometimes, though, there is no simple translation. Some contents may need to be combined to form the contents of the new field, or some processing may need to be performed on the contents of the source specification field to produce the required contents of the destination field.

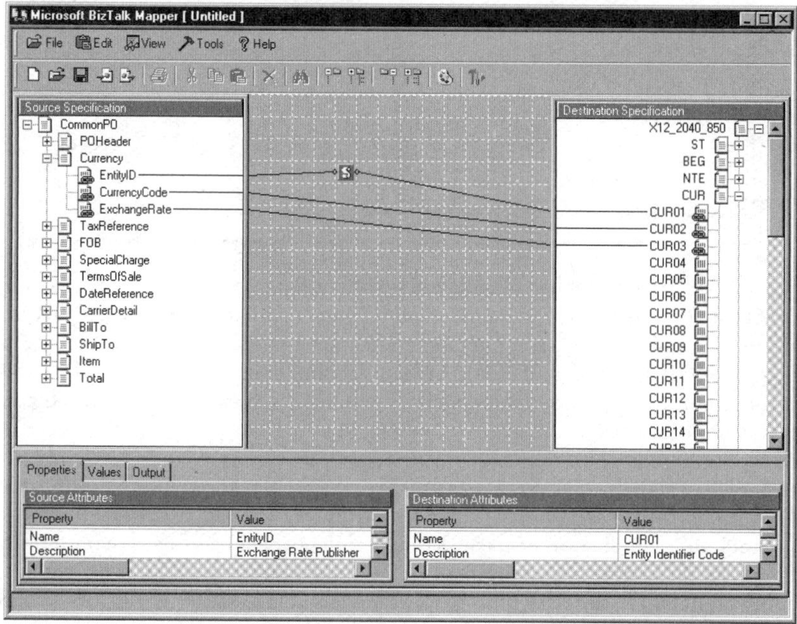

Intermediate processing can be performed in the transition between two specifications. This is accomplished through the application of pre-defined functions or operators furnished by BizTalk. More advanced processing can be provided by the user in terms of a short section of script code, dubbed a **functoid**. Functoids are implemented as script functions within the XSL style sheet, and are applied to the source fields to produce the destination field in the mapping.

When the desired mapping is complete, a programmer compiles the mapping using the Mapper. This results in an XSL style sheet. The runtime server process applies this stylesheet to an incoming message instance to produce a message instance that corresponds to the destination specification.

Configuring Workflow

In addition to designing specifications and maps, the developer of a BizTalk-style integration must configure the partners and agreements that make BizTalk work. This is done in terms of specifying the format of messages that pass between organizations and what happens when a message arrives at the server from a particular source bound for a particular destination. The tool for this is BizDesk, which lets you manage the business processing relationships that define your overall workflow.

BizTalk Server uses the agreements specified by the designer to route messages at runtime. The server stands as an intermediary between messages and their destination. Applications may be integrated with BizTalk through a COM API or by specifying a well-known protocol and location. In the latter case, BizTalk's components will monitor the protocol and location in order to intercept messages originating from legacy applications. This allows programmers to work with applications that cannot be modified.

Unfortunately, for Microsoft, they did not make it clear what BizTalk was about from the early days, as you can see, it incorporates many of the ideas we have met in this chapter already. It includes features such as the BizTalk repository of XML schemas and DTDs, it allows users to trade between parties using shared vocabularies, and will even transform the messages into another version for a recipient that requires a different vocabulary. In all it should prove to be a powerful tool that really does open up EDI style transactions to many smaller and medium sized enterprises.

Summary

In this chapter we have covered a lot of ground. From taking a quick look at how existing EDI applications work, to seeing how applications can make use of XML. We have seen that the problem of using XML in eBusiness is not just as simple as sharing a schema and sending messages in that schema between partners. For example, there will be many situations where we need to customize the DTD or other schema being used to incorporate rules for trading partners, we will not always be able to use supporting technologies (such as the DOM or XSLT) as easily as we may have hoped, and we need to consider what happens when we need to provide hooks for applications to work with.

Despite there being more problems to face than some may have hoped for, the popularity of XML in vendor's tools and software applications (that aim to achieve interoperability) has helped fuel the interest in the area, with more people getting involved in processes required for XML to be used in eBusiness.

We then went on to look at how some vertical industries have used XML to their advantage, and how their message might look. There are an ever increasing number of industries joining in the efforts to create XML schemas that will describe processes they need, as well as other things such as UML diagrams, database schemas, and software that will help users implement solutions.

Finally we looked at how some companies are helping markets communicate. Microsoft's BizTalk framework, not only helps vertical, but also horizontal and inter-company transactions, showing just how powerful XML can be in these situations. And hopefully all of the examples given look a lot easier to learn than the existing EDI solutions. Remember that the key to learning a new XML language is to have a good grasp of the basics. If you understand how to read and write XML documents, you are over half the way to understanding any new XML language for any business.

We have a good way to go in bringing millions of businesses online with eBusiness, hurdles that still need addressing and of course kinks to be worked out. In 1998 a well-respected industry analyst stated that there is a .8 chance that by the year 2002 a majority of new business exchanges will utilize XML.

The technology is well on the way to making this prediction a reality. To meet this prediction we need to focus on our vision of global eBusiness and ensure that the emerging complexity found in extended portions of new working drafts on XML do not derail the process of providing simple, consistent, light weight, easy-to-learn and broadly maintainable eBusiness systems. These e-commerce systems unlike their predecessor's, will include tight integration with languages (Java, VB, etc.), databases (All) and the operating system (Windows 2000), and in our work with XML technology we need to address *these* areas in addition to traditional exchanges.

We must participate in local area e-commerce users' groups, our industry initiatives. If you're already participating in an association and want to assure compliance to standards born now and in the future, join programs like Data Interchange Standards Association's Collaborative Services. If your company supplies XML tools, join vendor-based consortiums such as OASIS, RosettaNet or the many others. The problem for many vendors and small and medium sized enterprises is that they cannot afford to participate on a large national, let alone an international, level. Technology can assist us in this regard, tools that aid collaboration can help us leverage the little time and limited resources we have to share ideas and efforts on common across the board issues.

The bottom line is begin educating employees now, if your business nouns (information) and verbs (processes) aren't well defined. Define an enterprise architecture which is specific to your requirements, get hold of some tools, and begin now. There is no better time than now to leverage this critical technology for eBusiness.

Helpful Links:

XML/EDI Group: http://www.xmledi.org/
Bizcodes: http://www.bizcodes.org/
Data Interchange Standards Association: http://www.disa.org/
The World Wide Web Consortium (W3C): http://www.w3c.org/
Interactive Financial Exchange: http://www.ifxforum.org/
Open Travel Alliance: http://www.disa.org/opentravel.com/index.htm
RosettaNet: http://www.rosettanet.org
Electronic Business XML: http://www.ebxml.org/index.html

13

Styling XML

When communicating, humans use two main sensory channels: **hearing** and **sight**. As we have seen, XML separates data from its presentation rules. Thus, style languages for XML need to transform an original XML document into a collection of **rendition** objects for either our visual or aural perception system. As we are starting to see web applications reaching devices other than traditional browsers on desktop computers, there will be need for more flexible styling mechanisms than HTML offers. In this chapter, we will not only look at how we can style XML in traditional browsers; we will also see how we can create style sheets for other formats, such as print and aural browsers.

Style languages are strange beasts. Their underlying paradigm is **declarative** programming, where you mainly state 'what you want' instead of telling the system 'how to make the result you want to obtain'. At your disposal, you have a plethora of tools, some based on proprietary languages like Balise or Omnimark, and others based on standardized specifications like Cascading Style Sheets (CSS), eXtensible Stylesheet Language (XSL) or Document Style Semantic and Specification Language (DSSSL).

In this chapter, we will explore XML rendition or styling in two different style languages:

- CSS
- XSL

We will also take a brief look at DSSSL and Omnimark at the end of the chapter, as they are both used with XML. CSS and XSL are products of the W3C, and DSSSL is the product of the International Standards Organization (ISO). Meanwhile, Omnimark is a proprietary language, although it is freely available for download on the Web. While we are looking at XSL, we will see how it can be used to transform XML documents into HTML, VOXML, or XSL formatting objects (for print purposes). VOXML is the product of the VOXML consortium dedicated to the creation of voice browsers – if you are wondering why we might need this, just imagine your car radio or your cellular phone as a potential voice browser. But, before we take a look at any of these languages, let's have a look at some of the underlying theory.

Rendition location

The actual Web architecture is based on a client-server system. HTML browsers dominated the first wave of web clients, but now the second wave of web clients is reaching the market. These new kind of browsers are XML browsers: Internet Explorer (version 5 and up) is an XML document browser. The Mozilla (next generation Netscape browser being developed in the Open Source community) project is also creating an XML browser.

Rendition of an XML document can occur either on the server side or the client side. If the client's browser is an XML browser then the HTTP server has the very simple task of associating the right style sheet with the document (or the document may already contain the style sheet association) and sending it to the browser. When the client's browser is not an XML browser, however, then this document has to be transformed into a displayable document before being sent. Thus, the transformation of an XML document into a displayable entity can be carried out either by the XML browser or by the HTTP server.

Server side XML transformation

HTTP servers can be thought of as file servers, but unlike simple file servers their functionality can be expanded with server add-ons. These add-ons mostly take the form of script engines. The most popular ones like ASP, JSP, PHP, or Cold Fusion are template based.

To process XML, HTTP servers require XML processing add-ons – the simplest being one that is able to transform an XML file into an HTML document and then send this document to the browser for rendition (such as an XSLT engine). The more sophisticated add-ons are full XML repositories. As we saw in Chapter 9, the XML document is first parsed and transformed into an internal structure, and then a style engine will transform this internal structure into an HTML document using templates. However, in the case of sophisticated XML repositories, this parsing is unnecessary since the document is already parsed and stored in an internal format; the style engine then directly performs its function on the internal structure. Usually, servers that include a full XML repository have better performance than simple file based systems. But file-based systems can increase their performance by caching the XML documents that have already been transformed into HTML.

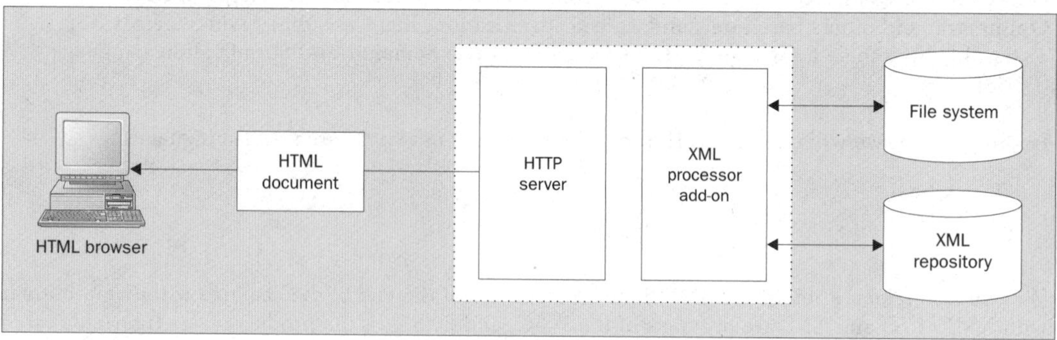

Client side XML transformation

When the client is an XML browser the task is a lot easier. Actually, almost any HTTP server can provide XML documents that can be rendered in these browsers.

The process is quite simple, the HTTP server sends the XML document to the browser. This then scans the received document for a particular construct, the "`processing-instruction`". As we will see later on, the processing instruction allows the browser to fetch the style sheet associated with the XML document and perform the document rendition.

Off course, your choice of style language is determined by the browser capabilities. Some XML browsers may only be able to process XML documents with CSS style sheet, others only with XSL.

Rendition Models

The two rendition models we will be looking at in this chapter are aural rendition and visual rendition. Because the aural rendition model implies a sequential placement of rendition objects, this also implies that an aural browser is a time dependent device. On the other hand, the visual rendition model implies spatial placement of rendition objects, so a visual browser is a space dependent device. So, let's look at some of the differences between the two.

Visual Rendition

Today, the most common portable information medium is a simple sheet of paper. However, if you think about the information you receive each day, the browser is constantly gaining popularity as a medium for sharing information. Despite the fact that a browser displays electronic information on a screen, there is another big difference between it and paper. Paper presents the reader with a fixed size page, while browsers give a variable sized page seen through a **viewport**, or window.

Browsers able to render XML documents are easily available, such as Microsoft Internet Explorer 5 (which is free to download). IE5 supports both CSS and XSL.

> **Note: IE5 CSS support is incomplete and its implementation of XSLT is not conformant to the W3C recommendation.**

In addition, the next incarnation of a Netscape browser, which is currently taking form as code developed by an open source project at http://www.Mozilla.org/, will support CSS and an implementation of XSL.

Both paper and the browser are substrates for visual rendition. We can say that they are the main **container** for visual **formatting objects**. The atomic entity of style languages is the **area**. In standard style languages, the area is a rectangular region. In this view of the world, a page is an area containing other areas. These rectangular areas containing other rectangular areas form a tree structure. Thus, a visual layout is a tree of formatting objects (rectangular areas) with the page at the top of the tree and the lower level formatting objects as children.

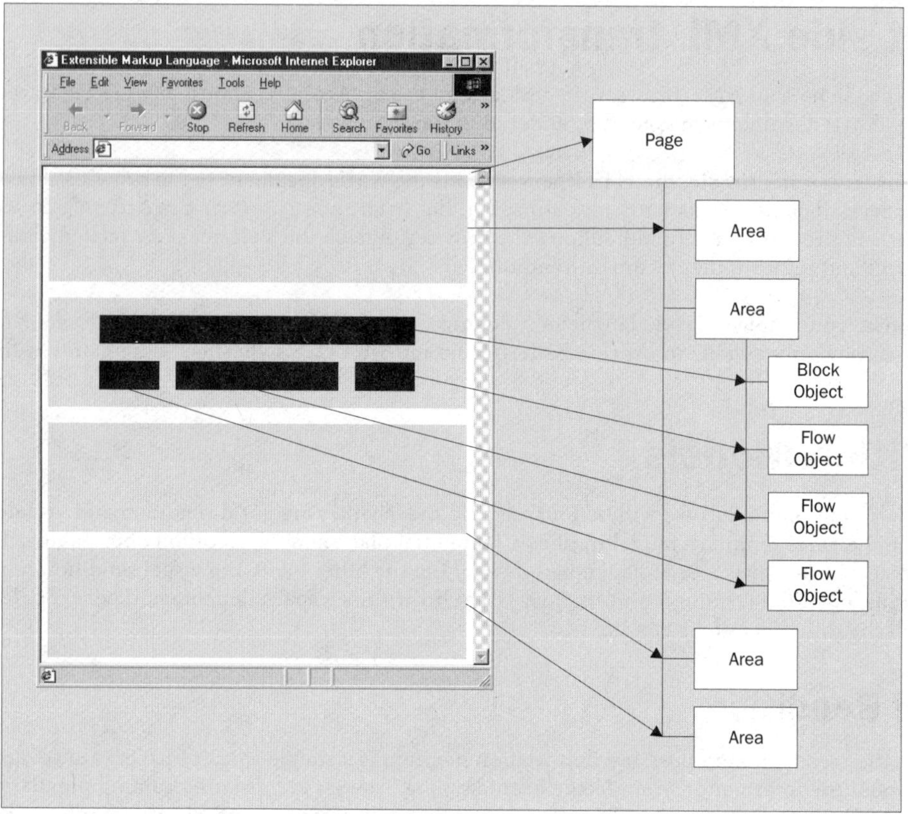

Depending on the level of sophistication of the style language, two layout models are proposed:

- Flow layout
- Fixed layout

A **flow** layout is a layout where formatting objects are laid on the substrate (a page or a scroll) one after the other. If the writing direction is from top to bottom and from left to right, then the objects are laid the same way – from top to bottom and from left to right. For example, paragraphs are laid vertically on top of each other and words/sentences are laid horizontally. Most of the time, there are formatting objects to be laid vertically and horizontally. For instance, the CSS style sheet language allows block objects to be laid vertically with a behavior similar to paragraphs, and inline objects to be laid horizontally with a behavior similar to words or sentences. Generally, objects laid vertically (for western writing orientation) contain the objects laid horizontally.

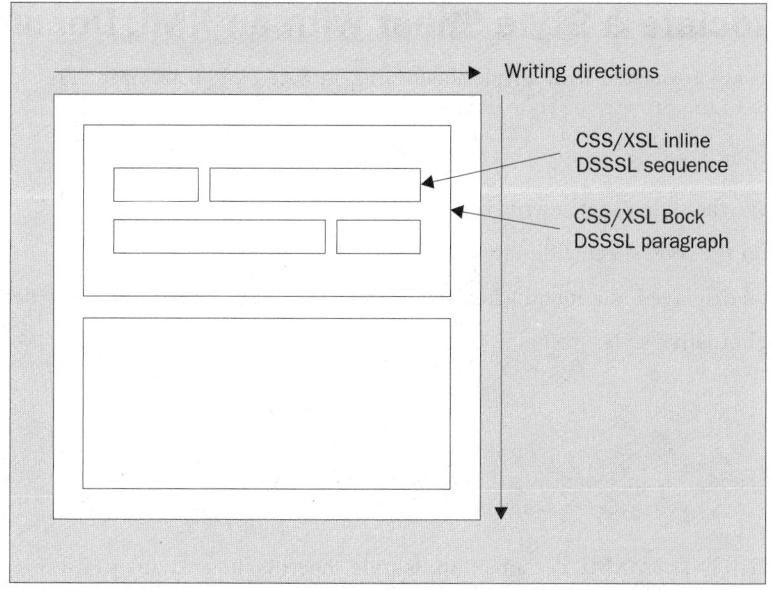

A **fixed** layout is a layout where formatting objects are laid on a page with a position. The area representing the document is then like a Cartesian universe, where each location can be uniquely identified by location coordinates. For instance, the CSS style language allows certain formatting objects to be laid at a specific position with `left` and `top` properties indicating the relative distance from the left and top of the container's borders. If the container is the document, then an object's fixed position is relative to the top and left borders of the document. If the container is an area, then the object's fixed position is relative to the area's top and left borders.

Aural Rendition

Aural browsers are less well known than their visual counterparts, and are largely still incubated in development labs. The main aural model is similar to the musical model. Sounds are organized sequentially with a **time duration**. But, unlike music, the sounds are more complex, because in this case a sound is a spoken word. Therefore, we usually call the atomic entity of an aural browser a **speech**, meaning a discourse made up of a series of words delimited by silences. Characteristics of a speech would be the tone, the gender of the voice, the rhythm, etc.

Several aural browsers have appeared recently in the developer's landscape, notably:

- Hewlett Packard's SpeechML browser
- IBM's VoiceXML browser

But, are aural browsers a lab hobby? We can answer this question with another one: Would you read while driving your car? An aural browser with speech commands could be used to render XML documents in your car. Thus, a news bulletin packaged in an XML news format could be rendered in your car with an aural browser.

How to Associate a Style Sheet with an XML Document

XML documents are associated with a style sheet using a processing instruction. This special type of element specifies to the browser or style engine:

Where to find the style sheet

What language the style sheet is written in

What medium the style sheet is designed for

The title to be displayed in a menu when several alternative style sheets are provided

If there are alternative style sheets

For example:

```
<?xml-stylesheet href="myStyleSheet.css" type="text/css"
title="CSS style" media="screen"?>
```

The element which links an XML document to its style sheets is the `xml-stylesheet` processing instruction. The W3C recommendation titled *Associating Style Sheets with XML documents Version 1.0* can be found at: http://www.w3.org/TR/xml-stylesheet/.

The attributes for this processing instruction are as follows:

Attribute	Description
`href`	Style sheet location. The value is a URI, and most of the time will be a URL.
`type`	The style sheet language, expressed as a MIME type. For instance, the CSS language MIME type is `text/css`, the DSSSL language MIME type is `text/dsssl`, and the XSL language MIME type is `text/xsl`.
`media`	The style sheet media target. This can be set to `screen`, `print`, `aural`, etc.
`title`	Provides a title for the style sheet. This title can be used by a style sheet engine to be displayed in a menu.
`alternate`	Can be `yes` or `no`. This indicates to the style engine if there are alternative style sheets for the same medium.

Rule-Based Languages

Most style languages are rule-based languages. What do we mean by rules? A rule is composed of two sections:

- The pattern matching section
- The action section

The pattern match section is an expression allowing the association between markup and some action. The action section is a small procedure or template.

As we saw in the transformation chapter, the process that goes on in rule-based style languages involves transforming the original XML document into a tree structure, then the tree's nodes are visited one at a time and matched to a particular rule. When a match occurs, the procedure is executed. In the case when the action part is a template, there is an implicit call to a rule or procedure that parses and outputs the content of the template, because a template may contain other elements that the processor needs to handle. In fact, the whole process we just described is the usual process of an XML rendition engine.

Having seen some of the common aspects of style languages, it is time to look at the first of the languages that this chapter will focus on: CSS. We will provide an overview of the language here, although there is a full list of CSS1 and CSS2 properties in Appendix F.

CSS

If you use HTML, you have probably encountered Cascading Style Sheets. Several browsers already include a partial or total CSS1 implementation, and more rarely a partial implementation of CSS2. CSS1 and 2 are both W3C recommendations, and can be found at: http://www.w3.org/TR/REC-CSS1 and http://www.w3.org/TR/REC-CSS2 respectively. The language is very similar to HTML based style instructions, and the specification is easy to follow.

The CSS Atom: the Box

If you could meet Democritus today (Greek philosopher 460-370 BC) and talked with him about CSS he would ask you "Where are the atoms?". To answer his question you may simply answer "With CSS everything is in a Box – so the atom is the box". This concept is referred to in the CSS recommendation document as the box model.

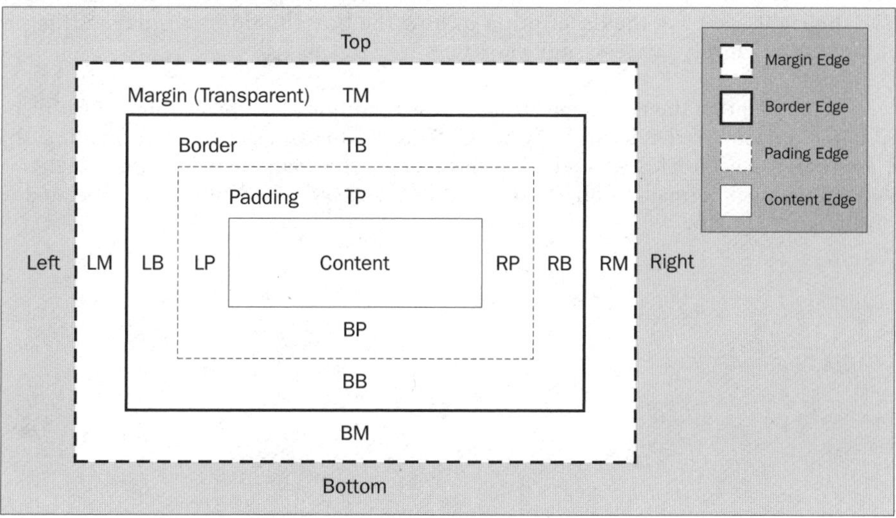

In the CSS world a box is a rectangular area with certain basic characteristics like **margin** and **border** dimensions. All boxes are fitted one into the other like Russian dolls. Some boxes contain other boxes, and some boxes are simply contained. This kind of construct could be translated into a tree of boxes or rectangular areas. The box tree is itself contained in a container box for either continuous media (such as in browsers, where the screen can scroll) or printed material (where the dimensions of the area are fixed).

How an XML Document's Elements are Linked to CSS Rules

Knowing that the CSS view of the world is through boxes, we need to look at how to associate the XML elements to these boxes. The answer is through rules. These rules consist of a set of properties linked to one or several element type(s). Each rule is composed of a **pattern match** part and a **procedure part** or **action**. In the CSS world, the pattern match part is also known as the **selector** and the procedure part as the **properties** collection. Thus, the CSS language is a rule-based language. Look at the following example of a CSS rule:

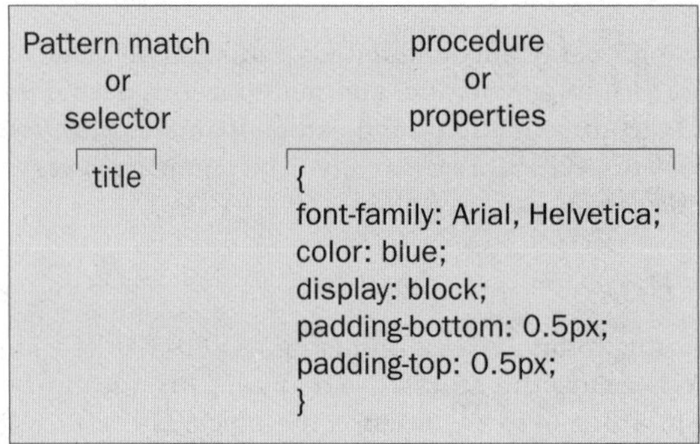
Pattern match
or
selector
procedure
or
properties
title
{
font-family: Arial, Helvetica;
color: blue;
display: block;
padding-bottom: 0.5px;
padding-top: 0.5px;
}

On the left, we have the pattern matching section (that is, the selector), which specifies the element name. On the right, we have the description of how the box should be displayed (the properties). We will look more closely at the syntax shortly.

CSS is very dependent on the document structure for rendition. The formatting objects tree is often identical to the document tree. Basically, what CSS does is to associate a CSS formatting object with specific properties to each XML element. For instance, in the example below, the `<ITEM>` element is associated with a block formatting object, the `<DESCRIPTION>` element is also associated with a block and so forth:

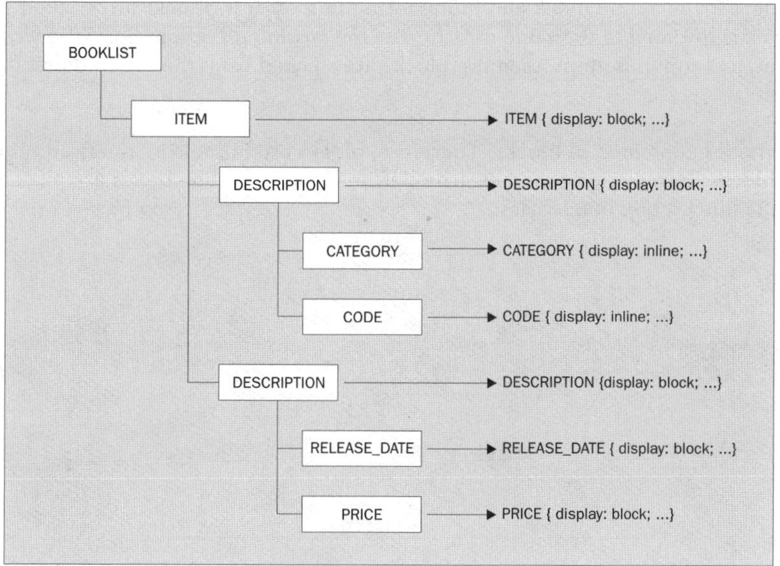

Now let's see what block and inline objects are.

CSS Visual Model

In CSS there are two main formatting objects:

- The block
- The inline object

However, if you are thinking in terms of items that can be displayed, then there are also items such as:

- The floating object
- The list
- The table

We could think in terms of a table, which has some specific characteristics; it can have headers, cells, rows, and columns. However, the model for such objects is not consistent in CSS, because the way in which we declare them varies. So, while block and inline flow objects are asserted as values of the `display` property, the float object is itself expressed as a property, which takes different values. So, in CSS the syntax differs from the visual model.

- Block: value (of the display property)
- Inline: value (of the display property)
- Table: value (of the display property)
- List: property
- Float: property

For the moment, let's focus on the block and inline formatting objects. Blocks are stacked one on top of the other. The stack is oriented in the same direction as the writing direction. So, if the writing direction is from left to right, and top to bottom, then the blocks are stacked from the top to the bottom within the container rectangle.

Inline objects are boxes contained in blocks. Therefore, blocks are inline containers and inline objects are contained in blocks. If the writing mode is from left to right, the inline boxes are placed one after the other within the block's box boundaries:

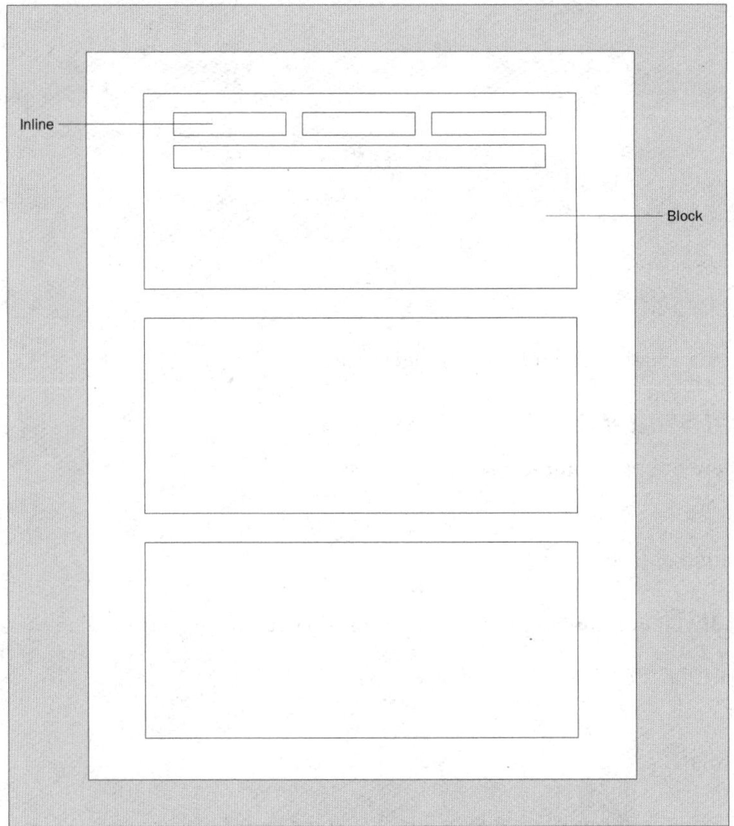

Most style languages are based on a flow rendition model. In this world, the formatting objects are simply displayed one after the other and the rendition follows the writing direction. CSS supports this model, but it also supports absolute positioning. A box could be positioned with a defined location or rendered after the last displayed box. Common uses of documents displayed with defined positions include forms where fields are displayed with an absolute position:

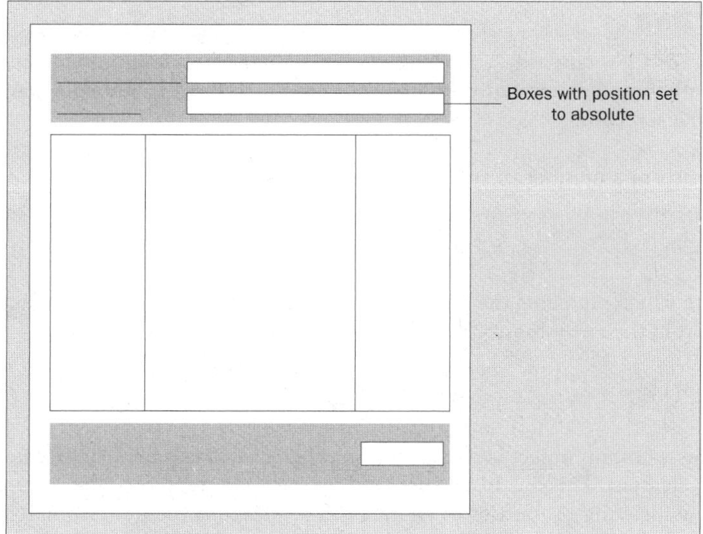

To include notes or images in a rendered page, an element could be set with the float property, which creates a special kind of box attached to the left or to the right of the containing box. The formatting flow lays the content around the floating object, as illustrated below:

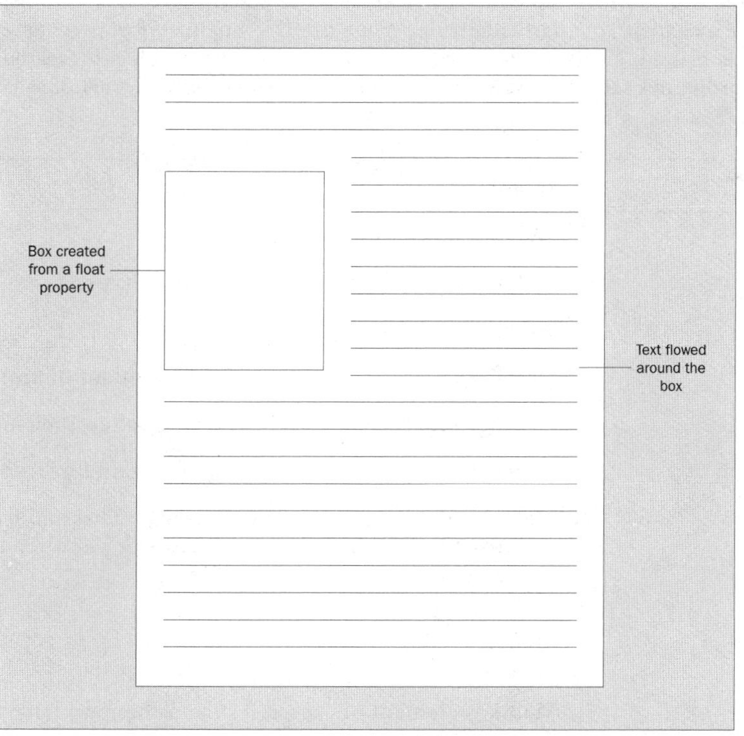

CSS Rule structure

If you know the C or C++ languages, the CSS structure might look familiar to you, although the resemblance is limited to the fact that rules are delimited with the { } characters, and that each property line is ended with a semi-colon.

A style sheet consists of a number of rules. Each rule takes the following syntax:

```
Selector { properties }
```

The selector states which elements the properties should be matched with and then applied to, while the properties are held in the curly brackets and take the following syntax:

```
Property = attribute: value;
```

Note that even the rendition object is declared as a property-value pair, whether it should be a block, a table or an inline element. This has to be specified for each element. So, when using the CSS style language, we are associating properties to elements. The selector, the pattern matching part of a CSS rule, indicates the element or elements to be matched against the rules, while the properties associated to this element – through the selector – are enclosed in curly brackets.

The Pattern Match Selector

So, any CSS rule begins with a selector. The selector is the pattern matching expression, which will link a particular XML element to a particular rule. When the CSS engine encounters an element matching a selector, the rule is fired. Firing a rule simply means that a rendition object is created and that this object gets its properties set by the rule's body. The table below shows the set of selector types supported by CSS2:

Pattern	Meaning
`*`	Matches any element.
`E`	Matches any `E` element (an element of type `E`).
`E,F`	Matches any `E` **or** `F` element.
`E F`	Matches any `F` element that is a descendant of an `E` element.
`E > F`	Matches any `F` element that is a child of an `E` element.
`E:first-child`	Matches element `E` when `E` is the first child of its parent.
`E:link` `E:visited`	Matches element `E` if `E` is the source anchor of a hyperlink of which the target has not yet visited (`:link`) or has already visited (`:visited`).

`E:active`
`E:hover`
`E:focus`
	Matches `E` during certain user actions.

`E:lang(c)`	Matches element of type `E` if it is in (human) language `c` (the document language specifies how language is determined).
`E + F`	Matches any `F` element immediately preceded by an element `E`.

Pattern	Meaning
`E[foo]`	Matches any `E` element with the `foo` attribute set (whatever the value).
`E[foo="warning"]`	Matches any `E` element whose `foo` attribute value is exactly equal to `"warning"`.
`E[foo~="warning"]`	Matches any E element whose `foo` attribute value is a list of space-separated values, one of which is exactly equal to `"warning"`.
`E[lang|="en"]`	Matches any `E` element whose `"lang"` attribute has a hyphen-separated list of values beginning (from the left) with `"en"`.
`E#myid`	Matches any `E` element with an `ID` equal to `myid`.

A selector is a chain of one or more simple selectors. As stated in the CSS2 specifications:

> *"A simple selector is either a* ***type selector*** *or* ***universal selector*** *followed immediately by zero or more* ***attribute selectors, ID selectors,*** *or* ***pseudo-classes,*** *in any order. The simple selector matches if all of its components match."*

A **type selector** is simply an XML element name, and is matched with any occurrences of this element in the XML document tree. The **universal selector** is the `*` character indicating a match with any element.

Attribute selectors allow more finely grained selection or pattern matching, by allowing precise selection down to the attribute, and even the attribute's value. For instance, if an element named `<TITLE>` has the `language` attribute set to "`English`" then the following rules could be used with this element:

```
TITLE {display: block;}
TITLE[language] {display: block;}
TITLE[language="English"] {display: block;}
```

The first rule matches all `<TITLE>` elements, even those not having the `language` attribute, and displays them as block level elements. The second rule matches any element having the `language` attribute with any kind of value. And finally, the last rule matches only the `<TITLE>` elements having the `language` attribute set to "`English`".

A much finer granular matching is achieved with the **ID selector**. This allows the rule to be matched with a particular element having a particular `ID`.

Normally, CSS rules are attached to an element based on its position in the document tree. **Pseudo classes** selectors, however, allow access to other types of nodes in the document tree. For instance the `first-child` pseudo class allows us to reach and attach a rule to the first child element of a particular element:

```
TITLE: first-child {...}
```

We can then associate a particular CSS rule to an object of the document tree without having to explicitly specify its name.

Pseudo elements are another type of interesting selector. For instance, it may be important to format the first line of a paragraph differently, or to set the first letter of a chapter with a larger font size. Here, the first line of the `<DESCRIPTION>` element's data content is selected and the rule's collection of properties is applied to the first line:

```
DESCRIPTION: first-line {...}
```

While in the following line of code the first letter of the `<DESCRIPTION>` element's data content is associated to the rule's property set:

```
DESCRIPTION: first-letter {...}
```

Simple selectors can be chained in a single selector expression as long as each simple selector is delimited by white space, >, or +.

An expression such as:

```
ITEM,TITLE
```

is a selector matching `<ITEM>` or `<TITLE>` elements. Thus, a comma can be also perceived as an implicit `or` logical expression.

For expressions such as:

```
ITEM > TITLE
```

it is only `<TITLE>` elements that are children of the `<ITEM>` element that are matched. Thus, if a `<TITLE>` element is found in a different location in the document type or document structure, the rule is not satisfied. For instance, if there is a `<TITLE>` element that is a child of the `<DOCUMENT>` element, then this element won't be matched with a rule having this kind of selector.

Finally, a selector such as:

```
ITEM + TITLE
```

will match only a `<TITLE>` element immediately preceded by the `<ITEM>` element. If, for example, the `<CATEGORY>` element is before the `<TITLE>` element, then the rule will not be matched.

We can also matched several elements with a single rule using a group of selectors in a comma-delimited list like so:

```
TITLE[language="English"], ITEM, DOCUMENT > BOOK
{
    ...
}
```

When CSS style sheets are used with HTML documents, the selectors are case insensitive. But, when used to render XML documents, CSS selectors are case sensitive – because the selectors are being used in the context of a case sensitive language.

There is not space to detail all of the properties in this chapter, however they are provided in Appendix F.

Media Types and Modular Style Sheets

A major characteristic associated with XML documents is the separation of data and presentation. A CSS style sheet is a means by which XML can be prepared for display. CSS allows rendition on several types of media:

Media Type	Description
`screen`	a screen device, for instance a browser
`print`	a print device like a printed book
`aural`	an aural device, for instance a speech synthesizer
`Braille`	a Braille device with tactile feedback
`embossed`	an embossed device, as created by a paged Braille printer
`projection`	a projection device
`tty`	a tty device, more commonly known as a teletype
`tv`	a TV

A CSS style sheet could contain style specifications for several kinds of media, for instance, a style specification for browsers, printers, and speech devices. Each target device is specified by the `@media` construct. The following expression associates CSS rules with a screen device (usually a browser):

```
@media screen { BOOKLIST {display :block;} }
```

As this shows, all rules targeted for a particular type of media are contained in the `@media` construct. In the same way that selectors can specify several elements to have the same rules, the selectors can be used for several media types:

```
@media screen, print { BOOKLIST {display: block;} }
```

Sometimes, however, it is necessary to split a style sheet into several files to add more modularity to the whole rendition specification, for example, storing the print style sheet in one file and the aural style sheet in another.

The `@import` construct allows you to import rules from other style sheets. The `@import` constructs should precede all the other CSS constructs in a style sheet document. The imported style sheets could be referred to with URLs:

```
@import url(booklist_aural.css);
```

It is possible to combine the @media and @import construct in the same expression, as in the following expressions:

```
@import url(booklist1.css) aural;
```

In the first expression the booklist1.css style sheet is imported and included in the implicit @media construct, which is in this case of type "aural". The media type is appended to the import reference:

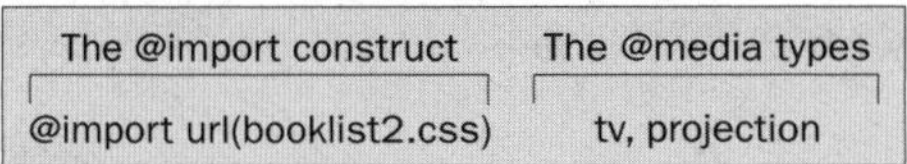

A Sample CSS Style Script

Enough theory, let's get on with an example. Throughout this chapter, we'll use the same XML document to be rendered successively with CSS, DSSSL and XSL. This document is a variation on the book catalog we have used in the rest of the book called booklist.xml:

```
<?xml version="1.0"?>
<BOOKLIST>
   <ITEM>
      <CODE>16-048</CODE>
      <CATEGORY>Scripting</CATEGORY>
      <RELEASE_DATE>1998-04-21</RELEASE_DATE>
      <TITLE>Instant JavaScript</TITLE>
      <PRICE>$49.34</PRICE>
   </ITEM>
   <ITEM>
   <CODE>16-105</CODE>
      <CATEGORY>ASP</CATEGORY>
      <RELEASE_DATE>1998-05-10</RELEASE_DATE>
      <TITLE>Instant Active Server Pages</TITLE>
      <PRICE>$23.45</PRICE>
   </ITEM>
   <ITEM>
      <CODE>16-041</CODE>
      <CATEGORY>HTML</CATEGORY>
      <RELEASE_DATE>1998-03-07</RELEASE_DATE>
      <TITLE>Instant HTML</TITLE>
      <PRICE>$34.23</PRICE>
   </ITEM>
</BOOKLIST>
```

Throughout this chapter, we'll also use the same kind of rendition. All scripts, when run, should display the same result, as shown below:

To obtain this result from our catalog example without any transformation on the original document is not feasible for two main reasons:

- We have to re-order the document's elements
- We also have to add new information for rendition purposes

For instance, the book's title should be at the beginning of each catalog item. Also, the Category, Release date, and Price strings should be added to help the reader identify each information type.

We cannot modify the original XML document for rendition using CSS, so the XML has to be transformed before it is styled for viewing. This implies that we re-order the elements and add new strings to the content. This is a perfect job for XSLT and its transformation capabilities.

Let's assume that our document has been transformed as previously explained in Chapter 9 into the following XML document; we have called it `trans_booklist.xml`:

```
<?xml version="1.0"?>
<?xml-stylesheet
   type="text/css"
   href="booklist.css"
   media="screen"?>
<BOOKLIST>
   <ITEM>
      <TITLE>Instant JavaScript</TITLE>
      <DESCRIPTION>
         <CATEGORY>Category: </CATEGORY>
         <CODE>(16-048)</CODE>
      </DESCRIPTION>
      <DESCRIPTION>
         <RELEASE_DATE>Release date: 1998-04-21</RELEASE_DATE>
         <PRICE>Price: $49.34</PRICE>
```

```
         </DESCRIPTION>
      </ITEM>
      <ITEM>
         <TITLE>Instant Active Server Pages</TITLE>
         <DESCRIPTION>
            <CATEGORY>Category: ASP</CATEGORY>
            <CODE>(16-105)</CODE>
         </DESCRIPTION>
         <DESCRIPTION>
            <RELEASE_DATE>release date: 1998-05-10</RELEASE_DATE>
            <PRICE>Price: $23.45</PRICE>
         </DESCRIPTION>
      </ITEM>
      <ITEM>
         <TITLE>Instant HTML</TITLE>
         <DESCRIPTION>
            <CATEGORY>Category: HTML</CATEGORY>
            <CODE>(16-041)</CODE>
         </DESCRIPTION>
         <DESCRIPTION>
            <RELEASE_DATE>release date: 1998-03-07</RELEASE_DATE>
            <PRICE>Price: $34.23</PRICE>
         </DESCRIPTION>
      </ITEM>
   </BOOKLIST>
```

Firstly, the association between the CSS style sheet and the XML document is through the `xml-stylesheet` processing instruction:

```
<?xml-stylesheet type="text/css" href="booklist.css" media="screen"?>
```

The first attribute, named `type`, specifies the type of style sheet and, in the case of CSS, should be set to the CSS MIME type, which is "`text/css`". The second attribute, `href`, is the link to the style sheet document's location. This attribute should be set to a URI (more commonly to a URL). Finally, the last attribute notifies the CSS engine that the rendition device is a screen device. For a printer, we would set the `media` attribute to "`print`".

Because Microsoft Internet Explorer 5 supports styling of XML documents with CSS, you can test the sample XML document linked to the following CSS style sheet and get the same result as the previous screen shot. Here is the CSS file that we will use to display our data in this format. It is called `booklist.css` and is available for download from http://www.wrox.com/ along with the rest of the code for the book:

```
@media screen, print
{
   ITEM
   {
      display: block;
      margin-left: 40pt;
      font-family: Times New Roman;
      font-size: 12pt;
      font-weight: 500;
```

```
        margin-bottom: 15pt;
        text-align: left;
        line-height: 12pt;
        text-indent: 0pt;
    }

    TITLE
    {
        display: block;
        font-family: Arial;
        font-weight: 700;
        font-size: 14pt;
    }

    DESCRIPTION
    {
        display: block;
    }

    CATEGORY
    {
        display: inline;
    }

    CODE
    {
        display: inline;
    }

    RELEASE_DATE
    {
        display: inline;
    }

    PRICE
    {
        display: inline;
    }
}
```

Because the style sheet processing instruction was set to link to this CSS, and the XML had already been transformed to include the extra text, the result will look like that we saw at the beginning of this section. So, let's have a look at some more of the CSS syntax.

The display Property

The `display` property indicates to a CSS interpreter whether the formatting object should be a block object, inline object, or table. A default context is automatically set to the rendered element. For instance, an element with the `display` property set to `block` will behave like a paragraph, and the formatting flow will break after this formatting object. If, however, the element has the `display` property set to `inline`, then this element behaves like a sentence or a word in a paragraph, and doesn't induce a break after its rendition. Finally, when an element uses `table` for the value of `display`, it sets the overall context for placing a table's rows and columns. A table may also result in a break in the normal formatting flow. So, to summarize, the three basic values for `display` are:

- `block` – behaves like a paragraph and causes a break in the normal rendition flow.
- `inline` – behaves like a word or a sentence. Inline formatting objects are appended one after the other (horizontally) and do not cause a break in the normal rendition flow.
- `table` – sets a table area that may or may not cause a break in the normal rendition flow.

The CSS table model is based on the HTML 4.0 table model. The table model is row oriented, which means that a table is defined by rows and columns, with columns deduced from the rows. A row is divided into cells. When a row is defined, cells compose the columns so that the first cell is in the first column, the second one the second column and so forth.

To produce tables or table parts, the display property may take one of these values:

Value	Description
`table`	Creates a box with a block behavior. Will create a formatting flow break.
`table-inline`	Creates a box with an inline behavior. This won't create a formatting flow break.
`table-row`	Specifies that an element is a row of cells.
`table-row-group`	Specifies that an element groups one or more rows.
`table-header-group`	Creates a table header. A table header group is displayed before other rows or groups.
`table-footer-group`	Creates a table footer. A table footer group is always displayed after other rows or groups.
`table-cell`	Specifies that an element represents a table's cells.
`table-caption`	Specifies a table's caption.

To illustrate the table behavior, let's position the elements from the example XML document we saw earlier, before it was transformed, and display it in a tabular format.

At the time of this writing, no browsers can illustrate table positioning with CSS level 2, so the figure below can give you an idea of the final rendition after the document has been processed by the sample CSS style sheet. (It has actually been reproduced in HTML 4.0, as the model is very similar; we will see the HTML code after the CSS style sheet.)

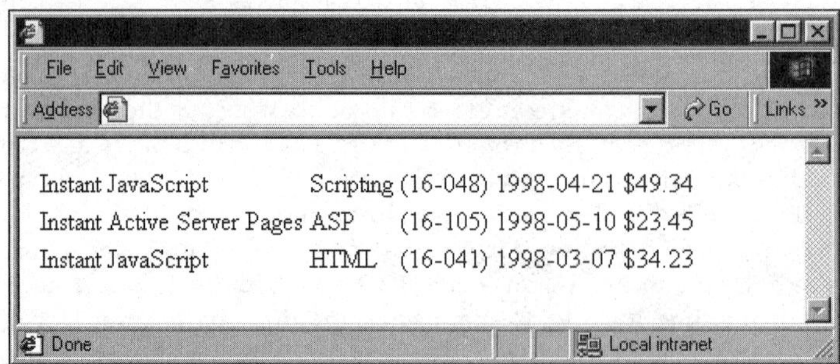

Here is the style sheet that would create such a table:

```
@media screen
{
   BOOKLIST     {display: table;}
   ITEM         {display: table-row;}
   TITLE        {display: table-cell;}
   CATEGORY     {display: table-cell;}
   CODE         {display: table-cell;}
   RELEASE_DATE {display: table-cell;}
   PRICE        {display: table-cell;}
}
```

The above CSS style sheet creates a table consisting of 3 rows and 5 columns. The `<BOOKLIST>` element creates a `table` formatting object with the matching rule containing the `display: table` property/value pair. Then, for each occurrence of the `<ITEM>` element, a row is created by the `display: table-row` property/value pair. This row has now to be filled with cells, which are created with the `display: table-cell` property/value associated with each of the `<TITLE>`, `<CATEGORY>`, `<CODE>`, `<RELEASE_DATE>` and `<PRICE>` elements.

As you can notice, the CSS model is very similar to the HTML 4.0 model. The same table created with HTML would have been:

```
<HTML>
<BODY>
   <TABLE>
      <TR>
         <TD>Instant JavaScript</TD>
         <TD>Scripting</TD>
         <TD>(16-048)</TD>
         <TD>1998-04-21</TD>
         <TD>$49.34</TD>
      </TR>
      <TR>
         <TD>Instant Active Server Pages</TD>
         <TD>ASP</TD>
         <TD>(16-105)</TD>
         <TD>1998-05-10</TD>
         <TD>$23.45</TD>
      </TR>
      <TR>
         <TD>Instant JavaScript</TD>
         <TD>HTML</TD>
         <TD>(16-041)</TD>
         <TD>1998-03-07</TD>
         <TD>$34.23</TD>
      </TR>
   </TABLE>
</BODY>
</HTML>
```

The position Property

The position property imposes a fixed position on a box. When the position property is set to anything except static, the element's box doesn't follow the normal rendition flow. Its position will be fixed in relation to a box container, and not relative to the last displayed box – overriding the default block behavior.

The position property can be set to one of the following different values:

Value	Description
static	The default behavior; normal flow.
relative	The box's position is calculated in accordance to the normal flow. It is positioned with an offset relative to the normal flow by the left, right, top, and bottom properties.
absolute	The box's position is set by the left, right, top, and bottom properties. Boxes positioned with the absolute value are left out of the normal flow. The box is positioned in accordance to the containing block.
fixed	Same behavior as for the absolute value, except that the box will not move. For example, in screen media, when the page is scrolled, the box stays in the same place relative to the viewport. In the case of a visual browser, this viewport is simply the browser's window.

It is important to notice that absolute positioning does not imply that the containing block's text will flow around the object with a position set to absolute. The following example, sample_position.xml, illustrates this:

```
<?xml version="1.0"?>
<?xml-stylesheet href="sample_position.css" type="text/css" media="screen"?>
<SAMPLE_POSITION>
   <TEXT>The position property imposes a fixed position to a box.
      When the position property is set to anything except static,
      the element's box doesn't follow the normal rendition flow. Its
      position will be fixed relatively to a box container, and not
      relative to the last displayed box - the default block behavior
      is overridden.
   </TEXT>
   <OVERLAP>
      box with position: absolute
   </OVERLAP>
</SAMPLE_POSITION>
```

Here is the associated style sheet, sample_position.css:

```
TEXT
{
   display: block;
   font-family: Arial;
   font-size: 10pt;
}
```

```
OVERLAP
{
   position: absolute;
   left: 60pt;
   top:20pt;
   background-color: white;
   font-weight: 700;
   font-size: 18 pt;
}
```

While this is not a very attractive example, the following illustration, nonetheless, shows clearly the CSS absolute positioning. The `<OVERLAP>` element's data content is displayed with a fixed position relative to the browser's top and left border:

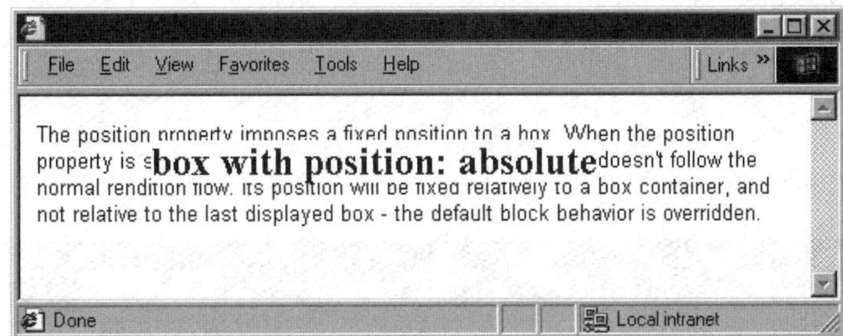

Even if the `<TEXT>` element is before the `<OVERLAP>` element in the `sample_position.xml` document, its content is displayed on top of the `<TEXT>` data content. Independently of the default formatting flow, the box associated with the `<OVERLAP>` element is displayed at an absolute position. In a browser, the absolute position is set relative to the document's borders with the top and left properties.

If we had used the relative positioning characteristics instead, then the `<OVERLAP>` element's data content would have been displayed with an offset relative to the bottom and left border of the `<TEXT>` element's data content (converted into a block object by a CSS rule). Let's see this; instead of the `<TEXT>` data content being displayed in the middle of the `<OVERLAP>` data content, it will be displayed after it, with an offset created by the `left` and `top` properties.

Here we have changed the style sheet processing instruction from the previous XML document and called it `sample_position2.xml`:

```
<?xml version="1.0"?>
<?xml-stylesheet href="sample_position2.css" type="text/css" media="screen"?>
<SAMPLE_POSITION>
   <TEXT>The position property imposes a fixed position to a box.
      When the position property is set to anything except static,
      the element's box doesn't follow the normal rendition flow. Its
      position will be fixed relatively to a box container, and not
      relative to the last displayed box - the default block behavior
      is overridden.
   </TEXT>
   <OVERLAP>
      box with position: relative
   </OVERLAP>
</SAMPLE_POSITION>
```

and here is its associated style sheet, `sample_position2.css`:

```
TEXT
{
   display: block;
   font-family: Arial;
   font-size: 10pt;
}

OVERLAP
{
   position: relative;
   left: 60pt;
   top:20pt;
   background-color: white;
   font-weight: 700;
   font-size: 18 pt;
}
```

Which lead to the following result:

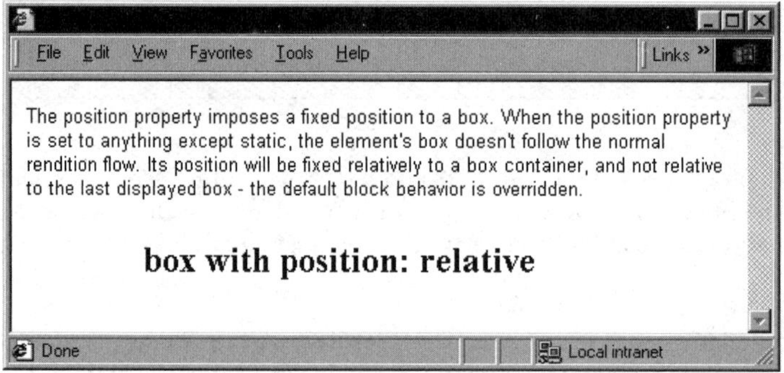

The following three figures illustrate the three kinds of positioning

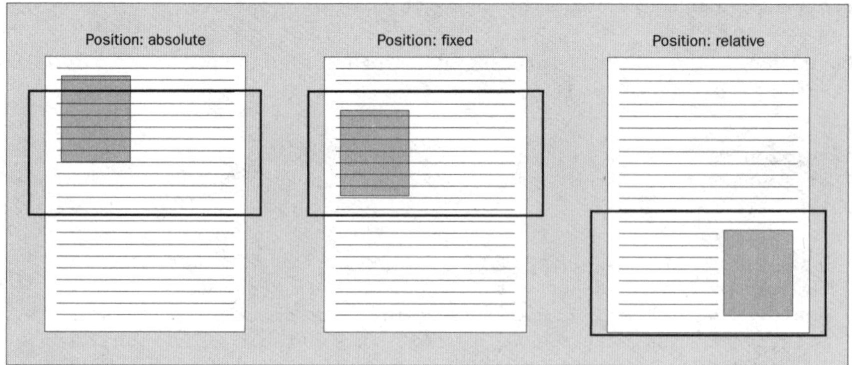

As you can see in the first figure (on the left) the gray area is an element converted into a formatting object with a position set to absolute. Thus, its position is absolute to the beginning of the document, which is the container. The window, illustrated by the overlapped rectangle, displays only a part of the element – the part contained in the window (viewport). As the document is scrolled in the viewport area, it becomes more or less visible.

In the second figure (in the middle), the position is fixed and thus offset not from the left and top borders of the document but from the top and left borders of the viewport (window). As we scroll the document, the gray area is always displayed at the same place.

Finally, the last figure (on the right) illustrates the relative position where the gray area is displayed with an offset relative to the left and bottom boundaries of the previous block.

Z-Order

Elements can be positioned absolutely not only in a two-dimensional space, but also in a three-dimensional space. Well, OK, it would be better to talk about **layers** here.

Imagine a rendered document with several layers of transparencies. Stretch your imagination further to see boxes laid on each transparency. The third dimension is the stack of transparencies. The Z dimension is a layered presentation where boxes can be overlapped. Each box stands in a stacking context. Each box in a stacking context is given a stack level integer (that may be negative); this integer indicates its position relative to the other boxes in the same context. Boxes with a larger stacking level are laid in front of other boxes having a lower level. For example, a box with a stacking level of 15 is nearer to the top than a box with a stacking level of 2.

Layers are particularly useful when you want to animate objects. With scripts able to manipulate the DOM and the element properties, it is possible to create an animated document with objects moving one on top of the other. For example, a slide show written as an XML document could be rendered with a CSS style sheet, and have animated paragraphs to add some pizzazz to the presentation. This third dimension or Z positioning is specified with the `z-index` property, for example:

```
OVERLAP
{
   display: block;
   z-index:-1;
   font-size: 10pt;
}
```

If no background color is specified, the overlapped boxes are transparent. If, however, a background color is specified for the overlapped box, then the displayed color is set by the `background-color` property.

The float Property

Another interesting property is the `float` property, where boxes are laid with a position relative to the left or to the right of the containing block. When an element is set with a float property it is attached to the left or right side of the containing box. In the following figure, two elements are rendered as float boxes. These are attached and displayed relative to the block box – not the document containing box. So, contrary to elements set with a `position: absolute` property/value, elements set with either a `float: right` or `float: left` property are positioned relative to the immediate containing box as shown here:

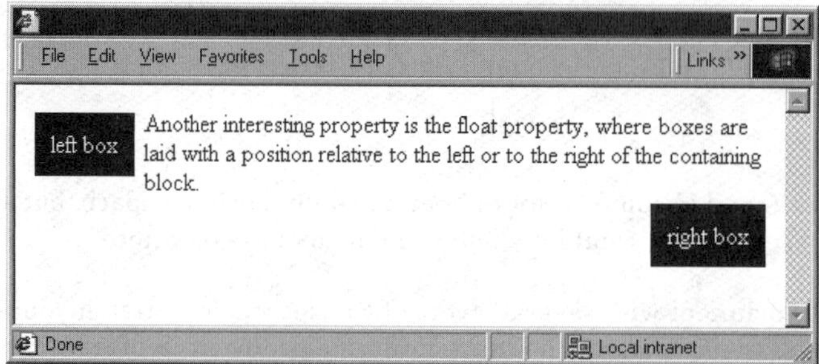

There are three basic properties that apply to boxes: `margin`, `border` and `padding`.

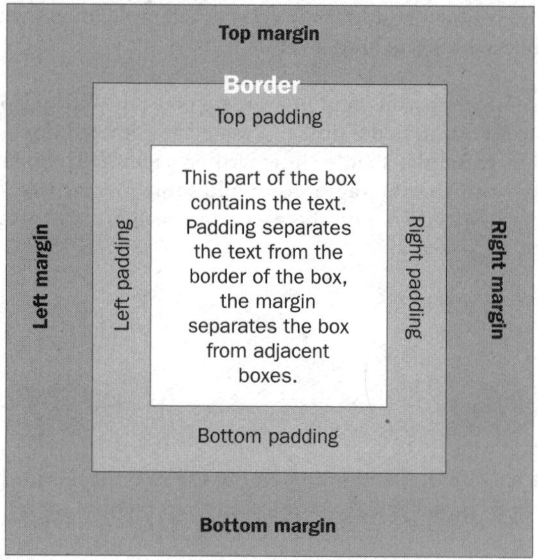

Each box has a border – even if this is not visible – which separates it from the edge of the canvas, or from adjacent boxes. The distance between the border and the outer edge of the adjacent box, or between the border and its containing box, is called its `margin`. The distance between the box and its border is its `padding`.

The XML code required for this, `float_sample.xml`, is as follows:

```
<?xml version="1.0"?>
<?xml-stylesheet type="text/css" href="float_sample.css" media="screen"?>
<FLOAT_SAMPLE>
   <PARAGRAPH>
      <LEFT_BOX>
         left box
      </LEFT_BOX>
         Another interesting property is the float property, where
         boxes are laid with a position relative to the left or to the
         right of the containing block.
      <RIGHT_BOX>
         right box
      </RIGHT_BOX>
   </PARAGRAPH>
</FLOAT_SAMPLE>
```

And here is the accompanying style sheet, `float_sample.css`:

```
LEFT_BOX
{
   float: left;
   margin-left:2pt;
   margin-top: 2pt;
   margin-right: 2pt;
   margin-bottom: 2pt;
   padding-top: 8pt;
   padding-left: 8pt;
   padding-right: 8pt;
   padding-bottom: 8pt;
   background-color: black;
   color: white;
}

RIGHT_BOX
{
   float: right;
   margin-left:2pt;
   margin-top: 2pt;
   margin-right: 2pt;
   margin-bottom: 2pt;
   padding-top: 8pt;
   padding-left: 8pt;
   padding-right: 8pt;
   padding-bottom: 8pt;
   background-color: black;
   color: white;
}

PARAGRAPH
{
   display: block;
}
```

The sequence of rendition events is as follows:

The paragraph element is encountered by the CSS rendition engine and is matched with the rule that has the `PARAGRAPH` selector. The paragraph context is set as a block object with a margin around it, but its content not displayed straight away.

The first thing the CSS engine encounters in the `<PARAGRAPH>` element is the `<LEFT_BOX>` element. This is matched with the rule that has the `LEFT_BOX` selector. The image context is set to be a floating box with a margin. The floating box is moved to the left as specified by the `float` property. The margin surrounding the float object is set with the `margin-top`, `margin-left`, `margin-right`, and `margin-bottom` properties. The `padding` properties set an area around the object displayed using `padding-top`, `padding-left`, `padding-right`, `padding-bottom` properties. The floating box is displayed with an offset position from the left and top borders of the containing box (the block context previously created by the `<PARAGRAPH>` element).

The CSS engine then gets the `<PARAGRAPH>` element's data content. The content is displayed flowing around the floating box. The gap between the floating box and the text is set by the `margin-right` and `margin-bottom` properties.

Interactive Behavior

Microsoft introduced behavioral extensions in Internet Explorer version 5. This is an added capability to CSS, which adds interactivity such as highlighting text. At the time of this writing, a working draft is available at http://www.w3.org/TR/becss. A behavior can be attached to any XML element. Unlike DHTML documents, usually XML documents do not include scripts, as this doesn't fit in with the concept of separating the data from the presentation (or the interaction). Behaviors can be associated with any XML elements in order to add interactivity to the rendered document. For instance, to highlight the `<TITLE>` element when the mouse cursor is on its rendered version, a behavior could be attached to the element as in the following example:

```
@media screen { TITLE {behavior: url(highlight.htc); }
```

In this case, the behavior could take the form of an **HTML component** (or HTC) containing some JavaScript.

An interesting feature mentioned in the latest behavioral extension working draft is the `@script` construct. This allows the inclusion of scripts in a style sheet. This is a very powerful construct, which could be useful for developers who already have some or a lot of experience with procedural languages like JavaScript, PerlScript, PythonScript, or VBScript. What advantages does scripting bring? Well, scripts can do a lot of handy things, such as manipulating the DOM, and attaching event handlers to events generated by the DOM nodes. This is not yet feasible with any DOM Level 1 compliant browser, but event support is part of the DOM Level 2 working draft. The document explaining the DOM event interfaces can be found at http://www.w3.org/TR/WD-DOM-Level-2/events.html. Adding event handling through DOM Level 2 interfaces could be tricky, but the `@script` CSS construct will make things a lot easier.

The script referred to or contained in the `@script` construct is similar to that in an HTML `<script>` element. The code not enclosed in a function or a procedure (or an object) is included in an implicit "main" function and this main function is executed when the style sheet is first loaded and parsed. Event handlers can be functions or procedures, and generally have names beginning with `On_`. For instance, an event handler attached to the `<TITLE>` element could be named `On_TitleClick()`. So, how do we link the event and the event handler? By adding a new property to the rule associated to an element. To attach an event handler to the `<TITLE>` element we would have a rule along the lines of:

```
TITLE
{
   display: block;
   color: red;
   OnClick:  "On_TitleClick(event)";
}
```

In this case the `OnClick` property in the `<TITLE>` element refers to the function called `On_TitleClick()`, which should be contained in the `@script` construct.

Another important point is that although we said that CSS cannot modify the XML document's structure, this is not necessarily true when the `@script` construct is implemented. Why? Because the browser may let the script manipulate the DOM, which may result in changes to the document's structure. Here is the sequence of events that a browser with behavioral extensions would follow:

- Parse the XML document and build a hierarchical structure (this structure is what is accessed by the DOM).
- Load and parse the CSS style sheet.
- Extract the `@script` construct content and give it to a script handler for parsing and execution (a JavaScript interpreter, for example).
- The script interpreter first executes the "main" (or the implicit "main"). The code can access the DOM, allowing it to manipulate each element of the document's structure.
- Attach a set of properties to each element in the structure. The matching is done via the selector's pattern matching capabilities.
- When the user interacts with the rendered document, events are fired and event handlers attached to elements are called – that is, a procedure or function included in the `@script` construct is called. The link between an element and an event handler is through one of the event properties, such as `OnClick`.

Now, with these new forthcoming additions, CSS is becoming more interesting with features such as:

- Behavioral extensions which bring document interactivity and document structure manipulation in much the same way as XSL, but with a procedural language like JavaScript, VBScript, PerlScript, PythonScript, or whatever is supported by the browser.
- An easy paradigm where properties are attached to elements.
- A simple syntax.

Concluding Thoughts on CSS

CSS is a very simple style language, which is quite easy to remember and use. Its major advantage is its simplicity. If you only need to render an XML document without any element transformation then CSS is the best fit. Its main drawbacks are the lack of more sophisticated rendition models, and its dependencies on the structure of processed XML documents. It also means that the processing application must understand XML – which is not the case for many browsers. If you need to get more independence between the document structure and the rendition format (as we do in our example) then XSL and DSSSL are better candidates. However, the work currently progressing offers promising capabilities and additions to the language.

So let's turn our attention to the other major styling language we will be using in this chapter: XSL.

XSL

The Extensible Stylesheet Language employs a very different way of rendering an XML document into displayable entities, compared with CSS. It is a lot more flexible, and can be used to transform XML into languages for different media. We have already met XSLT in Chapter 9, when we discussed transforming XML. In that chapter we illustrated how we can use XSLT to transform an XML document into HTML and into other XML document structures.

Transforming XML into HTML is an effective way of preparing XML for display on the Web, as it means that we are not limited to offering our pages to clients that use the latest browsers. This operation can be done on the server. And, as we saw earlier in this chapter, there are also times when we need to re-create an XML document into a different document type or document structure; again, XSL's transformation capabilities are an ideal candidate for this. We actually used XSLT to re-order the elements of the sample XML document that we have been using in this chapter back in Chapter 9, so that we could present it with a CSS style sheet. So, in the remainder of this chapter, we will look at how we can use XSL to create different presentation formats.

As we said at the beginning of the chapter, styling is not just about preparing a document for visual presentation on the Web. If we are to re-purpose our XML content for different uses, we need to be able to create different formats from the same source files. So, we shall look at how we can use XSL to present our sample XML document for display on-line, in print, and for an aural browser.

XSL is now divided into three different specifications:

- XPath – http://www.w3.org/TR/xpath
- XSLT – http://www.w3.org/TR/xslt
- XSLF – http://www.w3.org/TR/xsl

The XSLT specification focuses on XML document transformation, the XSLF specification is focused on formatting objects, and XPath is focused on accessing nodes from the XML hierarchical structure. As a bare minimum, an XSL engine should support the transformation part (XSLT) and XPath. XSLT will be probably more popular in browsers (such as IE5) than XSLF, because HTML elements could be used as formatting objects. XSLT can also be used with aural browsers, because their language is based on XML. The formatting objects of XSL are being implemented in print formatters, such as FOP (http://www.jtauber.com/fop/) or RenderX (http://www.renderx.com/), both of which allow transformation of XML documents into PDF. These implementations are useful in contexts where documents are to be prepared for the print media.

As we said at the beginning of this chapter, rendering XML is not just a matter of preparing XML documents to be viewed on the Web. At the moment, XSL has provisions for printed and on-line rendition, and can be used to transform XML documents into other markup languages, such as VOXML for aural browsing. So let's see where we use each of these approaches.

XSL Transformations

In Chapter 9 we saw how an XML document can be **transformed** into HTML, or into another XML document structure (such as XHTML, whose specifications can be found at: http://www.w3.org/TR/xhtml1/). The rendition with XSLT is independent of the document structure. To take another example, if a relational database server returns an XML document as the result of a query, a style sheet could produce layout objects or restructure the order of the elements before rendition.

In addition, we can use the same transformation principles we learned to create HTML and other XML document structures, to create the document in a number of other languages, such as VOXML (http://www.voxml.com), an application of XML that is used for aural rendition. These transformations are described in the XSLT (XSL Transformation) part of the XSL specification, found at http://www.w3.org/TR/xslt/.

XSL Formatting Objects

When we are dealing with printed material, the XML document can be transformed into XSL **formatting objects**. These are then, in most actual implementations, transformed into another format such as PDF in a separate process. This uses a different part of the XSL effort: XSLF. We should mention here that XSL formatting objects can be transformed not only into PDF, but specific implementations can also add other new formats to display the results of transformations – such as TeX, RTF, MIF, etc. The XSLF formatting objects are, as is the case for DSSSL formatting objects, independent of any particular rendition or formatting implementation. Thus, as is also the case for DSSSL, an XSLF engine can potentially transform an XML document into different output formats with a single style sheet.

XSL, as its name already advertises, is extensible. This means that new formatting objects could easily be added to the set already present in the language, removing the limitation that CSS has – a fixed set of formatting objects. The area of XSL formatting objects is still very much work in progress and, at the time of writing this chapter, it is not formalized into a W3C Recommendation. The latest working draft for XSL is available at http://www.w3.org/TR/WD-xsl/.

How XSLF Works

As with other rule-based languages, an XSL document (whether XSLT or XSLF) is a collection of rules made up of a pattern matching part and an action part. In XSL these rules are known as **templates**, so the atomic element of an XSL style sheet is a template. The pattern matching part of an XSL template is what is known as an **XPath** expression (as seen in Chapters 8 and 9).

Once the XPath expression has selected a document node it is associated with the content of the template. Because an XML document is being transformed into a result tree of XSL formatting objects, there is a need to match each element of the original XML document to a particular template. Also, when the original document is required to be transformed, several XSLT constructs are used in combination with XPath expressions to reach any node of the XML document transformed into a hierarchical structure.

An XPath expression allows us to reach any document node. XSLT constructs allow us to match nodes to templates, containing XSL formatting objects.

To better understand the process, let's explore the internals of an XSL engine.

As we saw in Chapter 9, an XSL processor that uses the DOM creates three trees:

- A source tree, holding the source XML document to be rendered
- A tree that holds the XSL style sheet
- A result tree, which is used to construct the resulting document

For each template in the tree holding the style sheet, and when an implicit or explicit `apply-template` construct is encountered, the processor finds a matching node in the source document tree. When it makes this match, the template's content is used as a base for the result that is written to the output tree. For instance, if the goal is to render the document in a browser, then the template may contain HTML constructs. For printed materials, the output will be XSL formatting objects, which can be transformed into graphic entities using print formatters for XSL, such as FOP – which, as already mentioned, produces PDF entities.

Rendering XML using XSL

In this section we will se how to transform our sample XML book list into an HTML version, into an aural version marked up in VOXML, and into a visual representation using PDF. We looked at the process of transforming XML documents using XSLT in more depth in Chapter 9, so this section just focuses on what we are doing to present the XML to the user, rather than the transformation process.

For the three following examples, we use the XML document shown below:

```
<?xml version="1.0"?>
<BOOKLIST>
   <ITEM>
      <CODE>16-048</CODE>
      <CATEGORY>Scripting</CATEGORY>
      <RELEASE_DATE>1998-04-21</RELEASE_DATE>
      <TITLE>Instant JavaScript</TITLE>
      <PRICE>$49.34</PRICE>
   </ITEM>
   <ITEM>
      <CODE>16-105</CODE>
      <CATEGORY>ASP</CATEGORY>
      <RELEASE_DATE>1998-05-10</RELEASE_DATE>
      <TITLE>Instant Active Server Pages</TITLE>
      <PRICE>$23.45</PRICE>
   </ITEM>
   <ITEM>
      <CODE>16-041</CODE>
      <CATEGORY>HTML</CATEGORY>
      <RELEASE_DATE>1998-03-07</RELEASE_DATE>
      <TITLE>Instant HTML</TITLE>
      <PRICE>$34.23</PRICE>
   </ITEM>
</BOOKLIST>
```

So, let's start off by creating the HTML version of this XML document, styled for use in a browser.

A Sample XSLT Style Sheet with HTML Visual Rendition Objects

We already looked at using XSLT to create XHTML documents in Chapter 9, which was about transformations. Here we will take another quick look at creating an HTML document. This is a simple way to transform XML into HTML and is a technique that can be used on the server to support clients that cannot read XML, solving one of the problems with CSS, which can only be used to render XML in an XML-aware browser.

An interesting feature of XSL is the ability to render the document's elements with a different order (something we saw already in the transformation chapter). For instance, in the example below, even if the `<TITLE>` element is not the first child of the `<ITEM>` element, it is displayed first because of the transformation capabilities of XSLT. Here is an example called `booklist.xsl`:

```
<?xml version="1.0"?>
<xsl:stylesheet xmlns:xsl="http://www.w3.org/TR/WD-xsl">

<xsl:template match="/">
   <html xmlns="http://www.w3.org/TR/xhtml1/strict">
      <head>
         <title>The book catalog</title>
      </head>
      <body>
         <xsl:apply-templates select="BOOKLIST/ITEM" />
      </body>
   </html>
</xsl:template>

<xsl:template match="ITEM">
   <xsl:apply-templates select="TITLE" />
      <DIV style="margin-left: 40pt;
         font-family: Times New Roman;
         font-size: 12pt;
         font-weight: 500;
         margin-bottom: 15pt;
         text-align: left;
         line-height: 12pt;
         text-indent: 0pt;" >
      <DIV>
         <SPAN>Category: </SPAN>
         <SPAN>
            <xsl:value-of select="CATEGORY"/>
         </SPAN>
         <SPAN> (</SPAN>
         <SPAN>
            <xsl:value-of select="CODE"/>
         </SPAN>
         <SPAN>)</SPAN>
      </DIV>
      <DIV>
         <SPAN>Release date: </SPAN>
         <SPAN>
```

```
            <xsl:value-of select="RELEASE_DATE"/>
         </SPAN>
         <SPAN>  -  Price: </SPAN>
         <SPAN>
            <xsl:value-of select="PRICE"/>
         </SPAN>
      </DIV>
   </DIV>
</xsl:template>

<xsl:template match="TITLE">
   <DIV style="margin-left: 40pt;
      font-family: Arial;
      font-weight: 700;
      font-size: 14pt;" >
      <SPAN>
         <xsl:value-of select="." />
      </SPAN>
   </DIV>
</xsl:template>

</xsl:stylesheet>
```

The above XSLT style sheet can be tested in IE5 by including a processing instruction in the sample XML document, just after the `<?xml version="1.0"?>` declaration. If you put the following processing instruction into the `booklist.xml` file:

```
<?xml-stylesheet type="text/xsl" href="booklist.xsl" media="screen"?>
```

then you should get the following result displayed in IE5:

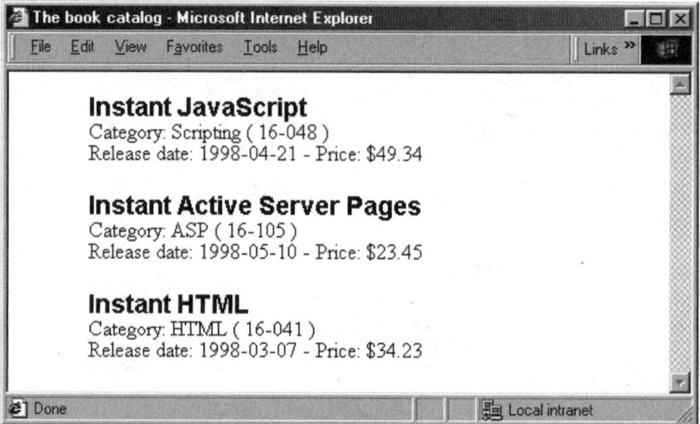

Note that while this stylesheet works in IE5, the version of XSL that it supports is not the same as the current working draft, our examples are written according to this working draft. So, let's take a look at how this style sheet works. The style sheet document is made up of a number of templates, each starting with the opening `<xsl:template>` tag and ending with the closing `</xsl:template>` tag. The `xsl:` part is the namespace for XSL, which prevents the processing application from confusing the `<template>` tag with any other element that may take the same name in the particular XML vocabulary. All XSL elements use this namespace.

The first template element takes the match attribute, which specifies the element to which the template should be applied. This is the selector. In this case, its value is the XML document's root element, indicated by the forward slash:

```
<xsl:template match="/">
```

This is actually an XPath expression, as laid out in the XPath working draft.

Within this template, we start producing the resulting HTML document, then we come across the xsl:apply-templates construct:

```
   <html xmlns="http://www.w3.org/TR/xhtml1/strict">
      <head>
         <title>The book catalog</title>
      </head>
      <body>
         <xsl:apply-templates select="BOOKLIST/ITEM" />
```

The instruction on the last line of this code section is used to apply any further templates specified at this position. The XPath expression "BOOKLIST/ITEM" means here that any template for the child <ITEM> elements of the <BOOKLIST> element will be matched. If you look at the remains of the first template:

```
      </body>
   </html>
</xsl:template>
```

we can see that we want the rest of the HTML elements to be written before we close the HTML document. So, when the processor reaches the <xsl:apply-templates /> element, we know that we want all other templates' content to be inserted in this location and replace the XSL construct with template content.

The second template is matched against all <ITEM> elements (as specified in the match attribute of the template element); these are then selected in the original XML document by the apply-templates construct:

```
<xsl:template match="ITEM">
   <xsl:apply-templates select="TITLE" />
```

Firstly the <TITLE> element is displayed, even if in the original document it is the fourth child element of <ITEM>. To display the <TITLE> element, the template matched to this element is applied. The template for <TITLE> is actually at the bottom of the style sheet:

```
<xsl:template match="TITLE">
   <DIV style="margin-left: 40pt;
      font-family: Arial;
      font-weight: 700;
      font-size: 14pt;" >
      <SPAN>
         <xsl:value-of select ="." />
      </SPAN>
   </DIV>
</xsl:template>
```

This has the effect of including a <DIV> element embellished with CSS properties. This <DIV> element contains a single <SPAN> with the content set to the <TITLE> element's content using the <xsl:value-of /> element. <xsl:value-of select ="."/> is effectively extracting the value of the element matching the select attribute. The "." expression, when used as a value for the select attribute, indicates that we want to select the value of the currently matched node (in this case the data content of the <TITLE> element). Thus, this whole template creates the first line of our display block (in exactly the same style as all the other examples in this chapter).

Having applied this template, the processor will move on to apply the rest of the last template, from the position where the <apply-templates /> in the last template was called.

```
<xsl:apply-templates select="TITLE" />
<DIV style="margin-left: 40pt;
   font-family: Times New Roman;
   font-size: 12pt;
   font-weight: 500;
   margin-bottom: 15pt;
   text-align: left;
   line-height: 12pt;
   text-indent: 0pt;" >
<DIV>
   <SPAN>Category: </SPAN>
   <SPAN>
      <xsl:value-of select="CATEGORY"/>
   </SPAN>
```

The rest of this template creates a <DIV> element – this is not in another template but in the template matched against the <ITEM> element. This last <DIV> contains inline HTML elements (such as <SPAN>). Some are simply strings that we insert in the resultant output and others are generated from the <xsl:value-of /> construct:

```
<SPAN>
   <xsl:value-of select="CATEGORY"/>
</SPAN>
```

So here the <SPAN> is created by extracting the data content (value) of the <CATEGORY> element. Just before this, we are writing out the legend for the elements content, in this case Category:

```
<SPAN>Category: </SPAN>
```

Having done the same thing for the code, this time putting it in parentheses, we finally add another <DIV> element with a strategy similar to the previous one. It includes the content of both the <RELEASE_DATE> and <PRICE> elements through the <xsl:value-of> construct respectively matched against the <RELEASE_DATE> and <PRICE> elements.

Unlike our CSS script, we have re-ordered the display of the XML document elements of our original document without having to re-organize the XML document itself first. Thus, XSL allows more rendition freedom and provides better independence of content and views.

Next, let's see how we create a version of this document that can be used for aural rendition.

A Sample XSLT Style Sheet with VOXML Aural Rendition Objects

The VOXML consortium led by Motorola provides an aural browser prototype and a VOXML SDK that developers can play with. The SDK and information about the VOXML project can be found at http://www.voxml.com. The VOXML project was motivated by the need to provide a common approach and broadly supported platform for voice applications, just as HTML provides for Web-based applications. VOXML applications take the form of dialogs. Navigation and input is produced via speech recognition of the end user's voice, and output is produced by text-to-speech technology or recorded audio.

The VOXML language is based on the XML format, and hence an XSLT document could be used to transform an original XML document into a VOXML application. Developing a VOXML application could be as easy as developing a Web-based application. An HTTP server can send the VOXML document to the aural user agent. The VOXML aplication is locally parsed and interpreted. The user interacts with the application through a microphone and headphones or speakers connected to the PC. Thus, a VOXML application server can be just an HTTP server, serving an XML document. The aural browser is dealing with the spech recognition and the text-to-speech processes.

VOXML applications are not solely limited to aural user agents but also could be running on a VOXML browser connected to the plain old telephone system. In this case, the input and output device is the telephone.

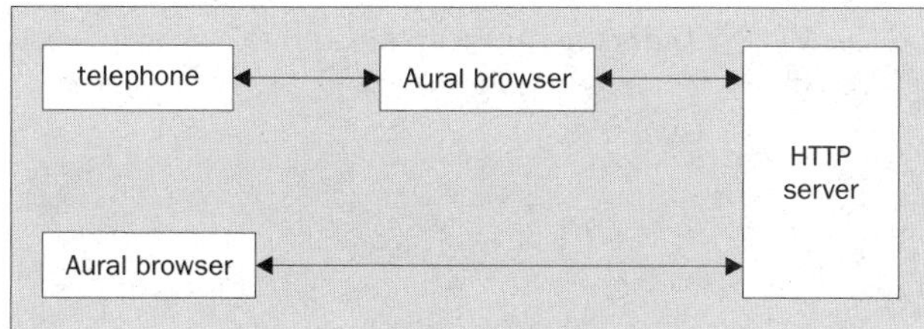

A white paper describing this architecture and a simple example is available at http://www.voxml.com/downloads/VoxMLwp.pdf.

Now, it's time to create a dialog between our potential user and a voice browser. The voice application that we'll create can be tested and improved with the VOXML SDK freely available for download from the VOXML consortium developer's web site located at: http://www.voxml.com/login.asp.

The original document can be transformed into VOXML with XT, an XSLT processor created by James Clark, which can be download at http://www.jclark.com/xml/xt.html (again, we used XT in Chapter 9 and appendix G tells you how to set it up). The resultant VOXML document can be interpreted with the VOXML simulator.

The figure below is the dialog displayed by the VOXML simulator. After having transformed your XML document into VOXML, you enter the URL for the transformed document. This document should have the `.vml` extension. Then you click on the enter button and all of a sudden, you'll see Merlin talking to you and waiting for an answer. You can reply to Merlin through a microphone or through the text at the bottom of the dialog. The response text area is provided in case you do not have a microphone.

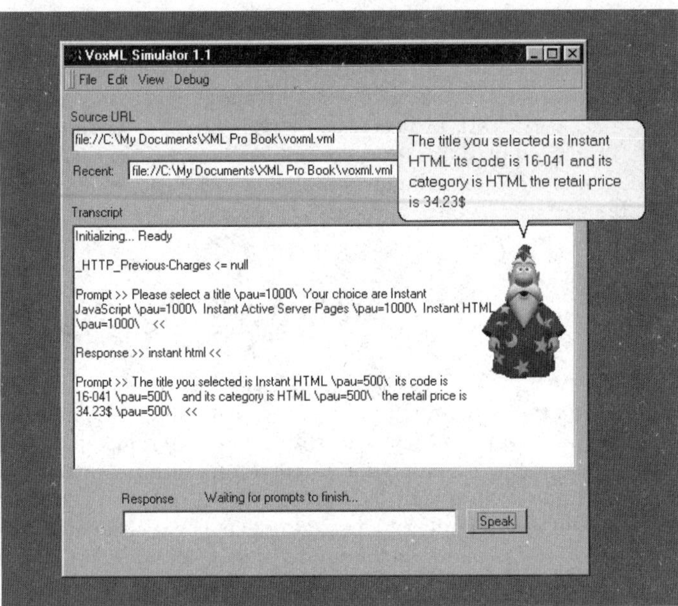

The document below is the VOXML document created with a XML to VOXML transformation using the XT processor. We'll see the style sheet in a moment.

```
<?xml version="1.0"?>
<DIALOG>
   <STEP NAME="init">
      <PROMPT>
         Please select a title<BREAK MSECS="1000"/>
      </PROMPT>
      <PROMPT>
         Your choices are: Instant JavaScript<BREAK MSECS="1000"/>
         Instant Active Server Pages<BREAK MSECS="1000"/>
         Instant HTML<BREAK MSECS="1000"/>
      </PROMPT>
      <INPUT TYPE="OPTIONLIST">
         <OPTION NEXT="#code:16-048">
            Instant JavaScript
         </OPTION>
         <OPTION NEXT="#code:16-105">
            Instant Active Server Pages
         </OPTION>
         <OPTION NEXT="#code:16-041">
            Instant HTML
         </OPTION>
      </INPUT>
   </STEP>
   <STEP NAME="code:16-048">
      <PROMPT>
         The title you selected is Instant JavaScript
         <BREAK MSECS="500"/>
      </PROMPT>
```

```
        <PROMPT>
           its code is 16-048<BREAK MSECS="500"/>
        </PROMPT>
        <PROMPT>
           its category is Scripting<BREAK MSECS="500"/>
        </PROMPT>
        <PROMPT>
           and the retail price is $49.34<BREAK MSECS="500"/>
        </PROMPT>
     </STEP>
     <STEP NAME="code:16-105">
        <PROMPT>
           The title you selected is Instant Active Server Pages
           <BREAK MSECS="500"/>
        </PROMPT>
        <PROMPT>
           its code is 16-105<BREAK MSECS="500"/>
        </PROMPT>
        <PROMPT>
           its category is ASP<BREAK MSECS="500"/>
        </PROMPT>
        <PROMPT>
           and the retail price is $23.45<BREAK MSECS="500"/>
        </PROMPT>
     </STEP>
     <STEP NAME="code:16-041">
        <PROMPT>
           The title you selected is Instant HTML
           <BREAK MSECS="500"/>
        </PROMPT>
        <PROMPT>
           its code is 16-041<BREAK MSECS="500"/>
        </PROMPT>
        <PROMPT>
           its category is HTML<BREAK MSECS="500"/>
        </PROMPT>
        <PROMPT>
           and the retail price is $34.23<BREAK MSECS="500"/>
        </PROMPT>
     </STEP>
  </DIALOG>
```

This document will give the user three options of books; if the user selects one, it will then tell them the title that they selected.

We won't go into the details of the VOXML language. These details are provided by the VOXML SDK. Instead, we will focus on the XSLT style sheet instead called `booklist_aural.xsl`:

```
<xsl:stylesheet version="1.0"
   xmlns:xsl="http://www.w3.org/1999/XSL/Transform">

<xsl:output method="xml"/>
```

```
<xsl:template match="/">
   <DIALOG>
      <xsl:apply-templates/>
   </DIALOG>
</xsl:template>

<xsl:template match ="BOOKLIST">
   <STEP NAME="init">
      <PROMPT>Please select a title<BREAK MSECS="1000" /></PROMPT>
      <PROMPT>
         Your choices are
         <xsl:for-each select="ITEM">
            <xsl:value-of select="TITLE"/><BREAK MSECS="1000" />
         </xsl:for-each>
      </PROMPT>
      <INPUT TYPE="OPTIONLIST">
         <xsl:for-each select="ITEM">
            <xsl:element name="OPTION">
               <xsl:attribute name="NEXT">
                  #code:<xsl:value-of select="CODE"/>
               </xsl:attribute>
               <xsl:value-of select="TITLE"/>
            </xsl:element>
         </xsl:for-each>
      </INPUT>
   </STEP>
   <xsl:apply-templates/>
</xsl:template>

<xsl:template match="ITEM">
   <xsl:element name="STEP">
      <xsl:attribute name="NAME">code:<xsl:value-of select="CODE"/>
      </xsl:attribute>
      <PROMPT>
         The title you selected is
         <xsl:value-of select="TITLE"/>
         <BREAK MSECS="500" />
      </PROMPT>
      <PROMPT>
         its code is
         <xsl:value-of select = "CODE"/>
         <BREAK MSECS="500" />
      </PROMPT>
      <PROMPT>
         its category is
         <xsl:value-of select="CATEGORY" />
         <BREAK MSECS="500" />
      </PROMPT>
      <PROMPT>
         and the retail price is
         <xsl:value-of select="PRICE" />
         <BREAK MSECS="500" />
      </PROMPT>
   </xsl:element>
</xsl:template>

</xsl:stylesheet>
```

Firstly we tell the XSLT engine that the intended output is XML, using the `xsl:output` construct. In the case of the XT engine, the format can be either XML or HTML.

Next we match the first template with the root node: the document node. Because we cannot introduce another XML processing instruction, we use the `xsl:processing-instruction` element to include the `<?xml version="1.0"?>` processing instruction.

Note: according to the XSLT recommendation, the XML declaration should not be created with a `processing-instruction` construct. The `xsl:output` construct with the `method` attribute set to `"xml"` should be sufficient to generate the appropriate XML declaration. We included a `processing-instruction` construct in the sample template because of the current XT limitations.

We enclose the `xsl:apply-templates` construct in the `<DIALOG>` element required by the VOXML engine (in the last example we enclosed this construct with the `<html>` element). This forces the XSLT engine to process all children nodes of the root node.

```
<DIALOG>
   <xsl:apply-templates/>
</DIALOG>
```

The second template is matched with the `<BOOKLIST>` element. The template contains a `<STEP>` element creating a dialog step for the VOXML engine. The `<PROMPT>` elements' content is rendered as speech. It enumerates the available titles contained in the book catalog. The enumeration is constructed with an `xsl:for-each` loop matched with any `<ITEM>` element child of the current template matched element which is the `<BOOKLIST>` element. For each `<ITEM>` element occurrence, the `<TITLE>` element's content is inserted in the `<PROMPT>` element with an `xsl:value-of` construct, and a `<BREAK>` element is appended before the `</PROMPT>` ending tag:

```
<PROMPT>
   Your choices are
   <xsl:for-each select="ITEM">
      <xsl:value-of select="TITLE"/><BREAK MSECS="1000" />
   </xsl:for-each>
</PROMPT>
```

The same technique is applied to the `<INPUT>` element. Several `<OPTION>` elements are included with an `xsl:for-each` loop matched with any `<ITEM>` elements. Because the `<OPTION>` element has to be created with data extracted from the XML document, we use the `xsl:element` construct in association with the `xsl:attribute` construct:

```
<xsl:for-each select="ITEM">
   <xsl:element name="OPTION">
      <xsl:attribute name="NEXT">
         #code:
         <xsl:value-of select="CODE"/>
      </xsl:attribute>
      <xsl:value-of select="TITLE"/>
   </xsl:element>
</xsl:for-each>
```

This loop produces the following output:

```
<OPTION NEXT="#code:16-048">Instant JavaScript</OPTION>
<OPTION NEXT="#code:16-105">Instant Active Server Pages</OPTION>
<OPTION NEXT="#code:16-041">Instant HTML</OPTION>
```

As usual, the template contains an `xsl:apply-templates` to force the XSLT engine to process all child nodes.

The third template is matched with the `<ITEM>` element. The template creates a `<STEP>` element with the `xsl:element` construct, and then its NAME attribute is created with `xsl:attribute`. This takes its value from the XML document with `xsl-value-of`, which appends the `<CODE>` data content to the "code:" content:

```
<xsl:element name="STEP">
   <xsl:attribute name="NAME">
      code:
      <xsl:value-of select="CODE"/>
   </xsl:attribute>
```

The subsequent `<PROMPT>` elements are created with data content extracted with the `xsl:value-of` construct:

```
<PROMPT>
   The title you selected is
   <xsl:value-of select="TITLE"/>
   <BREAK MSECS="500" />
</PROMPT>
```

The above statement creates the following output:

```
<PROMPT>
   The title you selected is Instant JavaScript
   <BREAK MSECS="500"/>
</PROMPT>
```

The VOXML example can be tested by firstly transforming the XML document into VOXML with XT, and then interpreting the VOXML document with the simulator included in the VOXML SDK.

A Sample XSLT Style Sheet with Formatting Objects

James Tauber created FOP to implement XML to PDF transformation using XSL formatting objects. The FOP package is a free download, which can be found at http://www.jtauber.com/fop/. A soon-to-be-released XSLF commercial package can be found at http://www.renderx.com.

The PDF format is based on a page model. A page could be printed or displayed on screen with the Adobe PDF viewer or the PDF plug-in.

The general structure of XSLF documents (which can be created by an XSLT transformation engine) begins with a root element of `<root>`. This has two sub-elements, a single `<fo:layout-master-set>` element, and one or more `<fo:page-sequence>` elements:

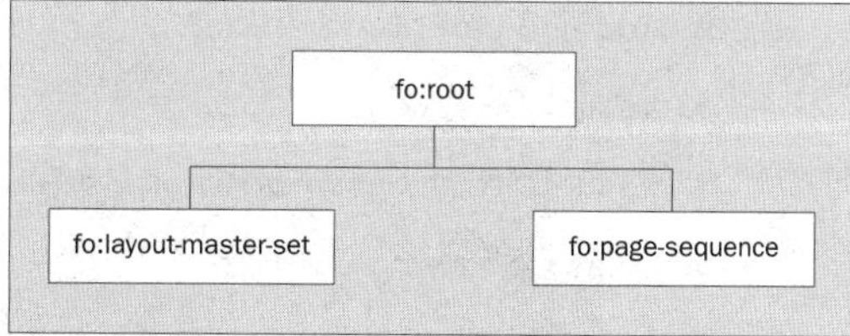

The `fo:layout-master-set` construct contains one or more `<fo:simple-page-master>` elements, which act as a template for the layout, while the `<fo:page-sequence>` elements hold the content of the document. These elements divide a page into 5 distinct regions:

- The body of a document (`xsl-body`)
- The region-before, or the header (`xsl-before`)
- The region-after, or the footer (`xsl-after`)
- The region-start, or left sidebar (`xsl-start`)
- The region-end, or right sidebar (`xsl-end`)

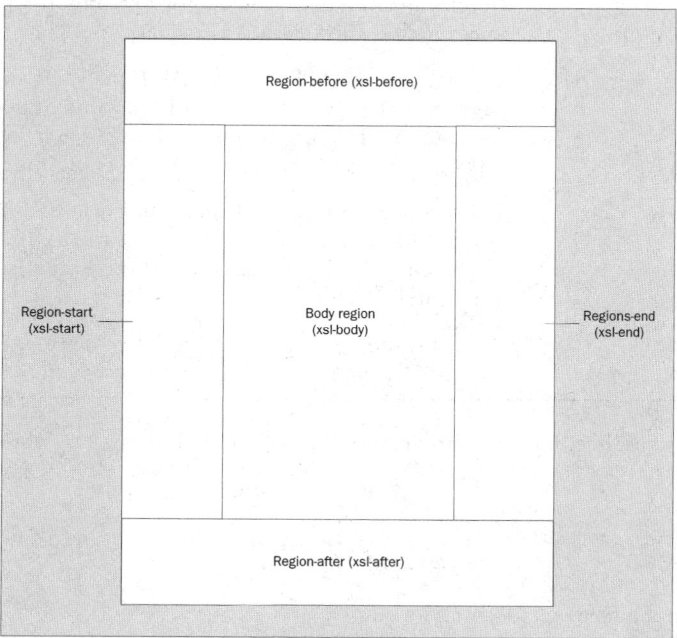

`fo:simple-page-master` has the following properties:

Property	Description
id	A unique element identifier.
margin-top	Same as CSS margin-top.
margin-bottom	Same as CSS margin-bottom.
margin-left	Same as CSS margin-left.
margin-right	Same as CSS margin-right.
margin	A shorthand property for setting margin-top, margin-right, margin-bottom, and margin-left of a block-area or inline-area.
page-master-name	Provides an identifying name for the page-master. This name is subsequently used by: fo:sequence-specifier-single, fo:sequence-specifier-repeating, and fo:sequence-specifier-alternating to request the use of this master to create a page instance.
page-height	Determines the page height. For example, the page could be set to 11 inches for a 8½ x 11 inch format.
page-width	Determines the page width. For example the page could be set to 8½ inches for a 8½ x 11 format.
reference-orientation	The content could be displayed in the same orientation as the page or be rotated. For example, a value of 90 would rotate the content 90 degrees counter-clockwise from the reference-orientation of the containing area.
size	This property specifies the size and orientation of a page box. For example if the value is set to "landscape", the page box is the same size as the target, and the longer sides are horizontal.
writing-mode	Indicates the writing direction. For example, this can be set to far east writing mode, which is right to left.

Here is a sample style sheet for transforming the catalog into XSL formatting objects called `booklist_FO.xsl`:

```
<xsl:stylesheet version="1.0"
   xmlns:xsl="http://www.w3.org/1999/XSL/Transform">

<xsl:template match="/">
   <fo:root xmlns:fo=http://www.w3.org/XSL/Format/1.0>

      <fo:layout-master-set>
         <fo:simple-page-master page-master-name="pagemaster-1">
            <fo:region-body
```

```
            column-count="1"
            reference-orientation="0"
            margin="1in" />
      </fo:simple-page-master>
   </fo:layout-master set>

   <fo:page-sequence>
      <fo:sequence-specification>
         <fo:sequence-specifier-single
            page-master-name="pagemaster-1"/>
      </fo:sequence-specification>

      <fo:static-content flow-name="xsl-before">
         <fo:block text-align="centered"
            font=36pt Times"
            font-weight="bold"
            space-after.optimum="6pt"
            color="red">Book Catalog</fo:block>
      <fo:static-content>

      <fo:static-content flow-name="xsl-after">
         <fo:block>
            <fo:block text-align="centered" font="10pt Times">
               <fo:page-number/>
            </fo:block>
         </fo:block>
      </fo:static-content>

      <fo:flow flow-name="xsl-body">
         <fo:block>
            <fo:display-sequence
               text-align="justified"
               font="1pica Times">
               <xsl:apply-templates/>
            </fo:display-sequence>
         </fo:block>
      </fo:flow>
   </fo:page-sequence>
  </fo:root>
</xsl:template>

<xsl:template match="ITEM">
   <fo:block space-before.optimum="9pt">
      <xsl:apply-templates select="TITLE" />
      <fo:block>
         <fo:inline-sequence>Category: </fo:inline-sequence>
         <fo:inline-sequence>
            <xsl:value-of select="CATEGORY"/>
         </fo:inline-sequence>
         <fo:inline-sequence> (</fo:inline-sequence>
         <fo:inline-sequence>
            <xsl:value-of select="CODE"/>
         </fo:inline-sequence>
         <fo:inline-sequence> )</fo:inline-sequence>
```

```
            <fo:block>
               <fo:inline-sequence>Release date: </fo:inline-sequence>
               <fo:inline-sequence>
                  <xsl:value-of select="RELEASE_DATE"/>
               </fo:inline-sequence>
               <fo:inline-sequence>-  Price: </fo:inline-sequence>
               <fo:inline-sequence>
                  <xsl:value-of select="PRICE"/>
               </fo:inline-sequence>
            </fo:block>
         </fo:block>
   </xsl:template>

   <xsl:template match="TITLE">
      <fo:block
         font=14pt Arial"
         font-weight="bold">
         <fo:inline-sequence>
            <xsl:value-of select ="." />
         </fo:inline-sequence>
      </fo:block>
   </xsl:template>
```

The template matching the root node produces a page master with a body region containing a single column. The `reference-orientation` is in the same orientation as the page (`portrait`) and the margin is 1 inch all around the body region:

```
<fo:layout-master-set>
   <fo:simple-page-master page-master-name="pagemaster-1">
      <fo:region-body
         column-count="1"
         reference-orientation="0"
         margin="1in" />
   </fo:simple-page-master>
</fo:layout-master set>
```

After a page master layout is created, the next step is to create a page sequence. The `<fo:page-sequence>` element contains an `<fo:sequence-specification>` element, zero or more `<fo:static-content>` elements, and an `<fo:flow>` element.

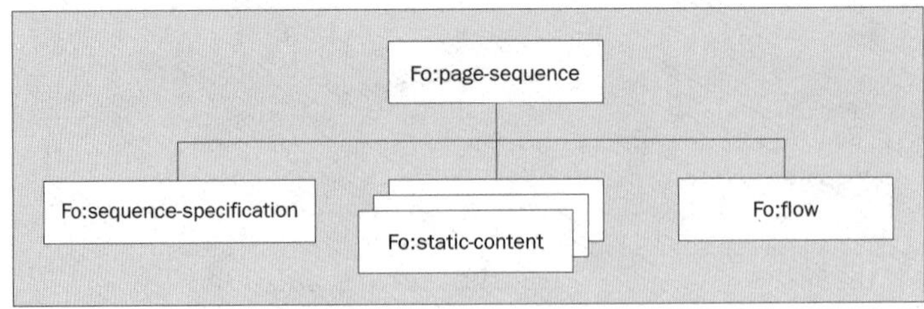

Basically, this element indicates to the XSL formatter how the pages will appear. Imagine that this element sets conditions applied by default to all subsequently rendered pages.

The <fo:sequence-specification> element contains one or more <fo:sequence-specifier-single>, <fo:sequence-specifier-repeating>, and <fo:sequence-specifier-alternating> elements.

In our example we used the <fo:sequence-specifier-single> element specifying to the XSL formatter that we are to use the page-master named "pagemaster-1" previously defined in the <fo:simple-page-master> element. This provides a template for pages to be rendered. In our case, pages will all have a 1 inch margin as mentioned in the page-master formatting object. By default, all pages are formatted in the same way:

```
<fo:sequence-specification>
   <fo:sequence-specifier-single
      page-master-name="pagemaster-1"/>
</fo:sequence-specification>
```

The <fo:sequence-specifier-alternative> element allows us to set different layouts for documents such as books, where pages have to be laid out differently. For example, one page-master can be used for even pages and another kind for odd pages. The <fo:sequence-specifier-repeating> element allows us to set a layout for the front page and a repeating sequence for subsequent pages.

In our pages we include two static content formatting objects: title and page number. This means that this static content will be included in all pages without any reference to the XML document content. This is like defining constants in a program.

Firstly, we create a static content for the title. The title is displayed before the document's body. This is specified by the flow-name property set to the "xsl-before" value. The title itself is created by a <fo:block> element which is centered, bold, red colored, displayed with a 36 pt Times font, and includes a space of size equal to 6 pt inserted below it. A XSL block is mostly similar to a CSS block object, and thus shares most of its properties:

```
<fo:static-content flow-name="xsl-before">
   <fo:block text-align="centered"
      font=36pt Times"
      font-weight="bold"
      space-after.optimum="6pt"
      color="red">Book Catalog</fo:block>
<fo:static-content>
```

In the example, we define a page number displayed after the body region. This is indicated by setting the flow-name property to "xsl-after". Another block formatting object is used to contain the page number, which is centered and rendered with a 10 pt Times font:

```
<fo:static-content flow-name="xsl-after">
   <fo:block>
      <fo:block text-align="centered" font="10pt Times">
         <fo:page-number/>
      </fo:block>
   </fo:block>
</fo:static-content>
```

Finally, we define the `<fo:flow>` element. This formatting object contains the XML document content. This is specified by setting the `flow-name` property to "`xsl-body`":

```
<fo:flow flow-name="xsl-body">
```

This element contains all the formatting objects associated to the XML document and consists of the document body.

Thus, we defined the basic overall layout for each page in a page master. The page master is used as a template in the `<fo:sequence-specification>` element. Then, we added a page number at the end of each page with the `<fo:static-content>` element. Finally, we defined the document body where all the flow objects associated with our XML document will be laid out.

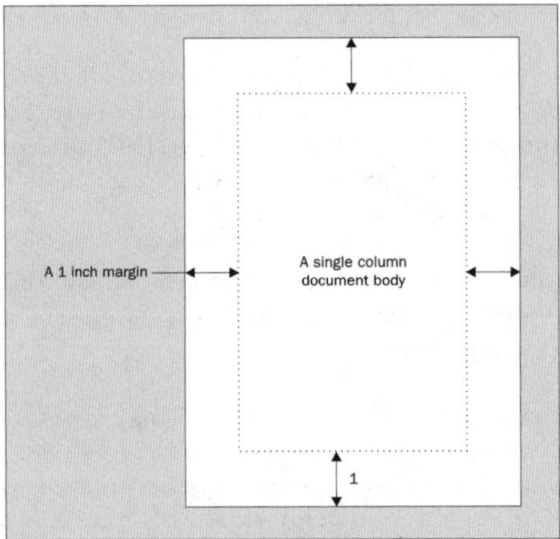

All elements contained in the body inherit their properties from the `<fo:display-sequence>` element. This specifies a set of properties inherited by all contained elements. Because we included the `<xsl:apply-templates>` element in it, and also because this construct is created in the root template, all other subsequent templates will replace the `xsl:apply-template` construct and inherit their default properties from the display-sequence element.

```
<fo:block>
   <fo:display-sequence
      text-align="justified"
      font="1pica Times">
      <xsl:apply-templates/>
   </fo:display-sequence>
</fo:block>
```

Each `<ITEM>` element is matched to a template creating a block for each instance of this element. The block is displayed with some space before it (9 pt). We added the "`optimum`" keyword to specify to the XSL formatter that the optimum value for the space is 9 pt – we could have mentioned a maximum or a minimum value:

```
<fo:block space-before.optimum="9pt">
```

This main block container contains three other blocks:

- The title
- The book's category and code
- The book's release date and price

The title is created by invoking the template associated to the <TITLE> element. This template contains an <fo:block> element which overrides some of the display-sequence properties:

```
<xsl:template match="ITEM">
   <fo:block space-before.optimum="9pt">
      <xsl:apply-templates select="TITLE" />

...

<xsl:template match="TITLE">
   <fo:block
      font=14pt Arial"
      font-weight="bold">
      <fo:inline-sequence>
         <xsl:value-of  select =" ."/>
      </fo:inline-sequence>
   </fo:block>
</xsl:template>
```

The other two block formatting objects displayed after the title contain <fo:inline-sequence> formatting objects with content extracted from the XML document through the <xsl:value-of> element. An inline-sequence formatting object is mostly similar to a CSS inline object.

Once you have created the transformed document, you can then use an application such as FOP to create a PDF version of the document.

Concluding Thoughts on XSL

XSLT is a clear winner; IE version 5 added XSLT to HTML+CSS transformation capability, and Mozilla XSLT support, at the time of writing, is a work in progress. So when browsers support a style language, and because XSLT is a powerful language, we have here ingredients for success.

I cannot say the same thing about XSLF (the formatting part of XSL). Its future depends on support built into XML authoring tools. But even if that is the case, if browsers do not support the language, it won't be as popular as XSLT. However, this language may fulfill the same niche as DSSSL (which we meet next) as a print styling language.

XSLT has also a lot of potential for server side transformations, since an XML document could be transformed into HTML+CSS for desktop browsers, into VOXML for aural browsers, and into WML for mobile phones and PDAs.

Having taken a look at CSS and XSL, we will now very briefly look at two other languages that you may choose to learn more about: DSSSL and Omnimark. We will briefly talk about each, and then show a sample of code that could be used with the booklist file so that you can get an idea of the syntax – there is not space to cover either of these in detail, however, you should get an idea of whether you should invest more time in learning about them.

DSSSL

DSSSL has been an ISO standard since 1996. The language is mainly composed of two parts:

- A style language
- A transformation language

The style language is very scalable and could be used as simply as CSS or with a full **expression** language. The expression language is a full programming language that allows you to do more elaborate processing on the XML document hierarchical model. Its visual model is based on flow objects independent of any particular implementation. For example, the DSSSL paragraph flow object could be mapped to an HTML `<P>` element, and a RTF `/par` object. It is a rule based language able to process SGML and XML documents. A lot of DSSSL features have been included in XSL.

DSSSL is often said to be hard to learn and complex. This is because of the powerful expression language that DSSSL includes. The expression language is a subset of LISP named **Scheme**. Programmers used to block-based procedural languages like C, C++, Basic, Pascal, etc. may have difficulty learning it. However, DSSSL can be used without the expression language, and in this case its difficulty level is about the same as CSS.

DSSSL expression language is well adapted to symbol manipulation. Very powerful style sheets can be constructed with the DSSSL style formatting objects and the scheme based expression language. Actually, DSSSL is usually used for print publication rather than on-line rendition. However, several server-side implementations are used to transform SGML or XML documents into HTML.

A DSSSL **Script** is used to process an XML document by first transforming it into a **GROVE**. The GROVE is the ISO equivalent of the W3C DOM. However, it is more of an abstract model, while the DOM is an API. We can say that the GROVE is probably nearer to W3C Information Sets than to the DOM. The GROVE is a data model and the DOM is an interface to this data model. So, when a GROVE or data structure is constructed, the DSSSL rules are pattern matched on the XML document elements. The DSSSL rule model is more complex than the one used in XSL, and includes several type of rule – whereas only one type is sufficient for XSL.

DSSSL could be used to transform XML documents. Its rendering model is as powerful as the XSL model, and provides independence between the XML document structure and its rendition. It is also possible to add new elements and strings, and to re-order elements for final output.

Unlike XSLF, which, at the time of this writing, is still work in progress, DSSSL is already used for day-to-day document processing. The first implementations were available from James Clark who wrote a program called Jade. Now the source is maintained by an international group of developers and Jade has become OpenJade, an open source project. OpenJade is a free download able to convert SGML or XML documents into HTML, SGML, XML, PDF, MIF, TeX, RTF, or Braille and is available at http://www.netfolder.com/DSSSL.

A Sample Style Script

In the example below, we could create the same result as we have done with XSL without having to transform the document before style processing, as we had to do with CSS. We will not go into the script in detail, but we will take a quick look at some of the basic concepts of DSSSL:

```
<!doctype style-sheet
   PUBLIC "-//Netfolder//DTD DSSSL library//EN" >
(root
   (make scroll
      (process-children)
   )
)

(element ITEM
   (make paragraph
      start-indent: 40pt
      font-family-name: "Times New Roman"
      font-size: 12pt
      font-weight: 'medium
      space-after: 15pt
      (process-matching-children "TITLE")
      (make paragraph
         font-weight: 'medium
         (literal "Category: ")
         (process-matching-children "CATEGORY")
         (literal " (")
         (process-matching-children "CODE")
         (literal ")")
      )
      (make paragraph
         (literal "Release date: ")
         (process-matching-children "RELEASE_DATE")
         (literal "  -  Price: ")
         (process-matching-children "PRICE")
      )
   )
)

(element TITLE
   (make paragraph
      font-family-name: "Arial"
      font-size: 14pt
      font-weight: 'bold
   )
)

(element CATEGORY
   (make sequence)
)

(element CODE
   (make sequence)
)
```

```
(element RELEASE_DATE
   (make sequence)
)

(element PRICE
   (make sequence)
)
```

The first rule creates a `scroll` formatting object. This represents the browser's scrollable view. The `root` element of this part of the style sheet refers to the XML document and not the root element. If we wanted to render the document onto a printed medium, then we would have used the `simple-page-sequence` formatting object.

The rule matched against the `<ITEM>` element is doing most of the job. First, a `paragraph` object is created. A `paragraph` is a rectangular area able to contain `sequence` objects. `Paragraphs` are similar to CSS `box` objects, and `sequence` objects are similar to `inline` objects.

The paragraph properties are called `characteristics`, and you have probably noticed they resemble CSS property names. The DSSSL construct:

```
(process-matching-children "TITLE")
```

instructs the style engine to fire the rule associated to the `<TITLE>` element. This latter creates a `paragraph` object contained in the previous one. Once this paragraph has been created, two other paragraphs are appended to it.

As we did with XSLT to HTML transformation, new content not present in the original document is added. This is accomplished through the `literal` formatting object, which is equivalent to a string. The content is included before producing the formatting object associated to the `<CATEGORY>` element:

```
(literal "Category: ")
(process-matching-children "CATEGORY")
```

If a set of elements share a common rule body, it is more convenient to use the following notation:

```
(element CATEGORY CODE RELEASE_DATE PRICE
   (make sequence)
)
```

This kind of construct is not part of the DSSSL ISO standard, but has been implemented in the OpenJade package to make life easier.

The DSSSL specifications are not a static entity, and this ISO style language is now entering a second edition phase. This is called the DSSSL-2 project and is an extension to improve upon the existing specification. Obviously, the actual specifications are maintained to assure stability of existing style sheets.

Concluding Thoughts on DSSSL

As you probably noticed, DSSSL is not necessarily harder to learn than XSLF, in fact it may even be simpler on certain facets. Of course, its expression language 'scheme' may not be as easy to understand for people used to procedural languages such as JavaScript. However, its formatting object construction mechanism is quite simple and very readable, maybe even more so than XSL. However, access to the GROVE nodes is less economical than using XPath.

Overall, DSSSL is a very powerful language probably more adapted to document processing for printed material than to on-line rendition, but it already has support in the print world.

Omnimark

Recently, the Omnimark language (created and produced by Omnimark Technologies) became available in the form of a free package. It can be downloaded from their site at http://www.omnimark.com. Because it can now be freely downloaded and used to produce HTML documents from XML documents, we'll take a very brief look at this simple language.

As with the languages we previously discussed, Omnimark is rule-based language. A rule is matched to an XML element with the Omnimark `element` construct. Unlike DSSSL, CSS, or XSL, it doesn't include a set of visual formatting objects, but uses a procedure named `output()`. The `output()` procedure takes a string as its parameter. This string can include any kind of expression, and could therefore be used to output documents for text based formatting languages like VOXML, HTML, TeX, and so on.

As with DSSSL or XSL, this language has a construct used to include the content produced by other rules. The `%c` expression means `content`, and is replaced by the output of rules matched with child elements of the current fired rule. For instance, the `<ITEM>` element is a child of the `<BOOKLIST>` element, so, if the rule matching the `<BOOKLIST>` element contains an output construct that has a parameter including a `%c` expression, then the content produced by the rule matching the `<ITEM>` element replaces the expression in the resultant document.

A Simple Omnimark Script

The following script is a bit different to other style sheet languages, although it is still rule based. Elements from the XML document are matched with an Omnimark rule. A rule, in its simplest form contains one or more `output` constructs. The desired result takes the form of a string:

```
down-translate with xml

element BOOKLIST
   output "<html>%n<head>%n" ||
      "<title>Transform with Omnimark<title>%n" ||
      "</head>%n<body>%c</body>%n</html>"

element ITEM
   output "<DIV style="margin-left: 40pt;%n" ||
      "font-family: Times New Roman;%n" ||
      "font-size: 12pt;%n" ||
      "font-weight: 500;%n" ||
      "margin-bottom: 15pt;%n" ||
```

```
        "text-align: left;%n" ||
        "line-height: 12pt;%n" ||
        "text-indent: 0pt;" >%n"

element TITLE
   output "<DIV style="margin-left: 40pt;%n" ||
        "font-family: Arial;%n" ||
        "font-weight: 700;%n" ||
        "font-size: 14pt;" >%n » ||
        "<SPAN>%c</SPAN>%n</DIV>%n"

element DESCRIPTION
   output "<DIV>%n%c%n</DIV>%n"

element ( CATEGORY | CODE | RELEASE_DATE | PRICE )
   output "<SPAN>%c</SPAN>"
```

You probably noticed that the output expressions contain some characters delimited by `%`. These are commands included in the output string. For example, the `%c` construct included in the rule:

```
element BOOKLIST
   output "<html>%n<head>%n" ||
      "<title>Transform with Omnimark<title>%n" ||
      "</head>%n<body>%c</body>%n</html>"
```

is the equivalent of the XSLT `apply-templates` construct. It indicates to the Omnimark engine that the other rules matching the `<BOOKLIST>` element's children will be inserted at this position in the resultant string.

Another construct, `%n`, indicates to insert an end of line (rather like `CR/LF` – a carriage return/line feed) so that the output stream will be more readable.

Concluding Thoughts on Omnimark

Apart from transformations, Omnimark is an easy to use language, but transformations are where XSLT shines. Still, for usual XML to HTML transformation and for people more used to procedural languages than to declarative languages, it is a tool worth mentioning.

Summary

In this chapter we have looked carefully at two styling languages, CSS and XSL, that can be used to present XML to users, and then taken a brief look at DSSSL and Omnimark, which can also be used with XML.

We saw that CSS1 and CSS2 are stable recommendations with parts already implemented in IE5, and in the future Mozilla browser. In addition, CSS3 is already on its way, improving the existing CSS model. These are currently ideal for viewing XML documents in XML- and CSS-aware browsers. Furthermore, the language is easy to use and learn, and will be familiar to existing HTML users.

Then we went on to look at XSL. At the time of writing XSLT and XPath had just become a recommendation at the W3C, so there will be a time lag before the major browser vendors implement the new standard (although they are sure to implement it eventually). In the mean time, there are other tools that will offer XSLT support. In addition the formatting objects effort was still underway, which will offer greater print support. However, XSLT is a strong general transformation tool. It allows us to create a number of formats for presentation, not necessarily requiring an XML-aware user-agent.

We also got a preview of the powerful DSSSL language, which can process either SGML or XML documents. This is based on an international standard due for revision soon, and we should expect a second generation DSSSL, which (we hope) will contain new features resulting from the knowledge gained in the last few years. Finally, we got a brief look at the Omnimark language. Even though this is a proprietary language, it is used everyday in a lot of situations and has been proven as a useful tool. Contrary to most proprietary languages, there is a free version available for download, and people used to procedural languages will be at home with this language.

Most of these tools are free downloads, so you can experiment with their limits and potential on your own:

- CSS: included in IE5 (http://www.microsoft.ie) and Mozilla (http://www.mizilla.org)
- XSLT: included in IE5, James Clark's XT (http://www.jclark.com/xml/xt.html) and SAXON (http://users.iclway.co.uk/mhkay/saxon)
- XSLF: James Tauber's FOP (http://www.jtauber.com/fop/)
- DSSSL: OpenJade (http://www.netfolder.com/DSSSL)
- Omnimark: Omnimark Corp (http://www.omnimark.com)

14

Wireless Application Protocol

Traditionally, when we think of browsing the Web, we think of browsers on desktop computers. This perception, however, is starting to change now that consumer devices such as mobile phones and personal digital assistants (or PDAs like the Palm Pilot and Psion Organizers) are also offering Web access. These devices, with their low bandwidth and small displays, require us to re-think the way web services are created and delivered. Although the market is currently immature, standards are emerging to offer a way of delivering services that is different from traditional browsing, or "surfing".

Mobile phone sales outstripped the number of desktop PCs sold in 1998, and many predict that this trend will continue well into the next century. With the high volume of devices offering different capabilities from desktop computers, the Internet will become an even more diverse place, where the ability to adapt services to a wide spectrum of clients will be essential for web services that wish to prevail.

In this chapter we will take a look at the problems that these new technologies present to web developers, and an emerging set of standards collectively known as the **Wireless Application Protocol** (**WAP**), which is designed for use on web enabled mobile phones and PDAs. The home for the WAP effort is http://www.wapforum.org/. We will also look at the technologies surrounding WAP, in particular how XML can form a strong base for providing content for these "platforms of the future", where networked services are not restricted to our desktops.

In order to address these future clients, we will also introduce an application of XML called **Wireless Markup Language** (WML). This is the language part of WAP used to mark up the data that is to be transported to these devices.

Specifically, in this chapter we will see:

- The challenges these new consumer devices pose to web developers
- How WAP enables us to serve web content to these new devices
- An introduction to the Wireless Markup Language
- A user-interface to search the Wrox book catalog on a mobile phone
- How XML content allows us to create pages for a variety of different platforms without creating parallel sites for each
- An introduction to WMLScript, the scripting language part of WAP

So, accepting that these new consumer devices will be a major force in the future of the Web, let's get on and see what challenges will face us in the wireless world.

Introducing the New Client

Compared to desktop computers, the new classes of web-enabled devices have limited hardware, software, and network capabilities. To provide an appropriate service to all Internet clients – from mobile phones to desktop computers – web servers must adapt their services based on the capabilities of the clients.

Today, most web servers basically provide the same service to all desktop clients. Some reproduce different parts of the web site for different browsers, one for recent versions of Internet Explorer, one for Netscape Navigator 4, and another for older browsers. To those who have experienced the headache of providing web pages that offer the same functionality in the different desktop browser versions, coping with these new generation clients may sound like a disaster in the making. As we shall see in the following section, called *Building Sites from the Ground up*, this need not be the case.

As diversity increases on the Internet, web servers must become more intelligent in their information delivery and offer the information the client wants, based on the capabilities of the device. Even though capabilities such as memory and processing power are likely to improve over time, because mobile phones and PDAs evolve in parallel to desktop computers, the capability gap between the two types of devices will prevail. This means that adapting web services to a wide spectrum of different devices will not be a temporary effort; it is the reality of the future Web.

Common traits of these new devices include:

- Smaller screens with low resolution
- Little memory and processing power available to run software and store applications
- Lower network bandwidth compared with wired networks

Due to differences in display capabilities and network bandwidth, we will need to adapt more than the presentation language to the specific device; the structure and content of the service is also likely to be different. For example, you may want to change a question such as "please enter your name" into "enter name" in the variant to be presented on a mobile phone.

In addition, these have spawned other areas of interest; different displays mean that we need to identify new usage patterns and different UI paradigms, for example. Also, the different technologies behind mobile devices allow new avenues for web applications, from location aware applications designed for use on the move, to new applications of push and voice technologies.

Since the market for consumer devices is growing at an amazing speed, the number of "legacy" devices will be large. To cover the entire spectrum of devices, content must be stored in a format that is independent of the fast evolution of presentation languages and device capabilities.

So, how do we address this problem of creating many different versions of a site? The answer is to build our web sites in a different way.

Building Sites from The Ground up

Until recently, web pages have primarily been written in HTML solely for display on desktop browsers, a language that effectively describes presentation for the desktop web browser. HTML's focus on presentation – as opposed to content – illustrates one of the major benefits of using XML in web development.

If we think about the web site in terms of "content", and mark up our data accordingly in XML, we can transform the same data into different formats. This means that it can effectively be re-purposed for different clients by changing what parts of, and how, the content is displayed. Much as we saw in Chapter 9, Manipulating XML, we can use XSL to transform the content of a site marked up using XML into different HTML versions, and also use it to transform the content into other presentation languages. This is the ideal approach for a web server that wishes to support more than the traditional web clients. The task of adapting the service to different devices becomes a matter of manipulating XML documents. (We will also explore another transformation technique in Case Study 3, which may be more suitable for large documents.)

By writing content in XML, templates can be used to adapt the service to various devices. We are building the site from the ground up: we build the content first (the heart of the site), and then transform the content for its various purposes. Supporting a new type of device, or a new version of a language, becomes a matter of creating new templates rather than replicating large amounts of documents stored in one particular version of a presentation language. This means that we can just offer the content that is suitable for each purpose – taking the limitations and new possibilities inherent in the new handheld devices into account, while still supporting desktop clients, although of course the data will be required in a different form.

If you consider a directory of restaurants, mobile devices will not be able to display the same amount of data about choices on one screen, so the way that the user navigates to the appropriate data may follow a different paradigm. The service, however, may also be extended to include a best route to get to the restaurant – based on the current location of the mobile user. Underneath it all, the need still remains to have the details of the restaurants marked up for use by whichever client.

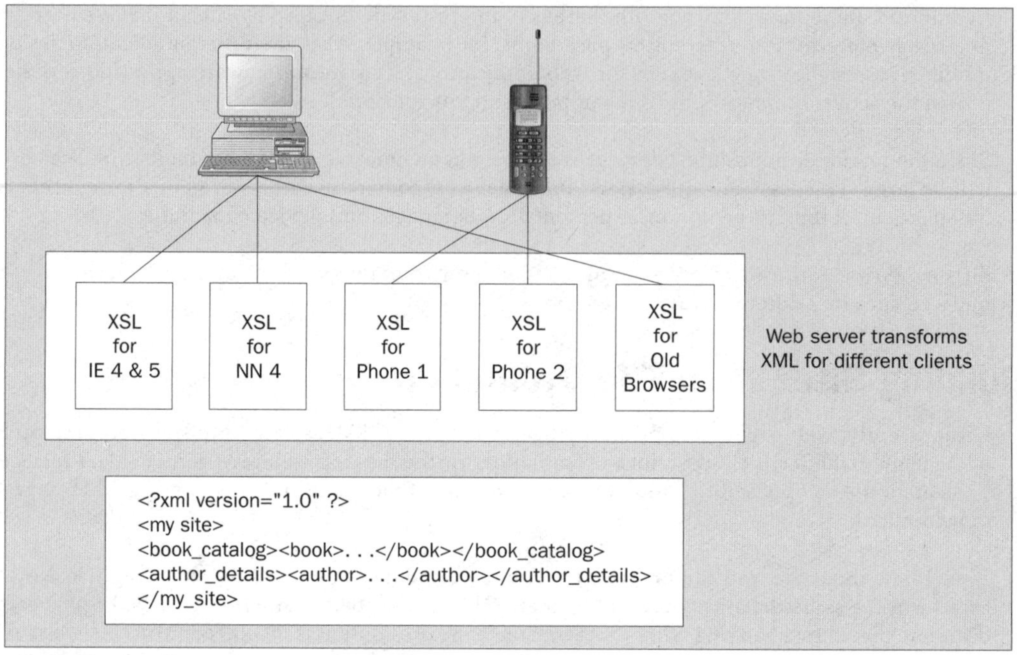

Getting Data to a Phone

In this chapter we will show how the Web, with the help of XML, can be extended to include wireless networks and devices. The existing rich set of features provided by HTML 4.0 is not ideally suited to these devices, and has kept the standard presentation language away from mobile phones and PDAs. Today, the following presentation languages exist for handheld clients:

- Various proprietary subsets of HTML (some with proprietary extensions)
- The Handheld Devices Markup Language (HDML)
- The Wireless Markup Language (WML)

Of the above three languages, WML has the most support from mobile phone manufacturers. WML was defined by the WAP Forum, founded in 1997 by Ericsson, Nokia, Motorola, and Phone.com. With over 250 members, the WAP Forum has been the most successful initiative to extend the Web to wireless networks. WAP provides content developers with a uniform interface to mobile phones all over the world, and to all different network standards.

HDML is a proprietary language defined by Phone.com and only supported by mobile phones with Phone.com browsers. One of the HTML subsets is "compact HTML", which was submitted to the W3C in early 1998. It has become very successful in Japan where it used in the "I-Mode" service that NTT DoCoMo provides (one of the world's largest network operators). In this chapter, however, due to its support by all the major phone manufacturers and the fact that it is an XML application, we focus on WML. In any case, "compact HTML" does not contain anything that isn't already in HTML. WML, however, is a small toolbox of interesting and new non-HTML features.

Although XML cannot make networks faster or the display of mobile phones bigger, by writing services in XML – rather than in, say, HTML – the same service can be transformed into an unlimited number of variants depending on the capabilities of the client (as reported in the request to the server). To do this well, however, requires not only an understanding of XML but also an understanding of the characteristics of the mobile phone as an Internet client.

This chapter describes aspects of wireless networks that content developers need to be aware of and the presentation language, WML. This application of XML, WML, just like HTML for desktop computers, is the interface to the display of the mobile phone.

WAP to the Rescue

WAP does not only consist of one specification; rather it is a suite of specifications, which will expand over time as technology progresses. The following specifications are approved as part of the WAP 1.1 specification suite. Don't let the size of the list put you off; content developers do not need to know about all of them, because WAP shields most developers from the underlying network and service provision details. They are nevertheless there, to ensure that software manufacturers provide appropriate software. We will not be looking at all of these here; rather we will just address those that are needed for serving pages to WAP-enabled devices.

- **Wireless Application Environment (WAE) Specification** – the overall application environment
- **Wireless Markup Language (WML) Specification** – the markup language that we will be transforming our XML into for transmission to mobile phones
- **Binary XML Content Format Specification** – the dictionary based compression scheme used to encode XML documents such as WML
- **WMLScript Language Specification** – an optimized script language similar to JavaScript that makes minimal demands upon memory and CPU usage
- **WMLScript Standard Libraries Specification** – the standard script libraries supported by all clients
- **WAP Caching Model Specification** – the browser's caching behavior and its relation to the browser's navigation history
- **Wireless Session Protocol (WSP) Specification –** the binary variant of the Internet HTTP protocol
- **Wireless Transaction Protocol (WTP) Specification** – the helper protocol to WSP that manages individual request-response transactions
- **Wireless Datagram Protocol (WDP) Specification** – the common interface to various wireless transport services
- **WAP over GSM USSD Specification** – the mapping of WDP onto USSD, which is a transport service used in GSM networks
- **Wireless Control Message Protocol (WCMP) Specification** – used for error reporting over networks that don't support the Internet Control Message Protocol
- **Wireless Transport Layer Security (WTLS) Specification –** for authentication and encryption

- **Wireless Telephony Application (WTA) Specification** – which will allow incoming and outgoing calls to be handled within WML and WMLScript, permitting trusted parties such as network operators to deploy combined voice call and Internet services – uses include automatically calling a number found in a yellow pages search, and visual interfaces to voicemail systems
- **Wireless Telephony Application Interface (WTAI) Specification** – the WMLScript library to telephony capabilities including the phone book and call logs

We will look how we implement WAP once we have looked at some of the issues that developers must get to grips with in order to create applications that are suited to this new environment.

Understanding the Wireless Environment

Enormous growth in wireless use has driven significant advances in the semiconductor business over the past ten years or so. As a result, phones and PDAs have become smaller and lighter. This trend is likely to continue at some pace, approaching some point where the display and keypad cannot get smaller.

In addition, the bandwidth offered by these mobile devices is lower than we are used to with **wireline** connections to the Internet (connections that use wires to carry data). A data call can have as low bandwidth as 9600 bps. **Latency** – the time it takes for a data packet to travel from one point to another – will also be an unwelcome part of the user's experience of the application, especially if the developer has not minimized the number of network round-trips the application requires.

What this means for the web developer is that a large majority of all users will have small phones with limited memory and processing power. Small devices also have smaller displays and keypads. So, successful applications will take these characteristics into account. In order to allow users to accomplish things quickly and with a minimal number of "clicks", at least the following parameters must be minimized: the amount of text the user has to type by hand, the amount of information to be displayed, the numbers of trips to the server, and the size of graphics. Meanwhile, the PDA market is likely to have comparatively increased facilities, such as processing power, and memory, so the divide in different devices will grow. On the other hand, users who buy a WAP phone in early 2000 will expect the built-in WML browser to access services for at least three years; that is, until 2003. In 2003, however, mobile phones and networks are expected to have become significantly more powerful than today. This "legacy problem" exists on the classic Web as well - an HTML browser from 1995 will not be able to display many of today's web sites - but since free browsers can be downloaded and installed from the network, the problem is not as big.

Developers will have to meet challenges of an ever-increasing variety of screen sizes, bandwidth availability, resolution, processing power, memory, keypad layout, languages, versions, etc.

Services

So, what sort of services can we expect to see on these mobile clients of the future? The possibilities are obviously endless – WAP could be used for anything that you may need to know while you are on the move, or anything you use an existing phone service for. Some of the more common examples of Web services for mobile phones and PDAs include:

- Yellow pages
- Stock quotes
- Booking airline flights
- Mobile banking facilities
- Groupware applications
- Address books
- Making dinner reservations

These services are different from browsing, or "surfing", as we know it, because the users will generally know the type of information they are looking for.

The key to a killer application for a wireless client is quick and simple access to the required information.

For developers this means that simplicity and a minimal use of network resources characterize a good service.

Online demonstration of WAP services are available from most of the WAP browser vendors, see end of this chapter for references.

Later in this chapter we will be developing an application that lets users look up authors from the catalog of Wrox books. Here is a screen shot of the application that we will develop later:

As you can see, here the information is kept very simple and is stripped down to the basics. Essentially, the user should get the information the user wants – multimedia presentations may satisfy desktop users with high-bandwidth connections, but will not be equally appreciated by the mobile user connected via low bandwidth (worse than dial-up) connection. In addition, wireless bandwidth is often more expensive than wire-based services. When developing services for mobile phones, one should pay close attention to bandwidth demands. Not only will "bandwidth conserving" applications run faster, they may also save the users money!

Here we are highlighting the current limitations of wireless technologies. As with other areas of Internet development, we will undoubtedly see services improve in capabilities and costs of calls fall.

As we mentioned earlier, we do not need to learn all of the WAP specifications, because WAP shields the content developer from the details of different network technologies. However, the application is not shielded from the characteristics of the wireless network. Next, let's take a closer look at the characteristics of wireless networks.

Wireless Networks

In order to understand how WAP works behind the scenes we must look at the traditional wire-based Internet. By looking at the problems faced when moving to wireless technologies we can see the solutions that WAP offers.

How Data is Passed Around the Internet

When the Internet was created, a series of protocols were defined that would operate simultaneously on a network. These protocols are known as the Internet Protocol Suite. The two most common protocols used within the suite are Transmission Control Protocol (TCP) which provides a connection-based reliable byte stream service, verifying the correct delivery of data from source to target, and Internet Protocol (IP) which provides the **packet** routing service.

Rather than always sending the whole of the data in one stream, IP is actually sending around smaller packets of information called **datagrams**. This prevents the need for a connection to the Internet all of the time; the connection is open only when there is a packet to transmit. If a package doesn't get through, the TCP will know and can act on this.

You can use a modem in a wireless network, just like in a wireline network. A modem establishes a continuous carrier over which the IP datagrams are transmitted. But since there often are long periods during a connection when no data is actually transmitted (for example, the user reads a document that has been downloaded), the modem must maintain the carrier even when there is no data to transmit. In an expensive wireless network this is not efficient, and networks that only transmit data when there is data to transmit are becoming increasingly popular. The most familiar wireless packet data networks are the **cellular digital packet data (CDPD)** and the **general packet radio service (GPRS)**. The CDPD system is deployed in the U.S. and in New Zealand, while the GPRS system has been developed as an extension to the **Global System for Mobile Communication (GSM)** standard; the predominant digital system for mobile phones in Europe, Asia, and parts of the U.S.

How the Data Gets Over the Air

Over the years, the wireless industry has adopted several incompatible technologies. First, there are analogue and digital systems. One of the most familiar analogue systems in the U.S. is AMPS, the standard analogue phone system. However, analogue systems are rapidly being replaced by new digital systems. In analogue networks each user gets a dedicated radio frequency. Since the number of frequencies available to network operators is limited, this is an expensive use of resources. One of the advantages of digital systems is that multiple users can access the same frequency simultaneously, which makes it possible for the phone operator to better utilize the network and make room for more voice and data. There are two different methods by which multiple users can access the same frequency:

- **Time division multiple access (TDMA)**
- **Code division multiple access (CDMA)**

The GSM standard is a TDMA system, but in the parts of the world where GSM isn't used, CDMA systems are becoming increasingly important. We don't have to know the details of how these systems work; indeed, one of the strongest motivations for WAP was to shield the application developer from the details of the different networks. Essentially, the application developer need only know that a given phone and network support WAP. The underlying "transport" or "bearer" networks needed to get data to and from the phones are implemented by the manufacturers to WAP standards. When the user accesses the Web from the browser, the phone will automatically connect to the network using one of these radio technologies.

As we will see later, WAP has adopted an application environment similar to the Web to make it as easy to write applications for wireless devices as it is to write applications for desktop computers connected to the Internet. Before WAP, services had to be created with different technologies depending on the network; in some networks it was impossible to add any services at all in addition to voice. In GSM, for example, many services are created with the SIM Application Toolkit. Services created with the SIM Applications Toolkit are installed into the smart card (SIM card) that every GSM phone has. For some categories of services, this is appropriate. But the services only work in GSM networks, are difficult to create and distribute, and cannot provide as sophisticated a user interface as a WAP browser can.

Additional Services on Wireless Networks

Wireless networks also provide some data services that are very different from the standard Internet protocols, such as the GSM SMS (short message service) and paging networks. The SMS service was originally intended as a paging service inside the GSM system, but is now, thanks to some innovative companies, often used as a general packet data service. An SMS "packet" is a maximum of 140 bytes and **latency** can be anything from two seconds up to several hours. The long latency is a result of the fact that SMS never was designed to be a general packet data network, but a short message service similar to a paging network.

Problems with Using TCP/IP on Wireless Networks

With a modem, TCP/IP – the standard suite of Internet protocols – *can* be used over wireless networks; but (as we have seen) the bandwidth available is a lot lower than wireline networks. This introduces a problem because mobility and an unpredictable radio environment often result in poor connectivity, resulting in the radio link going down temporarily. For example, the user may go out of radio coverage as a result of driving through a tunnel. While this does not affect the quality of a voice call, it would degrade the performance of a protocol such as TCP, which is built for a wireline network with stable connectivity. When the link goes down, TCP assumes that congestion has occurred in the network and responds by slowing down the transmission rate significantly; when the link comes back up again it takes time before TCP has restored the original high transmission speed. So, in wireless networks, TCP performance is not as good as in wireline networks. Optimizing TCP for wireless networks has occupied many research laboratories for the last couple of years. But despite some success, due to the large deployment of standard TCP/IP software and the fact that the resulting improvements in speed and reliability never have been significant, there is not yet a "wireless TCP" that has been able to replace the standard.

New network technologies promise the mobile user higher bandwidth. How high, however, and at what price, is uncertain. It remains to be seen whether the bandwidth heaven promised by the next generation of network technologies will be available to everyone for a reasonable price, or only to the few mobile professionals who can afford it. Radio spectrum frequencies are needed to transmit data across wireless networks. Transmitting more data requires more frequencies, but radio frequency is a limited natural resource, a problem that is not the same in the wireline world, where you just add more cables.

To summarize what has made it hard to create wireless applications:

- Many different network technologies provide different and incompatible methods for creating services
- There is both an inherent high latency and limited availability of the radio spectrum, which leads to bandwidth problems
- Due to coupling between data and radio frequencies, bandwidth hungry web services tend to be expensive and do not degrade gracefully
- Network services can vary depending on network provider and radio technology

How WAP Solves Problems with Wireless Networks

The purpose of the WAP Forum was to unify the member companies' proprietary technologies for mobile access to information on the Web. As already mentioned, the WAP Forum was founded in 1997 by Ericsson, Nokia, Motorola, and Phone.com. Today (January 2000) the WAP Forum has more than 250 members.

Before WAP Forum, web technologies had little success on wireless networks. As we have explained, many of the technologies of the classic Web are hard to digest by mobile phones. But the number of mobile phones in the world is increasing rapidly, as is the amount of information on the Web. Bringing the two markets together is the obvious next step. So, how does WAP allow mobile device users to access this web information despite the limitations of the receiving technology?

Web protocols such as HTTP and languages such as XML have been designed to be readable by humans. This makes development and testing simple and helps explain the success of these protocols. Unfortunately, they are network intensive and processing textual protocols requires a lot of string comparison and string manipulation. For example, if a web application were 10k, and the HTTP header information is around 100 or 200 bytes, this is not significant on the wired Internet. However, in the cut down wireless applications where a comparative application may be under 500 bytes in total, then a header of 200 bytes becomes significant.

To overcome these problems – low bandwidth, latency, etc. – and to hide the characteristics of the different wireless networks from the web server, WAP defines a gateway between the mobile phone and the web server hosting the web site. Between the WAP gateway and the web server the standard web protocols are used (XML, HTTP and TCP/IP). Between the mobile phone and the gateway, protocols defined by the WAP Forum are used. These are binary variants of the web protocols, that make web access from mobile phones possible, by compressing the volume of data. The gateway is responsible for translating between the protocols as shown in the following diagram:

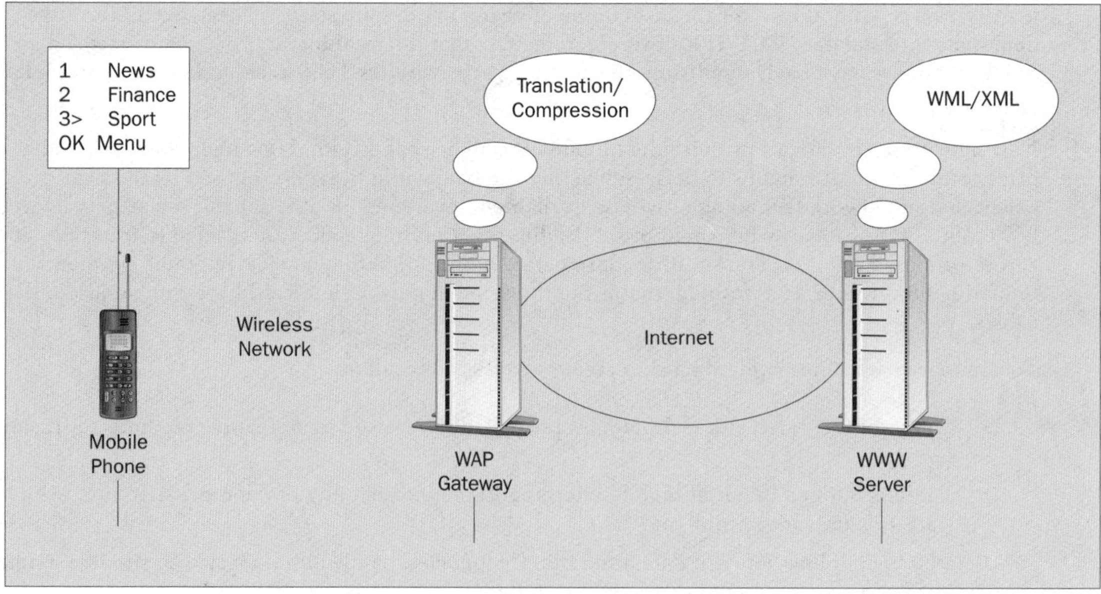

There is more in WAP than binary web protocols that provide these services between the WAP gateway and the mobile phone. We will come back to look at how we offer data in the WAP framework shortly, after we have looked at the protocols it offers.

The gateway may also perform additional functions such as transcoding between different character sets. A character set defines the mapping between characters and numbers. For example, the value 84 may be used to represent the character T. Different languages and countries may use different character sets.

The variant of HTTP used by WAP is the **Wireless Session Protocol** (**WSP**), which transfers information in a binary format, rather than a text based format. Unlike HTTP, it does not expect a connection-oriented protocol (TCP) as an underlying service, but can run over any kind of datagram service such as SMS and UDP (the datagram service on the Internet). Since datagram services are not reliable, WSP uses the transaction-oriented protocol WTP to manage each individual request-response transaction, and make retries when necessary. The difference between a binary protocol such as WSP and a text-based protocol such as HTTP is that if an HTTP header looks like this:

```
Accept-Language: en;q=0.7
```

a string of 25 ASCII characters, then the corresponding WSP header looks like this:

```
0x83 0x02 0x99 0x47
```

That is, four octets, where the mapping from text to binary values is defined in tables in the WSP specification. So, the amount of data that has to be transferred between the WAP gateway and the requesting client is a lot smaller. The WAP gateway is responsible for the translation between these two formats. As an application developer on the origin server, you should not have to think about this; it is all implemented by the WAP gateway. A similar text-to-binary translation is done for the actual WML code we write. For example, the following WML document:

```
<wml>
<card id="abc" ordered="true">
   <p>
      <do type="accept">
         <go href="http://xyz.org/s"/>
      </do>
      X: $(X)<br/>
      Y: $(&#x59;)<br/>
      Enter name: <input type="text" name="N"/>
   </p>
</card>
</wml>
```

is translated, in the WAP gateway, into something like this:

```
02 08 6A 04 'X' 00 'Y' 00 7F E7 55 03 'a' 'b' 'c' 00
33 01 60 E8 38 01 AB 4B 03 'x' 'y' 'z' 00 88 03
's' 00 01 01 03 ' ' 'X' ':' ' ' 00 82 00 26 03 ' ' 'Y'
':' ' ' 00 82 02 26 03 ' ' 'E' 'n' 't' 'e' 'r' ' ' 'n'
'a' 'm' 'e' ':' ' ' 00 AF 48 21 03 'N' 00 01 01 01 01
```

All XML tags and attributes have been replaced with binary values. Thus, the mobile phone does not see the real XML, it sees a sequence of binary values that represents the XML document that was received by the WAP gateway.

In addition to translating all HTTP headers that are present in the request and response messages into binary values, the WAP gateway offers other advantages. Many HTTP headers are the same in every message. The gateway can save the headers that do not change so that the browser does not have to send them over and over again and waste bandwidth. It can also offer support for 'push' communications, which means that it can send data to the mobile device, without it needing to request it. This is similar to the services offered by existing pagers, where news headlines and sports results can be transmitted (pushed) to the user.

So, having seen how we are able to transfer the data to mobile devices, and knowing some of the issues with providing services for these clients, we can look at the markup language that is used to convey the information to users.

Introducing WML

WML is an application of XML that incorporates a subset of XHTML elements, along with support for state and variables, validation of user's input, and a generic event model.

WML is only a small language compared to HTML 4.0, but it is adequate for the devices we will be developing for. Because we are dealing with smaller, lower resolution screens than desktop counterparts, many of the features of HTML are rendered unnecessary. WML does, however, add some extra features you do not find in HTML, such as variables to parameterize documents and state management, which allow for more efficient use of network resources.

Because WML is designed specifically for use with the small devices we have already spoken about, the following constraints were put in place to define the development of the specification:

- Small display and limited user facilities
- Narrowband network connection
- Limited memory and computational resources

These reflect the problems that we identified earlier in the chapter.

This section is an overview of the features of WML, especially those not found in HTML. Although the first version of WAP is stable, to keep up with an accelerating market, WAP is moving fast towards a second version. The WML version described in this section is version 1.1. One other point to note is that, if you are building your site from content written in XML, as we explained in the section on *Building Sites from the Ground up*, you will probably not be writing pages in WML; rather you will be transforming your existing data into WML using a transformation language such as XSLT. In any case, you still need to understand WML so that you can transform your XML into WML.

How to Get the First Document to the Phone

Just like all other resources on the Web, WML documents can be requested from URLs. And just like all HTML browsers, the WML browser will have some way of entering URLs into the browser. The exact mechanism to do this depends on the browser. Since typing in long URLs on the keypad of the phone is inconvenient, the browser vendors will provide the user with alternative mechanisms to configure the browser. In any case, the fact that the web browser is in the phone doesn't mean that you have to "call" web sites to get some content back. It all works just like the Web – it is the Web, after all.

The Structure of a WML Document

Instead of the HTML `<head>` and `<body>` document structure where the entire document is rendered at the same time as one web page, WML organizes information using a deck/card metaphor. The **deck** represents the set of **cards** that make up the resources of a particular URL (the deck is addressed just like an HTML page). The `<wml>` element transports one or more cards in the same document. (Cards are different from HTML frames, in that cards are not typically displayed at the same time like HTML frames are.) Including a set of cards in a deck saves network round-trips, compared to downloading many small documents separately. The following example shows the overall structure of a WML document:

```
<!DOCTYPE wml PUBLIC "-//WAPFORUM//DTD WML 1.1//EN"
          "http://www.wapforum.org/DTD/wml_1.1.xml">
<wml>

   <head>
   ...
   </head>

   <template>
   ...
   </template>

   <card>
      <p>
      ...
      </p>
   </card>

   <card>
      <p>
       ...
      </p>
   </card>
</wml>
```

Let's take a closer look at these sections. We start with the document prologue. The WAP gateway validates the document before it is passed down to the mobile phone, so the prologue must be present when the document reaches the gateway:

```
<!DOCTYPE wml PUBLIC "-//WAPFORUM//DTD WML 1.1//EN"
              "http://www.wapforum.org/DTD/wml_1.1.xml">
```

For the sake of brevity, the document prologue will not be shown in subsequent examples, although it is assumed that it is always present. Since the gateway validates the documents, documents that are not well-formed or valid will be rejected and not passed down to the client. So it is always wise to validate you documents before you post them on the wireless Web.

The prologue is followed by the root element, `<wml>`. The subsequent `<head>` and `<template>` elements are optional, so a minimal WML document can consist of only one `<card>` element.

The `<head>` element has the same function as the `<head>` element in HTML and contains meta-information about the document. Meta information is contained in the HTML `<meta>` element. The `<template>` element is used for elements that are shared by all cards. For example, it can be used to specify event bindings, such as `do` and `onevent` (which we meet shortly), which will apply to all cards in the deck. An element defined in a card can be specified to take precedence over an element of the same type in the template.

The `<card>` element is the most important element in WML. The cards hold text and input elements that specify the page content. Depending upon the size of the screen, each card can be presented in one screen, or a series of smaller screens if the device has a small screen. The following card contains two form fields that the user agent, depending on its capabilities, can display either as one screen with two form fields or two screens with one field on each:

```
<card id="author" title="Author search" newcontext="true" >
   <p mode="nowrap">
      <fieldset>
         First name:
         <input name="fname" type="text" title="Enter name"/>
      </fieldset>
      <fieldset>
         Last name:
         <input name="lname" type="text" title="Enter name" />
      </fieldset>
      <anchor>Done
           <go method="post" href="search">
              <postfield name="fname" value="$fname" />
              <postfield name="lname" value="$lname" />
           </go>
      </anchor>
   </p>
</card>
```

Each `<card>` element is identified by an `id` attribute, which allows users to navigate between the cards in a deck. When a deck is requested from a URL, the card `id` attribute is recognized as the **fragment identifier**. For example, http://www.wrox.com/wap/main.wml#author would display the card with the `author` identifier. If there is more than one card in the document, and no fragment identifier, the first card is processed first by the user agent (receiving application).

This is how cards often are used: one card, often the first, is used as the main card, while the rest of the cards contain some help information or sub-menus that will be presented to the user upon request. On an HTML web page, all this information would have been on the same page, or separated up into many web pages, and caused extra network round-trips to retrieve. A deck is really a container to transport many small web pages; which are cards.

The `title` attribute of the `<card>` element specifies the card's title. Some browsers display the `title` attribute in a similar way to HTML `<title>` elements in HTML browsers – at the top of the page. However, some browsers choose to treat the `title` attribute as the `title` attribute in HTML – as a tool-tip or title of the element. In any case you should use the `title` attribute since, no matter how it is presented, it will help the user. The code above will give the following display (the exact presentation depends on the phone model):

In phones with very small displays, the browser may break up one card into several smaller sections, called **fields**. There is no element that represents a field, but the WML specification states that if an `<input>` or `<select>` element is available, then a field is the text immediately before the element and the element itself. To make sure that the browser breaks the card at appropriate places in the content, use the `<fieldset>` element to encapsulate text and form controls that must be displayed together. The `ordered` attribute indicates the relationship between the fields in one card and can be used by the browser in the presentation of the card (it is ignored by most browsers).

The following table shows the elements and attributes available for document structure:

Element	Required	Attributes

`<wml>`	yes	`id`
		`class`
		`xml:lang`

`<head>`	optional	`id` `class`

`<template>`	optional	`id`
		`class`
		`onenterforward`
		`onenterbackward`
		`ontimer`

`<card>`	yes	`id`
		`class`
		`xml:lang`
		`title`
		`newcontext=(true|false)`
		`ordered=(true|false)`
		`onenterforward`
		`onenterbackward`
		`ontimer`

Common Attributes

Just like many other XML applications, WML has common attributes that are defined on most elements. In WML, they are the `id`, `class` and `xml:lang` attributes. The `id` attribute is, as its name suggests, an XML ID attribute type, providing a unique name for an element within a deck. The `class` attribute associates an element with one or more classes. So, many elements can be given the same class name, and all elements within a deck that share a class name are considered to be part of the same class. This is the same as in HTML, and is used to hook style sheet information onto the structure of the document – although style sheets have not been defined as part of the WAP specifications. A WAP browser can, of course, support style sheets anyway, but on most mobile phones of today there is not much a style sheet can do given the limited screen resources. Thus, the `class` attribute is reserved for future use. The `xml:lang` is the well-known XML attribute. In the following sections these common attributes will not be described again.

What's Inside WML?

Before we get started, here is an overview of the functions in WML:

- Meta information
- Basic text, tables, and presentation
- Timers
- Event handlers
- Variables
- Tasks and menus
- Templates
- Form data
- Images

Meta information, text, tables, presentation, forms, and images are well-known concepts to all HTML developers. The HTML `<a>` element is available for hyperlinks, the `<p>` element is available to structure text, and the most common form elements (`<input>` and `<select>`) are available with the same functionality.

New functions include the ability to use variables to enable a simple client-side template mechanism, and to maintain state between cards. A template is a document that can be reused with the same structure but with different data. Since state is maintained between cards, one card can display what the user entered in the previous card of the same deck. This is good when you want to confirm what the user entered, before the data is submitted to the server. The generic event handler, tasks, and timers are also new non-HTML functionality; however, W3C Recommendations with similar and more powerful features will be available in the future.

Meta Information

Meta information about a WML document is specified by using the <meta> element. This is the same as in HTML and should, just as in HTML, be used with some caution. Browsers are free to ignore the meta information, so if you don't know that a particular browser will accept the information you put into the element, you may clutter the document with unnecessary information. In HTML the <meta> element is, among other things, used to specify the character encoding of the document, but since WML is an XML application, as we have seen, the XML encoding declaration should be used for this purpose.

There is also an <access> element, which can be used to restrict access to the pages. The following table shows the elements for meta information:

Element	Attribute
<meta>	id
	class
	http-equiv
	name
	forua=(true|false) "false"
	content
	scheme
<access>	id
	class
	domain
	path

One non-standard usage of the <meta> element in HTML is to refresh a page after a specified time (by using the refresh directive), but in WML this can be done by using the <timer> element instead (as we will see in the section concerning events).

The forua attribute is a processing instruction to an intermediate agent (for example, the WAP gateway), and is not available on the HTML <meta> element. Some instructions are interesting only to the gateway. If the value of this attribute is "false", the default, an intermediate agent can remove the <meta> element and not pass it on to the client. Some browser vendors use the <meta> element with the name and content attributes for propriety functions.

The <access> element can be used to limit the access to the document. If no <access> element is specified everyone can access the document. If an <access> element is specified, the browser will only process the document if the referring URL – the URL of the link element from which the request for the document originates – matches the value of the domain and path attributes of the <access> element. The access domain is suffix-matched against the domain name portion of the referring URL and the access path is prefix-matched against the path portion of the referring URL. For example, if the access control attributes are:

```
domain="wrox.com"
path="/books"
```

the referring URL http://wrox.com/books/xml would be allowed to go to the deck, but the URL http://www.wapforum.org/books would not. The `<access>` element is not a replacement for security mechanisms such as HTTP authentication. However, it can be used to restrict access to only those documents that have a well-known initial state; for example, certain variables are available.

Basic Text, Tables, and Presentation

All the basic text and layout elements in WML are taken from HTML. Mostly attributes have been removed from elements. Here are the elements for basic text and layout.

Element	Attribute
Links	
`<a>`	`id`
	`class`
	`xml:lang`
	`href`
	`title`
Tables	
`<table>`	`id`
	`class`
	`xml:lang`
	`title`
	`align`
	`columns`
`<tr>`	`id`
	`class`
`<td>`	`id`
	`class`
Text Structure	
`<p>`	`id`
	`class`
	`xml:lang`
	`align`
	`mode`
` `	`id`
	`class`

Presentation	
<b>	id
	class
<u>	id
	class
<I>	id
	class
<big>	id
	class
<small>	id
	class
Phrasal	
<em>	id
	class
<strong>	id
	class

Most of these should be familiar to you, so we will only cover those that are different from HTML. One to note is the `<table>` element, as its `align` and `columns` attributes are WML specific. The `align` attribute is used to specify alignment information for all columns in the table. The required `column` attribute specifies the number of columns in the table. The value of the `align` attribute is a sequence of letters, where each letter represents one column:

Value of `align`	Meaning
"L"	left
"R"	right
"C"	center

For example, `"LLR"` means that the first two columns should be left aligned and the last column right aligned.

On the `<p>` element, the `mode` attribute is WML specific. It indicates how the text in the paragraph should be presented if the text in the paragraph does not fit into the display of the phone. If the `mode` is `"nowrap"` some browsers will use horizontal scrolling to display the text without wrapping the lines. If the mode is `"wrap"`, the text will be presented as in a normal HTML paragraph; word wrapping occurs where necessary. Note that the `align` attribute on the `<p>` element takes the values `left`, `right`, and `center`, and is used to align text inside a paragraph, (which is different from the `<table>` element).

Presentational elements such as <b>, <i>, and, <u> are available in WML. Headings, however, (the HTML <hn> elements) are not available in WML. Instead you have to use the presentational or phrasal elements to indicate headings. Although most mobile phones today with a WAP browser can display boldfaced text and italic fonts, and more will be able to do so in the future, you should not rely on the browser to honor these elements. Nor should you rely on presentational elements to convey semantic information. For example, if you use <big> as a heading, the browser is free to ignore the element if it cannot display big text, and will not know that the text is a *heading*. Also, avoid using underlined text, as it may look like a link in some browsers.

Navigation

Navigation is one of the hardest things to get right when you create applications for small devices. Here are some useful tips:

- Use the <a> and <br/> elements to create a list of navigation choices. If the number of choices exceeds nine, provide a "More..." link to continue with a new list.
- Always make sure that, in every card, the user always can navigate either back to the previous card or back to a well-known starting point. For example, in a complex menu hierarchy make sure the user always can get to the "main menu".
- Provide the user with quick-links back to well-known locations. The user should not have to press "back" ten times to get back to the "main menu".
- Use short names on links and avoid too many space characters.

The following example illustrates a list of navigation choices; the type of card most applications consists of:

```
<card id="main" title="WROX">
   <do type="prev" label="Back">
      <prev/>
   </do>
   <p mode="nowrap">
      <a href="#author">Search Author</a><br/>
      <a href="#title">Search Title</a><br/>
      <a href="#about">About</a><br/>
      <anchor>Done
         <go href="http://www.wrox.com/wap/index.wml" />
      </anchor>
   </p>
</card>
```

Using Timers

Timers can be used to help navigate between cards. The <timer> element can be used to generate an `ontimer` event after a specified time. The element has the following structure:

```
<timer name="V" value="Time" />
```

The `name` attribute specifies the name of a variable. The timer is set to the value of the variable, `V`. If no variable is specified, or the variable has no value, the timer is set to the value of the value attribute, *`Time`*. Time is specified in tenths of seconds.

The `<timer>` element is ideal for displaying a commercial message in a separate card or document for a short time, before the service is started. For example, when the user activates a link to a list of open restaurants, the first card that is loaded is one of a restaurant's logo, a few seconds later, the card with the list of restaurants is loaded; similar to the splash screens you get when loading programs, but used to advertise products or services. Other examples of where the `<timer>` element can be used include:

- Displaying a brief help text after a specified time. This feature is common on mobile phones; if the user is inactive for some time some help text is automatically displayed.
- Walking the user through a sequence of cards. For example, a long news story. If the user is inactive – does not press any keys – the service will automatically load the next card; that is, the next card we can assume the user would select next. Effectively, creating "hands-free" browsing.

Event Handlers

To capture an `ontimer` event either the `ontimer` event handler attribute or the `<onevent>` element must be used. The `ontimer` attribute is defined on the card element. The value of the attribute can be a URL or a fragment identifier. In the following example the `ontimer` event will trigger the loading of the next card:

```
<card id="about" title="WROX" ontimer="#about2">
   <timer value="100"/>
   <p mode="nowrap">
      <a href="#main">Done</a><br/>
Wrox Press aims to make programmers successful by sharing with them the
knowledge and experience of their professional peers.
   </p>
   <p>
      <a href="#main">Done</a>
      <a href="#about2">More</a>
   </p>
</card>

<card id="about2" title="WROX">
   <p mode="nowrap">
      <a href="#main">Home</a><br/>
      <a href="allbooks.wml">All Books</a><br/>
      <a href="http://www.wroxconferences.com">Conferences</a><br/>
      <a href="allauthors.wml">Authors</a><br/>
      <a href="support.wml">Support</a><br/>
      <a href="membership.wml">Membership</a><br/>
      <a href="contacts.wml">Contact Us</a><br/>
   </p>
</card>
```

In this example, the `ontimer` event is generated approximately 10 seconds after the first card is activated. Many developers find it convenient to use the event handler attribute, `ontimer`, on the card element. However, you can also use the `<onevent>` element to capture any event that has a name. In the following example the `<onevent>` element is located in the `<card>` element and used to capture an `ontimer` event:

```
      ...
    <onevent type="ontimer">
        <go href="#about2" />
    </onevent>
    <timer value="100" />
  ...
```

Event bindings can be specified with the `<onevent>` element, or as an event handler attribute. They can be specified both inside a `<card>` element and inside the `<template>` element. An event binding in a `<card>` element always overrides an event binding to the same event type in the `<template>` element. Similar rules for "shadowing" apply to the `<do>` element, as we will see in a later section.

Event Element	Attributes
`<timer>`	`id`
	`class`
	`name`
	`value`
`<onevent>`	`id`
	`class`
	`type`

In the section about *Tasks and Menus* we will come back to the `onevent` element, since its main usage is to bind a task to an event of a particular type.

Using Variables

Variables can be used to maintain state information across several documents. A variable is a name that has an associated value. The `<setvar>` element is used to bind a value to a variable:

```
<setvar name="N" value="V" />
```

The `name` attribute specifies the name of the variable, and the `value` attribute specifies the value. The `<setvar>` element can be used inside the `<onevent>` and `<do>` elements. Also, variable names are bound to a value via the `<input>` and `<select>` elements.

To include the value of a variable into the content the `$varname` or `$(varname)` notation is used (the latter preferred).

```
The timer is $(Timer).
```

The scope of a variable is a called a context. The `newcontext` attribute on the `card` element is used to create a new context. When a new context is created, all variables are cleared as well as the history list. So, you can use the `newcontext` attribute (as in the above example) to guarantee that some old variables which have been used by previous services will not interfere with your variables.

The following example illustrates how variables can be used to maintain state between cards:

```
<wml>
   <card id="card1" title="$title" >
      <onevent type="onenterforward">
         <refresh>
            <setvar name="title" value="Variables" />
         </refresh>
      </onevent>
      <onevent type="onenterbackward">
         <refresh>
            <setvar name="title" value="Try again" />
         </refresh>
      </onevent>
      <p>
         Name <input type="text" name="fname" title="Enter name" />
         <anchor>Done
            <go href="#card2"/>
         </anchor>
      </p>
   </card>

   <card id="card2" title="Variables" >
      <p>
      Your name is $(fname)?
      <anchor>Yes
         <go href="next.wml" />
      </anchor>
      <anchor>No
         <prev />
      </anchor>
      </p>
   </card>
</wml>
```

The title of the first card is a variable, `title`. When the user enters the first card the `title` variable is set to `"Variables"`. The user is asked to enter a name. The entered name is stored in the `fname` variable. When the user navigates to the second card, the value of the `fname` variable is included into the content and the user is asked to confirm that this was the name that was entered in the previous card. If the user selected no, the browser displays the first card again. However, in the navigation back from the second card to the first, the `<prev>` element generates an `onenterbackward` event, which, when captured in the first card, causes the `title` variable to be set to `"Try again"`. This use case is illustrated in the following pictures:

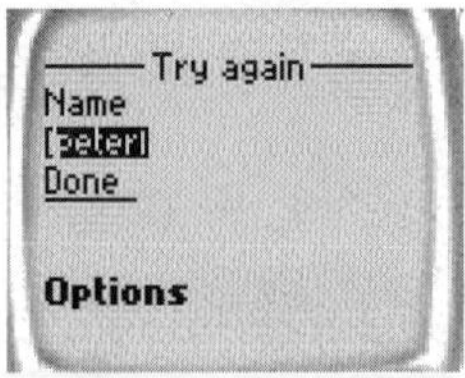

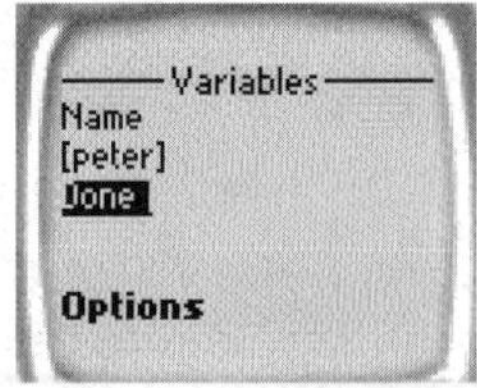

Since variables maintain state between cards, we use variables to ask the user for confirmation before the data is sent to the server, and the same card can be re-used with a different user interface without any script or extra network round-trips.

In the following example the `<setvar>` element is used to set the timeout for a timer. The timer's value is in the `T` variable and the current status is in the `Timer` variable. The variables are changed when the user enters the card, the timer times out, and when the user selects **Restart**:

```
<card title="Timer">
<onevent type="onenterforward">
  <refresh>
     <setvar name="Timer" value="Running" />
     <setvar name="T" value="10" />
  </refresh>
</onevent>
<onevent type="ontimer">
  <refresh>
     <setvar name="Timer" value="Timeout" />
     <setvar name="T" value="0" />
  </refresh>
</onevent>
<timer name="T" value="10" />
<do label="Restart" type="accept" >
  <refresh>
    <setvar name="Timer" value="Running" />
    <setvar name="T" value="10" />
  </refresh>
</do>
<p>
The timer is $(Timer).
</p>
</card>
```

Variable names are case sensitive and consist of a US-ASCII letter or underscore followed by zero or more letters, digits, or underscores, and the variable's value is treated as CDATA (so you cannot, for example, include markup in the variables).

Variables can be used inside elements that can contain plain text (PCDATA), and in the value of the following attributes:

- All `title` attributes
- All `value` and `ivalue` attributes
- All `href` and `src` attributes

- The `label` attribute on the `<do>` element
- The `name` attribute on the `<postfield>` and `<setvar>` elements
- The `alt` and `localsrc` attribute on the `<img>` element
- The event handler attributes `onpick`, `ontimer`, `onenterforward`, and `onenterbackward`

By appending a directive to the name of the variable, it can be specified whether the value should be URL-escaped, URL-unescaped, or left unchanged when the value of the variable is included into the content.

- Leave the value unchanged `$(varname:noesc)`
- URL-escape the value `$(varname:escape)`
- URL-unescape the value `$(varname:unesc)`

Since the `$` character is used to represent variables, to use the `$` character in character data or attribute values it must be escaped. The `$$` sequence is used as the escaping sequence and gets replaced by a single `$` character before the data is presented or the attribute value processed:

```
This is a dollar sign $$.
This is the value of the N variable $(N)
```

Tasks and Menus

In WML the developer has a certain degree of control over the browser's softkeys and menus. A softkey is a programmable control that the browser displays either as a separate menu, a separate key, or as part of the browser's menu. By using the `<do>` element, tasks such as navigation and refreshing variables can be assigned to softkeys and menus that are available on the browser. Tasks can also be made available inline by using the `<anchor>` element. The following elements are used to create menus and tasks:

Tasks	
Element	**Attributes**
`<anchor>`	`id`
	`class`
	`title`
`<do>`	`id`
	`class`
	`type`
	`label`
	`name`
	`optional= (true|false) "false"`

Tasks	
Element	**Attributes**
`<go>`	id
	class
	href
	sendreferer
	method= (post|get) "get"
	accept-charset
`<prev>`	id
	class
`<refresh>`	id
	class
`<noop>`	id
	class

Creating Menus and Softkeys – The <do> Element

By using the `<do>` element the content developer can specify menus associated with a card. How the menu is presented depends on the browser. In some browsers a link with the name menu or options is created to link the `<do>` elements to the content, in other browsers the menu is presented as a pop-up box, or as a list of buttons.

The `<do>` element represents a task, and the `label` attribute specifies the name. You are advised to use short names, less than 12 characters, and avoid space characters. When the element is selected the task is executed. A `<do>` element can, just like the `<onevent>` element, contain the task elements `<go>`, `<prev>`, `<refresh>`, and `<noop>`.

The following example creates a menu with two items:

```
<card id="form" title="Author search" newcontext="true">
   <do type="prev" label="Back">
      <prev/>
   </do>
   <do type="accept" label="Done" >
            <go method="post" href="search">
                  <postfield name="type" value="bio" />
                  <postfield name="fname" value="$fname" />
                  <postfield name="lname" value="$lname" />
            </go>
   </do>
   <p>
```

```
<fieldset>
         First name:
         <input name="fname" type="text" title="Enter name"/>
      </fieldset>
      <fieldset>
         Last name:
         <input name="lname" type="text" title="Enter name" />
      </fieldset>
   </p>
</card>
```

See the sections below for descriptions of the <go> and <prev> elements.

And here is a screen shot of what the Search form might look like:

The `<input>` and `<fieldset>` elements are the same as in HTML; we will take a closer look at these in the following section. The purpose of the `type` attribute on the `<do>` element is to help the browser to choose an appropriate presentation for the element. You should always specify a `type`. The `types` are specified in the WML specification:

Type	Description
`accept`	Positive acknowledgement (acceptance)
`prev`	Backward history navigation
`help`	Request for help. May be context-sensitive
`reset`	Clearing or resetting state
`options`	Context-sensitive request for options or additional operations
`delete`	Delete item or choice

The <go> Task

The `<go>` task element is used to navigate the browser to another resource or post data to a web server. It is used for many of the functions that in HTML are done by the `<form>` element. The following example shows how the `<go>` element can be used to post data to a web server when the user selects the `Done` menu item:

```
<do type="accept" label="Done" >
       <go method="post" href="search">
            <postfield name="fname" value="$fname" />
            <postfield name="lname" value="$lname" />
       </go>
</do>
```

The <postfield> is included in the <go> element to compose an HTTP post request. Also possible, although not shown in the above example, is to include one or many <setvar> elements inside the <go> element – that way, the variables will be made available to the destination resource.

When the <go> element is activated an onenterforward event is triggered and injected into the target resource.

The <prev> Task

The <prev> task element is used to navigate the browser to the last entry on the history list. The WML history is slightly different than a normal HTML browser history. The WML history is a list of old HTTP requests (URL, method, postdata, and headers) and not, as an HTML history is, a copy of exactly the resource as it was presented to the user. When you navigate back into the WML history, the requests will get re-submitted and the previous document will get fetched either from the network or the local cache. The following example will create a menu item that is a back key:

```
<do label="Back" type="prev">
   <prev/>
</do>
```

The <prev> element can contain <setvar> elements. So, it is possible to go back in history with new variable values.

When the <prev> element is activated an onenterbackward event is triggered and injected into the target resource.

The <noop> Task

The <noop> task element does absolutely nothing and the reason it exists is to provide a way by which a <do> element in the document's <template> can get overridden – "shadowed" – by a <do> element in a card. The following example illustrates this:

```
<wml>
<template>
   <do label="Back" name="prev" type="prev">
      <prev/>
   </do>
</template>
<card>
   <do name="prev" type="prev">
      <noop/>
   </do>
   <!-- This card will not display the "Back" key -->
</card>
<card>
   <!-- This card will display the "Back" key from the template -->
</card>
</wml>
```

If a <do> element inside a <card> element contains the <noop> task element, then the <do> element in the card will override any <do> element with the same name in the document's <template> element. Since the <noop> element does not do anything, the effect is that the template-level <do> element is disabled for the card. The <noop> task can also be used in the same way for event bindings with the <onevent> element.

The <refresh> Task

The <refresh> task element provides a mechanism to refresh variables with new values. In the following example, taken from the section about variables, the T and Timer variables will get new values when the Restart option is selected:

```
   <do label="Restart" type="accept" >
  <refresh>
    <setvar name="Timer" value="Running" />
    <setvar name="T" value="10" />
  </refresh>
</do>
```

The <do> element can be located inside a <card> or a <template>. When the card is processed the <do> elements in the template are concatenated with the <do> elements in the card. Unless, of course, the <do> element is overridden with a <noop> task as described above.

Accessing Tasks Inline – the <anchor> Element

Since the presentation of the <do> element is decided by the browser – some browsers displays it as softkeys and others as a menu – it can be difficult to create a service that looks the same on different browsers. As an alternative, or a complement, the <anchor> element can be used to include a task as a link inside the content.

In the following example the <anchor> element is used to submit the data to the server:

```
<card id="author" title="Author search" newcontext="true" >
   <p mode="nowrap">
      <fieldset>
         First name:
         <input name="fname" type="text" title="Enter name"/>
      </fieldset>
      <fieldset>
         Last name:
         <input name="lname" type="text" title="Enter name" />
      </fieldset>
      <anchor>Done
          <go method="post" href="search">
             <postfield name="type" value="bio" />
             <postfield name="fname" value="$fname" />
             <postfield name="lname" value="$lname" />
          </go>
      </anchor>
   </p>
</card>
```

The benefit of using the <anchor> element in the above card, instead of the <do> element, is that, as a developer, you know that the Done option will be displayed at the end of the card. If a <do> element is used, the presentation of the Done option is decided by the browser and will look different on different devices. To be one the safe side, you can use both a <do> element and a <anchor> element.

Client-side Templates

By using variables, WML documents can be used as local templates in the phone. This is similar to the way many web servers use templates when documents are generated dynamically. A template can be stored locally in the device and be shared by multiple services. For example, in a look-up service, the document that is used to present the data that comes back from the server can be a template. The template document contains all the structure, presentation, links, and help information that will be presented to the user together with the result. Thus, the card that is sent back from the server only has to contain the actual data. This is how it works.

First, we create the search form card, author, with all the structure, presentation, and additional links we want the user to see when the result is presented. Note that this deck also contains the card bio that is used to display the result:

```
<wml>
...
<card id="author" title="Author search" newcontext="true" >
   <p mode="nowrap">
      <fieldset>
         First name:
         <input name="fname" type="text" title="Enter name" />
      </fieldset>
      <fieldset>
         Last name:
         <input name="lname" type="text" title="Enter name" />
      </fieldset>
      <anchor>Done
          <go method="post" href="search">
             <postfield name="fname" value="$fname" />
             <postfield name="lname" value="$lname" />
          </go>
      </anchor>
   </p>
</card>

<card id="bio" title="Biography">
   <p mode="nowrap">
   <a href="#main" >Done</a>
   $(bio)
   <a href="#main" >Done</a>
   </p>
</card>
...
</wml>
```

This template card contains one variable: bio. When the bio card is presented, we want the variable name to get replaced by the data that was sent back from the server.

After the server has looked up the requested data, it sends back the following card, which contains the result but no text structure or presentation information, over the air to the client:

```
<card newcontext="true">
   <onevent type="onenterforward">
      <go href="main.wml#bio">
         <setvar name="bio" value="Peter Stark works as architect at Phone.com,
               Redwood City, Ca, and represents his company in the WAP Forum." />
      </go>
   </onevent>
</card>
```

The above card works like a trampoline. When processed by the user agent, the variable is set, and processing is moved to the template card, `bio`. This means that the card that is sent back from the server, over the air, can be of minimal size since it only contains the data; all structure information is already in the client. The `onenterforward` event was triggered by the link element that referred to this card. We will return to events and tasks later.

When the card has been processed and the `bio` variable has been substituted with its value, the `bio` card will become:

```
<card id="bio" title="Biography">
   <p mode="nowrap">
      <a href="#main" >Done</a>
         Peter Stark works as architect at Phone.com, Redwood City, Ca, and
         represents his company in the WAP Forum.
      <a href="#main" >Done</a>
   </p>
</card>
```

Note that the above "trampoline" card does not display any content. But it will anyway end up in the history list. This is a problem if the user navigates back; an empty card will be displayed. You can workaround this problem by not having a `<prev>` task – that is, a Back control – in the card that follows the empty one.

Form Data

The HTML form elements `<input>`, `<select>`, `<option>`, `<optgroup>`, and `<fieldset>` are available in WML and work in the same way as in HTML. Not all HTML attributes are available, however, and some attributes have been added. We have already seen how the `<go>` element and the `<postfield>` element are used to submit data to the server, andthat it is the `<go>` element that is used instead of the HTML `<form>` element. The differences between HTML forms and WML are described in this section. Firstly, here are the WML form elements, and their attributes:

Form fields	
Element	**Attributes**
`<select>`	`title`
	`name`
	`value`
	`iname`
	`ivalue`
	`multiple=(true|false) "false"`
	`tabindex`
`<input>`	`name`
	`type=(text|password) "text"`
	`value`
	`format`
	`emptyok=(true|false) "false"`
	`size`
	`maxlength`
	`tabindex`
	`title`
`<option>`	`value`
	`title`
	`onpick`
`<optgroup>`	`title`
`<fieldset>`	`title`

The <input> Element

To enhance input validation, two attributes have been added to the HTML `<input>` element. The `emptyok` attribute specifies whether a value is required for the input element or it can be left empty when the data is sent to the server. In the following example the user is required to enter a name before the data is submitted to the server:

```
Name<input name="N" emptyok="false" type="text" title="Enter name" />
```

Without the `emptyok` attribute it would be up to the server to check to see whether data has been typed in. By using the `emptyok` attribute, the check is performed in the client and network round-trips can be saved.

The `format` attribute specifies the format of the data expected by the user. In the following example the user is required to type in a telephone number of the format `12345-123`:

```
Name<input name="N" format="NNNNN\-3N" type="text" title="Enter name" />
```

The magic sequence of characters in the `format` attribute is defined in the WML specification and provided here for reference:

Value	Description
`A`	Entry of any upper-case alphabetic or punctuation character (upper-case non-numeric character).
`a`	Entry of any lower-case alphabetic or punctuation character (lower-case non-numeric character).
`N`	Entry of any numeric character.
`X`	Entry of any upper case character.
`x`	Entry of any lower-case character.
`M`	Entry of any character; the user agent may choose to assume that the character is upper-case for the purposes of simple data entry, but must allow entry of any character.
`m`	Entry of any character; the user agent may choose to assume that the character is lower-case for the purposes of simple data entry, but must allow entry of any character.
`*f`	Entry of any number of characters: `f` is one of the above format codes and specifies what kind of characters can be entered. Note: this format may only be specified once and must appear at the end of the format string.
`nf`	Entry of up to *n* characters where n is from 1 to 9; `f` is one of the above format codes (other than `*f` format code) and specifies what kind of characters can be entered. Note: this format may only be specified once and must appear at the end of the format string.
`\c`	Display the next character, `c`, in the entry field; allows escaping of the format codes as well as introducing non-formatting characters so they can be displayed in the entry area. Escaped characters are considered part of the input's value, and must be preserved by the user agent. For example, the stored value of the input `"12345-123"` having a mask `"NNNNN\-3N"` is `"12345-123"` and not `"12345123"`. Similarly, if the value of the variable named by the name attribute is `"12345123"` and the mask is `"NNNNN\-3N"`, the user agent must unset the variable since it does not conform to the mask.

The <select> Element

Another HTML form field that has been adopted by WML is the `<select>` element. It works as in HTML and can contain the `<option>` and `<optgroup>` elements.

The `onpick` attribute can be used to make the `<option>` element a link element; when the user selects the option the browser navigates to the URL specified in the attribute. However, you may want to avoid doing this because it can surprise the user (who thinks the select list is a select list and not a list of links), furthermore some browsers display the `<select>` element in a way that makes it inappropriate to use for navigation choices.

In the following example we use the `<select>` element let the user select the book category:

```
<card id="title" title="Title search" newcontext="true" >
   <p mode="nowrap">
       <fieldset>
       Word in title:
       <input name="title" type="text" title="Enter title"/>
       </fieldset>
       <fieldset>
       Category:
       <select name="cat" title="Select cat.">
       <option value="none">-none-</option>
       <option value="asp">ASP</option>
       <option value="cpp">C++</option>
       <option value="com">COM</option>
       <option value="dbs">Database</option>
       <option value="gnu">GNU/Linux</option>
       <option value="java">Java</option>
       <option value="vb">VB</option>
       <option value="xml">XML</option>
       </select>
       </fieldset>
      <anchor>Done
          <go method="post" href="search">
             <postfield name="type" value="books" />
             <postfield name="title" value="$title" />
             <postfield name="cat" value="$cat" />
          </go>
      </anchor>
   </p>
</card>
```

Note that we are using a `none` option in case the user does not want to select any category.

Forms are central in wireless applications. Almost every application follows the same pattern: the user is requested for some information and the result is sent back from a database. Popular applications for mobile phones consist almost always of dynamically generated content, and rarely of static documents such as "homepages" that are popular on the traditional Web.

Images

Although images are not what you would expect on a mobile phone, most WAP browsers support at least simple WAP bitmap images, WBMPs. The WBMP specification is available from the WAP Forum web site, http://www.wapforum.org/, but a little hard to find since it is only two pages and contained in a document called WAE Specification. Some browsers may also support standard web image formats such as GIF, in addition to WBMP.

To include an image into the document the HTML-like `<img>` element is used. One WML specific attribute has been added, the `localsrc` attribute. It used to include a local image rather than one from the web server on the network. The names of the local images, however, have not been specified in WAP so they are still proprietary, although work was underway at the time of writing to add names for local images. For the moment, to use the `localsrc` attribute you must check what images each WAP browser vendor supports. The following example will include the local image `book`, if it's available, otherwise it will request the `book.wbmp` image from the web server. The benefit of using the local image is that the browser does not have to go to the network to get it, saving network round-trips, and that image itself can be optimized to fit well into the user interface of the device.

```
<img localsrc="book" alt="A Book" src="/images/book.wbmp"/>
```

All other image attributes, `alt`, `src`, `vspace`, `hspace`, `align`, `height`, and `width`, are the same as the HTML ones with the same name. The following element and attributes are defined for images:

Images	
Element	**Attribute**
`<img>`	`alt`
	`src`
	`localsrc`
	`vspace`
	`hspace`
	`align`
	`height`
	`width`

Generating WML on the Server

For various reasons, services for small devices are often dynamic. Thus, you will not write static WML documents. Instead, you will almost always generate WML cards dynamically.

Of course we can use any technique that we use to create HTML or XML dynamically, be that ASP, JSP, CGI scripts, etc. But one tool that is ideally suited to generating our WML documents is the XSL Transformations (XSLT) language.

On the server we can use XSLT to generate the WML document from any XML source. Consider the result of a search coming back from the database as an XML document that contains the following:

```
<Author>
   <FirstName>Peter</FirstName>
   <MI>M</MI>
   <LastName>Stark</LastName>
   <Biographical>
      Peter Stark works as architect at Phone.com, Redwood City, Ca, and
      represents his company in the WAP Forum.
   </Biographical>
   <Portrait type="image/jpeg" href="stark.jpg"/>
   <Portrait type="image/vnd.wap.wbmp" href="stark.wbmp"/>
</Author>
```

Since we assume the mobile phone already has the document `main.wml` – otherwise it has to download it and put it into its local cache – all we need to send over the air is a minimal document that sets the `bio` variable. We have already seen this document when we demonstrated how the `onenterforward` event is used.

Here is the transformation sheet that generates the WML document:

```
<xsl:stylesheet xmlns:xsl="http://www.w3.org/1999/XSL/Transform">
<xsl:output method="xml" indent="yes"/>

<xsl:template match="Author">
<wml>
   <card newcontext="true">
      <onevent type="onenterforward">
         <go href="main.wml#bio">
            <setvar name="bio" value="{Biographical}" />
         </go>
      </onevent>
   </card>
</wml>
</xsl:template>

<xsl:template match="@*" >
   <xsl:apply-templates />
</xsl:template>

<xsl:template match="* | text()" >
   <xsl:apply-templates />
</xsl:template>

</xsl:stylesheet>
```

The image could have been transformed into a WBMP or GIF image, depending on the capability of the phone. This would of course have required a graphical library that could do the image translation.

Having looked at the theory behind WAP and WML, the markup language we use for WAP devices, we should see how we could put what we have learnt to use.

The WROX WML Application

This section summarizes the application we have created. It is a scaled down version of the WROX web site. The user can do the following:

- Get general information about WROX
- Lookup biography for an author based on first and/or last name
- Lookup a book title based on category and/or word in title

Here is the WML code:

```
<wml>

<template>
   <do type="prev" label="Back">
      <prev/>
   </do>
</template>

<card id="main" title="WROX">
   <onevent type="ontimer">
      <go href="#about" />
   </onevent>
   <timer value="100" />
   <p mode="nowrap">
      <a href="#author">Search Author</a><br/>
      <a href="#title">Search Title</a><br/>
      <a href="#about">About</a><br/>
   </p>
</card>

<card id="author" title="Author search" newcontext="true" >
   <p mode="nowrap">
      <fieldset>
         First name:
         <input name="fname" type="text" title="Enter name"/>
      </fieldset>
      <fieldset>
         Last name:
         <input name="lname" type="text" title="Enter name" />
      </fieldset>
      <anchor>Done
          <go method="post" href="search">
             <postfield name="type" value="bio" />
             <postfield name="fname" value="$fname" />
             <postfield name="lname" value="$lname" />
          </go>
      </anchor>
   </p>
</card>
```

```
<card id="bio" title="Biography">
   <do type="prev" >
      <noop/>
   </do>

   <p mode="nowrap">
      <a href="#main" >Done</a>
         $(bio)
      <a href="#main" >Done</a>
   </p>
</card>

<card id="title" title="Title search" newcontext="true" >
   <p mode="nowrap">
       <fieldset>
          Word in title:
          <input name="title" type="text" title="Enter title"/>
       </fieldset>
       <fieldset>
          Category:
          <select name="cat" title="Select cat.">
             <option value="none">-none-</option>
             <option value="asp">ASP</option>
             <option value="cpp">C++</option>
             <option value="com">COM</option>
             <option value="dbs">Database</option>
             <option value="gnu">GNU/Linux</option>
             <option value="java">Java</option>
             <option value="vb">VB</option>
             <option value="xml">XML</option>
          </select>
       </fieldset>
       <anchor>Done
          <go method="post" href="search">
             <postfield name="type" value="books" />
             <postfield name="title" value="$title" />
             <postfield name="cat" value="$cat" />
          </go>
      </anchor>
   </p>
</card>

<card id="book" title="Book">
   <p mode="nowrap">
      <a href="#main" >Done</a>
         $(book)
      <a href="#main" >Done</a>
   </p>
</card>


<card id="about" title="WROX" ontimer="#about2">
   <timer value="100"/>
   <p mode="nowrap">
      <a href="#main">Done</a><br/>
```

```
Wrox Press aims to make programmers successful by sharing with them the
          knowledge and experience of their professional peers.
   </p>
   <p>
      <a href="#main">Done</a>
      <a href="#about2">More</a>
   </p>
</card>

<card id="about2" title="WROX">
   <p mode="nowrap">
      <a href="#main">Home</a><br/>
      <a href="allbooks.wml">All Books</a><br/>
      <a href="http://www.wroxconferences.com">Conferences</a><br/>
      <a href="allauthors.wml">Authors</a><br/>
      <a href="support.wml">Support</a><br/>
      <a href="membership.wml">Membership</a><br/>
      <a href="contacts.wml">Contact Us</a><br/>
   </p>
</card>

</wml>
```

When the user looks up an author, a short biography will get returned and displayed in the bio card, as we have seen. In this card we are disabling the **Back** control since we do not want the user to navigate back to an empty card; the "trampoline" card, see the section on client-side templates. In case the biography is long, we have a `Done` anchor both in the beginning and at the end of the card.

If the user is inactive at the first card the application will automatically navigate to the `about` card, and provide the user with some commercial information about WROX.

When the user requests a book, and enters word in the title, the response is a list of all matches; for example:

```
<!DOCTYPE wml PUBLIC "-//WAPFORUM//DTD WML 1.1//EN"
          "http://www.wapforum.org/DTD/wml_1.1.xml">
<wml>
<template>
   <do type="prev" label="Back">
      <prev/>
   </do>
</template>
```

```
<card id="first" title="XML/Scripting">
   <p mode="nowrap">

   <a href="Details.asp?ISBN=1861002718">VBScript Programmer&#39;s
      Reference</a><br/>
   <a href="Details.asp?ISBN=1861002645">Professional Visual Interdev 6
      Programming</a><br/>
   <a href="Details.asp?ISBN=186100270X">Professional JavaScript</a><br/>
   <a href="Details.asp?ISBN=1861001746">IE5 Dynamic HTML Programmer&#39;s
      Reference</a><br/>
```

```
<a href="Details.asp?ISBN=1861002270">Designing Distributed Applications with
      XML, ASP, IE5, LDAP and MSMQ</a><br/>
   <a href="Details.asp?ISBN=1861001576">XML in IE5 Programmer&#39;s
      Reference</a><br/>
   <a href="Details.asp?ISBN=1861002289">Professional XML Design and
      Implementation</a><br/>
   <a href="#second">More...</a>

   <anchor>Done
      <go href="http://www.wrox.com/wap/index.wml" />
   </anchor>

   </p>
</card>

<card id="second" title="XML/Scripting">
   <p mode="nowrap">

   <a href="Details.asp?ISBN=1861002211">Implementing LDAP</a><br/>
   <a href="Details.asp?ISBN=1861001525">XML Applications</a><br/>
   <a href="Details.asp?ISBN=1861001894">JavaScript Objects</a><br/>
   <a href="Details.asp?ISBN=1861001657">Professional Style Sheets for HTML and
      XML</a><br/>
   <a href="Details.asp?ISBN=186100138X">Instant DHTML Scriptlets</a><br/>
   <a href="Details.asp?ISBN=1861001274">Instant JavaScript</a><br/>
   <a href="Details.asp?ISBN=1861001568">Instant HTML Programmer&#39;s Reference,
      HTML 4.0 Edition</a><br/>
   <a href="Details.asp?ISBN=1861000707">Professional IE4 Programming</a><br/>
   <a href="Details.asp?ISBN=1861000685">Instant IE4 Dynamic HTML Programmer&#39;s
      Reference - IE4 Edition</a><br/>
   <a href="Details.asp?ISBN=1861001193">Instant Netscape Dynamic HTML
      Programmer&#39;s Reference NC4 Edition</a><br/>
   <a href="Details.asp?ISBN=186100074X">Professional Web Site
      Optimization</a><br/>
   <a href="Details.asp?ISBN=1861000766">Instant HTML Programmer&#39;s
      Reference</a><br/>

   <anchor>Done
      <go href="http://www.wrox.com/wap/index.wml" />
   </anchor>

   </p>
</card>
</wml>
```

The list has been divided up into two cards to make it easier for the user to navigate. Note the More... option at the end of the first card. Also, every card provides a way for the user to get back to the starting point of the application. There is also a Back key available in every card, via the template.

Having taken a look at how we can markup our documents for the new generation of mobile devices, let's take a look at the scripting language for use with these clients.

WML Script

While WML allows us to mark up our documents for WAP-enabled devices, the WAP specifications include a scripting language called WMLScript to add more functionality to our pages. It is derived from the ECMAScript language (better known as JavaScript or JScript), and will look familiar to anyone that has programmed in this. Although not a proper subset of ECMAScript, it is a low-fat variant of the popular script language that most web developers are used to. First we will look at the basics and how to call script functions, then we will look at the libraries already provided.

Basics

In the following section I will assume you already know ECMAScript. Basic script language constructs such as `If` and `For` statements are not explained. Instead I will focus on the script function libraries that are available in the WAP browser, and how scripts and WML can work together.

WMLScript programs are not embedded inside the WML (as in HTML with the `<script>` element). Instead, script programs are always stored in separate files and are accessible via a URL.

Functions

WMLScript script programs are function oriented. There can be several functions in one file, so functions need to have unique names. To call a specific function in the file you need to use the URL of the file plus a fragment identifier with the function's name. The functions cannot be nested, so you cannot define one function inside another. And while all variables in a function are local, functions are often used to manipulate variables on the WML browser, which are global.

Variables

The data type of a variable is based on the most recent assignment. To declare a variable you use the `var` operator:

```
var wap = "Wireless Application Protocol";
```

Variable names are case-sensitive and can include alphabetic characters, digits, and the underscore character, but they cannot begin with a digit. If there is, like in the example above, an initial value, then the data type of that value is used as the initial data type for the variable. Variables also have local scope.

Byte Code

When the script passes the WAP gateway on its way down to the mobile phone, it gets compiled into byte-code and delivered as such to the phone. This is not the same byte-code as Java programs get compiled into, but the concept and reason for using byte-code are the same. Byte code is easier to digest and requires less bandwidth over the air.

How to Call Script Functions from WML

Since script functions can be located with a URL, they can be called from either of the link elements in WML: <go> or <a>.

```
<do type="accept">
   <go href="http://www.wrox.com/wmlscript#calculate($result, $1)" />
</do>
```

When the WML browser executes the above example, the <go> element points to a script function as the target resource. The script, however, will be executed in a separate context from the WML card, so variables in the script are not shared by the WML document. The control is returned to the WML document once the script has terminated. There is no return value from a script, but a script can manipulate variables in the WML document, as we will see shortly. If the target resource had been an ordinary WML document, the target would have replaced the current document.

Note that script functions are not added to the history list, so you cannot use <prev> to return to a script.

Libraries

You cannot do anything useful with WMLScript without the built-in standard libraries, but there are six standard libraries that should be supported by a WAP browser: `WMLBrowser`, `Dialogs`, `Lang`, `Float`, `String`, and `URL`.

By using the script libraries you can:

- Manipulate the state of the WML browser by setting and changing variables in the WML document
- Generate simple pop-up dialogs to ask the user for input, make a selection, or confirm an event
- Work with strings, floating numbers, and URLs
- Find out system properties such as whether floating point numbers are supported or not
- Generate random numbers
- Terminate the script in different ways

When you call a function of a script library you use the name of the library, followed by a ".", followed by the name of the function, and possibly any parameters. For example, to display an alert box, you do:

```
Dialogs.alert ("You have mail!");
```

The data types used in the functions are `Boolean`, `Float`, `Integer`, `String`, and `Invalid`. When both `Integer` and `Float` can be used, it is called a `Number`. And when the type does not matter, it is called `Any`. All of the functions have similar error handling: if any parameter is invalid (for example, of the wrong type), the function returns `Invalid`. Parameters are passed by value.

We will now take a closer look at the libraries.

Manipulating Browser's State – The WMLBrowser Library

The `WMLBrowser` library can be used to manipulate the state of the browser. The state of the browser comprises of the current list of variables, the current WML card, and the history list.

Handling Variables

The `setVar(`*`name`*`, `*`value`*`)` function is to bind the variable `name` to the `value`. The `getVar(`*`name`*`)` function retrieves the value of the variable *`name`*. If the browser does not have a variable that matches the *`name`*, an empty string is returned. The `refresh()` function updates the display. So, for example, if you have done a sequence of `setVar()` functions that affects the content that is currently displayed the changes will be visible to the user.

The following example implements a blinking Wrox logo. The function is triggered at a regular interval by using the `<timer>` element:

```
extern function repaint()
{
   var text = WMLBrowser.getVar("text");
   if (text == "Wrox")
      WMLBrowser.setVar("text", "");
   else
      WMLBrowser.setVar("text", "Wrox");
   WMLBrowser.refresh();
}
```

And this is the WML card from which the function is called:

```
<card id="card1" title="Intro" onenterforward="repaint.wmls#repaint()"
      ontimer="repaint.wmls#repaint()">
   <timer value="10" />
   <p align="center">
      <br/>
      <big>$text</big>
   </p>
</card>
```

The state of this application is maintained by the variables in the browser. The script executes operations on the browser by manipulating the variables. The above example could also be extended with more text, simple ASCII graphics or animation. By involving more than one card and perhaps using real WBMP or GIF images, the result can be a really nice "multimedia" introduction to your WAP service – even on a mobile phone.

The lifetime of variables in the WML document can be controlled by calling the `newcontext()` function, which clears all variables. This is especially useful if you want to make sure that you have initialized all variables before users start going through a sequence of cards.

Navigating Cards and Using the History

To make the browser navigate to a different location you can use the `go(url)` function, which can be a relative URL to the current document, while the previous location on the history can be reached by the `prev()` function. Subsequent calls to the `go()` and the `prev()` functions override each other. To find out the URL of the current card that is displayed by the browser, you can use the `getCurrentCard()` function. If the URL is relative to the URL of the current script, the returned value will be a relative URL, but if it is from a completely different web site it will be an absolute URL.

Using Dialogs

Using the `Dialogs` library from a script function you can trigger pop-up dialog boxes to ask the user for information or confirm an event. The actual dialogs may look different on different phones. Some browsers may use a small WML card to present the dialog, while others may have special dialog boxes.

To alert the user of an event, such as the result of a calculation, an error, or an invalid input value, you can use the simple `alert(text)` function. Or if you want the user to select between two different values, the `confirm(text, choiceOK, choiceNOK)` function is appropriate. The question is *`text`* and the choices are *`choiceOK`* and *`choiceNOK`*. The return value is a `Boolean`.

You can even ask the user to enter a value into a dialog box using the `prompt(text, defaultValue)` function, where *`defaultValue`* becomes the response to the *`text`*. The function will then return the entered value, which has the default value of *`defaultValue`*. For example, the following function asks the user about the name of an author:

```
extern function setname()
{
   var result = Dialogs.prompt("Who is the author?");
   WMLBrowser.setVar("name", result);
   WMLBrowser.go("#author");
}
```

The user's answer is set in the browser by using the "`name`" variable. We can then use two simple WML cards to call the script program and display the result:

```
<card id="intro" onenterforward="check.wmls#setname()" />
<card id="author"><p>$(name)</p></card>
```

Language Specific Functions

The `Lang` library is a mix of useful functions to convert between data types, getting system properties, and generate random numbers.

Some WAP browsers are not capable of supporting floating point numbers. You can call the `float()` function to find out whether the device your script is running on has support for floating point numbers (most browser have). The return value is a `Boolean` value; `true` means that floating point numbers are supported. You may also want to know the max and min *`Integer`* values on the device. The `maxInt()` returns the maximum, and `minInt()` the minimum. To check whether a particular value is an integer or can be converted into one, you call the `isInt(number)` function, and if the function returns `true`, you can call `parseInt(string)` function to convert the value into the corresponding integer. For example:

```
var y = isInt("13.13");     //Returns true
var y = parseInt("13.13"); //Returns "13"
```

The `isFloat(value)` and `parseFloat(string)` functions work the same way for floating point numbers.

And finally, you can get the character set that the device supports by calling the `characterSet()` function. The return value is the **MIBEnum** value assigned to the character set by the Internet Naming Authority (IANA); ISO-8859-1 has the number `4` and shift_JIS has the number `17`.

The `abs(number)`, `max(number1, number2)`, and `min(number1, number2)` functions do exactly what you expect them to.

You can also generate a positive random number by using the `random(value)` function; the value will be greater than or equal to 0 but less than or equal to `value`. To improve the randomness you can call the `seed(value)` function with an appropriate random seed value.

The last functions in the `Lang` library are the `abort(string)` and `exit(value)` functions. These functions will terminate the script program in the way you decide. The `abort(string)` function terminates with an error, the `exit(value)` terminates normally. Most browsers ignore the parameters in these functions.

Floating Point Numbers

The `Float` library is supported in devices that supports floating point numbers. The following functions are available:

- The `int(number)` function returns the integer part of the number.
- The `floor(number)` function returns the greatest integer value that is not greater than the number.
- The `ceil(number)` function returns the smallest integer value that is not less than the number.
- The `round(number)` function rounds off the number to the closest integer.
- The `sqrt(number)` function takes the square root of the number. The precision of the result depends on the device's capabilities.
- The `pow(number, number)` function raises the first number to the power of the second number. If the first parameter is a negative number, the second parameter must be an integer.
- The `maxFloat()` returns the maximum floating-point value available.
- The `minFloat()` returns the minimum floating-point value available.

The following script calls the above functions and uses a simple table in a WML card to display the results:

```
extern function Floatcheck()
{
   var a = Float.int("13.5");
   var b = Float.floor("13.5");
   var c = Float.ceil("13.5");
   var d = Float.round("13.5");
   var e = Float.sqrt("2,2");
   var f = Float.minFloat();
   var g = Float.maxFloat();

   WMLBrowser.setVar("a",a);
   WMLBrowser.setVar("b",b);
   WMLBrowser.setVar("c",c);
   WMLBrowser.setVar("d",d);
   WMLBrowser.setVar("e",f);
   WMLBrowser.setVar("g",g);
}
```

The script can be called from the following WML card:

```
<card id="card1" title="FloatCheck" >
   <onevent type="onenterforward">
      <go href="floatcheck.wmls#Floatcheck()" />
   </onevent>

   <p>
      <table columns="2" align="LR" >
         <tr><td>Float.int ("13.5")</td><td> => $a</td></tr>
         <tr><td>Float.floor ("13.5")</td><td> => $b</td></tr>
         <tr><td>Float.ceil ("13.5")</td><td> => $c</td></tr>
         <tr><td>Float.round ("13.5")</td><td> => $d</td></tr>
         <tr><td>Float.sqrt ("2,2")</td><td> => $e</td></tr>
         <tr><td>Float.minFloat ()</td><td> => $f</td></tr>
         <tr><td>Float.maxFloat ()</td><td> => $g</td></tr>
      </table>
   </p>
</card>
```

Strings

The `String` library is available to manipulate text strings.

Basics

The length of a string is returned by calling `length(string)`. The `isEmpty(string)` returns `True` if the string is empty, otherwise `False`. You can also access any single character from a string by calling the `charAt(string, index)` function. If you try to use an `index` that is out of range, an empty string will be returned. To get more than one character, you can use the `subString(string, startIndex, length)` function and get back a sub-string starting at `startIndex` and `length` number of characters forward.

Search and Replace

Sometimes you need to search for a particular string of characters. The `find(string, subString)` function returns the index of the first character in the `string` that matches the requested `subString`. A `-1` is returned if no match can be found. You can also replace text in a string by using the `replace(string, oldSubString, newSubString)` function. The result is a new string where all `oldSubStrings` have been replaced by the `newSubString`.

Elements

An "element" as we are using it in this context is not an XML element – it is text separated by a pre-defined separation string. The `elementAt(string, index, sepString)` function returns the element at the *index* position. The separation string is defined in *sepString*. The first element has index of `0`. To find the number of elements in a string you can call the `elements(string, sepString)` function. To insert an element into a set of elements, the `insertAt(string, elemString, number, sepString)` function can be used. It returns a new string with the new element. You can also replace one element at a specified index with another element. This is done by calling the `replaceAt(string, elemString, number, sepString)` function. Finally, you can remove an element by calling the `removeAt(string, number, sepString)` function.

URLs

The URL library is used to check whether a URL is valid, to request a particular part of a URL, to request the content from a URL, and for URL escape or unescape characters.

Parsing

A URL has the following format:

```
<scheme>://<host>:<port>/<path>;<params>?<query>#<fragment>
```

The following is a valid URL:

```
http://www.wrox.com:8080/wap/index.wml;3;2?author=peter#name
```

The `isValid(url)` function can be used to check whether a string is a valid URL.

There are also some functions you can use to request various parts of the URL:

- The `getScheme(url)` function returns the protocol used to access the server; in the above example, "http". If no protocol is specified, an empty string is returned.
- The `getHost(url)` function returns the hostname of the server; in the above example, "`www.wrox.com`". If no hostname is specified, an empty string is returned.
- The `getPort(url)` function returns the port number of the server; in the above example, "8080". If no port is specified, an empty string is returned.
- The `getPath(url)` function returns the location (a file or directory specification); in the above example, "/wap/index.wml". If no path is specified, an empty string is returned.
- The `getParameters(url)` function returns the parameters (rarely used); in the above example, "3;2". If no parameter is specified, an empty string is returned.

- The `getQuery(url)` function returns the query part; in the above example, "author=peter". If no query is specified, an empty string is returned.
- The `getFragment(url)` function returns the fragment part; in the above example, "name". If no fragment is specified, an empty string is returned.

The script program has a base URL that can be retrieved from the `getBase()` function. For example, a script program at "http://www.wrox.com/script.wmls" will have this URL as the base URL. When a script is invoked from a WML document, the WML document is called the "referrer". The URL of the referrer can be retrieved from the `getReferer()` function.

There are two types of URLs: absolute and relative. An absolute URL is a full URL such as "http://www.wrox.com/index.wml". A relative URL is a partial URL such as "/index.wml". The URL to which a relative URL is related is called the "base URL". The `resolve(baseURL, embeddedURL)` function can be used to create an absolute URL by combing a relative URL with its base URL. For example:

```
var absoluteURL = URL.resolve("http://www.wrox.com","index.wml");
```

will return "http://www.wrox.com/index.wml". The following example prompts the user for a URL (the script's base URL is used as default), parses the URL, and sets variables in the WML browser:

```
extern function parseUrl()
{
   WMLBrowser.newContext();

   var base = URL.getBase();

   var aUrl = Dialogs.prompt("Enter URL:", base);

   if (URL.isValid(aUrl))
   {
      var scheme = URL.getScheme(aUrl);
      var host   = URL.getHost(aUrl);
      var port   = URL.getPort(aUrl);
      var file   = URL.getPath(aUrl);
      var para   = URL.getParameters(aUrl);
      var query  = URL.getQuery(aUrl);
      var frag   = URL.getFragment(aUrl);

      WMLBrowser.setVar("scheme", scheme);
      WMLBrowser.setVar("host", host);
      WMLBrowser.setVar("port", port);
      WMLBrowser.setVar("path", file);
      WMLBrowser.setVar("parameters", para);
      WMLBrowser.setVar("query", query);
      WMLBrowser.setVar("frag", frag);
   }
   else
      Dialogs.alert("Invalid URL");

   WMLBrowser.refresh();
}
```

The WML document that invokes the above script may look something like the following:

```
<card id="show" onenterforward="parseurl.wmls#parseUrl" >
   <p>
      Scheme: $scheme <br/>
      Host: $host <br/>
      Port: $port <br/>
      Path: $path <br/>
      Parameters: $parameters<br/>
      Query: $query <br/>
      Fragment: $frag<br/>
   </p>
</card>
```

Requesting Data from the Server

`loadString(url, contentType)` can be used to load the content from a URL straight into a string variable. Only textual content is supported (media types that start with "`text/`"). In the following example the script downloads a data file with semicolon-separated values:

```
extern function getData()
{
   WMLBrowser.newContext();

   var absoluteUrl = URL.resolve(URL.getBase(), "data.txt");
   var data = URL.loadString(absoluteUrl, "text/plain");

   var title = String.elementAt(data,0,";");
   var fname = String.elementAt(data,1,";");
   var lname = String.elementAt(data,2,";");

   WMLBrowser.setVar("title", title);
   WMLBrowser.setVar("fname", fname);
   WMLBrowser.setVar("lname", lname);

   WMLBrowser.refresh();
}
```

The data file, `data.txt`, contains something like:

```
WAP;Peter;Stark
```

The data is returned as a string. If an error occurs, however, the HTTP error code is returned as an integer.

Escaping and Unescaping Characters

Finally, two functions are used to URL escape and unescape characters. Although a URL can contain any ISO Latin-1 character, it must be written using only the printable ASCII characters from the bottom half of the ISO Latin-1 character set. To represent non-ASCII characters a special character encoding is used. Also, several ASCII characters are disallowed in URLs and can be present only in the encoded form. Fortunately, the encoding is very simple:

```
%hh
```

The percentage sign indicates the start of the encoded character and the "hh" is hexadecimal code for the desired Latin-1 character.

The escapeString(*string*) function is used to encode a string with the URL character encoding. The unescapeString(*string*) function does the exact opposite; it decodes the string. The following function call:

```
URL.escapeString("http://www.wrox.com/index.wml?x=\u007f");
```

will return "http%3a%2f%2fwww.wrox.com%2fidex.wml%3fx%3d%7f".

Where to Get More Information

The WAP Forum has its own web site http://www.wapforum.org with all the specifications, news updates, and information about events and products related to WAP. Another good related site is the WAP Forum web site for developers, http://www.wapdevelopers.org, where you can test your WAP services and get a WAP logo.

Other good places to find information about WAP is on the web sites of the WAP browser vendors, for example:

Nokia, http://www.nokia.com/
Ericsson, http://www.ericsson.se/WAP/
Phone.com Inc., http://www.phone.com/

Apart from tools, specifications and tutorials the above web sites provide WAP developers kits. Just like in the desktop world there are well known differences between Internet Explorer and Netscape Navigator, there are differences between the various WAP browsers. Thus, one developer's kit will not be enough to make sure your WML documents look excellent on all phones.

Summary

In this chapter, we have introduced an XML application called Wireless Application Protocol, which is set to bring the Web to a number of mobile technologies. We have looked at the differences that these devices make to the way we develop pages due to the size of the screen, bandwidth available and processing power.

We looked at WML, the markup language for writing applications designed for mobile devices. As we have seen, much of it is similar to a cut down version of HTML. We also briefly looked at the scripting language that is provided with the WAP specifications, WMLScript, which is very similar to ECMAScript, which was based upon JavaScript.

We also saw how, if we are building pages from content in XML, we can transform XML into a number of other languages, such as different versions of HTML and other XML applications. So, rather than writing different versions of sites, it is possible to transform the underlying XML into applications for many different clients.

Hopefully this will have whetted your appetite for developing for the new generation of mobile devices that are set to increasingly populate the Web.

15

Case Study 1 – Data Duality

The work in this case study was developed to address the issue of data duality. There are many forms of data that we need to view in different ways. If you think about the spreadsheet paradigm, we can sort and view data by clicking on the top of a column. On the web, however, creating something like this in a pre-XML world was not an easy task. With XML, however, we can easily store XML on the client, and re-sort and order the data as we want.

The example developed in this chapter was originally written for a large insurance company. They required a system that would allow staff to edit details about forms (these were paper forms such as insurance claim forms, insurance application forms, etc., not HTML forms). Some people referred to the forms by their name, while others referred to them by a reference number. In an attempt to build a system that would require minimal training to deploy, rather than forcing the users to adopt one standard way of referring to the forms that they needed, we were to provide a system that allowed users to view the list of forms by either title or number.

The solution demonstrates the following techniques:

- Using ASP to create XML from a SQL Server database
- Using XSL to dynamically transform XML
- Using DHTML to collapse/expand an outline
- Using client-side scripting of the XML DOM to add/remove/update nodes

Business Need

It became apparent early in the design process that there would be a major challenge from a User Interface perspective. This was an e-commerce site that had paper forms as the products that could be ordered. The problem was that there was a duality about the forms: they had both names and numbers as identifiers.

There are many ways to solve this "data duality" issue in a web application using pre-XML technologies; some are more elegant than others. However, in the quest to provide an intuitive and elegant solution, we turned to XML.

System Requirements

We set the following design goals:

- Improve navigation method
- Provide the ability to search or request products either by name or by number
- Provide an extremely intuitive user interface
- Eliminate server round-trips where possible

We believed that if these goals were met, the project could be considered a success.

Design Time: Let the Games Begin

The original solution was developed for a system that was based on Microsoft technologies, with the site built on Microsoft Site Server. For illustration in this book, however, we are using a SQL Server database and ASP (the example will work perfectly well with either PWS on Windows 9x or Internet Information Server on Windows NT). As the target user base for this application was limited, and all in-house, we had the luxury of being able to mandate the browser requirements. We selected Microsoft's Internet Explorer 5 because it was the latest browser at the time.

We wanted to present a standard "table of contents on the left, data on the right" dual frame type of interface for the site administrators. These administrators could then click on the type of form they required from a contents menu in the left frame, and this would update the data displayed in the right frame, displaying details about the selected form such as form number, form name, form type, form description, etc. The administrator would be able to edit the form details in the right hand frame, or move to another form by clicking on a form in the left frame. The following screenshot illustrates the looks of the user interface:

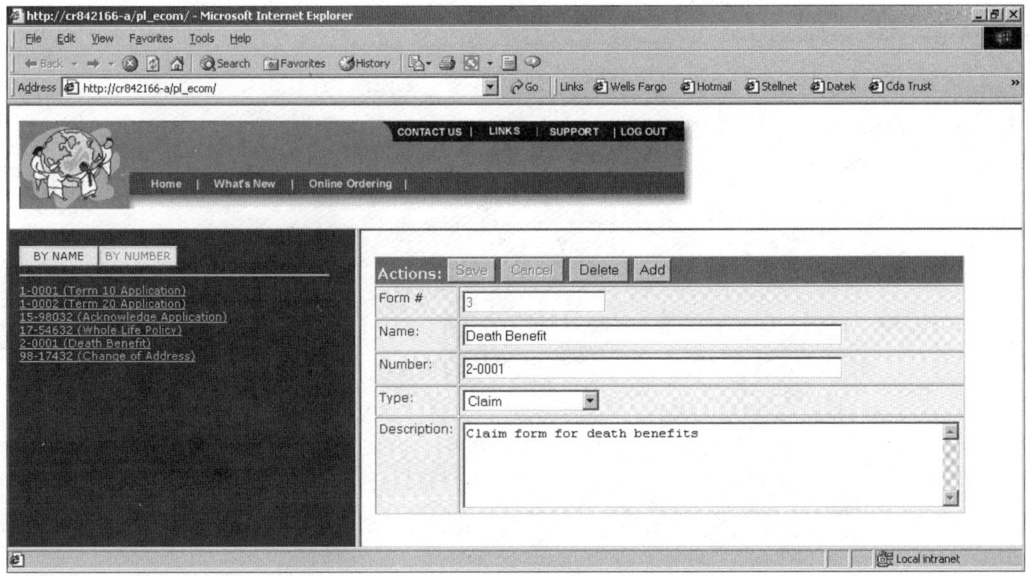

Given the duality of the key data – users could be looking for a form based on a name or a number – we would need two different tables of content: one for the form numbers, and another for the form titles. We could have gone the conventional route and used server-side ASP. In this scenario one ASP page would generate the 'by name' page, another would generate the 'by number' page. The drawbacks to this approach would be that two pages would need to be maintained, and changing views would require a round-trip to the server.

An improvement on that would have been to have a single page generate both views, and send them both to the client at once, but use DHTML to hide one of the views. While more elegant than the first solution, and obviating the need for a server round-trip, this solution would have duplicated the data being sent across the wire.

In search of a better way, we turned to XML and XSL. Ideally, we would send down the data only once and handle the rendering choices on the client. XML is ideal for this scenario.

Implementation Overview

In our XML solution, the user can click a button to change from one view to another, without the need for round-trips to the server. The data is sent to the client as XML once. When on the client, it can then be re-rendered as required by applying an XSL transformation to the XML data.

At a high level, these are the functional steps in the system:

1. ASP reads SQL Server product table and builds an XML stream
2. Client-side script loads XML document
3. Client-side script loads and applies XSL document

The following diagram shows the various pieces involved in the solution, as well as the relationships among them:

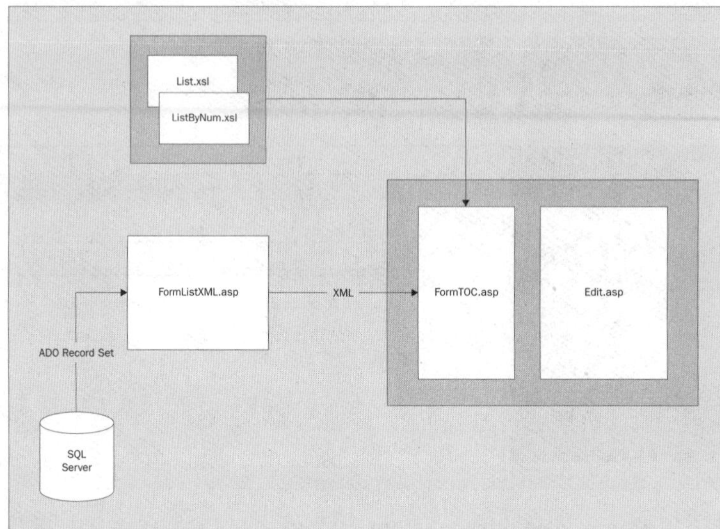

As we have just seen, this means that we will have two different views in the left-hand frame. The screen shot below illustrates both of these views:

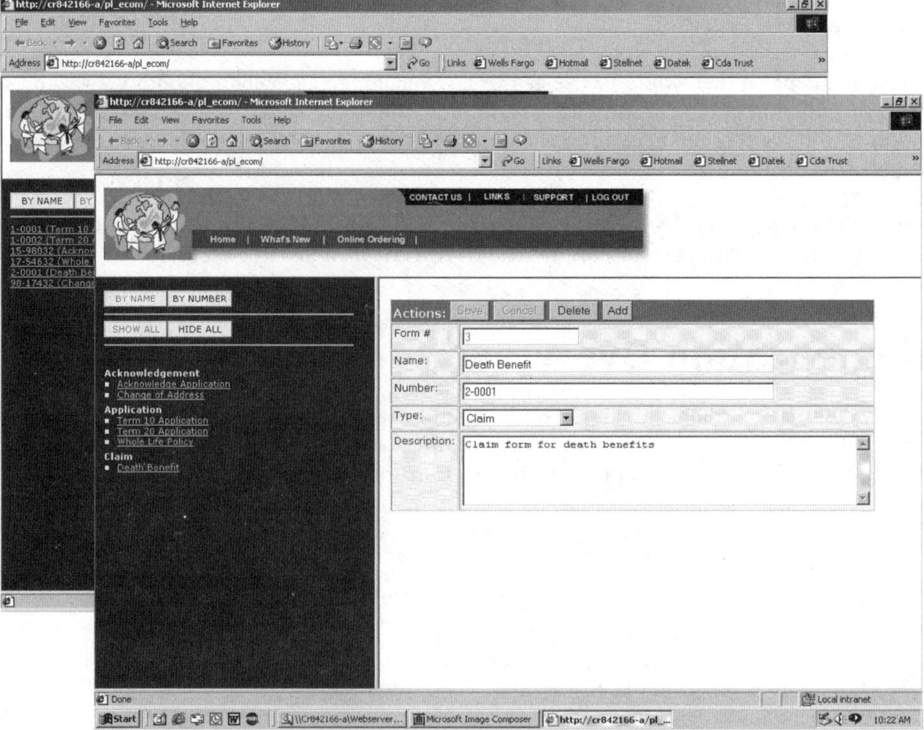

Setting Up the Database

The file required to set up the database for this case study is provided as part of the downloadable code for this book, in the form of a SQL script: `WroxProXMLForms.sql`.

To use this files, you first need to create a new database called `WroxProXMLForms` using the SQL Server Enterprise Manager. Next, if you are using SQL Server 7 then use the SQL Server Query Analyzer to run `WroxProXMLForms.sql` against the database you just created. In SQL Server 6.5, use the Tools | SQL Query Tool menu option and do the same thing. Back in Enterprise Manager you should see that the tables `ecom_form_type` and `ecom_product` have been created.

When you've done this, set up a System DSN called `WroxProXML` using the ODBC Data Sources control panel application.

Note that the file `edit.asp` included in the download is completely different from what was included in the original solution. In the original solution the role of that file was filled by several Site Server pages. Those pages were customized, and had calls in them to the various XML tree update functions presented later in this chapter.

XML-providing ASP

The first step in the chain is the `FormListXML.asp` ASP page that reads the data from the SQL Server tables, and returns an XML stream. The default return value from an ASP page is HTML, so we need to specify that the response will be XML. This is how:

```
<%Response.ContentType = "text/xml"%>
```

Once the response type has been set, anything outside of the ASP script tags, or written by an ASP `response.write`, will be considered XML and needs to be well-formed. Just to recap, this means that the generated document:

- must start with the XML declaration
- must have only one unique root element
- must have matching start and end tags
- must have properly nested tags

Any ASP page, such as our `FormListXML.asp`, that returns an XML stream must conform to those requirements or your browser (IE5) will report a parser error.

The XML we are generating will be in the following format:

```
<?xml version="1.0"?>
<FORMLIST TYPE="Insurance Forms">
   <FORMS TYPE="3rd Party Booklets and Article Reprints">
      <FORM>
         <FORMTITLE>NAIC - "Life Insurance Buyer's Guide"</FORMTITLE>
         <SKU>Product140</SKU>
         <FORMNUMBER>15-11297</FORMNUMBER>
      </FORM>
      <FORM>
         ...
      </FORM>
   </FORMS>
</FORMLIST>
```

In this case, a <FORMLIST> contains one or more <FORMS>, which is a grouping mechanism that groups the forms into specific 'types' (for example application forms). Within each <FORMS> branch, we can have one or more <FORM> entries, which contain the information about the actual forms themselves. The <FORMTITLE> and <FORMNUMBER> elements are self explanatory, and the <SKU> is a unique identifier for a form; this is required because the form number is not always unique.

So, let's have a look at the code for `FormListXML.asp`, which will generate this XML for us. We start, as we said, by setting the `ContentType` property of the ASP `Response` object to `"text/xml"`. We also set the expiration of the `Response` object to `-1`, preventing it from being cached on the browser:

```
<%
Response.ContentType = "text/xml"
Response.Expires = -1
%>
```

Having done this, we can start writing out our XML to the browser. The calling application will know that anything outside of the ASP delimiters is XML, because the `ContentType` property told them this in the HTTP headers. We start by writing the root element <FORMLIST> along with the `TYPE` attribute.

```
<?xml version="1.0"?>
<FORMLIST TYPE="Insurance Forms">
```

This will result in exactly this line being written back to the calling application, just as we expect with HTML tags that are outside the ASP delimiters.

So, we now have to set up a connection to the database; we will use ADO. It is simple to connect to the System DSN we created earlier:

```
<?xml version="1.0"?>
<FORMLIST TYPE="Insurance Forms">
<%
' Set up connection...
Set cnEcom = Server.CreateObject("ADODB.Connection")
cnEcom.Open "DSN=WroxProXML", "sa", ""
```

At the simplest level, in order to retrieve the information and create XML, we would create a recordset and iterate through it writing out the XML tags and contents. However, ASP can be somewhat sluggish with string manipulation, so as an optimization we hand off the string manipulation to SQL Server. This yields a somewhat cumbersome SQL statement, as shown below:

```
sSQL = "SELECT '<FORM><FORMTITLE>' + RTRIM(ep.name) + '</FORMTITLE><SKU>' + " & _
        "RTRIM(ep.sku) + '</SKU><FORMNUMBER>' + RTRIM(ep.number) + " & _
        "'</FORMNUMBER></FORM>', ep.form_type AS form_type_group, " & _
        "eft.form_type FROM ecom_product ep, ecom_form_type eft " & _
        "WHERE ep.form_type = eft.type_id ORDER BY eft.form_type"

Set rsForms = cnEcom.execute(sSQL)
```

Future versions of ADO and SQL Server will include better XML support, removing the need to do this sort of string concatenation. At this time, however, we are returning the XML tags for each individual form as part of the data from SQL Server.

This will give us a recordset that we will be able to step through to create our XML document. Each row in the record set will contain the entire XML tag for an individual form, as well as the form type for that form. The `form_type` is used to order and group the resulting XML, and also to populate the `"TYPE"` attribute of the `<FORMS>` tag.

Having done this, we open a loop to go through the results writing them out, with a closing `</FORMS>` tag for each record, and inserting a new opening tag with the `TYPE` attribute set. For each record we go through the following process:

```
thisFormType = ""
init = true
Do While Not rsForms.eof
   If thisFormType <> rsForms.fields(1) Then
      '// moving on to a new one...
      If not init Then
         '// we've already done some, we have to close the tag
         Response.Write "</FORMS>" & vbLF
      else
         init = false
      End if
      thisFormType = rsForms.fields(1)
      Response.Write "<FORMS TYPE=""" & _
         Server.HTMLEncode(Trim(rsForms.fields(2))) & """>"
   End if
```

Having created the XML for the record, we still have some characters left from the SQL statement, so we strip them:

```
   strThis = rsForms.fields(0)
   strThis = replace(strThis,""","""")
   strThis = replace(strThis,""",""""")
   strThis = replace(strThis,"&","&amp;")
   strThis = replace(strThis,"'","'")
```

Then we write the record back to the client, and loop through the recordset to find the next one:

```
        Response.Write strThis
        rsForms.moveNext
    Loop
    Response.Write "</FORMS>" & vbLF

    Set rsForms = nothing
    Set cnEcom = nothing
    %>
    </FORMLIST>
```

The following is the structure of our completed XML file (with some sample data), as viewed with Internet Explorer 5:

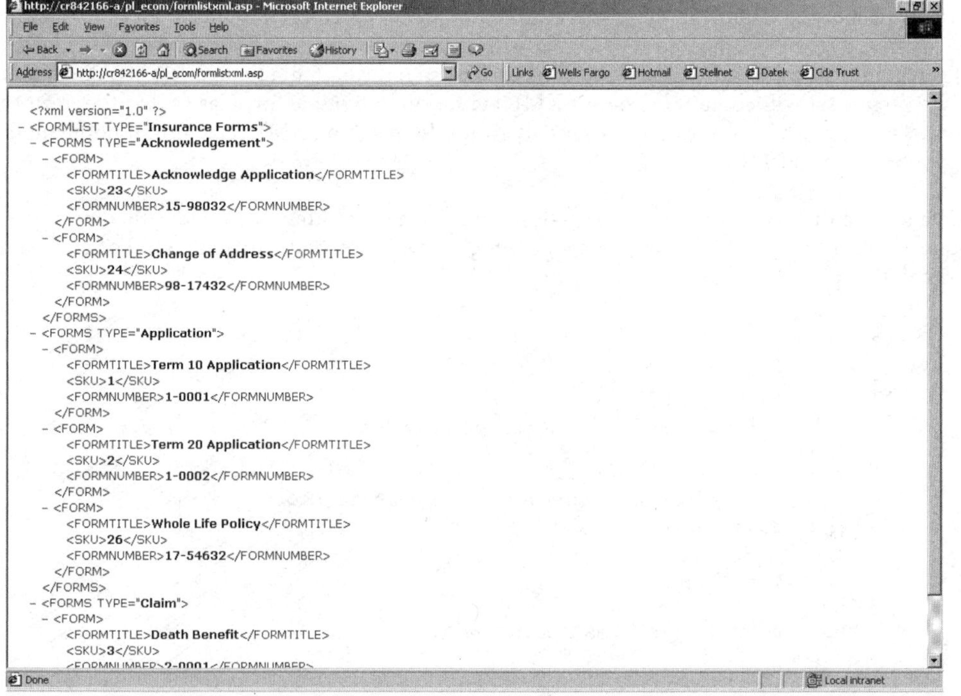

A convenient development trick is to save the resulting XML from the browser once you have the XML-creating ASP working properly. This will allow you to create test data for use while testing other pages that will rely on an XML-producing ASP (to do this, just choose 'File | Save As... " *while viewing the XML file in the browser). You can easily edit the test data with XML Notepad or your favorite ASCII editor. By using saved test data from an XML file you can work with a subset of your live data; you have removed a potential point of failure from the debugging process, and you know for certain what the data looks like without being concerned about the potentially complex SQL and underlying tables. I found this to be an extremely useful productivity enhancing technique.*

From a practical standpoint, it is easiest to debug an XML-providing ASP by itself, rather than as part of a more complete application. One nice feature of Internet Explorer 5 is the internal default XSL style sheet which will nicely render and indent an XML document that has not explicitly specified an XSL style sheet to be used to render it (as shown in the above screen shot). It also provides expand/collapse capabilities, and is a great way to examine your XML to ensure you're actually getting what you thought you were.

Having seen how we actually generate our XML from the database, let's take a look at how we call it, and how we display the forms that the administrator can edit.

Client-side Page

The client-side starting page, `default.asp`, creates a frameset that contains two frames; the left-hand side loads the page `FormTOC.asp` that generates the table of contents, and the right-hand frame loads the page `edit.asp` for the editing screen:

```
<frameset FRAMEBORDER="0" rows="120,*">
   <frame SRC="banner.asp">
   <frameset name="container" FRAMEBORDER="1" cols="350,*">
      <frame name="toc" SRC="FormTOC.asp">
      <frame name="mainbody" id="mainbody" SRC="edit.asp">
   </frameset>
</frameset>
```

The TOC Frame

`FormTOC.asp` is the page that contains our XML list of forms. It contains the logic that controls the application, so we will start with a discussion of this page. The page is essentially a "shell"; all of the work is accomplished through the scripts it contains. The body of the page only contains two buttons and a `<div>` element. The `xslresult` `<DIV>` is a placeholder; it will receive the results of the XML transformed using XSL:

```
<body>

  <button id="btnByName"
          onClick="changeXSL('<%=ByNameURL%>'); setButtons('<%=ByNameURL%>')"
          style="width:80">By Name</button>
  <button id="btnByNumber"
          onClick="changeXSL('<%=ByNumberURL%>'); setButtons('<%=ByNumberURL%>')"
          style="width:80">By Number</button>
  <hr>
  <div id="xslresult">
    <!-- resulting HTML will be inserted here -->
  </div>

</body>
```

Displaying the Two Views

We have seen that the forms have a dual nature (because they can be referred to by name or by number), so, in order to allow the user to switch between two views of the XML, we transform it using one of two XSL style sheets. In order for this transformation to take place, we need to create two instances of the DOM, using MSXML. One is used to store the XML that we have just created using `formlistxml.asp`, and the other holds the transformed content.

The first thing to happen when the `OnLoad()` event fires, is that a function called `init()` loads the XML we have just created. This is held in the XML DOM we call `source`. This then calls the `changeXSL()` function which chooses the appropriate structure for the view that we want. The other DOM is called `style`, and holds the result of the page once it has been transformed.

The transformed XML is then placed in between the `<DIV>` placeholders, where it is styled for presentation using the CSS style sheet that is used for the rest of the document.

Here is the code for the page in full; we shall examine it in more detail in a moment:

```
<%Response.Expires = -1%>

<%
Const ByNameURL = "list.xsl"
Const ByNumberURL = "listbynum.xsl"
%>

<html>
<head>
   <link REL="stylesheet" TYPE="text/css" HREF="list.css">
</head>

<script FOR="window" EVENT="onload">
   init();
</script>

<script>
var source;
var style;
var root;
var styleURL;

function init()
{
   // Do init stuff. Called by the parent frame.
   source = new ActiveXObject('Microsoft.XMLDOM');
   source.async = false;

   source.load('formlistxml.asp');

   // did the XML file load OK?
   if (source.parseError.errorCode != 0)
   {
```

```
      msg = 'Error loading data file.';
      msg += '\nDescription: ' + source.parseError.reason;
      msg += '\nSource text: ' + source.parseError.srcText;
   }

   root = source.documentElement;

   style = new ActiveXObject('Microsoft.XMLDOM');
   style.async = false;

   styleURL = ((typeof(styleURL)=='undefined') ? '<%=ByNumberURL%>' : styleURL );
   changeXSL(styleURL);
   setButtons('<%=ByNumberURL%>');
}

/*
*******************************
XML tree manipulation functions
*******************************
*/

function addBranch(sType)
{
   var newBranch = root.selectSingleNode("//FORMS").cloneNode(false);
   newBranch.setAttribute("TYPE", sType);
   root.selectSingleNode("//FORMLIST").appendChild(newBranch);

   return newBranch;
}

function addNode(oForm)
{
   // add a new node into the tree.
   // pick a node to use as a template...
   var newNode = root.selectSingleNode("//FORM").cloneNode(true);
   var insertPoint, newBranch;

   newNode.selectSingleNode("FORMTITLE").text = oForm.formTitle;
   newNode.selectSingleNode("FORMNUMBER").text = oForm.formNumber;
   newNode.selectSingleNode("SKU").text = oForm.sku;

   // find the node that corresponds to the parent for this form type
   insertPoint = root.selectSingleNode("//FORMS[@TYPE='" + oForm.formType + "']");

   if (insertPoint==null)
   {
      // couldn't find that form type, create a branch for it
      insertPoint = addBranch(oForm.formType);
   }
   insertPoint.appendChild(newNode);

   update();
}
```

```
function updateNode(oForm)
{
   // update an existing node
   var theNode = root.selectSingleNode('//FORM[SKU="' + oForm.sku + '"]');
   if (theNode==null)
   {
      // Should never get here. This would mean "node not found", so if
      // that happens just reload the tree
      parent.location.reload();
   }
   else
   {
      theNode.getElementsByTagName("FORMTITLE").item(0).text = oForm.formTitle;
      theNode.getElementsByTagName("FORMNUMBER").item(0).text = oForm.formNumber;

      var oldType = theNode.parentNode.attributes.item(0).text;
      var newType = oForm.formType;

      if (newType!=oldType)
      {
         // The form type has changed. We need to move it.

         // First create a clone...
         var theNewParent =
            root.selectSingleNode('//FORMS[@TYPE="' + newType + '"]');
         if (theNewParent==null)
         {
            // couldn't find that form type, create a branch for it
            theNewParent = addBranch(newType);
         }

         theNewParent.appendChild(theNode.cloneNode(true));

         // Now delete the original one...
         theNode.parentNode.removeChild(theNode);
      }
      update();
   }
}

function deleteNode(sFormno)
{
   // remove a node from the tree
   var theNode = root.selectSingleNode('//FORM[FORMNUMBER="' + sFormno + '"]');
   if (theNode==null)
   {
      // Should never get here. This would mean "node not found", so if
      // that happens just reload the tree
      document.location.reload();
   }
   else
   {
      theNode.parentNode.removeChild(theNode);
      update();
   }
}
```

```
/*
*********************
XSL-related Functions
*********************
*/

function update()
{
   // apply the XSL
   if (style.documentElement && source.documentElement)
   {
      document.all.item('xslresult').innerHTML = source.transformNode(style);
   }
}

function changeXSL(xsldoc)
{
   // load a new XSL
   styleURL = xsldoc;
   style.load(styleURL);
   update();

   if (xsldoc=='<%=ByNameURL%>')
   {
      hideAll('UL');
   }
}

/*
**************************************
Functions for the DHTML collapse/expand
**************************************
*/

function getChildElem(eSrc,sTagName)
{
   var cChildren = eSrc.children;
   var iLen = cChildren.length;
   for (var i=0; i < iLen; i++)
   {
      if (sTagName == cChildren[i].tagName)
      {
         return cChildren[i];
      }
   }
   return false;
}

function document.onclick()
{
   // expand/collapse
   var eSrc = window.event.srcElement;
   if ("clsHasChildren" == eSrc.className && (eChild = getChildElem(eSrc,"UL")))
   {
      eChild.style.display = ("block" == eChild.style.display ? "none" : "block");
```

```
    }
}

function showAll(sTagName)
{
   var cElems = document.all.tags(sTagName);
   var iNumElems = cElems.length;
   for (var i=1;i < iNumElems;i++) cElems[i].style.display = "block";
   document.all.btnShowAll.disabled = true;
   document.all.btnHideAll.disabled = false;
}

function hideAll(sTagName)
{
   var cElems = document.all.tags(sTagName);
   var iNumElems = cElems.length;
   for (var i=1;i < iNumElems;i++) cElems[i].style.display = "none";
   document.all.btnShowAll.disabled = false;
   document.all.btnHideAll.disabled = true;
}

/*
**************
Misc Functions
**************
*/

function setButtons(state)
{
   // set the disabled state of the buttons
   // ie: if already sorted by number, disable the button to allow you to do that
   document.all.btnByName.disabled = (state=='<%=ByNameURL%>');
   document.all.btnByNumber.disabled = (state=='<%=ByNumberURL%>');
}

function navigateTo(sSKU)
{
   // navigate to a new form
   var approved = true;
   if (window.parent.mainbody.dirty)
   {
      // the data has changed. Raise a warning.
      msg = 'You have made changes which have not been saved.';
      msg += '\n\nTo abort your changes, press OK.';
      msg += '\nTo resume editing, press Cancel.\n';
      if (!confirm(msg))
      {
         approved = false;
      }
   }

   if (approved)
   {
      // it's OK to move to another record
        sURL =  'edit.asp?sku='+sSKU;
        window.parent.mainbody.location.href = sURL;
```

```
    }
}

</script>

<body>

  <button id="btnByName"
          onClick="changeXSL('<%=ByNameURL%>'); setButtons('<%=ByNameURL%>')"
          style="width:80">By Name</button>
  <button id="btnByNumber"
          onClick="changeXSL('<%=ByNumberURL%>'); setButtons('<%=ByNumberURL%>')"
          style="width:80">By Number</button>
  <hr>
  <div id="xslresult">
    <!-- resulting HTML will be inserted here -->
  </div>

</body>

</html>
```

Having just seen the page, let's take a look at the functions that are at the heart of this page.

Function List

The following table lists the functions to manipulate the XML documents with their names and their purpose:

Function	Description
`init()`	Initialization code
`addNode()`	Add a new node to the XML tree
`updateNode()`	Update an existing node in the XML tree
`deleteNode()`	Remove a node from the XML tree
`update()`	Apply the XSL transformation and update the placeholder `<DIV>`
`changeXSL()`	Load a new XSL document

We also use the following miscellaneous functions:

Function	Description
`setButtons()`	Sets the enabled/disabled state of the buttons that are used to select the by name and by number views
`navigateTo()`	Accepts a form number and reloads the editing screen with the details for the selected form

In addition to the XML rendering, we also provide a DHTML expandable/collapsible outline of the by name view. The following are support functions for that purpose:

Function	Description
`showAll()`	Expand all tree branches and show all nodes
`hideAll()`	Collapse all tree branches and hide all nodes except for the first level nodes
`getChildElements()`	Retrieve the child nodes, if any, of a given tag
`document.onclick()` (event handler)	Check the class of a node, and expand/collapse it if it has children

We won't discuss the DHTML collapse/expand functions here, but they are included in the source code with the download. I will only discuss those functions that are key to the operation of the XML rendering.

Loading the XML List of Forms

As already mentioned, when the `onload` event fires in the browser, the following initialization code is run:

```
function init()
{
   // Do init stuff. Called by the parent frame.
   source = new ActiveXObject('Microsoft.XMLDOM');
   source.async = false;

   source.load('formlistxml.asp');

   // did the XML file load OK?
   if (source.parseError.errorCode != 0)
   {
      msg = 'Error loading data file.';
      msg += '\nDescription: ' + source.parseError.reason;
      msg += '\nSource text: ' + source.parseError.srcText;
   }

   root = source.documentElement;

   style = new ActiveXObject('Microsoft.XMLDOM');
   style.async = false;

   styleURL = ((typeof(styleURL)=='undefined') ? '<%=ByNumberURL%>' : styleURL );
   changeXSL(styleURL);
   setButtons('<%=ByNumberURL%>');
}
```

`FormListXML.asp` is, as we have seen, the name of the ASP page that creates the XML document from the database. The `init()` function creates a new instance of the Microsoft XML DOM and loads the XML document created by `FormListXML.asp` into it.

The `FormTOC.asp` page uses the following four page global variables:

Variable	Description
`Source`	The XML DOM which was loaded with the results of our ASP execution
`Style`	An XML DOM containing the currently loaded XSL
`Root`	A shortcut reference to the `source.documentElement`
`StyleURL`	Tracks which XSL style sheet is currently being used to render the XML

When the `init()` function runs, the `styleURL` is set to `list.xsl`, which is the default style sheet.

Before we look at how we apply XSL style sheets, let's take a look at the XSLs themselves.

Displaying the HTML

Using a client-side scripted approach to creating a page is very powerful, but has the downside that you can no longer just click View Source in the browser to see what your HTML looks like. If you need to see your HTML during development, simply add this button to the page:

```
<button onclick='alert(document.body.innerHTML);'>View Source</button>
```

The "view-by-number" XSL Style Sheet

The `ListByNum.xsl` file is the simpler of the two presented here. It produces a list of forms, in numerical order based on their form number, indicated by the `order-by` attribute of the `<xsl:for-each>` element. As a convenience, we also display the form name in parenthesis after the number. Note how the number itself is made into an HTML hyperlink to a JavaScript function (presented below):

```
<xsl:stylesheet xmlns:xsl="http://www.w3.org/TR/WD-xsl">
   <xsl:template match="/">
      <xsl:for-each select="//FORM" order-by="FORMNUMBER">
         <a>
            <xsl:attribute name="HREF">
               JavaScript:navigateTo('<xsl:value-of select="SKU" />');
            </xsl:attribute>
            <xsl:attribute name="TITLE">
               <xsl:value-of select="FORMTITLE" />
            </xsl:attribute>
            <xsl:value-of select="FORMNUMBER" />
            <span style="color:silver">
               (<xsl:value-of select="FORMTITLE" />)
            </span>
         </a>
         <br />
      </xsl:for-each>
   </xsl:template>
</xsl:stylesheet>
```

The resulting link with a JavaScript function looks like this:

```
<a HREF="JavaScript:navigateTo('sku')" TITLE="title">formnumber</a><br />
```

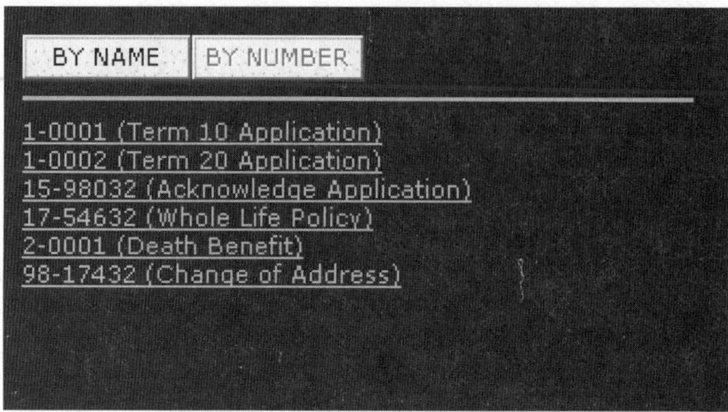

The XSL files set up URLs in the rendered HTML that reload the editing screen with the details of the selected form. This is accomplished by creating a call to the `navigateTo()` function, passing through the form number as a parameter. Both style sheets create the same calls to `navigateTo()`.

This brings us to a little design issue that can only happen in a stateless web application. It is possible for the user to start editing form details in the right-hand frame, and then attempt to navigate to another form prior to saving or canceling their changes. In order to detect this situation, we use a Boolean flag variable (`"dirty"`) in the main editing frame. The editing controls in that window will set the flag to `true` in their `onKeyDown` or `onChange` method (whichever is appropriate for that control) in order to indicate that the user has changed the data.

The `sku` is a unique identifier for a form (the form number is not unique), and it is what we use to navigate through the forms. All navigation is invoked from the `navigateTo()` function, found in `FormTOC.asp`. As we have just seen, as the XSL files step through the XML document, they set up hyperlinks that call the `navigateTo()` function, passing through the `SKU` for the `<form>` node being processed.

The `navigateTo()` function is also responsible for ensuring that the data in the right-hand editing window has not been changed by the user prior to navigating to another form; this is done by checking the value of the `dirty` variable in the parent window. If the data has not been changed or the user confirms that they want to move, then `navigateTo()` will load the new URL based on the SKU that was passed to it. If the data as been changed, we simply raise a warning to the user to say that they have not saved their changes. This gives the user the choice of ignoring the changes and continuing, or resuming their editing.

```
function navigateTo(sSKU)
{
   // navigate to a new form
   var approved = true;
   if (window.parent.mainbody.dirty)
   {
      // the data has changed. Raise a warning.
```

```
        msg = 'You have made changes which have not been saved.';
        msg += '\n\nTo abort your changes, press OK.';
        msg += '\nTo resume editing, press Cancel.\n';
        if (!confirm(msg))
        {
            approved = false;
        }
    }

    if (approved)
    {
        // it's OK to move to another record
        sURL =  'edit.asp?sku='+sSKU;
        window.parent.mainbody.location.href = sURL;
    }
}
```

The "view by name" XSL Style Sheet

This file is a bit more complex, as it has the `form type` grouping level which the `by-number` XSL style sheet did not have to worry about. In fact, if you refer back to the structure of the XML file presented at the beginning of this case study, you'll see that this is exactly the format we want to display the data in.

As we have seen in Chapter 9 on transforming XML, we can use XSL to output markup, even HTML tags. With the presentation of data we are doing here, I wanted to add the capability to collapse and expand all outlines, using DHTML. This is only relevant to the `by name` view which is created by `list.xsl`, which is why the code to create the collapse/expand buttons is in that template. This template is applied once, to the root of the XML document:

```
<xsl:template match="/">
    <BUTTON id="btnShowAll" ONCLICK="showAll('UL')" style="width:80">
        Show All
    </BUTTON>
    <BUTTON id="btnHideAll" ONCLICK="hideAll('UL')" style="width:80">
        Hide All
    </BUTTON>
    <hr />
    <UL><xsl:apply-templates select="FORMLIST/FORMS" /></UL>
</xsl:template>
```

The result of this will be the following well-formed HTML:

```
<BUTTON id="btnShowAll" ONCLICK="showAll('UL')" style="width:80">
    Show All
</BUTTON>
<BUTTON id="btnHideAll" ONCLICK="hideAll('UL')" style="width:80">
    Hide All
</BUTTON>
<hr />
<UL>the list of form generated by formListxml.asp</UL>
```

The next template is where the bulk of the work is done. This template is applied to each `<FORMS>` node, which you'll remember is the type of form. Each type of form becomes a "parent" in the rendered HTML for a list of forms that belong to that type. The child nodes are set up as HTML `<LI>` tags, which give them a nice bulleted display.

As was the case with the first style sheet, this one also sets up a hyperlink that is a call to the `navigateTo()` function:

```
<xsl:template match="FORMS">
   <LI CLASS="clsHasChildren">
      <xsl:value-of select="@TYPE" />
      <UL>
         <xsl:for-each select="FORM" order-by="FORMTITLE">
            <LI>
               <A>
                  <xsl:attribute name="HREF">
                     JavaScript:navigateTo('<xsl:value-of select="SKU" />');
                  </xsl:attribute>
                  <xsl:value-of select="FORMTITLE" />
               </A>
            </LI>
         </xsl:for-each>
         <xsl:if test="FORMS"><xsl:apply-templates /></xsl:if>
      </UL>
   </LI>
</xsl:template>
```

Invoking the XSL Style Sheets

Now that we've examined the XSL files, let's take a look at the function that applies them.

Pressing the by name or by number button causes the `changeXSL()` function to be called with the `xsldoc` parameter indicating which XSL file should be used to render the XML data. This function will call the `load()` method of the XML DOM instance which we stored in the style variable, causing the XSL file to be loaded. If we are changing to the by name view, we start with all the parent nodes collapsed:

```
function changeXSL(xsldoc)
{
   // load a new XSL
   styleURL = xsldoc;
   style.load(styleURL);
   update();

   if (xsldoc=='<%=ByNameURL%>')
   {
      hideAll('UL');
   }
}
```

This is the function that does all the work. This is where we are actually doing the XSL transformation. We take the XML document and transform it with the XSL. The resulting HTML string is stuffed into the xslresult <DIV>. The browser will re-render the newly changed <div>, which will display the formatted contents of our XML document.

```
function update()
{
   // apply the XSL
   if (style.documentElement && source.documentElement)
   {
      document.all.item('xslresult').innerHTML = source.transformNode(style);
   }
}
```

Problem: Keeping the Tree in Sync

The solution as presented so far works fine in a read-only situation, but this application is a maintenance application and as such will be used to edit data. This means that data which is included as part of our XML document, could be changed rendering our XML document obsolete.

There are two solutions to this dilemma: either we get a new copy of the data, forcing our ASP to re-generate the XML document, or we use the power of the XML DOM to update our copy of the XML document on the client.

I opted to use client-side script to keep our copy of the XML document updated on the client. Changes we need to be concerned about are:

- Additions (new forms)
- Deletions
- Changes to one or more of the fields in our XML document

Remember that the changes are made on the client, then the data is updated on the server, and finally we need to invoke client-side script to reflect those changes. We trigger the client-side XML updates by having Site Server add calls to our functions after it has saved the data changes in the full application; here this is done in `edit.asp`.

There is a bit of a risk in this design, because this is a non-transactional system. It is possible that a change gets made to the data, but for whatever reason that we don't get notified about it. Our XML data would now be out of sync with the underlying database data. I decided this was an acceptable risk in this case, as it is extremely unlikely to occur at all, it is not a mission critical system, and in the off chance that a de-synchronization did occur it could be "fixed" by refreshing the browser.

There are three functions we need to add on the client to update the XML document, one for each of the cases listed above. The `add()` and `change()` functions receive a JavaScript object called `oForm`, which I created as a transport mechanism for the form attributes (if you are not familiar with JavaScript, functions are treated as objects, to which you can add methods by simple assignment). Each `oForm` object has the following attributes:

- FormTitle
- FormNumber
- SKU

You'll notice that these are the same attributes we use in the XML. The oForm objects are created by the modified Site Server code and are passed in as a parameter to our add() and change() functions.

The addNode() function adds a new form to the XML tree. It does so by cloning an existing node, and updating it with the new values taken from the oForm object we passed in. The pattern match string //FORM selects the first <FORM> node:

```
function addNode(oForm)
{
   // add a new node into the tree.
   // pick a node to use as a template...
   var newNode = root.selectSingleNode("//FORM").cloneNode(true);
   var insertPoint, newBranch;

   newNode.selectSingleNode("FORMTITLE").text = oForm.formTitle;
   newNode.selectSingleNode("FORMNUMBER").text = oForm.formNumber;
   newNode.selectSingleNode("SKU").text = oForm.sku;
   ...
```

Once we have that, we can find the point in the tree to insert the new node by looking up the form type. In the event that it can't be found, we need to create a new branch. This could happen in the case where there are some form types that existed, but no forms of that type when we created the XML (for example, there was an Application form type in the type table, but no forms were tagged as being an Application).

After we have an insertion point, we add our new node as the first child of that point. The pattern match string //FORM[@TYPE='"+oForm.formType+"'] finds the first <FORM> node that has a type attribute with a value of oForm.formType:

```
   ...
   // find the node that corresponds to the parent for this form type
   insertPoint = root.selectSingleNode("//FORMS[@TYPE='" + oForm.formType + "']");

   if (insertPoint==null)
   {
      // couldn't find that form type, create a branch for it
      insertPoint = addBranch(oForm.formType);
   }
   insertPoint.appendChild(newNode);

   update();
}
```

The addBranch() function is responsible for inserting a new branch into our XML tree. It starts by doing a shallow clone (cloning a node but none of the child elements for that node) of a <FORMS> node (which is our by type grouping node). Next we set the TYPE attribute to the passed string, and then we append it to the FORMLIST root element:

```
function addBranch(sType)
{
   var newBranch = root.selectSingleNode("//FORMS").cloneNode(false);
   newBranch.setAttribute("TYPE", sType);
   root.selectSingleNode("//FORMLIST").appendChild(newBranch);

   return newBranch;
}
```

Updating a node is much the same as adding a new one, but we have a new logic wrinkle to consider and resolve. It is possible that the form type could have been changed. If that happens then we need to do more than just update an existing node, we need to remove the old node and re-create it as a child of the new parent in the XML tree:

```
function updateNode(oForm)
{
   // update an existing node
   var theNode = root.selectSingleNode('//FORM[SKU="' + oForm.sku + '"]');
   if (theNode==null)
   {
      // Should never get here. This would mean "node not found", so if
      // that happens just reload the tree
      parent.location.reload();
   }
   else
   {
      theNode.getElementsByTagName("FORMTITLE").item(0).text = oForm.formTitle;
      theNode.getElementsByTagName("FORMNUMBER").item(0).text = oForm.formNumber;

      var oldType = theNode.parentNode.attributes.item(0).text;
      var newType = oForm.formType;

      if (newType!=oldType)
      {
         // The form type has changed. We need to move it.

         // First create a clone...
         var theNewParent =
            root.selectSingleNode('//FORMS[@TYPE="' + newType + '"]');

         if (theNewParent==null)
         {
            // couldn't find that form type, create a branch for it
            theNewParent = addBranch(newType);
         }

         theNewParent.appendChild(theNode.cloneNode(true));

         // Now delete the original one...
         theNode.parentNode.removeChild(theNode);
      }
      update();
   }
}
```

The simplest of the update functions is the delete function. All we need to do is find the node and remove it from the tree. The pattern string `//FORM[FORMNUMBER="' + sFormno + '"]` means "get the `FORM` node that has a `FORMNUMBER` child element with a value of `sFormno`":

```
function deleteNode(sFormno)
{
   // remove a node from the tree
   var theNode = root.selectSingleNode('//FORM[FORMNUMBER="' + sFormno + '"]');
   if (theNode==null)
   {
      // Should never get here. This would mean "node not found", so if
      // that happens just reload the tree
      document.location.reload();
   }
   else
   {
      theNode.parentNode.removeChild(theNode);
      update();
   }
}
```

Note that after they have done their work, the functions that update the XML tree also call the `update()` function, which in turn re-applies the current XSL style sheet to our updated XML document.

Summary

In this case study we used XML to provide the end user with an enhanced functionality interface that would not have been readily achievable using older technologies.

We were faced with the problem of creating a user-interface that allowed users to view the same section of data referred to by one of two types of identifier: a name and a number. Rather than creating round trips to the server each time we wanted to change the view, we sent the data to the client once as XML, and then let the client manipulate the XML to create the view that we wanted.

We also needed to allow the user to update the data that they were viewing – these updates not only had to be effective on the client, but also on the server – again we used the power of the client workstation and updated the XML document in real time by adding, deleting and changing nodes.

In all, we met each of our design objectives, and the project was a success. If you think about it, there are several situations where this sort of application may be very helpful. After all, we might not inherently have different ways of referring to the same physical entity, but we might like to offer users different views of our data. Using a similar technique we can allow the client to re-sort this data, and there are many different times when we might want to do this, from sorting our book details in the examples we have already seen (say, by title, ISBN, author, etc.) to offering different views of details about football players (sorted by name, number, number of times they have been in the starting lineup etc.), each of these allowing the client to see the data the way they want, without the need to connect to the web server and download it again.

16

Case Study 2 – XML and Distributed Applications

XML is an excellent format for exchanging data between applications. This is especially important when we're dealing with loosely connected applications – like those that are Web-based. HTTP spans platforms when it comes to communications protocols. XML lets us do the same at the level of application data. With that in mind, let's construct a sample application and use it as a case study in the use of XML in Web applications.

This example is, of course, completely contrived. However, the design decisions made reflect the kinds of choices that actually get made when building software for corporations. We'll build an application using Active Server Pages, Internet Information Server, and Internet Explorer 5.0. We'll see what it is like to use XML and the DOM from a scripting language. More importantly, we'll get a glimpse of the kinds of problems that XML solves for us.

Our sample application is a programming team management tool. We want to be able to search for a particular programmer by name and get a list of performance reports for the projects on which he's worked. A user should be able to add new programmer records and performance reports for existing programmers. We'll use XML as the means of communicating data between the browser and the server. A combination of JavaScript in a Web page and server-side ASP JavaScript will implement the functionality of the application.

The whole point of adopting a new technology like XML is that it answers some needs that your current technology handles poorly. Needs like that imply problems where our desires for application features meet the current day computing environment. Before diving into the case study, then, let's look at the problems faced by Web developers. I'll present five guiding principles to help you solve these problems in your own work. XML, not surprisingly, is a big part of the solution.

Much of the material in this case study is adapted from Designing Distributed Applications *(Wrox Press, ISBN 1-861002-27-0). The origins and motivations of the weaknesses I summarize here are spelled out in detail in that book. The sample application presented later in this case study appears in a slightly different form in that book, where it serves as the starting point for an extended case study of my development principles. This case study is entirely self-contained. You will be able to gain an appreciation of XML in ASP applications from this case study without reference to my previous work.*

Where Are Our Present Weaknesses?

Web applications have proven extremely popular in recent years. Many, perhaps most, new applications are built using Web protocols and tools. It would seem that the Web is an outstanding computing environment. It is, of course, but it introduces some new challenges for programmers. If we do not plan for these challenges, then they will become major problems for us, weaknesses that cripple our ability to build robust applications. So, what are these weaknesses?

Dealing with Increased Complexity

Powerful sites addressing serious problems are easily as complicated as stand-alone applications. Moreover, they have the added complexities inherent in distributed systems. Unmanaged complexity is a weakness of distributed systems. Resources become less and less useful as knowledge of their meaning and capabilities is lost to later-deployed clients.

Because Web-based applications are easily fielded, requiring no one's permission to add to the Internet (other than the obvious requirement of obtaining a domain name), servers and services quickly blossom and mutate. Presumably someone understands what they can do, but there are many more clients who could use them who will never know these particular capabilities are available. Functions will be needlessly re-implemented again and again simply because no mechanism has been defined to advertise what is available. This is barely tolerable in the case of the public Internet; but it is a complete recipe for waste and disaster in a corporate intranet.

Inflexible Applications

Applications, even Web applications, are often written with a particular client in mind. Alter the needs of the client and you either have to re-write the server or create a new, highly similar service.

Duplication of Code

New applications often duplicate large bodies of existing code because of minor changes in needs and specifications. This duplication of code can be seen as wasteful.

Moves Towards Automated Web Tasks

Suppose we had a Web application that let a user perform some task by interacting with a browser-based interface. Now we want to make this an automated process – eliminate the manual intervention and connect two applications directly. We have a problem. Our previous server generated HTML for human consumption. Increasingly, though, we want to connect applications together without manual intervention. An example of this is Web-enabled business to business (B2B) commerce. Having a human user read and re-key the results at every step of a B2B process would eliminate many of the advantages of e-commerce. Such automated processes find HTML hard to process in a way that preserves the meaning of the data. HTML is primarily intended for visual styling, a task of little interest to an application that runs without human intervention.

Distributed Development and Implementation Teams

Disaster occurs when services are provided by some organization not under the control of the prospective client.

For example, you may be building an extranet supply chain application, in which case you must rely on an external partner for some of your application's services. When coordination is informal or nonexistent, services will move, change, and disappear. The administrative overhead of keeping pace with the changes rapidly snowballs. We need to add techniques and services that let us build flexible, robust, fault-tolerant distributed systems that can change over time along with our needs. More importantly, we need to do this without requiring human coordination.

Five Principles for Building Networked Applications

We can address any of the weaknesses using well-known techniques, so long as everyone involved with development agrees on the tools and technologies needed to implement the application. This sort of agreement is impractical on the Web. The solution, in my opinion, is to establish a very short list of common principles. The list must be short enough that everyone can agree without having to make major changes or technology commitments. I've come up with a list of five core principles.

These five principles will encompass the goals we need to achieve in developing applications that will promote the reuse of application code and the viability of applications in the face of changes in needs and applications.

So, here they are, our Five Principles of Building Cooperative Network Applications:

1. **Applications Will Be Built From Coarse-Grained Services** – applications will be implemented by coordinating the discrete results obtained from server-based modules that use various components to accomplish a specific problem or task.

2. **Services Will Be Discovered By Querying Directories** – applications will find the location and name of the services they need at runtime by querying a directory. They will ask not for a specific implementation, but rather for any service implementation that addresses a particular question, problem, or task.

3. **Services Will Be Provided As Self-Describing Data** – applications will deal with services by exchanging structured data written using an agreed upon syntax. The data will be written according to vocabularies defined for the problem or task that the service addresses.

4. **Services Will Be Enlisted On A Transient Basis** – applications will find and use services in a small number (preferably one) of round-trips, and will not require state to be held between round-trips. Neither application nor service will assume any long-term availability of the other partner in the exchange.

5. **Services Must Support Extension and Degrade Gracefully** – services must take future enhancement into account, both on the part of their own logic and exchange formats and those of other applications and services. When encountering a new version of exchange data, they should make as much use as possible of that data. Applications and services must never break if they do not receive exactly the format they expect.

Of course, these principles must observe what is readily practical, both in terms of current technology and the likelihood of heterogeneous platforms in the network. Some degree of cooperation and agreement between partners and developers will be required. We want to focus on implementing applications using these principles with currently available technology. So, let's consider each of these in turn and consider how to go about attaining these goals.

1. Applications Will Be Built From Course-Grained Services

Software components like COM components and controls, while useful tools, are reusable only in applications for platforms supporting the component technology in which they were built. There is no point in trying to use a COM component on a Unix platform, or a JavaBean on a non-Java server. (Of course, some Unix platforms have COM ports built for them, but generally speaking COM is a Windows technology.) In our case, where a development team will create just one part of an application, or where new clients are created for existing servers, we can't count on being able to use components in a way that spans the various tiers of our applications. Instead, we will turn to **services**. A service is an arbitrary collection of application code that is confined to one tier and accomplishes one well-defined task. It is bigger than a component; indeed, we will frequently use components to build services for reasons of productivity. A service is smaller than an application. Services model one useful part of a problem domain. If they are too small, the overhead of translating data to and from a neutral data format will place a burden on performance. If they are too big, services risk the problems of monolithic applications.

Compare our definition to that of services under Windows DNA or Windows NT. The services there are either applications that run using hooks into the operating system – a Windows 32 API service – or component frameworks like ActiveX Data Objects (ADO) for data retrieval. Both are bigger than a single component. ADO fails our definition only because it can rely on using a proprietary component technology across application boundaries. Apart from that, however, it would fit – it uses the interaction of several components to answer a specific problem: "Get me a result set based on a SQL query".

Often, a service will model some major object in the underlying business model – customers for a sales application, or a factory line for a manufacturing application, for example.

The kinds of services envisioned by our development principles are usually implemented as a server-side page or small group of cooperating pages. They are characterized by a well-known data format that represents the persistent state of the service's business objects. A collection of related objects might be offered to provide a wide range of functionality. For example, a service might offer HTML in addition to its data-only formats to permit its use by ultra-thin clients such as hand-held devices. The thin client would lose the benefit of being able to manipulate the data programmatically in exchange for not having to support the overhead of the data-only formats. While it could conceivably parse and manipulate HTML, that language is marked up for presentation, not semantic meaning. It would be easier to support a different exchange format than to try to use HTML as the basis of your data markup. In short, adding HTML support, a seemingly regressive move, allows simple platforms to participate in a limited fashion provided they support a standard Web browser. Services are always accessed via open protocols. By abstracting a major object this way, we retain some of the benefits of the object-oriented model, while reducing our dependency on proprietary component technologies.

Since a service is developed and maintained by a single organization, and hosted on a site under the control of that organization, we can use more proprietary technologies within the service to maximize our productivity. We expect to use component software within our services. (Often we will be providing a wrapper for some sort of legacy software or database to avoid major rewriting efforts.) We can utilize the full range of features of the host operating system and Web server to obtain the most value from our site. When we cross the line to another service or to a client, however, we understand we may be crossing organizational boundaries and we retreat to open standards and formats.

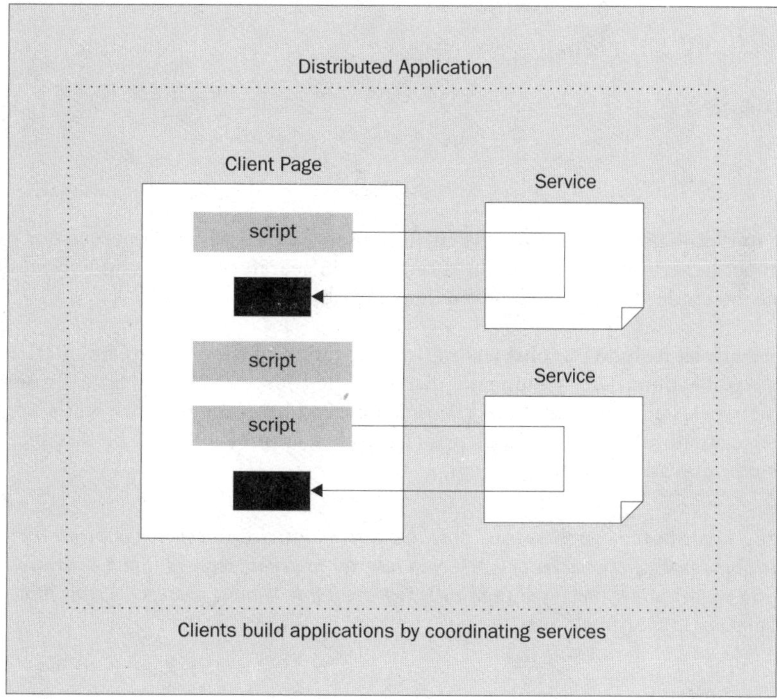

Our applications will be built from reusable services. Within services, we will rely on components. Applications use carefully defined interfaces to reach services, and services use interfaces to reach the components within themselves. We will therefore enjoy the benefits of encapsulation and delegation on both a large (service) and small (component) scale.

2. Services Will Be Discovered By Querying Directories

The network location of our services and the data formats they offer define access to our services. We must isolate these from any local conventions. While directories are still far from mature or widely deployed, we will make these the cornerstone of our service location strategy. They are pivotal to implementing location abstraction and dynamic discovery of resources. They are a resource that is useful only if visible to all users of the network. Consequently, we can safely assume that this service will receive managerial attention at the highest levels of the information systems organization. Its structure, and the location of its servers, will be the subject of much discussion and consensus building within an organization, and it is the one area where we can safely assume global agreement and understanding within the organization.

The directory will store more than just the location of our services. It must define the capabilities of the services in terms of the business problem they address.

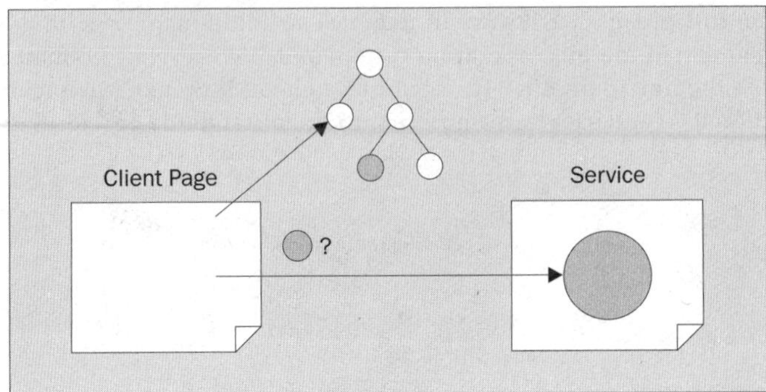

We must try to define useful directory structures and tools with which to peruse our directories. Every application must be written to browse our directories in search of information about desired services, so we should try to standardize this task as much as possible.

Directory services let us hide the physical network location of service implementations from using applications. Applications can dynamically discover the source of needed data – a service – at runtime. This allows network services to be added to and removed from the network while applications continue to run. If you scrupulously adhere to this principle, your applications will be flexible, surviving changes in the location and availability of resources.

> Designing Distributed Applications *provided a recommended scheme for implementing this principle that involved the names of XML vocabularies to denote services. Since directory services in general are not yet widely deployed (and therefore available to most readers), I have provided a stub implementation in the sample application.*

3. Services Will Be Provided As Self-Describing Data

Why do I make so much of data exchange formats? After all, I adhere to object-oriented methods as they are expressed in component software, and these methods try to shield the consumer of data from its format wherever possible. The exception is needed due to the fact that we are isolating components within a service as we have defined that term. When we hop across the platform boundaries between service pages and their clients, we must represent the object our service implements in a form readily accessible to *all* clients. Despite the advances in distributed object-based computing in recent years, this form remains static data structures.

We can define the characteristics of objects in terms of metadata, and each specific object instance will be represented by a data structure that conforms to that metadata definition. Since we want exceptional flexibility and robust response to errors (see principle 5, below), we shall use self-describing data, namely XML. That means that each discrete element of data is marked (tagged) as an element or attribute of an XML document. A consumer of the data will always know what data element it is processing (regardless of its expectations) and where the element ends, because the element is tagged with labels denoting what element it is. Any consumer that understands the vocabulary of the service is thus able to understand what the provider of the data is trying to communicate.

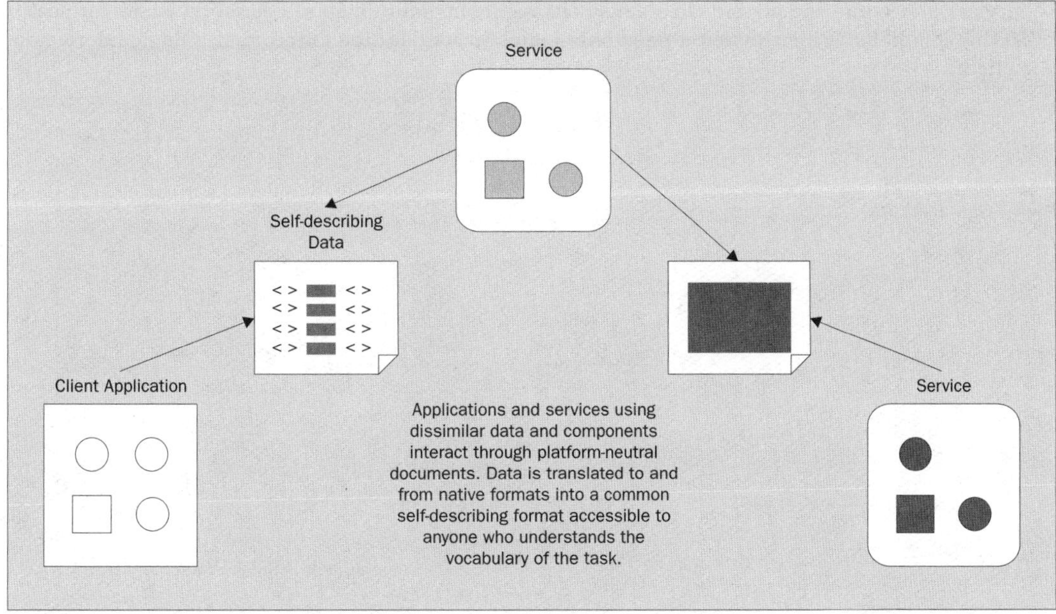

Traditionally, data is passed in a binary format where the structure of the data is shared by implication. That is, if two parties to a communication have the same message or operation in common, it is implied that they both understand the binary format of the data. The size, data type, and order of fields within a data structure are closely defined by design. Uncoordinated changes to data organization on the server break the client. You may have been part of a programming team working on a large client-server application in which parts of the application were assigned to different programmers. After writing the client to handle a particular data structure, you found your application broken one day. Upon investigation, you found that another programmer, responding to an enhancement request or bug report, had added a field or modified the length of an existing one without telling you. Your part of the program broke because of an arbitrary change in the data. Now imagine the server and its structures are shared by many programming teams widely separated in geographic space and time and you can see the potential for trouble.

The use of XML for data encoding minimizes this kind of trouble and maximizes the amount of useful sharing we can do. A consuming client or service can ignore changes it does not understand in a data structure. While we will have well-known vocabularies, we will also tag each field within a structure. Each field is clearly delimited with the name of the field. Thus, we will always be able to check for integrity on a field-by-field basis and ensure that our code is responding to the data it is actually receiving, not responding to data it *assumes* it is receiving.

4. Services Will Be Enlisted On A Transient Basis

We must design our applications so that any persistent state is maintained solely on the tier that is interested in the computation. That is, a shopping agent is the party interested in the identity of the shopper and the shopping list, so the agent should maintain this information, not the vendor services it accesses. This works with the stateless nature of HTTP, and also allows us to minimize the dependencies between machines on our networks.

Services may come and go and clients may change their requirements. Therefore, wherever possible, a service should be written so that it need only maintain state for the duration of a single interaction with a client.

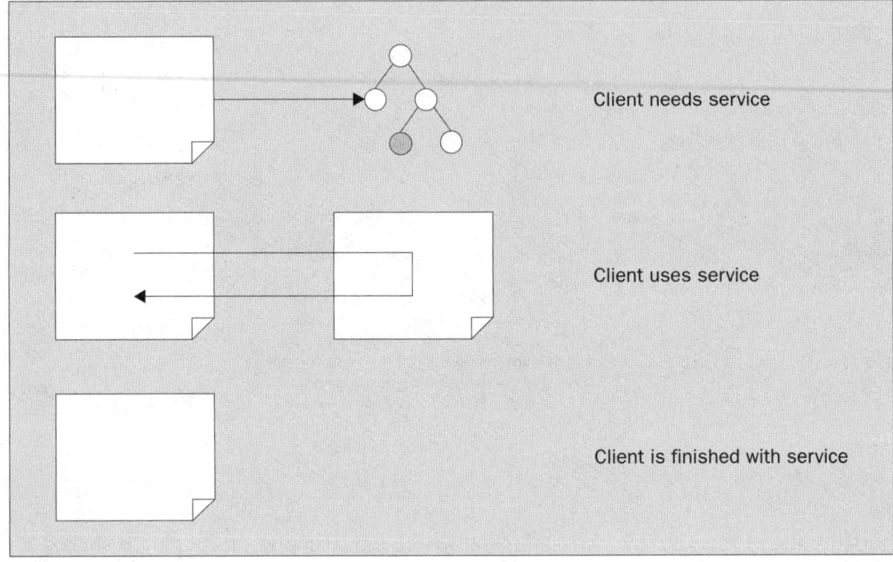

This will not always be possible, but it is the goal for which you must aim. Applications will be written as collections of clients that enlist services by making HTTP requests to obtain data. Once data is delivered, the association between the service and the client is assumed to be severed. Rather than put our efforts into ensuring state is properly maintained in a distributed system, we will devote ourselves to ensuring state need never be maintained. A client will obtain a cache of data sufficient for its needs.

From an organizational standpoint, this principle recognizes that differing development teams will change their priorities over time. An agreement reached today for maintaining state may not hold true tomorrow. This principle strives to eliminate the need for such agreements. We will limit the duration over which we must hold resources so as to minimize the chances of losing those resources while we need them. A prime example is accessing a busy Web site, which may go down or become overwhelmed while you are working with a page. If that page is a form into which you are entering information for a purchase, you will be quite unhappy when you submit the form and get no response. HTTP makes no guarantees about a resource, but the particular site's application implied long-term availability.

5. Services Must Support Extension and Degrade Gracefully

Remember that one of our underlying problems is that independent development teams are at work. Time, distance, and organizational boundaries separate these teams. We have to expect some errors in the implementation of the data format. Even without errors, differing versions of the data will be common in wide area networks as new implementations are released. The tagged nature of data in XML lets us write code that checks to see what is coming next and respond appropriately. Of course, if we use a validating parser, we can weed out these errors, but that may not be desirable. In some circumstances, we may want to turn validation off and accept well-formed XML with minor errors.

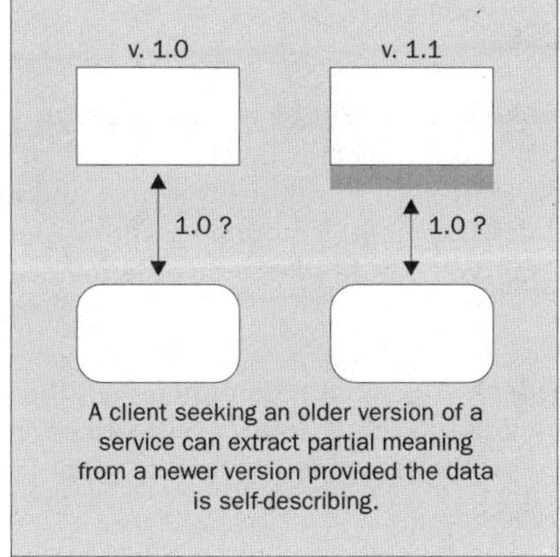

A client seeking an older version of a service can extract partial meaning from a newer version provided the data is self-describing.

Even if we insist on valid XML documents, we must still take an interest in this principle. Since different organizations have different views of common objects, we want to express our data in a way that will describe what pieces of data are held in common, and what pieces are peculiar to the offering organization. Similarly, data formats evolve over time, so we want to describe how the format has changed. That way, when a client accesses a service that offers data in a form slightly different from the form that the client would ideally like to see, it can still extract some information from the exchange. We will make use of XML's tagged, self-describing nature to express our problem vocabularies. Since it is written entirely in text, we can confidently assume that any computing platform we encounter will be able to read our data structures. It is possible to devise some conventions for specifying XML vocabularies that allow you to express collections, version evolution, and specialization of a general format. These conventions go beyond the rules for writing DTDs and schemas. Software written with an understanding of these conventions can implicitly recognize collections of data structures representing business objects, reconcile information to the particular version of the data it needs, and extract a general version of data when it receives a specialized form it does not recognize.

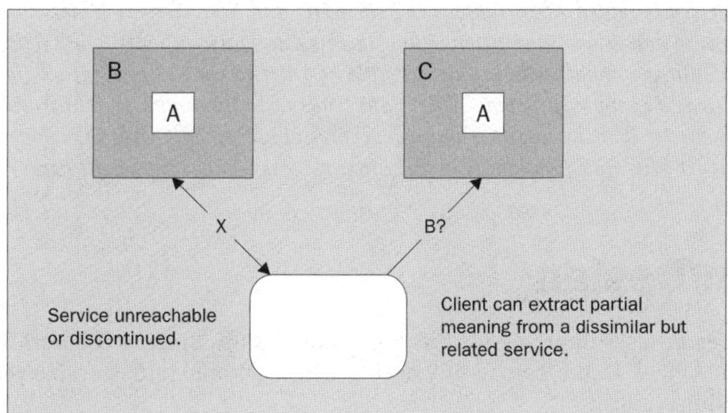

These are ambitious goals. One case study and one basic example aren't enough to illustrate and work through the ramifications of these principles. The case study on which we are about to embark will illustrate the fundamental techniques of using XML for the exchange of data in Web applications. Keep these principles in mind and consider how you might improve the code using the five principles. Along the way I'll provide some suggestions.

The Business Case

Suppose you are managing a small department of computer programmers. Each programmer is assigned to multiple projects over time. When a project is finished you write a brief note describing the programmer's performance on the project. Periodically you would like to review these notes to assess the programmer's professional development. You don't want to spend a lot of time and effort building the application to handle this, and you would like to be able to access the data from any computer on the network.

An intranet application seems ideal. Any system equipped with the company-standard browser (which for our purposes we are assuming is Internet Explorer 5.0) will be able to run the application. ASP and client-side scripting will let us rapidly prototype a system to meet your needs. The application will use JavaScript as its scripting language.

Having just learned the five development principles, you are eager to give them a try and see how they work in practice. If you remotely access the data using ADO from the client, you will be building technology dependencies into your data. If you use ADO on the server for data retrieval and generate HTML – the most common Web development technique for this problem – you will be restricting your server code to use with human users sitting in front of browsers. This means a manual step in the process. You decide to use ADO on the server and covert it to XML for transmission to the client. That way, you keep your data as data, not visual styling, until the last possible moment. Since you are using XML for the exchange format, the data is in a platform neutral format. Your ASP will take the form of a service. Your client will send a request (an XML document) to the server and receive a reply (another XML document) in return. You will locate this service by obtaining its URL each time you want to query it. In theory, the network administrator could move or replace the service between invocations without any client application being aware of the change. Clients will ask for the service's location by specifying the name of the XML vocabulary that they need to receive.

Microsoft has recently added XML support to both ADO and SQL Server. Unless the relational schema happens to match our conventions, though, this automatic support won't help. We will be composing XML programmatically in this example in order to use our conventions for expressing collections. This is a common problem. XML data tends to be hierarchical, which neatly expresses most business objects. Relational data, however, expresses hierarchy poorly though complex joins. The XML support Microsoft provides is useful in many cases, but is a poor fit here.

Application Design

The key to a successful user interface for this application is minimizing the number of pages the service representative must view. In the course of working with customers, the service representative will have to perform the following tasks:

- Query the system for programmer information (full name and job title)
- Add new staff programmers and update existing programmer records
- Query the system for project performance notes
- Enter a new performance note

We should be able to fit this onto one page, which we will split with a horizontal line. Above this line we will have a data-bound form displaying the information for one programmer. Below the line we will have a project performance history table, displaying in each cell the project name, project ID, and a text box containing the performance note. This is what the page will look like above the rule:

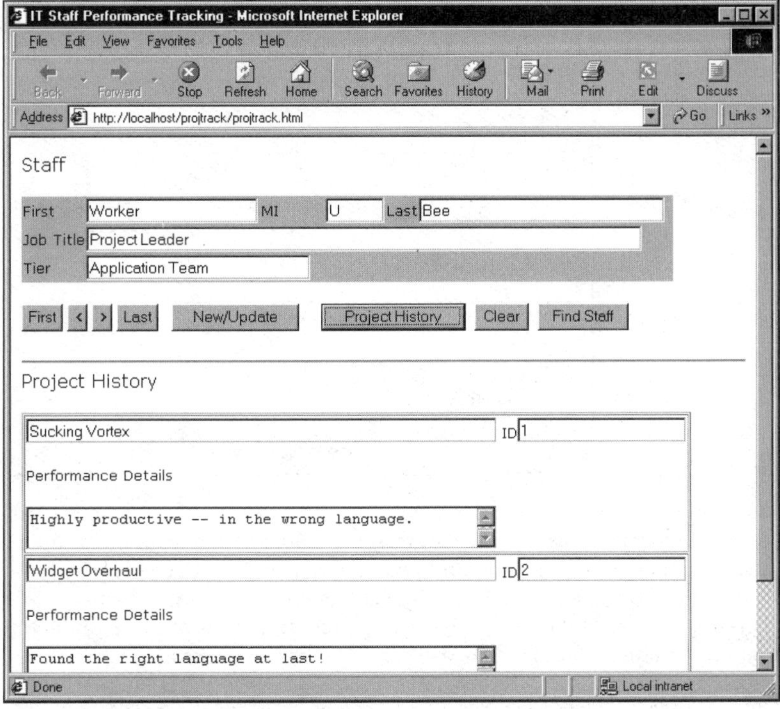

The four buttons in the lower left of the top half of the page allow users to navigate through multiple records to find the particular programmers whose performance they want to review. They allow users to display either the first or last programmer in the bound collection, or move forward or backward one programmer at a time. The elements in the programmer form will be bound to the XML returned from the server.

The remaining buttons allow us to perform the following functions:

- enter new programmers
- edit existing programmer information
- retrieve the project performance history for a programmer, to be displayed below the horizontal line on the page
- clear the programmer form in preparation for a search or new programmer data insertion
- search for an existing programmer's information

The lower portion of the page, shown below, allows users to view the performance history for a programmer, or to insert new performance reports:

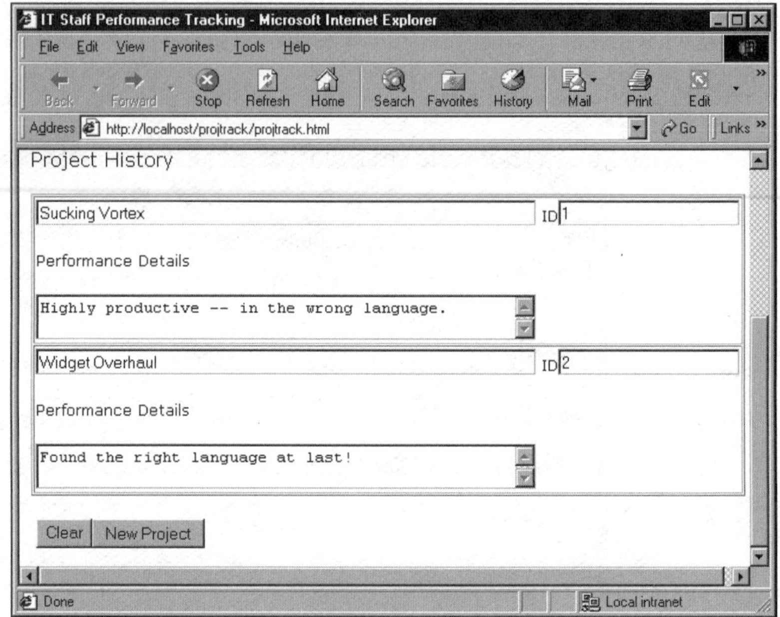

This application could be designed to bind directly to the database of programmer information. Our principles, however, encourage us to hide the details of data storage from the application. Instead, we should bind the elements to programmer and programmer performance history services. These services will operate directly with the database, but will exchange information with clients in the form of XML documents. This gives us freedom on the client-side to use methods other than data binding, as well as freedom on the server-side to change databases and database schemas.

If you wish to try out the application, you are encouraged to download the code and sample database from our Web site at http://www.wrox.com/*. The database includes programmer and programmer performance entries for programmers with the last names Genius, Authority, Doe, Smith, Typhoid, Calamity, Sullivan, Bee, and Greeley.*

How It All Fits Together

Here is the overall view of our application. We have a page, `ProjTrack.html`, which will be downloaded to the client. As a user works with the elements in the page, scripts will execute locally. These scripts will determine the location of the services they require. These services are implemented on a Web server as the ASP pages `Staff.asp` and `History.asp`. Requests are sent to the service as an XML document written according to the appropriate request vocabulary. The service parses the request, queries the database `projects.mdb`, and creates a new XML document in the response vocabulary based on the results of the query. The client receives the response, parses it, and displays the results in a data-bound DHTML form. Note that the server hides the details of data storage and retrieval from the client, and the client hides the issues of consuming and rendering the data from the service. Our principle of exchanging data in a platform-neutral way preserves our independence and consequently improves the possibility of reuse. You could, for example, replace the client, `ProjTrack.html`, with a report writing and summarization program and nothing would need to be changed on the server.

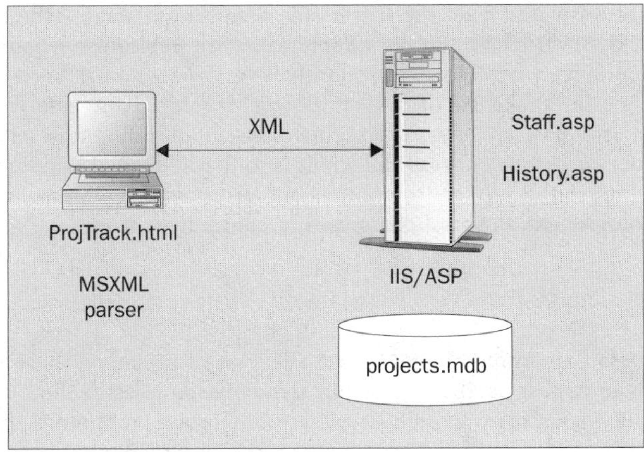

The Programmer Service Client

The client side of the application, which we saw above, consists of a single HTML page. A programming manager using the application need never leave this page. Nevertheless, there is a high degree of interactivity and communication with the server. The client queries each of two services to obtain data regarding programmers and programmer performance history. This data is encoded in two XML data vocabularies. Each vocabulary is paired with a query vocabulary. The client takes values from the form, encodes an appropriate query, and submits it to the proper service. When the data is returned, the XML is bound to the form. When a programming manager enters data on a new programmer, or writes a new performance report on an existing staff programmer, the application formats this information in the data vocabulary and submits it to the server.

Our system uses two classes of objects: `ITStaffers` and `ProjReports`. `ITStaffers` in the programming manager's view is specialized from the parent company's general `Staffer` class through the addition of a `Tier` property. This property indicates whether the programmer is primarily assigned to client, application logic, or data services tasks in the three-tier programming model. Ideally, then, the programmers developing the service that manages `ITStaffer` objects should write their server to handle both the `ITStaffer` and `Staffer` vocabularies. That way, the service can share the `Staffer` subset of `ITStaffer` information with any application that can process `Staffer` information. This follows from principle 5, which calls in part for services to degrade gracefully. Project Performance reporting history is unique to the IT department and their view of programmers. Since these reports are unique to `ITStaffers` it is useful to manage this data through another service rather than trying to fold it into the one handling `Staffers`.

> *Of course, as a practical matter, we are inventing this entire case study so there is no existing* `Staffer`*-processing code. Moreover, the specialization is minor. Consider, however, what the code would look like for a real-world view of staff members. They would have elaborate descriptions, certainly more than just a name and job title. Private information, like Social Security Numbers in the United States, would have special code protecting it from unauthorized use. Specializing the vocabulary to create* `ITStaffers` *would similarly involve nontrivial code. For example, we might maintain a list of programming languages the programmer knows and his proficiency level. In that case, we would make a clear separation in the code between* `Staffers` *and* `ITStaffers`.

Either way, the client is isolated from the server-side details of managing the data. As long as the client uses the techniques we developed in earlier chapters, we are free to use whatever database or file management techniques we wish. More importantly, everyone who has knowledge of the XML vocabularies we define can make use of the services we develop. Conversely, the servers are isolated from the techniques used by the client. Although we use data binding, the services are not required to support this. The data binding we use on the client is to the XML that is returned, not an ADO recordset. We could move the services to another operating system with no support for Windows data management technologies and the application would continue to work.

The Services

The services we develop are implemented with ASPs. Not surprisingly, these ASPs use ADO to access programmer data in an Access database, which is by far the simplest technique for our purposes. We are developing the whole system from scratch, so we are free to use technology that is friendly to our platform and efficient in terms of the requirements of the system. Many real-life organizations, however, will have legacy data residing on mainframe systems. They could use messaging or some proprietary API to access the data.

Both services follow a similar format. They extract the values passed in a form element named `XMLRequest`, parsing the XML and determining what vocabulary is being submitted. Programmers and project performance reports are packaged as collections according to our convention. Even though our particular client will only submit one programmer record or one performance report at a time, it is reasonable to pass collections of programmers and reports back and forth between clients and the services (in fact, this will be a common occurrence going from the server to the client). Once the server determines which vocabulary it is seeing it formats a SQL query, executes it, and returns data to the client as an XML document. In the case of a query, this will be a collection of zero or more Programmers or Project Performance Reports. In the case of a submission from the client, it will be a positive or negative acknowledgement to the client.

The ASPs are pure script and return nothing but XML. They contain no `HTML`, `HEAD`, or `BODY` elements. They make liberal use of MSXML and objects from ADO, but these are created dynamically. Consequently, they are more like small program fragments than Web pages.

Exchange Vocabularies

Our application will require four XML vocabularies for the exchange of data between the client and server. The client needs to be able to ask the server for programmers matching some criteria and for reports about a particular programmer. The server, in turn, will need to respond with collections of programmers matching a programmer query, and collections of reports matching a performance report query. In addition, the client will use the programmer and report collection vocabularies to push new programmers and reports to the server for storage.

Programmer Query

We've decided to allow applications to query the `ITStaffer` service by the programmer's last name, and staff ID. Since our user interface doesn't expose the staff ID, this particular client will always submit an empty element for that criterion. Here is a shell for a complete `StaffQuery document`:

```
<StaffQuery>
   <StaffID/>
   <LastName/>
</StaffQuery>
```

Although we won't be using a DTD to validate our documents, the shell above is more formally defined thus:

```
<!ELEMENT   StaffQuery    (StaffID, LastName)>
<!ELEMENT   StaffID       #PCDATA>
<!ELEMENT   LastName      #PCDATA>
```

Project Performance Query

In a large department, a staff query could result in multiple records being returned to the client application. Each will have a staff member ID, so we can be more precise when searching for the performance report records for a particular programmer. In fact, we need to be more precise to avoid mixing report records for several programmers. Here is the shell for the `ProjPerformanceQuery`:

```
<ProjPerformanceQuery>
   <StaffID/>
</ProjPerformanceQuery>
```

This corresponds to the following DTD:

```
<!ELEMENT   ProjPerformanceQuery    StaffID>
<!ELEMENT   StaffID     #PCDATA>
```

Programmer Response

Documents returned in response to a `StaffQuery` query will always consist of a `Collection` of one or more `ITStaffer` elements. As noted previously, `ITStaffer` is a specialization of `Staffer`. A `Staffer` element contains elements for the name, staff identifier, and job title of the staff member. The `ITStaffer` element contains an element for the programming tier assignment of the programmer as well as the `Staffer` element. All elements are mandatory. Here is a shell for a document containing one `ITStaffer` element:

```
<Collection>
   <ITStaffer>
      <Staffer>
         <StaffID/>
         <FirstName/>
         <MI/>
         <LastName/>
         <JobTitle/>
      </Staffer>
      <Tier/>
   </ITStaffer>
</Collection>
```

The DTD for this is a little unusual. We are going to use `Collection` as the document type. Strictly speaking, this should translate to one DTD, but we want to use `Collection` as a general purpose container for a variety of contained objects. Purists would say we need to declare a namespace for each use of `Collection`, but we won't be that strict here:

```
<!ELEMENT    Collection     (ITStaffer*)>
<!ELEMENT    ITStaffer      (Staffer, Tier)>
<!ELEMENT    Staffer        (StaffID, FirstName, MI, LastName, JobTitle)>
<!ELEMENT    StaffID        #PCDATA>
<!ELEMENT    FirstName      #PCDATA>
<!ELEMENT    MI             #PCDATA>
<!ELEMENT    LastName       #PCDATA>
<!ELEMENT    JobTitle       #PCDATA>
<!ELEMENT    Tier           #PCDATA>
```

Programmer Performance Report History Response

Performance report response documents, like `ITStaffer` documents, consist of collections of zero or more `ProjReport` elements, each of which must contain elements for the project name and ID, and an element containing the free-form textual details entered by the programming manager:

```
<Collection>
   <ProjReport>
      <ProjName/>
      <ProjID/>
      <PerformanceDetails/>
   </ProjReport>
</Collection>
```

Here is the variation of `Collection` that we are using:

```
<!ELEMENT    Collection           (ProjReport*)>
<!ELEMENT    ProjReport           (ProjName, ProjID, PerformanceDetails)>
<!ELEMENT    ProjName             #PCDATA>
<!ELEMENT    ProjID               #PCDATA>
<!ELEMENT    PerformanceDetails   #PCDATA>
```

Implementation

The programming team assigned to prototype this application familiarized themselves with our development philosophy before beginning. In addition to discerning the types of classes in the system and the XML vocabularies, the team latched onto the use of components. The team decided to use the `MSXML` DOM interfaces for parsing and manipulating the exchange data; the `IXMLHTTP` interface of `MSXML` to facilitate the transmission of an XML document via HTTP without leaving the page; and the XML DSO, again implemented by `MSXML`, for data binding. ADO is employed for the retrieval, insertion, and updating of relational data.

Locating Services

As mentioned previously, the right way – in terms of the five principles – to go when locating services is to ask a directory for the appropriate URL each time the client needs to post a query to the server. Presumably, the network administrator would list these services in the directory in terms of the names of the XML vocabularies they speak. In our case, `History.asp` would be associated with `ProjPerformanceQuery` and `PerformanceReport`. Since this is not a book about LDAP directories I've decided to provide a stub for that request. The client has a function, `GetASP()`, which takes a name and returns a URL sans http://:

```
function GetASP(svc)
{
   switch (svc)
   {
      case "Staff":
         return "localhost/ProjTrack/Staff.asp";
      case "StaffQuery":
         return "localhost/ProjTrack/Staff.asp";
      case "PerformanceReport":
         return "localhost/ProjTrack/History.asp";
      case "ProjPerformanceQuery":
         return "localhost/ProjTrack/History.asp";
   }
}
```

This section of code assumes you have created a virtual directory called `ProjTrack` to contain the application's resources, and that the directory resides on the same HTTP server that is hosting this page. Both assumptions are convenient for the purposes of this example. If you make other arrangements to run the code, be sure to change this section of code to accurately reflect this.

When we need a service URL, we call `GetASP()` with the name of the needed vocabulary as its parameter. We add the prefix "`http://`" to the value returned from `GetASP()`, and use the result as the URL for the `XMLHTTP` component. Thus, to send a request according to the `StaffQuery` vocabulary we need these two lines of code:

```
var sServer = "http://" + GetASP("StaffQuery");
xmlStaffd.Open("POST", sServer, false);
```

Since Designing Distributed Applications *did cover LDAP in general and the Windows 2000 ActiveDirectory, I provided a convention for listing services in the directory and two components that worked with that convention to implement the features in `GetASP()`. If you want to experiment with abstract location and don't have ActiveDirectory or some other LDAP directory service, you could try keeping URLs in a database. The drawback to this in actual production, of course, is that everyone has to be able to connect to the common database. If this is a concern, you might try encapsulating access to the database within a well-known ASP page that functions like our `GetASP()` function.*

It is understood that any service that supports a given data vocabulary, like `Staff`, also understands the complimentary query vocabulary, in our case `StaffQuery`. The query vocabularies are useless without their data vocabularies, and the data vocabularies are only useful without the query vocabularies when submitting data. With the understanding that query and data vocabularies are linked, we are free to ask for either when locating a service. Some programmers will find it natural to always ask for the data vocabulary, since that is what they are really interested in. Others will want to ask for whatever vocabulary they are about to send to the server, since that is what the service must process. The advantage to asking for the data vocabulary is that both parties are very clear on what will be returned to the client. Asking for the query vocabulary, however, ensures that the server can process what you are about to send up to the server. If there is any doubt that a particular query vocabulary is always paired with a specific data vocabulary, you should ask for the query vocabulary. Otherwise, clients should ask for the data vocabulary. This is a good place to keep things loose so that new applications can easily integrate older services.

Managing the Data Binding

Data binding will get quite a workout in `ProjTrack.html`. We use the technology to display both the programmer records and the performance report records in two forms on the page. The performance report form is a table, so we are calling on data binding to replicate a single template row as many times as is needed to display the performance history for a single programmer. This is not done just once. A typical user session will have a manager making multiple searches for programmers and histories, with insertions of programmers and performance reports interspersed. We have to take some care to make sure the binding is never broken.

To accomplish this, `ProjTrack.html` contains two data islands, one for each form. These are empty shells within the `BODY` element of the page:

```
<XML id=xmlStaff>
<Collection>
   <ITStaffer>
      <Staffer>
         <StaffID></StaffID>
         <FirstName></FirstName>
         <MI></MI>
         <LastName></LastName>
         <JobTitle></JobTitle>
      </Staffer>
      <Tier></Tier>
   </ITStaffer>
</Collection>
</XML>
<XML id=xmlProjs>
<Collection>
   <ProjReport>
      <ProjName></ProjName>
      <ProjID></ProjID>
      <PerformanceDetails></PerformanceDetails>
   </ProjReport>
</Collection>
</XML>
```

The form elements are bound at design time to the appropriate data island. This is the INPUT element for the first name on the customer form:

```
<INPUT id=firstNameText name=firstNameText dataFld=FirstName dataSrc=#xmlStaff>
```

Subsequently, we shall see that we need to manually manipulate the parse tree of the data islands and dynamically bind to the data. With this in mind, let's proceed to the specifics of our functional implementation.

Entering and Editing Programmers

We'll start by examining what happens when we use a service to add a new programmer into the database. Starting from a blank form, the manager fills in the information and clicks the button marked New/Update. Things begin to happen on the client side in the button click handler function, OnInsertClick(). The client begins to build a query document from the data provided by the user.

Client Side

The client will perform exactly the same actions to build the query document whether we are entering a completely new customer record or modifying an old one. We want to format a Collection document containing an ITStaffer element, which in turn contains the values of the fields in our form. There is one hidden INPUT element, staffIDText, which makes all the difference. If we are entering a new programmer, there is nothing in this field. If the server receives no text value in the StaffID element, it assumes this document represents a new programmer and assigns a value. The client, however, is indifferent. OnInsertClick() begins by retrieving the form element values and plugging them into the proper places in an XML document:

```
function OnInsertClick()
{
   var sReq = "";

   sReq = "<Collection><ITStaffer><Staffer><StaffID>"
         + staffIDText.value + "</StaffID>";
   sReq += "<FirstName>" + firstNameText.value +
         "</FirstName><MI>" + miText.value + "</MI>";
   sReq += "<LastName>" + lnameText.value +
         "</LastName><JobTitle>" + jobtitletext.value + "</JobTitle>";
   sReq += "</Staffer><Tier>" + tiertext.value +
         "</Tier></ITStaffer></Collection>";
```

Next we want to create an instance of MSXML's IXMLHTTP interface and use it to POST the document to a service supporting the ITStaffer vocabulary. However, there's a small issue to contend with. For simplicity, we are using the mime encoding for an HTML form. That means that the document we've just composed must have spaces converted to the literal %20 before transmission. Other non-alphanumeric characters are affected as well. We use the JavaScript String object's replace method to perform the conversion. This needs a regular expression parameter for the character we wish to find and replace. We create such a constant and call replace:

```
        var regExp = / /g;
        sReq = sReq.replace(regExp, "%20");
```

I've omitted the conversion for other atypical characters in the interest of simplicity. The form encoding makes life easy for us on the server as the ASP Request object can retrieve the XML document in one piece given the name of the form element, in our case `XMLRequest`, *whose value is the document. Some real-world problems may involve the frequent occurrence of non-alphanumeric characters. In that case, it might be easier to use another mime encoding.*

So far, our client has no idea where to send the information. We obtain a URL using the `GetASP()` utility function we saw earlier. We've previously established two instances of the `XMLHTTP` component with global scope. We'll use one, `xmlStaffd`, to process the posting of customer information. We complete the URL with the protocol identifier (`http://`) and use the steps `XMLHTTP` requires to cause a `POST` from `xmlStaffd`. These consist of specifying the `POST` operation and URL, setting the request header `Content-Type` appropriately, and sending off the request:

```
        var sServer = "http://" + GetASP("Staff");
        xmlStaffd.Open("POST", sServer, false);
        xmlStaffd.setRequestHeader("Content-Type",
                                   "application/x-www-form-urlencoded");
        xmlStaffd.Send("XMLRequest=" + sReq);
```

At this point, `xmlStaffd` contains a parsed XML document from the server. If the customer insertion went well, this document should read `<ACK/>` (representing 'acknowledged'). If we receive any other indication, we inform the user of an error:

```
        if (xmlStaffd.responseXML.documentElement.nodeName != "ACK")
           alert("Staff update was not accomplished due to a server problem.");
     }
```

This anticlimactic finish hides all the activity that took place on the server following our `POST`.

Server Side

Our service for the `ITStaffer` vocabulary is an ASP, `staff.asp`, which consists entirely of text. It begins by retrieving the root node of the document passed to it by the `XMLHTTP` component. Now, all the vocabularies it is prepared to deal with require some sort of database access, so we prepare ADO connection and recordset objects:

```
<%@ Language=JavaScript %>
<%

var dbConn, dbRecordSet;

/* Create a parser object and retrieve the XML search request
   from the server's Request object. */
```

```
var parser = Server.CreateObject("microsoft.xmldom");
parser.loadXML(Request.Form("XMLRequest").Item);

if (parser.readyState == 4 && parser.parseError == 0)
{
   // Establish a global connection
   dbConn = Server.CreateObject("ADODB.Connection");
   dbConn.Open("ProjTrack", "", "");
   dbRecordSet = Server.CreateObject("ADODB.RecordSet");
```

Under Windows 2000 and the latest version of the MSXML parser, the `load()` *method can accept a reference to any object that supports an* `IStream` *interface. This most notably includes an XML document object in MSXML. Consequently, the call to* `loadXML()` *with the value of the* `XMLRequest` *variable could more efficiently be replaced with the following:*

```
Parser.load(Request);
```

Windows and COM take care of the proper conversions for you. The result is that your server-side page receives an XML document object and can load it on the receiving side.

> **If you download the code from the Wrox Web site, don't forget to create a system DSN named `ProjTrack` that points to `projects.mdb` and has no user name or password.**

Determining What to Do

The service is prepared to respond to `StaffQuery` and `Collection` vocabulary documents. In the latter case, we need to look inside and see if the collection consists of `ITStaffer` objects. That's the case here:

```
   switch (parser.documentElement.nodeName)
   {
      case "StaffQuery":
         ProcessStaffQuery(parser.documentElement);
         break;
      case "Collection":
         // Receiving an update to SvcCustomer
         switch (parser.documentElement.childNodes(0).nodeName)
         {
            case "ITStaffer":
               ProcessStafferInsertion(parser.documentElement);
               break;
         }
         break;

      default:
         // Lack of ACK will signal db error,
         // empty collection doesn't spoil data binding
         Response.Write("<Collection/>");
   }
```

Putting Data into the Database

Whether we are adding a new programmer or updating an existing one, the ASP will be receiving elements for all the columns of the programmer table in the database. There are six of them. The first thing we want to do, then, is retrieve them and place them in an array of strings:

```
function ProcessStafferInsertion(collectionNode)
{
   var rsFrags = new Array("", "", "", "", "", "");

   // Assemble the values to insert or update
   for (var ni = 0; ni < collectionNode.childNodes.length; ni++)
   {
      switch (collectionNode.childNodes(ni).nodeName)
      {
         case "ITStaffer":
            // First child must be Staffer
            var staffNode = collectionNode.childNodes(ni).childNodes(0);
            for (var nk = 0; nk < staffNode.childNodes.length; nk++)
            {
               var sFragVal = staffNode.childNodes(nk).text
               switch (staffNode.childNodes(nk).nodeName)
               {
                  case "StaffID":
                     rsFrags[0] = sFragVal;
                     break;
                  case "FirstName":
                     rsFrags[1] = sFragVal;
                     break;
                  case "MI":
                     rsFrags[2] = sFragVal;
                     break;
                  case "LastName":
                     rsFrags[3] = sFragVal;
                     break;
                  case "JobTitle":
                     rsFrags[4] = sFragVal;
                     break;
               }
            } // end of Staffer loop
            // second child will be the tier assignment
            var tierNode = collectionNode.childNodes(ni).childNodes(1);
            sFragVal = tierNode.childNodes(0).text;
            rsFrags[5] = sFragVal;
            break; // ITStaffer case

      } // end of master switch statement
   } // end of master for - next loop
```

All the columns of our simple programmer table are string values. We'll keep things basic, as far as database retrieval goes, simply composing our SQL query through string concatenation. If your data includes a variety of data types, you will want to use a SQL query containing parameter placeholders, then use the ADO Parameter object to compose things by data type. This topic is covered in ADO 2.0 Programmer's Reference, *Wrox Press (ISBN 1-861001-83-5). We'll be focusing on the XML aspects of our topic in this case study.*

Recall our business rule regarding programmer IDs. We'll assign a unique number for new programmers. For this, we can use the `Autonumber` data type in Microsoft Access. Once assigned, we do not permit the ID to be modified. Consequently, the presence of a non-empty `StaffID` element tells us we are updating an existing programmer; its absence indicates a new programmer. Each case requires a different SQL query. A new programmer requires an `INSERT`, for example:

```
INSERT INTO members (FName, MI, LName, JobTitle, Tier) VALUES ("John", "A", "Doe",
"Senior Programmer , "Client");
```

An existing programmer change requires an `UPDATE` to an existing row:

```
UPDATE members SET FName="Jerome", MI="B", ..., Tier="Data" WHERE ID = "157";
```

Returning to `ProcessStafferInsertion()`, we check for the presence of a `StaffID` value and prepare the appropriate SQL command text:

```
if (rsFrags[0] == "")
{
   sCore = "INSERT INTO members (FName, MI, LName, JobTitle, Tier) VALUES (";
   sQuery = sCore + MakeStaffValues(rsFrags) + ");";
   DoQuery(sQuery);
}
else
{
   sCore = "UPDATE members SET ";
   var sConstraint = " WHERE ID = " + rsFrags[0];
   sQuery = sCore + MakeStaffSets(rsFrags) + sConstraint + ";";
   DoQuery(sQuery);
}
```

The first array entry, `rsFrags[0]`, contains the value, if any, for the `StaffID` element. `MakeStaffValues()` and `MakeStaffSets()` are utility functions that compose the column-based portion of their respective SQL commands using the values in `rsFrags`. `DoQuery()` is a utility function we use to execute the SQL command:

```
function DoQuery(sQuery)
{
   try
   {
      dbConn.Execute(sQuery);
      if (dbConn.Errors.Count > 0)
         Response.Write("<NACK/>");
      else
         Response.Write("<ACK/>");
   }
   catch(e)
   {
      Response.Write("<NACK/>");
   }
}
```

We use a `try...catch` block in the above code to avoid critical stops due to exceptions thrown by ADO. The `Errors` collection of the connection object indicates the presence or absence of problems with the command. If no problems were encountered, we expect to return the rowset and simply write `<ACK/>` back to the client to indicate success. If any problem is found, we send the negative acknowledgement, `<NACK/>`.

That takes us back to the point where we left the client. The next sections show the collected code for the client and server portions.

Complete Client Code for Programmer Insertion

The task of inserting a programmer took us through code that is highly representative of the rest of the application. It is worthwhile studying this code in some depth. For convenience, here is the complete source code for the client side of that task:

```
function OnInsertClick()
{
   var sReq = "";

   sReq = "<Collection><ITStaffer><Staffer><StaffID>" +
           staffIDText.value + "</StaffID>";
   sReq += "<FirstName>" + firstNameText.value + "</FirstName><MI>" +
            miText.value + "</MI>";
   sReq += "<LastName>" + lnameText.value + "</LastName><JobTitle>" +
           jobtitletext.value + "</JobTitle>";
   sReq += "</Staffer><Tier>" + tiertext.value +
           "</Tier></ITStaffer></Collection>";

   var regExp = / /g;
   sReq = sReq.replace(regExp, "%20");
   var sServer = "http://" + GetASP("Staff");
   xmlStaffd.Open("POST", sServer, false);
   xmlStaffd.setRequestHeader("Content-Type",
                              "application/x-www-form-urlencoded");
   xmlStaffd.Send("XMLRequest=" + sReq);
   if (xmlStaffd.responseXML.documentElement.nodeName != "ACK")
      alert("Staff update was not accomplished due to a server problem.");
}
```

Complete Server Code for Programmer Insertion

The main body of `staff.asp` is shared by all the tasks using this service. Many of the things we accomplished implementing programmer insertion will prove to be representative of the rest of this service. Here, then, is the complete server-side source code for programmer insertion:

```
<%@ Language=JavaScript %>
<%

var dbConn, dbRecordSet;

/* Create a parser object and retrieve the XML search request
   from the server's Request object. */
```

```
var parser = Server.CreateObject("microsoft.xmldom");
parser.loadXML(Request.Form("XMLRequest").Item);

// Configure the mime type to reflect XML
Response.ContentType="text/xml";

if (parser.readyState == 4 && parser.parseError == 0)
{
   // Establish a global connection
   dbConn = Server.CreateObject("ADODB.Connection");
   dbConn.Open("ProjTrack", "", "");
   dbRecordSet = Server.CreateObject("ADODB.RecordSet");

   // Check for the primary and secondary supported vocabularies
   switch (parser.documentElement.nodeName)
   {
      case "StaffQuery":
         ProcessStaffQuery(parser.documentElement);
         break;
      case "Collection":
         // Receiving an update to SvcCustomer
         switch (parser.documentElement.childNodes(0).nodeName)
         {
            case "ITStaffer":
               ProcessStafferInsertion(parser.documentElement);
               break;
         }
         break;

      default:
         // Lack of ACK will signal db error,
         // empty collection doesn't spoil data binding
         Response.Write("<Collection></Collection>");
   }
   // Clean up resources
   try
   {
      dbRecordSet.Close();
      dbConn.Close();
      dbConn = null;
      dbRecordSet = null;
   }
   catch (e)
   {
   }
}
else
   Response.Write("<Collection></Collection>");

parser = null;
```

```
function ProcessStafferInsertion(collectionNode)
{
   var rsFrags = new Array("", "", "", "", "", "");

   for (var ni = 0; ni < collectionNode.childNodes.length; ni++)
   {
      switch (collectionNode.childNodes(ni).nodeName)
      {
         case "ITStaffer":
            var staffNode = collectionNode.childNodes(ni).childNodes(0);
            for (var nk = 0; nk < staffNode.childNodes.length; nk++)
            {
               var sFragVal = staffNode.childNodes(nk).text
               switch (staffNode.childNodes(nk).nodeName)
               {
                  case "StaffID":
                     rsFrags[0] = sFragVal;
                     break;
                  case "FirstName":
                     rsFrags[1] = sFragVal;
                     break;
                  case "MI":
                     rsFrags[2] = sFragVal;
                     break;
                  case "LastName":
                     rsFrags[3] = sFragVal;
                     break;
                  case "JobTitle":
                     rsFrags[4] = sFragVal;
                     break;
               }
            } // end of Staffer loop
            // second child will be the tier assignment
            var tierNode = collectionNode.childNodes(ni).childNodes(1);
            sFragVal = tierNode.childNodes(0).text;
            rsFrags[5] = sFragVal;
            break; // ITStaffer case

      } // end of master switch statement
   } // end of master for - next loop

   var sCore, sQuery;
   if (rsFrags[0] == "")
   {
      sCore = "INSERT INTO members (FName, MI, LName, JobTitle, Tier) VALUES (";
      sQuery = sCore + MakeStaffValues(rsFrags) + ");";
      DoQuery(sQuery);
   }
   else
   {
      sCore = "UPDATE members SET ";
      var sConstraint = " WHERE ID = " + rsFrags[0];
      sQuery = sCore + MakeStaffSets(rsFrags) + sConstraint + ";";
      DoQuery(sQuery);
   }
}
```

Searching for Staff Programmers

Our programming managers won't always be modifying programmer records, of course. More typically, they'll want to review performance reports on existing programmers. This means they will have to retrieve records from the `ITStaffer` service. This is started in `ProjTrack.html`, with the button handler function `OnFindClick()`.

Client Side

We permit searches by some combination of staff ID and last name using the `StaffQuery` vocabulary. We once again make use of the global `XMLHTTP` component, `xmlStaffd`, to perform a `POST` of a query document:

```
function OnFindClick()
{
   var sReq = "";
   var sServer = "http://" + GetASP("StaffQuery");
   xmlStaffd.Open("POST", sServer, false);

   sReq = "XMLRequest=<StaffQuery><StaffID/><LastName>";
   sReq += lnameText.value + "</LastName>";
   sReq += "</StaffQuery>";

   var regExp = / /g;
   sReq = sReq.replace(regExp, "%20");
   xmlStaffd.setRequestHeader("Content-Type",
                              "application/x-www-form-urlencoded");
   xmlStaffd.Send(sReq);
   FixStaffBinding();
}
```

This is similar to what we did when sending a programmer record to the server. We compose an XML document, perform the mime encoding, and execute a `POST` using the component. In this case, however, we expect to receive zero or more `ITStaffer` objects in a `Collection` document. We need to manage the data binding, which we do in `FixStaffBinding()`:

```
function FixStaffBinding()
{
   while (xmlStaff.documentElement.childNodes.length > 1)
   {

xmlStaff.documentElement.removeChild(xmlStaff.documentElement.childNodes(1));
   }
   for (var ni = 0;
        ni < xmlStaffd.responseXML.documentElement.childNodes.length;
        ni++)
      xmlStaff.documentElement.appendChild(
         xmlStaffd.responseXML.documentElement.childNodes(ni).cloneNode(true));

   if (xmlStaff.documentElement.childNodes.length > 1)
   {
```

```
      xmlStaff.documentElement.removeChild(
         xmlStaff.documentElement.childNodes(0));
      xmlStaff.recordset.moveFirst();

      stafftable.dataFld="Staffer";
      stafftable.dataSrc="#xmlStaff";
      firstNameText.dataFld="FirstName";
      firstNameText.dataSrc="#xmlStaff";
      miText.dataFld = "MI";
      miText.dataSrc = "#xmlStaff";
      lnameText.dataFld = "LastName";
      lnameText.dataSrc = "#xmlStaff";
      jobtitletext.dataFld = "JobTitle";
      jobtitletext.dataSrc = "#xmlStaff";
      staffIDText.dataFld = "StaffID";
      staffIDText.dataSrc = "#xmlStaff";
      tiertext.dataFld = "Tier";
      tiertext.dataSrc = "#xmlStaff";
   }
```

This follows a pattern: delete all but the first child of the data island root node, append deep copies of the returned `ITStaffer` elements, then delete the remaining node from the original tree in the data island. Failing to do this causes the binding to fail, as we would otherwise be pulling the data out from under the XML DSO while it is in use. Once all that is done, we jog the data binding through code to set the `dataFld` and `dataSrc` attributes of each form element. At this point, the customer form displays the new values received from the service. Let's see what `staff.asp` had to do to obtain those values.

Server Side

We return to the main body of `staff.asp` to see where we go in response to the received document:

```
if (parser.readyState == 4 && parser.parseError == 0)
{
   // Establish a global connection
   dbConn = Server.CreateObject("ADODB.Connection");
   dbConn.Open("ProjTrack", "", "");
   dbRecordSet = Server.CreateObject("ADODB.RecordSet");

   switch (parser.documentElement.nodeName)
   {
      case "StaffQuery":
         ProcessStaffQuery(parser.documentElement);
         break;
      case "Collection":
         switch (parser.documentElement.childNodes(0).nodeName)
         {
            case "ITStaffer":
               ProcessStafferInsertion(parser.documentElement);
               break;
         }
         break;

      default:
         Response.Write("<Collection></Collection>");
   }
```

Retrieving Programmers

In the case under consideration, the ASP is receiving a document formed according to the `StaffQuery` vocabulary. Here is how we go about turning the XML query document into a SQL query:

```
function ProcessStaffQuery(staffNode)
{
   var sSelectCore = "SELECT FName, MI, LName, ID, JobTitle, Tier FROM Members";

   var sConstraint = "";

   sConstraint = MakeStaffConstraint(staffNode);
   if (sConstraint != "")
      sConstraint = " WHERE " + sConstraint;

   var sQuery = sSelectCore + sConstraint + ';';

   dbRecordSet = dbConn.Execute(sQuery);

   if (!dbRecordSet.BOF)
      dbRecordSet.MoveFirst();

   if (dbRecordSet.EOF)
      Response.Write("<Collection></Collection>");

   Response.Write("<Collection>");
   while (!dbRecordSet.EOF)
   {
      WriteStafferBody(dbRecordSet);
      dbRecordSet.MoveNext();
   }
   Response.Write("</Collection>");
}
```

We build a query, execute it, and then write out the resultant recordset values as XML. As with our previous example, we use string concatenation rather than `Parameter` objects to build the query. Here's an example of a completed SQL command corresponding to a `StaffQuery` document:

```
SELECT FName, MI, LNAME, ID, JobTitle, Tier FROM Members WHERE LName="Bee";
```

Our query vocabulary allows the inclusion of the programmer's ID number for generality of use. In our application, the ID is never displayed or entered manually, so this can never appear in a query arising from our client. Nevertheless, the service was built without knowledge of any particular client, so we include the code to handle that search parameter when building our SQL query.

Returning XML to the Client

Now that we have the result set, we have to write the values back to the client as XML so that they can be displayed. This occurs in `WriteStafferBody()`, which takes as its sole parameter the recordset we just obtained:

```
function WriteStafferBody(rsStaffers)
{
   Response.Write("<ITStaffer><Staffer>");
   Response.Write("<StaffID>" + rsStaffers("ID") + "</StaffID>");
   Response.Write("<FirstName>" + rsStaffers("FName") + "</FirstName>");
   Response.Write("<MI>" + rsStaffers("MI") + "</MI>");
   Response.Write("<LastName>" + rsStaffers("LName") + "</LastName>");
   Response.Write("<JobTitle>" + rsStaffers("JobTitle") + "</JobTitle>");
   Response.Write("</Staffer><Tier>" + rsStaffers("Tier") +
"</Tier></ITStaffer>");
}
```

Clearing the Programmer Form

It is useful to have a button that clears all entries in the programmer form, particularly when a manager using the application wants to issue a radically different search or enter a completely new programmer record. The programming task is one of putting the data binding back to an empty `ITStaffer` document. When the user clicks on the Clear button, we ask `MSXML` to load a document consisting entirely of elements with no textual contents, then perform our usual tree manipulation – deleting all but one child, appending the new elements, then deleting the last original node from the parse tree. This leaves the form elements bound to an XML document whose text elements are empty. As a result, nothing appears in the form:

```
function OnClearClick()
{
   var parser = new ActiveXObject("microsoft.xmldom");
   parser.loadXML("<Collection><ITStaffer><Staffer><StaffID/><FirstName/>
                   <MI/><LastName/><JobTitle/></Staffer><Tier/>
                   </ITStaffer></Collection>");
   if (parser.readyState == 4 && parser.parseError == 0)
   {
      while (xmlStaff.documentElement.childNodes.length > 1)
      {
         xmlStaff.documentElement.removeChild(
            xmlStaff.documentElement.childNodes(1));
      }
      for (var ni = 0; ni < parser.documentElement.childNodes.length; ni++)
         xmlStaff.documentElement.appendChild(
            parser.documentElement.childNodes(ni).cloneNode(true));
      if (xmlStaff.documentElement.childNodes.length > 1)
      {
         xmlStaff.documentElement.removeChild(
            xmlStaff.documentElement.childNodes(0));
         xmlStaff.recordset.moveFirst();
      }
   }
   parser = null;
}
```

Entering Programmer Performance Reports

We need to be able to enter brief reports about the performance of programmers on projects. `ProjTrack.html` performs this task from the button click handler function `OnInsertProj()`.

Client Side

We start by enforcing an important business rule: performance reports cannot exist without being tied to a programmer. We enforce this by looking for a staff ID in the hidden `INPUT` element named `staffIDText`. If it is not found, the form is either empty or a new programmer has not been submitted to the service. Either way, we shouldn't submit the performance report. If we pass this check, we want to compose a document in the `PerformanceReport` vocabulary and submit it the way we submitted `ITStaffer` documents. This vocabulary consists of a `Collection` containing one or more `PerformanceReport` elements. Our client will only ever submit one report at a time, but some clients might engage in batch transfers, so we've enabled the vocabulary to handle this. Let's have a look at `OnInsertProj()`:

```
function OnInsertProj()
{
   var sRequest;

   if (staffIDText.value != "")
   {
      sRequest  = "<Collection><PerformanceReport><StaffID>" +
                  staffIDText.value + "</StaffID>";
      sRequest += "<ProjID>" + projIDText.value +
                  "</ProjID><Comments>" + projDetail.value;
      sRequest += "</Comments></PerformanceReport></Collection>";
```

If a staff member ID is present, we collect the values from the form and make an XML document out of them. Let's proceed to the rest of `OnInsertProj()`, where we mime-prepare the document and perform an HTTP post:

```
      var regExp = / /g;
      sRequest = sRequest.replace(regExp, "%20");
      var sServer = "http://" + GetASP("PerformanceReport");
      xmlProjd.Open("POST", sServer, false);
      xmlProjd.setRequestHeader("Content-Type",
                  "application/x-www-form-urlencoded");
      xmlProjd.Send("XMLRequest=" + sRequest);
      OnStaffHistory();
   }
   else
      alert("We cannot add a service incident report without a staff member
            search.");
}
```

We've seen this before. It's virtually identical to the code we used to submit `ITStaffer` and `StaffQuery` documents. What's that call to `OnStaffHistory()` though? After submitting a performance report, the easiest way to refresh the client is to retrieve the programmer's entire performance report history. Performance report retrieval is our next task. Before we get to that, however, let's wrap up this task by looking at what happens on the server.

Server Side

A quick check with GetASP() shows that the PerformanceReport vocabulary is supported by an ASP named History.asp. The main body of that script is nearly identical to staff.asp. We retrieve the incoming document, set up some database resources, then switch according to the vocabulary of the incoming document. A PerformanceReport document, as we saw above, is part of a Collection. Here's the relevant part of the switch statement in History.asp's main body:

```
      ...
      case "Collection":
         switch (parser.documentElement.childNodes(0).nodeName)
         {
            case "PerformanceReport":
               ProcessPerformanceReport(parser.documentElement);
               break;
            default:
               Response.Write("<Collection></Collection>");
               break;
         }
         break;
      ...
```

Handling Performance Reports

ProcessPerformanceReport, in turn, composes a SQL query and submits it to the database. Again, we've included the flexibility to handle more than one call report per Collection document:

```
function ProcessPerformanceReport(collectionNode)
{
   var sDetails, sID, sProjID;

   for (var ni = 0; ni < collectionNode.childNodes.length; ni++)
   {
      switch (collectionNode.childNodes(ni).nodeName)
      {
         case "PerformanceReport":
            sDetails = collectionNode.childNodes(ni).childNodes(2).text;
            sProjID = collectionNode.childNodes(ni).childNodes(1).text;
            sID = collectionNode.childNodes(ni).childNodes(0).text;
            InsertPerfReport(sDetails, sID, sProjID);
            break;
      }
   }
}
```

We work through each child element of the Collection root. If it is a PerformanceReport – and who knows what crazy information a bad client might send? – we extract the detail text and the programmer and project IDs and send them off to InsertPerfReport(). That function compiles the SQL statement for one insertion and executes it.

Database Details for a Performance Report

We're not permitting managers to edit existing performance reports – the temptation to cover up unfavorable reviewers or favorable reviews for projects that subsequently failed would be too great! This has the happy effect of simplifying our programming. We don't have to worry about whether we need an `INSERT` or an `UPDATE`. All our commands related to the task of submitting performance reports will be `INSERT`s. An example of the kind of SQL we need looks like this:

```
INSERT INTO Details(ProjID, MemberID, Comments) VALUES ("6","157", "Worked hard,
had no clue.");
```

With that in mind, the rest of the code for inserting a new performance report should look familiar:

```
function InsertPerfReport(sComment, sStaffID, sProjID)
{
   var sCore = "INSERT INTO Details (ProjID, MemberID, Comments) VALUES ('";
   var sQuery = sCore + sProjID + "', '" + sStaffID + "', '" + sComment + "');";
   dbConn.Execute(sQuery);
   if (dbConn.Errors.Count > 0)
      Response.Write("<NACK/>");
   else
      Response.Write("<ACK/>");
}
```

After building the SQL text, we execute the query and look for errors. If none are found, we return the very short XML document `<ACK/>`.

> *The alert reader will note that this SQL INSERT puts a reference to a project into the* Details *table without ensuring there is a corresponding row in the* Projects *table. Since we are focusing on XML, not database issues, I'm taking a shortcut and omitting the issue of maintaining project information. If you want to extend this prototype into a real application, you should construct a page that lets you do this. You will also want to write triggers and perhaps stored procedures to assist you in maintaining the relational integrity of the database.*

Clearing the Performance Report History Form

This task, performed in response to clicking on the Clear button under the performance report history form, is functionally identical to the process we went through to clear the programmer form. We are resetting the parse tree for the data island named `xmlProjs` to a `Collection` document containing one `ProjReport` element. The `ProjReport` element and its children contain no textual values, only elements. Here is the source code to do this:

```
function OnClearProj()
{
   var parser = new ActiveXObject("microsoft.xmldom");
   parser.loadXML("<Collection><ProjReport><ProjName/>
                   <ProjID/><PerformanceDetails/></ProjReport></Collection>");
   if (parser.readyState == 4 && parser.parseError == 0)
   {
      while (xmlProjs.documentElement.childNodes.length > 1)
```

```
        {
            xmlProjs.documentElement.removeChild(
               xmlProjs.documentElement.childNodes(1));
        }
        for (var ni = 0; ni < parser.documentElement.childNodes.length; ni++)
            xmlProjs.documentElement.appendChild(
               parser.documentElement.childNodes(ni).cloneNode(true));
        if (xmlProjs.documentElement.childNodes.length > 1)
           xmlProjs.documentElement.removeChild(
               xmlProjs.documentElement.childNodes(0));
           xmlProjs.recordset.moveFirst();
        }
    }
}
```

Retrieving a Programmer's Performance History

There's just one feature left to implement, and that is retrieving all the existing performance reports for the programmer displayed on the page. This occurs in `ProjTrack.html` in the `OnStaffHistory()` handler. In this case, we are `POST`ing a `ProjPerformanceQuery` document to the server and receiving a `Collection` document containing zero or more `ProjReport` elements. After receiving the document from the service, we fix up the data binding.

Client Side

The job of composing the query document is fairly simple since we only need to send up the value of the `StaffID` field:

```
function OnStaffHistory()
{
   var sReq = "";
   if (staffIDText.value != "")
   {
      var sServer = "http://" + GetASP("ProjPerformanceQuery");
      xmlProjd.Open("POST", sServer, false);

      sReq = "XMLRequest=<ProjPerformanceQuery><StaffID>" +
             staffIDText.value + "</StaffID></ProjPerformanceQuery>";

      xmlProjd.setRequestHeader("Content-Type",
         "application/x-www-form-urlencoded");
      xmlProjd.Send(sReq);
      FixHistoryBinding();
   }
}
```

`FixHistoryBinding()` performs the dynamic fix-up we've seen several times in this case study. The only novelty here is that we are binding to a repeating HTML element. Each row of our table is matched to a `ProjReport` element by the XML DSO. `ProjTrack.html` merely has to provide a template consisting of one row. This is the table as it exists at design time:

```
<TABLE border=1 cellPadding=1 cellSpacing=1 width="75%"
              id=projTable name = "projTable">
  <TR>
    <TD>
      <P>
         <INPUT id=projName name=projName style="HEIGHT: 22px; WIDTH: 422px">
          
         <FONT face=Verdana size=2>ID
            <INPUT id=projIDText name=projIDText>
         </FONT>
      </P>
      <P><FONT face=Verdana size=2 >Performance Details</FONT></P>
      <P>
         <TEXTAREA id=projDetail name=projDetail
                   style="HEIGHT: 38px; WIDTH: 422px">
         </TEXTAREA>
      </P>
      </TD>
   </TR>
</TABLE>
```

The INPUT and TEXTAREA elements, projName, projIDText and projDetail, are bound dynamically when we retrieve any data. We remove all but the very first node from the existing document, leaving the first to prevent the binding from failing. Next, we append all the new nodes, and then delete the remaining node from the old document:

```
function FixHistoryBinding()
{
   while (xmlProjs.documentElement.childNodes.length > 1)
   {

xmlProjs.documentElement.removeChild(xmlProjs.documentElement.childNodes(1));
   }
   for (var ni = 0;
         ni < xmlProjd.responseXML.documentElement.childNodes.length;
         ni++)
      xmlProjs.documentElement.appendChild(
         xmlProjd.responseXML.documentElement.childNodes(ni).cloneNode(true));

      if (xmlProjs.documentElement.childNodes.length > 1)
         xmlProjs.documentElement.removeChild(
            xmlProjs.documentElement.childNodes(0));
      xmlProjs.recordset.moveFirst();

      projTable.dataSrc="#xmlProjs";
      projName.dataFld="ProjName";
      projIDText.dataFld = "ProjID";
      projDetail.dataFld="PerformanceDetails";
   }
```

Server Side

Once `History.asp` receives our query document, it switches on the root node:

```
case "ProjPerformanceQuery":
   ProcessHistoryQuery(parser.documentElement);
   break;
```

`ProcessHistoryQuery()` is responsible for converting our XML into a SQL `SELECT` statement. A sample SQL statement of this type would be:

```
SELECT Projects.ProjectName, Details.ProjID, Details.Comments FROM Details INNER
JOIN Projects ON Details.ProjID = Projects.ProjID WHERE Details.MemberID="6";
```

`ProcessHistoryQuery()` passes the bulk of the SQL text composition off to a function named `MakeHistConstraint()` (detailed below) before executing the query:

```
function ProcessHistoryQuery(histQNode)
{
   var sSelectCore = "SELECT Projects.ProjectName, Details.ProjID,
                      Details.Comments FROM Details INNER JOIN Projects ON
                      Details.ProjID = Projects.ProjID";

   var sConstraint = "";

   sConstraint = MakeHistConstraint(histQNode);
   if (sConstraint != "")
      sConstraint = " WHERE " + sConstraint;

   var sQuery = sSelectCore + sConstraint + ';';
   dbRecordSet = dbConn.Execute(sQuery);
```

Once it has issued the query, it must step through the recordset's results and write each row out as a member of a `Collection` document:

```
   if (!dbRecordSet.BOF)
      dbRecordSet.MoveFirst();

   if (dbRecordSet.EOF)
      Response.Write("<Collection></Collection>");

   // Write the collection root node and then the rest of the contents
   Response.Write("<Collection>");
   while (!dbRecordSet.EOF)
   {
      WriteHistBody(dbRecordSet);
      dbRecordSet.MoveNext();
   }
   Response.Write("</Collection>");
}
```

Here are our two helper functions, `MakeHistConstraint()` and `WriteHistBody()`. `MakeHistConstraint()` extracts the programmer ID passed in the query document and builds the heart of the SQL `WHERE` clause. `WriteHistBody()` is called from `ProcessHistoryQuery()` to convert the results of the database query into the XML document that is sent to the client:

```
function MakeHistConstraint(node)
{
   var sClause = "";
   var sID = "";
   for (var ni = 0; ni < node.childNodes.length; ni++)
   {
      switch (node.childNodes(ni).nodeName)
      {
         case "StaffID":
            if (node.childNodes(ni).text != "")
               sID = "Details.MemberID = " + node.childNodes(ni).text;
            break;
      }
   }
   sClause = sID;
   return sClause;
}

function WriteHistBody(rsCalls)
{
   Response.Write("<ProjReport><ProjName>");
   Response.Write(rsCalls("ProjectName"));
   Response.Write("</ProjName><ProjID>");
   Response.Write(rsCalls("ProjID"));
   Response.Write("</ProjID><PerformanceDetails>");
   Response.Write(rsCalls("Comments"));
   Response.Write("</PerformanceDetails></ProjReport>");
}
```

Lessons Learned

Now that we've completed the pilot project for the programming managers, we should grade our work against the principles of our development philosophy. The application meets the functional requirements for the project in a way that required minimal extra coding to preserve platform neutrality. We used platform specific technology – data binding for rich visual presentation – but shielded the server-side code from that implementation choice. Similarly, the server used ADO and a relational database, but the client was shielded from that. This brought us the possibility of reusing a great deal of code for other purposes. The server pages, in particular, could be used "as is" with other client applications.

Our work isn't perfect, however. The mistakes we made will serve to point out the value of our development principles.

Violations of the Development Philosophy

Data binding forced our programmers into coupling the `ITStaffer` vocabulary fairly tightly with the programmer form, and the `ProjReport` vocabulary with the performance report history table. We can't really call this a violation, at least in the absence of an accepted metadata standard. The use of data binding greatly simplified the programming task and gave us a compact user interface on the client. Nevertheless, changes to the vocabularies may break the client application.

We missed an opportunity for greater reuse when we failed to distinguish between `ITStaffer` and `Staffer` elements in our code. In this case, the differences were minor, so the additional code wasn't warranted. In a real-world case, however, we would want to build functions to handle the general `Staffer` vocabulary, then write other functions to handle the specialized `ITStaffer` vocabulary. The specialized functions would call on the work already implemented by the general case functions to process that general part of an `ITStaffer` document (the `Staffer` element).

Components

Development was greatly aided by the use of `MSXML` and its related interfaces, the XML DSO, and `IXMLHTTP`. Although this restricts us to Microsoft Internet Explorer 5.0 as the client browser, these components provided key functions that would have been expensive to replace with custom programming. Our particular application could have been completely executed on the server, with the ASP returning HTML. That approach, however, would have prevented reuse of the service implementation by other applications, particularly automated clients. We promoted reuse at the expense of significant client-side programming. We did, however, miss something. We have not created any components of our own. Specifically, our development philosophy called for using components on each tier, with component data being translated into XML to survive passage between platforms. Where are the components that go with `ITStaffer` and `ProjReport`?

An `ITStaffer` class could have been created in JavaScript as a pilot for a COM component. We might have used that for field validation or enforcing business rules. For example, we might check job titles against a corporate database of job classifications. Such a component would have been valuable on the server side of the application. This was impractical and unnecessary for the purposes of illustration, but in a real-world setting it would be important. As things stand, no other applications that make use of customers have anything they can reuse in terms of code except the scripts themselves. We have not produced anything that can be reused without editing the source code.

Reuse Potential

There are, however, two great resources coming out of this project that can be reused in the future: the two services represented by `History.asp` and `Staff.asp`. Their services are generalized and in accordance with our development philosophy, so any other application that needs these vocabularies will be able to call on them. That's the whole purpose of cooperative network applications. You develop services and publicize their availability through a directory listing. Client applications can use them because they are assured of a known interface. In this case, the interfaces consist of our XML vocabularies. These vocabularies are themselves reusable resources, provided they faithfully model some useful part of our business.

Summary

We took a look at the fundamentals of using XML with ASP. We saw that XML is well suited to ASP and dynamic generation of documents. Our approach used some platform-specific tools, mainly the `IXMLHTTP` interface of MSXML and data binding. If platform neutrality were an issue, we would need to move all the processing to the server, find platform neutral components, or produce different versions of the client pages for different browsers.

Along the way, we took a look at the problems that intranet and Internet applications introduce into common programming practice. These are:

- Dealing with increased complexity
- Inflexible applications
- Duplication of code
- Moves towards automated Web tasks
- Distributed development and implementation teams

I briefly stated my five principles for overcoming these weaknesses in Web development:

- Applications Will Be Built From Coarse-Grained Services
- Services Will Be Discovered By Querying Directories
- Services Will Be Provided As Self-Describing Data
- Services Will Be Enlisted On A Transient Basis
- Services Must Support Extension and Degrade Gracefully

Finally, we put the two together. XML proves to be an excellent enabling technology for implementing the five principles. ASP is similarly well-suited to building Web-based services. Overall, then, ASP and XML are an outstanding choice for building robust Web applications that meet the peculiar needs of loosely connected networks and the applications that run on them.

17

Case Study 3 – Book Catalog Information Service

In this case study we are going to create a powerful book catalog information service (BCIS) based upon SAX and XPath. The system will enable book publishers to upload XML catalog files that describe their books, and have those details filtered and delivered to subscribers of the system (via e-mail) in XML or HTML format. Both delivery formats will include URLs through which the books can be viewed and purchased online at Amazon.com. These URLs are built dynamically, based upon the book's ISBN and Amazon's current web site structure. They are not contained within the original source document, which means that the BCIS system could potentially include links to any number of online bookstores, possibly based on subscriber preferences.

The BCIS needs to be scalable and capable of processing XML catalog files of *any* size, so it uses a SAX parser for accessing all XML data content. As we discussed in the earlier chapters of the book, SAX parsers remove the need for loading an entire XML document into memory before processing, and at any one time they only keep a small portion of the document in memory – the exact amount of memory used depends upon element nesting within the document. This means that there is no upper limit on the size of files that can be processed, and the memory used during processing is negligible. Both of these points are important. If the system loaded documents into a DOM it would typically be limited by available memory, or would simply run very slowly due to paging.

The BCIS is based upon the publish/subscribe push paradigm: the publisher (server) delivers book details directly to the subscriber (client), rather than the subscriber requesting the information from the publisher. Subscribers to the BCIS can select two book categories (such as books related to ASP, XML, and so on) that are used to filter the information that will be delivered to them. So, if a publisher uploads a catalog file containing 8,000 books about gardening, 25,000 books about cars and only two about XML, a subscriber that has registered an interest in XML only will just receive information about the two XML books.

The publish/subscribe push paradigm has several key benefits that make it an attractive option for many applications:

- It saves the subscriber time, as it eliminates the need for 'polling' the publisher for changes.
- It allows the information publisher to save on precious resources and bandwidth, as servers don't have to process and serve up information requests that clients may just throw away (because nothing has changed).
- The publisher knows the subscriber is more likely to view the information, and doesn't have to rely on them remembering to go back to the original subscription source.

Probably the most popular applications of publish/subscribe services are currently newsletters and website update notifications. In both cases, the publisher knows the client is interested in the information they have to offer, or certain services they provide, so can e-mail the client information as pertinent events occur (such as new pages being added to a website). When the client receives the information, they can read it at their leisure and determine whether or not it is worth taking any action, such as following any hyperlinks that may have been included in the e-mail. Both of these types of application can also be built on the principles of filtering, transforming, and pushing XML data from a server to a client. This means that the BCIS has been written in a fashion that allows it to be easily adapted to support any type of information and delivery mechanism. For this reason, the design of the application may seem a little over complicated at first, but we hope you'll understand the rationale behind it by the time we've reached the end.

By the end of this chapter you will have seen:

- How to use a SAX parser in Visual Basic to process XML files of any size without using much memory. Note that, although we are using VB, I will ensure that you understand how the application could be implemented in any language, and will therefore explain any "VB-isms" that might seem a bit weird if you've have only ever programmed in C/C++ or Java before.
- An interesting alternative to XSLT that enables high performance, compiled style sheets by using native code for templates.
- How to develop an XML-based push application that can be adapted to suit many different applications.

The Book Catalog Information Service

There are three target customer types for the BCIS:

- **Subscribers** – Who use the service to receive information about books based upon two category filters. (The number of filters is an arbitrary number that has been chosen to reduce coding complexity for the purposes of this case study.)
- **Publishers** – Companies or individuals who want information about their books to be sent to subscribers.
- **Advertisers** – Companies like Amazon.com who sell books online, and will pay to have links to their website included in the information delivered to subscribers.

There is no reason why an advertiser couldn't also be a publisher, advertiser and/or subscriber etc.

We won't be looking at publishers very much in this case study. Effectively, they are the entities that create the XML catalog files that contain the book information processed by the system. As we'll see later, the interaction between the BCIS and subscriber in this case study simply involves copying the catalog file into a directory. This approach makes it easy for companies to publish information by simply FTPing XML files onto the BCIS server, but obviously means the system would need expanding should you decide to bill publishers for each book title that you distribute to a subscriber.

Advertisers are also given very little coverage, and the system we'll implement will only support a single advertiser that is hard-coded into the transformation code. You could of course expand this and include lots of companies.

Subscribers are the main focus of this case study, so lets take a closer look at how they fit into the bigger picture.

System Overview

This system overview for BCIS can be visualized as follows:

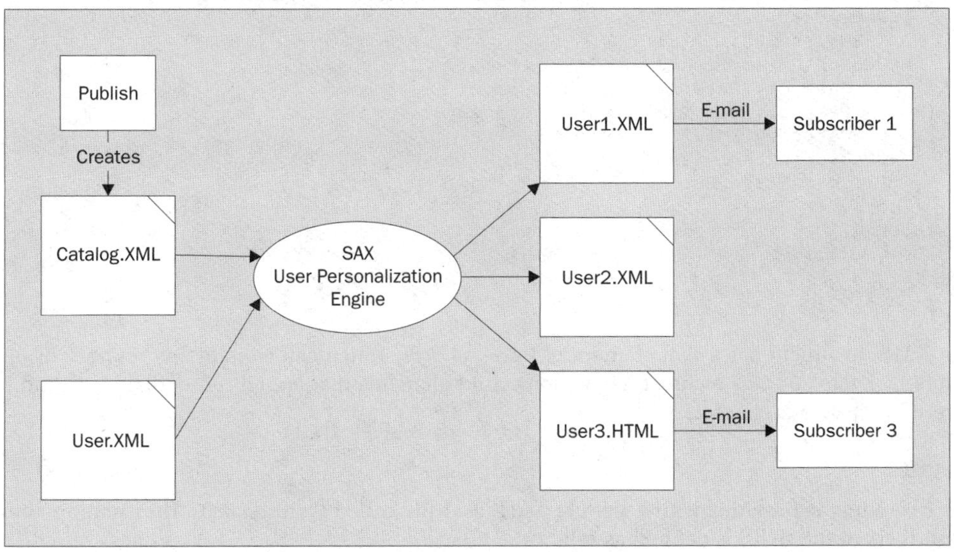

A publisher creates an XML file that lists all the information about books to be *filtered* and pushed out to subscribers (shown as `Catalog.XML`).

Subscribers and their personalization filters are defined in the file `Users.XML`. The system described in this chapter doesn't provide a UI for managing this file, so you will have to amend and edit this file manually (using something like notepad) to add additional details or change profiles.

The SAX user personalization engine loads the user information and transforms book information for each user based upon their settings, creating one output file for each user. Each transformed file is optionally e-mailed to the user in accordance with the publish/subscribe model we've already discussed.

XML File Formats

The subscriber and book information is kept in distinct (separate) XML files. The system doesn't use a DTD or schema to validate the files because the SAX parser used does not support validation. This doesn't really have a large impact on our case study, but it does mean you'd have to perform any validation (such as ensuring the root element name is correct etc.) yourself if you need that in systems you derive from this case study.

Catalog.XML

The case study is provided with a sample XML catalog called `Catalog.xml`, which is available for download along with the rest of the code for the book from http://www.wrox.com/. The book information file contained within this file uses the format we've seen throughout this book:

```
<Catalog>
<Book>
   <Title>IE5 XML Programmer's Reference</Title>
   <Authors>
      <Author>Alex Homer</Author>
   </Authors>
   <Publisher>Wrox Press, Ltd.</Publisher>
   <PubDate>August 1999</PubDate>
   <Abstract>Reference of XML capabilities in IE5</Abstract>
   <Pages>480</Pages>
   <ISBN>1-861001-57-6</ISBN>
   <RecSubjCategories>
      <Category>Internet</Category>
      <Category>Web Publishing</Category>
      <Category>XML</Category>
   </RecSubjCategories>
   <Price>$49.99</Price>
</Book>
<Book>
   ...
</Book>
</Catalog>
```

The XML document has a root element of `<Catalog>`, which can contain any number of `<Book>` elements. Each `<Book>` element has various child elements that are all self-explanatory and have been covered in previous chapters.

Users.XML

The case study is provided with a sample XML user file called `Users.XML`. Information about subscribers of the BCIS is defined as follows:

```
<?xml version="1.0" ?>
<!-- This file defines the register users for the book notification service -->
<Users>

   <User>
      <Name>Richard Anderson</Name>
      <OutputFile>c:\proxml\RJA.HTML</OutputFile>
      <Email>rja@arpsolutions.demon.co.uk</Email>
      <DeliveryFormat>HTML</DeliveryFormat>
      <Category1>XML</Category1>
      <Category2>ATL</Category2>
   </User>
```

```
    <User>
       <Name>Jon Duckett</Name>
       <OutputFile>c:\proxml\JD.HTML</OutputFile>
       <Email>jond@wrox.com</Email>
       <DeliveryFormat>HTML</DeliveryFormat>
       <Category1>ASP</Category1>
       <Category2>XML</Category2>
    </User>

    <User>
       <Name>Karli Watson</Name>
       <OutputFile>c:\proxml\KW.XML</OutputFile>
       <DeliveryFormat>XML</DeliveryFormat>
       <Category1>Java</Category1>
       <Category2>Web Server</Category2>
    </User>

 </Users>
```

The XML document has a root element of <Users>, which can contain any number of <User> elements. Each <User> element has various child elements (which can contain only text content):

Child Element	Description
<Name>	The name of the subscriber, used for logging purposes.
<OutputFile>	The name of the output file created when the transformation occurs.
<Email> (optional)	If present, the <OutputFile> is e-mailed to the user via this address.
<DeliveryFormat>	Specifies the transformation style sheet class that should be applied for the user. Values can either be XML or HTML.
<Category1>	The first category of book the user is interested in. This is matched against the catalog XML file using the XPath `/Catalog/Book/RecSubjCategories/Category`.
<Category2>	The second category of book the user is interested in. Matched as per <Category1>.

As a potential expansion idea for this case study you could extend it to support any number of category elements. I've only implemented two to make the code simpler.

The Delivery Formats

The BCIS allows subscribers to receive book information in either HTML or XML format. The HTML delivery format for a subscriber with category filters of ASP and ASP+ is shown here:

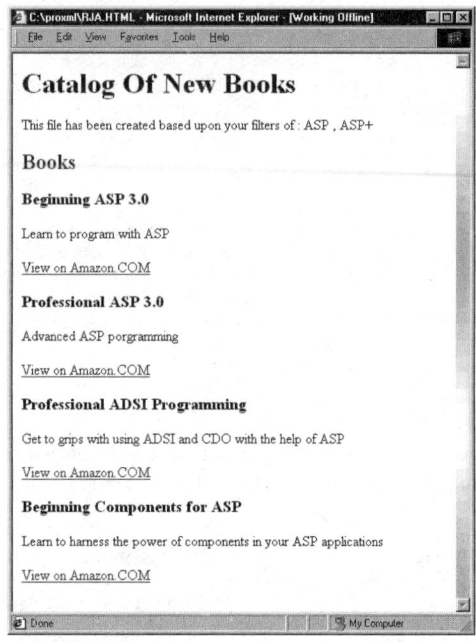

The transformation has created a fairly simple HTML output file, and indeed only shows two of the original XML input fields (title and abstract). It calculates the hyperlink to Amazon based a simple algorithm where any hyphens are removed from the ISBN number, which is then prefixed with `http://www.amazon.com/exec/obidos/ASIN/`.

The XML format is equally simple:

```
<?xml version="1.0" ?>
- <Catalog>
    <Notes>Filters: Java , Web Server</Notes>
  - <Books>
    - <Book>
        <Title>Professional Java XML</Title>
        <AmazonURL>http://www.amazon.com/exec/obidos/ASIN/1861002858</AmazonURL>
        <Abstract>Learn to utilize the powerful combination of Java and XML</Abstract>
      </Book>
    - <Book>
        <Title>Professional Site Server 3.0</Title>
        <AmazonURL>http://www.amazon.com/exec/obidos/ASIN/1861002696</AmazonURL>
        <Abstract>The definitive resource for Site Server</Abstract>
      </Book>
    </Books>
  </Catalog>
```

Both transformations are performed by VB class modules, as we'll discuss shortly.

Subscribers/Users

As we've discussed, subscribers are the most interesting entities in the BCIS case study as they define the filtering that is applied to the source catalog XML document, the format that is used for delivery (HTML or XML), and an optional e-mail address. Subscribers are modeled using the class `CUser`, and managed as a group using the class `CUserCollection`:

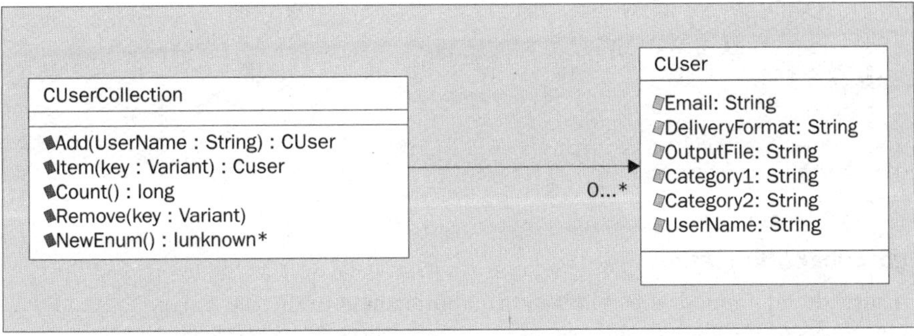

The notation used in this figure (and others in this chapter) is UML. To summarize quickly: a class is represented by a box divided into 3 sections. The top section shows the name of the class, the middle section shows properties (and their types), and the bottom section shows methods (along with their parameters and types). The arrows between boxes can indicate relationships such as ownership and containment, along with numbers to represent the cardinality of these relationships (one-to-one, one-to-many, etc.). In the figure above, `CUserCollection` *is shown containing zero or more* `CUser` *objects. For more information see* Instant UML *(ISBN: 1-861000-87-1).*

Publishers and advertisers are not modeled, because the system doesn't care who created the XML catalog file, and as we've discussed only links to Amazon are outputted. If we decided to extend the system and charge publishers per-user/book published, or support multiple advertisers, we would model them because they would then be equally important.

A Quick Note about VB Collections

As the BCIS is written using VB, all of the collection classes were created using the class builder add-in.

Although I've used class builder I generally rename the variable names it creates to use `m_` *rather than* `mvar` *and prefix the variables using Hungarian notation.*

I'm not going to explain any of the collection classes detailed in the design as their role in life is simple: they hold zero or more objects of the same class. However, for those of you how have not used VB before, I'll briefly discuss the `NewEnum()` method of the `CUserCollection` class.

This `NewEnum()` method enables us to write code using the `For...Each` syntax as follows:

```
Dim oUser as CUser
Dim oUserCollection as CUserCollection

For Each oUser in MyUserCollection
   MsgBox oUser.UserName
Next oUser
```

This is a fairly neat shorthand feature of VB that results in a very readable coding approach. The underlying implementation is based upon the COM interface `IEnumVARIANT`, and basically saves us from the traditionally slightly longer way of accessing items of a collection using an index:

```
Dim oUser as CUser
Dim oUserCollection as CUserCollection
Dim lIndex as long

For lIndex = 0 to oUser.Count
   Set oUser = oUserCollection.Item(lIndex)
   MsgBox oUser.UserName
Next lIndex
```

Loading Subscriber Information

As we've already mentioned, subscriber information is held in the file `Users.XML`. To transform this file into instances of the class `CUser` we use the class `CLoadUserInfo`:

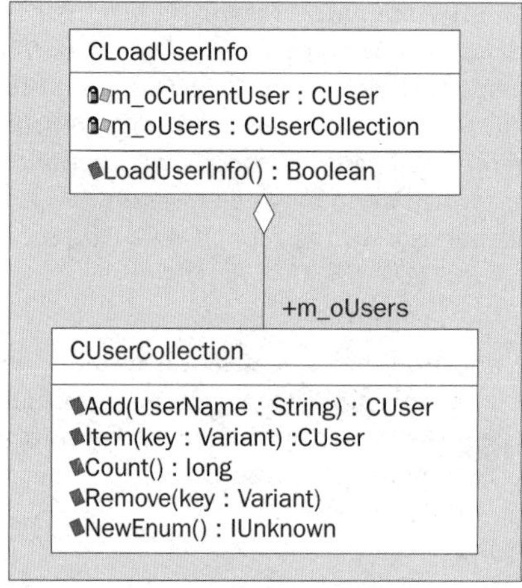

By invoking the `LoadUserInfo()` method of `CLoadUserInfo`, the `Users.XML` file is transformed into `CUser` objects which are placed in the `CUserCollection` stored in `m_oUsers`. XSLT obviously can't be used to achieve this transformation, so we use a SAX parser and a clever yet simple transformation engine based upon SAX/XPath that makes this conversion easy to implement. The transformation engine is implemented by the class `CSAXTransformEngine`.

As the transformation engine is based upon SAX, we don't have to load the XML file into a DOM. We simply react to certain events in SAX event stream and build our `CUser` objects. This removes the unnecessary operations of creating a DOM for the XML file, searching the DOM for the nodes and then destroying all the DOM nodes. This has two major advantages:

- We don't waste processing time and memory by creating DOM nodes and instantly destroying them once we've retrieved the data we need.
- We can process XML files of any size. No matter how big the user's file is, we are only constrained by the memory used by the `CUser` objects and not the DOM nodes. If you've ever tried loading a 20 megabyte file into a DOM before you'll know you generally need 3 or 4 times as much memory to load it, in this case around 80 megabytes. With SAX the memory footprint is usually only a couple of kilobytes for parsing, depending on the element nesting and character data within the file. This makes SAX very attractive for systems like BCIS that potentially have no upper limit on the size of the XML files they need to process.

The two major downsides of using SAX are:

- There is no random access to any data within the XML file except for that provided by the current event, or data that has been previously parsed saved in variables.
- There is no element-relative location or position indicator with events. For example, if the event `startElement` is received and the element name is `<Title>`, we can't determine whether this element is within another element (such as `<Book>`) unless we set some type of flag when we process that element to indicate the nesting. Of course, the relationship between a `<Book>` and a `<Title>` could be that of parent/child or ancestor/descendant. The more complex the nesting or relationships become, the more flags we need to keep.

More details of this tradeoff are given in the DOM and SAX chapters earlier in the book (Chapters 5 and 6).

We cannot easily address the first of these drawbacks, and the approach we take is simply to buffer information. Provided the XML file is not too complex this is not too much of a drawback. However, should you need to access information at the end of the XML file before processing that at the start you'll either have to parse the file twice, or rethink the structure the XML file and change any application that generates it.

The second problem, that of relative location, can easily be addressed by writing a SAX filter that maintains an element stack based upon calls to `startElement` and `endElement` as follows:

```
startDocument                               Stack = /

   startElement( "Books")                   Stack = /Books
      startElement("Book")                  Stack = /Books/Book
         startElement("Title")              Stack = /Books/Book/Title
            characters("ProXML")            Stack = /Books/Book/Title
         endElement("Title")                Stack = /Books/Book/Title
      endElement("Book")                    Stack = /Books/Book
   endElement( "Books")                     Stack = /Books

endDocument                                 Stack = /
```

As the SAX event `startElement` occurs we push the element name and effectively build up an XPath. As the SAX event `endElement` occurs we remove the element name. The stack initially contains "/" which is the root of the document. As the SAX events occur, the stack is built and the events are then extended with the XPath and passed on to the next handler. The net effect is that our classes process an event stream that looks more like this:

```
startDocument

   startElement("/Books")
      startElement("/Books/Book")
         startElement("/Books/Book/Title")
            characters("/Books/Book/Title", "ProXML")
         endElement("/Books/Book/Title)
      endElement("/Books/Book")
   endElement("/Books")

endDocument
```

You might start to think this looks a bit DOM-like, and in some respects you can argue it is, but the point to remember is that in the above stack we'll only ever have one instance of a book in memory, unlike the DOM where we'd potentially have thousands – and therefore very little free memory.

The BCIS is based upon a neat transformation technique that has been developed into a generic transformation engine as part of this case study. Rather than transformations being performed by an XSLT style sheet, it uses one or more classes that are invoked as the SAX events with certain patterns (XPaths) are matched in the SAX event stream. This approach provides the BCIS with great performance because the pseudo style sheet is compiled, and makes transforming a document using SAX event streams easier to process because you don't have to keep track of event nesting yourself.

The approach has more flexibility than plain XSLT because you can perform transformations using the power of whatever language you are used to developing in, which then allows operations such as database lookups (which are just not possible in *standard* XSLT). Another benefit I personally like a lot is that you don't have to concern yourself with the somewhat complex XSLT syntax when attempting more complex transformations, which should lead to productivity gains.

To understand the benefits and workings of the transformation engine, consider a typical SAX application:

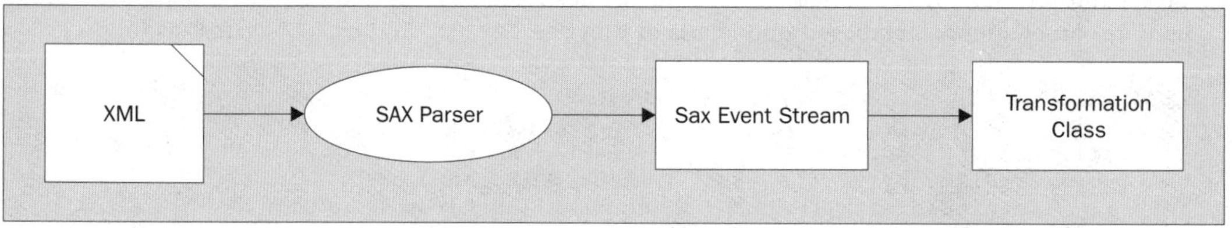

An XML file is parsed, and SAX events are processed by the class that implements the SAX `DocumentHandler` class. If the handler code were locating all the `<Book>` elements within `<Books>` the code would be written like this:

```
Bool m_bInBooks as Boolean

Private Sub m_oSAXParser_startElement(ByVal sName As String, _
                                ByVal pAttributeList As SAXLib.ISAXAttributeList)

   If sName = "Books" then
      m_bInBooks = true
   End if

   If sName = "Book" and m_bInBooks = true then
      MsgBox "We located a book"
   End if
End Sub

Private Sub m_oSAXParser_endElement(ByVal sName As String)
   If sName = "Books" then
      m_bInBooks = false
   End if
End Sub
```

The SAX event passes us the start tag name in `sName`, along with `pAttributeList` that gives us access to any attributes defined in the start tag. The code isn't terribly difficult, but locating an element that is more than one nested level deep will probably result in lots of state flags, messy code, and bugs. The other problem is that if we are searching for lots of elements the event handlers will soon grow and become somewhat monolithic. The introduction of an additional layer/filter to append an XPath to events as we discussed earlier makes the programming model a lot simpler:

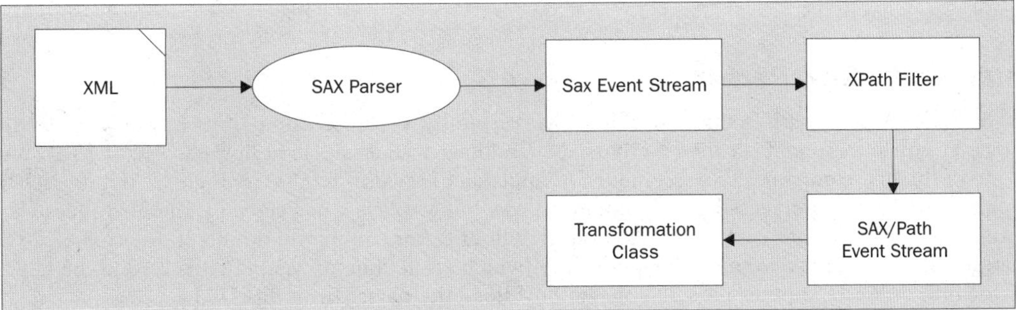

As somebody else maintains the element nesting for us (using the stack approach discussed) we can remove the need for any flags and simplify our code like this:

```
Private Sub m_oSAXParser_startElement(sXPath As String, _
                                      sElementName As String, _
                                      oAttribs As SAXLib.ISAXAttributeList)

   If sXPath = "/Books/Book" then
      MsgBox "We located a book"
   End if
End Sub
```

With this code we simply test against a complete XPath and we do not have to worry about setting flags in `startElement()`, and closing them in `endElement()`. The code is much simpler, and it is the basis upon which the transformations in this case study are performed. However, using XPaths does not resolve the problem of our event handlers becoming too big if we are searching for a large number of events. To resolve this we allow different class modules to handle SAX events based upon one or more XPaths:

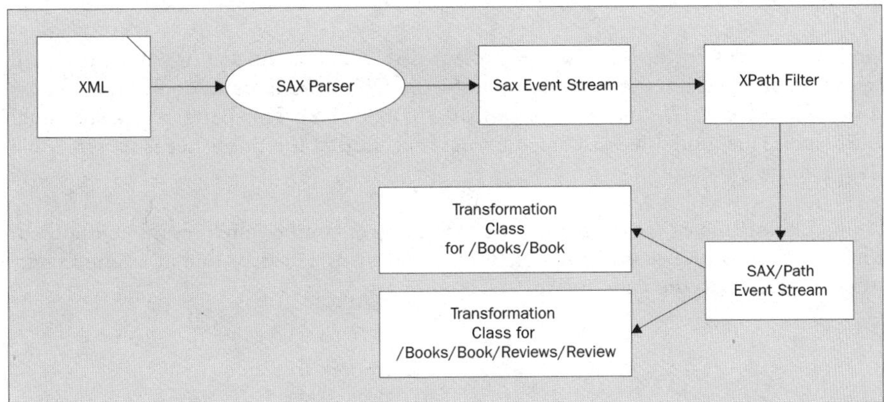

In this diagram one class is responsible for handling all SAX events with an XPath of /Books/Book, another class is responsible for process SAX events with an XPath of /Books/Book/Reviews/Review. The engine we implement allows for any number of XPaths to be processed by one class, but the same XPath can't be processed by more than one class.

At this point, we'll digress slightly and describe the SAX parser we are going to use in this case study, and get our hands dirty with some VB code. Once we've looked at how the parser is used, we'll crack on and create the BCIS.

Visual Basic SAX Parser

The SAX parser we use in this case study was created by Vivid Creations (http:/www.vivid-creations.com) and is called **ActiveSAX**. Vivid are well established in the world of XML, and were one of the first companies to implement SAX outside of Java (in C/C++, VB etc.) – in mid 1998. The parser is free for commercial/non-commercial use, but displays a nag screen if the file processed exceeds 10KB. For our case study purposes that limit is fine, but if you do intend to use SAX to process larger files you'll need to purchase a full-copy (which at the time of writing costs £99 in the U.K. or US$149) or locate another parser. You can download the parser from this URL: http://www.vivid-creations.com/sax/index.htm.

Using ActiveSAX

We'll create a simple application that demonstrates the usage of ActiveSAX by listing all the elements in an XML file. Note that this chapter does not give detailed coverage of the ActiveSAX parser.

> *More detailed coverage about ActiveSAX can be found on the Vivid website. Note that the download contains many other XML samples (both SAX and DOM) that you can refer to should you wish to learn more.*

First up, you'll need to download and install the Vivid ActiveSAX parser from the URL given above, install it, create a new Standard EXE VB project, and add a reference to the type library "Vivid Creations ActiveSAX".

Next, place a standard ListBox control onto the default form, then at the top of the code module for the form declare the variable m_oSAXParser as the type SAXParser:

```
Dim WithEvents m_oSAXParser As SAXParser
```

You'll notice we are using the WithEvents keyword, which is the way in which events from an object instance can be handled using connection points: the COM implementation of the **Observer** pattern as defined by Gamma *et al.* (*Design Patterns*, ISBN 0-201-63361-2). This pattern is pretty much the same as the publish/subscribe model we discussed earlier, except that the publisher is now an object, and the subscriber is some VB code.

Once defined, select the m_oSAXParser from the object combo, click on the method combo box, and select the events startElement, characters and endElement one at a time to add the subroutine prototypes to the code module:

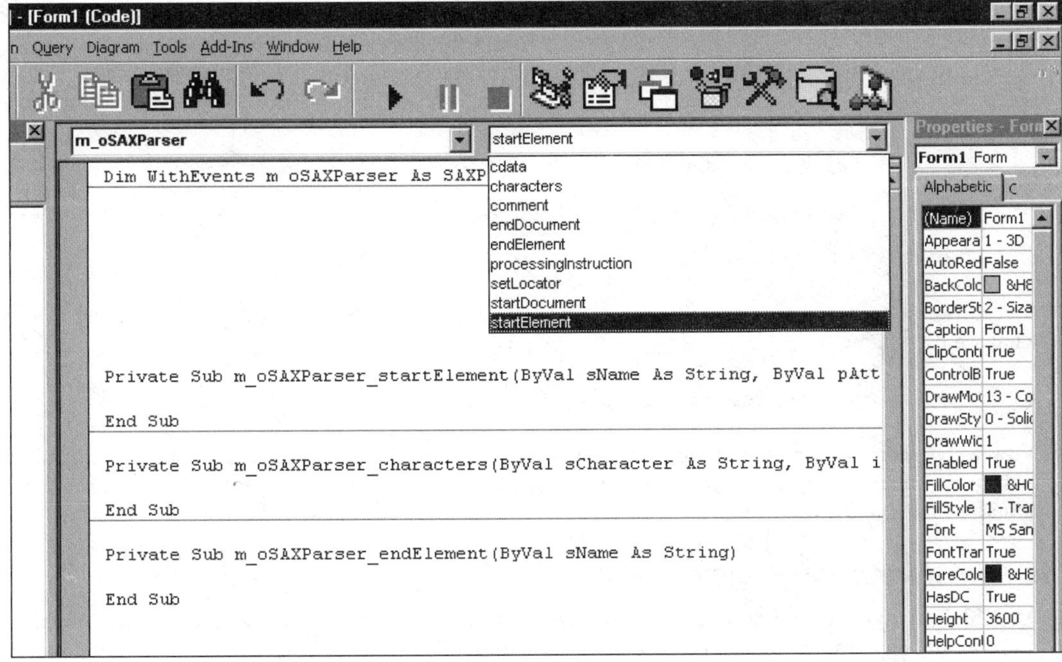

Modify the implementation of the three event handlers to look like this:

```
Private Sub m_oSAXParser_startElement(ByVal sName As String, _
                              ByVal pAttributeList As SAXLib.ISAXAttributeList)

   List1.AddItem "startElement:" & sName
End Sub

Private Sub m_oSAXParser_characters(ByVal sCharacters As String, _
                                ByVal iLength As Long)

   List1.AddItem "characters:" & sCharacters
End Sub

Private Sub m_oSAXParser_endElement(ByVal sName As String)
   List1.AddItem "endElement:" & sName
End Sub
```

For each handled event we write the event name to the list control along with the element name or character data.

Next, add the form load event handler as follows:

```
Private Sub Form_Load()
   Set m_oSAXParser = New SAXParser
   m_oSAXParser.parseString "<ProXML>Enjoy!</ProXML>"
End Sub
```

This code creates an instance of the SAX parser, then asks the parser to parse the text "<ProXML>Enjoy!</ProXML>". Run the code, and although I've increased the font size of my list control, the output you see should looks pretty similar to this:

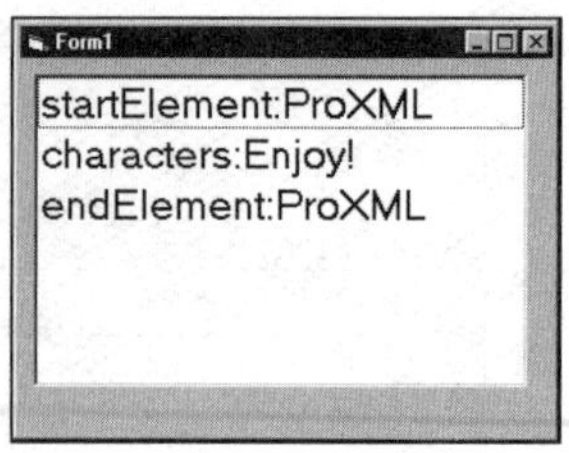

`LoadUserInfo` assumes the file `Users.XML` is in the current working directory.

If you want to, you can also make the parser process a file using the `parseFile()` method, which is what we'll use later:

```
m_oSAXParser.parseFile "c:\proxml\users.xml"
```

Now we've seen the parser we'll be using in action, and have discussed the SAX filter/transformation technique we are going to use to perform transformations, lets take a closer look at the other classes that actually implement everything.

The Transformation Engine Details

An XSLT style sheet is composed of templates and patterns. Each template effectively describes the markup and element content to be placed into the target file, and contains patterns that define an XPath that is used to drag information from the source document into the target. If we take the basic concepts of templates and patterns, we can build a transformation engine based upon them, whereby the template is some code contained within a class that is invoked when a given pattern (XPath) is matched against the XPath/SAX event stream discussed. For example:

```
Private Sub m_oSAXParser_startElement(sXPath As String, _
                                      sElementName As String, _
                                      oAttribs As SAXLib.ISAXAttributeList)

   If sXPath = "/Books/Book" then
      SomeClass.startElement sXPath, sElementName, oAttribs
   End if

   If sXPath = "/Books/Book/Reviews/Review" then
      AnotherClass.startElement sXPath, sElementName, oAttribs
   End if
End Sub
```

The mapping of events to class module applies to all SAX events, such as `endElement` and `characters`:

```
Private Sub m_oSAXParser_characters(sXPath as String, _
                                    ByVal sCharacters As String, _
                                    ByVal iLength As Long)

   If sXPath = "/Books/Book" then
      SomeClass.characters sXPath, sCharacters
   End if
```

```
    If sXPath = "/Books/Book/Reviews/Review" then
       AnotherClass.startElement sXPath, sElementName, oAttribs
    End if
End Sub
```

Obviously we don't want to write this repetitive matching and event forward code manually for every application we write, so we'll build this functionality into the BCIS transformation engine.

We've covered the basic functionality of the BCIS, so let's start to write the code to implement the system.

Creating the BCIS

Fire up and create a new Standard EXE project, and add a reference to the **Vivid ActiveSAX type library**.

SAX XPath Filter Interface – ITemplate

For the transformation engine to be able to generically invoke our template handlers, we need to define an interface (a VB class module that defines methods but has no implementation) that describes all the events a class module acting as a template can expect to receive. The transformation engine will use this interface to invoke the methods of the template handler without knowing what concrete class actually implements the interface.

Add a new class module and change its name to `ITemplate`, and add the following code:

```
Option Explicit

' start of the XPath

Sub startElement(sXPath As String, _
                 sElementName As String, _
                 oAttribs As SAXAttributeList)

End Sub

' characters within the XPath

Sub characters(sXPath As String, _
               sData As String)

End Sub

' end of the XPath

Sub endElement(sXPath As String, _
               sElementName As String)

End Sub

' start of document
```

```
Sub startDocument()

End Sub

' end of document

Sub endDocument()

End Sub
```

In Java or C/C++ you would just define an abstract class here.

Next, add a class module called `CXMLCatalogTransform` and add the line to the code module to tell VB it implements the `ITemplate` interface:

```
Implements ITemplate
```

Now that we've declared that the class module that implements an interface, the object combo contains an entry for `ITemplate`. Select it and you'll see the event combo lists all of its methods:

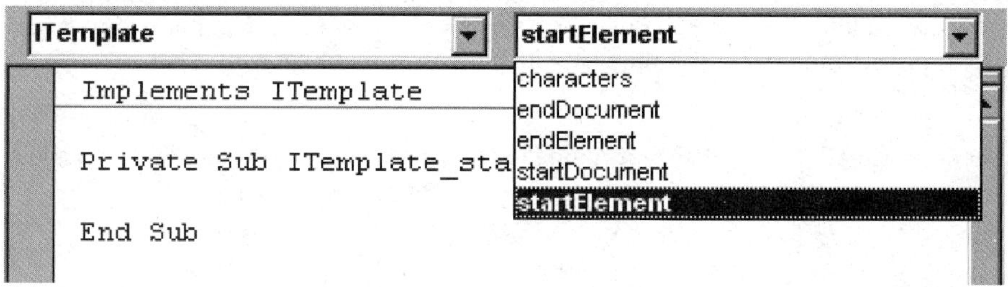

Select each of the methods in the event combo and VB should add the subroutine prototype to the class module:

```
Private Sub ITemplate_characters(sXPath As String, _
                                 sData As String)

End Sub

Private Sub ITemplate_endDocument()

End Sub

Private Sub ITemplate_endElement(sXPath As String, _
                                 sElementName As String)

End Sub

Private Sub ITemplate_startDocument()
```

```
End Sub

Private Sub ITemplate_startElement(sXPath As String, _
                                   sElementName As String, _
                                   oAttribs As SAXLib.ISAXAttributeList)

End Sub
```

Change the `characters()` method to include a message box displaying the event name and the passed XPath:

```
Private Sub ITemplate_characters(sXPath As String, _
                                 sData As String)
   MsgBox "CXMLCatalogTransform: xpath=" & sXPath & " data=" & sData
End Sub
```

Next, to demonstrate how polymorphism and interfaces work in VB, add the following subroutine to the code module for `Form1`:

```
Sub DummyCharactersEvent(oTemplate As ITemplate)
   oTemplate.characters "/Catalog/Book/Title", "ProXML"
End Sub
```

This routine is passed a reference to the interface, then invokes the `characters` event passing an XPath of `"/Catalog/Book/Title"` and some data, in this case `"ProXML"`. In the real BCIS these will be built based upon the XML source document, but for now we've simply hard-coded the values to demonstrate how the engine will work. The code that invokes the `characters` method does not know what *class* of object has implemented the interface, which means that it can polymorphically invoke the `characters` method of *any* class of object. This is very powerful, because new class modules for new XPaths can be added at any time without having to change the code. To demonstrate this, add a button to the form, double click on it and change the event handler like this:

```
Private Sub Command1_Click()
   Dim oXMLCatalogTransform As New CXMLCatalogTransform
   DummyCharactersEvent oXMLCatalogTransform
End Sub
```

The code creates an instance of our `CXMLCatalogTransform` class then invokes the subroutines to invoke the `characters` method of the `ITemplate` interface. If you run the project and click the button you should see the following message box, which is created by the instance of the `CXMLCatalogTransform` class:

The key point to note is that even though the `DummyCharactersEvent()` method accepts a parameter of the type `ITemplate`, VB asks the `CXMLCatalogTransform` object for the `ITemplate` interface and then invokes the function on our behalf. To show how powerful this is, add a class module called `CHTMLCatalogTransform`, copy all the code from `CXMLCatalogTransform` module but change the message box call in `ITemplate_characters()` as follows:

```
Private Sub ITemplate_characters(sXPath As String, _
                                  sData As String)
   MsgBox "CHTMLCatalogTransform: xpath=" & sXPath & " data=" & sData
End Sub
```

Go back to the event handler for the button, change the code to create an instance of this class and invoke `DummyCharacterEvents()` passing the newly created object:

```
Private Sub Command1_Click()
   Dim oXMLCatalogTransform As New CXMLCatalogTransform
   DummyCharactersEvent oXMLCatalogTransform

   Dim oHTMLCatalogTransform As New CHTMLCatalogTransform
   DummyCharactersEvent oHTMLCatalogTransform
End Sub
```

Run the project, click the button and you should see the original message box followed by the message box created by the `CHTMLCatalogTransform` class:

This shows that our simple function can invoke the same function of two different classes of object, and demonstrates the basic principles upon which the extensibility module for our transformation engine will work. Of course, the transformation engine will not be hard-coded, but instead will allow you to register an XPath and an associated template handler that is invoked when the XPath is detected within the SAX event stream.

Although we do not do it in this case study, you could quite easily move each transformation class module into its own ActiveX DLL, thereby creating a truly extensible system.

Pattern Matching

To associate XPaths with template handlers we use the classes `CPattern` and `CPatternCollection`. `CPattern` holds the XPath string, and also contains a reference to the template handler:

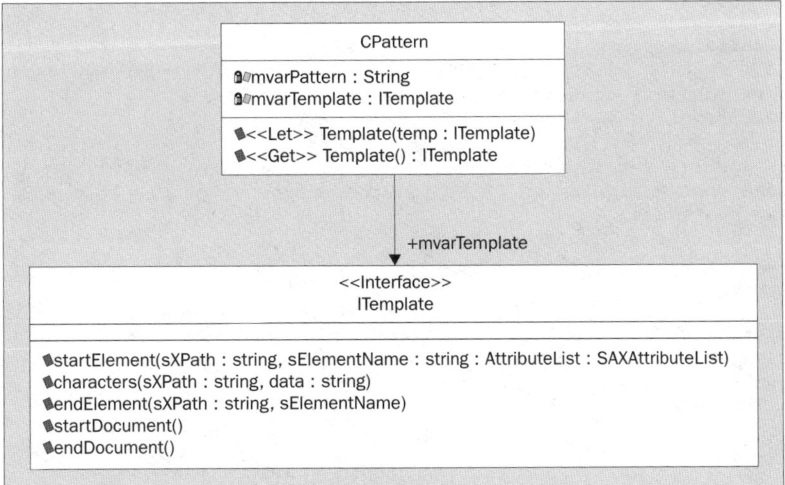

There is no reason why a single template handler could not be responsible for processing one or more patterns, and vice versa, but for this case study a pattern will only be associated with one template. Just to recap, the `CPattern` class is associated with the interface `ITemplate`, which removes the need for any reference to a concrete class – giving us great extensibility.

As with the `CUser` class, zero or more `CPattern` classes are held in the `CPatternCollection` class:

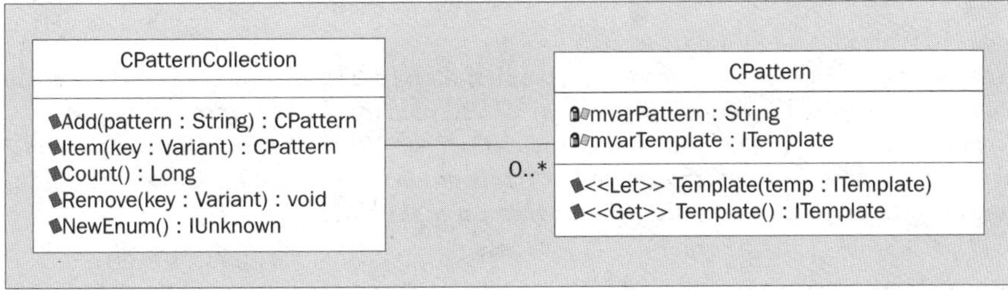

Creating CPattern and CPatternCollection

To create these classes we'll use the class builder.

If you haven't encountered this tool before, it is available through the Add-Ins *menu – you may need to use the* Add-In Manager *menu option to install it. The class builder is fairly self explanatory, and allows you to create classes with specified properties and methods very quickly – without worrying about typing errors so much. It provides a number of other useful functions, such as the quick creation of collections as we will see later, but the majority of these are beyond the scope of this chapter.*

Add the class module for `CPattern`, and use the class builder to add the properties and methods shown above. Update the project using *Ctrl-S* and your class module for `CPattern` should look like this (note that this code has been reformatted slightly, but only in terms of indentation and line-wrapping):

```
Option Explicit

'local variable(s) to hold property value(s)
Private m_Pattern As String 'local copy
'local variable(s) to hold property value(s)
Private m_Template As ITemplate 'local copy

Public Property Set Template(ByVal vData As ITemplate)
   ' used when assigning an Object to the property, on the left side of a
   ' Set statement.
   ' Syntax: Set x.Template = Form1
   Set m_Template = vData
End Property

Public Property Get Template() As ITemplate
   ' used when retrieving value of a property, on the right side of an assignment.
   ' Syntax: Debug.Print X.Template
   Set Template = m_Template
End Property

Public Property Let Pattern(ByVal vData As String)
   ' used when assigning a value to the property, on the left side of
   ' an assignment.
   ' Syntax: X.Pattern = 5
   m_Pattern = vData
End Property

Public Property Get Pattern() As String
   ' used when retrieving value of a property, on the right side of an assignment.
   ' Syntax: Debug.Print X.Pattern
   Pattern = m_Pattern
End Property
```

Note that I've manually added the line "`Option Explicit`" to all of the VB class modules. By adding that line, VB ensures that all variables are defined before they can be referenced/used. This is good practice, because otherwise VB will dynamically declare them when they are first used, which can lead to errors not being detected until runtime, and if you're only an only average speller like me that's a nightmare!

Create the `CPatternCollection` class by using the File | New | Collection menu option of the class builder, specifying `CPattern` as the Collection of parameter.

The transformation engine class will contain the patterns collection, and will provide an `AddPattern()` method for populating it:

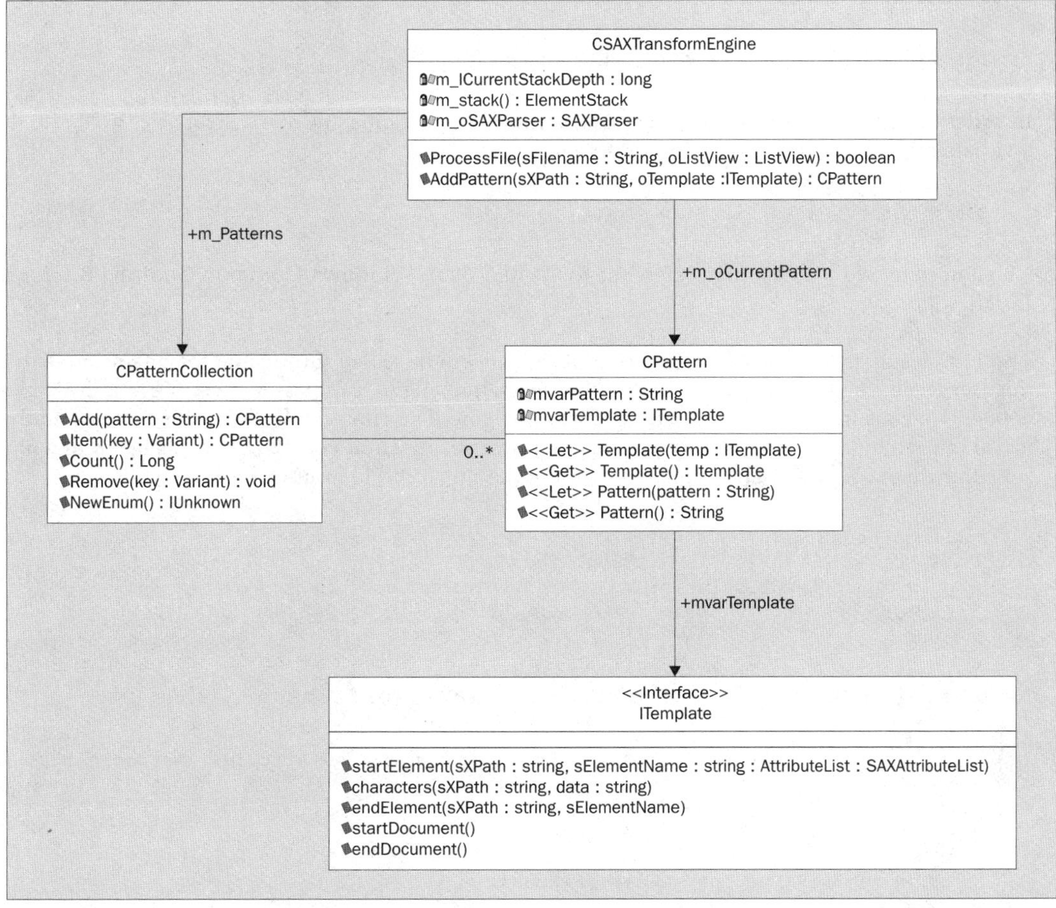

Add the class module `CSAXTransformEngine` and add a private member variable called `m_Patterns` of the type `CPatternCollection`, along with a method `AddPattern` used for indirectly populating it:

```
Private m_Patterns As New CPatternCollection

Function AddPattern(sXPath As String, oTemplate As ITemplate) As CPattern
   Set AddPattern = m_Patterns.Add(sXPath, oTemplate)
End Function
```

This pattern collection will be used by the transformation engine to determine if the various SAX events that occur whilst processing the source XML document should be routed to a template handler.

Adding the SAX Parser

Next, we need to integrate the SAX parser into the transformation engine class, so declare an instance of the SAX parser as before:

```
Dim WithEvents m_oSAXParser As SAXParser
```

In order to give the user feedback from the transformation engine and show errors etc. we'll also declare a variable for holding a reference to a list view:

```
Dim m_oListView As ListView
```

You'll need to add a component reference to the Microsoft Windows Common Controls 6.0 for the ListView.

The ListView is accessed by a logging routine, which will be called throughout the engine code to give the user feedback. The code that uses the transformation engine can pass a reference to a ListView it creates, which is then used by the transformation engine. I've chosen a ListView for this case study for visual impact, but by encapsulating the logging using this function you can easily change it to a file or something more suitable. The implementation of the `LogLine()` routine looks like this:

```
Sub LogLine(sLineToLog As String)
   If Not (m_oListView Is Nothing) Then
      m_oListView.ListItems.Add , , sLineToLog
   End If
End Sub
```

Next, we add the `ProcessFile()` method to the `CSAXTransformEngine` class:

```
Function ProcessFile(sFilename As String, oListView As ListView) As Boolean
   Dim bRC As Boolean
   Set m_oListView = oListView
   Set m_oSAXParser = New SAXParser

   bRC = m_oSAXParser.parseFile(sFilename)

   If bRC = False Then
      LogLine "  File is not well formed"
      ProcessFile = False
   Else
      ProcessFile = True
   End If
End Function
```

The `ProcessFile()` method causes the transformation engine to parse the specified file and invoke any template handlers based upon the patterns that have been added to the `CPatternCollection` using the `AddPattern()` method. The function stores the ListView in our `m_oListView` variable for access by the `LogLine()` subroutine (to give user feedback), creates an instance of the SAX parser and then asks it to parse the file. If the XML parsing fails for any reason, we tell the user by calling our `LogLine()` routine, which in turn adds an item to the ListView supplied in the `oListView` parameter.

To check this code works, let's update our form to include the ListView. At this point we'll add all the controls that will make up the final GUI, so we need to add component references to:

- Windows Tabbed Dialog Control 6.0
- Microsoft Internet Controls

Remove the command button we added to the form earlier along with the event handler code. Add a tab control (leave the default name VB gives it) that takes up around 2/3 of the form height, and place two command buttons and two text edit boxes as follows:

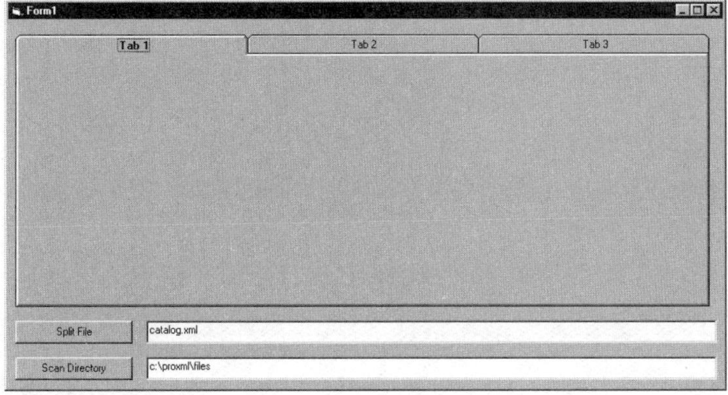

Note that I'm using the default names VB gives to almost all the controls you drop on the form, so don't worry about changing them unless it is specified in the text.

The button with the text Split File should be give the name `SplitFile` and the edit box next to it should be given the name `FileToProcess`.

The button with the text Scan Directory should be give the name `ScanDirectoy`; the edit box next to it should be given the name `ScanPath`.

Bring up the properties for the tab control, call the first tab Web View, the second tab Log Messages, and delete the third tab by bringing the tab controls property page, and reducing the tab count to 2. Select the first tab and drop a WebBrowser control onto it. Underneath this control place a combo box with the style `Dropdown List`:

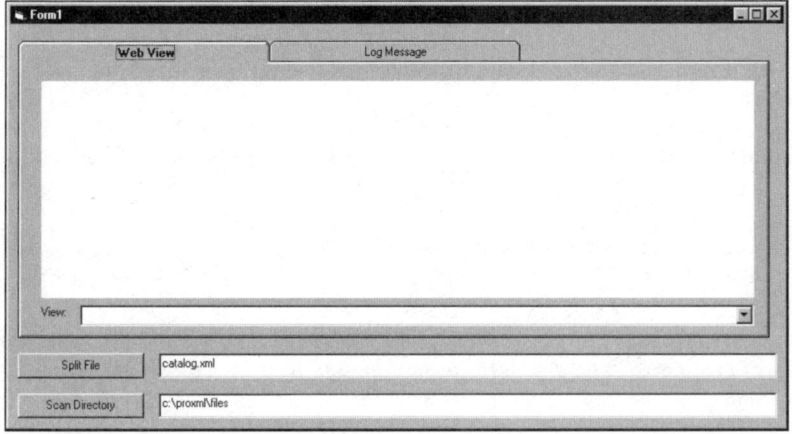

The web browser control will be used to view the transformation we create, with the combo box populated with all the filenames that are created by the transformation engine.

Select the second tab and drop a `ListView` control (not a `listbox`) on to it giving the control the name `LogWindow`:

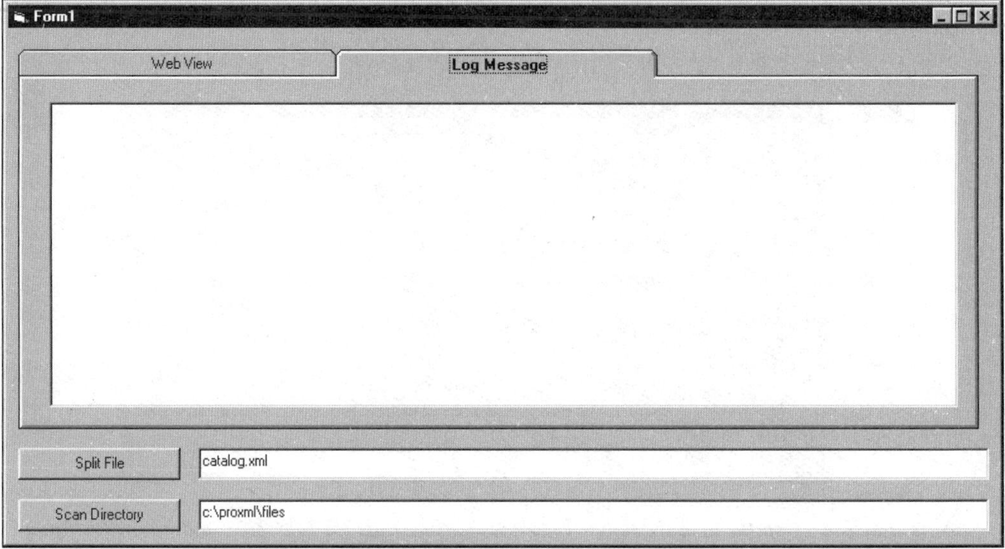

That's our GUI complete. The Split File button will enable us to ask the transformation engine to process a single XML file. The Scan Directory button will enable us to scan a directory for all XML files, and have each one processed.

Tracking Element Nesting to Create XPaths

The SAX transformation engine keeps track of the event nesting within the SAX event stream by using a simple array of `ElementStack` structures:

```
Private Type ElementStack
   sName As String
End Type
```

This stack will be used to build an XPath for each SAX event that is forwarded to a transformation class module's handlers.

Add this definition to the class module for `CSAXTransformEngine`, and below it place these two variables:

```
Dim m_lCurrentStackDepth As Long
Dim m_stack(100) As ElementStack
```

The array size of 100 is just an arbitrary value I've chosen that could be increased, decreased, or replaced by using `ReDim` depending upon your requirements. 100 should suffice for most XML documents.

When the engine first starts the current stack depth (`m_lCurrentStackDepth`) is set to zero, and is increase when a `startElement` event occurs:

```
Private Sub m_oSAXParser_startElement(ByVal sName As String, _
                                ByVal pAttributeList As SAXLib.ISAXAttributeList)
   ' Add this element to the stack

   m_stack(m_lCurrentStackDepth).sName = sName
   m_lCurrentStackDepth = m_lCurrentStackDepth + 1
End Sub
```

Just before the stack depth is increased, the name of the element is placed onto the stack.

The stack depth is decreased when an `endElement` event occurs:

```
Private Sub m_oSAXParser_endElement(ByVal sName As String)
   m_lCurrentStackDepth = m_lCurrentStackDepth - 1
End Sub
```

At any point in the event stream, the current XPath can be built by simply enumerating the stack. We do this using the `BuildXPath` function, that places the XPath into the variable `m_sCurXPath`:

```
Dim m_sCurXPath as String

' Builds an XPath based upon the current element nesting

Sub BuildXPath()
   Dim l As Long

   m_sCurXPath = "/"

   For l = 0 To m_lCurrentStackDepth - 1
      m_sCurXPath = m_sCurXPath + m_stack(l).sName
      If l <> m_lCurrentStackDepth - 1 Then
         m_sCurXPath = m_sCurXPath + "/"
      End If
   Next l
End Sub
```

`m_sCurXPath` is declared as a global variable, and is used when forwarding events like `characters` to template handlers.

To see the XPaths within the SAX event stream in the log window as they are built up, we need to call the `BuildXPath()` function from within the `m_oSAXParser_startElement()` method and write the `m_sCurXPath` to the log window using the `LogLine()` function:

```
Private Sub m_oSAXParser_startElement(ByVal sName As String, _
                                ByVal pAttributeList As SAXLib.ISAXAttributeList)
   ' Add this element to the stack

   m_stack(m_lCurrentStackDepth).sName = sName
   m_lCurrentStackDepth = m_lCurrentStackDepth + 1

   BuildXPath
   LogLine "Start: " & m_sCurXPath

End Sub
```

To see this code in action, double click the Split File button and add the following code to the event handler:

```
Private Sub SplitFile_Click()
   Dim oFP As CSAXTransformEngine

   ' Create the Transform Engine
   Set oFP = New CSAXTransformEngine

   oFP.ProcessFile Me.FileToProcess.Text, Me.LogWindow
End Sub
```

This creates an instance of the transformation class and invokes the `ProcessFile()` method, passing in the filename specified in the first edit box, and a reference to the ListView to which the engine will log the XPaths. To make the log messages added by the transformation engine readable, we need to modify the `Form_Load()` event to set the ListView view to `lvwReport` and add a column:

```
Private Sub Form_Load()
   LogWindow.View = lvwReport
   LogWindow.ColumnHeaders.Add , , "Message", Me.ScaleWidth
End Sub
```

If we don't do this, the default icon view will be used and the text won't be very legible.

SAX+XPATH in Action!

Run the form, specify the path to `catalog.xml` (included with the downloadable code for this chapter available from http://www.wrox.com/) and hit the Split File button. You should see all of the XPaths listed:

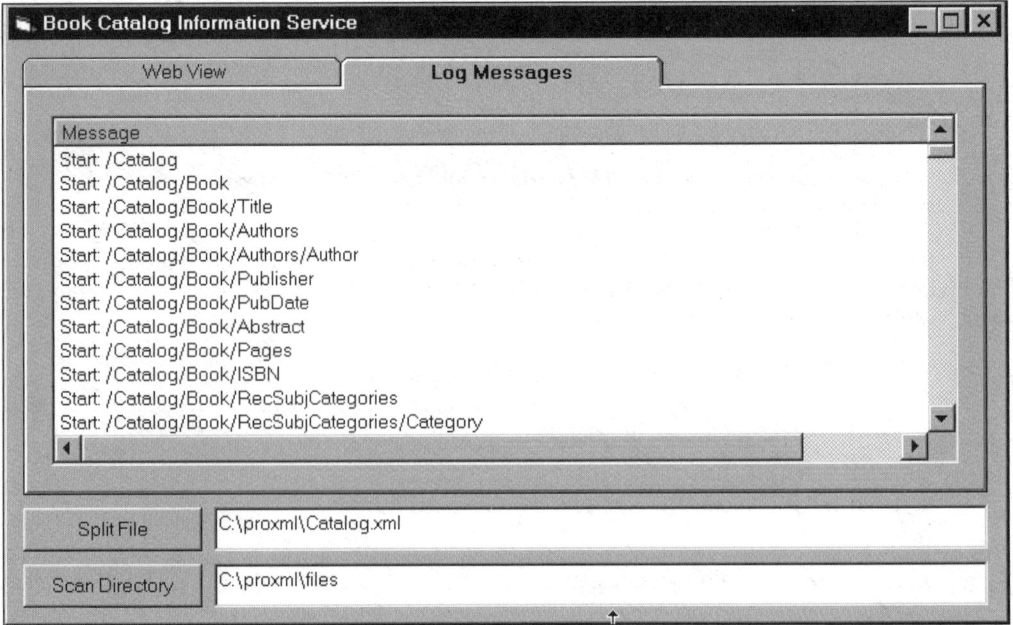

To get a more complete feel for the event stream, we'll modify `m_oSAXParser_endElement()` to display the XPath for an element when its close tag is reached:

```
Private Sub m_oSAXParser_endElement(ByVal sName As String)
   BuildXPath
   LogLine "End: " & m_sCurXPath

   m_lCurrentStackDepth = m_lCurrentStackDepth - 1
End Sub
```

And we'll also add the character event handler to log the XPath and character data:

```
Private Sub m_oSAXParser_characters(ByVal sCharacters As String, _
                                    ByVal iLength As Long)
   LogLine "characters: " & m_sCurXPath & " : " & sCharacters
End Sub
```

If we run the form again and parse the same file we can see a more complete picture of the SAX event stream extended with XPaths:

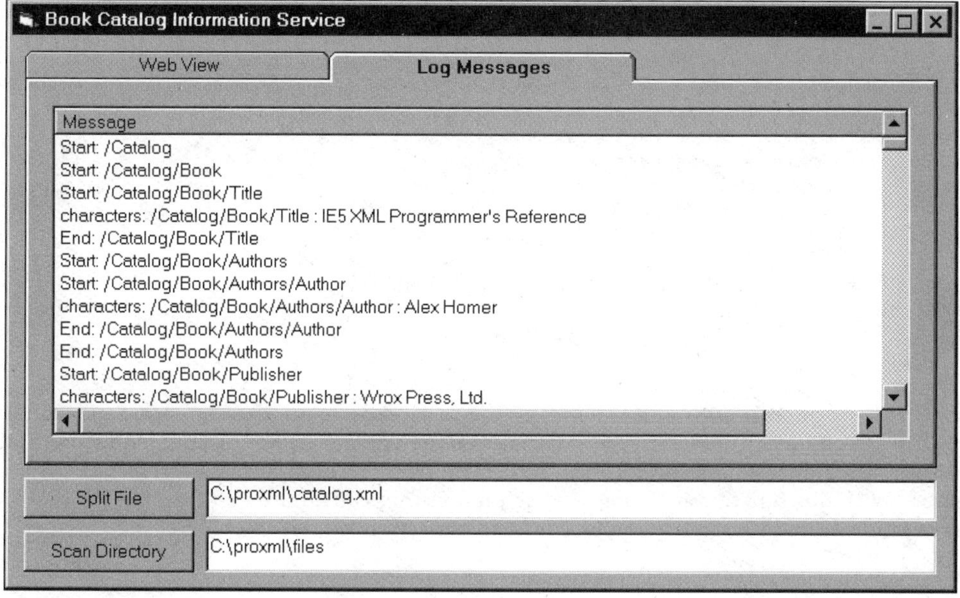

Checkpoint

Now we've seen:

- How the template handler class module functions can be invoked without any knowledge of the concrete class by using the `ITemplate` interface
- How we are going to associate XPaths with template handlers using `CPattern` and `CPatternCollection`
- How the SAX event stream is extended with an XPath

So it's time to link everything together.

MatchPatterns

The `MatchPatterns()` method is responsible for matching XPaths with template handlers by searching the `CPatternCollection` object held in the `m_Patterns` variable of `CSAXTransformEngine`. If a pattern is found, the `CPattern` object is placed in the member variable `m_oCurrentPattern`. Each of the SAX event handlers will check this variable, and unless the value is set to `Nothing`, it will forward the events to the associated template handler.

The pattern match code simply compares the current XPath against the `Pattern` property of the `CPattern` object. If they match *exactly*, or the Pattern property is "*" indicating it matches *all* XPaths the searching is successful. If you do use the "*" pattern make sure it is always the last item in the list, because searching stops once a match is found. The complete code for this method is shown here and should be added to the `CSAXTransformEngine` class:

```
Sub MatchPatterns()
   Dim Pattern As CPattern

   ' Build the current XPath
   BuildXPath

   '
   ' Match current XPath against configured template handlers
   '

   For Each Pattern In m_Patterns
      If m_sCurXPath = Pattern.Pattern Or Pattern.Pattern = "*" Then
         Set m_oCurrentPattern = Pattern
         Exit Sub   ' Searching ends!
      End If
   Next Pattern

   ' Clear the current pattern

   Set m_oCurrentPattern = Nothing
End Sub
```

The code calls the `BuildXPath()` function we've already seen, then enumerates each `CPattern` object in `m_Patterns` to determine if it matches the current XPath. If a match is found, the pattern is remembered and the routine exits. If no pattern is found, the current pattern variable is cleared. With this function in place, change the existing calls to `BuildXPath()` in the `startElement` and `endElement` event handlers as follows:

```
Private Sub m_oSAXParser_startElement(ByVal sName As String, _
                                ByVal pAttributeList As SAXLib.ISAXAttributeList)
   ' Add this element to the stack

   m_stack(m_lCurrentStackDepth).sName = sName
   m_lCurrentStackDepth = m_lCurrentStackDepth + 1

   MatchPatterns

   If Not (m_oCurrentPattern Is Nothing) Then
      m_oCurrentPattern.Template.startElement m_sCurXPath, sName, pAttributeList
   End If
End Sub
```

```
Private Sub m_oSAXParser_endElement(ByVal sName As String)
   MatchPatterns

   If Not (m_oCurrentPattern Is Nothing) Then
      m_oCurrentPattern.Template.endElement m_sCurXPath, sName
   End If
   m_lCurrentStackDepth = m_lCurrentStackDepth - 1
End Sub
```

Rather than logging the XPaths, these two event handlers now forward the event to the template handler associated with the current pattern if the `m_oCurrentPattern` object reference has been set. If the current pattern is not set, no action is taken. A similar change needs to be made to the characters event handler, except the `MatchPatterns()` method doesn't need to be called, because we know the element nesting only changes in the previous two events so the current path will already have been set:

```
Private Sub m_oSAXParser_characters(ByVal sCharacters As String, _
                                    ByVal iLength As Long)
   If Not (m_oCurrentPattern Is Nothing) Then
      m_oCurrentPattern.Template.characters m_sCurXPath, sCharacters
   End If
End Sub
```

For all this new code to compile, we need to add the `m_oCurrentPattern` variable definition to the `CSAXTransformClass` class module:

```
Dim m_stack(100) As ElementStack
Dim m_oListView As ListView
Dim m_oCurrentPattern As CPattern
Dim m_sCurXPath As String
```

In theory, we've now got the basics of the transformation engine implemented. To check it works, modify `SplitFile_Click()` to create an instance of the `CXMLCatalogTransform` class, and add an XPath pattern of `"/Catalog/Book/Title"` to the transformation engine using the `AddPattern()` method, passing a reference to the `CXMLCatalogTransform` object as the template handler:

```
Private Sub SplitFile_Click()
   Dim oFP As CSAXTransformEngine

   ' Create the Transform Engine
   Set oFP = New CSAXTransformEngine

   ' Create the XML catalog transform
   Dim oTransform As New CXMLCatalogTransform

   oFP.AddPattern "/Catalog/Book/Title", oTransform
   oFP.ProcessFile Me.FileToProcess.Text, Me.LogWindow
End Sub
```

Next, modify the CXMLCatalogTransform ITemplate_characters() event handler to display just the data and not the XPath, because we know the XPath will always be "/Catalog/Book/Title" – as that is what we specified to the AddPattern() call:

```
Private Sub ITemplate_characters(sXPath As String, sData As String)
   MsgBox sData
End Sub
```

Run the project as before and you should now see each book title in the XML file displayed in a message box. The transformation engine is providing us with all of the filtering of the XML source document, and only forwarding events with a specific XPath to the template handlers that we have defined. As can be seen from the characters event handler in the CXMLCatalogTransform class, this makes our code very simple and you're probably beginning to see the flexibility of this technique.

startDocument and endDocument

To finish off CSAXTransformEngine, we are going to implement the startDocument and endDocument SAX events and forward them to the template handlers just as we've done with startElement etc.

The startDocument event handler is invoked by the SAX parser when the processing of the XML document first starts. The code invokes the MatchPatterns() method to set the m_oCurrentPattern variable if a match is found. If a match is found we know it will always be "/" (the document root) because the stack will not yet contain any entries. If a pattern is found, the associated template handler's startDocument handler is invoked:

```
Private Sub m_oSAXParser_startDocument()
   MatchPatterns

   If Not (m_oCurrentPattern Is Nothing) Then
      If Not (m_oCurrentPattern.Template Is Nothing) Then
         m_oCurrentPattern.Template.startDocument
      End If
   End If
End Sub
```

The endDocument method is effectively identical except that the template handler's endDocument method is invoked:

```
Private Sub m_oSAXParser_endDocument()
   MatchPatterns

   If Not (m_oCurrentPattern Is Nothing) Then
      If Not (m_oCurrentPattern.Template Is Nothing) Then
         m_oCurrentPattern.Template.endDocument
      End If
   End If
End Sub
```

Load Subscriber Information from Users.XML

What we've really covered up to this point is the basic design of what the BCIS will do, and the implementation of the transformation engine. Now the transformation engine is written, we can use it to create the BCIS pretty quickly, with very little coding effort.

The first requirement is to load the subscriber information into memory. This tells the BCIS who it must send the book catalog information to, and what categories of book information each subscriber is interested in. To refresh your memory, the XML users file (`users.xml`, downloadable with the rest of the code) looks like:

```
<?xml version="1.0" ?>
<!-- This file defines the register users for the book notification service -->
<Users>

  <User>
    <Name>Richard Anderson</Name>
    <OutputFile>c:\proxml\RJA.HTML</OutputFile>
    <Email>rja@arpsolutions.demon.co.uk</Email>
    <DeliveryFormat>HTML</DeliveryFormat>
    <Category1>XML</Category1>
    <Category2>ATL</Category2>
  </User>
  ...

</Users>
```

As already discussed, the `CLoadUserInfo` class will load this file into the `CUserCollection`, resulting in each user being represented by a `CUser` object:

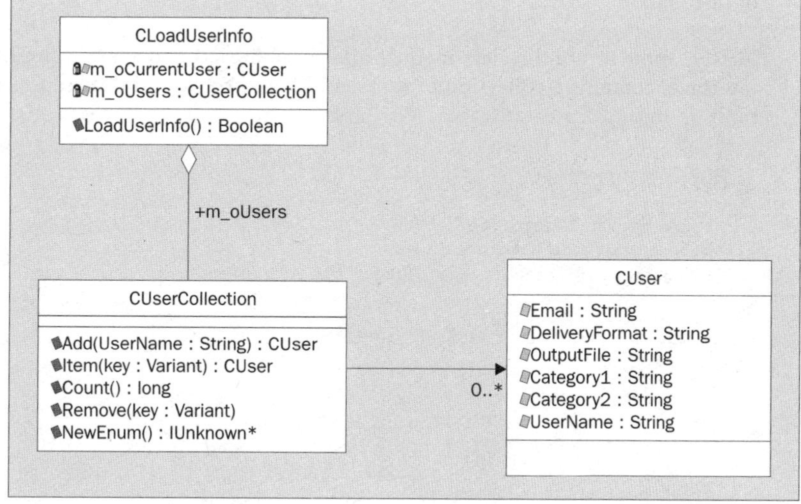

Add the class modules for `CUser` and `CUserCollection` just as we did with `CPattern` and `CPatternCollection` using the class builder. For the user class module you'll need to add the `String` properties `Email`, `DeliveryFormat`, `OutputFile`, `Category1`, `Category2`, and `UserName` as shown in the previous diagram. For the `CUserCollection` class module modify the `Add()` method of the `CUserCollection`, removing the `Category1`, `Category2`, `OutputFile`, `DeliveryFormat`, and `Email` parameters from the function prototype, and any references inside the function, so the code ends up like this:

```
Public Function Add(UserName As String, Optional sKey As String) As CUser
   'create a new object
   Dim objNewMember As CUser
   Set objNewMember = New CUser

   'set the properties passed into the method
   objNewMember.UserName = UserName
   If Len(sKey) = 0 Then
      mCol.Add objNewMember
   Else
      mCol.Add objNewMember, sKey
   End If

   'return the object created
   Set Add = objNewMember
   Set objNewMember = Nothing
End Function
```

We've removed all the parameters simply because they will not all be available when we initially create the `CUser` object, but class builder adds them because they are all properties of `CUser`. Each property will be set as XPaths are matched in the input stream inside the `ITemplate_characters()` method. For example, when the XPath "`/Users/User/Email`" is matched we'll set the `Email` property. The `CUser` object itself will be created when the XPath is "`/Users/User/Name`", when we'll also set the `UserName` property.

Add the class module `CLoadUserInfo`, but don't use class builder as we'll walk through the creation of this class.

Firstly, at the top of the class module add these lines that declare it implements the `ITemplate` interface, contains a collection of users, and keeps track of the current user (subscriber) profile being built up in `m_oCurrentUser`:

```
Option Explicit

Implements ITemplate
Dim m_oCurrentUser As CUser
Private m_oUsers As New CUserCollection
```

Next, add the `LoadUserInfo()` method:

```
Function LoadUserInfo() As Boolean
   Dim oFP As New CSAXTransformEngine
   Dim oPattern As CPattern

   ' Match all elements
   Set oPattern = oFP.AddPattern("*", Me)
   LoadUserInfo = oFP.ProcessFile("users.xml", Nothing)
End Function
```

As before this creates the transformation engine, registers a pattern and template handler (the template handler is the `CLoadUserInfo` class itself) and then asks for the file `Users.XML` to be processed. Unlike the previous template handler we've used the wildcard "`*`" pattern. This means that every single SAX event will be appended with an XPath and routed to the template handler. We've taken this approach because the XML file being processed is quite simple, and having multiple class modules just to load the user information would be overkill.

Next, add all of the empty event handlers for `ITemplate` as we've seen previously, then modify the `ITemplate_characters()` method as follows:

```
Private Sub ITemplate_characters(sXPath As String, sData As String)
   Select Case sXPath
      Case "/Users/User/Name"
         Set m_oCurrentUser = m_oUsers.Add(sData)

      Case "/Users/User/OutputFile"
         m_oCurrentUser.OutputFile = sData

      Case "/Users/User/Category1"
         m_oCurrentUser.Category1 = sData

      Case "/Users/User/Category2"
         m_oCurrentUser.Category2 = sData

      Case "/Users/User/Email"
         m_oCurrentUser.Email = sData

      Case "/Users/User/DeliveryFormat"
         m_oCurrentUser.DeliveryFormat = sData
   End Select
End Sub
```

This method then creates a new `CUser` object by calling the `Add()` method of `CUserCollection` when the XPath `"/Users/User/Name"` is matched, assigning the return object to `m_oCurrentUser`. For all of the other XPaths matched, the character data is copied into the property of the current user object as represented by `m_oCurrentUser`.

To enable other objects to access the loaded user information we add a property called `Users`:

```
Property Get Users() As CUserCollection
   Set Users = m_oUsers
End Property
```

To test out the `CLoadUserInfo` class add an event handler for the Scan Directory button and add the following code:

```
Private Sub ScanDirectory_Click()
   Dim oUser As CUser
   Dim oLoadUsers As New CLoadUserInfo
   oLoadUsers.LoadUserInfo

   For Each oUser In oLoadUsers.Users
      Me.LogWindow.ListItems.Add , , "User=" & oUser.UserName
   Next oUser
End Sub
```

Run the project and click the button and you'll see each of the user names listed within the log window as follows:

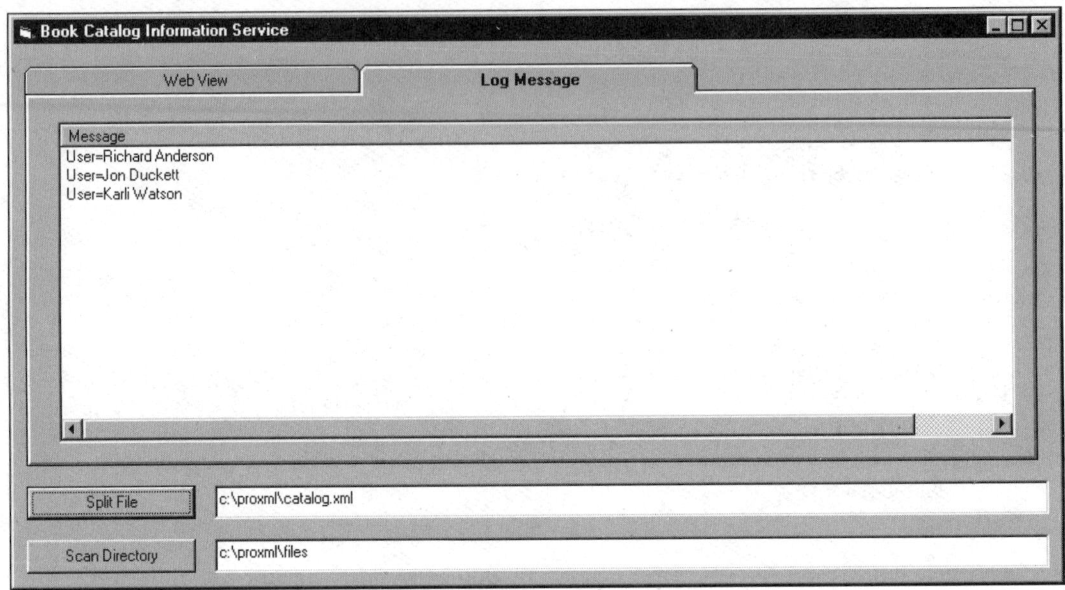

If you get an error, you need to double check that the `Users.xml` file parsed by `CLoadUserInfo` is in the current directory as the code used a relative path:

```
LoadUserInfo = oFP.ProcessFile("users.xml", Nothing)
```

Alternatively you can just qualify the path as shown below:

```
LoadUserInfo = oFP.ProcessFile("c:\proxml\users.xml", Nothing)
```

Now that we've loaded the user information, the next step is to transform the XML source document based upon each user's categories and preferred output format: XML or HTML. To do this we need to go back to the `CXMLCatalogTransform` and `CHTMLCatalogTransform` classes we implemented earlier and actually write the code to perform the transformations.

The XML to XML Transformation

The XML to XML transformation class, `CXMLCatalogTransform`, looks like this:

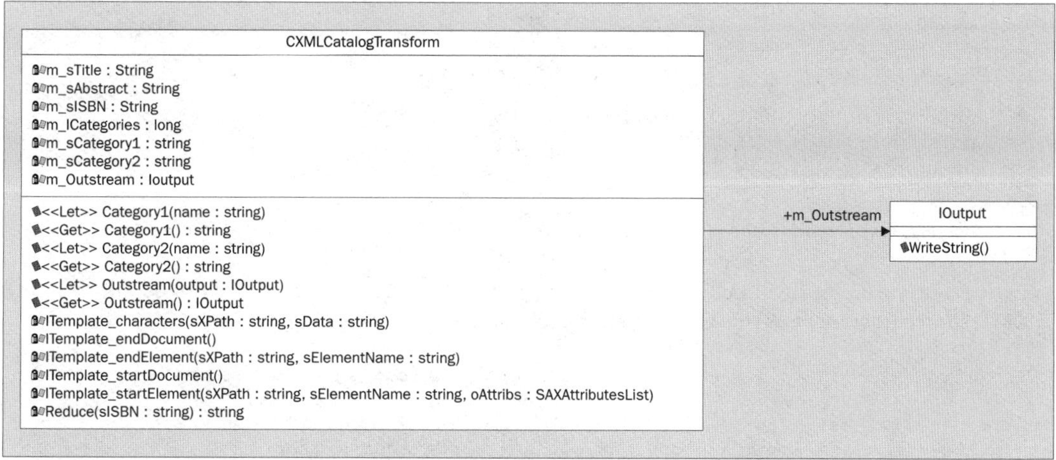

The properties `Category1` and `Category2` are set to tell the transformation class what book categories should be matched from the source XML document. Any books that do not match these categories are simply ignored. Books that match are written to the output stream.

Modify the code in the `CXMLCatalogTransform` module we created earlier, declaring the member variables and property access methods as follows (you could also do this with the class builder tool):

```
Option Explicit

Implements ITemplate

'
' Define temporary storage for book info
'

Dim m_sTitle As String
Dim m_sAbstract As String
Dim m_sISBN As String
Dim m_lCategories As Long
Private m_sCategory1 As String
Private m_sCategory2 As String
Private m_Outstream As IOutput

Public Property Set Outstream(ByVal vData As IOutput)
   Set m_Outstream = vData
End Property

Public Property Get Outstream() As IOutput
   Set Outstream = m_Outstream
End Property

Public Property Let Category2(ByVal vData As String)
   m_sCategory2 = vData
End Property

Public Property Get Category2() As String
   Category2 = m_sCategory2
End Property
```

```
Public Property Let Category1(ByVal vData As String)
   m_sCategory1 = vData
End Property

Public Property Get Category1() As String
   Category1 = m_sCategory1
End Property
```

The new implementations of the `ITemplate` *methods are shown over the following pages.*

The private variables `m_sTitle`, `m_sAbstract`, and `m_sISBN` are used to store details from the XML source document as the `ITemplate_characters` event handler is called:

```
Private Sub ITemplate_characters(sXPath As String, sData As String)
   ' Check filters
   If sXPath = "/Catalog/Book/RecSubjCategories/Category" Then
      If sData = m_sCategory1 Or sData = m_sCategory2 Then
         m_lCategories = m_lCategories + 1
      End If
   End If

   If sXPath = "/Catalog/Book/Title" Then
      m_sTitle = sData
   End If

   If sXPath = "/Catalog/Book/ISBN" Then
      m_sISBN = sData
   End If

   If sXPath = "/Catalog/Book/Abstract" Then
      m_sAbstract = sData
   End If
End Sub
```

The first XPath checked by the routine is `"/Catalog/Book/RecSubjCategories/Category"`. If this is found, the recommended category for the book is checked against the current filters. If a match is found then the variable `m_lCategories` is increased by one. Each book can have many recommended categories, so the `m_lCategories` variable is used to determine how many matches have been found for the current book. When the end of a book is detected in the `ITemplate_endElement()` method this variable is checked, and if it's not equal to zero then the book information is written to the output stream:

```
Private Sub ITemplate_endElement(sXPath As String, sElementName As String)
   If sXPath = "/Catalog/Book" Then
      If m_lCategories <> 0 Then
         m_Outstream.WriteString "<Book>"
         m_Outstream.WriteString "<Title>" & m_sTitle & "</Title>"
         m_Outstream.WriteString "<AmazonURL>" & _
            "http://www.amazon.com/exec/obidos/ASIN/" & Reduce(m_sISBN) & _
            "</AmazonURL>"
         m_Outstream.WriteString "<Abstract>" & m_sAbstract & "</Abstract>"
         m_Outstream.WriteString "</Book>"
      End If
   End If
End Sub
```

The first important point to note about this code is that we are building the output XML as text using simple `WriteString()` statements. Because we are using a SAX parser for processing the source document this makes a lot of sense. If we chose to create the output document using DOM objects we'd potentially run into memory problems for large output files, and we'd certainly use a lot more processor time because creating DOM objects has an associated overhead. Overall, this approach is far better for the BCIS and is around 3 times faster than using DOM objects.

This code does not check for XML reserved characters such as ampersands; you would need to do this for live production code.

We could have used a `Boolean` value rather than a `long` for the category matching, but I figured it might be nice for the user to be able define a minimum number of categories for a match. The `Reduce()` function, called when writing the URL for Amazon, simply ensures the ISBN does not contain hyphens – these do exist within the input stream, but are not compatible with the Amazon web site URLs. The code simply enumerates the input string removing any hyphens:

```
Function Reduce(ISBN As String) As String
   Dim l As Long
   Dim s As String

   For l = 1 To Len(ISBN)
      If Mid(ISBN, l, 1) <> "-" Then
         s = s + Mid(ISBN, l, 1)
      End If
   Next l

   Reduce = s
End Function
```

The link that is added for Amazon could be moved into a subroutine. Had we decided to support multiple advertisers I would have done this, but for only one entry the inline code is fine.

We need to ensure the `m_lCategories` variable is reset to zero when a new book is processed, so we reset it in the `ITemplate_startElement` method when the XPath `"/Catalog/Book/RecSubjCategories"` is detected. If we forgot to reset the counter, all books after the first successful match would appear in the output stream – which wouldn't make our subscribers very happy! As all book categories are defined as child elements of the `<RecSubjCategories>` element the approach taken here is a good way of resetting the value, although we could also reset the value in the `endElement` event handler. The code for resetting the value is shown here:

```
Private Sub ITemplate_startElement(sXPath As String, _
                                   sElementName As String, _
                                   oAttribs As SAXLib.ISAXAttributeList)
   ' If recommended subject categories start element:
   ' reset matched catagories count

   If sXPath = "/Catalog/Book/RecSubjCategories" Then
      m_lCategories = 0
   End If
End Sub
```

The approach of buffering various data elements from the input stream and then writing them out in one go is the only way in which SAX based *filtering* of XML data can work. It is not possible to seek back into the input stream (access events that have previously occurred), and if we started to write out elements to the output stream before we checked the book's categories matched the filter, we would have to somehow undo what we've written already – which is not a good approach. You could create the output for each book but write it to temporary variables (or a very small DOM), writing it out once your happy it matches the current filter, but the approach used here is fine for this case study.

The `m_Outstream` variable as shown earlier is a reference to the interface `IOutput`, which has a single method called `WriteString()`. By introducing the same polymorphic behavior we used with `ITemplate`, our transformation classes can write output to any media: files, memory, sockets, etc.

Add a class module called `IOutput` and change the code module so that it looks like this:

```
Option Explicit

Sub WriteString(sData As String)

End Sub
```

We'll implement this interface shortly.

All XML documents can only have one root element. So far we've only seen the code to write the `<Books>` elements, so we need to create the root element. We do this by implementing the `startDocument` and `endDocument` event handlers.

The `startDocument` event handler for `CXMLCatalogTransform` is written like this:

```
Private Sub ITemplate_startDocument()
   m_Outstream.WriteString "<?xml version='1.0' ?>"
   m_Outstream.WriteString "<Catalog>"
   m_Outstream.WriteString "<Notes>"
   m_Outstream.WriteString "Filters: " & m_sCategory1 & " , " & m_sCategory2
   m_Outstream.WriteString "</Notes>"
   m_Outstream.WriteString "<Books>"
End Sub
```

The XML declaration and root start tag is written out, along with the `<Notes>` element that details the filters used to create the file. The last line writes the start tag for the `<Books>` element, which contains all book matches.

The `endDocument` event handler fires when the end of source XML document is reached, so the code closes the `<Books>` element and the root element `<Catalog>`:

```
Private Sub ITemplate_endDocument()
   m_Outstream.WriteString "</Books>"
   m_Outstream.WriteString "</Catalog>"
End Sub
```

With the XML transformation class completed, we can add a method to our main form to help us invoke the XML to XML transformation for a given user, `PerformXMLToXMLTransform()`:

```
Sub PerformXMLToXMLTransform(oUser As CUser, sFilename As String)
   Dim oFP As CSAXTransformEngine
   Dim oPattern As CPattern
   Dim oTemplate As CXMLCatalogTransform
   Dim oFSO As New FileSystemObject

   ' Create the Transform Engine
   Set oFP = New CSAXTransformEngine

   ' Create the Template Class
   Set oTemplate = New CXMLCatalogTransform
   Set oTemplate.Outstream = Me

   ' Set the filters for this users transformation
   oTemplate.Category1 = oUser.Category1
   oTemplate.Category2 = oUser.Category2

   ' Match all elements
   Set oPattern = oFP.AddPattern("*", oTemplate)

   Set m_oOutStream = oFSO.CreateTextFile(oUser.OutputFile)
   oFP.ProcessFile sFilename, Me.LogWindow

   Me.Combo1.AddItem oUser.OutputFile

   m_oOutstream.Close
End Sub
```

The method takes a `CUser` object and the input XML file to process. The `CUser` object provides the details for transformation (such as the format and output filename). The code transformation engine is created, the template handler is created, and the template handler is given the output interface (`IOutput`) discussed earlier, to which it should write all output:

```
   Set oTemplate.Outstream = Me
```

As the code shows, the `IOutput` interface is implemented by the form, so we have to add the following line to the top of the main form:

```
Implements IOutput
```

And implement the write string method:

```
Private Sub IOutput_WriteString(sData As String)
   m_oOutstream.Write sData
End Sub
```

The `m_oOutstream` variable is defined as a `TextStream` object, which is part of the Microsoft Scripting Runtime type library, so you'll need to add a reference to that type library for the project. Once added, declare this object at the top of the form code module:

```
Dim m_oOutstream As Scripting.TextStream
```

This is then set just before the code invokes the process function of the transformation engine:

```
   Set m_oOutStream = oFSO.CreateTextFile(oUser.OutputFile)
   oFP.ProcessFile sFilename, Me.ListView1
```

Note that the output filename is specified by the user object, so is therefore defined on a per-user basis in the XML file.

The final interesting piece of code in `PerformXMLToXMLTransform()` sets up the category filters for the XML to XML transformation class by simply copying the categories from the user object:

```
oTemplate.Category1 = oUser.Category1
oTemplate.Category2 = oUser.Category2
```

With the ability to perform the XML transformation on a per-user basis by invoking the `PerformXMLtoXMLTransform()` method, we can now change the `SplitFile` click handler to perform a transformation for each subscriber who wants their received data in XML format:

```
Private Sub SplitFile_Click()
   Dim oUser As CUser

   Dim oLoadUsers As New CLoadUserInfo
   oLoadUsers.LoadUserInfo

   For Each oUser In oLoadUsers.Users
      Me.LogWindow.ListItems.Add , , "User=" & oUser.UserName
      If oUser.DeliveryFormat = "XML" Then
         PerformXMLToXMLTransform oUser, Me.FileToProcess.Text
      End If
   Next oUser
End Sub
```

If you run this code, you'll see that the XML transformation is performed for those subscribers who have their delivery format as XML, and you'll also notice that the web view tab combo will list the files that have been created:

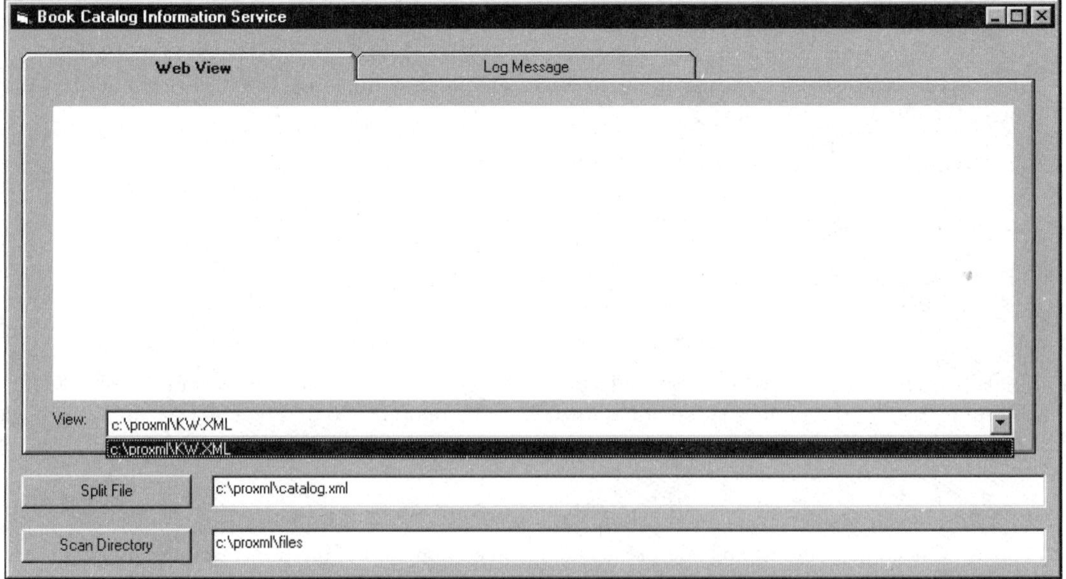

This combo is added to by the `PerformXMLToXMLTransform()` function:

```
Me.Combo1.AddItem oUser.OutputFile
```

The output filenames that are displayed are defined by the `OutputFile` element on `Users.XML`:

```
<?xml version="1.0" ?>
<!-- This file defines the register users for the book notification service -->
<Users>

   <User>
      <Name>Richard Anderson</Name>
      <OutputFile>c:\proxml\RJA.HTML</OutputFile>
      <Email>rja@arpsolutions.demon.co.uk</Email>
      <DeliveryFormat>HTML</DeliveryFormat>
      <Category1>ASP</Category1>
      <Category2>ASP+</Category2>
   </User>
```

However, if you select a filename from the combo nothing will happen as we've not yet implemented the change handler. To do this, implement the `click` handler for the `combobox` by adding the following code to the form, instructing the `webbrowser` control to navigate to the file:

```
Private Sub Combo1_Click()
   Me.WebBrowser1.Navigate Me.Combo1.Text
End Sub
```

If we then perform the transformation again by pressing the split file button, and select the `KW.XML` entry we'll see the XML file in the web browser control:

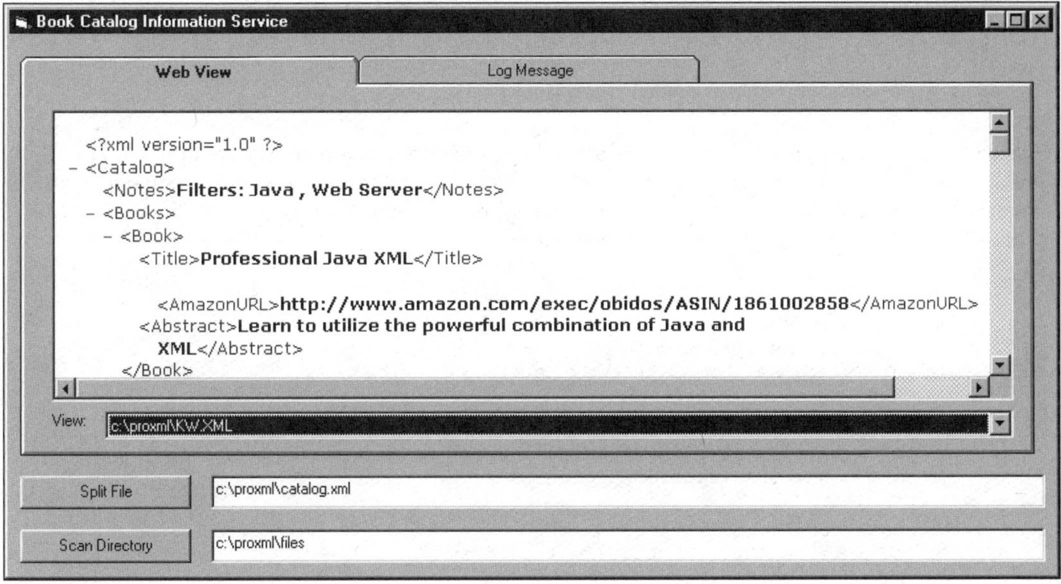

The XML to HTML Transformation

The XML to HTML transformation is implemented in an almost identical fashion to the XML to XML transformation, except that HTML is the output format. Because of this, I'll simply show the code here and not discuss it.

Delete the existing code in the class `CHTMLCatalogTransform` and replace it with the code from `CXMLCatalogTransform`. The lines that need changing, in the `startDocument`, `endDocument`, and `endElement` event handlers are highlighted below:

```
Private Sub ITemplate_endElement(sXPath As String, sElementName As String)
   If sXPath = "/Catalog/Book" Then
      If m_lCategories <> 0 Then
          m_Outstream.WriteString "<H3>" & m_sTitle & "</H3>"
          m_Outstream.WriteString "<P>" & m_sAbstract & "</P>"
          m_Outstream.WriteString "<A HREF=" & """" & _
             "http://www.amazon.com/exec/obidos/ASIN/" & _
             Reduce(m_sISBN) & """" & ">View on Amazon.com</A>"
      End If
   End If
End Sub

Private Sub ITemplate_startDocument()
   m_OutStream.WriteString "<HTML>"
   m_OutStream.WriteString "<H1>Catalog Of New Books</H1>"
   m_OutStream.WriteString "<P>"
   m_OutStream.WriteString "This file has been created based upon your " & _
                           "filters of : " & m_sCategory1 & " , " & m_sCategory2
   m_OutStream.WriteString "</P>"

   m_OutStream.WriteString "<H2>Books</H2>"
End Sub

Private Sub ITemplate_endDocument()
   m_OutStream.WriteString "</HTML>"
End Sub
```

As with the XML transformation we'll add a helper function to our form for creating the HTML output file. To do this, simply copy the `PerformXMLtoXMLTransform()` function, change its name to `PerformXMLtoHTMLTransform`, and change all reference to `CXMLCatalogTransform` to `CHTMLCatalogTransform` as shown below:

```
Sub PerformXMLToHTMLTransform(oUser As CUser, sFilename As String)
   Dim oFP As CSAXTransformEngine
   Dim oPattern As CPattern
   Dim oTemplate As CHTMLCatalogTransform
   Dim oFSO As New FileSystemObject

   ' Create the Transform Engine
   Set oFP = New CSAXTransformEngine

   ' Create the Template Class
   Set oTemplate = New CHTMLCatalogTransform
   Set oTemplate.OutStream = Me
```

```
    ' Set the filters for this users transformation
    oTemplate.Category1 = oUser.Category1
    oTemplate.Category2 = oUser.Category2

    ' Match all elements
    Set oPattern = oFP.AddPattern("*", oTemplate)

    Set m_oOutStream = oFSO.CreateTextFile(oUser.OutputFile)
    oFP.ProcessFile sFilename, Me.LogWindow

    Me.Combo1.AddItem oUser.OutputFile

    m_oOutStream.Close
End Sub
```

Now we've got both of the transformation classes and helper functions, we can change the `SplitFile_Click()` method to use either transformation depending upon our subscriber configuration details:

```
Private Sub SplitFile_Click()
    Dim oUser As CUser
    Dim oLoadUsers As New CLoadUserInfo
    oLoadUsers.LoadUserInfo

    For Each oUser In oLoadUsers.Users
        Me.LogWindow.ListItems.Add , , "User=" & oUser.UserName
        If oUser.DeliveryFormat = "XML" Then
            PerformXMLToXMLTransform oUser, Me.FileToProcess.Text
        Else
            PerformXMLToHTMLTransform oUser, Me.FileToProcess.Text
        End If
    Next oUser
End Sub
```

If we run the program again, we can now view the HTML output for our subscribers as shown here:

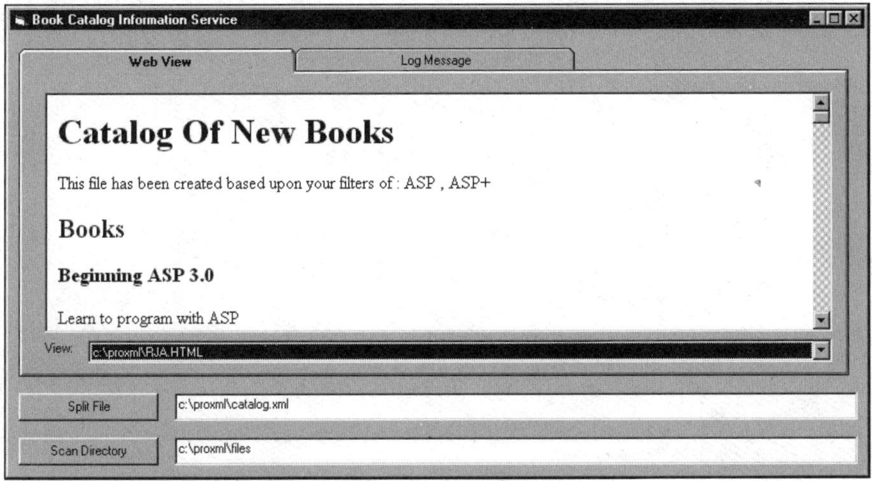

With the transformation in place all that is left to complete the BCIS is the mailing component and the scanning of directories to automatically detect and process multiple XML files.

Scan Directory Functionality

To implement the Scan Directory functionality we'll use the component provided by the Microsoft Scripting Runtime.

Double click on the Scan Directory button and change the click handler as follows:

```
Private Sub ScanDirectory_Click()
   Dim oFSO As New FileSystemObject
   Dim oFolder As Folder

   Set oFolder = oFSO.GetFolder(Me.ScanPath)

   Dim oFile As File
   Dim bRC As Boolean
   Dim sDestFile As String

   ' Process each file in the directory

   Me.LogWindow.ListItems.Add , , "Scanning directory " & Me.ScanPath

   For Each oFile In oFolder.Files
      If InStr(oFile.Name, ".xml") <> 0 Then
         Me.LogWindow.ListItems.Add , , oFile.Name
      End If
   Next oFile
End Sub
```

The code retrieves a `Folder` object based upon the current scan directory by using the `GetFolder()` method of the `FileSystemObject`. Once retrieved, each file within the folder is enumerated using the `For...Each` syntax. If the filename contains the text `".xml"` (the extension) we list the filename in the ListView:

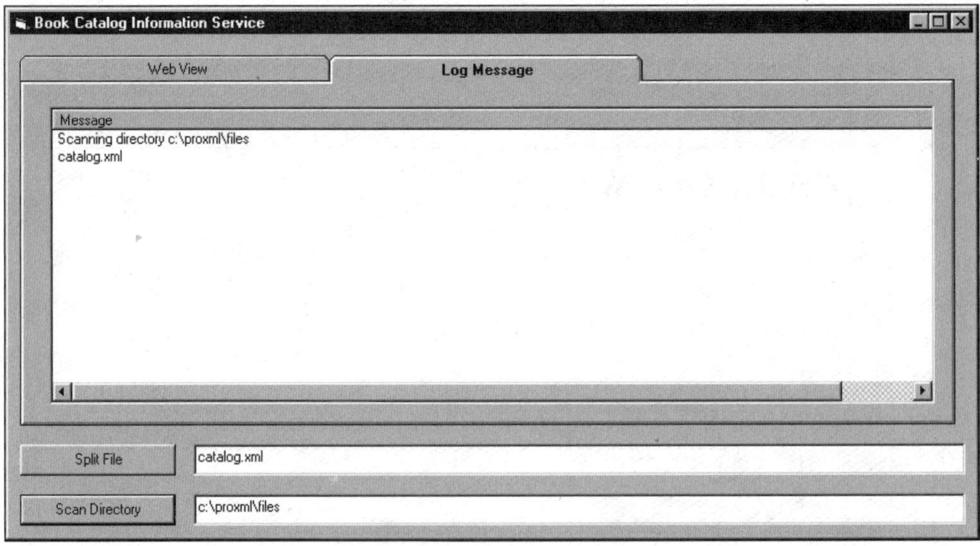

With the files being detected successfully we need to process each one. To do this we add the function `ProcessFile()` to the form. This function consists of the code from the split file click handler reworked to accept a filename rather than using the value from the edit box:

```
Private Sub ProcessFile(sFilename As String)
   Dim oUser As CUser
   Dim oLoadUsers As New CLoadUserInfo
   oLoadUsers.LoadUserInfo

   For Each oUser In oLoadUsers.Users
      Me.LogWindow.ListItems.Add , , "User=" & oUser.UserName
      If oUser.DeliveryFormat = "XML" Then
         PerformXMLToXMLTransform oUser, sFilename
      Else
         PerformXMLToHTMLTransform oUser, sFilename
      End If
   Next oUser
End Sub
```

We can call this function from within our scanning code, causing each file to be processed for each of our subscribers:

```
   For Each oFile In oFolder.Files
      If InStr(oFile.Name, ".xml") <> 0 Then
         Me.LogWindow.ListItems.Add , , oFile.Path
         ProcessFile oFile.Path
      End If
   Next oFile
```

> *Note that when scanning directories you should ensure that only valid XML catalog files are contained within them, otherwise your subscribers will receive empty XML or HTML files. In a real live system you'd have to improve the transformation class module interface to give some sort of feedback to say whether or not output has been created, and whether it is worth sending.*

If we run the project and specify a folder containing 10 XML catalog files, and our `Users.xml` file defines three subscribers, a total of 30 transformations will be performed. We could of course rework the code so only three transformations are performed, but this is left as an exercise for you if you decide to adopt this transformation approach. However, we have got one problem left to address. For each of our 3 users 10 transformations occur, but each transformation uses the same output filename. We need to do something with each transformation so it that is not lost before the next one is performed. For the BCIS the action we take is to e-mail the transformation to the user.

The Direct Mail Component

To deliver book information to subscribers I've used the Microsoft Collaboration Data Objects library. CDO support needs to be added to the project before the following code will compile, so select the type library "Microsoft CDO 1.21 Library" from the Project | References dialog. If you can't find the CDO type library, you'll need to install that component of Outlook from your Office CDs. Add the class `CSimpleMailer` and the `SendFile()` subroutine as follows:

```
Option Explicit

' Send a file to the specified email address

Function SendFile(sTo As String, sFilename As String) As Boolean
```

```
    Dim oSession As New Session
    Dim oMessage As Message
    Dim oRecipient As Recipient
    Dim oAttachments As Attachments

    ' Simple catch all error
    On Error GoTo failed

    ' Establish mapi session. You need to adjust this to match your mail profile
    oSession.Logon "Microsoft Outlook"

    ' Create a new message setting subject, text and attachment
    Set oMessage = oSession.Outbox.Messages.Add
    oMessage.Subject = "Automated Catalog Update Delivery"
    oMessage.Text = "Please find attached the lastest catalog filtered " & _
                    "especially for you!"

    ' Set the attachment
    oMessage.Attachments.Add "Catalog", , CdoFileData, sFilename

    ' Set the recipient
    Set oRecipient = oMessage.Recipients.Add(Name:=sTo, Type:=CdoTo)
    oRecipient.Resolve False

    ' Send the message and log off
    oMessage.Send
    oSession.Logoff

    SendFile = True
    Exit Function

failed:
    SendFile = False
End Function
```

You should replace the line:

```
oSession.Logon "Microsoft Outlook"
```

with a suitable string for your e-mail account, such as:

```
oSession.Logon "Karli Watson", "", True, True
```

Detailed syntax of this command is beyond the scope of this chapter.

> *For more information on CDO see* Professional CDO Programming *(ISBN: 1-861002-06-8) or* ADSI CDO Programming with ASP *(ISBN: 1-861001-90-8).*

With the class created for e-mailing files to our subscribers, we go back to the `ProcessFile()` function in the main form and modify it to use the mailer class to send the file if an e-mail address is configured for a subscriber:

```
Private Sub ProcessFile(sFilename As String)
   Dim oUser As CUser
   Dim oMailer As New CSimpleMailer
   Dim bRC As Boolean
   Dim oLoadUsers As New CLoadUserInfo
   oLoadUsers.LoadUserInfo

   For Each oUser In oLoadUsers.Users
      Me.LogWindow.ListItems.Add , , "User=" & oUser.UserName
      If oUser.DeliveryFormat = "XML" Then
         PerformXMLToXMLTransform oUser, sFilename
      Else
         PerformXMLToHTMLTransform oUser, sFilename
      End If

      ' If an email address is present e-mail the file to the user
      If oUser.Email <> "" Then
         bRC = oMailer.SendFile(oUser.Email, oUser.OutputFile)
         If bRC = True Then
            Me.LogWindow.ListItems.Add , , "E-mailed file to " & oUser.Email
         Else
            Me.LogWindow.ListItems.Add , , "Failed to e-mail file to " & _
               oUser.Email
         End If
      End If
   Next oUser
End Sub
```

The changes to code are that we've declared an instance of the mailer component, and after a transformation we check the `Email` property of the `CUser` object for the subscriber. If the e-mail address is present we e-mail the output to the subscriber and log a success/failure message depending on the return code from the `CSimpleMailer` class.

Next time we run the project and press the scan directory button to process data we'll see the e-mails sent in the log window:

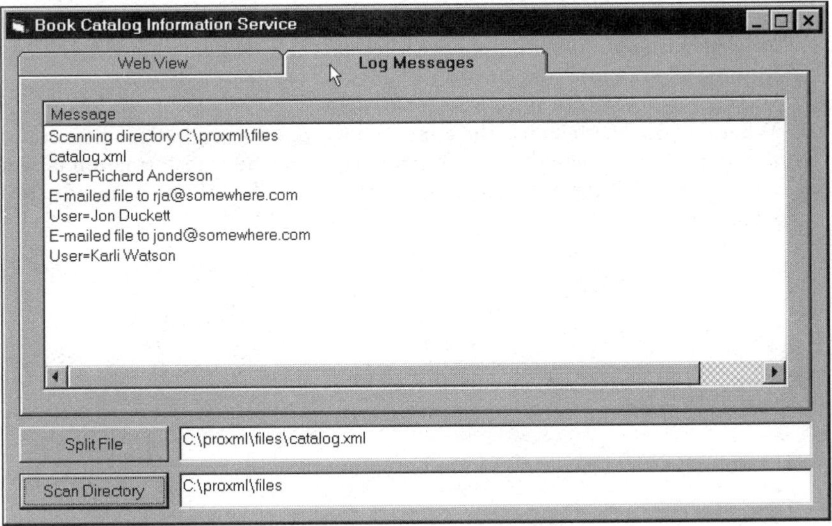

and each of the subscribers will see the output in their inbox:

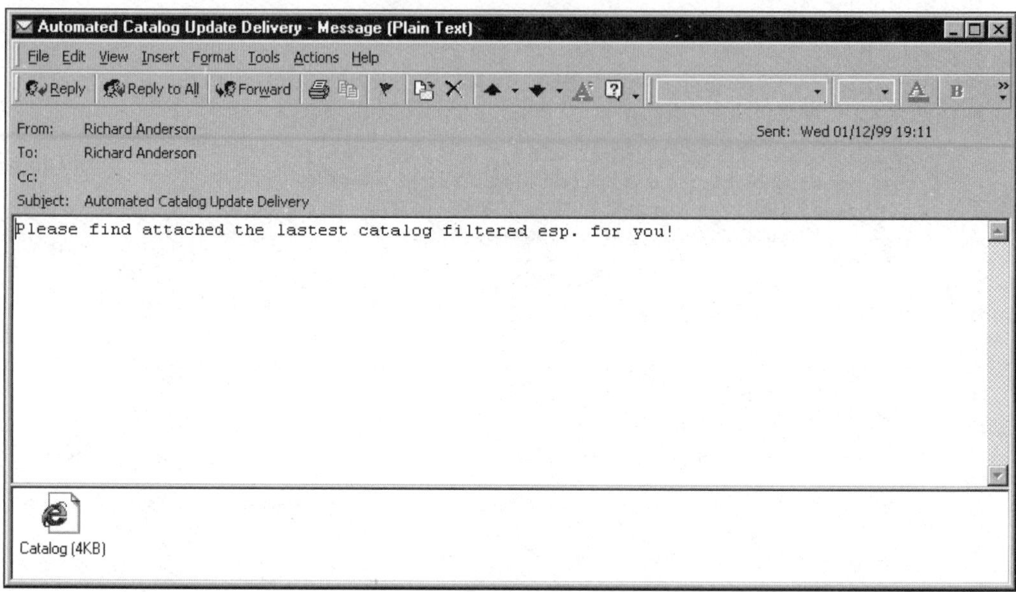

Most e-mail clients like Outlook will automatically launch the associated viewer, making HTML content easy to view.

Summary

In this chapter we've seen a way to transform XML data using VB class modules rather than XSLT. The approach is to build upon the principles of XSLT, which are not specific to VB, and can be implemented in other languages.

Whether you decide to use the approach we've outlined in this chapter or XSLT will depend a lot upon the applications you write. XSLT is a fairly powerful transformation language but it is limited by the current specification and can't easily perform database lookups or advanced one-file-in-multiple-file-out transformations.

18

Case Study 4 – SOAP

This is kind of painful for me. A long time ago in a galaxy far away (well, about eighteen months, in fact), I wrote a book called *Professional DCOM Application Development* (ISBN 1-861001-31-2). Despite the title, this book wasn't just about DCOM. In fact, it was a fairly general investigation about how to put together serious, enterprise-size applications based around *all* the technologies that have been emerging over the last few years from Microsoft, including MTS, MSMQ, ADSI, Microsoft Clusters and so on. Oh, and a bit about DCOM.

Trouble was, it had DCOM plastered all over the cover (mind you, these days it would have an extremely large picture of me on the cover, which would – frankly – be even worse). And whenever I met anyone who knew I'd written it, it usually wasn't very long before I got hauled into a debate about how practicable DCOM actually was. Occasionally, this was replaced by a polite enquiry as to why I wasn't using DCOM on the project that I was currently working on for them. Fair enough.

The reason for this, of course, is that DCOM, whilst being a really neat concept in theory (like, "Hey kids, why don't we build the system here, and then deploy it everywhere without making any changes to it?"), it isn't the universal panacea that it first appeared to be. It's a pretty heavyweight wire protocol, for one thing, and the versions on non-Windows platforms, whilst they do exist, inevitably lag behind the real thing. Crucially, you can't put DCOM through a firewall without talking very nicely with the networks people.

So this is why I was really excited when I heard about SOAP. The key thing about SOAP is that it's purely a wire protocol that doesn't mandate the use of any ORB technology (Microsoft or otherwise). It's also pretty good when it comes to handling firewalls. SOAP is described in more detail in Chapter 11, but here we're going to have a play with it to see how it works in practice. What I thought would be really cool would be to take one of the examples from my previous book, and re-implement it using SOAP, and see what it looked like. In this case study, we're going to use COM locally, plus SOAP, to implement a globally-oriented order entry application. We'll be coding the COM objects using Visual C++ 6.0 with ATL 3.0; if you're unfamiliar with this, I recommend Richard Grimes' *Beginning ATL 3 COM Programming* (ISBN 1-861001-20-7) and *Professional ATL COM Programming* (ISBN 1-861001-40-1). We'll be building two alternative servers – one on Windows NT (using Visual Studio C++ 6.0 and MFC) and one on Linux (using straight C) – just to show that it really is cross-platform. Where it's available, we'll use the DOM to parse the SOAP XML content, and, where it isn't, we'll roll our own.

To the Ends of the Earth

Those of you who have read *Professional DCOM Application Development* (and, if not, why not?) may remember a rather bizarre example involving record collectors in Ulaanbaatar ordering secondhand LPs featuring late sixties psychedelia from a host in Tierra del Fuego, thus:

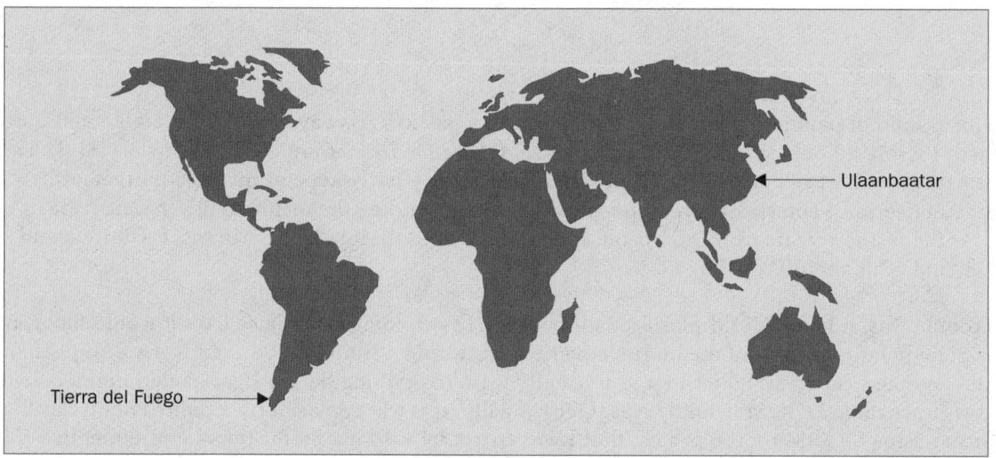

This example actually turned up in three (or possibly even four – I lost count) versions, demonstrating such things as basic field by field order entry with remote validation, marshaling by value for local validation and finally sending an order object over a reliable message queue using MSMQ. What we're going to do now is construct a version that uses SOAP.

Our order validation and entry COM object, `Order`, has a single interface, `IOrder`, which has five properties and one method. Each property corresponds to a field in the order, and has a slightly different validation requirement, as follows:

Field	Validation
`CustomerID`	Must be present, and be alphabetic
`Artist`	Must be present, and be alphabetic
`Title`	Must be present, and be alphanumeric
`Label`	May be blank; if present, must be alphabetic
`Price`	Must be valid dollar price

The single method, `Submit()`, simply writes the order details to a structured file (`c:\order.dat`). The code for this is in the project called `SimpleOrder`, and I don't propose to go into it in great detail here. If you're interested in looking into it further, *Professional DCOM Application Development* is still available from all good bookstores.

For the record, here is the code that implements the five properties and one method:

```
STDMETHODIMP COrder::put_CustomerID(BSTR newVal)
{
   HRESULT hResult = MandatoryAlphabetic(newVal);
   if (FAILED(hResult))
      return hResult;

   m_bstrCustomerID = newVal;
   return S_OK;
}

STDMETHODIMP COrder::put_Artist(BSTR newVal)
{
   HRESULT hResult = MandatoryAlphabetic(newVal);
   if (FAILED(hResult))
      return hResult;

   m_bstrArtist = newVal;
   return S_OK;
}

STDMETHODIMP COrder::put_Title(BSTR newVal)
{
   HRESULT hResult = MandatoryAlphanumeric(newVal);
   if (FAILED(hResult))
      return hResult;

   m_bstrTitle = newVal;
   return S_OK;
}

STDMETHODIMP COrder::put_Label(BSTR newVal)
{
   HRESULT hResult = OptionalAlphabetic(newVal);
   if (FAILED(hResult))
      return hResult;
```

```
    m_bstrLabel = newVal;
    return S_OK;
}

STDMETHODIMP COrder::put_Price(BSTR newVal)
{
    HRESULT hResult = MandatoryPrice(newVal);
    if (FAILED(hResult))
        return hResult;

    m_bstrPrice = newVal;
    return S_OK;
}

STDMETHODIMP COrder::Submit()
{
    CComPtr<IStorage> pStorage;
    HRESULT hResult = StgCreateDocfile(L"C:\\Order.dat",
                        STGM_SIMPLE| STGM_CREATE | STGM_READWRITE |
                        STGM_SHARE_EXCLUSIVE, 0, &pStorage);
    if (FAILED(hResult))
        return hResult;

    Write(pStorage, L"CustomerID", m_bstrCustomerID);
    Write(pStorage, L"Artist", m_bstrArtist);
    Write(pStorage, L"Title", m_bstrTitle);
    Write(pStorage, L"Label", m_bstrLabel);
    Write(pStorage, L"Price", m_bstrPrice);

    return S_OK;
}
```

As can be seen, each of the properties defines a single, validated field in the order, saving it to a local member variable, which is one of:

```
private:
    CComBSTR m_bstrCustomerID;
    CComBSTR m_bstrArtist;
    CComBSTR m_bstrTitle;
    CComBSTR m_bstrLabel;
    CComBSTR m_bstrPrice;
```

As defined in `Order.h`.

Next, the `Submit()` method writes these properties out to the order file. There are a number of helper methods, each of which handles a slightly different validation option:

Method	**Purpose**
`MandatoryAlphabetic()`	Checks that the value is not blank and is entirely alphabetic
`OptionalAlphabetic()`	Checks that the value is either blank or entirely alphabetic
`MandatoryAlphanumeric()`	Checks that the value is not blank and is entirely alphanumeric
`OptionalAlphanumeric()`	Checks that the value is either blank or entirely alphanumeric
`MandatoryPrice()`	Checks that the value is not blank and is a correctly-formatted price

The code for these methods is as follows:

```
HRESULT COrder::MandatoryAlphabetic(BSTR bstrValue)
{
   int length = SysStringLen(bstrValue);
   if (length == 0)
      return E_INVALIDARG;

   return OptionalAlphabetic(bstrValue);
}

HRESULT COrder::OptionalAlphabetic(BSTR bstrValue)
{
   int length = SysStringLen(bstrValue);

   for (int iChar = 0; iChar < length; iChar++)
   {
      if (!iswspace(bstrValue[iChar]) &&
          !iswalpha(bstrValue[iChar]))
         return E_INVALIDARG;
   }

   return S_OK;
}

HRESULT COrder::MandatoryAlphanumeric(BSTR bstrValue)
{
   int length = SysStringLen(bstrValue);
   if (length == 0)
      return E_INVALIDARG;

   return OptionalAlphanumeric(bstrValue);
}

HRESULT COrder::OptionalAlphanumeric(BSTR bstrValue)
{
   int length = SysStringLen(bstrValue);

   for (int iChar = 0; iChar < length; iChar++)
   {
      if (!iswspace(bstrValue[iChar]) &&
          !iswalnum(bstrValue[iChar]))
         return E_INVALIDARG;
   }

   return S_OK;
}

HRESULT COrder::MandatoryPrice(BSTR bstrValue)
{
   // Get the locale ID for the US with default sorting
   LCID lcid = MAKELCID(MAKELANGID(LANG_ENGLISH, SUBLANG_ENGLISH_US),
                        SORT_DEFAULT);
```

```
    // Define a variable to hold the returned currency
    CURRENCY cy = {0};

    // Convert the string to a currency value
    HRESULT hr = VarCyFromStr(bstrValue, lcid, 0, &cy);

    // If the function failed, bstrValue is not a valid currency
    if (FAILED(hr))
       return E_INVALIDARG;

    // Finally, check that the currency value is positive
    if (cy.int64 < 0)
       return E_INVALIDARG;

    return S_OK;
}
```

The last helper method, `Write()`, writes just one field out to the file:

```
void COrder::Write(IStorage* pStorage, LPOLESTR lpszField, CComBSTR& bstr)
{
   CComPtr<IStream> pStream;
   pStorage->CreateStream(lpszField, STGM_READWRITE |
                      STGM_SHARE_EXCLUSIVE, 0, 0, &pStream);

   bstr.WriteToStream(pStream);
}
```

In the original initial example, I had a simple Visual Basic client allowing the user to create a remote instance of this order object, populate the fields in a valid manner, and then submit it. I have decided to base the client application for this on the previous code, for two reasons: (1) I wanted to show that SOAP wasn't just applicable to web-based applications, and (2) I was lazy and had the code lying around anyway. (Guess which one is nearer the truth.)

So if we're going to use SOAP, what do we need?

A SOAP Opera

We need some kind of infrastructure to manage all this, and (this is the bit I really like) we're going to need a name for it. As you may imagine, SOAP is rapidly becoming a breeding ground for acronyms based around very bad puns. As an example, my original name, SUDS (standing for **S**imple **U**surper of **D**COM using **S**OAP) was quickly ruled out, for reasons which will become clear when the **S**OAP **U**niform **D**escription **S**emantics are released. Likewise, my first draft contained a joke that the first "SOAP dispensers" were likely to be on their way soon. Then I found out that this was in fact the preferred term. So it is with some trepidation that I unveil SOAP OPERA to the world. For what it's worth, OPERA probably stands for something like "**O**bject **P**rotocol **E**nabling **R**emote **A**ccess", but hey guys, it's just a name, right?

This is a somewhat simplified view of what the system looks like if we use pure DCOM:

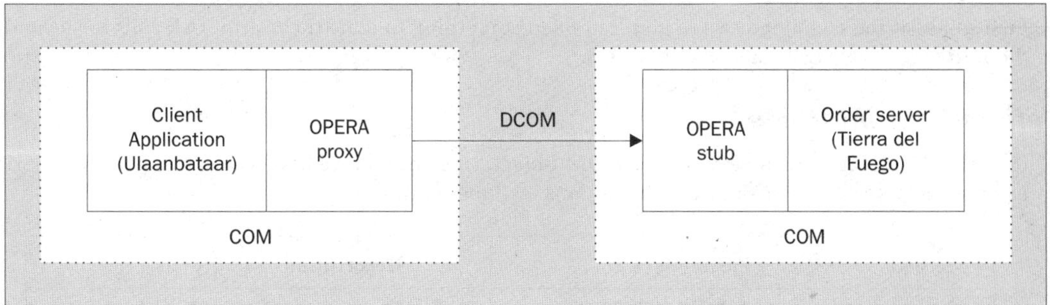

If we use SOAP, however, we'll need something like this:

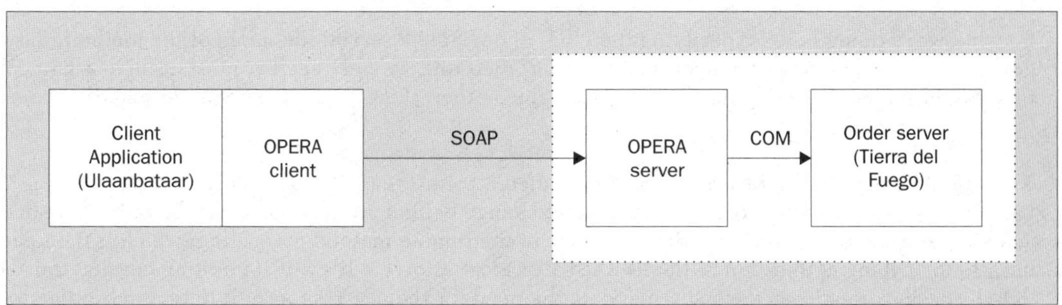

Here, the client application has to be slightly amended to use the OPERA client (although there's actually no reason why we couldn't provide it with a COM object that implemented the `IOrder` interface, and so use it without any changes at all). The OPERA client is an in-process COM object that implements a new interface, `IOpera`. We'll take a look at this in more detail in a minute. This exchanges SOAP calls with the OPERA server over in Tierra del Fuego. The OPERA server then instantiates COM order objects and invokes methods them using local COM. The order server itself remains exactly as it was in the original DCOM case, except that this time it is only accessed locally.

If we compare the two pictures, we can see that the COM proxy has been replaced by the OPERA client, the wire protocol has changed from DCOM to SOAP, and the COM stub has been replaced by the OPERA server. (Strictly speaking, the OPERA server still uses a COM proxy/stub to access the order server, but this is largely for code re-use purposes. If we were to re-implement the order server in-process this would no longer be the case.)

> *One last point. Experienced COM programmers may well be standing on their seats shouting "Custom Marshaling!" at this point. There is, of course, no reason why we couldn't implement* `IMarshal` *in our order object, so that every invocation of an* `IOrder` *method gets sent over to the server as a SOAP call that is completely transparently to the application. However, custom marshaling isn't really within the scope of this example, although interested readers are referred to Chapter 3 of "Professional DCOM Application Development", where this is discussed in some length.*

Let's take a look at how this works in practice.

The OPERA client

First of all, at the client end, we're going to need something to construct our SOAP calls for us and send them to our server. Let's take a look at this.

Defining our Interface

Our client is going to be a very simple COM object, `Opera`, that we'll *pretend* is completely generic. It has a single interface, `IOpera`, which contains just one method:

Method	Parameters	Description

`Exchange()`	`[in] BSTR URL`
	`[in] BSTR Method`
	`[in] VARIANT Argument`
		Exchange SOAP call with server.

So what we're doing here is specifying the URL of our SOAP server, the name of the method that we're going to invoke, and one argument. For all of our methods, we only need at most a single argument, so this should suffice. We don't need any return value, either. (Like I said, it's not a particularly generic implementation.)

You might be wondering why this method is called `Exchange()` if it doesn't have a return value. As it happens, there is actually a request/response exchange behind all this; however, the only thing that is actually returned by the server is the `HRESULT` of the remote method invocation, which is then passed back to the calling application as the `HRESULT` of `Exchange()`. It's worth pointing out that the V1.0 SOAP specification doesn't actually mandate the need for request/response. It defines a binding to HTTP, sure, but the actual protocol is transport-independent. There's absolutely no reason why you shouldn't use SOAP for one-way method calls – which opens up interesting possibilities for using it to provide a substrate for the likes of MSMQ.

Building the Client

Let's take a look at the code behind all this. We'll use ATL, and implement this as an in-process COM object. We use the ATL AppWizard to create the project, and the Object Wizard to add a simple object, making sure we check the box that says "Support ISupportErrorInfo". Then add the `Exchange()` method using the ClassView.

Here is the `Opera.h` header file:

```
// Opera.h : Declaration of the COpera

#ifndef __OPERA_H_
#define __OPERA_H_

#include "resource.h"       // main symbols
#import "msxml.dll"

/////////////////////////////////////////////////////////////////////////////
// COpera
```

```
class ATL_NO_VTABLE COpera :
   public CComObjectRootEx<CComSingleThreadModel>,
   public CComCoClass<COpera, &CLSID_Opera>,
   public ISupportErrorInfo,
   public IDispatchImpl<IOpera, &IID_IOpera, &LIBID_OPERACLIENTLib>
{
protected:
   int m_sock;

   HRESULT ConnectToHost(LPSTR lpszURL);
   HRESULT DisconnectFromHost();
   HRESULT ProcessContent(int nChar, LPSTR lpszContent);

public:
   COpera() : m_sock(-1)
   {
   }

   ~COpera()
   {
      if (m_sock != -1)
         DisconnectFromHost();
   }

DECLARE_REGISTRY_RESOURCEID(IDR_OPERA)

DECLARE_PROTECT_FINAL_CONSTRUCT()

BEGIN_COM_MAP(COpera)
   COM_INTERFACE_ENTRY(IOpera)
   COM_INTERFACE_ENTRY(IDispatch)
   COM_INTERFACE_ENTRY(ISupportErrorInfo)
END_COM_MAP()

// ISupportsErrorInfo
   STDMETHOD(InterfaceSupportsErrorInfo)(REFIID riid);

// IOpera
public:
   STDMETHOD(Exchange)(/*[in]*/ BSTR URL, /*[in]*/ BSTR Method,
                       /*[in]*/ VARIANT Argument);
};

#endif //__OPERA_H_
```

The highlighted code is the code that you will have to add, over and above that provided by the wizards and Class View. As you can see, I've added one or two helper methods, plus an `int` to hold a TCP/IP socket identifier, `m_sock`, and a reference to the MSXML library, in order to use Microsoft's DOM implementation. Which reminds me: we need to make a couple of additions to `DllMain` in the `OperaClient.cpp` file:

```
extern "C"
BOOL WINAPI DllMain(HINSTANCE hInstance, DWORD dwReason, LPVOID /*lpReserved*/)
{
   if (dwReason == DLL_PROCESS_ATTACH)
   {
      _Module.Init(ObjectMap, hInstance, &LIBID_OPERACLIENTLib);
      DisableThreadLibraryCalls(hInstance);
      WSADATA wsaData;
      if (WSAStartup (0x0101, &wsaData))
         return FALSE;
   }
   else if (dwReason == DLL_PROCESS_DETACH)
   {
      _Module.Term();
      WSACleanup();
   }
   return TRUE;    // ok
}
```

If we don't do this, all of our TCP/IP stuff won't work. What we're doing here is issuing the calls to start up WinSock (specifying that we need version 1.1) when our client application starts using the DLL, and to clean up when it detaches. An alternative to using WinSock would be to use WinInet, if you're happier with that.

The `Exchange()` method, as we've said above, is the one that carries out the SOAP exchange with the server. A typical exchange (say setting up the `CustomerID` property) might involve the following going from client to server:

```
POST /StockQuote HTTP/1.1
   Host: www.jpassoc.co.uk
   Content-Type: text/xml
   Content-Length: 300
   SOAPMethodName: www.jpassoc.co.uk/opera#put_CustomerID

   <SOAP:Envelope xmlns:SOAP="urn:schemas-xmlsoap-org:soap.v1">
      <SOAP:Body>
         <m:put_CustomerID xmlns:m="www.jpassoc.co.uk/opera">
            <argument>JMP</argument>
         </m:put_CustomerID>
      </SOAP:Body>
   </SOAP:Envelope>
```

and the following going back from server to client:

```
HTTP/1.1 200 OK
   Content-Type: text/xml
   Content-Length: 252

   <SOAP:Envelope xmlns:SOAP="urn:schemas-xmlsoap-org:soap.v1">
      <SOAP:Body>
         <m:put_CustomerIDResponse xmlns:m="www.jpassoc.co.uk/opera">
            <return>0</return>
         </m:put_CustomerIDResponse>
      </SOAP:Body>
   </SOAP:Envelope>
```

The Exchange() Method

Here's how the `Exchange()` method kicks off:

```
STDMETHODIMP COpera::Exchange(BSTR URL, BSTR Method, VARIANT Argument)
{
   size_t length = SysStringLen(URL);
   LPSTR lpszURL = new char[length + 1];
   wcstombs(lpszURL, URL, length);
   lpszURL[length] = 0;

   if (m_sock == -1)
   {
      HRESULT hResult = ConnectToHost(lpszURL);
      if (hResult != S_OK)
      {
         delete[] lpszURL;
         return hResult;
      }
   }
```

Here, we're using one of our helper methods to establish a connection to the server, if we don't have one already. We'll take a look at that method later. For now, let's carry on and take a look at what method call our application is invoking, and then extract the argument from the incoming `VARIANT`, building up the `MessageType` header as we do so:

```
   length = SysStringLen(Method);
   LPSTR lpszMethod = new char[length + 1];
   wcstombs(lpszMethod, Method, length);
   lpszMethod[length] = 0;

   char szCall[2000];

   sprintf(szCall,
           "SOAPMethodName: www.jpassoc.co.uk/opera#%s\r\n\r\n", lpszMethod);
   strcat(szCall,
          "<SOAP:Envelope xmlns:SOAP=\"urn:schemas-xmlsoap-org:soap.v1\">\r\n");
   strcat(szCall, "<SOAP:Body>\r\n");

   length = strlen(szCall);
   sprintf(&szCall[length],
           "          <m:%s xmlns:m=\"www.jpassoc.co.uk/opera\">\r\n", lpszMethod);

   char szArgument[100];

   switch (Argument.vt)
   {
      case VT_EMPTY:
         break;

      case VT_BSTR:
      {
         length = SysStringLen(Argument.bstrVal);
         wcstombs(szArgument, Argument.bstrVal, length);
         szArgument[length] = 0;
```

```
        length = strlen(szCall);
        sprintf(&szCall[length],
                "                    <argument>%s</argument>\r\n", szArgument);

        break;
    }

    default:
        delete[] lpszURL;
        delete[] lpszMethod;

        return AtlReportError(CLSID_Opera, "Variant type not supported",
                              IID_IOpera, E_NOTIMPL);
}
```

Well, you weren't really expecting a complete implementation, were you? Empty and String will do fine for us, thank you very much. Let's complete the POST by adding all the other headers (including that all-important `ContentType` header):

```
length = strlen(szCall);
sprintf(&szCall[length],
        "          </m:%s>\r\n      </SOAP:Body>\r\n</SOAP:Envelope>",
        lpszMethod);

length = strlen(szCall);

char szRequest[2000];
sprintf(szRequest, "POST /OperaServer HTTP/1.1\r\nHost: %s\r\nContent-Type: "
        "text/xml\r\nContent-Length: %d\r\n%s", lpszURL, length, szCall);

delete[] lpszURL;
delete[] lpszMethod;
```

And let's exchange request and response. Note that if this were a real application, we'd have to set a timer running in case the connection between us and the server breaks in mid-stream.

```
send(m_sock, szRequest, strlen(szRequest), 0);

char szResponse[20000];
int nChar = recv(m_sock, szResponse, sizeof(szResponse), 0);
```

Check that the socket hasn't been closed by the server:

```
if (nChar <= 0)
{
   DisconnectFromHost();
   return AtlReportError(CLSID_Opera, "Connection to server lost",
                         IID_IOpera, E_FAIL);
}
```

Now let's take a look at the response. We'll begin by removing the first line, as we're not particularly interested in it:

```
szResponse[nChar] = 0;
LPSTR lpszReturn = strstr(szResponse, "\r\n");

if (!lpszReturn)
   return AtlReportError(CLSID_Opera, "Incomplete response from server",
                         IID_IOpera, E_FAIL);

*lpszReturn = 0;

if (strcmp(szResponse, "HTTP/1.1 200 OK"))
   return AtlReportError(CLSID_Opera, "Bad response from server",
                         IID_IOpera, E_FAIL);
```

Here are a couple of interesting flags. The first one is only set when we've got all the headers we need for a valid SOAP call response. The second one is set if the server has sent back a `Connection: close` header. If we don't get this, we keep the connection open. This is because we are building up an order over in Patagonia, and we don't want to lose it. There is **state** over there. Actually, I have to admit that this is not nice, and I was sorely tempted to change the application so that the order was actually built up in the client before being sent over to the server at the end of the transaction. That way, we could keep the whole thing connectionless. However, my goal here was to emulate my original DCOM application as far as possible, except without the extra burden of the DCOM wire protocol. I leave it as an exercise to you, the reader, to change it so that it is completely connectionless. If there's enough demand, I might even post a connectionless version on my website, `www.jpassoc.co.uk`.

```
bool bSoap = false;
bool bClose = true;

HRESULT hResult = S_OK;

while (1)
{
   LPSTR lpszSegment = lpszReturn + 2;
   lpszReturn = strstr(lpszSegment, "\r\n");

   if (!lpszReturn)
   {
      hResult = AtlReportError(CLSID_Opera, "Non-SOAP response from server",
                               IID_IOpera, E_FAIL);
      break;
   }

   *lpszReturn = 0;

   if (!strncmp(lpszSegment, "Content-Type: ", 14))
   {
      if (!strcmp(&lpszSegment[14], "text/xml"))
         bSoap = true;
      else
      {
         hResult = AtlReportError(CLSID_Opera, "Non-SOAP response from server",
                                  IID_IOpera, E_FAIL);
         break;
      }
   }
   else if (!strncmp(lpszSegment, "Connection: ", 12))
   {
```

```
            if (!strcmp(&lpszSegment[12], "Keep-Alive"))
               bClose = false;
         }
         else if (!strncmp(lpszSegment, "Content-Length: ", 16))
         {
            if (!bSoap)
               hResult = AtlReportError(CLSID_Opera, "Non-SOAP response from server",
                                        IID_IOpera, E_FAIL);
            else
            {
```

Now, this is the point at which we know we've got content, and we've got a genuine SOAP response, so we invoke one of our helper methods to process it:

```
               int nChar = atoi(&lpszSegment[16]);
               hResult = ProcessContent(nChar, lpszReturn + 2);
            }

            break;
         }
      }
```

If we're finished with the order, close the socket; otherwise leave it open for the next call. (If the object gets released, it'll get closed anyway.)

```
      if (bClose)
         DisconnectFromHost();

      return hResult;
   }
```

The Helper Methods

Let's have a look at the helper methods. First of all, here's the connection method:

```
   HRESULT COpera::ConnectToHost(LPSTR lpszURL)
   {
      m_sock = socket(AF_INET, SOCK_STREAM, 0);

      int on = 1;
      setsockopt(m_sock, SOL_SOCKET, SO_REUSEADDR, reinterpret_cast<char*> (&on),
                 sizeof(on));

      struct sockaddr_in server;
      memset(&server, 0, sizeof(server));

      server.sin_family = AF_INET;
      server.sin_port = htons(80);

      struct hostent *pHost = gethostbyname(lpszURL);
```

```
    if (pHost)
       memcpy(&server.sin_addr, pHost->h_addr, pHost->h_length);
    else
    {
       server.sin_addr.s_addr = inet_addr(lpszURL);

       if (server.sin_addr.s_addr == 0)
       {
          DisconnectFromHost();
          return AtlReportError(CLSID_Opera, "Failed to translate host address",
                                IID_IOpera, E_FAIL);
       }
    }

    if (connect(m_sock, reinterpret_cast<struct sockaddr *> (&server),
        sizeof(server)) == -1)
    {
       char szError[256];
       sprintf(szError, "Failed to connect to host, error = %d\n",
               WSAGetLastError());

       DisconnectFromHost();

       return AtlReportError(CLSID_Opera, szError, IID_IOpera, E_FAIL);
    }

    return S_OK;
 }
```

Anyone who's familiar with TCP/IP programming will recognize much of this code. Most of it is taken up with converting the URL and port number into a server structure suitable for connecting to. Note that we are connecting to port 80 on the server machine – this is all part of SOAP's attempt to fool the firewall that we're actually doing web stuff. When SOAP starts achieving mass acceptance, it's actually quite likely that it will be put onto its own port, so that it can be separated out by the networks people, but for the time being, we'll stick to port 80.

The disconnection method is even simpler:

```
HRESULT COpera::DisconnectFromHost()
{
   closesocket(m_sock);
   m_sock = -1;

   return S_OK;
}
```

There's one more helper method that we need to look at before we leave the OPERA client, `ProcessContent()`, and this one's a bit more interesting. It's the one that actually processes the content of the response from the server.

There's no point, of course, in doing my own parsing here, since there is a perfectly satisfactory set of COM objects available to do this, in the Microsoft XML Document Object Model. Before we go into this, let's take a look at the kind of response we're likely to see. Here's an example of a response from the OPERA server:

```
<SOAP:Envelope xmlns:SOAP="urn:schemas-xmlsoap-org:soap.v1">
   <SOAP:Body>
      <m:put_CustomerIDResponse xmlns:m="www.jpassoc.co.uk/opera">
         <return>0</return>
      </m:put_CustomerIDResponse>
   </SOAP:Body>
</SOAP:Envelope>
```

So let's go ahead and parse it:

```
HRESULT COpera::ProcessContent(int nChar, LPSTR lpszContent)
{
   CComPtr<MSXML::IXMLDOMDocument> pXML;
   pXML.CoCreateInstance(__uuidof(MSXML::DOMDocument));

   CComBSTR bstrXML = lpszContent;
   VARIANT_BOOL success;
   success = pXML->loadXML(bstrXML.m_str);

   if (success != VARIANT_TRUE)
      return AtlReportError(CLSID_Opera, "Failed to parse XML", IID_IOpera,
                            E_FAIL);

   CComPtr<MSXML::IXMLDOMElement> pElem;
   XML->get_documentElement(&pElem);
```

Incidentally, if performance is likely to be an issue, we might consider avoiding using the DOM, especially considering the fact that we've not got a particularly complex XML structure here. If you're interested in how this might be done, the Linux implementation described later on shows this.

This is where we extract the method name (although in this case, we don't actually make use of it):

```
   CComBSTR bstrMethod;
   pElem->get_tagName(&bstrMethod);
```

Now let's extract the first child node:

```
   CComPtr<IXMLDOMNode> pChild;
   pElem->get_firstChild(&pChild);
```

Having got there, we're not interested in the tag (because we're going to assume that it's `return`), so we go straight to the text of it:

```
   CComBSTR bstrReturn;
   pChild->get_text(&bstrReturn);
```

And the result to return back to the calling application is simply what we get from the XML response:

```
    HRESULT hResult = _wtol(bstrReturn);

    return hResult;
}
```

And that's all we need to do for our client COM object. Before we look at the calling application, let's see what the server has to do.

The OPERA server

Our server has to receive and interpret HTTP commands, sent using TCP/IP as a transport mechanism. Put simply, it's going to have to look pretty much like a web server. So we're going to have to write a web server, right? Well, I think that this is one of those things that everyone should do at least once in their lives, if only because it helps make sense of a lot of the technology that underlies the web. Are you ready? Let's go...

Creating the Project

Actually, I lied. We're not really going to write a web server. We're going to write something that *looks* like a web server. We're going to build it using good old-fashioned MFC, because I happen to like MFC's socket classes, and it needs some sort of user interface; alternatively, we could use the WinSock control in Visual Basic, or the raw WinSock API from ATL. Before we start, however, we should make sure that we have switched off Internet Information Server or Personal Web Server, or anything else we have running on our machine that may have prior access to port 80. If we don't do this, we won't be able to have our own server listening on port 80. As I said earlier, it's quite likely that in the future, SOAP will have its own port defined for it, so you'll be able to run web servers and SOAP side by side. If you're not happy with switching off or re-directing your web server, you can of course pick any other available port for SOAP. You'll need to start by creating a dialog-based project using the MFC AppWizard, making sure that the sockets check box is checked.

We need a couple of classes for the socket stuff: a "main" class and a "client" class. The "main" one, `COperaMainSocket`, is the one from which we derive the object that listens on port 80 for incoming calls. When it accepts one of these, it creates a `COperaClientSocket` object. In actual fact, there's no reason why we couldn't put everything that any of the sockets does into one class, but my personal view is that this makes the whole thing less readable. Both of these classes derive from the standard MFC class `CAsyncSocket`.

The Main Socket Class

The "main" socket class overrides one standard method: `OnAccept()`. This is what the class definition looks like. Again, the highlighted lines are the ones which have been added after the MFC AppWizard has done its work:

```
///////////////////////////////////////////////////////////////////////////
// COperaMainSocket command target

class COperaMainSocket : public CAsyncSocket
{
// Attributes
public:

// Operations
public:
   COperaMainSocket();
   virtual ~COperaMainSocket();

// Overrides
public:
   // ClassWizard generated virtual function overrides
   //{{AFX_VIRTUAL(COperaMainSocket)
   //}}AFX_VIRTUAL

   // Generated message map functions
   //{{AFX_MSG(COperaMainSocket)
      // NOTE - the ClassWizard will add and remove member functions here.
   //}}AFX_MSG

// Implementation
protected:
   CObArray m_sockArray;

public:
   void Check();
};
```

The one new member variable is an object array that we'll use for storing pointers to our client socket objects. Here are the constructor and destructor for the class:

```
COperaMainSocket::COperaMainSocket()
{
}

COperaMainSocket::~COperaMainSocket()
{
   int nSock = m_sockArray.GetSize();

   for (int sock = 0; sock < nSock; sock++)
   {
      COperaClientSocket *pSocket =
         static_cast<COperaClientSocket *> (m_sockArray.GetAt(sock));
      delete pSocket;
   }

   m_sockArray.RemoveAll();
}
```

All we're doing here is clearing down the client socket array. The real action is in the `OnAccept()` override, which you should add via the MFC Class Wizard:

```
void COperaMainSocket::OnAccept(int nErrorCode)
{
   CWinApp *pWinApp = AfxGetApp();
   COperaServerDlg *pDialog = static_cast<COperaServerDlg *> (pWinApp-
>m_pMainWnd);

   int length = sizeof(SOCKADDR_IN);

   COperaClientSocket *pSocket = new COperaClientSocket();
   SOCKADDR_IN sockAddr;
   Accept(*pSocket, reinterpret_cast<SOCKADDR *> (&sockAddr), &length);

   m_sockArray.Add(pSocket);

   CString csAddress;
   unsigned int port;
   pSocket->GetPeerName(csAddress, port);

   CString csStatus;
   csStatus.Format("Accepting connection from %s", csAddress);
   pDialog->Status(csStatus);

   CAsyncSocket::OnAccept(nErrorCode);
}
```

All we do here is create a client socket to handle the traffic, accept the incoming TCP/IP call, and add it to our array. The rest of the code (from the declaration of `csStatus` onwards) is simply outputting some status information to the main dialog, `COperaServerDlg`, which we will see in a little while.

There's just one more method in the main socket class, and here it is:

```
void COperaMainSocket::Check()
{
   int nSock = m_sockArray.GetSize();

   for (int sock = 0; sock < nSock; sock++)
   {
      COperaClientSocket *pSocket =
         static_cast<COperaClientSocket *> (m_sockArray.GetAt (sock));

      if (!pSocket->m_bActive)
      {
         delete pSocket;
         m_sockArray.RemoveAt(sock);

         sock--;
         nSock--;
      }
   }
}
```

This is used to check to see if any client sockets have been closed. If one has, it is removed from the array. We need to do this because it's the client socket that gets notified of closure, not the main one. This method actually gets invoked on a timer from the main dialog. Again, we'll see this later, when we look at the code for `COperaServerDlg`.

The Client Socket Class

Now let's take a look at the client socket class. Remember, this is the class that handles the interactions with a single client. This has two overrides that can be added with the ClassView, `OnClose()` and `OnReceive()`. `OnClose()` gets invoked when the socket gets closed, and `OnReceive()` gets invoked when data is received by the socket. Here's the class definition:

```
#include <comdef.h>

#define SMARTPTR_TYPEDEF(x)  \
   typedef _com_ptr_t<_com_IIID<x, &IID_##x> > x##Ptr;

#include "..\SimpleOrder\SimpleOrder.h"

SMARTPTR_TYPEDEF(IOrder);

#import "msxml.dll"

///////////////////////////////////////////////////////////////////////////
// COperaClientSocket command target

class COperaClientSocket : public CAsyncSocket
{
// Attributes
public:

// Operations
public:
   COperaClientSocket();
   virtual ~COperaClientSocket();

// Overrides
public:
   // ClassWizard generated virtual function overrides
   //{{AFX_VIRTUAL(COperaClientSocket)
   virtual void OnClose(int nErrorCode);
   virtual void OnReceive(int nErrorCode);
   //}}AFX_VIRTUAL

   // Generated message map functions
   //{{AFX_MSG(COperaClientSocket)
      // NOTE - the ClassWizard will add and remove member functions here.
   //}}AFX_MSG

// Implementation
protected:
   IOrderPtr m_pOrder;

   void ReplyUnsupported();
   void ReplyBadRequest();
   void ProcessContent(int nChar, LPSTR lpszContent);

public:
   bool m_bActive;
};
```

Note the smart pointer stuff just before the definition (`#define SMARTPTR_TYPEDEF(x)` and so on) – we'll need that in order to access the order COM objects without having to go through the tedium of tracking reference counts. This isn't provided for us automatically in MFC as it is in ATL, so we have to do a little more work. Also, note again that the `#import` line sets up the smart pointers we need to access the MSXML COM objects.

The constructor and destructor are pretty unremarkable:

```
COperaClientSocket::COperaClientSocket() : m_bActive(true)
{
}

COperaClientSocket::~COperaClientSocket()
{
}
```

The `OnClose()` override is straightforward, too:

```
void COperaClientSocket::OnClose(int nErrorCode)
{
   CWinApp *pWinApp = AfxGetApp();
   COperaServerDlg *pDialog =
      static_cast<COperaServerDlg *> (pWinApp->m_pMainWnd);

   CString csStatus;

   if (nErrorCode)
      csStatus.Format("Closed with reason %d", nErrorCode);
   else
      csStatus.Format("Closed gracefully");

   pDialog->Status(csStatus);

   m_bActive = false;

   CAsyncSocket::OnClose(nErrorCode);
}
```

This outputs a suitable message to the main dialog, and then sets the active flag to `false`, so that the main socket's check method picks up the closure next time.

The real fun is in the `OnReceive()` override. Let's take a look:

```
void COperaClientSocket::OnReceive(int nErrorCode)
{
   CWinApp *pWinApp = AfxGetApp();
   COperaServerDlg *pDialog =
      static_cast<COperaServerDlg *> (pWinApp->m_pMainWnd);

   CString csStatus;

   if (nErrorCode)
   {
      csStatus.Format("OnReceive called with error code %d", nErrorCode);
      pDialog->Status(csStatus);
   }
   else
   {
```

After we've checked for a bad error status, we read in the contents of the request into a buffer. Strictly speaking, we should copy this into another cyclic buffer, and only process that when a complete line is received. TCP/IP doesn't respect message boundaries, and it is quite possible to receive half a message first, or even one and a half messages. However, for simplicity's sake, we'll assume that one and only one complete message has been received. The parsing of the message proceeds in a very similar manner to the `OperaClient` COM object:

```
      char szRequest[20000];
      int nChar = Receive(szRequest, sizeof(szRequest), 0);

      if (nChar > 0)
      {
         szRequest[nChar] = 0;
         pDialog->Status("Data received:");

         LPSTR lpszReturn = strstr(szRequest, "\r\n");

         if (!lpszReturn)
         {
            ReplyBadRequest();
            CAsyncSocket::OnReceive(nErrorCode);
            return;
         }

         *lpszReturn = 0;

         csStatus.Format("  %s", szRequest);
         pDialog->Status(csStatus);

         if (strcmp(szRequest, "POST /OperaServer HTTP/1.1"))
         {
            ReplyUnsupported();
            CAsyncSocket::OnReceive(nErrorCode);
            return;
         }

         bool bSoap = false;

         while (1)
         {
            LPSTR lpszSegment = lpszReturn + 2;
            lpszReturn = strstr(lpszSegment, "\r\n");

            if (!lpszReturn)
            {
               ReplyUnsupported();
               break;
            }

            *lpszReturn = 0;

            csStatus.Format("  %s", lpszSegment);
            pDialog->Status(csStatus);
```

```
            if (!strncmp(lpszSegment, "Content-Type: ", 14))
            {
               if (!strcmp(&lpszSegment[14], "text/xml"))
                  bSoap = true;
               else
               {
                  ReplyUnsupported();
                  break;
               }
            }
            else if (!strncmp(lpszSegment, "Content-Length: ", 16))
            {
               if (!bSoap)
               {
                  ReplyBadRequest();
                  break;
               }
               int nChar = atoi(&lpszSegment[16]);
               ProcessContent(nChar, lpszReturn + 2);

               break;
            }
         }
      }
   }

   CAsyncSocket::OnReceive(nErrorCode);
}
```

The principal differences between this code and that for the `OperaClient` COM object are that here the method `Receive()` is used instead of the raw `recv()` API call, and that error conditions are handled by messages sent back to the calling client, rather than being reported to the client using `AtlReportError()`.

As with the COM object, the real meat is in the `ProcessContent()` method:

```
void COperaClientSocket::ProcessContent(int nChar, LPSTR lpszContent)
{
   if (strncmp(lpszContent, "SOAPMethodName: www.jpassoc.co.uk/opera#", 40))
   {
      ReplyBadRequest();
      return;
   }

   LPSTR lpszMethod = &lpszContent[40];
   LPSTR lpszReturn = strchr(lpszMethod, '\r');

   if (!lpszReturn)
   {
      ReplyBadRequest();
      return;
   }

   *lpszReturn = NULL;
```

The first difference between the requirement here and that of the `OperaClient` COM object is that if we haven't got an order object already, we need to create one. Here we go:

```
if (m_pOrder == NULL)
   CoCreateInstance(CLSID_Order, NULL, CLSCTX_LOCAL_SERVER, IID_IOrder,
                    (void **) &m_pOrder);
```

Once that's out of the way, we can parse the content using XML DOM in a similar manner to last time:

```
MSXML::IXMLDOMDocumentPtr pXML;
CoCreateInstance(__uuidof(MSXML::DOMDocument), NULL, CLSCTX_INPROC_SERVER,
                 __uuidof(MSXML::IXMLDOMDocument), (void **) &pXML);

CString csXML = lpszReturn + 1;
BSTR bstrXML = csXML.AllocSysString();

VARIANT_BOOL success;
success = pXML->loadXML(bstrXML);

::SysFreeString(bstrXML);

MSXML::IXMLDOMElementPtr pElem;
pXML->get_documentElement(&pElem);

bool bClose = false;

HRESULT hResult = S_OK;
```

However, this time, we're actually going to invoke the methods as we get them. First of all, there's the one with no arguments:

```
if (!strcmp(lpszMethod, "Submit"))
{
   hResult = m_pOrder->Submit();
   bClose = true;
}
else
{
   MSXML::IXMLDOMNodePtr pChild;
   pElem->get_firstChild(&pChild);

   BSTR bstrArg;
   pChild->get_text(&bstrArg);
```

Then there's all the ones with a single argument:

```
   if (!strcmp(lpszMethod, "put_CustomerID"))
      hResult = m_pOrder->put_CustomerID(bstrArg);
   else if (!strcmp(lpszMethod, "put_Title"))
      hResult = m_pOrder->put_Title(bstrArg);
   else if (!strcmp(lpszMethod, "put_Artist"))
      hResult = m_pOrder->put_Artist(bstrArg);
   else if (!strcmp(lpszMethod, "put_Label"))
      hResult = m_pOrder->put_Label(bstrArg);
   else if (!strcmp(lpszMethod, "put_Price"))
      hResult = m_pOrder->put_Price(bstrArg);

   SysFreeString(bstrArg);
}
```

Finally, all we have to do is construct a SOAP response containing our result and send it:

```
    char szCallResponse[2000];

    strcpy(szCallResponse,
           "<SOAP:Envelope xmlns:SOAP=\"urn:schemas-xmlsoap-org:soap.v1\">\r\n");
    strcat(szCallResponse, "<SOAP:Body>\r\n");

    size_t length = strlen(szCallResponse);
    sprintf(&szCallResponse[length],
            "<m:%sResponse xmlns:m=\"www.jpassoc.co.uk/opera\">\r\n",
            lpszMethod);

    length = strlen (szCallResponse);
    sprintf(&szCallResponse[length], "            <return>%d</return>\r\n",
            hResult);

    length = strlen(szCallResponse);
    sprintf(&szCallResponse[length], "         </m:%sResponse>\r\n"
            "      </SOAP:Body>\r\n   </SOAP:Envelope>", lpszMethod);

    length = strlen(szCallResponse);

    char szResponse[2000];

    if (bClose)
       sprintf(szResponse, "HTTP/1.1 200 OK\r\nConnection: close\r\n"
               "Content-Type: text/xml\r\nContent-Length: %d\r\n%s",
               length, szCallResponse);
    else
       sprintf(szResponse, "HTTP/1.1 200 OK\r\nConnection: Keep-Alive\r\n"
               "Content-Type: text/xml\r\nContent-Length: %d\r\n%s",
               length, szCallResponse);

    Send(szResponse, strlen(szResponse), 0);
 }
```

There are two other helper methods, which are self-explanatory:

```
 void COperaClientSocket::ReplyUnsupported()
 {
    CWinApp *pWinApp = AfxGetApp();
    COperaServerDlg *pDialog =
         static_cast<COperaServerDlg *> (pWinApp->m_pMainWnd);
    pDialog->Status ("Replying \"Not supported\"");

    Send("HTTP/1.1 501 Not supported", 25, 0);
 }

 void COperaClientSocket::ReplyBadRequest()
 {
    CWinApp *pWinApp = AfxGetApp();
    COperaServerDlg *pDialog =
         static_cast<COperaServerDlg *> (pWinApp->m_pMainWnd);
    pDialog->Status("Replying \"Bad request\"");

    Send("HTTP/1.1 400 Bad request", 23, 0);
 }
```

Incidentally, there's no reason why a more sophisticated OPERA server couldn't just filter out and process the SOAP calls that were of interest to itself, and pass the rest on to another machine running a real web server.

The Main Dialog

Finally, we need to take a quick look at the main dialog. Apart from `OnInitDialog()`, there's one extra override: `OnTimer()`.

The dialog itself is very simple, consisting of an unsorted list box called `IDC_STATUS` and three buttons: `IDC_START`, `IDC_STOP` and `IDOK`:

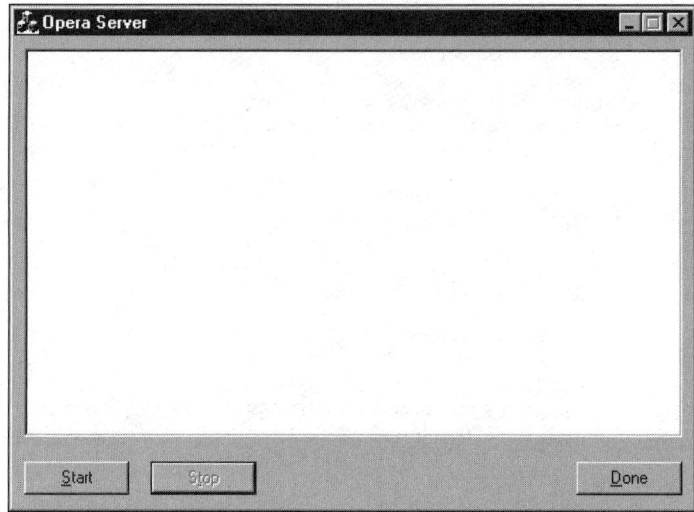

The first two buttons have `BN_CLICKED` methods associated with them, `OnStart()` and `OnStop()`. These can be added through the ClassView, along with a handler for `WM_TIMER` (`OnTimer()`), associated with the main dialog. Here's the class definition:

```
#define MAX_STATUS 1000

class COperaMainSocket;

//////////////////////////////////////////////////////////////////////////////
// COperaServerDlg dialog

class COperaServerDlg : public CDialog
{
// Construction
public:
   COperaServerDlg(CWnd* pParent = NULL);    // standard constructor

// Dialog Data
   //{{AFX_DATA(COperaServerDlg)
   enum { IDD = IDD_OPERASERVER_DIALOG };
      // NOTE: the ClassWizard will add data members here
   //}}AFX_DATA

   // ClassWizard generated virtual function overrides
   //{{AFX_VIRTUAL(COperaServerDlg)
   protected:
   virtual void DoDataExchange(CDataExchange* pDX);    // DDX/DDV support
   //}}AFX_VIRTUAL
```

```
// Implementation
public:
   void Status(CString csStatus);

protected:
   HICON m_hIcon;

   COperaMainSocket *m_pSocket;

   void Enable(int nID, BOOL bEnable);

   // Generated message map functions
   //{{AFX_MSG(COperaServerDlg)
   virtual BOOL OnInitDialog();
   afx_msg void OnSysCommand(UINT nID, LPARAM lParam);
   afx_msg void OnPaint();
   afx_msg HCURSOR OnQueryDragIcon();
   afx_msg void OnStart();
   afx_msg void OnStop();
   afx_msg void OnTimer(UINT nIDEvent);
   //}}AFX_MSG
   DECLARE_MESSAGE_MAP()
};
```

Let's see if there's anything interesting in the `OnInitDialog()` override:

```
BOOL COperaServerDlg::OnInitDialog()
{
   CDialog::OnInitDialog();

   // Add "About..." menu item to system menu.

   // IDM_ABOUTBOX must be in the system command range.
   ASSERT((IDM_ABOUTBOX & 0xFFF0) == IDM_ABOUTBOX);
   ASSERT(IDM_ABOUTBOX < 0xF000);

   CMenu* pSysMenu = GetSystemMenu(FALSE);
   if (pSysMenu != NULL)
   {
      CString strAboutMenu;
      strAboutMenu.LoadString(IDS_ABOUTBOX);
      if (!strAboutMenu.IsEmpty())
      {
         pSysMenu->AppendMenu(MF_SEPARATOR);
         pSysMenu->AppendMenu(MF_STRING, IDM_ABOUTBOX, strAboutMenu);
      }
   }

   // Set the icon for this dialog.  The framework does this automatically
   //  when the application's main window is not a dialog
   SetIcon(m_hIcon, TRUE);          // Set big icon
   SetIcon(m_hIcon, FALSE);       // Set small icon

   CoInitialize(NULL);

   SetTimer(1, 1000, NULL);

   return TRUE;  // return TRUE  unless you set the focus to a control
}
```

Nothing much there, apart from making sure that we've initialized COM, and setting the timer going to check that the sockets are still active. Remember, back when we were looking at the code for `COperaMainSocket`, we had a method that checked all the client sockets to see if they were still active? Well, this gets invoked by `COperaServerDlg`'s `OnTimer()` override:

```
void COperaServerDlg::OnTimer(UINT nIDEvent)
{
   if (m_pSocket)
      m_pSocket->Check();

   CDialog::OnTimer(nIDEvent);
}
```

So what happens when we start the OPERA server up by clicking on the Start button? Here's `OnStart()`:

```
void COperaServerDlg::OnStart()
{
   CString csStatus;

   m_pSocket = new COperaMainSocket();
   if (!m_pSocket->Create(80))
   {
      csStatus.Format("Failed to create socket, reason code %d",
                      m_pSocket->GetLastError());
      Status(csStatus);

      delete m_pSocket;
      m_pSocket = NULL;

      return;
   }

   if (!m_pSocket->Listen())
   {
      csStatus.Format("Failed to create socket, reason code %d",
                      m_pSocket->GetLastError());
      Status(csStatus);

      delete m_pSocket;
      m_pSocket = NULL;

      return;
   }

   Enable(IDC_START, FALSE);
   Enable(IDC_STOP, TRUE);
}
```

Again, this is pretty straightforward, in that all it basically involves is the creation of a main socket on port 80, followed by a listen. Once this is done, every time a new client connects, the `OnAccept()` override of `COperaMainSocket` will get invoked. `OnStop()` is even simpler:

```
void COperaServerDlg::OnStop()
{
    delete m_pSocket;
    m_pSocket = NULL;

    Enable(IDC_START, TRUE);
    Enable(IDC_STOP, FALSE);
}
```

All this enabling, by the way, is just to make sure that the right buttons are available at any time:

```
void COperaServerDlg::Enable(int nID, BOOL bEnable)
{
    CWnd *pWnd = GetDlgItem(nID);
    pWnd->EnableWindow(bEnable);
}
```

And just for completeness, here's the method that outputs information to the status list box:

```
void COperaServerDlg::Status(CString csStatus)
{
    CListBox *pStatus = static_cast<CListBox *> (GetDlgItem (IDC_STATUS));

    int count = pStatus->GetCount();
    if (count >= MAX_STATUS)
        pStatus->DeleteString(0);

    time_t now = time(NULL);
    struct tm *pTm = gmtime(&now);

    CString csFullStatus;
    csFullStatus.Format("%02d:%02d:%02d  %s", pTm->tm_hour, pTm->tm_min,
                        pTm->tm_sec, static_cast<LPCSTR> (csStatus));

    int index = pStatus->AddString(csFullStatus);
    pStatus->SetTopIndex(index);
}
```

A Quick Test

Before we connect to the client, let's have some fun by testing it stand-alone, running it, and connecting to it using Internet Explorer 5. That is, just click on Start, and while the server is running point your browser to `http://localhost/test`:

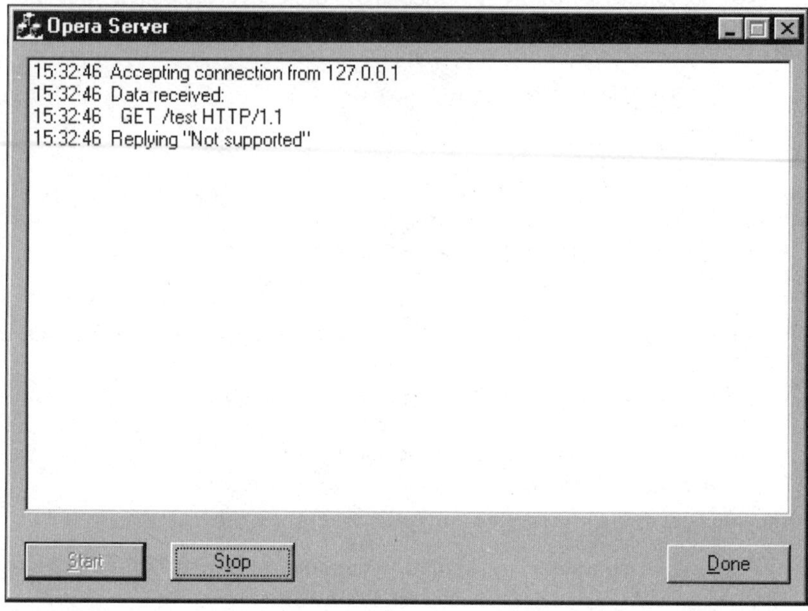

As we can see, Internet Explorer has established a connection with the local web server (in other words, OperaServer), and has sent it a GET request for "`test`". This is pretty much what we'd expect to happen so we're clear to try out our OPERA client. We'll leave the server running, ready to accept some real calls.

The Order Entry Application

For our actual order entry application, we're going to use precisely the same one as we did in *Professional DCOM Application Development*, with a few small changes. This is created using Visual Basic. Here's the one and only form, `frmOrderEntry`:

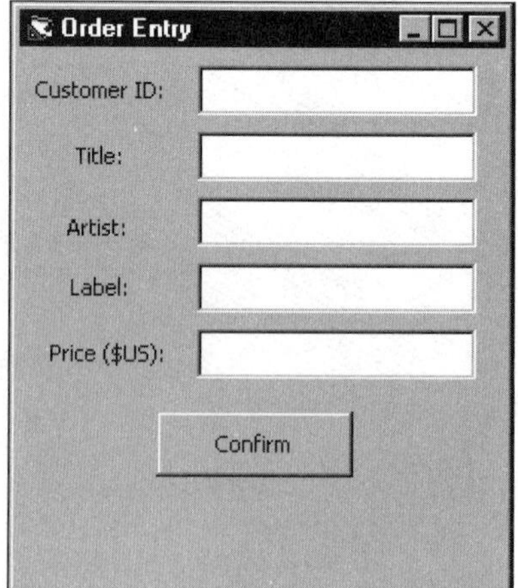

We have five text fields: `txtCustomer`, `txtTitle`, `txtArtist`, `txtLabel` and `txtPrice`. There's also a single command button, `cmdConfirm`, and (hidden away at the bottom of the form), a label, `lblError`.

Here's the Visual Basic code, with the changes from the original DCOM-oriented version highlighted:

```
Option Explicit
Const conHost = "laa-laa"
'Dim m_order As SIMPLEORDERLib.Order
Dim m_opera As OPERACLIENTLib.Opera

Private Sub HandleError(ctrl As MSForms.Control)
   If (Err.Number = 5) Then
      lblError.Caption = "Invalid input - please re-enter"
   ElseIf (Err.Number = &H80004005) Then
      lblError.Caption = "This field is mandatory"
   Else
      lblError.Caption = Err.Description
   End If
   ctrl.Tag = False
End Sub

Private Sub HandleSuccess(ctrl As MSForms.Control)
   lblError.Caption = ""
   ctrl.Tag = True
End Sub

Private Sub UserForm_Initialize()
'   Set m_order = New SIMPLEORDERLib.Order
   Set m_opera = New OPERACLIENTLib.Opera
End Sub

Private Sub txtCustomerID_Exit(ByVal Cancel As MSForms.ReturnBoolean)
On Error GoTo TryAgain
'   m_order.CustomerID = txtCustomerID.Text
   Call m_opera.Exchange(conHost, "put_CustomerID", txtCustomerID.Text)
   HandleSuccess txtCustomerID
   Exit Sub

TryAgain:
   HandleError txtCustomerID
   Cancel = True
End Sub

Private Sub txtTitle_Exit(ByVal Cancel As MSForms.ReturnBoolean)
On Error GoTo TryAgain
'   m_order.Title = txtTitle.Text
   Call m_opera.Exchange(conHost, "put_Title", txtTitle.Text)
   HandleSuccess txtTitle
   Exit Sub

TryAgain:
   HandleError txtTitle
   Cancel = True
End Sub
```

```
Private Sub txtArtist_Exit(ByVal Cancel As MSForms.ReturnBoolean)
On Error GoTo TryAgain
'    m_order.Artist = txtArtist.Text
   Call m_opera.Exchange(conHost, "put_Artist", txtArtist.Text)
   HandleSuccess txtArtist
   Exit Sub

TryAgain:
   HandleError txtArtist
   Cancel = True
End Sub

Private Sub txtLabel_Exit(ByVal Cancel As MSForms.ReturnBoolean)
On Error GoTo TryAgain
'    m_order.Label = txtLabel.Text
   Call m_opera.Exchange(conHost, "put_Label", txtLabel.Text)
   HandleSuccess txtLabel
   Exit Sub

TryAgain:
   HandleError txtLabel
   Cancel = True
End Sub

Private Sub txtPrice_Exit(ByVal Cancel As MSForms.ReturnBoolean)
On Error GoTo TryAgain
'    m_order.Price = txtPrice.Text
   Call m_opera.Exchange(conHost, "put_Price", txtPrice.Text)
   HandleSuccess txtPrice
   Exit Sub

TryAgain:
   HandleError txtPrice
   Cancel = True
End Sub

Private Sub cmdConfirm_Click()

   ' Make sure that all mandatory controls have been filled
   Dim ctrl As MSForms.Control
   For Each ctrl In Me.Controls
      If InStr(1, ctrl.Name, "txt", vbBinaryCompare) = 1 Then
         If ctrl.Tag <> "True" Then
            lblError = "This field is mandatory"
            ctrl.SetFocus
            Exit Sub
         End If
      End If
   Next ctrl

'    m_order.Submit
   Call m_opera.Exchange(conHost, "Submit", Empty)
   Unload Me
End Sub
```

Obviously, you'll need to change the value of conHost to match the name of the host where your server is running (or alternatively change the server name to laa-laa).

As you can see, what we've done is replace all the explicit DCOM calls with SOAP calls via the OPERA client (although if we'd implemented custom marshaling as we discussed back in the beginning of this chapter, we wouldn't even have had to do that). Let's see what happens when one of our clients in Ulaanbataar runs it up, assuming that our server is still running happily in Tierra del Fuego. Since we last looked at this, trends have changed in Mongolia, and late sixties psychedelia is seriously out of fashion. Instead, the thing that everyone just to have these days is a complete set of the limited edition CDs only available to members of the King Crimson Collectors' Club:

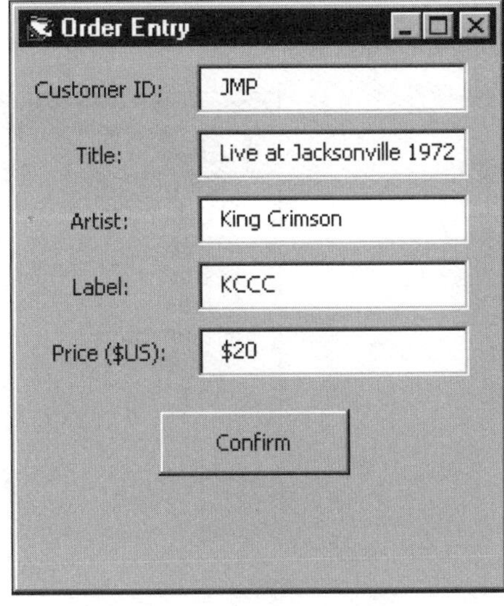

Well, I'd pay that much for it, anyway.

I'm assuming that the server is still running on host `laa-laa` following our experiment with Internet Explorer. So what do we see on the server? Here's the output:

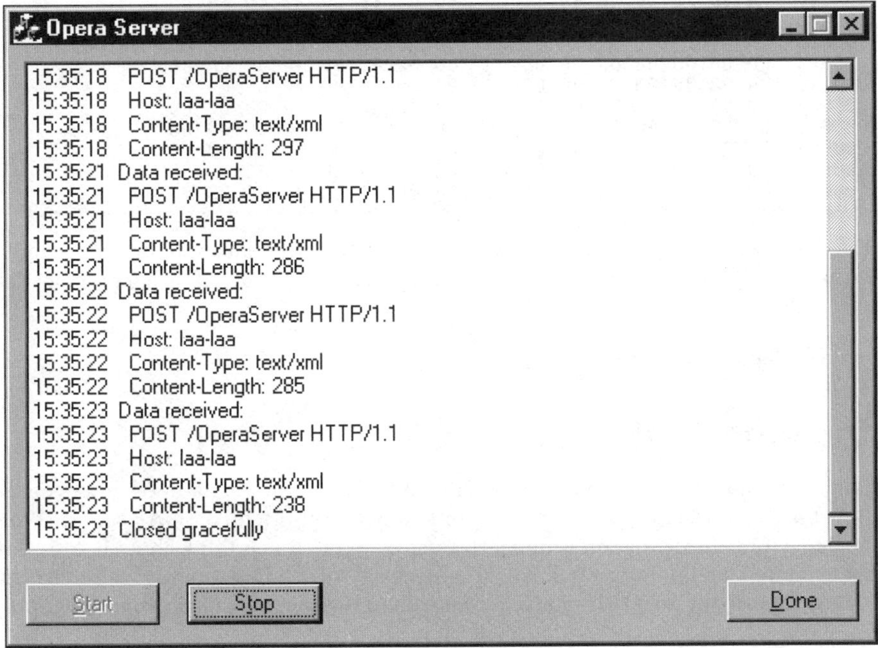

Which all looks pretty cool.

Before moving on, I guess we'd better take a look at the order file. We can use **dfview** for that, and here's what we see:

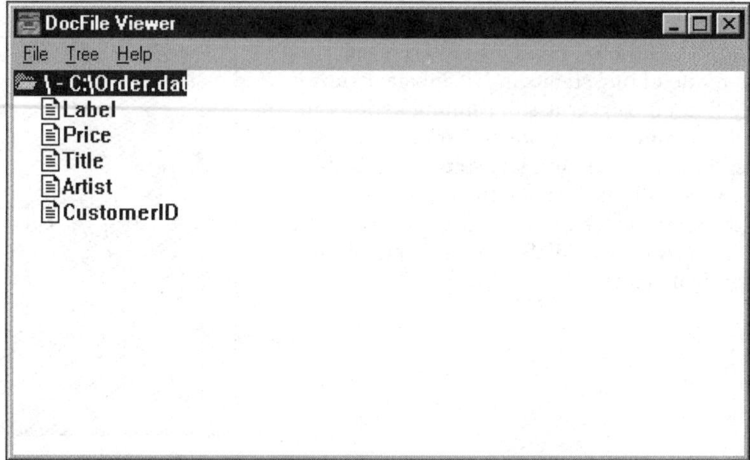

Double-click on the title, and we can see our entry right before our eyes:

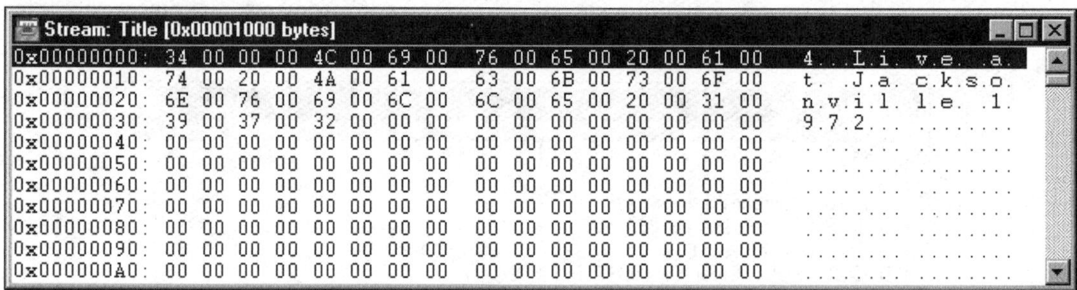

Now of course if we were writing all of this from scratch, rather than adapting an old application, we'd naturally be using XML as our file format. But you don't need to. SOAP is happy to let you do whatever you like.

So there's SOAP in action. One other thing...

Objects? What Objects?

On the Internet, famously, no-one knows you're a dog. What's more, no-one knows your server's a dog either. What if you haven't got a bright new shiny fully object-oriented SOAP server? What if you've just got a dodgy old Unix program running straight C? Well, if you think about it, SOAP doesn't really have that much to about objects at all. It's just a neat way of sending function calls through a firewall. Why not just capture those SOAP calls and direct them to function calls in your old C program?

So, yes, you really can clean up your old system with SOAP. Just for fun, I thought we might take a look at such an old system, coded up in good old-fashioned straight C (no, I couldn't bear to go back to Fortran or Cobol, I'm afraid – that would be a step too far for one of the first books of the new millennium). However, I think this one's still got retro appeal. Get out the flares and kipper ties, baby, as I present `ScumServer`. As the old saying goes, give a dog a bad name...

This little beauty was coded up to run on an old HP/UX system, which may well have stopped working by the time you read this, as I'm not currently convinced that it's Y2K compliant. Having got it working there, I transferred it to a slightly more trendy Linux system, where it proceeded to work just as well (after a couple of changes to get rid of some compiler warnings, and the addition of a call to `htons()` to convert the port number from host standard to network standard). Here we go.

We start off as ever, with the usual C header files, plus a few definitions that Unix doesn't provide for us:

```
#include <sys/socket.h>
#include <sys/time.h>
#include <netinet/in.h>
#include <errno.h>
#include <stdio.h>
#include <stdlib.h>
#include <string.h>

#define TRUE 1
#define FALSE 0

#define S_OK 0
#define E_INVALIDARG 0x80070057

#define FAILED(result) (result != S_OK)
```

This structure is the one that holds information about every incoming client socket (so it's sort of equivalent to `COperaClientSocket`). As well as this, it's also going to hold the current user's order details, so perhaps it's more of a session structure:

```
typedef struct tagSocket {
   struct tagSocket    *pNext;
   struct tagSocket    *pPrev;
   int          clientSock;
   char          *customerID;
   char          *artist;
   char          *title;
   char          *label;
   char          *price;
   } SOCKET;
```

This is the start of the linked list of socket structures:

```
SOCKET      sockHead = {NULL, NULL};
```

A few function prototypes (well actually, the compiler on this particular machine doesn't support full-blown function prototypes):

```
SOCKET* addSocket();
void    deleteSocket();
void    processRequest();
void    processContent();
```

```
void    replyUnsupported();
void    replyBadRequest();
int     put_CustomerID();
int     put_Artist();
int     put_Title();
int     put_Label();
int     put_Price();
int     submit();
int     isAlphabetic();
int     isAlphanumeric();
int     isPrice();
```

And here we go:

```
main(argc, argv)
int argc;
char **argv;
{
   int    mainSock;
   int    on;
   struct sockaddr_in address;
   struct timeval timeout;
   int    maxSock;
   fd_set readMask;
   int    addrLen;
   int    clientSock;
   int    nRead;
   char   buffer[2000];
   SOCKET *pSocket;
   SOCKET *pNextSock;
```

We start off by creating the socket, binding to it on port 80, and listening for incoming calls. Notice the use of `htons` to ensure that Linux gets the port number in the right format:

```
   mainSock = socket(AF_INET, SOCK_STREAM, 0);

   on = 1;
   setsockopt(mainSock,SOL_SOCKET, SO_REUSEADDR, (void *) &on,
              sizeof(on));

   address.sin_family = AF_INET;
   address.sin_addr.s_addr = INADDR_ANY;
   address.sin_port = htons(80);

   if (bind (mainSock, (struct sockaddr *) &address, sizeof(address)) < 0)
   {
       perror("Failed to bind to socket");
       exit(0);
   }

   listen(mainSock, 5);

   while (1)
   {
```

Here, we're preparing the all important `select` call. We're looking for read notifications on the main socket and on any client sockets that are connected. A read on the main socket is equivalent to an incoming call being signaled.

```
FD_ZERO(&readMask);
FD_SET(mainSock, &readMask);

maxSock = mainSock;

pSocket = sockHead.pNext;

while (pSocket)
{
   FD_SET(pSocket->clientSock, &readMask);

   if (maxSock < pSocket->clientSock)
      maxSock = pSocket->clientSock;

   pSocket = pSocket->pNext;
}

timeout.tv_sec = 0;
timeout.tv_usec = 100;

select(maxSock + 1, &readMask, (fd_set *) 0, (fd_set *) 0,
       &timeout);
```

Here, we're checking for an incoming call. If we have got one, we accept it, creating a new `SOCKET` structure and adding it to our linked list using the helper function `addSocket`:

```
if (FD_ISSET(mainSock, &readMask))
{
   addrLen = sizeof(struct sockaddr_in);
   clientSock = accept(mainSock, (struct sockaddr *) &address,
                       &addrLen);

   printf("Connection accepted\n");

   addSocket(clientSock);
}
```

Now we check for reads on our client sockets, by checking each one in the linked list:

```
pSocket = sockHead.pNext;

while (pSocket)
{
   pNextSock = pSocket->pNext;

   if (FD_ISSET(pSocket->clientSock, &readMask))
   {
      nRead = recv (pSocket->clientSock, buffer, sizeof(buffer), 0);
```

If there's nothing there, despite a read being signaled, the socket has either been closed, or an error has occurred, so we delete the socket structure. Otherwise, we process the request:

```
                if (nRead <= 0)
                   deleteSocket(pSocket);

                else
                {
                   buffer[nRead] = 0;
                   processRequest(pSocket, buffer);
                }
             }

             pSocket = pNextSock;
          }
       }
    }
```

That's it for the main() function. Here are a couple of helper functions which we need to handled the linked list stuff:

```
    SOCKET* addSocket(clientSock)
    int clientSock;
    {
       SOCKET *pSocket;

       printf("Adding new connection\n");

       pSocket = (SOCKET *) malloc(sizeof(SOCKET));
       memset(pSocket, 0, sizeof(SOCKET));

       pSocket->clientSock = clientSock;

       if (sockHead.pPrev)
       {
          pSocket->pPrev = sockHead.pPrev;
          (sockHead.pPrev)->pNext = pSocket;
       }
       else
       {
          pSocket->pPrev = &sockHead;
          sockHead.pNext = pSocket;
       }

       sockHead.pPrev = pSocket;

       return pSocket;
    }

    void deleteSocket(pSocket)
    SOCKET *pSocket;
    {
       printf("Deleting connection\n");
```

```
      (pSocket->pPrev)->pNext = pSocket->pNext;

      if (pSocket->pNext)
         (pSocket->pNext)->pPrev = pSocket->pPrev;
      else
         sockHead.pPrev = pSocket->pPrev;

      free(pSocket);
   }
```

Now for the meat of ScumServer. This code may be slightly familiar to you from COperaClientSocket. In fact, it's pretty much identical:

```
   void processRequest(pSocket, request)
   SOCKET *pSocket;
   char request[];
   {
      char *pReturn;
      int  bSoap;
      char *pSegment;
      int  nChar;

      printf("Data received:\n");

      pReturn = strstr(request, "\r\n");

      if (!pReturn)
      {
         replyBadRequest(pSocket);
         return;
      }

      *pReturn = 0;

      printf("  %s\n", request);

      if (strcmp(request, "POST /OperaServer HTTP/1.1"))
      {
         replyUnsupported(pSocket);
         return;
      }

      bSoap = FALSE;

      while (1)
      {
         pSegment = pReturn + 2;
         pReturn = strstr(pSegment, "\r\n");

         if (!pReturn)
         {
            replyUnsupported(pSocket);
            return;
         }
```

```
            *pReturn = 0;

            printf("   %s\n", pSegment);

            if (!strncmp(pSegment, "Content-Type: ", 14))
            {
               if (!strcmp(&pSegment[14], "text/xml"))
                  bSoap = TRUE;
               else
               {
                  replyUnsupported(pSocket);
                  break;
               }
            }
            else if (!strncmp(pSegment, "Content-Length: ", 16))
            {
               if (!bSoap)
               {
                  replyBadRequest(pSocket);
                  break;
               }
               nChar = atoi (&pSegment[16]);
               processContent (pSocket, nChar, pReturn + 2);

               break;
            }
         }
      }
```

However, the function that processes the XML content won't be, because we don't have any XML DOM to help us. We're going to have to parse the XML ourselves. Actually, this isn't quite as bad as it seems, as we're using a pretty small subset of XML, and we're not dealing with a very complex SOAP message structure.

```
   void processContent(pSocket, nChar, content)
   SOCKET *pSocket;
   int nChar;
   char content[];
   {
      char   *pMethod;
      char   *pReturn;
      char   *pXML;
      int    bClose;
      int    result;
      int    bArgument;
      char   *pElement;
      char   *pValue;
      char   callResponse[2000];
      size_t length;
      char   response[2000];
```

```
    if (strncmp (content, "SOAPMethodName: www.jpassoc.co.uk/opera#", 40))
    {
       replyBadRequest (pSocket);
       return;
    }

    pMethod = &content[40];
    pReturn = strchr (pMethod, '\r');

    if (!pReturn)
    {
       replyBadRequest (pSocket);
       return;
    }

    *pReturn = NULL;

    pXML = pReturn + 1;
```

Up to here, it's remarkably similar to `COperaClientSocket::ProcessContent`. However, from here on, we diverge for a little while, because this is the point at which `OperaServer` draws on the XML DOM:

```
    bClose = FALSE;
    result = S_OK;
```

If the method being invoked via OPERA happens to be `Submit()`, then we don't actually need to do any more parsing:

```
    if (!strcmp(pMethod, "Submit"))
    {
       result = submit(pSocket);
       bClose = TRUE;
    }
    else
    {
```

However, if one of the `put_` methods is being invoked, then we're going to have to extract the argument value. Let's use `strtok()` to extract the various elements of the XML. We're going to be in one of two states: waiting for the tag ("`<argument>`") and waiting for the argument itself. The flag `bArgument` is used to determine which:

```
       bArgument = FALSE;

       pElement = strtok(pXML, "<>\r\n");

       while (pElement)
       {
          if (bArgument)
          {
```

If we've got the tag, all we need to do is extract the argument itself, assuming that we haven't got a null value:

```
                if (!strcmp(pElement, "/argument"))
                   pValue = "";
                else
                   pValue = pElement;
```

Well, that's about it, really. We've got our argument value now, pointed to by `pValue`. So let's go ahead and invoke the required `put_` method:

```
                if (!strcmp(pMethod, "put_CustomerID"))
                   result = put_CustomerID(pSocket, pValue);
                else if (!strcmp(pMethod, "put_Title"))
                   result = put_Title(pSocket, pValue);
                else if (!strcmp(pMethod, "put_Artist"))
                   result = put_Artist(pSocket, pValue);
                else if (!strcmp(pMethod, "put_Label"))
                   result = put_Label(pSocket, pValue);
                else if (!strcmp(pMethod, "put_Price"))
                   result = put_Price(pSocket, pValue);
                break;
             }
```

And if we're still waiting for the tag, let's see if we've got it:

```
             else if (!strcmp (pElement, "argument"))
                bArgument = TRUE;
```

Now we move along to the next element in the XML:

```
             pElement = strtok(0, "<>\r\n");
          }
       }

       if (!pElement)
          replyBadRequest(pSocket);
```

Well, that wasn't too bad, was it? From here on, we're in familiar territory. This is pretty much identical to the equivalent code in `COperaClientSocket::ProcessContent`:

```
       strcpy(callResponse,
             " <SOAP:Envelope xmlns:SOAP=\"urn:schemas-xmlsoap-org:soap.v1\">\r\n");
       strcat(callResponse, "      <SOAP:Body>\r\n");

       length = strlen(callResponse);
       sprintf(&callResponse[length],
               "          <m:%sResponse xmlns:m=\"www.jpassoc.co.uk/opera\">\r\n",
               pMethod);
```

```
    length = strlen(callResponse);
    sprintf(&callResponse[length], "             <return>%d</return>\r\n",
            result);

    length = strlen(callResponse);
    sprintf(&callResponse[length], "          </m:%sResponse>\r\n"
            "       </SOAP:Body>\r\n    </SOAP:Envelope>",
            pMethod);

    length = strlen(callResponse);

    if (bClose)
       sprintf(response,
               "HTTP/1.1 200 OK\r\nConnection: close\r\n"
               "Content-Type: text/xml\r\nContent-Length: %d\r\n%s",
               length, callResponse);
    else
       sprintf(response,
               "HTTP/1.1 200 OK\r\nConnection: Keep-Alive\r\n"
               "Content-Type: text/xml\r\nContent-Length: %d\r\n%s",
               length, callResponse);

    send (pSocket->clientSock, response, strlen (response), 0);
 }
```

Here are two familiar-looking helper functions, which report error conditions back to the calling application:

```
 void replyUnsupported(pSocket)
 SOCKET *pSocket;
 {
    send(pSocket->clientSock, "HTTP/1.1 501 Not supported", 25, 0);
 }

 void replyBadRequest(pSocket)
 SOCKET *pSocket;
 {
    send(pSocket->clientSock, "HTTP/1.1 400 Bad request", 23, 0);
 }
```

And now we're into the equivalent of `SimpleOrder`. Here are the routines that set up the fields in the order:

```
 int put_CustomerID(pSocket, customerID)
 SOCKET *pSocket;
 char customerID[];
 {
    int result;

    result = isAlphabetic(customerID);

    if (FAILED(result))
       return result;
```

```
    pSocket->customerID = malloc(strlen(customerID) + 1);
    strcpy(pSocket->customerID, customerID);

    return S_OK;
}

int put_Artist(pSocket, artist)
SOCKET *pSocket;
char artist[];
{
    int result;

    result = isAlphabetic(artist);

    if (FAILED(result))
        return result;

    pSocket->artist = malloc(strlen(artist) + 1);
    strcpy(pSocket->artist, artist);

    return S_OK;
}

int put_Title (pSocket, title)
SOCKET *pSocket;
char title[];
{
    int result;

    result = isAlphanumeric(title);

    if (FAILED(result))
        return result;

    pSocket->title = malloc(strlen(title) + 1);
    strcpy(pSocket->title, title);

    return S_OK;
}

int put_Label(pSocket, label)
SOCKET *pSocket;
char label[];
{
    int result;

    result = isAlphabetic(label);

    if (FAILED(result))
        return result;

    pSocket->label = malloc(strlen(label) + 1);
    strcpy(pSocket->label, label);
```

```
    return S_OK;
}

int put_Price(pSocket, price)
SOCKET *pSocket;
char price[];
{
    int result;

    result = isPrice(price);

    if (FAILED(result))
        return result;

    pSocket->price = malloc(strlen(price) + 1);
    strcpy(pSocket->price, price);

    return S_OK;
}
```

This is the routine that submits the order (which in the case of this demo, simply involves writing the order details to a file):

```
int submit(pSocket)
SOCKET *pSocket;
{
    FILE *pOrder;

    pOrder = fopen("order.dat", "w+");

    fprintf(pOrder, "CustomerID:\t%s\n", pSocket->customerID);
    fprintf(pOrder, "Artist:\t%s\n", pSocket->artist);
    fprintf(pOrder, "Title:\t%s\n", pSocket->title);
    fprintf(pOrder, "Label:\t%s\n", pSocket->label);
    fprintf(pOrder, "Price:\t%s\n", pSocket->price);

    fclose(pOrder);

    return S_OK;
}
```

And, finally, here are the validation routines:

```
int isAlphabetic (value)
char value[];
{
    size_t nChar;
    int iChar;

    nChar = strlen(value);
```

```
    for (iChar = 0; iChar < nChar; iChar++)
    {
        if (!isspace(value[iChar]) && !isalpha (value[iChar]))
            return E_INVALIDARG;
    }

    return S_OK;
}

int isAlphanumeric(value)
char value[];
{
    size_t nChar;
    int iChar;

    nChar = strlen(value);

    for (iChar = 0; iChar < nChar; iChar++)
    {
        if (!isspace (value[iChar]) && !isalnum (value[iChar]))
            return E_INVALIDARG;
    }

    return S_OK;
}

int isPrice(value)
char value[];
{
    size_t nChar;
    int iChar;

    if (value[0] != '$')
        return E_INVALIDARG;

    nChar = strlen(value);

    for (iChar = 1; iChar < nChar; iChar++)
    {
        if (!isdigit(value[iChar]) && (value[iChar] != '.'))
        return E_INVALIDARG;
    }

    return S_OK;
}
```

If we run this up, we'll see that, as far as the client is concerned, it doesn't look any different from our nice bright shiny COM-based `OperaServer`. As before, you'll need to make sure that nothing else has got hold of port 80. This is what we see on the client:

```
Connection accepted
Adding new connection
Data received:
 POST /OperaServer HTTP/1.1
 Host: po
 Content-Type: text/xml
 Content-Length: 300
Data received:
 POST /OperaServer HTTP/1.1
 Host: po
 Content-Type: text/xml
 Content-Length: 306
Data received:
 POST /OperaServer HTTP/1.1
 Host: po
 Content-Type: text/xml
 Content-Length: 297
Data received:
 POST /OperaServer HTTP/1.1
 Host: po
 Content-Type: text/xml
 Content-Length: 286
Data received:
 POST /OperaServer HTTP/1.1
 Host: po
 Content-Type: text/xml
 Content-Length: 285
Data received:
 POST /OperaServer HTTP/1.1
 Host: po
 Content-Type: text/xml
 Content-Length: 238
Deleting connection
```

And this is what we see in the `order.dat` file:

```
CustomerID:  JMP
Artist:  King Crimson
Title:  The VROOOM Sessions 1994
Label:  KCCC
Price:  $15
```

So don't be misled by that O in SOAP. It means object in the very broadest sense of the word. The server here is coded in pure C, without any reference to objects.

Summary

So, what have we seen here? SOAP is a messaging protocol that can be used for packaging up method calls on remote objects. It's encoded in XML and uses HTTP as its transport (although this is not actually mandated by the specification, which merely defines a binding to HTTP). This makes it a neat way of tunneling through firewalls, especially when it uses a well-known port, such as 80. In future, it will almost certainly have its own standard port allocated to it.

Despite its name, SOAP doesn't actually require that the server that it communicates with is object-oriented in any way. In fact, it doesn't even require that the server treats the incoming SOAP messages as remote procedure calls at all. It's left completely up to the server to deal with each call as it sees fit.

So what's good about SOAP? Well, what's really neat is that it makes use of existing widespread technology to solve the general problem of how to standardize messaging protocols. Having established that, implementations for all sorts of applications will quickly emerge, and we can put all that messaging stuff onto one side as another problem solved.

Extensible Markup Language (XML) 1.0 Specification

This appendix is taken from the W3C Recommendation 10-February-1998 available at:

http://www.w3.org/TR/REC-xml

The appendix has also been edited in accordance with the list of errata of the 17-February-1999 posted at http://www.w3.org/XML/xml-19980210-errata

Editors:

Tim Bray (Textuality and Netscape) tbray@textuality.com
Jean Paoli (Microsoft) jeanpa@microsoft.com
C. M. Sperberg-McQueen (University of Illinois at Chicago) cmsmcq@uic.edu

Abstract

The Extensible Markup Language (XML) is a subset of SGML that is completely described in this document. Its goal is to enable generic SGML to be served, received, and processed on the Web in the way that is now possible with HTML. XML has been designed for ease of implementation and for interoperability with both SGML and HTML.

Status of this document

This document has been reviewed by W3C Members and other interested parties and has been endorsed by the Director as a W3C Recommendation. It is a stable document and may be used as reference material or cited as a normative reference from another document. W3C's role in making the Recommendation is to draw attention to the specification and to promote its widespread deployment. This enhances the functionality and interoperability of the Web.

This document specifies a syntax created by subsetting an existing, widely used international text processing standard (Standard Generalized Markup Language, ISO 8879:1986(E) as amended and corrected) for use on the World Wide Web. It is a product of the W3C XML Activity, details of which can be found at http://www.w3.org/XML. A list of current W3C Recommendations and other technical documents can be found at http://www.w3.org/TR.

This specification uses the term URI, which is defined by [Berners-Lee et al.], a work in progress expected to update [IETF RFC1738] and [IETF RFC1808].

The list of known errors in this specification is available at http://www.w3.org/XML/xml-19980210-errata.

Please report errors in this document to `xml-editor@w3.org`.

Extensible Markup Language (XML) 1.0

Table of Contents

Appendices

1. Introduction

Extensible Markup Language, abbreviated XML, describes a class of data objects called XML documents and partially describes the behavior of computer programs which process them. XML is an application profile or restricted form of SGML, the Standard Generalized Markup Language [ISO 8879]. By construction, XML documents are conforming SGML documents.

XML documents are made up of storage units called entities, which contain either parsed or unparsed data. Parsed data is made up of characters, some of which form character data, and some of which form markup. Markup encodes a description of the document's storage layout and logical structure. XML provides a mechanism to impose constraints on the storage layout and logical structure.

A software module called an **XML processor** is used to read XML documents and provide access to their content and structure. It is assumed that an XML processor is doing its work on behalf of another module, called the **application**. This specification describes the required behavior of an XML processor in terms of how it must read XML data and the information it must provide to the application.

1.1 Origin and Goals

XML was developed by an XML Working Group (originally known as the SGML Editorial Review Board) formed under the auspices of the World Wide Web Consortium (W3C) in 1996. It was chaired by Jon Bosak of Sun Microsystems with the active participation of an XML Special Interest Group (previously known as the SGML Working Group) also organized by the W3C. The membership of the XML Working Group is given in an appendix. Dan Connolly served as the WG's contact with the W3C. The design goals for XML are:

- XML shall be straightforwardly usable over the Internet.
- XML shall support a wide variety of applications.
- XML shall be compatible with SGML.
- It shall be easy to write programs which process XML documents.
- The number of optional features in XML is to be kept to the absolute minimum, ideally zero.
- XML documents should be human-legible and reasonably clear.
- The XML design should be prepared quickly.
- The design of XML shall be formal and concise.
- XML documents shall be easy to create.
- Terseness in XML markup is of minimal importance.

This specification, together with associated standards (Unicode and ISO/IEC 10646 for characters, Internet RFC 1766 for language identification tags, ISO 639 for language name codes, and ISO 3166 for country name codes), provides all the information necessary to understand XML Version 1.0 and construct computer programs to process it.

This version of the XML specification may be distributed freely, as long as all text and legal notices remain intact.

1.2 Terminology

The terminology used to describe XML documents is defined in the body of this specification. The terms defined in the following list are used in building those definitions and in describing the actions of an XML processor:

may

Conforming documents and XML processors are permitted to but need not behave as described.

must

Conforming documents and XML processors are required to behave as described; otherwise they are in error.

error

A violation of the rules of this specification; results are undefined. Conforming software may detect and report an error and may recover from it.

fatal error

An error which a conforming XML processor must detect and report to the application. After encountering a fatal error, the processor may continue processing the data to search for further errors and may report such errors to the application. In order to support correction of errors, the processor may make unprocessed data from the document (with intermingled character data and markup) available to the application. Once a fatal error is detected, however, the processor must not continue normal processing (i.e., it must not continue to pass character data and information about the document's logical structure to the application in the normal way).

at user option

Conforming software may or must (depending on the modal verb in the sentence) behave as described; if it does, it must provide users a means to enable or disable the behavior described.

validity constraint

A rule which applies to all valid XML documents. Violations of validity constraints are errors; they must, at user option, be reported by validating XML processors.

well-formedness constraint

A rule which applies to all well-formed XML documents. Violations of well-formedness constraints are fatal errors.

match

(Of strings or names:) Two strings or names being compared must be identical. Characters with multiple possible representations in ISO/IEC 10646 (e.g. characters with both precomposed and base+diacritic forms) match only if they have the same representation in both strings. At user option, processors may normalize such characters to some canonical form. No case folding is performed. (Of strings and rules in the grammar:) A string matches a grammatical production if it belongs to the language generated by that production. (Of content and content models:) An element matches its declaration when it conforms in the fashion described in the constraint "Element Valid".

for compatibility

A feature of XML included solely to ensure that XML remains compatible with SGML.

for interoperability

A non-binding recommendation included to increase the chances that XML documents can be processed by the existing installed base of SGML processors which predate the WebSGML Adaptations Annex to ISO 8879.

2. Documents

A data object is an **XML document** if it is well-formed, as defined in this specification. A well-formed XML document may in addition be valid if it meets certain further constraints.

Each XML document has both a logical and a physical structure. Physically, the document is composed of units called entities. An entity may refer to other entities to cause their inclusion in the document. A document begins in a "root" or document entity. Logically, the document is composed of declarations, elements, comments, character references, and processing instructions, all of which are indicated in the document by explicit markup. The logical and physical structures must nest properly, as described in "**4.3.2 Well-Formed Parsed Entities**".

2.1 Well-Formed XML Documents

A textual object is a well-formed XML document if:

- Taken as a whole, it matches the production labeled `document`.
- It meets all the well-formedness constraints given in this specification.
- Each of the parsed entities which is referenced directly or indirectly within the document is well-formed.

Document			
[1]	`document`	`::=`	`prolog element Misc*`

Matching the `document` production implies that:

- It contains one or more elements.
- There is exactly one element, called the **root**, or document element, no part of which appears in the content of any other element. For all other elements, if the **start-tag** is in the content of another element, the **end-tag** is in the content of the same element. More simply stated, the elements, delimited by start- and end-tags, nest properly within each other.

As a consequence of this, for each non-root element `C` in the document, there is one other element `P` in the document such that `C` is in the content of `P`, but is not in the content of any other element that is in the content of `P`. `P` is referred to as the **parent** of `C`, and `C` as a **child** of `P`.

2.2 Characters

A parsed entity contains **text**, a sequence of characters, which may represent markup or character data. A **character** is an atomic unit of text as specified by ISO/IEC 10646 [ISO/IEC 10646]. Legal characters are tab, carriage return, line feed, and the legal graphic characters of Unicode and ISO/IEC 10646. The use of "compatibility characters", as defined in section 6.8 of [Unicode], is discouraged.

Character Range				
[2]	`Char`	`::=`	`#x9 | #xA | #xD | [#x20-#xD7FF] | [#xE000-#xFFFD] | [#x10000-#x10FFFF]`	`/*any Unicode character, excluding the surrogate blocks, FFFE, and FFFF. */`

Production [2] is normative; in practical terms this means that newly added Unicode characters such as the Euro (`€ €`) are legal in XML documents.

The mechanism for encoding character code points into bit patterns may vary from entity to entity. All XML processors must accept the UTF-8 and UTF-16 encodings of 10646; the mechanisms for signaling which of the two is in use, or for bringing other encodings into play, are discussed later, in "**4.3.3 Character Encoding in Entities**".

2.3 Common Syntactic Constructs

This section defines some symbols used widely in the grammar.

`S` (white space) consists of one or more space (#x20) characters, carriage returns, line feeds, or tabs.

White Space		
[3]	`S ::=`	`(#x20 | #x9 | #xD | #xA)+`

Characters are classified for convenience as letters, digits, or other characters. Letters consist of an alphabetic or syllabic base character possibly followed by one or more combining characters, or of an ideographic character. Full definitions of the specific characters in each class are given in "**B. Character Classes**".

A **Name** is a token beginning with a letter or one of a few punctuation characters, and continuing with letters, digits, hyphens, underscores, colons, or full stops, together known as name characters. Names beginning with the string "`xml`", or any string which would match `(('X'|'x') ('M'|'m') ('L'|'l'))`, are reserved for standardization in this or future versions of this specification.

> ***NOTE**: The colon character within XML names is reserved for experimentation with name spaces. Its meaning is expected to be standardized at some future point, at which point those documents using the colon for experimental purposes may need to be updated. (There is no guarantee that any name-space mechanism adopted for XML will in fact use the colon as a name-space delimiter.) In practice, this means that authors should not use the colon in XML names except as part of name-space experiments, but that XML processors should accept the colon as a name character.*

An Nmtoken (name token) is any mixture of name characters.

<table>
<tr><th colspan="4">Names and Tokens</th></tr>
<tr><td>[4]</td><td>NameChar</td><td>::=</td><td>Letter | Digit | '.' | '-' | '_' | ':'
| CombiningChar | Extender</td></tr>
<tr><td>[5]</td><td>Name</td><td>::=</td><td>(Letter | '_' | ':') (NameChar)*</td></tr>
<tr><td>[6]</td><td>Names</td><td>::=</td><td>Name (S Name)*</td></tr>
<tr><td>[7]</td><td>Nmtoken</td><td>::=</td><td>(NameChar)+</td></tr>
<tr><td>[8]</td><td>Nmtokens</td><td>::=</td><td>Nmtoken (S Nmtoken)*</td></tr>
</table>

Literal data is any quoted string not containing the quotation mark used as a delimiter for that string. Literals are used for specifying the content of internal entities (EntityValue), the values of attributes (AttValue), and external identifiers (SystemLiteral). Note that a SystemLiteral can be parsed without scanning for markup.

<table>
<tr><th colspan="4">Literals</th></tr>
<tr><td>[9]</td><td>EntityValue</td><td>::=</td><td>'"' ([^%&"] | PEReference | Reference)* '"'
| "'" ([^%&'] | PEReference | Reference)* "'"</td></tr>
<tr><td>[10]</td><td>AttValue</td><td>::=</td><td>'"' ([^<&"] | Reference)* '"'
| "'" ([^<&'] | Reference)* "'"</td></tr>
<tr><td>[11]</td><td>SystemLiteral</td><td>::=</td><td>('"' [^"]* '"') | ("'" [^']* "'")</td></tr>
<tr><td>[12]</td><td>PubidLiteral</td><td>::=</td><td>'"' PubidChar* '"' | "'" (PubidChar - "'")* "'"</td></tr>
<tr><td>[13]</td><td>PubidChar</td><td>::=</td><td>#x20 | #xD | #xA | [a-zA-Z0-9] |
[-'()+,./:=?;!*#@$_%]</td></tr>
</table>

2.4 Character Data and Markup

Text consists of intermingled character data and markup. **Markup** takes the form of start-tags, end-tags, empty-element tags, entity references, character references, comments, CDATA section delimiters, document type declarations, and processing instructions.

All text that is not markup constitutes the **character data** of the document.

The ampersand character (&) and the left angle bracket (<) may appear in their literal form *only* when used as markup delimiters, or within a comment, a processing instruction, or a CDATA section. They are also legal within the literal entity value of an internal entity declaration; see "**4.3.2 Well-Formed Parsed Entities**". If they are needed elsewhere, they must be escaped using either numeric character references or the strings "&" and "<" respectively. The right angle bracket (>) may be represented using the string ">", and must, for compatibility, be escaped using ">" or a character reference when it appears in the string "]]>" in content, when that string is not marking the end of a CDATA section.

In the content of elements, character data is any string of characters which does not contain the start-delimiter of any markup. In a CDATA section, character data is any string of characters not including the CDATA-section-close delimiter, "]]>".

To allow attribute values to contain both single and double quotes, the apostrophe or single-quote character (') may be represented as "'", and the double-quote character (") as """.

<table>
<tr><th colspan="4">Character Data</th></tr>
<tr><td>[14]</td><td>CharData</td><td>::=</td><td>[^<&]* - ([^<&]* ']]>' [^<&]*)</td></tr>
</table>

2.5 Comments

Comments may appear anywhere in a document outside other markup; in addition, they may appear within the document type declaration at places allowed by the grammar. They are not part of the document's character data; an XML processor may, but need not, make it possible for an application to retrieve the text of comments. For compatibility, the string "--" (double-hyphen) must not occur within comments.

<table>
<tr><th colspan="4">Comments</th></tr>
<tr><td>[15]</td><td>Comment</td><td>::=</td><td>'<!--' ((Char - '-') | ('-' (Char - '-')))* '-->'</td></tr>
</table>

An example of a comment:

```
<!-- declarations for <head> & <body> -->
```

2.6 Processing Instructions

Processing instructions (PIs) allow documents to contain instructions for applications.

<table>
<tr><th colspan="4">Processing Instructions</th></tr>
<tr><td>[16]</td><td>PI</td><td>::=</td><td>'<?' PITarget (S (Char* - (Char* '?>' Char*)))? '?>'</td></tr>
<tr><td>[17]</td><td>PITarget</td><td>::=</td><td>Name - (('X' | 'x') ('M' | 'm') ('L' | 'l'))</td></tr>
</table>

PIs are not part of the document's character data, but must be passed through to the application. The PI begins with a target (PITarget) used to identify the application to which the instruction is directed. The target names "XML", "xml", and so on are reserved for standardization in this or future versions of this specification. The XML Notation mechanism may be used for formal declaration of PI targets.

2.7 CDATA Sections

CDATA sections may occur anywhere character data may occur; they are used to escape blocks of text containing characters which would otherwise be recognized as markup. CDATA sections begin with the string "<![CDATA[" and end with the string "]]>":

CDATA Sections			
[18]	CDSect	::=	CDStart CData CDEnd
[19]	CDStart	::=	'<![CDATA['
[20]	CData	::=	(Char* - (Char* ']]>' Char*))
[21]	CDEnd	::=	']]>'

Within a CDATA section, only the CDEnd string is recognized as markup, so that left angle brackets and ampersands may occur in their literal form; they need not (and cannot) be escaped using "<" and "&". CDATA sections cannot nest.

An example of a CDATA section, in which "<greeting>" and "</greeting>" are recognized as character data, not markup:

```
<![CDATA[<greeting>Hello, world!</greeting>]]>
```

2.8 Prolog and Document Type Declaration

XML documents may, and should, begin with an **XML declaration** which specifies the version of XML being used. For example, the following is a complete XML document, well-formed but not valid:

```
<?xml version="1.0"?>
<greeting>Hello, world!</greeting>
```

and so is this:

```
<greeting>Hello, world!</greeting>
```

The version number "1.0" should be used to indicate conformance to this version of this specification; it is an error for a document to use the value "1.0" if it does not conform to this version of this specification. It is the intent of the XML working group to give later versions of this specification numbers other than "1.0", but this intent does not indicate a commitment to produce any future versions of XML, nor if any are produced, to use any particular numbering scheme. Since future versions are not ruled out, this construct is provided as a means to allow the possibility of automatic version recognition, should it become necessary. Processors may signal an error if they receive documents labeled with versions they do not support.

The function of the markup in an XML document is to describe its storage and logical structure and to associate attribute-value pairs with its logical structures. XML provides a mechanism, the document type declaration, to define constraints on the logical structure and to support the use of predefined storage units. An XML document is **valid** if it has an associated document type declaration and if the document complies with the constraints expressed in it.

The document type declaration must appear before the first element in the document.

<table>
<tr><th colspan="4">Prolog</th></tr>
<tr><td>[22]</td><td>prolog</td><td>::=</td><td>XMLDecl? Misc* (doctypedecl Misc*)?</td></tr>
<tr><td>[23]</td><td>XMLDecl</td><td>::=</td><td>'<?xml' VersionInfo EncodingDecl? SDDecl? S? '?>'</td></tr>
<tr><td>[24]</td><td>VersionInfo</td><td>::=</td><td>S 'version' Eq ("'" VersionNum "'" | '"' VersionNum '"')</td></tr>
<tr><td>[25]</td><td>Eq</td><td>::=</td><td>S? '=' S?</td></tr>
<tr><td>[26]</td><td>VersionNum</td><td>::=</td><td>([a-zA-Z0-9_.:] | '-')+</td></tr>
<tr><td>[27]</td><td>Misc</td><td>::=</td><td>Comment | PI | S</td></tr>
</table>

The XML **document type declaration** contains or points to markup declarations that provide a grammar for a class of documents. This grammar is known as a document type definition, or **DTD**. The document type declaration can point to an external subset (a special kind of external entity) containing markup declarations, or can contain the markup declarations directly in an internal subset, or can do both. The DTD for a document consists of both subsets taken together.

A **markup declaration** is an element type declaration, an attribute-list declaration, an entity declaration, or a notation declaration. These declarations may be contained in whole or in part within parameter entities, as described in the well-formedness and validity constraints below. For further information, see "**4. Physical Structures**".

<table>
<tr><td>[28]</td><td>doctypedecl</td><td>::=</td><td>'<!DOCTYPE' S Name (S ExternalID)? S? ('[' (markupdecl | PEReference | S)* ']' S?)? '>'</td><td>[VC: Root Element Type]</td></tr>
<tr><td>[29]</td><td>markupdecl</td><td>::=</td><td>elementdecl | AttlistDecl | EntityDecl | NotationDecl | PI | Comment</td><td>[VC: Proper Declaration/PE Nesting]</td></tr>
<tr><td></td><td></td><td></td><td></td><td>[WFC: PEs in Internal Subset]</td></tr>
</table>

The markup declarations may be made up in whole or in part of the replacement text of parameter entities. The productions later in this specification for individual nonterminals (`elementdecl`, `AttlistDecl`, and so on) describe the declarations *after* all the parameter entities have been included.

Validity Constraint: Root Element Type

The `Name` in the document type declaration must match the element type of the root element.

Validity Constraint: Proper Declaration/PE Nesting
Parameter-entity replacement text must be properly nested with markup declarations. That is to say, if either the first character or the last character of a markup declaration (`markupdecl` above) is contained in the replacement text for a parameter-entity reference, both must be contained in the same replacement text.

Well-Formedness Constraint: PEs in Internal Subset
In the internal DTD subset, parameter-entity references can occur only where markup declarations can occur, not within markup declarations. (This does not apply to references that occur in external parameter entities or to the external subset.)

Like the internal subset, the external subset and any external parameter entities referred to in the DTD must consist of a series of complete markup declarations of the types allowed by the non-terminal symbol `markupdecl`, interspersed with white space or parameter-entity references. However, portions of the contents of the external subset or of external parameter entities may conditionally be ignored by using the conditional section construct; this is not allowed in the internal subset.

External Subset			
[30]	extSubset	::=	TextDecl? extSubsetDecl
[31]	extSubsetDecl	::=	(markupdecl | conditionalSect | PEReference | S)*

The external subset and external parameter entities also differ from the internal subset in that in them, parameter-entity references are permitted *within* markup declarations, not only *between* markup declarations.

An example of an XML document with a document type declaration:

```
<?xml version="1.0"?>
<!DOCTYPE greeting SYSTEM "hello.dtd">
<greeting>Hello, world!</greeting>
```

The system identifier "`hello.dtd`" gives the URI of a DTD for the document.

The declarations can also be given locally, as in this example:

```
<?xml version="1.0" encoding="UTF-8" ?>
<!DOCTYPE greeting [
  <!ELEMENT greeting (#PCDATA)>
]>
<greeting>Hello, world!</greeting>
```

If both the external and internal subsets are used, the internal subset is considered to occur before the external subset. This has the effect that entity and attribute-list declarations in the internal subset take precedence over those in the external subset.

2.9 Standalone Document Declaration

Markup declarations can affect the content of the document, as passed from an XML processor to an application; examples are attribute defaults and entity declarations. The standalone document declaration, which may appear as a component of the XML declaration, signals whether or not there are such declarations which appear external to the document entity.

<table>
<tr><th colspan="4">Standalone Document Declaration</th></tr>
<tr><td>[32]</td><td>SDDecl</td><td>::= S 'standalone' Eq (("'"
('yes' | 'no') "'") | ('"'
('yes' | 'no') '"'))</td><td>[VC: Standalone Document Declaration]</td></tr>
</table>

In a standalone document declaration, the value "yes" indicates that there are no markup declarations external to the document entity (either in the DTD external subset, or in an external parameter entity referenced from the internal subset) which affect the information passed from the XML processor to the application. The value "no" indicates that there are or may be such external markup declarations. Note that the standalone document declaration only denotes the presence of external *declarations*; the presence, in a document, of references to external *entities*, when those entities are internally declared, does not change its standalone status.

If there are no external markup declarations, the standalone document declaration has no meaning. If there are external markup declarations but there is no standalone document declaration, the value "no" is assumed.

Any XML document for which `standalone="no"` holds can be converted algorithmically to a standalone document, which may be desirable for some network delivery applications.

Validity Constraint: Standalone Document Declaration
The standalone document declaration must have the value "no" if any external markup declarations contain declarations of:

- attributes with default values, if elements to which these attributes apply appear in the document without specifications of values for these attributes, or
- entities (other than `amp`, `lt`, `gt`, `apos`, `quot`), if references to those entities appear in the document, or
- attributes with values subject to **normalization**, where the attribute appears in the document with a value which will change as a result of normalization, or
- element types with element content, if white space occurs directly within any instance of those types.

An example XML declaration with a standalone document declaration:

```
<?xml version="1.0" standalone='yes'?>
```

2.10 White Space Handling

In editing XML documents, it is often convenient to use "white space" (spaces, tabs, and blank lines, denoted by the nonterminal `S` in this specification) to set apart the markup for greater readability. Such white space is typically not intended for inclusion in the delivered version of the document. On the other hand, "significant" white space that should be preserved in the delivered version is common, for example in poetry and source code.

An XML processor must always pass all characters in a document that are not markup through to the application. A validating XML processor must also inform the application which of these characters constitute white space appearing in element content.

A special attribute named `xml:space` may be attached to an element to signal an intention that in that element, white space should be preserved by applications. In valid documents, this attribute, like any other, must be declared if it is used. When declared, it must be given as an enumerated type whose only possible values are "`default`" and "`preserve`". For example:

```
<!ATTLIST poem   xml:space (default|preserve) 'preserve'>
```

The value "`default`" signals that applications' default white-space processing modes are acceptable for this element; the value "`preserve`" indicates the intent that applications preserve all the white space. This declared intent is considered to apply to all elements within the content of the element where it is specified, unless overriden with another instance of the `xml:space` attribute.

The root element of any document is considered to have signaled no intentions as regards application space handling, unless it provides a value for this attribute or the attribute is declared with a default value.

2.11 End-of-Line Handling

XML parsed entities are often stored in computer files which, for editing convenience, are organized into lines. These lines are typically separated by some combination of the characters carriage-return (#xD) and line-feed (#xA).

To simplify the tasks of applications, wherever an external parsed entity or the literal entity value of an internal parsed entity contains either the literal two-character sequence "#xD#xA" or a standalone literal #xD, an XML processor must pass to the application the single character #xA. (This behavior can conveniently be produced by normalizing all line breaks to #xA on input, before parsing.)

2.12 Language Identification

In document processing, it is often useful to identify the natural or formal language in which the content is written. A special attribute named `xml:lang` may be inserted in documents to specify the language used in the contents and attribute values of any element in an XML document. In valid documents, this attribute, like any other, must be declared if it is used. The values of the attribute are language identifiers as defined by [IETF RFC 1766], "Tags for the Identification of Languages":

Language Identification			
[33]	LanguageID	::=	Langcode ('-' Subcode)*
[34]	Langcode	::=	ISO639Code | IanaCode | UserCode
[35]	ISO639Code	::=	([a-z] | [A-Z]) ([a-z] | [A-Z])
[36]	IanaCode	::=	('i' | 'I') '-' ([a-z] | [A-Z])+
[37]	UserCode	::=	('x' | 'X') '-' ([a-z] | [A-Z])+
[38]	Subcode	::=	([a-z] | [A-Z])+

The `Langcode` may be any of the following:

- a two-letter language code as defined by [ISO 639], "Codes for the representation of names of languages"
- a language identifier registered with the Internet Assigned Numbers Authority [IANA]; these begin with the prefix "`i-`" (or "`I-`")
- a language identifier assigned by the user, or agreed on between parties in private use; these must begin with the prefix "`x-`" or "`X-`" in order to ensure that they do not conflict with names later standardized or registered with IANA

There may be any number of `Subcode` segments; if the first subcode segment exists and the Subcode consists of two letters, then it must be a country code from [ISO 3166], "Codes for the representation of names of countries." If the first subcode consists of more than two letters, it must be a subcode for the language in question registered with IANA, unless the `Langcode` begins with the prefix "`x-`" or "`X-`".

It is customary to give the language code in lower case, and the country code (if any) in upper case. Note that these values, unlike other names in XML documents, are case insensitive.

For example:

```
<p xml:lang="en">The quick brown fox jumps over the lazy dog.</p>
<p xml:lang="en-GB">What colour is it?</p>
<p xml:lang="en-US">What color is it?</p>
<sp who="Faust" desc='leise' xml:lang="de">
  <l>Habe nun, ach! Philosophie,</l>
  <l>Juristerei, und Medizin</l>
  <l>und leider auch Theologie</l>
  <l>durchaus studiert mit heißem Bemüh'n.</l>
</sp>
```

The intent declared with `xml:lang` is considered to apply to all attributes and content of the element where it is specified, unless overridden with an instance of `xml:lang` on another element within that content.

A simple declaration for `xml:lang` might take the form:

```
xml:lang  NMTOKEN  #IMPLIED
```

but specific default values may also be given, if appropriate. In a collection of French poems for English students, with glosses and notes in English, the `xml:lang` attribute might be declared this way:

```
<!ATTLIST poem   xml:lang NMTOKEN 'fr'>
<!ATTLIST gloss  xml:lang NMTOKEN 'en'>
<!ATTLIST note   xml:lang NMTOKEN 'en'>
```

3. Logical Structures

Each XML document contains one or more **elements**, the boundaries of which are either delimited by start-tags and end-tags, or, for empty elements, by an empty-element tag. Each element has a type, identified by name, sometimes called its "generic identifier" (GI), and may have a set of attribute specifications. Each attribute specification has a name and a value.

Element				
[39]	`element`	`::=`	`EmptyElemTag`	
			`| STag content ETag`	`[WFC: Element Type Match ]`
				`[VC: Element Valid ]`

This specification does not constrain the semantics, use, or (beyond syntax) names of the element types and attributes, except that names beginning with a match to `(('X'|'x')('M'|'m')('L'|'l'))` are reserved for standardization in this or future versions of this specification.

Well-Formedness Constraint: Element Type Match
The `Name` in an element's end-tag must match the element type in the start-tag.

- ***Validity Constraint: Element Valid***
  An element is valid if there is a declaration matching `elementdecl` where the `Name` matches the element type, and one of the following holds:

- The declaration matches `EMPTY` and the element has no content.
- The declaration matches `children` and the sequence of child elements belongs to the language generated by the regular expression in the content model, with optional white space (characters matching the nonterminal `S`) between each pair of child elements.
- The declaration matches `Mixed` and the content consists of character data and child elements whose types match names in the content model.
- The declaration matches `ANY`, and the types of any child elements have been declared.

3.1 Start-Tags, End-Tags, and Empty-Element Tags

The beginning of every non-empty XML element is marked by a **start-tag**.

Start-tag				
[40]	`STag`	`::=`	`'<' Name (S Attribute)* S? '>'`	`[WFC: Unique Att Spec ]`

[41]	`Attribute`	`::=`	`Name Eq AttValue`	`[VC: Attribute Value Type ]`
				`[WFC: No External Entity References ]`
				`[WFC: No < in Attribute Values ]`

The `Name` in the start- and end-tags gives the element's **type**. The `Name-AttValue` pairs are referred to as the **attribute specifications** of the element, with the `Name` in each pair referred to as the **attribute name** and the content of the `AttValue` (the text between the `'` or `"` delimiters) as the **attribute value**.

Well-Formedness Constraint: Unique Att Spec
No attribute name may appear more than once in the same start-tag or empty-element tag.

Validity Constraint: Attribute Value Type
The attribute must have been declared; the value must be of the type declared for it. (For attribute types, see "3.3 Attribute-List Declarations".)

Well-Formedness Constraint: No External Entity References
Attribute values cannot contain direct or indirect entity references to external entities.

Well-Formedness Constraint: No < in Attribute Values
The replacement text of any entity referred to directly or indirectly in an attribute value (other than "`<`") must not contain a <.

An example of a start-tag:

```
<termdef id="dt-dog" term="dog">
```

The end of every element that begins with a start-tag must be marked by an **end-tag** containing a name that echoes the element's type as given in the start-tag:

End-tag			
[42]	`ETag`	`::=`	`'</' Name S? '>'`

An example of an end-tag:

```
</termdef>
```

The text between the start-tag and end-tag is called the element's **content**:

Content of Elements			
[43]	content	::=	(element | CharData | Reference | CDSect | PI | Comment)*

If an element is **empty**, it must be represented either by a start-tag immediately followed by an end-tag or by an empty-element tag. An **empty-element tag** takes a special form:

Tags for Empty Elements			
[44]	EmptyElemTag	::=	'<' Name (S Attribute)* S? '/>' [WFC: Unique Att Spec]

Empty-element tags may be used for any element which has no content, whether or not it is declared using the keyword `EMPTY`. For interoperability, the empty-element tag must be used, and can only be used, for elements which are declared `EMPTY`.

Examples of empty elements:

```
<IMG align="left"
 src="http://www.w3.org/Icons/WWW/w3c_home" />
<br></br>
<br/>
```

3.2 Element Type Declarations

The element structure of an XML document may, for validation purposes, be constrained using element type and attribute-list declarations. An element type declaration constrains the element's content.

Element type declarations often constrain which element types can appear as children of the element. At user option, an XML processor may issue a warning when a declaration mentions an element type for which no declaration is provided, but this is not an error.

An **element type declaration** takes the form:

Element Type Declaration				
[45]	elementdecl	::=	'<!ELEMENT' S Name S contentspec S? '>'	[VC: Unique Element Type Declaration]
[46]	contentspec	::=	'EMPTY' | 'ANY' | Mixed | children	

where the `Name` gives the element type being declared.

Validity Constraint: Unique Element Type Declaration
No element type may be declared more than once.

Examples of element type declarations:

```
<!ELEMENT br EMPTY>
<!ELEMENT p (#PCDATA|emph)* >
<!ELEMENT %name.para; %content.para; >
<!ELEMENT container ANY>
```

3.2.1 Element Content

An element type has **element content** when elements of that type must contain only child elements (no character data), optionally separated by white space (characters matching the nonterminal `S`). In this case, the constraint includes a content model, a simple grammar governing the allowed types of the child elements and the order in which they are allowed to appear. The grammar is built on content particles (`cp`s), which consist of names, choice lists of content particles, or sequence lists of content particles:

Element-content Models

[47]	`children`	`::=`	`(choice | seq) ('?' | '*' | '+')?`	
[48]	`cp`	`::=`	`(Name | choice | seq) ('?' | '*' | '+')?`	
[49]	`choice`	`::=`	`'(' S? cp ( S? '|' S? cp )* S? ')'`	[VC: Proper Group/PE Nesting]
[50]	`seq`	`::=`	`'(' S? cp ( S? ',' S? cp )* S? ')'`	[VC: Proper Group/PE Nesting]

where each `Name` is the type of an element which may appear as a child. Any content particle in a choice list may appear in the element content at the location where the choice list appears in the grammar; content particles occurring in a sequence list must each appear in the element content in the order given in the list. The optional character following a name or list governs whether the element or the content particles in the list may occur one or more (`+`), zero or more (`*`), or zero or one times (`?`). The absence of such an operator means that the element or content particle must appear exactly once. This syntax and meaning are identical to those used in the productions in this specification.

The content of an element matches a content model if and only if it is possible to trace out a path through the content model, obeying the sequence, choice, and repetition operators and matching each element in the content against an element type in the content model. For compatibility, it is an error if an element in the document can match more than one occurrence of an element type in the content model. For more information, see **Appendix E. Deterministic Content Models**.

Validity Constraint: Proper Group/PE Nesting

Parameter-entity replacement text must be properly nested with parenthesized groups. That is to say, if either of the opening or closing parentheses in a `choice`, `seq`, or `Mixed` construct is contained in the replacement text for a parameter entity, both must be contained in the same replacement text. For interoperability, if a parameter-entity reference appears in a `choice`, `seq`, or `Mixed` construct, its replacement text should not be empty, and neither the first nor last non-blank character of the replacement text should be a connector (`|` or `,`).

Examples of element-content models:

```
<!ELEMENT spec (front, body, back?)>
<!ELEMENT div1 (head, (p | list | note)*, div2*)>
<!ELEMENT dictionary-body (%div.mix; | %dict.mix;)*>
```

3.2.2 Mixed Content

An element type has **mixed content** when elements of that type may contain character data, optionally interspersed with child elements. In this case, the types of the child elements may be constrained, but not their order or their number of occurrences:

Mixed-content Declaration				
[51]	`Mixed`	`::=`	`'(' S? '#PCDATA' (S? '|' S? Name)* S? ')*'` `| '(' S? '#PCDATA' S? ')'`	[VC: Proper Group/PE Nesting] [VC: No Duplicate Types]

where the Names give the types of elements that may appear as children. The keyword PCDATA derives historically from the term "parsed character data".

Validity Constraint: No Duplicate Types
The same name must not appear more than once in a single mixed-content declaration.

Examples of mixed content declarations:

```
<!ELEMENT p (#PCDATA|a|ul|b|i|em)*>
<!ELEMENT p (#PCDATA | %font; | %phrase; | %special; | %form;)* >
<!ELEMENT b (#PCDATA)>
```

3.3 Attribute-List Declarations

Attributes are used to associate name-value pairs with elements. Attribute specifications may appear only within start-tags and empty-element tags; thus, the productions used to recognize them appear in "**3.1 Start-Tags, End-Tags, and Empty-Element Tags**". Attribute-list declarations may be used:

- To define the set of attributes pertaining to a given element type.
- To establish type constraints for these attributes.
- To provide default values for attributes.

Attribute-list declarations specify the name, data type, and default value (if any) of each attribute associated with a given element type:

Attribute-list Declaration			
[52]	`AttlistDecl`	`::=`	`'<!ATTLIST' S Name AttDef* S? '>'`
[53]	`AttDef`	`::=`	`S Name S AttType S DefaultDecl`

The `Name` in the `AttlistDecl` rule is the type of an element. At user option, an XML processor may issue a warning if attributes are declared for an element type not itself declared, but this is not an error. The `Name` in the `AttDef` rule is the name of the attribute.

When more than one `AttlistDecl` is provided for a given element type, the contents of all those provided are merged. When more than one definition is provided for the same attribute of a given element type, the first declaration is binding and later declarations are ignored. For interoperability, writers of DTDs may choose to provide at most one attribute-list declaration for a given element type, at most one attribute definition for a given attribute name in an attribute-list declaration, and at least one attribute definition in each attribute-list declaration. For interoperability, an XML processor may at user option issue a warning when more than one attribute-list declaration is provided for a given element type, or more than one attribute definition is provided for a given attribute, but this is not an error.

3.3.1 Attribute Types

XML attribute types are of three kinds: a string type, a set of tokenized types, and enumerated types. The string type may take any literal string as a value; the tokenized types have varying lexical and semantic constraints. The validity constraints noted in the grammar are applied after the attribute value has been normalized as described in **Section 3.3 Attribute-List Declarations**.

Attribute Types				
[54]	`AttType`	`::=`	`StringType | TokenizedType | EnumeratedType`	
[55]	`StringType`	`::=`	`'CDATA'`	
[56]	`TokenizedType`	`::=`	`'ID'`	[VC: ID]
			`| 'IDREF'`	[VC: One ID per Element Type]
			`| 'IDREFS'`	[VC: ID Attribute Default]
			`| 'ENTITY'`	[VC: IDREF]
			`| 'ENTITIES'`	[VC: IDREF]
			`| 'NMTOKEN'`	[VC: Entity Name]
			`| 'NMTOKENS'`	[VC: Entity Name]
				[VC: Name Token]
				[VC: Name Token]

Validity Constraint: ID

Values of type `ID` must match the `Name` production. A name must not appear more than once in an XML document as a value of this type; i.e., ID values must uniquely identify the elements which bear them.

Validity Constraint: One ID per Element Type

No element type may have more than one ID attribute specified.

Validity Constraint: ID Attribute Default

An ID attribute must have a declared default of `#IMPLIED` or `#REQUIRED`.

Validity Constraint: IDREF
Values of type IDREF must match the Name production, and values of type IDREFS must match Names; each Name must match the value of an ID attribute on some element in the XML document; i.e. IDREF values must match the value of some ID attribute.

Validity Constraint: Entity Name
Values of type ENTITY must match the Name production, values of type ENTITIES must match Names; each Name must match the name of an unparsed entity declared in the DTD.

Validity Constraint: Name Token
Values of type NMTOKEN must match the Nmtoken production; values of type NMTOKENS must match Nmtokens.

Enumerated attributes can take one of a list of values provided in the declaration. There are two kinds of enumerated types:

Enumerated Attribute Types				
[57]	EnumeratedType	::=	NotationType | Enumeration	
[58]	NotationType	::=	'NOTATION' S '(' S? Name (S? '|' S? Name)* S? ')'	[VC: Notation Attributes] [VC: One Notation per Element Type]
[59]	Enumeration	::=	'(' S? Nmtoken (S? '|' S? Nmtoken)* S? ')'	[VC: Enumeration]

A NOTATION attribute identifies a notation, declared in the DTD with associated system and/or public identifiers, to be used in interpreting the element to which the attribute is attached.

Validity Constraint: Notation Attributes
Values of this type must match one of the notation names included in the declaration; all notation names in the declaration must be declared.
Validity Constraint: One Notation per Element Type
No element type may have more than one NOTATION attribute specified.

Validity Constraint: Enumeration
Values of this type must match one of the Nmtoken tokens in the declaration.

For interoperability, the same Nmtoken should not occur more than once in the enumerated attribute types of a single element type.

3.3.2 Attribute Defaults

An attribute declaration provides information on whether the attribute's presence is required, and if not, how an XML processor should react if a declared attribute is absent in a document.

Attribute Defaults				
[60]	DefaultDecl	::=	'#REQUIRED' | '#IMPLIED'	
			| (('#FIXED' S)? AttValue)	[VC: Required Attribute]
				[VC: Attribute Default Legal]
				[WFC: No < in Attribute Values]
				[VC: Fixed Attribute Default]

In an attribute declaration, `#REQUIRED` means that the attribute must always be provided, `#IMPLIED` that no default value is provided. If the declaration is neither `#REQUIRED` nor `#IMPLIED`, then the `AttValue` value contains the declared **default** value; the `#FIXED` keyword states that the attribute must always have the default value. If a default value is declared, when an XML processor encounters an omitted attribute, it is to behave as though the attribute were present with the declared default value.

Validity Constraint: Required Attribute
If the default declaration is the keyword `#REQUIRED`, then the attribute must be specified for all elements of the type in the attribute-list declaration.

Validity Constraint: Attribute Default Legal
The declared default value must meet the lexical constraints of the declared attribute type.

Validity Constraint: Fixed Attribute Default
If an attribute has a default value declared with the `#FIXED` keyword, instances of that attribute must match the default value.

Examples of attribute-list declarations:

```
<!ATTLIST termdef
          id      ID      #REQUIRED
          name    CDATA   #IMPLIED>
<!ATTLIST list
          type    (bullets|ordered|glossary)  "ordered">
<!ATTLIST form
          method  CDATA   #FIXED "POST">
```

3.3.3 Attribute-Value Normalization

Before the value of an attribute is passed to the application or checked for validity, the XML processor must normalize it as follows:

- a character reference is processed by appending the referenced character to the attribute value
- an entity reference is processed by recursively processing the replacement text of the entity
- a whitespace character (#x20, #xD, #xA, #x9) is processed by appending #x20 to the normalized value, except that only a single #x20 is appended for a "#xD#xA" sequence that is part of an external parsed entity or the literal entity value of an internal parsed entity
- other characters are processed by appending them to the normalized value

If the declared value is not CDATA, then the XML processor must further process the normalized attribute value by discarding any leading and trailing space (#x20) characters, and by replacing sequences of space (#x20) characters by a single space (#x20) character.

All attributes for which no declaration has been read should be treated by a non-validating parser as if declared CDATA.

3.4 Conditional Sections

Conditional sections are portions of the document type declaration external subset which are included in, or excluded from, the logical structure of the DTD based on the keyword which governs them.

Conditional Section			
[61]	conditionalSect	::=	includeSect | ignoreSect
[62]	includeSect	::=	'<![' S? 'INCLUDE' S? '[' extSubsetDecl ']]>'
[63]	ignoreSect	::=	'<![' S? 'IGNORE' S? '[' ignoreSectContents* ']]>'
[64]	ignoreSectContents	::=	Ignore ('<![' ignoreSectContents ']]>' Ignore)*
[65]	Ignore	::=	Char* - (Char* ('<![' | ']]>') Char*)

Like the internal and external DTD subsets, a conditional section may contain one or more complete declarations, comments, processing instructions, or nested conditional sections, intermingled with white space.

If the keyword of the conditional section is INCLUDE, then the contents of the conditional section are part of the DTD. If the keyword of the conditional section is IGNORE, then the contents of the conditional section are not logically part of the DTD. Note that for reliable parsing, the contents of even ignored conditional sections must be read in order to detect nested conditional sections and ensure that the end of the outermost (ignored) conditional section is properly detected. If a conditional section with a keyword of INCLUDE occurs within a larger conditional section with a keyword of IGNORE, both the outer and the inner conditional sections are ignored.

If the keyword of the conditional section is a parameter-entity reference, the parameter entity must be replaced by its content before the processor decides whether to include or ignore the conditional section.

An example:

```
<!ENTITY % draft 'INCLUDE' >
<!ENTITY % final 'IGNORE' >

<![%draft;[
<!ELEMENT book (comments*, title, body, supplements?)>
]]>
<![%final;[
<!ELEMENT book (title, body, supplements?)>
]]>
```

4. Physical Structures

An XML document may consist of one or many storage units. These are called **entities**; they all have **content** and are all (except for the document entity, and the external DTD subset) identified by entity **name**. Each XML document has one entity called the **document entity**, which serves as the starting point for the XML processor and may contain the whole document.

Entities may be either parsed or unparsed. A **parsed entity's** contents are referred to as its replacement text; this text is considered an integral part of the document.

An **unparsed entity** is a resource whose contents may or may not be text, and if text, may not be XML. Each unparsed entity has an associated notation, identified by name. Beyond a requirement that an XML processor make the identifiers for the entity and notation available to the application, XML places no constraints on the contents of unparsed entities.

Parsed entities are invoked by name using entity references; unparsed entities by name, given in the value of `ENTITY` or `ENTITIES` attributes.

General entities are entities for use within the document content. In this specification, general entities are sometimes referred to with the unqualified term **entity** when this leads to no ambiguity. Parameter entities are parsed entities for use within the DTD. These two types of entities use different forms of reference and are recognized in different contexts. Furthermore, they occupy different namespaces; a parameter entity and a general entity with the same name are two distinct entities.

4.1 Character and Entity References

A **character reference** refers to a specific character in the ISO/IEC 10646 character set, for example one not directly accessible from available input devices.

Character Reference			
[66]	`CharRef ::=`	`'&#' [0-9]+ ';'`	
		`| '&#x' [0-9a-fA-F]+ ';'`	`[WFC:` Legal Character `]`

Well-Formedness Constraint: Legal Character

Characters referred to using character references must match the production for `Char`.

If the character reference begins with "`&#x`", the digits and letters up to the terminating `;` provide a hexadecimal representation of the character's code point in ISO/IEC 10646. If it begins just with "`&#`", the digits up to the terminating `;` provide a decimal representation of the character's code point.

An **entity reference** refers to the content of a named entity. References to parsed general entities use ampersand (`&`) and semicolon (`;`) as delimiters. **Parameter-entity references** use percent-sign (`%`) and semicolon (`;`) as delimiters.

Entity Reference				
[67]	Reference	::=	EntityRef | CharRef	
[68]	EntityRef	::=	'&' Name ';'	[WFC: Entity Declared] [VC: Entity Declared] [WFC: Parsed Entity] [WFC: No Recursion]
[69]	PEReference	::=	'%' Name ';'	[VC: Entity Declared] [WFC: No Recursion] [WFC: In DTD]

Well-Formedness Constraint: Entity Declared

In a document without any DTD, a document with only an internal DTD subset which contains no parameter entity references, or a document with "standalone='yes'", the Name given in the entity reference must match that in an entity declaration, except that well-formed documents need not declare any of the following entities: amp, lt, gt, apos, quot. The declaration of a parameter entity must precede any reference to it. Similarly, the declaration of a general entity must precede any reference to it which appears in a default value in an attribute-list declaration.

Note that if entities are declared in the external subset or in external parameter entities, a non-validating processor is not obligated to read and process their declarations; for such documents, the rule that an entity must be declared is a well-formedness constraint only if standalone='yes'.

Validity Constraint: Entity Declared

In a document with an external subset or external parameter entities with "standalone='no'", the Name given in the entity reference must match that in an entity declaration. For interoperability, valid documents should declare the entities amp, lt, gt, apos, quot, in the form specified in "**4.6 Predefined Entities**". The declaration of a parameter entity must precede any reference to it. Similarly, the declaration of a general entity must precede any reference to it which appears in a default value in an attribute-list declaration.

Well-Formedness Constraint: Parsed Entity

An entity reference must not contain the name of an unparsed entity. Unparsed entities may be referred to only in attribute values declared to be of type ENTITY or ENTITIES.

Well-Formedness Constraint: No Recursion

A parsed entity must not contain a recursive reference to itself, either directly or indirectly.

Well-Formedness Constraint: In DTD

Parameter-entity references may only appear in the DTD.

Examples of character and entity references:

```
Type <key>less-than</key> (&#x3C;) to save options.
This document was prepared on &docdate; and
is classified &security-level;.
```

Example of a parameter-entity reference:

```
<!-- declare the parameter entity "ISOLat2"... -->
<!ENTITY % ISOLat2
         SYSTEM "http://www.xml.com/iso/isolat2-xml.entities" >
<!-- ... now reference it. -->
%ISOLat2;
```

4.2 Entity Declarations

Entities are declared thus:

Entity Declaration			
[70]	EntityDecl	::=	GEDecl | PEDecl
[71]	GEDecl	::=	'<!ENTITY' S Name S EntityDef S? '>'
[72]	PEDecl	::=	'<!ENTITY' S '%' S Name S PEDef S? '>'
[73]	EntityDef	::=	EntityValue | (ExternalID NDataDecl?)
[74]	PEDef	::=	EntityValue | ExternalID

The `Name` identifies the entity in an entity reference or, in the case of an unparsed entity, in the value of an `ENTITY` or `ENTITIES` attribute. If the same entity is declared more than once, the first declaration encountered is binding; at user option, an XML processor may issue a warning if entities are declared multiple times.

4.2.1 Internal Entities

If the entity definition is an `EntityValue`, the defined entity is called an **internal entity**. There is no separate physical storage object, and the content of the entity is given in the declaration. Note that some processing of entity and character references in the literal entity value may be required to produce the correct replacement text: see "**4.5 Construction of Internal Entity Replacement Text**".

An internal entity is a parsed entity.

Example of an internal entity declaration:

```
<!ENTITY Pub-Status "This is a pre-release of the
 specification.">
```

4.2.2 External Entities

If the entity is not internal, it is an **external entity**, declared as follows:

External Entity Declaration				
[75]	ExternalID	::=	'SYSTEM' S SystemLiteral | 'PUBLIC' S PubidLiteral S SystemLiteral	
[76]	NDataDecl	::=	S 'NDATA' S Name	[VC: Notation Declared]

If the NDataDecl is present, this is a general unparsed entity; otherwise it is a parsed entity.

> ***Validity Constraint: Notation Declared***
> The Name must match the declared name of a notation.

The SystemLiteral is called the entity's **system identifier**. It is a URI, which may be used to retrieve the entity. Note that the hash mark (#) and fragment identifier frequently used with URIs are not, formally, part of the URI itself; an XML processor may signal an error if a fragment identifier is given as part of a system identifier. Unless otherwise provided by information outside the scope of this specification (e.g. a special XML element type defined by a particular DTD, or a processing instruction defined by a particular application specification), relative URIs are relative to the location of the resource within which the entity declaration occurs. A URI might thus be relative to the document entity, to the entity containing the external DTD subset, or to some other external parameter entity.

An XML processor should handle a non-ASCII character in a URI by representing the character in UTF-8 as one or more bytes, and then escaping these bytes with the URI escaping mechanism (i.e., by converting each byte to %HH, where HH is the hexadecimal notation of the byte value).

In addition to a system identifier, an external identifier may include a **public identifier**. An XML processor attempting to retrieve the entity's content may use the public identifier to try to generate an alternative URI. If the processor is unable to do so, it must use the URI specified in the system literal. Before a match is attempted, all strings of white space in the public identifier must be normalized to single space characters (#x20), and leading and trailing white space must be removed.

Examples of external entity declarations:

```
<!ENTITY open-hatch
         SYSTEM "http://www.textuality.com/boilerplate/OpenHatch.xml">
<!ENTITY open-hatch
         PUBLIC "-//Textuality//TEXT Standard open-hatch boilerplate//EN"
         "http://www.textuality.com/boilerplate/OpenHatch.xml">
<!ENTITY hatch-pic
         SYSTEM "../grafix/OpenHatch.gif"
         NDATA gif >
```

4.3 Parsed Entities

4.3.1 The Text Declaration

External parsed entities may each begin with a **text declaration**.

Text Declaration			
[77]	TextDecl	::=	'<?xml' VersionInfo? EncodingDecl S? '?>'

The text declaration must be provided literally, not by reference to a parsed entity. No text declaration may appear at any position other than the beginning of an external parsed entity.

4.3.2 Well-Formed Parsed Entities

The document entity is well-formed if it matches the production labeled `document`. An external general parsed entity is well-formed if it matches the production labeled `extParsedEnt`. An external parameter entity is well-formed if it matches the production labeled `extPE`.

Well-Formed External Parsed Entity			
[78]	`extParsedEnt`	`::=`	`TextDecl? content`
[79]	`extPE`	`::=`	`TextDecl? extSubsetDecl`

An internal general parsed entity is well-formed if its replacement text matches the production labeled `content`. All internal parameter entities are well-formed by definition.

A consequence of well-formedness in entities is that the logical and physical structures in an XML document are properly nested; no start-tag, end-tag, empty-element tag, element, comment, processing instruction, character reference, or entity reference can begin in one entity and end in another.

4.3.3 Character Encoding in Entities

Each external parsed entity in an XML document may use a different encoding for its characters. All XML processors must be able to read entities in either UTF-8 or UTF-16.

Entities encoded in UTF-16 must begin with the Byte Order Mark described by ISO/IEC 10646 Annex E and Unicode Appendix B (the ZERO WIDTH NO-BREAK SPACE character, #xFEFF). This is an encoding signature, not part of either the markup or the character data of the XML document. XML processors must be able to use this character to differentiate between UTF-8 and UTF-16 encoded documents.

Although an XML processor is required to read only entities in the UTF-8 and UTF-16 encodings, it is recognized that other encodings are used around the world, and it may be desired for XML processors to read entities that use them. Parsed entities which are stored in an encoding other than UTF-8 or UTF-16 must begin with a text declaration containing an encoding declaration:

<table>
<tr><th colspan="5">Encoding Declaration</th></tr>
<tr><td>[80]</td><td>EncodingDecl</td><td>::=</td><td colspan="2">S 'encoding' Eq ('"' EncName '"' | "'" EncName "'")</td></tr>
<tr><td>[81]</td><td>EncName</td><td>::=</td><td>[A-Za-z] ([A-Za-z0-9._] | '-')*</td><td>/*Encoding name contains only Latin characters */</td></tr>
</table>

In the document entity, the encoding declaration is part of the XML declaration. The `EncName` is the name of the encoding used.

In an encoding declaration, the values "`UTF-8`", "`UTF-16`", "`ISO-10646-UCS-2`", and "`ISO-10646-UCS-4`" should be used for the various encodings and transformations of Unicode / ISO/IEC 10646, the values "`ISO-8859-1`", "`ISO-8859-2`", ... "`ISO-8859-9`" should be used for the parts of ISO 8859, and the values "`ISO-2022-JP`", "`Shift_JIS`", and "`EUC-JP`" should be used for the various encoded forms of JIS X-0208-1997. XML processors may recognize other encodings; it is recommended that character encodings registered (as *charsets*) with the Internet Assigned Numbers Authority [IANA], other than those just listed, should be referred to using their registered names. Note that these registered names are defined to be case-insensitive, so processors wishing to match against them should do so in a case-insensitive way.

In the absence of information provided by an external transport protocol (e.g. HTTP or MIME), it is an error for an entity including an encoding declaration to be presented to the XML processor in an encoding other than that named in the declaration, or for an entity which begins with neither a Byte Order Mark nor an encoding declaration to use an encoding other than UTF-8. Note that since ASCII is a subset of UTF-8, ordinary ASCII entities do not strictly need an encoding declaration.

It is an error for a `TextDecl` to occur other than at the beginning of an external entity.

It is a fatal error when an XML processor encounters an entity with an encoding that it is unable to process.

Examples of encoding declarations:

```
<?xml encoding='UTF-8'?>
<?xml encoding='EUC-JP'?>
```

4.4 XML Processor Treatment of Entities and References

The table below summarizes the contexts in which character references, entity references, and invocations of unparsed entities might appear and the required behavior of an XML processor in each case. The labels in the leftmost column describe the recognition context:

Reference in Content
as a reference anywhere after the start-tag and before the end-tag of an element; corresponds to the nonterminal `content`.

Reference in Attribute Value
as a reference within either the value of an attribute in a start-tag, or a default value in an attribute declaration; corresponds to the nonterminal `AttValue`.

Occurs as Attribute Value
as a `Name`, not a reference, appearing either as the value of an attribute which has been declared as type `ENTITY`, or as one of the space-separated tokens in the value of an attribute which has been declared as type `ENTITIES`.

Reference in Entity Value
as a reference within a parameter or internal entity's literal entity value in the entity's declaration; corresponds to the nonterminal `EntityValue`.

Reference in DTD
as a reference within either the internal or external subsets of the DTD, but outside of an `EntityValue` or `AttValue`.

	Entity Type				Character
	Parameter	Internal General	External Parsed General	Unparsed	
Reference in Content	Not recognized	Included	Included if validating	Forbidden	Included
Reference in Attribute Value	Not recognized	Included in literal	Forbidden	Forbidden	Included
Occurs as Attribute Value	Not recognized	Forbidden	Forbidden	Notify	Not recognized
Reference in EntityValue	Included in literal	Bypassed	Bypassed	Forbidden	Included
Reference in DTD	Included as PE	Forbidden	Forbidden	Forbidden	Forbidden

4.4.1 Not Recognized

Outside the DTD, the `%` character has no special significance; thus, what would be parameter entity references in the DTD are not recognized as markup in `content`. Similarly, the names of unparsed entities are not recognized except when they appear in the value of an appropriately declared attribute.

4.4.2 Included

An entity is **included** when its replacement text is retrieved and processed, in place of the reference itself, as though it were part of the document at the location the reference was recognized. The replacement text may contain both character data and (except for parameter entities) markup, which must be recognized in the usual way, except that the replacement text of entities used to escape markup delimiters (the entities `amp`, `lt`, `gt`, `apos`, `quot`) is always treated as data. (The string "`AT&T;`" expands to "`AT&T;`" and the remaining ampersand is not recognized as an entity-reference delimiter.) A character reference is **included** when the indicated character is processed in place of the reference itself.

4.4.3 Included If Validating

When an XML processor recognizes a reference to a parsed entity, in order to validate the document, the processor must include its replacement text. If the entity is external, and the processor is not attempting to validate the XML document, the processor may, but need not, include the entity's replacement text. If a non-validating parser does not include the replacement text, it must inform the application that it recognized, but did not read, the entity.

This rule is based on the recognition that the automatic inclusion provided by the SGML and XML entity mechanism, primarily designed to support modularity in authoring, is not necessarily appropriate for other applications, in particular document browsing. Browsers, for example, when encountering an external parsed entity reference, might choose to provide a visual indication of the entity's presence and retrieve it for display only on demand.

4.4.4 Forbidden

The following are forbidden, and constitute fatal errors:

- the appearance of a reference to an unparsed entity.
- the appearance of any character or general-entity reference in the DTD except within an `EntityValue` or `AttValue`.
- a reference to an external entity in an attribute value.

4.4.5 Included in Literal

When an entity reference appears in an attribute value, or a parameter entity reference appears in a literal entity value, its replacement text is processed in place of the reference itself as though it were part of the document at the location the reference was recognized, except that a single or double quote character in the replacement text is always treated as a normal data character and will not terminate the literal. For example, this is well-formed:

```
<!ENTITY % YN '"Yes"' >
<!ENTITY WhatHeSaid "He said %YN;" >
```

while this is not:

```
<!ENTITY EndAttr "27'" >
<element attribute='a-&EndAttr;>
```

4.4.6 Notify

When the name of an unparsed entity appears as a token in the value of an attribute of declared type `ENTITY` or `ENTITIES`, a validating processor must inform the application of the system and public (if any) identifiers for both the entity and its associated notation.

4.4.7 Bypassed

When a general entity reference appears in the `EntityValue` in an entity declaration, it is bypassed and left as is.

4.4.8 Included as PE

Just as with external parsed entities, parameter entities need only be included if validating. When a parameter-entity reference is recognized in the DTD and included, its replacement text is enlarged by the attachment of one leading and one following space (#x20) character; the intent is to constrain the replacement text of parameter entities to contain an integral number of grammatical tokens in the DTD.

4.5 Construction of Internal Entity Replacement Text

In discussing the treatment of internal entities, it is useful to distinguish two forms of the entity's value. The **literal entity value** is the quoted string actually present in the entity declaration, corresponding to the non-terminal `EntityValue`. The **replacement text** is the content of the entity, after replacement of character references and parameter-entity references.

The literal entity value as given in an internal entity declaration (`EntityValue`) may contain character, parameter-entity, and general-entity references. Such references must be contained entirely within the literal entity value. The actual replacement text that is included as described above must contain the *replacement text* of any parameter entities referred to, and must contain the character referred to, in place of any character references in the literal entity value; however, general-entity references must be left as-is, unexpanded. For example, given the following declarations:

```
<!ENTITY % pub    "&#xc9;ditions Gallimard" >
<!ENTITY   rights "All rights reserved" >
<!ENTITY   book   "La Peste: Albert Camus,
&#xA9; 1947 %pub;. &rights;" >
```

then the replacement text for the entity "`book`" is:

```
La Peste: Albert Camus,
© 1947 Éditions Gallimard. &rights;
```

The general-entity reference "`&rights;`" would be expanded should the reference "`&book;`" appear in the document's content or an attribute value.

These simple rules may have complex interactions; for a detailed discussion of a difficult example, see "**D. Expansion of Entity and Character References**".

4.6 Predefined Entities

Entity and character references can both be used to **escape** the left angle bracket, ampersand, and other delimiters. A set of general entities (`amp`, `lt`, `gt`, `apos`, `quot`) is specified for this purpose. Numeric character references may also be used; they are expanded immediately when recognized and must be treated as character data, so the numeric character references "`<`" and "`&`" may be used to escape `<` and `&` when they occur in character data.

All XML processors must recognize these entities whether they are declared or not. For interoperability, valid XML documents should declare these entities, like any others, before using them. If the entities in question are declared, they must be declared as internal entities whose replacement text is the single character being escaped or a character reference to that character, as shown below.

```
<!ENTITY lt     "&#38;#60;">
<!ENTITY gt     "&#62;">
<!ENTITY amp    "&#38;#38;">
<!ENTITY apos   "&#39;">
<!ENTITY quot   "&#34;">
```

Note that the `<` and `&` characters in the declarations of "`lt`" and "`amp`" are doubly escaped to meet the requirement that entity replacement be well-formed.

4.7 Notation Declarations

Notations identify by name the format of unparsed entities, the format of elements which bear a notation attribute, or the application to which a processing instruction is addressed.

Notation declarations provide a name for the notation, for use in entity and attribute-list declarations and in attribute specifications, and an external identifier for the notation which may allow an XML processor or its client application to locate a helper application capable of processing data in the given notation.

Notation Declarations			
[82]	NotationDecl	::=	'<!NOTATION' S Name S (ExternalID | PublicID) S? '>'
[83]	PublicID	::=	'PUBLIC' S PubidLiteral

XML processors must provide applications with the name and external identifier(s) of any notation declared and referred to in an attribute value, attribute definition, or entity declaration. They may additionally resolve the external identifier into the system identifier, file name, or other information needed to allow the application to call a processor for data in the notation described. (It is not an error, however, for XML documents to declare and refer to notations for which notation-specific applications are not available on the system where the XML processor or application is running.)

4.8 Document Entity

The **document entity** serves as the root of the entity tree and a starting-point for an XML processor. This specification does not specify how the document entity is to be located by an XML processor; unlike other entities, the document entity has no name and might well appear on a processor input stream without any identification at all.

5. Conformance

5.1 Validating and Non-Validating Processors

Conforming XML processors fall into two classes: validating and non-validating.

Validating and non-validating processors alike must report violations of this specification's well-formedness constraints in the content of the document entity and any other parsed entities that they read.

Validating processors must report violations of the constraints expressed by the declarations in the DTD, and failures to fulfill the validity constraints given in this specification. To accomplish this, validating XML processors must read and process the entire DTD and all external parsed entities referenced in the document.

Non-validating processors are required to check only the document entity, including the entire internal DTD subset, for well-formedness. While they are not required to check the document for validity, they are required to **process** all the declarations they read in the internal DTD subset and in any parameter entity that they read, up to the first reference to a parameter entity that they do *not* read; that is to say, they must use the information in those declarations to *normalize* attribute values, *include* the replacement text of internal entities, and supply *default attribute values.* They must not process entity declarations or attribute-list declarations encountered after a reference to a parameter entity that is not read, since the entity may have contained overriding declarations.

5.2 Using XML Processors

The behavior of a validating XML processor is highly predictable; it must read every piece of a document and report all well-formedness and validity violations. Less is required of a non-validating processor; it need not read any part of the document other than the document entity. This has two effects that may be important to users of XML processors:

- Certain well-formedness errors, specifically those that require reading external entities, may not be detected by a non-validating processor. Examples include the constraints entitled Entity Declared, Parsed Entity, and No Recursion, as well as some of the cases described as forbidden in "**4.4 XML Processor Treatment of Entities and References**".
- The information passed from the processor to the application may vary, depending on whether the processor reads parameter and external entities. For example, a non-validating processor may not *normalize* attribute values, *include* the replacement text of internal entities, or supply *default attribute values*, where doing so depends on having read declarations in external or parameter entities.

For maximum reliability in interoperating between different XML processors, applications which use non-validating processors should not rely on any behaviors not required of such processors. Applications which require facilities such as the use of default attributes or internal entities which are declared in external entities should use validating XML processors.

6. Notation

The formal grammar of XML is given in this specification using a simple Extended Backus-Naur Form (EBNF) notation. Each rule in the grammar defines one symbol, in the form

```
symbol ::= expression
```

Symbols are written with an initial capital letter if they are defined by a regular expression, or with an initial lower case letter otherwise. Literal strings are quoted.

Within the expression on the right-hand side of a rule, the following expressions are used to match strings of one or more characters:

`#xN`
where `N` is a hexadecimal integer, the expression matches the character in ISO/IEC 10646 whose canonical (UCS-4) code value, when interpreted as an unsigned binary number, has the value indicated. The number of leading zeros in the `#xN` form is insignificant; the number of leading zeros in the corresponding code value is governed by the character encoding in use and is not significant for XML.

`[a-zA-Z]`, `[#xN-#xN]`
matches any character with a value in the range(s) indicated (inclusive).

`[^a-z]`, `[^#xN-#xN]`
matches any character with a value *outside* the range indicated.

`[^abc]`, `[^#xN#xN#xN]`
matches any character with a value not among the characters given.

`"string"`
matches a literal string matching that given inside the double quotes.

`'string'`
matches a literal string matching that given inside the single quotes.

These symbols may be combined to match more complex patterns as follows, where `A` and `B` represent simple expressions:

(**expression**)
`expression` is treated as a unit and may be combined as described in this list.

([-'()+,./:=?;!*#@$_%])
`characters matching this list are treated as an expression.`

A?
`matches A or nothing; optional A.`
A B
`matches A followed by B.`
A | B
`matches A or B but not both.`
A - B
`matches any string that matches A but does not match B.`
A+
`matches one or more occurrences of A.`
A*
`matches zero or more occurrences of A.`

Other notations used in the productions are:

/* ... */
comment.
[wfc: ...]
well-formedness constraint; this identifies by name a constraint on well-formed documents associated with a production.
[vc: ...]
validity constraint; this identifies by name a constraint on valid documents associated with a production.

Appendices

A. References

A.1 Normative References

(Internet Assigned Numbers Authority) *Official Names for Character Sets*, ed. Keld Simonsen et al. See ftp://ftp.isi.edu/in-notes/iana/assignments/character-sets.

IETF (Internet Engineering Task Force). *RFC 1766: Tags for the Identification of Languages*, ed. H. Alvestrand. 1995.

(International Organization for Standardization). *ISO 639:1988 (E). Code for the representation of names of languages.* [Geneva]: International Organization for Standardization, 1988.

(International Organization for Standardization). *ISO 3166-1:1997 (E). Codes for the representation of names of countries and their subdivisions -- Part 1: Country codes* [Geneva]: International Organization for Standardization, 1997.

ISO (International Organization for Standardization). *ISO/IEC 10646-1993 (E). Information technology -- Universal Multiple-Octet Coded Character Set (UCS) -- Part 1: Architecture and Basic Multilingual Plane.* [Geneva]: International Organization for Standardization, 1993 (plus amendments AM 1 through AM 7).

The Unicode Consortium. *The Unicode Standard, Version 2.0.* Reading, Mass.: Addison-Wesley Developers Press, 1996.

A.2 Other References

Aho, Alfred V., Ravi Sethi, and Jeffrey D. Ullman. *Compilers: Principles, Techniques, and Tools.* Reading: Addison-Wesley, 1986, rpt. corr. 1988.

Berners-Lee, T., R. Fielding, and L. Masinter. *Uniform Resource Identifiers (URI): Generic Syntax and Semantics.* 1997. (Work in progress; see updates to RFC1738.)

Brüggemann-Klein, Anne. Formal Models in Document Processing. Habilitationsschrift. Faculty of Mathematics at the University of Freiburg, 1993, available at `ftp://ftp.informatik.uni-freiburg.de/documents/papers/brueggem/habil.ps`.

Brüggemann-Klein, Anne, and Derick Wood. *Deterministic Regular Languages.* Extended abstract in A. Finkel, M. Jantzen, Hrsg., STACS 1992, S. 173-184. Springer-Verlag, Berlin 1992. Lecture Notes in Computer Science 577. Full version titled *One-Unambiguous Regular Languages* in Information and Computation 140 (2): 229-253, February 1998.

James Clark. Comparison of SGML and XML. See `http://www.w3.org/TR/NOTE-sgml-xml-971215`.

IETF (Internet Engineering Task Force). *RFC 1738: Uniform Resource Locators (URL)*, ed. T. Berners-Lee, L. Masinter, M. McCahill. 1994.

IETF (Internet Engineering Task Force). *RFC 1808: Relative Uniform Resource Locators*, ed. R. Fielding. 1995.

IETF (Internet Engineering Task Force). *RFC 2141: URN Syntax*, ed. R. Moats. 1997.

ISO (International Organization for Standardization). *ISO 8879:1986(E). Information processing -- Text and Office Systems -- Standard Generalized Markup Language (SGML).* First edition -- 1986-10-15. [Geneva]: International Organization for Standardization, 1986.

ISO (International Organization for Standardization). *ISO/IEC 10744-1992 (E). Information technology -- Hypermedia/Time-based Structuring Language (HyTime).* [Geneva]: International Organization for Standardization, 1992. *Extended Facilities Annexe.* [Geneva]: International Organization for Standardization, 1996.

B. Character Classes

Following the characteristics defined in the Unicode standard, characters are classed as base characters (among others, these contain the alphabetic characters of the Latin alphabet, without diacritics), ideographic characters, and combining characters (among others, this class contains most diacritics); these classes combine to form the class of letters. Digits and extenders are also distinguished.

Characters

[84] Letter ::= BaseChar | Ideographic

[85] BaseChar ::= [#x0041-#x005A] | [#x0061-#x007A] | [#x00C0-#x00D6] | [#x00D8-#x00F6] | [#x00F8-#x00FF] | [#x0100-#x0131] | [#x0134-#x013E] | [#x0141-#x0148] | [#x014A-#x017E] | [#x0180-#x01C3] | [#x01CD-#x01F0] | [#x01F4-#x01F5] | [#x01FA-#x0217] | [#x0250-#x02A8] | [#x02BB-#x02C1] | #x0386 | [#x0388-#x038A] | #x038C | [#x038E-#x03A1] | [#x03A3-#x03CE] | [#x03D0-#x03D6] | #x03DA | #x03DC | #x03DE | #x03E0 | [#x03E2-#x03F3] | [#x0401-#x040C] | [#x040E-#x044F] | [#x0451-#x045C] | [#x045E-#x0481] | [#x0490-#x04C4] | [#x04C7-#x04C8] | [#x04CB-#x04CC] | [#x04D0-#x04EB] | [#x04EE-#x04F5] | [#x04F8-#x04F9] | [#x0531-#x0556] | #x0559 | [#x0561-#x0586] | [#x05D0-#x05EA] | [#x05F0-#x05F2] | [#x0621-#x063A] | [#x0641-#x064A] | [#x0671-#x06B7] | [#x06BA-#x06BE] | [#x06C0-#x06CE] | [#x06D0-#x06D3] | #x06D5 | [#x06E5-#x06E6] | [#x0905-#x0939] | #x093D | [#x0958-#x0961] | [#x0985-#x098C] | [#x098F-#x0990] | [#x0993-#x09A8] | [#x09AA-#x09B0] | #x09B2 | [#x09B6-#x09B9] | [#x09DC-#x09DD] | [#x09DF-#x09E1] | [#x09F0-#x09F1] | [#x0A05-#x0A0A] | [#x0A0F-#x0A10] | [#x0A13-#x0A28] | [#x0A2A-#x0A30] | [#x0A32-#x0A33] | [#x0A35-#x0A36] | [#x0A38-#x0A39] | [#x0A59-#x0A5C] | #x0A5E | [#x0A72-#x0A74] | [#x0A85-#x0A8B] | #x0A8D | [#x0A8F-#x0A91] | [#x0A93-#x0AA8] | [#x0AAA-#x0AB0] | [#x0AB2-#x0AB3] | [#x0AB5-#x0AB9] | #x0ABD | #x0AE0 | [#x0B05-#x0B0C] | [#x0B0F-#x0B10] | [#x0B13-#x0B28] | [#x0B2A-#x0B30] | [#x0B32-#x0B33] | [#x0B36-#x0B39] | #x0B3D | [#x0B5C-#x0B5D] | [#x0B5F-#x0B61] | [#x0B85-#x0B8A] | [#x0B8E-#x0B90] | [#x0B92-#x0B95] | [#x0B99-#x0B9A] | #x0B9C | [#x0B9E-#x0B9F] | [#x0BA3-#x0BA4] | [#x0BA8-#x0BAA] | [#x0BAE-#x0BB5] | [#x0BB7-#x0BB9] | [#x0C05-#x0C0C] | [#x0C0E-#x0C10] | [#x0C12-#x0C28] | [#x0C2A-#x0C33] | [#x0C35-#x0C39] | [#x0C60-#x0C61] | [#x0C85-#x0C8C] | [#x0C8E-#x0C90] | [#x0C92-#x0CA8] | [#x0CAA-#x0CB3] | [#x0CB5-#x0CB9] | #x0CDE | [#x0CE0-#x0CE1] | [#x0D05-#x0D0C] | [#x0D0E-#x0D10] | [#x0D12-#x0D28] | [#x0D2A-#x0D39] | [#x0D60-#x0D61] | [#x0E01-#x0E2E] | #x0E30 | [#x0E32-#x0E33] | [#x0E40-#x0E45] | [#x0E81-#x0E82] | #x0E84 | [#x0E87-#x0E88] | #x0E8A | #x0E8D | [#x0E94-#x0E97] | [#x0E99-#x0E9F] | [#x0EA1-#x0EA3] | #x0EA5 | #x0EA7 | [#x0EAA-#x0EAB] | [#x0EAD-#x0EAE] | #x0EB0 | [#x0EB2-#x0EB3] | #x0EBD | [#x0EC0-#x0EC4] | [#x0F40-#x0F47] | [#x0F49-#x0F69] | [#x10A0-#x10C5]

Characters			
			| [#x10D0-#x10F6] | #x1100 | [#x1102-#x1103] | [#x1105-#x1107] | #x1109 | [#x110B-#x110C] | [#x110E-#x1112] | #x113C | #x113E | #x1140 | #x114C | #x114E | #x1150 | [#x1154-#x1155] | #x1159 | [#x115F-#x1161] | #x1163 | #x1165 | #x1167 | #x1169 | [#x116D-#x116E] | [#x1172-#x1173] | #x1175 | #x119E | #x11A8 | #x11AB | [#x11AE-#x11AF] | [#x11B7-#x11B8] | #x11BA | [#x11BC-#x11C2] | #x11EB | #x11F0 | #x11F9 | [#x1E00-#x1E9B] | [#x1EA0-#x1EF9] | [#x1F00-#x1F15] | [#x1F18-#x1F1D] | [#x1F20-#x1F45] | [#x1F48-#x1F4D] | [#x1F50-#x1F57] | #x1F59 | #x1F5B | #x1F5D | [#x1F5F-#x1F7D] | [#x1F80-#x1FB4] | [#x1FB6-#x1FBC] | #x1FBE | [#x1FC2-#x1FC4] | [#x1FC6-#x1FCC] | [#x1FD0-#x1FD3] | [#x1FD6-#x1FDB] | [#x1FE0-#x1FEC] | [#x1FF2-#x1FF4] | [#x1FF6-#x1FFC] | #x2126 | [#x212A-#x212B] | #x212E | [#x2180-#x2182] | [#x3041-#x3094] | [#x30A1-#x30FA] | [#x3105-#x312C] | [#xAC00-#xD7A3]
[86]	Ideographic	::=	[#x4E00-#x9FA5] | #x3007 | [#x3021-#x3029]
[87]	CombiningChar	::=	[#x0300-#x0345] | [#x0360-#x0361] | [#x0483-#x0486] | [#x0591-#x05A1] | [#x05A3-#x05B9] | [#x05BB-#x05BD] | #x05BF | [#x05C1-#x05C2] | #x05C4 | [#x064B-#x0652] | #x0670 | [#x06D6-#x06DC] | [#x06DD-#x06DF] | [#x06E0-#x06E4] | [#x06E7-#x06E8] | [#x06EA-#x06ED] | [#x0901-#x0903] | #x093C | [#x093E-#x094C] | #x094D | [#x0951-#x0954] | [#x0962-#x0963] | [#x0981-#x0983] | #x09BC | #x09BE | #x09BF | [#x09C0-#x09C4] | [#x09C7-#x09C8] | [#x09CB-#x09CD] | #x09D7 | [#x09E2-#x09E3] | #x0A02 | #x0A3C | #x0A3E | #x0A3F | [#x0A40-#x0A42] | [#x0A47-#x0A48] | [#x0A4B-#x0A4D] | [#x0A70-#x0A71] | [#x0A81-#x0A83] | #x0ABC | [#x0ABE-#x0AC5] | [#x0AC7-#x0AC9] | [#x0ACB-#x0ACD] | [#x0B01-#x0B03] | #x0B3C | [#x0B3E-#x0B43] | [#x0B47-#x0B48] | [#x0B4B-#x0B4D] | [#x0B56-#x0B57] | [#x0B82-#x0B83] | [#x0BBE-#x0BC2] | [#x0BC6-#x0BC8] | [#x0BCA-#x0BCD] | #x0BD7 | [#x0C01-#x0C03] | [#x0C3E-#x0C44] | [#x0C46-#x0C48] | [#x0C4A-#x0C4D] | [#x0C55-#x0C56] | [#x0C82-#x0C83] | [#x0CBE-#x0CC4] | [#x0CC6-#x0CC8] | [#x0CCA-#x0CCD] | [#x0CD5-#x0CD6] | [#x0D02-#x0D03] | [#x0D3E-#x0D43] | [#x0D46-#x0D48] | [#x0D4A-#x0D4D] | #x0D57 | #x0E31 | [#x0E34-#x0E3A] | [#x0E47-#x0E4E] | #x0EB1 | [#x0EB4-#x0EB9] | [#x0EBB-#x0EBC] | [#x0EC8-#x0ECD] | [#x0F18-#x0F19] | #x0F35 | #x0F37 | #x0F39 | #x0F3E | #x0F3F | [#x0F71-#x0F84] | [#x0F86-#x0F8B] | [#x0F90-#x0F95] | #x0F97 | [#x0F99-#x0FAD] | [#x0FB1-#x0FB7] | #x0FB9 | [#x20D0-#x20DC] | #x20E1 | [#x302A-#x302F] | #x3099 | #x309A

Table Continued on Following Page

Characters			
[88]	Digit	::=	[#x0030-#x0039] | [#x0660-#x0669] | [#x06F0-#x06F9] | [#x0966-#x096F] | [#x09E6-#x09EF] | [#x0A66-#x0A6F] | [#x0AE6-#x0AEF] | [#x0B66-#x0B6F] | [#x0BE7-#x0BEF] | [#x0C66-#x0C6F] | [#x0CE6-#x0CEF] | [#x0D66-#x0D6F] | [#x0E50-#x0E59] | [#x0ED0-#x0ED9] | [#x0F20-#x0F29]
[89]	Extender	::=	#x00B7 | #x02D0 | #x02D1 | #x0387 | #x0640 | #x0E46 | #x0EC6 | #x3005 | [#x3031-#x3035] | [#x309D-#x309E] | [#x30FC-#x30FE]

The character classes defined here can be derived from the Unicode character database as follows:

- Name start characters must have one of the categories Ll, Lu, Lo, Lt, Nl.
- Name characters other than Name-start characters must have one of the categories Mc, Me, Mn, Lm, or Nd.
- Characters in the compatibility area (i.e. with character code greater than #xF900 and less than #xFFFE) are not allowed in XML names.
- Characters which have a font or compatibility decomposition (i.e. those with a "compatibility formatting tag" in field 5 of the database -- marked by field 5 beginning with a "<") are not allowed.
- The following characters are treated as name-start characters rather than name characters, because the property file classifies them as Alphabetic: [#x02BB-#x02C1], #x0559, #x06E5, #x06E6.
- Characters #x20DD-#x20E0 are excluded (in accordance with Unicode, section 5.14).
- Character #x00B7 is classified as an extender, because the property list so identifies it.
- Character #x0387 is added as a name character, because #x00B7 is its canonical equivalent.
- Characters ':' and '_' are allowed as name-start characters.
- Characters '-' and '.' are allowed as name characters.

C. XML and SGML (Non-Normative)

XML is designed to be a subset of SGML, in that every valid XML document should also be a conformant SGML document. For a detailed comparison of the additional restrictions that XML places on documents beyond those of SGML, see [Clark].

D. Expansion of Entity and Character References (Non-Normative)

This appendix contains some examples illustrating the sequence of entity- and character-reference recognition and expansion, as specified in "**4.4 XML Processor Treatment of Entities and References**".

If the DTD contains the declaration

```
<!ENTITY example "<p>An ampersand (&#38;#38;) may be escaped
numerically (&#38;#38;#38;) or with a general entity
(&amp;amp;). </p>" >
```

then the XML processor will recognize the character references when it parses the entity declaration, and resolve them before storing the following string as the value of the entity "`example`":

```
<p>An ampersand (&#38;) may be escaped
numerically (&#38;#38;) or with a general entity
(&amp;amp;).</p>
```

A reference in the document to "`&example;`" will cause the text to be reparsed, at which time the start- and end-tags of the "p" element will be recognized and the three references will be recognized and expanded, resulting in a "p" element with the following content (all data, no delimiters or markup):

```
An ampersand (&) may be escaped
numerically (&#38;) or with a general entity
(&amp;).
```

A more complex example will illustrate the rules and their effects fully. In the following example, the line numbers are solely for reference.

```
1 <?xml version='1.0'?>
2 <!DOCTYPE test [
3 <!ELEMENT test (#PCDATA) >
4 <!ENTITY % xx '&#37;zz;'>
5 <!ENTITY % zz '&#60;!ENTITY tricky "error-prone" >' >
6 %xx;
7 ]>
8 <test>This sample shows a &tricky; method.</test>
```

This produces the following:

- in line 4, the reference to character 37 is expanded immediately, and the parameter entity "`xx`" is stored in the symbol table with the value "`%zz;`". Since the replacement text is not rescanned, the reference to parameter entity "`zz`" is not recognized. (And it would be an error if it were, since "`zz`" is not yet declared.)
- in line 5, the character reference "`<`" is expanded immediately and the parameter entity "`zz`" is stored with the replacement text "`<!ENTITY tricky "error-prone" >`", which is a well-formed entity declaration.
- in line 6, the reference to "`xx`" is recognized, and the replacement text of "`xx`" (namely "`%zz;`") is parsed. The reference to "`zz`" is recognized in its turn, and its replacement text ("`<!ENTITY tricky "error-prone" >`") is parsed. The general entity "`tricky`" has now been declared, with the replacement text "`error-prone`".
- in line 8, the reference to the general entity "`tricky`" is recognized, and it is expanded, so the full content of the "`test`" element is the self-describing (and ungrammatical) string *This sample shows a error-prone method.*

E. Deterministic Content Models (Non-Normative)

For compatibility, it is required that content models in element type declarations be deterministic.

SGML requires deterministic content models (it calls them "unambiguous"); XML processors built using SGML systems may flag non-deterministic content models as errors.

For example, the content model `((b, c) | (b, d))` is non-deterministic, because given an initial `b` the parser cannot know which `b` in the model is being matched without looking ahead to see which element follows the `b`. In this case, the two references to `b` can be collapsed into a single reference, making the model read `(b, (c | d))`. An initial `b` now clearly matches only a single name in the content model. The parser doesn't need to look ahead to see what follows; either `c` or `d` would be accepted.

More formally: a finite state automaton may be constructed from the content model using the standard algorithms, e.g. algorithm 3.5 in section 3.9 of Aho, Sethi, and Ullman [Aho/Ullman]. In many such algorithms, a follow set is constructed for each position in the regular expression (i.e., each leaf node in the syntax tree for the regular expression); if any position has a follow set in which more than one following position is labeled with the same element type name, then the content model is in error and may be reported as an error.

Algorithms exist which allow many but not all non-deterministic content models to be reduced automatically to equivalent deterministic models; see Brüggemann-Klein 1991 [Brüggemann-Klein].

F. Autodetection of Character Encodings (Non-Normative)

The XML encoding declaration functions as an internal label on each entity, indicating which character encoding is in use. Before an XML processor can read the internal label, however, it apparently has to know what character encoding is in use--which is what the internal label is trying to indicate. In the general case, this is a hopeless situation. It is not entirely hopeless in XML, however, because XML limits the general case in two ways: each implementation is assumed to support only a finite set of character encodings, and the XML encoding declaration is restricted in position and content in order to make it feasible to autodetect the character encoding in use in each entity in normal cases. Also, in many cases other sources of information are available in addition to the XML data stream itself. Two cases may be distinguished, depending on whether the XML entity is presented to the processor without, or with, any accompanying (external) information. We consider the first case first.

Because each XML entity not in UTF-8 or UTF-16 format *must* begin with an XML encoding declaration, in which the first characters must be '`<?xml`', any conforming processor can detect, after two to four octets of input, which of the following cases apply. In reading this list, it may help to know that in UCS-4, '<' is "`#x0000003C`" and '?' is "`#x0000003F`", and the Byte Order Mark required of UTF-16 data streams is "`#xFEFF`".

- `00 00 00 3C`: UCS-4, big-endian machine (1234 order)
- `3C 00 00 00`: UCS-4, little-endian machine (4321 order)
- `00 00 3C 00`: UCS-4, unusual octet order (2143)
- `00 3C 00 00`: UCS-4, unusual octet order (3412)

- `FE FF`: UTF-16, big-endian
- `FF FE`: UTF-16, little-endian
- `00 3C 00 3F`: UTF-16, big-endian, no Byte Order Mark (and thus, strictly speaking, in error)
- `3C 00 3F 00`: UTF-16, little-endian, no Byte Order Mark (and thus, strictly speaking, in error)
- `3C 3F 78 6D`: UTF-8, ISO 646, ASCII, some part of ISO 8859, Shift-JIS, EUC, or any other 7-bit, 8-bit, or mixed-width encoding which ensures that the characters of ASCII have their normal positions, width, and values; the actual encoding declaration must be read to detect which of these applies, but since all of these encodings use the same bit patterns for the ASCII characters, the encoding declaration itself may be read reliably
- `4C 6F A7 94`: EBCDIC (in some flavor; the full encoding declaration must be read to tell which code page is in use)
- other: UTF-8 without an encoding declaration, or else the data stream is corrupt, fragmentary, or enclosed in a wrapper of some kind

This level of autodetection is enough to read the XML encoding declaration and parse the character-encoding identifier, which is still necessary to distinguish the individual members of each family of encodings (e.g. to tell UTF-8 from 8859, and the parts of 8859 from each other, or to distinguish the specific EBCDIC code page in use, and so on).

Because the contents of the encoding declaration are restricted to ASCII characters, a processor can reliably read the entire encoding declaration as soon as it has detected which family of encodings is in use. Since in practice, all widely used character encodings fall into one of the categories above, the XML encoding declaration allows reasonably reliable in-band labeling of character encodings, even when external sources of information at the operating-system or transport-protocol level are unreliable.

Once the processor has detected the character encoding in use, it can act appropriately, whether by invoking a separate input routine for each case, or by calling the proper conversion function on each character of input.

Like any self-labeling system, the XML encoding declaration will not work if any software changes the entity's character set or encoding without updating the encoding declaration. Implementors of character-encoding routines should be careful to ensure the accuracy of the internal and external information used to label the entity.

The second possible case occurs when the XML entity is accompanied by encoding information, as in some file systems and some network protocols. When multiple sources of information are available, their relative priority and the preferred method of handling conflict should be specified as part of the higher-level protocol used to deliver XML. Rules for the relative priority of the internal label and the MIME-type label in an external header, for example, should be part of the RFC document defining the text/xml and application/xml MIME types. In the interests of interoperability, however, the following rules are recommended.

- If an XML entity is in a file, the Byte-Order Mark and encoding-declaration PI are used (if present) to determine the character encoding. All other heuristics and sources of information are solely for error recovery.
- If an XML entity is delivered with a MIME type of text/xml, then the `charset` parameter on the MIME type determines the character encoding method; all other heuristics and sources of information are solely for error recovery.
- If an XML entity is delivered with a MIME type of application/xml, then the Byte-Order Mark and encoding-declaration PI are used (if present) to determine the character encoding. All other heuristics and sources of information are solely for error recovery.

This algorithm does not work for UTF-7.

These rules apply only in the absence of protocol-level documentation; in particular, when the MIME types text/xml and application/xml are defined, the recommendations of the relevant RFC will supersede these rules.

G. W3C XML Working Group (Non-Normative)

This specification was prepared and approved for publication by the W3C XML Working Group (WG). WG approval of this specification does not necessarily imply that all WG members voted for its approval. The current and former members of the XML WG are:

Jon Bosak, Sun (Chair); James Clark (Technical Lead); Tim Bray, Textuality and Netscape (XML Co-editor); Jean Paoli, Microsoft (XML Co-editor); C. M. Sperberg-McQueen, U. of Ill. (XML Co-editor); Dan Connolly, W3C (W3C Liaison); Paula Angerstein, Texcel; Steve DeRose, INSO; Dave Hollander, HP; Eliot Kimber, ISOGEN; Eve Maler, ArborText; Tom Magliery, NCSA; Murray Maloney, Muzmo and Grif; Makoto Murata, Fuji Xerox Information Systems; Joel Nava, Adobe; Conleth O'Connell, Vignette; Peter Sharpe, SoftQuad; John Tigue, DataChannel

B

IE5 XML Document Object Model

This section contains a complete reference to the **Document Object Model** that is supported in Internet Explorer 5. This includes full support for the W3C version 1.0 DOM Recommendations, plus extensions specific to IE5. It is divided into four sections:

- **The Base DOM Objects**
- **The High-level DOM Objects**
- **IE5-Specific Parser Objects**
- **The DOM NodeTypes**

The Base DOM Objects

In Internet Explorer 5, all the nodes that appear in an XML document, with a couple of minor exceptions, are based on the `IXMLDOMNode` object. This represents the base `Node` object from which the specialist node objects, such as `Element`, `Attribute`, `Comment`, etc, inherit. There are three other base objects as well. The full list is:

- `Node` (the `IXMLDOMNode` object)
- `NodeList` (the `IXMLDOMNodeList` object)
- `NamedNodeMap` (the `IXMLDOMNamedNodeMap` object)

Node — the IXMLDOMNode Object

The IE5 IXMLDOMNode object extends the W3C DOM recommendations (which Microsoft implements as the IDOMNode object) by adding support for data types, namespaces, DTDs, and XML schemas. In the following tables, '**Ext**' indicates properties and methods that are extensions to the base W3C object model.

Node Properties

Name		Description
attributes		Returns a collection of the Attribute (or Attr) objects for this node as a NamedNodeMap object.
baseName	**Ext**	Returns the node name with any namespace removed. For example, in a node declared as <nspace:elemname> it returns the "elemname" part.
childNodes		Returns a NodeList containing all the child nodes of this node, for nodes that can have child nodes.
dataType	**Ext**	Sets or returns the data type for this node.
definition	**Ext**	For EntityReference nodes, returns the entry in the DTD or schema containing the definition for the entity, i.e. "<!ENTITY entityname 'entity value'>". For other nodes, returns null.
firstChild		Returns a reference to the first child node of this node.
lastChild		Returns a reference to the last child node of this node.
namespaceURI	**Ext**	Returns the URI for the namespace as a string. For example, in the namespace declaration xmlns:name="uri" it returns the "uri" part.
nextSibling		Returns a reference to the next sibling node of this node, i.e. the next node in the source data file at the same level of the hierarchy.
nodeName		Returns the name of the node, which will depend on the node type. See the list of **Node Types** at the end of this appendix for more details.
nodeTypeString	**Ext**	Returns the node type as a string. See the list of **Node Types** at the end of this appendix for more details.
nodeType		Returns the node type as a number. See the list of **Node Types** at the end of this appendix for more details.

Name		Description
nodeTypedValue	**Ext**	Sets or returns the strongly typed value of the node, expressed in its defined data type. If no data type has been defined for the node, its nodeValue is returned.
nodeValue		Sets or returns the value of the node as plain text.
ownerDocument		Returns the root node of the document that contains the node.
parentNode		Returns the parent node of this node, for nodes that can have parents.
parsed	**Ext**	Returns true if this node and all its descendants have been parsed and instantiated.
prefix	**Ext**	Returns the element namespace prefix as a string. For example, in a node declared as <nspace:elemname> it returns the "nspace" part.
previousSibling		Returns a reference to the previous sibling node of this node, i.e. the previous node in the source file at the same level of the hierarchy.
specified	**Ext**	Indicates whether the node value is explicitly specified or derived from a default value in the DTD or schema. Normally only used with attribute nodes.
text	**Ext**	Sets or returns the entire text content of this node and all its descendant nodes.
xml	**Ext**	Returns the entire XML content of this node and all its descendant nodes.

Node Methods

Name	Description
appendChild (new_node)	Appends the node object new_node to the end of the list of child nodes for this node.
cloneNode (recurse_children)	Creates a new node object that is an exact clone of this node, including all descendant nodes of this node if recurse_children is set to true.
hasChildNodes()	Returns true if this node has any child nodes.
insertBefore(new_node, this_node)	Inserts a new node object new_node into the list of child nodes for this node, to the left of the node object this_node or at the end of the list if this_node is omitted.
removeChild(this_node)	Removes the child node this_node from the list of child nodes for this node, and returns it.

Name		Description
replaceChild(new_node, old_node)		Replaces the child node old_node with the new child node object new_node, and returns the old child node.
selectNodes (pattern)	**Ext**	Applies a specified pattern to this node's context and returns a node list object containing matching nodes. The string pattern specifies the XSL pattern-matching operation to be used.
selectSingleNode (pattern)	**Ext**	Applies a specified pattern to this node's context and returns just the first node object that matches. The string pattern specifies the XSL pattern-matching operation to be used.
transformNode (stylesheet)	**Ext**	Processes this node and its children using an XSL style sheet specified in the stylesheet argument, and returns the resulting transformation. The style sheet must be either a Document node object, in which case the document is assumed to be an XSL style sheet, or a Node object in the xsl namespace, in which case this node is treated as a standalone style sheet fragment.

NodeList — the IXMLDOMNodeList Object

This object represents a collection (or list) of Node objects. The object list is 'live', meaning that changes to the document are mirrored in the list immediately. The IE5 extensions support iteration through the list in addition to indexed access. In the following tables, '**Ext**' indicates properties and methods that are extensions to the base W3C object model. (The base NodeList object is implemented in IE5 as IDOMNodeList).

NodeList Property

Name	Description
length	Returns the number of nodes in the node list.

NodeList Methods

Name		Description
item(index)		Returns the node at position index in the node list, where the first node is indexed zero.
nextNode()	**Ext**	Returns the next node object in the node list, or null if there are no more nodes.
reset()	**Ext**	Resets the internal pointer to the point before the first node in the node list. Prepares the list for iteration with the nextNode() method.

NamedNodeMap — the IXMLDOMNamedNodeMap Object

This object provides a collection of `Node` objects that allows access by name as well as by index. This collection is typically used with `attribute` objects rather than `element` or other node types, and is 'live' like the `NodeList` object. The IE5 extensions add support for namespaces, and iteration through the collection of attribute nodes. In the following tables, '**Ext**' indicates properties and methods that are extensions to the base W3C object model. This base object is implemented as `IDOMNamedNodeMap` by Microsoft.

NamedNodeMap Property

Name	Description
`length`	Returns the number of nodes in the named node map.

NamedNodeMap Methods

Name		Description
`getNamedItem(name)`		Retrieves the node object with the specified name. Typically used to retrieve attributes from an element.
`getQualifiedItem(base_name, namespace_uri)`	**Ext**	Returns the node object with the specified `base_name` and `namespace_uri` values.
`item(index)`		Returns the node at position index in the named node map, where the first node is indexed zero.
`nextNode()`	**Ext**	Returns the next node object in the named node map, or `null` if there are no more nodes.
`removeNamedItem(name)`		Removes the node object with the specified name from the named node map. Typically used to remove attributes from an element.
`removeQualifiedItem(base_name, namespace_uri)`	**Ext**	Removes the node object with the specified `base_name` and `namespace_uri` values from the named node map.
`reset()`	**Ext**	Resets the internal pointer to the point before the first node in the node list. Prepares the list for iteration with the `nextNode()` method.

Name	Description
setNamedItem (new_node)	Inserts the node object new_node into the named node map, updating the XML document. Any existing node with the same name is replaced with the new node. Typically used to update attribute values for an element.

The High-level DOM Objects

Because each type of node in an XML document differs in both obvious and subtle ways, specific objects are available for different types of nodes. Most inherit the properties and methods of the base Node (IXMLDOMNode) object, and add the specific properties and methods required for best tailoring the object to its purpose.

The specific objects are:

- Document (the IXMLDOMDocument object)
- DocumentType (the IXMLDOMDocumentType object)
- DocumentFragment (the IXMLDOMDocumentFragment object)
- Element (the IXMLDOMElement object)
- Attribute or Attr (the IXMLDOMAttribute object)
- Entity (the IXMLDOMEntity object)
- EntityReference (the IXMLDOMEntityReference object)
- Notation (the IXMLDOMNotation object)
- CharacterData (the IXMLDOMCharacterData object)
- CDATASection (the IXMLDOMCDATASection object)
- Text (the IXMLDOMText object)
- Comment (the IXMLDOMComment object)
- ProcessingInstruction (the IXMLDOMProcessingIntruction object)
- Implementation (the IXMLDOMImplementation object)

In addition to these, there are interfaces called IDOMDocument, IDOMDocumentType etc., which implement the W3C Recommendation, without the Microsoft extensions. These inherit from IDOMNode, which is the Microsoft implementation of the W3C Node object. The following tables repeat the base properties and methods, and add the node-specific ones. This provides a complete reference, with no need to check elsewhere which extra properties and methods the base objects provide in addition.

Document — the IXMLDOMDocument

The Document object is the root object for an XML document. In IE5, it is the object that is instantiated by creating a new ActiveX Object with the identifier "Microsoft.XMLDOM".

The IE5 IXMLDOMDocument object extends the base DOM document interface (implemented in IE5 by the IDOMDocument object) to include parser-specific functions. These include the ability to load documents asynchronously and control validation. The IXMLDOMDocument object also provides access to other IE5-specific objects such as parseError. In the following tables, '**Ext**' indicates properties and methods that are extensions to the base W3C object model.

Document Properties

Name		Description
async	**Ext**	Sets or returns whether asynchronous download of the XML data is permitted. Values are true (the default) or false.
attributes		Returns a collection of the Attribute (or Attr) objects for this node as a NamedNodeMap object.
baseName	**Ext**	Returns the node name with any namespace removed. For example, in a node declared as <nspace:elemname> it returns the "elemname" part.
childNodes		Returns a NodeList containing all the child nodes of this node, for nodes that can have child nodes.
dataType	**Ext**	Sets or returns the data type for this node.
definition	**Ext**	For EntityReference nodes, returns the entry in the DTD or schema containing the definition for the entity, i.e. "<!ENTITY entityname 'entity value'>". For other nodes, returns null.
doctype		Returns a reference to the DocumentType node specifying the DTD or schema for this document.
documentElement		Returns a reference to the outermost element of the document.
firstChild		Returns a reference to the first child node of this node.
implementation		Returns a reference to the Implementation object for the document. This object provides methods that are application-specific and document object model implementation independent.
lastChild		Returns a reference to the last child node of this node.

Name		Description
namespaceURI	**Ext**	Returns the URI for the namespace as a string. For example, in the namespace declaration xmlns:name="uri" it returns the "uri" part.
nextSibling		Returns a reference to the next sibling node of this node, i.e. the next node in the source data file at the same level of the hierarchy.
nodeName		Returns the name of the node, which will depend on the node type. See the list of **Node Types** at the end of this appendix for more details.
nodeTypeString	**Ext**	Returns the node type as a string. See the list of **Node Types** at the end of this appendix for more details.
nodeType		Returns the node type as a number. See the list of **Node Types** at the end of this appendix for more details.
nodeTyped Value	**Ext**	Sets or returns the strongly typed value of the node, expressed in its defined data type. If no data type has been defined for the node, its nodeValue is returned.
nodeValue		Sets or returns the value of the node as plain text.
ownerDocument		Returns the root node of the document that contains the node.
parentNode		Returns the parent node of this node, for nodes that can have parents.
parsed	**Ext**	Returns true if this node and all its descendants have been parsed and instantiated.
parseError	**Ext**	Returns a reference to the ParseError object that contains information about any errors encountered while parsing the document.
prefix	**Ext**	Returns the element namespace prefix as a string. For example, in a node declared as <nspace:elemname> it returns the "nspace" part.
preserve WhiteSpace	**Ext**	Specifies whether white space should be preserved. The default is false.
previous Sibling		Returns a reference to the previous sibling node of this node, i.e. the previous node in the source file at the same level of the hierarchy.

Name		Description
`readyState`	**Ext**	Indicates the current state of the XML document: `0 ("uninitialized")` - the object has been created but the `load()` has not yet been executed. `1 ("loading")` - the `load()` method is executing. `2 ("loaded")` - loading is complete and parsing is taking place. `3 ("interactive")` - some data has been read and parsed and the object model is now available. The data set is only partially retrieved and is read-only. `4 ("completed")` - document has been completely loaded. If successful the data is available read/write, if not the error information is available.
`resolveExternals`	**Ext**	Indicates whether external entities are resolved and the document is validated against external DTDs or schemas. The default is `false`.
`specified`	**Ext**	Indicates whether the node value is explicitly specified or derived from a default value in the DTD or schema. Normally only used with attribute nodes.
`text`	**Ext**	Sets or returns the entire text content of this node and all its descendant nodes.
`url`	**Ext**	Returns the URL of the last successfully loaded document, or `null` if the document was built from scratch in memory.
`validateOnParse`	**Ext**	Sets or returns whether the parser should validate the document. Takes the value `true` to validate or `false` (the default) to check only for 'well-formedness'.
`xml`	**Ext**	Returns the entire XML content of this node and all its descendant nodes.

Document Methods

Name		Description
`abort()`	**Ext**	Aborts a currently executing asynchronous download.
`appendChild(new_node)`		Appends the node object `new_node` to the end of the list of child nodes for this node.
`cloneNode(recurse_children)`		Creates a new node object that is an exact clone of this node, including all descendant nodes of this node if `recurse_children` is set to `true`.

Name		Description
createAttribute(attr_name)		Creates an Attribute node with the specified name.
createCDATASection(text)		Creates a CDATASection node containing text.
createComment(text)		Creates a Comment node containing text as the comment between the <!-- and --> delimiters.
createDocument_Fragment()		Creates an empty DocumentFragment node that can be used to build independent sections of a document.
createElement(tag_name)		Creates an Element node with the specified name.
createEntityReference(ref_name)		Creates an EntityReference node with the supplied name for the reference.
createNode (node_type, node_name, namespace_uri)	**Ext**	Creates any type of node using the specified node_type, node_name, and namespace_uri parameters.
createProcessing_Instruction(target, text)		Creates a ProcessingInstruction node containing the specified target and data.
createTextNode(text_data)		Creates a Text node containing the specified text data.
getElementsByTagName(tag_name)		Returns a NodeList of elements that have the specified tag name. If tag_name is "*" it returns all elements.
hasChildNodes()		Returns true if this node has any child nodes.
insertBefore(new_node, this_node)		Inserts a new node object new_node into the list of child nodes for this node, to the left of the node object this_node or at the end of the list if this_node is omitted.
load(url)	**Ext**	Loads an XML document from the location in url.
loadXML(string)	**Ext**	Loads a string that is a representation of an XML document.
nodeFromID(id_value)	**Ext**	Returns the node object whose ID attribute matches the supplied value.
removeChild(this_node)		Removes the child node this_node from the list of child nodes for this node, and returns it.
replaceChild(new_node, old_node)		Replaces the child node old_node with the new child node object new_node, and returns the old child node.
save(destination)	**Ext**	Saves the document to the specified destination, assuming the appropriate permissions are granted.

Name		Description
`selectNodes(pattern)`	**Ext**	Applies a specified pattern to this node's context and returns a node list object containing matching nodes. The string `pattern` specifies the XSL pattern-matching operation to be used.
`selectSingleNode (pattern)`	**Ext**	Applies a specified pattern to this node's context and returns just the first node object that matches. The string `pattern` specifies the XSL pattern-matching operation to be used.
`transformNode (stylesheet)`	**Ext**	Processes this node and its children using an XSL style sheet specified in the `stylesheet` argument, and returns the resulting transformation. The style sheet must be either a `Document` node object, in which case the document is assumed to be an XSL style sheet, or a Node object in the `xsl` namespace, in which case this node is treated as a standalone style sheet fragment.

Document Events

Name		Description
`ondataavailable`	**Ext**	The `ondataavailable` event occurs when data becomes available. When an asynchronous data load is in progress it allows processing in parallel with the download. The `readyState` property changes through several states to indicate the current status of the download.
`onreadystatechange`	**Ext**	The `onreadystatechange` event occurs when the value of the `readyState` property changes. This provides an alternative way to monitor the arrival of XML data when asynchronous loading is not used.
`ontransformnode`	**Ext**	The `ontransformnode` event is fired when a node is transformed through the `transformNode()` method of the `Node` object using an XSL style sheet.

DocumentType — the IXMLDOMDocumentType Object

This object contains information about the document type declaration or schema for the document. It is the equivalent of the `<!DOCTYPE>` node. In the following tables, '**Ext**' indicates properties and methods that are extensions to the base W3C object model. IE5 implements this base object as `IDOMDocumentType`.

DocumentType Properties

Name		Description
attributes		Returns a collection of the Attribute (or Attr) objects for this node as a NamedNodeMap object.
baseName	**Ext**	Returns the node name with any namespace removed. For example, in a node declared as <nspace:elemname> it returns the "elemname" part.
childNodes		Returns a NodeList containing all the child nodes of this node, for nodes that can have child nodes.
dataType	**Ext**	Sets or returns the data type for this node.
definition	**Ext**	For EntityReference nodes, returns the entry in the DTD or schema containing the definition for the entity, i.e. "<!ENTITY entityname 'entity value'>". For other nodes, returns null.
entities		Returns a node list containing references to the Entity objects declared in the document type declaration.
firstChild		Returns a reference to the first child node of this node.
lastChild		Returns a reference to the last child node of this node.
name		Returns the name of the document type (!DOCTYPE) for this document.
namespaceURI	**Ext**	Returns the URI for the namespace as a string. For example, in the namespace declaration xmlns:name="uri" it returns the "uri" part.
nextSibling		Returns a reference to the next sibling node of this node, i.e. the next node in the source data file at the same level of the hierarchy.
nodeName		Returns the name of the node, which will depend on the node type. See the list of **Node Types** at the end of this appendix for more details.
nodeTypeString	**Ext**	Returns the node type as a string, depending on the node type. See the list of **Node Types** at the end of this appendix for more details.
nodeType		Returns the node type as a number. See the list of **Node Types** at the end of this appendix for more details.
nodeTypedValue	**Ext**	Sets or returns the strongly typed value of the node, expressed in its defined data type. If no data type has been defined for the node, its nodeValue is returned.
nodeValue		Sets or returns the value of the node as plain text.

Name		Description
notations		Returns a node list containing references to the Notation objects present in the document type declaration.
ownerDocument		Returns the root node of the document that contains the node.
parentNode		Returns the parent node of this node, for nodes that can have parents.
parsed	**Ext**	Returns true if this node and all its descendants have been parsed and instantiated.
prefix	**Ext**	Returns the element namespace prefix as a string. For example, in a node declared as <nspace:elemname> it returns the "nspace" part.
previousSibling		Returns a reference to the previous sibling node of this node, i.e. the previous node in the source file at the same level of the hierarchy.
specified	**Ext**	Indicates whether the node value is explicitly specified or derived from a default value in the DTD or schema. Normally only used with attribute nodes.
text	**Ext**	Sets or returns the entire text content of this node and all its descendant nodes.
xml	**Ext**	Returns the entire XML content of this node and all its descendant nodes.

DocumentType Methods

Name	Description
appendChild (new_node)	Appends the node object new_node to the end of the list of child nodes for this node.
cloneNode(recurse_children)	Creates a new node object that is an exact clone of this node, including all descendant nodes of this node if recurse_children is set to true.
hasChildNodes()	Returns true if this node has any child nodes.
insertBefore(new_node, this_node)	Inserts a new node object new_node into the list of child nodes for this node, to the left of the node object this_node or at the end of the list if this_node is omitted.
removeChild (this_node)	Removes the child node this_node from the list of child nodes for this node, and returns it.
replaceChild (new_node, old_node)	Replaces the child node old_node with the new child node object new_node, and returns the old child node.

Name		Description
`selectNodes (pattern)`	**Ext**	Applies a specified pattern to this node's context and returns a node list object containing matching nodes. The string `pattern` specifies the XSL pattern-matching operation to be used.
`selectSingleNode (pattern)`	**Ext**	Applies a specified pattern to this node's context and returns just the first node object that matches. The string `pattern` specifies the XSL pattern-matching operation to be used.
`transformNode (stylesheet)`	**Ext**	Processes this node and its children using an XSL style sheet specified in the `stylesheet` argument, and returns the resulting transformation. The style sheet must be either a `Document` node object, in which case the document is assumed to be an XSL style sheet, or a Node object in the `xsl` namespace, in which case this node is treated as a standalone style sheet fragment.

DocumentFragment — the IXMLDOMDocumentFragment Object

A document fragment is a lightweight object that is useful for tree insert operations. A new document fragment can be created and elements added to it, then the entire fragment can be added to an existing document. It is also useful for storing sections of a document temporarily, such as when cutting and pasting blocks of elements. This object adds no new methods or properties to the base `IXMLDOMNode` object. In the following tables, '**Ext**' indicates properties and methods that are extensions to the base W3C object model. The unextended object is implemented in IE5 by the `IDOMDocumentFragment` object.

DocumentFragment Properties

Name		Description
`attributes`		Returns a collection of the `Attribute` (or `Attr`) objects for this node as a `NamedNodeMap` object.
`baseName`	**Ext**	Returns the node name with any namespace removed. For example, in a node declared as `<nspace:elemname>` it returns the "`elemname`" part.
`childNodes`		Returns a `NodeList` containing all the child nodes of this node, for nodes that can have child nodes.

Name		Description
dataType	**Ext**	Sets or returns the data type for this node.
definition	**Ext**	For EntityReference nodes, returns the entry in the DTD or schema containing the definition for the entity, i.e. "<!ENTITY entityname 'entity value'>". For other nodes, returns null.
firstChild		Returns a reference to the first child node of this node.
lastChild		Returns a reference to the last child node of this node.
namespaceURI	**Ext**	Returns the URI for the namespace as a string. For example, in the namespace declaration xmlns:name="uri" it returns the "uri" part.
nextSibling		Returns a reference to the next sibling node of this node, i.e. the next node in the source data file at the same level of the hierarchy.
nodeName		Returns the name of the node, which will depend on the node type. See the list of **Node Types** at the end of this appendix for more details.
nodeTypeString	**Ext**	Returns the node type as a string, depending on the node type. See the list of **Node Types** at the end of this appendix for more details.
nodeType		Returns the node type as a number. See the list of **Node Types** at the end of this appendix for more details.
nodeTypedValue	**Ext**	Sets or returns the strongly typed value of the node, expressed in its defined data type. If no data type has been defined for the node, its nodeValue is returned.
nodeValue		Sets or returns the value of the node as plain text.
ownerDocument		Returns the root node of the document that contains the node.
parentNode		Returns the parent node of this node, for nodes that can have parents.

Table Continued on Following Page

Name		Description
parsed	**Ext**	Returns true if this node and all its descendants have been parsed and instantiated.
prefix	**Ext**	Returns the element namespace prefix as a string. For example, in a node declared as <nspace:elemname> it returns the "nspace" part.
previousSibling		Returns a reference to the previous sibling node of this node, i.e. the previous node in the source file at the same level of the hierarchy.
specified	**Ext**	Indicates whether the node value is explicitly specified or derived from a default value in the DTD or schema. Normally only used with attribute nodes.
text	**Ext**	Sets or returns the entire text content of this node and all its descendant nodes.
xml	**Ext**	Returns the entire XML content of this node and all its descendant nodes.

DocumentFragment Methods

Name		Description
appendChild(new_node)		Appends the node object new_node to the end of the list of child nodes for this node.
cloneNode(recurse_children)		Creates a new node object that is an exact clone of this node, including all descendant nodes of this node if recurse_children is set to true.
hasChildNodes()		Returns true if this node has any child nodes.
insertBefore(new_node, this_node)		Inserts a new node object new_node into the list of child nodes for this node, to the left of the node object this_node or at the end of the list if this_node is omitted.
removeChild(this_node)		Removes the child node this_node from the list of child nodes for this node, and returns it.
replaceChild(new_node, old_node)		Replaces the child node old_node with the new child node object new_node, and returns the old child node.
selectNodes(pattern)	**Ext**	Applies a specified pattern to this node's context and returns a node list object containing matching nodes. The string pattern specifies the XSL pattern-matching operation to be used.

Name		Description
`selectSingleNode (pattern)`	**Ext**	Applies a specified pattern to this node's context and returns just the first node object that matches. The string `pattern` specifies the XSL pattern-matching operation to be used.
`transformNode (stylesheet)`	**Ext**	Processes this node and its children using an XSL style sheet specified in the `stylesheet` argument, and returns the resulting transformation. The style sheet must be either a `Document` node object, in which case the document is assumed to be an XSL style sheet, or a Node object in the `xsl` namespace, in which case this node is treated as a standalone style sheet fragment.

Element — the IXMLDOMElement Object

This object represents the elements in the document, and together with the `Attribute` and `Text` nodes, is likely to be one of the most common. Note that the text content of an `Element` node is stored in a child `Text` node. An `Element` node always has a `nodeValue` of `null`. In the following tables, '**Ext**' indicates properties and methods that are extensions to the base W3C object model. IE5 implements the unextended object through the `IDOMElement` interface.

Element Properties

Name		Description
`attributes`		Returns a collection of the `Attribute` (or `Attr`) objects for this node as a `NamedNodeMap` object.
`baseName`	**Ext**	Returns the node name with any namespace removed. For example, in a node declared as `<nspace:elemname>` it returns the "`elemname`" part.
`childNodes`		Returns a `NodeList` containing all the child nodes of this node, for nodes that can have child nodes.
`dataType`	**Ext**	Sets or returns the data type for this node.
`definition`	**Ext**	For `EntityReference` nodes, returns the entry in the DTD or schema containing the definition for the entity, i.e. "`<!ENTITY entityname 'entity value'>`". For other nodes, returns `null`.
`firstChild`		Returns a reference to the first child node of this node.
`lastChild`		Returns a reference to the last child node of this node.
`namespaceURI`	**Ext**	Returns the URI for the namespace as a string. For example, in the namespace declaration `xmlns:name="uri"` it returns the "`uri`" part.

Name		Description
nextSibling		Returns a reference to the next sibling node of this node, i.e. the next node in the source data file at the same level of the hierarchy.
nodeName		Returns the name of the node, which will depend on the node type. See the list of **Node Types** at the end of this appendix for more details.
nodeTypeString	**Ext**	Returns the node type as a string, depending on the node type. See the list of **Node Types** at the end of this appendix for more details.
nodeType		Returns the node type as a number. See the list of **Node Types** at the end of this appendix for more details.
nodeTypedValue	**Ext**	Sets or returns the strongly typed value of the node, expressed in its defined data type. If no data type has been defined for the node, its `nodeValue` is returned.
nodeValue		Sets or returns the value of the node as plain text.
ownerDocument		Returns the root node of the document that contains the node.
parentNode		Returns the parent node of this node, for nodes that can have parents.
parsed	**Ext**	Returns `true` if this node and all its descendants have been parsed and instantiated.
prefix	**Ext**	Returns the element namespace prefix as a string. For example, in a node declared as `<nspace:elemname>` it returns the "`nspace`" part.
previousSibling		Returns a reference to the previous sibling node of this node, i.e. the previous node in the source file at the same level of the hierarchy.
specified	**Ext**	Indicates whether the node value is explicitly specified or derived from a default value in the DTD or schema. Normally only used with attribute nodes.
tagName		Sets or returns the name of the element node; i.e. the text name that appears within the tag.
text	**Ext**	Sets or returns the entire text content of this node and all its descendant nodes.
xml	**Ext**	Returns the entire XML content of this node and all its descendant nodes.

Element Methods

Name	Description
`appendChild(new_node)`	Appends the node object new_node to the end of the list of child nodes for this node.
`cloneNode(recurse_children)`	Creates a new node object that is an exact clone of this node, including all descendant nodes of this node if `recurse_children` is set to `true`.
`getAttribute(attr_name)`	Returns the value of the attribute with the specified name.
`getAttributeNode(attr_name)`	Returns the attribute node with the specified name as an object.
`getElementsByTagName(name)`	Returns a node list of all descendant elements matching the specified name.
`hasChildNodes()`	Returns `true` if this node has any child nodes.
`insertBefore(new_node, this_node)`	Inserts a new node object new_node into the list of child nodes for this node, to the left of the node object `this_node` or at the end of the list if `this_node` is omitted.
`normalize()`	Combines all adjacent text nodes into one unified text node for all descendant element nodes.
`removeAttribute(attr_name)`	Removes the value of the attribute with the specified name, or replaces it with the default value.
`removeAttributeNode(attr_node)`	Removes the specified attribute node from the element and returns it. If the attribute has a default value in the DTD or schema, a new attribute node is automatically created with that default value and the `specified` property is updated.
`removeChild(this_node)`	Removes the child node `this_node` from the list of child nodes for this node, and returns it.
`replaceChild(new_node, old_node)`	Replaces the child node `old_node` with the new child node object new_node, and returns the old child node.

Name		Description
selectNodes (pattern)	Ext	Applies a specified pattern to this node's context and returns a node list object containing matching nodes. The string pattern specifies the XSL pattern-matching operation to be used.
selectSingleNode (pattern)	Ext	Applies a specified pattern to this node's context and returns just the first node object that matches. The string pattern specifies the XSL pattern-matching operation to be used.
setAttribute(attr_name, value)		Sets the value of the attribute with the specified name.
setAttributeNode (attr_node)		Adds the new attribute node to the element. If an attribute with the same name exists, it is replaced and the old attribute node is returned.
transformNode (stylesheet)	Ext	Processes this node and its children using an XSL style sheet specified in the stylesheet argument, and returns the resulting transformation. The style sheet must be either a Document node object, in which case the document is assumed to be an XSL style sheet, or a Node object in the xsl namespace, in which case this node is treated as a standalone style sheet fragment.

Attribute or Attr — IXMLDOMAttribute Object

This object represents an Attribute of an Element object. In the W3C DOM recommendations, the object name is Attr rather than Attribute, to avoid clashing with existing interface definition languages. An Attribute node has a name and a value, and attributes are normally manipulated through a NamedNodeMap object. In the following tables, '**Ext**' indicates properties and methods that are extensions to the base W3C object model. Microsoft implements the unextended object as IDOMAttribute).

Attribute Properties

Name		Description
attributes		Returns a collection of the Attribute (or Attr) objects for this node as a NamedNodeMap object.
baseName	Ext	Returns the node name with any namespace removed. For example, in a node declared as <nspace:elemname> it returns the "elemname" part.
childNodes		Returns a NodeList containing all the child nodes of this node, for nodes that can have child nodes.
dataType	Ext	Sets or returns the data type for this node.

Name		Description
`definition`	**Ext**	For `EntityReference` nodes, returns the entry in the DTD or schema containing the definition for the entity, i.e. "`<!ENTITY entityname 'entity value'>`". For other nodes, returns `null`.
`firstChild`		Returns a reference to the first child node of this node.
`lastChild`		Returns a reference to the last child node of this node.
`name`		Sets or returns the name of the attribute.
`namespaceURI`	**Ext**	Returns the URI for the namespace as a string. For example, in the namespace declaration `xmlns:name="uri"` it returns the "`uri`" part.
`nextSibling`		Returns a reference to the next sibling node of this node, i.e. the next node in the source data file at the same level of the hierarchy.
`nodeName`		Returns the name of the node, which will depend on the node type. See the list of **Node Types** at the end of this appendix for more details.
`nodeTypeString`	**Ext**	Returns the node type as a string, depending on the node type. See the list of **Node Types** at the end of this appendix for more details.
`nodeType`		Returns the node type as a number. See the list of **Node Types** at the end of this appendix for more details.
`nodeTypedValue`	**Ext**	Sets or returns the strongly typed value of the node, expressed in its defined data type. If no data type has been defined for the node, its `nodeValue` is returned.
`nodeValue`		Sets or returns the value of the node as plain text.
`ownerDocument`		Returns the root node of the document that contains the node.
`parentNode`		Returns the parent node of this node, for nodes that can have parents.
`parsed`	**Ext**	Returns `true` if this node and all its descendants have been parsed and instantiated.
`prefix`	**Ext**	Returns the element namespace prefix as a string. For example, in a node declared as `<nspace:elemname>` it returns the "`nspace`" part.
`previous Sibling`		Returns a reference to the previous sibling node of this node, i.e. the previous node in the source file at the same level of the hierarchy.

Name		Description
specified	**Ext**	Indicates whether the node value is explicitly specified or derived from a default value in the DTD or schema. Normally only used with attribute nodes.
tagName		Returns the name of the element that contains this attribute.
text	**Ext**	Sets or returns the entire text content of this node and all its descendant nodes.
xml	**Ext**	Returns the entire XML content of this node and all its descendant nodes.
value		Sets or returns the value of the attribute.

Attribute Methods

Name		Description
`appendChild(new_node)`		Appends the node object `new_node` to the end of the list of child nodes for this node.
`cloneNode(recurse_children)`		Creates a new node object that is an exact clone of this node, including all descendant nodes of this node if `recurse_children` is set to `true`.
`hasChildNodes()`		Returns `true` if this node has any child nodes.
`insertBefore(new_node, this_node)`		Inserts a new node object `new_node` into the list of child nodes for this node, to the left of the node object `this_node` or at the end of the list if `this_node` is omitted.
`removeChild(this_node)`		Removes the child node `this_node` from the list of child nodes for this node, and returns it.
`replaceChild(new_node, old_node)`		Replaces the child node `old_node` with the new child node object `new_node`, and returns the old child node.
`selectNodes(pattern)`	**Ext**	Applies a specified pattern to this node's context and returns a node list object containing matching nodes. The string `pattern` specifies the XSL pattern-matching operation to be used.
`selectSingleNode(pattern)`	**Ext**	Applies a specified pattern to this node's context and returns just the first node object that matches. The string `pattern` specifies the XSL pattern-matching operation to be used.

Name		Description
transformNode (stylesheet)	**Ext**	Processes this node and its children using an XSL style sheet specified in the stylesheet argument, and returns the resulting transformation. The style sheet must be either a Document node object, in which case the document is assumed to be an XSL style sheet, or a Node object in the xsl namespace, in which case this node is treated as a standalone style sheet fragment.

Entity — the IXMLDOMEntity Object

This object represents a parsed or unparsed entity as declared with an <!ENTITY...> element in the DTD. However, it does not provide a reference to the entity declaration. The W3C DOM recommendation does not define an object in version 1.0 that models the declaration of entities. In the following tables, '**Ext**' indicates properties and methods that are extensions to the base W3C object model. In IE5 the unextended object is implemented by the IDOMEntity object.

Entity Properties

Name		Description
attributes		Returns a collection of the Attribute (or Attr) objects for this node as a NamedNodeMap object.
baseName	**Ext**	Returns the node name with any namespace removed. For example, in a node declared as <nspace:elemname> it returns the "elemname" part.
childNodes		Returns a NodeList containing all the child nodes of this node, for nodes that can have child nodes.
dataType	**Ext**	Sets or returns the data type for this node.
definition	**Ext**	For EntityReference nodes, returns the entry in the DTD or schema containing the definition for the entity, i.e. "<!ENTITY entityname 'entity value'>". For other nodes, returns null.
firstChild		Returns a reference to the first child node of this node.
lastChild		Returns a reference to the last child node of this node.
namespaceURI	**Ext**	Returns the URI for the namespace as a string. For example, in the namespace declaration xmlns:name="uri" it returns the "uri" part.
nextSibling		Returns a reference to the next sibling node of this node, i.e. the next node in the source data file at the same level of the hierarchy.

Name		Description
`nodeName`		Returns the name of the node, which will depend on the node type. See the list of **Node Types** at the end of this appendix for more details.
`nodeTypeString`	**Ext**	Returns the node type as a string, depending on the node type. See the list of **Node Types** at the end of this appendix for more details.
`nodeType`		Returns the node type as a number. See the list of **Node Types** at the end of this appendix for more details.
`nodeTypedValue`	**Ext**	Sets or returns the strongly typed value of the node, expressed in its defined data type. If no data type has been defined for the node, its `nodeValue` is returned.
`nodeValue`		Sets or returns the value of the node as plain text.
`notationName`	**Ext**	Returns the name of the notation linked to the entity.
`ownerDocument`		Returns the root node of the document that contains the node.
`parentNode`		Returns the parent node of this node, for nodes that can have parents.
`parsed`	**Ext**	Returns `true` if this node and all its descendants have been parsed and instantiated.
`prefix`	**Ext**	Returns the element namespace prefix as a string. For example, in a node declared as `<nspace:elemname>` it returns the "`nspace`" part.
`previousSibling`		Returns a reference to the previous sibling node of this node, i.e. the previous node in the source file at the same level of the hierarchy.
`publicId`		Sets or returns the `PUBLIC` identifier value for this entity node.
`specified`	**Ext**	Indicates whether the node value is explicitly specified or derived from a default value in the DTD or schema. Normally only used with attribute nodes.
`systemId`		Sets or returns the `SYSTEM` identifier value for this entity node.
`text`	**Ext**	Sets or returns the entire text content of this node and all its descendant nodes.
`xml`	**Ext**	Returns the entire XML content of this node and all its descendant nodes.

Entity Methods

Name		Description
`appendChild(new_node)`		Appends the node object `new_node` to the end of the list of child nodes for this node.
`cloneNode(recurse_children)`		Creates a new node object that is an exact clone of this node, including all descendant nodes of this node if `recurse_children` is set to `true`.
`hasChildNodes()`		Returns `true` if this node has any child nodes.
`insertBefore(new_node, this_node)`		Inserts a new node object `new_node` into the list of child nodes for this node, to the left of the node object `this_node` or at the end of the list if `this_node` is omitted.
`removeChild(this_node)`		Removes the child node `this_node` from the list of child nodes for this node, and returns it.
`replaceChild(new_node, old_node)`		Replaces the child node `old_node` with the new child node object `new_node`, and returns the old child node.
`selectNodes(pattern)`	**Ext**	Applies a specified pattern to this node's context and returns a node list object containing matching nodes. The string `pattern` specifies the XSL pattern-matching operation to be used.
`selectSingleNode(pattern)`	**Ext**	Applies a specified pattern to this node's context and returns just the first node object that matches. The string `pattern` specifies the XSL pattern-matching operation to be used.
`transformNode(stylesheet)`	**Ext**	Processes this node and its children using an XSL style sheet specified in the `stylesheet` argument, and returns the resulting transformation. The style sheet must be either a `Document` node object, in which case the document is assumed to be an XSL style sheet, or a Node object in the `xsl` namespace, in which case this node is treated as a standalone style sheet fragment.

EntityReference — the IXMLDOMEntityReference Object

This object represents an entity reference node within the XML document. If the XML processor expands entity references while building the structure model, it's possible that no entity reference objects will appear in the tree, being replaced by the **replacement text** of the entity. In the following tables, '**Ext**' indicates properties and methods that are extensions to the base W3C object model. The object is implemented without extensions by Microsoft as the `IDOMEntityReference` object.

EntityReference Properties

Name		Description
`attributes`		Returns a collection of the `Attribute` (or `Attr`) objects for this node as a `NamedNodeMap` object.
`baseName`	**Ext**	Returns the node name with any namespace removed. For example, in a node declared as `<nspace:elemname>` it returns the "`elemname`" part.
`childNodes`		Returns a `NodeList` containing all the child nodes of this node, for nodes that can have child nodes.
`dataType`	**Ext**	Sets or returns the data type for this node.
`definition`	**Ext**	For `EntityReference` nodes, returns the entry in the DTD or schema containing the definition for the entity, i.e. "`<!ENTITY entityname 'entity value'>`". For other nodes, returns `null`.
`firstChild`		Returns a reference to the first child node of this node.
`lastChild`		Returns a reference to the last child node of this node.
`namespaceURI`	**Ext**	Returns the URI for the namespace as a string. For example, in the namespace declaration `xmlns:name="uri"` it returns the "`uri`" part.
`nextSibling`		Returns a reference to the next sibling node of this node, i.e. the next node in the source data file at the same level of the hierarchy.
`nodeName`		Returns the name of the node, which will depend on the node type. See the list of **Node Types** at the end of this appendix for more details.
`nodeTypeString`	**Ext**	Returns the node type as a string, depending on the node type. See the list of **Node Types** at the end of this appendix for more details.
`nodeType`		Returns the node type as a number. See the list of **Node Types** at the end of this appendix for more details.
`nodeTypedValue`	**Ext**	Sets or returns the strongly typed value of the node, expressed in its defined data type. If no data type has been defined for the node, its `nodeValue` is returned.

Name		Description
nodeValue		Sets or returns the value of the node as plain text.
ownerDocument		Returns the root node of the document that contains the node.
parentNode		Returns the parent node of this node, for nodes that can have parents.
parsed	**Ext**	Returns `true` if this node and all its descendants have been parsed and instantiated.
prefix	**Ext**	Returns the element namespace prefix as a string. For example, in a node declared as `<nspace:elemname>` it returns the "`nspace`" part.
previousSibling		Returns a reference to the previous sibling node of this node, i.e. the previous node in the source file at the same level of the hierarchy.
specified	**Ext**	Indicates whether the node value is explicitly specified or derived from a default value in the DTD or schema. Normally only used with attribute nodes.
text	**Ext**	Sets or returns the entire text content of this node and all its descendant nodes.
xml	**Ext**	Returns the entire XML content of this node and all its descendant nodes.

EntityReference Methods

Name	Description
appendChild (new_node)	Appends the node object `new_node` to the end of the list of child nodes for this node.
cloneNode(recurse_children)	Creates a new node object that is an exact clone of this node, including all descendant nodes of this node if `recurse_children` is set to `true`.
hasChildNodes()	Returns `true` if this node has any child nodes.
insertBefore(new_node, this_node)	Inserts a new node object `new_node` into the list of child nodes for this node, to the left of the node object `this_node` or at the end of the list if `this_node` is omitted.
removeChild(this_node)	Removes the child node `this_node` from the list of child nodes for this node, and returns it.
replaceChild(new_node, old_node)	Replaces the child node `old_node` with the new child node object `new_node`, and returns the old child node.

Name		Description
selectNodes (pattern)	**Ext**	Applies a specified pattern to this node's context and returns a node list object containing matching nodes. The string pattern specifies the XSL pattern-matching operation to be used.
selectSingleNode (pattern)	**Ext**	Applies a specified pattern to this node's context and returns just the first node object that matches. The string pattern specifies the XSL pattern-matching operation to be used.
transformNode (stylesheet)	**Ext**	Processes this node and its children using an XSL style sheet specified in the stylesheet argument, and returns the resulting transformation. The style sheet must be either a Document node object, in which case the document is assumed to be an XSL style sheet, or a Node object in the xsl namespace, in which case this node is treated as a standalone style sheet fragment.

Notation — the IXMLDOMNotation Object

This object represents a notation declared in the DTD or schema with a <!NOTATION...> element. In the following tables, '**Ext**' indicates properties and methods that are extensions to the base W3C object model. The unextended object is implemented as the IDOMNotation object in IE5.

Notation Properties

Name		Description
attributes		Returns a collection of the Attribute (or Attr) objects for this node as a NamedNodeMap object.
baseName	**Ext**	Returns the node name with any namespace removed. For example, in a node declared as <nspace:elemname> it returns the "elemname" part.
childNodes		Returns a NodeList containing all the child nodes of this node, for nodes that can have child nodes.
dataType	**Ext**	Sets or returns the data type for this node.
definition	**Ext**	For EntityReference nodes, returns the entry in the DTD or schema containing the definition for the entity, i.e. "<!ENTITY entityname 'entity value'>". For other nodes, returns null.
firstChild		Returns a reference to the first child node of this node.
lastChild		Returns a reference to the last child node of this node.

Name		Description
`namespaceURI`	**Ext**	Returns the URI for the namespace as a string. For example, in the namespace declaration `xmlns:name="uri"` it returns the `"uri"` part.
`nextSibling`		Returns a reference to the next sibling node of this node, i.e. the next node in the source data file at the same level of the hierarchy.
`nodeName`		Returns the name of the node, which will depend on the node type. See the list of **Node Types** at the end of this appendix for more details.
`nodeTypeString`	**Ext**	Returns the node type as a string, depending on the node type. See the list of **Node Types** at the end of this appendix for more details.
`nodeType`		Returns the node type as a number. See the list of **Node Types** at the end of this appendix for more details.
`nodeTypedValue`	**Ext**	Sets or returns the strongly typed value of the node, expressed in its defined data type. If no data type has been defined for the node, its `nodeValue` is returned.
`nodeValue`		Sets or returns the value of the node as plain text.
`ownerDocument`		Returns the root node of the document that contains the node.
`parentNode`		Returns the parent node of this node, for nodes that can have parents.
`parsed`	**Ext**	Returns `true` if this node and all its descendants have been parsed and instantiated.
`prefix`	**Ext**	Returns the element namespace prefix as a string. For example, in a node declared as `<nspace:elemname>` it returns the `"nspace"` part.
`previousSibling`		Returns a reference to the previous sibling node of this node, i.e. the previous node in the source file at the same level of the hierarchy.
`publicId`		Sets or returns the `PUBLIC` identifier value for this entity node.
`specified`	**Ext**	Indicates whether the node value is explicitly specified or derived from a default value in the DTD or schema. Normally only used with attribute nodes.
`systemId`		Sets or returns the `SYSTEM` identifier value for this entity node.
`text`	**Ext**	Sets or returns the entire text content of this node and all its descendant nodes.
`xml`	**Ext**	Returns the entire XML content of this node and all its descendant nodes.

Notation Methods

Name		Description
appendChild (new_node)		Appends the node object new_node to the end of the list of child nodes for this node.
cloneNode (recurse_children)		Creates a new node object that is an exact clone of this node, including all descendant nodes of this node if recurse_children is set to true.
hasChildNodes()		Returns true if this node has any child nodes.
insertBefore (new_node, this_node)		Inserts a new node object new_node into the list of child nodes for this node, to the left of the node object this_node or at the end of the list if this_node is omitted.
removeChild (this_node)		Removes the child node this_node from the list of child nodes for this node, and returns it.
replaceChild (new_node, old_node)		Replaces the child node old_node with the new child node object new_node, and returns the old child node.
selectNodes (pattern)	**Ext**	Applies a specified pattern to this node's context and returns a node list object containing matching nodes. The string pattern specifies the XSL pattern-matching operation to be used.
selectSingleNode (pattern)	**Ext**	Applies a specified pattern to this node's context and returns just the first node object that matches. The string pattern specifies the XSL pattern-matching operation to be used.
transformNode (stylesheet)	**Ext**	Processes this node and its children using an XSL style sheet specified in the stylesheet argument, and returns the resulting transformation. The style sheet must be either a Document node object, in which case the document is assumed to be an XSL style sheet, or a Node object in the xsl namespace, in which case this node is treated as a standalone style sheet fragment.

CharacterData — the IXMLDOMCharacterData Object

This object is the base for several higher-level objects including Text, CDATASection (which is inherited from the Text object) and Comment. It provides text information properties like length, and a range of text manipulation methods like substringData() that are used by these objects. The IE5 implementation of CharacterData follows the W3C recommendations for character data manipulation in the appropriate elements with the exception of those properties and methods marked with '**Ext**' in the following tables. The unextended W3C CharacterData object is implemented in IE5 by the IDOMCharacterData object.

CharacterData Properties

Name		Description
attributes		Returns a collection of the Attribute (or Attr) objects for this node as a NamedNodeMap object.
baseName	**Ext**	Returns the node name with any namespace removed. For example, in a node declared as <nspace:elemname> it returns the "elemname" part.
childNodes		Returns a NodeList containing all the child nodes of this node, for nodes that can have child nodes.
data		Contains this node's value, which depends on the node type.
dataType	**Ext**	Sets or returns the data type for this node.
definition	**Ext**	For EntityReference nodes, returns the entry in the DTD or schema containing the definition for the entity, i.e. "<!ENTITY entityname 'entity value'>". For other nodes, returns null.
firstChild		Returns a reference to the first child node of this node.
lastChild		Returns a reference to the last child node of this node.
length		Returns the number of characters for the data, i.e. the string length.
namespaceURI	**Ext**	Returns the URI for the namespace as a string. For example, in the namespace declaration xmlns:name="uri" it returns the "uri" part.
nextSibling		Returns a reference to the next sibling node of this node, i.e. the next node in the source data file at the same level of the hierarchy.
nodeName		Returns the name of the node, which will depend on the node type. See the list of Node Types at the end of this appendix for more details.
nodeTypeString	**Ext**	Returns the node type as a string. See the list of Node Types at the end of this appendix for more details.
nodeType		Returns the node type as a number. See the list of Node Types at the end of this appendix for more details.
nodeTypedValue	**Ext**	Sets or returns the strongly typed value of the node, expressed in its defined data type. If no data type has been defined for the node, its nodeValue is returned.
nodeValue		Sets or returns the value of the node as plain text.
ownerDocument		Returns the root node of the document that contains the node.

Name		Description
parentNode		Returns the parent node of this node, for nodes that can have parents.
parsed	**Ext**	Returns true if this node and all its descendants have been parsed and instantiated.
prefix	**Ext**	Returns the element namespace prefix as a string. For example, in a node declared as <nspace:elemname> it returns the "nspace" part.
previousSibling		Returns a reference to the previous sibling node of this node, i.e. the previous node in the source file at the same level of the hierarchy.
specified	**Ext**	Indicates whether the node value is explicitly specified or derived from a default value in the DTD or schema. Normally only used with attribute nodes.
text	**Ext**	Sets or returns the entire text content of this node and all its descendant nodes.
xml	**Ext**	Returns the entire XML content of this node and all its descendant nodes.

CharacterData Methods

Name	Description
appendChild(new_node)	Appends the node object new_node to the end of the list of child nodes for this node.
appendData(text)	Appends the string in the text argument to the existing string data.
cloneNode(recurse_children)	Creates a new node object that is an exact clone of this node, including all descendant nodes of this node if recurse_children is set to true.
deleteData(char_offset, num_chars)	Deletes a substring from the string data of the node, starting at char_offset and continuing for num_chars.
hasChildNodes()	Returns true if this node has any child nodes.
insertBefore(new_node, this_node)	Inserts a new node object new_node into the list of child nodes for this node, to the left of the node object this_node or at the end of the list if this_node is omitted.

Name		Description
insertData(char_offset, text)		Inserts the string in the text argument at the specified character offset within the data contained by the node.
removeChild(this_child)		Removes the child node this_node from the list of child nodes for this node, and returns it.
replaceChild(new_node, old_node)		Replaces the child node old_node with the new child node object new_node, and returns the old child node.
replaceData(char_ offset, num_chars, text)		Replaces the specified number of characters in the existing string data of the node, starting at the specified character offset, with the string in the text argument.
selectNodes(pattern)	**Ext**	Applies a specified pattern to this node's context and returns a node list object containing matching nodes. The string pattern specifies the XSL pattern-matching operation to be used.
selectSingleNode (pattern)	**Ext**	Applies a specified pattern to this node's context and returns just the first node object that matches. The string pattern specifies the XSL pattern-matching operation to be used.
substringData(char_ offset, num_chars)		Returns as a string the specified number of characters, starting at the specified character offset, from the data contained in the node.
transformNode (stylesheet)	**Ext**	Processes this node and its children using an XSL style sheet specified in the stylesheet argument, and returns the resulting transformation. The style sheet must be either a Document node object, in which case the document is assumed to be an XSL style sheet, or a Node object in the xsl namespace, in which case this node is treated as a standalone style sheet fragment.

Text — the IXMLDOMText Object

This object represents the text content of an element node or an attribute node. It is derived from the CharacterData object, and the CDATASection object is in turn inherited from it. In the following tables, '**Ext**' indicates properties and methods that are extensions to the base W3C object model; the W3C CDATASection object is implemented in IE5 by the IDOMText object).

Text Properties

Name		Description
attributes		Returns a collection of the Attribute (or Attr) objects for this node as a NamedNodeMap object.
baseName	Ext	Returns the node name with any namespace removed. For example, in a node declared as <nspace:elemname> it returns the "elemname" part.
childNodes		Returns a NodeList containing all the child nodes of this node, for nodes that can have child nodes.
data		Contains this node's value, which depends on the node type.
dataType	Ext	Sets or returns the data type for this node.
definition	Ext	For EntityReference nodes, returns the entry in the DTD or schema containing the definition for the entity, i.e. "<!ENTITY entityname 'entity value'>". For other nodes, returns null.
firstChild		Returns a reference to the first child node of this node.
lastChild		Returns a reference to the last child node of this node.
length		Returns the number of characters for the data, i.e. the string length.
namespaceURI	Ext	Returns the URI for the namespace as a string. For example, in the namespace declaration xmlns:name="uri" it returns the "uri" part.
nextSibling		Returns a reference to the next sibling node of this node, i.e. the next node in the source data file at the same level of the hierarchy.
nodeName		Returns the name of the node, which will depend on the node type. See the list of **Node Types** at the end of this appendix for more details.
nodeTypeString	Ext	Returns the node type as a string, depending on the node type. See the list of **Node Types** at the end of this appendix for more details.
nodeType		Returns the node type as a number. See the list of **Node Types** at the end of this appendix for more details.
nodeTypedValue	Ext	Sets or returns the strongly typed value of the node, expressed in its defined data type. If no data type has been defined for the node, its nodeValue is returned.

Name		Description
nodeValue		Sets or returns the value of the node as plain text.
ownerDocument		Returns the root node of the document that contains the node.
parentNode		Returns the parent node of this node, for nodes that can have parents.
parsed	**Ext**	Returns true if this node and all its descendants have been parsed and instantiated.
prefix	**Ext**	Returns the element namespace prefix as a string. For example, in a node declared as <nspace:elemname> it returns the "nspace" part.
previousSibling		Returns a reference to the previous sibling node of this node, i.e. the previous node in the source file at the same level of the hierarchy.
specified	**Ext**	Indicates whether the node value is explicitly specified or derived from a default value in the DTD or schema. Normally only used with attribute nodes.
text	**Ext**	Sets or returns the entire text content of this node and all its descendant nodes.
xml	**Ext**	Returns the entire XML content of this node and all its descendant nodes.

Text Methods

Name	Description
appendChild(new_node)	Appends the node object new_node to the end of the list of child nodes for this node.
appendData(text)	Appends the string in the text argument to the existing string data.
cloneNode(recurse_children)	Creates a new node object that is an exact clone of this node, including all descendant nodes of this node if recurse_children is set to true.
deleteData(char_offset, num_chars)	Deletes a substring from the string data of the node, starting at char_offset and continuing for num_chars.
hasChildNodes()	Returns true if this node has any child nodes.
insertBefore(new_node, this_node)	Inserts a new node object new_node into the list of child nodes for this node, to the left of the node object this_node or at the end of the list if this_node is omitted.

Name		Description
`insertData(char_offset, text)`		Inserts the string in the `text` argument at the specified character offset within the data contained by the node.
`removeChild(this_child)`		Removes the child node `this_node` from the list of child nodes for this node, and returns it.
`replaceChild(new_node, old_node)`		Replaces the child node `old_node` with the new child node object `new_node`, and returns the old child node.
`replaceData(char_offset, num_chars, text)`		Replaces the specified number of characters in the existing string data of the node, starting at the specified character offset, with the string in the `text` argument.
`selectNodes(pattern)`	**Ext**	Applies a specified pattern to this node's context and returns a node list object containing matching nodes. The string `pattern` specifies the XSL pattern-matching operation to be used.
`selectSingleNode(pattern)`	**Ext**	Applies a specified pattern to this node's context and returns just the first node object that matches. The string `pattern` specifies the XSL pattern-matching operation to be used.
`splitText(char_offset)`		Splits the node into two separate nodes at the specified character offset, then inserts the new node into the XML as a sibling that immediately follows this node.
`substringData(char_offset, num_chars)`		Returns as a string the specified number of characters, starting at the specified character offset, from the data contained in the node.
`transformNode(stylesheet)`	**Ext**	Processes this node and its children using an XSL style sheet specified in the `stylesheet` argument, and returns the resulting transformation. The style sheet must be either a `Document` node object, in which case the document is assumed to be an XSL style sheet, or a Node object in the `xsl` namespace, in which case this node is treated as a standalone style sheet fragment.

CDATASection — the IXMLDOMCDATASection Object

CDATA sections in a DTD or schema are used to 'escape' blocks of text that are not designed to be interpreted as markup. The are declared in the DTD using a `<!CDATA...>` element. The `IXMLDOMCDATASection` interface is inherited from the `IXMLDOMText` interface, and adds no extra methods or properties. In the following tables, '**Ext**' indicates properties and methods that are extensions to the base W3C object model. IE5 implements the unextended W3C object as the `IDOMCDATASection` object.

CDATASection Properties

Name		Description
attributes		Returns collection of the Attribute (or Attr) objects for this node as a NamedNodeMap object.
baseName	**Ext**	Returns the node name with any namespace removed. For example, in a node declared as <nspace:elemname> it returns the "elemname" part.
childNodes		Returns a NodeList containing all the child nodes of this node, for nodes that can have child nodes.
data		Contains this node's value, which depends on the node type.
dataType	**Ext**	Sets or returns the data type for this node.
definition	**Ext**	For EntityReference nodes, returns the entry in the DTD or schema containing the definition for the entity, i.e. "<!ENTITY entityname 'entity value'>". For other nodes, returns null.
firstChild		Returns a reference to the first child node of this node.
lastChild		Returns a reference to the last child node of this node.
length		Returns the number of characters for the data, i.e. the string length.
namespaceURI	**Ext**	Returns the URI for the namespace as a string. For example, in the namespace declaration xmlns:name="uri" it returns the "uri" part.
nextSibling		Returns a reference to the next sibling node of this node, i.e. the next node in the source data file at the same level of the hierarchy.
nodeName		Returns the name of the node, which will depend on the node type. See the list of **Node Types** at the end of this appendix for more details.
nodeTypeString	**Ext**	Returns the node type as a string, depending on the node type. See the list of **Node Types** at the end of this appendix for more details.
nodeType		Returns the node type as a number. See the list of **Node Types** at the end of this appendix for more details.
nodeTypedValue	**Ext**	Sets or returns the strongly typed value of the node, expressed in its defined data type. If no data type has been defined for the node, its nodeValue is returned.

Name		Description
nodeValue		Sets or returns the value of the node as plain text.
ownerDocument		Returns the root node of the document that contains the node.
parentNode		Returns the parent node of this node, for nodes that can have parents.
parsed	**Ext**	Returns true if this node and all its descendants have been parsed and instantiated.
prefix	**Ext**	Returns the element namespace prefix as a string. For example, in a node declared as <nspace:elemname> it returns the "nspace" part.
previousSibling		Returns a reference to the previous sibling node of this node, i.e. the previous node in the source file at the same level of the hierarchy.
specified	**Ext**	Indicates whether the node value is explicitly specified or derived from a default value in the DTD or schema. Normally only used with attribute nodes.
text	**Ext**	Sets or returns the entire text content of this node and all its descendant nodes.
xml	**Ext**	Returns the entire XML content of this node and all its descendant nodes.

CDATASection Methods

Name	Description
appendChild(new_node)	Appends the node object new_node to the end of the list of child nodes for this node.
appendData(text)	Appends the string in the text argument to the existing string data.
cloneNode(recurse_children)	Creates a new node object that is an exact clone of this node, including all descendant nodes of this node if recurse_children is set to true.
deleteData(char_offset, num_chars)	Deletes a substring from the string data of the node, starting at char_offset and continuing for num_chars.
hasChildNodes()	Returns true if this node has any child nodes.
insertBefore(new_node, this_node)	Inserts a new node object new_node into the list of child nodes for this node, to the left of the node object this_node or at the end of the list if this_node is omitted.

Name		Description
insertData(char_ offset, text)		Inserts the string in the text argument at the specified character offset within the data contained by the node.
removeChild(this_ child)		Removes the child node this_node from the list of child nodes for this node, and returns it.
replaceChild(new_ node, old_node)		Replaces the child node old_node with the new child node object new_node, and returns the old child node.
replaceData(char_ offset, num_chars, text)		Replaces the specified number of characters in the existing string data of the node, starting at the specified character offset, with the string in the text argument.
selectNodes(pattern)	**Ext**	Applies a specified pattern to this node's context and returns a node list object containing matching nodes. The string pattern specifies the XSL pattern-matching operation to be used.
selectSingleNode(pattern)	**Ext**	Applies a specified pattern to this node's context and returns just the first node object that matches. The string pattern specifies the XSL pattern-matching operation to be used.
splitText(char_ offset)		Splits the node into two separate nodes at the specified character offset, then inserts the new node into the XML as a sibling that immediately follows this node.
substringData(char_ offset, num_chars)		Returns as a string the specified number of characters, starting at the specified character offset, from the data contained in the node.
transformNode(stylesheet)	**Ext**	Processes this node and its children using an XSL style sheet specified in the stylesheet argument, and returns the resulting transformation. The style sheet must be either a Document node object, in which case the document is assumed to be an XSL style sheet, or a Node object in the xsl namespace, in which case this node is treated as a standalone style sheet fragment.

Comment - the IXMLDOMComment Object

Represents the content of an XML comment element. This object is derived from the IXMLDOMCharacterData object. In the following tables, '**Ext**' indicates properties and methods that are extensions to the base W3C object model. The unextended W3C Comment object is implemented in IE5 by the IDOMComment interface.

Comment Properties

Name		Description
attributes		Returns a collection of the Attribute (or Attr) objects for this node as a NamedNodeMap object.
baseName	**Ext**	Returns the node name with any namespace removed. For example, in a node declared as <nspace:elemname> it returns the "elemname" part.
childNodes		Returns a NodeList containing all the child nodes of this node, for nodes that can have child nodes.
data		Contains this node's value, which depends on the node type.
dataType	**Ext**	Sets or returns the data type for this node.
definition	**Ext**	For EntityReference nodes, returns the entry in the DTD or schema containing the definition for the entity, i.e. "<!ENTITY entityname 'entity value'>". For other nodes, returns null.
firstChild		Returns a reference to the first child node of this node.
lastChild		Returns a reference to the last child node of this node.
length		Returns the number of characters for the data, i.e. the string length.
namespaceURI	**Ext**	Returns the URI for the namespace as a string. For example, in the namespace declaration xmlns:name="uri" it returns the "uri" part.
nextSibling		Returns a reference to the next sibling node of this node, i.e. the next node in the source data file at the same level of the hierarchy.
nodeName		Returns the name of the node, which will depend on the node type. See the list of **Node Types** at the end of this appendix for more details.
nodeTypeString	**Ext**	Returns the node type as a string, depending on the node type. See the list of **Node Types** at the end of this appendix for more details.
nodeType		Returns the node type as a number. See the list of **Node Types** at the end of this appendix for more details.

Name		Description
nodeTypedValue	**Ext**	Sets or returns the strongly typed value of the node, expressed in its defined data type. If no data type has been defined for the node, its nodeValue is returned.
nodeValue		Sets or returns the value of the node as plain text.
ownerDocument		Returns the root node of the document that contains the node.
parentNode		Returns the parent node of this node, for nodes that can have parents.
parsed	**Ext**	Returns true if this node and all its descendants have been parsed and instantiated.
prefix	**Ext**	Returns the element namespace prefix as a string. For example, in a node declared as <nspace:elemname> it returns the "nspace" part.
previousSibling		Returns a reference to the previous sibling node of this node, i.e. the previous node in the source file at the same level of the hierarchy.
specified	**Ext**	Indicates whether the node value is explicitly specified or derived from a default value in the DTD or schema. Normally only used with attribute nodes.
text	**Ext**	Sets or returns the entire text content of this node and all its descendant nodes.
xml	**Ext**	Returns the entire XML content of this node and all its descendant nodes.

Comment Methods

Name	Description
appendChild(new_node)	Appends the node object new_node to the end of the list of child nodes for this node.
appendData(text)	Appends the string in the text argument to the existing string data.
cloneNode(recurse_children)	Creates a new node object that is an exact clone of this node, including all descendant nodes of this node if recurse_children is set to true.
deleteData(char_offset, num_chars)	Deletes a substring from the string data of the node, starting at char_offset and continuing for num_chars.
hasChildNodes()	Returns true if this node has any child nodes.

Name		Description
`insertBefore(new_node, this_node)`		Inserts a new node object `new_node` into the list of child nodes for this node, to the left of the node object `this_node` or at the end of the list if `this_node` is omitted.
`insertData(char_offset, text)`		Inserts the string in the text argument at the specified character offset within the data contained by the node.
`removeChild(this_child)`		Removes the child node `this_node` from the list of child nodes for this node, and returns it.
`replaceChild(new_node, old_node)`		Replaces the child node `old_node` with the new child node object `new_node`, and returns the old child node.
`replaceData(char_offset, num_chars, text)`		Replaces the specified number of characters in the existing string data of the node, starting at the specified character offset, with the string in the `text` argument.
`selectNodes(pattern)`	**Ext**	Applies a specified pattern to this node's context and returns a node list object containing matching nodes. The string `pattern` specifies the XSL pattern-matching operation to be used.
`selectSingleNode(pattern)`	**Ext**	Applies a specified pattern to this node's context and returns just the first node object that matches. The string `pattern` specifies the XSL pattern-matching operation to be used.
`substringData(char_offset, num_chars)`		Returns as a string the specified number of characters, starting at the specified character offset, from the data contained in the node.
`transformNode(stylesheet)`	**Ext**	Processes this node and its children using an XSL style sheet specified in the `stylesheet` argument, and returns the resulting transformation. The style sheet must be either a `Document` node object, in which case the document is assumed to be an XSL style sheet, or a Node object in the `xsl` namespace, in which case this node is treated as a standalone style sheet fragment.

ProcessingInstruction — the IXMLDOMProcessingInstruction Object

This element represents an instruction embedded in the XML within the '<?' and '?>' delimiters. It provides a way of storing processor-specific information within an XML document. The text content of the node is usually subdivided into the `target` (the text after the '<?' and up to the first white-space character) and the `data` content (the remainder up to the closing '?>'). In the following tables, '**Ext**' indicates properties and methods that are extensions to the base W3C object model. The W3C Recommendation for this object is implemented in IE5 by the `IDOMProcessingInstruction` object.

ProcessingInstruction Properties

Name		Description
`attributes`		Returns a collection of the `Attribute` (or `Attr`) objects for this node as a `NamedNodeMap` object.
`baseName`	**Ext**	Returns the node name with any namespace removed. For example, in a node declared as `<nspace:elemname>` it returns the "`elemname`" part.
`childNodes`		Returns a `NodeList` containing all the child nodes of this node, for nodes that can have child nodes.
`data`		Contains this node's value, which depends on the node type.
`dataType`	**Ext**	Sets or returns the data type for this node.
`definition`	**Ext**	For `EntityReference` nodes, returns the entry in the DTD or schema containing the definition for the entity, i.e. "`<!ENTITY entityname 'entity value'>`". For other nodes, returns `null`.
`firstChild`		Returns a reference to the first child node of this node.
`lastChild`		Returns a reference to the last child node of this node.
`length`		Returns the number of characters for the data, i.e. the string length.
`namespaceURI`	**Ext**	Returns the URI for the namespace as a string. For example, in the namespace declaration `xmlns:name="uri"` it returns the "`uri`" part.
`nextSibling`		Returns a reference to the next sibling node of this node, i.e. the next node in the source data file at the same level of the hierarchy.
`nodeName`		Returns the name of the node, which will depend on the node type. See the list of **Node Types** at the end of this appendix for more details.

Name		Description
nodeTypeString	**Ext**	Returns the node type as a string, depending on the node type. See the list of **Node Types** at the end of this appendix for more details.
nodeType		Returns the node type as a number. See the list of **Node Types** at the end of this appendix for more details.
nodeTypedValue	**Ext**	Sets or returns the strongly typed value of the node, expressed in its defined data type. If no data type has been defined for the node, its `nodeValue` is returned.
nodeValue		Sets or returns the value of the node as plain text.
ownerDocument		Returns the root node of the document that contains the node.
parentNode		Returns the parent node of this node, for nodes that can have parents.
parsed	**Ext**	Returns `true` if this node and all its descendants have been parsed and instantiated.
prefix	**Ext**	Returns the element namespace prefix as a string. For example, in a node declared as `<nspace:elemname>` it returns the "`nspace`" part.
previous Sibling		Returns a reference to the previous sibling node of this node, i.e. the previous node in the source file at the same level of the hierarchy.
specified	**Ext**	Indicates whether the node value is explicitly specified or derived from a default value in the DTD or schema. Normally only used with attribute nodes.
target		Specifies the application to which this processing instruction is directed. This is the text up to the first white-space character in the node content.
text	**Ext**	Sets or returns the entire text content of this node and all its descendant nodes.
xml	**Ext**	Returns the entire XML content of this node and all its descendant nodes.

ProcessingInstruction Methods

Name		Description
`appendChild(new_node)`		Appends the node object `new_node` to the end of the list of child nodes for this node.
`cloneNode(recurse_children)`		Creates a new node object that is an exact clone of this node, including all descendant nodes of this node if `recurse_children` is set to `true`.
`hasChildNodes()`		Returns `true` if this node has any child nodes.
`insertBefore(new_node, this_node)`		Inserts a new node object `new_node` into the list of child nodes for this node, to the left of the node object `this_node` or at the end of the list if `this_node` is omitted.
`removeChild(this_child)`		Removes the child node `this_node` from the list of child nodes for this node, and returns it.
`replaceChild(new_node, old_node)`		Replaces the child node `old_node` with the new child node object `new_node`, and returns the old child node.
`selectNodes(pattern)`	**Ext**	Applies a specified pattern to this node's context and returns a node list object containing matching nodes. The string `pattern` specifies the XSL pattern-matching operation to be used.
`selectSingleNode(pattern)`	**Ext**	Applies a specified pattern to this node's context and returns just the first node object that matches. The string `pattern` specifies the XSL pattern-matching operation to be used.
`transformNode(stylesheet)`	**Ext**	Processes this node and its children using an XSL style sheet specified in the `stylesheet` argument, and returns the resulting transformation. The style sheet must be either a `Document` node object, in which case the document is assumed to be an XSL style sheet, or a Node object in the `xsl` namespace, in which case this node is treated as a standalone style sheet fragment.

Implementation — the IXMLDOMImplementation Object

This object provides access to methods that are application-specific and independent of any particular instance of the document object model. It is a child of the `Document` object.

Implementation Method

Name	Description
`hasFeature(feature, version)`	Returns `true` if the specified version of the implementation supports the specified feature.

IE5-Specific XML Parser Objects

While the document object is quite tightly standardized as far as the structure of the document is concerned, there are other peripheral activities that any XML application must handle. This includes managing and reporting errors, originating and handling HTTP requests, and interfacing with style sheets. These are all application-specific tasks, and in IE5 are managed by three subsidiary objects:

- `ParseError` (the `IDOMParseError` object)
- `HttpRequest` (the `IXMLHttpRequest` object)
- `Runtime` (the `IXTLRuntime` object)

ParseError — the IDOMParseError Object

The properties of this object return detailed information about the last error that occurred while loading and parsing a document. This includes the line number, character position, and a text description. In the following table, all are marked '**Ext**' to indicate that the W3C recommendations do not cover this area of the DOM.

ParseError Properties

Name		Description
`errorCode`	**Ext**	Returns the error number or error code as a decimal integer.
`filepos`	**Ext**	Returns the absolute character position in the file where the error occurred.
`line`	**Ext**	Returns the number of the line in the document that contains the error.
`linepos`	**Ext**	Returns the character position of the error within the line in which it occurred.
`reason`	**Ext**	Returns a text description of the source and reason for the error, and can also include the URL of the DTD or schema and the node within it that corresponds to the error.
`srcText`	**Ext**	Returns the full text of the line that contains the error or an empty string if the error cannot be assigned to a specific line.
`url`	**Ext**	Returns the URL of the most recent XML document that contained an error.

HttpRequest — the IXMLHttpRequest Object

This object provides client-side protocol support for communication with HTTP servers. A client can use the `HttpRequest` object to send an arbitrary HTTP request, receive the response, and have the IE5 DOM parse that response. In the following table, all are marked '**Ext**' to indicate that the W3C recommendations do not cover this area of the DOM.

HttpRequest Properties

Name		Description
`readyState`	**Ext**	Indicates the current state of the XML document being loaded: `0 ("uninitialized")` - the object has been created but the `load()` has not yet been executed. `1 ("loading")` - the `load()` method is executing. `2 ("loaded")` - loading is complete and parsing is taking place. `3 ("interactive")` - some data has been read and parsed and the object model is now available. The data set is only partially retrieved and is read-only. `4 ("completed")` - document has been completely loaded. If successful the data is available read/write, if not the error information is available.
`responseBody`	**Ext**	Returns the response as an array of unsigned bytes.
`responseStream`	**Ext**	Returns the response as an `IStream` object.
`responseText`	**Ext**	Returns the response as an ordinary text string.
`responseXML`	**Ext**	Returns the response as an XML document. For security reasons, validation is turned off during this process to prevent the parser from attempting to download a linked DTD or other definition file.
`status`	**Ext**	Returns the status code sent back from the server as a long integer.
`statusText`	**Ext**	Returns the status text sent back from the server as a string.

HttpRequest Methods

Name		Description
`abort()`	**Ext**	Cancels a current HTTP request.
`getAllResponseHeaders()`	**Ext**	Returns all the HTTP headers as name/value pairs delimited by the carriage return-linefeed combination.
`getResponseHeader (header_name)`	**Ext**	Returns the value of an individual HTTP header from the response body as specified by the header name.
`open(method, url, async, userid, password)`	**Ext**	Initializes a request, specifying the HTTP method, the URL, whether the response is to be asynchronous, and authentication information for the request.
`send()`	**Ext**	Sends an HTTP request to the server and waits to receive a response.
`setRequestHeader (header_name, value)`	**Ext**	Specifies an HTTP header to send to the server.

Runtime — the IXTLRuntime Object

This object implements a series of properties and methods that are available within XSL style sheets. In the following table, all are marked '**Ext**' to indicate that the W3C recommendations do not cover this area of the DOM.

Runtime Properties

Name		Description
`attributes`	**Ext**	Returns a collection of the `Attribute` (or `Attr`) objects for this node as a `NamedNodeMap` object.
`baseName`	**Ext**	Returns the node name with any namespace removed. For example, in a node declared as `<nspace:elemname>` it returns the "`elemname`" part.
`childNodes`	**Ext**	Returns a `NodeList` containing all the child nodes of this node, for nodes that can have child nodes.
`dataType`	**Ext**	Sets or returns the data type for this node.
`definition`	**Ext**	For `EntityReference` nodes, returns the entry in the DTD or schema containing the definition for the entity, i.e. "`<!ENTITY entityname 'entity value'>`". For other nodes, returns `null`.

Name		Description
`firstChild`	**Ext**	Returns a reference to the first child node of this node.
`lastChild`	**Ext**	Returns a reference to the last child node of this node.
`namespaceURI`	**Ext**	Returns the URI for the namespace as a string. For example, in the namespace declaration `xmlns:name="uri"` it returns the `"uri"` part.
`nextSibling`	**Ext**	Returns a reference to the next sibling node of this node, i.e. the next node in the source data file at the same level of the hierarchy.
`nodeName`	**Ext**	Returns the name of the node, which will depend on the node type. See the list of **Node Types** at the end of this appendix for more details.
`nodeTypeString`	**Ext**	Returns the node type as a string. See the list of **Node Types** at the end of this appendix for more details.
`nodeType`	**Ext**	Returns the node type as a number. See the list of **Node Types** at the end of this appendix for more details.
`nodeTypedValue`	**Ext**	Sets or returns the strongly typed value of the node, expressed in its defined data type. If no data type has been defined for the node, its `nodeValue` is returned.
`nodeValue`	**Ext**	Sets or returns the value of the node as plain text.
`ownerDocument`	**Ext**	Returns the root node of the document that contains the node.
`parentNode`	**Ext**	Returns the parent node of this node, for nodes that can have parents.
`parsed`	**Ext**	Returns `true` if this node and all its descendants have been parsed and instantiated.
`prefix`	**Ext**	Returns the element namespace prefix as a string. For example, in a node declared as `<nspace:elemname>` it returns the `"nspace"` part.
`previousSibling`	**Ext**	Returns a reference to the previous sibling node of this node, i.e. the previous node in the source file at the same level of the hierarchy.

Name		Description
specified	**Ext**	Indicates whether the node value is explicitly specified or derived from a default value in the DTD or schema. Normally only used with attribute nodes.
text	**Ext**	Sets or returns the entire text content of this node and all its descendant nodes.
xml	**Ext**	Returns the entire XML of this node and all descendant nodes of this node.

Runtime Methods

Name		Description
`absoluteChildNumber (this_node)`	**Ext**	Returns the index of a specified node within its parent's `childNodes` list. Values start from `"1"`.
`ancestorChild Number(node_ name, this_node)`	**Ext**	Finds the first ancestor node of a specified node that has the specified name, and returns the index of that node within its parent's `childNodes` list. Values start from `"1"`. Returns `null` if there is no ancestor.
`appendChild(new_ node)`	**Ext**	Appends the node object `new_node` to the end of the list of child nodes for this node.
`childNumber (this_node)`	**Ext**	Finds the first node with the same name as the specified node within the specified node's parent's `childNodes` list (i.e. its siblings). Returns the index of that node or `null` if not found. Values start from `"1"`.
`cloneNode (recurse_ children)`	**Ext**	Creates a new node object that is an exact clone of this node, including all descendant nodes of this node if `recurse_children` is set to `true`.
`depth(start_node)`	**Ext**	Returns the depth or level within the document tree at which the specified node appears. The `documentElement` or root node is at level `0`.

Name		Description
`elementIndex_List(this_node, node_name)`	**Ext**	Returns an array of node index numbers for the specified node and all its ancestors up to and including the document root node, indicating each node's position within their parent's `childNodes` list. The ordering of the array starts from the root document node. When the `node_name` parameter is not supplied, the method returns an array of integers that indicates the index of the specified node with respect to all of its siblings, the index of that node's parent with respect to all of its siblings, and so on until the document root is reached. When the `node_name` parameter is specified, the returned array contains entries only for nodes of the specified name, and the indices are evaluated relative to siblings with the specified name. Zero is supplied for levels in the tree that do not have children with the supplied name. Although this method is included in the Microsoft documentation, it was not supported by IE5 at the time of writing.
`formatDate(date, format, locale)`	**Ext**	Formats the value in the date parameter using the specified formatting options. The following format codes are supported: m - Month (1-12) mm - Month (01-12) mmm - Month (Jan-Dec) mmmm - Month (January-December) mmmmm - Month as the first letter of the month d - Day (1-31) dd - Day (01-31) ddd - Day (Sun-Sat) dddd - Day (Sunday-Saturday) yy -Year (00-99) yyyy - Year (1900-9999) The locale to use in determining the correct sequence of values in the date. If omitted the sequence month-day-year is used.

Name		Description
`formatIndex (number, format)`	**Ext**	Formats the integer number using the specified numerical system. `1` - Standard numbering system `01` - Standard numbering with leading zeroes `A` - Uppercase letter sequence "`A`" to "`Z`" then "`AA`" to"`ZZ`". `a` - Lowercase letter sequence "`a`" to "`z`" then "`aa`" to "`zz`". `I` - Uppercase Roman numerals: "`I`", "`II`", "`III`", "`IV`", etc. `i` - Lowercase Roman numerals: "`i`", "`ii`", "`iii`", "`iv`", etc.
`formatNumber (number, format)`	**Ext**	Formats the value number using the specified format. Zero or more of the following values can be present in the format string: # (pound) – Display only significant digits and omit insignificant zeros. `0` (zero) – Display insignificant zeros in these positions. `?` (question) – Adds spaces for insignificant zeros on either side of the decimal point, so that decimal points align with a fixed-point font. You can also use this symbol for fractions that have varying numbers of digits. `.` (period) – Indicates the position of the decimal point. `,` (comma) – Display a thousands separator or scale a number by a multiple of one thousand. `%` (percent) – Display number as a percentage. `E` or `e` - Display number in scientific (exponential) format. If format contains a zero or # (hash) to the right of an exponent code, display the number in scientific format and inserts an "`E`" or "`e`". The number of `0` or # characters to the right determines the number of digits in the exponent. `E-` or `e-` Place a minus sign by negative exponents. `E+` or `e+` Place a minus sign by negative exponents and a plus sign by positive exponents.

Name		Description
`formatTime (time, format, locale)`	**Ext**	Formats the value in the time parameter using the specified formatting options. The following format codes are supported: `h` - Hours (0-23) `hh` - Hours (00-23) `m` - Minutes (0-59) `mm` - Minutes (00-59) `s` - Seconds (0-59) `ss` - Seconds (00-59) `AM/PM` - Add "`AM`" or "`PM`" and display in 12 hour format `am/pm` - Add "`am`" or "`pm`" and display in 12 hour format `A/P` - Add "`A`" or "`P`" and display in 12 hour format `a/p` - Add "`a`" or "`p`" and display in 12 hour format `[h]:mm` – Display elapsed time in hours, i.e. "`25.02`" `[mm]:ss` - Display elapsed time in minutes, i.e. "`63:46`" `[ss]` - Display elapsed time in seconds `ss.00` - Display fractions of a second The locale is used to determine the correct separator characters.
`hasChildNodes()`	**Ext**	Returns `true` if this node has any child nodes.
`insertBefore (new_node, this_node)`	**Ext**	Inserts a new node object `new_node` into the list of child nodes for this node, to the left of the node object `this_node` or at the end of the list if `this_node` is omitted.
`removeChild (this_node)`	**Ext**	Removes the child node `this_node` from the list of child nodes for this node, and returns it.
`replaceChild (new_node, old_node)`	**Ext**	Replaces the child node `old_node` with the new child node object `new_node`, and returns the old child node.
`selectNodes (pattern)`	**Ext**	Applies a specified pattern to this node's context and returns a node list object containing matching nodes. The string `pattern` specifies the XSL pattern-matching operation to be used.
`selectSingleNode (pattern)`	**Ext**	Applies a specified pattern to this node's context and returns just the first node object that matches. The string `pattern` specifies the XSL pattern-matching operation to be used.

Name		Description
transformNode (stylesheet)	Ext	Processes this node and its children using an XSL style sheet specified in the stylesheet argument, and returns the resulting transformation. The style sheet must be either a Document node object, in which case the document is assumed to be an XSL style sheet, or a Node object in the xsl namespace, in which case this node is treated as a standalone style sheet fragment.
uniqueID (this_node)	Ext	Returns the unique identifier for the specified node.

The DOM NodeTypes

Each node exposes its type through the nodeType property. In IE5, there is also a nodeTypeString property, which exposes the node type as a named string rather than an integer. This saves having to explicitly convert it each time. Each node type also has a named constant. These make up the IDOMNodeType enumeration.

IDOMNodeType Enumeration

The IDOMNodeType enumeration specifies the valid settings for particular DOM node types. This includes the range and type of values that the node can contain, whether the node can have child nodes, etc. Note that default string and numeric entities (such as &) are exposed as text nodes, rather than as entity nodes.

Named Constant	nodeType	nodeName	nodeValue	nodeTypeString(IE5)
NODE_ ELEMENT	1	tagName property	null	"element"

Can be the child of a Document, DocumentFragment, EntityReference, Element node.
Can have child nodes of type Element, Text, Comment, ProcessingInstruction, CDATASection, EntityReference.

NODE_ATTRIBUTE	2	name property	value property	"attribute"

Cannot be the child of any other node type. Only appears in other nodes' attributes node lists.
Can have child nodes of type Text, EntityReference.

NODE_TEXT	3	"#text"	content of node	"text"

Can be the child of an Attribute, DocumentFragment, Element, EntityReference node.
Cannot have any child nodes.

NODE_CDATA_SECTION	4	"#cdata-section"	content of node	"cdata section"

Can be the child of a DocumentFragment, EntityReference, Element node.
Cannot have any child nodes.

NODE_ENTITY_REFERENCE	5	entity reference name	null	"entity reference"

Can be the child of an Attribute, DocumentFragment, Element, EntityReference node.
Can have child nodes of type Element, ProcessingInstruction, Comment, Text, CDATASection, EntityReference.

NODE_ENTITY	6	entity name	null	"entity"

Can be the child of a DocumentType node.
Can have child nodes that represent the expanded entity, that is Text, EntityReference.

NODE_PROCESSING_INSTRUCTION	7	target property	content of node excluding target	"processing instruction"

Can be the child of a Document, DocumentFragment, Element, EntityReference node.
Cannot have any child nodes.

NODE_COMMENT	8	"#comment"	comment text	"comment"

Can be the child of a Document, DocumentFragment, Element, EntityReference node.
Cannot have any child nodes.

NODE_DOCUMENT	9	"#document"	null	"document"

Represents the root of the document so cannot be a child node.
Can have a maximum of one Element child node, and other child nodes of type Comment, DocumentType, ProcessingInstruction.

NODE_DOCUMENT_TYPE	10	doctype name	null	"document type"

Can be the child of the `Document` node only.
Can have child nodes of type `Notation`, `Entity`.

NODE_DOCUMENT_ FRAGMENT	11	"#document- fragment"	null	"document fragment"

Represents an unconnected document fragment, so cannot be the child of any node type.
Can have child nodes of type `Element`, `ProcessingInstruction`, `Comment`, `Text`, `CDATASection`, `EntityReference`.

NODE_NOTATION	1 2	notation name	null	"notation"

Can be the child of a `DocumentType` node only.
Cannot have any child nodes.

SAX 1.0: The Simple API for XML

This appendix contains the specification of the SAX interface. It is taken largely verbatim from the definitive specification to be found on http://www.megginson.com/sax/, with editorial comments added in italics.

The classes and interfaces are described in alphabetical order; within each class, the methods are also listed alphabetically.

The SAX specification is in the public domain: see the web site quoted above for a statement of policy on copyright. Essentially the policy is: do what you like with it, copy it as you wish, but no-one accepts any liability for errors or omissions.

The SAX distribution also includes three "helper classes":

- `AttributeListImpl` is an implementation of the `AttributeList` interface
- `LocatorImpl` is an implementation of the `Locator` interface
- `ParserFactory` is a class that enables you to load a parser identified by a parameter at run-time.

The documentation of these helper classes is not included here. For this, and for SAX sample applications, see the SAX distribution available from http://www.megginson.com.

Class Hierarchy

```
class java.lang.Object
      interface org.xml.sax.AttributeList
      class org.xml.sax.helpers.AttributeListImpl
            (implements org.xml.sax.AttributeList)
      interface org.xml.sax.DTDHandler
      interface org.xml.sax.DocumentHandler
      interface org.xml.sax.EntityResolver
      interface org.xml.sax.ErrorHandler
      class org.xml.sax.HandlerBase
            (implements org.xml.sax.EntityResolver,
                        org.xml.sax.DTDHandler,
                        org.xml.sax.DocumentHandler,
                        org.xml.sax.ErrorHandler)
      class org.xml.sax.InputSource
      interface org.xml.sax.Locator
      class org.xml.sax.helpers.LocatorImpl
            (implements org.xml.sax.Locator)
      interface org.xml.sax.Parser
      class org.xml.sax.helpers.ParserFactory
class java.lang.Throwable (implements java.io.Serializable)
      class java.lang.Exception
      class org.xml.sax.SAXException
      class org.xml.sax.SAXParseException
```

Interface org.xml.sax.AttributeList

An `AttributeList` is a collection of attributes appearing on a particular start tag. The Parser supplies the `DocumentHandler` with an `AttributeList` as part of the information available on the `startElement` event. The `AttributeList` is essentially a set of name-value pairs for the supplied attributes; if the parser has analyzed the DTD it may also provide information about the type of each attribute.

Interface for an element's attribute specifications.

The SAX parser implements this interface and passes an instance to the SAX application as the second argument of each `startElement` event.

The instance provided will return valid results only during the scope of the `startElement` invocation (to save it for future use, the application must make a copy: the `AttributeListImpl` helper class provides a convenient constructor for doing so).

An `AttributeList` includes only attributes that have been specified or defaulted: `#IMPLIED` attributes will not be included.

There are two ways for the SAX application to obtain information from the `AttributeList`. First, it can iterate through the entire list:

```
public void startElement (String name, AttributeList atts) {
  for (int i = 0; i < atts.getLength(); i++) {
    String name = atts.getName(i);
    String type = atts.getType(i);
    String value = atts.getValue(i);
    [...]
  }
}
```

(Note that the result of `getLength()` will be zero if there are no attributes.)

As an alternative, the application can request the value or type of specific attributes:

```
public void startElement (String name, AttributeList atts) {
  String identifier = atts.getValue("id");
  String label = atts.getValue("label");
  [...]
}
```

The `AttributeListImpl` helper class provides a convenience implementation for use by parser or application writers.

getLength public int getLength()	Return the number of attributes in this list. The SAX parser may provide attributes in any arbitrary order, regardless of the order in which they were declared or specified. The number of attributes may be zero. **Returns:** The number of attributes in the list.
getName public String getName(int index)	Return the name of an attribute in this list (by position). The names must be unique: the SAX parser shall not include the same attribute twice. Attributes without values (those declared #IMPLIED without a value specified in the start tag) will be omitted from the list. If the attribute name has a namespace prefix, the prefix will still be attached. **Parameters:** index - The index of the attribute in the list (starting at 0). **Returns:** The name of the indexed attribute, or null if the index is out of range.

Table Continued on Following Page

getType public String getType(int index)	Return the type of an attribute in the list (by position). The attribute type is one of the strings "CDATA", "ID", "IDREF", "IDREFS", "NMTOKEN", "NMTOKENS", "ENTITY", "ENTITIES", or "NOTATION" (always in upper case). If the parser has not read a declaration for the attribute, or if the parser does not report attribute types, then it must return the value "CDATA" as stated in the XML 1.0 Recommendation (clause 3.3.3, "Attribute-Value Normalization"). For an enumerated attribute that is not a notation, the parser will report the type as "NMTOKEN". **Parameters:** index - The index of the attribute in the list (starting at 0). **Returns:** The attribute type as a string, or null if the index is out of range.
getType public String getType(String name)	Return the type of an attribute in the list (by name). The return value is the same as the return value for getType(int). If the attribute name has a namespace prefix in the document, the application must include the prefix here. **Parameters:** name - The name of the attribute. **Returns:** The attribute type as a string, or null if no such attribute exists.

getValue public String getValue(int index)	Return the value of an attribute in the list (by position). If the attribute value is a list of tokens (IDREFS, ENTITIES, or NMTOKENS), the tokens will be concatenated into a single string separated by whitespace. **Parameters:** index - The index of the attribute in the list (starting at 0). **Returns:** The attribute value as a string, or null if the index is out of range.
getValue public String getValue(String name)	Return the value of an attribute in the list (by name). The return value is the same as the return value for getValue(int). If the attribute name has a namespace prefix in the document, the application must include the prefix here. **Parameters:** name - The name of the attribute. **Returns:** The attribute value as a string, or null if no such attribute exists.

Interface org.xml.sax.DocumentHandler

Every SAX application is likely to include a class that implements this interface, either directly or by subclassing the supplied class `HandlerBase`. See Chapter 6 for a full discussion of the various methods.

Receive notification of general document events

This is the main interface that most SAX applications implement: if the application needs to be informed of basic parsing events, it implements this interface and registers an instance with the SAX parser using the `setDocumentHandler` method. The parser uses the instance to report basic document-related events like the start and end of elements and character data.

The order of events in this interface is very important, and mirrors the order of information in the document itself. For example, all of an element's content (character data, processing instructions, and/or subelements) will appear, in order, between the `startElement` event and the corresponding `endElement` event.

Application writers who do not want to implement the entire interface can derive a class from HandlerBase, which implements the default functionality; parser writers can instantiate HandlerBase to obtain a default handler. The application can find the location of any document event using the Locator interface supplied by the Parser through the setDocumentLocator method.

characters
 	
public void characters(
    char ch[],
    int start,
    int length)
 	
throws SAXException
	Receive notification of character data.
	
	The Parser will call this method to report each chunk of character data. SAX parsers may return all contiguous character data in a single chunk, or they may split it into several chunks; however, all of the characters in any single event must come from the same external entity, so that the Locator provides useful information.
	
	The application must not attempt to read from the array outside of the specified range *and must not attempt to write to the array.*
	
	Note that some parsers will report whitespace using the ignorableWhitespace() method rather than this one (validating parsers must do so).
	
	Parameters:
	
	ch - The characters from the XML document.
	
	start - The start position in the array.
	
	length - The number of characters to read from the array.
	
	Throws: SAXException
	
	Any SAX exception, possibly wrapping another exception.

endDocument public void endDocument() throws SAXException	Receive notification of the end of a document. The SAX parser will invoke this method only once *for each document*, and it will be the last method invoked during the parse. The parser shall not invoke this method until it has either abandoned parsing (because of an unrecoverable error) or reached the end of input. **Throws**: SAXException Any SAX exception, possibly wrapping another exception.

endElement public void endElement(String name) throws SAXException	Receive notification of the end of an element. The SAX parser will invoke this method at the end of every element in the XML document; there will be a corresponding startElement() event for every endElement() event (even when the element is empty). If the element name has a namespace prefix, the prefix will still be attached to the name. **Parameters:** name - The element type name **Throws:** SAXException Any SAX exception, possibly wrapping another exception.
ignorableWhitespace public void ignorableWhitespace (char ch[], int start, int length) throws SAXException	Receive notification of ignorable whitespace in element content. Validating Parsers must use this method to report each chunk of ignorable whitespace (see the W3C XML 1.0 recommendation, section 2.10): non-validating parsers may also use this method if they are capable of parsing and using content models. SAX parsers may return all contiguous whitespace in a single chunk, or they may split it into several chunks; however, all of the characters in any single event must come from the same external entity, so that the Locator provides useful information. The application must not attempt to read from the array outside of the specified range. **Parameters:** ch - The characters from the XML document. start - The start position in the array. length - The number of characters to read from the array. **Throws:** SAXException Any SAX exception, possibly wrapping another exception.

Table Continued on Following Page

processingInstruction public void processingInstruction(String target, String data) throws SAXException	Receive notification of a processing instruction. The Parser will invoke this method once for each processing instruction found: note that processing instructions may occur before or after the main document element. A SAX parser should never report an XML declaration (XML 1.0, section 2.8) or a text declaration (XML 1.0, section 4.3.1) using this method. **Parameters:** target - The processing instruction target. data - The processing instruction data, or null if none was supplied. **Throws:** SAXException Any SAX exception, possibly wrapping another exception.
setDocumentLocator public void setDocumentLocator (Locator locator)	Receive an object for locating the origin of SAX document events. A SAX parser is strongly encouraged (though not absolutely required) to supply a Locator: if it does so, it must supply the Locator to the application by invoking this method before invoking any of the other methods in the DocumentHandler interface. The Locator allows the application to determine the end position[1] of any document-related event, even if the parser is not reporting an error. Typically, the application will use this information for reporting its own errors (such as character content that does not match an application's business rules). The information returned by the locator is probably not sufficient for use with a search engine. Note that the locator will return correct information only during the invocation of the events in this interface. The application should not attempt to use it at any other time. **Parameters:** locator - An object that can return the location of any SAX document event.

startDocument public void startDocument() throws SAXException	Receive notification of the beginning of a document. The SAX parser will invoke this method only once *for each document*, before any other methods in this interface or in DTDHandler (except for setDocumentLocator). **Throws**: SAXException Any SAX exception, possibly wrapping another exception.
startElement public void startElement (String name, AttributeList atts) throws SAXException	Receive notification of the beginning of an element. The Parser will invoke this method at the beginning of every element in the XML document; there will be a corresponding endElement() event for every startElement() event (even when the element is empty). All of the element's content will be reported, in order, before the corresponding endElement() event. If the element name has a namespace prefix, the prefix will still be attached. Note that the attribute list provided will contain only attributes with explicit values (specified or defaulted): #IMPLIED attributes will be omitted. **Parameters:** name - The element type name. atts - The attributes attached to the element, if any. **Throws:** SAXException Any SAX exception, possibly wrapping another exception.

Interface org.xml.sax.DTDHandler

This interface should be implemented by the application, if it wants to receive notification of events related to the DTD. SAX does not provide full details of the DTD, but this interface is available because without it, it would be impossible to access notations and unparsed entities referenced in the body of the document.

Notations and unparsed entities are rather specialized facilities in XML, so most SAX applications will not need to use this interface.

Receive notification of basic DTD-related events.

If a SAX application needs information about notations and unparsed entities, then the application implements this interface and registers an instance with the SAX parser using the parser's `setDTDHandler` method. The parser uses the instance to report notation and unparsed entity declarations to the application.

The SAX parser may report these events in any order, regardless of the order in which the notations and unparsed entities were declared; however, all DTD events must be reported after the document handler's `startDocument` event, and before the first `startElement` event.

It is up to the application to store the information for future use (perhaps in a hash table or object tree). If the application encounters attributes of type "`NOTATION`", "`ENTITY`", or "`ENTITIES`", it can use the information that it obtained through this interface to find the entity and/or notation corresponding with the attribute value.

The `HandlerBase` class provides a default implementation of this interface, which simply ignores the events.

notationDecl	Receive notification of a notation declaration event.
public void notationDecl (String name, String publicId, String systemId) throws SAXException	It is up to the application to record the notation for later reference, if necessary. If a system identifier is present, and it is a URL, the SAX parser must resolve it fully before passing it to the application. **Parameters:** name - The notation name. publicId - The notation's public identifier, or null if none was given. systemId - The notation's system identifier, or null if none was given. **Throws:** SAXException Any SAX exception, possibly wrapping another exception.

<table>
<tr><td>

unparsedEntityDecl

public void unparsedEntityDecl (
String name,
String publicId,
String systemId,
String notationName)

throws SAXException

</td><td>

Receive notification of an unparsed entity declaration event.

Note that the notation name corresponds to a notation reported by the notationDecl() event. It is up to the application to record the entity for later reference, if necessary.

If the system identifier is a URL, the parser must resolve it fully before passing it to the application.

Parameters:

name - The unparsed entity's name.

publicId - The entity's public identifier, or null if none was given.

systemId - The entity's system identifier (it must always have one).

notation - name The name of the associated notation.

Throws: SAXException

Any SAX exception, possibly wrapping another exception.

</td></tr>
</table>

Interface org.xml.sax.EntityResolver

When the XML document contains references to external entities, the URL will normally be analyzed automatically by the parser: the relevant file will be located and parsed where appropriate. This interface allows an application to override this behavior. This might be needed, for example, if you want to retrieve a different version of the entity from a local server, or if the entities are cached in memory on stored in a database, or if the entity is really a reference to variable information such as the current date.

When the parser needs to obtain an entity, it calls this interface, which can respond by supplying any `InputSource` *object.*

Basic interface for resolving entities

If a SAX application needs to implement customized handling for external entities, it must implement this interface and register an instance with the SAX parser using the parser's `setEntityResolver` method.

The parser will then allow the application to intercept any external entities (including the external DTD subset and external parameter entities, if any) before including them.

Many SAX applications will not need to implement this interface, but it will be especially useful for applications that build XML documents from databases or other specialized input sources, or for applications that use URI types other than URLs.

The following resolver would provide the application with a special character stream for the entity with the system identifier "`http://www.myhost.com/today`":

```
import org.xml.sax.EntityResolver;
import org.xml.sax.InputSource;

public class MyResolver implements EntityResolver {
    public InputSource resolveEntity (String publicId, String systemId)
    {
        if (systemId.equals("http://www.myhost.com/today")) {
            // return a special input source
            MyReader reader = new MyReader();
            return new InputSource(reader);
        } else {
            // use the default behaviour
            return null;
        }
    }
}
```

The application can also use this interface to redirect system identifiers to local URIs or to look up replacements in a catalog (possibly by using the public identifier).

The `HandlerBase` class implements the default behavior for this interface, which is simply always to return null (to request that the parser use the default system identifier).

resolveEntity	Allow the application to resolve external entities.
public InputSource resolveEntity(String publicId, String systemId) throws SAXException, IOException	The Parser will call this method before opening any external entity except the top-level document entity (including the external DTD subset, external entities referenced within the DTD, and external entities referenced within the document element): the application may request that the parser resolve the entity itself, that it use an alternative URI, or that it use an entirely different input source. Application writers can use this method to redirect external system identifiers to secure and/or local URIs, to look up public identifiers in a catalogue, or to read an entity from a database or other input source (including, for example, a dialog box). If the system identifier is a URL, the SAX parser must resolve it fully before reporting it to the application. **Parameters:** publicId - The public identifier of the external entity being referenced, or null if none was supplied. systemId - The system identifier of the external entity being referenced. **Returns:** An InputSource object describing the new input source, or null to request that the parser open a regular URI connection to the system identifier. **Throws:** SAXException Any SAX exception, possibly wrapping another exception. **Throws:** IOException A Java-specific IO exception, possibly the result of creating a new InputStream or Reader for the InputSource.

Interface org.xml.sax.ErrorHandler

You may implement this interface in your application if you want to take special action to handle errors. There is a default implementation provided within the `HandlerBase` *class.*

Basic interface for SAX error handlers

If a SAX application needs to implement customized error handling, it must implement this interface and then register an instance with the SAX parser using the parser's `setErrorHandler` method. The parser will then report all errors and warnings through this interface.

The parser shall use this interface instead of throwing an exception: it is up to the application whether to throw an exception for different types of errors and warnings. Note, however, that there is no requirement that the parser continue to provide useful information after a call to `fatalError` (in other words, a SAX driver class could catch an exception and report a `fatalError`).

The `HandlerBase` class provides a default implementation of this interface, ignoring warnings and recoverable errors and throwing a `SAXParseException` for fatal errors. An application may extend that class rather than implementing the complete interface itself.

error public void error(SAXParseException exception) throws SAXException	Receive notification of a recoverable error. This corresponds to the definition of "error" in section 1.2 of the W3C XML 1.0 Recommendation. For example, a validating parser would use this callback to report the violation of a validity constraint. The default behavior is to take no action. The SAX parser must continue to provide normal parsing events after invoking this method: it should still be possible for the application to process the document through to the end. If the application cannot do so, then the parser should report a fatal error even if the XML 1.0 recommendation does not require it to do so. **Parameters:** exception - The error information encapsulated in a SAX parse exception. **Throws:** SAXException Any SAX exception, possibly wrapping another exception.

fatalError public void fatalError(SAXParseException exception) throws SAXException	Receive notification of a non-recoverable error. This corresponds to the definition of "fatal error" in section 1.2 of the W3C XML 1.0 Recommendation. For example, a parser would use this callback to report the violation of a well-formedness constraint. The application must assume that the document is unusable after the parser has invoked this method, and should continue (if at all) only for the sake of collecting additional error messages: in fact, SAX parsers are free to stop reporting any other events once this method has been invoked. **Parameters:** exception - The error information encapsulated in a SAX parse exception. **Throws:** SAXException Any SAX exception, possibly wrapping another exception.
warning public void warning (SAXParseException exception) throws SAXException	Receive notification of a warning. SAX parsers will use this method to report conditions that are not errors or fatal errors as defined by the XML 1.0 recommendation. The default behaviour is to take no action. The SAX parser must continue to provide normal parsing events after invoking this method: it should still be possible for the application to process the document through to the end. **Parameters:** exception - The warning information encapsulated in a SAX parse exception. **Throws:** SAXException Any SAX exception, possibly wrapping another exception.

Class org.xml.sax.HandlerBase

This class is supplied with SAX itself: it provides default implementations of most of the methods that would otherwise need to be implemented by the application. If you write classes in your application as subclasses of HandlerBase, you need only code those methods where you want something other than the default behavior.

Default base class for handlers

This class implements the default behavior for four SAX interfaces: `EntityResolver`, `DTDHandler`, `DocumentHandler`, and `ErrorHandler`.

Application writers can extend this class when they need to implement only part of an interface; parser writers can instantiate this class to provide default handlers when the application has not supplied its own.

Note that the use of this class is optional.

In the description below, only the behavior of each method is described. For the parameters and return values, see the corresponding interface definition.

characters public void characters(char ch[], int start, int length) throws SAXException	By default, do nothing. Application writers may override this method to take specific actions for each chunk of character data (such as adding the data to a node or buffer, or printing it to a file).
endDocument public void endDocument() throws SAXException	Receive notification of the end of the document. By default, do nothing. Application writers may override this method in a subclass to take specific actions at the beginning of a document (such as finalizing a tree or closing an output file).
endElement public void endElement(String name) throws SAXException	By default, do nothing. Application writers may override this method in a subclass to take specific actions at the end of each element (such as finalizing a tree node or writing output to a file).

error public void error(SAXParseException e) throws SAXException	The default implementation does nothing. Application writers may override this method in a subclass to take specific actions for each error, such as inserting the message in a log file or printing it to the console.
fatalError public void fatalError(SAXParseException e) throws SAXException	The default implementation throws a SAXParseException. Application writers may override this method in a subclass if they need to take specific actions for each fatal error (such as collecting all of the errors into a single report): in any case, the application must stop all regular processing when this method is invoked, since the document is no longer reliable, and the parser may no longer report parsing events.
ignorableWhitespace public void ignorableWhitespace(char ch[], int start, int length) throws SAXException	By default, do nothing. Application writers may override this method to take specific actions for each chunk of ignorable whitespace (such as adding data to a node or buffer, or printing it to a file).
notationDecl public void notationDecl(String name, String publicId, String systemId)	By default, do nothing. Application writers may override this method in a subclass if they wish to keep track of the notations declared in a document.
processingInstruction public void processingInstruction(String target, String data) throws SAXException	By default, do nothing. Application writers may override this method in a subclass to take specific actions for each processing instruction, such as setting status variables or invoking other methods.

Table Continued on Following Page

resolveEntity public InputSource resolveEntity(String publicId, String systemId) throws SAXException	Always return null, so that the parser will use the system identifier provided in the XML document. This method implements the SAX default behavior: application writers can override it in a subclass to do special translations such as catalog lookups or URI redirection.
setDocumentLocator public void setDocumentLocator(Locator locator)	By default, do nothing. Application writers may override this method in a subclass if they wish to store the locator for use with other document events.
startDocument public void startDocument() throws SAXException	By default, do nothing. Application writers may override this method in a subclass to take specific actions at the beginning of a document (such as allocating the root node of a tree or creating an output file).
startElement public void startElement(String name, AttributeList attributes) throws SAXException	By default, do nothing. Application writers may override this method in a subclass to take specific actions at the start of each element (such as allocating a new tree node or writing output to a file).
unparsedEntityDecl public void unparsedEntityDecl(String name, String publicId, String systemId, String notationName)	By default, do nothing. Application writers may override this method in a subclass to keep track of the unparsed entities declared in a document.
warning public void warning(SAXParseException e) throws SAXException	The default implementation does nothing. Application writers may override this method in a subclass to take specific actions for each warning, such as inserting the message in a log file or printing it to the console.

Class org.xml.sax.InputSource

An `InputSource` object represents a container for the XML document or any of the external entities it references (technically, the main document is itself an entity). The `InputSource` class is supplied with SAX: generally the application instantiates an `InputSource` and updates it to say where the input is coming from, and the parser interrogates it to find out where to read the input from.

The `InputSource` object provides three ways of supplying input to the parser: a System Identifier (or URL), a `Reader` (which delivers a stream of Unicode characters), or an `InputStream` (which delivers a stream of uninterpreted bytes).

A single input source for an XML entity

This class allows a SAX application to encapsulate information about an input source in a single object, which may include a public identifier, a system identifier, a byte stream (possibly with a specified encoding), and/or a character stream.

There are two places that the application will deliver this input source to the parser: as the argument to the `Parser.parse` method, or as the return value of the `EntityResolver.resolveEntity` method.

The SAX parser will use the `InputSource` object to determine how to read XML input. If there is a character stream available, the parser will read that stream directly; if not, the parser will use a byte stream, if available; if neither a character stream nor a byte stream is available, the parser will attempt to open a URI connection to the resource identified by the system identifier.

An `InputSource` object belongs to the application: the SAX parser shall never modify it in any way (it may modify a copy if necessary).

If you supply input in the form of a `Reader` or `InputStream`, it may be useful to supply a system identifier as well. If you do this, the URI will not be used to obtain the actual XML input, but it will be used in diagnostics, and more importantly to resolve any relative URIs within the document, for example entity references.

InputSource	Zero-argument default constructor.
public InputSource()	
InputSource	Create a new input source with a system identifier.
public InputSource(	
String systemId)	Applications may use setPublicId to include a public identifier as well, or setEncoding to specify the character encoding, if known.
	If the system identifier is a URL, it must be full resolved.
	Parameters:
	systemId - The system identifier (URI).

Table Continued on Following Page

InputSource public InputSource(InputStream byteStream)	Create a new input source with a byte stream. Application writers may use setSystemId to provide a base for resolving relative URIs, setPublicId to include a public identifier, and/or setEncoding to specify the object's character encoding. **Parameters:** byteStream - The raw byte stream containing the document.
InputSource public InputSource(Reader characterStream)	Create a new input source with a character stream. Application writers may use setSystemId() to provide a base for resolving relative URIs, and setPublicId to include a public identifier. The character stream shall not include a byte order mark.
setPublicId public void setPublicId (String publicId)	Set the public identifier for this input source. The public identifier is always optional: if the application writer includes one, it will be provided as part of the location information. **Parameters:** publicId - The public identifier as a string.
getPublicId public String getPublicId ()	Get the public identifier for this input source. **Returns:** The public identifier, or null if none was supplied.

setSystemId public void setSystemId (String systemId)	Set the system identifier for this input source. The system identifier is optional if there is a byte stream or a character stream, but it is still useful to provide one, since the application can use it to resolve relative URIs and can include it in error messages and warnings (the parser will attempt to open a connection to the URI only if there is no byte stream or character stream specified). If the application knows the character encoding of the object pointed to by the system identifier, it can register the encoding using the setEncoding method. If the system ID is a URL, it must be fully resolved. **Parameters:** systemId - The system identifier as a string.
getSystemId public String getSystemId ()	Get the system identifier for this input source. The getEncoding method will return the character encoding of the object pointed to, or null if unknown. If the system ID is a URL, it will be fully resolved. **Returns:** The system identifier.
setByteStream public void setByteStream (InputStream byteStream)	Set the byte stream for this input source. The SAX parser will ignore this if there is also a character stream specified, but it will use a byte stream in preference to opening a URI connection itself. If the application knows the character encoding of the byte stream, it should set it with the setEncoding method. **Parameters:** byteStream - A byte stream containing an XML document or other entity.

Table Continued on Following Page

getByteStream public InputStream getByteStream()	Get the byte stream for this input source. The getEncoding method will return the character encoding for this byte stream, or null if unknown. **Returns:** The byte stream, or null if none was supplied.
setEncoding public void setEncoding(String encoding)	Set the character encoding, if known. The encoding must be a string acceptable for an XML encoding declaration (see section 4.3.3 of the XML 1.0 recommendation). This method has no effect when the application provides a character stream. **Parameters:** encoding - A string describing the character encoding.
getEncoding public String getEncoding()	Get the character encoding for a byte stream or URI. **Returns:** The encoding, or null if none was supplied.
setCharacterStream public void setCharacterStream(Reader characterStream)	Set the character stream for this input source. If there is a character stream specified, the SAX parser will ignore any byte stream and will not attempt to open a URI connection to the system identifier. **Parameters:** characterStream - The character stream containing the XML document or other entity.
getCharacterStream public Reader getCharacterStream()	Get the character stream for this input source. **Returns:** The character stream, or null if none was supplied.

Interface org.xml.sax.Locator

This interface provides methods that the application can use to determine the current position in the source XML document.

Interface for associating a SAX event with a document location

If a SAX parser provides location information to the SAX application, it does so by implementing this interface and then passing an instance to the application using the document handler's `setDocumentLocator` method. The application can use the object to obtain the location of any other document handler event in the XML source document.

Note that the results returned by the object will be valid only during the scope of each document handler method: the application will receive unpredictable results if it attempts to use the locator at any other time.

SAX parsers are not required to supply a locator, but they are very strong encouraged to do so. If the parser supplies a locator, it must do so before reporting any other document events. If no locator has been set by the time the application receives the `startDocument` event, the application should assume that a locator is not available.

getPublicId public String getPublicId()	Return the public identifier for the current document event. **Returns:** A string containing the public identifier, or null if none is available.
getSystemId public String getSystemId()	Return the system identifier for the current document event. If the system identifier is a URL, the parser must resolve it fully before passing it to the application. **Returns:** A string containing the system identifier, or null if none is available.
getLineNumber public int getLineNumber()	Return the line number where the current document event ends. Note that this is the line position of the first character after the text associated with the document event. In practice some parsers report the line number and column number where the event starts. **Returns:** The line number, or -1 if none is available.
getColumnNumber public int getColumnNumber()	Return the column number where the current document event ends. Note that this is the column number of the first character after the text associated with the document event. The first column in a line is position 1. **Returns:** The column number, or -1 if none is available.

Interface org.xml.sax.Parser

Every SAX parser must implement this interface. An application parses an XML document by creating an instance of a parser (that is, a class that implements this interface) and calling one of its parse() methods.

Basic interface for SAX (Simple API for XML) parsers.

All SAX parsers must implement this basic interface: it allows applications to register handlers for different types of events and to initiate a parse from a URI, or a character stream.

All SAX parsers must also implement a zero-argument constructor (though other constructors are also allowed).

SAX parsers are reusable but not re-entrant: the application may reuse a parser object (possibly with a different input source) once the first parse has completed successfully, but it may not invoke the parse() methods recursively within a parse.

parse public void parse(InputSource source) throws SAXException, IOException	Parse an XML document. The application can use this method to instruct the SAX parser to begin parsing an XML document from any valid input source (a character stream, a byte stream, or a URI). Applications may not invoke this method while a parse is in progress (they should create a new Parser instead for each additional XML document). Once a parse is complete, an application may reuse the same Parser object, possibly with a different input source. **Parameters:** source - The input source for the top-level of the XML document. **Throws:** SAXException Any SAX exception, possibly wrapping another exception. **Throws:** IOException An IO exception from the parser, possibly from a byte stream or character stream supplied by the application.

parse public void parse(String systemId) throws SAXException, IOException	Parse an XML document from a system identifier (URI). This method is a shortcut for the common case of reading a document from a system identifier. It is the exact equivalent of the following: `parse(new InputSource(systemId));` If the system identifier is a URL, it must be fully resolved by the application before it is passed to the parser. **Parameters:** systemId - The system identifier (URI). **Throws:** SAXException Any SAX exception, possibly wrapping another exception. **Throws:** IOException An IO exception from the parser, possibly from a byte stream or character stream supplied by the application.
setDocumentHandler public void setDocumentHandler(DocumentHandler handler)	Allow an application to register a document event handler. If the application does not register a document handler, all document events reported by the SAX parser will be silently ignored (this is the default behavior implemented by HandlerBase). Applications may register a new or different handler in the middle of a parse, and the SAX parser must begin using the new handler immediately. **Parameters:** handler - The document handler.

Table Continued on Following Page

setDTDHandler public void setDTDHandler(DTDHandler handler)	Allow an application to register a DTD event handler. If the application does not register a DTD handler, all DTD events reported by the SAX parser will be silently ignored (this is the default behavior implemented by HandlerBase). Applications may register a new or different handler in the middle of a parse, and the SAX parser must begin using the new handler immediately. **Parameters:** handler - The DTD handler.
setEntityResolver public void setEntityResolver(EntityResolver resolver)	Allow an application to register a custom entity resolver. If the application does not register an entity resolver, the SAX parser will resolve system identifiers and open connections to entities itself (this is the default behavior implemented in HandlerBase). Applications may register a new or different entity resolver in the middle of a parse, and the SAX parser must begin using the new resolver immediately. **Parameters:** resolver - The object for resolving entities.
setErrorHandler public void setErrorHandler(ErrorHandler handler)	Allow an application to register an error event handler. If the application does not register an error event handler, all error events reported by the SAX parser will be silently ignored, except for fatalError, which will throw a SAXException (this is the default behavior implemented by HandlerBase). Applications may register a new or different handler in the middle of a parse, and the SAX parser must begin using the new handler immediately. **Parameters:** handler - The error handler.

setLocale public void setLocale(Locale locale) throws SAXException	Allow an application to request a locale for errors and warnings. SAX parsers are not required to provide localization for errors and warnings; if they cannot support the requested locale, however, they must throw a SAX exception. Applications may not request a locale change in the middle of a parse. **Parameters:** locale - A Java Locale object. **Throws:** SAXException Throws an exception (using the previous or default locale) if the requested locale is not supported.

Class org.xml.sax.SAXException

This class is used to represent an error detected during processing either by the parser or by the application.

Encapsulate a general SAX error or warning

This class can contain basic error or warning information from either the XML parser or the application: a parser writer or application writer can subclass it to provide additional functionality. SAX handlers may throw this exception or any exception subclassed from it.

If the application needs to pass through other types of exceptions, it must wrap those exceptions in a SAXException or an exception derived from a SAXException.

If the parser or application needs to include information about a specific location in an XML document, it should use the SAXParseException subclass.

getMessage public String getMessage()	Return a detail message for this exception. If there is a embedded exception, and if the SAXException has no detail message of its own, this method will return the detail message from the embedded exception. **Returns:** The error or warning message.

Table Continued on Following Page

getException public Exception getException()	Return the embedded exception, if any. **Returns:** The embedded exception, or null if there is none.
toString public String toString()	Convert this exception to a string. **Returns:** A string version of this exception.

Class org.xml.sax.SAXParseException

Extends `SAXException`

This exception class represents an error or warning condition detected by the parser or by the application. In addition to the basic capability of SAXException, a SAXParseException allow information to be retained about the location in the source document where the error occurred. For an application-detected error, this information might be obtained from the Locator object.

Encapsulate an XML parse error or warning

This exception will include information for locating the error in the original XML document. Note that although the application will receive a `SAXParseException` as the argument to the handlers in the `ErrorHandler` interface, the application is not actually required to throw the exception; instead, it can simply read the information in it and take a different action.

Since this exception is a subclass of `SAXException`, it inherits the ability to wrap another exception.

SAXParseException public SAXParseException(String message, Locator locator)	Create a new SAXParseException from a message and a Locator. This constructor is especially useful when an application is creating its own exception from within a DocumentHandler callback. **Parameters:** message - The error or warning message. locator - The locator object for the error or warning.

SAXParseException public SAXParseException(String message, Locator locator, Exception e)	Wrap an existing exception in a SAXParseException. This constructor is especially useful when an application is creating its own exception from within a DocumentHandler callback, and needs to wrap an existing exception that is not a subclass of SAXException. **Parameters:** message - The error or warning message, or null to use the message from the embedded exception. locator - The locator object for the error or warning. e - Any exception
SAXParseException public SAXParseException(String message, String publicId, String systemId, int lineNumber, int columnNumber)	Create a new SAXParseException. This constructor is most useful for parser writers. If the system identifier is a URL, the parser must resolve it fully before creating the exception. **Parameters:** message - The error or warning message. publicId - The public identifer of the entity that generated the error or warning. systemId - The system identifer of the entity that generated the error or warning. lineNumber - The line number of the end of the text that caused the error or warning. columnNumber - The column number of the end of the text that cause the error or warning.
SAXParseException public SAXParseException(String message, String publicId, String systemId, int lineNumber, int columnNumber, Exception e)	Create a new SAXParseException with an embedded exception. This constructor is most useful for parser writers who need to wrap an exception that is not a subclass of SAXException. If the system identifier is a URL, the parser must resolve it fully before creating the exception. **Parameters:** message - The error or warning message, or null to use the message from the embedded exception. publicId - The public identifer of the entity that generated the error or warning. systemId - The system identifer of the entity that generated the error or warning. lineNumber - The line number of the end of the text that caused the error or warning. columnNumber - The column number of the end of the text that cause the error or warning. e - Another exception to embed in this one.

getPublicId public String getPublicId()	Get the public identifier of the entity where the exception occurred. **Returns:** A string containing the public identifier, or null if none is available.
getSystemId public String getSystemId()	Get the system identifier of the entity where the exception occurred. *Note that the term "entity" includes the top-level XML document.* If the system identifier is a URL, it will be resolved fully. **Returns:** A string containing the system identifier, or null if none is available.
getLineNumber public int getLineNumber()	The line number of the end of the text where the exception occurred. **Returns:** An integer representing the line number, or -1 if none is available.
getColumnNumber public int getColumnNumber()	The column number of the end of the text where the exception occurred. The first column in a line is position 1. **Returns:** An integer representing the column number, or -1 if none is available.

IE5 XML Schemas and Data Types

While XML documents can be successfully defined using a **Document Type Definition** (DTD), there is felt to be a requirement for a more flexible way of defining the structure of XML documents. It is also accepted that there needs to be a way for the data type to be indicated within the design of the XML document to make it easier for the handling of XML documents to be mechanized.

To this end, the W3C are – at the time of writing – working on a group of proposals that come under the general heading of **XML Schemas and Data Types**. This includes the proposed **Document Content Definition** (DCD) language. Internet Explorer 5 supports a reasonably standard implementation of XML Schemas and Data Types, as described in this reference section. This technology is still developing in IE5 and not all of the attributes listed here may work as described at the present time.

XML Schemas

An **XML Schema** is a description or definition of the structure of an XML document. The schema is itself written in XML. This makes it easier for newcomers to understand, when compared to the need to learn the SGML-like syntax of the Document Type Definition (DTD).

Internet Explorer 5 includes an implementation of XML Schemas that provides eight predefined elements for use in defining XML documents:

Name	Description
`Schema`	The overall enclosing element of the schema, which defines the schema name.
`ElementType`	Defines a type of element that will be used within the schema.
`element`	Defines an instance of an element declared for use within an `<ElementType>` element.
`AttributeType`	Defines a type of attribute that will be used within the schema.

Table Continued on Following Page

Name	Description
attribute	Defines an instance of an attribute declared for use within an <ElementType> element.
datatype	Defines the type of data that an attribute or element can contain.
description	Used to provide information about an attribute or element.
group	Used to collect elements together to define specific sequences of elements.

IE5 XML Schema Elements

This section describes each of the XML Schema elements in alphabetical order, complete with their attributes.

The attribute Element

The `<attribute>` element is used to define specific instances of an attribute that is used within an `<AttributeType>` or `<ElementType>` element.

Element Name	Attribute	Description
attribute	default	The default value for the attribute, used when required is "no". If required is "yes" then the value provided in the document must be the same as the default value.
	required	Specifies if a value for this attribute is required. Can be either "yes" or "no".
	type	Specifies the <AttributeType> of which the attribute is an instance.

The AttributeType Element

The `<AttributeType>` element is used to define a type of attribute that is used within elements in the schema. Specific instances of the attribute can be further specified using the `<attribute>` element.

Element Name	Attribute	Description
AttributeType	default	The default value for the attribute. If the attribute is an enumerated type, the value must appear in the list.
	dt:type	The data type that the attribute will accept.
	dt:values	A set of values that form an enumerated type, for example "roses carnations daisies"
	name	A unique string that identifies the <AttributeType> element within the schema and provides the attribute name.
	model	Defines whether the attribute can accept content that is not defined in the schema. The value "open" allows undefined content to appear, while the value "closed" allows only content defined in the schema to appear.
	required	Specifies if a value for this attribute is required. Can be either "yes" or "no". This and default are mutually exclusive when required is "yes".

The dt:type and dt:values are used in the same way as in the <datatype> element:

```
<AttributeType name="flowername"
               default="rose"
               dt:type="enumeration"
               dt:values="rose carnation daisy lilac" />
```

Note that, although dt is the usual namespace prefix for data types, we can replace it with a different prefix.

The datatype Element

The <datatype> element is used to define the type of data that an attribute or element can contain. At the time of writing, support for this element was particularly limited.

Element Name	Attribute	Description
datatype	dt:max	The maximum (inclusive) value that the element or attribute can accept.
	dt:maxExclusive	The maximum exclusive value that the element or attribute can accept, that is, the value must be less than this value.
	dt:maxlength	The maximum length of the element or attribute value. For strings this is the number of characters. For number and binary values this is the number of bytes required to store the value.
	dt:min	The minimum (inclusive) value that the element or attribute can accept.
	dt:minExclusive	The minimum exclusive value that the element or attribute can accept, that is, the value must be more than this value.
	dt:type	One of the specific or primitive data types listed at the end of this appendix.
	dt:values	For an enumeration, the list of values in the enumeration.

The description Element

The <description> element is used to provide information about an attribute or element.

Element Name	Attribute	Description
description	none	The descriptive text for the element or attribute.

The element Element

The <element> element is used to define specific instances of an element that is used within an <ElementType> element.

Element Name	Attribute	Description
element	type	The name of an element type defined in this or another schema, and of which this element is an instance.

Table Continued on Following Page

Element Name	Attribute	Description
element	minOccurs	Defines whether the element is optional in documents based on the schema. "0" denotes that it is optional and does not need to appear, while "1" denotes that the element must appear at least once. The default if omitted is "1".
	maxOccurs	Defines the maximum number of times that the element can appear at this point within documents based on the schema. "1" means only once, while "*" means any number of times. The default if omitted is "1".

The ElementType Element

The <ElementType> element is used to define a type of element that is used within the schema. Specific instances of the element can be further specified using the <element> element.

Element Name	Attribute	Description
ElementType	content	Defines the type of content that the element can contain. "empty" means no content, "textOnly" means it can contain only text (unless the model is "open"), "eltOnly" means it can contain only other elements and no free text, and "mixed" means it can contain any mixture of content.
	dt:type	One of the specific or primitive data types listed at the end of this appendix.
	model	Defines whether the element can accept content that is not defined in the schema. The value "open" allows undefined content to appear, while the value "closed" allows only content defined in the schema to appear.
	name	A unique string that identifies the <ElementType> element within the schema and provides the element name.
	order	Defines how sequences of the element can appear. The value "one" means that only one of the set of enclosed element elements can appear, "seq" means that all the enclosed elements must appear in the order that they are specified, and "many" means that none, any or all of the enclosed elements can appear in any order.

For examples of the content and order attributes, see the section on the <group> element next.

The group Element

The <group> element is used to collect series of <element> and/or <attribute> elements together so that they can be assigned a specific sequence in the schema. This can precisely control the order that they can appear in documents that are based on this schema.

Element Name	Attribute	Description
`group`	`minOccurs`	Defines whether the group is optional in documents based on the schema. "0" denotes that it is optional and does not need to appear, while "1" denotes that the group must appear at least once. The default if omitted is "1".
	`maxOccurs`	Defines the maximum number of times that the group can appear at this point within documents based on the schema. "1" means only once, while "*" means any number of times. The default if omitted is "1".
	`order`	Defines how sequences of the groups and element types contained in this group can appear. "one" means that only one of the set of enclosed groups or element types can appear, "seq" means that all the enclosed groups or element types must appear in the order that they are specified, and "many" means that none, any or all of the enclosed groups or element types can appear in any order.

The next example shows some of the ways that groups and element types can be used to define the ordering and appearance of elements in a document:

```
<ElementType name="first" content="empty" />
<ElementType name="second" content="textOnly" dt:type="string" />
<ElementType name="thirdEqual" content="empty" />

<ElementType name="third" content="eltOnly" order="many">
   <element type="thirdEqual" />
</ElementType>

<ElementType name="fallen" content="empty" />
<ElementType name="unplaced" content="empty" />
<ElementType name="last" content="empty" />

<ElementType name="raceorder" order="seq">

   <element type="first" />
   <element type="second" />
   <element type="third" />

   <group minOccurs="1" maxOccurs="1" order="one">
      <element type="fallen" />
      <element type="unplaced" />
      <element type="last" />
   </group>

</ElementType>
```

Because the main element `raceorder` has the attribute `order="seq"`, the `<first>`, `<second>` and `<third>` elements must appear at least once in the order shown. This also applies to the `group` element; however, of the three elements that are defined within the group, only one can occur in the document. So, the following combinations are some of the legal and valid possibilities:

```
<first />
<second>too slow again</second>
<third />
<fallen />
```

```
<first />
<second />
<third>
   <thirdEqual />
</third>
<unplaced />
<first />
<second>still too slow</second>
<third>
   <thirdEqual />
   <thirdEqual />
   <thirdEqual />
</third>
<last />
```

The Schema Element

The <Schema> element is the enclosing element of the schema. It defines the schema name and the namespaces that the schema uses.

Element Name	Attribute	Description
Schema	name	Defines a name by which the schema will be referred to.
	xmlns	Specifies the default namespace URI for the elements and attributes in the schema.
	xmlns:dt	Specifies the namespace URI for the datatype attributes in the schema.

```
<Schema name="myschema"
        xmlns="urn:schemas-microsoft-com:xml-data"
        xmlns:dt="urn:schemas-microsoft-com:datatypes">
```

As we noted above, the datatype namespace prefix does not have to be dt, but this is the usual value, and clearly indicates to a (human) reader that the attributes prefixed by it belong to the datatype namespace. However, the namespace definitions (the URN parts) *must* be as they appear here.

The IE5 XML Schema Structure

The following code shows the overall structure of an IE5 XML Schema, with the type of value expected for each attribute. Where elements can appear in more than one place, the subsequent occurrences have the attribute list removed to avoid excessive duplication:

```
<Schema name="schema_name"
        xmlns="namespace_URI"
        xmlns:dt="namespace_URI" >

   <AttributeType default="default_value"
                  dt:type="xml_data_type"
                  dt:values="enumerated_value_list"
                  name="name_or_id"
                  model="open"|"closed"
                  required="yes"|"no">
```

```
        <datatype dt:max="maximum_value"
                  dt:maxExclusive="maximum_value_exclusive"
                  dt:maxlength="maximum_length"
                  dt:min="minimum_value"
                  dt:minExclusive="minimum_value_exclusive"
                  dt:type="xml_data_type" />
                  dt:values="enumerated_value_list" />

        <description>description_text</description>

    </AttributeType>

    <AttributeType>
        ... etc ...
    </AttributeType>

    <ElementType content="empty"|"textOnly"|"eltOnly"|"mixed"
                 dt:type="xml_data_type"
                 model="open|"closed"
                 name="name_or_id"
                 order="one"|"seq"|"many" >

        <description>description_text</description>

        <datatype ... etc ... />

        <element type="element_type"
                 minOccurs="0"|"1"
                 maxOccurs="1"|"*" />

        <attribute default="default_value"
                   required="yes"|"no" />

        <attribute ... etc ... />

        <group minOccurs="0"|"1"
               maxOccurs="1"|"*"
               order="one"|"seq"|"many" >

            <attribute ... etc ... />

            <element ... etc ... />

        </group>

    </ElementType>

</Schema>
```

XML Datatypes

Data types are referenced from the data type namespace, which is declared within the XML `<Schema>` element of the schema using the `xmlns:`*datatypename* attribute.

The data types that are proposed by W3C, and supported in Internet Explorer 5, are shown in the next table, which includes all highly popular types and all the built-in types of popular database and programming languages and systems such as SQL, Visual Basic, C, C++ and Java. This table is taken from the W3C note at
http://www.w3.org/TR/1998/NOTE-XML-data/

Name	Parse type	Storage type	Example
`string`	`pcdata`	string (Unicode)	Ομωνυμα λεγαται ων ονομα μονον κοι νον, ο δε κατα τουνομα λογος της ουσιας ετερος, οι ον ζυον ο τε ανθροπος και το γεγραμμενον.
`number`	A number, with no limit on digits, may potentially have a leading sign, fractional digits, and optionally an exponent. Punctuation as in US English.	string	15, 3.14, -123.456E+10
`int`	A number, with optional sign, no fractions, no exponent.	32-bit signed binary	1, 58502, -13
`float`	Same as for `number`	64-bit IEEE 488	.314159265358979E+1
`fixed.14.4`	Same as `number` but no more than 14 digits to the left of the decimal point, and no more than 4 to the right.	64-bit signed binary	12.0044
`boolean`	`"1"` or `"0"`	bit	0, 1 (1=="true")
`dateTime.iso8601`	A date in ISO 8601 format, with optional time and no optional zone. Fractional seconds may be as precise as nanoseconds.	Structure or object containing year, month, hour, minute, second, nanosecond.	19941105T 08:15:00301
`dateTime.iso8601.tz`	A date in ISO 8601 format, with optional time and optional zone. Fractional seconds may be as precise as nanoseconds.	Structure or object containing year, month, hour, minute, second, nanosecond, zone.	19941105T 08:15:5+03
`date.iso8601`	A date in ISO 8601 format. (no time)	Structure or object containing year, month, day.	19541022
`time.iso8601`	A time in ISO 8601 format, with no date and no time zone.	Structure or object exposing day, hour, minute	

Name	Parse type	Storage type	Example
time.iso8601.tz	A time in ISO 8601 format, with no date but optional time zone.	Structure or object containing day, hour, minute, zone-hours, zoneminutes.	08:15-05:00
i1	A number, with optional sign, no fractions, no exponent.	8-bit binary	1, 255
i2	as above	16-bit binary	1, 703, -32768
i4	as above	32-bit binary	
i8	as above	64-bit binary	
ui1	A number, unsigned, no fractions, no exponent.	8-bit unsigned binary	1, 255
ui2	as above	16-bit unsigned binary	1, 703, -32768
ui4	as above	32-bit unsigned binary	
ui8	as above	64-bit unsigned binary	
r4	Same as number	IEEE 488 4-byte float	
r8	as above	IEEE 488 8-byte float	
float.IEEE.754.32	as above	IEEE 754 4-byte float	
float.IEEE.754.64	as above	IEEE 754 8-byte float	
uuid	Hexadecimal digits representing octets. Optional embedded hyphens should be ignored.	128-bytes Unix UUID structure	F04DA480-65B9-11d1-A29F-00AA00C14882
uri	Universal Resource Identifier	Per W3C spec	http://www.ics.uci.edu/pub/ietf/uri/draft-fielding-uri-syntax-00.txt http://www.ics.uci.edu/pub/ietf/uri/ http://www.ietf.org/html.charters/urn-charter.html
bin.hex	Hexadecimal digits representing octets	no specified size	

Table Continued on Following Page

Name	Parse type	Storage type	Example
`char`	String	1 Unicode character (16 bits)	
`string.ansi`	String containing only ASCII characters <= 0xFF.	Unicode or single-byte string.	This does not look Greek to me.

The dates and times above reading `iso8601`*xxx* actually use a restricted subset of the formats defined by ISO 8601. Years, if specified, must have four digits. Ordinal dates are not used. Of formats employing week numbers, only those that truncate year and month are allowed.

Primitive XML Data Types

The W3C also recommends tokenized data types for use in XML 1.0. These are sometimes referred to as **primitive types**. The primitive types supported in Internet Explorer 5 are:

Name	Description
`entity`	The XML `ENTITY` type.
`entities`	The XML `ENTITIES` type.
`enumeration`	An enumerated type, i.e. a list of permissible values.
`id`	The XML `ID` type.
`idref`	The XML `IDREF` type.
`idrefs`	The XML `IDREFS` type.
`nmtoken`	The XML `NMTOKEN` type.
`nmtokens`	The XML `NMTOKENS` type.
`notation`	A `NOTATION` type.
`string`	Represents a generic `String` data type.

E

IE5 XSL Reference

IE5 broadly supports the **Transformations** section of the working draft of XSL released by W3C on 16th December 1998, though there are some minor differences. It does *not* support the proposals for **Formatting Objects** or **Flow Objects**. This reference section details the XSL support available in IE5 final release.

XSL defines a set of XML elements that have special meaning within the `xsl` namespace (that is, each is prefixed with the `xsl` namespace identifier). These elements perform the transformation of the document into a new format. From here, under the W3C proposals, Formatting Objects would be used to define the actual output format for each element transformation. In IE5, we will generally use HTML within the transformations to define the new document format.

Bear in mind that XSL can also be used to transform *any* XML document into another (different) XML document, or into a document in almost any other format. This means, for example, that it can be used to transform an XSL stylesheet document into another XSL stylesheet document, or into some custom format that defines the styling in a way suited to some other application.

The IE5 XSL Elements

XSL in IE5 provides twenty elements that are used to create XSL stylesheets, or style sections within an XML document. The elements are:

Name	Description

`xsl:apply-templates`	Used inside a template to indicate that XSL should look for and apply another specific template to this node. The attributes are:
	`order-by="[+│-] `*`xsl-pattern`*`"`
	`select="`*`xsl-pattern`*`"`

`xsl:attribute`	Used to create a new `Attribute` node and attach it to the current element. The single attribute is: `name="`*`attribute-name`*`"`
`xsl:cdata`	Used to create a new `CDATASection` at this point in the output. Has no attributes.
`xsl:choose`	Used with the `xsl:when` and `xsl:otherwise` to provide a selection mechanism based on individual conditions for the same or different nodes. Similar to an `If...ElseIf...Else` construct. Has no attributes.
`xsl:comment`	Used to create a new `Comment` node at this point in the output. Has no attributes.
`xsl:copy`	Used to copy the current node in its entirety to the output. Has no attributes.
`xsl:define-template-set`	Used to define a set of templates that have a specific scope in the stylesheet. Has no attributes.
`xsl:element`	Used to create a new `Element` node at this point in the output. The single attribute is: `name="`*`element-name`*`"`
`xsl:entity-ref`	Used to create a new `EntityReference` node at this point in the output. The single attribute is: `name="`*`entity-reference-name`*`"`
`xsl:eval`	Used to evaluate a string expression and insert the result into the output. The string can be a mathematical or logical expression, an XSL function or a custom script function. The single attribute is: `language="`*`language-name`*`"`

Name	Description

`xsl:for-each`	Used to create a loop construct similar to a `For...Next` loop, allowing the same template to be applied to multiple more than one node. The attributes are:
	`order-by="[+|-] xsl-pattern"`
	`select="xsl-pattern"`

`xsl:if`	Used to create conditional branches within a template, in the same way as an `If...Then` construct, to allow a template to provide different output based on a condition. The single attribute is: `match="condition-pattern"`
`xsl:node-name`	Used to insert the name of the current node into the output as a text string. Has no attributes.
`xsl:otherwise`	*see* `xsl:choose` (above). Has no attributes.
`xsl:pi`	Used to create a new `ProcessingInstruction` node at this point in the output. The single attribute is: `name="processing-instruction-name"`
`xsl:script`	Used to define an area of the template that contains global variable declarations and script code functions. The single attribute is: `language="language-name"`

`xsl:stylesheet`	Used to define the 'root' element of an XSL stylesheet, the scripting language used, whether to preserve any white space in the input document when creating the output document, and a namespace declaration for the `xsl` prefix. The attributes are:
	`xmlns:xml="http://www.w3.org/TR/WD-xsl"`
	`language="language-name"`
	`indent-result="[yes|no]"` (default is `"no"`)
	NOTE: The namespace **must** be as shown here for XSL to work in IE5.

`xsl:template`	Used to define a template which containing contains the instructions for transforming the XML input into the output for nodes that match a specific pattern. The attributes are:
	`language="language-name"`
	`match="xsl-pattern"`

`xsl:value-of`	Used to evaluate an XSL pattern in the `select` attribute, and insert into the template as text the value of the matching node and its descendants. The single attribute is: `select="xsl-pattern"`
`xsl:when`	*see* `xsl:choose` (above). The single attribute is: `match="xsl-pattern"`

XSL Stylesheet Structure

The following shows the more common ways in which the XSL elements are used to construct an XSL style sheet, showing the kinds of structures that can be created. This isn't by any means the only combination, as most of the elements can be nested within most of the other elements. However, in general, each stylesheet will consist of one template that matches the root element in the document, followed by others that apply specific style and formatting to specific elements within the document.

```
<xsl:stylesheet xmlns:xsl="http://www.w3.org/TR/WD-xsl">

   <xsl:template match="...">
      <xsl:value-of select="..." />
      <xsl:eval> ...    </xsl:eval>
      <xsl:if match="..."> ... </xsl:if>
      <xsl:copy />

      <xsl:choose>
         <xsl:when match="..."> ... </xsl:when>
         <xsl:otherwise> ... </xsl:otherwise>
      </xsl:choose>

      <xsl:for-each select="...">
         <xsl:value-of select="..." />
         <xsl:eval> ... </xsl:eval>
         <xsl:if match="..."> ... </xsl:if>
         <xsl:copy />
         <xsl:apply-templates />
      </xsl:for-each>

      <xsl:apply-templates select="..." />
   </xsl:template>

   <xsl:define-template-set>
      <xsl:template match="..."> ... </xsl:template>
      <xsl:template match="..."> ... </xsl:template>
   </xsl:define-template-set>

   <xsl:script> ... </xsl:script>

</xsl:stylesheet>
```

Creating New Nodes in XSL

The XSL elements that create new nodes in the output document are `xsl:attribute`, `xsl:cdata`, `xsl:comment`, `xsl:element`, `xsl:entity-ref` and `xsl:pi`.

To create the XML node `<![CDATA[This is a CDATA section]]>` we could use:

```
<xsl:cdata>This is a CDATA section</xsl:cdata>
```

To create the XML node `<!ENTITY copy "©">` we could use:

```
<xsl:entity-ref name="copy">©</entity-ref>
```

To create the XML node `<!--This is the comment text-->` we could use:

```
<xsl:comment>This is the comment text</xsl:comment>
```

To create the XML node `<?WroxFormat="StartParagraph"?>` we could use:

```
<xsl:pi name="WroxFormat">StartParagraph</xsl:pi>
```

To create the XML element `<title>Instant JavaScript</title>` we could use:

```
<xsl:element name="title">Instant JavaScript</xsl:element>
```

and to add a `print-date` attribute to it we could use:

```
<xsl:attribute name="print_date">1998-02-07</xsl:attribute>
```

This gives us the XML result:

```
<title print_date="1998-02-07">Instant JavaScript</title>
```

XSL Stylesheet Runtime Methods

The `xsl:eval` element can be used to execute a number of built-in methods available in XSL in IE5. The `IXTLRuntime` object provides these methods:

Name	Description
`absoluteChildNumber (this_node)`	Returns the index of a specified node within its parent's `childNodes` list. Values start from `"1"`.
`ancestorChildNumber(node_name, this_node)`	Finds the first ancestor node of a specified node that has the specified name, and returns the index of that node within its parent's `childNodes` list. Values start from `"1"`. Returns `0` if there is no ancestor.
`childNumber (this_node)`	Returns the index of the specified node within its parent's `childNodes` list of children with the same name (that is, its index within the list of the node's identically named siblings) or `0` if not found. Values start from `"1"`.
`depth(start_node)`	Returns the depth or level within the document tree at which the specified node appears. The `XMLDocument` or root node is at level `0`.
`elementIndexList (this_node, node_name)`	Returns an array of node index numbers for the specified node and all its ancestors up to and including the document root node, indicating each node's position within their parent's `childNodes` list. The ordering of the array starts from the root document node. When the `node_name` parameter is not supplied, the method returns an array of integers that indicates the index of the specified node with respect to all of its siblings, the index of that node's parent with respect to all of its siblings, and so on until the document root is reached. When the `node_name` parameter is specified, the returned array contains entries only for nodes of the specified name, and the indices are evaluated relative to siblings with the specified name. Zero is supplied for levels in the tree that do not have children with the supplied name. Although this method is included in the Microsoft documentation, it was not supported by IE5 at the time of writing.

Name	Description
`formatDate(date, format, locale)`	Formats the value in the date parameter using the specified formatting options. The following format codes are supported: m - Month (1-12) mm - Month (01-12) mmm - Month (Jan-Dec) mmmm - Month (January-December) mmmmm - Month as the first letter of the month d - Day (1-31) dd - Day (01-31) ddd - Day (Sun-Sat) dddd - Day (Sunday-Saturday) yy -Year (00-99) yyyy - Year (1900-9999) The locale to use in determining the correct sequence of values in the date. If omitted the sequence month-day-year is used.
`formatIndex (number, format)`	Formats the integer number using the specified numerical system. 1 - Standard numbering system 01 - Standard numbering with leading zeros A - Uppercase letter sequence "A" to "Z" then "AA" to"ZZ". a - Lowercase letter sequence "a" to "z" then "aa" to "zz". I - Uppercase Roman numerals: "I", "II", "III", "IV", etc. i - Lowercase Roman numerals: "i", "ii", "iii", "iv", etc.
`formatNumber (number, format)`	Formats the value number using the specified format. Zero or more of the following values can be present in the format string: # (pound) – Display only significant digits and omit insignificant zeros. 0 (zero) – Display insignificant zeros in these positions. ? (question) – Adds spaces for insignificant zeros on either side of the decimal point, so that decimal points align with a fixed-point font. You can also use this symbol for fractions that have varying numbers of digits. . (period) – Indicates the position of the decimal point. , (comma) – Display a thousands separator or scale a number by a multiple of one thousand. % (percent) – Display number as a percentage. E or e - Display number in scientific (exponential) format. If format contains a zero or # to the right of an exponent code, display the number in scientific format and inserts an "E" or "e". The number of 0 or # characters to the right determines the number of digits in the exponent. E- or e- Place a minus sign by negative exponents. E+ or e+ Place a minus sign by negative exponents and a plus sign by positive exponents.

Table Continued on Following Page

Name	Description
`formatTime(time, format, locale)`	Formats the value in the time parameter using the specified formatting options. The following format codes are supported: `h` - Hours (0-23) `hh` - Hours (00-23) `m` - Minutes (0-59) `mm` - Minutes (00-59) `s` - Seconds (0-59) `ss` - Seconds (00-59) `AM/PM` - Add "`AM`" or "`PM`" and display in 12 hour format `am/pm` - Add "`am`" or "`pm`" and display in 12 hour format `A/P` - Add "`A`" or "`P`" and display in 12 hour format `a/p` - Add "`a`" or "`p`" and display in 12 hour format `[h]:mm` – Display elapsed time in hours, as in "`25.02`" `[mm]:ss` - Display elapsed time in minutes, as in "`63:46`" `[ss]` - Display elapsed time in seconds `ss.00` - Display fractions of a second The locale is used to determine the correct separator characters.
`uniqueID(this_node)`	Returns the unique identifier for the specified node.

As an example, this code transforms a number which is the content of the current element into Roman numerals using the built-in `formatIndex()` method:

```
<xsl:eval>
   intNumber=parseInt(this.text);
   formatIndex(intNumber, "i");
</xsl:eval>
```

Note that the content of the element must first be transformed from string format (which is the default for all XML content, unless we specify otherwise in the XML document's schema using data types).

The IE5 XSL Pattern-Matching Syntax

Using the elements described earlier, XSL can create a stylesheet document that contains one or more XSL `template` elements. These templates are applied to individual elements or sets of elements in the source document to create a particular section of the output document. To define which template applies to which of the source elements or nodes, a **pattern** is used. This pattern has one of two generic forms, and can define the node or nodes that match through:

- The **position** and **hierarchy** of the node or nodes within the source document
- The application of a **filter** that selectively targets one or more nodes

Node Position and Hierarchy

To select or match nodes (i.e. elements) through their position and hierarchy within the source document, we use a series of **path operators** to build up a pattern string. The path operators are:

Operator	Description
/	A forward slash is the **child** path operator. It selects elements that are direct children of the specified node, in much the same way as we use it to specify paths in a URL. For example, we use `book/category` to select all `<category>` elements that are children of `<book>` elements. To indicate the root node, we place this operator at the start of the pattern, for example: `/booklist/book`.
//	Two forward slashes indicate the **recursive descent** path operator. It selects all matching nodes at any depth below the current node (all descendants), for example: `booklist//title` to select all `<title>` elements that are descendants at any level of the `<booklist>` element. When it appears at the start of the pattern, it indicates recursive descent from the root node, that is, all elements in the document.
.	The period or 'full stop' is the **current context** path operator. It is used to indicate specifically the current node or 'context', for example: `.//title` to select all `<title>` elements at any level below the current element. The combination `./` always indicates the current context and is usually superfluous – for example `./book/category` is the same as `book/category`.
@	The 'at' operator is the **attribute** path operator. It indicates that this part of the pattern refers to attributes of the current element. For example, `book/@print_date` selects the `print_date` attributes of all `<book>` elements.
*	The asterisk is a **wildcard** path operator, and is used when we want to select all elements or attributes regardless of their name, for example `book/*` to select all child elements of all `book` elements, or `book/@*` to select all the attributes of all `<book>` elements.

Node Index Position

The path operators always return all elements or nodes that match the pattern. The node **index** can be used to specify a particular node within the set (or collection) of matching nodes, and the special XSL `end()` function can be used to specify the last node:

```
/booklist/book[0]      'first <book> element in root <booklist> element
/booklist/book[2]      'third <book> element in root <booklist> element
/booklist/book[end()] 'last <book> element in root <booklist> element
```

Note that the following three examples select different nodes within the same document:

```
book/category[2]          'second <category> element from all <book> elements
book[2]/category[2]       'second <category> element in second <book> element
(book/category)[2]        'second <category> element within the set of all ...
                          '... <category> elements from all <book> elements
```

In the last example, think of the pattern within the parentheses being applied first to create the set of all category elements from all book elements, followed by the index operator selecting just the second one.

XSL Filters and Filter Patterns

An **XSL filter** has the generic form `[operator pattern]` where `operator` is an optional **filter operator** that defines how the pattern is applied, and `pattern` is the required XSL **filter pattern** that selects one or more elements based on a range of criteria. One or more whitespace characters separate the filter operator and the filter pattern. The optional `operator` part can also consist of more than one filter operator expression if required. If omitted, any or all nodes that match the criteria in the filter pattern will be selected.

Filter Patterns

XSL filter patterns are very powerful, and offer an almost infinite number of pattern combinations. The following is a broad guide to the different kinds of ways that they can be used. The examples cover:

- Selecting by **child node name**
- Selecting by **node value**
- Selecting by **attribute existence**
- Selecting by **attribute value**
- Selecting by a **combination** of these

Selecting by Child Node Name

The position and hierarchy syntax we looked at earlier works by selecting elements based on their name as well as their position within the document. For example, `book/category` selects all `<category>` elements that are child elements of `<book>` elements. This is equivalent to the filter:

```
book[category]/category
```

because the filter `book/category` is actually a shorthand way of saying we want to select all `<book>` elements that have a `<category>` element (equivalent to `book[category]`), and then select the `<category>` element. A more useful way of using the longhand technique is when you want to specify a *different* child element to return. For example,

```
book[title]/category
```

means select only the `<category>` elements of books that have a `<title>` child element. To find all books that have both a `<category>` and a `<title>` child element, we use two filters:

```
book[title][category]
```

Selecting by Node Value

Extending the filter pattern that selects a node by its name, we can also select by value:

```
book[category = 'Scripting']
```

will select all `<book>` elements that have a `<category>` element with the value 'Scripting'. If we want to get the titles of books in this category, we would use:

```
book[category = 'Scripting']/title
```

To specify a value for the current element, we can include the period path operator. For example:

```
book/title[. = 'Instant JavaScript']
```

selects the title of the book 'Instant JavaScript'.

Selecting by Attribute Existence

The '@' attribute operator can also be used in a filter pattern to specify that the element must have a matching attribute:

```
book[@print_date]
```

selects only `book` elements that have a `print_date` attribute.

Selecting by Attribute Value

We can also specify the value that the attribute must have in order to match the pattern:

```
book[@print_date = '1998-05-02']
```

Selecting by a Combination of Methods

And, of course, we can combine all these methods to select exactly the element or node we require. For example:

```
book[@print_date = '1998-05-02']/title[. = 'Instant JavaScript']
```

to find the book titled 'Instant JavaScript' that was printed on 2nd May 1998, or:

```
/booklist//cover_design[issue = "final"]/*[@url = 'images']
```

to select all elements that:

- Have *any* name, but also have an attribute named `url` that has the value 'images' (from the `*[@url = 'images']` part);
- Are child elements of `cover_design` elements that themselves also have a child element named `issue` with the value 'final' (from the of `cover_design[issue = "final"]` part);
- Are descendants of the root `booklist` element (from the `/booklist//` part).

Note that the values of elements and attributes can be enclosed in single or double quotes.

Comparison Operators

The above examples all use the normal equality operator '=' to test if two values are equal. This works for numbers as well as strings. All XML values are strings by default, but IE5 casts them to appropriate data types before carrying out the comparison if possible. The data type chosen is based either on the content of the node value string, or on a **schema** (if one is present) that specifies the data type. This means that a comparison such as `[price = 29.95]` (without quotes around the numeric value) is perfectly valid.

If a schema is present and the content of the node cannot be cast into the type specified in the schema, for example if it contains characters that are illegal for that data type, such as letters in a numeric value, it is omitted from the set of matching nodes.

As well as the equality operator, there is a full set of other comparison operators:

Shortcut	Operator	Description
=	`$eq$`	Case-sensitive equality, for example `[price = 29.95]`
!=	`$ne$`	Case-sensitive inequality, for example `[category != 'Script']`
< *	`$lt$`	Case-sensitive less than, for example `[radius $lt$ 14.73]`
<= *	`$le$`	Case-sensitive less than or equal, for example `[age $le$ 18]`
>	`$gt$`	Case-sensitive greater than, for example `[name > 'H']`
>=	`$ge$`	Case-sensitive greater than or equal, for example `[speed >= 55]`
	`$ieq$`	Case-insensitive equality
	`$ine$`	Case-insensitive inequality
	`$ilt$`	Case-insensitive less than
	`$ile$`	Case-insensitive less than or equal
	`$igt$`	Case-insensitive greater than
	`$ige$`	Case-insensitive greater than or equal

* *Note that the '<' and '<=' operators cannot be used 'un-escaped' in XSL attributes, because these have to follow XML standards of well formed-ness. Instead, it is better to use the equivalent* `$lt$` *and* `$le$`. *Also note that all filter operator* ***names*** *(such as* `$eq$`*) are case sensitive, that is, they must be all lower-case.*

The shortcut operators perform exactly the same operation as the longer version, so the following are equivalent:

```
[category = 'Scripting']
[category $eq$ 'Scripting']
```

as are:

```
[category != 'Scripting']
[category $ne$ 'Scripting']
```

The case-insensitive operators have no shortcut operator syntax. They are useful, however, when you need to match irrespective of case. There is no `UCase` or `LCase` function included in XSL (unless you provide your own script function), so it saves having to do multiple tests, i.e.:

```
[category = 'html' $or$ category = 'HTML']
```

Instead, we just use:

```
[category $ieq$ 'html']
```

Logical Filter Operators

As well as single comparison tests, we can use logical operators to combine patterns to build up more complex ones (as seen in the final example in the previous section). The logical operators are:

Shortcut	Operator	Description
`&&`	`$and$`	Logical AND
`||`	`$or$`	Logical OR
	`$not$`	Negation, logical NOT

So, using these we can do things like selecting books that have a `<category>` element that is either 'Scripting' or 'HTML':

```
book/[category = 'Scripting' $or$ category = 'HTML']
```

or which have the title 'Instant JavaScript' (case-insensitive match), but are not in the category 'Scripting':

```
book/[category $ne$ 'Scripting' $and$ title $ieq$ 'Instant JavaScript']
```

The `$not$` operator simply changes the 'truth' of the match, so the following are equivalent, and match `<book>` elements which have a child `<category>` element with the value 'Scripting' but no child `<category>` element with the value 'HTML' (thus excluding `<book>` elements which have child `<category>` elements with both values):

```
book/[category = 'Scripting' $and$ category $ne$ 'HTML']
book/[category = 'Scripting' $and$ $not$ category = 'HTML']
```

Filter Set Operators

Remember that all the above examples of filter patterns that use comparison operators rely on the fact that the default filter action, if no operator is specified in the filter, is to return any or all nodes that match the pattern. However, there are ways that we can specify more exactly which of the matching elements we want, in a similar way to using an index to specify the first element. We use the **set** operators, `$any$` and `$all$`:

Operator	Description
`$all$`	Returns `True` only if the specified pattern matches all of the items in the collection.
`$any$`	Returns `True` if the specified pattern matches any of the items in the collection.

The easiest way to appreciate the difference is to think about the way that elements are selected. For an element named `<book>`, we can specify that we want it to be included in the results if it has a `<category>` child element with the value 'HTML' by using the pattern:

```
book[category = 'HTML']
```

However, this will only match the `<book>` element if the *first* `<category>` element has the value 'HTML'. If it doesn't have this value, even if other (later) child elements do, the `<book>` element will not be selected. However, if we use the pattern:

```
book[$any$ category = 'HTML']
```

we will get a match for this `<book>` element, because we specified that we want the `<book>` elements where *any* of the child elements has the value 'HTML'. If we use the alternative set operator, `$all$`, we are specifying that we only want to select `<book>` elements where *all* of their category child elements have the value 'HTML', not just the first one or any one or more of them. For the book to be included in the results, they must all have the value 'HTML':

```
book[$all$ category = 'HTML']
```

Of course, if the book only has one `<category>` child element, with the value 'HTML', all three of these filters will return this book element. The differences only appear when the pattern specifies elements with more than one matching child (or other) element.

XSL Built-In Methods

We saw one of the built-in methods of XSL earlier on when looking at selecting elements by their index. The last node in a collection of matching nodes is returned by the `end()` method:

```
booklist/category[end()]
```

The Information Methods

Other **information** methods are available to help isolate a specific node in a collection:

Name	Description
`end()`	Selects and returns the last node in a collection.
`index()`	Selects and returns the index (number) of the current node within its collection.
`nodeName()`	Selects and returns the tag name of the current node, including any namespace prefix.
`nodeType()`	Selects and returns as a number the type of the node (as used in the DOM).

Table Continued on Following Page

Name	Description
`date()`	Returns a value in date format.
`text()`	Selects and returns the text content of the current node.
`value()`	Returns a type cast version of the value of the current node.

The `value()` method is the default, so the following are equivalent:

```
book[category!value() = "Script"]
book[category = "Script"]
```

The exclamation mark operator (sometimes called the ***'bang'*** *operator) denotes that* `value()` *is a method of the* `<category>` *element. The normal use of a period here is not legal. It would be confused with the* ***current path*** *operator.*

The `index()` method is also optional when we want a specific element:

```
book[index() = 5]
book[5]
```

However, it is useful for selecting several elements, for example the fourth and fifth `<book>` elements only:

```
book[index() > 3 $and$ index() < 6]
```

The Collection Methods

It's also possible to select elements or other nodes using the **collection** methods supported by XSL in IE5:

Name	Description
`ancestor()`	Selects the ancestor node nearest to the current node that matches the pattern, starting at the parent node and working back up the document hierarchy. Returns a single element or `null` if none matches.
`attribute()`	Selects all attribute nodes of the current node, returning them as a collection. The optional parameter can specify the attribute name to match.
`comment()`	Selects and returns as a collection all child comment nodes.
`element()`	Selects all child element nodes of the current node, returning them as a collection. The optional parameter can specify the element name to match.
`node()`	Selects and returns as a collection all child nodes that are not attributes.
`pi()`	Selects and returns as a collection all child processing instruction nodes.
`textnode()`	Selects and returns as a collection all child text nodes.

As an example, we can select all of the comment elements within our <book> elements using:

```
book/comment()
```

The attribute() and element() methods accept a text parameter that can be used to limit the matching nodes:

```
book/attribute('print_date')
```

Of course, this is equivalent to the '@' operator we saw earlier, so these provide the same result:

```
book/attribute('print_date')
book/@print_date
```

And the element() method is equivalent to the earlier syntax as well – these two provide the same result:

```
book/element('category')
book/category
```

The ancestor() method also accepts a text parameter containing the pattern to be matched. For example:

```
ancestor(book/category)
```

will match the nearest <category> ancestor node which is a child of a <book> element. Note that this method cannot occur to the right of a '/' or '//' in the pattern, and that, unlike the attribute() and element() methods, the name of the node to be matched should not be placed in quotes.

Important Note

Remember that, of all of the XML-related technologies, XSL is probably the most volatile at the moment, in terms of changes that will come about in the language and syntax. There are subtle differences between the W3C working draft and Microsoft's implementation of XSL in IE5. You may wish to confine your development effort to experimental and induction projects until the future standards are more firmly established.

CSS Properties

This appendix lists the properties of CSS Level 2 (which includes all the properties of CSS1). However, not all these properties are implemented by IE5, although the level of support is likely to be increased with successive releases. As ever, to see if a property works, just try it!

I shall cover the properties under the same headings you'll find in the specification:

- Box Model
- Visual Formatting Model
- Visual Formatting Model Details
- Visual Effects
- Generated Content, Automatic Numbering and Lists
- Paged Media
- Colors and Backgrounds
- Font Properties
- Text Properties
- Tables
- User Interface
- Aural Style Sheets

The tables on the following pages list all the properties that can be applied to HTML and XML elements through a CSS style sheet. For more information about each of the properties, you should refer to the specification that may be found at http://www.w3.org/TR/1998/REC-CSS2/. You could also take a look at the Wrox Press title *Professional Style Sheets for HTML and XML* (1-861001-65-7).

Box Model

These properties are covered in section 8 of the CSS2 specification.

Property Name	Possible Values	Initial Value	Applies to	Inherited
`margin-top`	`<length> | <percentage> | auto` `<percentage>` refers to the parent element's width. Negative values are permitted.	0	All	No
`margin-right`	as above	0	All	No
`margin-bottom`	as above	0	All	No
`margin-left`	as above	0	All	No
`margin`	`[<length> | <percentage> | auto]{1,4}` If 4 values are given they apply to top, right, bottom, left, in that order. 1 value applies to all 4. If 2 or 3 values are given, the missing value is taken from the opposite side. `<percentage>` refers to the parent element's width. Negative values are permitted.	Undefined	All	No
`padding-top`	`<length> | <percentage>` `<percentage>` refers to the parent element's width. Negative values are *not* permitted.	0	All	No
`padding-right`	as above	0	All	No
`padding-bottom`	as above	0	All	No
`padding-left`	as above	0	All	No

Property Name	Possible Values	Initial Value	Applies to	Inherited
padding	[<length> | <percentage>]{1,4} If 4 values are given they apply to top, right, bottom, left, in that order. 1 value applies to all 4. If 2 or 3 values are given, the missing value is taken from the opposite side. <percentage> refers to the parent element's width. Negative values are *not* permitted.	0	All	No
border-top-width	thin | medium | thick | <length>	medium	All	No
border-right-width	thin | medium | thick | <length>	medium	All	No
border-bottom-width	thin | medium | thick | <length>	medium	All	No
border-left-width	thin | medium | thick | <length>	medium	All	No
border-width	[thin | medium | thick | <length>]{1,4} If 4 values are given they apply to top, right, bottom, left, in that order. 1 value applies to all 4. If 2 or 3 values are given, the missing value is taken from the opposite side.	Undefined	All	No
border-top-color	<color>	The element's color property	All	No
border-right-color	<color>	The element's color property	All	No

Table Continued on Following Page

Property Name	Possible Values	Initial Value	Applies to	Inherited
border-bottom-color	<color>	The element's color property	All	No
border-left-color	<color>	The element's color property	All	No
border-color	<color>{1,4} | transparent If 4 values are given they apply to top, right, bottom, left, in that order. 1 value applies to all 4. If 2 or 3 values are given, the missing value is taken from the opposite side.	The element's color property	All	No
border-top-style	none | hidden | dotted | dashed | solid | double | groove | ridge | inset | outset	none	All	No
border-right-style	none | hidden | dotted | dashed | solid | double | groove | ridge | inset | outset	none	All	No
border-bottom-style	none | hidden | dotted | dashed | solid | double | groove | ridge | inset | outset	none	All	No
border-left-style	none | hidden | dotted | dashed | solid | double | groove | ridge | inset | outset	none	All	No
border-style	[none | hidden | dotted | dashed | solid | double | groove | ridge | inset | outset]{1,4}	none	All	No
border-top	<border-top-width> || <border-top-style> || <color>	Undefined	All	No
border-right	<border-right-width> || <border-right-style> || <color>	Undefined	All	No

<table>
<tr><th>Property Name</th><th>Possible Values</th><th>Initial Value</th><th>Applies to</th><th>Inherited</th></tr>
<tr><td>border-bottom</td><td><border-bottom-width> || <border-bottom-style> || <color></td><td>Undefined</td><td>All</td><td>No</td></tr>
<tr><td>border-left</td><td><border-left-width> || <border-left-style> || <color></td><td>Undefined</td><td>All</td><td>No</td></tr>
<tr><td>border</td><td><border-width> || <border-style> || <color></td><td>Undefined</td><td>All</td><td>No</td></tr>
</table>

Visual Formatting Model

This is a new category of property in CSS2, and is covered in section 9 of the specification.

<table>
<tr><th>Property Name</th><th>Possible Values</th><th>Initial Value</th><th>Applies to</th><th>Inherited</th></tr>
<tr><td>display</td><td>block | inline | list-item | none | run-in | compact | marker | table | inline-table | table-row-group | table-column-group | table-header-group | table-footer-group | table-row | table-cell | table-caption | table-column</td><td>inline</td><td>All</td><td>No</td></tr>
<tr><td>position</td><td>static | relative | absolute | fixed</td><td>static</td><td>All (but not generated content)</td><td>No</td></tr>
<tr><td>top (box offsets)</td><td><length> | <percentage> | auto

<length>: the box offset is a fixed distance from the reference edge.

<percentage>: the box offset is a percentage of the containing block's width (for left or right) or height (for top and bottom).

auto: the value depends on which of the other box offset properties are auto as well.</td><td>auto</td><td>Positioned elements</td><td>No</td></tr>
</table>

Table Continued on Following Page

Property Name	Possible Values	Initial Value	Applies to	Inherited
`left` (*box offsets*)	*as above*	`auto`	Positioned elements	No
`bottom` (*box offsets*)	*as above*	`auto`	Positioned elements	No
`right` (*box offsets*)	*as above*	`auto`	Positioned elements	No
`float`	`left` | `right` | `none` Note: `float` removes inline elements from the line.	`none`	All but positioned elements and generated content	No
`clear`	`block` | `inline` | `list-item` | `none`	`none`	Block elements	No
`z-index`	`auto` | `<integer>`	`auto`	Positioned elements	No
`direction`	`ltr` | `rtl` `ltr`: left-to-right `rtl`: right-to-left	`ltr`	All	Yes
`unicode-bidi`	`normal` | `embed` | `bidi-override`	`normal`	All	No

Visual Formatting Model Details

This is another new section in CSS2, and is covered in section 10 of the CSS2 specification.

Property Name	Possible Values	Initial Value	Applies to	Inherited
`width`	`<length>` | `<percentage>` | `auto` `<percentage>` refers to parent element's width.	`auto`	All but non-replaced inline elements, table columns and column groups	No
`min-width`	`<length>` | `<percentage>`	Depends on user agent	All but non-replaced inline elements and table elements	No
`max-width`	`<length>` | `<percentage>` | `none`	`none`	All but non-replaced inline elements and table elements	No

Property Name	Possible Values	Initial Value	Applies to	Inherited
height	<length> | <percentage> | auto	auto	All but non-replaced inline elements, table rows and row groups	No
min-height	<length> | <percentage>	0	All but non-replaced inline elements and table elements	No
max-height	<length> | <percentage> | none	none	All but non-replaced inline elements and table elements	No
line-height	normal | <number> | <length> | <percentage> <number>:- line-height = font-size x num. <percentage> is relative to font-size.	normal	All	Yes
vertical-align	baseline | sub | super | top |text-top | middle | bottom |text-bottom | <percentage> | <length> <percentage> is relative to element's line-height property	baseline	Inline and table-cell elements	No

Visual Effects

This is a new category of property in CSS2. It is covered in section 11 of the specification.

Property Name	Possible Values	Initial Value	Applies to	Inherited
overflow	visible | hidden | scroll | auto	visible	Block-level and replaced elements	No
clip	<shape> | auto	auto	Block-level and replaced elements	No
visibility	visible | hidden | collapse | inherit	inherit	All	No

Generated Content, Automatic Numbering and Lists

Again, this is a new category of property in CSS2, covered in section 12 of the specification. In CSS2 it is possible to generate content in several ways:

- Using the content property in conjunction with the :before and :after pseudo-elements.
- In conjunction with the cue-before and cue-after aural properties
- Elements with a value of list-item for the display property

The style and location of generated content is specified with the :before and :after pseudo-elements. These are used in conjunction with the content property, which specifies what is inserted. Unsurprisingly, :before and :after pseudo-elements specify content before and after an element's document tree content. See the specification (section 12) for further details.

Property Name	Possible Values	Initial Value	Applies to	Inherited
content	[<string> | <uri> | <counter> | attr(X) | open-quote | close-quote | no-open-quote | no-close-quote]+	empty string	:before and :after pseudo-elements	No
quotes	[<string> <string>]+ | none	Depends on user agent	All	Yes
counter-reset	[<identifier> <integer>?]+ | none	none	All	No
counter-increment	[<identifier> <integer>?]+ | none	none	All	No

Property Name	Possible Values	Initial Value	Applies to	Inherited
marker-offset	<length> | auto	auto	Elements with the display property set to marker	No
list-style-type	disc | circle | square | decimal | decimal-leading-zero lower-roman | upper-roman | lower-greek | lower-alpha | upper-alpha | none | lower-latin |upper-latin | hebrew | armenian |georgian | cjk-ideographic |hiragana | katakana |hiragana-iroha | katakana-iroha	disc	Elements with the display property set to list-item	Yes
list-style-image	<uri> | none	none	List-items	Yes
list-style-position	inside | outside	outside	List-items	Yes

Paged Media

All the following paged media properties are new to CSS2 and are covered in section 13 of the specification.

Property Name	Possible Values	Initial Value	Applies to	Inherited
list-style	<list-style-type> || <list-style-position> || <list-style-image>	Undefined	List-items	Yes
size	<length>{1, 2} | auto | portrait | landscape	auto	Page context	N/A
marks (crop marks)	[crop || cross] | none	none	Page context	N/A
page-break-before	auto | always | avoid | left | right	auto	Block-level elements	No
page-break-after	auto | always | avoid | left | right	auto	Block-level elements	No

Table Continued on Following Page

<table>
<tr><th>Property Name</th><th>Possible Values</th><th>Initial Value</th><th>Applies to</th><th>Inherited</th></tr>
<tr><td>page-break-inside</td><td>avoid | auto</td><td>auto</td><td>Block-level elements</td><td>Yes</td></tr>
<tr><td>page (for using named pages)</td><td><identifier> | auto</td><td>auto</td><td>Block level elements</td><td>Yes</td></tr>
<tr><td>orphans</td><td><integer></td><td>2</td><td>Block-level elements</td><td>Yes</td></tr>
<tr><td>widows</td><td><integer></td><td>2</td><td>Block-level elements</td><td>Yes</td></tr>
</table>

Colors and Backgrounds

These properties (which are unchanged from CSS1) are in Section 12 of the CSS2 specification.

<table>
<tr><th>Property Name</th><th>Possible Values</th><th>Initial Value</th><th>Applies to</th><th>Inherited</th></tr>
<tr><td>color</td><td>keyword | numerical RGB specification</td><td>Depends on user agent</td><td>All</td><td>Yes</td></tr>
<tr><td>background-color</td><td><color> | transparent</td><td>transparent</td><td>All</td><td>No</td></tr>
<tr><td>background-image</td><td><uri> | none</td><td>none</td><td>All</td><td>No</td></tr>
<tr><td>background-repeat</td><td>repeat | repeat-x | repeat-y | no-repeat</td><td>repeat</td><td>All</td><td>No</td></tr>
<tr><td>background-attachment</td><td>scroll | fixed</td><td>scroll</td><td>All</td><td>No</td></tr>
<tr><td>background-position</td><td>[[<length> | <percentage>]{1,2} | [top | center | bottom] || [left | center | right]]</td><td>0%, 0%</td><td>Block and replaced elements</td><td>No</td></tr>
<tr><td>background</td><td>[<background-color> || <background-image> || <background-repeat> || <background-attachment> || <background-position>]</td><td>Undefined</td><td>All</td><td>No</td></tr>
</table>

Font Properties

These properties are unchanged in CSS2 from CSS1, and are covered in section 15 of the specification.

Property Name	Possible Values	Initial Value	Applies to	Inherited
font-family	[[<family-name> | <generic-family>],]* [<family-name> | <generic-family>] Use any font family name. <generic-family> values are: serif sans-serif cursive fantasy monospace	Depends on user agent	All	Yes
font-style	normal | italic | oblique	normal	All	Yes
font-variant	normal | smallcaps	normal	All	Yes
font-weight	normal | bold | bolder | lighter |100 | 200 | 300 | 400 | 500 | 600 |700 | 800 | 900	normal	All	Yes
font-stretch	normal | wider | narrower | ultra-condensed | extra-condensed |condensed | semi-condensed |semi-expanded | expanded |extra-expanded | ultra-expanded	normal	All	Yes
font-size	<absolute-size> | <relative-size> |<length> | <percentage> <absolute-size>: xx-small | x-small | small | medium |large | x-large | xx-large <relative-size>: larger | smaller <percentage>: In relation to parent element	medium	All	Yes

Table Continued on Following Page

<table>
<tr><th>Property Name</th><th>Possible Values</th><th>Initial Value</th><th>Applies to</th><th>Inherited</th></tr>
<tr><td>font-size-adjust</td><td><number> | none</td><td>none</td><td>All</td><td>Yes</td></tr>
<tr><td>font</td><td>[[<font-style> || <font-variant> || <font-weight>]? <font-size> [/<line-height>]? <font-family>] | caption | icon | menu | message-box | small-caption | status-bar</td><td>Undefined</td><td>All</td><td>Yes</td></tr>
</table>

Text Properties

The text properties are covered in section 16 of the CSS2 specification.

<table>
<tr><th>Property Name</th><th>Possible Values</th><th>Initial Value</th><th>Applies to</th><th>Inherited</th></tr>
<tr><td>text-indent</td><td><length> | <percentage></td><td>0</td><td>Block elements</td><td>Yes</td></tr>
<tr><td>text-align</td><td>left | right | center | justify | <string></td><td>Depends on user agent and writing direction</td><td>Block elements</td><td>Yes</td></tr>
<tr><td>text-decoration</td><td>none | [underline || overline || line-through || blink]</td><td>none</td><td>All</td><td>No</td></tr>
<tr><td>text-shadow</td><td>none | [<color> || <length> <length> <length>? ,]*[<color> || <length> <length> <length>?]</td><td>none</td><td>All</td><td>No</td></tr>
<tr><td>letter-spacing</td><td>normal | <length></td><td>normal</td><td>All</td><td>Yes</td></tr>
<tr><td>word-spacing</td><td>normal | <length></td><td>normal</td><td>All</td><td>Yes</td></tr>
<tr><td>text-transform</td><td>none | capitalize | uppercase | owercase</td><td>none</td><td>All</td><td>Yes</td></tr>
<tr><td>white-space</td><td>normal | pre | nowrap</td><td>normal</td><td>Block elements</td><td>Yes</td></tr>
</table>

Tables

All the `table` properties are new to CSS2 and can be found in section 17 of the specification.

Property Name	Possible Values	Initial Value	Applies to	Inherited
caption-side	top | bottom | left | right	top	Table-caption elements	Yes
border-collapse	collapse | separate	collapse	Table and in-line-table elements	Yes
border-spacing	<length>	0	Table and in-line-table elements	yes
table-layout	fixed | auto	auto	Table and in-line-table elements	No
empty-cells	show | hide	show	Table-cell elements	Yes
speak-header	once | always	once	Elements that have header information	Yes

User Interface

The user interface properties are new to CSS2 and can be found in section 18 of the specification.

Property Name	Possible Values	Initial Value	Applies to	Inherited
cursor	[[<uri>,]* [auto | crosshair | default | pointer | move | e-resize | ne-resize | nw-resize | n-resize | se-resize | sw-resize | s-resize | w-resize| text | wait | help]]	auto	All	Yes
outline	<outline-color> || <outline-style> || <outline-width>	See individual properties	All	No
outline-width	border-width	medium	All	No
outline-style	border-style	none	All	No
outline-color	border-color | invert	invert	All	No

Aural Style Sheets

These are a new addition in CSS2 and can be seen in further detail in section 19 of the specification.

<table>
<tr><th>Property Name</th><th>Possible Values</th><th>Initial Value</th><th>Applies to</th><th>Inherited</th></tr>
<tr><td>volume</td><td><number> | <percentage> | silent | x-soft | soft | medium | loud | x-loud</td><td>medium</td><td>All</td><td>Yes</td></tr>
<tr><td>speak</td><td>normal | none | spell-out</td><td>normal</td><td>All</td><td>Yes</td></tr>
<tr><td>pause-before</td><td><time> | <percentage></td><td>Depends on user agent</td><td>All</td><td>No</td></tr>
<tr><td>pause-after</td><td><time> | <percentage></td><td>Depends on user agent</td><td>All</td><td>No</td></tr>
<tr><td>pause</td><td>[[<time> | <percentage>]{1, 2}]</td><td>Depends on user agent</td><td>All</td><td>No</td></tr>
<tr><td>cue-before</td><td><uri> | none</td><td>none</td><td>All</td><td>No</td></tr>
<tr><td>cue-after</td><td><uri> | none</td><td>none</td><td>All</td><td>No</td></tr>
<tr><td>cue</td><td>[<cue-before> || <cue-after>]</td><td>Undefined</td><td>All</td><td>No</td></tr>
<tr><td>play-during</td><td><uri> mix? repeat? | auto | none</td><td>auto</td><td>All</td><td>No</td></tr>
<tr><td>azimuth</td><td><angle> | [[left-side | far-left | left | center-left | center | center-right | right | far-right | right-side] || behind] | leftwards | rightwards</td><td>center</td><td>All</td><td>Yes</td></tr>
<tr><td>elevation</td><td><angle> | below | level | above | higher | lower</td><td>level</td><td>All</td><td>Yes</td></tr>
<tr><td>speech-rate</td><td><number> | x-slow | slow | medium | fast | x-fast | faster | slower</td><td>medium</td><td>All</td><td>Yes</td></tr>
<tr><td>voice-family</td><td>[[<specific-voice> | <generic-voice>],]* [<specific-voice> | <generic-voice>]</td><td>Depends on user agent</td><td>All</td><td>Yes</td></tr>
<tr><td>pitch</td><td><frequency> | x-low | low | medium | high | x-high</td><td>medium</td><td>All</td><td>Yes</td></tr>
<tr><td>pitch-range</td><td><number></td><td>50</td><td>All</td><td>Yes</td></tr>
<tr><td>stress</td><td><number></td><td>50</td><td>All</td><td>Yes</td></tr>
<tr><td>richness</td><td><number></td><td>50</td><td>All</td><td>Yes</td></tr>
<tr><td>speak-punctuation</td><td>code | none</td><td>none</td><td>All</td><td>Yes</td></tr>
<tr><td>speak-numeral</td><td>digits | continuous</td><td>continuous</td><td>All</td><td>Yes</td></tr>
</table>

G

Installing XT

In order to run some of the XSLT and XPath examples in this book, you'll need to download and install XT. XT is a tool written by Jim Clark, an editor on the XSLT and XPath recommendations, and is intended to provide a reference implementation that your XSLT and XPath code may be tested with. It may be found at:

http://www.jclark.com/xml/xt.html

You'll need to install XT one of two ways, depending on your platform.

XT for Java

If you are in a non-Windows environment, or if you want to access the XT functionality from Java, you'll need to download the Java libraries. They may be found at

ftp://ftp.jclark.com/pub/xml/xt.zip

In order to use this library, you'll need to have a Java parser that supports SAX, such as XP. XP may also be downloaded from Jim Clark's page, at

http://www.jclark.com/xml/xp/index.html

Put the file `xt.jar` in your `CLASSPATH`, as well as your XML parser's `.jar` files. XT may then be executed with the command:

```
java -Dcom.jclark.xsl.sax.parser=your-sax-driver com.jclark.xsl.sax.Driver source
  stylesheet result name=value...
```

where:

Parameter	Description
`source`	The XML to be operated upon
`stylesheet`	The XSLT to be applied to the source document
`result`	The location of the output
`name=value`	Is a list of optional parameters (if you are using a parameterized stylesheet)

The XT libraries are also packaged as a servlet; for details on the use of this servlet, check Jim Clark's XT page at the URL mentioned above.

XT Packaged as a Win32 Executable

If you are running on the Windows platform, you may choose to download XT packaged as a Win32 executable. To use this version of XT, you must have Microsoft's Java VM installed on your machine (it comes with Internet Explorer). It may be downloaded from:

ftp://ftp.jclark.com/pub/xml/xt-win32.zip

To execute XT, use the command:

```
xt source stylesheet result name=value...
```

where the parameters mean the same as they do for the Java implementation.

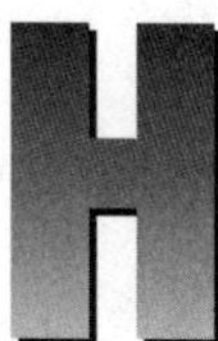

Support and Errata

One of the most irritating things about any computing book is when you find that bit of code you've just spent an hour typing simply doesn't work. You check it a hundred times to see if you've set it up correctly and then you notice the spelling mistake in the variable name on the book page. Of course, you can blame the authors for not taking enough care and testing the code, the editors for not doing their job properly, or the proofreaders for not being eagle-eyed enough, but this doesn't get around the fact that mistakes do happen.

We try hard to ensure no mistakes sneak out into the real world, but we can't promise that this book is 100% error free. What we can do is offer the next best thing by providing you with immediate support and feedback from experts who have worked on the book and try to ensure that future editions eliminate these gremlins. The following section will take you step by step through the process of posting errata to our web site to get that help. The sections that follow, therefore, are:

- Wrox Developers Membership
- Finding a list of existing errata on the web site

There is also a section covering how to e-mail a question for technical support. This comprises:

- What your e-mail should include
- What happens to your e-mail once it has been received by us

So that you only need view information relevant to yourself, we ask that you register as a Wrox Developer Member. This is a quick and easy process, that will save you time in the long run. If you are already a member, just update membership to include this book.

Wrox Developer's Membership

To get your FREE Wrox Developer's Membership click on Membership in the navigation bar of our home site – http://www.wrox.com. This is shown in the following screenshot:

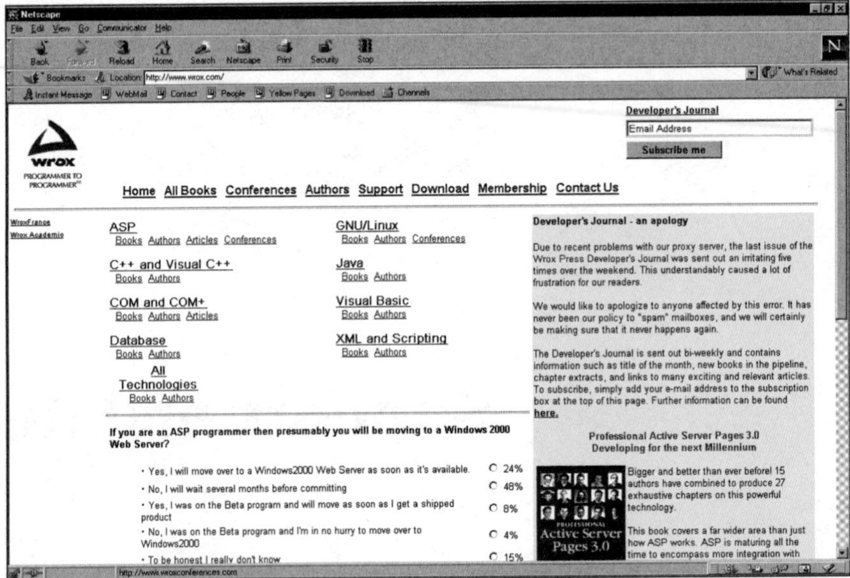

Then, on the next screen (not shown), click on New User. This will display a form. Fill in the details on the form and submit the details using the Register button at the bottom. Go back to the main Membership page, enter your details and select Logon. Before you can say 'The best read books come in Wrox Red' you will get the following screen:

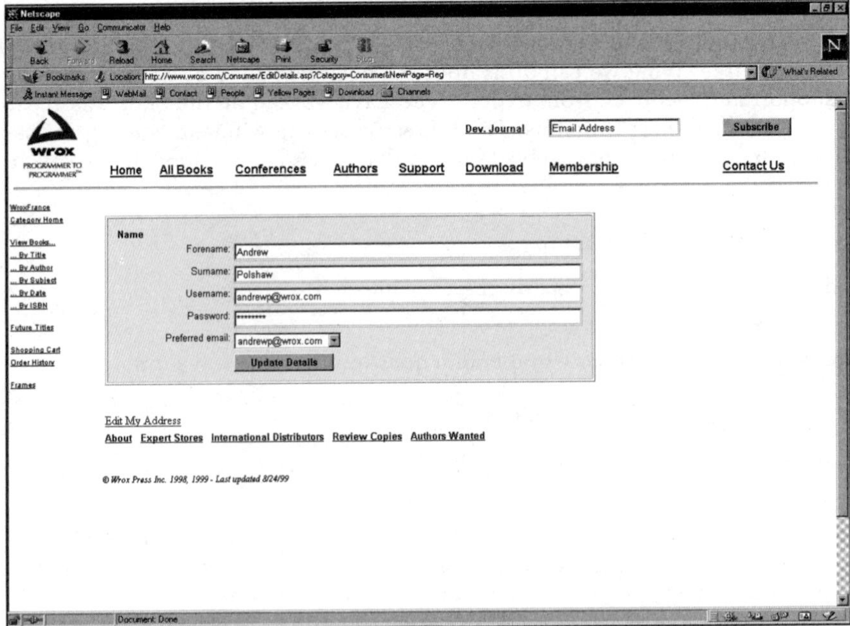

Finding an Errata on the Web Site

Before you send in a query, you might be able to save time by finding the answer to your problem on our web site – http:\\www.wrox.com.

Each book we publish has its own page and its own errata sheet. You can get to any book's page by clicking on Support from the top navigation bar.

From this page you can locate any book's errata page on our site. Select your book from the pop-up menu and click on it.

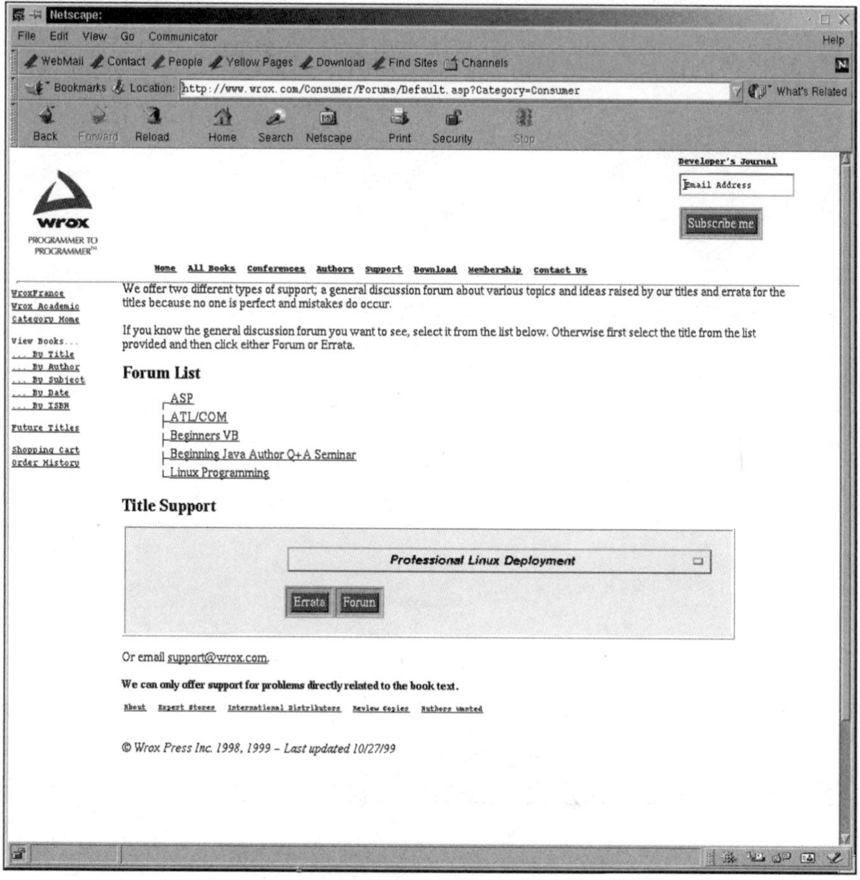

Then click on Errata. This will take you to the errata page for the book. Select the criteria by which you want to view the errata, and click the Apply criteria... button. This will provide you with links to specific errata. For an initial search, you are advised to view the errata by page numbers. If you have looked for an error previously, then you may wish to limit your search using dates. We update these pages daily to ensure that you have the latest information on bugs and errors.

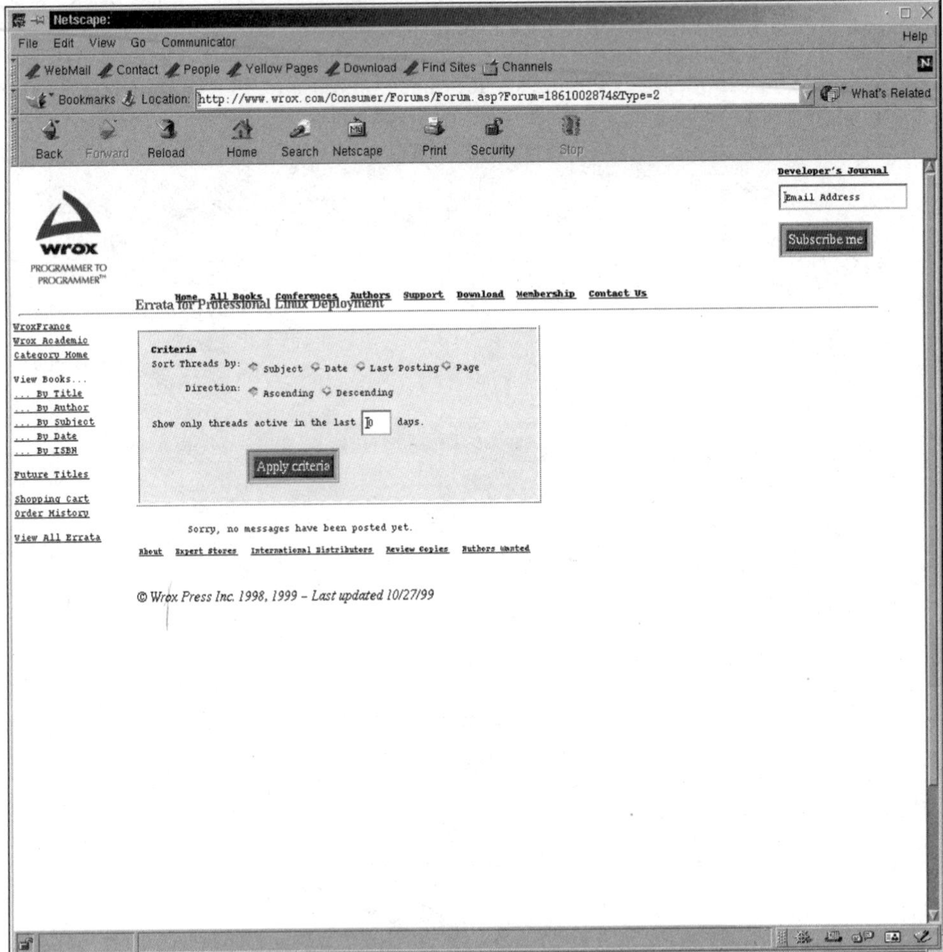

E-mail Support

If you wish to directly query a problem in the book with an expert who knows the book in detail then e-mail `support@wrox.com`, with the title of the book and the last four numbers of the ISBN in the subject field of the e-mail. A typical email should include the following things:

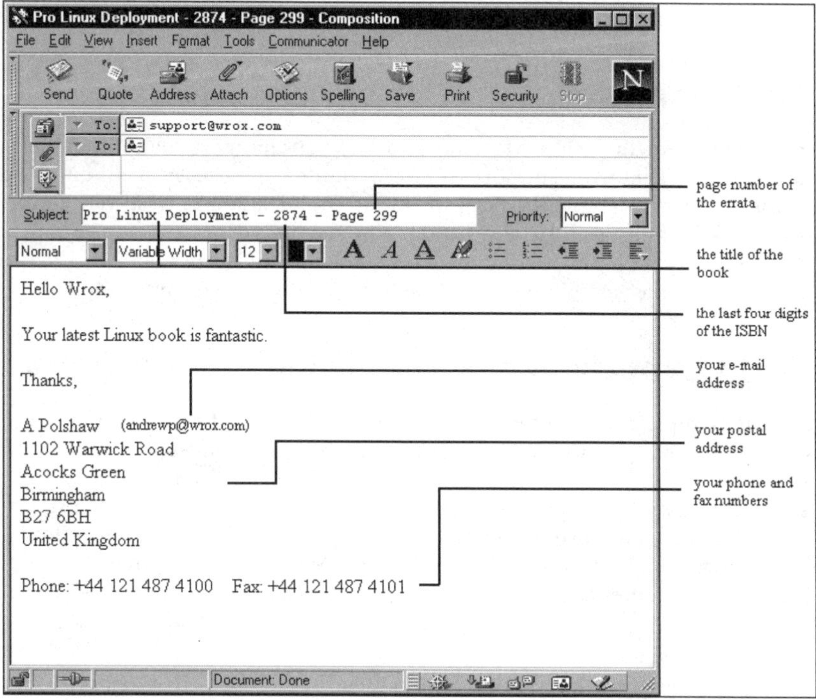

We won't send you junk mail. We need the details to save your time and ours. If we need to replace a disk or CD we'll be able to get it to you straight away. When you send an e-mail it will go through the following chain of support:

Customer Support

Your message is delivered to one of our customer support staff who are the first people to read it. They have files on most frequently asked questions and will answer anything general immediately. They answer general questions about the book and the web site.

Editorial

Deeper queries are forwarded to the technical editor responsible for that book. They have experience with the programming language or particular product and are able to answer detailed technical questions on the subject. Once an issue has been resolved, the editor can post the errata to the web site.

The Authors

Finally, in the unlikely event that the editor can't answer your problem, s/he will forward the request to the author. We try to protect the author from any distractions from writing. However, we are quite happy to forward specific requests to them. All Wrox authors help with the support on their books. They'll mail the customer and the editor with their response, and again all readers should benefit.

What We Can't Answer

Obviously with an ever-growing range of books and an ever-changing technology base, there is an increasing volume of data requiring support. While we endeavor to answer all questions about the book, we can't answer bugs in your own programs that you've adapted from our code. So, while you might have loved the help desk systems in our Linux book, don't expect too much sympathy if you cripple your company with a live adaptation you customized from Chapter 12. However, do tell us if you're especially pleased with the routine you developed with our help.

How to Tell Us Exactly What You Think

We understand that errors can destroy the enjoyment of a book and can cause many wasted and frustrated hours, so we seek to minimize the distress that they can cause.

You might just wish to tell us how much you liked or loathed the book in question. Or you might have ideas about how this whole process could be improved, in which case you should e-mail `feedback@wrox.com`. You'll always find a sympathetic ear, no matter what the problem is. Above all you should remember that we do care about what you have to say and we will do our utmost to act upon it.

Index

Symbols

A

C

D

E

F

G

H

I

N

O

X

Y

Z